PASTOR, CHURCH & LAW

Third Edition

PASTOR, CHURCH & LAW

Third Edition

Richard R. Hammar, J.D., LL.M., CPA

Christian Ministry Resources
Matthews, NC

ISBN # 1-880562-42-1
Library of Congress Catalog No. 99-06889

Published by CMR Press
Christian Ministry Resources
PO Box 1098
Matthews, NC 28106

(704) 821-3845
www.iclonline.com

Printed in the United States of America

to my beloved wife Christine,

and our children, Rachel, Ryan, Abe, and Holly

PREFACE TO FIRST EDITION

A few years ago I was asked to teach a course on church law at a local seminary. It was not until after I had accepted this invitation that I made an unexpected discovery—no comprehensive book on church law had been written in over fifty years. In retrospect, this discovery should not have been surprising. Churches and clergymen have long enjoyed a privileged position throughout our nation's history. In part, this status derived from the constitutional guarantee of religious freedom. But it derived as well from public deference.

In the latter half of the twentieth century, however, a profound change has occurred. Nearly every privilege enjoyed by churches and clergymen under federal, state, and local law has been challenged in the courts under the First Amendment's nonestablishment of religion clause. Many challenges have been successful. Churches and clergymen suddenly find themselves subject to many laws and regulations that formerly had not applied. The applicability of several other laws is an increasing possibility.

Predictably, much confusion and uncertainty surrounds the application of many of these laws. My objective in writing this book is to help reduce this confusion and uncertainty by providing seminary students, clergymen, attorneys, and accountants with a comprehensive yet readable analysis of the major laws affecting churches and clergymen. My intended audience is diverse. Yet, I have endeavored to present the materials in a manner that will be easily comprehended by those having no familiarity with the law. Technical materials and citations of authority are presented in footnotes, which will assist the attorney and accountant in further understanding and pursuing many of the subjects considered.

Although I have attempted to present the law as it is rather than confuse the reader with a dissertation on how it should be, I have not hesitated to express my opinion when I considered it appropriate. And although I have attempted to confine myself to a strictly legal analysis, I readily confess that I experienced a certain ambivalence in the presentation of some subjects, such as wrongful discharge of clergymen, defamation, or church property disputes, that are as much moral as legal problems.

I am indebted to many colleagues and students whose comments and suggestions led to valuable improvements in this text. Further suggestions and comments are invited. I am especially grateful for the contributions of Clyde L. Hawkins, CPA, who reviewed all of the chapters dealing with taxation, and whose comments were most instructive.

Finally, and most important, I express thanks to my beloved wife, Christine, for her patience and understanding.

Richard R. Hammar
May 1983

PREFACE TO SECOND EDITION

I had several reasons for writing this second edition to *Pastor, Church & Law*. First, I wanted to update materials in the original text that have been affected by changes and developments in the law. There have been hundreds of court decisions, statutes, and administrative rulings since the original text was published that directly impact churches and church leaders. These had to be addressed.

Second, in addition to incorporating developments, I wanted to expand the discussion of several subjects. Much of the text has been completely rewritten to provide more expanded coverage. Examples include the termination of clergy, clergy compensation, the clergy-penitent privilege, malpractice, social security coverage of clergy, the housing allowance, incorporation of churches, church records, the discipline and removal of church members, church property disputes, the application of federal payroll tax reporting requirements to churches, coverage of churches under the minimum wage law, termination of employees, copyright law, zoning law, judicial resolution of church disputes, theories of church legal liability, administration of private schools, and the first amendment religion clauses.

Third, I wanted to add subjects not covered in the original text. A casual reading of the table of contents will reveal many of these. Examples include the definition of the term *minister* for federal tax purposes, a clergy "employment contract checklist," confidentiality, immigration of alien ministers, diversion of church funds, state regulation of pastoral counselors, sexual seduction of church members by clergy, the Church Audit Procedures Act, ten sources of personal legal liability for church officers and directors, state laws providing limited immunity to uncompensated church officers and directors, a church's obligations under the immigration law, landmarking of church buildings, the application of the law of eminent domain to churches, the Civil Rights Restoration Act of 1987, the Americans with Disabilities Act, negligent selection and supervision of church workers, denominational legal liability, child abuse reporting obligations under state law, church child care facilities, and several new appendices.

Fourth, I wanted the text to reflect the changes in my own experience. Since the original text was published, I have become a CPA, written several additional books and articles, published a newsletter for church leaders and their advisers, participated in dozens of lawsuits involving churches and denominations, taught several seminary courses based on the book, conducted more than one hundred seminars for church leaders, and counseled with thousands of church leaders on legal and tax issues. The perspective that only these kinds of experiences can provide is reflected throughout the second edition. This is not the product of a theoretician or academic. It is the product of an active practitioner.

Finally, I wanted to provide a mechanism for keeping this text current for several years into the future. This challenge has been met, and this is one of the most exciting aspects of the second edition. *Pastor, Church & Law* will be supplemented bimonthly through appropriate cross-reference notations in many of the feature articles and case summaries appearing in my *Church Law & Tax Report* newsletter. This cross-referencing system is explained and illustrated fully in this text. With *Pastor, Church & Law*, and *Church Law & Tax Report*, readers can be assured of having the most up-to-date information available on virtually any legal topic affecting churches and clergy.

While the second edition is different from the original text in many ways, it retains the purpose of the original text—providing seminary students, clergy, attorneys, and accountants with a comprehensive yet readable analysis of the major laws affecting churches and clergy.

Richard R. Hammar, J.D., LL.M., CPA
August 1991

PREFACE TO THIRD EDITION

There were several considerations that led to the decision to write a new edition. Perhaps most importantly, I wanted to update materials in the original text that have been affected by developments in the law. Second, I wanted to add several subjects not covered in the original text. A casual reading of the table of contents will reveal many of these. Third, I wanted to remove all tax materials from the text. Tax issues for churches and clergy are addressed fully in my companion text, the annual *Church and Clergy Tax Guide*, and there simply was no reason to cover some of the same issues in both books. Of course, the removal of these materials left a big hole in the text, but it has been filled with new legal materials. Fourth, I wanted to make the text more user-friendly. I have added several tables, charts, examples, key points, tips, and references to other useful resources. In addition, each chapter begins with a brief summary, and a table of contents. The third edition will be a big book, but I think that most persons will find it to be very useable. Fifth, I wanted to focus on risk management. For most liability issues, I provide readers with specific recommendations on risk-reducing strategies. This is a very important new feature. Sixth, I have added "instructional aids" at the end of each chapter. These consist primarily of several practical questions that provide readers with an opportunity to apply the chapter text to realistic problems, most of which are based on my own experience in working with churches. As a result, the text can easily be used in seminary courses. These instructional aids also will make the text easy to use by denominational agencies that want applicants for credentials to have some knowledge of church law. Seventh, I have worked hard on creating an expanded index so that readers will more easily be able to find information. Also, the book will be available in the future on a CD-ROM with an excellent search engine that makes the location and retrieval of information almost instantaneous.

I want to give special recognition to my daughter, Rachel (Hammar) Fessler, who served as my editor on this project while at the same time planning her wedding. The final product is far better because of her efforts.

While the third edition is different from the original text in many ways, it retains the purpose of that text—providing clergy, church board members and officers, attorneys, accountants, and seminary students with a comprehensive yet readable analysis of the major laws affecting churches and clergy.

Richard R. Hammar, J.D., LL.M., CPA
December 1999

Special Note to Instructors and Denominational Leaders

An increasing number of seminaries are offering courses on church law, in recognition of the vital importance of this subject in the training of ministers. In addition, many denominational agencies are requiring candidates for ordination to complete a course on church law. The third edition will be readily useable as a textbook in both contexts.

seminaries

I have taught a 3-hour course on church law for several years. While instructors may differ on the materials to cover, my own suggestions are as follows:

(1) A 3-hour course. I will be covering the following chapters and sections in a 3-hour seminary course that I teach, in the following order: Chapters 1-4; Chapter 6; Sections 7-06 through 7-21; Sections 9-04, 9-05, and 9-09; Chapter 10; Chapter 11; Chapter 13; and Chapter 14. If time permits, I would like to spend a few class periods covering the following materials in my annual *Church and Clergy Tax Guide*: Chapter 1 (section D only); Chapters 2 and 3; Chapter 6; and Chapter 9. Emphasis is given to solving the problems in the "instructional aids" section at the end of each assigned chapter. By applying what they have learned from their reading to the typical factual situations described in the problems, students develop a practical, rather than an academic or theoretical, understanding of the materials.

(2) A 2-hour course. The text can be used in a 2-hour course in several ways. My own recommendation would be for the following materials to be covered: Chapters 1-4; Chapter 6; Sections 7-06 through 7-21; Chapter 10; Chapter 13 and Chapter 14.

denominational agencies

Denominational agencies can use the text as part of a continuing education program for ministers, or as part of the educational requirements for ordination. My recommendation would be that ministers, or ministerial applicants, be tested on the following materials: Chapters 1-4; Chapter 6; and Chapter 10.

TABLE OF CONTENTS

Chapter 7: Church Property 407

Chapter 10: CHURCH LEGAL LIABILITY 717

Part One

Law and the Pastor

1

DEFINITIONS AND STATUS

Chapter summary. *This chapter addresses the legal definitions of a number of important terms associated with clergy, including pastor, minister, and clergyman. A number of laws use these terms, and so it is important to understand their meaning. To illustrate, would a volunteer youth pastor who has no ministerial credentials be considered a "minister" for purposes of the clergy-penitent privilege? Would such a person be eligible to perform marriage ceremonies? What about eligibility for a housing allowance under federal tax law? These questions demonstrate the importance of understanding legal definitions. This chapter also addresses the important concept of ministerial status. Ministers may be either employees or self-employed, and this distinction is important in a number of contexts including income tax and social security reporting. In addition, some laws use the terminology of an ordained, commissioned, or licensed minister. The courts and government agencies have often expressed discomfort when called upon to define these terms, noting that they are not prepared to define ecclesiastical terminology. As we will see throughout this text, attempts by courts and government agencies to define ecclesiastical terms often are clumsy, naïve, and inadequate. Yet, the use of these terms in a number of statutes makes it necessary for the courts and agencies to define them.*

§ 1-01   Distinctions Between the Terms *Pastor, Clergy, Minister*

Key point 1-01. The terms pastor, clergy, and minister are used in a number of state and federal laws. Most courts construe these terms broadly, and disregard any distinctions among them. A few courts have construed these terms more narrowly, and attempt to distinguish them.

The terms *pastor, clergy,* and *minister* often are used interchangeably. Such usage is perfectly appropriate in most instances. Occasionally, however, it is important to distinguish among these terms, since many state and federal laws refer to only one or some of them. For example, the Military Selective Service Act provides that *[r]egular or duly ordained ministers of religion* shall be exempt from training and service.[1] Whether a representative of an organized religion may validly solemnize a marriage depends, in most states, upon his or her being characterized as a *clergy,* a *minister,* or a *priest.*[2] Confidential communications made to *clergymen, ministers,* and *priests* are considered privileged from disclosure in many states.[3] A few states specifically require *clergymen, ministers, priests,* or *rabbis* to report actual or reasonably suspected cases of child abuse to civil authorities.[4]

Clergymen and *ministers of the gospel* are excused from jury duty in many states.[5] The exemption is often conditioned upon the timely filing of an application for exemption. Federal law permits common carriers to grant reduced rates to *ministers of religion.*[6] The Immigration and Naturalization Act confers preferential "special immigrant" status upon alien *ministers* who have been engaged continuously in the ministry for two years immediately preceding their application for admission to the United States and whose services are needed by a domestic religious denomination.[7]

The Internal Revenue Code excludes rental or housing allowances, as well as the fair rental value of church-provided parsonages, from the gross income of a *minister of the gospel* for federal income tax purposes.[8] The Code also exempts *a duly ordained, commissioned, or licensed minister of a church in the exercise of his ministry* from self-employment taxes (if certain conditions are satisfied)[9] as well as from federal income tax withholding.[10] It treats such a person as self-employed for social security purposes,[11] and as an employee for purposes of church retirement plans.[12] A large number of states have adopted the federal provisions relating to the exemption of clergy from the tax withholding obligations. Accordingly, the term *duly ordained, commissioned, or licensed minister of a church in the exercise of his ministry* has relevance in the computation of state income taxes in many states.

A few courts have attempted to distinguish between the terms *pastor, clergy,* and *minister.* To illustrate, one court, in interpreting a state law exempting "buildings . . . actually occupied as a parsonage by the officiating clergymen of any religious corporation," held that an unordained youth minister was not a *clergy-*

---

[1]   50 U.S.C. App. § 456(g)(1).

[2]   For a summary of the laws of each state regarding solemnization of marriages by clergy, see Appendix 1.

[3]   For a summary of the laws of each state regarding the clergy privilege, see Appendix 2.

[4]   *See, e.g.,* CONN. GEN. STAT. § 17-38(b) ("clergyman"); MISS. CODE ANN. §§ 43-21-353 and 43-23-9 ("minister"); NEV. REV. STAT. § 432B.220(2)(d) ("clergyman," unless the information was obtained during a confession); N.H. REV. STAT. ANN. § 169-C:29 ("priest, minister, or rabbi"). *See also* § 4-08.

[5]   For a summary of the laws of each state regarding the eligibility of clergy for jury duty, see Appendix 3.

[6]   49 U.S.C. § 41511(b)(1).

[7]   8 U.S.C. § 1101(a)(27)(c).

[8]   I.R.C. § 107.

[9]   *Id.* at § 1402(e).

[10]   *Id.* at § 3401(a)(9).

[11]   *Id.* at §§ 1402(c)(4) and 3121(b)(8).

[12]   *Id.* at § 414(e)(3)(B).

man and thus was not entitled to have his residence exempted from state property taxation.[13] The court concluded that the term *clergyman* implies ordination and accordingly does not include an unordained youth minister. Another court drew a distinction between the terms *pastor* and *minister*.

> [T]here is a difference between a minister and a pastor. Pastor is defined in Webster's New International Dictionary, second edition [as] "the minister or priest in charge of a church or parish"; in Black's Law Dictionary, 4th Edition [as] "a minister of the Christian religion who has charge of a congregation or parish." Ecclesiastically, all pastors are ministers or priests, but all ministers or priests are not pastors. A minister has no authority to speak or act authoritatively for any local church, but its pastor does because he is the designated leader and top official of the local church.[14]

Many churches use the term *minister* with reference to any ordained or credentialed person, and reserve the term *pastor* for those ministers who serve in local churches. Accordingly, a missionary, seminary professor or administrator, or evangelist may be a minister but not a pastor. Some courts have observed that the term *minister* connotes a Protestant clergyman and not "a Jewish rabbi, Muslim imam . . . atheist or agnostic or a member of a religious sect which, like some divisions of Quakerism, lacks a formal clergy."[15]

Most courts and legislatures have given the terms *clergy*, *minister*, and *pastor* a broader interpretation, and have usually thereby disregarded any distinctions among them. To illustrate, Rule 505 of the Uniform Rules of Evidence, which addresses privileged communications between clergy and counselees and has been adopted by several states, defines *clergyman* as "a minister, priest, rabbi, accredited Christian Science practitioner, or other similar functionary of a religious organization." Similarly, a New York law pertaining to solemnization of marriages defined the phrase *clergyman or minister of any religion* to include pastors, rectors, priests, and rabbis.[16]

§ 1-02 Definition of the Terms *Pastor, Clergy,* and *Minister* — In General

> *Key point 1-02. While religious organizations may designate persons as ministers for their religious purposes free from any governmental interference, such a designation does not necessarily determine their legal or tax status.*

For the reasons summarized in section 1-01, it often is important to determine whether or not an individual is a minister for legal or tax purposes. This can be a difficult task, given the variety of staff positions in churches and other religious organizations. One court, in attempting to determine whether certain individuals were "ministers," quoted from an earlier decision of the United States Supreme Court: "Candor compels acknowledgment, moreover, that we can only dimly perceive the lines of demarcation in this extraordinarily sensitive area of constitutional law."[17] This same court made an additional and very important observation that has been repeated many times:

> While religious organizations may designate persons as ministers for their religious purposes free from any governmental interference, bestowal of such a designation does not control their extra-religious legal status.[18]

---

[13] Borough of Cresskill v. Northern Valley Evangelical Free Church, 312 A.2d 641 (N.J. 1973).

[14] Johnson v. State, 173 So.2d 824, 825-26 (Ala. 1964).

[15] Voswinkel v. City of Charlotte, 495 F. Supp. 588 (N.D.N.D. 1980).

[16] *See* Ravenal v. Ravenal, 338 N.Y.S.2d 324 (1972); *see also* In re Silversteins's Estate, 75 N.Y.S.2d 144 (1947); N.Y. Civ. Prac. Law § 4505 (Consol. 1999).

[17] E.E.O.C. v. Southwestern Baptist Theological Seminary, 651 F.2d 277, 283 (5th Cir. 1981), *cert. denied* 456 U.S. 905 (1982), quoting Lemon v. Kurtzman, 403 U.S. 602, 612 (1971).

This is an important point. No court will interfere with a church's decision to designate anyone as a minister. However, the courts are not bound by such ecclesiastical designations in defining the term "minister" for legal or tax purposes.

How have the civil courts defined the terms *pastor, clergy,* or *minister?* Before answering this question it must be acknowledged that attempts by the civil courts to define ecclesiastical terms often are awkward and inadequate. This is due in part to the fact that the meaning of such terms varies widely among religious groups, and even within the same group. To illustrate, it is common for religious denominations to recognize more than one category of ministry. The problem is compounded by the inexperience of judges in dealing with such terminology. The result is that judicial definitions of the terms *pastor, clergy,* and *minister* are not consistent or satisfactory. The United States Supreme Court observed more than a century ago that "[i]t is not to be supposed that the judges of the civil courts can be as competent in the ecclesiastical law and religious faith of all these bodies as the ablest men in each are in reference to their own."[19]

> ***Example.*** *The Tax Court has acknowledged the difficulties associated with any attempt by the civil courts to define ecclesiastical terms: "As a judicial body we are loath to evaluate ecclesiastical authority in the various religious disciplines."[20]*

It is important to recognize that courts do not define the terms *pastor, clergy,* and *minister* in a vacuum. Generally, the courts are called upon to define these terms in applying a specific law or rule. In deciding whether or not an individual is a *pastor,* member of the *clergy,* or *minister* for legal or tax purposes, the following three steps should be followed:

(1) Review the relevant statute to see if these terms are defined. As noted below, some statutes provide adequate definitions.

(2) Look at court decisions interpreting these terms under the relevant statute or rule.

(3) If no court decisions define these terms under the relevant statute, look at court decisions in other contexts.

Perhaps the best general definition of the term *clergy* was announced by a federal appeals court:

As a general rule, if the employee's primary duties consist of teaching, spreading the faith, church governance, supervision of a religious order, or supervision or participation in religious ritual and worship, he or she should be considered "clergy."[21]

Some courts have ruled that one need not be ordained to be a "minister."[22]

> ***Example.*** *A nun who served as a professor of canon law at the Catholic University of America was barred from bringing a sex discrimination claim against the University since she served in a "ministe-*

---

[18] *Id.*

[19] Watson v. Jones, 80 U.S. 679, 729 (1871).

[20] Haimowitz v. Commissioner, T.C. Memo. 1997-40 (1997).

[21] Rayburn v. General Conference of Seventh-Day Adventists, 772 F.2d 1164, 1169 (4th Cir. 1985), quoting Bagni, *Discrimination in the Name of the Lord: A Critical Evaluation of Discrimination by Religious Organizations,* 79 Colum. L. Rev. 1514, 1545 (1979).

[22] E.E.O.C. v. Southwestern Baptist Theological Seminary, 651 F.2d 277 (5th Cir. 1981), *cert. denied* 456 U.S. 905 (1982). The court noted that "one need not be ordained to be a minister." *Id.* at 284.

rial" position even though she was not an ordained priest. The court noted that the first amendment guaranty of religious freedom prevents the civil courts from resolving employment discrimination claims by ministers against religious employers, and that the so-called "ministerial exemption" is not limited to members of the clergy but "has also been applied to lay employees of religious institutions whose 'primary duties consist of teaching, spreading the faith, church governance, supervision of a religious order, or supervision or participation in religious ritual and worship.' " Employees whose positions are "important to the spiritual and pastoral mission of the church should be considered clergy." The court concluded that "the ministerial exception encompasses all employees of a religious institution, whether ordained or not, whose primary functions serve its spiritual and pastoral mission," and this included a nun who taught in the canon law department of the Catholic University. The court noted that the canon law department performs "the vital function of instructing those who will in turn interpret, implement, and teach the law governing the Roman Catholic Church and the administration of its sacraments."[23]

Example. *A federal district court in Ohio ruled that a church-operated school was subject to the Equal Pay Act (a part of the Fair Labor Standards Act).[24] The school, consisting of instruction from preschool through secondary levels, was operated by four congregations. The school adopted a policy of paying its teachers who qualified as a "head of household" an additional allowance of $1,500 per year. A "head of household" was defined as a teacher who was married with dependent children. The sponsoring churches adhered to the conviction that the Bible places the responsibility of the "head of a family" on the husband. Accordingly, the head of household allowance was not paid to a female unless her husband was either absent or unable to work. The Equal Employment Opportunity Commission ("EEOC") charged the school with violating the Equal Pay Act, and demanded that all employees be paid the head of household allowance (regardless of gender). The EEOC also ordered the school to pay "back pay" of $132,000 to female employees who had been denied the allowance in the past. The school maintained that (1) the Equal Pay Act did not apply since the school's alleged discrimination was not based on gender (but rather adherence to a religious principle), (2) the teachers were "ministers" and as such were not subject to the Act, and (3) application of the Act to the school employees violated the first amendment guaranty of religious freedom. The court rejected all of the school's defenses, and ruled in favor of the EEOC. The court began its opinion by noting that the provisions of the Equal Pay Act specifically apply to the employees of church-operated schools. The court then rejected each of the school's 3 defenses. In rejecting the school's first argument, the court insisted that the school's "head of household" allowance policy was in fact based on gender "albeit as a means of giving witness to a religious belief that men and women occupy different family roles." In rejecting the school's second argument, the court acknowledged that the teachers and administrators viewed themselves as teachers of the Christian faith who considered their work religious ministry and a religious calling. The court responded to this perception by noting that the school's "designation of these persons as 'ministers' for religious purposes does not determine their extra-religious legal status. There is no indication that any of the teachers are ordained ministers of the churches, nor do they perform sacerdotal functions. Although it appears undisputed that the principles of the Christian faith pervade the school's educational activities, this alone would not make a teacher or administrator a 'minister' for purposes of exempting that person from the [Fair Labor Standards Act's] definition of 'employee.'" In rejecting the school's third argument, the court concluded that "the compelling interests underlying the Equal Pay Act substantially outweigh its minimal impact on [the school's] religious beliefs . . . . [The school] remains free to practice its religious*

---

[23] E.E.O.C. v. Catholic University of America, 83 F.3rd 455 (D.C. Cir. 1996).
[24] E.E.O.C. v. Tree of Life Christian Schools, 751 F. Supp. 700 (S.D. Ohio 1990).

beliefs in ways that do not unlawfully discriminate in its wage scales on the basis of gender. Accordingly, the court finds the [school's] free exercise argument is without merit." In support of its decision, the court noted that while the school insisted that the Bible makes a distinction between the familial roles of men and women, "it concedes that the Bible does not mandate that men must be paid more than women for identical tasks."

Most courts have concluded that the terms *pastor, clergy,* and *minister,* when used in a legal context, connote a person who has been recognized as a minister by a church or denomination through a formal process rooted in ecclesiastical doctrine and practice, and who has been invested thereby with authority to perform some or all of the rites and practices of said church or denomination. Laws referring to pastors, clergy, and ministers are enacted for a purpose that assumes the dignity and unique role of the profession. For example, clergy typically are invested by law with authority to solemnize marriages and to maintain the confidences shared with them by those seeking spiritual counsel. It is understandable, then, that the courts have been reluctant to recognize as *clergy* or *ministers* those who seek such status through a simple and informal process unrelated to any recognized church or sect, particularly if the status was obtained for ulterior motives (such as tax savings).

Table 1-1 lists several examples of statutes that use the terms *pastor, clergy,* or *minister.* It also refers to those sections in this and a companion text where these statutes, along with their definition of the terms *pastor, clergy,* or *minister,* are addressed.

TABLE 1-1
CROSS-REFERENCE INDEX

context in which the terms *pastor, clergy,* or *minister* are used	where addressed
performance of marriage ceremonies	§ 3-04
exemption from military duty	§ 3-05
exemption from jury duty	§ 3-06
clergy-penitent privilege	§ 3-07
immigration of alien ministers	§ 3-10
unemployment benefits	R. HAMMAR, CHURCH AND CLERGY TAX GUIDE (Christian Ministry Resources, published annually)
Title VII of the Civil Rights Act of 1964	§ 8-06
federal income tax	R. HAMMAR, CHURCH AND CLERGY TAX GUIDE (Christian Ministry Resources, published annually)
social security	R. HAMMAR, CHURCH AND CLERGY TAX GUIDE (Christian Ministry Resources, published annually)

§ 1-03 Status — Employee or Self-Employed

It is often necessary to determine whether a minister or other religious worker is an employee or self-employed. The following paragraphs will illustrate the importance of this distinction.

§ 1-03.1 — Social Security

Key point 1-03.1. While most ministers are employees for federal income tax reporting purposes, they all are self-employed for social security purposes with respect to services they perform in the exercise of their ministry. This means that ministers are not subject to "FICA" taxes, even though they report their income taxes as employees and receive a W-2 from their church. Rather, they pay the "self-employment tax."

Social security taxes are collected under two separate tax systems. Under the Federal Insurance Contributions Act (FICA)[25], half the tax is paid by the employee and the other half is paid by the employer. Under the Self-Employment Contributions Act (SECA)[26] the total tax is paid by the self-employed person. Which tax applies to ministers and religious workers?[27]

1. Ministers

The Self-Employment Contributions Act provides that a "duly ordained, commissioned, or licensed minister of a church in the exercise of his ministry" is self-employed for purposes of social security[28] *even if he or she is considered to be an employee for income tax or other purposes.*

The Federal Insurance Contributions Act provides that the term *employment* does not include "service performed by a duly ordained, commissioned, or licensed minister of a church in the exercise of his ministry."[29]

In summary, for social security purposes, a duly ordained, commissioned, or licensed minister of a church is treated as a self-employed person with respect to services performed in the exercise of ministry. This is true even if a minister is an employee for income tax purposes. Accordingly, a minister reports and pays his or her social security taxes as a self-employed person (and not as an employee) with respect to services performed in the exercise of ministry.[30] A large number of churches withhold FICA taxes from ministers compensation, and pay the employer's share of FICA taxes with respect to ministers income. Such reporting is incorrect.

---

[25] I.R.C. §§ 3101 *et seq.*

[26] *Id.* at §§ 1401 *et seq.*

[27] For a full discussion of social security see R. Hammar, Church and Clergy Tax Guide (published annually by the publisher of this text).

[28] I.R.C. § 1402(c). *See also* Treas. Reg. § 1.1402(c)-5(a)(2), which provides that "a duly ordained, commissioned, or licensed minister of a church is engaged in carrying on a trade or business with respect to service performed by him in the exercise of his ministry . . . unless an exemption under section 1402(e) . . . is effective . . . ." Similarly, IRS Publication 517 specifies that "members of the clergy are treated as self-employed individuals in the performance of their ministerial services." *See also* IRS Publication 560. Treasury regulation 1.1402(c)-5(b)(2) provides that "service performed by a minister in the exercise of his ministry includes the ministration of sacerdotal functions and the conduct of religious worship, and the control, conduct, and maintenance of religious organizations (including the religious boards, societies, and other integral agencies of such organizations), under the authority of a religious body constituting a church or church denomination."

[29] I.R.C. § 3121(b)(8).

[30] I.R.C. § 3121(b)(8)(A).

It is important to emphasize that it is only with respect to *services performed in the exercise of ministry* that ministers are always deemed self-employed for social security purposes. This significant term is explained fully in a companion text (as is the definition of "minister").[31]

2. Nonminister Workers

Nonminister workers employed by churches and other religious organizations generally are treated the same for social security as they are for income tax reporting purposes.

> *Example. D is employed as a full-time office secretary by a church. D is not a minister. D is an employee for federal income tax reporting purposes, and should be treated by the church as an employee for social security.*

There is one major exception. Federal law allowed churches that had nonminister employees as of July of 1984 to exempt themselves from the employer's share of FICA taxes by filing a Form 8274 with the IRS by October 30, 1984. Many churches did so. The exemption was available only to those churches that were opposed for religious reasons to the payment of social security taxes. The effect of such an exemption is to treat all nonminister church employees as self-employed for social security purposes. Such employees must pay the self-employment tax (just like ministers). They are not exempt from social security taxes, as some church leaders have assumed. Churches hiring their first nonminister employee after 1984 have until the day before the due date for their first quarterly 941 form to file the exemption application. Churches can revoke their exemption by filing a Form 941 accompanied by full payment of FICA taxes for that quarter.

> *Example. A church filed a timely Form 8274, exempting itself from the employer's share of FICA taxes with respect to its 3 nonminister employees. The church does not withhold FICA taxes from the wages of its nonminister employees, but these employees must report their social security taxes though they are self-employed. This means that they pay the self-employment tax.[32]*

§ 1-03.2 — Income Taxes

> *Key point 1-03.2. Most ministers should report their federal income taxes as employees, because they will be considered employees under the tests currently used by the IRS and the Tax Court.*

The question of whether a minister is an employee or self-employed for federal income tax reporting purposes is an important one. The IRS thinks so too, for its audit guidelines for ministers state that "the first issue that must be determined is whether the minister is an employee or an independent contractor." Why is this distinction so important? Consider the following reasons:

(1) *Reporting compensation.* Employees report their compensation as wages on line 7 of Form 1040, while self-employed persons report compensation on Schedule C (of Form 1040).

(2) *Business expenses.* Employees deduct unreimbursed (and "nonaccountable" reimbursed) business expenses on Schedule A only if they itemize deductions *and* only to the extent that such expenses exceed 2% of adjusted gross income. Self-employed persons report their business expenses on Schedule C. Business expenses are in effect deductible whether or not the minister itemizes deductions, and are not subject to the 2% floor.

---

[31] See R. HAMMAR, CHURCH AND CLERGY TAX GUIDE (published annually by the publisher of this text).
[32] *Id.*

(3) *Adjusted gross income.* Adjusted gross income ordinarily will be higher if a minister reports income taxes as an employee, since unreimbursed (and "nonaccountable" reimbursed) business expenses are deductions *from* adjusted gross income. Self-employed persons deduct business expenses in computing adjusted gross income. Adjusted gross income is a figure that is important for many reasons. For example, the percentage limitations applicable to charitable contributions and medical expense deductions are tied to adjusted gross income.

(4) *W-2 or 1099?* Ministers working for a church or church agency should receive a Form W-2 each year if they are employees, and a Form 1099-MISC if they are self-employed (and receive at least $600 in annual compensation).

(5) *Tax-deferred annuities.* Favorable "tax-deferred annuities" (also known as "403(b) annuities") offered by nonprofit organizations (including churches) generally are available only to employees. However, they are available to ministers whether they report their federal income taxes as employees or self-employed.

(6) *Tax treatment of various fringe benefits.* Certain fringe benefits provided by a church on behalf of a minister are excludable from the minister's income only if he or she is an employee. Examples include medical insurance premiums paid by a church on behalf of its minister; group term life insurance (up to $50,000) provided by a church on behalf of a minister; amounts payable to employees on account of sickness, accident, or disability pursuant to an employer-financed plan; employer-sponsored "cafeteria plans" which permit employees to choose between receiving cash payments or a variety of fringe benefits.

(7) *Audit risk.* Self-employed persons face a much higher risk of having their tax returns audited.

The tests to apply in determining whether or not a minister or other church worker is an employee or self-employed for federal income tax reporting purposes are complex and beyond the scope of this text. They are addressed fully in a companion text.[33]

> **Observation.** *The IRS and the courts will apply the same tests used in determining the correct reporting status of ministers to determine the reporting status of nonminister church workers for income tax reporting purposes.*

§ 1-03.3 — Retirement Plans

> **Key point 1-03.3.** *A variety of tax-favored retirement plans are available to ministers and nonminister church workers. Some plans are available to both employees and self-employed workers, while others are available only to either employees or self-employed persons, but not both.*

A variety of retirement plans are available to ministers and nonminister church workers. Many of these plans are tax-favored, meaning that contributions to the plans made by or on behalf of a worker are partially or fully deductible for income tax purposes in the year of contribution, and the income (or appreciation) earned by the plan ordinarily is not taxable until distributed. The deferral of tax on income generated by the plan can result in rapid accumulations of wealth.

---

[33] *Id.*

Some retirement plans are available only to persons who report their federal income taxes as employees. The most common example of such a plan is a tax-sheltered annuity, sometimes called a "403(b) plan." Only employees may participate in such plans, although since 1997 ministers may participate whether they are employees or self-employed for income tax reporting purposes. Nonminister church workers who are self-employed are not eligible.

Some retirement plans are available only to persons who report their federal income taxes as self-employed. The most common example of such a plan is a "Keogh plan." Many retirement plans are available to both employees and self-employed workers. Examples include IRAs, simplified employee pensions, and rabbi trusts.

Retirement plans for ministers and nonminister church workers are addressed fully in a companion text.[34]

§ 1-03.4 — Legal Liability

Key point 1-03.4. Churches, like any employer, may be legally responsible for the negligence or other misconduct of employees committed within the course of their employment. This theory of liability generally is known as respondeat superior. It does not apply to self-employed workers.

The characterization of a minister (or other church worker) as an employee or self-employed is sometimes important in assessing legal liability. It is a well-established principle of law that an employer is responsible for the civil wrongs committed by an *employee* in the course of employment. This principle of employer liability for the misconduct and negligence of employees committed in the course of their employment generally is referred to as *respondeat superior* (the "superior responds").

If a minister or other church worker is considered to be self-employed, however, then the church is shielded from liability for his or her wrongs. To illustrate, if while driving recklessly on church business a minister injures a pedestrian, his or her church will be vicariously liable for the injury if an employer-employee relationship exists. If the minister is not an employee of the church, then the church will not be liable. The courts have come to both conclusions.[35]

Observation. The fact that a minister reports his or her federal income taxes as a self-employed person does not necessarily prevent church liability under the doctrine of respondeat superior. Some courts have construed the term employee very broadly to include those persons who are self-employed for federal income tax reporting purposes. On the other hand, other courts have construed the term employee more narrowly, and have ruled that ministers are not employees for purposes of respondeat superior even though they report their federal income taxes as employees.[36]

Example. A Catholic church was not legally responsible on the basis of respondeat superior for injuries caused by the negligent driving of a priest, since he was self-employed rather than an employee. The court based its decision on the following factors: (1) the priest's "day-to-day activities are within his own discretion and control"; (2) the priest is authorized under canon law to do whatever he feels necessary to carry out his duties; (3) he sets his own hours and vacation; (4) he makes out his own paycheck, and hires and fires non-clergy workers; (5) he has complete discretion in purchasing church supplies and paying bills out of parish funds; (6) his work requires a high level of skill and experience and is generally

---

[34] *Id.*
[35] *See generally* chapter 10, *infra.*
[36] *Id.*

done without supervision; and (7) he was driving his own car at the time of the accident and had obtained his own insurance on the vehicle. Under these facts, the court concluded that the priest was not an employee of the church, and accordingly the church was not responsible for his actions on the basis of respondeat superior.[37]

Example. *An elected but unpaid church official killed one person and injured another when the vehicle he was driving struck another vehicle. A court ruled that state and national denominational agencies were not legally responsible for the official's actions on the basis of respondeat superior, since he was not an employee or agent. The court looked to the following factors in deciding whether or not a person is an employee for purposes of respondeat superior: (1) whether or not the individual's performance is in the course of the employer's business; (2) whether or not the individual receives any compensation from the employer; (3) whether or not the employer supplied tools and a place of work in the normal course of the relationship; (4) whether the employer controls the details and quality of the work; (5) whether the employer controls the hours worked; (6) whether the employer selects the materials, tools and personnel used; (7) the length of employment; (8) the type of business; and (9) any pertinent agreements or contracts.[38]*

Under a related legal principle, the acts of an "agent" committed within the scope of an "agency relationship" are attributable to the "principal."[39] An agency relationship is similar to an employer-employee relationship, and it exists whenever two persons agree that one (the agent) will act on behalf of another (the principal) and be subject to the other's control.[40] An example would be an agent working for a real estate company. The agent and company agree that the agent will act on behalf of the company and be subject to its control. Under these circumstances an agency relationship exists and the company will be liable for the acts of the agent committed within the course of the agency relationship.

Many persons injured by the negligence or misconduct of a minister have sued the minister's church and even a parent denominational agency on the ground that the minister was an "agent" of the church and denominational agency. These cases are addressed in chapter 10 of this text.

§ 1-03.5 — Miscellaneous Federal and State Statutes

The applicability of numerous other federal and state statutes and regulations is dependent upon the existence of an employer-employee relationship. Some of the more important of these laws include the following: wage and hour legislation,[41] employment discrimination laws,[42] federal occupational safety and health legislation,[43] workers compensation,[44] and unemployment compensation.[45]

---

[37] Brillhart v. Scheier, 758 P.2d 219 (Kan. 1988).

[38] Nye v. Kemp, 646 N.E.2d 262 (Ohio App. 10 Dist. 1994).

[39] See chapter 10, *infra.*

[40] See RESTATEMENT (SECOND) AGENCY § 1 (1958): "Agency is the fiduciary relation which results from the manifestation of consent by one person to another that the other shall act on his behalf and subject to his control, and consent by the other so to act. The one for whom action is to be taken is the principal. The one who is to act is the agent." An official "comment" interpreting this language notes that "it is the element of continuous subjection to the will of the principal which distinguishes the agent from other fiduciaries and the agency agreement from other agreements."

[41] The Fair Labor Standards Act of 1938 exempts "professional employees" from the minimum wage and overtime pay provisions of the Act. Ministers are considered professional employees. See 29 C.F.R. § 541.301.

[42] See, e.g., Title VII of the Civil Rights Act of 1964, 42 U.S.C. §§ 2000e *et seq.*, and the Age Discrimination in Employment Act, 29 U.S.C. §§ 621-34.

[43] See the federal Occupational Safety and Health Act, 29 U.S.C. §§ 651 *et seq.*

[44] See, e.g., ILL. REV. STAT. ch. 48, §§ 138.1 *et seq.*; MO. REV. STAT. ch. 287; TEX. LABOR CODE title 5, chapters 401 *et seq.*

[45] See, e.g., ILL. REV. STAT. ch. 48, §§ 300 *et seq.*; MO. REV. STAT. ch. 288; TEX. LABOR CODE title 4, chapters 201 *et seq.*

TABLE 1-2
EMPLOYEE OR SELF-EMPLOYED STATUS
Selected Differences

issue	if an employee	if self-employed	how to decide if a worker is an employee or self-employed
social security	• employer and employee each pay FICA tax of 7.65% of employee wages (total tax of 15.3%) • ministers are never employees with regard to their ministerial duties (they do not pay FICA taxes) • nonminister church workers who are employees for income taxes are employees for social security (unless church filed a timely waiver from FICA taxes—in which case they are treated as self-employed for social security)	• pay 15.3% self-employment tax • ministers always are self-employed with regard to their ministerial duties • nonminister church workers who are self-employed for income taxes are self-employed for social security	use income tax tests
income taxes	• wages reported by employer on W-2 • wages reported by worker on line 7 (Form 1040) • unreimbursed and nonaccountable reimbursed expenses are deducted on Schedule A (subject to 2% floor) • low audit risk • some fringe benefits (such as employer paid medical insurance premiums and cafeteria plans) tax-free	• income reported by employer on 1099 • wages reported by worker on Schedule C and line 12 (Form 1040) • unreimbursed and nonaccountable reimbursed expenses are deducted on Schedule C • higher audit risk • some fringe benefits (such as employer paid medical insurance premiums and cafeteria plans) are taxable • church issues 1099 (if annual compensation is $600 or more)	IRS applies a 20-factor test, the Tax Court has adopted various tests—all focus on the degree of "control" exercised by the employer over the details of how the worker performs his or her job
retire-ment	• some retirement plans available only to employees (including tax-sheltered annuities or "403(b)" plans—for nonminister church staff)	• some retirement plans available only to self-employed (Keogh plans)	use income tax tests
legal liability	• employer is liable for misconduct of employees in course of their employment (respondeat superior)	• employer generally not liable for misconduct of self-employed workers	some courts follow income tax factors; others apply broader or narrower tests

§ 1.04 Status — Ordained, Commissioned, or Licensed

Key point 1-04. A number of federal and state statutes use the terms ordained, commissioned, or licensed minister. If these terms are defined by a statute, then this definition ordinarily controls even if it conflicts with the definitions adopted by a religious body. If they are not defined by statute, then the civil courts will define them based on applicable precedent.

It is sometimes important to determine whether a minister is ordained, commissioned, or licensed. To illustrate, the Internal Revenue Code exempts wages paid for services by "a duly ordained, commissioned, or licensed minister of a church" from income tax withholding;[46] permits a "duly ordained, commissioned, or licensed minister of a church" to apply for exemption from social security coverage under certain circumstances;[47] treats a "duly ordained, commissioned, or licensed minister of a church" as self-employed for social security purposes (if not exempt);[48] and excludes the costs of renting or maintaining a home (and the fair rental value of a church-provided parsonage) from the gross income of a "duly ordained, commissioned, or licensed minister of a church."[49]

The Military Selective Service Act exempts "duly ordained ministers" from training and service.[50] The Federal Unemployment Tax Act and many state unemployment laws exempt "service performed by a duly ordained, commissioned, or licensed minister" from unemployment compensation coverage.[51]

From a legal perspective, what is the meaning of an ordained, commissioned, or licensed minister? Unfortunately, this terminology is nowhere defined in the Internal Revenue Code for purposes of federal tax law. As one court has observed, the Code and regulations "do not attempt to say what a minister 'is,' but only what a minister 'does.'"[52] A few courts have given some hint as to the legal meaning of this terminology for federal tax purposes. In a case involving the eligibility of a Jewish cantor for a housing allowance, the Tax Court observed that while a housing allowance is available only to an "ordained, commissioned, or licensed minister," there is no requirement "that the ordination, commissioning, or licensing must come from some higher ecclesiastical authority. In a religious discipline having the lay democratic character of Judaism and lacking any central ecclesiastical organization, this ministerial authority can be conferred by the church or congregation itself." The requirement that a minister be "ordained, commissioned, or licensed," noted the court, "is to exclude self-appointed ministers" from the special tax provisions available to clergy.[53]

This case suggests that local churches may ordain, commission, or license clergy if they are not affiliated with any denomination or association of churches that credentials clergy. It is an open question whether a local church can ordain, commission, or license a minister if it is affiliated with a denomination that itself ordains, licenses, or commissions clergy (and there is no provision in the organizational documents of the denomination for the credentialing of clergy by local churches). Such churches often seek to ordain, commission, or license clergy solely for tax-savings purposes (i.e., to qualify a church worker for a housing allowance exclusion or for exemption from social security coverage). The Tax Court's decision in *Lawrence v. Commis-*

---

[47] *Id.* at § 1402(e).

[48] *Id.* at § 1402(c).

[49] *See generally* I.R.C. § 107; Treas. Reg. § 1.107; Rev. Rul. 78-301, 1978-2 C.B. 103; IRS Publication 517. Housing allowances are discussed in detail in R. HAMMAR, CHURCH AND CLERGY TAX GUIDE (published annually by the publisher of this text).

[50] 50 U.S.C. App. § 456(g)(1).

[51] *See, e.g.,* I.R.C. § 3309(b); MO. REV. STAT. § 288.034(9).

[52] Salkov v. Commissioner, 46 T.C. 190 (1966). *See also* Haimowitz v. Commissioner, T.C. Memo. 1997-40 (1997) ("[a]s a judicial body we are loath to evaluate ecclesiastical authority in the various religious disciplines").

[53] *Id. See also* Wingo v. Commissioner, 89 T.C. 922 (1987); Silverman v. Commissioner, 57 T.C. 727 (1972); Rev. Rul. 78-301, 1978-2 C.B. 103.

sioner is relevant in this context, since it warned that a local church's attempt to "commission" a minister was ineffective since the commissioning had been "nothing more than a paperwork procedure designed to help him get a tax benefit [a housing allowance exclusion] . . . without giving him any new status."[54] Other factors that will be relevant in determining whether a local church can ordain, commission, or license clergy in a way that will be recognized by the federal government include (1) whether or not the denomination has a tradition of local churches issuing ministerial credentials; (2) whether or not the local church's articles of incorporation empower it to confer ministerial credentials; and (3) whether or not a parent denomination recognizes the local church's issuance of ministerial credentials.

The Tax Court has observed that "the phrase 'ordained, commissioned, or licensed' is a disjunctive phrase such that a minister need only be ordained or commissioned or licensed to be a minister [for tax purposes]."[55] Further, the Court has noted that the terms "minister of the gospel" and "ordained, commissioned, or licensed" are rooted in Christian practice, and they are not meant to exclude the functional equivalents of ordained, commissioned, or licensed clergy in other religions and sects. For example, the Court has stated that "although 'minister of the gospel' is phrased in Christian terms, we are satisfied that Congress did not intend to preclude those persons who are the equivalent of 'ministers' in other religions."[56]

It is questionable whether an entity that is neither a church nor a religious denomination can ordain, commission, or license a minister for tax purposes, since these terms are so inextricably linked, in terms of history, practice, and etymology, with churches and religious denominations.

The classic legal definition of ordination (in a context other than federal tax law) was given by the Supreme Court of Connecticut in an early decision: "To ordain, according to the etymology and general use of the term, signifies to appoint, to institute, to clothe with authority. When the word is applied to a clergyman, it means that he has been invested with ministerial functions or sacerdotal power."[57] Similarly, one court has observed:

> A duly ordained minister, in general acceptation, is one who has followed a prescribed course of study of religious principles, has been consecrated to the service of living and teaching that religion through an ordination ceremony under the auspices of an established church, has been commissioned by that church as its minister in the service of God, and generally is subject to control or discipline by a council of the church by which he was ordained.[58]

The Military Selective Service Act defines *duly ordained minister of religion* as follows:

> [A]ny person who has been ordained, in accordance with the ceremony, ritual, or discipline of a church, religious sect, or organization established on the basis of a community of faith and belief, doctrines and practices of a religious character, to preach and to teach the doctrines of such church, sect, or organization and to administer the rites and ceremonies thereof in public worship, and who as his regular and customary vocation preaches and teaches the principles of religion and administers the ordinances of public worship as embodied in the creed or principles of such church, sect, or organization.[59]

---

[54] 50 T.C. 494 (1968).

[55] Wingo v. Commissioner, 89 T.C. 922 (1987).

[56] Salkov v. Commissioner, 46 T.C. 190 (1966); Silverman v. Commissioner, 57 T.C. 727 (1972).

[57] Kibbe v. Antram, 4 Conn. 134, 139 (1821).

[58] Buttecali v. United States, 130 F.2d 172, 174 (5th Cir. 1942).

[59] 50 U.S.C. App. § 466(g)(1). *But cf.* Yeoman v. United States, 400 F.2d 793 (10th Cir. 1968) (exemption from armed services for ministers available only to leaders of religious faiths, not to members in general); United States v. Dyer, 272 F. Supp. 965 (N.D. W. Va.

Webster's Third New International Dictionary defines *ordination* as "[investing] with ministerial or sacerdotal functions; [introduction] into the office of the Christian ministry by the laying on of hands or by other forms."

The legal definitions of *ordination* closely parallel those adopted by religious bodies themselves. Illustratively, *The Encyclopedia of the Lutheran Church* provides that "ordination is the solemn act of the church designating as ministers of the Gospel, and committing to them the holy office of the Word and Sacraments, certain ones who have been regularly called by God through the church to serve in a specific field or sphere of duty."[60] *The Episcopalian's Dictionary* defines *ordination* as "the ceremony in which an individual is commissioned and empowered for the work of the ministry."[61] The *Mennonite Encyclopedia* defines *ordination* of ministers as "an act of the church in which the minister-elect receives confirmation to his office by a ceremony of laying on of hands of a bishop and the intercession of the congregation, which gives him the right to lead the congregation in worship and life as pastor, to perform the duties of his office, whatever they may be, to preach the Word of God, to perform marriages, to ordain, to administer baptism and communion, to administer discipline, to administer the alms fund, etc."[62]

The Encyclopedia of World Methodism defines *ordination* as "the name for the solemn act whereby men are set apart for office in the Christian ministry."[63] *The Encyclopedia of Southern Baptists* defines *ordination* as "[t]he ceremony whereby those who have a vocation and have given some evidence of ability for the ministerial office are set apart for the work of their calling."[64]

If a statute or regulation pertaining to ordained ministers defines the term *ordained*, then the courts will apply this definition even if it conflicts with the definitions adopted by churches and other religious organizations. If a statute or regulation does not define the term *ordained*, then the courts ordinarily apply the most relevant judicial precedent in defining the term. They are not bound in such cases to defer to the definitions adopted by religious bodies themselves. To illustrate, a Jehovah's Witness was denied exemption from military service on the ground that he was not an "ordained minister" despite his claim that he was engaged "full time" in the ministry.[65] This is consistent with the general principle that ecclesiastical definitions and terminology cannot be affected by civil law and are absolute *in an ecclesiastical context*, but they may be superseded by statutory or judicial definitions in the limited context of civil law.

The term *licensed minister* is used by many religious bodies to denote a status inferior and preliminary to ordination. *Commissioning* is a procedure followed by some churches which do not recognize formal ordination. It is usually an investiture of authority to perform religious functions on behalf of a congregation, and thus is analogous to ordination. Some religious bodies commission missionaries, even though the prospective missionaries are already licensed or ordained. The IRS has held that for purposes of the Internal Revenue Code, commissioned or licensed ministers of religious bodies that provide for ordination will not be included within the term *ordained, commissioned, or licensed minister* unless they "perform substantially all the religious functions within the scope of the tenets and practices of their religious denominations" as an ordained minister.[66]

1967), *aff'd*, 390 F.2d 611 (4th Cir. 1968) (seminary education not a prerequisite to obtaining ministerial exemption); United States v. Hestad, 248 F. Supp. 650 (W.D. Wis. 1965) (Selective Service Act's definition of ordained takes precedence over definition adopted by particular cult).

[60] The Encyclopedia of the Lutheran Church 1857 (1965).

[61] H. Harper, The Episcopalian's Dictionary 116 (1974).

[62] The Mennonite Encyclopedia 73 (1959).

[63] The Encyclopedia of World Methodism 1817 (1974).

[64] Encyclopedia of Southern Baptists 1056 (1958).

[65] United States v. Hestad, 248 F. Supp. 650 (W.D. Wis. 1965).

[66] Rev. Rul. 78-301, 1978-2 C.B. 103. *See* R. Hammar, Church and Clergy Tax Guide (published annually by the publisher of this text).

INSTRUCTIONAL AIDS TO CHAPTER 1

Key Terms

clergy

duly ordained, commissioned, or licensed minister

employee

licensed minister

minister

pastor

ordained, commissioned, or licensed minister

ordination

self-employed

service performed in the exercise of ministry

Learning Objectives

- Understand the legal difference between the terms *pastor, clergyman,* and *minister.*

- Explain why it is important to define the terms *pastor, clergyman,* and *minister.*

- Name several statutes that use the terms *pastor, clergyman,* or *minister.*

- Explain how the civil courts determine the definition of a "minister" when a church's definition differs from the definition in a statute.

- Define the terms *employee* and *self-employed;* recognize the legal differences between these terms; and determine whether a minister is an employee or self-employed in several contexts including income tax and social security reporting.

- Understand the legal significance of the term *ordained, commissioned, or licensed.*

Definitions and Status

Short-Answer Questions

1. Rev. C, an ordained minister, is the full-time youth pastor at his church. As a youth pastor, is he eligible to perform marriage ceremonies under a state law that permits "clergy" to perform such ceremonies? How would a civil court most likely resolve this question?

2. Same facts as question 1, except Rev. C is licensed but not ordained.

3. Same facts as question 1, except Rev. C has no ministerial credentials. He is a part-time student at a local seminary and plans to become an ordained minister in the future.

4. Is a Jewish rabbi authorized to perform marriages under a state law that authorizes "ministers" to perform such ceremonies? How would a civil court most likely resolve this question?

5. Rev. D, an ordained minister, serves as music minister at her church. A choir member shares confidential information with her in the course of counseling. Is this communication protected from disclosure in court by the clergy-penitent privilege? Assume that state law extends the privilege to confidential communications made between "ministers" and counselees. How would a civil court most likely resolve this question?

6. A local congregation "ordains" its custodian as a "minister of administration." Is this legally permissible?

7. Same facts as question 6. Do you think the IRS would consider the "minister" to be eligible for a housing allowance? Why?

8. What three steps should be considered in deciding whether or not an individual is a "minister" for legal purposes?

9. List five situations in which it is important to define the term *minister.*

10. A church treats its minister as an employee for federal income tax reporting purposes. Should it treat the minister as an employee for purposes of social security? Explain.

11. List five reasons why it is important to determine whether a minister is an employee or self-employed for federal income tax reporting purposes.

12. Rev. A, the senior minister at his church, would like to establish a personal retirement fund. He has heard about Keogh plans and individual retirement accounts, and would like to contribute a portion of his church salary to one of these programs. In which of these two programs may he participate?

13. On his way to make hospital calls, Rev. S fails to stop his car at a red light and collides with another vehicle. The driver of the other vehicle is injured. Will Rev. S's church be legally responsible for the injuries? Explain.

14. A statute permits "ordained ministers" to perform wedding ceremonies. Is a minister who is licensed by a church that both ordains and licenses ministers legally qualified to perform wedding ceremonies? What factors would a court consider?

Discussion Questions

1. Rev. J files her income taxes as a self-employed person on the basis of theological convictions pertaining to the role and status of a minister. Her income tax return is audited, and the IRS asserts that she should have reported her income as an employee. Rev. J objects to being characterized as an employee. Who should have the right to determine Rev. J's status for income tax purposes? Why?

2. The Internal Revenue Code grants several benefits to *duly ordained, commissioned, or licensed ministers*. Who should have the authority to determine whether a particular minister is ordained, commissioned, or licensed? A church or religious denomination? The IRS? Why?

2

THE PASTOR-CHURCH RELATIONSHIP

Chapter summary. This chapter will acquaint you with the legal principles that apply to the three phases of a minister's relationship with a local church: (1) initiation of the relationship; (2) terms and conditions of the employment relationship, including the employment contract and compensation; and (3) termination of the relationship. Initiation of the pastor-church relationship varies from denomination to denomination and even from church to church within some denominations. Hierarchical denominations may exercise considerable control over local churches, and prescribe how a minister is to be selected. In congregational denominations, the local church is self-governing and has the authority to select its own ministers. This authority must be exercised in accordance with the church's constitution and bylaws. This is a very important principle of law, and it indicates the necessity of being familiar with a church's governing instruments. Sometimes clergy are asked to sign a contract of employment with their employing church. Such a contract generally will govern most aspects of the employment relationship. In most cases, however, no formal contract is ever signed. But even when no formal contract is ever signed, the courts "imply" a contract of employment once a minister begins performing duties on behalf of a church. The employment contract, whether actual or implied, gives the minister important legal rights. A minister is legally entitled to receive the compensation stated by his employment contract. If no formal contract exists, the minister is entitled to reasonable compensation for services rendered. In either case, the compensation received must not be unreasonably high, or the tax-exempt status of the church will be jeopardized. The termination of the pastor-church relationship presents more troublesome legal questions than either of the other two phases of the relationship. Whether and when a church can terminate a minister's employment is a legal question whose answer ordinarily depends upon the terms of the employment contract (if any), whether the minister was employed for a specified term or for an indefinite period, and terms of the church's constitution and bylaws. Again, it is crucial that a church follow the procedures set forth in its governing instrument in discharging a minister. If these procedures are not followed, the discharge may not be legally valid.

§ 2-01 Initiating the Relationship — In General

Key resource. *The selection of a minister is a critical decision for any church. An important resource for assisting church leaders with this task is the Selection and Screening Kit for Ministers. This kit includes a manual, ten application booklets containing all the forms you will need, and helpful interview booklets containing an extensive listing of questions to ask applicants. You can obtain this resource from the publisher of this text.*

The pastor-church relationship begins with the selection or appointment of the pastor. While the selection or appointment of a pastor is an ecclesiastical decision, it may have legal implications. For example, how is a pastor to be selected or appointed if a church's governing instrument does not address the issue? What are the legal consequences if the selection of appointment of a pastor is not in accordance with a church's governing instrument? Under what circumstances can a civil court review a church's selection or appointment of a pastor? These questions are addressed in the sections that follow. A related question is the liability of a church for the *negligent hiring* of a pastor. This important question is addressed in chapter 10.

§ 2-01.1 — Congregational Churches

Key point 2-01.1. *In congregational churches it is common for ministers to be selected by church members according to the procedures set forth in the church's governing instrument.*

Churches may be classified in terms of polity or organization as either *congregational* or *hierarchical.* Understanding the difference between these two basic types of church structure is important, since some aspects of the pastor-church relationship turn on this distinction. The United States Supreme Court has defined a *congregational* church as "a religious congregation which, by the nature of its organization, is strictly independent of other ecclesiastical associations, and so far as church government is concerned, owes no fealty or obligation to any higher authority."[1] The Supreme Court has defined a *hierarchical* church as "a subordinate member of some general church organization in which there are superior ecclesiastical tribunals with a general and ultimate power of control . . . over the whole membership of that general organization."[2] Many

---

[1] Watson v. Jones, 80 U.S. 679, 722 (1871).

[2] *Id.* at 722-23.

churches combine elements of both forms of polity.[3] For example, one court has noted that "a church may be hierarchical in terms of internal administration and discipline, and yet congregational as far as control and use of its property is concerned."[4]

In congregational churches the minister ordinarily is selected by the congregation itself according to the procedures set forth in the church's constitution, bylaws, or other governing instrument. If none of these documents addresses the subject, then the established practice of the church controls. Congregational churches often select their ministers either by majority vote of the church's membership or by the decision of the church's governing board.[5] Although either method is legally acceptable, most congregational or independent churches select their ministers by majority vote of the congregation's membership.

§ 2-01.2 — Hierarchical Churches

Key point 2-01.2. In hierarchical churches, ministers ordinarily are selected by church members or according to rules promulgated by a parent denomination.

Hierarchical churches generally select their ministers according to rules promulgated by a parent denomination. Some denominations give subordinate churches complete freedom in selecting ministers. Others dictate who will be the minister of each affiliated church. Many denominations provide for the selection of ministers by the combined efforts of both the denomination and the subordinate church.

When a hierarchical body or official selects a minister for a local congregation, the local congregation is without authority to affect or overrule that decision.

Example. A Methodist bishop acting pursuant to authority granted him by the Doctrines and Disciplines of the Methodist Church appointed a minister to serve a Methodist congregation in New Orleans, Louisiana. The congregation refused to recognize the bishop's appointment, and recognized instead a minister selected by congregational vote. In ruling in favor of the bishop, the court observed that the congregation was subject to the discipline of its denomination and accordingly had to recognize the appointment made by the bishop even though a majority of the congregation disapproved of it.[6]

Example. A Pennsylvania state appeals court ruled that a Lutheran Synod had the legal authority to dismiss the minister of a local church despite the protest of a majority of the congregation. When the congregation refused to recognize the Synod's designated pastor, the Synod sought and received a court order forbidding the performance of any further pastoral functions at the church by the dismissed

---

[3]   *See* Annot., 52 A.L.R.3d 324, 361 n.5 (1973).

[4]   Antioch Temple v. Parekh, 422 N.E.2d 1337, 1342 (Mass. 1981).

[5]   *See, e.g.,* Holiman v. Dovers, 366 S.W.2d 197 (Ark. 1963) (majority of members of Baptist church have right to select pastor); De Jean v. Board of Deacons, 139 A.2d 205 (Dela. 1958) (common practice in Baptist churches to select ministers by majority vote of congregation); Franklin v. Hahn, 275 S.W.2d 776 (Ky. 1955) (ministers in Christian Church selected by majority vote of congregation); Sherburne Village Baptist Society v. Ryder, 86 N.Y.S.2d 853 (1949) ("Under the usages and custom of the Baptist Church, the authority to employ or dismiss a minister lies not in the corporation, the trustees, or the deacons, but in the congregation itself."); Atkins v. Walker, 200 S.E.2d 641, 650 (N.C. 1973) ("[T]he congregation . . . had the right, by a majority vote, in a duly called and conducted meeting of the congregation . . . to call to its pastorate the man of its choice."); McCarther v. Pleasant Bethany Baptist Church, 195 S.W.2d 819 (Tex. 1946) (minister retained by action of board of deacons); Ex parte McClain, 762 S.W.2d 238 (Tex. App. 1988); First Baptist Church of Hope Hull v. Owens, 474 So.2d 638 (Ala. 1985).

[6]   Brooks v. Chinn, 52 So.2d 583 (La. 1951).

minister. The ousted minister refused to comply with the court order, which resulted in his being jailed for contempt of court.[7]

§ 2-01.3 — Compliance with a Church's Governing Instrument in the Selection of a Minister

Key point 2-01.3. Churches should comply with their governing instrument in the selection of a minister. If an unincorporated church has no governing instrument, or its governing instrument does not address elections, then the established practice of the church should be followed. Incorporated churches having no provision in their governing instrument addressing elections may be subject to the provisions of state nonprofit corporation law.

If a minister may be selected by vote of the congregation, it is important that the congregational vote be conducted pursuant to the church's constitution, bylaws, or other governing instrument. Failure to comply with the procedure set forth in a church's governing instrument in the selection of a minister may nullify the process. If an unincorporated church has no governing instrument, or its governing instrument does not address elections, then the established practice of the church should be followed. Incorporated churches having no provision in their governing instrument addressing elections may be subject to the provisions of state nonprofit corporation law. As an example, if an incorporated church has no governing instrument, and the applicable state nonprofit corporation law specifies quorum, notice, and voting requirements, then these requirements must be followed. If they are not, a congregational election may be voidable.

Example. A church's constitution and bylaws failed to define the "notice" requirements applicable to church membership meetings. As a result, it was bound by the notice provisions in state nonprofit corporation law. Since the church failed to comply with state law, its meeting was ruled invalid by a civil court.[8]

Most states have religious or nonprofit corporation laws that specify how elections are to be conducted.[9] The procedures specified by state law generally are effective only with respect to those matters not addressed in the corporation's constitution, bylaws, or other governing instrument.[10] Should an incorporated church's procedures for electing a minister conflict with provisions in state nonprofit corporation law, the church's procedures ordinarily will prevail.[11]

§ 2-01.4 — Civil Court Review of Clergy Selection Disputes — the General Rule of Non-Intervention

Key point 2-01.4. The selection of a minister is an ecclesiastical decision that the civil courts ordinarily will not review—even when it is alleged that a church failed to follow its own internal procedures in the selection of a minister, or the selection process was discriminatory.

What authority do the civil courts have to review church or denominational decisions regarding the selection of clergy? The United States Supreme Court has ruled that "[f]reedom to select the clergy, where no

---

[7] Trinity Lutheran Evangelical Church v. May, 537 A.2d 538 (Pa. Common. 1988).
[8] Bethlehem Missionary Baptist Church v. Henderson, 522 So.2d 1339 (La. App. 1988).
[9] *See, e.g.,* Ill. Rev. Stat. ch. 32, §§ 163a *et seq.*; Mo. Rev. Stat. chs. 352, 355; Tex. Stat. Ann. arts. 1396 *et seq.*
[10] *See generally* chapter 6, *infra.*
[11] *See* Rector, et al. v. Melish, 168 N.Y.S.2d 952 (1957).

improper methods of choice are proven, we think, must now be said to have federal constitutional protection as a part of the free exercise of religion against state interference."[12] This principle has been applied in several cases—even when it is alleged that a church failed to follow its own internal procedures in the selection of a minister, or the selection process was discriminatory. For example, one court concluded that it had no jurisdiction to determine whether or not an interim minister was improperly appointed since "[t]he appointment of a minister is a purely ecclesiastical matter which should not be subject to review by a civil or secular court."[13] In another case involving the selection of a minister within the United Methodist Church, a court observed:

[T]he appointment of a pastor is a purely subjective decision to be made by the empowered bishop to advance the purpose of the church organization. Appointment is undoubtedly an ecclesiastical matter to which judicial deference is mandated by the first amendment. *Whether or not the conference followed required procedure in appointing [the minister] is not for a civil court to consider, because it would entail scrutinizing the appointment decision-making process and reviewing the subjective criteria used by the church organization in reaching its decision.*[14]

Several courts have applied this fundamental principle, including a number of federal appeals courts. For example, the federal appeals court for the fifth circuit (covering the states of Louisiana, Mississippi, and Texas) ruled that since a minister is the "lifeblood" of the church, the assignment of a minister is inherently a matter of ecclesiastical concern.[15] The federal appeals court for the District of Columbia circuit ruled that the first amendment guaranty of religious freedom "precludes governmental interference with ecclesiastical hierarchies, church administration, *and appointment of clergy.*"[16] Other examples of federal appeals court and state court decisions are set forth below.

Example. The federal appeals court for the District of Columbia circuit refused to hear a claim by a Methodist minister that an annual conference of the United Methodist Church discriminated against him on account of age in refusing to appoint him to a suitable parish. The court emphasized that any determination regarding "whose voice speaks for the church" is a religious matter, and that the "evaluation of the gifts and graces of a minister must be left to ecclesiastical institutions." The pastor had argued that the refusal of civil courts to resolve controversies regarding the selection of clergy could lead to "the most egregious civil rights violations." For example, he suggested that under the court's rule of non-interference "the courts would be prevented from enforcing homicide statutes against churches that selected their pastors by making them play Russian roulette." The court rejected this claim, noting that the constitutional guaranty of religious freedom is subject to a "balancing" test. Clearly, the governmental interest in preserving life and preventing homicides would outweigh the interests of a church in selecting clergy through such means. The court noted that there may be other civil rights that outweigh a church's constitutionally protected right to select its clergy, but the federal policy of eliminating age discrimination is not one of them. The court stressed that the constitutional guaranty of religious freedom is at its apex when the church-pastor relationship is involved, and that non-clergy church employees are entitled to a lesser degree of protection. Further, "a church is always free to burden its activities

---

[12] Kedroff v. St. Nicholas Cathedral, 344 U.S. 94, 116 (1952).
[13] Wilkerson v. Battiste, 393 So.2d 195, 197 (La. App. 1980). *See also* Williams v. Palmer, 532 N.E.2d 1061 (Ill. App. 3rd Dist. 1988).
[14] Williams v. Palmer, 532 N.E.2d 1061 (Ill. App. 3rd Dist. 1988) (emphasis added). *See also* Kaufman v. Sheehan, 707 F.2d 355 (8th Cir. 1983).
[15] McClure v. Salvation Army, 460 F.2d 553 (5th Cir. 1972), *cert. denied*, 409 U.S. 896 (1972).
[16] King's Garden, Inc. v. FCC, 498 F.2d 51, 56 (D.C. Cir. 1974) (emphasis added).

voluntarily through contracts, and such contracts are fully enforceable." Therefore, a church can limit its authority to select or terminate a minister by contractual provisions.[17]

Example. *The federal appeals court for the fourth circuit (covering the states of Maryland, North Carolina, South Carolina, Virginia, and West Virginia) rejected a woman's claim that the failure of the Seventh Day Adventist church to appoint her to a particular pastoral position discriminated against her on the basis of sex and race. The court agreed that the government's interest in eradicating discrimination based on sex and race was of the highest order, but it nevertheless concluded that it was outweighed by a church's constitutionally protected right to choose its clergy. It observed that "the right to choose ministers without government restriction underlies the well-being of the religious community, for perpetuation of a church's existence may depend upon those whom it selects to preach its values, teach its message, and interpret its doctrines both to its own membership and to the world at large." The court emphasized that its ruling was limited to a church's right to select clergy, and that the government's interest in eliminating race and sex discrimination would outweigh a church's right to discriminate in decisions affecting non-clergy employees.*[18]

Example. *The federal appeals court for the first circuit (covering the states of Maine, Massachusetts, New Hampshire, and Rhode Island) ruled that "[h]owever a suit may be labeled, once a court is called upon to probe into a religious body's selection and retention of clergymen, the first amendment [guaranty of religious freedom] is implicated . . . . The relationship between an organized church and its ministers is its lifeblood. The minister is the chief instrument by which the church seeks to fulfill its purpose. Matters touching this relationship must necessarily be recognized as of prime ecclesiastical concern." The court concluded that any judicial review of decisions involving the selection or termination of clergy "would require judicial intrusion into rules, policies, and decisions which are unmistakably of ecclesiastical cognizance. They are, therefore, not the federal courts' concern. . . ."*[19]

Numerous state courts have followed the general rule of judicial non-intervention in controversies involving the selection of clergy. To illustrate, an Illinois appeals court dismissed a lawsuit brought by a Methodist minister against a Methodist conference for breach of contract and wrongful interference with contractual relations.[20] The minister claimed that despite his "good and satisfactory work" as pastor of a local church, he was assigned by the conference to another church which constituted "a severe demotion in terms of the number of church members, compensation, and opportunity for service." The court observed that

> the appointment of a pastor is a purely subjective decision to . . . advance the purpose of the church organization. Appointment is undoubtedly an ecclesiastical matter to which judicial deference is mandated by the first amendment. Whether or not the conference followed required procedure in appointing [the minister] is not for a civil court to consider, because it would entail

---

[17] Minker v. Baltimore Annual Conference of the United Methodist Church, 894 F.2d 1354 (D.C. Cir. 1990).

[18] Rayburn v. General Conference of Seventh Day Adventists, 772 F.2d 1164 (4th Cir. 1985).

[19] Natal v. Christian and Missionary Alliance, 878 F.2d 1575 (1st Cir. 1989).

[20] Williams v. Palmer, 532 N.E.2d 1061 (Ill. App. 3rd Dist. 1988) (emphasis added). *See also* Duffy v. California State Personnel Board, 283 Cal. Rptr. 622 (Cal. App. 3 Dist. 1991) (state's practice of allowing religious groups to select prison chaplains was "a safeguard against the doctrinal entanglement in religious issues prohibited by the establishment clause"); Wilkerson v. Battiste, 393 So.2d 195 (La. App. 1980); Antony v. Cardin, 398 N.Y.S.2d 215 (1977); Atkins v. Walker, 200 S.E.2d 641 (N.C. 1973); Braswell v. Purser, 193 S.E.2d 90 (N.C. 1972); Buchanan v. Second Tabernacle Missionary Baptist Church, 1996 WL 417135 (Ohio App. 1996) (civil court refused to review a clergy selection dispute since the church's governing instrument provided a procedure for appeal and this procedure had not been exercised).

scrutinizing the appointment decision-making process and reviewing the subjective criteria used by the church organization in reaching its decision.[21]

The court noted that the appropriate remedy for the minister was "to higher judicial tribunals within the church hierarchy," and if the minister "has made such appeal and been denied relief, this court must defer to the decision of the church." It also rejected the minister's contention that the so-called "neutral principles of law" approach gave the civil courts jurisdiction over this kind of dispute, since the neutral principles approach "has been used primarily for disputes over ownership of church property."

§ 2-01.5 — Civil Court Review of Clergy Selection Disputes — Limited Exceptions to the General Rule

Key point 2-01.5. A minority of courts are willing to review the selection of ministers in limited circumstances so long as they can do so without any inquiry into religious doctrine.

A few courts have been willing to resolve controversies involving the selection of clergy not involving religious discipline, faith, rule, custom, or law. For example, a minister may have been elected at a meeting which was not properly called. Some courts have concluded that there is no legitimate basis, constitutional or otherwise, for a civil court to refrain from resolving such a dispute. The Supreme Court has observed that the civil courts need not stay their hand in every case involving a church dispute, since "not every civil court decision jeopardizes values protected by the first amendment."[22] Further, the Supreme Court's recognition that churches have a constitutionally protected right to select clergy only pertains to instances "where no improper methods of choice are proven."[23] Accordingly, a number of courts have intervened in church disputes involving the selection of a minister if there has been an allegation of "improper methods of choice."

To illustrate, the constitution of a Lutheran church provided that "the candidate receiving the majority of all votes cast shall, *upon unanimous approval*, be declared elected." The church convened a congregational meeting to vote on a pastoral candidate, and the candidate received a majority of the votes cast (but not "unanimous approval"). The candidate was subsequently employed, and a group of dissidents filed a lawsuit in which they asked a civil court to enforce the church's constitutional requirement of "unanimous approval." While noting that the first amendment prohibits a court "from entangling itself in matters of church doctrine or practice," the court concluded that it could resolve controversies, such as this one, involving the interpretation "of an ambiguous provision in what amounts to a contract between the members of the congregation, dealing with a purely procedural question" and involving "no ecclesiastical or doctrinal issues." The court also noted that it found no "dispute resolution process" within the denomination to which it could defer.[24] Most courts define "doctrinal" issues broadly, thereby reducing considerably the number of clergy selection disputes they are willing to review.

Example. A minister of the African Methodist Episcopal Church (A.M.E. Church) filed a lawsuit claiming that his bishop failed to honor a promise to appoint him to a particular church. The minister claimed that when other ministers became aware that the bishop was going to appoint him as pastor of the church, they contacted the bishop and persuaded him not to follow through on his promise. The minister sued the other ministers for interfering with a contract, and the bishop for breaking his prom-

---

[21] *Id.* at 1065.

[22] Presbyterian Church in the United States v. Mary Elizabeth Blue Hull Memorial Presbyterian Church, 393 U.S. 440, 449 (1969).

[23] *See* note 12, *supra*, and accompanying text.

[24] Organization for Preserving the Constitution of Zion Lutheran Church v. Mason, 743 P.2d 848 (Wash. App. 1987).

ise. An Arkansas state appeals court noted that "it is not unconstitutional for civil courts to resolve legal disputes involving a church or minister so long as the court is not required to interpret church doctrine to render a decision." The minister claimed that he was asking a civil court to render a decision on the merits of his case without consulting A.M.E. doctrine or polity. The court concluded that it could not resolve the minister's claim against the bishop without consulting church doctrine: "It is impossible to decide the [claim against the bishop] without inquiring in to A.M.E. Church doctrine and polity and drawing conclusions as to what those doctrines provide. In order to [prevail the minister] must prove reasonable reliance on the alleged promise of [the bishop] to appoint him to the pastorship of [the church]. This necessarily requires inquiry into A.M.E. Church doctrine and polity to determine whether it is reasonable to rely on the promise of an A.M.E. Church bishop that he is going to appoint one to a specific pastorship. This requires the court to determine whether church doctrine gives bishops authority to promise appointments. Such an inquiry is impermissible under the first amendment."[25]

The general rule of judicial non-intervention in clergy selection disputes, and the limited exceptions, may be summarized as follows:

General rule. A church's right to select clergy is a constitutional right of the highest order. Accordingly, the civil courts generally will not resolve controversies regarding the selection of clergy.

Limited exceptions to the general rule. Some courts have created the following exceptions to the general rule:

(1) Violation of civil rights. Church decisions regarding the selection of clergy may be reviewed if a fundamental civil right is implicated that outweighs a church's constitutionally protected right to select clergy. At this time, no case has arisen that has presented a civil right of sufficient importance to outweigh a church's right to choose clergy free from judicial scrutiny. However, one court suggested that violation of the criminal law in some cases might present such a case. The right to be free from discrimination based on race, sex, and age—while of paramount importance—does not outweigh a church's right to select clergy in the manner it chooses.

(2) Contracts. Churches will be legally bound by their oral and written contracts. As a result, controversies regarding the selection of clergy may be reviewed by the civil courts if a contract right is involved. The Supreme Court has ruled that the courts may review contracts governing "the manner in which churches own property, *hire employees,* or purchase goods."[26] However, the mere assertion of a "breach of contract" will not be sufficient to trigger civil court review.[27]

(3) Nondoctrinal "procedural" disputes. A few courts have ruled that they have authority to resolve controversies involving the selection of clergy if there is a purely procedural dispute not involving religious discipline, faith, rule, custom, or law. An example would be an ambiguous provision in a church's bylaws concerning the notice to be given for a church business meeting at which a minister is selected. The United States Supreme Court seemed to sanction this exception when it noted that a church's constitutionally protected right to select clergy only pertains to instances "where no improper methods of choice are proven."[28]

---

[25] Belin v. West, 864 S.W.2d 838 (Ark. 1993).

[26] Jones v. Wolf, 443 U.S. 595, 606 (1979) (emphasis added).

[27] *See, e.g.,* Williams v. Palmer, 532 N.E.2d 1061 (Ill. App. 1988) (court refused to hear case despite pastor's claim of "breach of contract" and "interference with contractual relations").

[28] *See* note 12, *supra,* and accompanying text.

(4) Non-clergy staff. The courts are more willing to review controversies involving the selection of non-clergy church staff, since a church's constitutional right to select such employees is less substantial than the right to select clergy.

§ 2-01.6 — Negligent Selection

In recent years many churches and denominational agencies have been sued because of the misconduct of clergy. Many cases have involved sexual misconduct. In most of these cases, liability is based on negligent selection. That is, the church or denominational agency failed to exercise reasonable care in the selection of the minister. To illustrate, church employs a new youth minister without any investigation into his background. Within a few months the minister is charged with child molestation. Only then do church leaders learn that the minister left his previous church because of similar misconduct. The church may be sued on the basis of negligent selection — it failed to exercise reasonable care in the selection of the minister. This important topic is addressed in chapter 10, and more fully in the *Selection and Screening of Ministers* kit that is available from the publisher of this text.

> *Key Resource. Churches must exercise reasonable care in the selection of clergy in order to avoid potential liability based on negligent selection. A resource that will assist any church in the selection of clergy is the Selection and Screening of Ministers kit that is available from the publisher of this text. This kit includes ten application booklets containing key questions and reference forms; ten interview booklets containing nearly 200 additional questions to ask during a personal interview of pastoral candidates; and a helpful 100-page book that explains all of these resources in detail.*

§ 2-02   The Contract

> *Key point 2-02. The relationship between a minister and church is contractual in nature. The contract may be expressed in a signed document, or it may be implied. Either way, there are important legal consequences resulting from the contract.*

1. General Considerations

The relationship between a minister and church is based on contract. One court observed that "one becomes pastor of a church pursuant to a contract, made with the person or body having the authority to employ."[29] Another court noted that "just as a church can contract with persons outside the church membership, it can contract with its own pastor."[30] Often, a contract of employment will be implied between a church and its minister if no written agreement was signed. As one court observed, "[t]he absence of a written contract is completely immaterial; the conduct of the parties clearly indicates an agreement to retain [the] pastor until his dismissal by the church."[31]

Ascertaining when the contract between a minister and a church is created is important, for once a contract exists each party possesses rights which may be protected by law. If, for example, a church agrees to employ a minister, but reverses its decision before the minister begins his or her duties, has a contract been created? If so, the church may be liable for breach of contract. If not, the minister may be without a legal

---

[29] Walker v. Nicholson, 127 S.E.2d 564, 566 (N.C. 1962).
[30] Waters v. Hargest, 593 S.W.2d 364, 365 (Tex. 1979).
[31] Vincent v. Raglin, 318 N.W.2d 629 (Mich. 1982).

remedy. Similarly, is a contract created when a church offers a position to a minister who accepts the appointment, but who later repudiates it? If a contract did exist the church may have legal recourse against the minister for the costs incurred in seeking another minister.

Unfortunately, it is often difficult to ascertain whether or when a contract has been created, because a minister rarely signs a formal contract setting forth all of the terms of employment. Even when a minister and church attempt to execute a written agreement they may do so in a manner that is not legally enforceable. In one case, a church entered into the following contract with a prospective minister:

Section 1. Agreement on Salary. The First Party does hereby agree to pay the Second Party One Hundred Seventy-Five ($175) Dollars per week. All church engagements are counted as part of salary. This is a starting salary.

Section 2. Engagements. The Second Party cannot accept any outside engagements without first getting the approval of the First Party, even if it is a charitable affair.

Section 3. Length of Contract. This contract shall be a one (1) year contract with the option to terminate, if both parties mutually agree. This contract contains the entire agreement between the parties and supersedes any and all other agreements, verbal or written, and the first party shall not be bound by any agreement or representation other than those contained herein.

The church repudiated the agreement before the minister began his duties, and the minister sued the church for breach of contract. The court concluded that

in a contract for the performance of services by one party in consideration of the payment of money by the other party, the nature and character of the services to be performed as well as the place of performance and the amount to be paid must be certain and definite. The contract here contains no description of the nature and character of the services to be performed by the minister or when or where the duties are to be performed. It is so indefinite and vague that it is unenforceable.[32]

On the other hand, if the church's offer is in writing, and sets forth (1) the nature of the services to be performed, (2) compensation to be paid, and (3) the term of employment (which may be indefinite), an enforceable contract ordinarily will be created on the day the minister signs the agreement or mails an acceptance to the church. This assumes, of course, that the church had authority to make the offer and acted in conformity with its governing instrument.[33] On that date, all of the requirements for a valid and enforceable contract exist—an offer and an acceptance, an exchange of mutually beneficial promises, and a lawful purpose.[34] Some courts have ruled that the church or prospective minister may sue to enforce such a contract if the other party defaults, even if the minister never actually began to perform services under the contract. The contract of a minister who accepts the call of a hierarchical church includes all the canons and applicable rules set forth in the organizational documents of the parent hierarchical body.[35]

[32] McTerry v. Free For All Missionary Baptist Church, 200 S.E.2d 915, 916 (Ga. 1973).
[33] Most courts hold that acceptances are valid when deposited in the mail, assuming that the mail is an authorized means of acceptance. A minority of courts insist that actual delivery of the acceptance is necessary before a contract can be created. *See generally* Morrison v. Thoelke, 155 So.2d 889 (Fla. 1963); Reserve Insurance Co. v. Duckett, 238 A.2d 536 (Md. 1968); 1 A. CORBIN, CONTRACTS § 78 (1950 & Supp. 1999).
[34] *See generally* A. CORBIN, CONTRACTS vols. 1, 1A, and 2 (1950 & Supp. 1999).
[35] Olston v. Hollock, 201 N.W.2d 35 (Wis. 1972).

Most courts consider an agreement to work for a certain salary per week, month, or year to be so indefinite as to be terminable at will by either party.[36] A minister who agrees to work for a church for a stated annual salary is therefore not on that basis alone entitled to work for a full year. To illustrate, one church had its pastor sign a contract containing the following provision: "We promise and oblige ourselves . . . while you are dispensing spiritual blessings to us to pay you [a specified sum] yearly and every year so long as you continue the minister of the church . . . ." The minister claimed that this contract was a "contract for life." The court disagreed, noting that "a hiring on the basis of a yearly salary, if no period of employment is otherwise stated, is terminable, without cause, at the election of either employer or employee."[37]

If a valid contract exists between a church and its minister, then either party may be liable for breaching it. However, constitutional protections apply to the relationship between a church and its minister, and this has led most courts to refrain from resolving lawsuits brought by dismissed ministers claiming that their legal rights were violated.[38] Some courts have been willing to resolve such disputes if no inquiry into religious doctrine is required. In such cases it may become necessary to determine the legal remedies available to the dismissed minister. Consider the following illustration:

> **Example.** *Rev. G is hired by a church for a three-year term, and he is terminated by the church board after only one year because of the board's conviction that it can find someone "more effective." The board has no complaint with Rev. G's theology or personal conduct, and it considers his services to be adequate. The board simply feels that it can find someone "better." Rev. G cannot find another position for an extended period of time. He sues the church, seeking to be paid his stated compensation for the remaining two years of the contract term.*

Should a civil court accept such a case? Would the case interfere with the first amendment's guarantees of religious freedom and the nonestablishment of religion? Some courts have concluded that they do have the authority to hear such cases, since no inquiries into church doctrine or practice will be necessary. As one court has observed, the civil courts will involve themselves in a contractual dispute between a church and its pastor only if "the determination of the parties' rights can be accomplished by the application of neutral principles of law without the necessity of adjudicating matters of church doctrine or determining matters of church government in a hierarchical church."[39] Such courts have concluded that clergy who are dismissed prior to the expiration of a stated contract term are entitled to money damages.

Two additional factors must be considered. First, lawsuits brought by ministers who were dismissed prior to the end of the term of employment specified in an employment contract must be filed within the time period specified in the applicable statute of limitations—which begins to run upon the expiration of the contract term.[40] Second, wages not paid under the terminated contract will not necessarily be the measure of damages. The minister has a legal duty to *mitigate* the church's damages by accepting available alternative employment of the same or similar character.[41] If the minister diligently seeks alternative employment of the same or similar character, but none is available, he or she is entitled to sue for the full salary corresponding to the terminated portion of the employment term. If the dismissed minister does not seek other employment, then the church's liability will be reduced by the amount which the minister, with reasonable diligence, might

---

[36] 1 S. WILLISTON, CONTRACTS § 39 (1957 & Supp. 1999).

[37] Bethany Reformed Church v. Hager, 406 N.E.2d 93, 95 (Ill. 1980).

[38] *See* section 2-04, *infra.*

[39] Waters v. Hargest, 593 S.W.2d 364, 365 (Tex. 1979) (rule was mandated by first amendment).

[40] Rosenstock v. Congregation Agudath Achim., 164 S.E.2d 283 (Ga. 1968).

[41] *See generally* Annot., 44 A.L.R.3d 629 (1972).

have earned from other employment during the remaining contract term. If the minister finds work of the same or similar character during the remaining term of employment, then the church's liability will be reduced by the value of the compensation received by the minister from the new employer.

To illustrate, in one case a church discharged a minister who had served only four years of a seven-year term of employment. The discharged minister sued for breach of contract. In attempting to assess the proper monetary damages for breach of contract, the court observed:

> There is evidence . . . to the effect that . . . [the minister] saw . . . the secretary of the Gulf Coast
> Christian churches, and applied for a regular pastorate in some church, and none was available.
> The evidence also shows that [he] was advised that [there were] a number of calls for interim
> pastorates. The evidence is insufficient to show that [he] made any effort to obtain employment
> in any of such interim pastorates and it is difficult to ascertain from the record just what diligence
> [he] exercised to obtain employment. There is nothing in the record to the effect that [he] would
> not be able to obtain employment from the date the case went to trial to the time the contract
> would expire but for the wrongful termination thereof.[42]

Remedies other than money damages for breach of contract occasionally are recognized by the courts. One minister, who was physically ejected from his church by armed security guards hired by church trustees, was awarded injunctive relief prohibiting the trustees from interfering with his ministerial duties, and also received an award of monetary damages against the trustees and the security guards.[43] However, other courts have ruled that a wrongfully discharged minister may not sue to restrain his church from "breaching and terminating the contract." The appropriate remedy is a suit for breach of contract.[44]

The church, as an employer, has the right to dismiss a minister before the expiration of a specified term of office under either of two theories. First, a minister can be dismissed for committing a specific ground for dismissal specified in an employment contract or in the church's governing instrument. A church should not discharge a minister for misconduct without credible and convincing evidence. Churches should avoid the use of vague terminology in reciting the grounds for termination of employment in employment contracts or in the church's governing instrument. Terms such as *dishonesty, immorality, incompetence, inefficiency,* and *unbecoming conduct* should be avoided. The grounds should be stated with sufficient clarity that neither the minister nor the church will be in doubt as to their meaning. Some churches include a provision in their governing instrument specifying that the church's governing board will have the sole discretion to determine whether grounds for dismissal have occurred. This is a good practice, and it is likely one that the civil courts will honor.

Second, a church ordinarily may dismiss a minister prior to the expiration of a specified term of employment if the minister violates an implied condition of employment. Implied conditions of employment are not stated in the contract, but are reasonable inferences of the parties' unexpressed intentions and assumptions. One court has observed:

> The law implies a stipulation or undertaking by an employee in entering into a contract of employment
> that he is competent to perform the work undertaken and is possessed of the requisite skill and knowl-
> edge to enable him to do so, and that he will do the work of the employer in a careful manner. If he is

---

[42] Mayhew v. Vanway, 371 S.W.2d 90, 94 (Tex. 1963).
[43] Vincent v. Raglin, 318 N.W.2d 629 (Mich. 1982) (the trustees did not have authority to terminate the minister's services).
[44] *See, e.g.,* Bennett v. Belton, 436 S.W.2d 161 (Tex. 1968).

not qualified to do the work which he undertakes, if he is incompetent, unskillful or inefficient, or if he executes his work in a negligent manner or is otherwise guilty of neglect of duty, he may be lawfully discharged before the expiration of his term of employment.[45]

The courts have also held that an incapacitating illness of long duration or an intervening mental incapacity may also be sufficient grounds for termination of an employment contract before its expiration.[46]

It is not only the church that can breach an employment contract; a minister may as well. Again, the most frequent example is repudiation of the employer-employee relationship without justification prior to the expiration of a specified employment term. In such a case the church may be allowed to sue the former minister for the cost of obtaining the services of another minister, plus any other damages resulting directly from the minister's repudiation of the contract, provided that such damages were foreseeable at the time the contract was entered into.[47] Obviously, such cases are rare.

An employment contract, like any contract, may be rescinded where one party fraudulently induced the innocent party to enter into the contract. In one case, a synagogue sought to rescind a contract with a rabbi on the ground that it had been defrauded by the rabbi's failure to disclose a criminal record and disbarment as an attorney. The court, in holding in favor of the synagogue, observed:

> Arrangements between a pastor and his congregation are matters of contract subject to enforcement in the civil courts. Contracts in general are subject to rescission when they are obtained by fraud. . . . Legal fraud consists of a material misrepresentation of a presently existing or past fact made with knowledge of its falsity, with the intention that the other party rely thereon, and he does so rely to his damage.[48]

The court concluded that "a prior criminal record and disbarment from the practice of law must be disclosed by one seeking a rabbinical post involving the spiritual, religious and educational leadership of a religious congregation."

2. Clergy Employment Contract Checklist

What terms should be included in a minister's contract of employment? This will depend on the circumstances of each case. However, ministers and church boards should consider the following elements in structuring a minister's employment contract:

• *Names.* Legal names of each party.

• *Signatures of each party.* If the church is incorporated, then its president and secretary ordinarily are authorized to sign contracts on behalf of the church (they should be sure to sign in a representative capacity, indicating that they are signing on behalf of the church). If the church is unincorporated, state law will determine who should sign on behalf of the church. In some states, duly elected or appointed trustees may sign contracts on behalf of the church.

---

[45] Seco Chemicals, Inc. v. Stewart, 349 N.E.2d 733, 738-39 (Ind. 1976).
[46] Fisher v. Church of St. Mary, 497 P.2d 882 (Wyo. 1972).
[47] *See generally* Annot., 61 A.L.R.2d 1008 (1958 & Supp. 1999).
[48] Jewish Center v. Whale, 397 A.2d 712 (N.J. 1978), *aff'd*, 411 A.2d 475 (1980).

• *Characterize the minister as an employee or self-employed.* If self-employed, it would be helpful to cite the basis for this conclusion.

• *Job description.* Clergy are entitled to know what is expected of them and what is not. Many conflicts between ministers and church boards or congregations are based on differing assumptions as to the minister's responsibilities. These conflicts can be eliminated by a properly drafted job description.

• *Term.* State the term of employment and conditions for renewal. In some cases the term will be indefinite.

• *Discipline or dismissal.* Grounds for discipline or dismissal should be specified, as should any procedure that must be followed. This often is addressed in the bylaws of either the local church or a denominational agency. If so, it need not be mentioned in an employment contract.

Tip. It is advisable for the contract to state that it incorporates the provisions of the church's bylaws or other governing document.

• *Arbitration.* Churches and ministers should consider an arbitration clause committing them to use arbitration rather than the civil courts to resolve disputes.

• *Compensation.* Define the compensation of the minister. This is an important feature in any employment contract. A full discussion of this important issue, including salary surveys and several components of a compensation package, is contained in a companion text.[49]

§ 2-03   Compensation

Key point 2-03. Clergy compensation consists of a number of items that often are not well understood. Clergy compensation that is unreasonable in amount may jeopardize a church's tax-exempt status or trigger "intermediate sanctions" in the form of excise taxes that can be assessed against a recipient of unreasonable compensation.

There are four aspects to clergy compensation that should be understood by church leaders: (1) the definition of compensation; (2) the concept of reasonable compensation; (3) legal entitlement; and (4) compensation planning and strategies. Each of these four topics is addressed below.

Resources. The definition of compensation and the compensation planning are addressed fully in the following two companion resources—the annual Church and Clergy Tax Guide and the annual Compensation Handbook for Church Staff. You can obtain both resources from the publisher of this text.

1. DEFINITION OF COMPENSATION

It is important for church leaders to have a clear understanding of the definition of compensation. Such a definition is needed both for compensation planning and for income tax reporting. Unfortunately, many church leaders do not have a good understanding of this important term. A full analysis of the definition of clergy compensation is contained in a companion text.[50]

---

[49] *See* J. COBBLE AND R. HAMMAR, CHURCH COMPENSATION HANDBOOK (published annually by the publisher of this text).
[50] *See* R. HAMMAR, CHURCH AND CLERGY TAX GUIDE chapter 4 (published annually by the publisher of this text).

2. REASONABLE COMPENSATION

One of the conditions a church must meet in order to qualify for exemption from federal income taxes is that no part of its net earnings may "inure to the benefit of any private . . . individual."[51] The courts have held that although payment of "reasonable compensation" by a tax-exempt organization to its employees does not constitute the inurement of net earnings to the benefit of a private individual, the payment of unreasonably high salaries does.[52] As a result, church leaders should be familiar with the concept of reasonable compensation. A companion text defines this term in the context of current income tax regulations, IRS rulings, and court decisions.[53]

Few churches and other charities have lost their tax-exempt status because of the payment of unreasonable compensation. The IRS has been unwilling to impose so harsh a penalty upon an entire organization because a single individual receives excessive compensation. In 1996 Congress responded to this dilemma by giving the IRS authority to impose "intermediate sanctions" on individuals who receive excessive compensation from a charity. These sanctions are excise taxes that are levied against the recipient of the excessive compensation. In some cases the IRS can even impose sanctions against board members who authorized excessive compensation. Intermediate sanctions are discussed fully in a companion text.[54]

3. LEGAL ENTITLEMENT

A minister who works for a church without a written contract or with a contract that does not specify the compensation to be paid is entitled to receive reasonable compensation for services performed. If a church and its minister enter into a contract specifying the compensation to be paid, the minister is legally entitled to receive that compensation. One court has stated: "[T]he question of liability for the salary of a minister or pastor is governed by the principles which prevail in the law of contracts, and it is generally held that a valid contract for the payment of such a salary will be enforced."[55] As a result, if a church fails to pay a minister the full compensation specified in a written contract, the minister may be able to sue for breach of contract.

If the salary specified by contract is reduced by action of a church, the minister may immediately sue for breach of contract. But a minister who consents to a reduction in compensation will not be allowed to recover the loss.

Example. A church was unable to pay its minister the full salary specified by contract because of financial difficulties. The church and its minister mutually agreed to reduce the stated salary by nearly fifty percent. A court ruled that the minister could not later sue for the difference.[56]

Example. A minister waived full payment of his compensation by consenting to church budgets that reduced his salary, by voting for resolutions reducing his salary, and by returning a check to his church. A court ruled that he could not later recover the difference.[57]

---

[51] I.R.C. § 501(c)(3).

[52] *See, e.g.,* Harding Hospital, Inc. v. United States, 505 F.2d 1068 (6th Cir. 1974); Mabee Petroleum Corp. v. United States, 203 F.2d 872 (5th Cir. 1953).

[53] *See* R. HAMMAR, CHURCH AND CLERGY TAX GUIDE chapter 4 (published annually by the publisher of this text).

[54] *Id.*

[55] Way v. Ramsey, 135 S.E. 454, 455 (N.C. 1926).

[56] Norton v. Normal Park Presbyterian Church, 47 N.E.2d 526 (Ill. 1943).

[57] James v. Christ Church Parish, 185 P.2d 984 (Wash. 1947) (but as to later years, court held minister had not waived payment of contractual salary).

Example. The United States Tax Court denied a charitable contribution deduction to a minister for the portion of his church salary that he voluntarily canceled.[58]

The civil courts have been willing to resolve lawsuits by ministers for unpaid compensation despite a church's claim that such a controversy is purely ecclesiastical. In one case, a Catholic priest sued his diocese for wrongfully withholding his salary. The diocese maintained that the civil courts could not entertain suits involving the administration of church affairs and the relationship of a church to its minister, even with respect to salary, since these are matters of purely ecclesiastical concern. The court disagreed:

> It was not the intent of [the first amendment] and it has been so held in many cases, that civil and property rights should be unenforceable in the civil courts simply because the parties involved might be the church and members, officers, or the ministry of the church. It was not intended as a shield to payment of a just debt when the purpose of the first amendment is not being violated. Ministers have been awarded their salary in suits against the church.[59]

However, the courts also have ruled that they have no authority to review claims by clergy that their compensation is too low. To illustrate, a federal appeals court refused to resolve a lawsuit by Catholic priests who taught at a Catholic university and who claimed that the university's salary scale discriminated against them.[60] The court observed that "the salary scale for priests in a church-related institution clearly appears to be an internal matter of the religious institution affected. In other contexts, courts have traditionally refused to become involved in the resolution of internal religious questions."

Compensation paid to a minister must be in the amounts authorized by appropriate action. If a church authorizes a specified salary, and the church treasurer pays the minister an amount in excess of the authorized salary, the minister will have to account for the difference.[61]

If a minister receives cash gifts directly from church members, such gifts do not represent church compensation and do not reduce the church's obligation to pay a stated salary.[62]

One court has ruled that a minister could not sue the trustees of an unincorporated church to recover an unpaid salary since the trustees could not be personally liable.[63]

Ministers should scrupulously avoid any diversion of church funds to their own personal benefit in excess of their agreed upon compensation. Ministers should also avoid "commingling" their own funds with church assets. Diversions of church funds by clergy to their personal benefit have resulted in (1) a charge of embezzlement and fraudulent conversion;[64] (2) a tax fraud conviction for failure to report interest earned on an alleged "church account" that was used essentially for a minister's personal benefit;[65] and (3) the placing of a church in receivership by order of a state attorney general to prevent further diversion of church funds.[66]

---

[58] Winston v. Commissioner, 48 T.C.M. 55 (1984).

[59] Bodewes v. Zuroweste, 303 N.E.2d 509, 511 (Ill. 1973).

[60] Granfield v. Catholic University of America, 530 F.2d 1035 (D.C. Cir. 1976).

[61] Harrison v. Floyd, 97 A.2d 761 (N.J. 1953).

[62] *Id.*

[63] McCall v. Capers, 105 S.W.2d 323 (Tex. 1937).

[64] Commonwealth v. Nichols, 213 A.2d 105 (Pa. 1965).

[65] United States v. Moon, 718 F.2d 1210 (2nd Cir. 1983).

[66] Worldwide Church of God, Inc. v. California, 623 F.2d 613 (9th Cir. 1980). *See generally* section 4-09, *infra*; Comment, 73 J. Crim. L. & Criminol. 1204 (1982); Note, 53 So. Cal. L. Rev. 1277 (1980); Note, 6 West. St. L. Rev. 269 (1979).

4. Compensation Planning and Strategies

Clergy compensation planning is an important task that involves a consideration of several factors. A full analysis of clergy compensation planning, along with comprehensive survey data, is contained in a companion text.[67]

§2-04 Termination

Ministers may face termination in two ways. First, their employment with a local church may be terminated; and second, their ministerial credentials may be terminated by the church or denomination that issued them. A number of ministers have challenged their termination in court, usually on the basis of one or more of the following grounds:

(1) no act specified as a ground for dismissal in the employment contract or in church or denominational bylaws occurred

(2) the church or denomination failed to follow the procedure prescribed in its bylaws

(3) violation of a civil or property right

(4) breach of the employment contract

(5) emotional distress

(6) defamation

(7) fraud or collusion

Most courts have refused to review such claims, although some courts have agreed to do so in limited circumstances. Both views are summarized below.

§ 2-04.1 — Civil Court Review of Clergy Termination Disputes — the General Rule of Non-Intervention

Key point 2-04.1. Most courts have concluded that they are barred by the first amendment guarantees of religious freedom and nonestablishment of religion from resolving challenges by dismissed clergy to the legal validity of their dismissals.

1. Supreme Court Decisions

In the landmark case of *Watson v. Jones*,[68] the United States Supreme Court cited three grounds supporting the general rule of judicial nonintervention in clergy termination cases. First, the Court based the rule on the "implied consent" of church members to the exclusive jurisdiction of their church:

---

[67] *See* J. Cobble and R. Hammar, Church Compensation Handbook (published annually by the publisher of this text).

[68] 80 U.S. 679, 722 (1871) [hereinafter cited as *Watson*]. *See also* Bernard, *Churches, Members, and the Role of the Courts: Toward a Contractual Analysis*, 51 Notre Dame Lawyer 545 (1976); Dusenberg, *Jurisdiction of Civil Courts over Religious Issues*, 20 Ohio St. L.J.

All who unite themselves to such a body do so with an implied consent to its government, and are bound to submit to it. But *it would be a vain consent and would lead to the total subversion of such religious bodies, if anyone aggrieved by one of their decisions could appeal to the secular courts and have them reversed.* It is of the essence of these religious unions, and of their right to establish tribunals for the decision of questions arising among themselves, that those decisions should be binding in all cases of ecclesiastical cognizance subject only to such appeals as the organism itself provides for.[69]

Second, the Supreme Court suggested that the general rule of judicial nonintervention is based on the first amendment's religion clauses:

But it is a very different thing where a subject matter of dispute, strictly and purely ecclesiastical in its character—a matter over which the civil courts exercise no jurisdiction, *a matter which concerns theological controversy, church discipline, ecclesiastical government, or the conformity of the members of the church to the standards of morals required of them*—becomes the subject of its action. It may be said here, also, that *no jurisdiction has been conferred upon the tribunal* to try the particular case before it, or that, in its judgment, it exceeds the powers conferred upon it, or that the laws of the church do not authorize the particular form of proceeding adopted; and, in a sense often used in the courts, all of those may be said to be questions of jurisdiction. But it is easy to see that if the civil courts are to inquire into all these matters, the whole subject of doctrinal theology, the usages and customs, the written laws, and fundamental organization of every religious denomination may, and must, be examined into with minuteness and care, for they would become, in almost every case, the criteria by which the validity of the ecclesiastical decree would be determined in the civil court. This principle would deprive these bodies of the right of construing their own church laws . . . and would, in effect, transfer to the civil courts where property rights were concerned the decision of all ecclesiastical questions.[70]

Third, the Supreme Court noted that churches are much more qualified to resolve their own disputes (many of which turn on questions of doctrine and practice) than the civil courts:

Nor do we see that justice would be likely to be promoted by submitting those decisions to review in the ordinary judicial tribunals. Each of these large influential bodies . . . has a body of constitutional and ecclesiastical law of its own, to be found in their written organic laws, their books of discipline, in their collections of precedents, in their usage and customs, which to each constitute a system of ecclesiastical law and religious faith that tasks the ablest minds to become familiar with. It is not to be supposed that the judges of the civil courts can be as competent in the ecclesiastical law and religious faith of all these bodies as the ablest men in each are in reference to their own. It would therefore be an appeal from the more learned tribunal in the law which should decide the case, to one which is less so.[71]

---

508 (1959); Ellman, *Driven from the Tribunal: Judicial Resolution of Internal Church Disputes*, 69 CAL. L. REV. 1380 (1981); C. Esbeck, *Tort Claims Against Churches and Ecclesiastical Officers: The First Amendment Considerations*, 89 W. VA. L. REV. 22-23 (1986); Gilkey, *The Judicial Role in Intra-Church Disputes Under the Constitutional Guarantees Relating to Religion*, 75 W. VA. L. REV. 105 (1972); Patton, *The Civil Courts and the Churches*, 54 U. PA. L. REV. 391 (1906); Young and Tigges, *Into the Religious Thicket—Constitutional Limits on Civil Court Jurisdiction over Ecclesiastical Disputes*, 47 OHIO ST. L.J. 475 (1986).

[69] 80 U.S. (13 Wall.) 679, 729 (1871) (emphasis added).

[70] *Id.* (emphasis added). *See also* Kedroff v. St. Nicholas Cathedral, 344 U.S. 94 (1952) in which the Supreme Court observed that "[f]reedom to select clergy, where no improper methods of choice are proven, we think, must now be said to have federal constitutional protection as a part of the free exercise of religion against state interference."

[71] Watson v. Jones, 80 U.S. (13 Wall.) 679 (1872).

Similarly, the Supreme Court observed:

> The decisions of ecclesiastical courts, like every other judicial tribunal, are final, as *they are the best judges of what constitutes an offense against the word of God and the discipline of the church*. Any other than those courts must be incompetent judges of matters of faith, discipline, and doctrine; and civil courts, if they should be so unwise as to attempt to supervise their judgments on matters which come within their jurisdiction would only involve themselves in a sea of uncertainty and doubt which would do anything but improve either religion or good morals.[72]

In a 1928 case involving the authority of an ecclesiastical organization to discipline a minister, the United States Supreme Court observed:

> Because the appointment is a canonical act, it is the function of the church authorities to determine what the essential qualifications of a [clergyman] are and whether the candidate possesses them. In the absence of fraud, collusion, or arbitrariness, the decisions of the proper church tribunals on matters purely ecclesiastical, although affecting civil rights, are accepted in litigation before the secular courts as conclusive, because the parties . . . made them so by contract or otherwise.[73]

The Court's ruling in *Gonzalez* is significant, for it is a specific prohibition of civil court interference in the determinations of ecclesiastical bodies regarding the qualifications of clergy—*even if "civil rights" are involved*—absent fraud, collusion, or arbitrariness. As will be noted later, the Supreme Court subsequently eliminated arbitrariness and severely limited fraud and collusion as available grounds for civil court review.

In 1952, the Supreme Court in the *Kedroff* ruling[74] reaffirmed its pronouncement in *Watson* that civil courts have no authority to resolve "*questions of discipline, or of faith, or of ecclesiastical rule, custom, or law.*" The Court, referring to the *Watson* case, observed that "the opinion radiates, however, a spirit of freedom for religious organizations, and independence from secular control or manipulation, in short, *power to decide for themselves, free from state interference, matters of church government as well as those of faith and doctrine.* Freedom to select the clergy . . . we think must now be said to have federal constitutional protection as a part of the free exercise of religion against state interference." Significantly, the Court also observed:

> There are occasions when civil courts must draw lines between the responsibilities of church and state for the disposition or use of property. *Even in those cases when the property right follows as an incident from decisions of the church custom or law on ecclesiastical issues, the church rule controls.* This under our Constitution necessarily follows in order that there may be free exercise of religion.[75]

The *Kedroff* decision is important since it specifically holds that alleged deprivations or interference with "property rights" cannot serve as a basis for civil court review of ecclesiastical determinations regarding the qualifications or dismissal of clergy where "the property right follows as an incident from decisions of the church . . . on ecclesiastical issues." This important language should be read together with the Court's statement in the *Gonzalez* case that "the decisions of the proper church tribunals [on matters regarding the qualifications of clergy], *although affecting civil rights,* are accepted in litigation before the secular courts as conclu-

---

[72] *Id.* (emphasis added).
[73] Gonzalez v. Roman Catholic Archbishop, 280 U.S. 1, 16-17 (1928) (Justice Brandeis) (emphasis added) [hereinafter cited as *Gonzalez*].
[74] 344 U.S. 94 (1952).
[75] *Id.* at 120 (emphasis added).

sive," except under extraordinary circumstances described below. These two rulings indicate that dismissed clergy will not be able to have their dismissals reviewed by the civil courts merely because they claim that their civil or property rights have been violated.

In 1976, the Supreme Court addressed the legal right of a defrocked bishop to challenge his expulsion in civil court.[76] The Illinois Supreme Court, citing *Gonzalez*,[77] had reversed a decision of the Serbian Eastern Orthodox Diocese expelling the bishop. The court reasoned that the Diocese had not followed its own bylaws and accordingly its decision to expel was "arbitrary" and, on the basis of *Gonzalez*, subject to civil court review. In reversing the Illinois Supreme Court's ruling, the United States Supreme Court observed:

> The conclusion of the Illinois Supreme Court that the decisions of the [Diocese] were "arbitrary" was grounded upon an inquiry that persuaded the Illinois Supreme Court that the [Diocese] had not followed its own laws and procedures in arriving at those decisions. We have concluded that whether or not there is room for "marginal civil court review" under the narrow rubrics of "fraud" or "collusion" when church tribunals act in bad faith for secular purposes, no "arbitrariness" exception—in the sense of an inquiry whether the decisions of the highest ecclesiastical tribunal of a hierarchical church complied with church laws and regulations—is consistent with the constitutional mandate that civil courts are bound to accept the decisions of the highest judicatories of a religious organization of hierarchical polity on matters of discipline, faith, internal organization, or ecclesiastical rule, custom or law. For civil courts to analyze whether the ecclesiastical actions of a church judicatory are in that sense "arbitrary" must inherently entail inquiry into the procedures that canon or ecclesiastical law supposedly require the church adjudicatory to follow, or else into the substantive criteria by which they are supposedly to decide the ecclesiastical question. But this is exactly the inquiry that the first amendment prohibits . . . .[78]

The Supreme Court rejected an attempt by a defrocked bishop to force civil court review on the basis of an alleged deprivation of a "property right," since the alleged property right was incidental to the underlying issue of ecclesiastical discipline and "the civil courts must accept that consequence as the incidental effect of an ecclesiastical determination that is not subject to judicial abrogation, having been reached by the final church judicatory in which authority to make that decision resides."

Serbian is significant for the following reasons: (1) it reaffirmed the rule of judicial nonintervention in cases of ecclesiastical discipline over which an ecclesiastical organization has jurisdiction; (2) it rejected the claim that civil courts can justify intervention in cases of ecclesiastical discipline on the basis of alleged deprivation of "property rights," if the alleged deprivation is a mere incidental effect of the underlying disciplinary process; and (3) it categorically rejected civil court review of ecclesiastical disciplinary proceedings on the basis of "arbitrariness," and *defined arbitrariness as a failure by a church to follow its own rules and procedures.*

The Court based these conclusions on the following grounds: (1) civil courts are forbidden by the first amendment from engaging in "searching inquiry" into the organizational documents of religious organizations; (2) civil judges have no training, experience, or expertise in matters of ecclesiastical law or governance; and (3) "constitutional concepts of due process, involving secular notions of fundamental fairness or impermissible objectives," are not relevant to matters of ecclesiastical cognizance which typically "are reached and are to be accepted as matters of faith whether or not rational or measurable by objective criteria."

---

[76] Serbian Eastern Orthodox Diocese v. Milivojevich, 423 U.S. 696 (1976) [hereinafter cited as *Serbian*].
[77] *See* note 73, *supra*, and accompanying text.
[78] *Id.* at 712-713.

In summary, the United States Supreme Court over the past century has consistently held that the civil courts are prohibited from interfering in ecclesiastical controversies involving the termination of clergy. This is so even if an ecclesiastical determination results in an alleged deprivation of property, contract, or civil rights, and even if the ecclesiastical process was arbitrary in the sense that it was not in accordance with the church organization's own internal rules and procedures. While the Supreme Court has repudiated its 1928 ruling in *Gonzalez* to the extent that "arbitrariness" is no longer an available basis for civil court review of ecclesiastical determinations, it has left open "fraud" and "collusion" as possible grounds for review. However, the Court in *Serbian* severely limited the availability of "fraud and collusion" as grounds for civil court review by limiting their use to those occasions "when church tribunals act in bad faith for secular purposes." The mere assertion of fraud or collusion thus cannot invoke civil court review of ecclesiastical determinations regarding church discipline. A plaintiff also must establish that the alleged fraud or collusion was motivated by "bad faith for secular purposes." It would be extraordinary indeed to ever find a religious organization guilty of such conduct, and, understandably, none has ever been found to be so. The Supreme Court in *United States v. Ballard*,[79] anticipating the *Serbian* limitation, specifically held that frauds perpetrated by religious organizations are not redressable by the civil courts when matters of "religious faith or experience" are involved or implicated. The Court observed:

> Men may believe what they cannot prove. They may not be put to the proof of their religious doctrines or beliefs. Religious experiences which are as real as life to some may be incomprehensible to others. Yet the fact that they may be beyond the ken of mortals does not mean that they can be made suspect before the law. Many take their gospel from the New Testament. But it would hardly be supposed that they could be tried before a jury charged with the duty of determining whether those teachings contained false representations. The miracles of the New Testament, the Divinity of Christ, life after death, the power of prayer, are deep in the religious convictions of many. If one could be sent to jail because a jury in a hostile environment found those teachings false, little indeed would be left of religious freedom.[80]

Similarly, no court has ever found an ecclesiastical organization guilty of the *Serbian* definition of "collusion."

2. Selected Federal and State Court Decisions

The vast majority of lower federal courts and state courts[81] have followed the general rule of judicial

---

[79] 322 U.S. 78 (1944).

[80] *Id.* at 86-87.

[81] *See, e.g.,* First Baptist Church of Hope Hull v. Owens, 474 So.2d 638 (Ala. 1985); Foster v. St. John's Baptist Church, 406 So.2d 389 (Ala. 1981); Putman v. Vath, 340 So.2d 26 (Ala. 1976); In re Galilee Baptist Church, 186 So.2d 102 (Ala. 1966); Williams v. Cupp, 597 S.W.2d 855 (Ark. App. 1980); West v. Morris, 711 A.2d 1269 (D.C. 1998); United Methodist Church v. White, 571 A.2d 790 (D.C. App. 1990); Hemphill v. Zion Hope Primitive Baptist Church, 447 So.2d 976 (Fla. App. 1984); Covington v. Bowers, 442 So.2d 1068 (Fla. App. 1983); Epperson v. Myers, 58 So.2d 150 (Fla. 1952); Sanders v. Edwards, 34 S.E.2d 167 (Ga. 1945); Stony Island Church of Christ v. Stephens, 369 N.E.2d 1313 (Ill. App. 1977); Hatfield v. De Long, 59 N.E. 483 (Ind. 1901) (salary of expelled minister held not to be a property right); State ex rel. Hatfield v. Cummins, 85 N.E.2d 359 (Ind. 1908) (church membership is purely ecclesiastical, not a property or civil right); Ramsey v. Ahicks, 91 N.E. 344 (Ind. 1910) (church membership not a civil or valuable right); Sale v. First Regular Baptist Church, 17 N.W. 143 (Iowa 1883) (expulsion from religious corporation affects no property interest or civil right); Le Blanc v. Davis, 432 So.2d 239 (La. 1983); Quinn v. First Evangelical Baptist Church, 135 So. 753 (La. App. 1931); Sance v. Monroe, 39 So.2d 174 (La. App. 1949); Graffam v. Wray, 437 A.2d 627 (Me. 1981); Beulah Missionary Baptist Church v. Spann, 346 N.W.2d 911 (Mich. App. 1984); Vincent v. Raglin, 318 N.W.2d 629 (Mich. App. 1982); Blauert v. Schupmann, 63 N.W.2d 578 (Minn. 1954); Dees v. Moss Point Baptist Church, 17 So. 1 (Miss. 1895) (excommunication from church involves no property rights); Gray v. Ward, 950 S.W.2d 232 (Mo. 1997); Pounder v. Ashe, 63 N.W. 847 (Nebr. 1895) (church membership not a property right, nor is right to officiate as minister or resulting right to salary); Alicea v. New Brunswick Theological Seminary, 608 A.2d 218 (N.J. 1992) (seminary professor); Chavis v. Rowe, 459 A.2d 674 (N.J. 1983) (court dismissed lawsuit by

noninterference in ecclesiastical disputes involving the dismissal of clergy, and accordingly have ruled that the expulsion of a minister is an ecclesiastical matter that is not reviewable by the civil courts. To illustrate, a federal appeals court has observed that the "civil courts have long taken care not to intermeddle in internal ecclesiastical disputes" and that "it has thus become established that the decisions of religious entities about the appointment and removal of ministers and persons in other positions of similar theological significance are beyond the [ability] of civil courts."[82]

Examples of federal court and state court rulings illustrating this rule are set forth below. The examples are arranged topically on the basis of the various theories terminated ministers have used to invoke civil court review of their terminations.

(1) no act specified as a ground for dismissal in the employment contract or in church or denominational bylaws occurred

> **Example.** *The federal appeals court for the fifth circuit (covers the states of Louisiana, Mississippi, and Texas) dismissed a Methodist pastor's lawsuit arising from his claim that he had been expelled from his parish because of his wife's race. The pastor argued that the court should hear his claim since he was dismissed for reasons unrelated to religious belief or policy. The court ruled that there is no exception to the prohibition against judicial interference with matters of church administration, including the selection or dismissal of clergy. It concluded: "This case involves the fundamental question of who will preach from the pulpit of a church.... The bare statement of the question should make obvious the lack of jurisdiction of a civil court. That answer to that question must come from the church.... The people of the United States conveyed no power to Congress to vest its courts with jurisdiction to settle purely ecclesiastical disputes."[83]*

(2) "arbitrariness" (that is, the church or denomination failed to follow the procedure prescribed in its bylaws)

> **Example.** *A federal court in Michigan ruled that the first amendment prevents the civil courts from reviewing the validity of a religious denomination's dismissal of a minister.[84] A Seventh Day Adventist minister was dismissed by a regional denominational committee. He sued his denomination (the "Church"), alleging breach of contract and intentional infliction of emotional distress. The court granted the Church's request to dismiss the case. The court began its opinion by quoting Acts 18:15: "But if it be a question of words and names, and of your law, look ye to it; for I will be no judge of such matters." It then observed: "It is without question that the executive committee had the authority to terminate [the minister's] employment as a minister. In order to determine whether or not the committee followed its own rules and*

---

defrocked church officer despite claim that his civil, contract, and property rights were violated); Protestant Episcopal Church v. Graves, 391 A.2d 563 (N.J. Super. 1978), *aff'd* 417 A.2d 19 (1979); Waller v. Howell, 45 N.Y.S. 790 (1897) (church membership involves no civil right); Tibbs v. Kendrick, 637 N.E.2d 397 (Ohio App. 8 Dist. 1994) (court applied the rule of judicial nonintervention in clergy termination disputes to an attempt by church members to oust their minister); State v. Meagher, 1997 WL 180266 (Ohio App. 1997) (court applied the rule of judicial nonintervention in clergy termination disputes to an attempt by church members to oust their minister); Knotts v. Williams, 462 S.E.2d 288 (S.C. 1995); Nance v. Busby, 18 S.W. 874 (Tenn. 1892) (expulsion from church affects no pecuniary or civil right); Dean v. Alford, 994 S.W.2d 392 (Tex. App. 1999); Patterson v. Southwestern Baptist Theological Seminary, 858 S.W.2d 602 (Tex. App. 1993) ("the same rule is applicable to congregational systems, in that civil courts, with reference to the determination of matters that are ecclesiastical in nature, are to give deference to those officers in which are vested the authority to make such a determination"); Waters v. Hargest, 593 S.W.2d 364 (Tex. App. 1979); Bennett v. Belton, 436 S.W.2d 161 (Tex. App. 1968).

[82] Bell v. Presbyterian Church, 126 F.3d 328 (4th Cir. 1997).
[83] Simpson v. Wells Lamont Corporation, 494 F.2d 490 (5th Cir. 1974).
[84] Lewis v. Lake Region Conference of Seventh Day Adventists, 779 F. Supp. 72 (E.D. Mich. 1991).

procedures in discharging the [minister], the court would be involved in an inquiry into questions of ecclesiastical rule, custom, and law. [The minister does] not allege fraud or collusion. Consequently, the free exercise clause of the first amendment bars this court's further inquiry into this case."

Example. *The District of Columbia court of appeals ruled that the United Methodist Church could not be sued by a dismissed minister who sought to challenge his dismissal in a civil court.*[85] *The UMC filed a motion to dismiss the ex-minister's lawsuit, but a trial court rejected this motion. This decision was appealed immediately to a court of appeals, which ruled in favor of the UMC. The court of appeals began its opinion with a very important observation—the constitutional guaranty of religious freedom "grants churches an immunity from civil discovery and trial under certain circumstances in order to avoid subjecting religious institutions to defending their religious beliefs and practices in a court of law." Accordingly, a trial court's decision denying a church's claim of immunity from civil liability may be appealed immediately to prevent the church from having to endure a trial that may later be deemed improper. The importance of this conclusion cannot be overstated. Next, the court observed that the "United States Supreme Court has long held that, generally, civil courts are not a constitutionally permissible forum for review of ecclesiastical disputes" involving "matters of discipline, faith, internal organization, or ecclesiastical rule, custom or law." While there are "limited exceptions" to this general rule, no exception applies to disputes involving clergy dismissals. On the contrary, "the right to choose a minister without judicial intervention underlies the well-being of religious community, for perpetuation of a church's existence may depend upon those whom it selects to preach its values, teach its message, and interpret its doctrines both to its own membership and the world at large. Any attempt by the civil courts to limit the church's choice of its religious representatives would constitute an impermissible burden on the church's first amendment rights." Accordingly, the "courts have concluded that employment disputes concerning the status of pastors are inherently ecclesiastical and cannot constitutionally be subject to review." The court also rejected the dismissed minister's claim that his dismissal violated church procedures, since "a secular evaluation of procedures that ecclesiastical or canon law requires the church to follow is precisely the type of inquiry the first amendment prohibits." The court emphasized that churches are "not above the law," and that in some cases they may be legally liable for breaching an employment contract if the contract is in writing and the breach of contract claim can be clearly separated from ecclesiastical considerations.*

Example. *A Florida court ruled that the civil courts have no authority to intervene in a local church dispute involving the removal of a minister and the church's compliance with its own constitution.*[86] *Allegations of misconduct were made against the pastor of a local church. These allegations resulted in a dispute among congregational members regarding the retention of the pastor. The local church council (the governing board of the local church) referred these allegations to a denominational synod for investigation. The pastor filed a lawsuit asking a court to intervene. He claimed that the church council had not followed the church constitution in forwarding allegations of misconduct to the synod. In refusing to resolve the pastor's lawsuit, the court observed: "While the trial court is ordinarily empowered to adjudicate questions of Florida corporate law, a first amendment exception applies to matters of internal governance of a hierarchical religious organization." The court concluded that the pastor's lawsuit in this case "sought to inject the court into the internal governance of the Lutheran Church, a hierarchical religious organization . . . ." The pastor insisted that rulings by the United States Supreme Court required the civil courts to defer to the rulings of hierarchical bodies only if a final decision has*

---

[85] United Methodist Church v. White, 571 A.2d 790 (D.C. App. 1990).

[86] Franzen v. Poulos, 604 So.2d 1260 (Fla. App. 3 Dist. 1992). *Accord* New Mount Moriah Missionary Baptist Church, Inc. v. Dinkins, 708 So.2d 972 (Fla. App. 1998).

been rendered by the highest ecclesiastical authorities of a hierarchical church. The court disagreed: "That is plainly not the case. As the Serbian Eastern Orthodox decision clearly indicates, the judiciary is obliged to defer to the hierarchical church's internal decisional processes on matters of internal church discipline and government."

Example. *A Georgia court ruled that the first amendment guaranty of religious freedom prevented it from resolving a lawsuit brought by a minister challenging the legality of his removal by his church.[87] A church's constitution and bylaws specified that the pastor "shall be called for as long a period of time as mutual satisfaction shall prevail." A pastor was removed from office by a vote of the congregation at an annual membership meeting. The pastor challenged his removal, claiming that it did not conform to the rules set forth in the church constitution and bylaws. The pastor claimed that those rules mandated that the personnel committee or the board of deacons recommend the pastor's discharge to the congregation, which had not been done. A state appeals court affirmed the trial court's dismissal of the case, quoting from an earlier Supreme Court ruling: "Freedom to select the clergy, where no improper methods of choice are proven, we think, must now be said to have federal constitutional protection as a part of the free exercise of religion against state interference." The Georgia court concluded that the trial court "correctly determined that it lacked jurisdiction to consider the matter."*

Example. *A Texas appeals court ruled that a dismissed minister could not sue his denomination for wrongful dismissal. A regional denominational agency charged a minister with immoral conduct.[88] A few days before a scheduled ecclesiastical trial, the denominational agency dismissed the minister and revoked his ordination on the basis of his alleged efforts to intimidate and harass witnesses. The agency concluded that the minister had demonstrated "outrageous and blatant disregard for ethics and Christian principles." The minister sued his former denomination, alleging that it had failed to follow its internal rules in dismissing him and accordingly he had been denied "ecclesiastical due process." The court ruled that it had no jurisdiction to resolve an internal ecclesiastical dispute. It noted that the denomination's decision to dismiss the minister "was a purely ecclesiastical matter," and that the civil courts "are barred from entertaining claims that ecclesiastical procedures were arbitrary and thus violated fundamental due process rights." The court concluded by noting that the minister had been dismissed for his "blatant disregard of ethics and Christian principle," and that "a civil court cannot constitutionally intervene in this dispute because it is exactly the type of intervention the first amendment was designed to prevent."*

(3) violation of a civil, contract, or property right

Example. *The federal court of appeals for the first circuit (covers the states of Maine, Massachusetts, New Hampshire, and Rhode Island), in dismissing a minister's allegations that his termination violated various "contract and property rights," concluded that the first amendment guaranty of religious freedom prevents the civil courts from resolving such lawsuits "however a lawsuit may be labeled."[89] In other words, the fact that a dismissed minister alleges breach of contract, defamation, emotional distress, or similar "secular" theories of liability will not enable the civil courts to resolve what in essence is a dispute between a minister and his or her church or denomination. The court observed: "However a suit may be labeled, once a court is called upon to probe into a religious body's*

---

[87] Bledsoe v. Morningside Baptist Church, 501 S.E.2d 292 (Ga. App. 1998), quoting Kedroff v. St. Nicholas Cathedral, 344 U.S. 94 (1952).

[88] Green v. United Pentecostal Church International, 899 S.W.2d 28 (Tex. App. 1995).

[89] Natal v. Christian and Missionary Alliance, 878 F.2d 1575 (1st Cir. 1989).

selection and retention of clergymen, the first amendment [guaranty of religious freedom] is impli-cated . . . . The relationship between an organized church and its ministers is its lifeblood. The minister is the chief instrument by which the church seeks to fulfill its purpose. Matters touching this relationship must necessarily be recognized as of prime ecclesiastical concern." The court concluded: "At bottom, [the ex-minister's] complaint directly involves, and would require judicial intrusion into, rules, policies, and decisions which are unmistakably of ecclesiastical cognizance. They are, therefore, not the federal courts' concern. . . . The [church's] own internal guidelines and procedures must be allowed to dictate what its obligations to its members are without being subject to court intervention. It is well-settled that religious controversies are not the proper subject of civil court inquiry. Religious bodies must be free to decide for themselves, free from state interference, matters which pertain to church government, faith, and doctrine.[90]

Example. *The federal appeals court for the seventh circuit (covers the states of Illinois, Indiana, and Wisconsin) ruled that a black female could not sue her denomination on the basis of alleged race and sex discrimination for its decision to revoke her ministerial status.*[91] *After several years serving as a proba-tionary minister of the United Methodist Church, a black female applied for a promotion to the posi-tion of "clergy member in full connection" or "elder." A review panel of a Methodist Conference denied her request for a promotion and terminated her employment. The woman filed a lawsuit in federal court alleging that the United Methodist Church denied her promotion and fired her because of her race and sex and because of her opposition to the Church's discriminatory practices. The dismissed Methodist minister insisted that her lawsuit "only involves secular issues and will not require any entanglements over religious issues." The appeals court disagreed. It noted that "civil court review of ecclesiastical decisions of church tribunals, particularly those pertaining to the hiring or firing of clergy, are in themselves an extensive inquiry into religious law and practice, and hence forbidden by the first amendment." The court concluded: "[T]he free exercise [of religion] clause of the first amendment forbids a review of a church's procedures when it makes employment decisions affecting its clergy. . . . To accept [the dismissed minister's] position would require us to cast a blind eye to the overwhelming weight of precedent going back over a century in order to limit the scope of the protection granted to religious bodies by the free exercise clause."*

Example. *The federal appeals court for the eighth circuit (covers the states of Arkansas, Iowa, Minne-sota, Missouri, Nebraska, North Dakota, and South Dakota) ruled that a hospital chaplain could not sue the hospital for alleged age and sex discrimination following her dismissal.*[92] *The former chaplain was an ordained Episcopal priest who had served as chaplain of a church affiliated hospital for ten years. Following her dismissal, the former chaplain sued the hospital on the grounds that her dismissal (1) violated the federal Civil Rights Act of 1964, which prohibits certain employers from dismissing employees on the basis of their sex, and (2) violated the federal Age Discrimination in Employment Act, which bans discrimination in employment against persons 40 years of age and older on account of age. A federal appeals court rejected all of her claims. The court emphasized that the hospital was "without question a religious organization," and that the chaplain position "is primarily a ministerial position." The court concluded: "[W]e believe that the free exercise [of religion] clause of the first amendment also prohibits the courts from deciding cases such as this one. Personnel decisions by church-affiliated insti-tutions affecting clergy are per se religious matters and cannot be reviewed by civil courts, for to review such decisions would require the courts to determine the meaning of religious doctrine and canonical*

---

[90] *Id.* at 1577.
[91] Young v. Northern Illinois Conference of the United Methodist Church, 21 F.3d 184 (7th Cir. 1994).
[92] Scharon v. St. Luke's Episcopal Presbyterian Hospitals, 929 F.2d 360 (8th Cir. 1991).

law and to impose a secular court's view of whether in the context of the particular case religious doctrine and canonical law support the decision the church authorities have made. This is precisely the kind of judicial second-guessing of decision-making by religious organizations that the free exercise [of religion] clause forbids."

Example. *An Arizona court ruled that it was barred by the first amendment from resolving a dispute between a church and a priest concerning the termination of the priest's employment.[93] The court concluded: "[C]ivil courts must abstain from deciding ministerial employment disputes or reviewing decisions of religious judicatory bodies concerning the employment of clergy, because such state intervention would excessively inhibit religious liberty. Accordingly, secular courts will not attempt to right wrongs related to the hiring, firing, discipline or administration of clergy. he first amendment prohibits civil adjudication of [the priest's] breach of contract claim because his claim challenges church decisions involving the hiring and firing of its clergy. Review of [the] contract claims would have involved the trial court in matters of "internal church discipline, faith, and organization."*

Example. *A New Jersey court ruled that it had no authority to resolve a lawsuit brought by a priest against his diocese.[94] A Catholic priest was arrested and charged with several crimes. Two days later, he was suspended from all priestly functions by his bishop. The priest later sued his bishop and diocese, claiming that the bishop had breached a promise to pay for all legal fees incurred in his defense. The court ruled that it had no authority to resolve such a dispute. It acknowledged that "temporal matters of a church affecting civil, contract or property rights may be resolved in civil courts. Thus, secular courts may decide civil disputes between a religious body and its members or its clergy if those disputes involve purely secular issues and can be resolved without entanglement with matters of faith, discipline or doctrine." The priest argued that this was such a case, since the court need only apply neutral principles of contract law to determine whether or not the bishop made a commitment (to pay legal fees) that he did not honor. The court rejected the priest's assessment of the case, noting that it "ignores the relationship between the parties." It observed: "[The priest] relies both on [the bishop's] verbal promise of support and the church's preexisting similar duty. In order to reach the contention that defendants have not honored these obligations, a civil court would necessarily inquire into the nature (religious or secular) of these alleged obligations. This inquiry would, of course, involve a searching and detailed exploration of the doctrine and practice of the Roman Catholic Church in order to determine the existence of such obligations. Civil courts are enjoined from such inquiry by the first amendment . . . . Accordingly, a determination of [the priest's] claims would involve more than simply the secular questions of whether such promises were made and subsequently dishonored." Further, whether or not the bishop had the authority to bind the diocese by his alleged promises is "an ecclesiastical matter, requiring inquiry into the structure of the Roman Catholic Church regarding the relationship between a bishop and his diocese. An agency relationship between a bishop and his diocese may only be determined by reference to church law." In summary, the priest's claims "are replete with ecclesiastical issues, the resolution of which require impermissible court inquiry into the doctrine and practices of the Roman Catholic Church. These entanglements between religious and secular issues compel this court to refrain from exercising jurisdiction over this matter."*

(4) breach of the employment contract

Example. *A federal appeals court for the sixth circuit (covers the states of Kentucky, Michigan, Ohio, and Tennessee) ruled that the first amendment guaranty of religious freedom prevents the civil courts*

---

[93] Dobrota v. Free Serbian Orthodox Church, 952 P.2d 1190 (Ariz. App. 1998).
[94] McElroy v. Guilfoyle, 589 A.2d 1082 (N.J. Super. 1990).

from reviewing the decision of a denominational agency to dismiss a minister.[95] *A Seventh Day Adventist minister was employed by a denominational agency as a minister to a number of churches. Disputes arose between the minister and the agency over a number of issues including the agency's handling of church finances. The agency eventually dismissed the minister. Soon after the dismissal, the minister filed a lawsuit in federal court claiming that the agency was guilty of breach of contract and intentional infliction of emotional distress. The trial court dismissed the lawsuit, and the minister appealed. A federal appeals court upheld the dismissal of the lawsuit. The court observed that "the first amendment bars civil courts from reviewing decisions of religious judicatory bodies relating to the employment of clergy. Even when, as here, [a dismissed minister] alleges that the religious tribunal's decision was based on a misapplication of its own procedures and laws, the civil courts may not intervene." The court rejected the minister's claim that the "highest" church agency had not yet ruled on his dismissal and accordingly the civil courts were not barred from reviewing it. The court observed that this argument, "if upheld, would require a civil court to conduct a review of ecclesiastical law to determine which tribunal is the highest. This is exactly the sort of inquiry that the first amendment forbids."*

Example. *A Georgia court, in refusing to review a dismissed minister's claim that his dismissal constituted a "breach of contract," observed that "[t]he civil courts cannot take jurisdiction of an ecclesiastical issue even if the parties present it for resolution, because the first amendment [guaranty of religious freedom] prohibits such action by the civil judicial system. The entanglement of civil authority into ecclesiastical affairs which is prohibited by our fundamental law and which was one of the promptings of the creation of this nation is evident in this lawsuit. A priest sues his church, bringing into a civil court dispute over his termination as [priest]. He seeks monetary damages representing lost wages, consequential damages, interest and costs, claiming breach of an alleged civilly enforceable contract governing his call."*[96] *The court, in concluding that its resolution of such a dispute would impermissibly entangle it in ecclesiastical matters, noted that "[f]or the court to decide whether a binding civil contract was intended; for the court to construe the meaning of that contract if there is one, or leave to a jury its construction if ambiguity raises questions of fact; for the court or jury to determine whether canons or manual directives control; and most clearly, for a jury to decide whether [grounds existed] which warranted removal of the [priest]; all of these incursions into a religious controversy constitute a large leap beyond the constitutional boundary. Inextricably entangled is whether the priest's performance of his duties as a priest met with the requirements of his church as measured by ecclesiastical concerns."*

Example. *A Methodist minister sued the United Methodist Church claiming that a contractual relationship had been established between himself and the Church by virtue of the Book of Discipline which the minister characterized as the "employment manual" of the Church. He further claimed that the church violated the terms of his "employment contract" by failing to follow its Book of Discipline when it placed him on a forced leave of absence. The minister sought money damages against the Church. The Kentucky Supreme Court noted that decisions by the United States Supreme Court permit civil courts to resolve church property disputes on the basis of "neutral principles of law" (involving inspection of doctrinally neutral language in religious and legal documents). However, the court stressed that the neutral principles approach only applied to church property disputes and "should not be extended to religious controversies in the areas of church government, or order and discipline." The court continued: "This case does not involve a dispute over church property, but relates to [the minister's] status and employment as a minister of the church. It therefore concerns internal church discipline,*

---

[95] Lewis v. Seventh Day Adventists Lake Region Conference, 978 F.2d 940 (6th Cir. 1992).
[96] McDonnell v. Episcopal Diocese of Georgia, 381 S.E.2d 126 (Ga. 1989).

faith, and organization, all of which are governed by ecclesiastical rule, custom and law." The minister argued that the Church's decision to place him on a leave of absence was "arbitrary" in the sense that it was made in violation of the Book of Discipline, and accordingly it was not legally valid. In rejecting this position, the court quoted from the United States Supreme Court's decision in the Serbian case which prohibits clergy from challenging church decisions on the basis of "arbitrariness" (which it defined as a failure by the church to follow its own internal procedures or document). The court acknowledged that the United States Supreme Court has left open the question of whether disciplined clergy can sue their church as a result of decisions that are based on "fraud or collusion." However, the court concluded that there was no basis for intervention on these grounds: "Assuming, without deciding, that review is allowed for fraud or collusion, it is still only allowed for fraud or collusion of the most serious nature undermining the very authority of the decision-making body. Certainly there is no claim or showing of such fraud or collusion here." [97]

Example. *The Iowa Supreme Court dismissed a lawsuit brought by a former minister who claimed that a denominational agency violated his legal rights when it dismissed him. [98] The executive committee of each local "conference" of the Seventh-Day Adventist Church has authority over churches within the conference. This authority includes the right to hire ministers for local churches. The executive committee of the Iowa-Missouri Conference hired a minister who later served in a number of pastoral positions within the conference. A few years later the executive committee voted to terminate the minister's employment. This decision was made without providing the minister with any counseling, and he was given no opportunity to correct any problems associated with his ministry. He unsuccessfully challenged his dismissal within the church. He later filed a lawsuit in civil court, challenging his dismissal on numerous grounds including breach of contract, defamation, and infliction of severe emotional distress. The Iowa Supreme Court refused to resolve the dispute. It concluded: "We believe [the minister's] effectiveness as a minister was the essence of his termination. . . . [A] church's relationship with its ministers implicates internal church discipline, faith, and organization, all of which are governed by ecclesiastical rule, custom and law. The minister is the chief instrument by which the church seeks to fulfill its purpose. Matters touching this relationship must necessarily be recognized as of prime ecclesiastical concern. We agree with those courts that have determined that the first amendment requires secular tribunals to refuse to interfere with a church's relationship with its ministers. Accordingly, we decline to review any aspect of the executive committee's decision to terminate [the minister's] employment . . . ."*

Example. *A Minnesota court ruled that an assistant pastor who was dismissed by his employing church after the congregation voted to eliminate his position for financial reasons could not sue the church for breach of contract. [99] An ordained minister was hired as assistant pastor by a local church and was dismissed a few years later after the congregation voted to eliminate his position. The dismissed pastor sued his church and synod, claiming that he was terminated in retaliation for reporting certain information about the church's senior pastor. The dismissed pastor's contract claims were based on his "letter of call" and provisions of the church constitution regarding termination procedures. The court dismissed the case noting that "the first amendment precludes civil courts from resolving disputes involving churches if a resolution of the disputes cannot be made without extensive inquiry by civil courts into religious law and polity." The court rejected the former pastor's claim that "a pastor's breach of contract claim that does not necessarily entangle the court in matters of church doctrine would not be outside the court's jurisdiction." The court concluded that the former pastor's breach of contract claim is "based on*

---

[97] Music v. United Methodist Church, 864 S.W.2d 286 (Ky. 1993).
[98] Pierce v. Iowa-Missouri Conference of Seventh-Day Adventists, 534 N.W.2d 425 (Iowa 1995).
[99] Olson v. Luther Memorial Church, 1996 WL 70102 (Minn. App. 1996).

the letter of call and the church constitution. Resolution of these issues would require this court to interpret ecclesiastical documents regarding discipline, discharge, and proper expenditure of church funds and thus would be improper under the first amendment."

Example. *A Minnesota court ruled that the first amendment's "nonestablishment of religion" clause prevented it from resolving a dismissed minister's lawsuit against his former church.[100] Church leaders asked for the pastor's resignation as a result of congregational turmoil over theological and administrative issues. While waiting for a response, the church reduced his salary significantly due to financial difficulties. The pastor sued the church, claiming that it breached its contract with him and wrongfully discharged him by violating provisions of the church's constitution and the terms of his call. Specifically, he claimed that the large salary decrease breached his contract and in effect discharged him without following applicable church procedures. He argued that the church did not properly terminate his call because it did not cite any of the reasons for termination described in the church's constitution. The court rejected the pastor's claims: "[The pastor's] claims . . . relate to his appointment and discharge as a pastor and are fundamentally connected to issues of church governance. . . . The church constitution states that the church-pastor relationship can be terminated if the pastor is disqualified on grounds of doctrine, morality, or continued neglect of duty. [The pastor's] call letter discusses his spiritual obligations to the church, including to 'preach and teach the Word of God; to conduct public worship; to administer the sacraments; to provide pastoral care and leadership.' Judicial review of [the pastor's] claims, thus, would require an evaluation of scripture, doctrine, and moral principles. This is precisely the type of searching inquiry that intrudes into church doctrine and church administrative matters and engenders a prohibited relationship between the church and the judiciary."*

Example. *A Presbyterian minister left a pastoral position in Alaska and accepted a call as minister of a church in Tennessee. When he presented himself to the church to begin his duties, he was informed by church officials that because of derogatory information the church had received from a denominational official in Alaska the church would not hire him. The presbyter had informed church leaders that the minister was divorced, dishonest, unable to perform pastoral duties because of throat surgery, and that he had made an improper sexual advance to a church member in Alaska. The minister sued the presbyter for breach of contract, defamation, and interference with contract. A state supreme court ruled that it could not resolve the breach of contract claim since "employment disputes within churches are core ecclesiastical concerns outside the jurisdiction of the civil courts." The court observed: "The relationship between an organized church and its ministers is its lifeblood. . . . Matters touching this relationship must necessarily be recognized as of prime ecclesiastical concern. Just as the initial function of selecting a minister is a matter of church administration and government, so are the functions which accompany such a selection. In our society, jealous as it is of separation of church and state, one who enters the clergy forfeits the protection of the civil authorities in terms of job rights." As a result, the court concluded that the trial court correctly dismissed the minister's "breach of contract" claim, and that the minister "must rely upon administrative remedies the church provides for his contract claim, even if the church itself may be inadequate to provide a remedy." However, the court suggested that the minister's defamation and interference with contract claims could be resolved by the civil courts.[101]*

---

[100] Singleton v. Christ the Servant Evangelical Lutheran Church, 541 N.W.2d 606 (Minn. App. 1996).
[101] Marshall v. Munro, 845 P.2d 424 (Alaska 1993).

(5) emotional distress

Example. A Minnesota court ruled that the first amendment's "nonestablishment of religion" clause prevented it from resolving a dismissed minister's lawsuit against his former church.[102] The pastor claimed that the church's conduct and statements by church members caused him severe emotional distress. Specifically, he pointed to several statements regarding an intention to remove him from his position as pastor, several statements about his job performance, his removal from several church committees, submission of written "concerns" about his job performance, and the holding of church meetings without informing him or members of his family. The court noted that in order for the church to be guilty of intentional infliction of emotional distress the pastor had to prove that (1) the conduct was extreme and outrageous, (2) the conduct was intentional or reckless, (3) it caused emotional distress, and (4) the distress was severe. The court concluded that the pastor could not prove intentional infliction of emotional distress for two reasons. First, a court would have to conclude that the church "intended" to cause him distress. This would force the court to "review the motivations for the church's actions"—a prohibited inquiry since "the first amendment prohibits judicial inquiry into motivations for a church's pastoral employment decisions." Second, the pastor's claim for intentional infliction of emotional distress also failed because the church's actions "were not extreme and outrageous." The court observed that "conduct is extreme and outrageous if it is so atrocious that it passes the boundaries of decency and is utterly intolerable to the civilized community." The pastor had not met this difficult standard.

(6) defamation

Example. A minister who was dismissed after serving 40 years with the Christian and Missionary Alliance (CMA) sued the CMA claiming that his dismissal violated established procedures as well as various "contract and property rights," injured his reputation, and ruined his emotional health. A federal appeals court concluded that the first amendment guaranty of religious freedom prevents the civil courts from resolving lawsuits brought by dismissed ministers against former churches or denominations. The court observed: "However a suit may be labeled, once a court is called upon to probe into a religious body's selection and retention of clergymen, the first amendment [guaranty of religious freedom] is implicated . . . . The relationship between an organized church and its ministers is its lifeblood. The minister is the chief instrument by which the church seeks to fulfill its purpose. Matters touching this relationship must necessarily be recognized as of prime ecclesiastical concern." The court concluded: "At bottom, [the ex-minister's] complaint directly involves, and would require judicial intrusion into, rules, policies, and decisions which are unmistakably of ecclesiastical cognizance. They are, therefore, not the federal courts' concern. . . . The [church's] own internal guidelines and procedures must be allowed to dictate what its obligations to its members are without being subject to court intervention. It is well-settled that religious controversies are not the proper subject of civil court inquiry. Religious bodies must be free to decide for themselves, free from state interference, matters which pertain to church government, faith, and doctrine."[103]

Example. A denomination decided not to elevate a congregation to mission status, thereby cutting off all subsidies and in effect terminating the minister who served the congregation. The minister sued his de-

---

[102] Singleton v. Christ the Servant Evangelical Lutheran Church, 541 N.W.2d 606 (Minn. App. 1996). *See also* Bell v. Presbyterian Church, 126 F.3d 328 (4th Cir. 1997); Hutchison v. Thomas, 789 F.2d 392 (6th Cir. 1986), *cert. denied*, 107 S. Ct. 277 (1986).

[103] Natal v. Christian and Missionary Alliance, 878 F.2d 1575 (1st Cir. 1989). The court's decision is reinforced by the fact that it was upholding the lower court's order dismissing the lawsuit. Under federal law, a motion to dismiss may be granted only if the allegations in the plaintiff's complaint, accepted as true, state "no set of facts which might entitle the plaintiff to relief." The court's dismissal of this lawsuit under this minimal standard of review adds force to its conclusions.

nomination for defamation, alleging that denominational officials published both oral and written defamatory statements about him that damaged his reputation and professional status. The denomination claimed that the civil courts lacked jurisdiction to resolve religious disputes such as this. A federal district court in Minnesota agreed with the denomination and dismissed the lawsuit.[104] It noted that "the United States Supreme Court has determined that civil courts generally may not inquire into a religious organization's activities on matters of religious doctrine or authority and that courts lack subject matter jurisdiction over most disputes stemming from a religious organization's actions." The court quoted from a number of federal court rulings refusing to resolve lawsuits brought by dismissed ministers. The court rejected the minister's claim that resolving only a defamation claim would be permissible: "Although factual scenarios might exist where resolution of a defamation action against a religious organization would not require the court to undertake an inquiry in violation of the first amendment, this case does not present such a situation. [The minister's] defamation claim challenges [the denomination's] authority . . . to comment on [the minister's] actions and abilities as a . . . minister. Resolution of . . . the defamation claim would require the court to review the [denomination's] bases for terminating him, an ecclesiastical concern, and the veracity of the [denomination's] statements. The court determines that such an inquiry would implicate the concerns expressed in the first amendment. Based on that determination, the court concludes that it has no jurisdiction over this matter."

Example. *A Louisiana state appeals court, in refusing to hear a lawsuit (alleging defamation) brought by a dismissed minister against his denomination, referred to United States Supreme Court decisions limiting the authority of civil courts to hear such cases and concluded: "It would be ludicrous to believe that the constitutional principles upheld by the United States Supreme Court . . . could be satisfied by allowing this intrusion into the disciplinary proceedings of an ecclesiastical board. To allow defamation suits to be litigated to the fullest extent against members of a religious board who are merely discharging the duty which has been entrusted to them by their church could have a potentially chilling effect on the performance of those duties."[105]*

Example. *A Louisiana state appeals court dismissed a lawsuit brought by a dismissed minister against his denomination.[106] The minister, who had been dismissed for fiscal irresponsibility and other misbehavior, sued the state board of his denomination for defamation, wrongful disfellowship because of procedural irregularities by the denomination, and wrongful deprivation of a livelihood. The court held that all statements made at the board's disciplinary hearing, as well as the publication of the resolution of disfellowship announcing the board's decision, were privileged. This meant that the communications made by the denomination regarding the disciplinary action could not be defamatory without a finding "by clear and convincing evidence that the board or its members acted or spoke with malice." Malice in this context, as in other cases of defamation, requires not only that the statements made were in fact false, but also that the speakers knew that they were false or uttered them with a reckless disregard as to their truth or falsity. As in other contexts, this is a standard that is rarely proven. The court concluded that the minister's "loss of ministerial income must be accepted as a necessary consequence of his dismissal from ministry." Several other courts have rejected the claim of dismissed clergy that their dismissing church or denominational agency was defamatory.[107]*

[104] Farley v. Wisconsin Evangelical Lutheran Synod, 821 F. Supp. 1286 (D. Minn. 1993).
[105] McManus v. Taylor, 521 So.2d 449 (La. App. 1988).
[106] Joiner v. Weeks, 383 So.2d 101 (La. App. 1980).
[107] *See, e.g.,* Brewer v. Second Baptist Church, 197 P.2d 713 (Cal. 1948) (charges brought by church committee without malice and with reasonable belief in their truth); Crosby v. Lee, 76 S.E.2d 856 (Ga. 1957) (announcement of disciplinary results deemed privileged); Swafford v. Keaton, 93 S.E. 122 (Ga. 1919) (charges brought in good faith and in discharge of duty); Anderson v. Malm, 198 Ill. App. 58 (Ill. 1916) (words of presiding officer at expulsion hearing privileged as being in line of duty in relation to church discipline);

Example. An Ohio court dismissed a lawsuit brought by two dismissed ministers against their church and denomination, noting that the claims "necessarily concern internal church discipline governed by ecclesiastical rule, custom, and law."[108] The court continued: "Review of subjective judgments by religious officers and bodies, such as involuntary termination of pastors, necessarily requires inquiry into ecclesiastical matters. Civil courts cannot constitutionally intervene in such a dispute." In rejecting the claim of defamation against the church for publishing remarks critical of the pastors' ministry and financial dealings, the court concluded: "One who falsely and without a privilege to do so publishes a slander which ascribes to another conduct, characteristics, or a condition incompatible with the proper conduct of his lawful business, trade, or profession is liable to the other. However, inquiry by a civil court into the truth or falsity of the statements by [church officials] would require review of subjective judgments made by religious officers and bodies concerning [the co-pastors'] conduct of the pastorate and financial misdealings. Inquiry would be ecclesiastical in nature and constitutionally prohibited." The court acknowledged that the United States Supreme Court has authorized civil courts to resolve church property disputes by applying nondoctrinal "neutral principles of law." However, it emphasized that the "neutral principles doctrine has never been extended to religious controversies in the areas of church government, order and discipline." Accordingly, it had no application in a case involving pastoral termination.

Example. A Maryland court ruled that a former candidate for the priesthood could not sue his diocese or church officials for defamation.[109] The candidate entered seminary and pursued training in preparation for ordination as a priest. Less than a year before he was to be ordained, he was informed by a church official that he was being "released" from the diocese and as a result would never be considered for the priesthood. The candidate sued the archbishop on behalf of the diocese and various church officials, claiming that the decision to "release" him was based on defamatory information shared with the diocese. Specifically, the candidate claimed that a priest provided a reference to church officials in which he asserted that the candidate had engaged in "sexually motivated conduct" with certain staff members in a former parish. The candidate claimed that church officials repeated this information with knowledge that it was false and with an intent to harm his chances for ordination to the priesthood. He sought more than $2 million in damages. A trial court dismissed the case and the candidate appealed. A Maryland appeals court agreed that the case had to be dismissed. The court insisted that "the withdrawal of ecclesiastical controversies from civil jurisdiction has been a broad one." It referred to a Supreme Court decision declaring any dispute concerning "theological controversy, church discipline, ecclesiastical government, or the conformity of members of the church to the standard of morals required of them" to be beyond the authority of the civil courts to resolve. It concluded: "When the conduct complained of occurs in the context of, or is germane to, a dispute over the plaintiff's fitness or suitability to enter into or remain a part of the clergy . . . it is difficult to see how the forbidden inquiry could be avoided. Questions of truth, falsity, malice, and the various privileges that exist often take on a different hue when examined in the light of religious precepts and procedures that generally permeate controversies over who is fit to represent and speak for the church. . . . It is apparent from these allegations . . . that the very heart of the [lawsuit] is a decision by [the candidate's] clerical supervisors to prevent him from becoming a priest. The allegedly defamatory statements were made by them with that intent, thereby evidencing a determination on their part—whether valid and fair or invalid and unfair—that [the candidate] was not a suitable candidate for the priest-

---

Redgate v. Roush, 59 P. 1050 (Kan. 1900) (publication by church officers of expulsion of minister deemed privileged because standing in denomination of every minister is of common interest to every other minister); Butterworth v. Todd, 70 A. 139 (N.J. 1908) (announcing result of expulsion proceeding in good faith and within authority of church deemed privileged).

[108] Salzgaber v. First Christian Church, 583 N.E.2d 1361 (Ohio App. 1991).

[109] Downs v. Roman Catholic Archbishop, 683 A.2d 808 (Md. App. 1996).

hood. *That the offensive conduct was so directed is what brings this case squarely within the protective ambit of the first amendment."*

Example. *A Texas court ruled that a bishop and diocese could not be liable on the basis of defamation for statements made about a priest's status within the church.*[110] *A priest had a history of conflict with his diocese culminating in his association with a dissident Catholic sect. A parishioner asked the priest's bishop about the priest's standing in the Catholic Church, and was informed that "he is not in good standing with his diocese and does not enjoy the [authority] to function as a priest in [this] or any other diocese." The bishop advised another person that the priest was excommunicated, and not in good standing, and "says mass to a small number of people, including elderly women who have been deceived by him." The bishop later sent a memorandum to "all pastors" advising them to refrain from advertising or encouraging a mass being offered by the priest who was described as an "excommunicated priest who has left the Catholic Church." The priest sued the bishop and diocese, claiming that these communications were defamatory. A state appeals court disagreed. The court observed that the first amendment "forbids the government from interfering with the right of hierarchical religious bodies to establish their own internal rules and regulations." As a result, the civil courts cannot "intrude into the church's governance or religious or ecclesiastical matters, such as theological controversy, church discipline, ecclesiastical government, or the conformity of members to standards of morality." Furthermore, the court noted that "courts will not attempt to right wrongs related to the hiring, firing, discipline or administration of clergy. Although such wrongs may exist and may be severe, and although the administration of the church may be inadequate to provide a remedy, the preservation of the free exercise of religion is deemed so important a principle it overshadows the inequities which may result from its liberal application."*

Example. *A Minnesota court ruled that an assistant pastor who was dismissed by his employing church after the congregation voted to eliminate his position for financial reasons could not sue the church for defamation.*[111] *An ordained minister was hired as assistant pastor by a local church and was dismissed a few years later after the congregation voted to eliminate his position. The lawsuit alleged that a bishop of the synod falsely stated that the former pastor (1) was "on leave without call"; (2) had "physically threatened" him; (3) was a "troublemaker"; and (4) was "pathological" and "obsessive-compulsive." The former pastor further asserted that he had been warned by the bishop that he would not get another call unless he underwent counseling, and that the bishop called two other pastors and told them not to believe anything the former pastor said. The court concluded that such statements did not amount to defamation. It observed that "because these alleged defamatory statements relate to [the bishop's] reasons and motives for making employment decisions, such an inquiry is barred by the first amendment."*

(7) fraud or collusion

Example. *The federal appeals court for the sixth circuit (covers the states of Kentucky, Michigan, Ohio, and Tennessee) rejected the claim of a dismissed Methodist minister that his dismissal had been fraudulent, arbitrary, and a "collusive application of church disciplinary rules."*[112] *The minister also alleged defamation, infliction of emotional distress, and breach of contract. The appeals court, in affirming a lower court's summary judgment in favor of the church, ruled that civil court review of clergy dismissals "is*

---

[110] Tran v. Fiorenza, 934 S.W.2d 740 (Tex. App. 1996).
[111] Olson v. Luther Memorial Church, 1996 WL 70102 (Minn. App. 1996). *See also* Singleton v. Christ the Servant Evangelical Lutheran Church, 541 N.W.2d 606 (Minn. App. 1996).
[112] Hutchison v. Thomas, 789 F.2d 392 (6th Cir. 1986), *cert. denied*, 107 S. Ct. 277 (1986).

still only allowed for fraud or collusion of the most serious nature undermining the very authority of the decision-making body." Such exceptions, noted the court, are extremely rare and did not apply in this case. Significantly, the court also rejected summarily the minister's self-serving allegations of a deprivation of his "civil, contract, or property rights," since such rights, if they existed at all, were mere consequences of the underlying ecclesiastical determination and therefore could not afford an independent basis for civil court review. The court concluded with the following observation, which has been quoted by a number of other courts: "This case involves the fundamental question of who will preach from the pulpit of a church, and who will occupy the church parsonage. The bar statement of the question should make obvious the lack of jurisdiction of a civil court. The answer to that question must come from the church."

§ 2-04.2 — Civil Court Review of Clergy Termination Disputes — Limited Exceptions to the General Rule

Key point 2-04.2. Some courts are willing to resolve disputes over the termination of clergy if they can do so without any inquiry into religious doctrine.

Some courts have suggested that they have authority to review clergy terminations under one or more of the following circumstances:

1. FRAUD OR COLLUSION

As noted in the previous subsection, the United States Supreme Court has suggested that the civil courts can review clergy terminations if "fraud or collusion" are alleged.[113] However, the mere assertion that a dismissal was based on fraud or collusion will not suffice, since the Supreme Court has required that the alleged fraud or collusion be motivated "by bad faith for secular purposes."[114] It would be extraordinary indeed for a religious organization to be found guilty of such conduct, and understandably, none has ever been found to be so. Other courts have given the terms "fraud or collusion" a very narrow interpretation. To illustrate, a federal appeals court has noted that "[a]ssuming, without deciding, that review is allowed for fraud or collusion, it is still only allowed for fraud or collusion of the most serious nature undermining the very authority of the decision-making body."[115]

2. IMPROPER METHODS

The Supreme Court indicated in a 1952 decision that clergy dismissals can be reviewed by the civil courts if "improper methods of choice are proven."[116] The continuing validity of this exception is questionable, since in 1976 the Court specifically ruled that

whether or not there is room for "marginal civil court review" under the narrow rubrics of "fraud" or "collusion" when church tribunals act in bad faith for secular purposes, no "arbitrariness" exception—in the sense of an inquiry whether the decisions of the highest ecclesiastical tribunal of a hierarchical church complied with church laws and regulations—is consistent with the constitu-

---

[113] Gonzalez v. Roman Catholic Archbishop, 280 U.S. 1 (1928).

[114] Serbian Eastern Orthodox Diocese v. Milivojevich, 423 U.S. 696 (1976).

[115] Hutchison v. Thomas, 789 F.2d 392 (6th Cir. 1986), *cert. denied*, 107 S. Ct. 277 (1986). *See also* Music v. United Methodist Church, 864 S.W.2d 286 (Ky. 1993).

[116] Kedroff v. St. Nicholas Cathedral, 344 U.S. 94, 116 (1952) ("Freedom to select the clergy, *where no improper methods of choice are proven*, we think, must now be said to have federal constitutional protection . . . .").

tional mandate that civil courts are bound to accept the decisions of the highest judicatories of a religious organization of hierarchical polity on matters of discipline, faith, internal organization, or ecclesiastical rule, custom or law. For civil courts to analyze whether the ecclesiastical actions of a church judicatory are in that sense "arbitrary" must inherently entail inquiry into the procedures that canon or ecclesiastical law supposedly require the church adjudicatory to follow, or else into the substantive criteria by which they are supposedly to decide the ecclesiastical question. But this is exactly the inquiry that the first amendment prohibits . . . .[117]

According to this language, the civil courts can never review the dismissals of clergy in *hierarchical* denominations, even if a dismissed minister alleges that the denomination failed to follow prescribed procedure. As a result, if there is any basis for civil court review of clergy dismissals allegedly based on improper procedure, it would be in the context of *congregational* or independent churches. Even here, it is questionable whether or not civil court review would be consistent with the Supreme Court's 1976 ruling in the *Serbian* case.[118]

Some civil courts have been willing to review questions of proper procedure in clergy dismissal controversies. At best, such decisions are appropriate only if three conditions are satisfied: (1) the decision to dismiss a minister was made by a congregational church rather than a hierarchical church; (2) the dismissal violated applicable procedure; and (3) a civil court can resolve the dispute without inquiring into ecclesiastical doctrine or polity. To illustrate, the courts have ruled that the attempted discharge of a minister by congregational vote was invalid where the vote was conducted at an improperly called church meeting;[119] the meeting was "so beset with confusion that no business could have been legally transacted";[120] the notice of the meeting did not specify that a vote would be taken on the minister's termination;[121] and, the vote to terminate a minister's services was taken after the minister had properly dismissed the meeting.[122] Similarly, if a church's bylaws vest authority to remove a minister in the general membership, then the church board has no such authority.[123]

Some courts also have been willing to interpret ambiguous language in church constitutions and bylaws pertaining to termination of clergy. For example, one court resolved a church controversy over the number of votes needed to terminate a minister's services.[124] The bylaws specified that "three-fourths of the voting members present" could vote to terminate the minister's services. At a duly called meeting, the minister was voted out of office by more than three-fourths of the members present who voted. However, several members abstained from the vote, and accordingly the pastor argued that he had not been properly voted out of office since fewer than three-fourths of the total voting members present (including those who voted and those who

---

[117] Serbian Eastern Orthodox Diocese v. Milivojevich, 423 U.S. 696 (1976).

[118] *See, e.g.,* Patterson v. Southwestern Baptist Theological Seminary, 858 S.W.2d 602 (Tex. App. 1993) ("the same rule is applicable to congregational systems, in that civil courts, with reference to the determination of matters that are ecclesiastical in nature, are to give deference to those officers in which are vested the authority to make such a determination").

[119] First Union Baptist Church v. Banks, 533 So.2d 1305 (La. App. 1988) (meeting was "null and void"); In re Galilee Baptist Church, 186 So.2d 102 (Ala. 1966).

[120] *Id.*

[121] Bethlehem Missionary Baptist Church v. Henderson, 522 So.2d 1339 (La. App. 1988) (notice requirement in state nonprofit corporation law controlled since the church bylaws contained no notice provisions). *See also* St. John's Greek Catholic Hungarian Russian Orthodox Church v. Fedak, 233 A.2d 663 (N.J. 1967); Hayes v. Board of Trustees, 225 N.Y.S.2d 316 (1962). Where a church has no bylaw provisions dealing with dismissal of ministers, it has been held that a majority vote of the church's membership will warrant dismissal. This is so even if no notice was given that the dismissal of a minister was to be considered at a scheduled meeting, at least in the case where all members knew that the minister's continued employment would be discussed, and where the dismissed minister and his supporters did not object to the lack of notice. *See* Longmeyer v. Payne, 205 S.W.2d 263 (Mo. 1947).

[122] Brooks v. January, 321 N.W.2d 823 (Mich. App. 1982).

[123] Reddick v. Jones, 304 S.E.2d 389 (Ga. 1983); First Union Baptist Church v. Banks, 533 So.2d 1305 (La. App. 1988); Vincent v. Raglin, 318 N.W.2d 629 (Mich. App. 1982).

[124] Blanton v. Hahn, 763 P.2d 522 (Ariz. App. 1988).

did not) voted against him. The court concluded that the phrase "three-fourths of the voting members present" included those who voted as well as those who abstained, and accordingly the minister had not been properly dismissed. Another court agreed to determine whether proxy votes should be recognized in a meeting called to vote on the termination of a minister.[125]

A number of courts have been willing to determine whether or not a sufficient number of eligible members voted to dismiss a minister. In one case, a pastor ignored a congregational decision to terminate his services on the ground that most of those participating in the congregational vote were not lawful members. The pastor alleged that most of those voting against him had ceased to be members by their failure to abide by an unwritten church "rule" requiring that members attend church regularly and contribute to the church's support. Those who had been "disfellowshiped" claimed that they were aware of no such rule, and that they were never notified that their membership was in jeopardy. The court concluded that the expulsion of the church members was improper, since the alleged rule was of doubtful existence, and since the members were not given a hearing on their status.[126]

If a church's constitution or bylaws specify the manner by which a member may lose his membership, this will be controlling. For example, when a church's constitution specified that membership status could be severed only by "excommunication," and when no member voting to dismiss a minister had been excommunicated, the minister could not challenge his dismissal on the ground that several of the members voting against him had forfeited their membership through irregular attendance and inadequate support.[127] This was so despite the fact that the church's constitution also provided that "no one can . . . remain a member of this congregation . . . but such as partake of the Lord's Supper with due frequency . . . and contribute according to his ability toward the maintenance of the church." The court reasoned that the members' infrequent attendance and minimal support was justified by their belief that the pastor had deviated from the church's doctrines.

In another case, a minister challenged a congregational vote to dismiss him on the ground that many of the members who voted against him had lost their membership by holding separate services in another church under another minister. The court disagreed: "The constitution and bylaws nowhere specifically provide a procedure for determining whether a member has lost his membership because of his conduct or beliefs. However, we think it must be implied . . . that it is for the congregation to make this determination."[128]

3. Violation of a Civil, Contract, or Property Right Independent of the Disciplinary Process

A few courts have been willing to resolve clergy termination disputes if a civil, contract, or property right was allegedly violated that was independent of (rather than incident to) the disciplinary process and that required no inquiry into religious doctrine or polity. Few disputes satisfy these strict conditions. The key point is this: the alleged civil, contract, or property right must be independent of and not a consequence of an underlying ecclesiastical dispute involving ecclesiastical doctrine, polity, or discipline. As the Supreme Court itself has observed, there is no basis for civil court review if the alleged property right that was violated by a church's dismissal of a minister is "an incident from decisions of the church . . . on ecclesiastical issues."[129] Further, a number of courts have noted that the mere assertion that a civil, contract, or property right has been violated is not enough to warrant civil court intervention, for this often can be a spurious effort to

---

[125] Frankel v. Kissena Jewish Center, 544 N.Y.S.2d 955 (1989).
[126] Longmeyer v. Payne, 205 S.W.2d 263 (Mo. 1947).
[127] Blauert v. Schupmann, 63 N.W.2d 578 (Minn. 1954).
[128] Schumacher v. Giedt, 112 N.W.2d 898 (S.D. 1962).
[129] See note 74, supra, and accompanying text.

involve a court in an essentially ecclesiastical controversy.[130] To hold otherwise, according to the Supreme Court's decision in *Watson*,[131] "would lead to the total subversion of such religious bodies, if anyone aggrieved by one of their decisions could appeal to the secular courts and have them reversed."

Example. The federal appeals for the eighth circuit (covers the states of Arkansas, Iowa, Minnesota, Missouri, Nebraska, North Dakota, and South Dakota) ruled that a minister could not sue his denomination for allegedly failing to follow its bylaws in suspending him, but he could sue the denomination for defamation.[132] As one of its services for member churches, the Missouri Synod Lutheran Church (the "Synod") prepares and circulates personal information files on its ministers to churches interested in hiring pastors and advises them on the background and suitability of individual ministers. The Synod placed a document in a minister's file stating that his spouse had previously been married. The minister claimed that the Synod took this action without consulting him or verifying the accuracy of the information, and that the information in fact was untrue. The minister alleged that because churches within the Synod automatically disqualify a minister if his personal file shows that his spouse has been divorced, the Synod effectively excluded him from consideration for employment as a pastor by circulating this false information. He sued the Synod, seeking monetary damages for his loss of income during the time that the Synod circulated the false information about his spouse. A federal appeals court ruled that the minister could sue the Synod for defamation. It observed: "The first amendment proscribes intervention by secular courts into many employment decisions made by religious organizations based on religious doctrine or beliefs. Personnel decisions are protected from civil court interference where review by civil courts would require the courts to interpret and apply religious doctrine or ecclesiastical law. The first amendment does not shield employment decisions made by religious organizations from civil court review, however, where the employment decisions do not implicate religious beliefs, procedures, or law. . . . [The minister] claims that he was injured by the Synod's alleged libel, negligence, or intentional interference with his legitimate expectation of employment. The Synod has not offered any religious explanation for its actions which might entangle the court in a religious controversy in violation of the first amendment. [The minister] is entitled to an opportunity to prove his secular allegations at trial."

Example. An Ohio court ruled that a retired pastor could sue his former church for breaching its promise to pay him one-third of his former salary for the remainder of his life.[133] This was so despite the fact that the church's decision to discontinue the benefits was based in part on its dismissal of the former minister as a member of the church.

Example. An Idaho court ruled that it had authority to resolve a lawsuit by a dismissed minister challenging his dismissal.[134] A conflict arose within a local church between the minister and board. The minister attempted to dismiss most of the board members. The board members ignored this action and attempted to dismiss him. The minister insisted that his term was perpetual, and that the board could not dismiss him except for immorality or a lifestyle inconsistent with the standards of the church. He insisted that these grounds did not exist and accordingly that the board had no authority to terminate him. The board asked a court to prohibit the minister from conducting any further church business or coming on to church premises. The minister counter-sued the church board, claiming that it had wrongfully terminated him and breached his contract of employment. The court ruled in favor of the pastor. In rejecting the board's claim that the civil

---

[130] *See, e.g.,* Eddy ex rel. Pfeifer v. Christian Science Board of Directors, 379 N.E.2d 653 (Ill. App. 1978).

[131] *See* note 68, *supra,* and accompanying text.

[132] Drevlow v. Lutheran Church, Missouri Synod, 991 F.2d 468 (8th Cir. 1993).

[133] Brads v. First Baptist Church, 624 N.E.2d 737 (Ohio App. 2 Dist. 1993).

[134] Fellowship Tabernacle, Inc. v. Baker, 869 P.2d 578 (Idaho App. 1994).

courts could not resolve this dispute because it was ecclesiastical in nature, the court observed: "[W]e agree with [the church] that it is not the place of the [civil courts] to decide matters that are ecclesiastical in nature, we disagree that the doctrine applies to this case. The issues before the . . . court and jury involved an employment contract, its alleged breach, the various reasons asserted for the breach and the damages related to that breach. Simply because a church is involved in litigation does not make the matter ecclesiastical. [The church] argues that the reasons the board listed for discharging [the minister] were primarily ecclesiastical and for the . . . court to rule on those issues is beyond its jurisdiction as a court of law. The jury was not asked, however, to decide whether the asserted reasons for terminating [the minister] were objectively valid, nor whether the action taken by the board was an ecclesiastical punishment. Instead, the jury was asked to determine if the reasons the board listed were, in fact, why the church fired [the minister] and whether that action was proper under the church's own bylaws. The bylaws were not simply church rules governing religious doctrine and policy, but were, rather, the bylaws of an Idaho nonprofit corporation governing its corporate affairs. We conclude that there were no ecclesiastical questions decided by the jury or the . . . court."

Example. *An Ohio court ruled that the civil courts have the authority to resolve a lawsuit by a dismissed minister claiming that his denomination was responsible for paying legal fees he incurred in suing the denomination and defending himself against criminal sexual misconduct charges.[135] A trial court ruled that it was without jurisdiction to resolve what it perceived to be an internal ecclesiastical dispute, and the pastor appealed. A state appeals court reversed the trial court's decision, and ruled that the trial court did have the authority to resolve this controversy. The court acknowledged that the "Constitution prohibits any inquiry by the courts into religious doctrine or practice and, thus, courts have no role in determining ecclesiastical questions in the process of resolving church disputes." On the other hand, there is no constitutional prohibition against the civil courts resolving church disputes on the basis of nondoctrinal principles. The court noted that the denomination's constitution had provisions authorizing the payment of legal fees under limited circumstances, and that the trial court could determine whether these provisions required the denomination to pay the pastor's legal fees. It observed: "[W]here the dispute involves nondoctrinal contractual disputes, a civil court retains jurisdiction to hear the dispute. The indemnification clauses at issue in this case do not concern church doctrine, dogma or religious practice but, instead, pertain to the legal issue of whether or not [the minister] is entitled to indemnification for attorney fees he incurred in administrative and criminal proceedings against him. Thus, the issue in the case at hand is secular in nature and one to which basic contractual, legal principles may be applied. Simply because the litigants include religious bodies does not necessarily make all issues ecclesiastical in nature."*

§ 2-04.3 — Civil Court Review of Clergy Termination Disputes — "Exhaustion" of Ecclesiastical Remedies

The courts consistently have held that ministers who fail to "exhaust" their appeals within an ecclesiastical hierarchy are forbidden to seek redress in the civil courts.[136] This means that the courts will refuse to hear controversies involving the dismissal of a minister if the minister failed to pursue the remedies available within his or her church or denomination.

---

[135] Bennett v. Evangelical Lutheran Church in America, 647 N.E.2d 566 (Ohio App. 1994).

[136] *See, e.g.,* First Baptist Church v. State of Ohio, 591 F. Supp. 676 (S.D. Ohio 1983); Hickman v. Owens, 322 F. Supp. 1278 (D. Ga. 1971); United Pentecostal Church v. Morrison, 527 P.2d 1169 (Colo. App. 1974); Rodyk v. Ukrainian Autocephalic Orthodox Church, 328 N.Y.S.2d 685 (1972).

INSTRUCTIONAL AIDS TO CHAPTER 2

Terms

arbitrariness

breach of contract

civil, property, or contract rights

compensation

congregational

contract

fraud or collusion

good cause

hierarchical

polity

Learning Objectives

- Understand the legal aspects of the selection of clergy.

- Understand under what circumstances the civil courts will intervene in internal church disputes involving the selection of clergy.

- Explain why clergy and churches should enter into a contract of employment, and identify several important items to cover in such a contract.

- Define *unreasonable compensation*, and explain the significance of this concept to churches and clergy.

- Identify those circumstances in which the civil courts may intervene in internal church disputes involving the dismissal of a minister.

Short-Answer Questions

1. Explain the difference between a congregational and a hierarchical church.

2. Under what circumstances may a civil court intervene in a dispute regarding the *selection* of a minister? In which of the following situations might a civil court intervene (explain fully):

   a. A minister was ordained by a denomination that retains the authority to assign clergy to their pastoral positions. A 62-year-old minister was assigned to a small mission church. He sued his denomination, claiming that his civil rights were violated by such an "undesirable" assignment.

   b. A female minister sued her denomination, claiming that the denomination engaged in gender discrimination by assigning her to a small church.

   c. A church refuses to call a minister because he was not ordained by the denomination with which the church was affiliated.

   d. A church's bylaws require that a minister receive a "three-fourths vote" in order to be elected. The minister received a vote of 60%. The church board declared him elected, mistakenly believing that only a majority vote was required. Several months later, a member of the church discovered that a three-fourths vote was required, and he challenges the election in a civil court.

   e. A church's bylaws require that a minister receive a "majority vote" in order to be elected. The church has 100 members, and at a business meeting at which 60 members were present, Rev. C receives 40 votes. He is declared elected, since he received more than half of the votes of those members present and voting. A disgruntled member files a lawsuit in civil court challenging the election, claiming that the minister did not receive a majority vote of *all* the church membership.

   f. Only 35 members attend a church membership meeting that was called to select a new minister. The church's bylaws do not define a quorum. The members elect Rev. D as their minister. However, a group of members contest the election. They argue that the meeting was invalid since a quorum was not present. They note that the church is incorporated under a state nonprofit corporation law which defines a quorum as 20 percent of members. Since the church has 300 members the quorum requirement was not met. Those members who elected the pastor insist that state nonprofit corporation law can never invalidate an action taken at a church membership meeting.

   g. Same facts as the preceding example, except that the church's bylaws define a quorum as 25 members.

3. Calvary Church has no constitution or bylaws, and it is not affiliated with a denomination. In the past, it has selected its ministers by majority vote of church members attending a specially called business meeting. The pastor of Calvary Church resigns, and the trustees assert that they have as much authority as the church membership to select a replacement. Are they correct? Explain.

4. Peace Chapel is incorporated under a general nonprofit corporation law. The church's minister retires, and the church calls a special business meeting to vote on a new minister. The church membership was notified of the special meeting by public announcement in the course of a church service on the preceding Sunday. This procedure was mandated by the church's bylaws. During the business meeting, a church member points out that the state nonprofit corporation law calls for notice on each of the two Sundays preceding the date of the business meeting. Was the meeting legally called?

5. First Church employs Rev. R as its minister. Rev. R did not sign a contract. The constitution and bylaws of First Church do not specify Rev. R's term of office. Rev. R maintains that he has been hired "for life." Do you agree? Explain.

6. Faith Church employs Rev. J for a three-year term. In the second year of the term, the church membership votes to dismiss Rev. J because of recent statements in which he expressed doubts about a few fundamental doctrines of the church. Rev. J sues the church for breach of contract. Will he succeed? Explain.

7. Grace Church employs Rev. O for a five-year term. In the third year of the term, Rev. O suffers a stroke that leaves him with a speech impediment. The church wants to dismiss Rev. O, but he insists it cannot do so until his term is completed. The employment contract does not address the problem. If the dispute goes to court, who will prevail?

8. Describe the legal remedies available to a minister who is wrongfully dismissed by a church before the end of his term of employment.

9. A church is considering the hiring of a minister. Why would it be desirable for the church and the minister to sign an employment contract?

10. A church has decided to prepare an employment contract for a new minister. Why would the following terms be desirable:

    a. A job description.

    b. An arbitration clause.

    c. A housing allowance designation.

11. What is *unreasonable compensation*, and why should it be a concern to churches?

12. What are "intermediate sanctions"? Why are they relevant to clergy compensation planning?

13. Under what circumstances may a civil court intervene in a dispute regarding the *dismissal* of a minister by a local church or denomination? In which of the following situations might a civil court intervene (explain fully):

    a. A "hierarchical" denomination receives complaints about Rev. G, and it conducts an investigation and hearing. The denomination revokes the ministerial credentials of Rev. G. Rev. G files a lawsuit, alleging that the denomination did not follow its disciplinary procedure in conducting its investigation and in reaching its decision to dismiss him as a minister.

    b. Same facts as question 13a. Would it matter if Rev. G alleged that his civil, contract, or property rights were violated by the denomination's actions?

    c. Same facts as question 13a. Would it matter if Rev. G alleged that the denomination's actions were based on "fraud or collusion?"

    d. Same facts as 13a, except that the denomination is "congregational" in polity. Would this make any difference?

    e. A church conducts a special business meeting to vote on the dismissal of Rev. D. The church bylaws specify that the church must provide members with notice of any special business meeting on the two Sunday morning services immediately preceding the date of the special meeting. The special business meeting was announced only on one Sunday. Rev. D receives only 40% of the votes cast at the meeting (he needed a simple majority). Rev. D later challenges the church's actions in court.

    f. A church board votes to dismiss Rev. W. The church bylaws provide that only the church members can dismiss a minister. Rev. W challenges the board action in court.

    g. A church has 200 members. The church bylaws specify that a minister may be dismissed by a vote of "two-thirds of the church membership." At a special business meeting at which 80 members are present, 56 members (70% of those present) vote to dismiss the minister. The church board informs the minister that he has been dismissed. The minister files a lawsuit, alleging that he was not dismissed by a two-thirds vote of *all* the church's members, but rather only of those present at the meeting.

    h. A church votes to dismiss a minister. The minister contests the vote on the ground that many persons who were permitted to vote in the election were not valid members of the church.

    i. A church enters into a 3-year contract with Rev. L. The contract provides that Rev. L can be terminated only for doctrinal departure or incapacity. After serving for only 1 year, the church dismisses Rev. L. The basis for the dismissal was "ineffectiveness." Rev. L sues for damages.

    j. A denominational agency revokes the ordination of Rev. V, and lists Rev. V as "dismissed" in a denominational publication that is distributed to ministers. Rev. V sues the denomination for defamation.

    k. A minister is dismissed by a denominational agency. She fails to pursue the appeal procedure specified in her denomination's bylaws. Two years later she sues her denomination for wrongful dismissal.

Discussion Questions

    1. This chapter describes the legal remedies that are available to a minister who is dismissed by a church prior to the expiration of a stated term of employment. Do you believe that it is ever appropriate for a minister to seek such remedies in a court of law? Explain your position. Are there any alternatives? What steps could a church take to reduce the risk of civil litigation?

    2. There are several advantages to ministers entering into a contract of employment with their employing church. Yet, such contracts are rare. Why do you believe this is so?

3

AUTHORITY, RIGHTS, AND PRIVILEGES

Chapter summary. The increasing secularism of our society has led to a sharp reduction in the number of legal privileges enjoyed by ministers. Nevertheless, some important privileges remain. For example, ministers are exempted from jury duty in some states. They are exempted by federal law from military service. Ministers have the authority in all states to perform marriage ceremonies. And, confidential communications made to ministers acting in their professional capacity as spiritual advisers generally are protected against compelled disclosure in a court of law. This last privilege is a very important one. It means, for example, that clergy ordinarily cannot be compelled to disclose in a court of law statements made to them in confidence during spiritual counseling—even if the statements included a confession of criminal activity. Another important privilege is the exemption of pastoral counseling from laws prohibiting the unauthorized practice of psychology. This privilege is of increasing significance today because of the emphasis that is placed on counseling. These and other privileges are discussed in detail in this chapter. You should pay special attention to the conditions that must exist for these privileges to apply. This chapter also examines the nature and extent of a minister's legal authority. Does a minister have the legal authority to sign documents on behalf of his church or to preside at church meetings? Is the minister always the president of the church corporation? These and other pertinent questions will be explored.

§ 3-01   General Scope of a Minister's Authority

Key point 3-01. *In general, clergy have the legal authority to do those things specifically authorized in their employment contract, in their church's constitution or bylaws, or by specific delegation of authority from the church board or congregation.*

What authority do clergy possess by virtue of their office? In general, they have the authority to do those things specifically authorized in their employment contract, in the church's constitution or bylaws, or by specific delegation of authority from the church board or congregation. In addition, state law confers authority upon clergy to perform certain functions. Actions by clergy that are not authorized may be void. For example, one court invalidated a minister's attempted unilateral expulsion of 29 members of his church since neither the church charter nor bylaws authorized him to take such action.[1] The fact that a minister is invested with spiritual authority does not in itself create any legal authority.[2]

§ 3-02   Officer of the Church Corporation

Key point 3-02. *A minister has no legal right to serve as president of the church corporation unless authorized to do so in the church's governing documents.*

A minister has no inherent right to be the president of the church corporation. The office of president is one that is filled according to the charter and bylaws of the church. Although the minister is customarily named president of the corporation, this is not a legal requirement.

§ 3-03   Property Matters

A minister can engage in property transactions on behalf of a church only if authorized to do so.

---

[1]   Smith v. Riley, 424 So.2d 1166 (La. App. 1966).

[2]   *See, e.g.,* Mudd v. Goldblatt Bros. Inc., 454 N.E.2d 754 (Ill. App. 1983); Gospel Tabernacle Body of Christ Church v. Peace Publishers & Co., 506 P.2d 1135 (Kan. 1973).

Authority may be expressly granted in the church's charter or bylaws, but more frequently a church's board of directors or members vote to authorize the minister to represent the church in a specific transaction.[3]

If no authority over the business and property affairs of a church has been delegated to a minister, he or she may not lawfully act for the church in such matters. In one case a minister declared himself to be the absolute religious leader of a congregation and thereafter exercised complete control over all of the church's spiritual and business activities. The minister's conveyance of church properties was challenged by members of the congregation who questioned his authority in business matters. The court concluded that the minister's "proclaiming . . . of himself as the religious superior of the congregation may suffice to establish that fact in spiritual matters of his church, but it does not effect legal superiority in secular matters."[4] The court emphasized that there must be "clear and convincing" evidence of congregational acceptance of legal superiority by a minister over church business and property matters before such authority will be recognized by the courts. In a related case, a minister who was the sole trustee of a church was not permitted to convey church property for his own benefit.[5] And, when a minister attempted to lease church properties without authorization from the church board, the lease was found to have no legal effect.[6]

A church may of course ratify the unauthorized actions of its pastor. Ratification may be by express action of the congregation or church board, or it may be implied if the church has knowledge of unauthorized action but does nothing to repeal it.[7] To illustrate, if a minister commits some unauthorized act and the church knows of the act but does not object within a reasonable time, the church may be left without legal recourse.

Example. An Ohio court ruled that a home purchased by a church for its pastor was subject to a "purchase money resulting trust" in favor of the church and therefore the home could not be considered in a property settlement following the pastor's divorce.[8] The court concluded that when property is purchased by one person, but title is vested in another, the person holding title does so subject to a "purchase money resulting trust" in favor of the person who paid for the property—at least if the parties intended that the purchaser have some equitable interest in the property. The court pointed out that the church purchased the home and adjoining property as a site for a new church building. As a result, the pastor and his wife held title to the home in trust for the church, and the home was not marital property that could be divided between the pastor and his wife.

§ 3-04 Performance of Marriage Ceremonies

Key point 3-04. All states permit clergy to perform marriage ceremonies. However, some states permit only "ordained" or some other classification of clergy to perform marriage ceremonies. It is important for clergy to determine if they are legally authorized to perform marriages under applicable state law, and in addition to be aware of the legal qualifications for marriage and any license and reporting requirements prescribed by state law.

---

[3] Berymon v. Henderson, 482 N.E.2d 391 (Ill. App. 1985); Brooks v. January, 321 N.W.2d 823 (Mich. App. 1982).
[4] *Id.*
[5] Dawkins v. Dawkins, 328 P.2d 346 (Kan. 1958). *Accord* Biscegelia v. Bernadine Sisters, 560 N.E.2d 567 (Mass. App. 1990).
[6] American Legion v. Southwest Title Insurance Co., 207 So.2d 393 (La. 1968); Soho Center for Arts and Education v. Church of Saint Anthony, 541 N.Y.S.2d 396 (1989); Diocese of Buffalo v. McCarthy, 458 N.Y.S.2d 764 (1983).
[7] Hill v. Hill, 241 S.W.2d 865 (Tenn. 1951).
[8] Cayten v. Cayten, 659 N.E.2d 805 (Ohio App. 1995).

1. THE AUTHORITY OF MINISTERS TO PERFORM MARRIAGE CEREMONIES

A minister has the authority in all states to perform marriages.[9] This authority is granted by state law. State laws vary widely in defining those clergy who are authorized to perform marriages. Some states require that the minister be ordained;[10] others require that the minister be either licensed or ordained;[11] and others omit any specific reference to either licensure or ordination.[12]

It is the state, and not the minister or religious organization, that ordinarily will decide whether a minister is in fact "ordained" or "licensed" and therefore qualified to perform marriages under a state law requiring either ordination or licensure. To illustrate, ministers receiving ordination credentials through the mail-order Universal Life Church have been denied the right to perform marriage ceremonies under state laws permitting "ordained ministers" or even "ministers" to conduct such ceremonies.[13] The courts obviously are faced with a difficult task when they attempt to deny legal privileges to some ministers on the basis of principles that do not involve a judgment on the legitimacy of religious belief. The difficulty of such a task is reflected in the unsatisfactory attempts by the courts to explain the distinction between ministers who are eligible for certain legal privileges and those who are not.

In most states, it is a criminal offense for one to perform a marriage ceremony if he or she is not authorized to do so by state law. If a state law authorizes only ordained ministers to perform marriage ceremonies, an unordained minister will be criminally liable for performing a marriage. Criminal penalties for the unauthorized performance of a marriage ceremony generally include a small fine or short prison sentence.[14]

performance of marriages by nonresident ministers

Are ministers authorized to perform marriages in other states? To illustrate, what if a minister is asked to perform a marriage in another state for a friend or relative. Is the minister legally authorized to do so? The answer to this question will depend upon the law of the state in which the marriage will be performed. In many states, any minister is eligible to perform a marriage regardless of the minister's state of residence. Other states have enacted laws authorizing nonresident ministers to perform a marriage within the state if they are legally authorized to do so in their state of residence.[15]

Some states impose limitations on the authority of nonresident ministers to perform marriages. For example, one state law specifies that "the state secretary may authorize, subject to such conditions as he may determine, the solemnization of any specified marriage anywhere within the commonwealth by [a nonresident] minister of the gospel in good and regular standing with his church or denomination."[16]

---

9   The laws of all 50 states are summarized in Appendix 1.

10 *See, e.g.,* ARK. STAT. § 9-11-213.

11 *See, e.g.,* KAN. STAT. § 23-104a; TEX. FAMILY CODE ANN. title 1, § 1.83.

12 *See, e.g.,* ILL. REV. STAT. ch. 40, § 209 ("officiant in good standing with his religious denomination" who solemnizes a marriage "in accordance with the prescriptions of [his] religious denomination"); KY. REV. STAT. § 402.050 ("ministers of the gospel or priests of any denomination in regular communion with any religious society"); MO. REV. STAT. § 451.100 ("any clergyman, active or retired, who is in good standing with any church"); OKLA. STAT. title 43, § 7 ("an ordained or authorized preacher or minister of the Gospel, priest or other ecclesiastical dignitary of any denomination who has been duly ordained or authorized by the church to which he belongs to preach the Gospel").

13 Ravenal v. Ravenal, 338 N.Y.S.2d 324 (1972); Cramer v. Commonwealth, 202 S.E.2d 911 (Va. 1974).

14 *See, e.g.,* ILL. REV. STAT. ch. 38, § 32-6 ("class 4 felony" with imprisonment of one to three years); MO. REV. STAT. § 451.120 (up to $500 fine); OKLA. STAT. title 43, § 15 (fine of $100 to $500, imprisonment of thirty days to one year).

15 *See, e.g.,* MICH. STAT. ANN. § 551.7(1)(i).

16 MASS. GEN. LAWS CH. 207, § 39. *See also* OR. REV. STAT. § 106.120.

Ministers should not agree to perform a marriage in another state without first confirming that they are legally authorized to do so.

registration of ministers

Some states require ministers to register with a government agency before they are authorized to perform marriage ceremonies.[17] Prior to performing marriage ceremonies, ministers should know whether or not such a requirement exists.

2. LEGAL REQUIREMENTS

Every state has enacted legislation prescribing various requirements that must be satisfied in order for a lawful marriage to occur. While there is much variation among the states, some requirements are common. These include the following:

legal capacity

Each state prescribes those persons who are not permitted to marry, or who may marry only if certain conditions are satisfied. For example, persons who are related too closely are prohibited from marrying in all states, although the prohibited degree of relationship varies widely. Also, persons below a specified age are prohibited from marrying without the consent of one or both parents, or a court. Many states prohibit marriages between persons of the same gender; persons with a mental disability; and imprisoned felons. Persons with a living spouse are also barred from marrying. It is important for ministers to become familiar with their state's description of those persons who are authorized, and not authorized, to marry.

license

Most states forbid a minister from performing a marriage unless the couple has obtained a marriage license. In many states, such licenses are obtained from the county recorder's office. Licenses are obtained by completing and submitting an application to the appropriate government office, along with the applicable fee. License applications generally ask for biographical and residential information. Licenses usually are valid for only a specified period of time, and only in the county in which they were issued. Some states require a blood test as a condition to receiving a marriage license. Many states impose a "waiting period" of a few days after an application for a license has been submitted until the license may be issued.

> ***Key point.*** *Ministers should be familiar with the license requirements under local law, and share this information with engaged couples. Many counties publish pamphlets for engaged couples that summarize the license requirements. It would be a good practice for ministers to have a supply of these publications on hand.*

---

[17] *See, e.g.,* MN. STAT. § 517.05 ("ministers of any religious denomination, before they are authorized to solemnize a marriage, shall file a copy of their credentials of license or ordination with the court administrator of the district court of a county in this state, who shall record the same and give a certificate thereof. The place where the credentials are recorded shall be endorsed upon and recorded with each certificate of marriage granted by a minister"); N.Y. DOM. REL. LAW § 11-b ("Every person authorized by law to perform the marriage ceremony, before performing any such ceremonies in the city of New York, shall register his or her name and address in the office of the city clerk of the city of New York [and] every such person, before performing any marriage ceremonies subsequent to a change in his or her address, shall likewise register such change of address"); OR. REV. STAT. § 106.120 (marriages may be solemnized "by any minister of any church organized, carrying on its work and having congregations in this state, who is authorized by such church to solemnize marriages, and who has filed for record with the county clerk of the county in which the minister resides or in which the marriage is solemnized, evidence satisfactory to the county clerk that the minister has been so authorized").

Key point. Ministers may be criminally liable for marrying couples with expired licenses. Well in advance of a marriage, the minister should request a copy of the marriage license, and ensure that it does not expire prior to the wedding date.

the ceremony

State laws provide little guidance with regard to the content of the marriage ceremony itself. Most statutes simply state that ministers may perform marriages in accordance with their religious tradition and tenets. Many states permit members of religious sects to be married according to the rites and customs of their sect, even though such ceremonies may not otherwise be consistent with state marriage laws.[18] Such laws do not dispense with licensing and reporting requirements, however.

the marriage certificate

Most states require ministers to complete a marriage certificate after the solemnization of a marriage, and return it to the same government office that issues marriage licenses. A second certificate often is obtained, and is given to the married couple. State law generally prescribes the deadline for filing marriage certificates, and the penalty for not doing so.

Misspelling a name, inserting the wrong date, or having less than the required number of witness signatures on the marriage certificate will not affect the validity of the marriage. It is generally held that a marriage will be considered valid even though the minister fails to complete and return a marriage certificate. And, a marriage will be valid even though the minister performing the ceremony was not authorized to do so, at least if the parties did not know that the minister lacked authority.[19]

criminal penalties

Many states also impose criminal penalties upon ministers for the following acts:

1. failure to maintain a record of marriage ceremonies performed

2. failure to return promptly to the proper authorities a properly completed certificate of marriage and the license to marry

3. marrying persons without a marriage license, or with an expired license

4. marrying persons not legally capable of marrying (because of age, relationship, or some other disability specified by state law)

Key point. A state's right to regulate marriage and divorce is the same whether a marriage is performed in a church by a minister or in a civil ceremony by a judge. As a result, a state's divorce law can be applied to a Christian marriage performed in a church by a minister though one of the spouses maintains that the state's divorce law conflicts with his or her religious beliefs.[20]

---

[18] *See, e.g.,* ILL. REV. STAT. ch. 40, § 209; MO. REV. STAT. § 451.100.
[19] *See, e.g.,* UNIFORM MARRIAGE AND DIVORCE ACT § 206.
[20] Trickey v. Trickey, 642 S.W.2d 47 (Tex. App. 1982).

Example. An Arizona court upheld the validity of a marriage despite a number of technical violations of state law. A couple was issued a marriage license by a county clerk. While on vacation in Puerto Rico, the couple exchanged vows in a marriage ceremony performed by the pastor of a local church. The couple, the pastor, and two witnesses signed the marriage license after the ceremony. The couple then returned to Arizona, continued to reside there as husband and wife, and had one child. A few years later, the wife asked a court to annul the marriage on the following grounds: (1) the marriage was invalid in both Arizona and Puerto Rico because neither the Arizona marriage license nor any other was ever filed or recorded in either jurisdiction; (2) the marriage was solemnized by a Puerto Rican pastor rather than a duly licensed or ordained Arizona pastor; and (3) the couple went to a foreign country for solemnization of their marriage to evade Arizona marriage laws. A state appeals court rejected each of the wife's grounds for invalidating the marriage. In rejecting the wife's first argument, the court noted that a failure to return a marriage license to the county clerk may expose an officiating pastor to criminal liability, but it does not affect the validity of the marriage. In rejecting the wife's second argument, the court pointed out that Arizona law only required "duly licensed or ordained" clergy to perform marriages within the state. The law did not define the requirements for officiating clergy in other states or countries. In rejecting the wife's third argument, the court acknowledged that state law invalidated marriages obtained by Arizona residents in other states or countries solely to evade the requirements of Arizona law. However, the court concluded that the couple had traveled to Puerto Rico for a vacation, and only after arriving made the decision to get married. As a result, the foreign marriage was not an attempt to evade Arizona law.[21]

Example. A Tennessee court ruled that a marriage was valid despite the husband's claim that the officiating clergyman was not qualified to perform marriages and had failed to return a signed marriage license to the county clerk within three days of the marriage as required by law. An Iranian couple living in Tennessee obtained a marriage license from the county clerk's office. The man asked an acquaintance (the "officiant") to perform an Islamic "blessing" for the couple. A "blessing" is a formalized ceremony intended to hold out a couple as being married. The officiant was not an "imam" (an Islamic spiritual leader roughly equivalent to a pastor or priest), but he blessed the couple anyway. The husband kept the marriage license to establish the marriage in Iran, and so it was never filed with the county clerk as required by law. Problems arose within days of the marriage, and the husband sought to annul the marriage on the grounds that the officiant did not have the authority to perform the Islamic blessing, and the marriage license was not filed with the county clerk's office within three days of the marriage as required by law. A state appeals court rejected both arguments. The court pointed out that state law permitted "[a]ll regular ministers of the gospel of every denomination . . . having the care of souls" to solemnize marriages. It concluded that "the courts look to the tenets of the particular religion to determine whether a particular person is a regular minister having care of souls." The court noted that an expert in Islamic law had testified that Islam "has consistently rejected the distinction between clergy and laity," and that Islamic law "stipulates quite precisely that anyone with the requisite knowledge of Islamic law is competent to perform religious ceremonies, including marriage." Since the officiant in this case was familiar with Islamic law, he was qualified to perform blessings—even though he was not an imam. The court also concluded that the failure to return the marriage license to the county clerk within three days did not render the marriage invalid. The court noted that when the husband refused to file the original marriage license, the wife and the officiant had completed a second license and filed it with the county clerk several weeks after the blessing. While this was well beyond the three-day deadline, the court refused to invalidate the marriage on this basis. It pointed out that the clerk accepted

---

[21] Barbosa-Johnson v. Johnson, 851 P.2d 866 (Ariz. App. 1993).

the belated license, and that "Tennessee protects the institution of marriage by presuming that regularly solemnized marriages are valid."[22]

PREMARRIAGE LEGAL CHECKLIST

Here is a checklist of items to consider before performing a marriage:

• Am I legally qualified to perform a marriage according to the law of my state? Review your state's law in Appendix 1 at the end of this text. If in doubt, contact your local recorder's office or the office of the attorney general for an interpretation.

• Am I legally qualified to perform a marriage according to the law of another state? Ministers occasionally are asked to perform a marriage in another state. Review the other state's law in Appendix 1 at the end of this text. If in doubt, contact the recorder's office in the county where the marriage will occur, or the office of the attorney general in the other state.

• Is the engaged couple legally capable of marrying? You will need to check your state law for the legal qualifications for marriage. Every state lists certain conditions that will limit a person's legal right to marry, or even prohibit it. Common examples include persons who are below a specified age, or persons who are too closely related. During premarital counseling be sure to verify that the couple meets all of the eligibility requirements specified by your state's law.

• Be sure you explain to the couple the marriage license requirements prescribed by state law. Again, you need to be familiar with these. They can be obtained from your county recorder's office or the office of your state attorney general.

• Be sure that the couple has a valid marriage license with an expiration date later than the date of the marriage. Check the license several days or weeks prior to the wedding.

• Be sure that the marriage license is valid for the county in which the marriage will occur. Generally, a marriage license is valid only if the marriage occurs in the county in which the license was issued.

• Be sure you make a record of each marriage that you perform, in the manner prescribed by your state law.

• Be sure to complete a certificate of marriage (if required by state law), and return it to the appropriate government office.

• You may want to suggest that the couple be tested for any sexually transmitted diseases.

---

[22] Aghili v. Saadatnejadi, 958 S.W.2d 784 (Tenn. App. 1997).

§ 3-05 Exemption from Military Duty

Key point 3-05. "Regular or duly ordained ministers of religion" are exempt from military training and service if they apply for exemption. This exemption does not apply to registration requirements, and does not apply to ministerial students.

This section will review the registration requirement of the Selective Service Act, and discuss the exemption of clergy and the deferral of ministerial students from military training and service. The subjects of military chaplains and conscientious objectors also are reviewed.

1. REGISTRATION

The Selective Service Act specifies that

it shall be the duty of every male citizen of the United States . . . who, on the day or days fixed for the first or any subsequent registration, is between the ages of 18 and 26, to present himself for and submit to registration at such time or times and place or places, and in such manner, as shall be determined by proclamation of the President.[23]

Several Presidential proclamations have been issued over the years, specifying the times and places for military registration. The current proclamation specifies that "persons born on or after January 1, 1963, shall present themselves for registration on the day they attain the 18th anniversary of their birth or on any day within the period of 60 days beginning 30 days before such date." Persons register by reporting to a designated United States Post Office facility. Registration is a simple procedure requiring only verification of the registrant's identity (e.g., with a birth certificate) and mailing address.

Clergy and theology students (of the specified age) are not exempt from the registration requirement. Of course, this rule has very little significance since the current registration requirement applies to male citizens upon attaining the age of 18, and relatively few persons are either clergy or ministerial students on their 18th birthday. In the past, a number of clergy and ministerial students have claimed that the registration procedure violates their constitutional right to freely exercise their religion. This claim has been rejected by the federal courts in every case. To illustrate, a federal appeals court ruled that if "an individual's religious training and belief are so strong as to preclude even registration, his only alternative is to violate the law and accept the consequences come what may."[24]

The Selective Service regulations specify that it is the duty of every registrant who registered after July 1, 1980, to notify the Selective Service within 10 days of any change in their mailing address or permanent residence.[25] And, clergy or ministerial students who have been deferred or exempted from military training or service must notify the Service immediately of any changes in facts or circumstances relating to their exemption or deferral.

---

[23] 50 U.S.C. App. § 453(a).
[24] United States v. Schmucker, 815 F.2d 414 (6th Cir. 1987).
[25] 32 C.F.R. § 1621.1.

2. Exemption of Ministers from Military Training and Service

The Military Selective Service Act exempts "regular or duly ordained ministers of religion" from military training and service.[26] However, as noted above, ministers are *not* exempted from the Act's registration requirements. The Act defines the term *duly ordained minister of religion* as

a person who has been ordained, in accordance with the ceremonial [sic], ritual, or discipline of a church, religious sect, or organization established on the basis of a community of faith and belief, doctrines and practices of a religious character, to preach and to teach the doctrines of such church, sect, or organization and to administer the rites and ceremonies thereof in public worship, and who as his regular and customary vocation preaches and teaches the principles of religion and administers the ordinances of public worship as embodied in the creed or principles of such church, sect, or organization.[27]

The Act defines the term *regular minister of religion* as

one who as his customary vocation preaches and teaches the principles of religion of a church, a religious sect, or organization of which he is a member, without having been formally ordained as a minister of a religion, and who is recognized by such church, sect, or organization as a regular minister.[28]

The Selective Service regulations further specify that the term *regular or duly ordained minister of religion* does not include

(i) A person who irregularly or incidentally preaches and teaches the principles of a religion of a church, religious sect, or organization; or (ii) a person who has been duly ordained a minister in accordance with the ceremonial rite or discipline of a church, religious sect or organization, but who does not regularly, as a bona fide vocation, teach and preach the principles of a religion and administer the ordinances of public worship, as embodied in the creed or principles of his church, sect, or organization.[29]

Ministers satisfying the definition of "regular or duly ordained ministers of religion" are not automatically exempt from military training and service. They must apply for exemption. This is done by filing a written application with the Selective Service System requesting "4-D" classification. This is the classification that pertains to exempt clergy. The Selective Service regulations provide guidelines for evaluating ministers' exemption applications. These guidelines specify that the government cannot consider the "training or abilities" of an applicant or the applicant's "motive or sincerity" in becoming a minister. However, the regulations require the government to "be careful to ascertain the actual duties and functions" of each applicant. They further provide that

preaching and teaching the principles of one's sect, if performed part-time or half-time, occasionally or irregularly, are insufficient to establish eligibility for class 4-D. These activities must be regularly performed and must comprise the [applicant's] regular calling or full-time profession.

---

[26] 50 U.S.C. App. § 456(g)(1).
[27] 50 U.S.C. App. § 466(g)(1).
[28] 50 U.S.C. App. § 466(g)(2).
[29] 32 C.F.R. § 1645.1.

The mere fact of some secular employment on the part of an [applicant] requesting classification in class 4-D does not in itself make him ineligible for that class.[30]

The regulations further specify that a minister's application for exemption will be denied if the evidence "clearly shows" that the minister: (1) is not a regular minister or a duly ordained minister; or (2) is a duly ordained minister "but does not regularly as his bona fide vocation teach and preach the principles of religion and administer the ordinances of public worship"; or (3) is a regular minister of religion "but does not regularly, as his bona fide vocation, teach and preach the principles of religion"; or (4) is not recognized by a church, sect, or organization as a regular minister of religion; or (5) "he is a duly ordained minister of religion but does not administer the ordinances of public worship."[31]

Why are clergy exempt from military training and service? A federal appeals court explained the exemption as follows: "[M]inisters of religion are relieved of the duty of service not so much for their personal religious training and beliefs, but for the disruption of public worship and religious solace to the people at large which would be caused by their induction."[32]

The most important element in the definition of both ordained and regular ministers is the requirement that a minister's "customary vocation" be preaching and teaching the principles of his or her church or sect. The regulations (quoted above) recognize that ordained and regular ministers may have some secular employment. However, they also state that preaching or teaching that is "part-time or half-time, occasionally or irregularly, are insufficient" to establish exemption. The United States Supreme Court has ruled that the Act's definitions do "not preclude all secular employment," since many ministers who are employed by small churches must seek part-time secular employment in order to adequately support themselves.[33] The Court has held that a minister's vocation could be preaching and teaching the principles of his church although he supported himself by working five hours a week as a radio repairman.[34] Other cases make it plain that ministers may pursue minimal amounts of secular employment without jeopardizing their exemption from military service. Such cases suggest that full-time clergy who also work 5-10 hours per week in a secular job are eligible for the exemption.

On the other hand, ministers who spend substantial amounts of time in secular employment may not be entitled to the exemption. To illustrate, the following ministers were denied an exemption from military service on the ground that their customary vocation was not the ministry: a minister who worked 28 hours a week as a busboy and 30 hours a month as a minister;[35] a minister who worked 45 hours a week as a carpenter and 15 hours a month as a minister;[36] a minister employed full-time in secular employment and 14 hours a week in the ministry;[37] a minister employed full-time in secular employment and 10 hours a week in the ministry;[38] a minister who regularly performed ministerial work, but for only one-third of his total working hours;[39] and, a minister who worked a 40-hour per week secular job and who devoted only 12 or 13 hours per

---

[30] *Id.* at § 1645.7(c).

[31] *Id.* at § 1645.4.

[32] United States ex rel. Trainin v. Cain, 144 F.2d 944, 949 (2nd Cir. 1944), *cert. denied,* 323 U.S. 795 (1945).

[33] Dickinson v. United States, 346 U.S. 389 (1953).

[34] *Id.*

[35] Fore v. United States, 395 F.2d 548 (10th Cir. 1968).

[36] Leitner v. United States, 222 F.2d 363 (4th Cir. 1955).

[37] United States v. Burgueno, 423 F.2d 599 (9th Cir. 1970), *cert. denied,* 398 U.S. 965 (1970).

[38] *See generally* Annot., 1 A.L.R. FED. 607 (1969).

[39] United States v. Isenring, 419 F.2d 975 (7th Cir. 1969), *cert. denied,* 397 U.S. 1024 (1969).

month to ministerial duties.[40] One federal appeals court ruled that at least 160 hours per month should be devoted to ministry in order to qualify for the ministerial exemption.[41]

In summary, the cases and regulations make one thing very clear—clergy who work a full-time secular job will rarely if ever qualify for the ministerial exemption from military training and service, no matter how much time they devote to ministerial services. On the other hand, clergy who are employed on a full-time basis to perform ministerial services will not become ineligible for the exemption merely because they work a minimal number of hours (5-10) each week in a secular job.

It is clear that a minister need not be the sole or principal religious leader of a congregation in order to be eligible for an exemption. Assistant or associate ministers also are entitled to the exemption if they are either ordained or regular ministers.[42] The motivation of an individual in becoming a minister is irrelevant. Thus, a minister cannot be denied an exemption on the ground that his sole purpose in becoming a minister was to evade military service.[43] Further, the regulations prohibit the government from considering an applicant's lack of formal theological training in evaluating his or her application for exemption.[44] The definitions of *ordained* and *regular ministers* contained in the Selective Service Act will take precedence over the definitions adopted by a church or religious organization.[45] Further, ministers are entitled to the exemption if they meet the definition of either an ordained or regular minister, even if they have no college or seminary training.

The exemption of ministers from military training and service does not violate the "nonestablishment of religion" clause of the first amendment to the United States Constitution.[46] As one federal appeals court noted, the purpose of the exemption is not to benefit ministers, but rather "to assure religious leadership to members of [their] faith."[47]

3. Deferral of Ministerial Students from Military Training and Service

Until 1971, ministerial students were exempted from military training and service. That is, they were treated like clergy. In 1971, Congress amended the Selective Service Act to replace the ministerial student exemption with a *deferral* from military training or service. This deferral of course may mature into an exemption if the student completes his or her training and becomes an ordained or regular minister.

The Military Selective Service Act specifies that

[s]tudents preparing for the ministry under the direction of recognized churches or religious organizations, who are satisfactorily pursuing full-time courses of instruction in recognized theological or divinity schools, or who are satisfactorily pursuing full-time courses of instruction leading to their entrance into recognized theological or divinity schools in which they have been preenrolled, shall be deferred from training and service, but not from registration . . . .[48]

---

[40] United States v. Campbell, 439 F.2d 1087 (9th Cir. 1971).

[41] United States v. Kenstler, 377 F.2d 559 (3rd Cir. 1967).

[42] Wiggins v. United States, 261 F.2d 113 (5th Cir. 1958); United States v. Hull, 391 F.2d 257 (4th Cir. 1968), *cert. denied*, 392 U.S. 914 (1968).

[43] Rowell v. United States, 223 F.2d 863 (5th Cir. 1955).

[44] 32 C.F.R. § 1645.7.

[45] United States v. Novak, 475 F.2d 180 (7th Cir. 1973), *cert. denied*, 412 U.S. 930 (1973).

[46] United States v. Branigan, 299 F. Supp. 225 (S.D.N.Y. 1969).

[47] United States v. Bittinger, 422 F.2d 1032 (4th Cir. 1969).

[48] 50 U.S.C. App. § 456(g)(2).

The Selective Service regulations further explain the deferral of ministerial students by noting that

[i]n class 2-D shall be placed any [applicant] who is preparing for the ministry under the direction of a recognized church or religious organization; and (1) Who is satisfactorily pursuing a full-time course of instruction required for entrance into a recognized theological or divinity school in which he has been pre-enrolled or accepted for admission; or (2) Who is satisfactorily pursuing a full-time course of instruction in a recognized theological or divinity school; or (3) Who, having completed a theological or divinity school, is a student in a full-time graduate program or is a full-time intern, and whose studies are related to and lead toward entry into service as a regular or duly ordained minister of religion. Satisfactory progress in these studies as determined by the school in which the registrant is enrolled, must be maintained for qualification for the deferment.[49]

The regulations define a "recognized theological or divinity school" as a "theological or divinity school whose graduates are acceptable for ministerial duties either as an ordained or regular minister by the church or religious organization sponsoring a registrant as a ministerial student."[50]

The "deferral" of ministerial students is not automatic. Eligible students must request the deferral by submitting a written application for "2-D" status to their local Selective Service board. The regulations state that an application for deferral must be accompanied by "a statement from a church or religious organization that the [applicant] is preparing for ministry under its direction." The application for deferral also must contain a "certification" that the applicant (1) is satisfactorily pursuing a full-time course of study required for entrance into a recognized theological or divinity school, or (2) is satisfactorily pursuing a full-time course of study at a recognized theological or divinity school, or (3) is satisfactorily pursuing a full-time graduate program (following the completion of theological or divinity school) that "leads toward entry into service as a regular or duly ordained minister of religion," or (4) is a full-time intern "whose studies are related to and lead toward entry into service as a regular or duly ordained minister of religion."[51]

Part-time theology students are not entitled to deferral. Thus, one student who worked full-time in a secular job and who attended only two hours of classes each week was found to be subject to military training and service.[52]

A federal appeals court ruled that a Mennonite seminarian's constitutional right to religious freedom was not violated by a federal prosecution for his failure to register with the Selective Service System. The court observed that any burden on religious freedom was minimal since the religious objections could be raised after registration but before induction.

4. Military Chaplains

The federal government has made funds available for military chaplains since the Revolutionary War. In a recent year, government statistics revealed that the Army had 1,427 active-duty commissioned chaplains, 1,383 chaplain's assistants, 48 directors of religious education, and over 500 chapels. Of course, the Navy and Air Force have additional chaplains and facilities. Chaplains must meet educational requirements prescribed by the military, and be endorsed by an ecclesiastical endorsing agency. Chaplains currently represent more

---

[49] 32 C.F.R. § 1639.3(a).
[50] *Id.* at § 1639.1.
[51] *Id.* at § 1639.6.
[52] United States v. Bartelt, 200 F.2d 385 (7th Cir. 1952).

than 85 religious faiths, and each faith is assigned a "quota" of chaplains based on its relative size in the general civilian population.

Does the military chaplaincy program constitute a violation of the religious neutrality required by the first amendment's "nonestablishment of religion" clause? In 1985, a federal appeals court said no.[53] The court rejected the claim that the religious needs of military personnel could be accomplished at no expense to the government either through the use of civilian clergy or by using chaplains paid by religious denominations themselves. The court noted that 37 percent of Army personnel are stationed overseas and ordinarily do not have access to Christian clergy. With respect to military personnel stationed in the United States, the court observed that "local civilian clergy in the rural areas where most military camps are centered are inadequate to satisfy the soldiers' religious needs because they are too few in number for the task and are usually of different religious denominations from those of most of the nearby troops." In rejecting the claim that the military could operate with chaplains financed through denominational contributions, the court noted simply that there was no evidence that the various denominations would "be willing to pay their respective share of the $85 million required to operate a civilian chaplaincy."

The court emphasized that the purpose of the military chaplaincy program

is to make religion, religious education, counseling and religious facilities available to military personnel and their families under circumstances where the practice of religion would otherwise be denied as a practical matter to all or a substantial number. As a result, the morale of our soldiers, their willingness to serve, and the efficiency of the Army as an instrument for our national defense rests in substantial part on the military chaplaincy, which is vital to our Army's functioning.[54]

In further support of its decision upholding the constitutionality of the military chaplaincy program, the court also mentioned that civil courts ordinarily must defer to congressional determinations in military affairs, and that the same Congress that drafted the first amendment nonestablishment of religion clause authorized a paid chaplain for the Army. The court also noted that the first amendment guarantees the free exercise of religion, and it quoted with approval from an earlier opinion of a Supreme Court justice: "Spending federal funds to employ chaplains for the armed forces might be said to violate the establishment clause. Yet a lonely soldier stationed at some faraway outpost could surely complain that a government which did not provide him the opportunity for pastoral guidance was affirmatively prohibiting the free exercise of his religion."[55]

In conclusion, the military chaplaincy program does not violate the first amendment's nonestablishment of religion clause, and accordingly chaplains will continue to play a significant role in the armed forces.

5. CONSCIENTIOUS OBJECTORS

The Military Selective Service Act provides that no person who "by reason of religious training and belief is conscientiously opposed to participation in war in any form" shall be subject to combatant training and service in the armed forces.[56] One need not be a minister to qualify for conscientious objector status, and a person is not automatically entitled to such status because he or she is a minister.[57] The courts have greatly

---

[53] Katcoff v. Marsh, 755 F.2d 223 (2nd Cir. 1985).
[54] *Id.* at 237.
[55] Quoting Justice Stewart's dissenting opinion in Abingdon School District v. Schempp, 374 U.S. 203, 308 (1963).
[56] 50 U.S.C. App. § 456(j).
[57] United States v. Bryan, 263 F. Supp. 895 (N.D. Ga. 1967).

liberalized the meaning of "religious training and belief." The United States Supreme Court has held that conscientious objector status is properly available to any individual who is conscientiously opposed to war on the basis of "moral, ethical, or religious beliefs about what is right and wrong and [which are] held with the strength of traditional religious convictions."[58] Conscientious objector status is thus available to agnostics and even atheists, since belief in God is not a prerequisite to conscientious objector status.[59] Avowed humanists have been granted conscientious objector status.[60]

Conscientious objector status is available to an individual on the basis of religious conviction even though he is not a member of a religious society or organization.[61] And it is available even though an individual's opposition to war is based only partly on "religious training and belief." To receive conscientious objector status, one must be opposed to participation in war in any form. It is not enough that an individual is opposed merely to a particular war.[62] One may be entitled to conscientious objector status even though he is willing to use force in defense of self, home, or family.[63]

The Military Selective Service Act does provide that conscientious objectors may be compelled to perform noncombatant military service or civilian work contributing to the maintenance of the national health, safety, or interest.

Those sections of the Military Selective Service Act pertaining to conscientious objectors have been upheld against claims that they constitute a violation of the religious neutrality required by the first amendment's nonestablishment of religion clause,[64] and that they condone "involuntary servitude."[65]

§ 3-06   Exemption From Jury Duty

Key point 3-06. Clergy are exempt from jury duty in some states. Even if not exempt, clergy may be excused from jury duty on the basis of several grounds including hardship, prejudice, familiarity with the facts or one of the parties, and prior jury service in a similar case.

One has a right to have a jury decide questions of fact in most civil and criminal cases. This right is guaranteed by the United States Constitution and by most state constitutions. It also is recognized by many state and federal statutes. Associated with the right to trial by jury is the corresponding obligation of jury service. Every citizen has a duty to serve as a juror when called upon to do so, unless specifically exempted or excused.

In many states, ministers are exempted from the duty of jury service.[66] The exemption may be automatic, or it may be available only upon timely application. If the exemption is only available upon the filing of a timely application, a court generally is under no duty to inform a prospective juror of entitlement to an exemption—the burden is upon the prospective juror to affirmatively claim it.[67] Of course, exempted clergy have the right to waive the exemption and have their names placed on the list of eligible jurors.

---

[58] Welsh v. United States, 398 U.S. 333, 340 (1970).
[59] United States v. Wainscott, 496 F.2d 356 (4th Cir. 1974).
[60] United States v. Vlasits, 422 F.2d 1267 (4th Cir. 1970).
[61] United States v. Stock, 460 F.2d 480 (9th Cir. 1972).
[62] Gillette v. United States, 401 U.S. 437 (1971).
[63] Rosenfield v. Rumble, 515 F.2d 498 (1st Cir. 1975), *cert. denied,* 423 U.S. 911 (1975).
[64] *See generally* note 46 *supra.*
[65] United States v. Fallon, 407 F.2d 621 (7th Cir. 1969), *cert. denied,* 395 U.S. 908 (1969).
[66] The laws of all 50 states are summarized in Appendix 3.
[67] State v. Rogers, 324 So.2d 403 (La. 1975).

The exemption of ministers and various other occupations from the duty of jury service has been explained on the ground that "it is for the good of the community that their regular work should not be interrupted."[68] The exemption of ministers from jury duty has been upheld against the claim that such exemptions violate the first amendment's prohibition of the establishment of a religion.[69]

In those states in which a minister is not exempted from jury service, a minister often may be excused from service by showing that undue hardship or extreme inconvenience would result, or that the public good would be impaired. Such a decision is entirely within the discretion of the presiding judge. Obviously, a minister who is not exempted from jury service should be excused if there is a funeral to perform, several parishioners are in the hospital and in need of visitation, the church is engaged in the construction of a new facility, or there are urgent counseling needs.

A minister not otherwise exempt from jury service may be excused if properly challenged. A prospective juror may be challenged on the grounds of prejudice, direct interest in the litigation, previous knowledge of the facts, acquaintance with a party to the lawsuit, prior jury service in the same or a related case, or preconceived opinions about the lawsuit.

Persons whose religious beliefs prohibit them from serving on juries occasionally are excused from jury service.[70]

§ 3-07　The Clergy-Penitent Privilege

Every state[71] has a law making certain communications to clergy "privileged." This generally means that neither the minister nor the "penitent" can be forced to testify in court (or in a deposition or certain other legal proceedings) about the contents of the communication. The history of the clergy-penitent privilege was summarized by one court as follows:

> The priest-penitent privilege originated with the seal of confession. Under the Code of Canon Law of the Roman Catholic Church for a "confessor in any way to betray a penitent" was a crime. A confessor who directly violates the seal of confession incurs an automatic excommunication reserved to the Apostolic See. Traditionally, breaking the seal of confession "has been one of the most severely penalized offenses within the Code." The sanctity of the confession was recognized in English law from the Norman Conquest in 1066 until the English Reformation in the Sixteenth Century. After the Reformation, hostility towards the Catholic Church in England resulted in a refusal to recognize the privilege. When this country was founded, therefore, the privilege did not exist at common law. Accordingly, American courts required that the privilege be conferred by statute. Where no privilege existed, clergypersons were often compelled to testify

---

[68]　Rawlins v. Georgia, 201 U.S. 638 (1906) (Justice Holmes).

[69]　United States v. Butler, 611 F.2d 1066 (11th Cir. 1980), *cert. denied*, 449 U.S. 830 (1980).

[70]　In re Jenison, 125 N.W.2d 588 (Minn. 1963).

[71]　The statute or court rule recognizing the clergy-penitent privilege in each state is quoted verbatim in Appendix 2 (at the end of this book). For an excellent treatment of the history of the privilege, written by two clergymen who advocate a broad privilege, see W. Tiemann and J. Bush, The Right to Silence: Privileged Clergy Communications and the Law (1983). *See also* Callahan, *Historical Inquiry into the Priest-Penitent Privilege*, 36 Jurist 328 (1976); Mitchell, *Must Clergy Tell? Child Abuse Reporting Requirements versus the Clergy Privilege and Free Exercise of Religion*, 71 Minn. L. Rev. 723 (1986); Reese, *Confidential Communications to Clergy*, 24 Ohio St. L.J. 55 (1963); Smith, *The Pastor on the Witness Stand: Toward a Religious Privilege in the Courts*, 29 Cath. Law. 1 (1984); Yellin, *The History and Current Status of the Clergy-Penitent Privilege*, 23 Santa Clara L. Rev. 95 (1983); *see generally* J. Wigmore, Wigmore on Evidence §§ 2394-2396 (McNaughton rev. ed. 1961 & Supp. 1998); Annot., 71 A.L.R.3d 794; Annot., 49 A.L.R.3d 1205.

despite personal, moral, and religious objections. Although the Roman Catholic Church has the longest tradition of the sanctity of the confessional, for many other Christian denominations their "sincere dedication to secrecy is equally apparent." In the Episcopal Church, for example, the new Book of Common Prayer's rite, "The Reconciliation of a Penitent," warns that the secrecy of a confession is morally absolute for the confessor, and must under no circumstances be broken. Violators are subject to church discipline. The governing body of the American Lutheran Church also has adopted a resolution that the pastor hold inviolate and disclose to no one the confessions and communications made to him as a pastor without the specific consent of the person making the communication. Similarly, the Presbyterian Church in the U.S., the United Presbyterian Church, and the American Baptist Convention have adopted policy statements strongly affirming the inviolability of religious confidentiality.

The prospect of clergy going to jail to comply with their religious beliefs rather than disclosing a penitent's confession resulted in various religious groups bringing pressure on state legislatures to enact a clergyperson privilege. Thus, the origin of the priest-penitent privilege as well as the moving force behind the enactment of the statutory privilege was to protect the clergyperson from being forced against his or her will to reveal confidences. Now almost all states have clergyperson-penitent privileges.[72]

What is the current justification for this rule, that "contravenes the fundamental principle that the public has a right to every man's evidence"?[73] The United States Supreme Court has observed that "the priest-penitent privilege recognizes the human need to disclose to a spiritual counselor, in total and absolute confidence, what are believed to be flawed acts or thoughts and to receive priestly consolation and guidance in return."[74] A federal appeals court judge stated the justification for the privilege as follows:

Sound policy—reason and experience—concedes to religious liberty a rule of evidence that a clergyman shall not disclose in a trial the secrets of a penitent's confidential confession to him, at least absent the penitent's consent. Knowledge so acquired in the performance of a spiritual function . . . is not to be transformed into evidence to be given to the whole world. . . . The benefit of preserving these confidences inviolate overbalances the possible benefit of permitting litigation to prosper at the expense of the tranquility of the home, the integrity of the professional relationship, and the spiritual rehabilitation of a penitent. The rules of evidence have always been concerned not only with truth but with the manner of its ascertainment.[75]

A state court explained the privilege as follows:

Communicant-clergyman confidentiality benefits the individual communicant, the clergy, and society. The individual benefits from unfettered freedom of religion in his use of the confessional; his perceived ability to communicate with God through an emissary; the therapeutic value in obtaining psychological and physical relief from fear, tension, and anxiety; and in his exercise of a fundamental right to privacy. The clergy benefits in being able to safely draw out a communicant's innermost thoughts and feelings with the assurance that confidences are protected by public policy. Id. The church as an institution benefits in enjoying recognition of its prestigious place in

---

[72] State v. Szemple, 640 A.2d 817 (N.J. 1994).

[73] United States v. Bryan, 339 U.S. 323, 331 (1950).

[74] Trammel v. United States, 445 U.S. 40, 51 (1980).

[75] Mullen v. United States, 263 F.2d 275, 280 (D.C. Cir. 1958) (Fahy, J., concurring).

society. The judiciary benefits by avoiding direct confrontations with the clergy. There is the realization that requiring the clergy to testify will not necessarily produce testimony. The concept of jailing a clergyman for adhering to the absolute duty imposed upon him by deep religious beliefs is offensive.[76]

Not every communication made to a minister is privileged and thereby protected from disclosure. The typical statute applies only to (1) communications (2) confidentially made (3) to a minister (4) acting in his or her professional capacity as a spiritual adviser. To illustrate, Rule 505 of the Uniform Rules of Evidence, which has been adopted by several states, provides:

(a) *Definitions.* As used in this rule:

(1) A "clergyman" is a minister, priest, rabbi, accredited Christian Science Practitioner, or other similar functionary of a religious organization, or an individual reasonably believed so to be by the person consulting him.

(2) A communication is "confidential" if made privately and not intended for further disclosure except to other persons present in furtherance of the purpose of the communication.

(b) *General Rule of Privilege.* A person has a privilege to refuse to disclose and to prevent another from disclosing a confidential communication by the person to the clergyman in his professional character as a spiritual adviser.

(c) *Who May Claim the Privilege.* The privilege may be claimed by the person, by his guardian or conservator, or by his personal representative if he is deceased. The person who was the clergyman at the time of the communication is presumed to have authority to claim the privilege but only on behalf of the communicant.

Some states add a fifth requirement—the communication made in confidence to a clergyman must be made "in the course of discipline." Before addressing the five elements of the clergy-penitent privilege, it should be noted that there is some variation in the definition of the privilege from state to state. As one court has observed, "The numerous state clergy-privilege statutes are not identical and they provide varying treatment of the privilege."[77] Clergy must be familiar with the definition of the privilege in their own state, and it is for this reason that the full text of the clergy-penitent privilege (for all fifty states) is set forth in Appendix 2.

§ 3-07.1 — A "Communication"

> ***Key point 3-07.1.*** *In order for the clergy-penitent privilege to apply there must be a "communication." A communication includes verbal statements, but it also may include nonverbal acts that are intended to transmit ideas. Mere observations generally are not considered to be communications.*

The privilege against divulging confidential communications extends only to actual communications between an individual and a clergyman. Communications obviously include verbal statements, but they also

---

[76] Simpson v. Tennant, 871 S.W.2d 301 (Tex. App. Houston 1994). *See also* Church of Jesus Christ of Latter-Day Saints v. Superior Court, 764 P.2d 759 (Ariz. App. 1988) (the clergy-penitent privilege is a response "to the urgent need of people to confide in, without fear of reprisal, those entrusted with the pressing task of offering spiritual guidance so that harmony with one's self and others can be realized").

[77] State v. Szemple, 640 A.2d 817 (N.J. 1994).

can include nonverbal forms of communication. One court ruled that the delivery of a gun to a minister constituted a "privileged communication" that was not admissible in court. A New York City police officer who also served as assistant pastor of a local church was approached one evening (while in civilian clothes on the church grounds) by an elderly man who addressed the minister by name and stated that he had something at home that he wanted to give him. A few minutes later, the individual returned, and was escorted into an office where he handed the minister a plastic bag containing a .38 caliber revolver. Not wanting to the leave the gun on church premises overnight, the minister flagged a patrol car that was passing by the church, and handed the gun to the officer driving the vehicle. A few months later, the minister was accused of violating several police department regulations in the proper disposition of the gun. The minister claimed that the incident could not give rise to any disciplinary action since it was a "privileged communication" under New York law and therefore could not be used in any legal proceeding. A state appeals court reversed this ruling, and dismissed the charges. The court concluded that the gun had been delivered to the minister in his capacity as a minister, and that the manner in which the gun was delivered constituted a "confidential" nonverbal communication. The court found it significant that the elderly gentleman had gone to the church with the gun rather than to a police facility, and that the minister was wearing civilian clothes.[78] Another court ruled that the act of a murder suspect in displaying a gun to a minister was a "communication." The court reasoned that the word *communication* is not limited to conversation but includes "any act by which ideas are transmitted from one person to another."[79]

Acts that are not intended to "transmit ideas" are not deemed communications. Some courts have ruled that a minister's personal impressions of a person's mental capacity are not privileged,[80] nor are a minister's personal observations of the demeanor or reactions of another.[81] In a case involving a challenge to the will of an elderly decedent, a minister who testified concerning the speech, hearing, and sight of the decedent was held not to have "waived" the privilege since he only testified concerning personal "observations." He therefore was permitted to claim the privilege with respect to confidential communications he had with the decedent.[82] And a minister who assumed the custody of a two-month-old child was permitted to testify concerning the child's condition and the conduct of the child's parents, since this testimony related only to observations and not to communications arising out of spiritual counseling.[83]

There is no reason why communications transmitted by telephone should not be privileged, if they satisfy the conditions specified by state law. What about correspondence? Should a letter to a minister be privileged? One federal court ruled that a letter written by a prisoner to a priest, requesting the priest to get in contact with an FBI agent and have him visit the prisoner, was not privileged.[84] The court observed, "The letter contains no hint that its contents were to be kept secret, or that its purpose was to obtain religious or other counsel, advice, solace, absolution, or ministration. It merely requested assistance by putting [the prisoner] in touch with the agent and explained [his] purpose and plan in asking this." Under the circumstances, the court concluded that the letter was not confidential. However, the court's decision strongly suggests that a letter written to a minister may be privileged if it (1) seeks religious counsel, and (2) indicates on its face that its contents are to be kept secret.

---

[78] Lewis v. New York City Housing Authority, 542 N.Y.Y.2d 165 (1989).

[79] Commonwealth v. Zezima, 310 N.E.2d 590 (Mass. 1974).

[80] Buuck v. Kruckeberg, 95 N.E.2d 304 (Ind. 1951). *Contra* Boyles v. Cora, 6 N.W.2d 401 (Iowa 1942).

[81] State v. Kurtz, 564 S.W.2d 856 (Mo. 1978). *See also* State v. Winn, 828 P.2d 879 (Idaho 1992) (pastor could testify regarding the demeanor of a woman who counseled with him and who was later charged with murdering her son); State v. Orfi, 511 N.W.2d 464 (Minn. App. 1994).

[82] Snyder v. Poplett, 424 N.E.2d 396 (Ill. App. 1981).

[83] Jones v. Department of Human Resources, 310 S.E.2d 753 (Ga. App. 1983).

[84] United States v. Wells, 446 F.2d 2 (2nd Cir. 1971).

One court ruled that the clergy-penitent privilege covered personal records of a deceased church member that were in the possession of the pastor.[85]

Example. A New Jersey court ruled that some documents maintained by a Catholic Archdiocese were not subject to disclosure in a civil lawsuit.[86] Two adult brothers sued a priest and their church and an archdiocese as a result of injuries they allegedly suffered when they were sexually molested by the priest some thirty years before. The brothers claimed that the church and archdiocese were legally responsible for the priest's actions on the basis of negligent selection and negligent supervision. The brothers asked the archdiocese to turn over all documents contained in the files of its "vicar for priests," along with any other documents regarding sexual misconduct by any priest from the 1960s to the present. The archdiocese insisted that it was protected from turning over these documents on the basis of the clergy-penitent privilege and the first amendment guaranty of religious freedom. In particular, the archdiocese asserted that the files of the vicar for priests "were of a confidential nature of the highest order" because "the vicar for priests serves as a confidant to priests in need. Accordingly, all priests who confide in the vicar for priests do so with an expectation of privacy and confidentiality. The relationship is the same as a confessional matter with any other penitent. Through the vicar for priests, priests in distress seek counsel and support regarding matters related to the stresses and tension involved in ministry." The court concluded that documents in the vicar's files containing statements made by the offending priest to the vicar "are protected by the privilege," since "it is undisputed that the vicar was acting in his professional character, or as a spiritual adviser, when, or if [the offending priest] confided in him respecting the alleged sexual assaults or any other personal or professional matter. . . . Priests confide in the vicar with the expectation of privacy and confidentiality; the relationship is the same as a confessional matter with any other penitent. Priests in distress seek counsel and support regarding matters related to the stresses and tensions involved in their ministry. Thus . . . [the vicar] received such communications in confidence as a "confidant to priests in need." Thus, so long as [the offending priest's] communications to the vicar were "confessions" or otherwise made with the expectation of confidentiality, these communications are protected against disclosure." The court cautioned that not every document in the vicar's files was necessarily privileged. Only those documents reflecting "communications made in confidence" to the vicar while he was acting as a spiritual counselor were protected by the privilege.

Example. A Texas court ruled that a minister did not have to disclose the identity of a person who spoke with him in confidence about the cause of an accident that injured a young child on church premises.[87] A 3-year-old girl suffered a broken neck and was rendered quadriplegic and respirator-dependent for life when unsecured "monkey bars" fell on her while she was using them on church property. The girl's parents sued the church and a denominational agency. Their attorneys took the minister's deposition, and asked him if he had any knowledge about the accident. The minister admitted that he had spoken with someone about the accident, but insisted that the identity of the person and the substance of the conversation were both protected from disclosure by the clergy-penitent privilege. The parents claimed that a person's identity is not a "communication" at all, but a mere "observation" that is not privileged. The court disagreed. It concluded that the privilege was broad enough to protect clergy from disclosing the identity of counselees as well as what counselees share. It pointed out that the child's parents were "no worse off being denied the identity of the communicant since that information would not have existed but for the privilege. . . . Communications that are made because of the privilege and which the law assumes never could have been made without the privilege remain private. Nothing is hidden that the rest of the world would have reasonably expected to be available."

---

[85] State v. Franklin, 226 S.E.2d 896 (S.C. 1976).

[86] Corsie v. Camanalonga, 721 A.2d 733 (N.J. Super. 1998).

[87] Simpson v. Tennant, 871 S.W.2d 301 (Tex. App. Houston 1994).

Example. A federal court in Virginia ruled that the clergy-penitent privilege applied to a pastoral counselor's written notes.[88] A woman was injured when a can fell from a top shelf in a grocery store and struck her. She sued the grocery store for damages. The grocery store attempted to subpoena all of the counseling records maintained on the woman by a pastoral counseling service that she had consulted. The grocery store claimed that it was entitled to see the counseling records since the woman referred to her religious counseling in support of her claim that her injuries had caused severe emotional distress. It also asserted that the clergy-penitent privilege only protects "testimony" and not written records. The court concluded that "to compel the production of these documents would render meaningless the clear protection against disclosure of confidential communications to the clergy. . . ." It added, "[The counselor's] notes would reveal the substance of [the woman's] confidential communications to [her]. Consequently, the counselor's testimony as a witness in the civil trial would no longer be needed . . . . Thus, a party seeking disclosure of such confidential communications could easily subvert the protections provided by the statute in cases in which a prudent clergyperson had documented the counseling. This court holds, therefore, that the protection of [the privilege] provided to clergy . . . also extends to their disclosure, in any civil action, of documents that contain the substance of that testimony."

Example. A Texas court suggested that letters written to clergy may be protected by the clergy-penitent privilege.[89] A woman was prosecuted for the murder of her husband. A jury rejected her alibi defense that she was with her pastor at the time of the murder. The prosecution, in rebutting the woman's alibi defense, introduced into evidence two letters written by the woman to her pastor in which she urged him to testify that she was with him at the time of the murder. The letters warned the pastor that if he did not agree to testify that she had been with him at the time of the murder, she would "be forced" to disclose "the full truth" about their "personal relationship." The pastor, who denied any inappropriate relationship with the woman, took the letters to the police. He later testified in court that the woman had not been with him at the time of the murder. The woman was convicted of murder, and appealed her conviction on the ground that the letters she wrote to the pastor were protected by the clergy-penitent privilege and should not have been introduced into evidence at her trial. A court rejected this claim. It observed, "[N]ot every private conversation with or letter to a member of the clergy is privileged. The privilege extends only to communications that are addressed to a clergyman in his professional capacity. The [trial court] found that the [woman's] letters were not written to the pastor in his professional character as a spiritual adviser. There is nothing in either letter than can remotely be characterized as a request for spiritual guidance or consolation. The letters were nothing more than open threats to destroy the pastor's reputation if he did not provide [her] with an alibi, and could as easily have been addressed to any other man with whom [she] had or could claim to have had a "personal relationship."

§ 3-07.2 — Made in Confidence

Key point 3-07.2. In order for the clergy-penitent privilege to apply there must be a communication that is made in confidence. This generally means that there are no other persons present besides the minister and counselee who can overhear the communication, and that there is an expectation that the conversation will be kept secret.

To be entitled to the privilege against the disclosure of confidential communications made to a minister, a communication must be made in confidence. This generally is interpreted to mean that a communication must be made under circumstances which indicate that it would forever remain a secret. Otherwise, the

---

[88] Blough v. Food Lion, Inc., 142 F.R.D. 622 (E.D. Va. 1992).
[89] Easley v. State, 837 S.W.2d 854 (Tex. App. 1992).

privilege does not apply. Thus, statements made to a minister in the presence of other persons generally will not be privileged.

To illustrate, in each of the following situations the communication was not "confidential" and therefore not privileged: statements made by a murder suspect to his minister in the presence of a church elder;[90] statements made by a church member to his minister in the presence of his minister's wife;[91] a confession by a church member to his minister in the presence of two other persons;[92] and a confession made to a minister by a prisoner in the obvious presence of a prison guard.[93]

Statements made by a suspected rapist to a minister immediately following a Sunday morning worship service three days before the rape were not privileged since they were not made in confidence. The minister testified that the conversation had occurred while "many people were hanging around as they usually do" following a service, and that "we [the minister and the accused] talked with quite a number of people." The accused claimed that the prosecution erred in allowing the statements made by the accused to the minister to be introduced in court, since such statements were the product of the "clergy-penitent" privilege. The court rejected this claim, noting that only *confidential* communications made to a minister acting in his or her professional capacity as a spiritual adviser are privileged from disclosure in a court of law, and that the statements made by the accused in this case were not privileged. It concluded that "the record supports the trial court's finding that the conversation had not taken place in private and therefore was not a privileged confidential communication."[94]

If the presence of a third person is legally required (*e.g.*, a prisoner who cannot communicate with a minister unless a guard is present), the privilege *may* apply.[95] A few courts have concluded that communications made to a minister in the presence of elders, deacons, or other church officers are privileged if the communication involved a confession of sin made in the course of a disciplinary proceeding.[96] And, a few state laws extend the clergy-penitent privilege to situations in which other persons are present "in furtherance of the communication."[97]

Statements made to a minister by a spouse during marriage counseling may be privileged despite the presence of the other spouse, and a few state laws specifically so provide.[98] In other states, the same will be true because of liberal interpretations of state law.[99] Certainly, the objective of the privilege (as noted above)

[90] Perry v. State, 655 S.W.2d 380 (Ark. 1983).
[91] State v. Melvin, 564 A.2d 458 (N.H. 1989). The *Melvin* case involved a confession of child abuse. In permitting the prosecutor to compel the testimony of the minister regarding the member's confession, the court observed that "generally, *the presence of a third party during a privileged conversation operates to destroy the privilege*" because the communication is not "confidential." The father argued that the clergy-penitent privilege should apply in cases where a third party is present (such as a pastor's spouse) who is "assisting or working under the supervision of the licensed minister." The court disagreed, noting that the state law recognizing the privilege did not recognize such an exception. *See also* State v. West, 345 S.E.2d 186 (N.C. 1986) (confession made by rapist to pastor in presence of pastor's wife was not privileged).
[92] State v. Berry, 324 So.2d 822 (La. 1975).
[93] United States v. Webb, 615 F.2d 828 (9th Cir. 1980).
[94] State v. Hedger, 768 P.2d 1331 (Ida. 1989).
[95] People v. Brown, 368 N.Y.S.2d 645 (1974). In the *Brown* case, a prisoner refused to confess to a murder during interrogation, but then telephoned his minister, in the presence of a guard, and blurted out "Bishop Hicks, praise the Lord, I need your prayers, I have killed a man."
[96] *See, e.g.*, Reutkemeier v. Nolte, 161 N.W. 290 (Iowa 1917). Such decisions are of questionable value, and no reliance should be placed on them.
[97] For example, the states of Florida, Mississippi, Oregon, and Wisconsin have such laws. *See generally* Appendix 2 at the end of this book.
[98] The states of Alabama, New Jersey, and the District of Columbia extend the privilege to marriage counseling involving both spouses.
[99] *See, e.g.*, Spencer v. Spencer, 301 S.E.2d 411 (N.C. App. 1983).

applies to marital counseling involving one or both spouses perhaps as much as in any other context. Ordinarily, however, statements made to a minister in the presence of deacons, elders, church members, or any other persons will not be privileged, unless specifically recognized by state law.[100] Statements made to a minister in the course of friendly, informal conversation ordinarily are not privileged, since the circumstances do not suggest that the conversation will be kept in confidence.[101] Communications made to a minister with the understanding that he or she will transmit them to a third party obviously lack confidentiality, and are not considered privileged.[102]

In summary, privileged communications to a minister must not only be made in private, but they also must be made with an express or implied understanding that they will never be disclosed. The substance of the communication, the place where it is made, and the relationship, if any, between the minister and the one making the communication, are all factors to be considered.

Example. An Idaho court ruled that a hospital chaplain could testify in court regarding incriminating statements made to him by the father of an abused child.[103] The father took the child to a hospital emergency room, and disclosed to the chaplain that he had "shook him too hard." The father was charged with abuse, and the chaplain was called as a witness. A state appeals court concluded that the father's conversation with the chaplain was not privileged since the father's statements were not made privately with an intent that there be no further disclosure. The court pointed out that the circumstances surrounding the discussion between the father and the hospital chaplain "compel the conclusion that the communication was not made in private. For example, [the chaplain] testified at trial that the door to the room where the parties spoke was open and that hospital staff were going back and forth just outside the room. Additionally . . . [the chaplain] testified that he could hear what was being said outside of the room; that no effort was made to prevent others from hearing his conversation with [the father]; and that [the chaplain] was not asked to close the door or to keep the matters confidential." Further, the child's mother testified that the chaplain never represented that the conversations would be kept confidential. The court also noted that the father had mentioned to other hospital staff members that he had shaken the child."

Example. A Minnesota court ruled that statements made by a murder suspect to a hospital chaplain were privileged, but not statements made by the suspect after his grandmother entered the room because he "could not have intended confidentiality at that moment."[104]

Example. The Montana Supreme Court ruled that statements made by a child molester to lay leaders in his church were not protected from disclosure by the clergy-penitent privilege.[105] A father (the "defendant") was charged with sexually abusing his nine-year-old stepdaughter. He pleaded not guilty to the charge, and a trial date was set. While awaiting trial, the defendant and his wife divorced, but both began attending the same church. The church allows its members to confess their sins to one another, but no church member has the authority to formally forgive sins. Rather, the church believes forgiveness only comes from God. After an evening church service which both the defendant and his former wife attended, the two of them and the stepdaughter encountered each other in a restaurant parking lot. The

---

[100] Milburn v. Haworth, 108 P. 155 (Colo. 1910).

[101] Angleton v. Angleton, 370 P.2d 788 (Idaho 1962).

[102] United States v. Wells, 446 F.2d 2 (2nd Cir. 1971); Bottoson v. State, 443 So.2d 962 (Fla. 1983) (murder suspect handed written confession to two ministers intending that it be relayed to the prosecutor's office); Naum v. State, 630 P.2d 785 (Okla. App. 1981).

[103] State v. Gardiner, 898 P.2d 615 (Idaho App. 1995).

[104] State v. Orfi, 511 N.W.2d 464 (Minn. App. 1994).

[105] State v. MacKinnon, 957 P.2d 23 (Mont. 1998).

defendant began talking with his stepdaughter, and apologized to her, presumably in an attempt to prevent her from testifying against him. Concerned with the nature of this conversation, the former wife suggested that they continue the conversation inside the restaurant in the presence of a married couple from church who were also present. This couple served as "lay leaders" in the church, although they were not ordained ministers. The conversation continued in the back of the lobby area of the restaurant with everyone sitting on chairs. During this conversation the defendant admitted to sexually molesting his stepdaughter. At the defendant's criminal trial, the court allowed the lay leaders to testify concerning the defendant's comments during their conversation in the restaurant. Largely as a result of this evidence, the defendant was convicted of child molestation. He appealed his conviction, claiming that the statements he made in the restaurant were protected from disclosure by the clergy-penitent privilege, and that the lay leaders should not have been allowed to testify regarding them. He insisted that the lay leaders were functioning in their professional character as clergy during the conversation at the restaurant, and in the course of discipline enjoined by the church. Further, because of the "religious setting" of the meeting, he assumed that his statements would be kept confidential. The state supreme court ruled that the conversation was not protected by the clergy-penitent privilege. The court concluded that even if the lay leaders were "clergy" (it declined to resolve this question), the statements made in their presence by the defendant were not privileged since they were not directed at them in their "professional character" as clergy "acting in their religious roles . . . pursuant to the practice and discipline of the church." To the contrary, the defendant "was not making a confession to [them] for the purpose of receiving forgiveness or for spiritual or religious counseling, guidance, admonishment or advice." The court pointed out that the restaurant meeting was a continuation of the defendant's conversation with his former wife and stepdaughter which began after evening church services. Since the former wife felt uncomfortable facing the defendant by herself as he attempted to "set things right" with his former stepdaughter, she asked him to continue their conversation inside the restaurant, and she also asked the two lay leaders (without explaining the subject of their conversation) to serve as "facilitators" while she and the defendant and stepdaughter talked. The court noted that the conversation continued in the back of the lobby area of the restaurant, a public place, with everyone sitting on chairs. No representations of confidentiality were made during the conversation. The court concluded, "[The defendant] had no reasonable expectation that his statements would be held in confidence. [He] did not seek and the [lay leaders] did not make any representations of confidentiality. Instead, [he] made his statements in a public place to his ex-wife and stepdaughter in the presence of the [two lay leaders]."

Example. *A New Jersey court ruled that a letter written by a murderer to his pastor, and left in plain view in his home after he killed 5 members of his family, was not protected from disclosure in court by the clergy-penitent privilege since it was not considered "confidential."[106] The court observed, "Defendant's invocation of the clergy-communicant privilege is insupportable. It is clear both from the very terms of [New Jersey law] and the history of the privilege that it protects confidential communications only. The letter to [the pastor], left for anyone to find and read, cannot be considered to have been made with a reasonable expectation of confidentiality."*

Example. *A Texas appeals court ruled that statements made to a hospital chaplain by the spouse of a patient were privileged despite the presence of a doctor and nurse.[107] The court rejected the chaplain's claim that the clergy-penitent privilege was "waived" because of the presence of other persons during the conversation. It noted that the clergy-penitent privilege does not require the absence of any persons other than the minister and the counselee. Rather, it defines a privileged communication as one that is "not*

---

[106] State v. List, 636 A.2d 1054 (N.J. Super. A.D. 1993).
[107] Nicholson v. Wittig, 832 S.W.2d 681 (Tex. App. 1992).

intended for further disclosure except to other persons present in furtherance of the purpose of the communication." The court observed, "[The privilege] contemplates that individuals other than a chaplain may be present at the time the confidential communications are made. In the present case, both a surgeon . . . and the director of nurses were present while [the wife] was communicating with the chaplain. . . . It is difficult to conceptualize a hospital setting that affords complete privacy to a chaplain and a communicant in circumstances where a family member is undergoing surgery. Common experience tells us that, more often than not, the chaplain will be assisting the family by affording company and comfort in the waiting room of a surgical suite, recovery room, or intensive care unit. Various hospital personnel and physicians are periodically bringing news of what is transpiring. Often, these personnel are also explaining, encouraging, or comforting the family. Family members of other patients are present. If this court were to decide that the presence of a surgeon and of the director of nurses waived the privilege, hospitals would need to furnish clergy-communicant conference facilities outside every waiting room. Such a narrow interpretation of [the privilege] was not intended, especially where the rule expressly acknowledges that others may be present while the communications are made."

Example. *A Washington court ruled that the clergy-penitent privilege applied to confidential statements made to a pastor, and that the privilege was not waived when the pastor disclosed the communications to two others.[108] A distraught mother contacted a pastor and asked him to meet with her son. The pastor, who was not acquainted with either the mother or son, drove to the son's apartment where he was introduced by the mother as "the preacher." The mother remained in the apartment during the pastor's "spiritual" consultation with her son which lasted about an hour. The pastor met with the son on at least two other occasions before the son turned himself over to the police. One meeting took place at an army medical center, where the son was accompanied by his mother, wife, and several others, and the other at a friend's home. The pastor later shared the substance of the son's communications with two colleagues. The son was later charged with second degree murder for the death of his three-month-old son. The state alleged that the son caused the child's death by violently shaking him, and it asked the trial court to determine whether the clergy-penitent privilege applied to the son's statements to the pastor. The state asserted that the son's conversations with the pastor were not privileged because they were not confidential. It noted that the mother was in the apartment during the pastor's initial meeting with her son, and that other individuals were present during the pastor's other visits with him. Further, the pastor shared the contents of the son's communications with two of his colleagues. The court noted that whether a communication is confidential "turns on the communicant's reasonable belief that the conversation would remain private." The court pointed out that while the mother was present in the apartment, there was no proof that she was in the room the entire time that her son spoke with the pastor. To the contrary, the pastor claimed that he spoke confidentially with the son at his apartment outside of the mother's presence. The pastor also insisted that he spoke privately with the son during each of his other meetings with him, even though others were present for part of the time. The court concluded that those portions of the conversations that occurred outside of the presence of any third person were privileged. It cautioned that the son's communications to the pastor "are confidential only to the extent the conversations were outside the presence of others."*

Many states have enacted clergy privilege statutes or rules based directly on Rule 505 of the Uniform Rules of Evidence, which defines a "confidential" communication as one that is made "privately and not intended for further disclosure except to other persons present in furtherance of the purpose of the communication." In such states it is more likely that the presence of other persons will not affect the privileged status

---

[108] State v. Martin, 959 P.2d 152 (Wash. App. 1998).

of a conversation between a minister and counselee so long as the presence of the other persons is somehow "in furtherance of the purpose of the communication." To illustrate, some clergy do not engage in opposite sex counseling without a third person being present. Will the presence of such a third person mean that statements made to the minister are not privileged (because they are no longer confidential)? Such a conclusion is certainly possible. But in states with a clergy-penitent privilege based on Rule 505 of the Uniform Rules of Evidence, the argument could be made that the presence of the third person in such a situation is "in furtherance of the purpose of the communication," particularly if the church board adopted a resolution prohibiting opposite sex counseling by clergy without a third person being present.

§ 3-07.3 — To a Minister

Key point 3-07.3. In order for the clergy-penitent privilege to apply there must be a communication that is made to a minister.

Clergy-penitent privilege laws generally limit the privilege to confidential communications made to clergymen, priests, or ministers of the gospel. Communications made to nuns,[109] an elder and deacon in the Christian Church,[110] lay religious counselors,[111] "lay ministers,"[112] unordained, self-proclaimed ministers,[113] and a "born-again" police officer who was a former deacon in his church,[114] are not privileged because they are not made to a member of the clergy. But communications made to lay religious counselors whose services are necessary because of the number of people requiring counseling,[115] to elders in the Presbyterian Church,[116] and to a pastoral counselor in a nonprofit counseling center not affiliated with a church[117] have been deemed privileged.

A federal appeals court ruled that the IRS could not be prevented from inspecting church records on the basis of the clergy-penitent privilege since the term *clergyman* applies only to natural persons and not to church corporations.[118]

Example. The Illinois Supreme Court ruled that statements made by a murder suspect to his brother were not protected from disclosure in court by the clergy-penitent privilege since the brother was not a recognized minister.[119] The court acknowledged that the brother became a minister of the "Church of the Second Coming" while serving in the United States Army overseas. However, it noted that "there was no ordination procedure in this nondenominational church" and that "one became a minister by receiving one's call from God and by being confirmed by the pastor." When the brother returned to the United States, he became a police officer and began attending a Baptist church because there were no "Church of the Second Coming" congregations.

---

[109] In re Murtha, 279 A.2d 889 (N.J. 1971); Masquat v. Maguire, 638 P.2d 1105 (Okla. 1981) (privilege did not apply since nun was consulted in her capacity as a hospital administrator and "not in her capacity as a 'clergyman'"). *Contra* Eckmann v. Board of Education, 106 F.R.D. 70 (E.D. Mo. 1985).

[110] Knight v. Lee, 80 Ind. 201 (1881).

[111] State v. Buss, 887 P.2d 920 (Wash. App. 1995) ("nonordained church counselors"); People v. Diercks, 411 N.E.2d 97 (Ill. 1980).

[112] Farner v. Farner, 480 N.E.2d 251 (Ind. App. 1985).

[113] State v. Hereford, 518 So.2d 515 (La. App. 1987).

[114] State v. Welch, 448 So.2d 705 (La. App. 1984). *See also* Banks v. State, 725 So.2d 711 (Miss. 1998).

[115] In re Verplank, 329 F. Supp. 433 (C.D. Cal. 1971).

[116] Cimijotti v. Paulsen, 219 F. Supp. 621 (N.D. Iowa 1963), *appeal dismissed*, 323 F.2d 716 (8th Cir. 1963).

[117] Blough v. Food Lion, Inc., 142 F.R.D. 622 (E.D. Va. 1992).

[118] United States v. Luther, 481 F.2d 429 (9th Cir. 1973) (the court so held because no evidence was presented in favor of extending the privilege to church corporations).

[119] People v. McNeal, 677 N.E.2d 841 (Ill. 1997).

Key point. Some state clergy-penitent privilege laws contain unusual rules. For example, the Mississippi clergy-penitent privilege specifies that "a clergyman's secretary, stenographer, or clerk shall not be examined without the consent of the clergyman concerning any fact, the knowledge of which was acquired in such capacity." Familiarity with your state's clergy-penitent privilege is essential. See Appendix 2 for the clergy-penitent privilege statutes and rules for each state as of the date of publication of this text.

§ 3-07.4 — Acting in a Professional Capacity as a Spiritual Adviser

Key point 3-07.4. In order for the clergy-penitent privilege to apply there must be a communication that is made to a minister acting in a professional capacity as a spiritual adviser.

Most clergy-penitent privilege laws require that the communication be made to a minister acting in a professional capacity as a spiritual adviser. Certainly there can be no expectation of confidentiality—and therefore no privilege—unless a statement is made to a minister acting in such a capacity.

If a statement is made to a minister as a mere friend, the privilege does not apply. To illustrate, a murder suspect's incriminating admissions made to a clergyman who was a friend and frequent companion were held not to be privileged. The court reasoned that the statements had been made to the clergyman as a friend and not as a professional spiritual adviser.[120] Statements made by a murder suspect to a minister were not privileged since the suspect (1) was not a church member, (2) had entered a minister's home to conceal himself from the police, (3) did not seek spiritual counseling and did not request that their conversation be kept confidential, and (4) the minister did not believe the conversation was confidential. The court reasoned that the facts did not establish the confidential nature of the statements or that the minister was acting in his professional capacity as a spiritual adviser.[121]

In another case, statements made to a clergyman by an individual who was attempting to sell him a watch were held not to be privileged.[122] And, statements made to a priest who worked as an executive in a secular business (while on a leave of absence from the priesthood) were not privileged since they were not made to a minister acting in his professional capacity as a spiritual adviser.[123]

A New York court addressed the issue of privileged communications to clergy in an important decision. An individual entered an office building in New York City, pulled a gun, ordered several people to lie on the floor, and fired at least one shot. He later left the building and went to a nearby Catholic church. The church secretary informed the priest that there was a man in the office who wanted to see him. The priest met the individual in the church sanctuary a short time later. The individual appeared very distraught, and informed the priest that his mother was a member of the parish and that she was a saint, and that he had done something very bad. Upon further questioning by the priest, the individual disclosed the criminal actions he had taken earlier in the day. The priest advised the individual that if he had not hurt anyone he "would be better off" turning himself in to the police. While the individual began to pray, the priest slipped outside and ran to a police headquarters a

---

[120] Burger v. State, 231 S.E.2d 769 (Ga. 1977). *See also* People v. Police, 651 P.2d 430 (Colo. App. 1982); Wainscott v. Commissioner, 562 S.W.2d 628 (Ky. 1978) (murderer, speaking to pastor as friend rather than as spiritual adviser, told him where murder weapon was located); People v. Carmona, 606 N.Y.S.2d 879 (Ct. App. 1993) ("not every communication between a cleric and a congregant will justify application of the privilege," and "the privilege may not be invoked to enshroud conversations with wholly secular purposes solely because one of the parties to the conversation happened to be a religious minister"); Fahlfelder v. Commonwealth, 470 A.2d 1130 (Pa. 1984) (minister consulted in his capacity as a parole rehabilitation counselor and not a spiritual adviser).

[121] Lucy v. State, 443 So.2d 1335 (Ala. App. 1983).

[122] State v. Berry, 324 So.2d 822 (La. 1975).

[123] United States v. Gordon, 493 F. Supp. 822 (S.D.N.Y. 1980).

block away. On his way, he yelled to several police officers that there was a man in the church with a gun. The officers went into the church, removed the gun from the individual and placed him under arrest. The individual was later indicted by a grand jury in part because of the conversation between the priest and the accused in the church. The individual sought a court order dismissing the indictment on the ground that it was based on privileged communications between himself and the priest. The court observed that "not every communication between a clergyman and a penitent is considered privileged." To be privileged, the conversation with the clergyman "must have been made to him in his or her professional character as a spiritual adviser." The court concluded that the accused "was seeking some type of spiritual advice from [the priest] and had the reasonable expectation that his conversation with the priest was to be kept secret. Therefore, [the priest] was not at liberty to testify before the grand jury as to his conversation with [the accused]."[124]

Another New York court ruled that a priest's testimony in a criminal hearing was not "privileged" since the information shared with the priest by a criminal suspect was not communicated in the course of spiritual counseling.[125] The court acknowledged that there was a difference of opinion as to why the suspect had spoken with the priest. The suspect claimed that he spoke with the priest solely to ask him to contact an attorney on his behalf. On the other hand, the priest testified that the suspect sought him out in order to apologize personally to him for burglarizing his home. The court concluded that only those communications made to a minister while acting in his or her professional role as a spiritual adviser are privileged from disclosure in a court of law. Under either the suspect's or the priest's account of the communication, it was not privileged since the priest had not been sought out for spiritual counsel or advice. Accordingly, it was appropriate to admit the priest's testimony over the defendant's objection.

A California court ruled that confidential statements made by a church treasurer to an Episcopalian priest were not "penitential communications" exempted by law from involuntary disclosure in a civil court. Late one night, the treasurer arranged a meeting with the priest after informing him that she "had done something almost as bad as murder." The treasurer, after requesting that their conversation be kept confidential, informed the priest that she had embezzled nearly $30,000 in church funds from a church account. The priest, with the permission of the treasurer, sought the assistance of the church wardens and vestry. A short time later the vestry decided that the embezzlement had to be reported to the local police. Even though the treasurer reimbursed the church for the full amount taken, she was prosecuted for embezzlement and found guilty. The treasurer appealed her conviction on the ground that it had been based on her confidential statements to the priest, which she alleged were protected by the clergy-penitent privilege. The court concluded that the statements made by the church treasurer to the priest were not privileged since they involved a "problem-solving entreaty" by the treasurer rather than "a request to make a true confession seeking forgiveness or absolution—the very essence of the spiritual relationship privileged under the statute." That is, the treasurer sought out the priest not for spiritual counseling, but to disclose her embezzlement and to seek his counsel on how to correct the problem. Further, the court observed (despite testimony to the contrary) that while Episcopalian priests have a duty to maintain the secrecy of a confession by a penitent seeking God's forgiveness, there is no corresponding duty with respect to statements made to a priest in the course of ordinary "pastoral counseling." The court also emphasized that the treasurer had "released" the priest from his assurance of confidentiality by consenting to his disclosure of the facts of the case to the church wardens and vestry. Unfortunately, the court's decision contradicts the very purpose of the privilege. Church members in California may be dissuaded from seeking pastoral counseling now that there is no assurance that communications made in confidence in the course of such counseling sessions are privileged from involuntary disclosure in a court of law. Such a crabbed interpretation of California law is unwarranted, and hopefully will be rejected by the state supreme court and by other appeals courts in the state.[126]

---

[124] People v. Reyes, 545 N.Y.S.2d 653 (1989).
[125] People v. Schultz, 557 N.Y.S.2d 543 (N.Y. 1990).

One court ruled that statements made by a murder suspect to a minister regarding his intent to kill his wife were not privileged since they were not made by the suspect "in professing religious faith or seeking spiritual comfort or guidance."[127]

A Pennsylvania court ruled that statements made by a murder suspect to a minister were not "privileged" since they were not made to the minister while acting in his professional role as a spiritual adviser.[128] In 1966, a 10-year-old girl and her 6-year-old friend were playing by a creek near their homes. A man approached the children, and asked them to help him "catch minnows" around a bend in the stream. He offered them chewing gum if they would accompany him. The 6-year-old declined the invitation, but the 10-year-old girl went with the man. A search for the girl was launched when she failed to return home for lunch. Her body was discovered, with her throat slashed, behind some bushes a few hundred yards from where the children had been playing. A small, plastic "sheriff's badge" was found under her body. An intensive search was conducted, and several suspects were questioned, but no arrests were made. Twenty-two years later, a man was arrested in the same community for indecent exposure. The court appointed a local minister to counsel with the individual. While he was not an active member of the minister's church, he and his wife occasionally attended services there. During a counseling session, the individual informed the minister that he was guilty of the murder of the girl 22 years before, and he asked the minister to accompany him to the police station where he would confess to the crime. The minister also noticed that the individual had a plastic sheriff's badge in his pocket. Largely on the basis of this new evidence, a murder prosecution was commenced, and the individual was convicted of first degree murder.

The murderer appealed his conviction on the ground that the statements he had made to the minister were protected by the clergy-penitent privilege, and accordingly should not have been introduced in evidence during the trial. A state appeals court rejected this claim, and upheld the murder conviction. The court concluded that the clergy-penitent privilege did not apply in this case since "the circumstances in which the statements were made were not religious, in that nothing spiritual or in the nature of forgiveness ever was discussed." The court emphasized that "our legislature did not intend a *per se* privilege for any communication to a clergyman based on his status. We therefore look to the circumstances to determine whether [the murderer's] statements were made in secrecy and confidence to a clergyman in the course of his duties." The court noted that the minister had been appointed by the court to counsel with the murderer concerning his indecent exposure conviction, and that it was the minister who sought out the murderer. The court observed:

> [The murderer] never sought [the minister] in a confessional role; further, there was no evidence that [the minister] was acting in any capacity other than that of counselor. Thus, the statements were not motivated by religious considerations or in order to seek the forgiveness of God. Accordingly, they were not made to [the minister] in the course of his duties as a minister. Instead, they were made because he was a court-appointed counselor. Further, [the murderer] never was a member of the church. Under these circumstances, we conclude that the fact that [the minister] is ordained was not relevant to [the murderer's] statements to him and there is no basis to conclude that his statements were made confidentially or for religious, penitent purposes.[129]

---

[126] People v. Edwards, 248 Cal. Rptr. 53 (Cal. App. 1st Dist. 1988).

[127] Burger v. State, 231 S.E.2d 769 (Ga. 1977). *Accord* Ball v. State, 419 N.E.2d 137 (Ind. 1981). Both of these cases involved murder prosecutions. Perhaps the courts felt that the privilege should be construed more narrowly in this context since the societal need for evidence is correspondingly greater due to the gravity of the crime.

[128] Commonwealth v. Patterson, 572 A.2d 1258 (Pa. Super. 1990).

[129] *Id.* at 1262.

Accordingly, the clergy-penitent privilege did not apply, and the minister could testify regarding the murderer's confession. Further, the court stressed that "we categorically reject the allegation that this privilege extends to openly-displayed objects, as was the toy sheriff's badge."

Many, perhaps most, of the communications made to clergy are *not* made to them in their professional capacity as spiritual advisers. They are made by church members and nonmembers alike at church functions, following church services, in committee rooms, in hospital rooms, at funeral homes, in restaurants, on street corners, and at social and recreational events. Such communications ordinarily are not privileged, since other persons typically are present, and it is difficult to conclude that the "counselee" sought out the minister in his or her professional capacity as a spiritual adviser. This is not a necessary conclusion, since it is entirely possible that such conversations, even if they begin as a purely social exchange, could become spiritual in nature. In other words, by the end of a conversation the "counselee" may well be communicating with the minister because of his or her status as a spiritual adviser. There is no reason why such a conversation should not be privileged, assuming that the other requirements are satisfied. On the other hand, even strictly private conversations may be made for purposes other than spiritual advice, and thus are not privileged.

A minister (or court) may need to ascertain the objective of a conversation in determining whether a communication is privileged. Was the minister sought out primarily for spiritual advice? Were the statements of a type that could have been made to anyone? Where did the conversation take place? Was the conversation pursuant to a scheduled appointment? What was the relationship between the minister and the person making the communication? These are the kinds of questions which help to clarify the purpose of a particular conversation, thereby determining the availability of the privilege.

> *Tip.* *The applicability of the clergy-penitent privilege can be enhanced if a minister simply asks a person during a counseling session whether he or she intends for the conversation to be privileged and confidential. If the counselee responds affirmatively, then there is little doubt that the courts will conclude that the privilege applies. Clergy should bear this point in mind in the course of their counseling. If, during a conversation with a member (wherever it may occur), it appears to a minister that the other person may intend for the conversation to be confidential and privileged, the minister should confirm this understanding verbally. If the minister is ever called to testify in court concerning the conversation, this verbal confirmation should resolve most questions regarding the applicability of the clergy-penitent privilege.*

> *Example.* *A hospital chaplain could testify in court regarding incriminating statements made to him by the father of an abused child.[130] The father took the child to a hospital emergency room, and disclosed to the chaplain that he had "shook him too hard." The father was charged with abuse, and the chaplain was called as a witness. A state appeals court concluded that the father's conversation with the chaplain was not privileged since the chaplain "acted as a conduit between the hospital and patients or their families" and therefore "his role was not simply one of a spiritual adviser."*

> *Example.* *Statements made by a church member to three church officials were not protected by the clergy-penitent privilege.[131] Two adults drowned during a tragic accident while camping with another adult and five minors in a national park. A lawsuit was brought against the United States government by the families of the victims. The government later asked for a copy of a tape recording that was made in a church shortly after the accident, in which the sole surviving adult gave an account of the accident*

---

[130] State v. Gardiner, 898 P.2d 615 (Ida. App. 1995).
[131] Ellis v. United States, 922 F. Supp. 539 (D. Utah 1996).

to three church leaders. The church leaders called for the meeting in order to obtain a first hand account of the trip so they could respond properly to the media and address the needs of family members. The church refused to provide the government with a copy of the tape on the ground that it was protected from disclosure by the clergy-penitent privilege. The court noted that "not all confidential communications to a cleric are protected." Rather, the communication "must be in the cleric's religious capacity and must be pertinent to religion and not just church administration or information." The court concluded that the statements made by the adult survivor to the three church officials did not meet this test. The court acknowledged that the survivor believed that the meeting was in part for "counseling," and that it occurred on church premises and involved three ministers. While these facts suggested that the statements were privileged, they were outweighed by a number of other facts, including the following: (1) the survivor did not seek out the counseling but was invited to share his account of the accident with church officials; (2) church officials considered the meeting to be an "information exchange" rather than a confession or personal counseling session; and (3) there was evidence that some of the comments shared during the meeting were later disclosed to others. The court concluded, "Although the communication is at times moving and in some places poignant and stirring, it was not ecclesiastical or religious. It was not a communication for doctrinal, spiritual, or religious purposes. It was a communication to impart and report about an event for purposes of informing and acquainting the listener to what had happened. The church leaders did not receive the communication within the religious role of clerics, but as clerics performing an attendant executive function. The communication is not within the clergy privilege and must be disclosed."

Example. Statements made by a burglary suspect to a minister were not protected by the clergy-penitent privilege since they were not made to the minister acting in his professional capacity as a spiritual adviser.[132] The suspect was charged with burglarizing his former girlfriend's home. At his trial, the former girlfriend's minister testified regarding a previous telephone conversation with the suspect. The minister mentioned the burglary, and the suspect replied, "Well, to tell you the truth, I was only trying to scare the hell out of her." The suspect sought to have this statement excluded from evidence on the basis of the clergy-penitent privilege. The court ruled that this privilege did not apply because the suspect "failed to show he made this statement to [the minister] acting in a capacity as [the suspect's] spiritual adviser. Neither the fact that [the suspect] initiated the telephone call nor that the communication could be construed as a penitent statement in confession to a crime overcomes the absence of this essential element of the privilege."

Example. A man was convicted of sexually molesting his young stepdaughter.[133] The trial court permitted a priest to testify about a conversation he had with the father. Among other things, the father informed the priest (with regard to the allegations of sexual abuse) that he "did it" only once and would not "do it" again, and that the incident happened because he and his stepdaughter both had a mutual need for comfort and consolation. The father appealed his conviction, claiming that his statements to the priest were privileged and should not have been disclosed at his trial. The appeals court disagreed: "[The father] did not seek out the priest for spiritual advice, but was responding to the latter's request to see him for the purpose of informing him of the allegations that had been made against him by his wife and stepdaughter, and to warn him that the authorities would be advised unless he quit his job at the day-care center. As the priest was clearly not acting or purporting to act as [the father's] spiritual adviser, the communication was not privileged."

---

[132] State v. Nunez, 647 A.2d 1007 (Vt. 1994).
[133] In the Matter of N and G Children, 574 N.Y.S.2d 696 (A.D. 1 Dept. 1991).

Example. Statements made by a criminal defendant to a minister were not protected by the clergy-penitent privilege since the minister informed the defendant that he would not be his counselor.[134] A man was prosecuted for criminal sexual assault against his eleven-year-old stepdaughter. The stepdaughter testified that her stepfather had sexual intercourse with her more than 100 times, on virtually every occasion when the child's mother "left the house." The child was so traumatized that she attempted suicide. The stepfather was found guilty and sentenced to prison. At the trial, the prosecution relied in part on the testimony of a minister. The minister testified that the stepfather had contacted him three times by telephone, seeking counsel and advice. The minister told the stepfather during their second conversation that he would not be his counselor, since the stepfather had lied to him. Under the minister's theology, these lies prevented him from entering into a counseling relationship with the stepfather. The minister testified that during their third conversation, the stepfather admitted to having had sexual intercourse with his stepdaughter on "twenty-five to fifty" occasions. The stepfather argued on appeal that the minister should not have been permitted to testify because of the clergy-penitent privilege. He claimed that the privilege applied because he contacted him "to confess and for spiritual guidance, and the conversation was in confidence as no third party was present." A state appeals court disagreed. It observed that the minister told the stepfather that he would not be his counselor. Therefore, the stepfather's statements to the minister "were not obtained by the minister in his professional character or as a spiritual adviser."

Example. Statements made by a criminal suspect to his minister were privileged, and accordingly not admissible as evidence in a court of law.[135] A burglary suspect made incriminating statements to his minister, which were admitted at trial. The trial court reasoned that the statements to the minister were not privileged since they were not made to him in his professional capacity. Rather, they "emanated from the closeness of the relationship between them." The suspect was convicted, and he appealed his conviction on the ground that the state's clergy-penitent privilege was violated. A state appeals court agreed. It observed, "We conclude that the requirements of the statute are met to establish the communications are privileged. [The minister] is a licensed minister of the gospel . . . and the information was communicated by the defendant in a confidential manner [to the minister] who was acting in his professional capacity in the furtherance and discharge of his functions as a minister. The minister initiated the contact and transported the defendant to a motel and inquired `are you having problems?' The minister accompanied the defendant to the motel room and explained he intended to give `comfort to him' since the defendant was `really burdened down.' [The minister] further testified he didn't distinguish between being the defendant's minister or friend on that occasion. . . . Clearly, the minister inquired of defendant's troubles, consoled him, and counseled him to put his faith in God and the defendant felt the minister was God's emissary. The evidence [does not support] the trial judge's determination that the [conversation] between the defendant and the minister was due to their friendship."

Example. A church member sexually molested three boys. The boys and their families were members of the same church. The molester invited one of the boys to his home to "try on some Boy Scout uniforms," and molested him. Another boy was molested by the same person in the sound room at the church. In each case, the molestation consisted of touching the boys' genitals, either directly or through their clothing. The parents of two of the boys informed their pastor of the molestation. The pastor promptly pulled the molester out of a choir rehearsal and asked him to come to his office. The pastor confronted the individual with the allegations, and the molester admitted that they were true. The molester was later prosecuted criminally. His confession to the pastor was introduced as evidence over his objection that it

---

[134] People v. Bole, 585 N.E.2d 135 (Ill. App. 1991).
[135] State v. Boling, 806 S.W.2d 202 (Tenn. App. 1990).

was protected from disclosure by the clergy-penitent privilege. On the basis of this and other evidence, he was convicted on three counts of molestation and was sentenced to the state penitentiary. The molester appealed his conviction, arguing that the trial court erred in allowing the pastor to testify regarding their conversation in his office. The molester pointed out that he was a member of the church; that he had counseled with the pastor on numerous occasions in the past, and the pastor had assured him that their conversations were private; and that his confession was made in confidence. A state supreme court ruled that the clergy-penitent privilege did not apply to the molester's confession.[136] The court observed, "We find it significant . . . that the pastor sought out the molester to confront him with the allegations of sexual abuse conveyed to him by the parents of two of the victims. Although the pastor had counseled with the molester on previous occasions . . . the pastor did not consider this to be a counseling session at all, but disciplinary in nature. The attendant circumstances support the trial court's decision that this was an accusatory situation initiated by the pastor that did not encompass spiritual counseling, thereby precluding the molester from excluding the pastor's testimony at trial. . . . The molester's communication was not made to the pastor in his professional character as a spiritual adviser . . . ."

Example. *A murder suspect was convicted of the second degree murder of his wife on the basis of the testimony of two ministers. The suspect was a good friend of one of the ministers. This minister testified that the suspect came to him "as a friend" and confessed to murdering his wife. He did not ask for forgiveness and there was no discussion of a spiritual nature. The minister later related the confession to his wife, because he simply could not believe it. He testified in court that as a minister he would not have discussed the information he got from the suspect with anyone else had the suspect come to him as a penitent to confess and seek forgiveness. The other minister also was a friend of the suspect. He testified that he called the suspect and asked him if he had shot his wife. The suspect admitted that he had. There was no discussion of a need for spiritual guidance or forgiveness. The defendant appealed his conviction on the ground that the statements to the ministers were protected by the clergy-penitent privilege and accordingly should not have been used in court. A Louisiana appeals court rejected this defense and affirmed the conviction. It concluded that the defendant's testimony "was not that he sought privileged spiritual advice and guidance from the reverends in their capacity as ministers of the church, but that he made no confessions to anyone." Accordingly, it was inappropriate for him to assert on appeal that the testimony of the ministers should have been excluded on the basis of the clergy-penitent privilege.[137]*

§ 3-07.5 — In the Course of Discipline

Key point 3-07.5. *In some states the clergy-penitent privilege only applies to communications made to a minister in the course of "discipline." While most courts interpret this requirement broadly to cover statements made in the course of spiritual counsel and advice, others have interpreted it narrowly to apply only to confessions made to Catholic priests.*

Several state laws limit the clergy-penitent privilege to communications made to a minister "in the course of discipline enjoined by the rules or practice" of his or her church. Some courts have interpreted this language strictly. As a result they apply the privilege only to communications "made in the understood pursuance of that church discipline which gives rise to the confessional relation, and, therefore, in particular to confessions of sin only, not to communications of other tenor."[138]

---

[136] Magar v. State, 826 S.W.2d 221 (Ark. 1992). *But see* People v. Burnidge, 664 N.E.2d 656 (Ill. App. 1996) ("The fact that the [counselee] did not instigate the counseling and that he was counselor for the youth group at the church did not destroy the privilege.").

[137] State v. Mayer, 589 So.2d 1145 (La. App. 1991).

[138] In re Estate of Soeder, 220 N.E.2d 547, 568-69 (Ohio 1966).

The courts generally have construed the term *discipline* broadly, extending the privilege to all confidential communications made to clergy acting in their professional capacity as spiritual advisers. In a leading case, one court, in interpreting the phrase *in the course of discipline enjoined by the rules or practice of the religious body to which he belongs,* observed:

> The word "discipline" . . . has no technical legal meaning. . . . The "discipline enjoined" includes the "practice" of all clergymen to be trained so as to . . . concern themselves in the moral training of others, and to be as willing to give spiritual aid, advice, or comfort as others are to receive it . . . . So it is in the course of "discipline enjoined" by the "practice" of their respective churches that the clergyman is to show the transgressor the error of his way; to teach him the right way; to point the way to faith, hope, and consolation; perchance, to lead him to seek atonement. . . . It is important that the communication be made in such spirit and within the course of "discipline," and it is sufficient whether such "discipline" enjoins the clergyman to receive the communication or whether it enjoins the other party . . . to deliver the communication. Such practice makes the communication privileged, when accompanied by the essential characteristics. . . . The fundamental thought is that one may safely consult his spiritual adviser. . . . When any person enters that secret chamber, this statute closes the door upon him, and civil authority turns away its ear.[139]

One court recognized that a narrow interpretation of the requirement that confidential communications be made "in the course of discipline enjoined by the rules or practice" of a church would largely restrict the privilege to the Roman Catholic Church, since most Protestant denominations have no formalized system of "discipline."[140] Another court labeled any such limitation of the privilege to the clergy of one denomination an "absurdity."[141] Such an interpretation, favoring the clergy of one sect, would present serious constitutional problems, since the first amendment prevents states from passing laws which arbitrarily favor one sect to the disadvantage of others.[142] In 1982, the United States Supreme Court ruled that "when we are presented with a state law granting a denominational preference, our precedents demand that we treat such a law as suspect" and that it be invalidated unless it (1) is justified by a compelling governmental interest, and (2) is closely fitted to further that interest.[143] This standard could not be satisfied by a state law recognizing the privileged status of confidential communications only in the context of one or a few religious organizations to the exclusion of all others.

Courts in most states broadly interpret the requirement that the confidential communication be made in the course of discipline, and extend the privilege to any communication made in confidence to clergy acting in their professional capacity as spiritual advisers. Such an interpretation is not only permissible in view of the lack of any technical legal definition of the term, but it is also a socially desirable interpretation since it encourages and promotes spiritual counseling. Some of the more recent clergy-penitent privilege statutes have avoided any reference to the term *discipline.* Rule 505 of the Uniform Rules of Evidence, which has been adopted in several states, provides that the privilege extends to any confidential communication made "to a clergyman in his professional character as spiritual adviser." There is no reference to "discipline."[144]

---

[139] In re Swenson, 237 N.W. 589 (Minn. 1931).

[140] In re Estate of Soeder, 220 N.E.2d 547 (Ohio 1966).

[141] In re Swenson, 237 N.W. 589 (Minn. 1931).

[142] Everson v. Board of Education, 330 U.S. 1 (1947); *see generally* Stoyles, *The Dilemma of the Constitutionality of the Priest-Penitent Privilege—The Application of the Religion Clauses,* U. Pitt. L. Rev. 27 (1967).

[143] Larson v. Valente, 456 U.S. 228 (1982).

[144] Simpson v. Tennant, 871 S.W.2d 301 (Tex. App. Houston 1994).

Some states protect *confessions* from compulsory disclosure in court. This term generally has been broadly interpreted. One court observed that "the 'confession' contemplated by the statute has reference to a penitential acknowledgment to a clergyman of actual or supposed wrongdoing while seeking religious or spiritual advice, aid, or comfort, and . . . it applies to a voluntary 'confession' as well as to one made under a mandate of the church."[145]

Another court provided a broad definition of the term *confession*.[146] It ruled that a bishop did not have to disclose in a civil trial information shared with him by a father who was guilty of abusing his adopted child. An adult woman sued her adoptive father, alleging that he had sexually abused her throughout her childhood. As a result of his conduct, the father sought advice from a bishop of his church. The church later convened a disciplinary hearing at which the father was excommunicated. The daughter subpoenaed documents from the church pertaining to any communications her father had with the bishop regarding his conduct. The bishop opposed this request on the ground that the information sought by the daughter was protected from disclosure by the clergy-penitent privilege. The daughter insisted that any communications made by her father to the bishop were not privileged since they were not made in the context of a "confession" as required by the applicable clergy-penitent privilege statute. The court agreed with the bishop that the statements made by the father were privileged. It refused to narrowly interpret the word "confession" to mean a penitential confession to a member of the clergy, since such an interpretation would limit the privilege to the Catholic Church. The court observed that such an interpretation would favor one sect over all others, making it unconstitutional. Further, the court noted that the word "confession" is used in several ways, including to simply "disclose or acknowledge" something, and it insisted that this broader interpretation is more sensible and realistic:

> [A] constricted interpretation of the privilege does not take into account the essential role that clergy in most churches perform in providing confidential counsel and advice to their communicants in helping them to abandon wrongful or harmful conduct, adopt higher standards of conduct, and reconcile themselves with others and God. . . . In counseling parishioners in religious and moral matters, clergy frequently must deal with intensely private concerns, and parishioners may be encouraged, and even feel compelled, to discuss their moral faults. As one commentator has stated, "Because most churches do not set aside formal occasions for special private encounters labeled 'confession,' less formal consultation must be privileged if the privilege is not in effect to be limited to Roman Catholics."

The court concluded that "the term 'confession' need not be construed to apply only to penitential communications and that a broad construction of that term is necessary to take into account the essential religious role clergy play in dealing with the wrongdoing of parishioners."

While the court interpreted the word "confession" broadly, it did caution that the clergy-penitent privilege still requires that the communication be confidential and in the course of discipline. In deciding if a conversation with a minister is "confidential" and in the course of "discipline," the court suggested that the following factors be considered:

> [W]hether the [location] of the communication indicates an intent that the communication be confidential, whether the conversation was casual in nature or undertaken by the cleric and the parishioner with a sense that the parishioner's moral conduct was at issue, and whether persons not concerned with the subject matter were present. A communication that does not take place in

---

[145] In re Swenson, 237 N.W. 589 (Minn. 1931).
[146] Scott v. Hammock, 870 P.2d 947 (Utah 1994).

private or that is made in the presence of others not intimately and directly concerned with the issue may indicate that the parties involved did not intend the conversation to be confidential. . . . Likewise, statements made to a cleric in a social context are not privileged because the statements are not made to the cleric in the course of his or her professional responsibilities or in a religious context.

The court concluded that statements made by the father to the bishop were privileged, even though some of them occurred in the father's home, since "the bishop communicated with [the father] in the bishop's clerical role with regard to spiritual or religious matters."

Some courts have interpreted the term *confession* more narrowly.[147]

Example. A Washington court ruled that the clergy-penitent privilege applied to confidential statements made to a pastor.[148] A distraught mother contacted a pastor and asked him to meet with her son. The pastor, who was not acquainted with either the mother or son, drove to the son's apartment where he was introduced by the mother as "the preacher." The mother remained in the apartment during the pastor's "spiritual" consultation with her son, which lasted about an hour. The pastor met with the son on at least two other occasions before the son turned himself over to the police. One meeting took place at an army medical center, where the son was accompanied by his mother, wife, and several others, and the other at a friend's home. The pastor later shared the substance of the son's communications with two colleagues. The son was later charged with second degree murder for the death of his three-month-old son. The state alleged that the son caused the child's death by violently shaking him. The prosecutor asked the trial court to determine whether the clergy-penitent privilege applied to the son's statements to the pastor. The trial court ruled that the privilege did not apply since the son had not sought out the pastor as a matter of church "discipline." An appeals court agreed. The court conceded that the Washington clergy-penitent privilege applies only to "confessions," but it concluded that the son's statements to the pastor were confessions because the pastor "considered those communications to be such." The court also noted that the privilege refers to confessions that are made in the course of church discipline. The court interpreted this requirement to refer to "the rules or practices of the religion to which the clergy member belongs." It continued, "The statute does not require that the communicant be enjoined by his or her religion to confess or to seek spiritual counseling. Rather, the statute requires only that the clergy member receiving the confidential communication be enjoined by the practices or rules of the clergy member's religion to receive the confidential communication and to provide spiritual counsel." The court concluded that the pastor in this case "felt enjoined by his religion to receive [the son's] penitential communications and to provide [him] with spiritual counsel." As a result, the pastor's religion "constrains him to provide confessors with spiritual counsel and the opportunity for redemption. It is a duty that the pastor must fulfill based upon the tenets of his faith."

§ 3-08   The Clergy-Penitent Privilege — Miscellaneous Issues

There are a number of miscellaneous issues associated with the clergy-penitent privilege that are addressed in the following subsections.

---

[147] State v. Buss, 887 P.2d 920 (Wash. App. 1995).
[148] State v. Martin, 959 P.2d 152 (Wash. App. 1998). *But see* State v. Buss, 887 P.2d 920 (Wash. App. 1995).

CHECKLIST — DOES THE CLERGY-PENITENT PRIVILEGE APPLY?

Does the clergy-penitent privilege apply to a particular statement or conversation? Consider the following:

Step 1. Is there a "communication"? If so, go to step 2. If not, stop here. The clergy-penitent privilege does not apply. Usually, a "communication" refers to an oral conversation. But it can include correspondence and even gestures or other physical acts if intended to transmit ideas.

Step 2. Was the communication made in confidence? If so, go to step 3. If not, stop here. The clergy-penitent privilege does not apply. A communication is confidential if there is an expectation that it will not be revealed. In some states the presence of a third person prevents a communication from being confidential.

Step 3. Was the communication made to a minister? If so, go to step 4. If not, stop here. The clergy-penitent privilege does not apply.

Step 4. Was the communication made to a minister acting in a professional capacity as a spiritual adviser? If so, go to step 5. If not, stop here. The clergy-penitent privilege does not apply. Generally, this requirement is met if a person seeks out a minister for spiritual counsel or confession.

Step 5. Are you legally authorized to assert the privilege? If so, go to step 6. If not, stop here. The clergy-penitent privilege does not apply. In most states both the minister and counselee may assert the privilege, but in some states the privilege may be claimed only by the counselee.

Step 6. Have all additional legal requirements been met? If so, go to step 7. If not, stop here. The clergy-penitent privilege does not apply. You will need to review your state clergy-penitent privilege statute to identify any additional legal requirements that may apply. Some states require that the communication be made in the course of spiritual "discipline." While this is defined broadly to include spiritual counsel by most courts, this is not always true. Some courts have applied this language exclusively to confessions to Catholic priests.

Step 7. Has the privilege been waived by the counselee? If not, go to step 8. If so, stop here. The clergy-penitent privilege does not apply. A privilege may be waived if a counselee discloses to others the same information shared in confidence with a minister.

Step 8. Did the counselee confess to or disclose one or more incidents of child abuse? If not, and if all of the conditions summarized in the preceding steps have been satisfied, then the clergy-penitent privilege probably applies. To be certain, check with an attorney licensed to practice law in your state. If the counselee did confess to or disclose one or more incidents of child abuse, then you may be legally required to report this information to the civil authorities. Check with your state child abuse reporting law, and a local attorney, to be sure. Some states do not abrogate the privilege if child abuse is disclosed.

§ 3-08.01 — Clergy-Parishioner Relationship

Key point 3-08.01. The courts have not required that a counselee be a church member in order for communications to a minister to qualify for the clergy-penitent privilege. However, church membership is a factor that the courts have considered in deciding if the privilege applies to a particular communication.

Most courts that have addressed the question have concluded that a person need not be a member of a minister's church in order to invoke the clergy-penitent privilege.[149] As a result, even though the person making the communication is not a member of the minister's church, his or her confidential communications to the minister generally will be privileged. This certainly is the correct view, since the purpose underlying nondisclosure of confidential communications made to clergy applies with equal force to all who seek out a minister in confidence for spiritual guidance and help.[150]

§ 3-08.02 — Marriage Counseling

Key point 3-08.02. *The clergy-penitent privilege may apply to communications made to a minister in the course of marriage counseling, even when both spouses are present.*

Some courts have had difficulty in deciding whether the clergy-penitent privilege applies to statements made to clergy in the course of marriage counseling when both spouses are present. Most courts have assumed that statements made to a minister in the course of marriage counseling are made to the minister in his or her professional capacity as a spiritual adviser, and in the course of discipline.[151] The problem is whether or not such communications can be "confidential" when both spouses are present. Some courts have concluded that such communications can be privileged so long as all of the requirements of the privilege are satisfied. One court observed that the presence of both spouses during marital counseling with a minister "did not destroy the confidential nature of the admissions the husband made during marriage counseling—to attempt reconciliation of the parties in a troubled marriage reinforces the confidential nature of communications made during those sessions."[152] Some courts have reached the opposite conclusion.[153] A few state laws specifically extend the privilege to marital or family counseling sessions even if both spouses are present.[154]

Rule 505 of the Uniform Rules of Evidence, which has been adopted by several states, specifies that "a communication is confidential if made privately and not intended for further disclosure *except to other persons present in furtherance of the purpose of the communication.*" This language can be interpreted to preserve the privilege despite the presence of both spouses during marriage counseling.

§ 3-08.03 — Who May Assert the Privilege

Key point 3-08.03. *In most states either the minister or counselee can assert the clergy-penitent privilege, although the minister can do so only on behalf of the counselee. This means that the minister cannot independently assert the privilege if the counselee chooses not to do so.*

In most states, both the person who made the communication and the minister to whom it was made may claim the privilege. Rule 505 of the Uniform Rules of Evidence, which has been adopted by several states,

---

[149] Kohloff v. Bronx Savings Bank, 233 N.Y.S.2d 849 (1962).

[150] Professor Wigmore has listed four preconditions to the existence of any privilege: (1) the parties assumed that the communication would forever be kept secret; (2) communications would often not be made if the privilege did not exist; (3) in the opinion of the community, the secrecy of a particular kind of communication (*e.g.*, confidential communications to clergy) should be preserved; (4) the injury which would attend elimination of the privilege outweighs the benefits to justice. 8 J. WIGMORE, EVIDENCE § 2396 (McNaughton ed. 1961 & Supp. 1998). These conditions would apply equally to church members and nonmembers.

[151] People v. Pecora, 246 N.E.2d 865 (Ill. 1969), *cert. denied*, 397 U.S. 1028 (1970); Kruglikov v. Kruglikov, 217 N.Y.S.2d 845 (1961), *appeal dismissed*, 226 N.Y.S.2d 931 (1962).

[152] Spencer v. Spencer, 301 S.E.2d 411 (N.C. App. 1983).

[153] Simrin v. Simrin, 43 Cal. Rptr. 376 (Cal. 1965).

[154] *See* notes 84 and 85, *supra*, and accompanying text.

specifies that "the privilege may be claimed by the person, by his guardian or conservator, or by his personal representative if he is deceased. The person who was the clergyman at the time of the communication is presumed to have authority to claim the privilege but only on behalf of the communicant."

Many states permit the person who made the communication to prevent the minister or any other person from disclosing the communication.[155] In some states, only the penitent or "counselee" may assert the privilege, not the minister. See Appendix 2 for the full text of the clergy-penitent privilege in all fifty states.

Example. A member of a church informed three church officials that he had sexually molested a number of children. The mother of one of the victims sued the church, arguing that its negligence in not reporting the molester to civil authorities and in carelessly counseling with him had contributed to the molestation of her daughter. The molester later confessed to at least 33 acts of child molestation, and freely disclosed to the police the confessions that he had made earlier to the church officials. The mother sought to compel the church officials to testify regarding the confessions as part of her attempt to demonstrate that the officials had been aware of the risks posed by the molester and had been negligent in failing to report him to the authorities. This request was opposed by the church officials, who claimed that the confessions made to them were shielded from disclosure in court by the clergy-penitent privilege. The court ruled that under Arizona law the clergyman-penitent privilege "belongs to the communicant, not the recipient of a confidential communication," and accordingly only the molester could assert it. The court rejected the church's claim that the church officials to whom the confessions were made could independently assert the clergy-penitent privilege as a means of avoiding the obligation to testify.[156]

Many state laws give the minister the right to claim the privilege only on behalf of the penitent, meaning that if the penitent waives the privilege and agrees to testify, the minister cannot assert the privilege independently. This is the approach taken by Rule 505 of the Uniform Rules of Evidence. In other states, the minister can assert the privilege independently of the penitent.

§ 3-08.04 — When to Assert the Privilege

Key point 3-08.04. The clergy-penitent privilege does not excuse ministers from appearing in court or at a deposition.

The clergy-penitent privilege does not excuse ministers (or counselees) from appearing in court. Rather, it excuses them from disclosing a privileged communication in court against their will. The proper time to assert the privilege is in court (or at a deposition) when asked to disclose communications protected by the privilege. Of course, ministers do not technically "object" to such a question. The attorney for one of the parties to the underlying legal action ordinarily will object to the question in order to prevent the minister from disclosing the privileged communication. In some cases no objection is made. In such a case ministers are free to inform the judge that they prefer not to answer the question on the ground that it seeks privileged information.

---

[155] *See, e.g.,* Uniform Rules of Evidence § 505.
[156] Church of Jesus Christ of Latter-Day Saints v. Superior Court, 764 P.2d 759 (Ariz. App. 1988).

§ 3-08.05 — Waiver of the Privilege

Key point 3-08.05. *In most states a counselee can waive the clergy-penitent privilege by disclosing the privileged communication to someone other than the minister. In some states the minister also may waive the privilege.*

The clergy-penitent privilege can be "waived" if a minister or counselee voluntarily discloses a privileged communication to another person. If the privilege is waived it no longer protects communications against compelled disclosure in a court of law or judicial proceeding. To illustrate, one court ruled that a counselee waived any privilege when he disclosed to the police the substance of confidential communications he had made to his minister.[157] There is some variation among the states regarding a waiver of the privilege. One court observed that the "states are split on the issue of who holds the power to waive the clergyperson-penitent privilege."[158] Most states allow the counselee to waive the privilege, but in some states only the minister can do so.[159]

Example. *A couple waived the clergy-penitent privilege by alleging damages to their "marital relationship" in a medical malpractice lawsuit. To refute the claim of marital injury, a physician sought to obtain the counseling records of a Roman Catholic priest to whom the couple had gone for marriage counseling. The priest refused to comply on the ground that such records were protected by the clergy-penitent privilege. The court concluded that by alleging damage to their marital relationship the couple had "waived the privilege of their communication with [the priest] during his counseling with them, solely as to their marital problems. Insofar as other communications with [the priest occurred] not pertaining to marriage counseling, the privilege remains intact."[160]*

Example. *Statements made by an imprisoned pastor to another pastor were not protected by the clergy-penitent privilege because he "consented" to their disclosure.[161] A pastor was imprisoned while awaiting trial on several counts of child molestation. While in prison, he was visited by another pastor who met with him to provide comfort and solace. The two prayed together. At the pastor's trial, the visiting pastor testified that the accused pastor stated that he knew that his behavior was wrong, but he "couldn't quit." The visiting pastor also testified that the accused pastor gave him permission to "use [their conversation in] any way that [he thought] would be helpful" to others. The pastor was found guilty of several counts of molestation, and received a prison sentence of 50 to 110 years. The pastor appealed his conviction, in part because his conversation with the visiting pastor was protected by the clergy-penitent privilege and therefore should not have been disclosed. The court concluded that the communications in this case were not privileged since it was clear that the pastor "consented to the testimony and therefore waived the confidentiality of the communication" by giving the visiting pastor permission to use their conversation in any way that he thought would be helpful to others.*

Example. *Children of a deceased woman could not waive the clergy-penitent privilege with regard to documents given by their mother to her priest in the course of an ecclesiastical annulment proceeding. The court conceded that some privileges, including the attorney-client and physician-patient privileges, can be waived by a deceased person's heirs. However, the court concluded that "[t]he legislative concern for the inviolability of the communications in this case is more substantial than*

---

[157] Church of Jesus Christ of Latter-Day Saints v. Superior Court, 764 P.2d 759 (Ariz. App. 1988).
[158] State v. Szemple, 640 A.2d 817 (N.J. 1994).
[159] State v. Martin, 959 P.2d 152 (Wash. App. 1998) (only the counselee can waive the privilege under Washington law).
[160] Ziske v. Luskin, 524 N.Y.S.2d 145 (1987).
[161] State v. Potter, 748 S.E.2d 742 (W. Va. 1996).

that expressed in most [other privileges]." The court noted that the clergy-penitent privilege statute "contains no list of exceptions" as do other privileges. As a result, the civil courts should be "cautious in accepting any argument that the representatives of the [deceased wife], especially when they are not disinterested persons, may waive the privilege, a right that [the deceased wife] had but never exercised."[162]

Example. *A minister was free to waive the clergy-penitent privilege and testify in court regarding a confession made to him by a murderer, even though the murderer did not consent to the disclosure. The minister visited with the murderer (the "defendant") in prison on 19 occasions. On one occasion the defendant confessed to the minister that he had killed 3 persons. The minister later testified at the defendant's trial, and disclosed the defendant's confession. The defendant claimed that his confession to the minister was protected by the clergy-penitent privilege and should not have been disclosed in court. A state supreme court ruled that the confession was privileged, but that the minister had the unilateral right to waive the privilege and disclose the confession in court. The court noted that the purpose of the privilege was to protect ministers from being forced to disclose confidential communications in court and "to curb the potential manipulations of a penitent who, through waiver, could compel a clergyperson to reveal communications that were given purposely to mislead."[163]*

One court, citing Roman Catholic and Episcopal clergy, observed that "complex issues" are raised when clergy are bound by an absolute obligation of silence "unwaivable by a penitent."[164]

§ 3-08.06 — The Privilege in Federal Courts

Key point 3-08.06. *Federal courts generally apply state clergy-penitent privilege statutes.*

In 1972 the United States Supreme Court adopted a set of rules of evidence for use in federal courts.[165] Congress later suspended implementation of these rules pending a thorough review. In 1975, Congress enacted into law a revised version of the Federal Rules of Evidence, incorporating several changes in the rules as originally proposed by the Supreme Court. One of the most significant modifications pertained to privileged communications. The Supreme Court had proposed nine specific privileges for use in the federal courts, including the clergy-parishioner, attorney-client, husband-wife, and psychotherapist-patient privileges. Congress, however, deleted all of the Supreme Court's specific rules of privilege and replaced them with a single principle:

> [T]he privilege of a witness . . . shall be governed by the principles of the common law as they may be interpreted by the courts of the United States in the light of reason and experience. However, in civil actions and proceedings, with respect to an element of a claim or defense as to which state law supplies the rule of decision, the privilege of a witness . . . shall be determined in accordance with state law.[166]

---

[162] Ryan v. Ryan, 642 N.E.2d 1028 (Mass. 1994).

[163] State v. Szemple, 640 A.2d 817 (N.J. 1994).

[164] Church of Jesus Christ of Latter-Day Saints v. Superior Court, 764 P.2d 759 (Ariz. App. 1988) ("once the penitent has waived the privilege, his penitential need is unserved and the public's evidentiary need disserved by permitting a clergyman to assert the privilege independently").

[165] 56 F.R.D. 184 (1972).

[166] Fed. R. Evid. 501.

§ 3-08.07 — Constitutionality of the Privilege

Key point 3-08.07. The clergy-penitent privilege is not required by the first amendment guaranty of religious freedom.

Often, a communication made to a minister will fail one or more of the requirements for a valid privilege, yet the minister or the person making the communication will argue that the first amendment's guaranty of religious freedom prohibits compelled disclosure of the communication. To illustrate, in one case a Catholic nun who was not eligible for the privilege argued that the first amendment protected her from being compelled to testify regarding communications made to her by a murder suspect. The court, in rejecting the nun's claim, observed that "this case calls for a balancing of interests—that of the state in enforcing the power of the grand jury to inquire into the commission of a crime, and that of [the nun] who claims she responds to a call of conscience. In the particular circumstances of this case the latter must give way to the former."[167]

Another court, in rejecting a priest's claim that requiring a bishop to disclose unprivileged records relating to the priest violated the first amendment, observed: (1) disclosure of the documents pertaining to the priest would not interfere with the bishop's "right to believe as he chooses and to engage in the religious observances of his faith"; (2) no impermissible "entanglement" between church and state would result; (3) information in the possession of a church "has always been subject to civil process"; and (4) there would be no need for the clergy-penitent privilege if the first amendment's "free exercise of religion" clause protected information in the possession of a church from civil process.[168]

§ 3-08.08 — Child Abuse Reporting

Key point 3-08.08. Clergy who are mandatory reporters of child abuse are excused from a duty to report in many states if they learn of the abuse in the course of a conversation covered by the clergy-penitent privilege. Some state child abuse reporting laws do not contain this exception.

Ministers who are mandatory reporters of child abuse under state law are under a profound ethical dilemma when they receive information about abuse in the course of a confidential counseling session that is subject to the clergy-penitent privilege. They have to chose between fulfilling their legal obligation to report, or honoring their ecclesiastical duty to maintain the confidentiality of privileged communications. A number of states have attempted to resolve this dilemma by specifically exempting clergy from the duty to report child abuse if the abuse is disclosed to them in the course of a privileged conversation. Other states, while not specifically excluding clergy from the duty to report, do provide that information protected by the clergy-penitent privilege is not admissible in any legal proceeding regarding the alleged abuse.

Not every communication made to a minister is protected by the clergy-penitent privilege. Generally, only confidential communications shared with a minister acting in a professional capacity as a spiritual adviser are covered. Ministers who live in a state that exempts them from reporting child abuse if they learned of it in the course of a privileged communication must be familiar with the requirements of the clergy-penitent privilege under state law.

While no court has addressed the issue directly, it is possible that clergy having religious opposition to disclosing confidences may be able to defend a failure to report a confession (or indication) of child abuse on

---

[167] In re Murtha, 279 A.2d 889, 894 (N.J. 1971).
[168] Pagano v. Hadley, 100 F.R.D. 758 (D. Del. 1984).

the basis of the first amendment's guaranty of religious freedom. This position would be the strongest for those clergy whose churches or denominations have taken specific positions prohibiting disclosure of confessions or confidential communications as a matter of ecclesiastical doctrine or practice. Even here, it is possible that a civil court would conclude that the state's interest in obtaining information about child abuse is so compelling that it supersedes the constitutional guaranty of religious freedom. Generally, religious freedom may be limited or abridged by a state law or practice that is supported by a compelling governmental interest.[169] One commentator noted that the first amendment guaranty of religious freedom outweighs the state's interest in uncovering cases of child abuse if a minister's failure to disclose is based on the established dogma or practice of his or her church or sect.[170]

The issue of child abuse reporting is discussed fully in chapter 4.

Example. A Texas court noted that the duty to report child abuse in Texas "is sweeping and makes no exceptions for clergy, physicians, mental health professionals or teachers." The statute reads simply: "A person having cause to believe that a child's physical or mental health or welfare has been or may be adversely affected by abuse or neglect by any person shall report [the suspected abuse]." The court noted that a minister is more "likely to learn of child abuse, which he is obligated by law to report," given the nature of the profession. However, the court also observed that the Texas child abuse reporting law does not contain any exemption for ministers who receive reports of abuse in the context of confidential counseling sessions. In other words, the clergy-penitent privilege is presumably no defense to a failure to report.[171]

DOES THE CLERGY-PENITENT EXCUSE CLERGY FROM REPORTING CHILD ABUSE?

It is common for ministers to learn of child abuse in the course of counseling. Should they report the abuse to civil authorities, or respect the confidentiality of the conversation? This is a difficult question. The following considerations may help in reaching an informed decision:

- *Are you a mandatory reporter under your state's child abuse reporting law?* A mandatory reporter has a legal obligation to report known or reasonably suspected incidents of child abuse to designated civil authorities. Ministers are mandatory reporters in many states. Be sure to check your state's child abuse reporting law.

- *Does the clergy-penitent privilege apply?* In many states, clergy who are mandatory reporters of child abuse are excused from the duty to report if they learn of the abuse in the course of a conversation that is protected by the clergy-penitent privilege. Did you learn of child abuse in the course of a privileged conversation? If so, you may be excused from the duty to report. Be sure to check your state's child abuse reporting law to see if such an exception exists.

- *If you are not a mandatory reporter.* If you are not a mandatory reporter you cannot be criminally liable for failing to report child abuse. However, this does not necessarily relieve you of civil liability. As a result, you still may want to report the abuse.

- *Moral obligation.* Be sure to consider the moral as well as the legal issues. What are the consequences if you elect not to report the child abuse? Is it possible that the victim will continue to be abused? If so, do you have a moral obligation to intervene?

---

[169] *See generally* chapters 12-14, *infra.*

[170] Mitchell, *Must Clergy Tell? Child Abuse Reporting Requirements Versus the Clergy Privilege and Free Exercise of Religion*, 71 MINN. L. REV. 723 (1986).

[171] Texas Department of Human Services v. Benson, 893 S.W.2d 236 (Tex. App. 1995). The court refused to address this question directly since the minister had not asked it to do so.

Example. Two teenage girls were sexually molested at their church by a "youth counselor." The counselor later informed his pastor of his actions. The pastor arranged a meeting between the counselor, the victim, and the victim's parents. The counselor apologized to the victim and her parents at the meeting. None of the participants at that meeting said anything to indicate that his statements would be revealed in public. The pastor then referred the counselor to an associate pastor for further counsel. After speaking with the youth counselor, the associate pastor became concerned that he was required to report the incident. He contacted a state child welfare agency and was informed that as a pastor he was not required to report, but as a psychologist he was required to report. He later reported the abuse. His report led to criminal charges being filed against the youth counselor who was later convicted on two counts of aggravated criminal sexual abuse. The youth counselor appealed his conviction, claiming that the state improperly compelled the associate pastor to report the abuse in violation of the clergy privilege. A state appeals court agreed with the youth counselor that the clergy-penitent privilege applied to his conversations with both pastors and accordingly he had been improperly informed by the state that he should report the abuse. The court noted that ministers are not mandatory reporters under the Illinois child abuse reporting law, and as a result "the clergy privilege is applicable."[172]

Example. An Alaska appeals court ruled that a minister who reported an incident of child abuse was barred by the clergy-penitent privilege from testifying in court. A man sexually molested a 4-year-old child who had been placed in his care for an evening. The molester sought help through counseling with a minister. After learning of the individual's sexual relations with a child, the minister reported the incident to the authorities. State troopers investigated the report, and the molester was prosecuted. The molester claimed that the troopers' investigation, and the subsequent prosecution, were based entirely on information he provided to his minister in the course of confidential counseling. As such, it was protected by the clergy-penitent privilege and could not be basis for a criminal prosecution. A trial judge agreed that the statements made to the minister were covered by the clergy-penitent privilege. On that basis, the judge ruled that the minister could not be called as a witness to testify regarding the statements made to him by the molester in the course of their confidential counseling session. On the other hand, the judge ruled that the minister had a legal obligation to report the abuse, and this duty was not affected by the clergy-penitent privilege. The molester appealed the trial judge's ruling, and an appeals court concluded that the trial court's decision was correct. The Alaska clergy-penitent privilege applies "at all stages of all actions, cases, and proceedings." This is broad language, meaning that the privilege is not confined to "in court" testimony. The court concluded, however, that the minister's "report of sexual abuse was made in an out-of-court statement that was unrelated to any action, case, or proceeding then pending. For this reason, although it divulged confidential communications between [the molester and the minister], the report did not amount to a violation of the . . . clergy privilege." In summary, the court concluded that the clergy-penitent privilege applies only to pending "actions, cases, or proceedings," and accordingly it prevents a minister from testifying in court regarding a conversation protected by the privilege. However, the privilege does not excuse a minister from making a report of child abuse (and thereby initiating an official investigation) since at the time of a report there ordinarily is no pending legal action.[173]

§ 3-08.09 — Confidentiality

Key point 3-08.09. Clergy can be liable for disclosing communications shared with them in confidence to others without the permission of the counselee.

---

[172] People v. Burnidge, 664 N.E.2d 656 (Ill. App. 1996).
[173] Walstad v. State, 818 P.2d 695 (Alaska App. 1991).

The concepts of privilege and confidentiality are closely related. Generally, "confidentiality" refers to a duty not to disclose to *anyone* the substance of communications shared in confidence. While the impropriety of disclosing confidential information is universally acknowledged, few clergy have been found legally accountable for unauthorized disclosures. This is because, until recently, the duty of clergy to preserve confidences was considered to be moral rather than legal in nature. However, in recent years some clergy have been sued for divulging confidences.

> *Tip. Be sure to distinguish between the concepts of privilege and confidentiality. The clergy-penitent privilege provides that clergy cannot be compelled to disclose in court the content of communications shared with them in confidence while acting as a spiritual adviser. The related concept of confidentiality imposes upon clergy a duty not to disclose to others any communications shared with them in confidence.*

To illustrate, a bishop who confessed to church leaders that he had committed adultery sued his church when church leaders disclosed the confession without the bishop's consent.[174] The bishop had specifically asked his church leaders to keep his confession in confidence, and they promised to do so. A short time later, the female church member who was the other party to the affair confessed to a church leader who promised to keep her confession in confidence. The church leaders allegedly disclosed these confidences to a local church's board of elders, and to numerous other persons. One of the church leaders allegedly disclosed the confidences to the assembled congregation in a Sunday worship service, and then proceeded to "excommunicate" the bishop and "cast his spirit" from the church. A family counselor to whom the female member had also made a confession and obtained a promise of confidentiality also allegedly disclosed the information to others. And, the bishop alleged that one of the church leaders disclosed his confession to a "gathering of local priests, ministers, pastors, and guests."

As a result of these disclosures, the bishop and the female church member were shunned by friends, family, and members of their local church and denomination. The two sued the church and various church officials, alleging invasion of privacy, breach of fiduciary duty, false imprisonment, emotional distress, and malpractice. The church countered by arguing that the civil courts lacked jurisdiction over the controversy since "the conduct complained of is ecclesiastical in nature." A state appeals court ruled that the church could be sued for emotional distress and related claims, and it ordered the case to proceed to trial. The court began its opinion by noting that "religious disputes can take a number of forms . . . and do not always result in immunity from liability." The court acknowledged that the civil courts may not intervene in disputes over church doctrine, but it was not willing to accept the trial court's summary conclusion that this dispute in fact involved church doctrine. It observed:

> The trial court was not told, and we do not know, whether it is a canon of [the church's] belief that confessions (penitential or not) are revealed to the congregation . . . ; whether it is church practice for the substance of a confession to be shared among church officials; or whether it is consistent with church doctrine to reveal the substance of a confession to anyone outside the church, and if so, under what circumstances.

Even if church doctrine prescribed the disclosure of confidences, this would not end the analysis, for certain types of behavior may be regulated or subjected to legal liability by state law, even if rooted in religious doctrine, so long as the state has a compelling interest that justifies the burden on religious conduct. For example, "under the banner of the first amendment provisions on religion, a clergyman may not with impu-

---

[174] Snyder v. Evangelical Orthodox Church, 264 Cal. Rptr. 640 (Cal. App. 1989).

nity defame a person, intentionally inflict serious emotional harm on a parishioner, or commit other torts." In other words, the first amendment guaranty of religious freedom does not necessarily insulate clergy from liability for their actions.

The court acknowledged that it could find no previous case in which "a counselee or communicant has sought to hold a religious officer liable in tort for [an unauthorized disclosure of confidential communications]." However, it saw no reason why clergy and church leaders should not be held legally accountable for injuries they inflict when they disclose confidential information to others without consent.

Tip. Clergy who disclose confidential information shared with them in counseling sessions may be exposing themselves, as well as their church, to legal liability on the basis of malpractice, invasion of privacy, breach of fiduciary duty, and infliction of emotional distress. This conclusion may apply even when clergy share confidential information in order to discipline a member for violating church standards. The point is this—would members disclose confidential information if they suspected that their minister would report it to the church board or congregation in order to discipline them? Clearly, the answer is "no." Therefore, it is essential for clergy to refrain from disclosing information obtained during confidential counseling sessions—even if it relates to a person's qualifications or eligibility for membership. Of course, the church board can still discipline the individual, but not on the basis of any information shared with the minister in the course of a confidential counseling session. Another alternative is for a minister to obtain the permission of the counselee to share confidential information with the board or with some other person. If this permission is obtained (in writing), this will serve as a defense in the event that the minister is later sued for disclosing the information.

Example. A woman (the "victim") was referred to a pastor for counseling because of his many years of counseling experience. The victim later joined the pastor's church, and continued to meet with him for counseling, relating to him highly personal and private matters including the fact that her father had sexually molested both her and a sister. The victim's sister attended the same church, and married the pastor's son. The marriage between the sister and the pastor's son deteriorated after the sister learned that her husband was having an affair with another woman. When the pastor's son publicly blamed his wife for the breakup of their marriage, the victim met with the pastor to defend her sister and to present evidence showing that the husband (the pastor's son) was the one who had been unfaithful. The pastor responded by defending his son to the church board and congregation. He informed both the board and congregation that the sister could not be believed because her family was "incestuous" and "dysfunctional." The victim and her sister sued the pastor and the church on a number of grounds, including invasion of privacy, defamation, malpractice, and breach of fiduciary duty. The court concluded that the pastor offered "no good reason for insulating a counselor from liability for betraying clients' confidences to their detriment merely because the counselor is a clergy member and unlicensed, and the counseling as well as wrongful disclosure takes place in a religious setting."[175]

Example. A Michigan court ruled that a minister could not be sued for breaching a "duty of confidentiality" by disclosing to the congregations information that was communicated to him by a member in the course of a confidential counseling session.[176] A church member (the "plaintiff") confessed to his pastor that he had previously committed adultery with prostitutes. The pastor decided to communicate this information to the entire congregation, including the member's wife, family, and friends. The

---

[175] Barnes v. Outlaw, 937 P.2d 323 (Ariz. App. 1996).
[176] Smith v. Calvary Christian Church, 592 N.W.2d 713 (Mich. App. 1998).

pastor insisted that he did not believe in confidential communications and that church doctrine required exposing sins to the congregation. The member claimed that the pastor had been motivated not by religious doctrine but by ill will and the intent to humiliate him and create dissension within his family. The disgraced member sued his pastor and church, alleging that the pastor's disclosure amounted to a breach of the duty of confidentiality. The plaintiff insisted that the clergy-penitent privilege imposes upon clergy a "duty of confidentiality," and that clergy who disclose confidences without permission may be sued for breaching this duty. The court disagreed, noting that the clergy-penitent privilege is a "rule of evidence that did not create a cause of action for disclosure of private or privileged communications."

Example. *A New York court ruled that two rabbis could be sued for divulging information shared with them by a counselee in a conversation protected by the clergy-penitent privilege.[177] A woman obtained counseling, individually, from two rabbis. During her counseling sessions, she revealed information of an extremely personal and confidential nature. The woman later brought a lawsuit seeking to divorce her husband and obtain custody of their four minor children. In the course of this lawsuit, the woman's husband introduced an affidavit from each of the rabbis to support his claim for custody of the children. In the affidavits the rabbis disclosed some of the confidential information that had been shared with them in confidence by the woman. The woman immediately sued both rabbis, claiming that they violated the clergy-penitent privilege. The court ruled that ministers who breach the clergy-penitent privilege by disclosing information shared with them in confidence may be sued by the counselee for breaching a fiduciary duty of confidentiality. The court further concluded that imposing liability on clergy in such cases does not violate the first amendment guaranty of religious freedom.*

§ 3-08.10 — Disclosure of Criminal Activity to Civil Authorities

Key point 3-08.10. *The clergy-penitent privilege does not prevent clergy from disclosing confidential communications to the police. Rather, it prevents clergy from disclosing the content of privileged communications in court. Clergy who choose to inform the police about information shared with them in confidence are providing no more than a "tip." The police will need to confirm the information through their own investigation, since the minister will be prevented by the privilege from disclosing the information in court.*

Clergy sometimes feel morally obligated to inform the police about a confession of criminal activity made to them in confidence. They often resist doing so, however, out of a desire to honor the confidential nature of the communication. One consideration that may be helpful in resolving this dilemma is the fact that the minister's disclosure of the information to the civil authorities will constitute little more than an unsubstantiated "tip." The minister will be prevented by the privilege from disclosing the information in court, and so the authorities will need to confirm the minister's account through their own investigation. In many cases the identity of the minister is never disclosed.

Example. *The body of a woman was found at a church camp. A few weeks later, another woman went to the home of a local pastor and confessed that she had killed her. When the woman left, the pastor called the police and advised them of the confession. Based entirely on this information, the police arrested the woman, obtained a confession from her, and charged her with murder. The woman was later found guilty of second degree murder. The woman appealed her conviction, claiming that her arrest had been unlawful since it was based on the improper and unauthorized disclosure of her privi-*

---

[177] Lightman v. Flaum, 687 N.Y.S.2d 562 (Sup. 1999).

leged communication with the pastor. A state appeals court disagreed, noting simply that "the clergy-man-penitent privilege is an evidentiary rule proscribing the revelation of privileged communications at a trial when the privilege is asserted by the protected party. Here, revelation of [the woman's] confession to the police provided probable cause for her arrest and subsequent prosecution." In other words, if the woman's conversation with the pastor was privileged, the legal effect of this would be to prevent the pastor from testifying in court about the conversation. The privilege does not apply in making a decision whether or not the police have probable cause to make an arrest. As a result, the woman's arrest was lawful, as was her conviction.[178]

§ 3-08.11 — Church Records

Key point 3-08.11. *The clergy-penitent privilege does not prevent clergy from disclosing confidential communications to the police. Rather, it prevents clergy from disclosing the content of privileged communications in court. Clergy who choose to inform the police about information shared with them in confidence are providing no more than a "tip." The police will need to confirm the information through their own investigation, since the minister will be prevented by the privilege from disclosing the information in court.*

What if your church were served with a subpoena demanding that various financial records, membership records, and a pastor's counseling notes be turned over to an attorney? How would you react? Many church leaders consider such demands to be inappropriate, and resist turning over internal church records. Is this a legally appropriate response? Does the law exempt churches from having to turn over internal church records in response to a subpoena? These are important questions for which there has been little direction from the courts.

One of the leading cases is a decision by the Pennsylvania Supreme Court.[179] An individual (the "defendant") was charged with the murder of a Roman Catholic priest. The priest was found shot to death in the defendant's home. The defendant admitted that he shot the priest, but he insisted that he did so in self-defense. In attempting to prove that he acted in self-defense, the defendant subpoenaed documents from the local Catholic Diocese. Specifically, the defendant requested the priest's personnel records and the Diocese's records concerning the priest's alleged alcohol and drug abuse and sexual misconduct. The defendant insisted that these documents could help prove that he acted in self-defense because of the priest's past violent conduct.

The Diocese turned over some documents but refused to turn over any records kept in its "secret archives." According to the Diocese, its secret archives contain copies of all written communications between the bishop and his priests and notes of any oral communications between the bishop and priests that are considered to be confidential. The Diocese asked the court to excuse it from turning over the following categories of documents: (1) All reports, letters, and other documents pertaining to any allegations of misconduct or other disciplinary action regarding the priest. (2) Copies of any reports pertaining to any sexual misconduct by the priest. (3) Copies of all personal records, correspondence, diaries, or similar documents maintained by the priest, whether such documents were maintained at his former parish or other locations. (4) Copies of any reports pertaining to any alcohol or other substance abuse or treatment by the priest from 1986 to 1989. The Diocese claimed that these records had to be exempted from the defendant's subpoena on the basis of the Pennsylvania clergy-penitent privilege and the first amendment guaranty of religious freedom.

---

[178] People v. Ward, 604 N.Y.S.2d 320 (A.D. 3 Dept. 1993).
[179] Commonwealth v. Stewart, 690 A.2d 195 (Pa. 1997). *Accord* Niemann v. Cooley, 637 N.E.2d 943 (Ohio App. 1994).

The trial court denied the Diocese's request for a blanket exemption of these documents from the defendant's subpoena. However, the court did concede that some of the documents might be protected from disclosure by the clergy-penitent privilege. Since it was not clear whether any of the documents were protected by the privilege, the trial judge ordered the documents turned over to him for a confidential review to determine if the privilege applied. The Diocese appealed the trial court's ruling to the state supreme court.

The court first addressed the Diocese's claim that the documents in question were protected from disclosure by the clergy-penitent privilege. It noted that privileges are narrowly interpreted and are "not favored" since "exceptions to the demand for every man's evidence are not lightly created nor expansively construed, for they are in derogation of the search for truth." Therefore, privileges should be recognized "only to the very limited extent that permitting a refusal to testify or excluding relevant evidence has a public good transcending the normally predominant principle of utilizing all rational means for ascertaining the truth."

It then addressed the question of whether internal church documents can be protected by the privilege. More specifically, could the Diocese refuse to turn over the documents in question on the ground that they are protected from disclosure by the privilege? The Diocese asserted that all of the documents in question would have been obtained in confidence by the Bishop or other clergy in the course of their duties and were maintained in the confidential diocesan archives. The Diocese filed an affidavit that stated in part:

> The bishop fulfills [his] duties in conjunction with his priests, over whom he exercises hierarchical authority. Thus, a bishop maintains a special relationship with his priests. He provides primary support and guidance for them concerning their spiritual lives and the faithful performance of their mission within the Church. Free, frank and confidential communication between the bishop and his priests must be protected so that the bishop can fulfill his obligations to his priests and the faithful under the prescriptions of Canon Law. A bishop must be able to candidly discuss with a priest his character, talents, spiritual life, health, and pastoral or familial problems and concerns in order to be able to assign the priest to compatible duties and to provide him with appropriate guidance in the conduct of his affairs and ministry to the faithful.

The court did not agree that this affidavit demonstrated that the documents were privileged:

> The affidavit refers only to the hierarchical structure of the Roman Catholic Church and in general terms to the Bishop's duties. The affidavit fails to indicate whether the precise information subject to the discovery request was, in fact, acquired by the Bishop or Diocesan representatives secretly and in confidence while acting in their capacity as confessors or spiritual advisors. We cannot assume that all communications with or between members of the clergy occur in confidence and for confessional or spiritual purposes.

In particular, the court noted that the affidavit failed to explain why the priest's personnel records, correspondence, diaries, and other similar documents were protected by the privilege. In addition, "the Diocese has not demonstrated how any letters, reports or records relating to allegations of misconduct or substance abuse of [the priest], particularly documents reflecting investigations of misconduct or disciplinary actions, fall within the protection of the privilege."

Because the Diocese failed to demonstrate that the documents were protected by the clergy-penitent privilege, the trial court "properly directed the Diocese to produce the documents to the trial court" for a confidential review.

The court concluded that "to the extent the requested documents reflect relevant disciplinary action, investigations of misconduct, substance abuse treatment or non-confessional admissions of misconduct by [the priest], they are discoverable."

The court rejected the Diocese's argument that disclosure of its archival documents violated its right to the free exercise of religion as protected by the federal and state constitutions. The court did not question the fact that the Diocese's refusal to produce documents in violation of canon law "is rooted in a sincerely held religious belief." However, it concluded that this burden on the Diocese's religious freedom "furthers a compelling governmental interest by the least restrictive means available." It noted that "a defendant in a criminal case has a right to discover material evidence, and the state has a compelling interest in pursuing the truth in a criminal matter." And, although a confidential review of the documents by the trial judge to determine whether any are privileged "may cause a limited exposure of privileged information to the trial court, a court order limiting discovery to relevant, non-privileged documents advances this compelling governmental interest in the least restrictive way." As a result, "the compelled production of documents for [confidential] review and the discovery of documents deemed relevant and non-privileged does not impermissibly intrude upon the Diocese's exercise of its religious beliefs and practices."

§ 3-08.12 — Death of the Counselee

Key point 3-08.12. The clergy-penitent privilege may continue to protect communications made to a minister even after the counselee's death.

The United States Supreme Court issued an opinion in 1998 suggesting that the clergy-penitent privilege may survive a counselee's death.[180] While the case involved the attorney-client privilege, the court's reasoning applies equally to the clergy-penitent privilege. The case involved several pages of notes taken by an attorney during a meeting with President Clinton's counsel Vince Foster. Following Foster's suicide, an independent counsel subpoenaed the attorney's notes. The attorney refused to turn over his notes, claiming that they were protected from disclosure by the attorney-client privilege. The independent counsel insisted that the privilege no longer applied after the client's death. A federal appeals court ruled in favor of the independent counsel, and the case was appealed to the Supreme Court, which concluded that the attorney-client privilege survives the death of the client. The court observed, "[W]e think there are weighty reasons that counsel in favor of posthumous application. Knowing that communications will remain confidential even after death encourages the client to communicate fully and frankly with counsel. While the fear of disclosure, and the consequent withholding of information from counsel, may be reduced if disclosure is limited to posthumous disclosure in a criminal context, it seems unreasonable to assume that it vanishes altogether. Clients may be concerned about reputation, civil liability, or possible harm to friends or family. Posthumous disclosure of such communications may be as feared as disclosure during the client's lifetime."

The court added that the privilege survives the life of a client even in noncriminal matters:

Clients consult attorneys for a wide variety of reasons, only one of which involves possible criminal liability. Many attorneys act as counselors on personal and family matters, where, in the course of obtaining the desired advice, confidences about family members or financial problems must be revealed in order to assure sound legal advice. The same is true of owners of small businesses who may regularly consult their attorneys about a variety of problems arising in the course

---

[180] Swidler & Berlin v. United States, 118 S. Ct. 2081 (1998).

of the business. These confidences may not come close to any sort of admission of criminal wrongdoing, but nonetheless be matters which the client would not wish divulged.

§ 3-09   Visiting Privileges at Penal Institutions

Many states allow ministers to enter correctional institutions for purposes of religious counseling and instruction. However, much discretion is given to prison authorities in deciding the conditions under which such visits will be allowed. It is customary to allow a prisoner to visit with a minister prior to the infliction of the death penalty, and some states provide for the presence of clergy at executions.

The first amendment does not forbid outsiders from entering prisons in order to conduct religious services and to "witness" to prisoners, at least if prisoners are not forced to participate.[181] The practice of many prisons in employing chaplains has also been upheld against the claim that it constitutes a violation of the first amendment's "nonestablishment of religion" clause.[182]

Example. A federal appeals court ruled that a prosecutor violated the legal rights of a priest by secretly tape recording a penitential conversation between the priest and an inmate at a county jail.[183] A Catholic priest occasionally administered the sacrament of penance to inmates of a local county jail. On one occasion, he met with an inmate who was a suspect in the murder of three young persons. Unknown to the priest, his conversation with the inmate was being secretly recorded by the prosecuting attorney's office. The priest and archbishop brought a lawsuit in federal court claiming that the secret recording (and retention of the tape) violated the first amendment guaranty of religious freedom, the fourth amendment protection against unreasonable searches and seizures, the Religious Freedom Restoration Act (RFRA), and the federal Wiretapping Act. The court ruled that the prosecutor's act of secretly taping a confidential communication between the inmate and priest violated the federal Religious Freedom Restoration Act and the fourth amendment prohibition against unreasonable searches and seizures. The court observed, "[T]he history of the nation has shown a uniform respect for the character of sacramental confession as inviolable by government agents interested in securing evidence of crime from the lips of criminal. . . . All fifty states have enacted statutes granting some form of testimonial privilege to clergy-communicant communications. Neither scholars nor courts question the legitimacy of the privilege, and attorneys rarely litigate the issue. It would be strange if a privilege so generally recognized could be readily subverted by the governmental recording of the privileged communication and the introduction of the recording into evidence."

§ 3-10   Immigration of Alien Ministers

Federal immigration law gives preferential treatment to certain classes of aliens. Under certain conditions, ministers are entitled to "special immigrant" status and therefore may be admitted to the United States without the numerical limitations that ordinarily apply to immigrants. To be entitled to this special immigrant status, a minister must establish that (1) for at least two years immediately preceding the time of application for admission to the United States, he or she was engaged continuously in carrying on the vocation of a minister; (2) he or she seeks to enter the United States solely for the purpose of carrying on the vocation of

---

[181] Campbell v. Cauthron, 623 F.2d 503 (8th Cir. 1980).
[182] Theriault v. Silber, 547 F.2d 1279 (5th Cir. 1977), *cert. denied,* 434 U.S. 871 (1977).
[183] Mockaitis v. Harcleroad, 104 F.3d 1522 (9th Cir. 1997).

a minister; and (3) his or her services are needed by a religious denomination having a bona fide organization in the United States.[184] The minister's spouse and dependent children also receive special immigrant status.

These requirements are strictly construed. In one case, a Turkish clergyman of the outlawed Bektashi faith sought special immigrant status as a "minister." His application was denied by the Immigration and Naturalization Service on the ground that the applicant had not functioned as a minister for two years immediately preceding the time of his application for admission to the United States, despite the applicant's claim that he had been unable to function as a minister because the Turkish government had outlawed his sect.[185]

The Immigration and Naturalization Service has held that the term *minister* as used in the Immigration and Naturalization Act means a person duly authorized by a recognized religious denomination having a bona fide organization in the United States to conduct religious worship and to perform other duties usually performed by a regularly ordained clergyman of that denomination. Therefore, the Service has held that an ordained "minister of music" was not a "minister" since her education was primarily in music and not theology, she never officiated at weddings or funerals, she never performed preaching or visitation functions although she allegedly had the authority to do so, and she did not have two continuous years of ministry experience immediately preceding the filing of her application for admission to the United States.[186]

§ 3-11 Miscellaneous Benefits

Ministers are eligible for various benefits under federal tax laws. Most important, they are permitted to exclude from their gross income the cost of owning or maintaining a residence; they can elect (if certain conditions are met) to be exempt from social security; they are not subject to federal income tax withholding (even if they report their federal income taxes as employees); and they are not considered to be "employees" subject to federal unemployment taxes.[187] Most states similarly exempt ministers from unemployment taxes and income tax withholding. Several states exempt parsonages from property taxes, although nearly all of such states require that a parsonage be owned by the church and not by the minister in order to be qualified for the exemption.

Several states exempt ministration to the sick by prayer from the prohibition against unauthorized practice of medicine and exempt ministers from the penalties imposed upon persons who practice psychology without a license.[188] As a result, a minister ordinarily is not in violation of law when he or she prays for the sick. But if a minister persuades a sick person to forego medical treatment and rely completely upon prayer for recovery, the minister may be responsible for any adverse consequences which could have been prevented by conventional medical treatment.

The Interstate Commerce Act permits common carriers to provide transportation without charge or at discounted rates to "a minister of religion."[189] Various states likewise permit common carriers to provide free or discounted transportation to ministers.

---

[184] 8 U.S.C. § 1101(a)(27)(c).

[185] First Albanian Teqe Bektashiane in America v. Sahli, 231 F. Supp. 516 (E.D. Mich. 1964).

[186] Re Rhee, I & N Interim Decision No. 2682 (1982).

[187] *See* R. Hammar, Church and Clergy Tax Guide chapters 9 and 11 (published annually by the publisher of this text).

[188] *See, e.g.,* Tex. Health Code Ann. title 71, §§ 4504, 4512c.

[189] 49 U.S.C. § 10723.

INSTRUCTIONAL AIDS TO CHAPTER 3

Terms

confidential communications

confidentiality

conscientious objector

customary vocation

discipline

duly ordained ministers of religion

privilege

ratification

regular ministers of religion

Learning Objectives

- Describe a minister's legal authority.

- Identify the legal requirements that clergy must follow in performing marriage ceremonies.

- Explain the status of clergy, and theology students, under the Selective Service Act.

- Understand the nature and purpose of the clergy-penitent privilege, and apply it to a variety of factual circumstances.

- Understand whether or not a minister has a legal duty to report known or reasonably suspected cases of child abuse to state authorities.

Short-Answer Questions

1. Rev. T is the senior minister of First Church. Is he entitled to chair church business meetings? Assume that the church bylaws do not address the matter.

2. Rev. C, the minister of Faith Church, learns that a homeowner who lives next door to the church is about to sell her home for $80,000. Rev. C would like the church to buy the property for future expansion, and he immediately calls the homeowner and states that "the church will buy your home for $90,000." The homeowner accepts this offer. At its next-meeting, the church board refuses to authorize the purchase because it feels that $90,000 is too much to pay for the property. The seller wants to enforce the contract. Result?

3. Same facts as question 2, except that the church board takes no action approving or disapproving the sale. Title is transferred to the church, and the church begins using the property. Is the church bound by the purchase even if the church board later decides to repudiate the transaction?

4. Rev. B recently performed his first wedding. He did not know that the couple were second cousins, or that they had not obtained a marriage license. Rev. B also was not aware of a requirement to complete and return a marriage certificate to civil authorities. Is this marriage valid? Is Rev. B subject to any legal penalties? Explain.

5. The following questions pertain to the status of ministers under the Selective Service Act:

a. Explain the registration responsibilities of male citizens under the Selective Service Act.

b. Do the registration requirements apply to ministers or students preparing for the ministry?

c. D is an 18-year-old male who plans to pursue theological training at the college level immediately after graduation from high school. He is opposed to registration on the basis of his religious convictions, and believes that the registration requirement would violate the first amendment guaranty of religious freedom. Is he correct? Explain.

d. Rev. L is the full-time minister of a local church. Is he automatically exempt from mandatory military training and service (in the event of a draft)? Explain.

e. W is a full-time seminary student. Is he automatically exempt from mandatory military training and service (in the event of a draft)?

f. Rev. S serves as minister of a small rural congregation. To help support himself, he works twenty hours a week as a car salesman. Is he exempt from military training and service? Explain.

g. J is an agnostic who is opposed to the current defense policies of the United States. In the event of a national draft, would he be eligible for conscientious objector status?

6. Rev. W receives a notice to appear for jury service on June 10. She has a funeral on that day. May she be excused from jury service? How?

7. While playing golf with Rev. C, a church member confesses to an unsolved crime. Is this confession privileged? Explain.

8. A church member discusses a personal problem with a deacon in the church library following a worship service. Is this conversation privileged? Explain.

9. A church member discussed a personal problem with her minister over the telephone. Is this conversation privileged? Explain.

10. A church member makes certain admissions to Rev. T in the presence of a friend. Are these admissions privileged? Explain.

11. A member of First Church suggests to a friend that he contact Rev. A for counseling. The friend is not a member of First Church. Are statements made by the friend to Rev. A privileged? Explain.

12. A member and her husband seek marital counseling from their pastor. Are statements made during counseling sessions privileged? Explain.

13. Rev. G suspects that the church treasurer has embezzled church funds. He calls the treasurer into his office, and confronts him with the evidence. The treasurer confesses. Are statements made by the treasurer during this meeting privileged? Explain.

14. Who is entitled to claim the privilege against disclosure of confidential communications, and when must the privilege be claimed?

15. Trinity Church receives a subpoena demanding that it produce certain financial records in court. Can it refuse to respond on the basis that the documents are privileged? Explain.

16. Rev. M counseled privately with a church member about a personal problem. In a subsequent lawsuit, he is called to the witness stand and questioned about the counseling session. He is asked to "describe the demeanor" of the church member during their conference. The member's attorney objects to this question on the ground that it seeks privileged information. How should the judge rule? Explain.

17. A church member informs Rev. H during a counseling session that her husband has been sexually abusing their minor child. Does Rev. H have a legal duty to report this information to the state? Is it privileged?

18. A church member confesses to the pastor during a counseling session to moral failure. The pastor later communicates this information to the church board and to other members of the church. Have the pastor's actions placed him in legal jeopardy? Explain.

19. Jack meets with his minister to discuss a church project that he is coordinating. Are statements made by Jack during this meeting protected by the clergy-penitent privilege? Explain.

20. Same facts as question 19, except that at the end of the meeting Jack informs the minister that he has "something else" to tell him. He recounts how he embezzled funds from the church while counting offerings over the past several months. Are these statements protected by the clergy-penitent privilege? Explain.

21. A church member is audited by the IRS, and her charitable contributions to her church are questioned. The IRS issues a subpoena to the church, requesting disclosure of the woman's contribution records for the past three years. Are these documents protected from disclosure by the clergy-penitent privilege? Explain.

22. A church dismisses an employee. The former employee later sues the church, alleging that her dismissal was discriminatory and wrongful. She serves a subpoena on the church, demanding disclosure of her personnel file and any other internal church record pertaining to her dismissal. Are these documents protected from disclosure by the clergy-penitent privilege? Explain.

23. A pastor, along with his church and a denominational agency, are sued by a woman who claims that the pastor took advantage or her emotional vulnerability during a counseling relationship by engaging in sexual relations. The woman serves a subpoena on the denominational agency, demanding disclosure of any former disciplinary actions or allegations of misconduct involving the pastor. Are any of these documents protected from disclosure by the clergy-penitent privilege? Explain.

24. A minor is sexually molested by a volunteer church worker. The minor's parents sue the church. They serve a subpoena on the church demanding disclosure of any screening form or application used by the church when it began using the volunteer worker, in addition to any policies the church has adopted pertaining to the screening and supervision of youth activities and workers. Are these documents protected from disclosure by the clergy-penitent privilege? Explain.

25. A woman seeks out her pastor for marriage counseling. The woman discontinues the counseling after several sessions, and later sues her husband for a divorce. The husband serves a subpoena on the church, demanding that the pastor turn over all of the counseling notes that he compiled while counseling the woman. Are these documents protected from disclosure by the clergy-penitent privilege? Explain.

Discussion Questions

1. Do you agree that ministers should be excused in some cases from the civil obligations of jury and military service? Why?

2. Assume that you are a minister and that a stranger visits you and confesses to a serious and unsolved crime. Would you inform the police about the conversation? Why or why not? Under what circumstances, if any, do you feel that ministers are justified in violating the confidence of those who come to them for counseling?

4

LIABILITIES, LIMITATIONS, AND RESTRICTIONS

Chapter summary. While ministers continue to enjoy a few legal privileges because of their status, they are treated no differently than other citizens for purposes of most laws and regulations. As a result, they can be sued, and they are subject to government regulations. The more common forms of legal liability, and several important regulatory requirements, are addressed in this chapter. These include negligence, defamation, undue influence, malpractice, contracts, securities, failure to report child abuse, diversion of church funds, counseling, and sexual misconduct. As you read the text you will realize that the widespread belief that ministers enjoy a privileged legal status is largely a misconception. The importance of this chapter should be apparent. Ministers are being sued today in increasing numbers for a wide variety of reasons. A thorough understanding of this chapter will help you, or your minister, to avoid many of the kinds of behavior that may result in legal liability.

Ministers may be sued for a variety of reasons. Some of the theories of liability are new and in the process of formation. Others are well-established. In this chapter the more common theories of legal liability will be reviewed.

§ 4-01   Negligence

The most common basis of legal liability for ministers is negligence. Negligence is conduct which creates an unreasonable and foreseeable risk of harm to another person, and which does in fact result in injury. Negligent conduct need not be and usually is not intentional. It may consist either of a specific act or failure to act. It may be helpful to think of negligence as carelessness.

Although negligence can arise in many ways, it is most often associated with carelessness in the operation of an automobile. But a minister may create unreasonable risks of harm to others in countless other ways, such as entrusting a dangerous article to one who, because of inexperience or immaturity, cannot safely handle it; authorizing a children's activity or retreat without adequate adult supervision; knowing of a dangerous condition on the church property but failing to warn members and visitors; failing to take reasonable action to have ice and snow removed from the church's sidewalks and parking lot; or failing to have an excessively slippery floor made safe.

Even if a minister's conduct or failure to act creates an unreasonable risk of harm to others, and harm does in fact result, the minister may assert various defenses which may prevent liability. One defense is *contributory negligence*. Contributory negligence is simply negligence on the part of the injured party that contributes to the injury. Obviously, if the victim is negligent, and except for his or her negligence the accident would not have occurred, the party whose negligence directly caused the accident cannot be fully accountable for the injury.

Traditionally, contributory negligence on the part of a victim was a complete defense to liability. Such a rule proved to be inequitable, however, for it entirely insulated from legal liability the party whose negligence directly caused the injury. To remedy this situation, most states have adopted "comparative negligence" laws. These laws seek to apportion damages and liability on the basis of the relative fault of the parties involved. Under the doctrine of comparative negligence, negligence victims who were themselves contributorily negligent will not necessarily be denied recovery. Instead, their recovery will be reduced in proportion to their fault. Comparative negligence laws vary widely. Some states have adopted "pure" comparative negligence. Such laws allow a proportionate recovery to all negligence victims, including those whose own contributory negligence was equal to or greater than the negligence of the person directly causing the injury. Other states have adopted a "fifty percent" rule, under which victims may recover proportionate damages only if their contributory negligence was less than fifty percent of the combined negligence resulting in their injuries.

Another defense to negligence is the doctrine of *assumption of risk*. Under this doctrine, persons who voluntarily expose themselves to a known and appreciated danger created by the negligence of another will not be allowed to recover damages for injuries that occur. Assumption of risk is distinct from contributory negligence and ordinarily is not affected by comparative negligence laws.

Another defense to negligence is *imputed negligence*. Under certain circumstances the law permits the negligence of one party to be imputed to another, even though the other was not negligent. The most common example involves the negligence of employees committed in the course of employment. The negligence of employees acting in the course of their employment is imputed to their employers. Courts and attorneys refer to this as the *respondeat superior* doctrine (i.e., the "superior responds" for the damages its employees cause). The reason for this rule has been stated as follows:

> The losses caused by the negligence of employees, which as a practical matter are sure to occur in the conduct of the employer's enterprise, are placed upon the enterprise itself, as a required cost of doing business. They are placed upon the employer because, having engaged in an enterprise which will, on the basis of past experience, involve harm to others through the [negligence] of employees, and sought to profit by it, it is just that he, rather than the injured plaintiff, should bear them; and because he is better able to absorb them and to distribute them, through prices, rates or liability insurance, to society, to the community at large.[1]

If a minister is an employee of the church for which he or she works, then the minister's negligence may be imputed to the church. The potential legal liability of churches (and denominational agencies) for the negligence of clergy is discussed fully in chapter 10. For now, simply note the following four considerations.

(1) A church may be legally responsible for the negligence of its minister committed within the scope of employment.

(2) The church will be liable only if the minister is an employee rather than self-employed.

(3) A minister's reporting status for federal income tax reporting purposes is of limited significance. The courts often ignore this status completely when deciding if a worker is an employee or self-employed for purposes of imputing liability to an employer under the respondeat superior doctrine. Further, many ministers who report their income taxes as self-employed would probably be reclassified as employees by the IRS if audited.

(4) The justification for imputing an employee's negligence to an employer (discussed above) does not apply as forcefully to a church, which, unlike many business corporations, is not necessarily "better able to absorb [legal judgments] and to distribute them, through prices, rates or liability insurance, to society, to the community at large." It is perhaps reasonable to require businesses to "pass along" the cost of their employees' negligence to consumers through price adjustments. But how does a church "pass along" such costs to the public?

(5) The fact that a minister's negligence may be imputed to his or her employing church does not necessarily shield the minister from personal liability. Negligent ministers ordinarily are personally liable for their negligence and can be sued directly by their "victims." It is common for the victim of a minister's negligence to sue both the minister individually and the minister's employing church. The fact that the church may be liable in no way shields the minister from personal liability. And, if for any reason the suit against the church is dismissed, the minister may be solely liable. While unlikely, in some states a church could require a minister to indemnify or reimburse it for damages paid as a result of imputed negligence.

§ 4-02   Defamation — In General

> **Key point 4-02.** *Defamation consists of (1) oral or written statements about another person; (2) that are false; (3) that are "published" (that is, communicated to other persons); and (4) that injure the other person's reputation.*

---

[1] W. Prosser, Torts § 69 (5th ed. 1984).

Defamation consists of the following elements:

(1) oral or written statements about another person

(2) that are false

(3) that are "published" (that is, communicated to other persons), and

(4) that injure the other person's reputation

If the words are oral, the defamation is sometimes called *slander.* If the words are written, the defamation may be referred to as *libel.* Although this terminology is still widely used, there is a tendency to refer to both slander and libel as defamation.

Defamation involves injury to another's reputation rather than feelings. To illustrate, the courts have held that it is defamatory to say of another that he refuses to pay his just debts, that he is immoral, about to be divorced, a hypocrite, a liar, a scoundrel, a crook, or a swindler.[2] In each instance, a court concluded that the victim's esteem or reputation had in fact been adversely affected. But not every derogatory statement is defamatory. For example, one court ruled that it was not defamatory for a religious official to tell a minister that she should have consulted with her religious superiors before choosing a particular minister as her co-pastor since the denomination had "been after [him] for a long time." The court found these remarks to be "wholly lacking in defamatory content" and "not capable of a defamatory meaning."[3] Other statements that the courts have ruled are not defamatory include newspaper articles describing ex-members' criticisms of a church;[4] derogatory statements contained in a letter to a minister when the person who sent the letter had no reason to believe that the minister would share it with others;[5] and a newspaper article referring to a minister as the "former pastor" of a church.[6]

§ 4-02.1 — Pastors Who are Sued For Making Defamatory Statements

Key point 4-02.1. *Ministers may be liable for making defamatory statements if a civil court can resolve the dispute without any inquiry into church doctrine or polity.*

Ministers may be liable for defamation if they communicate false statements to other persons that injure the reputation of another. To illustrate, in one case a minister publicly stated that a member of his congregation had a "vile spirit and utter disrespect for leadership," and declared that another member had associated himself with a pastor who "under the role of minister of Jesus, is one of Satan's choicest tools." A court found such remarks to be defamatory.[7] In another notable case, a Roman Catholic archbishop was found guilty of defaming a priest by publicly referring to him as an "irresponsible and insane" person who was "morally blind" and "disobedient to the laws of the church."[8]

---

[2] *See generally* Annot., 87 A.L.R.2d 453 (1963).

[3] Joiner v. Weeks, 383 So.2d 101, 103 (La. 1980).

[4] Missouri Church of Scientology v. Adams, 543 S.W.2d 776 (Mo. 1976) (court refused to decide whether a church "can maintain an action for libel on the basis of statements as to its tenets and practices in the light of the First Amendment to the United States Constitution").

[5] Bretz v. Mayer, 203 N.E.2d 665 (Ohio 1963) (defamation requires that the defamatory statements be published or publicly disseminated).

[6] Nichols v. Item Publishers, 113 N.Y.S.2d 701 (1952).

[7] Brewer v. Second Baptist Church, 197 P.2d 713 (Cal. 1948).

Here are a number of other cases in which ministers were sued for defamation:

Example. A minister left a pastoral position in Alaska and accepted a call as minister of a church in Tennessee. When he presented himself to the church to begin his duties, he was informed by church officials that because of derogatory information the church had received from a denominational official (a "presbyter") in Alaska, the church would not hire him. The presbyter had informed church leaders that the minister was divorced, dishonest, unable to perform pastoral duties because of throat surgery, and that he had made an improper sexual advance to a church member in Alaska. The minister sued the presbyter for defamation and interference with contract. A state supreme court ruled that it could resolve these claims without violating the first amendment guaranty of religious freedom. It rejected the presbyter's contention that these claims involved pastoral qualifications (a "core ecclesiastical concern"). With regard to the defamation claim, a court would simply have to determine whether or not the presbyter made the statements attributed to him. There would be "no need to determine if [the pastor] was qualified to be a pastor or what those qualifications may be." [9]

Example. A minister wrote an article in a church publication that addressed the church's newly developed doctrine on divorce and remarriage. The article contained statements that allegedly defamed the former spouse of a prominent church official. The court concluded that "our accommodation of the competing interests of our society--one protecting reputation, the other, the free exercise of religion—requires that we hold that in order for a plaintiff to recover damages for defamatory remarks made during the course of a doctrinal explanation by a duly authorized minister, he or she must show, by clear and convincing evidence, that the defamation was made with 'constitutional malice,' that is, with knowledge that it was false or with reckless disregard of whether it was false or not." Such a rule, observed the court, "strikes an appropriate balance between our citizens' reputational interests and our society's interest in protecting the right to free exercise of religion." The court rejected the church's claim that the constitutional guaranty of religious freedom prevents ministers from ever being sued for defamatory statements made in the course of doctrinal explanations. Such suits are constitutionally permissible, concluded the court, but a plaintiff has the difficult burden of proving "malice" by "clear and convincing evidence." [10]

Example. A conflict arose in a local Lutheran church between a pastor and some members of the congregation. A denominational official intervened in an attempt to resolve the problem. The official prepared a report to the church council that stated, "A significant number of members have experienced the pastor as being aloof; as being the boss; as being dogmatic; as not being open to the persons who disagree or have different viewpoints, even to the point of feeling that they are dismissed from friendship; as not always hearing what the other person is trying to say; as having particular difficulty in appreciating women as equals; as one who talks negatively about persons to others (behind their backs), sometimes close to the point of breaking confidentiality." The pastor alleged that this statement was defamatory, as was a bishop's disclosure to members of the congregation that the pastor was going to a psychiatric hospital for treatment. The court dismissed the lawsuit, concluding that it was an ecclesiastical dispute even though no specific church doctrine was involved. The court observed, "The matters in this case concern the intimate relationship between a pastor and his congregation. In an attempt to resolve an inner church conflict, Lutheran leadership investigated congregational attitudes toward [the pastor]. The investigation was done in accordance with the constitutional provisions of the church. The

---

8   Hellstern v. Katzer, 79 N.W. 429 (Wis. 1899).
9   Marshall v. Munro, 845 P.2d 424 (Alaska 1993).
10 McNair v. Worldwide Church of God, 242 Cal. Rptr. 823 (2d App. Dist. 1987).

alleged defamatory statements were made in connection with the mediation process and strictly within the confines of the church. There can be no doubt that the matters in this case concerned the minister's current and future employment relationship with the church. As such, they are matters of ecclesiastical concern, over which this court has no jurisdiction. Wisdom mandates that we refrain from dictating to a congregation that if they are unhappy with their religious leader they cannot freely speak their mind."[11]

Example. *A Catholic priest became upset when he suspected that a monument company that did work at a church cemetery was guilty of using church utilities without paying for them. He wrote a letter to the owner of the monument company which stated, in part, "Stated simply, your workers entered our property, and used [church] utilities without permission, and that is theft. I could have them arrested and charged, for your information." A copy of the letter was sent to the diocese. A week later, the priest published the following statement in a church newsletter (that was mailed to 362 families): "For your information, I have been obliged [to inform the monument company] that it is forbidden . . . to perform work of any kind in [the cemetery]. The company has persisted in ignoring my cemetery policies, and has a 'come as you please, go as you please' attitude and uses our electrical utilities without permission. The utilities come out of cemetery funds (e.g., your pocket)." The monument company sued the priest, the local church, and the diocese when it learned of the statement in the newsletter. A trial court ruled in favor of the defendants, and the company appealed. A state appeals court also rejected the claim of defamation. The court observed that "a statement which imputes the commission of a crime to another is defamatory per se and as a result, falsity and malice are presumed, but not eliminated as requirements." The court concluded that the statements by the priest in the letter and church newsletter were false, but that they were not defamatory since the priest made them with a reasonable belief that they were true and accordingly they were not made with "malice."*[12]

Example. *A youth pastor who made statements to members of his congregation about an alleged affair between an associate pastor and a church employee was found guilty of defamation. While the employee was on a church-sponsored trip to the Holy Land (led by the associate minister), the youth minister entered her office to look for a file he needed. While there, he discovered a file containing personal notes from the associate pastor to the employee. The notes confirmed the youth pastor's growing suspicion that the two were engaged in a sexual relationship. He immediately shared the notes with the associate pastor's wife, and offered specific details of when and where he believed the two had met privately. The associate pastor's wife discussed the allegations with her husband, and concluded that the relationship was not sexual in nature. The youth pastor accepted the wife's decision, and retracted his allegations. He apologized to the associate pastor and the female employee for the pain he had caused them, and promised never to repeat his suspicions again. Despite his promise, the youth pastor soon repeated his suspicions to members of the drama group, and in very little time the entire congregation was aware of the allegations. The church convened a special committee that investigated the matter and dismissed the employee. Subjected to scorn in her church and unable to find a job commensurate with her skills, the former employee sued the youth pastor for defamation of character. She also sued the church, claiming that by dismissing her it had "ratified" the youth pastor's allegations. A jury ruled in favor of the former employee, and this verdict was affirmed by a state appeals court. The court acknowledged that a plaintiff suing a "public figure" (such as a pastor) for defamation of character must prove not only that the pastor publicized false statements that injured the plaintiff's reputation, but also that the defendant acted with "malice." Malice means that the youth pastor either knew that the statements he uttered were false, or that he uttered them with a reckless disregard as to their truth or falsity. The court*

---

[11] Yaggie v. Indiana-Kentucky Synod, 860 F. Supp. 1194 (W.D. Ky. 1994).
[12] Redmond v. McCool, 582 So.2d 262 (La. App. 1991).

concluded that the youth pastor acted with malice—since he had repeated statements that he had acknowledged were not true.[13]

Example. *A minister wrote a letter to another minister, recommending that a foreign missionary's endorsement be withdrawn. In the letter, the minister stated that the missionary in question was a liar; that he failed to pay his debts; that he was engaged in a program of destruction, hatred, and "tyrancy"; that his nature was to rule as a dictator; that his aim was to divide and split the churches; and that he was carrying out Satan's plan of division and destruction. The court concluded that such allegations could be defamatory. However, it concluded that communications made by one minister to another minister involving matters of common concern enjoy a "qualified privilege." This means that they will not be considered defamatory unless they are made with legal malice. The court defined legal malice as either knowledge that a statement is false or a reckless disregard concerning the truth or falsity of a statement. Since the court could not say that the statements concerning the missionary were known by the minister to be false or were made with a reckless disregard concerning their truth or falsity, it denied the missionary's motion for a verdict in his behalf.[14]*

Example. *A minister was found guilty of defaming a former member by publicly referring to him as a "lost sheep" who had attempted to put the minister "out of the church."[15]*

These examples suggest that ministers should refrain from making public remarks that might diminish the reputation, respect, goodwill, or esteem of other persons. However, if a minister does communicate a disparaging remark about another, he or she may be able to assert one or more defenses to a charge of defamation. These defenses are described later in this section.

§ 4-02.02 — Pastors Who Are Victims of Defamation

Key point 4-02.02. *Ministers are considered "public figures" and as a result they cannot be defamed unless the person making an otherwise defamatory remark did so with malice. In this context, malice means that the person making the defamatory remark either had actual knowledge that it was false or made it with a reckless disregard as to its truth or falsity.*

Since a landmark Supreme Court ruling in 1964,[16] it has become much more difficult for *public figures* to prove defamation. The courts reason that when people voluntarily thrust themselves into the public eye, they must expect to be the target of criticism. In addition to the other elements of defamation summarized in the preceding section, public figures must prove that defamatory statements were made with *malice.* Although few courts have addressed the question, it is likely that ministers will be deemed to be public figures. As a result, they will be required to show more than damage to their reputation to establish defamation. They also must demonstrate that the allegedly defamatory remark was made with *malice.* In this context malice means either actual knowledge that the remark was false or a reckless disregard as to its truth or falsity.

The courts have found that it is defamatory to publicly accuse a minister of willful deceit, a greatly confused mind, and the grossest type of moral misconduct;[17] heresy and disturbing the peace of the church;[18] low

---

[13] St. Luke Evangelical Lutheran Church v. Smith, 568 A.2d 35 (Md. 1990).

[14] Murphy v. Harty, 393 P.2d 206 (Ore. 1964).

[15] Servatius v. Pichel, 34 Wis. 292 (1876).

[16] New York Times Co., v. Sullivan, 376 U.S. 254 (1964).

[17] Stewart v. Ging, 327 P.2d 333 (N.M. 1958).

moral character and scandalous and evil conduct that was so bad that it could not be described publicly;[19] lying, hatred, "tyrancy," failure to pay debts, and satanic motives;[20] adultery or fornication;[21] improper handling of church finances;[22] ineptness in administrative ability;[23] and being unable to keep his word for 24 hours.[24]

Similarly, the courts have held that it is defamatory to say of a minister that "there has not to our knowledge appeared in public within the memory of the present generation of North Carolinians a more ignorant man,"[25] or that "I would not have anything to do with him or touch him with a ten foot pole."[26] Some of these cases were decided before the Supreme Court's decision in 1964 requiring public figures to prove malice in order to sue for defamation. However, it now should be assumed that ministers will be deemed to be public figures and as a result they will have to prove malice as a precondition to winning a defamation suit.[27]

Key point. *It was much easier for ministers to prove defamation prior to 1964. Since 1964, "public figures" (including ministers) must prove malice in addition to the other elements of defamation. This often is very difficult to do. As a result, little weight should be given to cases decided before 1964 in which ministers were successful in proving defamation.*

Example. *A Louisiana court ruled that a pastor could sue a former employee for defaming him by spreading false allegations of sexual misconduct.[28] A woman (the "defendant") was employed as choir director. Shortly after she came to work, she claimed that the pastor started engaging in inappropriate sexual contact with her. The defendant told her husband, and then told the pastor that if he did not stop touching her, she would tell his wife and denominational officials. The defendant claimed that the pastor continued to badger her, so she told the organist, a church member, and the pastor-parish relations committee. The pastor steadfastly denied all allegations of wrongful conduct. During this time the congregation began hearing about the accusations, and rumors started spreading. In an attempt to defuse the rumors, the pastor-parish relations committee read a statement to the congregation to the effect that the defendant had made allegations against the pastor, that the pastor-parish relations committee had conducted an investigation, and that there was no factual support for the allegations. A denominational agency, after a full review of all the evidence, issued a statement exonerating the pastor. Church attendance, membership, and financial support to the church plummeted as a result of the defendant's allegations. The pastor was forced to leave his post and move to a different part of the state. The defendant later sued the former pastor and church. After filing her lawsuit, the defendant discussed her claims on two local television stations and in a newspaper. A year later, the pastor sued the defendant for defamation of character. A state appeals court began its opinion by noting that in order for ministers to win a defamation claim, they must prove the public and malicious disclosure of false allegations, resulting in an injury to reputation. The court defined "malice" as "the lack of reasonable*

[18] Creekmore v. Runnels, 224 S.W.2d 1007 (Mo. 1949).
[19] Loeb v. Geronemus, 66 So.2d 241 (Fla. 1953).
[20] Murphy v. Harty, 393 P.2d 206 (Ore. 1964).
[21] Haynes v. Robertson, 175 S.W. 290 (Mo. 1915).
[22] Curtis v. Argus Co., 156 N.Y.S. 813 (1916).
[23] Lathan v. Journal Company, 140 N.W.2d 417 (Wis. 1966).
[24] Boling v. Clinton Cotton Mills, 161 S.E. 195 (S.C. 1931).
[25] Pentuff v. Park, 138 S.E. 616 (N.C. 1927).
[26] Cole v. Millspaugh, 126 N.W. 626 (Minn. 1910).
[27] *See, e.g.,* Washington v. New York News, Inc., 322 N.Y.S.2d 896 (1971) (gossip column article stating that a minister had attended a nightclub performance at which one of his choir members was performing was a matter of public interest and was not made with malice, so minister's claim of defamation was denied).
[28] Steed v. St. Paul's United Methodist Church, 728 So.2d 931 (La. App. 1999).

belief in the truth of the words." However, when words accuse a person of criminal conduct, they are presumed to be false and malicious, and defamation is assumed. The court noted that "the record amply supports the finding that [the defendant's] words were defamatory. [The pastor's] reputation was diminished to the point that he was transferred from [his church] and in fact relocated in the southeast portion of the state, an extraordinary move necessary to distance him from the scandal. A rational juror could find, more probably than not, that his reputation, and his ability to serve as a minister in north Louisiana, were damaged by [the defendant's] accusations. Moreover, [her] charges that [he] grabbed her, tried to kiss her, and physically blocked her from leaving his office, amount to accusations of at least simple battery. Additionally, by accusing him of sexual harassment, [the defendant] launched allegations which by their nature tended to injure his personal and professional reputation." Even though malice was assumed because the defendant accused the pastor of criminal behavior, the court noted that the defendant's own testimony provided additional proof of malice. Specifically, she admitted in court that when she told the television reporters that the pastor had grabbed her thigh, she was incorrect. Further, "the general absence of evidence to support her allegations could persuade a rational juror that [she] had no reasonable belief that her statements were true."

Example. A New York court ruled that a religious teacher was not a "public figure" and therefore could more easily sue an organization that allegedly defamed him in one of its publications.[29] A nonprofit organization existed to provide education and support to women who were victims of sexual abuse. One of its representatives allegedly mailed letters to several members of a religious organization informing them that a number of their religious leaders had "sexually coerced and exploited" scores of women during the previous twenty-five years. One leader sued the organization for defamation. The organization claimed that a religious leader is a "public figure," and as such cannot establish defamation without proving "malice." The court concluded that the religious leader was not a public figure: "There is no proof that [the religious leader] has achieved general fame or notoriety or assumed a role of especial prominence in the affairs of society." Further, the leader had not "voluntarily injected himself into the vortex of the particular public controversy at issue in order to influence the outcome and thus is not a limited issue public figure."

Ministers who fail to prove one or more of the elements of defamation will fail to recover any damages in court. For example, a statement, no matter how derogatory, cannot be defamatory if it does not injure the reputation of a minister, if it is not publicized to others, or if it in fact is true.

The courts generally have rejected allegations of dismissed clergy that their dismissals caused them to be "defamed." This issue is addressed in chapter 2.

Dismissed church members also have had difficulty persuading civil courts to resolve their claims of defamation. This issue is addressed in chapter 6. Some disciplined ministers have sued their denomination for defamation as a result of statements published in denominational publications concerning the discipline. These cases are addressed in chapter 10.

---

[29] Sovik v. Healing Network, 665 N.Y.S.2d 997 (A.D. 1997).

Table 4-1
Elements of Defamation

non-public figure	public figure
(1) oral or written statement	(1) oral or written statement
(2) concerning another person	(2) concerning another person
(3) the statement is false	(3) the statement is false
(4) the statement is publicized (made public through communication to other persons)	(4) the statement is publicized (made public through communication to other persons)
(5) injury to reputation	(5) injury to reputation
	(6) the person making the defamatory statement did so with "malice," meaning that he or she either knew the statement was false, or made it with a reckless disregard as to its truth or falsity

§ 4-02.03 — Defenses

Key point 4-02.03. *A number of defenses are available to one accused of defamation. These include truth, statements made in the course of judicial proceedings, consent, and self-defense. In addition, statements made to church members about a matter of common interest to members are protected by a "qualified privilege," meaning that they cannot be defamatory unless they are made with malice. In this context, malice means that the person making the statements knew that they were false or made them with a reckless disregard as to their truth or falsity. This privilege will not apply if the statements are made to nonmembers.*

There are a number of defenses to defamation. The more common examples are summarized below.

1. TRUTH

The maxim that truth is an "absolute defense" to defamation is correct in most states. If an allegedly defamatory remark is true, it is simply not regarded as defamatory by most courts. This defense is based on the principle that the dissemination of truth should not be restricted by the fear of defamation lawsuits. In recent years, courts have devised a new tort ("invasion of privacy") to punish statements which, though true, disclose private facts about another person in a way that would be highly offensive to a reasonable person. As a result, while truth is a defense to defamation, it does not necessarily insulate one from all legal liability.

2. JUDICIAL PROCEEDINGS

Remarks uttered during the course of judicial proceedings generally cannot be defamatory.

3. CONSENT

Persons who consent to defamatory communications generally cannot later claim that they were defamed. For example, persons who consent to a current or former employer providing a letter of reference to a prospective employer generally cannot claim that the letter of reference was defamatory. The consent, to be effective, must of course be voluntary and knowing. Similarly, if a minister agrees to submit an issue to binding arbitration, he or she cannot later assert that the arbiter's decision is defamatory.

> **Example.** *The qualifications of an individual engaged in the business of testing garments for shatnes (a mixture of wool and linen in one garment prohibited by Mosaic law) were questioned by another person engaged in the same business. Both parties agreed to submit the question of qualifications to a tribunal of three rabbis. The tribunal ultimately decided that the person whose qualifications had been questioned was in fact not qualified to test for shatnes. The disqualified party refused to honor this ruling, which caused the complaining party to publish circulars informing the public of the decision of the rabbis. The disqualified party charged that the circulars were defamatory, but a court disagreed on the ground that the parties had voluntarily agreed to be bound by the decision of the rabbis which was "in the nature of a common law award in arbitration [that] acts as a bar to relitigating essentially the same issue."* [30]

4. Self-defense

Many courts have allowed victims of defamation to respond to the defamation in a manner which, if viewed independently, might constitute defamation. The victim must be careful to confine his or her remarks to the defamatory statements.

5. Matters of "Common Interest"

Many courts have concluded that the law should encourage members of churches and other organizations to share with each other about matters of mutual concern without undue concern about being sued for defamation. As a result, these courts have ruled that church members are protected by a *qualified privilege* when sharing with other church members about matters of mutual concern or common interest. This means that such communications cannot be defamatory unless made with malice. Malice in this context means that the person who made the allegedly defamatory remark knew that it was false, or made it with a reckless disregard as to its truth or falsity. This is a difficult standard to prove, which means that communications between church members will be defamatory only in exceptional cases. The same rule has been applied by a number of courts to statements made in the course of church disciplinary proceedings.

One court explained the qualified privilege as follows:

A privilege will be granted to statements that occur under circumstances wherein any one of several persons having a common interest in a particular subject matter may reasonably believe that facts exist that another, sharing that common interest, is entitled to know. . . . This privilege is termed conditional or qualified because a person availing himself of it must use it in a lawful manner and for a lawful purpose. The effect of the privilege is to justify the communication when it is made without actual malice. Thus, when a statement is privileged, Texas law requires a showing of actual malice to overcome that privilege. Actual malice means with knowledge that the statement was false or with reckless disregard of whether it was false. Reckless disregard requires proof that a false defamatory statement was made with a high degree of awareness of its probable falsity. Generally, when publication is made under circumstances creating a qualified

---

[30] Berman v. Shatnes Laboratory, 350 N.Y.S.2d 703 (1973).

privilege, the plaintiff has the burden to prove malice. . . . Malice exists when the evidence shows that the speaker entertained serious doubts as to the truth of his statements.[31]

Tip. Church leaders occasionally communicate potentially defamatory statements to their congregations. Examples include statements concerning suspected embezzlement by a church employee, allegations of sexual misconduct by a staff member or volunteer, or explanations of why a church employee was dismissed. Before making any statements to the congregation in such cases, church leaders should consider the following points:

• Such statements may be defamatory.

• Such statements will not be protected by the qualified privilege if nonmembers are present when they are made.

• Such statements may be protected by a qualified privilege if they are made to members only. This means that church leaders take steps to ensure that only members are present when the statements are made. This can be accomplished in a number of ways. For example, a special meeting of members is called and only persons whose names are on the church's current list of active voting members are admitted. As an additional precaution, members present at such a meeting should be asked to adopt a resolution of confidentiality, agreeing not to discuss the information with any non-member under any circumstances. Persons dissenting from this vote should be excused from the meeting. Alternatively, the statements are set forth in a letter that is sent to active voting members (with the notation "privileged and confidential" on both the letter and envelope).

• Consult with an attorney before making any potentially defamatory statement to the congregation (in a meeting or through correspondence).

To illustrate, statements made under the following circumstances have been held not to be defamatory: a communication made between officers of a church or denomination on any subject in which they both have an interest;[32] communications between members of a religious organization concerning the conduct of other members or officers;[33] charges made against a church member during a church investigation into his character;[34] reading a sentence of excommunication of a church member in the presence of a church congregation;[35] an article in a publication produced by a religious denomination describing difficulties in missions work in an area under the control of a particular minister;[36] charges made by an officer of a church against the church's minister;[37] and disparaging statements made by several church members concerning their minister during a church disciplinary proceeding.[38]

Example. Church board members who wrote a letter asking their pastor to resign on account of his failing health were not guilty of defamation. The letter requested that the pastor either retire or resign and stated that if he did not elect one of these alternatives, the deacons would recommend to the church

---

[31] Hanssen v. Our Redeemer Lutheran Church, 938 S.W.2d 85 (Tex. App. 1997).
[32] Church of Scientology v. Green, 354 F. Supp. 800 (S.D.N.Y. 1973).
[33] Willenbucher v. McCormick, 229 F. Supp. 659 (D. Colo. 1964).
[34] Cimijotti v. Paulsen, 219 F. Supp. 621 (N.D. Iowa 1963), *appeal dismissed,* 323 F.2d 716 (8th Cir. 1963).
[35] *Id.*
[36] Herndon v. Melton, 105 S.E.2d 531 (N.C. 1958).
[37] Browning v. Gomez, 332 S.W.2d 588 (Tex. 1960).
[38] Joiner v. Weeks, 383 So.2d 101 (La. App. 1980).

congregation that his services as pastor be terminated. The pastor responded to the deacons' request by informing them that he would neither retire nor resign. The deacons then called for a special meeting of the congregation and distributed copies of the letter they had sent the pastor. At this meeting, the congregation requested that the pastor retire and approved the terms and conditions of his retirement package. The pastor retired at this meeting. He later sued the board of deacons for defamation. A state appeals court ruled that even if the letter signed by the deacons was defamatory, it was protected by a "qualified privilege" since it "concerned various church interests" including the pastor's perceived inability to perform his pastoral duties, it was written by members of the congregation (the deacons), and communicated exclusively to other members of the church. The court stressed that there was no evidence that any nonmembers "were either given or otherwise received a copy of the letter." The court concluded that the pastor failed to prove that the deacons acted with malice, and as a result the letter was not defamatory. It observed, "While it is true that the deacons consulted neither [the pastor's] doctors nor the church records immediately prior to drafting the letter, we see no reason why the deacons would be required to consult these specific sources to establish the truth of their statements. Numerous other sources of information were available to them for this purpose. For instance, several of the deacons testified that they came to the conclusion that [the pastor's] health was affecting the leadership of the church through their conversations with members of the congregation, their independent observations of his performance, and repeated discussions during official meetings regarding the deteriorating financial condition and membership of the church. Thus, the deacons did have a factual foundation for their opinion concerning the effect of [the pastor's] health on his performance as pastor and did not act in reckless disregard as to the truth or falsity of their statements in the letter." [39]

Caution. *In many states the "qualified privilege" is an "affirmative defense" that may be lost if it is not asserted in an answer to a lawsuit. If your church is sued for defamation as a result of statements shared with members, be sure that your attorney is aware of this rule and raises the qualified privilege as an affirmative defense in the answer to the lawsuit.*

Example. *A prominent televangelist communicated statements critical of the moral character of a local pastor to other pastors, churches, and the public at large. The pastor sued the televangelist, claiming that he had been defamed. A Louisiana court noted that the pastor's lawsuit alleged defamatory statements occurring outside his church and denomination after he had been formally dismissed as a minister. It ruled that "there is a serious question as to whether the first amendment's protection would extend to those statements allegedly made to the press, the general public, and pastors of other denominations." The court rejected the televangelist's claim that he was entitled to publicize statements regarding the pastor to the "church at large" (referring to all Christians of whatever persuasion).[40]*

Example. *An Ohio appeals court ruled that a former teacher at a church-operated school could not sue school officials for defamation since the allegedly defamatory statements made by the school officials concerned a matter of "common interest" and accordingly were privileged. A teacher at a church-operated school was convicted of contributing to the delinquency of a minor for providing alcohol to one of his students. He advised school officials of his conviction, and was permitted to remain on the faculty both as a teacher and yearbook adviser. A few years later, his teaching contract was not renewed. A priest was hired to replace him as teacher and yearbook adviser. When the former teacher continued to associate with student members of the yearbook staff, two priests (who served as administrators at the school) contacted the parents of two of these students and informed them that the former teacher had*

---

[39] Mosley v. Evans, 630 N.E.2d 75 (Ohio App. 11 Dist. 1993).
[40] Gorman v. Swaggart, 524 So.2d 915 (La. App. 1988).

155

been convicted of "corrupting a minor," implied that he was a homosexual, and recommended that they not permit their sons to associate with such a person. The former teacher learned of these statements and sued the priests for defamation. A state appeals court ruled that the statements made by the priests were not defamatory since they were protected by a qualified privilege. The court defined defamation as a false oral or written statement made about another person that injures his or her reputation. However, it concluded that the remarks made by the priests concerning the former teacher were protected by a qualified privilege, and that there was no proof of malice. The court noted that malice "cannot be inferred from evidence of intent to injure, ill will or personal spite . . . [r]ather, the evidence must demonstrate with convincing clarity that the defendants were aware of a high probability of falsity." [41]

Example. *A Texas appeals court ruled that statements made by church leaders during a church investigation were not defamatory. It observed, "Statements made in the context of a church investigatory proceeding are protected by a qualified privilege. If a qualified privilege exists, the defamed party has the burden of establishing that the privilege has been abused. A qualified privilege is abused when the person uttering the statement knows the matter to be false or does not act for the purpose of protecting the interest for which the privilege exists."* [42]

Example. *A Texas court ruled that a church was not liable for defaming a former secretary as a result of statements made to church members claiming that she had misappropriated church funds. A church operated a private school. Its minister of education, who also served as principal of the school, resigned after admitting that he misappropriated church funds, destroyed church records, forged signatures, and committed other criminal acts. He later pleaded guilty to criminal charges for his admitted conduct in misappropriating school funds. He informed the church that a woman who served as a secretary at the school participated in the misappropriations. After an audit confirmed the principal's accusations, the church asked the secretary to resign. The church published (1) a letter to its members claiming that the secretary misappropriated school funds; (2) a letter to the school children's parents claiming that the secretary deposited tuition funds into the wrong accounts and later used the funds for her personal benefit; destroyed checks, financial records, and bank records; forged signatures; covered up these indiscretions; received seventy dollars extra per pay period for nearly two years as well as other undocumented "reimbursements"; and (3) a report to the church members reporting the secretary's resignation and claiming that she deposited tuition funds into the wrong accounts and then used the funds to support programs and individuals outside of and over the budget adopted by the congregation. At a meeting of church members, church officials orally accused the secretary of depositing tuition funds into the wrong account and then using the funds for her personal benefit or for other people or projects as she and the principal saw fit; destroying checks, bank records, and financial records; forging signatures; and covering up many of these indiscretions. The secretary later sued the church and the individual members of the church audit committee, claiming that the church's actions defamed her, placed her in a false light, and inflicted emotional distress. A state appeals court ruled that the secretary had not been defamed because the church was protected by a qualified privilege and she failed to prove malice: "All of the members of [the church] have a common interest in the church's use of their financial contributions to the church; thus, the members have a common interest in information about those funds. The members who made the statements in question reasonably believed that the misappropriation took place and that the board, the members, and the parents shared a common interest in the use of the funds and information about those funds. [The church] reasonably believed that these people were entitled to know of the misappropriation. [It] had a duty to perform for the board, the members, and the parents. [It] made the*

---

[41] McCartney v. Oblates of St. Francis de Sales, 609 N.E.2d 216 (Ohio App. 6 Dist. 1992).
[42] Kelly v. Diocese of Corpus Christi, 832 S.W.2d 88 (Tex. App. Corpus Christi 1992).

communications without actual malice. [The principal] confessed his and [the secretary's] involvement, and [he] later pleaded guilty to criminal charges. [The church's] audit confirmed all of [his] statements. [The secretary] never swore under oath in an affidavit in opposition to summary judgment that the statements were lies. [She] kept the misappropriated funds in a shoe box in her closet and returned the funds when accused. [The principal] testified that the statements were true. [The secretary] admits receiving personal benefit from the misappropriation of funds. [She] admits she destroyed records. [The church] neither entertained serious doubts as to the truth of the statements nor made these statements with a high degree of awareness of their probable falsity. The communications appeared accurate, [the church] reasonably believed [the principal], and church members and parents who received information had an interest in the funds and information about the funds."[43]

6. Mitigating Factors

Although technically not defenses to a charge of defamation, public retraction of a defamatory statement or proof that the allegedly defamed individual provoked a defamatory statement will be admissible for the purpose of mitigating or minimizing damages.

§ 4-03 Undue Influence

Key point 4-03. *A gift to a church or minister may be challenged on the ground that the recipient unduly influenced the donor into making the gift. There are several factors the courts will consider in deciding whether or not undue influence occurred, including the age and mental health of the donor, and the presence of independent legal advice. Undue influence generally must be proven by "clear and convincing" evidence.*

If the recipient of a gift unduly influenced the donor into making the gift, the donor may have the gift canceled. This rule applies both to direct gifts made during one's lifetime and to gifts contained in documents (such as wills) which take effect at the donor's death. Undue influence is more than persuasion or suggestion. It connotes total dominion and control over the mind of another. As one court noted, "undue influence is that influence which, by force, coercion or overpersuasion destroys the free agency" of another.[44]

Undue influence generally must be inferred from the circumstances surrounding a gift, since it seldom can be proven directly. Circumstances commonly considered in determining whether a donor was unduly influenced in the making of a gift include the following:

- whether the gift was the product of hasty action

- whether the gift was concealed from others

- whether the person or organization benefited by the gift was active in securing it

- whether the gift was consistent or inconsistent with prior declarations and planning of the donor

- whether the gift was reasonable rather than unnatural in view of the donor's circumstances, attitudes, and family

---

[43] Hanssen v. Our Redeemer Lutheran Church, 938 S.W.2d 85 (Tex. App. 1997).

[44] In Matter of Soper's Estate, 598 S.W.2d 528, 538 (Mo. 1980).

- the donor's age, physical condition, and mental health

- whether a confidential relationship existed between the donor and the recipient of the gift

- whether the donor had independent advice[45]

Most courts have held that undue influence must be proven by "clear and convincing" or "clear and satisfactory" evidence. Proof by a mere preponderance of the evidence will not suffice.[46] However, some courts have ruled that a "presumption" of undue influence may arise when a gift is made by a church member directly to his or her minister, or when an attorney who drafts a will leaving a gift to a church is a member of the same church. This presumption is rebuttable.

Here are some examples of cases in which the courts have canceled a gift to a church or minister on the basis of undue influence:

Example. A federal appeals court ruled that an heiress could revoke a substantial contribution she had made to a church because she had been the victim of undue influence. The heiress to a large family fortune began attending a church in Massachusetts. She became intimately involved with the church and many of its related ministries, and made three large contributions to the church. The first contribution (stock in the family business worth $1 million) was made because of her belief that the gift would "cure" the severe headaches experienced by the pastor's wife. After making the gift, the pastor allegedly informed the donor that his wife had been "cured" when in fact she continued to suffer from migraine headaches. Because of this event, the donor came to believe that large gifts could "affect events on earth." Later, when advised by church officials that a particular missionary was being kept a prisoner in Romania and that "they're probably pulling out his fingernails by now," the donor informed the pastor that she intended to make a $5 million gift to the church to bring about the missionary's release. In fact, church officials knew that the missionary had been released several days earlier, but this information was not disclosed to the donor. She was simply told that her gift had "worked a miracle." The donor also made a $500,000 gift to the church in an attempt to resolve her marital difficulties. Eventually, the donor was taken by concerned family members to religious "deprogrammers" who persuaded her to terminate her association with the church. She then sued the church, demanding a return of her gifts on the ground that they had all been the product of "undue influence" and accordingly were void. The federal appeals court, applying Massachusetts law, observed that gifts to charity can be revoked on the basis of undue influence, and that undue influence involves three elements: (1) a person who is susceptible to being influenced, (2) deception or improper influence is exerted, and (3) submission to the "overmastering effect of such unlawful conduct." The court stressed that "it generally takes less to establish undue influence when a confidential relation exists between the parties." Such a confidential relationship, the court concluded, existed between the donor and the pastor. The court found the following factors to be relevant in determining whether undue influence occurred: (1) the donor's age, and mental and physical health; (2) "disproportionate gifts made under unusual circumstances"; (3) inexperience with financial matters; (4) attempts by the recipient of the funds to "isolate the donor from her former friends and relatives"; (5) whether or not the donor acted with or without "independent and disinterested advice." The court rejected the donor's claim that the $1 million gift had been the result of undue influence, since general statements by the pastor and other church officials that large gifts would "do great works" were "too amorphous to show undue influence." However, the court found that the $5

---

[45] In re Estate of McCauley, 415 P.2d 431 (Ariz. 1966).
[46] *See generally* 25 AM. JUR. 2D *Duress and Undue Influence* § 48 (1966 & Supp. 1999).

million and $500,000 gifts were the result of undue influence and ordered them canceled. The court observed that all three elements of undue influence were present. First, the donor was susceptible to undue influence. Second, the pastor had knowingly deceived her into believing that the missionary was in great danger when he knew that the missionary had been released from Romania several days earlier. Third, the donor clearly "submitted" to the pastor's misrepresentation. The court quoted with approval the United States Supreme Court's admonition that "nothing we have said is intended even remotely to imply that under the cloak of religion persons may, with impunity, commit frauds upon the public."[47]

Example. An Arkansas court invalidated a will that left all of a decedent's assets to a cult leader. The leader had convinced the decedent that he had supernatural powers, that he could transmigrate, did not have to eat or perform other bodily functions, and had the power to heal. He refrained from displaying his powers openly, however, because it would cause people to "focus on his miracles rather than upon his teachings." The leader also warned the decedent that "bad things" would happen to her if she did not give more and more of her money to him. She began giving up to 75 percent of her earnings as a nurse to the leader, executed a will leaving her entire estate to him, and assigned several life insurance policies to him. After her untimely death in an accident, a lawsuit was filed on behalf of her minor child seeking to invalidate the will and life insurance beneficiary designations on the basis of undue influence. The lawsuit alleged that the decedent had been so unduly influenced by the leader that her actions were not the product of her own free will and therefore should be invalidated. The court agreed that the decedent had been unduly influenced by the cult leader, and accordingly invalidated the transfer of assets to him. It noted that the leader was a very skillful manipulator of emotionally immature and dependent persons, and that he "virtually enslaved" the decedent through manipulation of her mind and emotions.[48]

Example. A 70-year-old invalid dying from cancer was visited several times a week by a pastor of her church. Three days before her death, the pastor persuaded her to execute a will leaving most of her property to him. The pastor's personal attorney was called upon to draft the instrument. Two days later, the pastor attempted to have the donor give him additional property by a deed of gift, but by this time the donor was in a stupor and was physically unable to sign her name. She died a day later. The gift to the pastor was challenged on the ground that it was the product of undue influence. The court concluded that undue influence was established by the age and feeble mental and physical condition of the donor, the involvement of the pastor in procuring the gift to himself, the confidential "clergyman-parishioner" relationship that existed between the pastor and the donor, and the lack of any independent advice.[49]

Example. Gifts to an Episcopal rector and his church were invalidated on the basis of undue influence since the donor was a 76-year-old woman suffering from arteriosclerosis, senility, and severe loss of memory.[50]

Example. The Oklahoma Supreme Court ruled that an assignment of property to a church was invalid since the donor lacked mental capacity and the church exerted undue influence on the donor in making the gift. An 81-year-old woman signed a legal document assigning the bulk of her estate to a church, and on the same day signed a will that named the church as her primary beneficiary. A relative later

---

[47] In re The Bible Speaks, 869 F.2d 628 (1st Cir. 1989).

[48] Carpenter v. Horace Mann Life Insurance Co., 730 S.W.2d 502 (Ark. App. 1987).

[49] In re Miller's Estate, 60 P.2d 492 (Cal. 1936).

[50] Tallahassee Bank and Trust Co. v. Brooks, 200 So.2d 251 (Fla. App. 1967). *See also* Hensley v. Stevens, 481 P.2d 694 (Mont. 1971) (gift to minister held to be product of undue influence and fraud since minister induced gift by falsely representing that he would reconvey a portion of the property to the donor's husband but never did).

challenged the assignment on the grounds that the donor had been unduly influenced by the church in making the gifts. The state supreme court invalidated the assignment of property on the basis of undue influence. It noted that when a confidential relationship exists between a donor and a beneficiary, only "slight evidence" of undue influence is required to set aside a gift. The court also noted that when an attorney acting on behalf of a donor in preparing a will or assignment is also the primary beneficiary, "there is a presumption that undue influence existed and the beneficiary bears the burden of showing the contrary." In this case, the attorney for the church prepared the assignment and will that the donor signed, though he never met with her personally. Accordingly, the court concluded that there was a presumption of undue influence. The court observed that the presumption of undue influence can be overcome by showing that the donor had the benefit of independent advice from some disinterested third party. However, no such independent advice was sought or received by the donor in this case. The court concluded that "it is clear that [the donor] did not receive the quality of independent advice called for by our case law. . . . If, as the [church's] attorney testified, it is not unusual for him as agent of the church to be asked to draw up instruments donating or leaving gifts to the church, he should have advised the donor to seek independent advice in order to avoid conflict of interest, undue influence, and the appearance of impropriety." [51]

Example. *The Oklahoma Supreme Court ruled that a provision in a deceased church member's will leaving the bulk of her estate to her church was invalid since it was a product of the pastor's "undue influence." A 96-year-old woman died, leaving the bulk of her estate to the Baptist church she had attended for the last several years of her life. For many years, the woman suffered from alcoholism and during the 1970's her health and living conditions deteriorated. From 1980 to 1983 the pastor of a local Baptist church became closely acquainted with her and visited with her in her home several times. By 1984 all of the woman's friends were members of this church. The pastor arranged for several of them to regularly assist the woman by cleaning her home. Through this process the woman became very dependent upon the pastor and reposed great trust in him. Although in 1983 the woman attended several sessions of an estate planning seminar at her church, she failed to make the last session where a "will information guide" was distributed. In 1984, when the woman was 89 years of age, the pastor brought her a copy of the "will information guide" and spent several hours assisting her in cataloging her assets. The pastor later asked a church member who was an attorney to contact the woman and discuss her will's preparation. This attorney had not represented the woman in any other legal matters. Before the attorney drafted the will he had one 15-minute telephone conversation with her in which he discussed the contents of her estate using the "will information guide" provided him by the pastor. A few weeks later the woman was taken to the attorney's office by a church member. She reviewed her will and signed it. All of the subscribing witnesses were church members chosen by the pastor. Seven years after the will was signed the woman died. Her nephew claimed that the gift to the church should not be honored since it was based on "undue influence." The supreme court invalidated the gift on the basis of undue influence. The court applied a "2-prong test" to determine whether undue influence invalidates a provision in a will: First, does a "confidential relationship" exist between the deceased and another person; and second, did the stronger party in the relationship assist in the preparation of the weaker person's will. Factors to be considered in applying this 2-prong test include (1) whether the person charged with undue influence was not a natural object of the maker's bounty; (2) whether the stronger person was a trusted or confidential advisor or agent of the will's maker; (3) whether the stronger person was present or active in the procurement or preparation of the will; (4) whether the will's maker was of advanced age or impaired faculties; (5) whether independent and disinterested advice regarding the*

---

[51] Matter of the Estate of Carano, 868 P.2d 699 (Okla. 1994).

will was given to its maker. The court rejected the pastor's claim that he could not have unduly influenced the woman since he received nothing under her will.[52]

Example. *A gift by a 79-year-old single woman to her church was invalidated because the evidence demonstrated that the church's minister visited the donor daily and preyed upon her fear that other churches in the community might exceed her own in size and prosperity.*[53]

In the great majority of cases, however, gifts to churches have been upheld despite the claim that they were the product of undue influence. To illustrate, in one case, a court in upholding a gift to a church observed:

If a determined old lady, who knows her own mind and without consulting her children, carries out her own wishes in that regard and buys an annuity contract, can have her wishes held for naught and the contract set aside . . . then no such annuity can stand in this state against such attack. The entire evidence discloses that the conduct of the officer of this church or organization was above reproach, for, even after she sought them out and asked for the investment, they did not press the matter, but gave her every opportunity to seek other advice and change her desires.[54]

Similarly, a gift of property by an 82-year-old single woman to a Catholic church to assure the saying of masses for deceased members of her family was upheld despite the claims of her nearest relatives that such was not her real intention and that she had been unduly influenced by the church without her family's knowledge or consent. In upholding the validity of the gift, the court noted the following factors: (1) the donor's desire to make provision for the saying of masses for her family preceded the date of the gift; (2) the donor's will, which had been executed prior to the gift to the church, left nothing to surviving family members; (3) the donor did not conceal the gift; (4) there was no evidence that the donor was in a weakened condition of mind or body at the time of the gift; and (5) she reaffirmed the gift in subsequent letters, one of which was written five years after the day of the gift.[55]

Other courts have rejected a charge of undue influence where a donor, though 90 years of age, was well-educated and predisposed to making a gift to her church;[56] where an elderly donor had long considered making a gift to his church and was not close to his parish priest;[57] where an elderly donor was mentally competent and experienced in business affairs, and was the first to suggest making a gift to his church;[58] where a donor's lifetime gifts to her church and minister left her with ample assets for her own support, were not the result of active solicitation by her minister, and were acknowledged with satisfaction several times by the donor during her life;[59] where a donor frequently gave to her church, was capable of making independent business decisions, and was not close to any of her relatives;[60] and where an 84-year-old single woman left the bulk of her estate to a minister who was a friend and not the minister of the church she attended.[61]

Here are some additional examples of cases in which the courts have rejected attempts by donors (or their heirs) to invalidate gifts to religious institutions on the basis of undue influence:

[52] Suagee v. Cook, 897 P.2d 268 (Okla. 1995).
[53] Whitmire v. Kroelinger, 42 F.2d 699 (W.D.S.C. 1930).
[54] Wixson v. Nebraska Conference Association of Seventh-Day Adventists, 241 N.W. 532 (Neb. 1932).
[55] Guill v. Wolpert, 218 N.W.2d 224 (Neb. 1974).
[56] Klaber v. Unity School of Christianity, 51 S.W.2d 30 (Mo. 1932).
[57] Coughlin v. St. Patrick's Church, 209 N.W. 426 (Iowa 1926).
[58] Severson v. First Baptist Church, 208 P.2d 616 (Wash. 1949).
[59] Lindley v. Lindley, 356 P.2d 455 (N.M. 1960).
[60] Umbstead v. Preachers' Aid Society, 58 N.E.2d 441 (Ind. 1944).
[61] Succession of Easterly, 563 So.2d 1006 (La. App. 1990).

Example. The Arkansas Supreme Court upheld the validity of a will that left a large portion of an elderly widow's estate to a Baptist university. The decedent's surviving heirs argued that the will was invalid since the decedent lacked mental capacity at the time the will was executed. To support their claim, the heirs alleged that at the time she executed her will the decedent was in a state of grief over the loss of her husband and was manifesting eccentric behavior. In addition, the heirs argued that the decedent had never expressed an interest in the university during her lifetime. Such evidence, concluded the court, fell far short of that required to establish mental incapacity.[62]

Example. A South Carolina court rejected a claim that an elderly decedent's will, which left the bulk of her estate to the Lutheran Church in America (LCA), was the product of "undue influence" and accordingly invalid. The decedent executed her first will at the age of 78. This will left 10 percent of her estate to her local church, 40 percent to various relatives, and 50 percent to another charity. At the age of 87, the decedent began changing her will. The fourth and final amendment of her will, executed when she was 88 years old, placed the bulk of her estate in a charitable trust, the income from which was distributed to the LCA. The final will was challenged by a beneficiary whose share of the estate had been reduced. The beneficiary argued that the final will was invalid since it had been the product of undue influence. The court acknowledged that undue influence can invalidate a will, but it denied that the decedent's final will had been the result of undue influence. The court observed that undue influence must be proven by the person challenging a will, and that it consists of "influence amounting to coercion destroying free agency on the part of the [decedent]" so that the will was the result of "force and fear." The court, in rejecting the allegation of undue influence, observed that the final version of the decedent's will had been executed "when she was in reasonably good health, and during her latter years [when] she continued to work in her yard, talk with her neighbors, do some cooking and go to a grocery store . . . ." In short, she still possessed sufficient independence and health to support the conclusion that "she was the ultimate decision maker." Accordingly, the allegation of undue influence was rejected and the validity of the will upheld.[63]

Example. A Washington state court ruled that a sizable gift to a church in a decedent's will was not the product of undue influence. A devout church member ("Mary") who was retired and unmarried was diagnosed to be suffering from terminal cancer. She was scheduled to have surgery, followed by outpatient treatment as part of an experimental cancer program. On the evening before her surgery, Mary told a friend ("Judy") that "I am not afraid to die, but I'm afraid of all the things I have to do before I die, like make a will." Judy offered to call an attorney the next day. On the day of the surgery, Judy called her attorney, who was unable to prepare a will that day. He suggested that Judy purchase a "will kit" from a stationery store. Judy went to an Office Depot store and purchased a kit. Mary read the instructions that came with the kit and began discussing her desires with Judy. The day after the surgery, Judy retyped the language from the will kit onto her home computer, and inserted the information Mary had given her. Over the next couple of days, Mary made a few minor revisions to the document and then signed a final version in the presence of three witnesses. A few days later, Mary told some friends that she had just prepared her will, and that most of her estate would go "to the kingdom, for the Lord's work." She also confided that some of her family members might not be happy with her decisions. The friends later testified that Mary, though weak, was strong-willed and resolute. The will left a portion of the estate to family members, but the bulk of the estate went to her church and a parachurch ministry operated by Judy and her husband. Mary died a few weeks after she signed her will. Her will was admitted to probate, and it was immediately challenged by a brother who claimed that the will was invalid since it was the product of

---

[62] Baerlocker v. Highsmith, 730 S.W.2d 237 (Ark. 1987).
[63] First Citizens Bank & Trust v. Inman, 370 S.E.2d 99 (S.C. App. 1988).

undue influence. The court began its opinion by noting, "A will procured by undue influence is invalid. Undue influence must be proven by the contestants of a will, using clear, cogent, and convincing evidence. Influence becomes undue only when it overcomes the will of the testator, when the act of making the will is the result of such coercion that free agency is destroyed. Not every influence exerted over a person can be characterized as undue influence. Generally, influence exerted by giving advice, arguments, persuasions, solicitations, suggestions or entreaties is not considered undue unless it be so importunate, persistent or coercive and operates to subdue and subordinate the will of the testator and take away his or her freedom of action." The court concluded that the brother had failed to prove by "clear, cogent, and convincing evidence" that Mary's will had been the product of undue influence. The court characterized Mary as "a generous woman, prone to intense involvement" with her church and various other religious ministries. The court acknowledged that Judy and her husband took Mary into their home and cared for her while she was ill, showing her many acts of kindness, but concluded that they had "exerted no undue influence over the disposition contained in her will."

Persons who would challenge a gift made to a church on the basis of undue influence must not delay in seeking redress for an unreasonable length of time, since unreasonable delay will bar any recovery.[64]

In summary, ministers should refrain from soliciting gifts to themselves from aged or mentally infirm church members, and should be very cautious in soliciting gifts for the church. However, gifts to a church ordinarily will be valid if a minister merely suggests and does not actively solicit a gift, the donor is mentally competent, the donor was predisposed to conveying the gift, and the donor had independent advice and assistance in implementing the gift.

Many wills leaving substantial portions of estates to churches and other charities have been challenged by "disinherited heirs" on the basis of undue influence. Persons bringing such lawsuits often recognize that they have a weak case, but they sue anyway, hoping that the church will quickly "settle" with them in order to avoid the potential "adverse publicity" associated with such lawsuits. After all, what church wants to be accused publicly of coercing elderly members into making gifts to the church? If your church receives a gift under a will that is challenged on the basis of undue influence, be sure to bear in mind a couple of considerations. First, undue influence usually is very difficult to prove, particularly when the decedent was in reasonably good mental and physical health at the time the will was executed. Second, in many states, undue influence must be proven by "clear and convincing evidence"—a more difficult burden of proof than the ordinary "preponderance of the evidence" standard. A church that becomes aware that an elderly or infirm person is considering leaving a portion of his or her estate to the church can reduce the possibility of undue influence even further by ensuring that the person obtains the independent counsel of an attorney in drafting the will or trust. Ideally, the attorney should not be a member of the same church. Finally, church leaders should recognize that they have a moral obligation to assist in implementing the estate plans of deceased members so long as they are satisfied that no improper influence was exercised. If a former member in fact intended that a portion of his or her estate be distributed to the church, and church leaders too quickly succumb to threats of attorneys hired by disgruntled family members, then they have violated a sacred trust.

---

[64] Nelson v. Dodge, 68 A.2d 51 (R.I. 1949).

§ 4-04 Invasion of Privacy

Key point 4-04. *Many states recognize "invasion of privacy" as a basis for liability. Invasion of privacy may consist of any one or more the following: (1) public disclosure of private facts; (2) use of another person's name or likeness; (3) placing someone in a "false light" in the public eye; or (4) intruding upon another's seclusion.*

In recent years the subject of invasion of privacy has achieved considerable attention. Actually, the term *invasion of privacy* encompasses four separate kinds of conduct. Some states recognize some or all of these varieties of invasion of privacy.[65]

1. PUBLIC DISCLOSURE OF PRIVATE FACTS

Those who give publicity to the private life of another are subject to liability for invasion of privacy if the matter publicized is of a kind that would be highly offensive to a reasonable person and is not of legitimate concern to the public.[66] The key elements of this form of invasion of privacy are (1) publicity, (2) of a highly objectionable kind, (3) given to private facts about another. *Publicity* is defined as a communication to the public at large, or to so many persons that the matter is substantially certain to become one of public knowledge. It is not an invasion of privacy to communicate a fact concerning another's private life to a single person or even to a small group of persons.[67] But a statement made to a large audience, such as a church congregation, does constitute "publicity."

The facts that are publicly disclosed must be *private*. There is no liability if one merely repeats something that is a matter of public record or has already been publicly disclosed. Thus, a minister who makes reference in a sermon to the prior marriage or prior criminal acts of a particular church member has not invaded the member's privacy, since such facts are matters of public record. Many other facts—such as dates of birth, military service, divorce, licenses of various kinds, pleadings in a lawsuit, ownership of property, and various debts—are matters of public record. References to such facts ordinarily will not invade another's privacy.

The matter that is communicated must be such that a reasonable person would feel justified in feeling seriously aggrieved by its dissemination.

This type of invasion of privacy is perhaps the most significant for ministers, since ministers typically are apprised of many private facts about members of their congregations, and they have innumerable opportunities to divulge such information. Ministers must exercise caution in divulging private facts about members of their congregations, even when the communication is positive in nature and contains information that is factually true (and accordingly would not be defamatory). For example, a minister publicly comments on the sordid immorality of a recent convert to his church, intending his remarks to be complimentary. He nonetheless has publicized private facts about the member under circumstances that may be highly offensive. The minister under these circumstances may well have invaded the privacy of the church member.

---

[65] Some states do not recognize all four kinds of invasion of privacy. *See, e.g.,* Mulinix v. Mulinix, 1997 WL 585775 (unpublished, Minn. App. 1997) (invasion of privacy not recognized in Minnesota); Hanssen v. Our Redeemer Lutheran Church, 938 S.W.2d 85 (Tex. App. 1997) ("false light" invasion of privacy not recognized in Texas).

[66] RESTATEMENT (SECOND) OF TORTS § 652D.

[67] *Id.* at § 652D comment "a".

Example. A Michigan court ruled that a minister may invade the privacy of a church member by disclosing to the congregations information that was communicated to him by the member in the course of a confidential counseling session.[68] A church member (the "plaintiff") confessed to his pastor that he had previously committed adultery with prostitutes. The pastor decided to communicate this information to the entire congregation, including the member's wife, family, and friends. The pastor insisted that he did not believe in confidential communications and that church doctrine required exposing sins to the congregation. The member claimed that the pastor had been motivated not by religious doctrine but by ill will and the intent to humiliate him and create dissension within his family. The disgraced member sued his pastor and church, alleging that the pastor's disclosure amounted to an invasion of privacy. The court noted that invasion of privacy may consist of a number of different offenses, including public disclosure of embarrassing private facts. In order for the plaintiff to prove this kind of invasion of privacy, he would have to establish (1) the disclosure of information, (2) that is highly offensive to a reasonable person, and (3) that is of no legitimate concern to the public. The court concluded that "a jury must determine whether a public disclosure involves embarrassing private facts." It concluded, "[W]e believe that plaintiff has pleaded that [the pastor] disclosed to the congregation plaintiff's previous contacts with prostitutes, that this information was of no legitimate concern to the public and was conveyed to the congregation with the intent to embarrass plaintiff and cause him severe emotional distress. Whether [the pastor's] conduct was sufficiently outrageous or extreme is a question best left to the jury." The court cautioned that it was assuming that the plaintiff was not a member of the church as of the date of the pastor's disclosure. If the plaintiff were a member on that date, then the court insinuated that the first amendment would prevent it from resolving any "intentional tort claims."

2. USE OF ANOTHER'S NAME OR LIKENESS

Another type of *invasion of privacy* is defined as the unauthorized use of another's name or likeness for personal or commercial advantage. To illustrate, if a company uses a child's name or picture in its advertisements without consent of the child or the child's parents, the company has invaded the child's privacy. The person whose name or likeness is used need not be a public figure. Churches may commit this type of invasion of privacy by publishing a picture of a person without his or her consent.

3. FALSE LIGHT IN THE PUBLIC EYE

One who gives publicity to a matter that places another before the public in a "false light" is subject to liability for invasion of that person's privacy. However, the false light in which the person was placed must be highly offensive to a reasonable person, and it must have been publicized either with a knowledge that it was false or with a reckless disregard concerning its truth or falsity.[69]

A minister who ascribes beliefs or positions to others that they do not in fact hold may have invaded their privacy.[70] In preparing sermons or articles, ministers must be careful not to attribute to other persons opinions, statements, or beliefs that are not in fact held.

Example. An Oregon court ruled that a pastor was guilty of invading the privacy of a church member and his wife by making public statements placing them in a false light.[71] A church member's three

---

[68] Smith v. Calvary Christian Church, 592 N.W.2d 713 (Mich. App. 1998).

[69] *Id.* at § 652E (1977).

[70] *See, e.g.,* F.G. v. MacDonell, 696 A.2d 697 (N.J. 1997) (minister placed female church member in "false light" by the way he informed the congregation of a sexual relationship between the woman and another pastor).

[71] Muresan v. Philadelphia Romanian Pentecostal Church, 962 P.2d 711 (Or. App. 1998).

children were injured when the car they were driving was struck by the daughter of another church member. The pastor informed the church board, and the congregation itself, that the father whose children were injured was having his children pretend to be injured in order to obtain a larger settlement from the other driver's insurance company. Neither the pastor, nor any other church member, ever investigated the facts to ascertain the extent of damage done to the car or the injuries suffered by the passengers. The pastor did not know whether the children, in fact, were injured by the accident. The children's parents sued the pastor, claiming that he had defamed them and invaded their privacy. They also sued the church as the pastor's employer. The jury determined that the pastor's statements placed the parents in a false light by repeatedly accusing them of falsifying their children's condition to obtain a larger insurance settlement. The court defined "false light" invasion of privacy as follows: "One who gives publicity to a matter concerning another that places the other before the public in a false light is subject to liability to the other for invasion of his privacy, if (a) the false light in which the other was placed would be highly offensive to a reasonable person, and (b) the actor had knowledge of or acted in reckless disregard as to the falsity of the publicized matter and the false light in which the other would be placed."[72] The pastor insisted that he could not be liable for "false light" invasion of privacy because the parents failed to prove the element of publication. According to the pastor, to prevail on a false light invasion of privacy claim, the parents had to establish that he published false information about them "to the public at large." The court disagreed, noting that publication is established by proof that "the false information reached or was sure to reach either the public generally or a large number of persons in [the parents'] work community." In this case, "there was evidence that plaintiffs' entire community of friends, relatives and acquaintances were members of the church and that [the pastor] made false statements about [them] in church meetings of hundreds of members at a time. We conclude that the evidence was sufficient as to the element of publication." The pastor also claimed that the parents failed to prove the element of malice, which he insisted requires evidence of actual intent to harm. Once again, the court disagreed. It noted that "in this case, there is evidence that [the pastor] repeatedly made false statements with no regard for their truth or falsity."

4. Intruding Upon Another's Seclusion

One who intentionally intrudes upon either the solitude or private affairs of another is subject to liability for invasion of privacy if the intrusion would be highly offensive to a reasonable person.[73] This is committed if one without consent enters another's home, inspects another's private records, eavesdrops upon another's private conversation, or makes persistent and unwanted telephone calls to another. In some cases, it can be committed by unauthorized entry into a hospital room. To illustrate, a minister who enters a hospital room without consent and peers behind a closed screen may have invaded the privacy of the patient.

5. Defenses

There are a number of defenses available to ministers who are accused of invasion of privacy. These include consent by the alleged victim; statements made in judicial proceedings; statements that are required by law; or statements that are exchanged between husband and wife or attorney and client. Further, statements relating to a matter of common interest—such as statements between members of a church relating to the qualifications of church officers and members—generally cannot serve as the basis for invasion of privacy.

---

[72] Restatement (Second) of Torts § 652E.
[73] Id. at § 652B.

6. THE PRIVACY ACT OF 1974

Considerable confusion surrounds the scope of the Privacy Act of 1974. The Privacy Act was enacted to permit persons (1) to know of any records about them the government is collecting, maintaining, and distributing; (2) to prevent government records about them from being used without consent and for purposes other than those for which the records were first acquired; and (3) to correct and amend such records if necessary. The Privacy Act applies only to records maintained by the federal government and some federal contractors. It has no relevance to church records.

The Freedom of Information Act requires that federal agencies promptly make available to any person upon request any identifiable record, subject to various exceptions.[74] The Act also mandates the publication of certain categories of agency information in the Federal Register, and requires that various other kinds of records be made available for public inspection and copying. The purpose of the Act is to promote public access to the information in the possession of federal agencies. Several states have enacted similar laws applying to state agencies. None of these laws applies to churches or other nonprofit religious organizations.

7. "SUNSHINE" LAWS

Related to the Privacy Act are the various public meeting or "sunshine" laws that have been enacted by the federal government[75] and several states.[76] Such laws typically provide that meetings of all governmental bodies will be open to the public unless specifically exempted. One court has held that a state public meeting law applied to a private, nonprofit corporation organized to perform a governmental function and supported almost exclusively by tax revenues.[77] It is unlikely that such laws will ever be amended or construed to apply to churches and religious organizations.

Example. A New Jersey court allowed a woman to sue a pastor of her church for invasion of privacy for informing the congregation about a sexual relationship she had with another pastor of the same church.[78]

Example. Three female church members claimed that their pastor sexually harassed and abused them over a period of several months. The district superintendent of a state denominational agency (the "Conference") learned of the allegations, and asked the three women to appear before a "staff-parish relations committee" of their church. At the meeting each woman was given an opportunity to describe the pastor's allegedly inappropriate behavior. After hearing the accusations against their pastor, the committee gave the pastor a vote of "no confidence" and submitted the charges to the Conference for a full review. The pastor then requested six weeks' paid vacation followed by a leave of absence, and the committee granted his request. The pastor spoke to the church congregation the following Sunday, and explained he was taking a paid vacation. The women claimed that the Conference and district superintendent invaded their privacy by the following actions: (1) they asked the women to appear before a church committee to disclose their accusations; (2) they permitted the pastor to make some final remarks to the congregation, at which time he made it appear that he was being falsely accused; (3) they "acquiesced" in the decision of the staff-parish relations committee to permit the pastor to go on paid vacation after his final service, and this further implied that the women's charges were groundless; and (4) they

---

[74] 5 U.S.C. § 552(a)(3).

[75] 5 U.S.C. § 552b.

[76] *See generally* Annot., 38 A.L.R.3d 1070 (1971 & Supp. 1999).

[77] Seghers v. Community Advancement, Inc., 357 So.2d 626 (La. 1978).

[78] F.G. v. MacDonell, 677 A.2d 258 (N.J. Super. 1996).

failed to inform the congregation of the true reason for the pastor's resignation. A South Carolina court ruled that neither the Conference nor the district superintendent was guilty of invasion of privacy. In concluding that there had been no "public disclosure of private facts" the court observed, "[The women] made their disclosures expecting and intending that both the committee and [Conference] would act on those complaints. [They] therefore intended that their complaints should become public to the limited extent that occurred under these circumstances." With regard to the women's claim that the Conference and district superintendent invaded their privacy by publicly placing them in a "false light," the court simply noted that no South Carolina case has recognized this theory of liability. And, even if it were to be recognized, neither the Conference nor district superintendent did anything to "give rise to such a claim under these circumstances."[79]

§ 4-05   Clergy Malpractice

Key point 4-05. *Most courts have rejected clergy malpractice as a basis for liability in all cases. A few courts have found clergy guilty of malpractice for engaging in sexual misconduct with an adult or minor, or if they engage in "non-religious" counseling.*

Malpractice generally is defined as a failure to exercise an accepted degree of skill in the performance of professional duties that results in injury to another. In the past, malpractice suits were restricted almost exclusively to doctors and lawyers—a doctor prescribed the wrong medication or made a faulty diagnosis; a lawyer missed a pleading deadline or made an error in a title search. But in recent years a small number of malpractice suits have been brought against ministers.

1. THE NALLY CASE

In the most significant ruling addressing "clergy malpractice," the California Supreme Court ruled that a church and certain of its ministers were not legally responsible for the death of a suicide victim who had been a member of the church and who had counseled with the ministers.[80] In 1973, while attending college, Kenneth Nally became depressed after breaking up with his girlfriend. He often talked about the absurdity of life, the problems he had with his girlfriend and with his family, and he occasionally mentioned suicide. Though raised in a Roman Catholic home, Nally converted to Protestantism and in 1974 began attending Grace Community Church in Sun Valley, California, and became active in various church programs and ministries.

At the time of the events in question, the church employed about 50 pastoral counselors to serve a congregation of over 10,000 persons. Pastoral counseling, according to the church's 1979 annual report, was "a very important part" of the church's ministry. The church offered its counseling services not only to members, but also to large numbers of nonmembers. In 1979, the annual report noted that about half of the persons seeking counseling were nonmembers. A church publication entitled the "Guide for Biblical Counselors" noted that a number of symptoms and disorders fell within the pastoral counselor's domain, including "drug abuse, alcoholism, phobias, deep depression, suicide, mania, nervous breakdown, manic-depressive disorder and schizophrenia." The Guide devoted separate sections to a number of disorders, including suicide, with hypothetical questions and answers. For example, one question read: "You mean I could counsel with an extreme problem like a suicidal tendency or nervous breakdown or something like that?" The answer

---

[79] Brown v. Pearson, 483 S.E.2d 477 (S.C. App. 1997).
[80] Nally v. Grace Community Church, 253 Cal. Rptr. 97 (1988).

read: "With the proper understanding of God's Word to diagnose and treat the problems, this could not only be done occasionally but could become the rule."

The church taught that the Bible is the fundamental Word of God containing truths that must govern Christians in their relationship with God and the world at large, and in their own lives. As a result, pastoral counseling was essentially religious in nature. The church's senior pastor testified that "we just respond as pastors, so what we do is on a spiritual level, and a biblical level or a prayer level."

Nally was aware of the church's professed ability in treating severe depression and suicidal symptoms. He had been a student in one of the church's courses on biblical counseling (which used the Guide as a text) and sought out formal and informal pastoral counseling from the church during each of his several suicidal crises. Early in 1979, Nally again became depressed after his breakup with another girlfriend. He confided in his mother that he "could not cope." His mother had him see a general medical practitioner who prescribed a strong anti-depressant drug but who did not refer Nally to a psychiatrist. By late February of 1979, Nally's depression did not appear to be subsiding. He was examined by another physician, and spoke briefly with one of the church's pastoral counselors during a drop-in counseling session.

On March 11, Nally attempted to take his life by consuming an overdose of the antidepressant drug that had previously been prescribed for him. He was rushed to a hospital and his life was saved. His parents, concerned about their friends' reactions to their son's suicide attempt, asked the attending physician to inform others that Nally had been hospitalized for pneumonia. On March 12, two of the church's pastors visited Nally at the hospital. Nally, still drowsy from the drug overdose, informed them that he was sorry he had not succeeded in his suicide attempt. The pastors assumed that the hospital staff was aware of Nally's unstable mental condition, and accordingly they did not discuss Nally's "death wish" with anyone else. A few days later, a staff psychiatrist examined Nally and recommended that he commit himself to a psychiatric hospital. When Nally and his father expressed reluctance at the thought of formal commitment, the psychiatrist agreed to release Nally for outpatient treatment. However, he warned Nally's father that it would "not be unusual" for a suicidal patient to repeat his suicide attempt. Nally was released the next day, and moved in with one of the church's pastors because he "didn't want to return home." The pastor encouraged Nally to keep his appointments with the hospital psychiatrist, and arranged to have him examined by a physician who attended the church. This physician concluded that Nally was a continuing threat to himself, and recommended commitment to a psychiatric hospital. Nally rejected this advice, and the psychiatrist later called Nally's father to recommend immediate commitment. This plea was rejected by Nally's parents, his mother saying, "No, that's a crazy hospital. He's not crazy."

A few days later, Nally met with another of the church's pastors, and asked "whether Christians who commit suicide would nevertheless be saved." The pastor assured Nally that "a person who is once saved is always saved," but warned Nally that "it would be wrong to be thinking in such terms." A few days later, Nally moved back home. He was examined by two physicians, at least one of whom recommended commitment in a psychiatric hospital. Nally then saw another pastor of the church, who recommended that Nally see a particular psychologist. Nally did so, and was referred to a psychological clinic. Nally visited the clinic and met with a registered psychologist's assistant. A few days later, Nally met with a former girlfriend who rejected an apparent marriage proposal by telling Nally "I can't marry you when you are like this. You have got to pull yourself together." Three days later, on April 1, 1979, Nally committed suicide by shooting himself in the head with a shotgun.

Nally's parents filed a lawsuit naming the church and four of its pastors as defendants. The parents alleged that the pastors were responsible for the death of Nally on the basis of "clergyman malpractice." Specifically, they alleged that

- the church was negligent in the training and selection of its spiritual counselors, and in not referring Nally to medical professionals

- the pastors failed to make themselves available to Nally following his first suicide attempt, and "actively and affirmatively dissuaded and discouraged him from seeking further professional psychological or psychiatric care," and

- the pastors were guilty of "outrageous conduct" for teaching "certain Protestant religious doctrines that conflicted with Nally's Catholic upbringing" and which "exacerbated Nally's pre-existing feelings of guilt, anxiety, and depression."

With regard to the third allegation, the parents alleged that the pastors' counseling was "outrageous" because they "taught or otherwise imbued Nally, whom they knew to be depressed and having entertained suicidal thoughts, with the notion that if he had accepted Jesus Christ as his personal savior, he would still be accepted into heaven if he committed suicide." As proof of their charge, the parents referred to the counseling session in which Nally had been informed that a Christian who commits suicide would nevertheless be "saved" since "a person who is once saved is always saved."

The parents also relied on a short passage taken from a 12-part tape recorded series by one of the pastors entitled "Principles of Biblical Counseling" that was recorded several months after Nally's death. The tape recorded passage stated that "suicide is one of the ways the Lord takes home a disobedient believer. We read that in the Bible. . . . Suicide for a believer is the Lord saying, 'Okay, come on home. Can't use you anymore on earth. If you're not going to deal with those things in your life, come on home.'" The parents also cited an occasion when Nally's father opened the office door of one of the pastors and found Nally in the midst of a counseling session and on his knees crying. They also referred to a statement of the church's senior pastor that spiritual counseling (such as he gave Nally) could potentially cause "the deepest depression." The trial court granted the church and pastors a summary judgment, and the parents appealed to a California state appeals court. The appeals court reversed the summary judgment, concluding that a legitimate question existed on the issue of outrageous conduct. The trial court again ruled in favor of the church and its pastors, concluding that "there is no compelling state interest to climb the wall of separation of church and state and plunge into the pit on the other side that certainly has no bottom." The state court of appeals again reversed, noting that "nontherapist counselors," both religious and secular, have a duty to refer suicidal persons to psychiatrists or other physicians qualified to prevent suicide. That ruling was then submitted to the state supreme court for review.

The California Supreme Court rejected the court of appeals conclusion that a pastor has a legal duty to refer suicidal persons to medical professionals. It acknowledged that in a few previous rulings it had found hospitals and staff psychiatrists responsible for the deaths of suicide victims confined in hospital psychiatric wards. However, the court concluded that such cases were limited to "the limited context of hospital-patient relationships where the suicidal person died while under the care and custody of hospital physicians who were aware of the patient's unstable mental condition." Such cases were of no relevance to churches and clergy "not involved in a supervised medical relationship" with a suicidal person.

In rejecting the main contention of Nally's parents—that the church and its pastors were negligent in failing to refer Nally to medical professionals—the court observed:

> Nally was examined by five physicians and a psychiatrist during the weeks following his [first] suicide attempt. [The church and its pastors] correctly assert that they arranged or encouraged many of these visits and encouraged Nally to continue to cooperate with all doctors. In addition, following Nally's overdose attempt, [a physician] warned [Nally's parents] that Nally remained suicidal and that they should encourage him to see a psychiatrist on his release from the hospital. [Nally's parents] also rejected [two other physicians'] suggestions that Nally be institutionalized because, according to [the parents], their son was "not crazy." Nevertheless, we are urged that mere knowledge on the part of the [church and its pastors] that Nally may have been suicidal at various stages in his life should give rise to a duty to refer. Imposition of a duty to refer Nally necessarily would imply a general duty on all nontherapists to refer all potentially suicidal persons to licensed medical practitioners. . . . While under some circumstances counselors may conclude that referring a client to a psychiatrist is prudent and necessary, our past decisions teach that it is inappropriate to impose a duty to refer—which may stifle all gratuitous or religious counseling—based on foreseeability alone. Mere foreseeability of the harm or knowledge of the danger is insufficient to create a legally cognizable special relationship giving rise to a legal duty to prevent harm.[81]

The court emphasized that "neither the legislature nor the courts have ever imposed a legal obligation on persons to take affirmative steps to prevent the suicide of one who is not under the care of a physician in a hospital." On the contrary, "the [California] legislature has exempted clergy from the licensing requirements applicable to marriage, family, child and domestic counselors and from the operation of statutes regulating psychologists. In so doing, the legislature has recognized that *access to the clergy for counseling should be free from state imposed counseling standards, and that 'the secular state is not equipped to ascertain the competence of counseling when performed by those affiliated with religious organizations'* " (emphasis added).

In further support of its conclusion that clergy have no duty to "refer" suicidal persons to medical professionals, the court observed that "because of the differing theological views espoused by the myriad of religions in our state and practiced by church members, it would certainly be impractical, and quite possibly unconstitutional, to impose a duty of care on pastoral counselors. Such a duty would necessarily be intertwined with the religious philosophy of the particular denomination or ecclesiastical teachings of the religious entity."

The court also rejected the contention of Nally's parents that the "outrageous conduct" of the church and its pastors was responsible for Nally's death. Nally's parents based their charge of outrageous conduct largely on a segment of a tape recording produced by one of the pastors (quoted above). In rejecting the relevance of this recording, the court observed:

> In 1981, 18 months after Nally's suicide, [one of the church's pastors] taught a series of classes on biblical counseling. The class sessions included question and answer periods that were tape recorded. During one session, a student questioned [the pastor] on whether a person who committed suicide could be "saved." [The pastor] replied, in a manner consistent with Reformation Protestant theology views regarding sin, grace and faith, that a person neither acquires salvation by his own works nor forfeits salvation by the commission of subsequent sins. [Nally's parents] sought to introduce the tape recording at trial on the basis that it provided inferential proof of

---

[81] *Id.* at 108.

[the pastor's] advice to Nally during three counseling sessions in 1979. . . . [T]he tape does not tend to prove that [the church or its pastors] in any way encouraged Nally to commit suicide or acted recklessly in disregard of Nally's emotional state prior to his suicide. . . . [W]hat was said in an extemporaneous answer, which did not precisely reflect the thoughts of [the pastor], given almost two years after [Nally's suicide] is at best marginally relevant to prove what was said at the time in question.[82]

Two of the court's seven justices concluded that the church and its pastors *did* have a limited duty "to recognize the limits of their own competence to treat an individual, such as Nally, who exhibited suicidal tendencies, and once having recognized such symptoms, to advise that individual to seek competent professional medical care." However, these two justices also concluded that the church and its pastors did *not* breach this duty of care, and their actions did not "contribute in any legally significant respect to his suicide."

What is the impact of the *Nally* case on churches and clergy? Consider the following points:

1. The *Nally* case is binding only in the state of California. Courts in other states are free to disregard it. However, decisions of the California Supreme Court generally are treated with great respect by other state courts, and often are followed. The fact that the California Supreme Court unanimously ruled in favor of the church and its pastors should make the *Nally* decision especially compelling elsewhere. In summary, while it is likely that the *Nally* decision will be followed by other state courts, such a result is not certain.

2. In California, and other states that follow the *Nally* decision, nontherapist clergy will not have a "duty to refer" suicidal or emotionally disturbed persons to medical professionals. Of course, clergy in such states may voluntarily choose to recommend that a suicidal counselee contact a medical professional for assistance.

3. Some churches employ pastoral counselors who are licensed counselors or psychologists. In some cases, clergy who are licensed counselors or psychologists have opened their own private counseling practices independent of any church. While the court did not specifically address the liability of such counselors, it did cite with approval an earlier California state appeals court decision that suggested that a psychiatrist might be legally responsible for failing to take appropriate measures to prevent the death of an imminently suicidal patient.[83] It is possible that this ruling might extend to clergy in California who are licensed counselors, psychologists, or psychiatrists.

4. Clergy in California and elsewhere may be liable for "clergy malpractice" on the basis of theories of liability other than a failure to refer suicidal persons to medical professionals. For example, a number of persons have attempted to sue clergy for sexual molestation of minors, or seduction of a church member during the course of counseling. In some cases, the plaintiffs allege that such conduct constitutes "clergy malpractice." As a result, the *Nally* case does not necessarily eliminate lawsuits alleging clergy malpractice, even in the state of California.

5. Despite the result in the *Nally* case, churches should purchase "clergy malpractice" or counseling liability insurance for their pastoral staff. There are two reasons for doing so. First, this type of insurance is inexpensive, and in light of the *Nally* decision should become even less costly. Second,

---

[82] *Id.* at 112.
[83] Bellah v. Greenspan, 146 Cal. Rptr. 535 (1981).

while it is very unlikely that a minister will be successfully sued for malpractice in counseling, it is entirely possible that a minister may be sued. Counseling liability insurance will cover the costs of defending the lawsuit, and will pay any settlement or judgement up to the policy limits. In other words, while clergy who are sued for counseling malpractice will almost certainly prevail in court, the cost of a successful legal defense can easily amount to several tens of thousands of dollars. A counseling liability insurance policy ordinarily will pay these costs.

2. OTHER CASES REJECTING CLERGY MALPRACTICE

In the *Nally* case, the California Supreme Court based its rejection of clergy malpractice on two grounds. First, by exempting clergy from the licensing requirements that apply to other counselors, the state legislature recognized that "the secular state is not equipped to ascertain the competence of [pastoral] counseling." Second, "it would certainly be impractical, and quite possibly unconstitutional, to impose a duty of care on pastoral counselors" since such a duty "would necessarily be intertwined with the religious philosophy of the particular denomination or ecclesiastical teachings of the religious entity." A number of other courts, in rejecting clergy malpractice as a basis for legal liability, have relied on either or both of these grounds. To illustrate, a Colorado court, in concluding that a pastor and his employing church were not responsible for the pastor's sexual misconduct with a counselee on the basis of clergy malpractice, observed:

[The courts of this state have] joined substantially all of the other courts that have passed upon the issue in rejecting the notion that a claim will lie against a pastoral counselor or the pastor's church based upon the pastor's failure to observe any particular standard of care in providing the counseling; no claim for "clergy malpractice" can be asserted. The judicial rejection of such a claim has been based, in large part, upon the effect that recognition of such a claim would have upon the right of religious expression guaranteed by the first amendment. In order to adjudicate a claim based upon the "malpractice" of a religious counselor, courts would first have to establish the degree of skill and learning normally exercised by members of the clergy in similar circumstances and, then, to determine whether such standard had been violated. . . . To attempt to require members of the clergy to comply with such a standard, however, could very well restrict their right freely to exercise and practice their religion.[84]

A Texas court, in refusing to recognize "clergy malpractice" as a basis for liability, made the following observation:

Because the [civil courts] must abstain from ecclesiastical disputes involving questions of doctrine or practice, state courts have rejected uniformly claims for clergy malpractice. This is because such a claim requires definition of the relevant standard of care. Defining that standard could embroil courts in establishing the training, skill, and standards applicable for members of the clergy in a diversity of religions with widely varying beliefs. Furthermore, defining such a standard would require courts to identify the beliefs and practices of the relevant religion and then to determine whether the clergyman had acted in accordance with them. Thus, as these courts have correctly concluded, to recognize a claim for clergy malpractice would require courts to identify

---

[84] DeBose v. Bear Valley Church of Christ, 890 P.2d 214 (Colo. App. 1994). *See also* Schieffer v. Catholic Archdiocese, 508 N.W.2d 907 (Neb. 1993) ("[s]o far as we have been able to determine, no jurisdiction to date has recognized a claim for clergy malpractice"); Bladen v. First Presbyterian Church, 857 P.2d 789 (Okla. 1993) ("[c]laims for clergy malpractice for improper sexual conduct have so far been rejected by the courts").

and apply the teachings of a particular faith, thereby making the judiciary responsible for deter-mining what conduct and beliefs are part of a particular religion.[85]

A federal court in New York refused to find a pastor guilty of malpractice on the basis of his alleged sexual seduction of a church member he had counseled for several years. A woman (the "victim") began a counseling relationship with a pastor when she was a child of 12. The relationship continued for nearly 30 years. The victim alleged that the pastor engaged in repeated sexual contact with her over the years, and that she terminated the relationship with him only after seeing a psychotherapist who convinced her that the pastor's behavior had been wrong. The victim later sued the pastor, claiming that his acts amounted to clergy malpractice. The court dismissed this claim, along with all of the victim's other claims of liability against the pastor and her former church. In addressing the claim of malpractice, the court observed:

> The court must address the real issue here—clergy malpractice . . . . Whether an independent tort denominated "clergy malpractice" exists has become a frequently litigated issue in the courts of this nation. . . . And the fact is that neither the legislature nor the courts of New York have upheld or authorized a claim for clergy malpractice. . . . Nor is this likely in New York. . . . [The pastor, church, presbytery, and denomination] concede, as they must, that tort claims can be maintained against clergy, for such behavior as negligent operation of the Sunday School van, and other misconduct not within the purview of the first amendment, because unrelated to the religious efforts of a cleric. Claims of malpractice stand on a different footing. While the clergy of most denominations do provide counseling to youths and other members of their congregations, when they do so it is normally part of their religious activities; in so doing, they do not thereby become subject to the same standards of liability for professional malpractice which would apply, for example, to a state-licensed psychiatrist or a social worker. That there is no recorded instance of a New York court upholding an action for clergy malpractice, in this most litigious of states, speaks to this point, and loudly.

> It would be impossible for a court or jury to adjudicate a typical case of clergy malpractice, without first ascertaining whether the cleric, in this case a Presbyterian pastor, performed within the level of expertise expected of a similar professional (the hypothetical "reasonably prudent Presbyterian pastor"), following his calling, or practicing his profession within the community. As the California Supreme Court has held in *Nally v. Grace Community Church of the Valley:* "Because of the differing theological views espoused by the myriad of religions in our state and practiced by church members, it would certainly be impractical, and quite possibly unconstitu-tional, to impose a duty of care on pastoral counselors. Such a duty would necessarily be inter-twined with the religious philosophy of a particular denomination or ecclesiastical teachings of the religious entity." This court agrees with *Nally,* and regards the unconstitutionality as more than possible. It is real. . . . Any effort by this court to instruct the trial jury as to the duty of care which a clergyman should exercise, would of necessity require the court or jury to define and express the standard of care to be followed by other reasonable Presbyterian clergy of the commu-nity. This in turn would require the court and the jury to consider the fundamental perspective and approach to counseling inherent in the beliefs and practices of that denomination. This is as unconstitutional as it is impossible. It fosters excessive entanglement with religion.

> It may be argued that it requires no excessive entanglement with religion to decide that reason-ably prudent clergy of any sect do not molest children. The difficulty is that this court, and the

---

[85] Sanders v. Casa View Baptist Church, 134 F.3d 331 (5th Cir. 1998).

New York courts whose authority we exercise here, must consider not only this case, but the next case to follow, and the ones after that, before we embrace the newly invented tort of clergy malpractice. This places us clearly on the slippery slope and is an unnecessary venture, since existing laws against battery, and the criminal statute against sexual abuse if timely invoked, provide adequate protection for society's interests. Where could we stop? Assume a severely depressed person consults a storefront preacher, unaffiliated with any of the mainstream denominations, but with them, equally protected by the first amendment. The cleric consults with our hypothetical citizen, reminds him of his slothful life, and that he is a miserable sinner; recommends prayer and fasting and warns of the Day of Judgment. Our depressed person becomes more so, and kills himself and a few more people. These deaths are followed by lawsuits. As to a licensed psychiatrist or social worker, our lay courts should have no trouble adjudicating a claim of professional malpractice on these facts. As to a clergyman, it would be both impossible and unconstitutional to attempt to do so.

The court concluded that since clergy malpractice was not recognized in New York, it had no choice but to dismiss the lawsuit against the pastor.[86]

The Colorado Supreme Court refused to recognize the theory of "clergy malpractice" in a case involving the seduction of a female church member by a Catholic priest.[87] The woman had claimed that the priest "negligently performed his duty as a marital counselor." The court viewed this theory as a claim of malpractice, which it defined as "any professional misconduct, unreasonable lack of skill or fidelity in professional or fiduciary duties, evil practice, or illegal or immoral conduct." Since a priest was involved, the court characterized the malpractice claim as a claim of "clergy malpractice." However, the court ruled that the lower courts had properly dismissed this claim since "to date no court has acknowledged the existence of such a tort" and it raises "serious first amendment issues." The court acknowledged that psychologists and psychiatrists may be sued for malpractice if they engage in sexual relations with counselees. However, a Colorado statute specifically excluded clergy from the list of counselors who can be sued for malpractice on the basis of such conduct, and accordingly the court ruled that the priest could not be sued for malpractice.

An Illinois court ruled that a husband whose wife was seduced by her pastor could not sue the pastor, or denominational agencies, for malpractice. The former husband asserted that (1) the pastor had approximately 11 years experience in preaching and counseling; (2) his professional counseling experience included marriage counseling, faith counseling, and general family counseling; (3) he "held himself out as a skilled professional in matters of counseling"; (4) the pastor and denominational agencies "encouraged congregants to seek counseling from the church and its clergy before seeking secular professionals in order to promote unity, closeness and interdependence within members of the congregation in accordance with stated church doctrine"; and (5) the pastor "was acting within the scope and parameters of his employment duties on behalf of the church defendants and in furtherance of stated church doctrine when he counseled" the husband and wife. A state appeals court rejected the former husband's claim that the pastor and bishop were guilty of clergy malpractice:

Our courts have refused to entertain [clergy malpractice] claims because the first amendment's free exercise clause prohibits courts from considering claims requiring the interpretation of religious doctrine. To permit claims for clergy malpractice would require courts to establish a stan-

---

[86] Schmidt v. Bishop, 779 F. Supp. 321 (S.D.N.Y. 1991). *See also* Jones by Jones v. Trane, 591 N.Y.S.2d 927 (Sup. 1992) ("It is when what is sought is an evaluation of a member of the clergy while acting as a spiritual counselor that courts have refrained from undertaking to define a standard of care.").

[87] Destefano v. Grabian, 763 P.2d 275 (Colo. 1988).

dard of reasonable care for religious practitioners practicing their respective faiths, which necessarily involves the interpretation of doctrine.

The former husband insisted that if the pastor and bishop could not be sued for malpractice, they could be sued for "psychotherapy malpractice." The court disagreed, at least to the extent that this claim was in reality alleging malpractice by the pastor and bishop in their roles as clergy. If, on the other hand, the former husband was addressing conduct outside of the performance of ministerial duties, then his claims could be redressed by a civil court. The court observed:

In essence, the plaintiff's complaint alleges that [the pastor], while counseling him in accordance with duties established by church doctrine, breached his duty as a professional marriage counselor. We believe there is an inherent contradiction in this core allegation which exposes the problem with claims of malpractice against members of the clergy, even when couched in terms of professional or psychotherapy malpractice. . . .

The plaintiff's complaint does not allege that [the pastor] is either a licensed social worker, licensed psychotherapist or a licensed marriage counselor or that he held himself out as one. Indeed, during the time when the plaintiff's claims accrued, the statutes in force authorizing the licensing of and the establishment of standards for practitioners of these professions specifically exempted religious practitioners from their ambit, so long as they do not hold themselves out as qualified under the acts. Furthermore, to the extent Illinois has, subsequent to the alleged actions involved in this case, statutorily recognized an action for sexual exploitation within the confines of a psychotherapeutic relationship, it has limited recovery under that act to the victims of the exploitation and, in addition, excluded "counseling of a religious nature" from the definition of "psychotherapy." Finally, although the plaintiff does allege that [the pastor] mishandled psychotherapeutic principles, such as the transference phenomenon, he does not allege that [the pastor] had either formal training in and knowledge of these principles or any counseling training outside of his training by the [church]. Indeed, the plaintiff's allegations presuppose that a pastor is under the same ethical obligations the state imposes upon therapists it licenses. We cannot impose such obligations on a church within the constricts of the first amendment.

The complaint does allege that the pastor held himself out as a "skilled professional" in matters of counseling, but it also admits that [he] counseled in accordance with stated church doctrine and encouraged members to seek counseling within the church "before seeking secular professionals." The plaintiff alleged that [the pastor] provided marriage counseling to him in accordance with church doctrine. That is not the same as a situation in which a plaintiff alleges that "a particular church . . . also offers purely secular counseling as a service to members of its congregation or to a broader segment of the population in need of such services." We believe that given the particular facts alleged by the plaintiff, a trial court would be required to investigate the nature of counseling, as well as the training of counselors, within this particular church. That is not permitted in Illinois or in any other jurisdiction. This area requires . . . that a bright line be drawn between those claims actionable and those which impinge on first amendment guarantees. In the factual context of this case, we believe that "line" requires us to uphold the trial judge's ruling. At core, the plaintiff has alleged that [the pastor] is a very bad counselor who tried during counseling sessions to hide an illicit affair with the plaintiff's wife. Yet, according to the complaint, he was performing the counseling itself in the context of duties imposed upon him as a cleric by church doctrine. And, as the plaintiff concedes, this case is about the counseling. We believe that to permit the plaintiff's claims would effectively erase the bright line [discussed above]. Accordingly, the trial judge did not err in dismissing the count for psychotherapy malpractice against [the pastor].

As to the former husband's allegations of malpractice against the bishop, the court noted that (1) in response to the husband's request that the bishop render counseling services to him as a result of the pastor's activities, the bishop responded that the plaintiff should seek professional counseling; (2) the husband failed to demonstrate that he and the bishop ever entered into a counseling relationship; and (3) the husband approached the bishop within the context of his duties as the head of the church, and as such any communications that occurred between them would not be the basis for civil liability.[88]

A New York court ruled that a church and diocese could not be sued on the basis of malpractice for the alleged sexual misconduct of a priest. The priest allegedly molested a minor pupil at a church-operated secondary school. A state appellate court rejected the malpractice claim, noting that malpractice is based on negligent rather than intentional behavior, and that the sexual assault alleged in this case was an intentional act. The court also pointed out that "we are unaware of any authority supporting the proposition that sexual abuse by a member of the clergy is cognizable as clergy malpractice." The court referred to the *Nally* case.[89]

The Ohio Supreme Court refused to recognize the alleged tort of "clergy malpractice" in a case involving the sexual seduction of a wife during marital counseling. A husband and wife who had been experiencing marital problems went to a minister for counseling. They selected him because "he held himself out to the public . . . as a minister and counselor trained and able to provide counseling for marital difficulties." During the final three or four weeks of counseling, the minister allegedly engaged in consensual sexual relations with the wife. These relations, and the counseling, ended when the husband learned of the affair. The husband, who was later divorced from his wife, sued both the minister and his church. The suit against the minister alleged "clergy malpractice" among other theories of liability. The Ohio Supreme Court dismissed all of the husband's claims. It concluded that the minister could not be guilty of clergy malpractice since malpractice implies negligent conduct, and the minister's actions were intentional in nature. The court observed:

> The reluctance of courts to embrace the tort of clergy malpractice may be attributed to the many, and often complex, questions that arise under it. For example, what exactly are the "professional services" rendered by a cleric? And does the standard of the professional vary with the ecclesiastical office? In other words, is a rabbi, priest, pastor, or lay elder held to the same standard of care regardless of training or wide variances in the authority and obligation of religious offices? Also, where a "professional service," such as the marriage counseling involved in this case, is not unique to the cleric, should the cleric be held to the same duty of care as secular counselors? Finally if a legal duty is imposed on clergy to perform or not to perform in a particular way, will this clash with the religious beliefs of some faiths and thus violate the free exercise clause of the first amendment to the United States Constitution?[90]

In another ruling, the Ohio Supreme Court, in rejecting clergy malpractice as a basis for liability in a case involving sexual misconduct by a minister with a counselee, noted that if a minister's behavior "fits within an established category of liability, such as fraud, duress, assault, or battery, it would be redundant to

---

[88] Amato v. Greenquist, 679 N.E.2d 446 (Ill. App. 1997).
[89] Joshua S. v. Casey, 615 N.Y.S.2d 200 (A.D. 1994).
[90] Stock v. Pressnell, 527 N.E.2d 1235 (Ohio 1988).

simultaneously hold the cleric liable for clergy malpractice; to avoid a redundant remedy . . . any functional theory of clergy malpractice needs to address incidents of the clergy-communicant relationship not already [the basis of legal liability]." Since the plaintiff's claim of clergy malpractice was based entirely on facts that also supported claims of battery, fraud, and the intentional infliction of emotional distress, the court refused to recognize any claim of clergy malpractice.[91]

The Oklahoma Supreme Court rejected clergy malpractice as a basis for liability in a case brought by a husband for "bad advice" he had received from a minister. The court concluded:

> Once a court enters the realm of trying to define the nature of advice a minister should give a parishioner serious first amendment issues are implicated. We decline to determine the nature of the advice a minister must give during counseling sessions with a parishioner, and we decline to recognize a claim for bad advice from a minister under the facts before us.[92]

A Utah court refused to recognize "clergy malpractice" as a basis for legal liability.[93] A minister who used church funds to send a 17-year-old boy to visit his brother was sued by the boy's mother. The mother alleged a variety of wrongs, including clergy malpractice and intentional infliction of emotional distress. A trial court granted the minister and church a summary judgment, and the mother appealed. A state appeals court agreed with the trial court, and summarily rejected the mother's claims. In rejecting the mother's charge of clergy malpractice, the court observed:

> [The mother] admits that no court has recognized clerical malpractice as a cause of action, but argues that such malpractice exists here, not because [the minister], who had not been trained as a counselor, improperly counseled [the boy], but because he failed to refer [the boy] to trained professionals or others who could assist in resolving the family conflicts. In other words, [the mother] wishes to impose a duty upon [the minister] to make further inquiry into the alleged family conflicts, and then, if beyond his expertise, refer [the boy] to others who are qualified to treat such problems. Under the present circumstances, charging lay clergy with this duty of care goes too far because it approaches the same level of care imposed upon trained professionals in medicine and psychology.[94]

The court quoted with approval from the *Nally* case (discussed earlier in this chapter): "Because of the differing theological views espoused by the myriad of religions in our state and practiced by church members, it would certainly be impractical, and quite possibly unconstitutional, to impose a duty of care on pastoral counselors. Such a duty would necessarily be intertwined with the religious philosophy of the particular denomination or ecclesiastical teachings of the religious entity." The Utah appeals court agreed with the California Supreme Court's refusal to recognize clergy malpractice as a basis for legal liability, and refused to impose upon clergy a duty to refer parishioners experiencing emotional trauma to medical professionals. The court also rejected all of the other theories of legal liability alleged by the mother.

A Missouri appellate court left unanswered the question of whether a cause of action for *clergy malpractice* should be recognized in that state. The court observed that to "avoid a redundant remedy," the concept of clergy malpractice must address conduct that is not already the basis for legal action. For example, clergy

---

[91] Byrd v. Faber, 565 N.E.2d 584 (Ohio 1991).
[92] Bladen v. First Presbyterian Church, 857 P.2d 789 (Okla. 1993).
[93] White v. Blackburn, 787 P.2d 1315 (Utah App. 1990).
[94] *Id.* at 1317.

malpractice should not be expanded to cover such areas as defamation, infliction of emotional distress, interference with contract, or invasion of privacy, since all of these are already well-recognized legal theories. Clergy malpractice, concluded the court, must be limited to negligent counseling. However, the court acknowledged that recognizing a cause of action against a minister for improper counseling may well violate the constitutional guaranty of religious freedom.[95]

3. Other Cases Recognizing Clergy Malpractice

A few courts have recognized malpractice claims against clergy in either or both of the following two situations:

(1) sexual misconduct with an adult or minor

(2) "non-religious" counseling

To illustrate, a Colorado court, in concluding that a pastor and his employing church were not responsible for the pastor's sexual misconduct with a counselee on the basis of clergy malpractice, observed:

> [W]hile the services performed by a therapeutic counselor and those provided through pastoral counseling often overlap, so long as the cleric providing pastoral counseling is not held out as a therapeutic counselor, the standards of care applicable to therapeutic counseling cannot be applied to a pastoral counselor.[96]

An Arizona court ruled that a pastor and his church could be sued on the basis of "therapist" malpractice as a result of the pastor's disclosure of confidential information shared with him by a counselee during counseling. The counselee sought out the pastor to help her through emotional difficulties and depression "because of his 40 years counseling experience." The pastor relied on several cases rejecting clergy malpractice claims because of first amendment concerns about determining a standard of care for pastors. The court concluded that these cases were not relevant because the victim sued the pastor for therapist malpractice rather than clergy malpractice, and her claim was based on a psychological therapist's duty not to disclose confidential information revealed in counseling sessions. The court noted that "the inclusion of biblical passages on the chart [used by the pastor] did not convert the session into religious counseling, especially when the purpose of the meeting was not to provide her with religious or spiritual guidance, the church's precepts and practices were not part of the counseling, and [the victim] was not a church member when she sought help from [the pastor]." The court concluded, "[The pastor and church] offer no good reason for insulating a counselor from liability for betraying clients' confidences to their detriment merely because the counselor is a clergy member and unlicensed, and the counseling as well as wrongful disclosure takes place in a religious setting."[97]

A federal appeals court concluded that two female church employees could sue the minister who had seduced them since he had "held himself out" as a qualified marital counselor. The minister's duties did not include counseling, and he knew that he was not responsible for providing spiritual counseling to church members. He also knew that the church had a written policy of referring church members in need of non-pastoral counseling to a licensed professional counselor. Nevertheless, the minister began counseling with two women

---

[95] Hester v. Barnett, 723 S.W.2d 544 (Mo. App. 1987). Note that this case was decided prior to the California Supreme Court's decision in the *Nally* case.

[96] DeBose v. Bear Valley Church of Christ, 890 P.2d 214 (Colo. App. 1994).

[97] Barnes v. Outlaw, 937 P.2d 323 (Ariz. App. 1996).

after assuring them that he was qualified by both education and experience to provide marital counseling. The women assumed that he was authorized by the church to provide counseling. The minister entered into a sexual relationship with both women, and hired both of them as church employees. When the women learned that they both were having affairs with the same minister, they informed a church deacon. The minister resigned, and the two women were dismissed. The women later sued the minister for malpractice. The court refused to recognize a claim for clergy malpractice, but it did conclude that the women could sue the minister for malpractice as a "marriage counselor." The former minister insisted that he could not be guilty of malpractice as a marriage counselor unless his counseling was purely secular in nature. And, since he occasionally discussed scripture in his counseling sessions with the two women, his counseling was not purely secular. The court disagreed, noting that the minister's marriage counseling was "essentially secular" in nature and that this was enough for him to be guilty of malpractice as a marriage counselor.

The court concluded that the first amendment did not prevent the former minister from being sued for malpractice as a marriage counselor or for breach of fiduciary duties "not derived from religious doctrine." It explained its reasoning as follows:

> [B]ecause the jury found that [the former minister] held himself out as possessing the education and experience of a professional marriage counselor, his counseling activities with the [two women] were judged, not by a standard of care defined by religious teachings, but by a professional standard of care developed through expert testimony describing what a reasonably prudent counselor would have done under the same or similar circumstances.[98]

Another federal appeals court ruled that a church and denominational agency were not legally responsible for a pastoral counselor's sexual contacts with a female counselee. However, it concluded that the pastor could be sued for professional negligence with regard to purely secular counseling, and could be liable with respect to such counseling under a state law imposing liability on "psychotherapists" for engaging in sexual contact with counselees. A woman alleged that a pastor told her that she needed "secular psychological" and not religious counseling, and that he was qualified to provide it. The pastor allegedly assured the woman that such treatment was included in his job description at the church. The woman attended counseling sessions with the pastor at his office in the church for more than two years. Over time the pastor increased the frequency and length of the sessions. The woman claimed that he told her that "religion does not apply here. Your problems are so deep you need more psychological treatment from me." She stated that she became very involved in the therapy and attached to the pastor. He allegedly represented to her that he was a capable, trained professional on whom she could rely to assist her with her personal problems. However, the pastor eventually gave the woman an ultimatum: "I have been giving to you, and I need something back for my services. You must give back to me or I will not work with you anymore." From that date on the woman claimed that her therapy sessions began with sexual relations with the pastor.

The woman later sued her pastor, church, and a denominational agency. She asserted that the pastor was responsible for her injuries on the basis of professional negligence, breach of fiduciary duty, negligent infliction of emotional distress, and violation of the Sexual Exploitation of Psychotherapy Act. A federal appeals court ruled that the woman could sue the pastor for professional negligence. It acknowledged that no court has permitted clergy to be sued for malpractice, but it limited such cases to the context of religious counseling. The court observed:

---

[98] Sanders v. Casa View Baptist Church, 134 F.3d 331 (5th Cir. 1998).

Therefore, if a complaint alleges that the psychological services that were provided were "secular" in nature, or that the provider held himself out to be providing the services of a psychological counselor, the negligence claim cannot be characterized as one for clergy malpractice. Tort claims for behavior by a cleric that does not require the examination of religious doctrine are cognizable. Under these circumstances, the claim is for professional malpractice by a psychological counselor, not clergy malpractice.[99]

A New Jersey court allowed a woman to sue her church for clergy malpractice as a result of a sexual relationship that was initiated by her pastor. The woman's lawsuit alleged that she had sought counseling from a pastor of her church, and that the pastor became aware of her emotional vulnerabilities and exploited them by inducing her to engage in sexual acts with him. The woman filed a complaint with a "standing committee on clergy ethics" of her denomination, and the committee later determined that the minister had "violated his pastoral relationship" with the victim by engaging in "inappropriate sexual behavior toward her." The committee "sanctioned" the minister. The woman then sued her church, claiming that the pastor's actions amounted to clergy malpractice. A state appeals court ruled that the woman could sue the church for clergy malpractice. The court acknowledged that a number of courts have rejected liability based on clergy malpractice, but it refused to reach the same conclusion. It observed that "malpractice" is nothing more than the negligent performance of a professional service and "a deviation from the standards of performance applicable to the professional service in question." The court expressed concern over potential first amendment violations when civil courts apply the concept of malpractice to members of the clergy. However, it was unwilling to conclude (as many other courts have done) that the first amendment bars recognition of civil liability for clergy malpractice in all cases. It concluded, "In the present case, it is unlikely that [the church] will assert that sex with a counselee by a pastoral counselor is sanctioned by or somehow involves tenets of the . . . church, or would otherwise create an entanglement with religious beliefs or rituals of first amendment concern."[100]

§ 4-06 Contract Liability

Key point 4-06. Clergy who sign legal documents in their own name with no indication that they are signing in a representative capacity on behalf of their church may be personally liable on the document.

Whether clergy will be personally liable on contracts they sign depends upon two factors: (1) whether their employing church is disclosed in the contract, and (2) whether they sign in a representative capacity, such as "Rev. John Smith, President." If both elements are observed, generally a minister will not be personally liable for the contract. The church's identity usually is disclosed by listing the church as one of the parties to the contract. Clergy who sign a contract on behalf of a church without disclosing their title or office will not be personally liable if the church is identified in the contract and the circumstances clearly reveal that they signed in an official capacity.[101] This view, however, is not universally accepted. As a result, ministers should be careful to disclose their representative capacity when signing a contract on behalf of a church, and clearly identify the church in the body of the contract as the party to the agreement.

One legal authority has stated that "if there is no disclosure of the [corporation] in the body of the contract, the mere appending of words descriptive of the signer as, for example, the word 'president,' would not be sufficient of itself to relieve the signer of individual liability."[102]

---

[99] Dausch v. Rykse, 52 F.3d 1425 (7th Cir. 1994).
[100] F.G. v. MacDonell, 677 A.2d 258 (N.J. Super. 1996).
[101] Kenneally v. First National Bank of Anoka, 400 F.2d 838 (8th Cir. 1968), *cert. denied*, 393 U.S. 1063 (1969).
[102] FLETCHER CYC. CORP. § 3034 (1978 & Supp. 1999).

The above discussion assumes that the contract was authorized by appropriate church action. If a minister signs a contract that has not been so authorized, the general rule is that he or she will be personally liable on the contract. The church, of course, can "ratify" an unauthorized contract, in which case the church becomes liable for it.

In many cases it is unclear whether a minister in fact has been authorized to sign a contract on behalf of the church. This obviously is a very important question, for clergy who sign contracts without authorization may be personally liable. Clergy should be certain that the contract has been duly authorized by appropriate action and that they are authorized to sign. The church's charter and bylaws must be reviewed, as well as resolutions of the church board and pertinent state laws. To illustrate, many churches have adopted bylaws requiring that disposition of church property be authorized only by congregational vote. Even if the board of deacons or trustees of such a church independently approves the disposition of church property, any subsequent contract of sale would be unauthorized. And even if the church congregation has approved the sale in a church business meeting, the minister should be satisfied that all of the procedural requirements for such a meeting—such as notice and quorum—have been met.

> **Tip.** *Clergy should refrain from signing contracts unless they are certain that (1) the contract has been properly authorized; (2) they are authorized to sign on behalf of the church; (3) the church is clearly identified in the contract as the party to the agreement; and (4) the minister signs in a "representative capacity" (for example, as "authorized agent" or "president").*

In no event should clergy assume that they are authorized to enter into contracts on behalf of their church simply by virtue of their position. One court observed:

> The mere proclaiming of [oneself] as the religious superior of the congregation may suffice to establish that fact in spiritual matters of his church, but it does not effect legal superiority in secular matters. There must be clear and convincing evidence of congregational acknowledgement of and acquiescence in the concept of legal superiority and authority over church business and property matters.[103]

A minister of an unincorporated church who signs a contract on behalf of the church may be personally liable on the contract even if the church is identified in the contract and the minister signs in a representative capacity. Several courts have concluded that ministers and trustees of unincorporated churches who sign contracts on behalf of their churches will be personally liable on them.[104]

> **Example.** *A corporate officer signed a check in the amount of $43,000 on behalf of his company. The company's name was imprinted on the check, so there was no doubt that it was an obligation of the company. However, the officer's signature did not indicate that he was signing in a "representative capacity"—that is, as a representative of the company rather than in his personal or individual capacity. A bank dishonored the check on the basis of insufficient funds, and the recipient sued the officer directly. The officer insisted that he could not be personally liable for the amount of the check, since the company's name had been imprinted on it. The court disagreed. It referred to a state law specifying that*

---

[103] Gospel Tabernacle Body of Christ Church v. Peace Publishers & Co., 506 P.2d 1135, 1138 (Kan. 1973). *See also* American Legion v. Southwest Title and Insurance Co., 207 So.2d 393 (La. 1968), *reversed on other grounds*, 218 So.2d 612 (La. 1969) (lease entered into by minister without knowledge of church was held to be a "nullity"); Hill v. Hill, 241 S.W.2d 865 (Tenn. 1951).

[104] *See, e.g.*, I.W. Phillips & Co. v. Hall, 128 So. 635 (Fla. 1930); Abrams v. Brent, 362 S.W.2d 155 (Tex. 1962); Mitterhausen v. South Wisconsin Conference Assoc. of Seventh-Day Adventists, 14 N.W.2d 19 (Wis. 1944).

an authorized representative who signs his or her name to an instrument "is personally obligated if the instrument names the [company] represented but does not show that the representative signed in a representative capacity." In summary, the officer was personally liable for payment of the check even though the company's name was imprinted on it, since the officer did not indicate clearly that he was signing in a representative capacity.[105]

§ 4-07 Securities Law Violations

Key point 4-07. *Clergy may violate state securities laws in a number of ways, including the sale of securities without registering as an agent, and the commission of fraudulent practices.*

Laws regulating the sale of securities have been enacted by the federal government and by all 50 states. The term *security* is defined very broadly by such laws. The Uniform Securities Act, which has been adopted by a majority of the 50 states, defines a security as

any note; stock; treasury stock; bond; debenture; evidence of indebtedness; certificate of interest or participation in any profit-sharing agreement; collateral trust certificate; preorganization certificate or subscription; transferable share; investment contract; voting trust certificate; certificate of deposit for a security; certificate of interest or participation in an oil, gas, or mining title or lease or in payments out of production under such a title or lease; or in general any interest or instrument commonly known as a "security" . . . .

This definition is broad enough to include many instruments used in church fundraising efforts.

Securities laws were enacted to protect the public against fraudulent and deceptive practices in the sale of securities and to provide full and fair disclosure to prospective investors. To achieve these purposes, most securities laws impose the following conditions on the sale of securities:

1. registration of proposed securities with the federal or state government in advance of sale

2. filing of sales and advertising literature with the federal or state government

3. registration of agents and broker-dealers who will be selling the securities

4. prohibition of fraudulent practices

Ministers may be directly impacted by their state's securities law in at least two ways. First, if they are engaged in selling their church's securities (or offering them for sale), they may be required to register as an "agent" or "salesperson." Second, they are prohibited from engaging in any form of fraudulent practice in connection with the offer or sale of securities.

1. AGENT REGISTRATION

The Uniform Securities Act, which has been adopted by a majority of states, provides that "it is unlawful for any person to transact business in this state as a broker-dealer or agent unless he is registered under this

---

[105] Hind-Marsh v. Puglia, 665 So.2d 1091 (Fla. App. 1995).

act." Registration generally involves the filing of a detailed application with the state securities commission, payment of the prescribed fee, and, in many states, the successful completion of a securities law examination. The "Church Bond Guidelines," prepared by the North American Securities Administrators Association (NASAA) and adopted by several states, specify that the Uniform Securities Act requires that

> any person, including an officer or director of the issuer, who wishes to offer or sell church bonds must either be a registered representative of a licensed securities broker-dealer, or alternatively must file for registration as an agent with the administrators of the states in which he intends to sell securities pursuant to section 201 of the Act. This is true even if the church bonds themselves are exempt from registration under . . . the Act. Any person who sells church bonds without compliance with the agent registration provisions of the Act could also be liable under both the civil and criminal sections of the Act.

Some states exempt the sellers of church securities from the agent registration requirements. The majority, however, require registration—and only a few of these states waive the examination requirement. The NASAA church bond guidelines specify that "an administrator may waive the testing requirements for a securities agent's license, provided, however, that the offering is substantially in compliance with" the church bond guidelines.

> **Key point.** *Ministers who contemplate making offers or sales of securities should assume that they must register as an agent until they receive adequate assurance that they are exempt. Even those ministers who do not plan on offering or selling securities directly should note that virtually any promotion of church securities, no matter how indirect, may trigger the agent registration requirements.*

Section 410 of the Uniform Securities Act provides that any person who offers or sells a security in violation of the agent registration requirement is

> liable to the person buying the security from him, who may sue either at law or in equity to recover the consideration paid for the security, together with interest at the rate of six percent per year from the date of payment, costs, and reasonable attorneys' fees, less the amount of any income received on the security, upon the tender of the security, or for damages if he no longer owns the security.

Section 410 further provides that the employer of an unregistered agent is also liable. Thus, both a minister and his or her employing church will be liable under this section if the minister sells church securities in violation of an agent registration provision.

2. THE PROHIBITION OF FRAUDULENT ACTIVITIES

The term *fraud* is defined above. Neither federal nor state securities laws exempt ministers from the prohibition of fraudulent activities in the offer or sale of securities. As noted above, the term "fraud" is defined broadly, and this can result in unexpected liability for securities fraud.

> **Example.** *To help promote the sale of church notes, a minister assures his congregation during a sermon that the notes are as safe "as the Rock of Gibraltar" since they were issued on behalf of the church. This statement may constitute securities fraud.*

Example. A minister was found guilty of engaging in fraudulent practices through failing to disclose to investors of church securities that he had $116,000 in unsatisfied debts, that he had incurred $700,000 in unsatisfied debts on behalf of a previous church through the sale of securities, and that the church's financial statements were in error.[106]

In a leading case, a federal appeals court upheld the conviction of a pastor for securities fraud. A church began selling to investors what it called "certificates of deposit." The pastor allegedly told potential purchasers that the certificates of deposit would be used to finance the improvement or expansion of the church and to build a retirement complex. He represented or caused others to represent that the church would pay certificate holders between 12 and 16 percent interest on a quarterly basis and that interest payments would continue until the maturity of the certificate (5 years after the date of issuance). He further promised that, when the certificate matured, the investor would be entitled to repayment of the principal plus the balance of any outstanding interest. The pastor further informed investors that they would not have to pay income taxes on the interest payments they received from the church and that the investment was safe because it was backed by the assets of the church.

The church raised over $1.6 million dollars from the sale of the certificates to 90 investors, 27 of whom were church members. The pastor took a significant portion of the certificate proceeds for his personal use. Among other things, he purchased 4 airplanes, a house for his mother, sports cars and passenger trucks, and made a down payment on his daughter's house. The pastor resigned when his actions were uncovered, and the church filed for bankruptcy protection.

The pastor was later prosecuted for 12 counts of securities fraud under federal law, including the following:

- The pastor made "false and fraudulent representations and material omissions" in the sale of the certificates of deposit.

- The pastor "converted approximately $900,000 of [certificate] funds to the personal benefit of himself and family members."

- The pastor told potential purchasers that the certificates of deposit would be used to finance the improvement or expansion of the church and to build a retirement complex.

- The pastor represented or caused others to represent that the church would pay certificate holders between 12 and 16 percent interest on a quarterly basis and that interest payments would continue until the maturity of the certificate (5 years after the date of issuance).

- The pastor further promised that when the certificate matured, the investor would be entitled to repayment of the principal plus the balance of any outstanding interest.

- The pastor told investors that they would not have to pay income taxes on the interest payments they received from the church.

- The pastor told investors that their investments were safe because they were backed by the assets of the church.

---

[106] Order of Florida Comptroller No. 78-1-DOS (February 17, 1978).

- At no time did the pastor tell investors that the money from the sale of certificates was to be used for the personal expenses of the pastor and his family.

The pastor was convicted on all counts and sentenced to five years in prison. He appealed his conviction to a federal appeals court on the ground that the government's investigation and prosecution violated his first amendment right to the free exercise of religion. The federal appeals court rejected the pastor's defense and affirmed his conviction. It began its opinion by noting that

[the pastor] does not maintain that the tenets of his religion require him to undertake securities fraud [or] that by outlawing securities fraud [the federal securities law] impermissibly burdened his first amendment right to practice his religion freely. Instead, he asserts that "[t]he ability to determine what is an appropriate use of church money is at the heart of the charges brought against" him, and that "[a]llowing the Court, or a branch of the United States Government, to make that determination violated [his] constitutionally protected free exercise of religion."

The pastor insisted that the first amendment guaranty of religious freedom assured pastors of the right to determine the appropriate use of church money without government interference. The court disagreed. The court stressed that the trial court's conviction of the pastor for securities fraud

had absolutely nothing to do with reviewing the church's internal allocation of funds, nor did it implicate any issue of religious polity. Instead, [the pastor's] offense pertained solely to the way in which he procured the "church" funds in the first place. [The pastor] obtained the money by, among other things, making fraudulent misrepresentations and omissions of material fact in the sale of the certificates of deposit. Those misrepresentations and omissions are objectively demonstrable actions the pastor undertook as an individual. [He] was convicted not because the government or the court decided that the church had spent its money unwisely, but because [the pastor] did not spend the certificate money in the way that he promised the investors he would, and because he lied to the investors about their ability to recover their investment principal upon certificate maturity.

Hence, neither the [government's] investigation into the pastor's conduct, nor the [trial court's] adjudication of his guilt, required any governmental foray into the realm of religious law or any repudiation of an ecclesiastical tribunal's decision. [The pastor's] first amendment challenge to his conviction is without merit.

The pastor also claimed that his prison sentence had been improperly increased by the court. Under federal sentencing guidelines a court may increase a prison sentence for "breach of a position of trust." In order for a court to increase a prison term on this basis, it must find that (1) the defendant occupied a position of trust, and (2) the defendant abused his position in a manner that significantly facilitated the commission or concealment of the offense. The sentencing guidelines state that "[t]he position of trust must have contributed in some substantial way to facilitating the crime and not merely have provided an opportunity that could as easily have been afforded to other persons. This adjustment, for example, would not apply to an embezzlement by an ordinary bank teller." The appeals court concluded that the pastor had abused a position of trust and therefore the increase in his prison sentence was warranted. It observed:

Because [the pastor] was the church's financial decisionmaker, church-member investors and church personnel trusted him to be the sole, unsupervised manager of the church's finances. This position of trust allowed the pastor to control the church's bank accounts and misapply the certificate funds clandestinely. Because [the pastor] was the church's pastor and spiritual leader, his congregation undoubtedly trusted him to further the church's religious mission. [The pastor's] position of trust allowed him to use his authority to mislead church-member investors into believing that the church needed the certificate funds for building projects and to persuade them to invest their money for the good of the church and its endeavors. The [trial court] therefore correctly determined that [the pastor] occupied and abused a position of trust.

Key point. An unexpected consequence of the pastor's securities fraud was that he was also guilty of income tax invasion. He failed to realize that by treating the investors' monies as his own personal funds he was in effect receiving taxable income that he failed to report.

The subject of church liability for securities law violations is addressed in another chapter.[107]

§ 4-08   Failure to Report Child Abuse

Key point 4-08. Every state has a child abuse reporting law that requires persons designated as mandatory reporters to report known or reasonably suspected incidents of child abuse. Ministers are mandatory reporters in many states. Some states exempt ministers from reporting child abuse if they learned of the abuse in the course of a conversation protected by the clergy-penitent privilege. Ministers may face criminal and civil liability for failing to report child abuse.

It is common for ministers to learn that a minor is being abused. This can occur in a number of ways, including a confession by the perpetrator, or a disclosure by a friend or relative of the victim or perpetrator. Often, ministers want to resolve such matters internally through counseling with the victim or the alleged offender, without contacting civil authorities. Such a response can have serious legal consequences, including the following: (1) Ministers who are *mandatory reporters* under state law face possible criminal prosecution for failing to comply with their state child abuse reporting law; (2) some state legislatures have enacted laws permitting child abuse victims to sue ministers for failing to report child abuse; and (3) some courts have permitted child abuse victims to sue ministers for failing to report child abuse. Each of these theories of liability is addressed below.

1. CRIMINAL LIABILITY

All fifty states have enacted child abuse reporting statutes in an effort to protect abused children and prevent future abuse.[108] *Child abuse* is defined by most statutes to include physical abuse, emotional abuse, neglect, and sexual molestation. A *child* ordinarily is defined as any person under the age of 18 years. Some states specifically limit the definition of "child abuse" to abuse that is inflicted *by a parent or other person legally responsible for the minor's care.* Such a statute, if interpreted narrowly, might not require clergy to report incidents of abuse inflicted by teachers, child care workers, custodians, associate ministers, adolescents, or volunteer youth workers—even if they otherwise are under a mandatory duty to report child abuse under state law.

All fifty states enumerate categories of persons who are under a legal duty to report abuse to designated civil authorities. In most states, such "mandatory reporters" must report both actual and reasonably suspected

---

[107] *See* § 9-04, *infra.*
[108] *See generally* I. SLOAN, CHILD ABUSE: GOVERNING LAW & LEGISLATION (1983); Mitchell, *Must Clergy Tell? Child Abuse Reporting Requirements Versus the Clergy Privilege and Free Exercise of Religion,* 71 MINN. L. REV. 723 (1987).

cases of child abuse. Failure to do so is a crime (usually a misdemeanor). Some states define *mandatory reporters* to include any person having a reasonable belief that child abuse has occurred. Obviously, clergy will be mandatory reporters under these statutes. The remaining states define *mandatory reporters* by referring to a list of occupations which generally includes physicians, dentists, hospital employees, nurses, coroners, school employees, nursery school workers, law enforcement officers, and licensed psychologists. Ministers are specifically identified as mandatory reporters under a few of these statutes.[109] But even if they are not, they may be mandatory reporters if they fall within a listed classification, such as school or child care workers and administrators, or counselors. In summary, many clergy have a mandatory duty to report child abuse. Clergy should not assume that they have no duty to report.

Clergy who are not mandatory reporters under their state law generally are considered "permissive reporters," meaning that they may report cases of abuse to the designated civil authorities but are not legally required to do so.

Ministers who are mandatory reporters of child abuse under state law are under a profound ethical dilemma when they receive information about child abuse in the course of a confidential counseling session that is subject to the clergy-penitent privilege. They have to chose between fulfilling their legal obligation to report, or honoring their ecclesiastical duty to maintain the confidentiality of privileged communications. A number of states have attempted to resolve this dilemma by specifically exempting clergy from the duty to report child abuse if the abuse is disclosed to them in the course of a communication protected by the clergy-penitent privilege.[110] Other states, while not specifically excluding clergy from the duty to report, do provide that information protected by the clergy-penitent privilege is not admissible in any legal proceeding regarding the alleged abuse.[111] Some state child abuse reporting statutes do not list the clergy-penitent privilege among those privileges that are abolished in the context of child abuse proceedings.[112] The intent of such statutes may be to excuse clergy from the testifying in such cases regarding information they learned in the course of a privileged communication.

Even if the clergy-penitent privilege applies in the context of child abuse reporting, it is by no means clear that the privilege will be a defense to a failure to report, since (1) the information causing a minister to suspect that abuse has occurred may not have been privileged (that is, it was not obtained in confidence, or it was not obtained during spiritual counseling); and (2) a privilege ordinarily applies only to courtroom testimony or depositions, and not to a statutory requirement to report to a state agency.

Unfortunately, the failure by many states to recognize the clergy-penitent privilege in the context of child abuse reporting disregards the therapeutic purpose of the privilege. Many child abusers will be discouraged from seeking spiritual counsel if the privilege does not assure the confidentiality of their communications. This will only compound the problem. If, on the other hand, the privilege were preserved, many child abusers would seek out ministers for spiritual counseling, and the underlying causes of such behavior could be isolated and in some cases corrected.

---

[109] *See, e.g.,* CONN. GEN. STAT. § 17-38(b) ("clergyman"); MISS. CODE ANN. §§ 43-21-353 and 43-23-9 ("minister"); NEV. REV. STAT. § 432B.220(2)(d) ("a clergyman, practitioner of Christian Science or religious healer, unless he has acquired the knowledge of the abuse or neglect from the offender during a confession"); N.H. REV. STAT. ANN. § 169-C:29 ("priest, minister, or rabbi").

[110] *See, e.g.,* ARIZ. REV. STAT. § 13-3620A; FLA. REV. STAT. § 415.512; KY. REV. STAT. § 620.050(2); LA. REV. STAT. § 14:403B(4)(b); MD. CODE § 5-705(a)(3); MINN. STAT. § 626.556(3)(a)(1); MONT. CODE § 41-3-201(4)(b); NEV. REV. STAT. § 432B.220(2)(d); OR. REV. STAT. § 418.750; S.C. CODE § 20-7-550; UTAH CODE § 62A-4-503(2). The clergy-penitent privilege is addressed fully in chapter 3.

[111] *See, e.g.,* ARK. STAT. § 12-12-511; KY. REV. STAT. § 620.050(2); PA. STAT. TITLE 23, § 6381(c); S.C. CODE § 20-7-550.

[112] *See, e.g.,* IND. REV. STAT. § 31-6-11-8; N.C. STAT. § 7A-551; TENN. REV. STAT. § 37-1-411; VA. STAT. § 63.1-248.11.

Every state grants legal immunity to reporters of child abuse. This means that a reporter cannot be sued simply for reporting child abuse. However, several states require that the report be based on "reasonable cause to believe" that abuse has occurred.[113] The purpose of extending legal immunity to reporters obviously is to encourage child abuse reporting. However, several studies indicate that numerous false reports have also been encouraged.[114] Such studies have raised serious legal questions concerning the propriety of legal immunity. One expert has observed that the many false reports "invite the intolerable situation of falsely accusing large numbers of parents of abuse."[115] Persons who maliciously transmit false reports are subject to civil liability in most states and criminal liability in some.

Persons who are legally required to report generally make their report by notifying a designated state agency by telephone and confirming the telephone call with a written report within a prescribed period of time. The reporter generally is required to (1) identify the child, the child's parents or guardians, and the alleged abuser by name, and provide their addresses; (2) give the child's age; and (3) describe the nature of the abuse. Most states have toll-free numbers that receive initial reports of child abuse.

While persons who are legally required to report child abuse are subject to criminal prosecution for failure to do so, instances of actual criminal prosecution are rare. However, some clergy have been prosecuted for failing to file a report when they were in a mandatory reporting classification and they had reasonable cause to believe that abuse had occurred. Criminal penalties for failing to file a report vary, but typically involve short prison sentences and small fines.

2. CIVIL LIABILITY BASED ON STATUTE

A few states have enacted statutes that create civil liability for failure to report child abuse.[116] In these states, victims of child abuse can sue adults who failed to report the abuse. Not only are adults who fail to report abuse subject to possible criminal liability (if they are mandatory reporters), but they also can be sued for money damages by the victims of abuse. In each state, the statute only permits victims of child abuse to sue *mandatory reporters* who failed to report the abuse. No liability is created for persons who are not mandatory reporters as defined by state law.

---

[113] The courts generally have interpreted "reasonable cause to believe" very liberally, thereby reducing the risk of being sued for making a report that turns out to have been false. *See, e.g.*, Cream v. Mitchell, 264 Cal. Rptr. 876 (Cal. App. 1989) (a doctor who misdiagnosed chicken pox as venereal disease, and reported his diagnosis to the state, was found to have had a reasonable suspicion of abuse); Thomas v. Chadwick, 274 Cal. Rptr. 128 (Cal. App. 4 Dist. 1990) (a doctor who misdiagnosed a congenital defect as child abuse, and who reported his diagnosis to the state, was immune from liability).

[114] *See, e.g.*, A. SUSSMAN & S. COHEN, REPORTING CHILD ABUSE AND NEGLECT: GUIDELINES FOR LEGISLATION (1975) (56% of all reports are valid).

[115] R. Light, *Abused and Neglected Children in America: A Study of Alternative Policies*, 43 HARVARD EDUCATIONAL REVIEW 556, 569 (1973).

[116] *See, e.g.*, ARK. CODE § 12-12-504(b) ("[a]ny person . . . required by this subchapter to make notification of suspected child maltreatment who willfully fails to do so, shall be civilly liable for damages proximately caused by that failure"); COLO. STAT. § 19-3-304(4)(b) (any person who is a mandatory reporter of child abuse and who willfully fails to report known or reasonably suspected incidents of abuse "shall be liable for damages proximately caused thereby"); IOWA CODE § 232.75 ("[a]ny person . . . required . . . to report a suspected case of child abuse who knowingly fails to do so is civilly liable for the damages proximately caused by such failure"); MICH. COMP. LAWS § 722.633 ("[a] person who is required by this act to report an instance of suspected child abuse or neglect and who fails to do so is civilly liable for the damages proximately caused by the failure"); MONT. CODE § 41-3-207 ("[a]ny person . . . required by law to report known or suspected child abuse or neglect who fails to do so or who prevents another person from reasonably doing so is civilly liable for the damages proximately caused by such failure or prevention"); N.Y. SOC. SERV. § 420 ("[a]ny person . . . required by this title to report a case of suspected child abuse or maltreatment who knowingly and willfully fails to do so shall be civilly liable for the damages proximately caused by such failure"); R.I. GEN. LAWS § 40-11-3 (a mandatory reporter who fails to report a reasonably suspected incident of child abuse "shall be civilly liable for the damages proximately caused by that failure").

Key point. Persons who are "mandatory" child abuse reporters in some states can be sued by victims of child abuse for failure to comply with state child abuse reporting requirements. These lawsuits may be brought in some states many years after the failure to report. It is possible that other state legislatures will enact laws giving victims of child abuse the legal right to sue mandatory reporters who failed to comply with their reporting obligations. It is also possible that the courts in some states will allow victims to sue mandatory reporters (and perhaps those who are not mandatory reporters) for failing to report child abuse even if no state law grants them the specific right to do so. These potential risks must be considered when evaluating whether or not to report known or suspected incidents of child abuse.

3. CIVIL LIABILITY BASED ON COURT RULINGS

Several courts have refused to allow child abuse victims to sue ministers on the basis of a failure to comply with a child abuse reporting law. A few courts have reached the opposite conclusion.

Example. A California appeals court upheld the conviction of two pastors for failing to report an incident of child abuse. A girl was sexually molested by her stepfather, and informed two pastors of her church who also served as president and principal of a church-operated school the girl attended. The pastors did not report the abuse to civil authorities, even though as school administrators they were mandatory child abuse reporters, because they wanted to handle the matter within the church. They viewed the matter as "a pastoral one" involving the girl's inability to forgive her stepfather. The pastors also insisted that they considered the stepfather's actions to be a sin rather than child abuse, and that as pastors they were required to follow the scriptures concerning the discipline of a fellow Christian. A jury found the pastors guilty of violating the state child abuse reporting law, and a state appeals court upheld the convictions. The court rejected the pastors' claim that their conviction amounted to a violation of the first amendment guaranty of religious freedom by forcing them to report incidents of abuse rather than "handling problems within the church." The court concluded, "The mere fact that a [minister's] religious practice is burdened by a governmental program does not mean an exception accommodating that practice must be granted. The state may justify an inroad on religious liberty by showing it is the least restrictive means of achieving some compelling state interest. Here, if [the pastors] are held to be exempt from the mandatory requirements of the [child abuse reporting law] the act's purpose would be severely undermined. There is no indication teachers and administrators of religious schools would voluntarily report known or suspected child abuse. Children in those schools would not be protected. The protection of all children cannot be achieved in any other way." [117]

Example. An Indiana appeals court ruled that an adult who had been abused as a minor could sue his pastor on the basis of negligence for failing to report the abuse. A minor (the "victim") was sexually abused by his foster father and a number of other adults. When he was an adult, the victim sued a minister who had knowledge of the abuse but failed to report it to the authorities. He claimed that the minister was legally responsible for his injuries on the basis of a negligent failure to report. The court noted that negligence consists of the following elements: a duty to exercise reasonable care with respect to another, a breach of that duty, and injury to the other. In determining whether or not one has a duty to exercise reasonable care with respect to another, the court considered three factors—the existence of a "special relationship," the foreseeability of injury, and public policy. The court concluded that it often will be foreseeable that a victim of child abuse will suffer further injury if the abuse is not reported. It also conceded that public policy does not support the imposition of legal liability on adults who fail to

---

[117] People v. Hodges, 13 Cal. Rptr.2d 412 (Cal. Super. 1992).

report incidents of child abuse absent a state law creating such liability. In short, the second factor often supports the recognition of a duty, while the third factor often does not. This makes the first factor (the existence of a special relationship) determinative. The court acknowledged that no satisfactory definition of a "special relationship" exists. However, it concluded that such a relationship may have existed between the victim and the pastor, as a result of the following allegations made by the victim: (1) he met the pastor when he was fourteen years of age; (2) over the next four years he spoke with the pastor more than fifty times; (3) he sought help from the pastor concerning the sexual abuse he was suffering from his foster father and others; and (4) the pastor did provide some counsel to him regarding his abuse. The court concluded, "[The pastor] knew of the alleged abuse and could have reasonably foreseen that it would continue absent adult intervention. In addition, there is a genuine issue of material fact as to whether [he] enjoyed a special relationship with [the victim]. When the level of interaction or dependency between an abused child and an adult results in a special relationship, the adult necessarily assumes a greater responsibility for that child. The special relationship imbues to the child a sense of security and trust. For the child, the stakes are high. For the adult, making a good faith report to a local child protection service is neither burdensome nor risky. In such circumstances, the adult is committing an even greater disservice to the child when the adult fails to make a report of the alleged abuse."[118]

Example. *The Iowa Supreme Court ruled that a priest was not legally responsible for damages suffered by a victim of child abuse as a result of his decision not to report the abuse to civil authorities. A child (the victim) and her parents met with their parish priest on a number of occasions for family counseling. The priest was not a licensed counselor. The victim did not tell the priest that her father had sexually abused her but did tell him that he had "hurt" her. The physical and sexual abuse of the victim stopped when her father left home when she was in eighth grade. The victim attempted suicide a month later. The victim later sued her former priest and church. She claimed that the priest failed to report her abuse to the civil authorities, and that as a result the abuse continued and her injuries were aggravated. She conceded that the priest was not aware that abuse had occurred, but she insisted that he should have been aware of the abuse based on her statement to him that her father had "hurt her." A trial court dismissed the claim against the priest on the ground that he was not a mandatory child abuse reporter under state law and as a result had no duty to report the abuse even if he suspected it. The state supreme court affirmed the trial court's decision. This case demonstrates that members of the clergy are not necessarily mandatory child abuse reporters under a state law that makes "counselors" mandatory reporters. And, it illustrates that clergy who are not mandatory reporters, and who fail to report an incident of child abuse, will not necessarily be liable for the victim's injuries.[119]*

Example. *A Texas court ruled that ministers who are mandatory child abuse reporters under state law cannot be sued by child abuse victims on account of their failure to report. A 12-year-old boy was sexually molested by the children's music director at his church. At first, the victim told no one. However, over the next few years the victim told 5 pastors in his church about the molestation. Although pastors are "mandatory reporters" of child abuse under Texas law, none of them reported the allegations to civil authorities or to the victim's parents. The victim sued his church when he was an adult. He claimed that the church was responsible for his injuries because of its "inadequate response" to his "cries for help," and because of the failure by the 5 pastors to report the abuse to civil authorities. The court concluded that the church was not liable for the victim's injuries on account of the 5 pastors' failure to comply with the state child abuse reporting law. The 5 pastors in this case were mandatory reporters under Texas law, and the victim*

---

[118] J.A.W. v. Roberts, 627 N.E.2d 802 (Ind. App. 5 Dist. 1994).

[119] Wilson v. Darr, 553 N.W.2d 579 (Iowa 1996).

claimed that their failure to report his allegations of abuse made them and the church legally responsible for his injuries. The court disagreed, noting that the state child abuse reporting law is a criminal statute and that "nothing in the statute indicates that it was intended to create a private cause of action."[120]

Example. *The Washington state supreme court ruled that an ordained minister could not be prosecuted criminally for failing to file a report despite his knowledge that a child was being abused. The minister was informed by a female counselee that her husband had sexually abused their minor child. The minister discussed the matter with both the husband and daughter in an attempt to reconcile the family, but filed no report with civil authorities within 48 hours as required by state law. The minister was prosecuted and convicted for violating the state child abuse reporting statute. He received a deferred sentence coupled with one year's probation and a $500 fine, and in addition was required to complete a "professional education program" addressing the ramifications of sexual abuse. The minister appealed his conviction, and the state supreme court reversed the conviction and ruled that the state child abuse reporting statute could not apply to clergy acting in their professional capacity as spiritual advisers. The court noted that the state legislature's 1975 amendment of the Washington child abuse reporting statute deleting a reference to "clergy" among the persons under a mandatory duty to report known or reasonably suspected cases of child abuse "relieved clerics from the reporting mandate. Logically, clergy would not have been removed from the reporting class if the legislature still intended to include them." The court further observed, "Announcing a rule that requires clergy to report under all circumstances could serve to dissuade parishioners from acknowledging in consultation with their ministers the existence of abuse and seeking a solution to it. . . . [But] simply establishing one's status as clergy is not enough to trigger the exemption in all circumstances. One must also be functioning in that capacity for the exemption to apply. . . . Thus we hold as a matter of statutory interpretation that members of the clergy counseling their parishioners in the religious context are not subject to the reporting requirement [under the state child abuse reporting law]." However, the court concluded that two "religious counselors" who were not ordained or licensed ministers could be prosecuted criminally for failure to report incidents of abuse that had been disclosed to them. The court concluded that the criminal conviction of the non-clergy "religious counselors" did not violate the first amendment guaranty of religious freedom.[121]*

Example. *A federal district court in Wisconsin ruled that a church was not legally responsible for the molestation of a young boy by a teacher at the church's school. It rejected the victim's claim that the church was responsible on the basis of a failure to report the abuse to civil authorities as required by state law. The court conceded that the school administrator had "reasonable cause to suspect" that one of his teachers had committed child sexual abuse, and was obligated to alert the authorities under the state child abuse reporting law. However, the court emphasized that the church's breach of its duty to report the suspected abuse to civil authorities could not have been the cause of the victim's injuries since the victim could not prove that any of the acts of molestation occurred after the time a child abuse report should have been filed.[122]*

---

[120] Marshall v. First Baptist Church, 949 S.W.2d 504 (Tex. App. 1997).

[121] State v. Motherwell, 788 P.2d 1066 (Wash. 1990). *See also* Wilson v. Darr, 553 N.W.2d 579 (Iowa 1996), in which the Iowa Supreme Court observed, "The legislature did not include members of the clergy among those that are required to report child abuse under [state law]. Because it is common knowledge that clergymen engage in activities within a religious context that might unearth abusive situations, that omission must be deemed to have been a conscious choice to exclude this profession from the reporting requirements of the statute."

[122] Kendrick v. East Delavan Baptist Church, 886 F. Supp. 1465 (E.D. Wis. 1995).

STEPS CLERGY SHOULD TAKE AFTER RECEIVING AN ALLEGATION OF CHILD ABUSE

Clergy who learn of allegations of child abuse should consult with a local attorney and address the following questions:

• Am I a mandatory or a permissive reporter under state law?

• If the allegations are true, do they constitute child abuse as defined under state law? Remember, in some states the definition of child abuse is limited to abuse inflicted by a parent or person responsible for a child's care.

• Do I have reasonable cause to believe that abuse has occurred? Be sure to interpret this broadly. An alleged offender's denial of any wrongdoing does not preclude reasonable cause. Remember, offenders typically deny any wrongdoing.

• Did I receive the information in the course of spiritual counseling? If so, does the clergy-penitent privilege protect me from disclosing this information? In a few states, it does.

• How severe was the abuse? Evaluate the severity of the alleged abuse and the possible existence of other victims of the same perpetrator.

• Did the alleged abuse involve pedophilic behavior (sexual contact with a pre-adolescent child)? If so, respond aggressively since pedophilia is considered to be incurable and many pedophiles have hundreds of victims over the course of a lifetime.

• Do I have any risk of civil liability under state law if I choose not to report the abuse? It is possible that abuse victims will be permitted to sue clergy who fail to report (even if they are not mandatory reporters) if their injuries are aggravated and perpetuated because of the failure to report.

• Should I candidly (but anonymously) discuss the available evidence with the state agency that receives child abuse reports to determine whether the agency believes that a report should be filed?

• Should I try to persuade the informant to report the abuse? If the informant is unwilling, offer to accompany him or her to the police station or state agency that receives reports of abuse. If this does not work, then ask for the informant's permission to file a report yourself.

• Can child abuse be reported to law enforcement officials in my state? Some states permit this. If you are in such a state, and you have a law enforcement officer in your congregation, consider reporting to that person.

---

§ 4-09   Diversion of Church Funds

Key point 4-09. Clergy who divert church funds to their personal use face possible criminal and civil liability.

Church income ordinarily consists of designated and undesignated contributions, interest on bank accounts, gain on investments, and rent from church-owned properties. Some churches have income from the rendition of services, such as the operation of child care facilities, private schools, or counseling services. Church income, from whatever source, is held by the church in trust for the church's religious and charitable purposes. Such a trust may be express, as when a donor contributes funds for a specified purpose, or implied, as when funds are contributed without designation regarding their use or constitute rents, interest income, service income, or gains.[123]

The principle that church funds and assets are held in trust for the religious and charitable uses of the church is codified in the Internal Revenue Code, which conditions the exemption of churches from federal income taxation on several factors, including the following: (1) none of a church's net earnings inures to the benefit of a private individual, except for the payment of reasonable compensation for services rendered, and (2) a church is organized and operated exclusively for religious purposes.[124]

Ministers who divert church funds to their own benefit in excess of their stated compensation may be personally liable on the basis of several legal theories, including breach of trust, embezzlement, fraud, conversion, securities law violations, and theft. In addition, the tax-exempt status of their church may be jeopardized, and a state investigation could result. Diversion of church funds by a minister can be intentional, but often is inadvertent. For example, diversion of church funds by clergy to compensate themselves for travel or entertainment expenses allegedly incurred on behalf of a church may be considered improper if done without proper authorization.

There have been many notable cases of ministers being found guilty of diversion of church funds. To illustrate, the Founding Church of Scientology lost its exemption from federal income taxation in 1969 because of unexplained payments to its founder in the form of loans and reimbursement of expenses in excess of his salary, even though the amounts of such payments were small. The court observed that Congress, "when conditioning the exemption upon 'no part' of the earnings being of benefit to a private individual, specifically intended that the amount or extent of benefit should not be the determining factor."[125]

The Reverend Sun Myung Moon was convicted of tax fraud for failure to report interest income on certain bank accounts that were held in his name, despite his allegation that he held the funds as "trustee" for the Unification Church.[126] The court concluded, "[T]he government presented evidence . . . that Moon controlled the [bank] accounts, . . . held them in his name, considered [them] his own, used the accounts in a seemingly personal manner, and was regarded by other Church figures as owning the assets personally. . . . Because he owned the assets, he should have reported the interest . . . on his tax return. Since he failed to do so, his returns were false."[127] The court rejected Moon's "messiah defense" that the church was exempt from paying taxes on its income and therefore he was too since he was "potentially the new messiah" and therefore personified the church and was indistinguishable from it.

In another case, a church had three checking accounts. Two of the accounts were in the church's name and required checks to be signed by the minister and two other persons. The third account was in the name of the minister, and only his signature was required for withdrawals. Over the course of many years, funds

---

[123] *See generally* G. Bogert, The Law of Trusts and Trustees § 371 (1977 & suppl. 1999).
[124] I.R.C. § 501(c)(3).
[125] Founding Church of Scientology v. United States, 412 F.2d 1197, 1202 (Ct. Cl. 1969), *cert. denied*, 397 U.S. 1009 (1970).
[126] United States v. Moon, 718 F.2d 1210 (2nd Cir. 1983).
[127] *Id.* at 1222.

from many sources were deposited in each of the accounts and withdrawn for various purposes. The minister was charged with embezzlement and fraudulent conversion to his own use of certain funds in the checking account that was in his name.[128]

In summary, ministers ordinarily should not permit church funds or assets to be placed in their names; bank checking and savings accounts should require the signature of two unrelated persons; ministers should not pay for their personal or business expenses out of church funds without written authorization; and they should not accept favorable loans and other financial benefits out of church funds in excess of their stated compensation without the advice of legal counsel.[129]

§ 4-10 State Regulation of Psychologists and Counselors

Key point 4-10. Every state strictly regulates the practice of both psychology and counseling. However, pastoral counseling within a church to members of the congregation does not constitute the unauthorized practice of either psychology or counseling. Clergy who establish counseling ministries outside of this limited context may be liable for the unauthorized practice of either psychology or counseling.

One of the principal functions of most ministers is acting as a counselor. Many ministers spend several hours each week in counseling sessions with church members and others. Some ministers have left the pastoral ministry to open full-time counseling ministries independent of their church. Some churches employ associate ministers with special training specifically in counseling. Do state laws regulating the practice of psychology or counseling apply in any of these situations?

All fifty states have enacted statutes regulating the practice of psychology.[130] These statutes prohibit persons from practicing psychology or representing that they are psychologists unless they are certified or licensed by the state. The purpose of such statutes is to protect the public against "charlatans and quacks who, despite inadequate training and professional experience, guarantee easy solutions to psychological problems."[131]

Psychologist regulation statutes fall into two general categories. *Certification laws* do not prevent persons from practicing psychology, but rather prohibit use of the title "psychologist" or any of its derivatives by persons who are not certified psychologists. *Licensure laws* prohibit the practice of psychology by anyone who is not a licensed psychologist. Certification laws have been criticized for not adequately protecting the public against unqualified practitioners. Licensure statutes have been criticized as being too restrictive. A typical certification statute provides:

No person shall, without a valid, existing certificate of registration as a psychologist issued by the [state] attach the title "psychologist" to his name and under such title render or offer to render services to individuals, corporations, or the public for remuneration or a fee; or render or offer to render to individuals, corporations, or the public, services if the words "psychological," "psychologic," "psychologist," or "psychology" are used to describe such services by the person or organization offering to render or rendering them.[132]

---

[128] Commonwealth v. Nichols, 213 A.2d 105 (Pa. 1965).
[129] *See generally* Comment, 73 J. CRIM. L. & CRIMINOL. 1204 (1982).
[130] *See generally* Note, *State Regulation of Psychologists*, 58 WASH. U. L. Q. 639 (1980).
[131] National Psychologist Association v. University of New York, 203 N.Y.S.2d 821 (1960).
[132] ILL. REV. STAT. ch. 111, § 5303.

Certification is obtained from state authorities through an application process. Applicants ordinarily must demonstrate that they are at least 21 years of age, of good moral character, and a citizen of the United States. In addition, they must have earned a specified degree in psychology and have practiced psychology for a minimum number of years.

Licensure statutes prohibit any person from engaging in the practice of "psychology" without a valid license. A typical licensing statute provides, "No person shall practice as a psychologist . . . unless he is validly licensed and registered."[133] Licensing statutes differ in their definition of the phrase "practice of psychology." Some statutes define the term broadly. For example, one statute provides:

The "practice of psychology" . . . is defined as rendering to individuals, groups, organizations, or the public any psychological service involving the application of principles, methods, and procedures of understanding, predicting and influencing behavior, such as the principles pertaining to learning, perception, motivation, thinking, emotion, and interpersonal relationships; the methods and procedures of interviewing, counseling, behavior modification, and psychotherapy; of constructing, administering, and interpreting tests of mental abilities, aptitudes, interests, attitudes, personality characteristics, emotion, and motivation; and of assessing public opinion.[134]

Other statutes define *practice of psychology* more narrowly.[135]

All licensing statutes exempt certain activities from the definition of *practice of psychology*. Exemptions vary from state to state, but the following exemptions are common: (1) professional activities of lawyers, physicians, clergymen, social workers, sociologists, and counselors; (2) activities of government employees in the ordinary course of their employment; (3) activities of a student, intern, or resident in psychology, pursuing a course of study at an accredited university; (4) educational activities of teachers in public and private schools, or the authorized duties of guidance counselors.[136]

---

[133] Mo. Rev. Stat. § 337.015.
[134] *Id. See also* Colo. Rev. Stat. § 12-43-108; Ga. Ann. Code § 84-3101; Ky. Rev. Stat. § 319.010; Okla. Stat. Ann. Title 59, § 1352.
[135] *See, e.g.*, Ariz. Rev. Stat. Ann. § 32-2061; Minn. Stat. Ann. § 148.81; N.Y. Educ. Law § 7601.
[136] For examples of statutes that exempt certain activities of clergy from the "practice of psychology," *see, e.g.*, Ark. Stat. Ann. § 17-96-103 ("nothing in this chapter shall be construed to limit the professional pursuits of . . . clergymen . . . from full performance of their professional duties"); Ill. Ann. Stat. ch. 111, § 5353 ("duly recognized members of any bona fide religious denomination shall not be restricted from functioning in their ministerial capacity provided they do not represent themselves as being clinical psychologists or providing clinical psychological services"); Kan. Stat. Ann. § 74-5344 ("nothing contained in this act shall be construed to prevent qualified . . . ministers . . . from doing work of a psychological nature consistent with their training and consistent with any code of ethics of their respective professions so long as they do not hold themselves out to the public by any title or description of services incorporating the words 'psychologic,' 'psychological,' 'psychologist' or 'psychology'"); Ky. Rev. Stat. Ann. § 319.015 ("nothing in this chapter shall be construed to limit . . . a duly ordained minister, priest, rabbi, Christian Science practitioner, or other clergyman from carrying out his responsibilities while functioning in his ministerial capacity within a recognized religious organization serving the spiritual needs of its constituency, provided he does not hold himself out as a psychologist"); Mo. Rev. Stat. § 337.045 ("nothing in sections 337.010 to 337.090 shall in any way limit qualified members of other professional groups such as . . . clergymen . . . from doing work of a psychological nature consistent with their training and consistent with any code of ethics of their respective professions"); Okla. Stat. title 59, § 1353 ("the provisions of the Psychologists Licensing Act shall not apply to qualified members of other professions, including but not limited to . . . pastoral counselors doing work of a psychological nature consistent with their training and consistent with the code of ethics of their respective professions provided they do not hold themselves out to the public by any title or description incorporating the work psychological, psychologist, or psychology"); Tenn. Code Ann. § 63-11-206 ("nothing in this chapter shall be construed to limit the professional pursuits of teachers in public and private schools, [or] clergymen . . . from full performance of their professional duties"); Tex. Rev. Civ. Stat. Ann. art. 4512c ("nothing in this Act shall be construed to apply to . . . duly ordained religions [sic] doing work of a psychological nature consistent with their training and consistent with any code of ethics of their respective professions, provided they do not represent themselves by any title or in any manner prohibited by this Act").

An application for a license to practice psychology must satisfy various requirements. Ordinarily, these are similar to the requirements for obtaining a certificate, and generally include a minimum age (typically 21), good moral character, being a resident of the state and citizen of the United States, professional experience of a prescribed duration, and the prescribed academic degree. Some states require that the academic degree be a doctoral degree based on a program of studies that were primarily psychological. Others permit a masters degree in psychology plus a longer number of years of professional experience.[137]

Several states have combined certification and licensure statutes. Such statutes prohibit anyone from practicing psychology without a license, and also prohibit use of the term *psychology* or any of its derivatives by any person who is not a licensed psychologist.[138]

Can persons engage in "counseling" if they are not licensed to practice psychology? Counseling certainly would come within an expansive definition of the term *practice of psychology*, and thus would appear to be a prohibited practice. Some courts have reached this conclusion. In one case, a state board of psychological examiners obtained a court order barring an individual who had not applied for or received a license to practice psychology from engaging in the practice of counseling. A state appeals court upheld the court order prohibiting the counselor from engaging in the practice of counseling.[139] This case resulted in the enactment of a separate licensing statute for counselors.

The validity of psychologist licensing laws has been challenged in several cases. Such statutes have been upheld despite the claims that (1) they are unconstitutionally vague; (2) they violate due process of law; (3) boards of psychologist examiners unconstitutionally combine prosecutorial and adjudicative powers; (4) they arbitrarily deny licenses to persons holding doctorate degrees in disciplines related to psychology such as vocational rehabilitation and guidance counseling; and (5) they constitute an unconstitutional delegation of legislative authority to administrative agencies without adequate standards for the agency to follow.[140]

In conclusion, ministers who are employed full-time in a pastoral ministry by a church congregation are free to counsel with church members and others in the course of their employment with their church. The same rule ordinarily will apply to ministers who are hired by a church specifically for a counseling ministry. In neither case, however, may a minister use the term *psychology* or any of its derivatives in connection with such counseling ministry unless he or she is in fact a licensed psychologist. Ministers who establish a full-time or part-time *counseling* ministry independent of a church ordinarily should not engage in professional counseling unless (1) they are specifically exempted from the prohibition against the unlicensed practice of psychology; (2) their state board of psychologist examiners does not prosecute unlicensed counselors; (3) the term *practice of psychology* is not defined broadly enough (under applicable state law) to include counseling; or (4) their state has a professional counselor licensing statute under which the counselor is licensed or exempt.

Finally, many churches maintaining counseling ministries do not charge for such services but do require counselees to make a "contribution" to the church. Such contributions, often based on the number of hours of counseling, ordinarily are deductible only to the extent that they exceed the fair market value of the counseling services received in exchange.[141]

---

[137] *See, e.g.,* MO. REV. STAT. § 337.020; OKLA. STAT. ANN. title 59, § 1362.

[138] *See, e.g.,* MO. REV. STAT. § 337.015; KY. REV. STAT. § 319.005.

[139] *See* note 130, *supra.*

[140] *Id.*

[141] *See, e.g.,* Hernandez v. Commissioner, 109 S. Ct. 2136 (1989); Rev. Rul. 76-232, 1976-1 C.B. 62. *See also* Triune of Life Church, Inc. v. Commissioner 85 T.C. 45 (1985), *aff'd,* (unpublished decision of the 3rd Circuit, June 3, 1986).

§ 4-11   Sexual Misconduct

A number of clergy have been sued for engaging in sexual relations with adult counselees or minors. To illustrate, many cases have involved sexual relations between male clergy and female counselees. The woman later sues the minister for intentional infliction of emotional distress, battery, and malpractice, among other theories of liability. Suing clergy for sexual misconduct presents certain problems for adult victims. First, clergy often will assert the "consent" defense—meaning that the "victim" consented to the relationship and accordingly should not be permitted to sue. Victims will allege that a minister's unique position of authority and respect overcame their free will and made their conduct non-consensual. Second, any theory of liability based on intentional behavior by a minister is potentially excluded from coverage under the church's general liability insurance policy. If a minister's conduct is excluded from insurance coverage, and the minister has little if any financial resources, then the victim will be left without a remedy unless she can sue the minister's church or denomination. However, lawsuits brought by victims of clergy sexual misconduct against a minister's employing church or denomination have been rejected by the courts in most cases unless the victim can prove that the church or denomination had actual knowledge of previous incidents of sexual misconduct by the same minister and did nothing to monitor or restrict the minister's activities. The issue of church or denominational liability for clergy sexual misconduct is addressed fully in chapter 10. Third, the first amendment guaranty of religious freedom affords some protection for clergy conduct. Fourth, the abolition by most states of any liability for "seduction" or "alienation of affections" may restrict if not eliminate lawsuits brought against clergy based upon sexual misconduct.

Ministers can be liable in such cases on the basis of a number of legal principles. These principles, along with possible defenses, are summarized below.

§ 4-11.1 — Theories of Liability

Key point 4-11.1. Clergy who engage in sexual contact with an adult or minor are subject to civil liability on the basis of several legal theories. They also are subject to criminal liability.

1. Malpractice

Some courts have found clergy liable on the basis of malpractice for sexual misconduct with an adult or minor. These cases are addressed in section 4-05 of this chapter.

2. Fiduciary Duty

A few courts have concluded that clergy, in some situations, owe a "fiduciary duty" toward members of their congregation, and that they can be liable for breaching this duty when they engage in sexual misconduct with a member of their congregation. For example, a few courts have concluded a fiduciary duty arises when clergy "hold themselves out" to their church and community as a skilled marriage counselor. Most of these cases have occurred in one state—Colorado.

Example. A federal appeals court ruled that a pastor who had engaged in sexual relations with two female church employees who had sought him out for marriage counseling could be sued by the women for breaching a fiduciary duty he owed them. This case suggests that clergy who act as marriage counselors may be deemed fiduciaries, and as such they are held to a very high standard of ethical behavior with regard to those they counsel. This duty is breached when a counselor engages in sexual relations with a counselee. The court also ruled that it may be breached by "betraying confidences" obtained in a "relation of trust" (such as a counseling relationship). In other words, apart from the sexual misconduct, the former minister was liable to the two women for disclosing confidences he obtained during counseling sessions with them. This aspect of the ruling illustrates the importance of maintaining the confidentiality of information shared during counseling sessions. Disclosing such information without permission may lead to legal liability based on a breach of the counselor's fiduciary duties.[142]

Example. *The Colorado Supreme Court ruled that a victim of clergy sexual misconduct could sue the minister for breaching his fiduciary duty. A married couple who were experiencing marital problems sought marriage counseling from their parish priest. The husband and wife were both Catholics and "had faith and confidence" in their priest. During the course of counseling, the priest developed an intimate relationship with the wife that contributed directly to the dissolution of her marriage. The wife alleged that the priest, as one who held himself out to her as a professional and trained marriage counselor, breached his "fiduciary duty" to her. The court noted that a marriage counselor has a "fiduciary duty" toward a counselee to act "with utmost good faith and solely for the benefit of" the counselee. The court concluded that the priest violated his fiduciary duty toward the wife if the allegations in her complaint were true.[143]*

Example. *The Colorado Supreme Court ruled that an Episcopal diocese and bishop were responsible for a pastor's sexual misconduct with a female member of the congregation who had sought him out for counseling. The court concluded that the bishop and diocese breached their "fiduciary duty" to the victim. The court noted that a fiduciary relationship exists when there is a special relationship of trust, confidence and reliance between two persons, and when one of them assumes a duty to act in the other's best interests. The court acknowledged that the clergy-parishioner relationship "is not necessarily a fiduciary relationship." However, the clergy-parishioner relationship often involves "the type of interaction that creates trust and reliance" and in some cases will constitute a fiduciary relationship. The court concluded that a fiduciary relationship existed between the bishop and the victim on the basis of the following factors: (1) The bishop was in a superior position and was able to exert substantial influence over the victim. An unequal relationship between two parties can be evidence of a fiduciary relationship, since the party with the greater influence and authority often assumes a duty to act in the dependent party's best interests. (2) The bishop, in his meeting with the victim, served as a counselor to the victim and not as a representative of the diocese. If he was acting only as a representative of the diocese, he failed to convey that fact to the victim and led her to believe that he was acting in her interest. The court concluded that the bishop and diocese had breached their fiduciary duty to the victim by not acting in her "utmost good faith" (by taking no action to help her, not assisting her in understanding that she was not solely responsible for the sexual relationship, and not recommending counseling for her).[144]*

Example. *A Colorado court ruled that a minister could be sued by a woman with whom he had sexual contacts. A woman (the victim) attended a church for a few years, and began to volunteer her services for a variety of activities including the remodeling of a classroom. She engaged in these volunteer services on the recommendation of a therapist who suggested that she work in a "safe environment" to overcome her fears of the workplace. The victim's volunteer work caused her to come in contact with her minister after normal working hours. On one occasion the minister approached her while she was remodeling a*

---

[142] Sanders v. Casa View Baptist Church, 134 F.3d 331 (5th Cir. 1998).
[143] Destefano v. Grabian, 763 P.2d 275 (Colo. 1988).
[144] Moses v. Diocese of Colorado, 863 P.2d 310 (Colo. 1993).

classroom, began caressing her back, and told her "I love you Dianne, you mean so much to me." Following this incident the victim became physically ill and cried. A few days later, the minister called the victim into his office where the two of them sat next to each other on a small couch. The minister again caressed her and expressed his love for her. Following a third incident, the victim informed two other women in the church about the minister's behavior, and one responded, "Oh my God, not you too." The victim later sued the minister, claiming that he had breached his fiduciary duty toward her. A state appeals court rejected the claim that no fiduciary relationship existed between the victim and the minister. The court noted that the minister had counseled the victim on personal and intimate matters, and that such counseling was enough to establish a fiduciary relationship.[145]

Example. The Colorado Supreme Court ruled that a pastor who molested a young boy could be sued for his behavior on the basis of a breach of a fiduciary duty. A 7-year-old boy (the "victim"), who was experiencing emotional trauma, was encouraged by his pastor to enter into a counseling relationship with him. The boy's mother approved, and the counseling sessions lasted for a number of years. From the very first counseling session the victim claimed that the pastor engaged in sexual contact with him, including having him sit on the pastor's lap while the pastor massaged his thighs and genitals. While these "massages" were occurring the pastor would tell the victim that "your father loves you, your mother loves you, God loves you, and I love you." Two other adult males claimed that the pastor had engaged in similar behavior with them when they were minors, including a physical inspection of their genitals to see if they had been "properly circumcised." The court ruled that the victim could sue the pastor for breaching a fiduciary duty.[146]

Example. An Oregon state appeals court ruled that a victim of clergy sexual misconduct could sue her minister.[147] The woman sued the minister for "breach of confidential relationship." The woman alleged that her minister abused his pastoral and counseling relationships with her by "manipulating" her into having sexual relations with him. She claimed to have suffered sexual abuse, extreme emotional distress, physical illness, loss of sleep and memory, clinical depression, and loss of her "ability to trust other adults, to trust authority, and to deal with religion and faith in God." A state appeals court concluded that the woman's lawsuit stated facts which, if proven true, could possibly result in legal liability. The court concluded that the facts alleged in the lawsuit stated a claim for breach of confidential relationship. It rejected the minister's argument that the claims against him were really an attempt to sue him for "seduction"—a legal theory that had been eliminated by the Oregon legislature in 1973. The fact that the minister allegedly used seduction as a means of breaching his confidential relationship with the woman, and to intentionally cause her emotional distress, did "not convert her claim into one for seduction."

Most courts have refused to hold ministers liable for their sexual misconduct on the basis of a fiduciary duty. In some cases this is because the court refuses to recognize breach of fiduciary duty as a basis for legal liability. In other cases, the ministers did not hold themselves out as marriage counselors or engage in other behavior giving rise to a fiduciary duty.

Example. A Florida court ruled that it was barred by the first amendment from resolving a woman's claim that her priest and church were responsible on the basis of a breach of a fiduciary duty for the priest's acts of sexual misconduct.[148] The woman had sought out a priest for marital counseling and

---

[145] Winkler v. Rocky Mountain Conference, 923 P.2d 152 (Colo. App. 1995).
[146] Bear Valley Church of Christ v. DeBose, 928 P.2d 1315 (Colo. 1996).
[147] Erickson v. Christenson, 781 P.2d 383 (Or. App. 1989).
[148] Doe v. Evans, 718 So.2d 286 (Fla. App. 1998).

alleged that the priest engaged in sexual contacts with her. The woman sued her church and diocese, claiming that they were aware of prior incidents involving sexual misconduct during counseling by the same priest. Despite this knowledge, nothing was done to address the problem. She claimed that the priest breached a fiduciary duty by becoming romantically involved with her, and that the church and diocese had a fiduciary relationship with her (because she reported the priest's misconduct to them) that was breached. A state appeals court concluded that resolving the woman's breach of fiduciary duty claims (against the priest, church, and diocese) would constitute excessive entanglement between church and state in violation of the first amendment: "Taking the allegations of [her] complaint as true, [she] alleged the church defendants owed her a fiduciary duty, yet definition of that duty necessarily involves the secular court in church practices, doctrines, and belief. To establish a breach of the fiduciary duty allegedly owed to [her] by the church defendants, [she] would need to establish the church remained inactive in the face of her allegations against [the priest]. However, the church's policies undoubtedly differ from the rules of another employer, and may require the nonsecular employer to respond differently when faced with such allegations. When a secular court interprets church law, policies, and practices it becomes excessively entangled in religion. We align ourselves with those courts finding a first amendment bar to a breach of fiduciary duty claim as against church defendants, concluding resolution of such a claim would necessarily require the secular court to review and interpret church law, policies, and practices."

Example. *An Illinois court ruled that a husband whose wife was seduced by her pastor could not sue the pastor for breach of a fiduciary duty. The court noted that Illinois law prohibits "the recognition of an action for breach of fiduciary duty premised upon the counseling relationship between a cleric and a church member with whom the cleric had been sexually involved." The court further noted that courts in a few states have reached the opposite conclusion, but it insisted that "when a parishioner lodges such a claim, religion is not merely incidental to a plaintiff's relationship with a defendant, it is the foundation for it. . . . The fiduciary relationship is inescapably premised upon the cleric's status as an expert in theological and spiritual matters."* [149]

Example. *The Nebraska Supreme Court ruled that a priest was not liable on the basis of a breach of any fiduciary duty for his sexual contacts with a woman who had come to him for counseling. The woman claimed that the priest had a fiduciary obligation to refrain from doing anything that might harm her relationship with her husband and children, and that he breached this duty. The court acknowledged that "[s]everal cases have allowed recovery on the theory of breach of fiduciary duty with regard to sexual misconduct of a member of the clergy with a parishioner." However, it stressed that this theory of liability has been rejected by other courts because of "constitutional difficulties with regard to defining a standard of care."* [150]

Example. *A federal court in New York refused to find a pastor liable for his alleged sexual seduction of a church member he had counseled for several years.[151] The woman sued the pastor on the basis of an alleged breach of a fiduciary duty. The court noted that this basis of liability was simply a variation of clergy malpractice. It pointed out that neither the state legislature nor any court had recognized clergy malpractice as a basis for liability, and therefore the woman's lawsuit had to be dismissed.*

---

[149] Amato v. Greenquist, 679 N.E.2d 446 (Ill. App. 1997).
[150] Nebraska Supreme Court issues an important ruling; Schieffer v. Catholic Archdiocese, 508 N.W.2d 907 (Neb. 1993).
[151] Schmidt v. Bishop, 779 F. Supp. 321 (S.D.N.Y. 1991). *Accord* Langford v. Roman Catholic Diocese, 677 N.Y.S.2d 436 (A.D. 1998).

Example. The Ohio Supreme Court rejected a woman's attempt to sue her church and pastor for injuries she allegedly suffered because of a sexual relationship with her pastor.[152] A husband and wife who had been experiencing marital problems went to a Lutheran minister for counseling. They selected him because "he held himself out to the public . . . as a minister and counselor trained and able to provide counseling for marital difficulties." During the final three or four weeks of counseling, the minister allegedly engaged in consensual sexual relations with the wife. These relations, and the counseling, ended when the husband learned of the affair. The husband, who was later divorced from his wife, sued both the minister and his church. The suit against the minister alleged a breach of fiduciary duty, among other things. The state supreme court dismissed all of the husband's claims. It noted that the breach of fiduciary claim, like the husband's other claims, had to be dismissed since they all sought damages based on the minister's seduction of the wife, and as such were barred by the state law prohibiting lawsuits based on "alienation of affections."

Example. The Oklahoma Supreme Court ruled that a pastor was not liable on the basis of a breach of a fiduciary duty for sexual contacts he had with a woman during counseling. In rejecting this basis of liability, the court noted that only "[o]ne court has followed this view" and that "[o]ther courts have declined to use this fiduciary or trust theory for various reasons." The court concluded that "[w]e need not determine if the fiduciary theory applies to the facts before us, because . . . the underlying conduct at issue does not invade a legally recognized right of the husband. . . . We conclude that the husband's claims arising from the affair are not cognizable." The court noted that the Oklahoma legislature had abolished the torts of alienation of affections.[153]

3. EMOTIONAL DISTRESS ("OUTRAGEOUS CONDUCT")

Some clergy who have engaged in sexual misconduct have been sued by their victims on the basis of intentional infliction of emotional distress (sometimes referred to as "outrageous conduct"). This is a very difficult wrong to prove. The elements of an intentional infliction of emotional distress claim are (1) the defendant acted intentionally or recklessly; (2) the conduct was extreme and outrageous; (3) the actions of the defendant caused the victim emotional distress; and (4) the emotional distress suffered by the victim was extreme and severe. Generally, liability is proven "only when the conduct has been so outrageous in character, and so extreme in degree, as to go beyond all possible bounds of decency, and to be regarded as atrocious, and utterly intolerable in a civilized community."[154] One court has further explained that

> [t]here must be substantial evidence of extreme conduct: It has not been enough that the defendant has acted with an intent which is tortious or even criminal, or that [he or she] has intended to inflict emotional distress, or even that [his or her] conduct has been characterized by malice, or a degree of aggravation that would entitle the plaintiff to punitive damages for another tort.[155]

Example. The Colorado Supreme Court ruled that a victim of clergy sexual misconduct could sue the minister for intentional infliction of emotional distress (or "outrageous conduct"). The court concluded

---

[152] Stock v. Pressnell, 527 N.E.2d 1235 (Ohio 1988).

[153] Bladen v. First Presbyterian Church, 857 P.2d 789 (Okla. 1993).

[154] Hanssen v. Our Redeemer Lutheran Church, 938 S.W.2d 85 (Tex. App. 1997). *See also* Bear Valley Church of Christ v. DeBose, 928 P.2d 1315 (Colo. 1996); Doe v. Hartford Roman Catholic Diocesan Corporation, 716 A.2d 960 (Conn. Super. 1998); Singleton v. Christ the Servant Evangelical Lutheran Church, 541 N.W.2d 606 (Minn. App. 1996); Brown v. Pearson, 483 S.E.2d 477 (S.C. App. 1997). Most courts refer to section 46 of the Restatement (Second) of Torts, a respected legal treatise.

[155] John v. Estate of Hartgerink, 528 N.W.2d 539 (Iowa 1995).

that the wife could sue the priest for outrageous conduct if she could establish that the priest was guilty of "extreme and outrageous conduct" that intentionally caused the wife "severe emotional distress."[156]

Example. *An Illinois court ruled that a husband whose wife was seduced by her pastor could sue the pastor for intentionally inflicting emotional distress as a result of marital counseling he performed for the husband without disclosing the affair. The court noted that for the pastor to be guilty of intentional infliction of emotional distress, the former husband had to prove facts "establishing that the [pastor's] conduct was extreme and outrageous and that [he] either intended his conduct to inflict severe emotional distress or knew that there was a high probability that the conduct would cause such distress." Such a basis of liability exists "only where the conduct complained of is so outrageous as to go beyond all bounds of decency, and to be regarded as atrocious, and utterly intolerable in a civil community." The court noted that the former husband had sought counseling from the pastor "concerning his failing marriage," and it concluded that the pastor "acted in an extreme and outrageous manner by counseling the [husband] while [he] was involved with [the wife] and by counseling in a manner designed to covertly undermine the couple's marriage."[157]*

Example. *The Nebraska Supreme Court ruled that a priest could not be sued for infliction of emotional distress by a woman with whom he engaged in sexual relations. The woman alleged that the conduct of her priest was outrageous and extreme and caused her severe emotional distress. As a direct result of that conduct, the woman allegedly suffered severe and permanent emotional injury and incurred current and future medical expenses. She also claimed that she had lost faith in the Catholic Church and in God. The court observed that intentional infliction of emotional distress requires proof of the following three elements: (1) intentional or reckless conduct; (2) the conduct is so outrageous in character and so extreme in degree as to go beyond all possible bounds of decency and is to be regarded as atrocious and utterly intolerable in a civilized community; and (3) the conduct caused emotional distress so severe that no reasonable person should be expected to endure it. In rejecting this theory of liability the court observed, "A sexual relationship between two consenting adults is not outrageous conduct such as to give rise to a claim for intentional infliction of emotional distress. This seems especially true given the fact that the [woman and the priest] engaged in an approximate 7-year sexual relationship."[158]*

Example. *An Oregon state appeals court ruled that a victim of clergy sexual misconduct could sue her minister.[159] The woman sued the minister for "intentional infliction of emotional distress." The woman alleged that her minister abused his pastoral and counseling relationships with her by "manipulating" her into having sexual relations with him. She claimed to have suffered sexual abuse, extreme emotional distress, physical illness, loss of sleep and memory, clinical depression, and loss of her "ability to trust other adults, to trust authority, and to deal with religion and faith in God." A state appeals court concluded that the woman's lawsuit stated facts which, if proven true, could possibly result in legal liability. The court concluded that the facts alleged in the lawsuit stated a claim for intentional infliction of emotional distress by the minister. It rejected the minister's argument that the claims against him were really an attempt to sue him for "seduction"—a legal theory that had been eliminated by the Oregon legislature in 1973. The fact that the minister allegedly used seduction as a means of breaching*

---

[156] Destefano v. Grabian, 763 P.2d 275 (Colo. 1988).

[157] Amato v. Greenquist, 679 N.E.2d 446 (Ill. App. 1997).

[158] Nebraska Supreme Court issues an important ruling; Schieffer v. Catholic Archdiocese, 508 N.W.2d 907 (Neb. 1993).

[159] Erickson v. Christenson, 781 P.2d 383 (Or. App. 1989).

his confidential relationship with the woman, and to intentionally cause her emotional distress, did "not convert her claim into one for seduction."

4. ASSAULT AND BATTERY

Clergy who engage in inappropriate sexual contacts with others may be subject to civil and criminal liability for their actions. Assault and battery not only are crimes, but they also are intentional torts (meaning that they can be the basis for civil lawsuits seeking money damages).

5. SEXUAL HARASSMENT

Sexual harassment is a form of "sex discrimination" prohibited by Title VII of the Civil Rights Act of 1964. Equal Employment Opportunity Commission (EEOC) regulations define sexual harassment as follows:

Unwelcome sexual advances, requests for sexual favors, and other verbal or physical conduct of a sexual nature constitute sexual harassment when (1) submission to such conduct is made either explicitly or implicitly a term or condition of an individual's employment, (2) submission to or rejection of such conduct by an individual is used as the basis for employment decisions affecting such individual, or (3) such conduct has the purpose or effect of unreasonably interfering with an individual's work performance or creating an intimidating, hostile, or offensive working environment.

This definition confirms the conclusion reached by numerous state and federal courts that sexual harassment includes *at least two separate types of conduct:*

*   *"quid pro quo" harassment*, which refers to conditioning employment opportunities on submission to a sexual or social relationship, and

*   *"hostile environment" harassment*, which refers to the creation of an intimidating, hostile, or offensive working environment through unwelcome verbal or physical conduct of a sexual nature.

Many states have enacted similar statutes. Clergy may be personally liable for sexual harassment under some of these laws. The liability of a church for a minister's acts of sexual harassment is addressed in chapter 9.

Example. An Ohio appeals court ruled that a minister could be sued for his alleged acts of sexual harassment.[160] A woman served some ten years as parish secretary of a church prior to the arrival of a new minister. Soon after the arrival of the new minister, the secretary began alleging that the minister was engaging in acts of sexual harassment against her. Initially, the secretary contacted the bishop of the diocese with her complaint. He promised to make an investigation and apparently did, but concluded that, although he believed she was sincere in her allegations, there was nothing that he could do because the minister denied any wrongdoing, and the bishop felt he could not resolve the credibility issue. The bishop did, during the investigation, order the work hours of the minister and secretary to be so staggered that they would not be working at the same time. After hearing that the bishop would take no further action, the woman wrote to the minister in question, the standing committee of the diocese, the vestry, the warden, and the bishop in an attempt to resolve what she called "this terrible problem."

---

[160] Davis v. Black, 591 N.E.2d 11 (Ohio App. 1991).

Upon receipt of this letter, the minister called the chancellor of the diocese, who advised him to fire the secretary. The minister thereafter was instructed by the vestry of the church to notify the congregation that the secretary had been fired and to give a reason. Accordingly, the minister published in the parish newsletter a statement that the secretary had been engaging in an open malicious endeavor to discredit him. Following her dismissal, the former secretary filed a lawsuit against the minister, her church, and the diocese. She based her lawsuit on several legal grounds, including sexual harassment. A state appeals court ruled that there was sufficient evidence of sexual harassment by the minister to allow the case to proceed to trial.

6. Criminal and Statutory Liability

Sexual contact between clergy and a counselee may constitute a crime under state law. Many states have enacted legislation making it a crime for "psychotherapists" to engage in sexual contact with a counselee, and some of these laws define the term *psychotherapist* to include clergy.[161] Other states have enacted legislation giving counselees a statutory right to sue counselors for sexual misconduct.

Example. *A federal appeals court ruled that a pastor could be liable under a state law imposing liability on "psychotherapists" for engaging in sexual contact with counselees.[162] A woman sued a pastoral counselor alleging that the counselor had engaged in sexual relations with her. The court permitted the woman to sue the pastor for violating the Illinois Sexual Exploitation in Psychotherapy Act. This Act permits counselees to sue a psychotherapist for sexual contact. While the Act excludes "counseling of a spiritual or religious nature" from liability, the court noted that this exclusion would not apply to purely "secular" counseling by a pastor.*

Example. *A Minnesota appeals court ruled that a minister could be criminally liable for sexually seducing a female counselee.[163] The minister was approached by a married female church member who desired counseling. At the conclusion of one counseling session that explored the subject of grief, the pastor gave the woman a brief hug. The following week she asked the pastor if they were engaged in "normal counseling," and he replied that he loved her. The session ended with the two engaged in hugging and passionate kissing. Two days later, the woman went back to clarify that their relationship would remain "platonic" and non-sexual. At that meeting, the two engaged in hugging and kissing. The pastor gave the woman a rose as a symbol that their relationship would forever remain "pure and chaste from afar" and that he would "maintain her virginity." A month later, the two went to a motel and engaged in sexual intercourse for the first time. The woman testified that the pastor assured her that it was a "good" sexual encounter because he was unselfish. He also informed her that sex between a counselor and counselee was a felony in Minnesota. The two engaged in sexual intercourse on at least*

---

[161] *See, e.g.,* Iowa Code § 709.15 (makes "sexual abuse by a counselor or therapist" a crime, and defines "counselor or therapist" to include a "member of the clergy" who "provides or purports to provide mental health services"); Minn. Stat. § 609.345 (makes it a felony for a "psychotherapist" to engage in "sexual contact" with a counselee during a counseling session, or at any time if the counselee is "emotionally dependent upon the psychotherapist" or the sexual contact occurred by means of "therapeutic deception," and defines "psychotherapist" to include clergy who engage in counseling activities); N.D. Cent. Code § 12.1-20-06.1 (makes it a felony for a therapist to have sexual contact with a counselee and defines the term "therapist" to include a "member of the clergy" who engages in counseling or any other effort to treat a mental or emotional condition); Tex. Civ. Pract. & Rem. Code, title 4, § 81.001 et seq. (makes "sexual exploitation" of a patient by a "mental health services provider" a felony, and defines a mental health services provider to include a "member of the clergy" not engaged in "religious, moral, or spiritual counseling, teaching, and instruction"); Wis. Stat. § 940.22 (makes "sexual contact" between a "therapist" and a counselee a felony offense, and defines "therapist" to include a "member of the clergy" who engages in counseling or any other effort to treat a mental or emotional condition).

[162] Dausch v. Rykse, 52 F.3d 1425 (7th Cir. 1994).

[163] State v. Dutton, 450 N.W.2d 189 (Minn. App. 1990).

two other occasions over the next few months. The woman testified that the pastor assured her that sexual contact and intercourse was consistent with her "treatment" because it would remove her inhibitions about sex and "set her free" from her sexual "hang-ups." The pastor was later prosecuted for criminal sexual contact under a state law prohibiting sexual contact by a "psychotherapist" with an "emotionally dependent" patient, or sexual contact by a psychotherapist with a patient occurring by means of "therapeutic deception." A jury convicted the pastor on four felony counts, and he appealed. In upholding the conviction, a state appeals court concluded that the pastor was a psychotherapist since he had assumed the role of a counselor, and that he had in fact committed both sexual contact and sexual intercourse with an "emotionally dependent" patient, and that the sexual contact and intercourse occurred because of "therapeutic deception."

Example. *A minister was sentenced to two consecutive life sentences for 3 acts of rape and 8 first-degree sexual offenses perpetrated on 4 women. The minister professed his innocence during his trial, but the prosecutor introduced into evidence several "love letters" the minister had written to at least one of the victims, along with several pornographic magazines and videos found in the minister's apartment. The magazines and videos were introduced by the prosecutor to rebut the minister's attempt to portray himself as an exemplary "family man" and minister. A North Carolina appeals court rejected the minister's claim that the 2 consecutive life sentences constituted "cruel and unusual punishment" in violation of the Constitution. This case illustrates the significant criminal liability that clergy face for acts of sexual misconduct. Of course, this is in addition to civil liability.[164]*

7. "Loss of Consortium" or Alienation of Affections

This basis of liability has been consistently rejected by the courts. It is discussed below under "defenses to liability."

§ 4-11.02 — Defenses to Liability

Key point 4-11.02. *Clergy who are sued for sexual misconduct may be able to assert one or more defenses.*

1. Consent

The courts have reached different conclusions regarding the legal effect of a person's "consent" to a sexual relationship with a minister. Some courts have concluded that sexual relations between two consenting adults cannot be the basis for liability. Other courts have reached the opposite conclusion, usually on the ground that the pastor's unique authority and status precludes voluntary consent.

Several courts have referred to section 892A of the *Restatement of Torts* (a respected legal treatise), which provides:

(1) One who effectively consents to conduct of another intended to invade his interests cannot recover in an action of tort for the conduct or for harm resulting from it.

(2) To be effective, consent must be

---

[164] State v. Woodard, 404 S.E.2d 6 (N.C. App. 1991).

(a) by one who has the capacity to consent or by a person empowered to consent for him, and

(b) to the particular conduct, or to substantially the same conduct.

(3) Conditional consent or consent restricted as to time, area or in other respects is effective only within the limits of the condition or restriction.

(4) If the actor exceeds the consent, it is not effective for the excess.

(5) Upon termination of consent its effectiveness is terminated, except as it may have become irrevocable by contract or otherwise, or except as its terms may include, expressly or by implication, a privilege to continue to act.

An official comment in the *Restatement of Torts* further explains this language:

Except in the case of persons whom the law protects for reasons of policy, such as those who are mentally immature or otherwise incompetent, no one suffers a legal wrong as the result of an act to which, unaffected by fraud, mistake or duress, he freely consents or to which he manifests apparent consent. This principle is expressed in the ancient legal maxim, volenti non fit injuria, meaning that no wrong is done to one who consents. . . .

To be effective, the consent must be given by one who has the capacity to give it or by a person empowered to consent for him. If the person consenting is a child or one of deficient mental capacity, the consent may still be effective if he is capable of appreciating the nature, extent and probable consequences of the conduct consented to, although the consent of a parent, guardian or other person responsible is not obtained or is expressly refused. If, however, the one who consents is not capable of appreciating the nature, extent or probable consequences of the conduct, the consent is not effective to bar liability unless the parent, guardian or other person empowered to consent for the incompetent has given consent, in which case the consent of the authorized person will be effective even though the incompetent does not consent; or unless there is a privilege to take emergency action . . . .

Example. *A Colorado court ruled that consent is not a defense to a pastor's sexual contacts with a minor. It observed that such a defense would be "premised on the assumption that a child is capable of giving the kind of consent the law should recognize to a sexual relationship with an adult religious counselor." The court insisted that "a child is in no position to exercise independent judgment and evaluate on an equal basis the consequences of such a relationship." The court also rejected the argument that the victim became capable of consenting to the relationship as she matured, since this "ignores that dependence, transference, and the resulting vulnerability do not cease merely because a child physically matures while sexual abuse in secrecy by an adult in a position of trust continues unabated."* [165]

Example. *The Nebraska Supreme Court ruled that a priest could not be sued by a woman with whom he engaged in sexual relations since her consent to the relationship was a complete bar to any recovery. The court observed, "What is involved in this case is conduct between consenting adults. There is no allegation that the [priest] used force or fraud to accomplish his sexual relations with the [woman]." The court continued, "In tort law, consent ordinarily bars recovery for intentional interferences with*

---

[165] Bohrer v. DeHart, 943 P.2d 1220 (Colo. App. 1996).

person or property. . . . [I]t is a fundamental principle of common law that 'to one who is willing, no wrong is done.'" The court concluded that "[a] sexual relationship between two consenting adults is not outrageous conduct such as to give rise to a claim for intentional infliction of emotional distress. This seems especially true given the fact that the [woman and the priest] engaged in an approximate 7-year sexual relationship." The court referred to section 892A of the Restatement of Torts (a respected legal treatise), which provides, "One who effectively consents to conduct of another intended to invade his interests cannot recover in an action of tort for the conduct or for harm resulting from it." An official comment in the Restatement of Torts further explains this language: "Except in the case of persons whom the law protects for reasons of policy, such as those who are mentally immature or otherwise incompetent, no one suffers a legal wrong as the result of an act to which, unaffected by fraud, mistake or duress, he freely consents or to which he manifests apparent consent." [166]

2. Statute of Limitations

Every state has enacted various "statutes of limitation" that prescribe the deadlines for filing legal claims. Clergy who are sued for sexual misconduct often assert that the lawsuit must be dismissed because it was filed after the deadline prescribed by the applicable statute of limitations expired. Some courts have recognized this defense.[167] Other courts (and some legislatures) have extended the statute of limitations deadline in cases of sexual misconduct, recognizing that in some cases victims are not fully capable of associating the misconduct with their emotional injuries until many years after the statute of limitations deadline has expired.

Example. A Maryland court ruled that a 34-year-old adult's lawsuit against two priests who molested him when he was a minor was barred by the statute of limitations. The victim was repeatedly molested by the two priests while serving as an altar boy over a period of 6 years. The victim claimed that it was not until he was 33 years old when his marriage was "falling apart" that he first became aware that he had been injured as a result of the priests' actions. He sued the priests the next year. A state appeals court concluded that the victim's lawsuit was barred by the Maryland statute of limitations, which requires personal injury lawsuits to be filed within 3 years of the date a victim "knew or, with due diligence, reasonably should have known of the wrong." The victim claimed that he was aware of the priests' conduct but did not appreciate the offensiveness of it or realize that he had been harmed until he began experiencing marital difficulties, and therefore the statute of limitations should not start running until that date. A state appeals court disagreed, concluding that "if any memory of sexual abuse suffered during childhood survives into adulthood, the statute of limitations begins to run when the victim reaches the age of majority." Further, "even if no memory at all survives into adulthood, the limitations period still begins to run on the date the victim reaches the age of majority." [168]

Example. A federal court in New York refused to find a pastor liable for his alleged sexual seduction of a church member he had counseled for several years.[169] The woman sued the pastor some 30 years after the pastor began engaging in sexual contact with her. The court noted that the statute of limitations for negligence and malpractice, under New York law, is 3 years. Since the alleged malpractice first occurred nearly 30 years ago, the woman's claims obviously were barred by the statute of limitations. The woman attempted to avoid the application of the statute of limitations in three ways, each of which was rejected by the court. First, she asked the court to apply the "delayed discovery" doctrine. By this she

---

[166] Nebraska Supreme Court issues an important ruling; Schieffer v. Catholic Archdiocese, 508 N.W.2d 907 (Neb. 1993).
[167] *See, e.g.,* Doe v. Maskell, 679 A.2d 1087 (Md. 1996).
[168] Doe v. Archdiocese of Washington, 689 A.2d 634 (Md. App. 1997).
[169] Schmidt v. Bishop, 779 F. Supp. 321 (S.D.N.Y. 1991).

meant that the statute of limitations should not start until a person "knows or should have known of the injury and the defendant's role in causing that injury." The court acknowledged that some states have adopted such a rule, particularly in the context of child sexual abuse cases. It noted that "the argument for a delayed discovery rule in this context, simply stated, is that victims of child sexual abuse often do not realize until years later either that they have been abused at all or the scope of their injuries." However, the court rejected this view: "Persuasive though this argument may be, there is not authority for the adoption of such a rule in child sex abuse cases in New York. . . . [The New York courts] have steadfastly declined to alter the traditional New York rule that the statute of limitations commences to run when a cause of action accrues, even though the plaintiff is unaware that he has a cause of action." Next, the woman argued that the pastor should be prohibited from relying on the statute of limitations because of his "misrepresentations." The court agreed that the statute of limitations can be suspended if a party's fraud or "active concealment" prevents a plaintiff from filing a timely claim. However, it disagreed that this rule applied in the present case, since the pastor had done nothing to prevent the woman from filing a timely lawsuit. Finally, the woman argued that the statute of limitations should be suspended because she "was under duress." The court rejected this claim as well, since "it is extremely doubtful whether any reasonable juror could find that [she] was under constant legal duress for a 31-year period, during most of which she lived half a continent away from the [pastor]."

Example. *The Ohio Supreme Court dismissed a lawsuit brought by a 25-year-old man who had been repeatedly molested as a minor by a church choir director. The victim had been molested by his church choir director on nearly 300 occasions over a period of 3 years (from 1981 through 1984) when he was between 15 and 18 years of age. He turned 18 in July of 1984. In July of 1991, shortly after his 25th birthday, the victim filed a lawsuit against the choir director and his church. This was long after the applicable statute of limitations had expired, but the victim insisted that he did not "discover" the nature and extent of his injuries until he sought psychological help as an adult. The court ruled that the statute of limitations began to run on the victim's 18th birthday and not when he claimed to have "discovered" that his emotional injuries were caused by the abuse. The court observed, "Here, the facts clearly establish that at the time [the victim] reached the age of majority, [he] knew that he had been sexually abused by [the choir director]. [The choir director] allegedly initiated homosexual conduct with [the victim] on two hundred to three hundred separate occasions without [his] consent. During the period of sexual abuse, [the victim] was fourteen to seventeen years of age. . . . [U]pon reaching the age of majority, [the victim] knew that he had been sexually abused, and he knew the identity of the perpetrator. Although [he] may not have discovered the full extent of his psychological injuries until [later] the fact that [he] was aware upon reaching the age of majority that he had been sexually abused by [the choir director] was sufficient to trigger the commencement of the statute of limitations for assault and battery."* [170]

3. First Amendment

Does the first amendment guaranty of religious freedom protect clergy from being sued as a result of their sexual misconduct? Most courts have said that it does not, although a few courts have reached the opposite conclusion.

Example. *The Colorado Supreme Court ruled that an Episcopal diocese and bishop were responsible for a pastor's sexual misconduct with a female member of the congregation who had sought him out for*

---

[170] Doe v. First United Methodist Church, 629 N.E.2d 402 (Ohio 1994).

counseling. It rejected the bishop's claim that the first amendment's guaranty of religious freedom prevented a civil court from addressing the victim's claims. The court acknowledged that the first amendment prevents civil courts from resolving controversies involving church doctrine. However, the court insisted that churches have no absolute immunity from being sued in cases not involving doctrine: "Civil actions against clergy members and their superiors that involve claims of a breach of fiduciary duty, negligent hiring and supervision, and vicarious liability are actionable if they are supported by competent evidence in the record. . . . [The victim's] claims in this case do not involve disputes within the church and are not based solely on ecclesiastical or disciplinary matters . . . . Our decision does not require a reading of the Constitution and Canons of the Protestant Episcopal Church or any other documents of church governance. Because the facts of this case do not require interpreting or weighing church doctrine and neutral principles of law can be applied, the first amendment is not a defense against [the victim's] claims."[171]

Example. *The Colorado Supreme Court ruled that a pastor who molested a young boy could be sued for his behavior, and that the first amendment guaranty of religious freedom was no defense. The pastor had argued that any touching of the victim that might have occurred was not designed to satisfy any sexual desires, but was intended to facilitate the minor's communication with God. The court concluded that the pastor's "massage technique" was not entitled to constitutional protection as an exercise of religion: "Although his ultimate goal . . . was for counselees to receive help from God in resolving their problems . . . his choice to use massage with children had no biblical, doctrinal, or spiritual basis . . . . Despite the religious setting, the described massage technique simply reflects [the pastor's] choice of a relaxation and communication method between himself and his counselees."[172]*

Example. *An Illinois court ruled that a pastor could be sued by a woman he had sexually seduced during marriage counseling, and that the lawsuit was not barred by the first amendment guaranty of religious freedom. The court acknowledged that "[a] court's authority to resolve disputes involving a church is narrowly circumscribed by the first amendment's guarantee that the right to the free exercise of religion will not be abridged." However, "where doctrinal controversy is not involved in a church dispute, mandatory deference to religious authority is not required by the first amendment, and the court may choose from a variety of approaches in resolving the dispute." It noted that the courts can resolve disputes over control of church property so long as they can do so on the basis of "neutral principles of law" requiring no examination of religious doctrine. The court applied the same "neutral principles of law" approach in this case involving alleged church liability for the sexual misconduct of its pastor.[173]*

Example. *A Minnesota appeals court ruled that the first amendment guaranty of religious freedom was no defense to a minister's criminal conviction for engaging in sexual contact with a vulnerable counselee.[174] The court ruled that no constitutional right protects a pastor who engages in sexual activity as part of religious counseling. The court observed, "These statutes are meant to protect vulnerable persons and allow them to reposit trust in those who can help them. The legislature has recognized the emotional devastation that can result when a psychotherapist takes advantage of a patient."*

---

[171] Moses v. Diocese of Colorado, 863 P.2d 310 (Colo. 1993).
[172] Bear Valley Church of Christ v. DeBose, 928 P.2d 1315 (Colo. 1996).
[173] Bivin v. Wright, 656 N.E.2d 1121 (Ill. App. 1995).
[174] State v. Dutton, 450 N.W.2d 189 (Minn. App. 1990).

Example. The Ohio Supreme Court rejected a woman's attempt to sue her church and pastor for injuries she allegedly suffered because of a sexual relationship with her pastor.[175] A husband and wife who had been experiencing marital problems went to a Lutheran minister for counseling. They selected him because "he held himself out to the public . . . as a minister and counselor trained and able to provide counseling for marital difficulties." During the final three or four weeks of counseling, the minister allegedly engaged in consensual sexual relations with the wife. These relations, and the counseling, ended when the husband learned of the affair. The husband, who was later divorced from his wife, sued both the minister and his church. The suit against the minister alleged a breach of fiduciary duty, among other things. The state supreme court dismissed all of the husband's charges against the minister. The court began its decision by acknowledging that clergy are not immune from legal liability for their actions. It observed that "religious leaders have been held liable for obtaining gifts and donations of money by fraud; for undue influence in the transfer of property; for the kidnapping of a minor; for unlawful imprisonment; and for homosexual assault." The first amendment guaranty of religious freedom did not prevent liability in these cases, and did not protect the minister in the present case, since "we find it difficult to conceive of pastoral fornication with a parishioner or communicant as a legitimate religious belief or practice in any faith."

The court next addressed the question of "whether a member of the clergy, who holds himself out as being trained and capable of conducting marital counseling, is immune from any liability for harm caused by his counseling by virtue of the first amendment" guaranty of religious freedom. Both the priest and the diocese argued that the first amendment required the dismissal of the lawsuit since "the performance of pastoral duties by a Catholic priest, including sacramental counseling of parishioners, is a matter of ecclesiastical cognizance and policy with which a civil court cannot interfere." The court acknowledged that "marital counseling by a cleric presents difficult questions" and "may implicate first amendment rights." However, it concluded that the priest could not argue that his conduct was protected by the constitutional guaranty of religious freedom since "when the alleged wrongdoing of a cleric clearly falls outside the beliefs and doctrine of his religion, he cannot avail himself of the protections afforded by the first amendment." In particular, the court noted that "sexual activity by a priest is fundamentally antithetical to Catholic doctrine," and "by definition is not an expression of a sincerely held religious belief."

4. INSURANCE

Clergy who are sued as a result of sexual misconduct often assume that the church's insurance policy will provide a legal defense and pay for any judgment or settlement up to the insurance limits. Such an assumption may be incorrect, since most insurance policies exclude coverage for any "intentional" or criminal acts, and some exclude coverage for sexual misconduct. As a result, a number of clergy have had to retain and pay for their own attorney, and pay any judgment or settlement attributable to their misconduct.

Key point. Ministers who engage in sexual misconduct may be guilty of a number of "intentional wrongs" including battery, breach of a fiduciary duty, and intentional infliction of emotional distress. Generally, intentional wrongs are not covered under a church's liability insurance policy, and so ministers who commit such acts may find that they must pay for their own attorney and any portion of a judgment or settlement attributable to their conduct.

---

[175] Stock v. Pressnell, 527 N.E.2d 1235 (Ohio 1988).

Example. A Colorado court ruled that a church insurance policy could not be tapped to pay a judgment rendered against a minister in a sexual misconduct case. A woman sued her former minister and her church on the basis of injuries she suffered as a result of the minister's sexual misconduct. A jury ruled that the minister was liable for the woman's injuries and awarded a monetary judgment in her favor. The minister insisted that the judgment against him was covered under a church insurance policy. A state appeals court disagreed. The court noted that "if the meaning of the insurance policy is expressed in plain, certain, and readily understandable language, it must be enforced as written." The church's insurance policy provided, "The company will pay on behalf of the insured all sums which the insured shall become legally obligated to pay as damages because of injury to any person arising out of sexual misconduct or sexual molestation which occurs during the policy period." Exclusions to the policy, however, specifically provided that the insurance did not apply "[t]o any person who personally participated in any act of sexual misconduct or sexual molestation." The minister claimed that by denying coverage to the perpetrator of the sexual misconduct, the exclusion rendered any coverage under the policy for sexual misconduct "illusory." The court disagreed, noting that coverage existed under the policy for the church. The court also rejected the minister's claim that the insurance company had "waived" its right to deny coverage by providing a defense to the minister under a "reservation of rights."[176]

Example. A Minnesota appeals court ruled that a church insurance policy did not require the insurance company to defend a pastor who was sued by a woman he had seduced. The court also ruled that the insurance company would not have to pay any portion of a jury verdict against the pastor. The pastor turned the lawsuit over to the church's insurance company, assuming that the insurer would defend him and pay any verdict against him up to the policy limits. The insurer rejected the pastor's request, and informed him that it would neither defend him against the claims of the lawsuit nor pay any portion of a verdict attributable to his misconduct. The pastor sued the insurance company in an attempt to force it to defend him. A state appeals court noted that the church's insurance policy specified that the insurer was liable for any personal injury "caused by an occurrence to which this insurance applies." The policy defined the term "occurrence" as an act that "results in bodily injury . . . neither expected nor intended." The court concluded that the pastor's repeated sexual exploitation of the victim resulted in personal injuries that were both "expected and intended," and accordingly they did not constitute an "occurrence" for which insurance coverage was available. The court observed, "We conclude [that the victim's] allegations that [the pastor] used his authority as a pastor and counselor to facilitate his sexual abuse of a psychologically vulnerable person creates an inference of an intent to injure and relieves [the insurance company] of its duty to defend."[177]

5. Elimination of "Loss of Consortium" and "Alienation of Affection" Claims

A number of courts have concluded that a husband whose wife is seduced by a pastor cannot sue the pastor since any basis for liability was effectively abolished when "alienation of affections" was eliminated as a basis for liability by the state legislature.[178]

Example. A Louisiana appeals court ruled that a husband whose wife had allegedly been seduced by his pastor could not sue the pastor or his church. The court noted that the state of Louisiana abolished the tort of "alienation of a wife's affections" in 1927, and that this prevented the husband from suing his priest for

---

[176] Church Mutual Insurance Company v. Klein, 940 P.2d 1001 (Colo. App. 1996).
[177] Houg v. State Farm Fire and Casualty Company, 481 N.W.2d 393 (Minn. App. 1992).
[178] See, e.g., Cherepski v. Walters, 913 S.W.2d 761 (Ark. 1996); R.E.R. v. J.G., 552 N.W.2d 27 (Minn. App. 1996).

clergy malpractice. However, the court stressed that it was not addressing the issue of whether or not a wife who is seduced by a priest can maintain a lawsuit for clergy malpractice. Second, the court rejected the husband's claim that the priest was guilty of intentional infliction of emotional distress, since such a claim may only be brought by the intended victim (in this case, the wife). The court also concluded that the four minor children could not sue the priest for alienation of their mother's affections.[179]

Example. *The Nebraska Supreme Court ruled that a husband could not sue a priest for "loss of consortium" as a result of the priest's sexual relationship with the man's wife. The husband claimed that as a result of the priest's actions he had lost the care and comfort of his wife and had been deprived of her comfort and companionship and incurred pain, suffering, and mental anguish. The court rejected this theory of liability, noting that it was essentially a claim for "alienation of affection" and that such claims are specifically prohibited by a Nebraska statute.[180]*

Example. *The Oklahoma Supreme Court ruled that a pastor was not liable on the basis of "seduction" for sexual contacts he had with a woman during counseling. In rejecting this basis of liability, the court noted that the state legislature had abolished any liability for seduction. A state statute provides that the "seduction of any person of sound mind and legal age is hereby abolished as a civil cause of action in this state." It concluded that "[w]e are not at liberty to recognize a cause of action by the wife against her minister for engaging in a consensual sexual affair."[181]*

6. DUPLICATE VERDICTS

Victims of clergy sexual misconduct usually sue not only the offending pastor, but also the church that employed the pastor. In some cases the jury awards a victim money damages against the pastor and church separately. To illustrate, a jury determines that both a pastor and church are legally responsible for injuries suffered by a victim of the pastor's sexual misconduct. The jury awards the victim $200,000 in damages, to be split evenly between the pastor and church. In such a case the argument can be made that the verdicts are "duplicative," meaning that the jury's award of damages against the pastor and church for the same alleged wrongs results in "duplication of damages" since the actions of the church did not result in any additional harm to the victim beyond what had been caused by the pastor.[182]

---

[179] Greene v. Roy, 604 So.2d 1359 (La. App. 3 Cir. 1992).

[180] Nebraska Supreme Court issues an important ruling; Schieffer v. Catholic Archdiocese, 508 N.W.2d 907 (Neb. 1993).

[181] Bladen v. First Presbyterian Church, 857 P.2d 789 (Okla. 1993).

[182] *See, e.g.,* Bohrer v. DeHart, 943 P.2d 1220 (Colo. App. 1996).

INSTRUCTIONAL AIDS TO CHAPTER 4

Terms

assumption of risk

child abuse

comparative negligence

contributory negligence

defamation

imputed negligence

intentional infliction of emotional distress

invasion of privacy

malpractice

mandatory reporter

negligence

outrageous conduct

permissive reporter

Privacy Act of 1974

publicity

securities

sunshine laws

undue influence

Learning Objectives

- Understand the legal concept of negligence, and its application to clergy and churches.

- Define the term *defamation*, and explain its application to clergy both as plaintiffs and defendants in civil litigation.

- Define the term *undue influence*, and explain its significance to churches and clergy.

- Explain the four varieties of *invasion of privacy*, and their relevance to clergy.

- Define the term *malpractice*, and describe the application of the term to a variety of clergy practices.

- Understand the application of securities law to clergy who offer or sell church securities to church members as a means of raising funds.

- Describe the status of clergy under state child abuse reporting laws, and the consequences of a failure to report known or reasonably suspected incidents of abuse.

- Understand the legal consequences to a minister in the event the minister engages in sexual contact with an adult or minor member of the congregation.

Short-Answer Questions

1. Define the term *negligence*. Give three examples of negligent conduct.

2. Rev. N, while driving home from work, is involved in an accident with another vehicle. Both drivers were issued citations for violating traffic laws. The driver of the other vehicle was seriously injured, and she sues Rev. N and Rev. N's employing church. Answer each of the following questions:

    a. Does the conduct of Rev. N constitute negligence?

    b. In a state that recognizes comparative negligence, would either Rev. N or the church be liable?

    c. Is the church legally responsible for the other driver's injuries? If so, on the basis of what legal theory?

    d. Is the church's liability affected by the fact that Rev. N reports his income taxes as a self-employed person?

3. The following questions pertain to the *respondeat superior* doctrine:

   a. Define *respondeat superior.*

   b. What are the 3 requirements for this rule to apply?

   c. What is the basis for this rule?

   d. Do the courts apply this rule to charitable organizations? Should they?

4. In an effort to prevent the re-election of Rev. B at a church business meeting, a member publicly asserts that "Rev. B was married and divorced on at least two occasions in the past, and was convicted for driving while intoxicated." While the member based this statement on rumors he had heard, the substance of the remark was true. Has the member defamed Rev. B? Explain.

5. Define *legal malice.* When must it be proven in a defamation case?

6. An accusation is brought to the board of Trinity Church that Rev. D has had an adulterous affair with a member of the congregation. The board confronts Rev. D with this rumor, and he acknowledges that it is true. The board dismisses Rev. D from his position with the church, and reads a statement to the congregation during morning worship services on the following Sunday which informs the congregation that Rev. D "is guilty of adultery." Rev. D believes that the public reading of this statement constituted defamation. Did it? Explain fully.

7. A mother informs her pastor and members of the church board that a volunteer youth worker sexually molested her son during an overnight church activity. The youth worker threatens to sue the mother for defamation. There were no witnesses to the alleged incident; however, the mother took her son to a physician who confirmed that sexual molestation had occurred. The women's accusations, if true, would mean that the youth worker committed a crime (aggravated child molestation) under state law. What is the legal significance of this fact?

8. A denomination that ordains clergy has the authority to discipline and dismiss clergy for violations of church teachings. Clergy who are dismissed are identified by name under a column reading "dismissed" in a monthly denominational publication that is distributed to affiliated clergy. Could this practice constitute defamation? Why or why not?

9. A church board decides to dismiss a member on the basis of his confessed violations of the church's moral teachings. The chairman of the church board reads a prepared statement to the congregation during a Sunday morning worship service, informing the church of the nature of the member's moral indiscretions and of the board's decision to dismiss him. Answer the following questions:

   a. Does the reading of the statement to the congregation constitute defamation? Why or why not?

   b. Could the reading of the statement to the congregation create legal liability for the church on the basis of any other legal theory? Explain.

c. Assume that the member did not confess, but rather denied his guilt, and that the board determined that he was guilty on the basis of the testimony of only one other person. Would the reading of the statement under these circumstances constitute defamation? Explain.

10. An associate minister at First Church is dismissed because of conduct violating the church's moral teachings. The dismissed minister seeks a position at Second Church. The church board at Second Church writes the minister of First Church, asking for a letter of recommendation. The minister promptly writes a letter recounting the facts that led to the dismissal. Does this conduct constitute defamation of the former minister? Would it constitute invasion of the former minister's privacy? What steps should the minister of Second Church have taken to reduce the risk of legal liability under these circumstances?

11. At a church board meeting, the membership of G is discussed. The board asks member A to attend, and A testifies about certain conduct on the part of G. As a result of this testimony, G is dismissed from the membership of the church. G sues A for defamation. Result?

12. J has attended a local church for several months. She has an infant child, and both J and her child have tested positive to the AIDS virus. J informs the pastor of this fact during a counseling session. The pastor advises the church nursery workers that the child has AIDS. Has the pastor defamed J or her child? Has he invaded their privacy?

13. During a sermon, Rev. T describes the criminal activities that a church member had been engaged in prior to his conversion as an example of the ability of the Gospel to change lives. Has Rev. T defamed the member? Has he invaded the member's privacy?

14. M has attended the same church for over fifty years. She now is confined to a convalescent home. Throughout her life, she gave liberally to the church, and often stated that she wanted to leave a portion of her estate to the church. Her minister visits her each week. Shortly before her death, she signed a deed conveying her former home to the church. She did not discuss this gift with her attorney or tax adviser. Her children, who live in another state, challenge the gift on the ground that it was the product of undue influence. Answer the following questions:

a. Define *undue influence.*

b. What factors will a court consider in deciding whether or not undue influence has occurred?

c. Which of these factors support a finding of undue influence in this case?

d. Which of these factors support a finding of no undue influence in this case?

e. What is the likely ruling of a court?

f. What is the standard of proof that ordinarily is required to establish undue influence? Why is this a relevant consideration in deciding whether or not undue influence has occurred?

g. The woman's heirs retain an attorney who sends a letter to the pastor, threatening to sue the church for undue influence if it does not immediately renounce all claim to the gift. The pastor, fearing the negative publicity that might result from such a lawsuit, is seriously considering agreeing to the attorney's demand. Identify at least two considerations that would support a decision to reject the attorney's demand.

h. What steps can a church take to reduce the likelihood of undue influence claims?

15. A church member insists that the "Privacy Act" gives church members the legal right to inspect any church record. Is this a correct assumption? Explain.

16. K is a married woman who begins attending a local church by herself. After several months, she becomes a member of the church. On several occasions, she counsels with Rev. R, a pastor of her church, regarding marital problems she his having, and her husband's refusal to attend church with her. Within a year after joining the church, K divorces her husband. K's former husband sues the Rev. R, claiming that he committed clergy malpractice. Specifically, K's former husband alleges that the content of Rev. R's counseling directly resulted in the divorce. What is the likelihood that Rev. R will be found liable for clergy malpractice under these facts? Explain.

17. E is a young woman who has attended a local church for several years. She is suffering from a severe emotional disorder, and she counsels at length with Rev. B, the senior pastor of her church. E eventually commits suicide, and her family sues Rev. B for malpractice. Answer fully the following questions:

    a. What factors would a court probably consider in deciding whether or not Rev. B is guilty of malpractice?

    b. Assume that Rev. B urged E on several occasions to see a psychologist or psychiatrist, but that she rejected this advice. Would this evidence be relevant in deciding if Rev. B was guilty of malpractice?

    c. Assume that Rev. B did not suggest to E that she visit a psychologist or psychiatrist, and in fact discouraged her from doing so. Would this evidence be relevant in deciding if Rev. B was guilty of malpractice?

    d. What is the most likely decision of a court in this case? Give reasons.

    e. Would it matter if Rev. B is a licensed counselor or psychologist who is a full-time pastoral counselor at the church?

18. Should a church obtain malpractice insurance for its clergy and counselors? Why or why not?

19. Rev. W decides that the church needs a new van, and so she enters into a contract to purchase a van. She signs the contract in her own name, without any reference to the church or to the fact that she was signing on behalf of the church.

    a. Is Rev. W personally liable on this contact? Why or why not?

    b. Is the church liable on the contract? Why or why not?

    c. What steps should church leaders take to be sure that they will not be personally liable on legal documents that they sign on behalf of their church?

20. In an effort to raise $500,000 to finance construction of a new sanctuary, a local church decides to issue promissory notes to church members. The minister encourages members to purchase the notes, and assures them of the safety of such an investment. Several members purchase notes, but they receive no prospectus or offering circular. Has the minister acted in an unlawful manner? Explain fully.

21. List 5 examples of securities fraud.

22. Rev. Y is informed by a member during counseling that the member's husband is sexually molesting their minor child. Does Rev. Y have a duty to report this information to the state? What three factors must be considered in answering this question?

23. A church nursery attendant informs Rev. T following a morning worship service that a particular child has suspicious bruising. Rev. T thanks the attendant, but decides not to do anything about the information. Does Rev. T have a duty to report this information to the state? What three factors must be considered in answering this question?

24. A teenage girl informs Rev. H that her stepfather has been molesting her. Does Rev. H have a duty to report this information to the state? What three factors must be considered in answering this question?

25. Same facts as question 24. Assume that Rev. H is not a mandatory reporter under state law. Does this mean that she should not report the allegation to the state? List several factors that Rev. H should consider in making this decision.

26. Same facts as question 24. Assume that Rev. H is a mandatory reporter. List at least two legal risks that she assumes by not reporting the allegations to the state.

27. Assume that a minister learns of child abuse during a confidential counseling session. Does the clergy-penitent privilege excuse the minister from reporting the abuse to the state?

28. Does the first amendment guaranty of religious freedom protect clergy from reporting (to the state) cases of child abuse that they learn of during confidential counseling sessions?

29. A local church employs an ordained minister as its "minister of counseling." The minister is not a licensed counselor or psychologist under state law. The minister counsels in an office in the church, and counsels only with church members or with persons who attend the church. Does this practice violate state laws requiring counselors and psychologists to be licensed?

30. Rev. G sexually seduces a female church member during marital counseling. Answer the following questions:

    a. If the member sues Rev. G, what will be the most likely theories of liability?

    b. Will Rev. G's church be legally responsible for the member's damages? Why or why not?

    c. If the church is sued, will its liability policy cover an out-of-court settlement or jury verdict?

    d. Rev. G insists that the woman "consented" to the relationship. Will this be an effective defense? Explain.

    e. Does Rev. G face potential criminal liability?

    f. Assume that the woman does not file her lawsuit until ten years after the relationship. Is she automatically prevented from any recovery on the basis of the statute of limitations?

Discussion Questions

1. Do you agree that a church should be held legally accountable for the negligence of its ministers and employees committed in the course of their employment? Why?

2. A minister visits an elderly church member in a convalescent home on several occasions. Shortly before his death, the member executed a will leaving half of his estate to the church. Following the member's death, one of his children informs the minister that the heirs are prepared to contest the will in court on the basis of undue influence unless the church voluntarily renounces its gift. The minister never suggested that the member make the gift, but there were no witnesses to any of his several visits with the member. It is the opinion of the church's attorney that the church has a sixty percent chance of winning the case. The church board is considering renouncing the gift to avoid unfavorable public opinion, since it is certain that the case will be discussed in the local newspaper. Do you believe that the church should renounce the gift or defend itself in court? Why?

3. A minister sells church securities without having registered as a securities salesman. He also makes a number of unfounded and incorrect representations about the securities, and encourages several members to invest even though they were not in a financial position to do so. A complaint is filed with the state securities commission. The commission investigates the charges, and threatens to prosecute the minister. Do you believe that the government should have the authority to regulate the sale of church securities? Explain.

Part Two
Law and the Church

DEFINITIONS

Chapter summary. What is a church? This question is the central focus of this chapter. While the answer may seem obvious, a definition of the term "church" is a surprisingly complex task. For example, does a church include a church-operated school or nursing home, a denomination, a religious organization that conducts commercial activities, a small group of persons who meet in a home for religious study? These are but a few of the issues that have confronted the courts. The term "church" appears several times in the Internal Revenue Code. However, the term is never defined. Presumably, Congress fears that any definition will be either too expansive (and encourage tax fraud) or too restrictive (and hurt legitimate churches). There is little doubt that the proliferation of "mail order churches" has caused the courts and the IRS to interpret the term "church" more narrowly. The IRS has created a list of fourteen criteria that characterize a church. As you will see, these criteria are extremely narrow, and would not apply to many legitimate churches (including the original churches described in the New Testament Book of Acts). The definition of the term "church" is also relevant in the contexts of zoning and property tax exemptions. Can a church that is located in an area zoned for residential and church uses build a school on its property? Can it construct an activities building? A softball field? A radio station? Does a state law that exempts churches from property taxes apply to church schools? To a vacant lot owned by a church? To a church-owned religious camp ground? Such illustrations demonstrate the importance and complexity of the question addressed in this chapter. These are the very kinds of issues that have generated heated litigation, pitting churches against government agencies. This chapter was intentionally placed at the beginning of Part Two of the text, which is concerned with the relationship between law and the church. Obviously, one must have a clear idea of what the church is before moving on to the remaining chapters in Part Two. Be sure you understand thoroughly the materials presented in this chapter before moving on to chapter 6.

Since many state and federal laws use the term *church*, it is important to define the term with precision. To illustrate, the Internal Revenue Code uses the term *church* in many contexts, including the following:

1. charitable giving limitations[1]

2. church pension plans under the Employee Retirement Income Security Act of 1974 (ERISA)[2]

3. church "retirement income accounts"[3]

4. deferred compensation plans[4]

5. ineligibility of churches for using an "expenditure test" for determining permissible lobbying activities[5]

6. unrelated business taxable income[6]

7. unrelated debt-financed income[7]

8. exemption from the necessity of applying for recognition of tax-exempt status[8]

9. treatment of church employees for social security purposes if church waives employer FICA coverage[9]

10. unemployment tax exemptions[10]

11. exemption from filing annual information returns[11]

12. exemption from filing returns regarding liquidation, dissolution, or termination[12]

13. restrictions on the examination of financial records[13]

14. election to waive the employer's obligation to pay social security and Medicare taxes on nonminister employees[14]

The Internal Revenue Code occasionally uses the term *church* in connection with the term *minister*. For example, service performed by a duly ordained, commissioned, or licensed minister of a church is expressly

---

[1] I.R.C. § 170(b)(1)(A)(i).
[2] *Id.* at §§ 410(d), 414(e).
[3] *Id.* at § 403(b)(9).
[4] *Id.* at §§ 414 and 457.
[5] *Id.* at § 501(h).
[6] *Id.* at § 512.
[7] *Id.* at § 514.
[8] *Id.* at § 508(c).
[9] *Id.* at § 1402(j).
[10] *Id.* at § 3309(b)(1).
[11] *Id.* at § 6033(a)(2)(A).
[12] *Id.* at § 6043(b)(1).
[13] *Id.* at § 7605(c).
[14] *Id.* at § 3121(w).

exempted from federal employment taxes,[15] unemployment taxes,[16] income tax withholding requirements,[17] and self-employment taxes (if a valid waiver has been timely filed).[18] Despite these many references to the term *church*, the Internal Revenue Code contains no adequate definition of the term.[19]

In addition, federal law (1) imposes penalties on anyone who "intentionally defaces, damages, or destroys" a church or who "intentionally obstructs, by force or threat of force, any person in the enjoyment of that person's free exercise of religious beliefs, or attempts to do so";[20] (2) prescribes the position and manner of display of the United States flag in church buildings;[21] (3) imposes penalties upon persons who cross state lines to avoid prosecution for damaging or destroying church buildings, or who refuse to testify in any criminal proceeding relating to such an offense;[22] (4) describes the benefits available to churches under the National Flood Insurance Act;[23] (5) exempts churches from the "price discrimination" provisions of the Robinson-Patman Act;[24] and (6) provides for the employment of chaplains and the conduct of religious services at military installation.[25]

Many state and local laws contain specific references to the term *church*. Examples include laws pertaining to zoning, nonprofit corporations, state and local revenue, the use of church buses, the desecration of church buildings, the sale of intoxicating liquors within a specified distance from a church, building codes, property ownership, workers compensation, and interference with church services.

Every law that uses the term *church* raises definitional questions. As one court observed:

[The term *church*] can mean an organization for religious purposes. It can also have the more physical meaning of a place where persons regularly assemble for worship. . . . [I]f "church" is interpreted to mean a place where persons regularly assemble for worship, does this include merely sanctuaries, chapels, and cathedrals, or does it also include buildings adjacent thereto such as parsonages, friaries, convents, fellowship halls, Sunday schools, and rectories?[26]

The courts have attempted to define the term *church* in various ways. Some of the definitions include:

- A body or community of Christians, united under one form of government by the profession of the same faith, and the observance of the same rituals and ceremonies.[27]

---

[15] *Id.* at § 3121(b)(8).

[16] *Id.* at § 3309(b)(2).

[17] *Id.* at § 3401(a)(9).

[18] *Id.* at § 1402(e).

[19] *See generally* Whelan, *"Church" in the Internal Revenue Code: The Definitional Problems*, 45 FORDHAM L. REV. 885 (1977); Worthing, *"Religion" and "Religious Institutions" under the First Amendment*, 7 PEPPERDINE L. REV. 313 (1980); Note, *Toward a Constitutional Definition of Religion*, 91 HARV. L. REV. 1056 (1978).

[20] 18 U.S.C. § 247. Damages to church property must exceed $10,000. The penalties for violating this section include fines and a prison sentence of up to life (if a death results), up to ten years (if "serious bodily injury" results), or up to one year in all other cases. Section 247(d) specifies that "no prosecution for any offense described in this section shall be undertaken by the United States except upon the notification in writing of the Attorney General or his designee that in his judgment a prosecution by the United States is in the public interest and necessary to secure substantial justice."

[21] 36 U.S.C. § 175(k).

[22] 18 U.S.C. § 1074.

[23] 42 U.S.C. § 4013(b)(1)(C).

[24] 15 U.S.C. § 13c.

[25] 10 U.S.C. § 6031.

[26] Guam Power Authority v. Bishop of Guam, 383 F. Supp. 476, 479 (D. Guam 1974).

[27] McNeilly v. First Presbyterian Church, 137 N.E. 691 (1923).

- An organization for religious purposes, for the public worship of God.[28]

- The term [church] may denote either a society of persons who, professing Christianity, hold certain doctrines or observances which differentiate them from other like groups, and who use a common discipline, or the building in which such persons habitually assemble for public worship.[29]

- A church consists of its land and buildings, its trustees and its congregation (the people who more or less regularly attend its religious services), as well as of its faith, doctrine, ritual and clergy.[30]

- At a minimum, a church includes a body of believers or communicants that assembles regularly in order to worship. Unless the organization is reasonably available to the public in its conduct of worship, its educational instruction, and its promulgation of doctrine, it cannot fulfill this associational role.[31]

- Among some ten definitions of "church" given by the lexicographers, two have gotten into the law books generally. One is "A society of persons who profess the Christian religion." The other is "The place where such persons regularly assemble for worship."[32]

- A church is a building consecrated to the honor of God and religion, with its members united in the profession of the same Christian faith.[33]

- A Christian youth organization having no official connection with any denominational church body was a church since it "proclaims Christianity, conducts services for the worship of the Christian God and provides for the administration of the Christian sacraments to its assembled members.[34]

- The ordinary meaning of the term contemplates a place or edifice consecrated to religious worship, where people join together in some form of public worship.[35]

- The word "church" . . . includes at a minimum any religious organization which, as the whole of its activities, advocates and teaches its particular spiritual beliefs before others with a purpose of gaining adherents to those beliefs and instructing them in the doctrine which those beliefs comprise.[36]

- The term "church" means a voluntary organization of people for religious purposes who are associated for religious worship, discipline and teaching and who are united by the profession of the same faith, holding the same creed, observing the same rites, and acknowledging the same ecclesiastical authority.[37]

[28] Bennett v. City of LaGrange, 112 S.E. 482 (1922).
[29] First Independent Missionary Baptist Church v. McMillan, 153 So.2d 337 (Fla. App. 1963), quoting Baker v. Fales, 16 Mass. 488 (1820).
[30] Eastern Orthodox Catholic Church v. Adair, 141 N.Y.S.2d 772 (1955).
[31] American Guidance Foundation v. United States, 490 F. Supp. 304 (D.D.C. 1980).
[32] Church of the Holy Faith v. State Tax Commission, 48 P.2d 777 (N.M. 1935).
[33] Wiggins v. Young, 57 S.E.2d 486 (Ga. 1950).
[34] Young Life Campaign v. Patino, 176 Cal. Rptr. 23 (Cal. App. 1981) (an excellent discussion of the definition of *church*).
[35] In re Upper St. Clair Township Grange, 152 A.2d 768 (Pa. 1959).
[36] Christian Jew Foundation v. State, 653 S.W.2d 607 (Tex. App. 1983) (an excellent discussion of the term *church*, rejecting a proposed definition by the state of Texas as unconstitutionally preferring some churches over others).
[37] State v. Lynch, 265 S.E.2d 491 (N.C. App. 1980).

Definitions

- The "plain, ordinary, and popular meaning of the word *church* includes a building in which people assemble for the worship of God and for the administration of such offices and services as pertain to that worship, a building consecrated to the honor of God and religion, and a place where persons regularly assemble for worship."[38]

- The term church includes "a building consecrated to the honor of a religion would likewise include buildings in which people assemble for non-Christian worship, such as a mosque, a synagogue, or a temple."[39]

- A church . . . in general terms, is an assemblage of individuals who express their adherence to a religion.[40]

Courts most often are called upon to define the term *church* in the context of tax exemptions and zoning ordinances. Does a particular organization qualify for an exemption from federal income taxes or state property or sales taxes? May an organization construct a new facility in an area zoned exclusively for residential and "church" use? The definitions the courts have given to the term *church* in these two contexts will be considered individually.

§ 5-01   Tax Legislation — Federal

Federal tax law uses many terms to describe religious organizations. It is important to comprehend the meaning of these terms in order to determine the applicability of various tax provisions. All of these terms are addressed below.

§ 5-01.01 — Churches

Key point 5-01.01. The IRS has adopted a 14-criteria test for use in determining whether or not a particular entity is a church for purposes of federal tax law. This test is theologically flawed, and is subject to challenge.

As noted above, the Internal Revenue Code contains several references to the term *church*, but provides no adequate definition. This is understandable, since a definition that is too narrow potentially interferes with the constitutional guaranty of religious freedom, while a definition that is too broad will encourage abuses in the name of religion. The United States Supreme Court has noted that "the great diversity in church structure and organization among religious groups in this country . . . makes it impossible, as Congress perceived, to lay down a single rule to govern all church-related organizations."[41] Nevertheless, the Code contains some limited attempts to define churches and related organizations.

Prior to 1970, the income tax regulations specified that the term *church* included

a religious order or religious organization if such order or organization (a) is an *integral part* of a church, and (b) is engaged in carrying out the functions of a church, whether as a civil law

---

[38] Calvary Baptist Church v. Coonrad, 163 Neb. 25, 77 N.W.2d 821 (1956).
[39] Latenser v. Intercessors of the Lamb, Inc., 553 N.W.2d 458 (Neb. 1996).
[40] The Way International v. Limbach, 552 N.E.2d 908 (Ohio 1990).
[41] St. Martin Evangelical Lutheran Church v. South Dakota, 451 U.S. 772, 782 n.12 (1981).

corporation or otherwise. In determining whether a religious order or organization is an integral part of a church, consideration will be given to the degree to which it is connected with, and controlled by, such church. A religious order or organization shall be considered to be engaged in carrying out the functions of a church if its duties include the ministration of sacerdotal functions and the conduct of religious worship. . . . What constitutes the conduct of religious worship or the ministration of sacerdotal functions depends on the tenets and practices of a particular religious body constituting a church.[42]

This language implied that a church is an organization whose "duties include the ministration of sacerdotal functions and the conduct of religious worship."

Section 3121(w) of the Code, which permits churches and church-controlled organizations to exempt themselves from the employer's share of social security and Medicare taxes (if certain conditions are met), defines the term *church* as follows:

For purposes of this section, the term "church" means a church, a convention or association of churches, or an elementary or secondary school which is controlled, operated, or principally supported by a church or by a convention or association of churches. For purposes of this subsection, the term "qualified church-controlled organization" means any church-controlled tax-exempt organization described in section 501(c)(3), other than an organization which—(i) offers goods, services, or facilities for sale, other than on an incidental basis, to the general public, other than goods, services, or facilities which are sold at a nominal charge which is substantially less than the cost of providing such goods, services, or facilities; and (ii) normally receives more than 25 per cent of its support from either (I) governmental sources, or (II) receipts from admissions, sales of merchandise, performance of services, or furnishing of facilities, in activities which are not unrelated trades or businesses, or both.[43]

In 1974, the IRS proposed, but never adopted, the following definition of a "church" as part of proposed regulations addressing charitable contributions:

A church or convention or association of churches is . . . an organization of individuals having commonly held religious beliefs, engaged solely in religious activities in furtherance of such beliefs. The activities of the organization must include the conduct of religious worship and the celebration of life cycle events such as births, deaths and marriage. The individuals engaged in the religious activities of a church are generally not regular participants in activities of another church, except when such other church is a parent or subsidiary organization of their church.[44]

In the context of charitable contribution deductions, the Code defines the term *church, or convention or association of churches* as a "church, or convention or association of churches."[45]

These definitions clearly are inadequate, and provide very little help in applying the many Code sections pertaining to churches. The IRS has attempted to fill this definitional vacuum by compiling a list of fourteen "criteria" which presumably characterize a church:

[42] Treas. Reg. § 1.511-2(a)(3)(ii) (emphasis added).
[43] I.R.C. § 3121(w)(3).
[44] Quoted in GCM 37116 (1977).
[45] Treas. Reg. § 1.170A-9(a).

1. a distinct legal existence

2. a recognized creed and form of worship

3. a definite and distinct ecclesiastical government

4. a formal code of doctrine and discipline

5. a distinct religious history

6. a membership not associated with any other church or denomination

7. an organization of ordained ministers

8. ordained ministers selected after completing prescribed studies

9. a literature of its own

10. established places of worship

11. regular congregations

12. regular worship services

13. Sunday schools for religious instruction of the young

14. schools for the preparation of ministers

No single factor is controlling, although all fourteen may not be relevant to a given determination.[46]

These criteria have been recognized by a number of courts.

Example. *The first federal court to recognize the IRS "fourteen criteria" test involved a claim by a husband and wife that they and their minor child constituted a church. The family insisted that it was a church since the father often preached and disseminated religious instruction to his son; the family conducted "religious services" in their home; and the family often prayed together at home. A federal court agreed with the IRS that the family was not a church, basing its decision on the fourteen criteria. In commenting upon the fourteen criteria, the court noted that "[w]hile some of these are relatively minor, others, e.g., the existence of an established congregation served by an organized ministry, the provision of regular religious services and religious education for the young, and the dissemination of a doctrinal code, are of central importance. The means by which an avowedly religious purpose is accomplished separates a 'church' from other forms of religious enterprise." In concluding that the family was not a church, the court observed: "At a minimum, a church includes a body of believers or communicants that assembles regularly in order to worship. Unless the organization is reasonably available to the*

---

[46] The fourteen criteria seem to have originated in a 1959 IRS ruling that found the Salvation Army to be a church. *See* Rev. Rul. 59-129, 1959-1 C.B. 58, and GCM 37116 (1977).

public in its conduct of worship, its educational instruction, and its promulgation of doctrine, it cannot fulfill this associational role."[47]

Example. *The IRS ruled that a religious organization was properly exempt from federal income taxes as a "church." The organization in question was established to develop an ecumenical form of religious expression that would "unify western and eastern modes of religious practice" and place greater significance on the mystical aspects of religious truth. Some twenty or so persons met for an hour each week in the church's facilities, and were asked to pay dues of $3 each month and subscribe to the church's ten precepts. A "Sunday school" was provided for children of members and nonmembers, and literature was produced. The IRS concluded that this organization was properly exempt from federal income taxes as a church, since it satisfied a majority of the fourteen criteria. The IRS observed that "the organization meets most of the fourteen criteria . . . . It is fully incorporated and has a fully distinct legal existence. It has a creed and form of worship recognized by its members. Although it is still in a developing stage, it has a definite and distinct ecclesiastical government . . . . It has a formal code of doctrine and discipline as evidenced by the ten precepts . . . . While it has a history of only a few years because it is a relatively new organization, its members have documented its growth and major changes. It has what could be called an organization of ordained ministers . . . a literature of its own . . . an established place of worship . . . a regular congregation . . . and regular services including Sunday school." The IRS noted that the church did not have a "membership not associated with any other church or denomination" since members were not required to sever their ties with other churches. However, a failure to meet this factor was "overcome" by the presence of the remaining thirteen factors.[48]*

Example. *A federal appeals court, in rejecting an individual's claim that he was exempt from federal taxes since he was a "church," relied directly on the fourteen criteria. The individual maintained that after "much Bible study" he had concluded that "if you believe you are a church and you are practicing your religion to your point of view, then you can have tax exempt status because churches are exempt." He pointed out that the Internal Revenue Code contains no definition of the term church, and that churches are not required to file applications for exemption from federal income tax. The court, in rejecting the taxpayer's "tax-exempt" status, observed that "it is obvious that one person cannot free all his taxable income from all tax liabilities by the simple expedient of proclaiming himself a church and making some religious contributions. Common sense makes this clear." If this were not so, "there would likely be an overabundance of one-person churches paying no income taxes, and leaving to the rest of us the payment of their fair share of the expense of running the government. That attitude hardly seems like an act of churchly charity to one's neighbors." The court concluded its opinion by observing: "Every year with renewed vigor, many citizens seek sanctuary in the free exercise [of religion] clause of the first amendment. They desire salvation not from sin or from temptation, however, but from the most earthly of mortal duties—income taxes. Any salvation sought from income taxes in this court is denied."[49]*

Example. *The United States Tax Court ruled that a religious organization formed to "spread the message of God's love and hope throughout the world" and to "provide a place in which those who believe in the existence of God may present religious music to any persons interested in hearing such"*

---

[47] American Guidance Foundation v. United States, 490 F. Supp. 304 (D.D.C. 1980). *See also* Lutheran Social Service of Minnesota v. United States, 758 F.2d 1283 (8th Cir. 1985); Church of the Visible Intelligence that Governs the Universe v. Commissioner, 4 Cls. Ct. 55 (Ct. Cl. 1983).

[48] Technical Advice Memorandum 8833001.

[49] United States v. Jeffries, 854 F.2d 254 (7th Cir. 1988).

[50] Spiritual Outreach Society v. Commissioner of Internal Revenue, 58 T.C.M. 1284 (1990), *aff'd,* 927 F.2d 335 (8th Cir. 1991).

was not a church.[50] *The organization maintained an outdoor amphitheater on its property, at which musical programs and an occasional "retreat" or "festival" were conducted about twelve times each year. No other regularly scheduled religious or musical services were conducted. Most of the musical events were held on Saturdays so that persons could attend their own churches on Sundays. Musical services consisted of congregational singing of religious music. A minister always opened and closed these events with prayer. While it did not charge admission to its events, there was a published schedule of "donations" that were similar to admissions charges. The organization also maintained a chapel on its property that was open to the public for individual prayer. The organization applied to the IRS for recognition of tax exempt status on the ground that it was a church. Eventually, the IRS rejected the organization's exemption application on the ground that it was not a church. In reaching its decision, the IRS noted that the organization failed most of the fourteen criteria used by the IRS in identifying churches. The organization maintained that it met a majority of these criteria, and appealed to the Tax Court. The Tax Court agreed with the IRS, and ruled that the organization was not a church. Significantly, it refused to accept the fourteen criteria as the only test for determining whether or not a particular organization is a church. It did concede, however, that the fourteen criteria are helpful in deciding such cases. The court noted that the organization met at least a few of the fourteen criteria, and that some would not be relevant to "a newly-created rural organization." On the other hand, the court noted that the organization had no ecclesiastical government, formal creed, organization of ordained clergy, seminary, or Sunday school for the training of youth. Further, it did not produce its own religious literature (it sold literature produced by other religious organizations). The court concluded by noting that "[w]hile a definitive form of ecclesiastical government or organizational structure may not be required, we are not persuaded that musical festivals and revivals (even if involving principally gospel singing . . .) and gatherings for individual meditation and prayer by persons who do not regularly come together as a congregation for such purposes should be held to satisfy the cohesiveness factor which we think is an essential ingredient of a 'church.'" This case is significant, since it represents the first time that the Tax Court has acknowledged that the fourteen criteria used by the IRS in identifying churches are not an exclusive test that must be used in all cases.*

Example. *A state supreme court ruled that "all fourteen factors need not be answered affirmatively in favor of there being a church for a religious organization to be classified as a church. Neither must there necessarily be a numerical majority. Mechanical evaluation is not the process to be used. Rather, the facts of each case are to be considered in their respective context and considered in light of these factors . . . ."*[51]

These examples demonstrate the continuing viability of the fourteen criteria. Nevertheless, these criteria are troubling because they are so restrictive that many if not most bona fide churches fail to satisfy several of them. In part, the problem results from the apparent attempt by the IRS to draft criteria that apply to both local churches and religious denominations. To illustrate, few if any local churches would meet the seventh, ninth, and fourteenth criteria, since these ordinarily would pertain only to religious denominations. In addition, many newer, independent churches often will fail the first and fifth criteria and may also fail the second, third, fourth, sixth, and eighth. It is therefore possible for a legitimate church to fail as many as ten of the fourteen criteria. The original Christian churches described in the New Testament Book of Acts easily would have failed a majority of the fourteen criteria.[52]

---

[51] Nampa Christian Schools, Foundation v. State, 719 P.2d 1178 (Idaho 1986).

[52] *See generally* S. SCHLATTER, THE CHURCH IN THE NEW TESTAMENT PERIOD (P. Levertoff trans. 1955); R. SCHNECKENBURG, THE CHURCH IN THE NEW TESTAMENT (1965); E. SCHWEIZER, CHURCH ORDER IN THE NEW TESTAMENT (1961); E. SCHWEIZER, THE CHURCH AS THE BODY OF CHRIST (1964).

The criteria clearly are vague and inadequate. Some apply exclusively to local churches, others do not. And the IRS does not indicate how many criteria an organization must meet in order to be classified as a church, or if some criteria are more important than others. The vagueness of the criteria necessarily means that their application in any particular case will depend on the discretionary judgment of a government employee. This is the very kind of conduct that the courts repeatedly have condemned in other contexts as unconstitutional. To illustrate, the courts consistently have invalidated municipal ordinances that condition the constitutionally protected interests of speech and assembly upon compliance with criteria that are so vague that decisions essentially are a matter of administrative discretion. The United States Supreme Court has held that "[it] is a basic principle of due process that an enactment is void for vagueness if its prohibitions are not clearly defined. . . . A vague law impermissibly delegates basic policy matters to [government officials] for resolution on an *ad hoc* and subjective basis with the attendant dangers of arbitrary and discriminatory application."[53] This same reasoning also should apply in the context of other fundamental constitutional rights, such as the first amendment right to freely exercise one's religion. The IRS should not be permitted to effectively limit the right of churches and church members to freely exercise their religion on the basis of criteria that are as vague as the fourteen criteria listed above, and whose application in a particular case is essentially a matter of administrative discretion.

The criteria also are constitutionally suspect on the related ground of "overbreadth." The Supreme Court "has repeatedly held that a governmental purpose to control or prevent activities constitutionally subject to state regulation may not be achieved by means which sweep unnecessarily broadly and thereby invade the area of protected freedoms. The power to regulate must be so exercised as not, in attaining a permissible end, unduly to infringe the protected freedom. Even though the governmental purpose be legitimate and substantial, that purpose cannot be pursued by means that broadly stifle fundamental personal liberties when the end can be more narrowly achieved."[54] Congress and the IRS undoubtedly have the authority to identify those churches that are not qualified for the tax benefits afforded by federal law, but they may not do so on the basis of criteria that sweep so broadly as to jeopardize the standing of legitimate churches. The courts understandably find the task of defining the term *church* perplexing. But they should avoid referring to the fourteen criteria as support for their conclusions, particularly in cases involving "mail-order churches" and other obvious shams for which the definitional question is not in doubt.

The IRS has successfully challenged a variety of tax-evasion schemes that have operated under the guise of a church. These schemes usually involve some or all of the following characteristics: An individual forms his own church, assigns all or a substantial part of his income to the church, takes a vow of poverty, declares himself to be the minister, retains control over all church funds and property, designates a substantial housing allowance for himself, and reports the income that he has assigned to his church as a charitable contribution deduction on his federal tax return. In most cases the church has no building other than the personal residence of the "minister," and it conducts few if any religious activities. Since the minister often purchases his credentials and church charter by mail, such schemes commonly are referred to as mail-order churches. The IRS consistently has refused to recognize such entities as entitled to exemption from federal income taxation. This determination often is based on the fact that the net earnings of the alleged church "inure" to the benefit of private individuals, not because the organization is not a church.

A number of federal courts have defined the term *church* without reference to the fourteen criteria, and have concluded that the term may include a private elementary and secondary school maintained and operated by a church,[55] a seminary,[56] and conventions and associations of churches.[57]

---

[53] Grayned v. City of Rockford, 408 U.S. 104, 108-09 (1972).
[54] N.A.A.C.P. v. Alabama, 377 U.S. 288, 307-08 (1964).

The United States Supreme Court has held that some church-controlled organizations that are not separately incorporated may be regarded for tax purposes as part of the church itself.[58]

Example. The IRS ruled that an evangelistic association was not a church. The most prominent feature of the association's ministry was the series of religious meetings held in various cities around the world. Each meeting followed a pattern virtually identical to that of thousands of other Christian church services, including prayer, music, an offering, announcements regarding the association's ministry, and further meetings and readings from the Bible. Each service culminated with the message that those present should commit or recommit their lives to Christ, followed by an invitation. All of those who made decisions for Christ in the meetings were encouraged to join a local church. The association published a variety of religious books and tracts in furtherance of its teaching ministry. The association asked the IRS to rule that it was a church or a convention or association of churches, and thereby exempt from filing annual information returns (Form 990) with the IRS. The IRS declined to do so. It observed that "the association is not a convention or association of churches as it is completely independent from and, to the best of our knowledge, has no continuing relationship with any other religious organizations." The IRS also concluded that the association was not a church. It reviewed several other rulings addressing the definition of a church, and concluded that there was "one common thread"—whether or not "the organization had (or did not have) a distinct congregation whose members did not maintain affiliation with other churches." While the IRS conceded that this one factor was not determinative, it did find it significant that the association did not have a distinct congregation and that those attending its services maintained or acquired affiliation with other churches. Further, the association was essentially interdenominational and did not "seek converts other than to the principles of Christianity generally." The IRS concluded: "While it has a distinct legal existence and arguably a recognized creed and form of worship, it does not have a definite and distinct ecclesiastical government, a formal code of doctrine and discipline, or a distinct religious history. While it has ordained ministers, the association apparently does not prescribe courses of study leading to their ordination and in fact does not ordain them itself. Of course, these ministers have no distinct congregations to which they minister. While the association does publish and distribute [a magazine, it] has no distinct scripture and no established place of worship. It does not conduct regular religious services as its conduct of such services is dependent on invitations from other religious organizations. Finally, it has no Sunday schools and no schools for the preparation of its ministers. We think it evident that the association has relatively few of the characteristics normally associated with a church."[59]

Example. The Tax Court ruled that an interdenominational organization that existed to perform dental work in foreign countries as a means of promoting "the Gospel of the Lord Jesus Christ, around the world, and the evangelization of the world on the basis of the principles of the Protestant Faith," was not a church. The organization conducted regular services in the United States and provided various churches with speakers and literature concerning its activities. The members of the organization were all trained in the Bible and church work. While many of its members were ordained ministers, the organization did not conduct a seminary or Bible School. All members were required to be licensed

---

[55] St. Martin Evangelical Lutheran Church v. South Dakota, 451 U.S. 772 (1981).

[56] EEOC v. Southwestern Baptist Theological Seminary, 651 F.2d 277 (5th Cir. 1981).

[57] De La Salle Institute v. United States, 195 F. Supp. 891 (N.D. Cal. 1961); Senate Report 2375, 81st Congress, 2d Session, p. 27.

[58] St. Martin Evangelical Lutheran Church v.South Dakota, 451 U.S. 772 (1981) (the Court declined to rule on the status of separately incorporated, church-controlled organizations). *See also* Treas. Reg. § 1.6033-2(g)(5)(iv), example 6; Lutheran Social Service of Minnesota v. United States, 758 F.2d 1283 (8th Cir. 1985).

[59] GCM 37116 (1977).

dentists. The court determined that a more limited concept was intended for the term "church" than that denoted by the term "religious organization." It stated that Congress did not intend "church" to be used in a generic or universal sense but rather in the sense of a "denomination" or "sect." The court added that a group need not necessarily have an organizational hierarchy or maintain church buildings to constitute a "church." In holding that the organization was not a church, the court emphasized that (1) the organization's individual members maintained their affiliation with various churches; (2) the organization was interdenominational and did not seek converts other than to the principles of Christianity generally; (3) the organization did not ordain its own ministers; and (4) the conducting of religious services by its members was not conclusive per se that the organization was a church.[60]

Example. *A federal court, in revoking the tax-exempt status of a religious organization because of its extensive lobbying activities, commented on the organization's status as a church. It noted that the organization was founded and administered by an ordained minister; that other ordained ministers were employed by the organization and were empowered to perform all sacerdotal functions on its behalf; that the organization conducted numerous religious revivals in various churches throughout the United States sponsored by local congregations, and it also held regular Sunday services; and, that it conducted annual conventions, leadership schools, and summer sessions for the young. Although the organization's status as a "church" was not in issue, the court noted that the organization's "structure, its practices, precepts, and activities provide all the necessary elements of and is legally defined a church in the ordinary accepted meaning of the term and as used in the Internal Revenue Code of 1954, its amendments and applicable regulations. . . . [The organization's] followers together with its ordained pastors constitute a congregation the same as any local church."[61]*

Example. *A federal district court interpreted the meaning of the term "church" in the context of the unrelated business income tax (prior to the application of this tax to churches). The court noted that the unrelated business income tax was imposed upon the income of religious corporations other than churches or conventions or associations of churches. It noted that every church or convention or association of churches was obviously a religious organization, but questioned whether the converse was true—whether every religious organization was a church. The court pointed out that Congress would in all probability not have drawn a new word into the statute unless it meant thereby to express a different idea. There could be no sound reason to use the term "church" in the statute, unless there was an intention to express a more limited idea than is conveyed by "religious organization." The court also pointed out that the legislative history underlying the unrelated business income tax "constantly drew the distinction between churches and religious organizations under church auspices and that not all religious activities tended to make an organization a church. Rather, the legislative history imparted a restrictive interpretation to the word "church." The court employed a "common sense" approach in determining whether a particular organization constituted a church: "To exempt churches, one must know what a church is. Congress must either define church or leave the definition to the common meaning and usage of the word; otherwise, Congress would be unable to exempt churches." The court concluded that an incorporated religious teaching order that performed no sacerdotal functions was not a church, and that the income derived by the order from the ownership and operation of a separately incorporated winery was not the income of a church, despite the fact that both corporations were formed under church auspices.[62]*

---

[60] Chapman v. Commissioner, 48 T.C. 358 (1967).

[61] Christian Echoes National Ministry, Inc. v. United States, 470 F.2d 848 (10th Cir. 1972) (quoting from a district court opinion in the same case).

[62] De La Salle Institute v. United States, 195 F. Supp. 891 (N.D. Cal. 1961).

§ 5-01.02 — Mail Order Churches

Key point 5-01.02. *A "mail order church" is a sham organization that is created in order to reduce or eliminate the founder's tax liability. Often, such organizations purchase a "church charter" through the mail from an organization that also offers ministerial "credentials." Such organizations are not recognized as "churches" by the IRS.*

In recent years, many taxpayers have attempted to exclude all or part of their income from federal taxation through the creation of a mail order church. The IRS *Exempt Organizations Handbook* addresses the subject of mail order churches as follows:

> The term "mail order church" refers to organizations set up pursuant to "church charters" purchased through the mail from organizations that claim that the charters and other "ministerial credentials" can be used to reduce or eliminate an individual's federal income tax liability. Organizations selling these documents represent that an individual can form a tax-exempt church by purchasing a "church charter." The individual, who controls the purported church, and determines how its money will be spent, then contributes up to 50 percent of his or her income to the "church," claiming a charitable contribution deduction . . . . Alternatively, the individual may take a "vow of poverty," under which the individual's assets and income are transferred to the church. The individual then claims that his or her income is not includable in gross income for federal tax purposes nor subject to employment taxes or income tax withholding. Under either of these alternatives, the assets and income transferred to the church are in turn used to pay the personal living expenses of the founder.[63]

The IRS has challenged the tax-exempt status of several mail order churches on the ground that they fail to meet one or more of the prerequisites of exempt status. The IRS often asserts that mail order churches are ineligible for tax-exempt status since they are not organized or operated exclusively for exempt purposes. This assertion often is based on the following provision in the income tax regulations:

> An organization is not organized or operated exclusively for one or more [exempt purposes] unless it serves a public rather than a private interest. Thus, to meet [this] requirement . . . it is necessary for an organization to establish that it is not organized or operated for the benefit of private interests such as designated individuals, the creator or his family, shareholders of the organization, or persons controlled, directly or indirectly, by such private interests.

A church that exists primarily to serve the private interests of its creator is not serving a public interest and therefore is not organized or operated for exempt purposes. Such a finding will be made whenever a church exists primarily as a means for handling the personal financial transactions of its founder.

Example. *In Revenue Ruling 81-94,[64] the IRS denied exempt status to a mail order church founded by a nurse. Following a vow of poverty, the nurse had transferred all of her assets, including her home and automobile, to her church and assigned her secular income to the church's checking account. In return, all of her expenses, such as her home mortgage and all outstanding credit card balances, were assumed by the church. The nurse also was provided with a full living allowance sufficient to maintain her*

---

[63] IRS Exempt Organizations Handbook § 344.7 (1988).

[64] Rev. Rul. 81-94, 1981-1 C.B. 330. The IRS has stated that its position regarding mail order churches is set forth in this ruling. IRS Exempt Organizations Handbook § 344.7 (1988).

previous standard of living. The church permitted her to use the home and automobile for personal uses. While the church's charter stated that it was organized exclusively for religious and charitable purposes, including a religious mission of healing the spirit, mind, emotions, and body, the church conducted few if any religious services and performed virtually no religious functions. The IRS concluded that the church existed primarily as a vehicle for handling the nurse's personal financial transactions and thus it was operated for the private interests of a designated individual rather than for a public interest.[65]

The IRS often asserts that a mail order church is ineligible for exempt status since its net earnings inure to the benefit of private individuals. A church cannot be exempt from federal income taxes if any part of its net earnings inures to the benefit of a private individual (other than as reasonable compensation for services rendered). Prohibited inurement may be indicated by a number of circumstances, including the following: (1) compensation paid by an exempt organization is excessive in light of services rendered; (2) the value of services performed and of the corresponding compensation paid cannot be established objectively; (3) payments are not compensation for services rendered; (4) material benefits are provided in addition to regular wages; (5) compensation is based on a percentage of a church's gross receipts; (6) substantially all of a church's gross receipts come from its minister and are returned to him or her in the form of compensation and reimbursement of personal expenses; or (7) a church exists primarily to facilitate the personal financial transactions of its founder.

To illustrate, inurement has been found in the following contexts: church ministers received fees, commissions, royalties, loans, a personal residence, and a car, in addition to ordinary wages;[66] a church devised a formula for determining the percentage of its gross receipts that would be payable to its minister, under which formula the minister received 63 percent of the church's gross receipts in one year and 53 percent in the next;[67] a boilermaker was ordained and chartered as "a church personally" by a mail order organization, took a vow of poverty, continued to work full time in secular employment, assigned his salary to his church account over which he maintained complete control, paid all of his personal expenses out of the church account, and claimed the maximum charitable contribution deduction for the amounts he transferred to the church account;[68] a married couple was ordained by and received a church charter from a mail order organization, established a church in their home, conducted religious services for between 3 and 10 persons, paid all of their secular income to the church, and received such income back in the form of compensation and a housing allowance;[69] a married couple took a vow of poverty and established a religious order in which they and their children were the only members, assigned all of their secular income to the order, and claimed a charitable contribution deduction for the income assigned;[70] a taxpayer was ordained by and received a church charter

---

[65] *See also* New Life Tabernacle v. Commissioner, 44 T.C.M. 309 (1982); Solander v. Commissioner, 43 T.C.M. 934 (1982); Self v. Commissioner, 41 T.C.M. 1465 (1981); Basic Bible Church v. Commissioner, 74 T.C. 846 (1980); Southern Church of Universal Brotherhood Assembled, Inc. v. Commissioner, 74 T.C. 1223 (1980).

[66] Founding Church of Scientology v. Commissioner, 412 F.2d 1197 (Ct. Cl. 1969), *cert. denied,* 397 U.S. 1009 (1970).

[67] People of God Community v. Commissioner, 75 T.C. 127 (1981). The court concluded that "paying over a portion of gross earnings to those vested with the control of a church organization constitutes private inurement . . . ."

[68] Hall v. Commissioner, 41 T.C.M. 1169 (1981). *See also* McGahen v. Commissioner, 76 T.C. 468 (1981).

[69] Church of the Transfiguring Spirit v. Commissioner, 76 T.C. 1 (1981). In all of the following cases, individuals were ordained by and received a church charter from a mail order organization, established a church in their homes, conducted few if any religious services, assigned their secular income to the church checking account out of which they paid most of their personal expenses, and attempted to claim the maximum charitable contribution deduction allowable for the income assigned. An IRS finding of inurement was upheld in each case. Basic Unit Ministry of Schurig v. Commissioner, 670 F.2d 1210 (D.C. Cir. 1982); Solander v. Commissioner 43 T.C.M. 934 (1982); Riemers v. Commissioner 42 T.C.M. 838 (1981); Southern Church of Universal Brotherhood Assembled v. Commissioner, 74 T.C. 1223 (1980); Bubbling Well Church of Universal Love v. Commissioner, 74 T.C. 531 (1980); Rev. Rul. 81-94, 1981-12 I.R.B. 15.

[70] Greeno v. Commissioner, 42 T.C.M. 1112 (1981); Granzow v. Commissioner, 739 F.2d 266 (7th Cir. 1984).

from a mail order organization, established a church in his home, declared himself and two others to be its ministers, assigned all of his secular income to the church, and received substantially all of it back in the form of wages, a housing allowance, loans, and travel allowances;[71] a church made substantial cash grants to its officers without provision for repayment;[72] and a mail order church could not support substantial payments made to its founder.[73]

Predictably, standards that are comprehensive enough to deal effectively with the abuses of mail order churches may be sufficiently broad to affect adversely some legitimate churches. For example, the Tax Court denied exempt status to a church having 56 members that conducted regular evangelistic worship services, performed baptisms, communion services, weddings, and burials; whose beliefs included the infallibility of the Bible; and whose pastor testified that "we do not have a creed but Christ; no law but love, no book but the Bible."[74] The IRS contended that the church was not entitled to exempt status since it had not established that (1) its charter or bylaws provided for the distribution of church property to another exempt organization upon dissolution, (2) it was operated exclusively for religious purposes, (3) it was operated for public rather than private interests, and (4) its net earnings did not inure to the benefit of private individuals. In another case, the Tax Court observed: "Until recent years, a mere declaration that an organization was a church was almost enough to assure its treatment as such under the revenue laws. The cynical abuse of the church concept for tax purposes in recent years, however, has made necessary the same critical analysis of organizations claiming exemption on that ground as organizations engaged in admittedly secular activities." [75]

> **Key point.** *Churches, like any other exempt organization, have the burden of proving that they meet each of the prerequisites to exempt status. The burden of proof is not on the IRS to disprove eligibility for exempt status. Many mail order churches have been denied exempt status because they could not prove that they in fact were organized or operated exclusively for exempt purposes or that none of their net earnings inured to the benefit of private individuals.*

Many mail order church schemes involve the assignment of a founder's secular income to his church's checking account, and the founder's claiming the largest allowable charitable contribution deduction on his or her federal income tax return. Since a charitable contribution deduction is available only to donors who make contributions to an exempt organization, the deductibility of charitable contributions to mail order churches often is challenged by the IRS. Unless taxpayers can prove that their contributions were made to a church that satisfies the prerequisites to exempt status listed in section 501(c)(3) of the Internal Revenue Code, their deductions will be disallowed. Occasionally, the IRS challenges a charitable contribution to a mail order church on the ground that such a transfer does not constitute a contribution.

---

[71] Unitary Mission Church v. Commissioner, 74 T.C. 507 (1980). Besides finding the amount of ministerial wages paid by the church to be excessive, the court observed that housing allowances also may be so excessive as to constitute unreasonable compensation. In either case, inurement occurs. The court rejected the church's argument that the First Amendment prohibits the courts from inquiring into the reasonableness of church salaries, at least where such inquiries involve no analysis of religious doctrine. *See also* Universal Life Church v. Commissioner, 83 T.C. 292 (1984); Church of Ethereal Joy v. Commissioner, 83 T.C. 20 (1984); Self-Realization Brotherhood, Inc. v. Commissioner, 48 T.C.M. 344 (1984).

[72] Church in Boston v. Commissioner, 71 T.C. 102 (1978).

[73] Bubbling Well Church of Universal Love v. Commissioner, 74 T.C. 531 (1980). *See also* Truth Tabernacle v. Commissioner, 41 T.C.M. 1405 (1981).

[74] Truth Tabernacle v. Commissioner, 41 T.C.M. 1405 (1981). *But cf.* Truth Tabernacle, Inc. v. Commissioner of Internal Revenue, T.C. Memo. 1989-451.

[75] Church of Ethereal Joy v. Commissioner, 83 T.C. 20, 27 (1984). An excellent summary of the abuses of mail order churches is contained in the congressional history to the Church Audit Procedures Act.

To illustrate, in Revenue Ruling 78-232,[76] the IRS disallowed a charitable contribution deduction for any part of a taxpayer's secular income that he assigned to his mail order church's checking account, since

> [s]ection 170 of the Code provides . . . a deduction for charitable contributions to or for the use of [exempt] organizations . . . . Section 170(c)(2) of the Code provides, in part, that the term "charitable contribution" means a contribution or gift to or for the use of a corporation organized and operated exclusively for religious or other charitable purposes, no part of the net earnings of which inures to the benefit of any private shareholder or individual.

> The term "charitable contribution," as used in section 170 of the Code, has been held to be synonymous with the word "gift." A gift for purposes of section 170 is a voluntary transfer of money or property that is made with no expectation of procuring a commensurate financial benefit in return for the transfer. It follows that if the benefits the donor can reasonably expect to obtain by making the transfer are sufficiently substantial to provide a quid pro quo for it, then no deduction under section 170 is allowable.

> In the instant case the money deposited by the taxpayer in the . . . church account was used or available for use for the taxpayer's benefit. . . . Accordingly, the amount of the salary checks deposited by the taxpayer in the bank account maintained in the name of the . . . church is not deductible as a "charitable contribution" under section 170 of the Code.

The Tax Court has observed that "our tolerance for taxpayers who establish churches solely for tax avoidance purposes is reaching a breaking point. Not only do these taxpayers use the pretext of a church to avoid paying their fair share of taxes, even when their brazen schemes are uncovered many of them resort to the courts in a shameless attempt to vindicate themselves."[77] Similarly, a federal appeals court has lamented that "we can no longer tolerate abuse of the judicial review process by irresponsible taxpayers who press stale and frivolous arguments, without hope of success on the merits, in order to delay or harass the collection of public revenues or for other nonworthy purposes."[78] The court ordered a mail order church to pay the government's costs and attorneys' fees incurred in contesting the church's claim of exemption, and warned that in the future it would "deal harshly" with frivolous tax appeals involving mail order churches. Other courts have sustained additions to tax for negligence or intentional disregard of tax laws pursuant to section 6653(a) of the Code.[79]

There are many potentially adverse consequences that can befall the founder of a mail order church. These include civil fraud penalties, criminal penalties, sanctions and costs of up to $25,000 for claiming a frivolous position, and substantial understatement penalties.[80] In addition, as part of its Illegal Tax Protester Program, the IRS has developed guidelines to assist its agents in "detecting, processing, examining and investigating" mail order churches.[81] Further, the IRS *Internal Revenue Manual* instructs agents to

> be especially alert to possible fraud when examining organizations identified under the Illegal Tax Protester Program. Fraudulent practices that have been uncovered in such cases include:

---

[76] Rev. Rul. 78-232, 1978-1 C.B. 69 (citations omitted).

[77] Miedaner v. Commissioner, 81 T.C. 272 (1982).

[78] Granzow v. Commissioner, 739 F.2d 265 (7th Cir. 1984).

[79] *See, e.g.,* Hall v. Commissioner, 729 F.2d 632 (9th Cir. 1984); Davis v. Commissioner, 81 T.C. 806 (1983).

[80] All of these penalties are discussed in R. HAMMAR, CHURCH AND CLERGY TAX GUIDE chapter 1 (published annually by the publisher of this text).

[81] INTERNAL REVENUE MANUAL § 7(10)75.6 (1988).

(a) Keeping a double set of books;

(b) Giving of false information/documents to the examining specialist;

(c) Concealing or destroying financial records;

(d) Closing out checking and savings accounts at banks and thereafter conducting financial affairs in cash;

(e) Disguising income from an unrelated trade or business as nontaxable income;

(f) Controlling and using funds in the church bank accounts by the reputed minister for his/her own benefit;

(g) Using funds claimed as contributions to the church for personal use of the reputed minister; and

(h) Falsifying application forms which are signed under penalties of perjury.[82]

The IRS is strictly construing the requirements of section 501(c)(3) when assessing the eligibility of a mail order church for exempt status, and it is threatening criminal prosecution of taxpayers who persist in using these tax evasion schemes.

Mail order clergy encounter difficulties in other contexts as well. For example, they have been denied eligibility to conduct marriage ceremonies by some states.[83]

§ 5-01.03 — Other Religious Organizations

Key point 5-01.03. Federal tax law refers to several kinds of religious organizations in addition to churches, including conventions or associations of churches, integrated auxiliaries of churches, integral parts of a church, and qualified church-controlled organizations. It is important to define these terms in order to determine whether or not special tax rules apply.

The Internal Revenue Code, income tax regulations, and IRS rulings refer to a number of church-related organizations, including *conventions or associations of churches, integrated auxiliaries of a church, integral agencies of a religious organization, integral parts of a church, qualified church controlled organizations, religious and apostolic organizations,* and *religious orders.* These terms will be defined in the paragraphs that follow.

1. Convention or Association of Churches

The term *convention or association of churches* appears several times in the Internal Revenue Code. Conventions and associations of churches are exempted from the requirements of applying for tax-exempt status,[84] filing annual information returns,[85] and filing returns regarding dissolution.[86] Unfortunately, there is no

---

[82] *Id.* at § 7(10)75.7 (1988).
[83] *See* section 3-04, *supra.*
[84] I.R.C. § 508(c)(1)(A).
[85] *Id.* at § 6033(a)(2)(A)(i).
[86] *Id.* at § 6043(b)(1).

adequate definition of the term. The income tax regulations define *a convention or association of churches* as "a convention or association of churches."[87] One court has observed that the phrase *convention or association of churches* was inserted in the Internal Revenue Code to relieve the concerns of congregational and independent churches that the term *church* included hierarchical religious denominations but not conventions or associations of "congregational" or independent churches.[88] Therefore, the term *convention or association of churches* pertains to the organizational structures of congregational churches.

2. INTEGRATED AUXILIARY

The term *integrated auxiliary* occasionally appears in the Internal Revenue Code and income tax regulations in connection with the term *church*. Integrated auxiliaries of churches are exempted from the requirements of applying for tax-exempt status,[89] filing annual information returns,[90] and filing returns regarding dissolution.[91]

IRS regulations[92] define the term *integrated auxiliary* to include an organization that is described in section 501(c)(3) of the Code, and that satisfies *both* of the following two tests:

Test 1 — affiliated with a church or convention or association of churches. The regulations specify that an organization is affiliated with a church or a convention or association of churches if it meets any one or more of the following three conditions: (1) it is covered by a group exemption letter; (2) it is operated, supervised, or controlled by a church or convention or association of churches; or (3) relevant facts and circumstances show that it is so affiliated. The regulations specify that the factors to be considered include:

(1) The organization's enabling instrument (corporate charter, trust instrument, articles of association, constitution, or similar document) or bylaws affirm that the organization shares common religious doctrines, principles, disciplines, or practices with the church or convention or association of churches.

(2) The church or convention or association of churches has authority to appoint or remove or to control the appointment or removal of at least one of the organization's officers or directors.

(3) The church or convention or association of churches receives reports, at least annually, on the financial and general operations of the organization.

(4) The corporate name of the organization indicates an institutional relationship, which relationship is affirmed by the church or convention or association of churches or a designee thereof; or if the corporate name of the organization does not indicate an institutional relationship, this institutional relationship is affirmed by the church, or convention or association of churches, or designee thereof.

(5) In the event of dissolution, the assets are required to be distributed to the church or convention or association of churches or to an affiliate thereof within the meeting of this regulation.

---

[87] Treas. Reg. § 1.170A-9(a).
[88] Lutheran Social Service of Minnesota v. United States, 758 F.2d 1283 (8th Cir. 1985).
[89] I.R.C. § 508(c)(1)(A).
[90] *Id.* at § 6033(a)(2)(A)(i).
[91] *Id.* at § 6043(b)(1).
[92] Treas. Reg. § 1.6033-2(h)

(6) Any other relevant fact or circumstance.[93]

The regulations state that the absence of one or more of these factors "does not necessarily preclude classification of an organization as being affiliated with a church or convention or association of churches."

Test 2 — internal support test. An organization satisfies the second test *unless it both*

(1) offers admissions, goods, services, or facilities for sale, other than on an incidental basis, to the general public (except goods, services, or facilities sold at a nominal charge or substantially less than cost), *and*

(2) normally receives more than 50 percent of its support from a combination of governmental sources; public solicitation of contributions (such as through a community fund drive); and receipts from the sale of admissions, goods, performance of services, or furnishing of facilities in activities that are not unrelated trades or businesses.

Note that the second disqualifying test refers to "public solicitation of contributions." The regulations suggest that this test is not met if an organization solicits funds primarily from churches and donors of a specific denomination. This conclusion is supported by the following example that is set forth in the regulations which define integrated auxiliaries:

Example. Organization A is described in sections 501(c)(3) and 509(a)(2) and is affiliated . . . with a church. Organization A publishes a weekly newspaper as its only activity. On an incidental basis, some copies of Organization A's publication are sold to nonmembers of the church with which it is affiliated. Organization A advertises for subscriptions at places of worship of the church. Organization A is internally supported, regardless of its sources of financial support, because it does not offer admissions, goods, services, or facilities for sale, other than on an incidental basis, to the general public. Organization A is an integrated auxiliary.

This example confirms the understanding expressed above that organizations that do not offer their services for sale to the general public and that do not engage in public solicitation of contributions satisfy the internally supported test. The example demonstrates that religious organizations that solicit and receive contributions *solely from affiliated churches* are not engaged in public solicitation of contributions and are internally supported.

The income tax regulations contain the following additional example:

Example. Organization B is a retirement home described in sections 501(c)(3) and 509(a)(2). Organization B is affiliated . . . with a church. Admission to Organization B is open to all members of the community for a fee. Organization B advertises in publications of general distribution appealing to the elderly and maintains its name on non-denominational listings of available retirement homes. Therefore, Organization B offers its services for sale to the general public on more than an incidental basis. Organization B receives a cash contribution of $50,000 annually from the church. Fees received by Organization B from its residents total $100,000 annually. Organization B does not receive any government support or contributions from the general public. Total support is $150,000 ($100,000 + $50,000), and $100,000 of that total is from receipts from the performance of services (two-thirds of total support). Therefore,

---

[93] *Id.*

Organization B receives more than 50 percent of its support from receipts from the performance of services. Organization B is not internally supported and is not an integrated auxiliary.

This example illustrates that some church-affiliated institutions will not be deemed internally supported and therefore will not be integrated auxiliaries.

In general, the philosophy of the IRS is that if an organization is "internally supported" by a church or religious denomination then there is no compelling reason why that organization should file annual information returns (Form 990) or an application for exemption from federal income tax (Form 1023). On the other hand, if an organization is not internally supported by a church or denomination, and is supported through public donations or the sale of products or services, then there is a compelling interest in having the public accountability that annual information returns and applications for exemption can provide (both of these forms are available for public inspection).

Key point. *The regulations specify that "men's and women's organizations, seminaries, mission societies, and youth groups" that are described in section 501(c)(3) and that meet the "affiliation" test described above "are integrated auxiliaries of a church regardless of whether such an organization meets the internal support requirement."*

3. INTEGRAL AGENCIES

The term *integral agency* occasionally appears in the Internal Revenue Code and associated regulations and refers to agencies that are integrally connected with churches and associations or conventions of churches. For example, ordained, commissioned, or licensed ministers are eligible for the housing allowance exclusion if they are engaged in the "administration and maintenance of religious organizations and their integral agencies."[94] In a revenue ruling, the IRS has listed the following criteria to be considered in determining whether a church-related institution is an integral agency of a religious organization:

1. whether the religious organization incorporated the institution

2. whether the corporate name of the institution indicates a church relationship

3. whether the religious organization continuously controls, manages, and maintains the institution

4. whether the trustees or directors of the institution are approved by or must be approved by the religious organization or church

5. whether trustees or directors may be removed by the religious organization or church

6. whether annual reports of finances and general operations are required to be made to the religious organization or church

7. whether the religious organization or church contributes to the support of the institution, and

---

[94] Treas. Reg. § 1.107-1(a).

8. whether, in the event of dissolution of the institution, its assets would be turned over to the religious organization or church.[95]

The IRS has stated that the absence of one or more of these characteristics will not necessarily be determinative in a particular case, and, that if the application of these eight criteria in a particular case does not clearly support an affirmative or negative answer, "the appropriate organizational authorities are contacted for a statement, in light of the criteria, whether the particular institution is an integral agency, and their views are carefully considered."[96]

Example. Rev. T is an ordained minister employed in an administrative capacity by a nursing home. The institution is affiliated with, but not controlled by, a religious denomination. Although the old age home had a corporate name which implied a church relationship and its articles of incorporation directed that upon dissolution all assets would be turned over to the sponsoring denomination, these facts were not sufficient to support a finding that the home was an integral agency of the denomination. Rev. T's administrative services in the control, conduct, and maintenance of the institution are not services performed in the exercise of ministry. Accordingly, he does not qualify for a housing allowance or any of the other special rules summarized above.[97]

Example. A college was ruled to be an integral agency of a church because of the following factors: (1) the board of directors of the college was indirectly controlled by the church because each board member had to be a member in good standing of the congregation; (2) every teacher was a member in good standing of the congregation; (3) the majority of students were members of the church; (4) all subjects taught at the college, whether in natural science, mathematics, social science, languages, etc., were taught with emphasis on religious principles and religious living; (5) the college had a department which performed all the functions for ministerial training that a seminary offers. Accordingly, ordained ministers employed in teaching or administrative positions at the college were engaged in the exercise of ministry and were eligible for a housing allowance.[98]

Example. Rev. F is an ordained minister who serves as a professor of religion at Texas Christian University. He occasionally officiates at weddings, preaches sermons, and performs other sacerdotal functions, but these activities are not part of his employment at the University. The University has a close relationship with the Christian Church (Disciples of Christ), but the Church does not control or manage the University either directly or indirectly. In fact, the University only satisfies the last of the 5 factors listed in Revenue Ruling 70-549 (see preceding examples). In addition, the University satisfies only two of the eight criteria cited in Revenue Ruling 72-606 (quoted above). Accordingly, the University is not an integral agency of the Church, and Rev. F is not eligible for any of the special provisions discussed above (including a housing allowance). Since he was not working for an integral agency of a church, he had to satisfy all three elements of the definition of "service performed by a minister in the exercise of his ministry" in order to qualify. He failed to satisfy all three elements with respect to his employment by the University.[99]

---

[95] Rev. Rul. 72-606, 1972-2 C.B. 78. *See also* R. HAMMAR, CHURCH AND CLERGY TAX GUIDE chapter 11 (published annually by the publisher of this text).
[96] *Id.*
[97] Rev. Rul. 72-606, 1972-2 C.B. 78. *See also* IRS Letter Ruling 8329042.
[98] Rev. Rul. 70-549, 1970-2 C.B. 16. *See also* Technical Advice Memorandum 9033002, and IRS Letter Rulings 7907160, 8004087, 80929145, 8922077, 9144047, and 9608027.
[99] Flowers v. United States, 82-1 USTC ¶ 9114 (N.D. Tex. 1981).

4. Integral Part of a Church

Prior to 1970, the income tax regulations specified that the term *church* included a religious organization that was an *integral part of a church*.[100] This term has no further relevance in light of the obsolescence of this regulation. The term does not occur elsewhere.

5. Qualified Church-controlled Organization

The term *qualified church-controlled organization* is used a few times in the Internal Revenue Code. For example, such organizations are exempt from the nondiscrimination rules that apply to tax-sheltered annuities under Code section 403(b),[101] and they are eligible for exemption from the employer's share of social security and Medicare taxes if certain conditions are satisfied.

A qualified church-controlled organization is defined by the Code as

> any church-controlled tax-exempt organization described in section 501(c)(3), other than an organization which (i) offers goods, services, or facilities for sale, other than on an incidental basis, to the general public, other than goods, services or facilities which are sold at a nominal charge which is substantially less than the cost of providing such goods, services, or facilities; and (ii) normally receives more than 25% of its support from either (I) governmental sources, or (II) receipts from admissions, sales of merchandise, performance of services, or furnishing of facilities, in activities which are not unrelated trades or businesses, or both.[102]

Clearly, local churches, church denominations, and church-controlled elementary and secondary schools are qualify as "church-controlled organizations." While it is less clear, it is reasonably certain that seminaries and Bible colleges also qualify. The committee report on the Tax Reform Act of 1986, in construing the term "qualified church-controlled organization," noted that it included "the typical seminary, religious retreat center, or burial society, regardless of its funding sources, because it does not offer goods, services, or facilities for sale to the general public." The committee report also noted that the term "qualified church-controlled organization" includes

> a church-run orphanage or old-age home, even if it is open to the general public, if not more than 25% of its support is derived from the receipts of admissions, sales of merchandise, performance of services, or furnishing of facilities (in other than unrelated trades or businesses) or from governmental sources. The committee specifically intends that the [term "qualified church-controlled organization" will not include] church-run universities (other than religious seminaries) and hospitals if both conditions (i) and (ii) exist.

6. Religious or Apostolic Associations or Corporations

The Code exempts *religious or apostolic associations or corporations* from federal income taxation if they

> have a common treasury or community treasury, even if such associations or corporations engage in business for the common benefit of the members, but only if the members thereof include (at

---

[100] Treas. Reg. § 1.511-2(a)(3)(ii) (emphasis added).
[101] I.R.C. §§ 403(b)(1)(D), 403(b)(12)(B).
[102] I.R.C. § 3121(w)(3)(B).

the time of filing their returns) in their gross income their entire pro rata shares, whether distributed or not, of the taxable income of the association or corporation for such year. Any amount so included in the gross income of a member shall be treated as a dividend received.[103]

Religious or apostolic associations and corporations must file a Form 1065 each year, stating the items of gross income and deductions, along with a statement listing the names and addresses of each member and the amount of his or her distributive share of the organization's taxable income.[104]

The IRS has issued guidance on the definition of the term *religious order*.[105] The Internal Revenue Code exempts from self-employment taxes, FICA taxes, and federal income tax withholding, compensation received for services performed by a member of a religious order in the exercise of duties required by the order. Neither the Code nor the income tax regulations defines the term *religious order*. To provide some certainty regarding the definition of a religious order, the IRS has published seven characteristics that traditionally have been associated with religious orders. The IRS came up with this list by reviewing the court decisions that have addressed the issue. From now on, the IRS will use the following characteristics in determining whether or not an organization is a religious order:

> (1) The organization is described in section 501(c)(3) of the Code. (2) The members of the organization vow to live under a strict set of rules requiring moral and spiritual self-sacrifice and dedication to the goals of the organization at the expense of their material well-being. (3) The members of the organization, after successful completion of the organization's training program and probationary period, make a long-term commitment to the organization (normally, more than two years). (4) The organization is, directly or indirectly, under the control and supervision of a church or convention or association of churches, or is significantly funded by a church or convention or association of churches. (5) The members of the organization normally live together as part of a community and are held to a significantly stricter level of moral and religious discipline than that required of lay church members. (6) The members of the organization work or serve full-time on behalf of the religious, educational, or charitable goals of the organization. (7) The members of the organization participate regularly in activities such as public or private prayer, religious study, teaching, care of the aging, missionary work, or church reform or renewal.

The IRS has clarified that "generally, the presence of all the above characteristics is determinative that the organization is a religious order" and that

> the absence of one or more of the other enumerated characteristics is not necessarily determinative in a particular case. Generally, if application of the above characteristics to the facts of a particular case does not clearly indicate whether or not the organization is a religious order, the [IRS] will contact the appropriate authorities affiliated with the organization for their views concerning the characteristics of the organization and their views will be carefully considered.[106]

---

[103] I.R.C. § 501(d). *See also* Riker v. Commissioner, 244 F.2d 220 (9th Cir. 1957); Rev. Rul. 78-100, 1978-1 C.B. 162; Rev. Rul. 77-295, 1977-2 C.B. 196; Rev. Proc. 72-5, 1972-1 C.B. 709.

[104] I.R.C. 6104(b) specifies that a religious or apostolic association's annual Form 1065 is not subject to public inspection.

[105] Rev. Proc. 91-20, I.R.B. 1991-10, 26.

[106] *Id. See also IRS Letter Ruling 9219012* (an organization was a religious order though it did not satisfy one of the 7 criteria) and *IRS Letter Rulings 9418012 and 9630011* (evangelical organizations were religious orders though they were not directly or indirectly under the control and supervision of a church or convention or association of churches or significantly funded by a church or convention or association of churches).

Example. A federal court rejected a church's claim that its employees' wages were exempt from federal tax withholding because they qualified for the exemption available to members of "religious orders."[107] The court defined a "religious order" as "a religious body typically an aggregate of separate communities living under a distinctive rule, discipline or constitution; a monastic brotherhood or society."

Tip. Few organizations will meet the current IRS definition of a religious order. Yet, a number of organizations are basing their "exemption" from tax withholding on their status as religious orders. Such organizations should carefully review the IRS definition and be sure that it is satisfied.

There is little if any justification for the confusing number of terms employed by the Internal Revenue Code and the income tax regulations in describing church-related organizations. Such terminology suggests a confusion on the part of Congress and the IRS in dealing with church-related organizations. An even more troubling concern is the largely discretionary authority of the IRS to interpret these ambiguously defined or undefined terms.

In summary, there clearly is a need for Congress to (1) reduce the unnecessarily confusing number of terms used in the Internal Revenue Code to describe and define church-related organizations; (2) sufficiently clarify the remaining definitions so as to eliminate discretionary application by the IRS; and (3) demonstrate a greater deference to the legitimate perceptions of bona fide churches concerning those entities that are sufficiently related as to come within the definition of the term *church*.

§ 5-02   Tax Legislation — State

Key point 5-02. The term "church" is used in a number of state tax laws, including property tax exemption statutes. State courts have struggled to provide an adequate definition..

Several state courts have attempted to define the term *church* in the process of interpreting state tax exemptions. To illustrate, in one case a religious radio station argued that it was exempt from state sales and use taxes since it was a church.[108] The radio station's corporate purpose was "to exalt the Lord Jesus Christ and to maintain facilities for the worship of God and for the teaching and preaching of the Gospel." The station actively engaged in religious activities, including broadcasting of predominantly religious programming, missions promotion, child evangelism, establishment of Bible study groups, and personal counseling. In addition, the station owned an auditorium that was used frequently for interdenominational worship services and related programs. The state tax commissioner challenged the station's exemption on the ground that it was not a church. In particular, the commissioner argued that the radio station could not be a church since it did not have a body of communicants gathered together in an order, or united under one form of government." The court, acknowledging that the term *church* "is not susceptible to a precise definition," summarily concluded that the radio station was entitled to the exemption since it "exhibited the essential qualities of a church," despite the fact that it did not have a definite congregation.

In another case,[109] a county tax assessor determined that a private residence was not a church, despite the homeowners' contention that monthly meetings of the eleven-member Ideal Life Church were held in the home

---

[107] Eighth Street Baptist Church v. United States, 291 F. Supp. 603 (D. Kan. 1968); *see also*, Bethel Baptist Church v. United States, 822 F.2d 1334 (3rd Cir. 1987); United States v. Philadelphia Yearly Meeting of the Religious Society of Friends, 91-1 U.S.T.C. ¶ 50,042 (E.D. Pa. 1990); Schultz v. Stark, 554 F. Supp. 1219 (D. Wis. 1983); Goldsboro Christian Schools, Inc. v. United States, 436 F. Supp. 1314 (D.S.C. 1976).

[108] Maumee Valley Broadcasting Assoc. v. Porterfield, 279 N.E.2d 863 (Ohio 1972). *But see* G.C.M. 38982.

[109] Ideal Life Church v. County of Washington, 304 N.W.2d 308 (Minn. 1981).

and the church had received a charter from the mail-order Universal Life Church. The tax assessor's determination was upheld by the state supreme court, which quoted with approval the reasoning of a lower court in the same case:

> [T]he proper test for determination of a "church" depends upon an analysis of all the facts and circumstances of each particular case. In the present action the following factors . . . lead to the clear conclusion that Petitioner is not a "church" . . . .
>
> 1. In substance, the preconceived and primary, if not the sole motive behind petitioner's organization and operation was tax avoidance in favor of the private individuals who control the corporation . . . .
>
> 2. Petitioner's doctrine and beliefs, such as they are, are intentionally vague and non-binding upon its members.
>
> 3. Petitioner's members freely continue to practice other religions.
>
> 4. Petitioner has no formally trained or ordained ministry.
>
> 5. Petitioner has no sacraments, rituals, education courses or literature of its own.
>
> 6. Petitioner has no liturgy, other than simple meetings which resemble mere social gatherings or discussion groups rather than religious worship.
>
> 7. Petitioner is not an institution which advances religion (as that term is commonly understood) as a way of life for all men.
>
> 8. Petitioner does not require a belief in any Supreme Being or beings.[110]

Another court upheld the property tax exemption of a 65-acre tract of land containing a religious hermitage and retreat center. While noting that the property was "not a church in the narrow sense," the court concluded that a church is more than merely an edifice affording people the opportunity to worship God. . . . To limit a church to being merely a house of prayer and sacrifice would, in a large degree, be depriving the church of the opportunity of enlarging, perpetuating and strengthening itself and the congregation."[111]

One court has held that an evangelistic association is not a church and thus is not exempt from unemployment insurance payroll taxes.[112] The court noted that the evangelistic association was exempt from federal income tax, was established for avowedly religious purposes, conducted worship services in cities throughout the country, had a mailing list in excess of 25,000 persons, and relied upon contributions for its support. However, the association could not be deemed a church since "there was no group of believers who had voluntarily bound themselves together in an organized association for the purpose of shared and regular

---

[110] *Id.* at 315. *But see* State v. American Fundamentalist Church, 530 N.W.2d 200 (Minn. 1995), in which the Minnesota Supreme Court, while not overruling its 8-factor test, noted that it should be applied together with a "subjective" test that looks to the sincerity of an organization's religious belief to be sure that it is not "cloaking a secular enterprise with the legal protections of religion." The 8-factor test was rejected by the Wisconsin Supreme Court in Waushara County v. Graf, 480 N.W.2d 16 (Wis. 1992).

[111] Order of Conventuals v. Lee, 409 N.Y.S.2d 667, 669 (1978).

[112] Vic Coburn Evangelistic Assoc. v. Employment Division, 582 P.2d 51 (Ore. 1978). *See also* Alton Newton Evangelistic Assoc., Inc. v. South Carolina Employment Security Commission, 326 S.E.2d 165 (S.C. 1985).

worship." Another court ruled that an interdenominational Christian youth organization that conducted religious services and administered sacraments was a church and thus was exempt from payment of unemployment taxes.[113] The court concluded that a comprehensive definition of the term *church* was not possible. Instead, the court opted for a functional approach—if an organization performs church functions, such as the conduct of worship and the promulgation of a creed, it will be deemed a church.

Other state courts have ruled that (1) a separately incorporated religious school operated by a group of local churches was not a church for purposes of unemployment law;[114] and (2) a Christian foundation that propagated its beliefs through written publications and radio broadcasts rather than through face-to-face communications, and that was not affiliated with any church or denomination, was a "church" for purposes of a state unemployment law.[115]

§ 5-03 Zoning law

The civil courts often have been called upon to define the term *church* in the context of zoning laws. There rarely is a question about the status of a building used by a congregation for regular worship services. However, many churches do much more than conduct worship services. Some operate a preschool, elementary or secondary school, homeless shelter, recreational building, camp, bookstore, counseling center, or radio station. Can these kinds of activities be conducted on property that is zoned for "church" use?

§ 5-03.01 — Churches

> **Key point 5-02.01.** *Local zoning laws generally allow "churches" in residential areas. The courts have struggled with applying this term to various activities and organizations other than traditional congregations meeting in a building for regular worship services.*

Many other courts have been asked to decide whether a particular use of property comes within the definition of a *church* under municipal zoning laws. The following activities and uses have been held to come within that definition: use of a home across the street from a church for women's fellowship meetings and religious education classes;[116] a single-family residence used by the United Presbyterian Church as a religious coffeehouse for university students;[117] a priest's home, convent, and parochial school;[118] a 24-acre tract of land containing a large mansion that was used as a synagogue and a meeting place for the congregation's social groups and youth activities;[119] a kindergarten, play area, and parochial school;[120] a 37-acre estate used by an Episcopal church as a religious retreat and center for religious instruction;[121] and a private school operated by a Baptist church.[122]

---

[113] Young Life Campaign v. Patino, 176 Cal. Rptr. 23 (1981).

[114] Nampa Christian Schools Foundation v. State Department of Employment, 719 P.2d 1178 (Ida. 1986). The court concluded that the school was exempt under another provision of the unemployment law which exempted an organization operated primarily for religious purposes and which is operated or principally supported by a church or group of churches.

[115] Christian Jew Foundation v. State, 653 S.W.2d 607 (Tex. App. 1983).

[116] Twin-City Bible Church v. Zoning Board of Appeals, 365 N.E.2d 1381 (Ill. 1977).

[117] Synod of Chesapeake, Inc. v. Newark, 254 A.2d 611 (Del. 1969).

[118] Board of Zoning Appeals v. Wheaton, 76 N.E.2d 597 (Ind. 1948).

[119] Community Synagogue v. Bates, 154 N.Y.S.2d 15 (1956).

[120] Diocese of Rochester v. Planning Board, 154 N.Y.S.2d 849 (1956).

[121] Diocese of Central New York v. Schwarzer, 199 N.Y.S.2d 939 (1960), *aff'd*, 217 N.Y.S.2d 567 (1961).

[122] City of Concord v. New Testament Baptist Church, 382 A.2d 377 (N.H. 1978). *Accord* Alpine Christian Fellowship v. Pitkin County, 870 F. Supp. 991 (D. Colo. 1994).

Other courts have concluded that certain uses of property do not constitute a church in the context of zoning laws. To illustrate, one court has held that an area restricted to residential and church uses could not accommodate temporary, open-air camp meetings.[123] The court observed that not every place in which religious services are conducted is a church. It inferred that a church at the least must consist of "a building set apart for public worship," and thus could not include camp meetings. Another court held that a dwelling of 16 bedrooms and 12 bathrooms occupied by 25 people comprising four different families, all members of the American Orthodox Catholic Church, was not a church or parish house even though religious instruction was given daily for one hour to the children and three times a week to the adults.[124] The court reasoned that "the principal use of the building . . . is that of a dwelling for residential purposes" and that "the incidental religious instruction provided to the families does not change this fact."

Other courts have held that the following activities were not *churches* for purposes of zoning laws: a 28-acre tract used by a Jewish foundation for a conference center, leadership training center, and children's retreat;[125] a private school operated by a local Baptist church;[126] a religious school not operated or controlled by a church;[127] camp meetings;[128] a parish house used for Sunday school, choir practice, and church committee meetings;[129] a religious retreat house;[130] a dwelling of sixteen bedrooms and twelve bathrooms occupied by twenty-five persons comprising four different families, all members of the American Orthodox Catholic church;[131] a child-care center operated in a minister's residence;[132] a single-family residence used for organized religious services;[133] and a college.[134] Similarly, when a farmers' organization purchased a church building for meetings promoting agriculture and "higher ideals of manhood, womanhood, and citizenship," a court concluded that the building no longer could be considered a church.[135] "A church," observed the court, "[is] a place or edifice consecrated to religious worship, where people join together in some form of public worship."

> **Example.** *A New York court ruled that a city zoning board acted improperly in denying a homeowner's application to use his home as a church. The court noted that "the inclusion of churches among uses permitted in the [residential] zoning district is tantamount to a legislative determination that the use is in harmony with the general zoning plan and will not be detrimental to the surrounding area. It is presumed that a religious use will have a beneficial effect in a residential area." However, this presumption may be "rebutted with evidence of a significant impact on traffic congestion, property values, municipal services and the like." The zoning board's refusal to allow the homeowner to use his home as a church was improper since it was "based on conclusory findings and not upon substantial evidence of significant adverse effects."[136]*

---

[123] Portage Township v. Full Salvation Union, 29 N.W.2d 297 (Mich. 1947).

[124] People v. Kalayjian, 352 N.Y.S.2d 115 (1973). *See also* Heard v. Dallas, 456 S.W.2d 440 (Tex. 1970) (child care center operated in minister's residence held not to be a "church").

[125] State ex rel. B'Nai B'rith Foundation v. Walworth County, 208 N.W.2d 113 (Wis. 1973).

[126] Abram v. City of Fayetteville, 661 S.W.2d 371 (Ark. 1984).

[127] Chaminade College v. City of Creve Coeur, 956 S.W.2d 440 (Mo. App. 1997).

[128] Portage Township v. Full Salvation Union, 29 N.W.2d 297 (Mich. 1947).

[129] Newark Athletic Club v. Board of Adjustment, 144 A. 167 (N.Y. 1928).

[130] Independent Church of the Realization of the Word of God, Inc. v. Board of Zoning Appeals, 437 N.Y.S.2d 443 (1981).

[131] People v. Kalayjian, 352 N.Y.S.2d 115 (1973).

[132] Heard v. Dallas, 456 S.W.2d 440 (Tex. 1970).

[133] Grosz v. City of Miami Beach, 721 F.2d 729 (5th Cir. 1983); State v. Cameron, 460 A.2d 191 (N.J. App. 1983).

[134] Fountain Gate Ministries, Inc. v. City of Plano, 654 S.W.2d 841 (Tex. App. 1983).

[135] In re Upper St. Clair Township Grange No. 2032, 152 A.2d 768 (Pa. 1959).

[136] Neddermeyer v. Ontario Planning Board, 548 N.Y.S.2d 951 (1989).

Example. A Connecticut court ruled that a convent and chapel constituted a "church" for purposes of zoning law despite the operation of a bookstore and audiovisual center on the premises. The court concluded that the convent and chapel, by themselves, clearly satisfied the definition of a church. The fact that a bookstore and audiovisual center were also operated on the premises did not affect this conclusion, since the books and materials were religious and educational in nature and were sold to support the order's missionary and instructional purposes. The court quoted from a 1943 decision of the United States Supreme Court: "The mere fact that religious literature is sold rather than donated does not transform evangelism into a commercial enterprise." Further, the court concluded that the definition of "church" must be "regarded broadly for zoning purposes in order to avoid serious constitutional questions." The court rejected the claim that the convent and chapel should not be allowed in a residential neighborhood since they "would be a detriment to the neighborhood by increasing traffic congestion." The court observed that the intersection where the order planned to construct the convent and chapel "carried a daily traffic volume of over 18,000 cars," and that the construction of the convent and chapel "would draw approximately twenty [additional] cars per day." This case will be of interest to the many churches that operate bookstores on their premises.[137]

Example. A North Carolina court ruled that a church-owned house used by a church for social events was not a "church" for purposes of a local zoning law. The zoning law permitted "churches" in a city's historic district. A church owned a house in the historic district that was used for such purposes as bridge club, social gatherings, community functions, and occasional choir practices and religious instruction. The church planned to sell the home to an individual who wanted to use the home for a "bed and breakfast" establishment. The city informed the purchaser that such a use would not be permitted. The purchaser argued that the church's use of the home was also a "nonconforming" use that was allowed by the city and that could be continued by future owners. A court agreed that the home, as used by the church, was "nonconforming" since it was not a church. The court noted that the term "church" is not defined in the zoning law. It continued: "The expression "church" ordinarily embraces three basic and related definitions: (1) a building set apart for public worship; (2) a place of worship of any religion; and (3) the organization of Christianity or of an association of Christians worshipping together." The city zoning commission insisted that the third definition applied in this case—a church is an organization for religious purposes. The commission claimed that the term "church" cannot be limited to a building where religious services are held, but must also include any building owned and used by a church. The court rejected this sweeping definition, noting that it "would produce the unreasonable result that every building owned by a church or 'organization for religious purposes' would qualify as a 'church' for purposes of the ordinance. . . . [W]e believe the plain and ordinary meaning of 'church' . . . to be 'a building set apart for public worship.'"[138]

Example. The use of a two-story residence and smaller buildings on the premises qualified as a church within the meaning of a zoning ordinance, when the use of the buildings included daily religious ceremonies, prayers, lectures, and a public feast held each Sunday.[139]

Example. A Catholic religious order was formed for the purpose of intercessory prayer. The order purchased a tract of land including a large home. The home contained a chapel which could accommodate as many as 50 worshippers. It was used to conduct seminars on prayer. These events usually involved between 20 and 30 participants. The home also was used for worship services, and as a residence for several members of the order. The tract was subject to a "restrictive covenant" that prohib-

---

[137] Daughters of St. Paul v. Zoning Board of Appeals, 549 A.2d 1076 (Conn. App. 1988).

[138] Hayes v. Fowler, 473 S.E.2d 442 (N.C. App. 1996).

[139] Marsland v. International Society for Krishna Consciousness, 66 Haw. 119, 657 P.2d 1035 (1983).

ited it from being used for any purpose other than a church and certain other uses. Neighbors filed a lawsuit, claiming that the order's use of the property was in violation of the restrictive covenant. A court agreed, concluding that the order was not using the property as a church. The court based its conclusion on ten factors: (1) the order did not have rules, regulations, or discipline; (2) there was no priest assigned to the order; (3) there was no regular public mass or worship on the grounds; (4) for the most part, the residents attended their own parishes for mass; (5) the grounds were not open to the public for mass and other related church activities on a regular basis; (6) the order had no parish lines or jurisdictional limits; (7) the order's name did not include the word "church"; (8) the IRS recognized the order as an educational organization and not as a church; (9) the Catholic Church does not ordain females as priests; and (10) the order did not have any official recognition within the Catholic Church. A state appeals court reversed the trial court's decision, and ruled that the order's use of its property constituted a church. The court noted that the "plain, ordinary, and popular meaning of the word church includes a building in which people assemble for the worship of God and for the administration of such offices and services as pertain to that worship, a building consecrated to the honor of God and religion, and a place where persons regularly assemble for worship." The court concluded that the order's use of its property "having a priest assigned to it living on its grounds and holding daily religious services open to the public, is, under any definition, a use consistent with the plain, ordinary, and popular meaning of a church or use incident to a church."[140]

Example. *The Supreme Court of Ohio, in concluding that a religious organization was exempt from state sales tax as a church, observed, "It has adherents. It adopts the Bible as the main source of its dogma, it propagates a comprehensive set of religious objectives and beliefs which attempt to answer its adherents' religious concerns, and it conducts services . . . . It employs ministers who preside at sacramental ceremonies, operates schools to train ministers, and sends forth missionaries to spread its beliefs."[141]*

Example. *The Arkansas Supreme Court concluded that the word "church" in a state law prohibiting the sale of liquor within 200 yards of a church "means the place where a body of people or worshipers associate together for religious purposes." This definition included a congregation of forty members, thirteen of whom were active, that met for religious services every Sunday morning.[142]*

Example. *A Texas court concluded that a proposed building that was to devote 2,400 square feet to healing and prayer rooms but only 600 square feet to a "church proper" was not a church.[143]*

Example. *A Texas court ruled that even though an Episcopal vicar conducted religious worship and training in his rectory, this did not change what was essentially a day nursery into a "church" exempt from zoning regulations.[144]*

Example. *A federal court in Texas ruled that a small area used for religious purposes in a prison was not a "church" for purposes of a local ordinance banning any sexually oriented business within 1,000 feet of a "church." The ordinance defined a church as "a building in which persons regularly assemble for religious worship and activities intended primarily for purposes connected with such worship or for propagating a particular form of religious belief." The court concluded that the space used for religious*

---

[140] Latenser v. Intercessors of the Lamb, Inc., 553 N.W.2d 458 (Neb. 1996).
[141] The Way International v. Limbach, 552 N.E.2d 908 (Ohio 1990).
[142] Arkansas A.B.C. v. Person, 832 S.W.2d 249 (Ark. 1992).
[143] Coe v. City of Dallas, 266 S.W.2d 181 (Tex. App. 1953).
[144] Heard v. City of Dallas, 456 S.W.2d 440 (Tex. App. 1970).

worship within the prison did not satisfy this definition since it was a very small area of the prison; it was not used exclusively for religious purposes; it occasionally was shifted to different locations within the facility; and did not constitute a "building" as required by the ordinance.[145]

§ 5-03.02 — Accessory Uses

***Key point 5-02.02.** Local zoning laws generally allow "churches" in residential areas. The courts generally have extended this term to various "accessory uses" that are needed for a church to carry out its mission and purposes.*

Many zoning laws permit uses that are "accessory" to a permitted use. As one court has observed:

A church is more than merely an edifice affording people the opportunity to worship God. Strictly religious uses and activities are more than prayer and sacrifice and all churches recognize that the area of their responsibility is broader than leading the congregation in prayer. Churches have always developed social groups for adults and youth where the fellowship of the congregation is strengthened with the result that the parent church is strengthened. To limit a church to being merely a house of prayer and sacrifice would, in a large degree, be depriving the church of the opportunity of enlarging, perpetuating, and strengthening itself and the congregation.[146]

To illustrate, one court upheld a church's right to construct a recreational complex on property adjacent to its sanctuary despite the claim of neighboring landowners that the complex was not a church and thus should not be permitted in a residential district.[147] The court concluded that the term *church* "is broader than the church building itself" and must be interpreted to include "uses customarily incidental or accessory to church uses . . . if reasonably closely related, both in distance and space, to the main church purpose." The court upheld the use of the recreational complex since the activities conducted on the field were an integral part of the church's overall program.

Other courts have found that the following uses were accessory to a permitted church use and therefore were appropriate in a residential district: a church activities building and playground,[148] a kindergarten play area,[149] a parking lot,[150] residential use of church buildings by members,[151] a home for parochial school teachers,[152] a school,[153] a neon sign constructed on church property to inform the public as to the time of worship services,[154] a center for performing arts,[155] and a sanctuary or shelter for the homeless.[156]

---

[145] Hooters, Inc. v. City of Texarkana, 897 F. Supp. 946 (E.D. Tex. 1995).

[146] Cash v. Brookshire United Methodist Church, 573 N.E.2d 692 (Ohio App. 1988).

[147] Corporation of the Presiding Bishop v. Ashton, 448 P.2d 185 (Ida. 1968).

[148] Board of Zoning Appeals v. New Testament Bible Church, Inc., 411 N.E.2d 681 (Ind. 1980).

[149] Diocese of Rochester v. Planning Board, 154 N.Y.S.2d 849 (1956).

[150] Mahrt v. First Church of Christ, Scientist, 142 N.E.2d 567 (Ohio 1955), *aff'd*, 142 N.E.2d 678 (Ohio 1955).

[151] Havurah v. Zoning Board of Appeals, 418 A.2d 82 (Conn. 1979).

[152] Board of Zoning Appeals v. New Testament Bible Church, Inc., 411 N.E.2d 681 (Ind. 1980).

[153] City of Concord v. New Testament Baptist Church, 382 A.2d 377 (N.H. 1978); Westbury Hebrew Congregation, Inc. v. Downer, 302 N.Y.S.2d 923 (1969); Diocese of Rochester v. Planning Board, 154 N.Y.S.2d 849 (1956).

[154] Parkview Baptist Church v. Pueblo, 336 P.2d 310 (Colo. 1959).

[155] North Shore Hebrew Academy v. Wegman, 481 N.Y.S.2d 142 (1984).

[156] St. John's Evangelical Lutheran Church v. City of Hoboken, 479 A.2d 935 (N.J. App. 1983); Lubavitch Chabad House of Illinois, Inc. v. City of Evanston, 445 N.E.2d 343 (Ill. App. 1982); Greentree at Murray Hill Condominium v. Good Shepherd Episcopal Church, 550 N.Y.S.2d 981 (1989).

Not every use of church property, however, will be so approved. The following uses of church property have been disallowed on the ground that they were not accessory to permitted church use: parking of a church bus on church property,[157] a ritualarium constructed by a Jewish synagogue,[158] a 301-foot radio transmission tower that was more than ten times higher than neighboring residences,[159] and a school.[160]

Example. A city enacted a zoning ordinance permitting only single-family dwellings, churches, schools, libraries, and farms in areas classified as "residential." A church purchased seven acres of undeveloped land in a residential zone and constructed a church building, parking lot, and recreational complex consisting of two softball diamonds. The softball diamonds were surrounded by banks of high-intensity electric lights, which made nighttime games possible. Several neighbors complained of the bright lights, noise, dust, traffic, and stray softballs. The city discontinued electrical service to the softball fields, defending its action on the ground that the lighted softball fields were not a permissible activity in a residential zone. The church sued the city, arguing that the softball fields were a legitimate extension of the church itself, and therefore were permissible. The court agreed with the church: "The activities conducted on this field are an integral part of the church program and are sufficiently connected with the church itself that the use of this property for recreational purposes is permissible." The court emphasized that "the term 'church' is broader than the church building itself" and must be interpreted to include "uses customarily incidental or accessory to church uses . . . if reasonably closely related, both in substance and in space, to the main church purpose."[161]

Example. An Ohio appeals court ruled that a church could use its property to conduct a "Little League" baseball program, despite the claim of a neighbor that such use violated local zoning law. The church maintained that one of its fundamental tenets was that worship involves not only religious services, but also reaching out to the community through sponsorship of activities such as scouting and Little League. The church property was located in a residential zone, which permitted churches and "church use." A trial court agreed with the neighbor that the operation of a baseball program on church property was not a permitted use of church property in an area zoned for "church use." A state appeals court reversed this decision and permitted the baseball program to continue. The court observed: "The trial court appears to suggest that a church is only a building and any use of the building or land adjacent must be necessary to the operation of that building as a church. We disagree." The Ohio court concluded that "activities such as sponsoring a Little League baseball program on land owned by, and adjacent to, the [church] are incidental to, and form a part of, the public worship program of [the church] and are permitted under the city zoning ordinances as a church use." The court emphasized that zoning ordinances must be construed "in favor of the property owner" (whose use of property is being questioned) and "in favor of the free use of property."[162]

Example. The Missouri Supreme Court ruled that a church-run child care center is a permissible activity on church property zoned exclusively for church or residential purposes. The court acknowledged that the zoning ordinance did not allow child care facilities in the neighborhood in which the church was located, but it concluded that such an activity was a permissible "accessory" use. The court

---

[157] East Side Baptist Church v. Klein, 487 P.2d 549 (Colo. 1971).
[158] Sexton v. Bates, 85 A.2d 833 (N.J. 1951), *aff'd*, 91 A.2d 162 (N.J. 1952).
[159] Gallagher v. Zoning Board of Adjustment, 32 Pa. D. & C.2d 669 (Pa. 1963).
[160] Damascus Community Church v. Clackamas County, 610 P.2d 273 (Ore. 1980), *appeal dismissed*, 450 U.S. 902 (1981).
[161] Corporation of the Presiding Bishop v. Ashton, 448 P.2d 185, 189 (Ida. 1968).
[162] Cash v. Brookshire United Methodist Church, 573 N.E.2d 692 (Ohio App. 1988). The court rejected the neighbor's claim that the property's ineligibility for a property tax exemption prevented it from being considered an accessory use of the church.

observed: "The day care program is subordinate to the principal use of the church. It was created by the governing body of the church and funded by the church. The governing body determined the curriculum for the program and hired a director. The record shows that the church operates the day care to attract new members to the church and accomplish its mission of preaching the gospel and serving the community. Similarly, the day care is subordinate in area to the principal building and use of the church. The day care service contributes to the comfort and convenience of the church parishioners by providing child care for them. The day care proper is located on the same lot as the church and it is located in the same zoning district." Accordingly, the child care center was an accessory use of the church under Missouri law and was a permissible use of church property. [163]

Example. *A New York state court ruled that a church could operate a homeless shelter despite the complaints of neighboring residents. In response to a citywide need for emergency shelters for thousands of homeless, a church in New York City opened its doors to groups of 10 homeless men for temporary emergency shelter 3 nights each week. The church was part of a network of some 380 churches and synagogues in the city that provide more than 400,000 individual nights of temporary shelter annually. The city provides the churches and synagogues with beds, linens, clothing, toiletries, and cleaning supplies, and inspects shelters for compliance with health and safety regulations. Homeless men are transported to the church from a "drop-in center," and arrive at 9:30 PM. They are picked up by bus the following morning at 6:00 AM. From the time of their arrival until their departure the next morning, the men are continually supervised and are not allowed to congregate in the street. The church's minister asserted that sheltering the homeless is an important part of the church's religious mission. Neighboring luxury condominium owners sought a court order preventing the church from continuing its homeless shelter. They complained that the shelter violated city zoning laws, and constituted a public nuisance. The court began its opinion by observing that the lawsuit "concerns the extent, if any, to which the court may or should be brought in as arbiter of a dispute involving the right of a church and its parishioners to exercise their religion and to practice Christian charity by temporarily sheltering the homeless, and the rights of some adjacent property [owners] who fear crime, drug sales, prostitution and a [decrease] in their property values." The court acknowledged that churches may only be used for religious and social purposes, but it noted that "it has long been held that a church or synagogue may be used for accessory uses and activities which go beyond just prayer and worship." The court concluded that a church's operation of a shelter for the homeless is a legitimate "accessory use" of a church, since it "is a use which is clearly incidental to, and customarily found in connection with," a church. Therefore, a church's operation of a homeless shelter did not violate the city's zoning laws.* [164]

Example. *A Pennsylvania state court ruled that a local zoning board acted improperly in refusing to allow a church to use a portion of its property for counseling services. The church sought a permit allowing it to convert a building containing the church offices into a counseling center. The church offered extensive pastoral counseling services to members and non-members alike. A zoning board denied the church's request on the ground that professional counseling was not a permitted use in a residential district (in which the church was located). The board expressed the view that "the counseling sought to be offered was of a secular nature and not directly related to the church's function." The*

---

[163] City of Richmond Heights v. Richmond Heights Presbyterian Church, 764 S.W.2d 647 (Mo. 1989). *Accord* Shim v. Washington Township Planning Board, 689 A.2d 804 (N.J. Super. 1997) ("What is clear from this modern trend is that a church's ministry is not confined to prayer or dissemination of its religious beliefs. Religious institutions consider day care centers as part of their spiritual mission, not necessarily in advancing their religious teachings, but by providing a valuable community service. Grounded on this broad-based commitment, we are persuaded that a church-operated day care center is . . . an incidental use of church facilities.")

[164] Greentree at Murray Hill Condominium v. Good Shepherd Episcopal Church, 550 N.Y.S.2d 981 (Sup. 1989).

church challenged this ruling in court, and won. The court ruled that the church's properties could lawfully be used for counseling since "counseling is an integral part of the church's activities" and therefore was a permissible "church use."[165]

Example. *The Alabama Supreme Court ruled that a church could not create a parking lot on land located across the street from the church. A church purchased land across the street from the church building in order to expand its parking facilities. Neighboring landowners complained that such a use of the property was not permitted by local zoning law. A local zoning board ruled in favor of the church. It reasoned that churches were permitted uses in the area in question, and that a church parking lot should be permitted as an "accessory use" by a church. The neighbors appealed to a state appeals court, which reversed the decision of the zoning board and prohibited the church from establishing the parking lot. The case was then appealed to the state supreme court, which agreed with the appeals court that the parking lot should not be allowed. The court noted that the local zoning ordinance defined an accessory use as a use "on the same lot with" the principal use or structure. The court concluded that "the definition of accessory use in the ordinance is consistent with the general rule that the accessory use must be located on the same lot as the building to which it is accessory." Since the proposed parking lot was across the street from the church, it was not "on the same lot" and accordingly could not be permitted as an accessory use.*[166]

Example. *A federal appeals court ruled that a county did not violate a church's constitutional right to religious freedom by denying it a zoning variance to operate a homeless shelter on its premises. A church became concerned with the problem of homelessness in its community. Homeless people were living in vacant lots under unsanitary conditions. In response to this community crisis, the church converted a building on its premises into a shelter for the homeless. The shelter created considerable distress among some residents of the community who were concerned about health and safety problems associated with the shelter. A zoning board later ordered the church to close the shelter on the ground that it was not a permitted use of the church's property under the county zoning ordinance and the church had not been granted a variance. The church sued the county arguing that closing the shelter would violate its first amendment right to freely exercise its religion. Specifically, the church argued that sheltering the homeless is an essential aspect of the Christian faith. A federal appeals court ruled that no constitutional rights had been violated by the county's action.*[167]

---

[165] Church of the Savior v. Zoning Hearing Board, 568 A.2d 1336 (Pa. Common. 1989). *See also* Needham Pastoral Counseling Center, Inc. v. Board of Appeals, 557 N.E.2d 43 (Mass. App. 1990).

[166] Ex parte Fairhope Board of Adjustments and Appeals, 567 So.2d 1353 (Ala. 1990).

[167] First Assembly of God v. Collier County, 20 F.3d 419 (11th Cir. 1994). The court relied almost entirely on a 1993 decision of the United States Supreme Court in which the Court struck down a municipal ordinance that prohibited ritualistic animal sacrifices by the Santeria religion. The Supreme Court observed: "In addressing the constitutional protection for free exercise of religion, our cases establish the general proposition that a law that is neutral and of general applicability need not be justified by a compelling governmental interest even if the law has the incidental effect of burdening a particular religious practice." Church of the Lukumi Babaluaye, Inc. v. City of Hialeah, 113 S. Ct. 2217 (1993). The federal appeals court concluded that the county zoning law that prohibited the operation of homeless shelters without a variance was a "neutral law of general applicability," and accordingly it was valid even if it burdened the church's exercise of its religion. *Accord* Daytona Rescue Mission, Inc. v. City of Daytona Beach, 885 F. Supp. 1554 (M.D. Fla. 1995). *But see* Capital City Rescue Mission v. City of Albany, 652 N.Y.S.2d 388 (N.Y. 1997).

INSTRUCTIONAL AIDS TO CHAPTER 5

Terms

accessory use

church

convention or association of churches

integral agency

integrated auxiliary

qualified church-controlled organizations

religious or apostolic associations

religious orders

religious organizations

Learning Objectives

- Identify several references to the term *church* in the Internal Revenue Code.

- Summarize some of the more common judicial interpretations of the term *church*.

- Familiarity with the fourteen characteristics of a church developed by the IRS.

- Recognize several other terms used in the Internal Revenue Code, including *conventions or associations of churches, integrated auxiliaries of a church, integral agencies of a religious organization, integral parts of a church, qualified church-controlled organizations,* and *religious orders.*

- Describe the importance of the definition of the term *church* in the context of zoning laws.

- Describe the importance of the definition of the term *church* in the context of state property tax exemption laws.

Short-Answer Questions

1. T, an electrician, obtains ministerial credentials after completing several correspondence school courses. He begins a Bible study group in his home. The group meets twice weekly for religious instruction and worship. Offerings are taken which go directly to T. Is T's home a church for purposes of local zoning law? Explain.

2. What is *integrated auxiliary of a church*? Why would it be advantageous for an organization affiliated with a church to be considered an integrated auxiliary?

3. Is a church-controlled college an *integral agency* of the church? What difference does it make?

4. A local church, seeking to eliminate its payroll tax reporting obligations, attempts to characterize its eight nonminister employees (including secretarial, clerical, accounting, and custodial personnel) as a *religious order*. Will this arrangement eliminate the church's payroll tax reporting obligations? Explain.

5. A church begins a private elementary school. The church separately incorporates the school. Is the school exempt from federal income taxes? Explain.

6. J, an attorney, purchases ministerial credentials from a mail order organization. She declares her home to be a church, and begins to conduct weekly services before her family and a few friends. She contributes half of her income to the church as a charitable contribution, and excludes from her gross income a housing allowance. Will the IRS recognize J's home to be a church? Why or why not?

7. Grace Church purchases an undeveloped 10-acre tract of land as a future building site. The land is located several miles from the present location of Grace Church. Will this tract be exempt from property taxation as a *church*?

8. Does a religious denomination have to apply for exemption from federal income taxes? Does a local church? Explain.

9. First Church conducts a child care program and an elementary school at its facility. Neighbors complain to the city that the neighborhood is not zoned for school or preschool activities (it is zoned only for residential and church uses). Do the church's child care and school activities come within the definition of the term *church*? Explain.

10. Explain the significance of the term *accessory use* in the context of zoning law.

11. A zealous tax collector asserts that the parking lot of First Church is subject to property taxation since it obviously is not a church. What arguments could the church make to maintain the tax-exempt status of its parking lot?

Discussion Questions

1. The Internal Revenue Code uses the term *church* in many contexts, yet it contains no definition of the term. Why do you suppose that Congress (which drafted the Code) failed to provide a definition?

2. Refer to the criteria developed by the IRS for determining whether a particular organization is a church. Do you think that these criteria are reasonable? Can you think of legitimate churches that might not satisfy this test?

6

ORGANIZATION AND ADMINISTRATION

Chapter summary. Chapter 6 is one of the most important chapters in this text. In this chapter, you will study the legal aspects of church organization and administration. The chapter begins with a review of both the unincorporated and incorporated forms of organization. Should a church be incorporated? What advantages are there? Are there any disadvantages? These are issues of fundamental importance. Church records raise a number of important legal questions. For example, under what circumstances can church members inspect church records? What church records are subject to their inspection? Can the IRS inspect church records? If so, what protections are available to churches? These questions are all addressed in this chapter. Churches may have a number of reporting requirements under state and federal law, including the filing of an annual corporate report, applications for exemption from various taxes, payroll tax reporting obligations, and the annual certification of racial nondiscrimination (for churches that operate a preschool, or an elementary or secondary school). These reporting requirements are addressed in this chapter. The selection, authority, removal, and personal liability of church officers, directors, and trustees present complex legal questions that are discussed in detail in this chapter. For example, how may a church remove a director prior to the expiration of a term of office? What about the filling of vacancies? When may church directors or trustees be personally liable for their actions on behalf of a church? You will learn the answers to these and many other questions. The selection, authority, and removal of church members also raise difficult questions. Who are the legal members of a church? Can members lose their church membership through non-attendance or lack of support? How can a church remove a member? Do dismissed members have a legal right to challenge their dismissals in court? Each of these problems will be analyzed in detail. Church business meetings also present a variety of legal questions that are fully addressed in this chapter. How should a church give notice of its business meetings? What is a quorum? Who can vote? What is the effect of procedural irregularities? What body of parliamentary law applies? You also will study the nature and extent of a church's legal authority, and the procedures employed in merging, consolidating, and dissolving churches.

More than one hundred years ago, the United States Supreme Court observed that "[t]he right to organize voluntary religious associations to assist in the expression and dissemination of any religious doctrine . . . is unquestioned."[1] Generally, churches have organized themselves as either corporations or unincorporated associations. This chapter will explore the essential features of both forms of organization, discuss the advantages and disadvantages of each, and summarize the incorporation process. This chapter also will address several issues of church administration, including reporting requirements; the protection of church names; the selection, authority, and personal liability of officers and directors; the selection and dismissal of church members; annual and special membership meetings; and dissolution.

§ 6-01   Unincorporated Associations

In general, any church that is not a corporation is an unincorporated association. The term *unincorporated association* is defined as any group "whose members share a common purpose, and . . . who function under a common name under circumstances where fairness requires the group be recognized as a legal entity."[2] One court has observed:

A church or religious society may exist for all the purposes for which it was organized independently of any incorporation of the body . . . and, it is a matter of common knowledge that many do exist and are never incorporated. For the promotion of religion and charity, they may subserve

---

[1]   Watson v. Jones, 80 U.S. (13 Wall.) 679 (1872).
[2]   Barr v. United Methodist Church, 153 Cal. Rptr. 322, 328 (1979), *cert. denied*, 444 U.S. 973 (1980).

all the purposes of their organization, and generally, need no incorporation except incidentally to further these objects.[3]

§ 6-01.1 — Characteristics

Key point 6-01.1. Unincorporated associations have no legal existence and as a result cannot sue or be sued, hold title to property, or enter into contracts. Some states have modified or eliminated some or all of these limitations.

Traditionally, unincorporated associations had no legal existence. This fact had many important consequences. First, an association could not own or transfer property in its own name; second, an association could not enter into contracts or other legal obligations; and third, an association could not sue or be sued.

The inability to sue or be sued had many important ramifications. It meant, for example, that a church association could not sue its members. If a church member's negligence caused fire damage to a church building, neither the church nor the church's insurance company could sue the member.[4] It also meant that a church association could not be sued by its members. In one case, a church member who was injured because of the negligence of her church was denied recovery against the church on the ground that a member of an unincorporated church is engaged in a joint enterprise and may not recover from the church any damages sustained through the wrongful conduct of another member.[5]

> *Example. A Pennsylvania court ruled that a member of an unincorporated church cannot sue the church for injuries sustained on church property.[6] A church member was injured when she slipped and fell while leaving Christmas services. She sued her church, alleging that the church board had been negligent in failing to provide adequate lighting, handrails, and stripes on the stairs where the accident occurred. In dismissing the lawsuit, The court observed, "[T]he members of an unincorporated association are engaged in a joint enterprise, and the negligence of each member in the prosecution of that enterprise is imputable to each and every other member, so that the member who has suffered damages through the tortious conduct of another member of the association may not recover from the association for such damages." The court concluded, "[The victim] was a member of the association and thus any negligence of her fellow members is imputed to her and she cannot recover in tort. . . . [The victim] was a member of the church, an unincorporated association, at all times material to this case. As a member of the association . . . the decision not to place a handrail, lights, and stripes on the stairway is attributed to her. She cannot recover in tort because any negligence of the board is attributable to her.*

Such rulings may leave members of unincorporated churches without a legal remedy for injuries sustained because of the negligence of other members. This certainly is a matter that should be considered seriously by any church wishing to remain unincorporated. Such churches should apprise their members that if they are injured during any church activity because of the actions of another member, they may have no legal right to compensation or damages from the church or other members—even if the church maintains liability insurance that otherwise would be available.

---

[3] Murphy v. Taylor, 289 So.2d 584, 586 (Ala. 1974), quoting Hundley v. Collins, 32 So. 575 (Ala. 1901).

[4] Employers Mutual Casualty Co. v. Griffin, 266 S.E.2d 18 (N.C. 1980).

[5] Goard v. Branscom, 189 S.E.2d 667 (N.C. 1972), *cert. denied*, 191 S.E.2d 354 (1972).

[6] Zehner v. Wilkinson Memorial United Methodist Church, 581 A.2d 1388 (Pa. Super. 1990). *See also* Crocker v. Barr, 367 S.E.2d 471 (S.C. App. 1988)´ ("a member of a voluntary unincorporated association . . . cannot maintain an action in tort against the association for injuries suffered by the member because of the negligence of fellow members").

The traditional legal disabilities associated with unincorporated status, particularly the potential personal liability of every member for the acts of other members in the course of the association's activities (discussed below), rendered the unincorporated association form of organization highly undesirable for churches and most other nonprofit organizations. Many states have enacted laws that remove some or all of these traditional disabilities.[7] As a result, while most states still prohibit an association from owning or transferring title to property in its own name, many states permit an association to hold or transfer title to property in the name of "trustees" acting on behalf of the association.[8] Some states permit unincorporated associations to sue and be sued in the association name.[9] Other states permit some members of an association to bring suit as representatives of the entire membership.[10] Some courts, under limited circumstances, permit an association to bring suit in its own name as representative of its members. One court has held that a church association may bring suit on behalf of its members when "(a) its members would otherwise have standing to sue in their own right; (b) the interests it seeks to protect are germane to the organization's purpose; and (c) neither the claim asserted nor the relief requested requires the participation of individual members in the lawsuit."[11] Many states permit associations to enter into contracts.

Unless state law provides otherwise, unincorporated associations remain incapable of suing or being sued, holding or transferring title to property, and entering into contracts and other legal obligations. In those states where some or all of the traditional legal disabilities persist, an association generally may act only through its membership.[12]

> ***Example.*** *The Indiana Supreme Court ruled that members of an unincorporated church can sue their church for injuries they suffer on church property or in the course of church activities.[13] A church member (the "victim") attended a meeting of a local "Toastmasters" chapter that had rented a portion of the church for the evening. Both members and non-members of the church attended the function. Over the course of the evening, some snow and ice accumulated in the parking lot of the church. After spending about two hours inside, the victim left the church and walked toward her automobile. As she neared her car, she slipped and fell. An associate pastor saw her fall and immediately drove her to the hospital, where she received treatment for a broken arm. The associate pastor later commented to the church's business manager that the parking lot had been slick on his way into the church earlier that evening and was still slippery on his way out when he saw the victim fall. The victim later sued her church and its 9-member board of trustees for her personal injuries, alleging negligence for failure to properly maintain the parking lot, failure to inspect the parking lot for dangerous conditions, failure to remove the snow and ice from the parking lot, and failure to warn her of the dangerous conditions. The trustees and church pointed out that the church was unincorporated, and as a result the victim could not sue them. A trial court agreed, applying the traditional rule that a member of an unincorporated association cannot sue the association for the negligence of another member. The supreme court reversed*

---

[7] *See generally* Kauper & Ellis, *Religious Corporations and the Law,* 71 MICH. LAW REV. 1500 (1973); Barr v. United Methodist Church, 153 Cal. Rptr. 322 (1979), *cert. denied,* 444 U.S. 973 (1980).

[8] Kauper & Ellis, *supra* note 7, at 1542; Adams v. Bethany Church, 361 So.2d 510 (Ala. 1978); Ervin v. Davis, 199 S.W.2d 366 (Mo. 1947); African Methodist Episcopal Church v. Independent African Methodist Episcopal Church, 281 S.W.2d 758 (Tex. 1955).

[9] *See, e.g.,* Enterprise Lodge v. First Baptist Church, 264 So.2d 153 (Ala. 1972); Adams v. Bethany Church, 361 So.2d 510 (Ala. 1978). Of course, in such states there is no reason why members should be personally liable for the obligations of the church. *See* note 7, *supra,* and accompanying text.

[10] Rock Zion Baptist Church v. Johnson, 47 So.2d 397 (La. 1950).

[11] Church of Scientology v. Cazares, 638 F.2d 1272, 1279 (5th Cir. 1981).

[12] *See, e.g.,* Trinity Pentecostal Church v. Terry, 660 S.W.2d 449 (Mo. App. 1983) (unincorporated religious association was "without capacity to hold and pass title to real estate under Missouri law").

[13] Hanson v. Saint Luke's United Methodist Church, 704 N.E.2d 1020 (Ind. 1998).

the trial court's decision, and ruled that the victim could sue the church. It conceded that under the "traditional rule" a member of an unincorporated association may not sue the association itself for injuries suffered as a result of the acts of the association or its members. However, the court concluded that the traditional rule had to be abolished, and that members should be allowed "to bring tort actions against the unincorporated associations of which they are part." It listed the following considerations to justify its decision, "(1) it is inherently unfair to require an injured member, who is one of a number of equally faultless members, to bear a loss incurred as a result of the association's activities; (2) there is no reason to limit the availability of the insurance that associations can, and presumably often do, obtain to avoid unexpected liabilities of the members as a result of exposure to third party claims." The court cautioned that an injured member's right to sue his or her unincorporated church was subject to some important limits. Most importantly, "while a member may now sue an unincorporated association in tort, she may only reach the association's assets. If she wishes to reach the assets of any individual, she must name that individual as a party and prove that individual's fault, as always. As a result, individual members, including officers and trustees, may not be held vicariously liable for a judgment against the association."

Example. *The South Carolina Supreme Court ruled that a church member could sue his unincorporated church for injuries sustained while repairing the church sound system. The member volunteered to enter the church attic to repair the sound system. While in the attic, he fell through the ceiling and landed on a concrete floor some ten feet below. The victim sued his church, alleging that its negligence was the cause of his injuries. The supreme court ruled that the injured member could sue the church, even though it was unincorporated.*[14]

Example. *The Texas Supreme Court ruled that a member of an unincorporated church could sue the church for injuries she sustained when she slipped and fell on a wet linoleum floor. The court acknowledged that the longstanding rule in Texas had been that the members of an unincorporated church could not sue the church for injuries inflicted by fellow church members. It noted that this historic rule was based on the notion that the members of unincorporated churches are engaged in a "joint venture" and that the negligence of one is imputed to all the others, including a fellow member who is injured by the negligence. The court repudiated this rule, noting that it had been abandoned by most other states. The court concluded, "Why should a church member be precluded from suing an association in tort when a paid workman would be allowed to maintain an action for the very same injury. . . ? We are unable to discern a defensible reply to this query. Consequently, we hold that a member of an unincorporated charitable association is not precluded from bringing a negligence action against the association solely because of the individual's membership in the association. Any assets of the unincorporated charitable association, held either by the association or in trust by a member of the association, may be reached in satisfaction of a judgment against the association."*[15]

§ 6-01.2 — Personal Liability of Members

Key point 6-01.2. The traditional rule is that members of an unincorporated association are personally liable for the acts of other members committed within the course of association activities. Some courts have modified or rejected this rule.

---

[14] Crocker v. Barr, 409 S.E.2d 368 (S.C. 1992).

[15] Cox v. Thee Evergreen Church, 836 S.W.2d 167 (Tex. 1992). A dissenting justice noted that "a majority of jurisdictions follow the rule that a member of an unincorporated association injured due to the tortious conduct of another member cannot sue the association. . . . The court may have wrongly implied that the rule exempting unincorporated associations from liability is a waning doctrine. In fact, most jurisdictions still adhere to it."

Since an association could not sue or be sued, it generally was held that an association's members were personally responsible for the acts of other members or agents of the association committed in the course of the association's business.[16] One court stated the general rule as follows:

[T]he members of an unincorporated association are engaged in a joint enterprise, and the negligence of each member in the prosecution of that enterprise is imputable to each and every other member, so that the member who has suffered damages to his person, property, or reputation through the tortious conduct of another member of the association may not recover from the association for such damage although he may recover individually from the member actually guilty of the tort.[17]

This rule is particularly relevant in Virginia and West Virginia, since churches are prohibited by law from incorporating in these states. The Virginia legislature has addressed this issue by enacting a statute specifying that "no member of any church, synagogue or religious body shall be liable in tort or contract for the actions of any officer, employee, leader, or other member of such church, synagogue or religious body solely because of his membership in such church, synagogue or religious body. Nothing in this section shall prevent any person from being held liable for his own actions."[18]

Example. A Texas appeals court suggested that the members of an unincorporated church could be sued individually in a "class action" for the church's fraudulent acts. The church used property that was owned by another person. A portion of the property was subject to an unpaid tax liability which created a defect in the title. A church employee allegedly informed the owner that he would help her clear this title defect by representing her before the local taxing authorities and by informing her if and when the property was to be sold to satisfy the tax liability. Instead, the church allegedly bought the property at a tax foreclosure sale without communicating this fact to the owner. The owner immediately filed a lawsuit. Since the church was unincorporated, she claimed that the individual members of the church were personally responsible for the church's alleged breach of the rental contract and the misconduct of the church in purchasing the property at the foreclosure sale. The owner attempted to sue all of the church's members by filing a class action lawsuit naming all of the members as defendants. The appeals court began its opinion by observing, "An unincorporated association is a voluntary group of persons, without a charter, formed by mutual consent for the purposes of promoting a common enterprise. An unincorporated association is not liable on its contracts, which are regarded as the liability of the individuals who sign them. . . . Members of an unincorporated association are individually liable for tortious acts of agents or employees of the association if the tort is committed within the scope of their authority." Further, the personal liability of individual members was affected by the fact that state law permits unincorporated organizations to be sued directly. However, the court concluded that the owner had not met all of the procedural requirements for filing a class action lawsuit, and remanded the case to the trial court. In summary, while the court dismissed the owner's attempt to bring a class action lawsuit against the members of an unincorporated church, it did so on the basis of an easily corrected technicality.[19]

Example. An Indiana appeals court ruled that the individual members of an unincorporated nonprofit association were personally responsible for a contract entered into by the association. The association

---

[16] *See generally* Kauper & Ellis, *Religious Corporations and the Law*, 71 MICH. LAW REV. 1500 (1973).

[17] Williamson v. Wallace, 224 S.E.2d 253, 254 (N.C. 1976).

[18] VA. CODE § 8.01-220.1:3.

[19] Hutchins v. Grace Tabernacle United Pentecostal Church, 804 S.W.2d 598 (Tex. App. 1991).

rented a convention facility for a fund-raising banquet. The bill for the event came to $16,000, but the association paid only $2,000. The convention center sued two of the association's members personally for the balance. The members claimed that they could not be liable for the association's debts, but a state appeals court disagreed. The court observed, "[T]he common law is well settled that a member of an association which does not conduct business for profit becomes liable for obligations incurred on behalf of the association within the scope of the authority of the agent attempting to create the liability." The court quoted with approval from a leading treatise on contract law: "Insofar as the obligation was created in a manner authorized by [the association's] articles of agreement or bylaws, the individual members are liable, presumably jointly." Williston on Contracts § 308. The court also quoted with approval from a legal encyclopedia: "[Members of unincorporated nonprofit associations] are jointly and severally liable as principals on contracts made by, from or in the name of, the association for the purpose of promoting its objects, to which they have given either assent or subsequent ratification." 6 American Jurisprudence 2nd, Associations and Clubs, § 46. The court noted that "other states have uniformly applied the common law" rule, as does Indiana. Accordingly, "members of a not-for-profit unincorporated association are liable for the obligations incurred by the association under a contract if the members authorize the contract or subsequently ratify its terms."[20]

Example. *A Connecticut appeals court ruled that individual members of an unincorporated association could be sued personally as a result of negligence or other misconduct of fellow members. The court observed, "Persons who associate together for some common nonbusiness purpose without a corporate franchise from the state are merely an aggregation of individuals, not a separate legal entity. . . . A voluntary association for tort liability purposes remains an aggregation of individuals who may be held personally liable in tort for certain of its activities."[21]*

Example. *The Texas Supreme Court ruled that the members of an unincorporated association are not necessarily responsible for the misconduct of their fellow members. A police officer was injured while attempting to carry away a protester at an abortion clinic. He later sued twelve other persons who were engaged in the protest. The supreme court ruled that the twelve protesters were not personally liable for officer's injuries. It noted that "even if the demonstrators constituted an unincorporated association, we have never held that they are automatically liable for the actions of other members of the association." The court further noted that "imposing liability on individuals on the sole basis that a member of the group to which they belong has committed a [wrong] in the pursuit of the group's goals would pose serious threats to the right of free association." The court concluded, "We believe that the liability of members of a group should be analyzed in terms of the specific actions undertaken, authorized or ratified by those members. Therefore, regardless of whether there was an unincorporated association here, we reject the lower court's intimation that the existence of such an association might alone form the basis for imposing tort liability on all members for the acts of some." Note, however, that the court did not grant members of unincorporated associations absolute immunity from personal liability. The court pointed out that members can be personally liable on the basis of "specific actions undertaken, authorized or ratified."[22]*

---

[20] Victory Committee v. Genesis Convention Center, 597 N.E.2d 361 (Ind. App. 3 Dist. 1992).

[21] Company v. Sena, 619 A.2d 489 (Conn. Super. 1992).

[22] Juhl v. Airington, 936 S.W.2d 640 (Tex. 1996). In a case addressing the question of whether or not members of an unincorporated church can sue the church for injuries they sustain, the Texas Supreme Court avoided the issue of the personal liability of individual members of unincorporated churches for the negligence or misconduct of other members. It simply noted that this lawsuit had not named any individual church members as defendants and accordingly there was no need to address this broader issue. It did mention, however, that "protection is afforded by the simple act of incorporation." Cox v. Thee Evergreen Church, 836 S.W.2d 167 (Tex. 1992).

Example. An Illinois court ruled that members of an unincorporated association were not responsible for the alleged defamatory statements made by other members of the association, since they had not authorized or ratified the statements and the association was not organized for profit. The persons who claimed to have been defamed by certain members of the association claimed that all of the members of an unincorporated association are legally responsible for the acts of their fellow members, on the basis of both partnership and agency law. A state appeals court disagreed. It concluded that members of an unincorporated association can be liable for the acts of other members only if the association is a "for profit" entity. Since the association in this case was a nonprofit entity, the members could not be liable for the actions of other members. The court concluded that members of a nonprofit unincorporated association cannot be legally responsible for the misconduct of other members "without their direct participation, authorization, or subsequent ratification."[23]

Tip. As noted later in this chapter, incorporation is a simple and relatively inexpensive process. Of course, it requires the assistance of an attorney. Unfortunately, many church leaders do not know if their church is incorporated. Many assume that it is. This can be a dangerous assumption if in fact the church is not incorporated, since it may mean that the members are personally responsible for the liabilities of the church. It is essential for church leaders to confirm whether or not their church is incorporated. This easily can be done by contacting the office of the secretary of state in your state capital. Representatives of the office of secretary of state ordinarily will tell you over the telephone whether or not your church is incorporated. If you are informed that your church is incorporated, then you may wish to ask for a certificate of good standing (the name of this document varies somewhat from state to state) that confirms the corporate status of your church. You also should request a certified copy of your charter (article of incorporation), to be sure that you have a copy of the document on file with the state.

Tip. Calling the office of the secretary of state is important even if you think that your church is incorporated, since the corporate status of many churches has "lapsed" through failure to file annual reports with the state. In many states, church corporations must file relatively simple annual reports with the state. In a surprisingly large number of cases, churches do not file these reports. In some states, the failure to file these reports will cause the church's corporate status to lapse. As a result, it is a prudent practice for churches to confirm each year with the office of their secretary of state that they are in fact a corporation in good standing.

Although the Internal Revenue Code restricts tax-exempt status to corporations, community chests, funds, and foundations organized and operated exclusively for religious and other charitable purposes,[24] the IRS construes the term *corporations* to include unincorporated associations.[25] The inclusion of unincorporated associations within the definition of the term *corporations* is a well-established principle of federal tax law. Section 7701(a)(3) of the Internal Revenue Code defines *corporation* to include associations, and the federal courts for many years have held that associations possessing at least three of the four principal corporate characteristics of centralized control, continuity, limited personal liability, and transferability of beneficial interests are to be treated as corporations.[26] The exemption available to religious and charitable corporations under the Internal Revenue Code accordingly should be available to most unincorporated associations that meet all of the other conditions for exempt status.

---

[23] Joseph v. Collins, 649 N.E.2d 964 (Ill. App. 1995).
[24] I.R.C. § 501(c)(3).
[25] Treas. Reg. § 1.501(c)(3)-1(b)(2); IRS Publication 557.
[26] *See, e.g.*, Smith's Estate v. Commissioner, 313 F.2d 724 (8th Cir. 1963).

§ 6-01.3 — Creation and Administration

Key point 6-01.3. A church is an unincorporated association if it is not a corporation in good standing under state law. This status can occur in a number of ways, including the following: (1) a church never was incorporated; (2) a church was incorporated, but the period of duration specified in its charter has expired; or (3) a church was incorporated, but its corporate status lapsed under state law because of its failure to submit annual reports to the office of the secretary of state.

In general, an unincorporated association is created by the voluntary association of two or more individuals under a common name for a particular purpose. The creation of an unincorporated association ordinarily does not require compliance with state laws, although several states have enacted laws allowing associations to organize in a more formal way.[27] Such laws typically confer many of the rights and privileges enjoyed by corporations upon associations that choose to formally organize.

It is customary and desirable for the members of an unincorporated association to adopt rules for the internal management of the affairs of the association. Although these rules usually are called bylaws, they occasionally are called articles of association, constitution, or charter. Such terminology is not important.[28] In this chapter, the rules and regulations of an unincorporated association will be referred to as bylaws. The bylaws of an unincorporated association typically contain provisions dealing with meetings; election, qualification, and tenure of officers and trustees; qualification and acceptance of members; the acquisition and transfer of property; the status of property upon the dissolution of the association; and the rights and duties of members among themselves and with the association.

The bylaws of an unincorporated association constitute a contract between the association and its members, and that the rights and duties of members, as between themselves and in their relation to the association in all matters affecting its internal government and the management of its affairs, are measured by the terms of such bylaws.[29] By becoming a member an individual agrees to be bound by the association's bylaws, and to have his rights and duties determined by them.[30]

The members of an unincorporated association may vote to incorporate their organization and transfer title to all properties to the new corporation. A minority of the unincorporated association's members are without authority to block such a transfer.[31]

§ 6-02 Corporations

The legal disabilities connected with the unincorporated association form of organization cause many churches to incorporate. Unlike many unincorporated churches, church corporations are capable of suing and being sued, entering into contracts and other legal obligations, and holding title to property. Perhaps most important, the members of a church corporation ordinarily are shielded from personal liability for the debts and misconduct of other members or agents of the church.

---

[27] Kauper & Ellis, *supra* note 7, at 1541 n.213.
[28] Cunningham v. Independent Soap & Chemical Workers, 486 P.2d 1316 (Kan. 1971).
[29] Savoca Masonry Co., Inc. v. Homes & Son Construction Co., Inc., 542 P.2d 817, 820 (Ariz. 1975).
[30] Libby v. Perry, 311 A.2d 527 (Me. 1973).
[31] Jacobs v. St. Mark's Baptist Church, 415 So.2d 251 (La. App. 1982).

The Uniform Unincorporated Nonprofit Association Act (1996)

In 1996 the National Conference on Commissioners on Uniform State Laws released the "Uniform Unincorporated Nonprofit Association Act" and recommended that state legislatures enact it. A few states have enacted the Act into law, and others no doubt will do so in the future. The purpose of the Act was described as follows:

"At common law an unincorporated association, whether nonprofit or for-profit, was not a separate legal entity. It was an aggregate of individuals. . . . This approach obviously created problems. A gift of property to an unincorporated association failed because no legal entity existed to receive it. . . . Proceedings by or against an unincorporated association presented similar problems. If it were not a legal entity, each of the members needed to be joined as party plaintiffs or defendants. . . . Unincorporated associations, not being legal entities, could not be liable in tort, contract, or otherwise for conduct taken in their names. On the other hand, their members could be. . . . The unincorporated nonprofit association is now governed by a hodge-podge of common law and state statutes governing some of their legal aspects. No state appears to have addressed the issues in a comprehensive, integrated, and internally consistent manner. This Act deals with a limited number of the major issues relating to unincorporated nonprofit associations in an integrated and consistent manner."

One of the most important features of the Act is its treatment of the personal liability of members. The Act provides that members of an unincorporated association are not liable for the contracts of the association or for the wrongs of other members (or of the association itself), assuming that they did not participate personally. The key provision specifies:

"A nonprofit association is a legal entity separate from its members for the purposes of determining and enforcing rights, duties, and liabilities in contract and tort. . . . A person is not liable for a breach of a nonprofit association's contract merely because the person is a member, is authorized to participate in the management of the affairs of the nonprofit association, or is a person considered to be a member by the nonprofit association. A person is not liable for a tortious act or omission for which a nonprofit association is liable merely because the person is a member, is authorized to participate in the management of the affairs of the nonprofit association, or is a person considered as a member by the nonprofit association. A tortious act or omission of a member or other person for which a nonprofit association is liable is not imputed to a person merely because the person is a member of the nonprofit association, is authorized to participate in the management of the affairs of the nonprofit association, or is a person considered as a member by the nonprofit association."[32]

The Act also clarifies that individual members can "assert a claim against the nonprofit association." In other words, members of an unincorporated church are not barred from suing the church for injuries they sustain as a result of the church's negligence.

---

[32] Uniform Unincorporated Nonprofit Association Act § 6 (1996).

Two forms of church corporation are in widespread use in the United States. By far the more common form is the membership corporation, which is composed of and controlled by church members. Several states also recognize trustee corporations. The trustees of a trustee corporation constitute and control the corporation. A few states also permit certain officers of hierarchical churches to form a *corporation sole*,[33] which is a corporation consisting of a single individual.

In a few states, churches are not permitted to incorporate. For example, the constitutions of both Virginia and West Virginia prohibit the issuance of a charter of incorporation to "any church or religious denomination." The validity of such provisions is suspect under the prevailing construction of the first amendment's religion clauses by the United States Supreme Court, for they deny churches a valuable benefit available generally to nonreligious charitable and noncharitable organizations (*i.e.,* protection of members against personal liability) without a sufficiently compelling justification. Unsuccessful attempts have been made in both of these states to amend their constitutions to repeal the prohibition against church incorporation.

Some have maintained that churches should never incorporate since incorporation constitutes a "subordination" of a church to the authority of the state. Such a view reflects a fundamental misunderstanding regarding the legal status of corporations. The term *corporation* has been defined "as an association of persons to whom the sovereign has offered a franchise to become an artificial, juridical person, with a name of its own, under which they can act and contract, sue and be sued, and who have . . . accepted the offer and effected an organization in substantial conformity with its terms."[34] A corporation, then, is entirely distinct from its members and should not be confused with them. A church that incorporates is not "subordinating itself" to the state. Rather, it is subordinating merely the artificial corporate entity to the state, and it is free to terminate that entity at any time. Similarly, under some corporation laws, the state can terminate the corporate status of church corporations that fail to file annual reports. But the termination of the church corporation under such conditions certainly does not mean that the church itself is dissolved, for the church is completely independent of the artificial corporate entity and survives its demise. On the contrary, many church corporations have been terminated by operation of law because of noncompliance with the annual reporting requirements, yet church leaders and members alike remain oblivious to the fact.

One court acknowledged that "a church does not lose its ecclesiastical function, and the attributes of that function, when it incorporates. It does not, by incorporating, lose its right to be governed by its own particular form of ecclesiastical government. *Incorporation acts merely to create a legal entity to hold and administer the properties of the church.*"[35] Another court has observed that "[t]he law recognizes the distinction between the church as a religious group devoted to worship, preaching, missionary service, education and the promotion of social welfare, and the church as a business corporation owning real estate and making contracts. . . . The former is a matter in which the state or the courts have no direct legal concern, while in the latter the activities of the church are subject to the same laws as those in secular affairs."[36] The United States Supreme Court has ruled that the first amendment guaranty of religious freedom assures churches "an independence from secular control or manipulation, in short, power to decide for themselves, free from state interference, matters of church government as well as those of faith and doctrine."[37]

---

[33] *See generally* Kauper & Ellis, *supra* note 7, at 1538-41.

[34] Mackay v. New York, N.H. & H.R. Co., 72 A. 583 (1909) (this definition is still frequently cited by the courts).

[35] Providence Baptist Church v. Superior Court, 243 P.2d 112 (Cal. 1952).

[36] Gospel Tabernacle Body of Christ Church v. Peace Publishers & Co., 506 P.2d 1135 (Kan. 1973).

[37] Kedroff v. St. Nicholas Cathedral, 344 U.S. 94 (1952) (the Court ruled that a New York statute transferring control over Russian Orthodox churches in the United States from the Patriarch of Moscow to the governing authorities of the Russian Orthodox Church in America "violates our rule of separation between church and state"). *See also* People v. Wood, 402 N.Y.S.2d 726 (1978) ("The purpose of the Religious Corporations Law is not to determine the ecclesiastical jurisdiction . . . .").

One legal scholar has observed that "the distinctiveness of the corporate entity from the members . . . is inherent in and exemplified by other corporate attributes, which could not be conceded were they one and the same, e.g., the transfer of shares and change in membership without change in the corporation [and] the right to sue and be sued in the corporate name. . . ."[38] The distinctiveness of the corporate entity from its members is also the basis for the limitation of personal liability of members for the acts of the corporation. This limitation of personal liability is not an example of social irresponsibility that should be avoided by churches. On the contrary, it is a recognition of the fact that church members should not be personally responsible for the wrongdoing of other members or agents over which they had no control.

> *Key point. Clergy having theological opposition to church incorporation should consider letting the church membership determine whether or not to incorporate the church. Church members who are apprised of the potential personal liability they have for the obligations of their unincorporated church may well not share their pastor's theology on this issue.*

In summary, churches wanting to avail themselves of the benefits of the corporate form of organization should not be dissuaded by unwarranted fears of governmental control. In the unlikely event that an incorporated church ever does believe that it is being "unduly controlled" by the state, it can easily and quickly rectify the problem by voluntarily terminating its corporate existence. A number of courts have specifically held that incorporation of a church under a state corporation law does not subject the church to any greater degree of civil scrutiny.[39]

§ 6-02.1 — The Incorporation Process

> *Key point 6-02.1. In many states, churches can incorporate either under the Model Nonprofit Corporation Act or under an alternative statute that was adopted prior to the enactment of the Act. Some alternative statutes involve the filing of a petition with a local court. Often, these alternative statutes contain far less detail than the model Act. Some states have enacted statutes that regulate the incorporation of specific religious organizations.*

Although procedures for the incorporation of churches vary from state to state, most states have adopted one or more of the following procedures:

1. Model Nonprofit Corporation Act

The Model Nonprofit Corporation Act, which has been adopted in whole or in part by several states,[40] provides a uniform method of incorporation for several kinds of nonprofit organizations, including religious, scientific, educational, charitable, cultural, and benevolent organizations. The procedure consists of the following steps: (1) preparation of duplicate articles of incorporation setting forth the corporation's name, period of duration, address of registered office within the state, name and address of a registered agent, purposes, and names and addresses of the initial board of directors and incorporators; (2) notarized signature of the duplicate articles of incorporation by the incorporators; and (3) submission of the prescribed filing fee and duplicate articles of incorporation to the secretary of state. The secretary of state reviews the articles of incorporation to ensure compliance with the Act. If the articles of incorporation are satisfactory, the secretary of

---

[38] Fletcher Cyc. Corp. § 25 (perm. ed. 1990).

[39] *See, e.g.,* Bourgeois v. Landrum, 387 So.2d 611 (La. App. 1980), *rev'd on other grounds,* 396 So.2d 1275 (La. 1981).

[40] Fletcher Cyc. Corp. § 2.65, n.2 (Perm. ed. 1990).

state endorses both duplicate copies, files one in his or her office, and returns the other along with a certificate of incorporation to the church.[41] The church's corporate existence begins at the moment the certificate of incorporation is issued.[42] After the certificate of incorporation has been issued, the Act specifies that an organizational meeting of the board of directors shall be held at the call of a majority of the incorporators for the purpose of adopting the initial bylaws of the corporation and for such other purposes as may come before the meeting.[43]

The incorporators and directors can be the same persons in most states. Many states require at least three directors. Incorporators and directors must have attained a prescribed age and be citizens of the United States. They ordinarily do not have to be citizens of the state in which the church is incorporated.

The Model Nonprofit Corporation Act governs many aspects of a nonprofit corporation's existence. As one court has observed, "[i]f a church or religious group elects to incorporate under the laws of this state, then the courts have the power to consider and require that the corporation thus formed comply with state law concerning such corporations."[44] Some of the issues addressed by the Act include meetings of members, notice of meetings, voting, quorum, number and election of directors, vacancies, officers, removal of officers, books and records, merger or consolidation with other organizations, and dissolution. In most of these matters, a corporation is bound by the Act's provisions only if it has not provided otherwise in its articles of incorporation or bylaws. In other words, most of the Act's provisions apply "by default." For example, a corporation may stipulate in its bylaws the percentage of members constituting a quorum, but if it fails to do so the Act provides that a quorum consists of ten percent of the voting membership.[45] Similarly, the Act provides that directors shall serve for one-year terms unless a corporation's articles of incorporation or bylaws provide otherwise.[46]

Key point. One court has observed that "in a conflict between the general procedures outlined in the [state nonprofit corporation law] and the specific procedures contained in the church bylaws, we must defer to the church bylaws."[47]

Example. A court ruled that proxy voting had to be recognized in a church election since the Model Nonprofit Corporation Act required it and the church had not provided otherwise in its articles or bylaws. The court rejected the church's claim that requiring it to recognize proxy votes violated the constitutional guaranty of religious freedom. The court observed that a church could easily avoid the recognition of proxy votes by simply amending its charter or bylaws to expressly prohibit this form of voting.[48]

Example. The Arkansas Supreme Court ruled that the provisions of the state nonprofit corporation law could not be applied to a church if doing so would violate church doctrine. As part of what the court described as a dispute of "a longstanding, ongoing, and heated nature," certain church members sought

---

[41] MODEL NONPROFIT CORPORATION ACT § 30.
[42] *Id.* at § 31.
[43] *Id.* at § 32.
[44] Lozanoski v. Sarafin, 485 N.E.2d 669, 671 (Ind. App. 1985). *See also* Board of Trustees v. Richards, 130 N.E.2d 736, 739 (Ohio App. 1954) ("if the church law is repugnant to the specific statutory enactments, the church law must yield to the civil law").
[45] *Id.* at § 16.
[46] *Id.* at § 18.
[47] Green v. Westgate Apostolic Church, 808 S.W.2d 547 (Tex. App. 1991).
[48] Herning v. Eason, 739 P.2d 167 (Alaska 1987). *See also* Frankel v. Kissena Jewish Center, 544 N.Y.S.2d 955 (1989), in which a New York court concluded that the state "Not-For-Profit Corporation Law" permits proxy voting unless prohibited by the corporation's charter or bylaws.

to obtain various financial records of the church as part of a concerted effort to oust the current church leadership. When church elders rejected the members' request, the members incorporated the church under a state nonprofit corporation law making the "books and records" of a corporation subject to inspection "by any member for any proper purpose at any reasonable time." Church elders continued to reject the members' request for inspection, whereupon the members asked a state court to recognize their legal right to inspection under state corporation law. The elders countered by arguing that application of state corporation law would impermissibly interfere with the religious doctrine and practice of the church, contrary to the constitutional guaranty of religious freedom. Specifically, the elders argued that according to the church's "established doctrine," the New Testament "places within the hands of a select group of elders the sole responsibility for overseeing the affairs of the church," and that this authority is "evidenced by biblical admonitions to the flock to obey and submit to them that have rule over the flock." The Arkansas Supreme Court agreed that "application of our state corporation law would almost certainly impinge upon the doctrine of the church" as described by the elders, and accordingly would violate the constitutional guaranty of religious freedom. The court concluded that if the application of a state law would conflict with the "doctrine, polity, or practice" of a church, then the law cannot be applied to the church without a showing of a "compelling state interest." No such showing was made in this case, the court concluded, and therefore the state law giving members of nonprofit corporations the legal right to inspect corporate records could not be applied to the church.[49]

Certain provisions of the Act may not be altered by a corporation. For example, the Act mandates that corporations have a minimum of three directors.[50] Although a corporation may require more than three directors, it may not require less. The Act also prohibits corporations from making loans to officers or directors.[51]

The Act requires all nonprofit corporations to file an annual report with the secretary of state's office.[52] A few states have amended this provision to require reports less frequently, such as once every two years. The report is filed on a form provided by the secretary of state, and ordinarily sets forth the name of the corporation, the address of the corporation's registered office in the state of incorporation, the name of the registered agent at such address, the names and addresses of the directors and officers, and a brief statement of the nature of the affairs the corporation is actually conducting. A nominal fee must accompany the report.

States that have adopted the Act differ with regard to the penalties imposed upon corporations that fail to file the annual report by the date prescribed. The Act itself imposes a nominal fine ($50) on corporations that fail to comply with the reporting requirement. Many states have followed this provision, but others call for the cancellation of a corporation's certificate of incorporation. Cancellation of a certificate of incorporation has the effect of terminating the existence of a corporation. This is an extraordinary penalty, generally available only after the secretary of state's office has sent the corporation a written notice of the impending cancellation. If a corporation fails to respond to the written notice, the secretary of state issues a certificate of cancellation, which is the legal document terminating both the certificate of incorporation and the corporation's legal existence. Many states permit reinstatement of terminated corporations. Reinstatement generally is available upon the filing of a formal application within a prescribed time. Because of the potentially adverse consequences resulting from a cancellation of a church's corporation charter, church leaders should periodically check with the office of their secretary of state to ensure that the church is a corporation in good standing.

---

[49] Gipson v. Brown, 749 S.W.2d 297 (Ark. 1988).
[50] *Id.* at § 18.
[51] *Id.* at § 27. This important topic is discussed in more detail in section F of this chapter.
[52] Model Nonprofit Corporation Act § 81.

Many churches will find that they are not, either because they failed to file an annual return, or because their corporation was created for a specified period of time that has expired.

In 1987, the American Bar Association's Subcommittee on the Model Nonprofit Corporations Law of the Business Law Section adopted the "Revised Model Nonprofit Corporation Act." The revised Act, which has been adopted by a few states,[53] is based on the "Revised Model Business Corporations Act." It likely will be adopted by many states in the years to come. One of the important features of the revised Act is the division of nonprofit corporations into three classifications—(1) public benefit corporations, (2) mutual benefit corporations, and (3) religious corporations.[54] Special rules apply to each classification. This is the first recognition of the unique status of religious corporations in a "model" nonprofit corporations law.

Other new features of the revised Act include the following:

(1) Members. The definition of "members" is clarified. A corporation is required to compile a listing of eligible voters in advance of each annual or special membership meeting, and this list must be available for inspection. However, the Act specifies that "the articles or bylaws of a religious corporation may limit or abolish the rights of a member . . . to inspect and copy any corporate record."[55]

(2) Religious doctrine. The revised Act specifies that "[i]f religious doctrine governing the affairs of a religious corporation is inconsistent with the provisions of this Act on the same subject, the religious doctrine shall control to the extent required by the Constitution of the United States or the constitution of this state or both."[56]

(3) Duration. There is a presumption of perpetual duration unless the articles of incorporation specifically provide otherwise.[57]

(4) Emergency actions of board. The board of directors is empowered to act in an "emergency" though a quorum of the board is not present.[58]

(5) Personal liability. The Act specifies that "[a] member of a corporation is not, as such, personally liable for the acts, debts, liabilities, or obligations of the corporation."[59]

(6) Removal of members. Detailed procedures apply to the suspension or expulsion of members, but these procedures do not apply to religious corporations (they apply only to public benefit corporations and mutual benefit corporations).[60]

(7) Delegates. A corporation "may provide in its articles or bylaws for delegates having some or all of the authority of members."[61]

---

[53] Fletcher Cyc. Corp. § 2.75.05 (Perm. ed. 1990).

[54] Model Revised Nonprofit Corporation Act § 2.02(a).

[55] *Id.* at § 7.20.

[56] *Id.* at § 1.80. This is the same conclusion reached by the Arkansas Supreme Court in Gipson v. Brown, 749 S.W.2d 297 (Ark. 1988). *See* note 49, *supra*, and accompanying text.

[57] *Id.* at § 3.02.

[58] *Id.* at § 3.03. The Act specifies that "[a]n emergency exists for purposes of this section if a quorum of the corporation's directors cannot readily be assembled because of some catastrophic event."

[59] *Id.* at § 6.12.

[60] *Id.* at § 6.21.

[61] *Id.* at § 6.40.

(8) Court-ordered meetings. Civil courts are empowered to call meetings of a corporation upon the application of any member if the corporation fails to conduct an annual or special meeting within a pre-scribed number of days after a specified meeting.[62] A court also may determine those persons who constitute members for purposes of any such meeting, and may "enter other orders necessary to accomplish the purpose or purposes of the meeting."

(9) Action of members without a meeting. Unless prohibited by the corporate charter or bylaws, members are permitted to act without a meeting if 80 percent or more of the membership agrees to a proposed action in a signed writing. Similarly, members may act by "written ballot" without calling a meeting if such action is not prohibited by the corporate charter or bylaws.[63]

(10) Notice of meetings. The Act specifies that "[u]nless one-third or more of the voting power is present in person or by proxy, the only matters that may be voted upon at an annual or regular meeting of members are those matters that are described in the meeting notice."[64]

(11) At least three directors. The board of directors must consist of at least three directors.[65]

(12) Removal of directors. The Act specifies a procedure for removing directors from office, but permits religious corporations to provide otherwise in their charters or bylaws.[66]

(13) Duties of board members. The Act imposes specific "standards of conduct" upon each officer and director of a nonprofit corporation. These include the performance of an officer's or director's official duties "in good faith, with the care an ordinarily prudent person in a like position would exercise under similar circumstances, and in a manner the director [or officer] reasonably believes to be in the best interests of the corporation."[67]

(14) Indemnification. The Act contains detailed indemnification rules.[68]

(15) Inspection of records. The Act gives each member the right to inspect (and copy) corporate records "at a reasonable time and location" if a member "gives the corporation written demand at least five business days before the date on which the member wishes to inspect and copy." Corporate records include the articles of incorporation, bylaws, board resolutions, minutes of membership meetings, all written communications to members within the preceding three years, a list of the names and addresses of directors and officers, and the current annual report submitted to the secretary of state. Some limitations apply. Further, the Act provides that "the articles or bylaws of a religious corporation may limit or abolish the right of a member under this section to inspect and copy any corporate record."[69]

(16) Membership list. The Act specifies that "[e]xcept as provided in the articles or bylaws of a religious corporation, a corporation upon written demand from a member shall furnish that member its latest annual financial statements . . . ."[70]

---

[62] *Id.* at § 7.03.
[63] *Id.* at §§ 7.04 and 7.08.
[64] *Id.* at § 7.22.
[65] *Id.* at § 8.03.
[66] *Id.* at §§ 8.08 and 8.10.
[67] *Id.* at §§ 8.30 and 8.42.
[68] *Id.* at §§ 8.50 through 8.58.
[69] *Id.* at §§ 16.01 through 16.05.
[70] *Id.* at § 16.20.

Some churches prefer not to incorporate under the Model Nonprofit Corporation Act (or the Revised Model Nonprofit Corporation Act). This decision ordinarily is based on one or more of four considerations. First, churches do not want to be bothered with the annual reporting requirements. Although these requirements normally are not burdensome, they must be rigidly followed if a church is to avoid fines, and in some states, the loss of its corporate status. Second, many churches regard the Model Nonprofit Corporation Act as too restrictive since it regulates virtually every aspect of corporate organization and administration. The Act does specify that most of its provisions are applicable only if a corporation has not provided otherwise in its articles of incorporation or bylaws. However, churches often are unwittingly controlled by the Act through their failure to adopt articles or bylaws dealing with particular aspects of organization and administration that are addressed in the Act. Some churches of course consider this to be an advantage, for it means that there will be authoritative direction on most questions of church administration. Third, the Act was based largely on the Model Corporation Act for business corporations, and therefore fails to adequately recognize the substantial differences between nonprofit and for-profit enterprises.[71] Fourth, some clergy maintain that churches should not incorporate as "nonprofit" organizations since this would suggest that they are "unprofitable" or of no social or spiritual benefit. In this regard, one court has observed that the term *not-for-profit* refers only to monetary profit and does not include "spiritual profit," and therefore a church properly can be characterized as "not-for-profit" even though it "receives some type of profit from its public works in the form of the feeling of achievement and satisfaction the contributors derive from their good work or the enhancement of the image of the organization and its members in the eyes of the community."[72]

Here is one additional point about incorporating under the Model Nonprofit Corporation Act or the Revised Model Nonprofit Corporation Act. Remember that many of the provisions of both laws apply "by default"—meaning that they will apply unless a church has provided otherwise in its articles of incorporation or bylaws. Churches that are incorporated under either of these laws, or that are considering doing so, must carefully review the language of the law to be sure they understand the applicable provisions. Any desired changes must be made in the church's articles or bylaws.

It is important to distinguish between the terms *nonprofit* and *tax-exempt*. Nonprofit corporations generally are defined to include any corporation whose income is not distributable to its members, directors, or officers. The fact that an organization incorporates under a state's nonprofit corporation law does not in itself render the corporation exempt from federal, state, or local taxes. Exemption from tax generally is available only to those organizations that have applied for and received recognition of tax-exempt status. In some cases the law recognizes the tax-exempt status of certain nonprofit organizations and waives the necessity of making formal application for recognition of exempt status. For example, "churches, their integrated auxiliaries, and conventions or associations of churches" are deemed to be exempt from federal income tax without the need for filing an application for exemption.[73] In summary, unless a nonprofit corporation applies for and receives recognition of tax-exempt status or is expressly recognized by law to be exempt from tax without the necessity of making formal application, it will not be considered tax-exempt.

> *Tip. Churches need not be incorporated to be exempt from federal income tax. However, one court has observed that "while not a prerequisite for exemption, a showing that [an organization seeking a property tax exemption as a church] is incorporated as a church or religious association will lend credence to that organization's claim that it is a bona fide church or religious association."[74]*

---

[71] Revised Model Nonprofit Corporation Act is based directly on the Revised Model Business Corporation Act, and uses the same numbering system. However, the revised Act in several places attempts to take into account the unique status of religious corporations.

[72] United States v. 564.54 Acres of Land, More or Less, 576 F.2d 983, 989 (3rd Cir. 1978). *See also* People ex rel. Meiresonne v. Arnold, 553 P.2d 79 (Colo. 1976).

[73] I.R.C. § 508(c).

[74] Waushara County v. Graf, 480 N.W.2d 16 (Wis. 1992).

2. Special Statutes

Several states have adopted statutes that pertain exclusively to the incorporation and administration of specific religious denominations. Such statutes typically apply only to churches affiliated with specified denominations or religions. Some of the states that provide for the incorporation of churches of specified denominations also have general nonprofit corporation laws. Churches generally can elect to incorporate under either the general nonprofit or the special religious corporation law.[75]

Such statutes have been upheld against the claim that they "entangle" the state in religious matters contrary to the "nonestablishment of religion clause" of the first amendment to the United States Constitution.[76] The Supreme Court has upheld the validity of such statutes,[77] and has approved reference to them as a permissible way to resolve church property disputes.[78]

3. Court-Approved Corporations

Some states allow churches to incorporate by submitting articles of incorporation or articles of agreement to a local state court for approval. If the court determines that the church is organized for religious purposes and its objectives are consistent with the laws of the state, a certificate of incorporation is issued, which ordinarily is filed with the local recorder's office and with the secretary of state. This form of incorporation provides a minimum of state control over the operation of church corporations, since ordinarily no annual reporting is required, and the corporation law regulates only a few areas of corporate organization and administration.

4. Religious Corporation Laws

Many states have adopted general laws pertaining to the incorporation and administration of religious corporations without any specific reference to particular denominations or religions. Incorporation under such statutes ordinarily is simpler than incorporating under the general nonprofit corporation law. Typically, a church may incorporate under a general religious corporation statute by adopting articles setting forth the church's name, address, purposes, and the names and addresses of church officers and directors, and filing the articles with the county recorder, a court, or the secretary of state.

Churches are free to incorporate under either the Model Nonprofit Corporation Act or a general religious corporation law in those states where both forms of incorporation are available. One court rejected the claim that churches must incorporate under a state's general religious corporation law.[79] Obviously, a church that incorporates under the Model Nonprofit Corporation Act rather than under a general religious corporation law will be governed by the Model Act.

5. "De Facto" Corporations

Even if a church fails to comply with one or more technical requirements of incorporation, it will be considered a *de facto corporation* if the following three requirements are satisfied:

---

[75] Bible Presbyterian Church v. Harvey Cedars Bible Conference, 202 A.2d 455 (N.J. 1964); Rector, Church Wardens & Vestrymen v. Committee to Preserve St. Bartholomew's Church, 445 N.Y.S.2d 975 (1982).

[76] Smith v. Church of God, 326 F. Supp. 6 (D. Md. 1971). Bennison v. Sharp, 329 N.W.2d 466 (Mich. App. 1982).

[77] Maryland and Virginia Eldership of Churches of God v. Church of God at Sharpsburg, 396 U.S. 367 (1970).

[78] Jones v. Wolf, 443 U.S. 595 (1979).

[79] Bible Presbyterian Church v. Harvey Cedars Bible Conference, Inc., 202 A.2d 455 (N.J. 1964).

(1) a special act or general law under which a corporation may lawfully exist, (2) a bona fide attempt to organize under the law and colorable compliance with the statutory requirements, and (3) actual use or exercise of corporate powers in pursuance of such law or attempted organization.[80]

To illustrate, when church trustees failed to sign a certificate of incorporation as required by state law, and the certificate was duly filed with the proper state authorities and remained on file without challenge for over thirty years, a court rejected the contention that the church was not a corporation.[81] Once the de facto status of a corporation is established, it may be attacked only by the state in a *quo warranto* proceeding.

§ 6-02.2 — Charters, Constitutions, Bylaws, and Resolutions

Key point 6-02.2. Churches are subject to the provisions of their governing documents, which generally include a charter and a constitution or bylaws (in some cases both). A charter is the state-approved articles of incorporation of an incorporated church. Most rules of internal church administration are contained in a constitution or bylaws. Specific and temporary matters often are addressed in resolutions. If a conflict develops among these documents, the order of priority generally is as follows—charter, constitution, bylaws, and resolutions.

It is important for church leaders to be familiar with the terms *charter, constitution, bylaws*, and *resolution*. The United States Supreme Court has observed that "[a]ll who unite themselves to [a church] do so with an implied consent to its government, and are bound to submit to it."[82] A church's "government" generally is defined in its charter, constitution, bylaws, resolutions, and practice. In addition, numerous courts have observed that the articles of incorporation and bylaws of a church constitute a "contract" between the congregation and its members.[83]

1. Charters and Articles of Incorporation

The application for incorporation that is filed with the secretary of state generally is called the *articles of incorporation* or *articles of agreement*. This document, when approved and certified by the appropriate government official, is commonly referred to as the corporate *charter*.[84] It is often said that the corporate charter includes by implication every pertinent provision of state law.[85]

Church charters typically set forth the name, address, period of duration, and purposes of the corporation; the doctrinal tenets of the church; and the names and addresses of incorporators and directors.

The income tax regulations require that the assets of a church pass to another tax-exempt organization upon its dissolution.[86] The IRS has stated that the following paragraph will satisfy this requirement if contained in a church corporation's articles of incorporation:

Upon the dissolution of the corporation, assets shall be distributed for one or more exempt purposes within the meaning of section 501(c)(3) of the Internal Revenue Code, or corresponding section of

---

[80] Trustees of Peninsular Annual Conference of the Methodist Church, Inc. v. Spencer, 183 A.2d 588, 592 (Del. 1962).

[81] *Id.*

[82] Watson v. Jones, 80 U.S. 679 (1871).

[83] *See, e.g.*, Lozanoski v. Sarafin, 485 N.E.2d 669 (Ind. App. 1985).

[84] FLETCHER CYC. CORP. § 164, n.21 (perm. ed. 1993).

[85] *Id.*

[86] Treas. Reg. § 1.501(c)(3)-1(b)(4).

any future federal tax code, or shall be distributed to the federal government, or to a state or local government, for a public purpose. Any such assets not so disposed of shall be disposed of by the Court of Common Pleas of the county in which the principal office of the corporation is then located, exclusively for such purposes or to such organization or organizations, as said Court shall determine, which are organized and operated exclusively for such purposes.[87]

It would be very unusual for a church to use this suggested language without modification. Most churches prefer to specify the religious organization to which their assets will be distributed in the event of dissolution rather than leaving this determination to a judge's discretion. There is no assurance, under the suggested IRS language, that a dissolved church's assets would even go to another religious organization. For example, a judge could transfer a dissolved church's assets to a city or state government, or to a non-religious charitable organization, under the IRS language. Of course, churches wishing to designate a religious organization in their dissolution clauses should condition the distribution upon that organization's existence and tax-exempt status at the time of the distribution.

Tip. It is doubtful that inclusion of a dissolution clause in a church's bylaws will be acceptable to the IRS, and such a practice should be avoided.

The Internal Revenue Manual and IRS Publication 557 both require that an appropriate dissolution clause appear in a church's articles of incorporation. However, the IRS has conceded that no dissolution clause is required if state law requires that the assets of a dissolved church corporation (or other charitable corporation) be distributed to another tax-exempt organization.[88] The IRS has stated that this special provision does not apply to unincorporated churches, since no state "provides certainty by statute or case law, for the distribution of assets upon the dissolution of an unincorporated nonprofit association. Therefore, any unincorporated nonprofit association needs an adequate dissolution provision in its organizing document . . . ."[89]

The IRS also suggests that the following two paragraphs be placed in a church corporation's articles of incorporation:

Said corporation is organized exclusively for charitable, religious, and educational purposes, including, for such purposes, the making of distributions to organizations that qualify as exempt organizations under section 501(c)(3) of the Internal Revenue Code, or the corresponding section of any future federal tax code.

No part of the net earnings of the corporation shall inure to the benefit of, or be distributable to its members, trustees, officers, or other private persons, except that the corporation shall be authorized and empowered to pay reasonable compensation for services rendered and to make payments and distributions in furtherance of the purposes set forth in [these articles]. No substantial part of the activities of the corporation shall be the carrying on of propaganda, or otherwise attempting to influence legislation, and the corporation shall not participate in, or intervene in

[87] IRS Publication 557. An abbreviated version of this language, which also is acceptable to the IRS, appears in Rev. Proc. 82-2, 1982-1 C.B. 367.
[88] In Rev. Proc. 82-2, 1982-3 I.R.B. 9, the IRS held that a dissolution clause is not required in the articles of incorporation of nonprofit corporations incorporated under the nonprofit corporation laws of Arkansas, California, Louisiana, Massachusetts, Minnesota, Missouri, Ohio, and Oklahoma, since such laws contain adequate dissolution provisions that apply to any organization incorporated under them. *But see* IRS Announcement 82-91 (Missouri has two charitable corporation statutes, and only one contains an adequate dissolution provision).
[89] INTERNAL REVENUE MANUAL § 322.3(13).

279

(including the publishing or distribution of statements) any political campaign on behalf of or in opposition to any candidate for public office. Notwithstanding any other provision of these articles, the corporation shall not carry on any other activities not permitted to be carried on (a) by a corporation exempt from Federal income tax under section 501(c)(3) of the Internal Revenue Code, or the corresponding provision of any future federal tax code, or (b) by a corporation contributions to which are deductible under section 170(c)(2) of the Internal Revenue Code, or corresponding section of any future federal tax code.[90]

Inclusion of the preceding paragraphs in a church's articles of incorporation helps to ensure the continued recognition of its tax-exempt status.[91]

Tip. Ordinarily, it is advisable for a church to state its purposes in its articles of incorporation in terms of "charitable, religious, and educational" activities, since this will allow the greatest operational flexibility and will minimize problems. For example, if a church wishes to establish an elementary school, its authority to do so will be indisputable if its purposes are "charitable, religious, and educational." Similarly, a church clearly has the authority to build a nursing home or homeless shelter if its purposes are "charitable, religious, and educational," since care for the aged and poor are without question a charitable function. Church leaders may be convinced that education and care for the aged and poor are religious functions, but the IRS does not necessarily agree with this conclusion.

The state law under which a church is incorporated will specify the procedure to be followed in amending the corporate charter. Generally, a charter amendment must be filed with and approved by the state official who approved the charter.

Example. The Washington Supreme Court ruled that a church's board of elders was powerless to amend the church's articles of incorporation without the pastor's approval. The church's articles of incorporation specified that neither the articles nor the bylaws could be amended without the pastor's approval. After allegations of sexual misconduct on the part of the pastor surfaced, the board of elders decided to conduct hearings into the matter. At the conclusion of these hearings, the board adopted a resolution placing the pastor on "special status." This meant that he could resume his duties as pastor of the church, but he would not be permitted to be alone with any females. This decision was announced to the church congregation in a special meeting. The pastor refused to accept this special status or to honor the board's decision. Instead, he announced to the congregation that he was not under the authority of the elders and that he would resume his role of pastor without restriction. The board convened a meeting with the pastor in an attempt to reach a compromise. When it was clear that no agreement was possible, the board members voted to amend the articles by removing the provision requiring the pastor to approve all amendments to the articles. They also voted to remove the pastor from office because of his breach of his "fiduciary duties" to the corporation. The pastor immediately filed a lawsuit asking a civil court to determine whether or not the elders had the authority to amend the articles without his approval. The state supreme court ruled in favor of the pastor. It reasoned that the articles clearly specified that they could not be amended without the pastor's approval, and that as a result the elders' attempt to amend the articles without the pastor's approval was null and void. The court observed, "Neither of the parties has called to our attention any case

---

[90] IRS Publication 557. The IRS states in Publication 557 that "[i]f reference to federal law in articles of incorporation imposes a limitation that is invalid in your state, you may wish to substitute the following for the last sentence of the preceding paragraph: 'Notwithstanding any other provision of these articles, this corporation shall not, except to an insubstantial degree, engage in any activities or exercise any powers that are not in furtherance of the purposes of this corporation.'"

[91] *See* R. Hammar, Church and Clergy Tax Guide chapter 11 (published annually by the publisher of this text).

holding that any corporation law in the country, profit or nonprofit, prohibits a provision in the articles of incorporation requiring the concurrence of a special individual to amend the articles." The court agreed that the church's articles "might well, in retrospect, be viewed by some as an improvident provision," but it concluded that "it is not the function of this court . . . to protect those who freely chose to enter into this kind of relationship."[92]

2. Constitutions and Bylaws

Articles of incorporation rarely contain rules for the internal government of the corporation. For this reason, it is desirable and customary for churches to adopt rules of internal administration. One court has observed that "it has been uniformly held that religious organizations have the right to prescribe such rules and regulations as to the conduct of their own affairs as they may think proper, so long as the same are not inconsistent with . . . the law of the land."[93] Such rules ordinarily are called bylaws, although occasionally they are referred to as a constitution or a "constitution and bylaws." The terms *bylaws* and *constitution* often are used interchangeably. Technically, however, the terms are distinguishable—*bylaws* referring generally to the rules of internal government adopted by a corporation, and *constitution* referring to the supreme law of a corporation.[94] Correctly used, the term *constitution* refers to a body of rules that is paramount to the bylaws. It may refer to the charter or to a document separate and distinct from both the charter and bylaws. Church corporations that differentiate between a constitution and bylaws ordinarily do so on the basis of the relative importance of the provisions assigned to either document. Often, more important provisions are assigned to the constitution, which is made more difficult to amend because a greater majority vote is required than for amendments to the bylaws. Routine items are assigned to the bylaws, which is more easily amended because of a lesser voting requirement.

It makes no sense for a church corporation to have both a "constitution" and a separate set of "bylaws" unless the constitution is made superior to the bylaws either by express provision or by a more restrictive amendment procedure. Identifying a single body of rules as the "constitution and bylaws" without any attempt to distinguish between the two is a common but inappropriate practice. Obviously, the best practice would be to set forth the corporation's purposes and beliefs in the corporate charter, and to have a single body of rules for internal government identified as bylaws.

At a minimum, church bylaws should cover the following matters: (1) qualifications, selection, and expulsion of members; (2) time and place of annual business meetings; (3) the calling of special business meetings; (4) notice for annual and special meetings; (5) quorums; (6) voting rights; (7) selection, tenure, and removal of officers and directors; (8) filling of vacancies; (9) responsibilities of directors and officers; (10) method of amending bylaws; and (11) purchase and conveyance of property.[95] Other matters that should be considered for inclusion with church bylaws include (12) adoption of a specific body of parliamentary procedure; (13) a clause requiring disputes between church members, or between a member and the church itself, to be resolved through mediation or arbitration; (14) a clause specifying how contracts and other legal documents are to be approved and signed; (15) signature authority on checks; (16) "bonding" of officers and employees who handle church funds; (17) an annual audit by independent certified public accountants; (18) an indemnification clause; (19) specification of the church's fiscal year; and (20) "staggered voting" of directors (a portion of the board is elected each year—to ensure year-to-year continuity of leadership).

---

[92] Barnett v. Hicks, 792 P.2d 150 (Wash. 1990).
[93] Ohio Southeast Conference of Evangelical United Brethren Church v. Kruger, 243 N.E.2d 781, 787 (Ohio 1968).
[94] Fletcher Cyc. Corp. § 4167, n.21 (perm. ed. 1992).
[95] *See generally* the Model Nonprofit Corporation Act Bylaws.

The power to enact and amend bylaws is vested in the members, unless the charter or bylaws grants this authority to some other body. Occasionally, trustees or directors are given the authority to enact and amend bylaws. Procedures to be followed in amending the bylaws should be and usually are set forth in the bylaws. Such procedures must be followed.

Church bylaws often contain ambiguous language, and this can result in both confusion and internal disputes. It is essential for church bylaws to be reviewed periodically by the board, or a special committee, to identify ambiguities and propose modifications. Will the civil courts interfere in a church dispute over the meaning of ambiguous bylaw provisions? Generally, the civil courts have been willing to interpret contested terminology in church bylaws so long as the inquiry does not involve questions of religious doctrine or polity.

Example. An Arizona court agreed to interpret a clause in a church's bylaws specifying that "a pastor may be terminated by the church congregation . . . but only if . . . the vote equals or exceeds three-fourths of the voting members present." A church voted to oust its pastor at a duly called meeting by a vote of 18 of the 26 members present (the remaining 8 members did not vote). The pastor refused to acknowledge that the vote resulted in his dismissal, since less than "three-fourths of the voting members present" had voted to dismiss him (18 is only 70 percent of 26). Several disgruntled members of the congregation disagreed with this interpretation, and petitioned a court for a ruling recognizing that the congregational vote had resulted in the dismissal of the pastor. The members argued that the phrase "three-fourths of the voting members present" should be interpreted to mean three-fourths of the individuals who actually cast votes at the business meeting rather than three-fourths of all members actually present and eligible to vote. Since all 18 of the persons who actually voted at the meeting voted to dismiss the pastor, 100 percent of the votes were cast in favor of dismissal. A state appeals court ruled that the pastor had not been lawfully dismissed in the meeting in question. The court relied on Robert's Rules of Order, which had been adopted by the church (in its bylaws) as the governing body of parliamentary procedure, as support for its conclusion that the phrase "three-fourths of the voting members present" means three-fourths "of the individuals present and eligible to vote." Accordingly, the pastor had not been dismissed by the congregational vote since less than three-fourths of the members present and eligible to vote had voted to dismiss him.[96]

Example. The Iowa Supreme Court suggested that it was barred by the first amendment guaranty of religious freedom from resolving a dispute involving the interpretation of church bylaws.[97] A group of church members filed a lawsuit claiming that the pastor and other members had violated the church bylaws in several ways, including the following: (1) Placed some members on "probation" when no such status was recognized by the bylaws; (2) terminated longtime members without cause; (3) allowed the minister and his wife to take money from the church treasury and funds for their own personal and private use; (4) appointed members to leadership positions illegally; (5) refused to honor a proper request for a meeting of the congregation called for the purpose of exploring the relationship of the church and its minister; (6) leased church property to private individuals; (7) disposed of property belonging to the church to private individuals; (8) eliminated church committees; (9) held illegal meetings; (10) violated church spending limits. The pastor's attorney filed a motion to dismiss the case, arguing that the first amendment guaranty of religious freedom prevents the civil courts from resolving such disputes. The trial court agreed, and dismissed the lawsuit. The disgruntled members appealed. The state supreme court began its ruling by noting that "civil courts are precluded by the first amendment from deciding doctrinal issues," including "membership in a church organization or church dis-

---

[96] Blanton v. Hahn, 763 P.2d 522 (Ariz. App. 1988).
[97] Holmstrom v. Sir, 590 N.W.2d 538 (Iowa 1999).

cipline," and that "the courts have no jurisdiction over, and no concern with, purely ecclesiastical questions and controversies, including membership in a church organization, but they do have jurisdiction as to civil, contract, and property rights which are involved in or arise from a church controversy."

Example. *A church's constitution provided that "the candidate receiving the majority of all votes cast shall, upon unanimous approval, be declared elected." The church convened a congregational meeting to vote on a pastoral candidate, and the candidate received a majority of the votes cast (but not "unanimous approval"). The candidate was subsequently employed, and a group of dissidents filed a lawsuit asking a civil court to enforce the church's constitutional requirement of "unanimous approval." While noting that the first amendment prohibits a court "from entangling itself in matters of church doctrine or practice," a Washington state court concluded that it could resolve controversies, such as this one, involving the interpretation "of an ambiguous provision in what amounts to a contract between the members of the congregation, dealing with a purely procedural question" and involving "no ecclesiastical or doctrinal issues." The court also noted that it found no "dispute resolution process" within the denomination to which it could defer.*[98]

3. Resolutions

Corporate resolutions are not bylaws. A resolution is an informal and temporary enactment for disposing of a particular item of business, whereas bylaws are rules of general applicability. For example, a minister's "housing allowance" generally is designated by his or her church board in a resolution. A church's business expense reimbursement policy or medical insurance reimbursement plan ordinarily appear in resolutions of the church board.

4. Reconciling Conflicting Language

Occasionally, conflicts develop among provisions in a corporation's charter, constitution, bylaws, and resolutions. The general rule is that provisions in a corporate charter take precedence over conflicting provisions in a corporation's constitution, bylaws, or resolutions.

Example. *A federal appeals court ruled that a local church's articles of incorporation took priority over a conflicting provision in a denominational "Book of Discipline" which the court viewed as the "functional equivalent" of the local church's bylaws. In 1991 the African Union Methodist Protestant Church (the "national church") adopted a "church property" resolution specifying that "the title to all property, now owned or hereafter acquired by an incorporated local church . . . shall be held by or conveyed to the corporate body in its corporate name, in trust for the use and benefit of such local church and of the African Union Methodist Protestant Church." The property resolution was incorporated into the national church's governing Book of Discipline. At the same 1991 meeting of the national church, another resolution was adopted authorizing pastors "to sign official documents pertaining to the individual local church." On the basis of these resolutions, the national church directed a number of pastors to sign a quitclaim deed transferring title to their church's property to the national church. One church, whose property was deeded to the national church by its pastor pursuant to such a directive, voted unanimously to secede from the national church and then challenged the legality of the transfer in court.*

[98] Organization for Preserving the Constitution of Zion Lutheran Church v. Mason, 743 P.2d 848 (Wash. App. 1987). A dissenting judge, quoting several passages of scripture (Numbers 11:16-17; Matthew 9:35-38; 28:18-20; John 20:19-23; Acts 6:2-7; 2 Corinthians 3:6; Ephesians 4:7-12; Hebrews 5:1-10) characterized the selection of clergy as an ecclesiastical process in which the civil courts may never interfere.

Table 6-1
Provisions Commonly Found in Governing Documents

charter	constitution	bylaws	resolutions
• name • address • duration • purposes • names and addresses of initial board members • dissolution clause	[many churches only use bylaws, and not bylaws plus a constitution; this column assumes that a church has both documents] • doctrinal tenets (and any other matter whose amendment is subject to a greater voting requirement)	• qualifications, selection, and discipline of members • time and place of annual business meetings • calling of special business meetings • notice for annual and special meetings • quorum • voting rights • selection, tenure, and removal of officers and directors • filling of vacancies • responsibilities of directors and officers • method of amending bylaws • purchase and conveyance of property • adoption of a specific body of parliamentary procedure • a clause requiring disputes between church members, or between a member and the church itself, to be resolved through mediation or arbitration • a clause specifying how contracts and other legal documents are to be approved and signed • signature authority on checks • "bonding" of officers and employees who handle church funds • an annual audit by independent certified public accountants • an indemnification clause • specification of the church's fiscal year • "staggered voting" of directors (a portion of the board is elected each year —to ensure year-to-year continuity of leadership)	• housing allowances for clergy • accountable business expense reimbursement arrangement • clergy compensation package

A federal appeals court ruled that the pastor's attempt to deed his church's property to the national church had to be invalidated. It based this conclusion on a provision in the local church's articles of incorporation that permitted conveyances of church property only upon a vote of at least two-thirds of the church's members. The court noted that this provision conflicted with the national church's "property resolutions" that were incorporated into its Book of Discipline. However, the court concluded that the Book of Discipline "functioned" as the local church's bylaws, and it concluded that whenever there is a conflict between a church's articles of incorporation and its bylaws, the articles of incorporation prevail. As a result, the pastor was bound by the requirement in the articles of incorporation rather than the Book of Discipline since "provisions of a corporation's charter or articles of incorporation enjoy priority over contradictory or inconsistent bylaws."[99]

Example. *A church charter provided for seven trustees and the church's bylaws called for nine. A California court ruled that the charter provision took priority over the provision in the church bylaws.*[100]

Example. *A Florida court ruled that a church board properly removed a pastor without a congregational vote, since this was the procedure specified in the church's articles of incorporation.*[101] *A church's board of deacons voted to terminate their pastor's employment pursuant to the following provision in the church's articles of incorporation: "With respect to the hiring of a . . . pastor . . . the sole responsibility for both hiring and firing said individuals shall rest with the deacons, as more fully set out in the bylaws of this not for profit corporation." The bylaws contained a similar provision. However, when several members of the congregation objected to the board's decision, the board decided to submit the question of the pastor's removal to the church membership at a specially called business meeting. The membership voted to retain the pastor. The board ignored this vote, and attempted to enforce its previous decision to remove the pastor by seeking a court order. The pastor, on the other hand, argued that the board had "amended" the bylaws when it permitted the membership vote, and therefore the vote was valid and the pastor was retained. A state appeals court agreed with the board that the pastor had been properly removed. It noted that the state nonprofit corporation law requires that any new bylaws must be consistent with the articles of incorporation. As a result, the pastor's argument that the board "amended" the bylaws by calling a meeting of the membership to vote on the pastor's retention had to be rejected, since such an "amendment" would be in direct violation of the articles of incorporation which allow a pastor to be removed only by the board.*

Example. *A New Jersey court ruled that "religious and quasi-religious societies may adopt a constitution and bylaws for the regulation of their affairs, if conformable and subordinate to the charter and not repugnant to the law of the land . . . ."*[102]

If the constitution is separate and distinct from the bylaws and is of superior force and effect either by expressly so providing or by reason of a more difficult amendment procedure, then provisions in a corporation's constitution take precedence over conflicting provisions in the bylaws.[103] To illustrate, where a church constitution specified that a pastor was to be elected by a majority vote of the church membership and the bylaws called for a two-thirds vote, the constitution was held to control.[104] Resolutions of course are inferior to, and thus may not contradict, provisions in a corporation's charter, constitution, and bylaws.

Example. *The Georgia Supreme Court ruled that a provision in the state nonprofit corporation law mandating annual membership meetings did not take priority over a provision in a church's bylaws calling for membership meetings once every four years. The members of a church filed a lawsuit in civil*

---

[99] Scotts African Union Methodist Protestant Church v. Conference of African Union First Colored Methodist Protestant Church, 98 F.3d 78 (3rd Cir. 1996).

[100] Morris v. Richard Clark Missionary Baptist Church, 177 P.2d 811 (Cal. 1947).

[101] New Mount Moriah Missionary Baptist Church, Inc. v. Dinkins, 708 So.2d 972 (Fla. App. 1998).

[102] Leeds v. Harrison, 87 A.2d 713, 720 (N.J. 1952).

[103] Fletcher Cyc. Corp. § 4195 (perm. ed. 1992).

[104] Pelzer v. Lewis, 269 A.2d 902 (Pa. 1970).

court seeking to compel their church to conduct an annual membership meeting. The members relied upon a provision in the state nonprofit corporation law specifying that a nonprofit corporation "shall hold a meeting of members annually at a time stated in or fixed in accordance with the bylaws." The church's bylaws called for a membership meeting once every four years. The state supreme court ruled that state nonprofit corporation law did not override the church's own bylaws and therefore the church was required to conduct meetings only once every four years. The court observed that the state nonprofit corporation law itself specifies that if any of its provisions is inconsistent with religious doctrine governing a nonprofit corporation's affairs on the same subject, "the religious doctrine shall control to the extent required by the Constitution of the United States or the Constitution of this state or both." As a result, the issue "is whether the frequency with which the church's membership meets is a matter of religious doctrine having constitutional precedence over inconsistent statutory provisions of [the nonprofit corporation law]." The court noted that the church in this case was "hierarchical" in nature, and that the members had very limited authority to direct church affairs. It concluded, "[A]n annual meeting as contemplated by [the nonprofit corporation law] would be totally inconsistent with the church's fundamental religious freedom, as a hierarchical religious body, to determine its own governmental rules and regulations. Members have no legal right to wrest the governing of the church from [church officials] by obtaining court-ordered annual meetings conducted in accordance with [nonprofit corporation law]."[105]

Tip. *Incorporated churches are free to adopt bylaws addressing issues of internal administration, and these bylaws generally take precedence over conflicting provisions in state nonprofit corporation law. In other words, state nonprofit corporation law may be viewed in most cases as a "gap filler"—filling gaps in a church's bylaws. For example, if an incorporated church's bylaws do not address how vacancies on the board are to be filled, or do not define a quorum, the nonprofit corporation law will "fill the gaps."*

§ 6-03 Church Records

Key point 6-03. *State nonprofit corporation laws generally require incorporated churches to maintain certain kinds of records. The federal tax code also requires churches to maintain specified records.*

Each church should maintain the following records: (1) correct and complete books and records of account, (2) minutes of the proceedings of its members, (3) minutes of the proceedings of its board of directors, (4) resolutions of its board of directors, (5) minutes of the proceedings of committees, and (6) a current list of voting members. These documents, in addition to the corporate charter, constitution, bylaws, certificate of incorporation, and business correspondence, constitute the records of a church corporation. The Model Nonprofit Corporation Act, under which many churches are incorporated, states:

Each corporation shall keep correct and complete books and records of account and shall keep minutes of the proceedings of its members, board of directors and committees having any of the authority of the board of directors; and shall keep at its registered office or principal office in this State a record giving the names and addresses of its members entitled to vote. All books and records of a corporation may be inspected by any member, or his agent or attorney, for any proper purpose at any reasonable time.[106]

---

[105] First Born Church of the Living God, Inc. v. Hill, 481 S.E.2d 221 (Ga. 1997).
[106] MODEL NONPROFIT CORPORATION ACT § 25.

Table 6-2
Priority Among Governing Documents in Congregational Churches

Note: when attempting to resolve any question of church administration in a "congregational" church, relevant provisions in the following sources of authority generally are applied in the following order of priority.

document	order of priority
charter	• the highest order of priority • its provisions take priority over any other source of authority • start with the charter when attempting to resolve a question of administration; if it doesn't address the matter, then proceed on to the next order of priority until an answer is found
constitution	• the second highest order of priority • takes priority over all other sources of authority except the charter, assuming that it is made superior to the bylaws either by express provision or by a greater voting requirement to amend
bylaws	• the third highest order of priority • takes priority over all other sources of authority except the charter and constitution (assuming the constitution is made superior to the bylaws)
parliamentary law	• the fourth highest order of priority (assuming that a specific body of parliamentary law has been adopted) • takes priority over all other sources of authority if specifically adopted in the church bylaws, except the charter, constitution, and bylaws
state nonprofit corporation law	• the fifth highest order of priority • its provisions generally apply only if the church has not provided otherwise in its charter, constitution, or bylaws (including rules of parliamentary law adopted by the bylaws) • state nonprofit corporation laws ordinarily make a few provisions mandatory despite a bylaw or charter provision to the contrary
resolutions	• the sixth highest order of priority • resolutions can provide guidance in the event that the charter, constitution, bylaws, parliamentary law, and applicable state nonprofit corporation law do not address an issue
established custom	• the seventh highest order of priority • only applies if the custom is established by long and consistent use • it can provide guidance on questions for which an established custom exists, and no higher source of authority applies
majority rule	• the last order of priority; the only basis for resolving issues not addressed in any other manner

The "Revised Model Nonprofit Corporation Act," which has been adopted in a few states (and which no doubt will be adopted by several more), specifies:

(a) A corporation shall keep as permanent records minutes of all meetings of its members and board of directors, a record of all actions taken by the members or directors without a meeting, and a record of all actions taken by committees of the board of directors . . . .

(b) A corporation shall maintain appropriate accounting records.

(c) A corporation or its agent shall maintain a record of its members in a form that permits preparation of a list of the name and address of all members, in alphabetical order by class, showing the number of votes each member is entitled to cast.

(d) A corporation shall maintain its records in written form or in another form capable of conversion into written form within a reasonable time.

(e) A corporation shall keep a copy of the following records at its principal office:

(1) its articles or restated articles of incorporation and all amendments to them currently in effect;

(2) its bylaws or restated bylaws and all amendments to them currently in effect;

(3) resolutions adopted by its board of directors relating to the characteristics, qualifications, rights, limitations and obligations of members or any class or category of members;

(4) the minutes of all meetings of members and records of all actions approved by the members for the past three years;

(5) all written communications to members generally furnished within the past three years, including the financial statements furnished for the past three years under section 16.20;

(6) a list of the names and business or home addresses of its current directors and officers; and

(7) its most recent annual report delivered to the secretary of state . . . .[107]

Churches incorporated under statutes other than the Model Nonprofit Corporation Act (or the revised Act) and unincorporated churches often are under no legal obligation to maintain records.

All records should be as complete as possible, which means that each record should be dated and indicate the action taken, the persons present, and the voting results if any. It is often helpful to include a brief statement of the purpose for each action if it would not otherwise be clear. The secretary of the board of directors usually is the custodian of the corporate records, while accounting records customarily are maintained by the treasurer.

---

[107] REVISED MODEL NONPROFIT CORPORATION ACT § 16.01.

The income tax regulations state that "any person subject to tax . . . shall keep such permanent books of account or records, including inventories, as are sufficient to establish the amount of gross income, deductions, credits, or other matters required to be shown by such person in any return of such tax . . . ."[108]

§ 6-03.1 — Inspection

Key point 6-03.1. Church members generally have no right to inspect church records unless such a right is conferred by state nonprofit corporation law, a church's charter or bylaws, state securities law (if the church has issued securities), or a subpoena. Church records enjoy no privilege against disclosure, with the exception of documents that are protected by the clergy-penitent privilege under state law.

Can church members inspect church records? If so, which records can be inspected and under what circumstances? What about nonmembers? Generally, there is no inherent right to inspect church records. Such a right must be granted in some legal document such as a church's bylaws or state nonprofit corporation law. Some of the possible justifications for a right of inspection are reviewed in this section.

1. Nonprofit Corporation Law

Section 25 of the Model Nonprofit Corporation Act, previously quoted, gives members of an incorporated church the right to inspect corporate records for any proper purpose at any reasonable time. The Revised Model Nonprofit Corporation Act gives members broad authority to inspect corporate records, but specifies that "[t]he articles or bylaws of a religious corporation may limit or abolish the right of a member . . . to inspect and copy any corporate records."[109]

Can a church incorporated under the Model Nonprofit Corporation Act refuse a member's request to inspect church records on the ground that such a right conflicts with the church's constitutional guaranty of religious freedom? The courts have reached conflicting answers to this question.

Example. One court ruled that members of a church incorporated under the Model Nonprofit Corporation Act do not have a right to inspect church records if doing so would "impinge upon the doctrine of the church." When church elders rejected members' requests to inspect church records, the members incorporated the church under a state nonprofit corporation law making the "books and records" of a corporation subject to inspection "by any member for any proper purpose at any reasonable time." When church elders continued to reject the members' request for inspection, the members asked a state court to recognize their legal right to inspection under state law. The elders countered by arguing that application of state corporation law would impermissibly interfere with the religious doctrine and practice of the church, contrary to the constitutional guaranty of religious freedom. Specifically, the elders argued that according to the church's "established doctrine," the New Testament "places within the hands of a select group of elders the sole responsibility for overseeing the affairs of the church," and

---

[108] Treas. Reg. § 1.6001-1(a).

[109] Revised Model Business Corporations Act § 16.02. Some of the special provisions under the revised Act include: (1) ordinarily, a member must give the corporation written notice at least five business days before the date of inspection; (2) the right to inspect includes the right to make copies; (3) the corporation may charge a reasonable fee for the duplicating expenses; (4) for certain types of records, a member's request for inspection must be "in good faith and for a proper purpose," and the member must describe with "reasonable particularity the purpose of the records the member desires to inspect," and the records must be directly related to such purpose; and (5) a member's agent or attorney has the same inspection and copying rights as the member. In addition, the revised Act empowers the civil courts to order a corporation to grant a member's request for inspection.

that this authority is "evidenced by biblical admonitions to the flock to obey and submit to them that have rule over the flock." The state supreme court agreed that "application of our state corporation law would almost certainly impinge upon the doctrine of the church" as described by the elders, and accordingly would violate the constitutional guaranty of religious freedom. The court concluded that if the application of a state law would conflict with the "doctrine, polity, or practice" of a church, then the law cannot be applied to the church without a showing of a "compelling state interest." No such showing was made in this case, the court concluded, and therefore the state law giving members of nonprofit corporations the legal right to inspect corporate records could not be applied to the church.[110]

Other courts have rejected the claim that the first amendment insulates church records from inspection by members. To illustrate, members of one church sought a court order authorizing them to examine the church's financial records. The church was incorporated under the state's general nonprofit corporation law, which gave members the right to inspect corporate records at any reasonable time. The church and its pastor objected to the inspection on the ground that the first amendment prohibits the courts from involving themselves in church affairs. The court disagreed with this contention, concluding that "first amendment values are plainly not jeopardized by a civil court's enforcement of a voting member's right to examine these records."[111]

> ***Example.*** *A Louisiana court ruled that an incorporated church had to allow members to inspect church records. Four members asked for permission to inspect the following records of their church: (1) bank statements; (2) the check register and cancelled checks for all the church's bank accounts; (3) the cash receipts journal; and (4) monthly financial reports. The pastor denied the members' request. The members then sought a court order compelling the church to permit them to inspect the records. The pastor insisted that such an order would interfere with "internal church governance" in violation of the first amendment. A state appeals court ruled that allowing the members to inspect records, pursuant to state nonprofit corporation law, would not violate the first amendment. The court quoted from an earlier Louisiana Supreme Court ruling: "A voting member of a nonprofit corporation has a right to examine the records of the corporation without stating reasons for his inspection. Since the judicial enforcement of this right does not entangle civil courts in questions of religious doctrine, polity, or practice, the first amendment does not bar a suit to implement the statutory right. First amendment values are plainly not jeopardized by a civil court's enforcement of a voting member's right to examine these records. No dispute arising in the course of this litigation requires the court to resolve an underlying controversy over religious doctrine."[112]*

It is doubtful that most courts would permit churches incorporated under the model Act to refuse members' requests to inspect church records on the basis of the first amendment guaranty of religious freedom. The statutory right of inspection is a "neutral law of general applicability" that is presumably constitutional without the need for demonstrating a compelling state interest.[113] As a result, church leaders should not assume that the first amendment permits them to deny inspection rights given to members under state corporation law.

A right of inspection, however, generally applies only to *members*. Persons who are not members of a church generally have no right to demand inspection of church records under nonprofit corporation law.

---

[110] Gipson v. Brown, 749 S.W.2d 297 (Ark. 1988). A "compelling state interest" no longer is required with respect to "neutral laws of general applicability," according to the United States Supreme Court's decision in Employment Division v. Smith, 494 U.S. 872 (1990).

[111] Burgeois v. Landrum, 396 So.2d 1275, 1277-78 (La. 1981).

[112] Jefferson v. Franklin, 692 So.2d 602 (La. App. 1997). The court quoted from the Louisiana Supreme Court's decision in Burgeois v. Landrum, 396 So.2d 1275 (La. 1981), referred to in the text.

[113] Employment Division v. Smith, 110 S. Ct. 1595 (1990).

Example. Some of the members of a charitable organization incorporated under the state nonprofit corporation law demanded to see various corporate records. Their request was denied by corporate officers, and the members sued. A state appeals court ruled that the members had a broad right to inspect the corporation's records. The court noted that the state nonprofit corporation law specified that "all books and records of a corporation may be inspected by any member . . . for any proper purpose at any reasonable time." The court continued, "The [member] has the burden to establish he has a proper purpose to inspect the corporation's records. A proper purpose is shown when a shareholder has an honest motive, is acting in good faith, and is not proceeding for vexatious or speculative reasons; however, the purpose must be lawful in character and not contrary to the interests of the corporation. A proper purpose is one that seeks to protect the interests of the corporation and the [member] seeking the information. . . . [A member's] right to inspect a corporation's books and records must be balanced against the needs of the corporation depending on the facts of the case. Proof of actual mismanagement is not required; a good faith fear of mismanagement is sufficient to show proper purpose. The [member] is not required to establish a proper purpose for each record he requests. Once that purpose has been established, the [member's] right to inspect extends to all books and records necessary to make an intelligent and searching investigation and from which he can derive any information that will enable him to better protect his interests."[114]

Example. An Ohio court ruled that a member of a nonprofit corporation did not have a legal right to inspect corporate records. A nonprofit organization was incorporated under an Ohio statute that gives members a legal right to inspect "all corporate records . . . for any reasonable and proper purpose and at any reasonable time." A member of a nonprofit corporation asked to inspect (1) minutes of the board; (2) financial records; and (3) membership records. His stated purpose was to determine whether or not he had been secretly "excommunicated" from the organization. The member sued the corporation when it refused to respond to his request. A court ruled that the member was not entitled to inspect any of the records in question. It noted that Ohio nonprofit corporation law "requires that two elements be met before the books and records of a nonprofit corporation can be examined: (1) the person requesting the records must be a member of the organization; and (2) the member must have a reasonable and proper purpose for wanting to see the corporate books." The court concluded that the member had no legal right to inspect the corporation's records. On the one hand, if he in fact were not a member, then he would fail the first requirement (only members have a legal right to inspect corporate records). On the other hand, if he in fact was still a member, then he failed the second requirement since there would be no "reasonable and proper purpose" in inspecting corporate records to ascertain this fact.[115]

Example. The Texas Supreme Court ruled that a state nonprofit corporation law that granted a limited right to inspect corporate records did not mandate the disclosure of donor records.[116] The Texas Nonprofit Corporation Act specifies that nonprofit corporation "shall maintain current true and accurate financial records with full and correct entries made with respect to all financial transactions of the corporation." It further specifies that "[a]ll records, books, and annual reports of the financial activity of the corporation shall be kept at the registered office or principal office of the corporation . . . and shall be available to the public for inspection and copying there during normal business hours." Based on these provisions, a group of persons demanded that a charity turn over documents revealing the identities of all donors and the amounts of donors' annual contributions. The charity resisted this request, claiming that the inspection right provided under the nonprofit corporation law did not refer to inspec-

---

[114] Meyer v. Board of Managers, 583 N.E.2d 14 (Ill. App. 1 Dist. 1991).
[115] Nozik v. Mentor Lagoons Yacht Club, 678 N.E.2d 948 (Ohio App. 1996).
[116] In re Bacala, 982 S.W.2d 371 (Tex. 1998).

tion or disclosure of donor lists, and that even if it did, such a provision would violate the first amendment freedom of association. The state supreme court ruled that the right of inspection did not extend to donor lists. It noted that "the statute does not expressly require that contributors' identities be made available to the public." And, it found that the intent of the legislature in enacting the inspection right "was not to force nonprofit corporations to identify the exact sources of their income; rather, it was to expose the nature of the expenditures of that money once received from the public and to make nonprofit organizations accountable to their contributors for those expenditures." As a result, the statute "can be upheld as constitutional when interpreted as not requiring disclosure of contributors' names."

Tip. *The Privacy Act and Freedom of Information Act have no application to religious organizations. They do not provide church members with any legal basis for inspecting church records.*

2. CHURCH CHARTER OR BYLAWS

A right of inspection may be given by the bylaws or charter of a church corporation or association.

3. STATE SECURITIES LAW

Churches that raise funds by issuing securities (*i.e.,* bonds or promissory notes) may be required by state securities laws to allow investors—whether members or not—to inspect the financial statements of the church.

INSPECTION OF CHURCH RECORDS

Do church members have a legal right to inspect church records as a result of state nonprofit corporation law? Consider the following:

- Most state nonprofit corporation laws give members a limited right to inspect corporate records.

- The right of inspection is not absolute. It only exists if a church is incorporated under a state nonprofit corporation law that gives members such a right.

- The right of inspection only extends to members.

- The right of inspection only extends to those records specified in the statute creating the right.

- Most such laws provide that the member may inspect documents only "for a proper purpose" at a "reasonable time."

- Some courts have ruled that the right of inspection is limited by considerations of privacy, privilege and confidentiality.[117] That is, some documents may be protected from disclosure by legitimate considerations of privacy (such as an employee's health records); privilege (such as communications protected by the clergy-penitent privilege); or confidentiality (such as reference letters submitted by persons who were given an assurance of confidentiality).

- Any decision to withhold documents from a member should be made with the advice of an attorney.

---

[117] *See, e.g.,* Lewis v. Pennsylvania Bar Association, 701 A.2d 551 (Pa. 1997).

4. SUBPOENA

Members and nonmembers alike may compel the production (*i.e.*, disclosure) or inspection of church records as part of a lawsuit against a church if the materials to be produced or inspected are relevant and not privileged. For example, Rule 34 of the Federal Rules of Civil Procedure, adopted by several states and used in all federal courts, specifies that any party to a lawsuit

> may serve on any other party a request (1) to produce and permit the party making the request, or someone acting on his behalf, to inspect and copy, any designated documents . . . which are in the possession, custody or control of the party upon whom the request is served; or (2) to permit entry upon designated land or other property in the possession or control of the party upon whom the request is served for the purpose of inspection . . . .

Similarly, Rule 45(b) of the Federal Rules of Civil Procedure states that a subpoena may command the person to whom it is directed "to produce the books, papers, documents, or tangible things designated therein . . . ." Rule 45 also stipulates that a subpoena may be quashed or modified if it is "unreasonable and oppressive." Federal, state, and local government agencies are also invested with extensive investigative powers, including the right to subpoena and inspect documents. However, this authority generally may not extend to privileged or irrelevant matters.

Since church records are not inherently privileged, they are not immune from production or inspection. Although most states consider confidential communications to be privileged when they are made to clergy acting in their professional capacity as a spiritual adviser, several courts have held that the privilege does not apply to church records.

> **Example.** *In upholding an IRS subpoena of the records of a religious corporation over its objection that its records were privileged, a federal court observed that the "contention of violation of a penitent-clergyman privilege is without merit. A clergyman must be a natural person."[118]*

> **Example.** *The Ohio Supreme Court, in upholding the admissibility of a church membership registration card over an objection that it was privileged, noted that "this information by any flight of the judicial imagination cannot conceivably be considered as a confession made to [a clergyman] in his professional character in the course of discipline . . . and, of course, is not privileged."[119]*

> **Example.** *A New York court ruled that a church's books and records were subject to government inspection as part of an investigation into alleged wrongdoing in soliciting contributions.[120] The state attorney general received reports that the church forced residents of its homeless shelter to "panhandle" contributions on the streets in exchange for room, board, and 25 percent of the moneys collected. There also were allegations that most of the contributions were appropriated for the personal benefit of the church's founder. Accordingly, the attorney general issued a subpoena to the church, directing it to make available for inspection its (1) books and records, (2) leases and deeds, (3) minutes of its governing body*

---

[118] United States v. Luther, 481 F.2d 429, 432 (9th Cir. 1973) (the court did state that its holding would not prevent "a later determination at a time when the issue is properly raised and supported by a proper showing"). *See also* Abrams v. Temple of the Lost Sheep, Inc., 562 N.Y.S.2d 322 (Sup. Ct. 1990); Abrams v. New York Foundation for the Homeless, Inc., 562 N.Y.S.2d 325 (Sup. Ct. 1990).

[119] In re Estate of Soeder, 220 N.E.2d 547, 572 (Ohio 1966).

[120] Abrams v. New York Foundation for the Homeless, Inc., 562 N.Y.S.2d 325 (Sup. Ct. 1990); Abrams v. Temple of the Lost Sheep, Inc., 562 N.Y.S.2d 322 (Sup. Ct. 1990).

and the names and addresses of all directors, officers, and trustees, and (4) copies of all materials used to solicit contributions. The church refused to respond to this subpoena on the ground that it violated its "religious rights." In rejecting the church's claim, the court observed, "There is no doubt that the attorney general has a right to conduct investigations to determine if charitable solicitations are free from fraud and whether charitable assets are being properly used for the benefit of intended beneficiaries." It makes no difference whether or not the organization soliciting the donations is a church or other religious organization, since "religious corporations . . . are still within the attorney general's subpoena power, and investigations by the attorney general of alleged fraudulent behavior may proceed based upon law and the public interest against fraudulent solicitations by so-called religious groups." The court emphasized that the attorney general's investigation did not prevent the church or its members "from practicing their religious activity, nor is it disruptive to such activity."[121]

Example. *A Pennsylvania court ruled that a church cannot avoid inspection of its records in a civil lawsuit by placing them in a location that it designates as a "secret archive." A plaintiff filed a lawsuit against a priest and diocese on account of damages suffered as a result of the priest's acts of child molestation. The plaintiff issued a subpoena to the diocese seeking disclosure of various church documents concerning alleged sexual misconduct with minor male children by priests assigned to the diocese; the complete personnel files of specified priests; and documents kept by the diocese in its secret archives. The diocese refused to produce any documents contained in its secret archives. A state appeals ordered the diocese to turn over the requested information. The court concluded that the requested information was clearly relevant to the lawsuit, and not privileged. It acknowledged that Pennsylvania law contains a "priest-penitent privilege," which protects clergy from disclosing in court any confidential communications made to them while acting in their role as a confessor or counselor. However, the court insisted that "this privilege protects priest-penitent communications; it does not protect information regarding the manner in which a religious institution conducts its affairs or information acquired by a church as a result of independent investigations not involving confidential communications between priest and penitent." The court concluded, "We hold . . . that where the only action required of a religious institution is the disclosure of relevant, non-privileged documents to an adversary in civil litigation, such action, without more, poses no threat of governmental interference with the free exercise of religion. . . . [T]he relevant inquiry is not whether the church gives a file a particular name, but whether disclosure of the information requested from that file interferes with the exercise of religious freedom."[122]*

Example. *The Pennsylvania Supreme Court ruled that the clergy-penitent privilege did not excuse a Roman Catholic diocese from turning over internal documents pertaining to a priest in response to a subpoena. An individual (the "defendant") was charged with the murder of a Roman Catholic priest. The defendant admitted that he shot the priest, but he insisted that he did so in self-defense. In attempting to prove that he acted in self-defense, the defendant subpoenaed documents from the local Catholic Diocese. Specifically, the defendant requested the priest's personnel records and the Diocese's records concerning the priest's alleged alcohol and drug abuse and sexual misconduct. The defendant insisted that these documents could help prove that he acted in self-defense because of the priest's past violent conduct. The Diocese turned over some documents but refused to turn over any records kept in its "secret archives." It insisted that documents in its secret archives were protected from disclosure by the clergy-penitent privilege since they had been obtained in confidence by the bishop or other clergy in the course of their duties. The court*

---

[121] *Id.* at 328.

[122] Hutchison v. Luddy, 606 A.2d 905 (Pa. Super. 1992). *Accord* Niemann v. Cooley, 637 N.E.2d 943 (Ohio App. 1 Dist. 1994). *But see* State v. Burns, 830 P.2d 1318 (Mont. 1992) (Montana Supreme Court ruled that a priest's personnel file maintained by a diocese did not have to be disclosed in response to a subpoena).

disagreed, noting that there was no proof that the secret records reflected communications between members of the clergy in confidence and for confessional or spiritual purposes.[123]

§ 6-03.2 — "Accountings" of Church Funds

Key point 6-03.2. *Most courts have viewed requests by church members for an "accounting" of church funds to be an internal church matter over which the civil courts have no jurisdiction.*

Do church members, or a government agency or officer, have the right to demand an accounting of church funds? The courts have reached conflicting answers to this question.

Example. A group of church members who had contributed funds to their church demanded that the church give an "accounting" of the use of the contributed funds. When the church refused, the members turned to the courts for relief. A trial judge ordered an immediate accounting, as well as annual audits "forever," and required the church to disclose the contents of a church safety deposit box to the complaining members. The church appealed, arguing that the civil courts had no jurisdiction over a church, and even if they did, they had no authority to order accountings or annual audits. A Florida court, in upholding the trial judge's ruling regarding an accounting and inspection of the church's safety deposit box, observed that "we are of the opinion that this is not an improper interference by the government into a church, or ecclesiastical, matter. When the members of the church decided to incorporate their body under the laws of the state of Florida, they submitted themselves to the jurisdiction of the state courts in all matters of a corporate nature, such as accounting for funds." However, the court reversed the trial judge's order requiring annual audits forever, since "we cannot agree it is proper to order annual, ad infinitum, audits of the books" of a church.[124]

Example. The Supreme Judicial Court of Maine ruled that a state has the authority to demand an accounting of church trust funds. In 1939, a wealthy individual made a gift of a substantial amount of stock to a church, subject to the following two conditions: (1) the church was to use the trust fund for "charitable uses and purposes," and (2) the church was not to sell or transfer the stock for a period of fifty years. In 1983, after faithfully observing the terms of the trust for forty-four years, the church sought court permission to sell the stock. It noted that the value of the stock had fallen sharply and the rate of return was substantially less than could be achieved with other investments. The court permitted the church to sell the stock (then valued at $733,000) in order to protect the trust fund. In 1987, the state attorney general received information suggesting that the church was not carrying out the terms of the trust. The attorney general asked the church for an accounting of the trust fund. When the church refused to comply, the attorney general sought a court order compelling the church to provide an accounting. The church argued that the first amendment guaranty of religious freedom protected the church from complying with the demand for an accounting. The court rejected the church's position. It noted that the attorney general had the legal authority to ensure that the church was complying with the trust purpose, and this authority included the right to demand an accounting of trust funds. In rejecting the church's first amendment argument, the court observed, "The attorney general is not attempting to inquire into the financial affairs of the church, or impose a regulatory scheme, but only to obtain the information necessary for him to fulfill his statutory obligation to the public. Because we find that the trust is a public trust, separate and distinct from the church, the court ordered accounting can be

---

[123] Commonwealth v. Stewart, 690 A.2d 195 (Pa. 1997).
[124] Matthews v. Adams, 520 So.2d 334 (Fl. App. 1988).

accomplished by application of neutral principles of law and therefore, does not impinge upon the church's first amendment freedoms."[125]

Example. *The Oklahoma Supreme Court refused to permit a number of dismissed church members to inspect church records or demand an accounting of church funds. Five members of a local church became concerned over the way their pastor and church board were conducting church business. The members filed a lawsuit asking a civil court to issue an order giving them access to the church's financial records. The members were immediately dismissed by a unanimous vote of the church at a hastily called business meeting. The supreme court refused to permit them to inspect the church's financial records. The former members insisted that they needed access to these records to prove that church leaders diverted church funds to uses that were not authorized by the church. The court observed, "Some of their claims alleging diversion of church property to non-church uses may have been capable of invoking civil judicial relief, and some may not have been. . . . We need not, however, address the extent to which their claims were cognizable when they filed suit, because their expulsion mooted any claims they had as to the diversion of church property to non-church uses." In other words, non-members no longer have "standing" to use the courts to protect their former church from an alleged diversion of funds to unauthorized uses. Only members can sue to protect church assets.*[126]

Example. *An Illinois court ruled that it lacked jurisdiction to resolve a lawsuit brought by church members who demanded an accounting of church funds. Six members of a church filed a lawsuit asking the court to order an accounting of church funds as a result of what they perceived to be financial irregularities involving their minister. A state appeals court declined the members' request. It observed, "It is eminently clear that the basis of this lawsuit is to have the courts examine the way the church is managing its financial affairs; to substitute the prudence of a court's judgment for that of the [minister] who is entrusted by church doctrine to exercise such judgment; to impose court supervision over all financial matters of an entire religious faith; and to have a court interfere with the proper succession in the hierarchy of a religious faith. These matters, however, are beyond the realm of judicial jurisdiction."*[127]

Example. *A court in the District of Columbia ruled that the first amendment guaranty of religious freedom prevents the civil courts from resolving internal church disputes over accounting and reporting practices, except in limited circumstances. The court acknowledged that the first amendment guaranty of religious freedom greatly restricts the authority of the civil courts to resolve internal church disputes, including those involving alleged accounting or reporting irregularities. However, the court concluded that the first amendment would not bar the civil courts from resolving such disputes if they could do so on the basis of clear, objective accounting and reporting criteria requiring no inquiry into religious doctrine— assuming that a church in fact had adopted them. A civil court could enforce such rules since it "would not have a role in deciding what principles apply to the church; the court merely would be asked to apply, without ecclesiastical judgment or intrusion, a previously prescribed, authoritative, nondiscretionary, and clear, policy." The court gave eight examples of accounting and reporting irregularities that the civil courts cannot resolve: (1) What should be the collection, tithing, or offering practices of the church? (2) Should the church pursue pledges from—or take any other particular type of action affecting—members who neglect to remit their obligations? (3) What cash management and investment decisions should be made? (4) Who in the church establishes its spending priorities? (5) Should the pastor have one or more discretionary funds? (6) Should there be an audit committee, and if so, should its membership be internal,*

---

[125] Attorney General v. First United Baptist Church, 601 A.2d 96 (Me. 1992).
[126] Fowler v. Bailey, 844 P.2d 141 (Okla. 1992).
[127] Rizzuto v. Rematt, 653 N.E.2d 34 (Ill. App. 1995).

external, or both, and how many members of each type should there be? (7) Should the church maintain any of its funds as imprest accounts useable only for specified purposes, or should church finances be operated as a general account? (8) For each of the above questions, who makes the decision? The civil courts cannot resolve these questions since they cannot do so without delving into church doctrine and polity.[128]

§ 6-03.3 — Public Inspection of Tax-Exemption Applications

Key point 6-03.3. *Federal law requires tax-exempt organizations to provide a copy of their application for exemption (and supporting materials) upon request. There is no exemption for churches, although many churches have not applied for recognition of tax-exempt status and therefore will have no documents to provide in response to such a request. Many churches are covered by a denominational agency's "group exemption" ruling. Such churches must provide a copy of the group ruling in response to a request for a copy of their tax exemption application.*

Generally, "exempt organizations" (including churches and religious denominations) must make available a copy of the following materials in response to a request from a member of the public: (1) the exemption application form (Form 1023) submitted to the IRS; (2) any supporting documents submitted with the exemption application, including legal briefs or a response to questions from the IRS; and (3) any letter or document issued by the IRS with respect to the exemption application (such as a favorable determination letter or a list of questions from the IRS about the application).[129]

An exempt organization is not required to provide a photocopy of its exemption application to a requester, but is required to have on hand a copy available for inspection. The organization may have an employee present in the room during the inspection, but must allow the requester to take notes freely during the inspection or must allow the requester to photocopy the document on the requester's own photocopying equipment "within reasonable constraints of time and place." Alternatively, if a requester prefers his or her own copy *and the organization does not object* to making a photocopy to give to the requester, the organization may make the copies on its own equipment and charge the requester $1 for the first page and 15 cents for each additional page plus any actual postage costs. The required information "should normally be available on the day of the request for inspection and during the normal business hours of the organization's office."

An organization that fails to comply with a request for inspection may be assessed a penalty of $10 per day up to a maximum of $5,000. A willful failure to comply may result in a penalty of $1,000. The IRS notice also provides that "if an organization filed its application before July 15, 1987, it is required to make available a copy of its application only if it had a copy of the application on July 15, 1987."

Many churches never filed an exemption application with the IRS because they are covered by a "group exemption" obtained by their denomination. If such a church receives a request for inspection of its exemption application, it "must acquire from the parent organization a copy of those documents that were submitted to the IRS by the parent organization . . . and make the material available to the requester in a reasonable amount of time." Alternatively, the requester may obtain the information directly from the parent organization.

If an exempt organization maintains one or more "regional or district offices," the exemption application (and related materials) "shall be made available at each such district or regional office as well as at the principal

---

[128] Bible Way Church v. Beards, 680 A.2d 419 (D.C. App. 1996)
[129] IRS Notice 88-120, 1988-2 C.B. 4541.

office." This rule will be relevant to many religious denominations. Churches and religious denominations should be aware of these new requirements, since some undoubtedly will be receiving requests for inspection.

§ 6-03.4 — Government Inspection of Donor and Membership Lists

Key point 6-03.4. Church donor and membership lists are subject to government inspection, so long as the government has a compelling interest in obtaining this information.

Whether the government has the right to compel religious organizations to release the *names of members and contributors* is a hotly contested issue. In 1958, the United States Supreme Court ruled that the freedom to associate with others for the advancement of beliefs and ideas is a right protected by the first amendment against governmental infringement, whether the beliefs sought to be advanced are political, economic, religious, or cultural.[130] The Court acknowledged that the right of association is nowhere mentioned in the first amendment, but it reasoned that such a right must be inferred in order to make the express first amendment rights of speech and assembly more secure. The court concluded that an order by the State of Alabama seeking to compel disclosure of the name of every member of the National Association for the Advancement of Colored People in Alabama constituted an impermissible restraint upon members' freedom of association, since on past occasions revelation of the identity of its rank-and-file members has exposed these members to economic reprisal, loss of employment, threat of physical coercion, and other manifestations of public hostility. Under these circumstances, we think it apparent that compelled disclosure of [the NAACP's] Alabama membership is likely to affect adversely the ability of [the NAACP] and its members to pursue their collective effort to foster beliefs which they admittedly have the right to advocate, in that it may induce members to withdraw from the Association and dissuade others from joining it . . . ."[131]

It is clear that governmental actions that may have the effect of curtailing the freedom of association are subject to the closest scrutiny. Yet the courts have made it clear that the right to associate is not absolute; a "significant interference" with the right may be tolerated if the government (1) avoids unnecessary interference, (2) demonstrates a sufficiently important interest, and (3) employs the least intrusive means of achieving its interests.[132]

The Supreme Court has observed that "[d]ecisions . . . must finally turn, therefore, on whether [the government] has demonstrated so cogent an interest in obtaining and making public the membership lists . . . as to justify the substantial abridgement of associational freedom which such disclosures will effect. Where there is a significant encroachment upon personal liberty, the state may prevail only upon showing a subordinating interest which is compelling."[133]

Government demands for the production and inspection of membership and contributor lists frequently are approved on the ground that a compelling governmental interest exists.

Example. A federal appeals court upheld the enforcement of an IRS summons seeking the name of every individual who had contributed property other than securities to Brigham Young University (BYU) during a three-year period.[134] Before issuing the summons, the IRS had audited the returns of 162

---

[130] National Association for the Advancement of Colored People v. Alabama, 357 U.S. 449 (1958).
[131] *Id.* at 462-63.
[132] Cousins v. Wigoda, 419 U.S. 477, 488 (1975).
[133] Bates v. Little Rock, 361 U.S. 516, 524 (1960).
[134] United States v. Brigham Young University, 679 F.2d 1345 (10th Cir. 1982).

taxpayers who had contributed property to the university during the years in question. In each instance the amount of the contribution claimed by the taxpayer was overvalued, and in many cases grossly overvalued. As a result, the IRS surmised that many other contributors had overvalued their contributions as well. The university challenged the summons on the ground that the IRS was without a reasonable basis for believing that the remaining contributors had overvalued their contributions. The university further asserted that the information sought was readily available to the IRS through its own files, and that enforcement of the summons would infringe upon the contributors' freedom of association under the first amendment. The court, in upholding the summons, observed that "having previously examined the returns of some 162 donors of gifts in kind to BYU and having found that all were overvalued, the IRS has established a reasonable basis for believing that some of the remaining donors of in kind gifts may have also overvalued their gifts."[135]

Example. *The Federal Communications Commission (FCC) received complaints that a religious broadcaster was not expending contributed funds as indicated in over-the-air solicitations. As part of its investigation, the FCC ordered the broadcaster to divulge the names of all contributors and the amount of each contribution. The broadcaster refused to comply on the ground that such information was protected by the first amendment freedoms of religion and association. An FCC administrative tribunal ruled that under the circumstances the agency had a compelling interest in obtaining disclosure of the names of contributors and the amounts of contributions, and that this interest outweighed the freedoms of religion and association. A federal appeals court affirmed this determination on the grounds that (1) the government has a compelling interest in preventing the diversion of funds contributed for specific, identified purposes, especially when such funds are obtained through the use of the public airwaves, which, by congressional mandate, must be operated in the public interest; (2) the allegations of diversion of funds were made by a former employee and therefore they were entitled to a greater inference of reliability; (3) the government's investigation was narrow and avoided unnecessary interference with the free exercise of religion; and (4) the government's request for records was necessary to serve its compelling interest in investigating the alleged diversion of funds.[136]*

Example. *A New York court ruled that the constitutional guaranty of religious freedom did not excuse a church from producing its records in response to a grand jury subpoena. During a tax investigation, the state attorney general subpoenaed several records and documents from a church. The church challenged the validity of the subpoena on the ground that disclosure of the documents would violate the constitutional rights of the church and its members. Church representatives argued that disclosure of the records would reveal the identities of contributors to the church in violation of the church's belief (based on Matthew 6:1-4) that "charity should be given in secrecy." The court rejected the church's claim. It noted that "it is hard to conceive that release of charge or credit account records, or records of employees' travel expense accounts, would have any likelihood whatsoever" of violating any religious beliefs or tenets of the church. The court agreed that the disclosure of some records would violate contributor's constitutional guaranty of religious freedom. It cited cash receipts records and bank statements. The court further agreed that disclosure of records revealing the charitable recipients of church funds (e.g., canceled checks and bank statements) also might violate the church's rights. However, the church would be required to disclose these records if the state could prove that the alleged violation of the church's rights was outweighed by a "compelling state interest to which the information sought is substantially related" and that the "state's ends may not be achieved by less restrictive means." The court concluded*

---

[135] *Id.* at 1349.
[136] Scott v. Rosenberg, 702 F.2d 1263 (9th Cir. 1983).

that such was the case here, since the church's records were sought in connection with an investigation into tax-related offenses including underreporting of compensation paid to officers and employees and diversion of church funds to nonreligious purposes, and "it is by now well settled that enforcement of a state's revenue laws constitutes a compelling governmental interest."[137]

Example. *A California court ruled that the right to associational privacy extends to private lawsuits as well as governmental investigations, and thus a litigant has no right to compel disclosure of the membership list of a church unless he can establish a compelling state interest justifying disclosure.[138]*

It is not clear whether the government needs to prove a "compelling interest" in order to inspect church membership or donor records following the Supreme Court's 1990 decision in the *Smith* case.[139] In *Smith*, the Court ruled that "neutral laws of general applicability" are presumably valid without the need for demonstrating a "compelling state interest." Statutes that give government agencies a broad authority to collect information (including church membership or donor information) may well be deemed "neutral laws of general applicability" by the courts. But this does not necessarily mean that such agencies can inspect church records without proof of a compelling state interest. In the *Smith* case the Supreme Court observed that the compelling government interest test applies if a neutral and generally applicable law burdens not only the exercise of religion, but also some other first amendment right (such as the right of association, described above). The Court observed, "The only decisions in which we have held that the first amendment bars application of a neutral, generally applicable law to religiously motivated action have involved not the free exercise clause alone, but the free exercise clause in conjunction with other constitutional protections, such as freedom of speech and of the press . . . ." In other words, if a neutral and generally applicable law or governmental practice burdens the exercise of religion, then the compelling governmental interest standard can be triggered if the religious institution or adherent can point to some other first amendment interest that is being violated. In many cases, this will not be hard to do.

If the identities of all members or contributors are not reasonably relevant to a particular governmental investigation, the government's interest in disclosure will not be sufficiently compelling to outweigh the constitutionally protected interests of members and contributors.[140]

Tip. Neither the Privacy Act of 1974 nor the Freedom of Information Act applies to church records.

§ 6-03.5 — The Church Audit Procedures Act

Key point 6-03.5. *The Church Audit Procedures Act provides churches with a number of important protections in the event of an IRS inquiry or examination. However, there are some exceptions.*

Section 7602 of the Internal Revenue Code gives the IRS broad authority to examine or subpoena the books and records of any person or organization for the purposes of (1) ascertaining the correctness of any federal tax return, (2) making a return where none has been filed, (3) determining the liability of any person or organization for any federal tax, or (4) collecting any federal tax. This authority has been held to apply to churches.[141]

---

[137] Full Gospel Tabernacle, Inc. v. Attorney General, 536 N.Y.S.2d 201 (1988). *See also* Abrams v. Temple of the Lost Sheep, Inc., 562 N.Y.S.2d 322 (Sup. Ct. 1990); Abrams v. New York Foundation for the Homeless, Inc., 562 N.Y.S.2d 325 (Sup. Ct. 1990).

[138] Church of Hakeem, Inc. v. Superior Court, 168 Cal. Rptr. 13 (1980).

[139] Employment Division v. Smith, 110 S. Ct. 1595 (1990).

[140] *See, e.g.,* Savola v. Webster, 644 F.2d 743 (8th Cir. 1981); Familias Unidas v. Briscoe, 619 F.2d 391 (5th Cir. 1980).

[141] *See, e.g.,* United States v. Coates, 692 F.2d 629 (9th Cir. 1982); United States v. Dykema, 666 F.2d 1096 (7th Cir. 1981); United States v. Freedom Church, 613 F.2d 316 (1st Cir. 1979).

As part of the Tax Reform Act of 1969, Congress amended section 511 of the Internal Revenue Code to extend the federal tax on the unrelated business income of tax-exempt organizations to churches and religious denominations. In general, unrelated business income constitutes income from a regularly carried on trade or business not substantially related to the exempt purposes of a tax-exempt organization. The amendment of section 511 represented a major change in the treatment of churches and denominations, previously exempt from most federal taxes, including unrelated business income taxes. The Tax Reform Act of 1969 also added section 7605(c) to the Internal Revenue Code:

> No examination of the *books of account* of a church or convention or association of churches shall be made to determine whether such organization may be engaged in the carrying on of an unre-lated trade or business or may be otherwise engaged in activities which may be subject to [the tax on unrelated business income] unless the Secretary (such officer being no lower than a principal internal revenue officer for an internal revenue region) [1] believes that such organization may be so engaged and [2] so notifies the organization in advance of the examination. No examination of the *religious activities* of such an organization shall be made except to the extent necessary to determine whether such organization is a church or a convention or association of churches, and no examination of the *books of account* of such an organization shall be made other than to the extent necessary to determine the amount of tax imposed by this title.[142]

Because amended section 511 created new tax liability for churches and denominations, the addition of section 7605(c) was considered necessary to protect such organizations from excessive tax audits by IRS agents investigating unrelated business activities. Accordingly, the first sentence of section 7605(c) shielded the *books of account* of churches and denominations from any IRS examination for the purpose of determin-ing any unrelated business income tax liability unless the IRS (1) had some basis for believing that such an organization was engaged in an unrelated trade or business, and (2) notified the organization in advance of the examination.

Prior to 1985, some churches argued that section 7605(c) prohibited any IRS examination of church records not undertaken to determine whether a church was engaged in an unrelated trade or business. While it is true that section 7605(c) was enacted primarily in response to the application of the unrelated business income tax to churches and religious organizations, it certainly did not suggest that churches and religious denominations could not be examined under any other circumstances. Churches and denominations, for example, remained liable for withholding and paying employment taxes on nonminister employees and for the payment of certain excise taxes; and they were subject to the IRS examination power to ensure that they were properly complying with such requirements. Section 7605(c) did not negate such authority. On the contrary, the second sentence of that section specifically recognized the authority of the IRS to examine (1) the *religious activities* of a church or denomination to the extent necessary to determine if it were in fact entitled to tax-exempt status, and (2) the *books of account* of a church or denomination to the extent necessary "to determine the amount of tax imposed" under any internal revenue law (including income, employment, and excise taxes). The view that section 7605(c) acknowledged the preexisting authority of the IRS to exam-ine the activities and records of churches and denominations to ensure compliance with income, employ-ment, and excise taxes and entitlement to tax-exempt status was endorsed by the courts[143] and legislative history,[144] and was embodied in the income tax regulations.[145]

---

[142] I.R.C. § 7605(c) (emphasis added).

[143] *See, e.g.*, United States v. Coates, 692 F.2d 629 (9th Cir. 1982); United States v. Dykema, 666 F.2d 1096 (7th Cir. 1981); United States v. Life Science Church of America, 636 F.2d 221 (8th Cir. 1980); United States v. Holmes, 614 F.2d 985 (5th Cir. 1980); United States v. Freedom Church, 613 F.2d 316 (1st Cir. 1979).

Section 7605(c) was criticized for its failure to provide adequate guidelines and for its insensitivity to the unique protections afforded churches by the first amendment's free exercise of religion clause. Such criticism led to the repeal of section 7605(c) in the Tax Reform Act of 1984 and the enactment of the Church Audit Procedures Act as section 7611 of the Internal Revenue Code. Section 7611 imposes detailed limitations on IRS examinations of churches for tax years beginning in 1985 or thereafter. The limitations can be summarized as follows:

1. Church tax inquiries. The IRS may begin a *church tax inquiry* (defined as any inquiry to determine whether a church is entitled to tax-exempt status as a church or is engaged in an unrelated trade or business) only if (a) an *appropriate high-level Treasury official* (defined as a regional IRS commissioner or higher official) *reasonably believes* on the basis of written evidence that the church is not exempt[146] (by reason of its status as a church), may be carrying on an unrelated trade or business, or is otherwise engaged in activities subject to taxation; and (b) the IRS sends the church written *inquiry notice* containing an explanation of the following: (1) the specific concerns which gave rise to the inquiry, (2) the general subject matter of the inquiry, and (3) the provisions of the Internal Revenue Code that authorize the inquiry and the applicable administrative and constitutional provisions, including the right to an informal conference with the IRS before any examination of church records, and the First Amendment principle of separation of church and state.

2. Church tax examinations. The IRS may begin a *church tax examination* of the church records or religious activities of a church only under the following conditions: (a) the requirements of a church tax inquiry have been met, and (b) an *examination notice* is sent by the IRS to the church at least fifteen days *after* the day on which the inquiry notice was sent, and at least fifteen days *before* the beginning of such an examination, containing the following information: (1) a copy of the inquiry notice, (2) a specific description of the church records and religious activities which the IRS seeks to examine, (3) an offer to conduct an informal conference with the church to discuss and possibly resolve the concerns giving rise to the examination, and (4) a copy of all documents collected or prepared by the IRS for use in the examination and the disclosure of which is required by the Freedom of Information Act.

3. Church records. Church records (defined as all corporate and financial records regularly kept by a church, including corporate minute books and lists of members and contributors) may be examined only to the extent necessary to determine the liability for and amount of any income, employment, or excise tax.

4. Religious activities. Religious activities may be examined only to the extent necessary to determine whether an organization claiming to be a church is in fact a church.

5. Deadline for completing church tax inquiries. Church tax inquiries not followed by an examination notice must be completed not later than ninety days after the inquiry notice date.[147] Church tax inquiries and church tax examinations must be completed not later than two years after the examination notice date.[148]

---

[144] H.R. Rep. No. 413, 91st Cong., 1st Sess. (1969).

[145] Treas. Reg. § 301.7605-1(c).

[146] Since only organizations that are exempt from federal income tax ordinarily are qualified recipients of deductible charitable contributions, an IRS inquiry into the deductibility of contributions to a particular church is the equivalent of an inquiry into the church's tax-exempt status.

[147] The ninety-day limitation can be suspended for the same reasons listed in the preceding footnote.

[148] The two-year limitation can be suspended (a) if the church brings a judicial proceeding against the IRS, (b) if the IRS brings a judicial proceeding to compel compliance by the church with any reasonable request for examination of church records or religious activities, (c) for any period in excess of twenty days (but not more than six months) in which the church fails to comply with any reasonable request by the IRS for church records, or (d) if the IRS and church mutually agree.

6. Written opinion of IRS legal counsel. The IRS can make a determination based on a church tax inquiry or church tax examination that an organization is not a church that is exempt from federal income taxation or that is qualified to receive tax-deductible contributions, or that otherwise owes any income, employment, or excise tax (including the unrelated business income tax), only if the appropriate regional legal counsel of the IRS determines in writing that there has been substantial compliance with the limitations imposed under section 7611 and approves in writing of such revocation of exemption or assessment of tax.

7. Statute of limitations. Church tax examinations involving tax-exempt status or the liability for any tax other than the unrelated business income tax may be begun only for any one or more of the *three most recent taxable years* ending before the examination notice date. For examinations involving unrelated business taxable income, or if a church is proven not to be exempt for any of the preceding three years, the IRS may examine relevant records and assess tax as part of the same audit for a total of *six years* preceding the examination notice date. For examinations involving issues other than revocation of exempt status or unrelated business taxable income (such as examinations pertaining to employment taxes), no limitation period applies if no return has been filed.

8. Limitation on repeat inquiries and examinations. If any church tax inquiry or church tax examination is completed and does not result in a revocation of exemption or assessment of taxes, then no other church tax inquiry or church tax examination may begin with respect to such church *during the five-year period beginning on the examination notice date* (or the inquiry notice date if no examination notice was sent) unless such inquiry or examination is (a) approved in writing by the Assistant Commissioner of Employee Plans and Exempt Organizations of the IRS, or (b) does not involve the same or similar issues involved in the prior inquiry or examination. The five-year period is suspended if the two-year limitation on the completion of an examination is suspended.

9. Exceptions. The limitations upon church tax inquiries and church tax examinations do not apply to

a. inquiries or examinations pertaining to organizations other than churches[149]

b. any case involving a knowing failure to file a tax return or a willful attempt to defeat or evade taxes[150]

c. criminal investigations

d. the tax liability of a contributor to a church, or inquiries regarding assignment of income to a church or a vow of poverty by an individual followed by a transfer of property[151]

---

[149] The term *church* is defined by section 7611 as any organization claiming to be a church, and any convention or association of churches. The term does not include separately incorporated church-affiliated schools or other separately incorporated church-affiliated organizations.

[150] The Conference Committee Report to the Tax Reform Act of 1984 contains the following information: "In Fiscal Year 1983, the IRS closed 6,612 examinations involving alleged church tax avoidance schemes, assessing $23,803,200 in taxes and penalties (an average assessment of $3,600 per return) and leaving a calendar year-end inventory of 15,296 church tax avoidance cases (in addition to approximately 200 criminal investigations). In the first six months of Fiscal 1984 alone . . . the IRS assessed $25,620,178 in taxes and penalties in 5,498 cases relating to church tax avoidance schemes. The conferees specifically intend that nothing in the church audit procedures will inhibit IRS inquiries, examinations, or criminal investigations of tax protestor or other tax avoidance schemes posing as religious organizations, including (but not limited to) tax avoidance schemes posing as mail-order ministries or storefront churches . . . ."

[151] *See, e.g.,* St. German of Alaska Eastern Orthodox Catholic Church v. Commissioner, 840 F.2d 1087 (2nd Cir. 1988); United States v. Coates, 692 F.2d 629 (9th Cir. 1982); United States v. Life Science Church of America, 636 F.2d 221 (8th Cir. 1980); United States v. Holmes, 614 F.2d 895 (5th Cir. 1980); United States v. Freedom Church, 613 F.2d 316 (1st Cir. 1979).

e. routine IRS inquiries, including

(1) the filing or failure to file any tax return or information return by the church;

(2) compliance with income tax or FICA tax withholding;

(3) supplemental information needed to complete the mechanical processing of any incomplete or incorrect return filed by a church;

(4) information necessary to process applications for exempt status, letter ruling requests, or employment tax exempt requests; or

(5) confirmation that a specific business is or is not owned by a church.

10. Remedy for IRS violations. If the IRS has not complied substantially with (a) the notice requirements, (b) the requirement that an appropriate high-level Treasure official approve the commencement of a church tax inquiry, or (c) the requirement of informing the church of its right to an informal conference, the church's exclusive remedy is a stay of the inquiry or examination until such requirements are satisfied.

The fact that the IRS has authority to examine *church records* and the *religious activities* of a church or religious denomination does not necessarily establish its right to do so. The courts have held that an IRS summons or subpoena directed at church records must satisfy the following conditions to be enforceable:

1. It is issued in good faith. Good faith in this context means that (a) the investigation will be conducted pursuant to a legitimate purpose, (b) the inquiry is necessary to that purpose, (c) the information sought is not already within the IRS' possession, and (d) the proper administrative steps have been followed.[152]

2. It does not violate the church's first amendment right to freely exercise its religion. An IRS subpoena will not violate a church's first amendment rights unless it substantially burdens a legitimate and sincerely held religious belief, and is not supported by a compelling governmental interest that cannot be accomplished by less restrictive means. This is a very difficult test to satisfy, not only since few churches can successfully demonstrate that enforcement of an IRS summons or subpoena substantially burdens an actual religious tenet, but also because the courts have ruled that maintenance of the integrity of the government's fiscal policies constitutes a compelling governmental interest that overrides religious beliefs to the contrary.[153]

3. It does not create an impermissible entanglement of church and state.[154]

---

[152] In United States v. Powell, 379 U.S. 48 (1964), the United States Supreme Court held that in order to obtain judicial enforcement of a summons or subpoena the IRS must prove "that the investigation will be conducted pursuant to a legitimate purpose, that the inquiry may be relevant to the purpose, that the information sought is not already in the Commissioner's possession, and that the administrative steps required by the Code have been followed . . . ." *Powell* did not involve an IRS examination of church records. In United States v. Holmes, 614 F.2d 985 (5th Cir. 1980), a federal appeals court held that section 7605(c) narrowed the scope of the second part of the *Powell* test from mere relevancy to necessity in the context of church records since it required that an examination of church records be limited "to the extent necessary." The "necessity test" should apply to church inquiries or examinations conducted under section 7611 since the same language is employed. United States v. Church of Scientology, 90-2 U.S.T.C. ¶ 50,349 (D. Mass. 1990).

[153] *See, e.g.,* St. German of Alaska Eastern Orthodox Catholic Church v. Commissioner, 840 F.2d 1087 (2nd Cir. 1988); United States v. Coates, 692 F.2d 629 (9th Cir. 1982); United States v. Life Science Church of America, 636 F.2d 221 (8th Cir. 1980); United States v. Holmes, 614 F.2d 895 (5th Cir. 1980); United States v. Freedom Church, 613 F.2d 316 (1st Cir. 1979).

Further, federal law provides that if the IRS wants to *retroactively* revoke the tax-exempt status of a church, then it must show either that the church "omitted or misstated a material fact" in its original exemption application, or that the church has been "operated in a manner materially different from that originally represented."[155]

Although IRS authority to examine and subpoena church records is very broad, it has limits. To illustrate, one subpoena was issued against all documents relating to the organizational structure of a church since its inception; all correspondence files for a three-year period; the minutes of the officers, directors, trustees, and ministers for the same three-year period; and a sample of every piece of literature pertaining to the church.[156] A court concluded that this subpoena was "too far reaching" and declared it invalid. It noted, however, that a "properly narrowed" subpoena would not violate the first amendment. Another federal court that refused to enforce an IRS subpoena directed at a church emphasized that "the unique status afforded churches by Congress requires that the IRS strictly adhere to its own procedures when delving into church activities."[157] The court also stressed that the safeguards afforded churches under federal law prevent the IRS from "going on a fishing expedition into church books and records."

The limitations of section 7611 are illustrated by the following examples:

Example. First Church receives substantial rental income each year from several residential properties it owns in the vicinity of the church. The IRS has learned of the rental properties and would like to determine whether the church is engaged in an unrelated trade or business. It sends the church an inquiry notice in which the only explanation of the concerns giving rise to the inquiry is a statement that "you may be engaged in an unrelated trade or business." This inquiry notice is defective since it does not specify the activities which may result in unrelated business taxable income.

Example. The IRS receives a telephone tip that First Church may be engaged in an unrelated trade or business. A telephone tip cannot serve as the basis for a church tax inquiry since such an inquiry may commence only if an appropriate high-level Treasury official reasonably believes on the basis of written evidence that a church is not tax-exempt, is carrying on an unrelated trade or business, or otherwise is engaged in activities subject to taxation.

Example. The IRS sends First Church written notice of a church tax inquiry on March 1. On March 10 of the same year it sends written notice that it will examine designated church records on April 15. The examination notice is defective. While it was sent at least 15 days before the beginning of the examination, it was sent less than 15 days after the date the inquiry notice was sent. The church's only remedy is a stay of the examination until the IRS sends a valid examination notice.

---

[154] *See generally* United States v. Coates, 692 F.2d 629 (9th Cir. 1982); United States v. Grayson County State Bank, 656 F.2d 1070 (5th Cir. 1981); United States v. Freedom Church, 613 F.2d 316 (1st Cir. 1979); *but cf.* Surinach v. Pesquera de Busquets, 604 F.2d 73 (1st Cir. 1979) (subpoena issued against Catholic schools in Puerto Rico violated the first amendment, since no compelling governmental interest justified the investigation); EEOC v. Southwestern Baptist Theological Seminary, 651 F.2d 277 (5th Cir. 1981) (application of 1964 Civil Rights Act's reporting requirements to seminary did not violate first amendment).

[155] Treas. Reg. § 601.201(n)(6)(i). *See* United States v. Church of Scientology of Boston, 90-2 U.S.T.C. ¶ 50,349 (D. Mass. 1990).

[156] United States v. Holmes, 614 F.2d 985 (5th Cir. 1980). *See also* United States v. Trader's State Bank, 695 F.2d 1132 (9th Cir. 1983) (IRS summons seeking production of all of a church's bank statements, correspondence, and records relating to bank accounts, safe deposit boxes, and loans held to be overly broad).

[157] United States v. Church of Scientology of Boston, 90-2 U.S.T.C. ¶ 50,349 (D. Mass. 1990).

Example. An IRS inquiry notice does not mention the possible application of the first amendment principle of separation of church and state to church audits. Such a notice is defective. A church's only remedy is a stay of the inquiry until the IRS sends a valid inquiry notice.

Example. An IRS examination notice specifies that the "religious activities" of First Church will be examined as part of an investigation into a possible unrelated business income tax liability. Such an examination is inappropriate since the religious activities of a church may be examined by the IRS under section 7611 only to the extent necessary to determine if a church is in fact a bona fide church entitled to tax-exempt status.

Example. The IRS sends First Church written notice of a church tax inquiry on August 1. As of October 20 of the same year, no examination notice had been sent. The church tax inquiry must be concluded by November 1.

Example. The IRS sends an examination notice to First Church on September 1. On November 1 of the same year, as part of its examination, the IRS requests several documents that it reasonably believes are necessary. The church refuses to disclose the documents, and the IRS seeks a court order compelling disclosure. Such an order is issued on October 1. The two-year limitation on completing church examinations is suspended during the legal proceeding instituted by the IRS, and therefore the examination need not be terminated.

Example. In 1999, the IRS conducts an examination of the tax-exempt status of First Church. It concludes that the church was properly exempt from federal income taxation. In 2002, the IRS commences an examination of First Church to determine if it is engaged in an unrelated trade or business, and if it has been withholding taxes from nonminister employees. Such an examination is not barred by the prohibition against repeated examinations within a five-year period, since it does not involve the same or similar issues.

Example. First Church knowingly fails to withhold federal income taxes from wages paid to its nonminister employees despite its knowledge that it is legally required to do so. The limitations imposed upon the IRS by section 7611 do not apply.

Example. The IRS commences an examination of a separately incorporated private school that is controlled by First Church. The limitations of section 7611 do not apply.

§ 6-04   Reporting Requirements

Churches may be subject to a number of reporting requirements under state and federal law. The more common requirements are summarized in this section.

§ 6-04.1 — State Law

Key point 6-04.1. Churches may have a number of reporting requirements under state law. One of the most important is the filing of an annual corporate report with the office of secretary of state. This requirement applies to incorporated churches in many states. Failure to comply with this requirement can cause the church's corporate status to lapse.

1. ANNUAL CORPORATE REPORT

Many state nonprofit corporation laws require the filing of an annual report with the office of secretary of state. Generally, this report calls for the name of the corporation, the address of its registered office in the state of incorporation and the name of its registered agent at such address, a brief statement of the nature of the affairs that the corporation is actually conducting, and the names and addresses of the current directors and officers. A nominal fee usually must accompany the report. Annual reports are prepared on forms provided by the secretary of state's office. Failure to file the annual reports may result in a small monetary fine, or in some states to loss of corporate status. The corporate status of many churches has been terminated through inadvertent disregard of the annual reporting requirements, though such churches and their members typically are unaware of their unincorporated status. This obviously can lead to unfortunate consequences, including the potential personal legal liability of members for the obligations of the church—the very risk that most churches seek to avoid through incorporation.[158] Churches should periodically (i.e., every year or so) check with the secretary of state's office to ensure that they are "in good standing." Most states issue certificates of good standing to corporations for a nominal fee.

> *Example. The Supreme Judicial Court of Massachusetts upheld an action by the secretary of state revoking the corporate status of 11,000 nonprofit corporations that failed to file their annual corporate reports as required by state law. Massachusetts nonprofit corporation law specifies: "If the corporation fails to submit its [annual report] for two successive years, the state secretary shall give notice thereof by mail, postage prepaid, to such corporation in default. Failure of such corporation to submit the required [report] within ninety days after the notice of default has been given shall be sufficient cause for the revocation of its charter by the state secretary." Pursuant to this statute, the secretary of state revoked the corporate status of 11,000 nonprofit corporations in Massachusetts that failed to file their annual reports for two consecutive years. These revocations were all preceded by the required notice to the lapsed corporations. The president of a nonprofit corporation whose charter had been revoked filed a lawsuit challenging the actions of the secretary of state. The court ruled in favor of the secretary of state, noting that "it is undisputed that there was sufficient cause to revoke the charters of the corporations since they did not file acceptable annual reports for two consecutive years."[159]*

> *Example. A New Mexico appeals court ruled that a charitable organization's corporate status "lapsed" when it failed to submit an annual corporate report to the secretary of state, and that the organization's property automatically passed to the organization described in its dissolution clause. A charitable organization was incorporated as a nonprofit corporation in 1957. In 1969, the state corporation commission issued an order dissolving the corporation because of its failure to file annual corporate reports for three years. The dissolved corporation later attempted to "re-incorporate," using the same directors, place of business, and federal tax identification number. The directors assumed that the property of the old corporation automatically vested in the new corporation upon its creation. A state appeals court disagreed. The court concluded that "dissolution of a corporation is tantamount to corporate death and effectively terminates the existence of the corporation," and that "after dissolution, a corporation is without power to dispose of its property, except as specifically authorized by law or judicial order." The court noted that under state law (as it existed at the time of the corporation's dissolution in 1969) a nonprofit corporation's corporate existence "dissolved" or lapsed upon its failure to file an annual corporate report with the secretary of state within one year of the due date. Since the corporation's corporate*

---

[158] Shakra v. Benedictine Sisters of Bedford, 553 A.2d 1327 (N.H. 1989).
[159] Brattman v. Secretary of the Commonwealth, 658 N.E.2d 159 (Mass. 1995).

status lapsed as a matter of law in 1969, it was without power to dispose of its property following its dissolution. The court noted that "in the absence of a statute specifying the method of distribution of the assets of a dissolved corporation, the articles of incorporation of the corporation control and are its fundamental and organic law." As a result, the court concluded that the corporation's assets (at the time of its dissolution) passed to the organization described in the "dissolution clause" contained in its corporate charter. In conclusion, the court ruled that the assets of the dissolved corporation did not pass to the successor corporation, but rather went to the organization described in the dissolved corporation's "dissolution clause."[160]

2. New Hire Reporting

Churches are required to report information about "new hires" to a designated state agency pursuant to the Personal Responsibility and Work Opportunity Reconciliation Act, which was enacted by Congress in 1996. These requirements are addressed in section 8-22.

3. Other State Reports

Many states have attempted to regulate charitable solicitations by requiring charitable organizations to register with a state agency prior to soliciting donations. Many states require, in addition to the initial registration, the filing of annual reports. Churches and other religious organizations are exempted from the registration and reporting requirements of most charitable solicitation laws. This subject is covered in detail in chapter 9.

Some states impose additional reporting requirements on churches. For example, New York requires some churches to seek court approval before selling, mortgaging, or leasing property, and to notify the state attorney general prior to any such transaction.

Example. A New York court upheld the validity of a state law imposing requirements on the sale, mortgage, or lease of church property. New York law specifies that "a religious corporation shall not sell, mortgage or lease for a term exceeding five years any of its real property without applying for and obtaining leave of the court . . . ." New York law also requires several "congregational" (and some hierarchical) churches to notify the state attorney general prior to the sale, mortgage, or lease of their property. A church that violated these requirements argued that they not only violated the first amendment's ban on the establishment of religion but also violated the first amendment's guaranty of religious freedom by involving the government in the internal decisions of churches. The court acknowledged that the New York law discriminated among religions by only requiring "congregational" churches, and some hierarchical churches, to notify the attorney general while exempting most hierarchical churches. However, it concluded that this discriminatory treatment did not violate the establishment clause since it was based on a compelling government interest ("protecting members of religious corporations by safeguarding the potentially substantial proceeds from sales of property, and ensuring that the proceeds are properly disbursed"). The court noted that the hierarchical churches that are exempted from the notice requirement are required to obtain the consent of their top executive officer before seeking court approval. It concluded that the notice requirement applied to those churches, whether congregational or hierarchical, whose structure "does not assure that its members have an opportunity to review the sale of real property." The court also rejected the church's claim that the law in question violated the first

---

[160] Matter of the Will of Coe, 826 P.2d 576 (N.M. App. 1992).

amendment's guaranty of religious freedom, noting that "any inquiry by the attorney general involves only the terms of a real estate transaction; it involves no inquiry into religious beliefs nor does it involve the regulation or prohibition of conduct undertaken for religious reasons."[161]

§ 6-04.2 — Federal Law

Key point 6-04.2. *A church may have a number of reporting obligations under federal law, including annual information returns to employees and self-employed workers (W-2 and 1099 forms), the quarterly employer's tax return (Form 941), the unrelated business income tax return (Form 990-T), and the annual certification of racial nondiscrimination (Form 5578).*

Federal law imposes several reporting requirements on charitable organizations. Among them are the following:

1. APPLICATION FOR RECOGNITION OF TAX-EXEMPT STATUS

Most organizations seeking recognition of exemption from federal income tax must file an application with the IRS. This is done either on IRS Form 1023 or 1024, depending on the nature of the applicant. Churches, their integrated auxiliaries, and conventions or associations of churches are exempted by law from payment of federal income tax and therefore they are not required to file an application with the IRS.[162] Such organizations nevertheless may find it advantageous to obtain IRS recognition of exempt status since this would avoid the need of substantiating their tax-exempt status each time the IRS questions the deductibility of contributions made by a member or adherent. A church may obtain recognition of exemption in either of two ways: (1) by filing a Form 1023 with the IRS, or (2) by being a member of a convention or association of churches that has obtained a "group-exemption ruling" from the IRS.

If a church independently applies for and receives IRS recognition of exemption, it must notify the IRS of any material changes in its sources of support, purposes, character, or methods of operation. Churches that are included in the group exemption ruling of a convention or association of churches must annually notify their convention or association of any changes in their purposes, character, or methods of operation.[163]

2. ANNUAL INFORMATION RETURNS

Section 6033 of the Internal Revenue Code requires most tax-exempt organizations to file an annual information return with the IRS. The annual information return is IRS Form 990. This form sets forth an exempt organization's gross income, expenses, disbursements for exempt purposes, assets and liabilities, net worth, contributions received (including the names and addresses of substantial contributors), and compensation paid to certain employees. Section 6033 provides a "mandatory exemption" for (1) "churches, their integrated auxiliaries, and conventions and associations of churches"; (2) certain religious and charitable organizations whose annual gross receipts normally do not exceed $5,000; and (3) the "exclusively religious activities of any religious order." Form 990 itself specifies that the following organizations are exempt from

---

[161] Greek Orthodox Archdiocese v. Abrams, 618 N.Y.S.2d 504 (Sup. 1994). The court's conclusion is questionable, since it was attempting (without a shred of supporting evidence) to distinguish between churches on the basis of whether their membership has an opportunity to review property transactions.

[162] I.R.C. § 508(c)(1)(A).

[163] The procedures for obtaining an exemption from federal income taxes are discussed in R. HAMMAR, CHURCH AND CLERGY TAX GUIDE (published annually by the publisher of this text).

the annual information return requirement: (1) "a church, an interchurch organization of local units of a church, a convention or association of churches, an integrated auxiliary of a church (such as a men's or women's organization, religious school, mission society, or youth group)"; (2) "a school below college level affiliated with a church or operated by a religious order"; (3) "a mission society sponsored by or affiliated with one or more churches or church denominations, if more than one-half of the society's activities are conducted in, or directed at, persons in foreign countries"; (4) "an exclusively religious activity of any religious order"; (5) "an organization whose annual gross receipts are normally $25,000 or less."

3. TAX ON UNRELATED BUSINESS INCOME

Even though a church is recognized as tax-exempt by the IRS, it still may be liable for tax on its *unrelated business income*, that is, income from a regularly carried on trade or business that is not substantially related to the purposes constituting the basis for the church's exemption. A church that has $1,000 or more in gross income from an unrelated trade or business must file an IRS Form 990-T. In computing unrelated business taxable income, churches are entitled to deduct all reasonable and necessary expenses directly associated with the unrelated business.[164]

4. EMPLOYMENT TAXES

Every employer, including organizations exempt from federal income tax, that pays taxable wages to employees is responsible for withholding, depositing, paying, and reporting federal income tax, social security and Medicare tax, and federal unemployment tax unless specifically exempted by law. Churches are exempted from paying federal and state unemployment taxes on their employees.[165]

A church's obligation to withhold federal income tax and social security (and Medicare) tax from employees' wages, and to deposit such withheld taxes and periodically report the amounts withheld to the IRS, generally are referred to as a church's "payroll tax obligations." Compliance with the various payroll tax obligations represents perhaps the most significant reporting obligation for most churches. This is so for two very important reasons. First, the payroll reporting obligations apply to most churches. Second, there are substantial penalties for failing to comply with these requirements. For example, the church, and possibly some church board members individually, may be responsible for the payment of these taxes if they are not withheld from employee wages. Accordingly, it is essential for the church board to familiarize itself with the church's payroll tax reporting obligations, and to be certain that these obligations are being properly discharged. This is not as easy as it sounds, for several reasons. First, churches often use volunteer treasurers or bookkeepers who serve for limited terms and are unable to devote their full time and attention to such matters. This has a tendency of making church accounting practices sloppy. Second, a surprisingly large number of church leaders continue to assume that they are immune from legal obligations that apply to everyone else because they represent the church. Third, the payroll tax reporting procedures are complex. In fact, one private organization presented its annual "most incomprehensible government regulation" award to tax code provisions dealing with payroll tax reporting requirements. These rules are complex, and they are even more complex in the context of church reporting—since special rules apply.

All of a church's payroll tax reporting obligations are addressed in a companion text.[166]

---

[164] The tax on unrelated business income is addressed in R. HAMMAR, CHURCH AND CLERGY TAX GUIDE (published annually by the publisher of this text).

[165] I.R.C. § 3306(c)(6). The application of unemployment taxes to churches and other religious organizations is addressed in R. HAMMAR, CHURCH AND CLERGY TAX GUIDE (published annually by the publisher of this text).

[166] R. HAMMAR, CHURCH AND CLERGY TAX GUIDE (published annually by the publisher of this text).

5. Information Returns

Churches must issue annual "information returns" to (1) all employees who were paid wages, and (2) any self-employed person to whom the church paid annual compensation of at least $600. These information returns are referred to as the W-2 and 1099-MISC forms, respectively. In addition, churches are required to issue a 1099-INT form to each person who was paid $600 or more in interest income during any one year (a $10 rule applies to certain forms of interest payments). These rules are considered fully in a companion text.[167]

6. Annual Certification of Racial Nondiscrimination

No doubt one of the most widely disregarded federal reporting obligations applicable to churches is the annual certification of racial nondiscrimination (IRS Form 5578). Any church that operates, supervises, or controls a "private school" must submit a Form 5578 each year to the IRS certifying that it operates its school in a racially nondiscriminatory manner. The term *private school* is defined in the instructions to Form 5578 to include "an educational organization which normally maintains a regular faculty and curriculum and normally has a regularly enrolled body of pupils or students in attendance at the place where its educational activities are regularly carried on. The term includes primary, secondary, preparatory, or high schools, and colleges and universities, whether operated as a separate legal entity or as an activity of a church . . . . The term also includes preschools . . . ." This important reporting obligation is discussed fully in a companion text.[168]

7. Returns Regarding Dissolution or Termination

Section 6043 of the Internal Revenue Code requires a corporation to file a return (Form 966) within 30 days after the adoption of any resolution or plan concerning the dissolution of the corporation. Churches, their integrated auxiliaries, and conventions and associations of churches, however, are exempted by section 6043 from this reporting requirement.

8. EEOC Reports

Title VII of the Civil Rights Act of 1964 prohibits employers from discriminating in any employment decision—including hiring, discharge, compensation, and the terms, conditions, or privileges of employment—on the basis of race, color, religion, sex, or national origin.[169] Title VII applies to every employer, including churches, having 15 or more employees for at least 20 weeks in a year. Part-time employees are to be included in making the calculation. The Act does exempt religious organizations, including churches, from the prohibition against discrimination based on religion, and the United States Supreme Court upheld the constitutionality of this provision in 1987.[170]

The Equal Employment Opportunity Commission (EEOC), an agency created by Congress to enforce Title VII of the Civil Rights Act of 1964, requires all employers, including religious organizations, having 100 or more employees to submit annually an Employer Information Report. This report is prepared on Standard Form 100, which is also known as Employer Information Report EEO-1. Among other things, this report provides the EEOC with the racial composition of the employer's work force.

---

[167] *Id.*

[168] *Id.*

[169] 42 U.S.C. § 2000e-2(a). *See generally* chapter 10, *infra.*

[170] Corporation of Presiding Bishop of the Church of Jesus Christ of Latter Day Saints v. Amos, 483 U.S. 327 (1987).

§6-05   Church Names

Key point 6-05. A church name is a valuable property right that is protected by the legal principle of unfair competition. Protection also is available under federal trademark law.

Occasionally, a new church will acquire a name that is so similar to the name of another church in the same community that public confusion is likely to result. For example, a new congregation calling itself Calvary Presbyterian Church establishes a church in a community already having a Presbyterian church called "Calvary Church." A confusion of names may occur in other ways, such as a new sect or religious denomination acquiring a name similar to that of an existing one, or a local church withdrawing from a denominational organization but continuing to employ a name associating itself with the denomination. In any of these situations, does the preexisting church body have any legal basis for stopping further use of the similar name by the other church or religious organization?

The courts have long protected the names of existing commercial enterprises against unauthorized use of confusingly similar names by other commercial organizations.[171] In many instances, the courts are simply enforcing state corporation laws that, in most states, prohibit new corporations from using names that are identical or confusingly similar to those of existing organizations.[172] Other courts have emphasized that such name protection statutes are merely embodiments of the underlying common law of unfair competition, which protects existing corporate names independently of any provisions in state corporate laws.[173]

The courts have consistently protected the names of nonprofit corporations as well on the basis of one or more of the following theories: (1) the applicable nonprofit corporation statute contains a provision protecting the preexisting names of nonprofit corporations in much the same way as business corporation statutes protect the names of business corporations;[174] (2) extension of the name protection provided by business corporation statutes to nonprofit corporations when the state nonprofit law does not specifically provide such protection;[175] (3) the common law of unfair competition;[176] and (4) trademark protection.

In states having a name protection statute protecting the names of religious corporations, a church's name generally will be protected against later use of the same or a confusingly similar name in either of two

---

[171] *See, e.g.,* Couhigs' Pestaway Co., Inc. v. Pestaway, Inc., 278 So. 2d 519 (La. 1973); Virginia Manor Land Co. v. Virginia Manor Apartments, Inc., 282 A.2d 684 (Pa. 1971); Annot., 115 A.L.R. 1241 (1938).

[172] *See, e.g.,* ILL. REV. STAT. ch. 32, § 157.9 ("The corporate name . . . [s]hall not be the same as, or deceptively similar to, the corporate name or assumed name of any domestic corporation existing under any Act of this State or of any foreign corporation authorized to transact business in this State . . . ."); KAN. STAT. ANN. § 17-6002 ("The articles of incorporation shall set forth . . . [t]he name of the corporation which . . . shall be such as to distinguish it upon the records in the office of the secretary of state from the names of other corporations and partnerships organized, reserved or registered under the laws of this state . . . ."); KY. REV. STAT. § 271A.040 ("The corporate name . . . [s]hall not be the same as, or deceptively similar to, the name of any domestic corporation existing under the laws of this state or any foreign corporation authorized to transact business in this state . . . ."); MO. REV. STAT. § 351.110 ("The corporate name . . . [s]hall not be the same as, or deceptively similar to, the name of any domestic corporation existing under any law of this state or any foreign corporation authorized to transact business in this state . . . .").

[173] Massachusetts Mutual Life Ins. Co. v. Massachusetts Life Ins. Co., 218 N.E.2d 564, 570 (Mass. 1966) ("It is our view, however, that the corporate name protection statute is a statutory declaration and clarification of a portion of the extant common law of unfair competition . . . ."); Virginia Manor Land Co., v. Virginia Manor Apartments, Inc., 282 A.2d 684, 687 (Pa. 1971) ("[t]he right of the corporation to the exclusive use of its own name exists at common law, and includes the right to prohibit another from using a name so similar to the corporate name as to be calculated to deceive the public").

[174] *See, e.g.,* ILL. REV. STAT. ch. 32, § 163a(6); MODEL NONPROFIT CORPORATION ACT § 7(b).

[175] First Congressional District Democratic Party Organization v. First Congressional District Democratic Organization, Inc., 177 N.W.2d 224 (Mich. 1970).

[176] Oklahoma District Council of the Assemblies of God v. New Hope Assembly of God, 597 P.2d 1211 (Okla. 1979).

ways: (1) the state official charged with the duty of reviewing applications for incorporation can reject the application of an organization whose name is either identical or deceptively similar to the name of an existing corporation; or (2) if the state official chooses to recognize the corporate status of an organization whose name is either identical or deceptively similar to that of an existing corporation, the offended corporation may sue to stop further use of the name.

As noted above, a church may also seek legal protection of its name through the law of unfair competition. *Unfair competition* is a civil wrong created to protect existing organizations from the deceptive or unfair practices of competitors. It is entirely separate and distinct from trademark law. Among other things, unfair competition means the use of a name that is either identical with or confusingly similar to that of a preexisting organization. As one court has observed:

> In the law of unfair competition, a corporate or trade name used in connection with the business to which it relates may become an asset of great value. When it does, it partakes of the nature of a property right, and equity will enjoin the appropriation and use of such name if confusion of identity is likely to result.[177]

Courts have consistently protected charitable as well as business organizations from unfair competition. In a leading case one court observed:

> We hold that the common law principles of unfair competition protecting business corporations against another's use of the same or similar name are applicable to charitable or religious associations and corporations. . . . The right to this protection rests generally upon the fact that the use of identical or similar terms or names is likely to result in confusion or deception.[178]

To successfully establish that the name chosen by another organization constitutes unfair competition, a church must demonstrate

1. Prior use of the name.

2. Subsequent use of the same or a confusingly similar name by another religious organization.

3. The church with prior use of the name will be injuriously affected by continued use of the same or a confusingly similar name by the other religious organization. It has been held that anything that diverts members or donations from one church to another causes injury. Thus, injury generally will be established by the unauthorized use of a name identical or confusingly similar to that of a preexisting corporation.

4. The church with prior use of the name did not delay for an unreasonable time in seeking to enjoin further use of the same or a confusingly similar name by the other religious organization.[179]

Generic or highly generalized names are not protected from misappropriation under the doctrine of unfair competition unless a secondary meaning has been established. A generic name acquires a secondary meaning through such continued use that it is commonly associated with a particular church or religious

---

[177] *Id.* at 1214.
[178] *Id.* at 1215. *See also* National Board of YWCA v. YWCA of Charleston, 335 F. Supp. 615 (D.S.C. 1971).
[179] *See generally* Annot., 37 A.L.R.3d 277 (1971).

organization in the public mind. Proof of a secondary meaning is a question of fact to be established on a case-by-case basis.

To illustrate, the General Conference of the Seventh-Day Adventists sued the "Seventh-Day Adventist Congregational Church" (located in Kealakekua, Hawaii) and its pastor for trademark infringement and unfair competition. A trial court ruled in favor of the denomination, and ordered the local church to discontinue using a name including the term *Seventh-Day Adventist* or *SDA*, or representing to others that it was connected in any way with the Seventh-Day Adventist denomination. The local church refused to comply with this order on the ground that the denomination's trademark was invalid since it was "generic." The court found the church to be in contempt of court for ignoring its order, and set a fine of $500 per day until the church and its pastor agreed to comply. The church and pastor appealed this decision, and a federal appeals court agreed that the trial court's ruling in favor of the denomination was improper.[180] The court reasoned that the church and its pastor had raised a significant issue (the validity of the denomination's trademark) that should have been heard by a jury. The appeals court noted that "a trademark's function is to identify and distinguish the goods and services of one seller from another." A trademark, however, is always "subject to the defense that it is generic." A "generic" trademark is "one that tells the buyer what the product is, rather than from where, or whom, it came." Generic marks are not eligible for trademark protection since they do "not indicate the product of service's origin, but is the term for the product or service itself." The church and pastor claimed that the name "Seventh-Day Adventist" is generic since it refers to a religion rather than to a particular church organization. They asserted, "The phrase Seventh-Day Adventist is not theirs alone, as they would like to claim, for it describes a system or set of Bible based Christian beliefs, doctrines, and standards. One therefore is not necessarily Seventh-Day Adventist because of what organization he may be affiliated with, but rather he is a Seventh-Day Adventist because of what he believes."

The appeals court concluded that the denomination's claim of trademark infringement would fail if the local church and its pastor could prove that the name "Seventh-Day Adventist" is generic. On the other hand, if the denomination could establish that its name was not generic, then it would win its trademark infringement suit if it could prove a "likelihood of confusion" caused by the church's continued use of a name similar to that of the denomination. In deciding whether or not there is a likelihood of confusion, a court should consider the following factors: (1) the strength of the denomination's name; (2) the similarity of the parties' goods or services; (3) similarity of the two names; (4) evidence that persons actually have been confused by the similarity of names; (5) marketing methods used; (6) the likely degree of care the public would take in differentiating between the names; (7) the intent of the local church in using the similar name; and (8) likelihood of "expansion of product lines" (i.e., will the local church benefit at the expense of the denomination). The local church claimed that it had "never in any way sought to deceive or confuse anyone in regard to our name," and that its use of the word "Congregational" in its name effectively distinguished it from the Seventh-Day Adventists. The case was sent back to the trial court to determine whether or not the denomination's name is generic, and if not, whether the local church's use of its present name created a "likelihood of confusion."

A local church congregation that votes to disaffiliate from a parent denomination may lose the right to use the denominational name. One court has observed:

> The local name of a church is of great value, not only because business is carried on and property held in that name, but also because millions of members associate with the name the most sacred

---

[180] General Conference Corporation of Seventh-Day Adventists v. Seventh-Day Adventist Congregational Church, 887 F.2d 228 (9th Cir. 1989).

of their personal relationships and the holiest of their family traditions. And, since the right to use the name inheres in the institution, not in its members . . . when they cease to be members of the institution, use by them of the name is misleading and, if injurious to the institution, should be enjoined.[181]

In some cases the name of a church or religious organization can be protected under federal trademark law. *Trademark* is defined by the federal Trademark Act as "any word, symbol, or device, or any combination thereof adopted and used by a manufacturer or merchant to identify his goods and distinguish them from those manufactured and sold by others."[182] Trademark protection is thus available to any church or religious organization that uses a particular name to identify goods or services it offers to the public. For example, if a religious denomination publishes religious literature for its churches, and affixes its name to such literature, the name identifies the goods and therefore is eligible for trademark registration. Similarly, if a church establishes a counseling center, correspondence school, private elementary or secondary school, nursing home, radio or television station, or magazine that is identified by the church's name, the name may be entitled to trademark protection.

Of course, trademark protection is not available for a name or mark that so resembles a mark already registered with the Patent and Trademark Office, or previously used by another organization and not abandoned, as to be likely to cause confusion or to deceive. There are two ways of determining whether a proposed name conflicts with a preexisting name that is entitled to protection. First, a commercial search service can be retained which, for a fee, will render an opinion on the availability of a specified name. Second, an application for registration can be filed with the Patent and Trademark Office in Washington, D.C. Although the Patent and Trademark Office takes several months to evaluate an application, it eventually will notify the applicant whether its proposed name or mark conflicts with a preexisting mark.

"Descriptive" and highly generalized names and marks are not eligible for registration unless a secondary meaning can be established. A secondary meaning is established by proof of public association of a generic name or mark with a particular church or religious organization. So-called "generic" marks may not be capable of trademark protection even if a secondary meaning is present. The distinction between descriptive and generic marks is a close one that has caused the courts considerable difficulty.

An application for trademark registration is a relatively simple procedure consisting of the following elements:

1. Preparation of a written application stating the applicant's name, address, state of incorporation or organization; the goods or services in connection with which the name or mark is used; the class of goods or services according to the official international classification system; the date of the first use of the name or mark on or in connection with the goods or services; the date of the first use of the name or mark as a trademark "in commerce"; the mode or manner in which the mark is used on or in connection with the goods.

2. A drawing of the mark, unless the mark consists solely of a name—in which case the name may be typed in capital letters on a piece of paper.

3. Five specimens of the goods bearing the name or mark. No specimens are required for names or marks associated with services.

---

[181] Carnes v. Smith, 222 S.E.2d 322, 329 (Ga. 1976) (citations omitted).
[182] 15 U.S.C. § 1127.

4. The required filing fee.

If a church name is not used in connection with any specific goods or services, trademark protection is unavailable.

§ 6-06   Officers, Directors, and Trustees — In General

Churches and religious organizations can conduct their temporal and spiritual affairs only through individuals. State laws generally require that church corporations appoint an initial board of directors which in turn elects the corporation's first president, secretary, and treasurer. The initial board of directors adopts a set of bylaws that specifies the term of office of both officers and directors and sets forth the procedure for electing successors. Directors of church corporations occasionally are called trustees. This terminology is perfectly appropriate if it is intended to suggest that the business and spiritual oversight of the church is delegated "in trust" to such individuals, or if it is required by law.[183] However, it often happens that such terminology is simply a holdover from a church's pre-incorporation status when title to church property was held in the name of church trustees (since unincorporated churches historically were incapable of holding title in their own name). If this is the case, the continued use of the title *trustee* can be misleading. Incorporated churches that retain the use of the term *trustee* should be careful to refrain from listing the names of the trustees as either the transferor or transferee on a deed.

Unincorporated churches generally elect officers, consisting of a president, secretary, and treasurer. This is especially true of unincorporated churches that are permitted by law to hold title to property in their own name. Those churches that are still required by law to hold title in the names of trustees should add the words "or their successors" following the names of the church trustees in deeds, mortgages, and other legal documents. This will avoid problems in the event that the named trustees are deceased or otherwise unavailable at some future date when the church wants to sell its property.

Directors of church corporations occasionally are called *deacons*, although it is common for churches to have both directors and deacons—directors having oversight of the temporal affairs of the church and deacons having oversight of the spiritual.[184]

The Model Nonprofit Corporation Act specifies that a corporation shall have a president, one or more vice-presidents, a secretary, a treasurer, and such other officers or assistant officers as the corporation deems necessary. The Act permits the same person to hold two or more offices except the offices of president and secretary. The term *officer* occasionally is interpreted broadly to include directors. Normally, however, a church president, secretary, treasurer, and vice-president (if any) are the only officers of the church.

There are no legal requirements regarding the number of trustees an unincorporated association must appoint or elect. Some states require that church corporations have a minimum number of directors.[185]

§ 6-06.1 — Election or Appointment

Key point 6-06.1. *Churches select their officers and directors in various ways. For example, it is common for members of a church board to be elected by the church's membership, while officers are elected*

---

[183] Osnes v. Morris, 298 S.E.2d 803 (W. Va. 1982).
[184] Hayes v. Board of Trustees, 225 N.Y.S.2d 316 (1962).
[185] MODEL NONPROFIT CORPORATION ACT § 18.

by the board. The civil courts generally refrain from resolving disputes involving the selection of church officers and directors on the ground that the first amendment guaranty of religious freedom prevents them from becoming involved in ecclesiastical disputes.

It is customary for directors and trustees to be elected by the church membership and for officers to be elected by the board of directors or trustees. However, this is not always the case. For example, it is common for directors to nominate officers who are then elected by the voting membership.

Unless stated otherwise in either the bylaws or state law, officers, directors, and trustees are elected by a majority vote of the congregation's membership. To illustrate, one court ruled that the congregation, and not the board of deacons, had the exclusive authority to elect a treasurer when the church constitution or bylaws did not grant this authority to the board of deacons.[186]

Many churches have adopted a "staggered system" of electing directors whereby a minority (often a third) of the directors are elected at each annual meeting. This normally is accomplished by classifying directors in the bylaws according to tenure: the first class holding office for one year, the second class for two years, and the third class for three years. Thereafter successors for each class of directors are elected for three-year terms. This system helps to ensure that a majority of the board at all times will be experienced. Unless forbidden by charter, bylaw, or statute, directors or officers may succeed themselves in office.

Vacancies occurring in any office or on the board of directors or board of trustees are filled according to applicable provisions in state law or in the church's charter or bylaws. Church bylaws often permit vacancies in the board of directors to be filled by the board itself except for vacancies created by an increase in the number of directors. Vacancies typically are filled only for the unexpired term of the predecessor in office.

If the filling of vacancies is not provided for by state law or a church's charter or bylaws, there is no alternative but to await the next annual meeting of the congregation or to call a special meeting of the congregation expressly for the purpose of filling the vacancy for the unexpired term.

A minister it not entitled to serve as president of a church or even as a director or trustee unless specifically authorized in the church's charter or bylaws.[187]

Incorporated and unincorporated churches must follow the procedures in their charter or bylaws and in applicable state laws regarding the election or appointment of church officers, directors, and trustees. The courts have differed, however, as to the legal remedies available in the event that such internal procedures are not followed. Some courts have been willing to intervene in internal church controversies regarding the selection of officers and directors. To illustrate, members of a church were allowed to challenge in court the legality of a congregational election of directors that allegedly did not conform to the procedural requirements in the church bylaws.[188] And, when a board of directors sought to perpetuate itself in office by refusing to call an election, church members were allowed to obtain legal redress because the state law under which the church was incorporated required annual elections of directors.[189]

---

[186] Gervin v. Reddick, 268 S.E.2d 657 (Ga. 1980).

[187] Allen v. North Des Moines Methodist Episcopal Church, 102 N.W. 808 (Iowa 1905).

[188] Wilkerson v. Battiste, 393 So.2d 195 (La. 1980); Trinity Pentecostal Church v. Terry, 660 S.W.2d 449 (Mo. App. 1983). *See also* In re Uranian 1st Gnostic Lyceum Temple, 547 N.Y.S.2d 63 (N.Y. App. 1989).

[189] Burnett v. Banks, 279 P.2d 579 (Cal. 1955); Smith v. Riley, 424 So.2d 1166 (La. App. 1982).

Example. The Virginia Supreme Court intervened in an internal church dispute concerning the term of office of church trustees. For nearly 70 years, the trustees of an Episcopal church's endowment fund served life terms. A dispute then arose, and the church's vestry sought a court ruling on the trustees' term of office. The court concluded that the trustees' term of office was one year on the basis of a provision in the Virginia nonprofit corporation law specifying that "in the absence of a provision in the articles of incorporation fixing a term of office, the term of office for a director shall be one year." Since the court found no provision in the articles of incorporation "fixing a term of office," it concluded that state law mandated a one-year term. In support of its conclusion, the court observed that "had the organizers intended to take the unusual step of providing life terms for trustees, they surely would have done so in unmistakable fashion." It further noted that the articles of incorporation required "not less than three" trustees to be "vestrymen of the church." And, since the terms of the church's vestrymen were limited to three years, there were at least three trustees (at any given time) who could not serve life terms. The court found this to be "unmistakable evidence of the organizers' intention not to fix the trustees' terms of office at life." Since no provision in the articles of incorporation specified a life term (or any other term), the nonprofit corporation law fixed the trustees' term at one year.[190]

Example. An Illinois court intervened in a dispute involving the dismissal of local church trustees by the regional diocese of the American-Bulgarian Eastern Orthodox Church. The diocese selected other church members to govern the church, and ordered the discharged trustees to deliver the church's assets and records over to the newly appointed trustees. When the discharged trustees refused to comply with these mandates, the newly appointed trustees filed suit. A state appeals court ruled in favor of the former trustees. The court began its opinion by observing that "the state has a cognizable interest in the peaceful resolution of internal church disputes which are concerned with control or ownership of church property, and the civil courts have general authority to resolve such controversies." However, "when doctrinal or polity issues arise in the determination of a property dispute, the courts must defer to the resolution reached by the church's highest ecclesiastical authority." If doctrinal issues are not involved, "the first amendment does not require that the state adopt a rule of compulsory deference to religious authorities in resolving property disputes. Instead, the state courts may choose from a variety of approaches." One of these, the neutral principles approach, allows a court to determine who owns or controls church property by applying objective legal principles to church documents and records. The Illinois court applied the "neutral principles" approach and concluded that it was not compelled to rule in favor of the diocese. Only when a church property dispute (or any other internal church dispute) involves doctrine or polity is a civil court compelled to defer to determinations of religious hierarchies. This was not such a case, concluded the court. The appeals court remanded the case to the trial court with instructions to resolve the dispute on the basis of "neutral principles of law."[191]

Example. A Louisiana court ruled that provisions in a church charter listing the requirements of church membership did not apply to members of the church board. A pastor attempted to disqualify three deacons from voting on an important issue because they no longer qualified as church members under a provision in the church charter requiring members to tithe. A state appeals court rejected the pastor's argument that the three deacons had forfeited their right to vote by virtue of the fact that they failed to tithe. The court pointed out that the tithing requirement applied only to church members—

---

[190] St. John's Protestant Episcopal Church Endowment Fund, Inc. v. Vestry of St. John's Protestant Episcopal Church, 377 S.E.2d 375 (Va. 1989). This case illustrates the important principle that questions of church administration may be resolved by state nonprofit corporation law if the church is incorporated under the general nonprofit corporation law and the church's articles of incorporation do not address a particular matter.

[191] Aglikin v. Kovacheff, 516 N.E.2d 704 (Ill. App. 1987).

and not to members of the board of deacons. It observed that the church charter "sets forth requirements for corporate membership exclusively; thus, individual directors need not comply with [the charter's] assessment requirements to maintain their status as voting members of the deacon board." Instead, the court concluded that the church's board members were governed by another provision in the church's charter stipulating that "the persons elected deacons of the church shall automatically become members of the board of directors."[192]

Example. *A Missouri court ruled that it could determine whether two board members of a religious organization were qualified to serve, since it could do so without considering religious doctrine. A synagogue created a subsidiary corporation and transferred all of its property to the subsidiary in an attempt to protect its assets from liability. The subsidiary was incorporated as a nonprofit corporation under state law. Its bylaws specified that board members had to be members of the synagogue. A dispute arose among members of the subsidiary's board, and two board members filed a lawsuit against other board members, and attempted to oust other board members and install new ones. In response to these actions, the board voted to expel the two dissident members. The two dissidents refused to honor this vote, but they did nothing to challenge it. The board then asked a court to determine that the dissidents were not qualified to serve as directors since they were no longer members of the congregation as required by the bylaws, and to remove them from office. A state appeals court acknowledged that it had no authority to resolve ecclesiastical matters, and that "the removal or expulsion from a congregation is a matter for an ecclesiastical tribunal to decide and its decision thereon is binding and not reviewable by the civil courts." However, in this case the two dissidents had already been removed, and their removal was not the issue. Rather, the court was asked to determine whether or not the dismissed board members were eligible to continue serving on the board. The court concluded that "to resolve the matter does not require the court to become entangled in religious doctrine or unconstitutionally interfere with a religious body's affairs."[193]*

Some courts have refused to intervene in such disputes even if the selection of church officers or directors allegedly violated a church's charter or bylaws. These courts have relied primarily on the following language from a 1976 decision by the United States Supreme Court:

The conclusion of the Illinois Supreme Court that the decisions of the [Diocese] were "arbitrary" was grounded upon an inquiry that persuaded the Illinois Supreme Court that the [Diocese] had not followed its own laws and procedures in arriving at those decisions. We have concluded that *whether or not there is room for "marginal civil court review" under the narrow rubrics of "fraud" or "collusion" when church tribunals act in bad faith for secular purposes, no "arbitrariness" exception— in the sense of an inquiry whether the decisions of the highest ecclesiastical tribunal of a hierarchical church complied with church laws and regulations—is consistent with the constitutional mandate that civil courts are bound to accept the decisions of the highest judicatories of a religious organization of hierarchical polity on matters of discipline, faith, internal organization, or ecclesiastical rule, custom or law.* For civil courts to analyze whether the ecclesiastical actions of a church judicatory are in that sense "arbitrary" must inherently entail inquiry into the procedures that canon or ecclesiastical law supposedly require the church adjudicatory to follow, or else into the substantive criteria by which they are supposedly to decide the ecclesiastical question. But this is exactly the inquiry that the first amendment prohibits . . . .[194]

---

[192] Chimney Ville Missionary Baptist Church v. Johnson, 665 So.2d 730 (La. App. 1995).
[193] Beth Hamedrosh Hagodol Cemetery v. Levy, 923 S.W.2d 439 (Mo. App. 1996).
[194] Serbian Eastern Orthodox Diocese v. Milivojevich, 426 U.S. 696, 712-13 (1976) (emphasis added).

Example. A New York court ruled that it had no authority to interfere with a Baptist church's appointment of "lifetime" deacons, though it could prohibit the appointment of lifetime trustees by the same church. An incorporated Baptist church adopted bylaws that made certain individuals "lifetime deacons." These deacons were invested with virtually absolute authority over the church's affairs. The bylaws also called for the election of trustees, and while trustees were given authority over the "legal and financial matters" of the church, they were subject to the control of the deacons. A dispute arose within the church over the seemingly unlimited authority of the deacons. A group of dissident members filed a lawsuit asking a court to rule that lifetime appointments of deacons are not permissible under state law. The court refused. It began its opinion by observing that the civil courts have no authority to resolve issues relating to a church's "spiritual" affairs, but that they can "with great reluctance" resolve church disputes relating to "temporal" affairs such as property. The court concluded that the selection and tenure of deacons is a spiritual rather than a temporal matter, and accordingly the courts were without authority to resolve disputes involving such issues. It observed, "The office of deacon has primarily a ministerial function and, in large measure, deals with the spiritual well being of the church and its members. In this function, the court will not interfere with the constitution and bylaws of this church. While this may be outside the mainstream of current Baptist practice, it is not impermissible. The life tenure of certain named deacons is clear in the bylaws and as to them cannot be disputed." On the other hand, the court concluded that trustees occupy a "temporal" rather than a spiritual position, and accordingly it would be appropriate for the civil courts to resolve internal church disputes pertaining to the selection or tenure of trustees.[195]

Example. Maryland's highest court ruled that an arbitration award addressing the composition of a church's board of trustees was not reviewable by the civil courts since any review would require an interpretation of religious doctrine. The court concluded that "in many instances, issues of church polity will be inextricably intertwined with secular issues in contested church elections," and that the civil courts may not "wander into the theological thicket in order to render a decision."[196]

This rule of judicial non-intervention in disputes concerning internal church government has been applied by some courts, since 1976, to disputes involving the selection of church officers and directors. To illustrate, a Pennsylvania court declined to rule on which of two warring factions of church trustees rightfully held office.[197] A minister in a local church had ousted several trustees from office, replacing them with new trustees more loyal to himself. The ousted trustees alleged that the minister lacked the authority to replace them, and that they accordingly were still the lawful church board. The court, noting that civil courts must "defer" to churches and their own ecclesiastical organizations regarding any question of "discipline, faith, ecclesiastical rule, custom, or law," held that the question of a minister's authority to replace church trustees involves ecclesiastical law and therefore must be resolved by the church itself. It ordered the trial court to identify the highest body within the church empowered to decide the issue. The issue of judicial intervention in internal church disputes is considered in detail in chapter 9.

§ 6-06.2 — Authority

Key point 6-06.2. Officers and directors must be legally authorized to act on behalf of their church. Legal authority can be express, implied, inherent, or apparent. In addition, a church can ratify the unauthorized actions of its officers or directors, but this is not required.

---

[195] Ward v. Jones, 587 N.Y.S.2d 94 (Sup. 1992).
[196] American Union of Baptists v. Trustees of the Particular Primitive Baptist Church, 644 A.2d 1063 (Md. 1994).
[197] Atterberry v. Smith, 522 A.2d 683 (Pa. App. 1987).

1. OFFICERS

It is often said that church officers may perform only those acts for which they have authority, and that the authority of church officers is similar to that exercised by officers of private corporations.[198] The legal authority of a corporate officer may derive from four sources: express, implied, inherent, and apparent authority. The most basic kind of authority possessed by a church officer consists of *express authority* deriving from those powers and prerogatives conferred by statute, charter, bylaw, or resolution. Statutes occasionally confer certain powers upon the officers of church corporations, but by far the greatest sources of express authority are a church's charter, bylaws, and resolutions. Article V of the Model Nonprofit Corporation Bylaws lists the powers of corporate officers as follows:

President. The President shall be the principal executive officer of the corporation and shall in general supervise and control all of the business affairs of the corporation. He shall preside at all meetings of the Board of Directors. He may sign, with the Secretary or any other proper officer of the corporation authorized by the Board of Directors, any deeds, mortgages, bonds, contracts, or other instruments which the Board has authorized to be executed, except in cases where the signing and execution thereof shall be expressly delegated by the Board of Directors or by these bylaws or by statute to some other officer or agent of the corporation; and in general shall perform all duties incident to the office of President and such other duties as may be prescribed by the Board of Directors from time to time.

Vice President. In the absence of the President or in the event of his inability or refusal to act, the Vice President (or, in the event that there be more than one Vice President, the Vice Presidents in the order of their election) shall perform the duties of the President, and when so acting, shall have all powers of and be subject to all the restrictions upon the President. Any Vice President shall perform such other duties as from time to time may be assigned to him by the President or by the Board of Directors.

Treasurer. If required by the Board of Directors, the Treasurer shall give a bond for the faithful discharge of his duties in such sum and with such surety or sureties as the Board of Directors shall determine. He shall have charge and custody of and be responsible for all funds and securities of the corporation; receive and give receipts for moneys due and payable to the corporation from any source whatsoever, and deposit all such moneys in the name of the corporation in such banks, trust companies or other depositories as shall be selected in accordance with the provisions of . . . these bylaws; and in general perform all the duties incident to the office of Treasurer and such other duties as from time to time may be assigned to him by the President or by the Board of Directors.

Secretary. The Secretary shall keep the minutes of the meetings of the Board of Directors in one or more books provided for that purpose; see that all notices are duly given in accordance with the provisions of these bylaws or as required by law; be custodian of the corporate records and of the seal of the corporation and see that the seal of the corporation is affixed to all documents, the execution of which on behalf of the corporation under its seal is duly authorized in accordance with the provisions of these bylaws . . . and in general perform all duties incident to the office of Secretary and such other duties as from time to time may be assigned to him by the President or by the Board of Directors.

---

[198] Lewis v. Wolfe, 413 S.W.2d 314 (Mo. 1967).

Officers also possess *implied authority* to perform all those acts that are necessary in performing an express power. The law essentially implies the existence of such authority, without which the express powers would be frustrated. To illustrate, the courts have held that express authority to manage a business includes the power to enter into contracts and to make purchases on behalf of the company. Authority to sell property has been held to include the power to execute a mortgage necessary for the sale of the property. And, authority to borrow money has been held to include the power to execute a guaranty.

Certain powers often are said to be *inherent* in a particular office, whether or not expressly granted in an organization's charter, bylaws, or resolutions. For example, it commonly is said that the president has inherent authority to preside at meetings of the corporation, that the vice-president has inherent authority to act as president if the president is absent or incapacitated, that the secretary has inherent authority to maintain the corporate seal and records and to serve as secretary in all corporate meetings, and that the treasurer has inherent authority to receive money for the corporation.[199]

Officers occasionally possess *apparent authority*, that is, authority that has not actually been granted by the corporation but which the corporation through its actions and representations leads others to believe has been granted.[200] The doctrine of apparent authority rests on the principle of estoppel, which forbids persons or organizations to give an officer or agent an appearance of authority that does not in fact exist and to benefit from such misleading conduct to the detriment of one who has relied on it.

Transactions entered into by church officers acting without authority are invalid. To illustrate, one court concluded that a land sales contract executed by a church secretary and treasurer was not legally enforceable.[201] The court observed that the officers of a corporation "have only those powers conferred on them by the bylaws of the corporation or by the resolution of the directors." Neither the bylaws of the church nor any resolution by the board vested the secretary and treasurer with authority to enter into contracts on behalf of the church. Another court rejected the validity of a land sales contract executed by an officer of an unincorporated religious organization.[202] The court emphasized that the officer had no actual or implied authority to sign contracts, and it concluded that "[t]rustees or similar officers of unincorporated religious organizations must have the consent of their organization in order to convey its property. . . . [We] see no evidence that [the officer] had obtained any authorization or consent for the proposed land sale from any membership group."

Corporations can "ratify" the unauthorized acts of their officers and directors by consenting to them. Ratification generally is held to consist of three elements: acceptance by the corporation of the benefits of the officer's action, full knowledge of the facts, and circumstances or affirmative conduct indicating an intention to adopt and approve the unauthorized action. Ratification may not occur before an unauthorized action, and must take place within a reasonable time after such action. Ratifications generally are considered to be irrevocable. Only that body possessing the power to perform or authorize an officer's unauthorized action has the power to ratify it. This generally is the board of directors. Ratification can be express, such as by formal, recorded action of the board of directors, or it can be implied from the acts and representations of the board. Implied ratification often occurs when a corporation knows or should have known of an unauthorized act and does nothing to repudiate it. Thus, when a church's parish committee should have known of various mort-

---

[199] FLETCHER CYC. CORP. § 441 (perm. ed. 1990); Note, *Inherent Powers of Corporate Officers: Need for a Statutory Definition*, 61 HARV. L. REV. 867 (1948).

[200] Continental-Wirt Electronics Corp. v. Sprague Electric Co., 329 F. Supp. 959 (E.D. Pa. 1971).

[201] Daniel Webster Council v. St. James Association, 533 A.2d 329 (N.H. 1987).

[202] Shakra v. Benedictine Sisters of Bedford, 553 A.2d 1327 (N.H. 1989). *Accord* Biscegelia v. Bernadine Sisters, 560 N.E.2d 567 (Mass. App. 1990).

gages executed by the church's minister on behalf of the church but did nothing to disavow them, it was held to have ratified them by implication.[203]

Section 8.45 of the Revised Model Nonprofit Corporation Act specifies:

Any contract or other instrument in writing executed or entered into between a corporation and any other person is not invalidated as to the corporation by any lack of authority of the signing officers in the absence of actual knowledge on the part of the other person that the signing officers had no authority to execute the contract or other instrument if it is signed by any two officers in category 1 [*i.e.*, the presiding officer of the board and the president] or by one officer in category 1 [see above] and one officer in category 2 [*i.e.*, a vice president, the secretary, treasurer and executive director].

Example. *The Mississippi Supreme Court ruled that a church was legally bound by the misrepresentation of its financial secretary. The church signed a contract with a local contractor for the construction of a building at a cost of $1.2 million. From the start, payments under the contract were late. The contractor eventually informed the church that construction would be stopped until payments were brought up to date and the church placed in escrow sufficient monies to pay the balance of the contract. The church brought payments up to date, and then the church's financial secretary provided the contractor with a letter stating that the church had placed monies in escrow sufficient to pay the balance of the contract. On the basis of this representation, the contractor resumed construction and continued to work until it was informed that no further funds were available. The contractor sued the church for the balance due on the contract (nearly $500,000), claiming that the financial secretary's letter was false and fraudulent, that the financial secretary was an agent of the church, and that the church was responsible for its agent's acts. The state supreme court ruled in favor of the contractor. The church insisted that it had not been aware of its financial secretary's letter, that it did not condone fraud, and that it was an "innocent party." While it acknowledged that the financial secretary was an agent of the church, it claimed that the church could not be responsible for an act of its agent that was unauthorized and contrary to the church's teachings against fraud. The court did not agree. It noted that a church can be responsible for the unauthorized acts of an agent under the theory of "apparent agency" if the following three conditions are satisfied: (1) actions by the church indicating that the agent has authority, (2) reasonable reliance on those actions, and (3) a detrimental change in position as a result of that reliance. The court concluded that all three of these conditions were satisfied in this case, and accordingly that the church was liable for the misrepresentations of its financial secretary.*[204]

2. Directors and Trustees

Like officers, the authority of directors and trustees is to be found primarily in the express provisions of state law or in a church's charter or bylaws. In addition, directors and trustees will be deemed to have implied authority to do those things that are necessary to fulfill their express powers, and they will be clothed with apparent authority when a church through its actions or representations leads others to believe that authority to perform a particular act has been granted.[205] There is one significant difference between officers and directors with respect to authority—while one or two corporate officers often have authority to act on behalf of the corporation in certain matters, directors *never* have authority, acting individually or in small groups, to bind

---

[203] Perkins v. Rich, 429 N.E.2d 1135 (Mass. 1982).

[204] Christian Methodist Episcopal Church v. S & S Construction Company, Inc., 615 So.2d 568 (Miss. 1993).

[205] Straughter v. Holy Temple of Church of God in Christ, 150 So.2d 124 (La. App. 1963).

the corporation. Directors can only act as a board, not as individuals. Accordingly, a director has no authority, acting alone, to purchase equipment or land, hire employees, or otherwise make legally binding commitments on behalf of the corporation. One or two officers, however, may be vested with this authority.

The United States Supreme Court has stated that "the first place one must look to determine the powers of corporate directors is in the relevant state's corporation law. Corporations are creatures of state law . . . and it is state law which is the font of corporate directors' powers."[206] The Model Nonprofit Corporation Act states that "the affairs of a corporation shall be managed by a board of directors."[207] Many states that have not adopted the Act have similar provisions in their religious or nonprofit corporation laws. Most state laws thus confer general managerial authority upon the directors or trustees of incorporated churches. This authority often is very broad, even to the point of empowering the board to act on behalf of the church in the ordinary business of the corporation without the necessity of obtaining the consent or approval of the membership. Thus, the board of a church corporation ordinarily has the authority to enter into contracts; elect officers; hire employees; authorize notes, deeds, and mortgages; and institute and settle lawsuits. The powers of the board, however, may be limited by church charter, bylaw, or resolution. The boards of unincorporated churches generally derive little or no authority from state law.

The courts often have held that a church board occupies a position similar to the managing directors of a business corporation, at least with respect to the temporal affairs of a church, and that the board has authority to act only at regularly assembled meetings.[208] Accordingly, when four out of seven directors met informally and agreed to change the location of an annual church meeting, the election of directors at such a meeting was invalid.[209] Another court observed that "only when acting as a board may trustees of a religious corporation perform or authorize acts binding on the corporation," and therefore the attempt by an individual trustee of a church to employ an attorney on behalf of the church was invalidated.[210] The Revised Model Nonprofit Corporation Act confers upon the board of directors limited "emergency powers" (pertaining to the amendment of bylaws, selection of successors to incapacitated officers, relocation of the corporation's principal office, and notice and quorum requirements).[211]

Directors and trustees may not perform acts not authorized either by state law or the church's charter or bylaws. To illustrate, one court ruled that if a church charter gives the board of trustees authority to institute lawsuits in the corporation's name only after being directed to do so by a majority vote of the church membership, then a lawsuit instituted by the board itself without congregational approval is unauthorized.[212] Another court ruled that the trustees of a church corporation do not possess the authority to adopt bylaws for the church unless the charter or constitution of the church specifically gives them such authority.[213] The Washington Supreme Court ruled that a church's board of elders was powerless to amend the church's articles of incorporation without the pastor's approval.[214] The church's articles of incorporation specified that neither the articles nor the bylaws could be amended without the pastor's approval. The church board members met without the pastor and voted to amend the articles by removing the provision requiring the pastor to approve all amendments to the articles. The pastor immediately filed a lawsuit asking a civil court to determine

---

[206] Burks v. Lasker, 441 U.S. 471, 478 (1979).

[207] MODEL NONPROFIT CORPORATION ACT § 16.

[208] Coates v. Parchman, 334 S.W.2d 417 (Mo. 1960).

[209] Id.

[210] Krehel v. Eastern Orthodox Catholic Church, 195 N.Y.S.2d 334, 336 (1959), aff'd, 221 N.Y.S.2d 724 (1961).

[211] REVISED MODEL NONPROFIT CORPORATION ACT §§ 2.07 and 3.03.

[212] Honey Creek Regular Baptist Church v. Wilson, 92 N.E.2d 419 (Ohio 1950).

[213] Lewis v. Wolfe, 413 S.W.2d 314 (Mo. 1967).

[214] Barnett v. Hicks, 792 P.2d 150 (Wash. 1990).

whether or not the elders had the authority to amend the articles without his approval. A trial court ruled in favor of the elders, and the pastor appealed.

The state supreme court ruled in favor of the pastor. It reasoned that the articles clearly specified that they could not be amended without the pastor's approval, and that as a result the elders' attempt to amend the articles without the pastor's approval was null and void. The court observed, "Neither of the parties has called to our attention any case holding that any corporation law in the country, profit or nonprofit, prohibits a provision in the articles of incorporation requiring the concurrence of a special individual to amend the articles." The court agreed that the church's articles "might well, in retrospect, be viewed by some as an improvident provision," but it concluded that "it is not the function of this court . . . to protect those who freely chose to enter into this kind of relationship."

Example. A South Carolina court ruled that a former trustee of a Baptist church who resigned his membership lacked the legal authority to act on behalf of the church. In 1952 a couple deeded property to a new Baptist church in the name of three trustees. One of the trustees (the "trustee") attended this church for three or four years but then stopped attending. Some 40 years later, this former trustee learned that the church was for sale, and he demanded the keys from the current pastor. The former trustee pointed out that he was the only surviving trustee, and that his name still appeared on the deed and accordingly he had the legal authority to determine whether or not the church could be sold. The pastor claimed that the former trustee's authority ended when he left the church nearly 40 years before, and also when the church was incorporated in 1965 (following its incorporation the church could hold legal title to its property in the name of the corporation, and no longer needed to hold title in the name of trustees). A state appeals court ruled in favor of the pastor. It observed that the former trustee had abandoned his membership in the church when he quit attending services some 40 years before and began attending other churches. The court then addressed the issue of the legal authority of a church trustee: "Although [the former trustee] was named as a trustee for the church, the deed to him and the other trustees does not purport to create a property interest in him, except to the extent he, as trustee, held legal title for the church and would benefit as a member of the church. . . . [T]he trustees of a church hold the property solely for the congregation whose officers they are at the time of the conveyance. While legal title to the property may be in the trustees, the use of the property is controlled by the discipline of the church in general. Moreover, the duly elected trustees of a church hold office only for the term for which they are elected and until their successors are elected." Finally, the court pointed out that "generally, congregational forms of church government provide that one may not be a trustee without being a member of the church," and that because the former trustee "abandoned his membership in [the church] he likewise forfeited his right to remain a trustee of the church."[215]

Example. A New York court ruled that an unincorporated nonprofit organization was not bound by three promissory notes executed by its treasurer without authorization. The treasurer executed three promissory notes totaling $260,000 to a creditor who later sued the organization and its treasurer for nonpayment. A state appeals court ruled that the nonprofit organization could not be liable for payment of the notes since it had not authorized the treasurer to issue them. It observed, "[S]ince a voluntary, unincorporated association has no existence separate and apart from its members, an association is not liable on the contracts of its officers, agents, or individual members in the absence of prior authorization or ratification with full knowledge of the facts by its members. The authority of a member or officer of an unincorporated association to bind the association will not be presumed or implied from

---

[215] Brock v. Bennett, 443 S.E.2d 409 (S.C. App. 1994).

the existence of a general power to attend to or transact the business, or promote the objects for which the association was formed, except where the debt contracted is necessary for its preservation. Once the authority of an agent is put in issue, it must be shown that the purported agent of the association had authority to incur any obligation on the association's behalf. The court acknowledged that the creditor served as chairman of the organization's executive committee, and in that capacity directed the treasurer to execute the promissory notes. However, this did not make the organization liable on the notes since the creditor *"failed to show that [the treasurer] was authorized to execute the promissory notes, and that the debt was necessary for the [organization's] preservation."*[216]

§ 6-06.3 — Meetings

Key point 6-06.3. *Church boards generally can act only in a meeting that is duly called pursuant to the church's governing documents. Many state nonprofit corporation laws permit church boards to act by written consent, or by conference telephone call.*

The general authority to manage church affairs generally is vested in the directors or trustees, and their acts are binding on the corporation only when done as a board at a legal meeting. Neither a minority nor a majority of the board has the authority to meet privately and take action binding upon the corporation. The reason for this rule has been stated as follows: "The law believes that the greatest wisdom results from conference and exchange of individual views, and it is for this reason that the law requires the united wisdom of a majority of the several members of the board in determining the business of the corporation."[217]

This rule of course has exceptions. For example, some state nonprofit corporation laws permit directors to take action without a meeting if they all submit written consents to a proposed action.[218] And some states permit directors to conduct meetings by conference telephone call. The entire board of directors of course can take action at a duly convened meeting to ratify an action taken by a minority or majority of the board acting separately and not in a legal meeting.

The corporate bylaws ordinarily specify that regular meetings of the directors or trustees shall occur at specified times and at a specified location. The designation in the bylaws of the time and place for regular meetings of the board generally will be considered sufficient notice of such meetings. In addition, special meetings may be convened by those officers or directors who are authorized by the bylaws to do so. The bylaws ordinarily require that notice of a special meeting be communicated to all directors at a prescribed interval before the meeting. The notice also must be in the form prescribed by the bylaws.

A meeting of the directors or trustees will not be legal unless a *quorum* is present. A quorum refers to that number or percentage of the total authorized number of directors that must be present in order for the board to transact business. The bylaws typically state the quorum requirements. In the absence of a bylaw provision, the number of directors constituting a quorum ordinarily will be determined by state nonprofit corporation law (for incorporated churches). In many states, a majority of the board will constitute a quorum in the absence of a bylaw or statutory provision to the contrary. Some nonprofit corporation laws specify that a quorum may not consist of less than a certain number. If vacancies in the board reduce the number of directors to less than a quorum, some statutes permit the board to meet for the purpose of filling vacancies.[219]

---

[216] Barrett v. Republican State Committee, 625 N.Y.S.2d 769 (A.D. 4 Dept. 1995).

[217] Trethewey v. Green River Gorge, 136 P.2d 999, 1012 (Wash. 1943).

[218] Section 8.22 of the Revised Model Nonprofit Corporation Act permits such action unless the articles or bylaws provide otherwise.

[219] MODEL NONPROFIT CORPORATION ACT § 19.

Board meetings are often informal. The president of the corporation generally presides at such meetings, and the secretary keeps minutes. Actions of the board may be in the form of a resolution, although this is not necessary since it has been held that actions taken by the board and recorded in the minutes constitute corporate actions as effectively as a formal resolution.[220]

If a board meeting does not comply with the requirements in the corporation's bylaws or in state law, it will be invalid, and its actions will have no legal effect. Thus, meetings will be invalid and ineffective if notice requirements are not satisfied, unless all of the directors waive the defect in notice either verbally or implicitly by their attendance without objection at the meeting. Meetings will also be invalid if quorum requirements are not satisfied, and an action taken by the board even at a duly called meeting will be invalid if it was adopted by less than the required number of votes.

§ 6-06.4 — Removal

Key point 6-06.4. *Church officers and directors can be removed from office in the manner authorized by the church's governing documents. It is common for church bylaws to give the membership the authority to remove officers and directors who engage in specified misconduct or change their doctrinal position.*

A corporation possesses the inherent power to remove an officer, director, or trustee for *good cause.*[221] To illustrate, one court ruled that the members of a nonprofit corporation may remove directors from office at a meeting called for this purpose, at any time.[222] Another court held that a church congregation has the inherent authority to remove a director for good cause even though the church bylaws did not address the issue.[223] In the context of church corporations, good cause ordinarily will consist of material doctrinal deviation, conduct deemed unacceptable behavior by established church custom and practice, incompetency, or incapacity. The church membership itself, and not the board, generally has the authority to remove directors or trustees for cause. Officers elected by the board ordinarily may be removed by the board.[224] Officers or directors removed for cause generally have no right to compensation (if any) for the unexpired term of office.

A church has no authority to remove an officer or director without cause prior to the expiration of a stated term of office unless a bylaw or statute specifically grants such authority. But officers or directors elected for an unspecified term generally may be removed at any time with or without cause by the body that elected them. And, when the term of an officer or director expires, a church congregation can fill the vacancy without proving that good cause exists for not reelecting the individual.[225]

State nonprofit corporation laws usually provide for removal of officers and directors. For example, section 18 of the Model Nonprofit Corporation Act states that a director may be removed by any procedure set forth in the corporation's articles of incorporation, and section 24 specifies that an officer may be removed by the persons authorized to elect or appoint such officer whenever in their judgment it serves the best interests of the corporation.

---

[220] Fletcher Cyc. Corp. § 419 (perm. ed. 1990).

[221] Rodyk v. Ukrainian Autocephalic Orthodox Church, 296 N.Y.S.2d 496 (1968), *aff'd*, 328 N.Y.S.2d 685 (1972).

[222] First Union Baptist Church v. Banks, 533 So.2d 1305 (La. App. 1988).

[223] Mangum v. Swearingen, 565 S.W.2d 957 (Tex. 1978).

[224] Beth Hamedrosh Hagodol Cemetery v. Levy, 923 S.W.2d 439 (Mo. App. 1996) ("the body which appoints a director may also remove a director").

[225] Morris v. Richard Clark Missionary Baptist Church, 177 P.2d 811 (Cal. 1947).

Provisions in state law or a church's bylaws for removal of officers and directors must be followed. Thus, if a statute specifies that any ten members of a church can call for a congregational meeting for the purpose of removing directors from office, any action taken at a meeting called by only eight members will be ineffective.[226] And, if a church votes to remove certain officers at a meeting conducted in violation of church bylaws, the removal of the officers will be without effect.[227]

It is the general rule that provisions in statutes, charters, or bylaws calling for an officer or director to serve for a prescribed term and until his or her successor is chosen do not prevent an officer or director from resigning. A resignation is complete upon its receipt by the corporation even though the corporate charter states that the office is to be held until a successor is elected and qualified.[228] Furthermore, the resignation of an officer or director will be effective even if not accepted at a formal meeting of the board of directors, at least if the board knew of the resignation and acquiesced in it.[229]

Example. The Alabama Supreme Court ruled that the dismissal of two church elders by a minister and his supporters was not legally effective since the church's established procedures were not followed. The minister convened a meeting of 27 church members (out of a total of 162) at which a vote was taken to "disfellowship" the elders. The elders were not notified of this meeting. An announcement was made after the next Sunday morning service that the elders had been removed "because of their willful and persistent violation of scripture in taking [the minister] to court." The elders challenged their dismissal in court. The state supreme court concluded that the dismissal of the elders violated this established procedure in a number of respects and accordingly was invalid. As a result, the court reinstated the elders and directed the minister to vacate the parsonage and discontinue conducting services on behalf of the church. The court concluded, "Clearly, the civil court will not review acts of church discipline or membership expulsion where there is no question as to the invasion of civil or property rights. However, the court has jurisdiction to review an expulsion from a religious society to determine whether the expelling organization acted in accordance with its own regulations, or to determine whether it acted in accordance with the principles of natural justice."[230]

Example. An Illinois court concluded that it had no authority to resolve an internal church dispute regarding the membership of a church's board of deacons. A local congregation adopted bylaws that conflicted with the provisions of the hierarchical denomination with which it was affiliated. The church elected deacons under its bylaws, and these individuals later were deposed by the denomination. A lawsuit was brought to determine the legal authority of the deposed deacons. The deposed deacons argued that the court should resolve this dispute since it did not involve "doctrinal matters" and could be resolved on the basis of non-doctrinal "neutral principles of law." The court disagreed. It observed, "In our opinion, resolution of the questions of who the true members of the board of deacons . . . are and which bylaws govern it would require this court to delve, impermissibly, into matters of church doctrine and polity." It rejected the dismissed deacons' claim that this case involved secular issues that could be resolved using neutral principles of law. In rejecting this contention the court observed, "[T]he real questions presented here are: Who governs? And by what rules? Stated otherwise, which of the factions should be recognized as the true members of the board of deacons?"[231]

---

[226] Miles v. Wilson, 181 N.Y.S.2d 585 (1958).

[227] Tybor v. Ukrainian Autocephalic Orthodox Church, 151 N.Y.S.2d 711 (1956).

[228] Koven v. Saberdyne Systems, Inc., 625 P.2d 907 (Ariz. 1980).

[229] Anderson v. K.G. Moore, Inc., 376 N.E.2d 1238 (Mass. 1978), *cert. denied*, 439 U.S. 1116 (1979).

[230] Shearry v. Sanders, 621 So.2d 1307 (Ala. 1993).

[231] St. Mark Coptic Orthodox Church v. Tanios, 572 N.E.2d 283 (Ill. App. 1991).

Example. *The Supreme Judicial Court of Massachusetts ruled that the first amendment prevented it from resolving an internal church dispute regarding the authority of a denominational official to dismiss members of a local church board.*[232] *The court conceded that the civil courts can resolve church property disputes on the basis of "neutral principles of law" involving no inquiry into doctrine or policy. However, this was not a property case: "Here the dispute is not one of property as such . . . . The conflict here began when a majority of the parish corporation passed a vote of no confidence in the [pastor], hardly a question of property. The dispute blossomed to encompass wider questions of church governance, including the method of selection of members of the [board]. . . . What is at stake here is the power to exert religious authority."*

Example. *A Missouri court ruled that it was prevented by the first amendment guaranty of religious freedom from resolving a lawsuit brought by ousted church officers challenging the legal validity of their removal.*[233] *As a result of internal conflicts a church amended its bylaws so that it was governed by six officers. These six persons soon divided into two opposing groups of three officers, which led to a stalemate on many issues. One of these groups attempted to appoint a seventh member to the board, and then these four persons ousted the other three officers. The three ousted officers sued the remaining officers, claiming that their ouster was invalid. They argued that the contest was between two factions within a nonprofit corporation disagreeing over which group was the duly elected and qualified officers of the church, and this issue was not a "purely ecclesiastical" matter that was off limits to the civil courts. The matter could be resolved simply by reviewing the church's bylaws. The other group of officers insisted that the dispute was an ecclesiastical matter. They asserted that whether an individual is properly appointed or removed as an officer of a church is subject to ecclesiastical, not corporate, law and therefore "callings, ordinations and removals" of such positions are not within the jurisdiction of the civil courts. A trial court agreed with this position, and dismissed the case. The ousted officers appealed. They claimed that when the church incorporated under state law it submitted to the state courts' jurisdiction in all matters of a corporate nature. As a result, the courts could determine if the four officers who ousted them did so in accordance with the church's bylaws. They insisted that they were raising questions of authority to act, and whether proper corporate procedures were followed in accordance with the bylaws. The other group of officers claimed that the act of ousting the leaders of a religious body has long been an ecclesiastical matter because "the officers of a religious society are to be determined according to the discipline of that society, and civil courts will not review the decision of a competent ecclesiastical body upon a question involving the election of officers." This group also asserted that it is inconsistent with the American concept of the relationship between church and state to permit civil courts to determine ecclesiastical questions. A state appeals court concluded that the first amendment prevented the civil courts from resolving the ousted members' claims. The court concluded that this dispute was far more than a disagreement over the meaning and application of corporate bylaws. The "ultimate issue" was whether or not the ouster of church officers was proper. The court noted that "there is no way that can be a non-ecclesiastical issue."*

§ 6-07   Officers, Directors, and Trustees — Personal Liability

Traditionally, the officers and directors of nonprofit corporations performed their duties with little if any risk of personal legal liability. In recent years, a number of lawsuits have attempted to impose personal

---

[232] Parish of the Advent v. Protestant Episcopal Diocese, 688 N.E.2d 923 (Mass. 1997).
[233] Rolfe v. Parker, 968 S.W.2d 178 (Mo. App. 1998).

liability on such officers and directors. In some cases, directors are sued because of statutes that provide limited legal immunity to churches (discussed in section 6-08).

As a general rule, directors are not responsible for actions taken by the board prior to their election to the board (unless they vote to ratify a previous action). Similarly, directors ordinarily are not liable for actions taken by the board after their resignation. Again, they will continue to be liable for actions that they took prior to their resignation.

A number of state laws permit nonprofit corporations to amend their bylaws to indemnify directors for any costs incurred in connection with the defense of any lawsuit arising out of their status as directors.

The more common theories of liability are summarized below.

§ 6-07.01 — Tort Liability

Key point 6-07.01. Church board members may be personally liable for their own torts (conduct causing personal injury to another). This is so whether or not the church is incorporated.

Perhaps the most common basis of legal liability relates to the commission of torts. A "tort" is a civil wrong, other than a breach of contract, for which the law provides a remedy. Common examples include negligence (e.g., careless operation of a church-owned vehicle), defamation, fraud, copyright infringement, and wrongful termination of employees. It is the general rule that the directors and officers of a nonprofit corporation do not incur personal liability for the corporation's torts merely by reason of their official position. Rather, they will be liable only for those torts that they commit, direct, or participate in, even though the corporation itself may also be liable. To illustrate, directors in some cases may be personally liable if they (a) knowingly permit an unsafe condition to exist on church property that results in death or injury; (b) cause injury as a result of the negligent operation of a vehicle in the course of church business; (c) negligently fail to adequately supervise church activities resulting in death or injury; (d) terminate an employee for an impermissible or insufficient reason; (e) utter a defamatory remark about another individual; (f) authorize an act that infringes upon the exclusive rights of a copyright owner; (g) engage in fraudulent acts; (h) knowingly draw checks against insufficient funds; or (i) knowingly make false representations as to the financial condition of the church to third parties who, in reliance on such representations, extend credit to the church and suffer a loss. In all such cases, the director must personally commit, direct, or participate in the tort. Therefore, a director ordinarily will not be liable for the torts committed by other board members without his or her knowledge or consent. Obviously, board members having any question regarding the propriety of a particular action being discussed at a board meeting should be sure to have their dissent to the proposed action registered in the minutes of the meeting.

§ 6-07.02 — Contract Liability

Key point 6-07.02. Church board members may be personally liable for contracts they sign if they do so without authorization, or if they fail to indicate that they are signing as a representative of the church.

Church board members may be personally liable on contracts that they sign in either of two ways. First, a board member may be personally liable on a contract that he signs without authority. Second, a board member may be personally liable on a contract that he is authorized to sign but which he signs in his own name without any reference to the church or to his representational capacity. To prevent this inadvertent assumption of liability, board members who are authorized to sign contracts (as well as any other legal document) should be careful to indicate the church's name on the document and clearly indicate their own representational capacity (agent, director, trustee, officer, etc.).

§ 6-07.03 — Breach of the Fiduciary Duty of Care

Key point 6-07.03. Church board members have a fiduciary duty to use reasonable care in the discharge of their duties, and they may be personally liable for damages resulting from their failure to do so.

The board members of business corporations are under a duty to perform their duties "in good faith, in a manner they reasonably believe to be in the best interests of the corporation, and with such care as an ordinarily prudent person in a like position would use under similar circumstances." This duty commonly is referred to as the "prudent person rule" or the "duty of due care." In recent years, some courts have extended this duty to the board members of nonprofit corporations. To illustrate, a federal district court ruled that the directors of a nonprofit corporation breached their fiduciary duty of care in managing the corporation's funds.[234] For nearly 20 years, management of the corporation had been dominated almost exclusively by two officers, whose decisions and recommendations were routinely adopted by the board. The corporation's finance committee had not convened in more than 11 years. Under these facts, the court concluded:

> Total abdication of [a director's] supervisory role, however, is improper . . . . A director who fails to acquire the information necessary to supervise . . . or consistently fails even to attend the meetings . . . has violated his fiduciary duty to the corporation . . . . A director whose failure to supervise permits negligent mismanagement by others to go unchecked has committed an independent wrong against the corporation.[235]

A ruling of the bankruptcy court in the PTL ministry bankruptcy case addressed the liability of directors and officers.[236] The court agreed with the bankruptcy trustee that televangelist Jim Bakker (as both an officer and director) had breached his legal duty of care to PTL. It quoted a South Carolina statute (PTL was located in South Carolina) that specifies the duty of care that a director or officer owes to his or her corporation:

> A director or officer shall perform his duties as a director or officer, including his duties as a member of any committee of the board of directors upon which he may serve, in good faith, in the manner he reasonably believes to be in the best interest of the corporation and of its shareholders, and with such care as an ordinary prudent person in a like position would use under similar circumstances.[237]

The court, in commenting upon this provision, observed:

> Good faith requires the undivided loyalty of a corporate director or officer to the corporation and such a duty of loyalty prohibits the director or an officer, as a fiduciary, from using this position of trust for his own personal gain to the detriment of the corporation. In this instance, there are no shareholders of the corporation; however, even though there are no shareholders, the officers and directors still hold a fiduciary obligation to manage the corporation in its best interest and not to the detriment of the corporation itself.[238]

---

[234] Stern v. Lucy Webb Hayes National Training School for Deaconesses & Missionaries, 381 F. Supp. 1003 (D.D.C. 1974).
[235] *Id.* at 1014.
[236] Heritage Village Church and Missionary Fellowship, Inc., 92 B.R. 1000 (D.S.C. 1988).
[237] *Id.* at 1014-1015, quoting S.C. STAT. ANN. § 33-13-150(a).
[238] *Id.* at 1015.

The court concluded that "the duty of care and loyalty required by [Bakker] was breached inasmuch as he (1) failed to inform the members of the board of the true financial position of the corporation and to act accordingly; (2) failed to supervise other officers and directors; (3) failed to prevent the depletion of corporate assets; and (4) violated the prohibition against self-dealing."

With respect to Bakker's defense that his actions had been "approved" by the board, the court observed that Bakker "exercised a great deal of control over his board" and that "a director who exercises a controlling influence over co-directors cannot defend acts committed by him on the grounds that his actions were approved by the board." The court acknowledged that officers and directors cannot be "held accountable for mere mistakes in judgment." However, it found that "the acts of [Bakker] did not constitute mere mistakes in judgment, but constituted gross mismanagement and a neglect of the affairs of the corporation. Clearly the salaries, the awards of bonuses and the carte blanche exercised over PTL checking accounts and credit cards were excessive and without justification and there was lack of proper care, attention and circumspection to the affairs of the corporation. [Bakker] breached [his] duty to manage and supervise . . . ."

In support of its conclusions, the court cited numerous findings, including the following: (a) Bakker failed to require firm bids on construction projects though this caused PTL substantial losses; (b) capital expenditures often greatly exceeded estimates, though Bakker was warned of the problem; (c) Bakker rejected warnings from financial officers about the dangers of debt financing; (d) many of the bonuses granted to Bakker were granted "during periods of extreme financial hardship for PTL"; (e) Bakker "let it be known that he did not want to hear any bad news, so people were reluctant to give him bad financial information"; (f) "it was a common practice for PTL to write checks for more money than it showed in its checkbook; the books would often show a negative balance, but the money would eventually be transferred or raised to cover the checks written—this 'float' often would be three to four million dollars"; (g) most of the events and programs at PTL that were made available to the public were operated at a loss; since 1984, "energy was placed into raising lifetime partner funds rather than raising general contributions"; (h) Bakker "during the entire period in question, failed to give attention to financial matters and the problems of raising money and cutting expense."

Though at the time of Bakker's resignation in 1987 PTL had outstanding liens of $35 million, and general contributions were in a state of decline, "millions of dollars were being siphoned off by excessive spending." Such spending, noted the court, "is shocking to the conscience to the extent that it is unbelievable that a religious ministry would be operated in such a manner." The court concluded that "Mr. Bakker, as an officer and director of PTL . . . approached the management of the corporation with reckless indifference to the financial consequences of [his] acts. While on the one hand [he was] experiencing inordinate personal gain from the revenues of PTL, on the other hand [he was] intentionally ignoring the extreme financial difficulties of PTL and, ironically, [was], in fact, adding to them." To illustrate, Bakker accepted huge bonuses at times of serious financial crisis at PTL. "Such conduct," noted the court, "demonstrates a total lack of fiduciary responsibility to PTL."[239] The court emphasized that *"trustees and corporate directors for not-for-profit organizations are liable for losses occasioned by their negligent mismanagement."*[240]

Lawsuits against nonprofit directors for breach of their "duty of care" are still rare. Directors of churches and religious organizations can reduce the risk of liability even further by (a) attending all of the meetings of the board and of any committees on which they serve; (b) thoroughly reviewing all interim and annual financial statements and reports, and seeking clarification of any irregularities or inconsistencies; (c) affirma-

---

[239] *Id.* at 1013.
[240] *Id.* at 1015.

tively investigating and rectifying any other problems or improprieties; (d) thoroughly reviewing the corporate charter, constitution, and bylaws; (e) dissenting from any board action with which they have any misgivings, and insisting that their objection be recorded in the minutes of the meeting; and (f) resigning from the board if and when they are unable to fulfill these duties. As one court has observed, "the law has no place for dummy directors."

Example. An Ohio court refused to allow church members to sue board members personally for breaching their fiduciary duties by failing to oust a pastor who allegedly had engaged in financial improprieties. It observed, "[I]nquiry into the relationship between the trustees and the congregation in matters concerning the pastorship would require the courts to consider each party's view of who should preach from the pulpit. Review of such matters would further require the court to determine the issue of whether the trustees' performance of their duties met the standards of the congregation and would therefore involve an inquiry into ecclesiastical concerns. Therefore . . . civil courts lack . . . jurisdiction to entertain such matters. . . . [We] hold that the lower court has no jurisdiction over the claims brought by the individual members of the congregation seeking to . . . hold the board liable for breach of fiduciary duty to the congregation."[241]

Example. A New York appeals court ruled that directors of a charitable trust could be sued for breaching their fiduciary duties. A child of the founder of the trust filed a lawsuit seeking to remove 8 of the trust's 11 directors. He asserted that the 8 directors breached their fiduciary duties, mismanaged the trust's investments, and negligently selected the trust's investment advisor. The court ruled that the 8 directors could be sued. It noted that "it is well established that, as fiduciaries, board members bear a duty of loyalty to the corporation and may not profit improperly at the expense of their corporation." In this case, the lawsuit alleged that the 8 directors breached their fiduciary duties by investing a substantial portion of the trust's assets in speculative securities and in the stock of a company with direct ties to the directors. The court concluded that the "business judgment rule" (which protects directors from any liability for their reasonable and good faith decisions) did not apply in this case, since it was not available "when the good faith or oppressive conduct of the officers and directors is in issue."[242]

Example. A Minnesota court dismissed a lawsuit brought by Lutheran pastors against a denominational pension board for allegedly breaching their fiduciary duty to participants by not investing in companies that did business in South Africa. The Evangelical Lutheran Church in America (ELCA) established a board of pensions in 1988 to manage and operate a pension fund for Lutheran pastors and lay employees "exclusively for the benefit of and to assist in carrying out the purposes of the ELCA." The ELCA adopted the position that the system of apartheid in South Africa was so contrary to Lutheran theology that it had to be rejected as a matter of faith. The ELCA passed a resolution to "see that none of our ELCA pension funds will be invested in companies doing business in South Africa." A dissenting group of Lutherans opposed the ELCA's decision to use its assets as a political weapon and asked to withdraw their pension funds. When their request was denied they sued the board of pensions and the ELCA, claiming that both groups had violated their fiduciary duties to participants in the pension program by elevating social concerns over sound investment strategy. A state appeals court dismissed the lawsuit on the ground that a resolution of the lawsuit would require the court to interpret religious doctrine in violation of the first amendment's nonestablishment of religion clause. The court concluded that the "ELCA enacted the [apartheid] policy in an effort to further its social and doctrinal goals . . . . Accordingly, any review of the Board of Pensions' [investment policy] would entangle the court in reviewing church doctrine and policy."[243]

---

[241] State v. Meagher, 1997 WL 180266 (Ohio App. 1997).
[242] Scheuer Family Foundation, Inc. v. 61 Associates, 582 N.Y.S.2d 662 (A.D. 1 Dept. 1992).
[243] Basich v. Board of Pensions, 540 N.W.2d 82 (Minn. App. 1995).

§ 6-07.04 — Breach of the Fiduciary Duty of Loyalty

Key point 6-07.04. Church board members have a fiduciary duty of loyalty to their church, and they may be personally liable for breaching this duty by participating in board decisions that place the interests of one or more board members above the interests of the church itself.

Directors of nonprofit corporations have a fiduciary duty of loyalty to the corporation. This duty generally requires that any transaction between the board and one of its directors be (a) fully disclosed, (b) approved by the board without the vote of the interested director, and (c) fair and reasonable to the corporation. In most cases, a director breaches the duty of loyalty only through some secret or undisclosed interest in a transaction with the corporation. To illustrate, a director who owns a business (e.g., insurance, real estate, furnishings) may violate the duty of loyalty by inducing the board to enter into a transaction with his company without fully disclosing to the board his personal interest in the transaction. Additionally, the director ordinarily should abstain from voting on the transaction, and the transaction should be fair and reasonable to the corporation.

§ 6-07.05 — Violation of Trust Terms

Key point 6-07.05. Church board members may be personally liable for diverting designated funds or trust funds to some other purpose.

Church officers and directors may be legally accountable for violating the terms or restrictions of properties and funds held in trust by the church. To illustrate, the trustees of one church were sued by church members when they attempted to sell church assets contrary to the restrictions specified in the church charter.[244] The original charter of the church stated that it was formed "for the purpose of religious worship . . . at the corner of Fifth Street and E Street, Southeast, in the City of Washington." In 1982, after the safety of the historic church building became an issue, the pastor and board of trustees decided to close the church and move to a new location. For at least ten years prior to the sale of the church property, relations between the board of trustees and a segment of the congregation became increasingly hostile. After the sale of the church building, a group of the dissidents filed a lawsuit alleging that the trustees and pastor had violated their fiduciary duty as trustees to hold church properties for the purposes specified in the corporate charter (i.e., to conduct religious worship "at the church building on the southeast corner of Fifth Street and E Street"). The dissidents claimed they were attempting to "salvage the historic old Mount Jezreel church building." The dissidents pointed out that title to the church's properties was in the name of the trustees who held church properties "in trust" for the members of the congregation, and that church members were "trust beneficiaries" who could sue the trustees for improper or unauthorized transactions with respect to those properties.

A trial court dismissed the lawsuit, but an appeals court ruled in favor of the dissidents. The appeals court observed:

Although title to the church property is vested in the trustees or directors, the property itself is held in trust for the uses and purposes named and no other. Because the church was incorporated for the purpose of religious worship, and because the property was held in trust for that purpose, the members of the congregation are indeed the beneficiaries of the trust. As such, they have standing to sue the trustees in the event that the trust property is used or disposed of in a manner

---

[244] Mt. Jezreel Christians Without a Home v. Board of Trustees of Mount Jezreel Baptist Church, 582 A.2d 237 (D.C. App. 1990).

contrary to the stated purposes of the trust. . . . We therefore hold that, as a general principle, bona fide members of a church have standing to bring suit as trust beneficiaries when there is a dispute over the use or disposition of church property.[245]

The same principle may apply to board members who authorize the diversion of designated funds from their intended purposes or projects. For example, assume that a member donates $10,000 to a church's new building fund, and that the church later decides not to build a new facility. Can the church board divert the $10,000 to another use, or must it return the funds to the donor? Or, assume that the church raises several contributions totaling $250,000 for a new building fund and later decides to abandon the project. Does the board have an obligation to track down all of the donors and offer to return their contributions?

Church board members may be liable for diverting designated gifts to other purposes only if someone has the legal right to enforce the original designation. Some courts have ruled that the donor has such a right, but others have not. Even if a donor cannot enforce a designated gift, this does not make it unenforceable. In most states the following persons are authorized to enforce a designated gift: (1) the state attorney general; (2) a donor who reserves a right to enforce a designated gift in a written instrument; or (3) a trustee of a written trust that contains the designated gift.

> **Example.** *The Connecticut Supreme Court ruled that donors who make designated gifts to charity ordinarily do not have a legal right to enforce their designations.[246] A foundation contributed $250,000 to a university with the stipulation that the funds be used to provide scholarships to needy students in the nursing program. A few years later the university closed its nursing school. The foundation sued the university, and asked a court to order the university to segregate the gift from its general fund and set it aside once again for the gift's original purpose. If that purpose could no longer be fulfilled, then the foundation asked the court to compel the university to return the gift. The court ruled that donors who make designated gifts to charity have no legal right to enforce their designations unless they specifically reserve the right to do so. The court acknowledged that a designated contribution is held in trust by a charity for the specified purpose. And, while the donor cannot enforce a designated gift, there are others who can. These include the state attorney general, a trustee of a written trust, or anyone with a "special interest" in the enforcement of the designation.*

Since designated gifts generally can be enforced by someone (even if not the donor), church board members may be legally responsible for diverting designated gifts to other purposes. As a result, it is essential for church leaders to consult with a local attorney before using a donor's designated funds for some other purpose. To reduce the risk of personal liability, church leaders should consider the following precautions if they decide to use designated gifts for other purposes:

• *Donors can be identified.* If donors can be identified, they should be asked if they want their contributions returned or retained by the church and used for some other purpose. Ideally, donors should communicate their decision in writing to avoid any misunderstandings. Churches must provide donors with this option in order to avoid violating their legal duty to use designated funds only for the purposes specified. Of course, churches should advise these donors that they may need to file amended tax returns if they claimed a charitable contribution deduction for their contributions in a prior year.

---

[245] *Id.* at 239 (citations omitted).
[246] Herzog Foundation v. University of Bridgeport, 699 A.2d 995 (Conn. 1997).

Key point. Often, donors prefer to let the church retain their designated contributions rather than go through the inconvenience of filing an amended tax return.

• *Donors cannot be identified.* A church may not be able to identify all donors who contributed to the building fund. This is often true of donors who contributed small amounts, or donors who made anonymous cash offerings to the building fund. In some cases, designated contributions were made many years before the church abandoned its building plans, and there are no records that identify donors. Under these circumstances the church has a variety of options. One option would be to address the matter in a meeting of church members. Inform the membership of the amount of designated contributions in the church building fund that cannot be associated with individual donors, and ask the church members to take an official action with regard to the disposition of the building fund. In most cases, the church membership will authorize the transfer of the funds to the general fund. Note that this procedure is appropriate only for that portion of the building fund that cannot be traced to specific donors. If donors can be identified, then use the procedure described above.

Other options are available. Churches should be sure to consult with a local attorney when deciding how to dispose of designated funds if the specified purpose has been abandoned.

• *Some donors can be identified, and some cannot.* In most cases, some of the building fund can be traced to specific donors, but some of it cannot. Both of the procedures summarized above would have to be used.

Key point. This discussion has focused on building funds. The same analysis is relevant to contributions that designate any other specific purpose or activity. Other examples include contributions designating a new organ, a missions activity, or a new vehicle.

• *Uniform Management of Institutional Funds Act (UMIFA).* This Act is designed to provide the boards and trustees of charitable organizations (including churches) with guidance in handling *institutional funds*. The Act defines an institutional fund as a fund that is "not wholly expendable by the institution on a current basis under the terms of the applicable gift instrument." An official interpretation of the Act, adopted by its drafters, further clarifies that

> an endowment fund is an institutional fund . . . which is held in perpetuity or for a term and which is not wholly expendable by the institution. Implicit in the definition is the continued maintenance of all or a specified portion of the original gift. . . . If a governing board has the power to spend all of a fund but, in its discretion, decides to invest the fund and spend only the yield or appreciation therefrom, the fund does not become an endowment fund under this definition . . . .

According to these provisions, the Act would not apply to church building funds (or other designated funds) that exist for a specific project requiring the expenditure of the entire fund. However, some churches have established perpetual endowment funds that will meet the Act's definition of an institutional fund. These churches should be familiar with the key provisions of the Act. An introductory note to the Act states:

> It is established law that the donor may place restrictions on his largesse which the donee institution must honor. Too often, the restrictions on use or investment become outmoded or wasteful or unworkable. There is a need for review of obsolete restrictions and a way of modifying or adjusting them. The Act authorizes the governing board to obtain the acquiescence of the donor to a release of restrictions and, in the absence of the donor, to petition the appropriate court for relief in appropriate cases.

The Act contains the following relevant provisions:

§ 7. (a) With the written consent of the donor, the governing board may release, in whole or in part, a restriction imposed by the applicable gift instrument on the use or investment of an institutional fund.

(b) If written consent of the donor cannot be obtained by reason of his death, disability, unavailability, or impossibility of identification, the governing board may apply in the name of the institution to the [appropriate] court for release of a restriction imposed by the applicable gift instrument on the use or investment of an institutional fund. The [attorney general] shall be notified of the application and shall be given an opportunity to be heard. If the court finds that the restriction is obsolete, inappropriate, or impracticable, it may by order release the restriction in whole or in part. A release under this subsection may not change an endowment fund to a fund that is not an endowment fund.

(c) A release under this section may not allow a fund to be used for purposes other than the educational, religious, charitable, or other eleemosynary purposes of the institution affected.

(d) This section does not limit the application of the doctrine of *cy pres*.

An official comment to this section of the Act contains the following additional guidance:

One of the difficult problems of fund management involves gifts restricted to uses which cannot be feasibly administered or to investments which are no longer available or productive. There should be an expeditious way to make necessary adjustments when the restrictions no longer serve the original purpose. . . . This section permits a release of limitations that imperil efficient administration of a fund or prevent sound investment management if the governing board can secure the approval of the donor or the appropriate court.

Although the donor has no property interest in a fund after the gift, nonetheless if it is the donor's limitation that controls the governing board and he or she agrees that the restriction need not apply, the board should be free of the burden. . . . If the donor is unable to consent or cannot be identified, the appropriate court may upon application of a governing board release a limitation which is shown to be obsolete, inappropriate or impracticable.

This section of the Act, which remains largely unknown to church leaders and their advisers, provides important guidance in the event that the purpose of a perpetual endowment fund is frustrated and the church would like to expend the gift for another purpose.

Example. *The Connecticut Supreme Court ruled that the Uniform Management of Institutional Funds Act (UMIFA) does not give donors the authority to enforce designated gifts to charity. The court acknowledged that UMIFA permits a charity to avoid an obsolete designation in a gift without resort to the courts by obtaining the donor's consent: "With the written consent of the donor, the governing board may release, in whole or in part, a restriction imposed by the applicable gift instrument on the use or investment of an institutional fund." However, the court pointed out that the drafters of UMIFA made the following official comments: "It is established law that the donor may place restrictions on his largesse which the donee institution must honor. Too often, the restrictions on use or investment become* *outmoded or wasteful or unworkable. There is a need for review of obsolete restrictions and a way of modifying or adjusting them. The Act authorizes the governing board to obtain the acquiescence of the donor to a release of restrictions and, in the absence of the donor, to petition the appropriate court for relief in appropriate cases. . . . The donor has no right to enforce the restriction, no interest in the fund and no power to change the [charitable] beneficiary of the fund. He may only acquiesce in a lessening of a restriction already in effect."* The court noted that these *"clear comments regarding the power of a donor to enforce restrictions on a charitable gift"* were based on a concern by the drafters of UMIFA *that donors would be exposed to "potential adverse tax consequences" if UMIFA "was interpreted to provide donors with control over their gift property after the completion of the gift."* The court explained this concern as follows: *"The drafters' principal concern in this regard was that the matter of donor restrictions not affect the donor's charitable contribution deduction for the purposes of federal income taxation. In other words, the concern was that the donor not be so tethered to the charitable gift through the control of restrictions in the gift that the donor would not be entitled to claim a federal charitable contribution exemption for the gift."* In resolving these concerns, the drafters of UMIFA clearly stated their position as follows: *"No federal tax problems for the donor are anticipated by permitting release of a restriction. The donor has no right to enforce the restriction, no interest in the fund and no power to change the [charitable] beneficiary of the fund. He may only acquiesce in a lessening of a restriction already in effect."* The court concluded, *"[W]e find no support in any source for the proposition that the drafters of UMIFA intended that a donor or his heirs would supplant the attorney general as the designated enforcer of the terms of completed and absolute charitable gifts. Indeed, it would have been [inconsistent] for the drafters of UMIFA to strive to assist charitable institutions by creating smoother procedural avenues for the release of restrictions while simultaneously establishing standing for a new class of litigants, donors, who would defeat this very purpose by virtue of the potential of lengthy and complicated litigation."*

• *The "cy pres" doctrine.* Note that Section 7(c) of the Uniform Management of Institutional Funds Act (quoted above) specifies that the Act does not limit the application of the *cy pres* doctrine. This is a potentially significant provision. The "cy pres" doctrine (which has been adopted by most states) generally specifies that if property is given in trust to be applied to a particular charitable purpose, and it is or becomes impossible or impracticable or illegal to carry out the particular purpose, and if the donor manifested a more general intention to devote the property to charitable purposes, the trust will not fail but the court will direct the application of the property to some charitable purpose which falls within the general charitable intention of the donor.

Consider the following illustration, based on a ruling by the Iowa Supreme Court.[247] An elderly man drafted a will in 1971 that left most of his estate "in trust" to his sisters, and upon the death of the surviving sister, to a local Congregational church with the stipulation that the funds be used "solely for the building of a new church." The man died in 1981, and his surviving sister died in 1988. Since the Congregational church had no plans to build a new sanctuary, it asked a local court to interpret the will to permit the church to use the trust fund not only for construction of a new facility but also "for the remodeling, improvement, or expansion of the existing church facilities" and for the purchase of real estate that may be needed for future church construction. The church also asked the court for permission to use income from the trust fund for any purposes that the church board wanted. The state attorney general, pursuant to state law, reviewed the church's petition and asked the court to grant the church's requests. However, a number of heirs opposed the church's position, and insisted that the decedent's will was clear, and that the church was attempting to use the trust funds "for purposes other than building a new church." They asked the court to distribute the trust fund to the decedent's lawful heirs.

---

[247] Matter of Trust of Rothrock, 452 N.W.2d 403 (Iowa 1990).

The local court agreed with the church on the ground that "gifts to charitable uses and purposes are highly favored in law and will be most liberally construed to make effectual the intended purpose of the donor." The trial court's ruling was appealed by the heirs, and the state supreme court agreed with the trial court and ruled in favor of the church. The supreme court began its opinion by observing that "it is contrary to the public policy of this state to indulge in strained construction of the provisions of a will in order to seek out and discover a basis for avoiding the primary purpose of the [decedent] to bestow a charitable trust." The court emphasized that the "cy pres" doctrine clearly required it to rule in favor of the church. Applying the cy pres rule, the court concluded:

> The will gave the property in trust for a particular charitable purpose, the building of a new church. The evidence clearly indicated that it was impractical to carry out this particular purpose. Furthermore, the [decedent] did not provide that the trust should terminate if the purpose failed. A trust is not forfeited when it becomes impossible to carry out its specific purpose, and there is no forfeiture or reversion clause.[248]

The court concluded that the trial court's decision to permit the church to use the trust fund for the remodeling, improvement, or expansion of the existing church facilities "falls within the [decedent's] general charitable intention." Accordingly, the trial court's decision represented a proper application of the cy pres rule.

Another court ruled that church funds earmarked by a donor for a specific purpose could be used by the church for other, related purposes.[249] In 1911, a Quaker church established a fund for the care and maintenance of its graveyard, and began soliciting contributions for the fund. By 1988, the fund had increased to nearly $200,000, and had annual income far in excess of expenses. In 1985, the church discussed the possibility of using the excess income for purposes other than graveyard maintenance, and ultimately expressed a desire to use excess income from the fund for general church purposes (including upkeep and maintenance of church properties). A church trustee who administered the fund took an unbending position that the fund could not be used for any purpose other than graveyard maintenance. The church and trustee thereupon sought an opinion ("declaratory judgment") from a local court as to the use of the fund for other purposes.

The trial court ruled that the excess income could be used for general church purposes other than graveyard maintenance, and the trustee appealed the case to a state appeals court on the ground that the trial court's decision "conflicts with the express intent of the donors." The appeals court agreed with the trial court on the basis of the "cy pres" doctrine. The court observed that the cy pres doctrine was created "for the preservation of a charitable trust when accomplishment of the particular purpose of the trust becomes impossible, impractical, or illegal." The court concluded that "if income from a charitable trust exceeds that which is necessary to achieve the donor's charitable objective, cy pres may be applied to the surplus income since there is an impossibility of using the income to advance any of the charitable purposes of the [donor]." Therefore, to the extent that the graveyard fund in question "exceeds maintenance and preservation costs, application of cy pres is appropriate since there is an impossibility of using the excess income to advance the particular purpose expressed by the donors."

The only remaining question was whether or not the donors manifested an intention to devote excess income to a charitable purpose more general than graveyard maintenance. The court concluded that the donors to the graveyard fund in fact manifested such an intent:

---

[248] *Id.* at 406.

[249] Sharpless v. Medford Monthly Meeting of the Religious Society of Friends, 548 A.2d 1157 (N.J. Super. 1988).

Since the donations were made for the perpetual maintenance of a graveyard, it is logical to assume that the donors expected excess income would be used . . . "to strengthen the very institution to which [they] entrusted their money" to permit it to survive in perpetuity in order to carry out the donors' intent. A contrary result, that the income be held in the trust and accumulate in perpetuity for maintenance of the graveyard, is both illogical and contrary to the probable intent of the donors. The only sensible conclusion to be reached is that the donors did not intend that the trusts would grow while the [church] itself may cease to exist because of lack of funds. We are also convinced that use of the funds for general meeting purposes is sufficiently similar to the particular purpose of the [donors] to apply the cy pres doctrine.[250]

The court emphasized that only trust income in excess of graveyard expenses could be applied for general church purposes, and that the church's bylaws required an annual audit of the fund by certified public accountants.

§ 6-07.06 — Securities Law

Key point 6-07.06. Federal and state securities laws make board members personally liable for acts of fraud committed by an organization in connection with the offer or sale of securities. These laws apply to churches, and as a result church board members may be liable for fraudulent practices occurring in connection with the offer or sale of church securities.

Section 410(b) of the Uniform Securities Act (adopted in about 40 states) imposes civil liability on every officer or director of an organization that (a) offers or sells unregistered, nonexempt securities; (b) uses unlicensed agents in the offer or sale of its securities (unless the agents are specifically exempted from registration under state law); or (c) offers or sells securities by means of any untrue statement of a material fact or any omission of a material fact. In recent years, a number of churches have violated some or all of these requirements. Such violations render each officer and director of the church potentially liable. Section 410(b) does provide that an officer or director of an organization that sells securities in violation of any of the three provisions discussed above is not liable if he "sustains the burden of proof that he did not know, and in the exercise of reasonable care could not have known of the existence of the facts by reason of which the liability is alleged to exist."

§ 6-07.07 — Wrongful Discharge of an Employee

Key point 6-07.07. Church board members may be personally liable if they participate in a decision to terminate an employee in a way that violates the employee's legal rights.

In the past, employment agreements of *unspecified* duration were considered to be terminable at the will of either the employer or the employee. No "cause" was necessary. In recent years, the courts of a number of states have permitted discharged "at will" employees to sue their former employer on the basis of one or more legal theories, including: (a) wrongful discharge in violation of public policy (e.g., employee terminated for filing a workmen's compensation claim, or for reporting illegal employer activities); (b) intentional infliction of emotional distress (e.g., discharge accompanied by extreme and outrageous conduct); (c) fraud (e.g., employee accepts job in reliance on employer misrepresentations); (d) defamation (e.g., malicious and false statements made by previous employer to prospective employers); (e) breach of contract terms (e.g., employer made oral represen-

---

[250] *Id.* at 1160 (citations omitted).

tations, or written representations contained in a contract of employment or employee handbook, that were not kept). Directors may be personally liable to the extent that they participate in such activities.

§ 6-07.08 — Willful Failure to Withhold Taxes

Key point 6-07.08. Church board members who have authority to sign checks or make financial decisions on behalf of a church may be personally liable for a willful failure by the church to withhold federal payroll taxes, or to deposit or pay over withheld taxes to the IRS.

The officers and directors of a church or other nonprofit organization can be personally liable for the amount of payroll taxes that are not withheld or paid over to the government. To illustrate, a church-operated charitable organization failed to pay over to the IRS withheld income taxes and the employer's and employees' share of FICA taxes for a number of quarters in both 1984 and 1985. Accordingly, the IRS assessed a penalty in the amount of 100 percent of the unpaid taxes ($230,245.86) against *each* of the four officers of the organization pursuant to section 6672 of the Internal Revenue Code, which specifies that "any person required to collect . . . and pay over any [FICA or income] tax who willfully fails to collect such tax . . . or willfully attempts in any manner to evade or defeat any such tax or the payment thereof, shall, in addition to other penalties provided by law, be liable to a penalty equal to the total amount of the tax evaded, or not collected, or not accounted for and paid over."

The officers challenged the validity of the IRS actions. A federal district court in New York observed that federal law requires employers to withhold FICA and income taxes from the wages of their employees, and to hold the withheld taxes as a "special trust fund" for the benefit of the United States government until paid or deposited.[251] If an employer fails to make the required payments, "the government may actually suffer a loss because the employees are given credit for the amount of the taxes withheld regardless of whether the employer ever pays the money to the government." Accordingly, "section 6672 of the Code supplies an alternative method for collecting the withheld taxes. Pursuant to this section, the government may assess a penalty, equal to the full amount of the unpaid tax, against a person responsible for paying over the money who willfully fails to do so." The court observed that a person is liable for the full amount of taxes under section 6672 if "(1) he or she was under a duty to collect, account for, and pay over the taxes (i.e., a 'responsible person'), and (2) the failure to pay the taxes was 'willful.'"

The court concluded that the four officers of the church-related charitable organization satisfied both requirements, and accordingly that they were personally liable for the unpaid taxes under section 6672. The officers were "responsible persons" since (a) they were directors as well as officers, (b) they had the authority to sign checks (including payroll checks), and (c) they were involved in "routine business concerns such as corporate funding, bookkeeping, salaries, and hiring and firing." The fact that a nonprofit organization was involved, and that the officers donated their services without compensation, did not relieve them of liability. The court also ruled that the officers acted "willfully" and accordingly met the second requirement of section 6672. It defined "willful action" as "voluntary, conscious and intentional—as opposed to accidental—decisions not to remit funds properly withheld to the government." There need not be "an evil motive or an intent to defraud." The court specifically held that "the failure to investigate or to correct mismanagement after having notice that withheld taxes have not been remitted to the government is deemed to be willful conduct." Further, the court concluded that payment of employee wages and other debts with the knowledge that the payment of payroll taxes is "late" constitutes willful conduct.

---

[251] Carter v. United States, 717 F. Supp. 188 (S.D.N.Y. 1989).

This case demonstrates that church officers and directors can be *personally liable* for the payment of income taxes and FICA taxes that they fail to withhold, account for, or pay to the government. It does not matter that they serve without compensation, so long as they satisfy the definition of a "responsible person" and act willfully. Many church officers and directors will satisfy the definition of a "responsible person," and such persons can be personally liable for unpaid payroll taxes if they act under the liberal definition of "willfully" described above. Clearly, church leaders must be knowledgeable regarding a church's payroll tax obligations, and insure that such obligations are satisfied.

§ 6-07.09 — Exceeding the Authority of the Board

> *Key point 6-07.09. Church board members may be personally liable for actions they take that exceed the authority vested in them by the church's governing documents.*

Occasionally, it is asserted that the directors of a nonprofit corporation have exceeded their authority or power. Some courts have held that directors of nonprofit corporations have a fiduciary relationship with the members of the corporation that requires them to follow the corporate charter and bylaws. For example, one court held that directors who attempted to amend the bylaws of a nonprofit corporation without the knowledge or approval of the membership violated their fiduciary duty to the corporation: "[I]n seeking to disenfranchise the members of the corporation, some or all of the officers and directors of the corporation failed to meet their fiduciary obligation to the members."

§ 6-07.10 — Loans to Directors

> *Key point 6-07.10. Church board members may be personally liable, under state nonprofit corporation law, for loans they authorize for any officer or director of the church.*

The Model Nonprofit Corporations Act, as well as various other laws under which some churches are incorporated, prohibit the board from making loans (out of corporate funds) to either directors or officers. Directors who vote in favor of such loans can be liable for them in the event that the loan is unauthorized or otherwise impermissible. Church boards must check the state law under which they are incorporated before considering any loans to a minister.

§ 6-08 Immunity Statutes

> *Key point 6-08. State and federal laws provide limited immunity to uncompensated officers and directors of churches and other charities. This means that they cannot be personally liable for their ordinary negligence. However, such laws contain some exceptions. For example, officers and directors may be personally liable for their gross negligence or their willful or wanton misconduct.*

Most states have enacted laws limiting the liability of church officers and directors. In some states, these laws protect all church volunteers. In some cases, the statute may protect only officers and directors of churches that are incorporated under the state's general nonprofit corporation law. The most common type of statute immunizes *uncompensated* directors and officers from legal liability for their ordinary negligence committed within the scope of their official duties. These statutes generally provide no protection for "willful and wanton" conduct or "gross negligence."

"Compensation" ordinarily is defined to exclude reimbursement of travel expenses incurred while serving as a director or officer. Churches that compensate their directors and officers over and above the reimbursement of travel expenses should reconsider such a policy if they are located in a state that grants limited immunity to uncompensated officers and directors. Obviously, these statutes will not protect ministers who receive compensation from their church.

> *Tip. Churches should consider adopting an appropriate resolution clarifying that a minister's annual compensation package is for ministerial duties rendered to the church, and not for any duties on the church board. Like any other church officer or director, the minister serves without compensation. Such a provision, if adopted, might qualify the minister for protection under the legal immunity law. It is worth serious consideration.*

Statutes immunizing the directors and officers of nonprofit organizations from liability do not prevent the organization itself from being sued on the basis of the negligence of an officer or director. The immunity statutes only protect the officers or directors themselves. Many of the immunity statutes apply only to the directors and officers of organizations exempt from federal income tax under section 501(c) of the Internal Revenue Code. Some of them appear to apply only to *incorporated* organizations.

Why have states enacted such laws? The primary reason is to encourage persons to serve as directors of nonprofit organizations. In the past, many qualified individuals have declined to serve as directors of such organizations out of a fear of legal liability. The immunity statutes respond directly to this concern by providing directors of nonprofit organizations with limited immunity from legal liability.

> *Example. A Colorado court ruled that a denominational agency could be sued by a woman with whom a minister had sexual contacts, and that a state statute providing limited immunity to uncompensated officers and directors of nonprofit corporations was not a defense.[252] The statute specifies, "No member of the board of directors of a nonprofit corporation or nonprofit organization shall be held liable for actions taken or omissions made in the performance of his duties as a board member except for wanton and willful acts or omissions."[253] The court concluded that this provision did not apply in this case, since there was no evidence that the agency "accomplished its work through unpaid volunteers."*

> *Example. The Minnesota Supreme Court rejected the argument that a state limited immunity statute only protected board members when acting collectively as a board.[254] It acknowledged that "it is a longstanding tenet of corporation law that a member of the board has no authority to act individually unless specifically authorized by the corporate bylaws or articles of incorporation." However, the court noted that the statute protects more than directors. It also protects officers, trustees, members, and agents, and these individuals (unlike directors) can act individually rather than collectively. The court concluded that "a director acting outside the specific scope of his or her duty as a member of the board will receive the statute's protection so long as the director is acting on behalf of the nonprofit corporation."*

> *Example. A New York court ruled that a "charitable immunity" law granting limited legal immunity to the uncompensated directors of a nonprofit organization did not protect a church's trustees from liability for the sexual misconduct of their minister. An unincorporated church and its trustees were sued as a result of their minister's alleged rape of a number of minor females in the church. Among other*

---

[252] Winkler v. Rocky Mouton Conference, 923 P.2d 152 (Colo. App. 1995).
[253] Colo. Rev. Stat. § 13-21-116.
[254] Rehn v. Fischley, 557 N.W.2d 328 (Minn. 1997).

things, the lawsuit alleged that the church and trustees were responsible for the victims' suffering as a result of their "negligent supervision" of the minister's actions. In their defense, the trustees relied on a state law granting uncompensated directors of nonprofit organizations limited immunity from liability for their actions. The court rejected this defense for two reasons: "The [trustees] did not present presumptive evidence of uncompensated status in that they did not present an affidavit of a chief financial officer of the [church]. Further, there is a reasonable probability that the specific conduct of such [trustees] constitutes gross negligence. If the [trustees] did act as the [victims] allege, they may be found to have proceeded in reckless disregard of the consequences of their acts."[255]

Example. The Wisconsin Supreme Court ruled that a state law providing limited immunity to the uncompensated officers and directors of nonprofit corporations only provided protection for acts arising from one's status as an officer or director.[256] A church-sponsored relief agency needed some plumbing work done. Its director negotiated and signed a contract with a plumbing company. The name of the relief agency was mentioned prominently in the contract, as was the fact that the director was signing in his capacity as director

---

Gross Negligence

Church leaders should be familiar with the concept of gross negligence, for the following three reasons:

(1) Punitive damages. Courts can award "punitive damages" for conduct that amounts to gross negligence. Punitive damages are damages awarded by a jury "in addition to compensation for a loss sustained, in order to punish, and make an example of, the wrongdoer." They are awarded when a person's conduct is particularly reprehensible and outrageous. This does not necessarily mean intentional misconduct. Punitive damages often are associated with reckless conduct or conduct creating a high risk of harm. To illustrate, in one case a punitive damage award was based on the fact that church officials repeatedly and knowingly placed a priest in situations where he could sexually abuse boys and then failed to supervise him and disclose his sexual problem. Clearly, church officials did not intend for the priest to molest anyone. But, under the circumstances, the jury concluded that the church's actions were sufficiently reckless to justify an award of punitive damages. Church leaders must understand that reckless inattention to risks can lead to punitive damages, and that such damages may not be covered by the church's liability insurance policy. It is critical to note that many church insurance policies exclude punitive damages. This means that a jury award of punitive damages represents a potentially uninsured risk. Accordingly, it is critical for church leaders to understand the basis for punitive damages, and to avoid behavior which might be viewed as grossly negligent.

(2) Loss of limited immunity under state law. State and federal laws provide uncompensated officers and directors of nonprofit corporations (including churches) with immunity from legal liability for their ordinary negligence. This is an important protection. However, such laws do not protect officers and directors from liability for their gross negligence.

(3) Personal liability. Church leaders who are guilty of gross negligence are more likely to be sued personally than if their behavior is merely negligent. Indifference by church leaders to information that clearly demonstrates improper behavior by a staff member or volunteer worker can be viewed by a court as gross negligence, and this will make it more likely that the church leaders will be sued personally.

---

[255] Karen S. v. Streiferdt, 568 N.Y.S.2d 946 (A.D. 1 Dept. 1991).
[256] Benjamin Plumbing, Inc. v. Barnes, 470 N.W.2d 888 (Wis. 1991).

Table 6-3
Personal Liability of Church Officers, Directors, and Trustees

theory of liability	definition	examples
tort	conduct that injures another's person or property	• negligent operation of a church vehicle • negligent supervision of church workers and activities • copyright infringement • wrongful termination of employees
contract	executing a contract without authorization, or with authorization but without any indication of a representative capacity	• a church board member signs a contract without indicating he is signing in a representative capacity, on behalf of a named church • a church board member signs a contract without authorization
breach of the fiduciary duty of care	every officer or director has a fiduciary duty of due care to the corporation; a breach of this duty can result in liability	• failure to attend board meetings; question irregularities; review the church's financial records; and dissenting from questionable actions
breach of the fiduciary duty of loyalty	every officer or director has a fiduciary duty of loyalty to the corporation; a breach of this duty can result in liability	• a church board votes in favor of a contract with a member of the board (unless the conflict is fully disclosed, the contract is fair to the church, and is approved by a disinterested majority of the board)
violation of trust terms	board members may be liable for violating or disregarding the terms of an express trust	• a donor contributes money to a church's building fund, and the church board approves the use of the fund for other purposes unrelated to a building (cf. cy pres doctrine)
securities law	selling securities without registering as an agent (if required by state law); engaging in fraudulent activities in the offer or sale of church securities	• church board members sell church securities to members of the congregation without registering as an agent under state securities law • church board members make unfounded guarantees in the sale of church securities. • church board members make material misrepresentations of fact, or fail to disclose material facts, in the offer or sale of church securities
wrongful discharge of employees	dismissing without "good cause" an employee hired for a definite term of employment prior to the expiration of the term; dismissing an "at will" employee in violation of public policy	• a church board dismisses an employee prior to the end of a 2-year term, without good cause • a church board dismisses an "at will" employee for refusing to backdate tax records
willful failure to withhold taxes	section 6672 of the Internal Revenue Code imposes a 100 percent penalty upon any "responsible person" who willfully fails to withhold federal payroll taxes, or who withholds them but fails to pay them over to the government	• a church treasurer uses withheld federal taxes to meet a church's payroll obligations
exceeding the authority of the board	church board members may be accountable for taking action they are not authorized to perform	• a church board purchases real estate on behalf of the church (without congregational approval as required by the church charter)
loans to directors	many state nonprofit corporation laws specify that church board members may be liable for approving a loan to an officer or director	• a church board approves a $15,000 loan to the senior minister to enable him to make the down payment on a home

VOLUNTEER PROTECTION ACT

In 1997 Congress enacted the Volunteer Protection Act (42 U.S.C. § 14501) based on the following findings: (1) the willingness of volunteers to offer their services is deterred by the potential for liability actions against them; (2) as a result, many nonprofit organizations have been adversely affected by the withdrawal of volunteers from boards of directors and service in other capacities; and (3) due to high liability costs and unwarranted litigation costs, volunteers and nonprofit organizations face higher costs in purchasing insurance, through interstate insurance markets, to cover their activities.

The Act clarifies that it "preempts the laws of any state to the extent that such laws are inconsistent with this [Act] except that this [Act] shall not preempt any state law that provides additional protection from liability relating to volunteers or to any category of volunteers in the performance of services for a nonprofit organization or governmental entity."

Here is a summary of the Act's main provisions:

• No volunteer of a nonprofit organization shall be liable for harm caused by an act or omission of the volunteer on behalf of the organization or entity if—(1) the volunteer was acting within the scope of the volunteer's responsibilities in the nonprofit organization or governmental entity at the time of the act or omission; (2) if appropriate or required, the volunteer was properly licensed, certified, or authorized by the appropriate authorities for the activities or practice in the state in which the harm occurred, where the activities were or practice was undertaken within the scope of the volunteer's responsibilities in the nonprofit organization or governmental entity; (3) the harm was not caused by willful or criminal misconduct, gross negligence, reckless misconduct, or a conscious, flagrant indifference to the rights or safety of the individual harmed by the volunteer; and (4) the harm was not caused by the volunteer operating a motor vehicle, vessel, aircraft, or other vehicle for which the state requires the operator or the owner of the vehicle, craft, or vessel to possess an operator's license or obtain insurance.

• The Act provides no protection to nonprofit organizations themselves.

• Punitive damages may not be awarded against a volunteer unless the victim proves by clear and convincing evidence that the harm was caused by the volunteer's willful or "criminal misconduct, or a conscious, flagrant indifference to the rights or safety of the individual harmed."

of the agency. The agency was unable to pay the plumbing bill, and the plumbing company sued the director personally. The director claimed that he was immune from liability on the basis of a state law protecting uncompensated officers and directors of nonprofit corporations for "monetary liabilities arising from a breach of, or failure to perform, any duty resulting solely from his or her status as a director or officer." The court disagreed. It noted that a director "cannot be granted immunity unless his liability related solely to his status as a director." In this case, however, the director's contractual liability to the plumbing company "stems from his position as an agent to a partially disclosed corporate principal and not from his status as a director."

§ 6-08.1 — Directors and Officers Insurance

Key point 6-08.1. *Directors and officers insurance provides coverage for various acts committed by board members in the course of their official duties. Such insurance may provide coverage for claims that are excluded under a church's general liability policy. It also may cover acts not protected by the federal and state limited immunity laws.*

Should churches obtain "directors and officers" insurance coverage for the members of their board? Does the enactment of the Volunteer Protection Act (and corresponding state laws) make such insurance unnecessary? Not at all. The legal protection provided by these laws is not absolute. They do not apply if a board member receives any form of compensation (other than travel expense reimbursements), and they do not apply if a board member is accused of gross negligence. Directors and officers insurance will provide coverage for such exceptions. Just as importantly, the insurance company is responsible for providing legal representation in the event a director or officer is sued directly.

Example. *An Alabama court ruled that a church's "directors and officers" insurance policy covered a lawsuit brought against a pastor for improperly obtaining money from an elderly member.[257] The daughter of an elderly church member was appointed guardian of her mother's property. The daughter sued the minister of her mother's church, claiming that he improperly obtained funds from her mother by means of conversion, fraud, and undue influence. The minister notified the church's "directors and officers" insurer of the lawsuit and asked the insurer to provide him with a legal defense. The insurer asked a court to determine whether or not the minister's actions were covered under the insurance policy. The court concluded that the insurer had a legal duty to provide the minister with a defense of the lawsuit. It noted that the church's insurance policy provided coverage for officers and directors (including the minister in this case) in any lawsuit brought against them by reason of alleged dishonesty on their part unless a court determined that the officer or director acted with deliberate dishonesty. Since the minister had not yet been found guilty of "deliberate dishonesty," he was covered under the insurance policy. The court acknowledged that if the minister was found to have acted with deliberate dishonesty in the daughter's lawsuit, the insurer would have no duty to pay any portion of the judgment or verdict.*

§ 6-09   Members — In General

It is often important to determine which persons comprise the membership of a church since the church's charter and bylaws, and in some cases state nonprofit corporation law, generally vest considerable authority in the members.[258] In congregational churches, the members typically elect and depose directors and ministers, authorize the purchase and sale of property, adopt and amend the charter or bylaws, and approve budgets. Church members in hierarchical churches typically possess some or all of these powers.

---

[257] Graham v. Preferred Abstainers Insurance Company, 689 So.2d 188 (Ala. App. 1997).

[258] *See generally* W. TORPEY, JUDICIAL DOCTRINES OF RELIGIOUS RIGHTS IN AMERICA (1948) (while this text is obsolete in most respects, it presents a principled analysis that is of continuing utility); Bernard, *Churches, Members and the Role of the Courts: Toward a Contractual Analysis*, 51 NOTRE DAME LAWYER 545 (1976) (provides useful suggestions regarding judicial involvement in church membership determinations); Ellman, *Driven from the Tribunal: Judicial Resolution of Internal Church Disputes*, 69 CALIF. L. REV. 1380 (1981) (contending that churches must engage in limited involvement in internal church disputes, ideally through construction of doctrinally-neutral internal church "contractual" documents).

§ 6-09.1 — Selection and Qualifications

Key point 6-09.1. *The procedure for selecting members generally is defined by a church's governing documents. The civil courts have refrained from resolving disputes over the selection of members on the ground that the first amendment guaranty of religious freedom prevents them from deciding whether or not individuals satisfy the requirements for church membership.*

The essence of the relation between members and a church consists of an agreement between the parties, a profession of faith, adherence to the doctrines of the church, and submission to its government.[259] The membership of a church is typically determined by reference to the church charter and bylaws and to any applicable state corporation law. It is well-settled that (1) the right to determine the qualifications for membership belongs to the church, (2) a determination as to who are "members in good standing" is an ecclesiastical question relating to the government and discipline of a church, and (3) a church's decision about either matter is binding on the courts.[260]

To illustrate, when two purported members of a church sought an accounting of church funds and the church defended its noncompliance on the ground that the plaintiffs were not members in good standing, a court deferred to the church's determination that the plaintiffs were not members and dismissed the case.[261] The court observed that membership in a religious society is an ecclesiastical matter to be determined by the church, not the courts. The United States Supreme Court has stated the general rule of judicial nonintervention in the ecclesiastical affairs of churches, including membership determinations, as follows:

> But it is a very different thing where a subject matter of dispute, strictly and purely ecclesiastical in its character—a matter over which the civil courts exercise no jurisdiction—a matter which concerns theological controversy, church discipline, ecclesiastical government, or the conformity of the members of the church to the standard of morals required of them—becomes the subject of its action. It may be said here, also, that no jurisdiction has been conferred on the tribunal to try the particular case before it, or that, in its judgment, it exceeds the powers conferred upon it, or that the laws of the church do not authorize the particular form of proceeding adopted; and, in a sense often used in the courts, all of those may be said to be questions of jurisdiction. But it is easy to see that if the civil courts are to inquire into all these matters, the whole subject of the doctrinal theology, the usages and customs, the written laws, and fundamental organization of every religious denomination may, and must, be examined into with minuteness and care, for they would become, in almost every case, the criteria by which the validity of the ecclesiastical decree would be determined in the civil court.[262]

The Supreme Court has also held that religious freedom encompasses the "power of [religious bodies] to decide for themselves, free from state interference, matters of church government as well as those of faith and

---

[259] Freshour v. King, 345 P.2d 689 (Kan. 1959); Henson v. Payne, 302 S.W.2d 44 (Mo. 1956); Second Baptist Church v. Mount Zion Baptist Church, 466 P.2d 212 (Nev. 1970); Western Conference of Original Free Will Baptists v. Creech, 123 S.E.2d 619 (N.C. 1962).

[260] Rodyk v. Ukrainian Autocephalic Orthodox Church, 296 N.Y.S.2d 496 (1968), *aff'd*, 328 N.Y.S.2d 685 (1972). *See also* Stewart v. Jarriel, 59 S.E.2d 368 (Ga. 1950); Fast v. Smyth, 527 S.W.2d 673, 676 (Mo. 1975) ("the determination of who are qualified members of a church is an ecclesiastical matter"); Eisenberg v. Fauer, 200 N.Y.S.2d 749 (1960); Presbytery of Beaver-Butler v. Middlesex, 489 A.2d 1317 (Pa. 1985) ("the view of a court as to who are heretics among warring sects is worth nothing, and must count as nothing if our cherished diversity of religious views is to prevail").

[261] Taylor v. New York Annual Conference of the African Methodist Episcopal Church, 115 N.Y.S.2d 62 (1952).

[262] Watson v. Jones, 80 U.S. 679, 733-34 (1871).

doctrine."[263] And, the Court has stated that "religious controversies are not the proper subject of civil court inquiry."[264] This rule is often followed even when it is alleged that a church deviated from its own charter or bylaws in making a membership determination.[265]

A number of courts, however, have been willing to review church determinations involving members as long as no "strictly and purely ecclesiastical" question is presented. For example, some courts have been willing to review such determinations (1) if the church determination was the product of fraud or collusion;[266] (2) if civil, contract, or property rights of members are affected;[267] or (3) if a legitimate dispute occurs over the meaning of the criteria for membership.[268] The issue of judicial intervention in internal church disputes involving membership determinations is covered later in this section.

Example. A Pennsylvania court refused to order church officials to explain why they refused to admit a person as a member. A member asked his church to transfer his membership to another church pursuant to an established church procedure. The minister of the second church rejected the transfer of membership without explanation. The member filed a lawsuit asking a court to order church officials to "show cause" why he should not be admitted as a member. A state appeals court ruled that the civil courts are bound by the first amendment guaranty of religious freedom to accept the decisions of religious organizations on matters of "discipline, faith, internal organization, and ecclesiastical rule, custom, and law." On the other hand, the civil courts can intervene in church disputes that do not implicate such concerns. The court concluded that this case, which involved an individual's right to membership in a church, was the kind of ecclesiastical matter that was beyond the authority of the civil courts to resolve. It observed, "[M]embership in a congregation is purely an ecclesiastical matter subject to the church rules and controlled by the decisions of the appropriate church tribunals in so far as they do not contravene the civil law. The heart of [the member's] case is that he desires to become a member in [another church]. Accordingly, it is clear that this case involves a purely ecclesiastical matter."[269]

Example. A Pennsylvania court ruled that it was barred by the first amendment from resolving a lawsuit by an individual who wanted to be admitted as a member of a church. The court relied upon

[263] Kedroff v. St. Nicholas Cathedral, 344 U.S. 94, 116 (1952).
[264] Serbian Eastern Orthodox Diocese v. Milivojevich, 426 U.S. 696, 713 (1976).
[265] Evans v. Shiloh Baptist Church, 77 A.2d 160 (Md. 1950); Jenkins v. New Shiloh Baptist Church, 56 A.2d 788 (Md. 1948).
[266] Gonzalez v. Roman Catholic Archbishop, 280 U.S. 1 (1929). The United States Supreme Court has stated that "arbitrariness" is no longer a basis for civil court review of the ecclesiastical determinations of churches. Serbian Eastern Orthodox Diocese v. Milivojevich, 426 U.S. 696 (1976).
[267] Carden v. La Grone, 169 S.E.2d 168, 172 (Ga. 1969) ("a court of equity will not interfere with the internal management of a religious society where property rights are not involved"); Third Missionary Baptist Church v. Garrett, 158 N.W.2d 771, 776 (Iowa 1968) ("[i]t is a general rule recognized here and in foreign jurisdictions that ordinarily the courts have no jurisdiction over, and no concern with, purely ecclesiastical questions and controversies, including membership in a church organization, but they do have jurisdiction as to civil, contract, and property rights which are involved in or arise from a church controversy"); Mitchell v. Albanian Orthodox Diocese, 244 N.E.2d 276, 278-79 (Mass. 1969) ("courts do not interfere in a controversy that is exclusively or primarily of an ecclesiastical nature. Where civil or property rights or the construction of legal instruments are involved, however, the courts have been less reluctant to interfere"); Fast v. Smyth, 527 S.W.2d 673, 676 (Mo. 1975) ("the determination of who are qualified members of a church is an ecclesiastical matter. There is, however, a well recognized exception to this general rule in this state. Civil courts will review ecclesiastical matters where necessary to protect the property, contracts, or civil rights of members").
[268] Smith v. Riley, 424 So.2d 1166 (La. App. 1982) (in the absence of any evidence to the contrary, the term *members* as used in a church charter includes females); Second Baptist Church v. Mount Zion Baptist Church, 466 P.2d 212 (Nev. 1970) (where church bylaws stipulated that failure to attend church or make financial contributions "without a reasonable excuse" resulted in termination of membership, the court resolved church dispute concerning the meaning of "without a reasonable excuse"); Honey Creek Regular Baptist Church v. Wilson, 92 N.E.2d 419 (Ohio 1950) (court agreed to hear church dispute concerning the issue of whether "extending the right hand of fellowship" was a requirement of church membership).
[269] Gundlach v. Laister, 625 A.2d 706 (Pa. Cmwlth. 1993).

what it called the "deference rule" which "provides that civil courts are bound to accept the decisions of the highest judicatories of a religious organization of hierarchical polity on matters of discipline, faith, internal organization, or ecclesiastical rule, custom or law."[270]

§ 6-09.2 — Authority

Key point 6-09.2. *Church members have such legal authority as is vested in them by their church's governing documents, and in some cases by state nonprofit corporation law.*

In churches with a congregational form of government, the general rule is that a majority of the members represent the church and have the right to manage its affairs and to control its property for the use and benefit of the church, and that the law will protect such authority at least as it relates to civil, contract, or property rights.[271] One court has stated the rule as follows: "[T]he courts will give effect to the action of the majority of members of a congregational or independent religious organization . . . insofar as regards civil or property rights when they have acted in harmony with church rules, customs and practices at a meeting properly called."[272]

The United States Supreme Court similarly has observed that "[m]ajority rule is generally employed in the governance of religious societies."[273] Other courts have held that a majority of a church's membership has the authority to sell a parsonage and acquire a new one;[274] to oust a minority group that had wrongfully and violently seized possession of the church building;[275] to call a meeting of the church;[276] to expel members;[277] to disaffiliate from one denomination and associate with another;[278] to adopt bylaws;[279] to authorize church activity and direct or control disposition of church property;[280] and to select and remove a minister.[281] The general authority possessed by the members of a congregational church exists whether the church is incorporated or unincorporated. However, state corporate law may grant the members of an incorporated church additional specific powers. For example, the Model Nonprofit Corporation Act, which has been adopted in whole or in part in a majority of states, specifies that "all books and records of a corporation may be inspected by any member, or his agent or attorney, for any proper purpose at any reasonable time."[282]

The authority of a majority of members in a church with a congregational form of government is limited. It is often stated that church members have only such authority as is vested in them by the church's charter or bylaws or by state corporation law. In a leading case, a court rejected a demand by several church members that their church conduct a meeting at which the pastor and trustees would give a complete ac-

---

[270] In re St. Clement's Church, 687 A.2d 11 (Pa. Common. 1996).

[271] Mitchell v. Dickey, 173 S.E.2d 695 (Ga. 1970); Wright v. Smith, 124 N.E.2d 363 (Ill. 1955); McHargue v. Feltner, 325 S.W.2d 349 (Ky. 1959).

[272] Willis v. Davis, 323 S.W.2d 847, 849 (Ky. 1959).

[273] Jones v. Wolf, 443 U.S. 595, 607 (1979).

[274] McHargue v. Feltner, 325 S.W.2d 349 (Ky. 1959).

[275] Mitchell v. Dickey, 173 S.E.2d 695 (Ga. 1970).

[276] Willis v. Davis, 323 S.W.2d 847 (Ky. 1959).

[277] Smith v. Lewis, 578 S.W.2d 169 (Tex. App. 1979); Moorman v. Goodman, 157 A.2d 519 (N.J. 1960).

[278] Foss v. Dykstra, 342 N.W.2d 220 (S.D. 1983); Douglass v. First Baptist Church, 287 P.2d 965 (Colo. 1955).

[279] First Baptist Church v. State of Ohio, 591 F. Supp. 676 (S.D. Ohio 1983); Lewis v. Wolfe, 413 S.W.2d 314 (Mo. 1967).

[280] Mt. Jezreel Christians Without a Home v. Board of Trustees of Mount Jezreel Baptist Church, 582 A.2d 237 (D.C. App. 1990) ("[w]e therefore hold that, as a general principle, bona fide members of a church have standing to bring suit as trust beneficiaries when there is a dispute over the use or disposition of church property"); Pilgrim Evangelical v. Lutheran Church-Missouri Synod Foundation, 661 S.W.2d 833 (Mo. App. 1983); Blair v. Blair, 396 S.E.2d 374 (S.C. App. 1990).

[281] LeBlanc v. Davis, 432 So.2d 239 (La. 1983).

[282] MODEL NONPROFIT CORPORATION ACT § 25.

counting of the affairs of the church, since neither the church's charter nor bylaws conferred such authority upon the membership. The court concluded that the members "have only such powers, if any, in the management of the affairs of the corporation as may be conferred upon them by the charter and bylaws."[283] On the other hand, while no court has reached this conclusion, it would seem reasonable to regard a church's bylaws, like the United States Constitution, as a "delegated powers" instrument. The tenth amendment to the Constitution states that "[t]he powers not delegated to the United States by the Constitution, nor prohibited by it to the States, are reserved to the States, respectively, or to the people." In essence, the citizens have delegated certain powers to the federal government in the Constitution, reserving unto themselves all powers not specifically delegated. Similarly, it could be said that the members who organize a church delegate various powers to the church and its officers, directors, and committees, and that any powers not specifically delegated are reserved unto the membership.

The charter and bylaws of many congregational churches limit the authority of a simple majority of members. For example, some require that sales or purchases of property, elections of ministers, and amendments to the charter or bylaws be by a two-thirds or three-fourths vote of the church membership.

The courts generally will disregard the authority of a church's members when property rights or civil liberties protected under state or federal law are violated. As one court has observed, the rights that exist by virtue of state or federal law "cannot be overridden by a majority rule of any organization—church or otherwise."[284]

Members are under no compulsion to adhere to the tenets of their church, but they cannot impose their beliefs upon a majority that rejects them.[285] Members of course have the right to withdraw from one church and join another.[286] But members who withdraw or whose membership is terminated by action of the church no longer possess any authority. They have no interest in church property, and they cannot represent members in any legal action against the church.[287]

It is often stated that when persons become a member of a church, they do so upon the condition of submission to its ecclesiastical jurisdiction, and however much they may be dissatisfied with the exercise of that jurisdiction, they have no right to invoke the supervisory power of a civil court so long as their property, contract, or civil rights are not affected.[288] Nor may a member deny the existence of a church's bylaws.[289]

Church members generally have no personal interest in church property since title ordinarily is vested in the trustees of unincorporated churches and in the church itself if the church is incorporated. If a church acquires property by a deed naming the church as grantee, the conveyance is to the church and constitutes no benefit or interest to any individual member.[290] Prior to 1969 the courts commonly ruled that church property was held in trust for the use and benefit of those members adhering to the original tenets of the church, and thus a majority of the members could not abandon the tenets of the church and retain the right to use the

---

[283] First Baptist Church v. State of Ohio, 591 F. Supp. 676 (S.D. Ohio 1983); Evans v. Shiloh Baptist Church, 77 A.2d 160, 163 (Md. 1950). *See also* Katz v. Singerman, 127 So.2d 515 (La. 1961).

[284] Stansberry v. McCarty, 149 N.E.2d 683, 686 (Ind. 1958). *See also* Serbian Eastern Orthodox Diocese v. Ocokoljich, 219 N.E.2d 343 (Ill. 1966).

[285] Katz v. Singerman, 127 So.2d 515 (La. 1961).

[286] Trett v. Lambeth, 195 S.W.2d 524 (Mo. 1946); Brady v. Reiner, 198 S.E.2d 812 (W. Va. 1973).

[287] Stewart v. Jarriel, 59 S.E.2d 368 (Ga. 1950); Brady v. Reiner, 198 S.E.2d 812 (W. Va. 1973).

[288] Stewart v. Jarriel, 59 S.E.2d 368 (Ga. 1950).

[289] State ex rel. Morrow v. Hill, 364 N.E.2d 1156 (Ohio 1977).

[290] Presbytery of Cimarron v. Westminster Presbyterian Church, 515 P.2d 211 (Okla. 1973).

church's property so long as a single member adhered to the original doctrines of the church.[291] This rule was abolished by the United States Supreme Court in 1969.[292]

Members of churches affiliated with an ecclesiastical hierarchy generally are subject to the same limitations on their authority discussed above in connection with members of congregational churches, but in addition they are limited by the bylaws and tribunals of the parent denomination.[293]

Example. A Georgia court ruled that church members could obtain a court order blocking a church's planned disposition of its assets, and appointing a receiver to oversee the church's property. A church board (consisting of the pastor, the pastor's son-in-law, and a third person) decided to sell the church property for $725,000 because of low attendance. The pastor was to receive a lump sum gift of $100,000 out of these proceeds, and title to the parsonage. The remaining sale proceeds, after payment of debts, were to be used for religious activities with the pastor having control of the funds. Some of the church members brought a lawsuit against the pastor and the church in which they sought the appointment of a receiver to take control of the church's assets. The pastor opposed this action, claiming that (1) the court's exercise of jurisdiction over this dispute was prohibited by the first amendment's guaranty of religious freedom; (2) the members who brought the lawsuit lacked "standing" to do so since they did not represent a majority of the church's members; and (3) the first amendment prohibits the appointment of a receiver over church assets. The appeals court rejected all of these claims. The court concluded that the trial court's exercise of jurisdiction over this dispute was permissible since "the property dispute here was capable of resolution by reference to neutral principles of law . . . without infringing upon any first amendment values." Next, the court rejected the pastor's claim that the members who brought the lawsuit lacked "standing" to do so. It noted that the members who brought the lawsuit "had standing in this action alleging a diversion of the church property from the purpose for which the church and its assets had been devoted." In rejecting the pastor's contention that the first amendment prohibits a civil court from appointing a receiver over church assets, the court observed, "Under [state] law the superior court has full power to liquidate the assets and affairs of a nonprofit corporation when it is established that the acts of the directors or those in control of the corporation are illegal or fraudulent, the assets are being misapplied or wasted, or where the corporation is unable to carry out its purposes."[294]

§ 6-10   Members — Discipline and Dismissal

Do the civil courts have the authority to review internal church determinations regarding the discipline or dismissal of members? Some courts have strictly avoided any intervention in such disputes, while others have been willing to intervene in limited circumstances. This section will review representative decisions of both positions.

---

[291] Wright v. Smith, 124 N.E.2d 363,365 (Ill. 1955) ("[c]ourts will raise and enforce an implied trust so that the majority faction cannot effect a fundamental change of doctrine").

[292] In Presbyterian Church in the United States v. Mary Elizabeth Blue Hull Memorial Presbyterian Church, 393 U.S. 440 (1969), the Supreme Court held that civil courts could no longer construe or apply religious doctrine in resolving church property disputes. *See generally* chapter 9, *infra.*

[293] Presbytery of Cimarron v. Westminster Presbyterian Church, 515 P.2d 211 (Okla. 1973).

[294] Crocker v. Stevens, 435 S.E.2d 690 (Ga. App. 1993). *But see* Hines v. Turley, 615 N.E.2d 1251 (Ill. App. 1993) (persons who did not satisfy the church bylaws' definition of *member* lacked standing to challenge their church's disposition of assets).

[295] 80 U.S. 679, 722 (1871).

§ 6-10.1 — Judicial Nonintervention

Key point 6-10.1. According to the majority view, the civil courts will not resolve disputes challenging a church's discipline of a member since the first amendment guaranty of religious freedom prevents them from deciding who are members in good standing of a church.

In *Watson v. Jones,*[295] the United States Supreme Court developed a framework for the judicial review of ecclesiastical disputes that has persisted essentially unchanged until today, more than a century later. The Court began its landmark opinion by acknowledging that "religious organizations come before us in the same attitude as other voluntary associations for benevolent or charitable purposes, and their rights of property, or of contract, are equally under the protection of the law, and the actions of their members subject to its restraints." Though recognizing in principle the authority of civil courts to address the "rights of property, or of contract" of ecclesiastical organizations or officers, the Court proceeded to severely limit this authority. Most importantly, the Court held that "whenever the *questions of discipline, or of faith, of ecclesiastical rule, custom, or law* have been decided by the highest church judicatory to which the matter has been carried, the legal tribunals must accept such decisions as final, and as binding on them . . . ."

In 1872, one year after the *Watson* decision, the Supreme Court emphasized that it had "*no power to revise or question ordinary acts of church discipline,* or of excision from membership," nor to "decide who ought to be members of the church, nor whether the excommunicated have been regularly or irregularly cut off."[296] Many courts have followed this rule of judicial "non-intervention," concluding that the discipline and dismissal of church members is exclusively a matter of ecclesiastical concern and thus the civil courts are without authority to review such determinations. This position generally is based upon the first amendment guarantees of religious freedom and the nonestablishment of religion, or upon the fact that by joining the church a member expressly or implicitly consents to the authority of the church to expel members.[297] As noted in the preceding section, the United States Supreme Court has held that all who unite themselves with a religious organization do so with implied consent to its bylaws and procedures.[298] Another court has noted, "A party having voluntarily assented to becoming a member of the local church thereby subjects himself to the existing rules and procedures of said church and cannot deny their existence."[299] It is therefore held that a church may promulgate rules governing the expulsion or excommunication of its members, and such rules bind the church's members.

There is little doubt that the civil courts are now required to accept the determinations of *hierarchical churches* concerning ecclesiastical discipline. In 1976, the United States Supreme Court ruled that

the first and fourteenth amendments permit hierarchical religious organizations to establish their own rules and regulations for internal discipline and government, and to create tribunals for adjudicating disputes over these matters. When this choice is exercised and ecclesiastical tribunals are created to decide disputes over the government and direction of subordinate bodies, the Constitution requires that civil courts accept their decisions as binding upon them.[300]

---

[296] Bouldin v. Alexander, 82 U.S. (15 Wall.) 131, 139-40 (1872) (emphasis added).

[297] *See generally* Nunn v. Black, 506 F. Supp. 444 (W.D. Va. 1981), *aff'd*, 661 F.2d 925 (4th Cir. 1981), *cert. denied*, 102 S. Ct. 1008 (1982); Simpson v. Wells Lamont Corp., 494 F.2d 490 (5th Cir. 1974); Konkel v. Metropolitan Baptist Church, Inc., 572 P.2d 99 (Ariz. 1977); Macedonia Baptist Foundation v. Singleton, 379 So.2d 269 (La. 1979); St. John's Creek Catholic Hungarian Russian Orthodox Church v. Fedak, 213 A.2d 651 (N.J. 1965), *rev'd on other grounds*, 233 A.2d 663 (N.J. 1967).

[298] Watson v. Jones, 80 U.S. 679, 729 (1871).

[299] State ex rel. Morrow v. Hill, 364 N.E.2d 1156, 1159 (Ohio 1977).

[300] Serbian Eastern Orthodox Diocese v. Milivojevich, 426 U.S. 696, 724-25 (1976).

The Supreme Court further noted, in the same decision, that

> [w]e have concluded that whether or not there is room for "marginal civil court review" under the narrow rubrics of "fraud" or "collusion" when church tribunals act in bad faith for secular purposes, no "arbitrariness" exception—in the sense of an inquiry whether the decisions of the highest ecclesiastical tribunal of a hierarchical church complied with church laws and regulations—is consistent with the constitutional mandate that civil courts are bound to accept the decisions of the highest judicatories of a religious organization of hierarchical polity on matters of discipline, faith, internal organization, or ecclesiastical rule, custom or law. For civil courts to analyze whether the ecclesiastical actions of a church judicatory are in that sense "arbitrary" must inherently entail inquiry into the procedures that canon or ecclesiastical law supposedly require the church adjudicatory to follow, or else into the substantive criteria by which they are supposedly to decide the ecclesiastical question. But this is exactly the inquiry that the first amendment prohibits . . . .[301]

Permitting civil courts to review the membership determinations of hierarchical churches would "undermine the general rule that religious controversies are not the proper subject of civil court inquiry."[302] In other words, the fact that a hierarchical church's determination regarding membership status was "arbitrary" (in the sense that it violated the church's own internal rules) is *not* a justification for civil court review. This extraordinary rule demonstrates the Court's commitment to church autonomy in the context of membership determinations involving hierarchical churches.

Membership determinations based on "fraud or collusion" *may* constitute a basis for marginal civil court review. The Court left this question unanswered. However, it did note that the concepts of *fraud* or *collusion* both involve "church tribunals [acting] in bad faith for secular purposes." It is virtually inconceivable that such a standard could ever be established, particularly in view of the higher evidentiary standard ("clear and convincing evidence") that generally applies to allegations of fraud.

What is a "hierarchical church"? One legal authority defines "hierarchical" and "congregational" churches as follows:

> At least three kinds of internal structure, or "polity," may be discerned: congregational, presbyterial, and episcopal. In the congregational form each local congregation is self-governing. The presbyterial polities are representative, authority being exercised by laymen and ministers organized in an ascending succession of judicatories—presbytery over the session of the local church, synod over the presbytery, and general assembly over all. In the episcopal form power reposes in clerical superiors, such as bishops. Roughly, presbyterial and episcopal polities may be considered hierarchical, as opposed to congregational polities, in which the autonomy of the local congregation is the central principle.[303]

Do the civil courts have authority to review the membership determinations of *congregational churches*? It is here that some courts have limited the Supreme Court's 1976 ruling to hierarchical churches and intervened. Such cases are reviewed in the next section. However, a number of courts have been unwilling to intervene in the membership determinations of congregational churches. Some courts have concluded that

---

[301] *Id.* at 713.
[302] *Id.* at 713.
[303] Note, *Judicial Intervention in Disputes Over the Use of Church Property*, 75 HARV. L. REV. 1142, 1143-44 (1962).

the principle enunciated by the Supreme Court in its 1976 decision in *Milivojevich*[304] is broad enough to apply to congregational churches. For example, a federal district court in Virginia ruled that "[i]t is clear that the fact that the local church may have departed arbitrarily from its established expulsion procedures in removing [members] is of no constitutional consequence [citing *Milivojevich*]."[305] A federal district court in Ohio acknowledged that "[i]t is not altogether clear whether the Supreme Court, if confronted with an internal dispute within a congregational church, would follow the [*Milivojevich*] analysis in all respects."[306] However, the court concluded that "because the 'hands off' policy espoused by the [Supreme Court in *Milivojevich*] is of constitutional dimension, we find it difficult to justify the application of a different standard where a congregational church is involved." The court concluded that (1) church discipline is an ecclesiastical matter in a congregational church,[307] and (2) "unless the internal disciplinary decisions of [a congregational church] are tainted by fraud or collusion, or constitute an extreme violation of the rights of a disciplined member, civil court inquiry with respect to the underlying reasons for church disciplinary action is constitutionally impermissible."

A federal district court in the District of Columbia, while acknowledging that *Milivojevich* involved a hierarchical church, concluded that "[we] can discern no justification for refusing to apply the first amendment analysis and reasoning of the Supreme Court and lower federal court case law involving hierarchical churches to [the membership determinations of a congregational church]."[308] The court noted that membership determinations typically involve standards of membership that are intrinsically ecclesiastical. For example, in this case, the congregational church's bylaws specified that "members are expected . . . to be faithful in all duties essential to the Christian life." The court could not contemplate "any criterion for membership that could more directly implicate ecclesiastical considerations protected by the first amendment . . . ." It concluded that the church's

> *own internal guidelines and procedures must be allowed to dictate what its obligations to its members are without being subject to court intervention.* It is well-settled that religious controversies are not the proper subject of civil court inquiry. *Religious bodies must be free to decide for themselves, free from state interference, matters which pertain to church government, faith and doctrine.*[309]

Some courts have expressed concern that the rule of judicial non-intervention may lead to injustice without a remedy. For example, one Supreme Court justice has observed that "[i]f the civil courts are to be bound by any sheet of parchment bearing the ecclesiastical seal and purporting to be a decree of a church court, they can easily be converted into handmaidens of arbitrary lawlessness."[310] It also has been noted that "[w]hen a faction of the church arrogates authority to itself, disrupts the organization and sets at naught well-defined rules of church order, there is no recourse left for those who desire their rights settled through orderly processes but resort to the courts."[311]

---

[304] *See* note 300, *supra*, and accompanying text.

[305] Nunn v. Black, 506 F. Supp. 444 (W.D. Va. 1981), *aff'd*, 661 F.2d 425 (4th Cir. 1981), *cert. denied*, 454 U.S. 1146 (1982). The court noted that the church apparently was part of a "larger religious society," but that the society had "no structured decision-making process."

[306] First Baptist Church v. State of Ohio, 591 F. Supp. 676 (S.D. Ohio 1983).

[307] The court noted that the Supreme Court in *Milivojevich* observed that "questions of church discipline . . . are at the core of ecclesiastical concern."

[308] Burgess v. Solid Rock Baptist Church, 734 F. Supp. 30 (D.D.C. 1990).

[309] *Id.* at 34 (emphasis in original), quoting Dowd v. Society of St. Columbans, 861 F.2d 761, 764 (1st Cir. 1988).

[310] Serbian Eastern Orthodox Diocese v. Milivojevich, 426 U.S. 696, 727 (1976) (Justice Rehnquist, dissenting). Justice Rehnquist also observed, in the same opinion, that "[t]o make available the coercive powers of civil courts to rubber-stamp ecclesiastical decisions of hierarchical religious associations, when such deference is not accorded similar acts of secular voluntary associations, would . . . itself create far more serious problems under the Establishment Clause." *Id.* at 734.

Example. An Ohio court ruled that it could not resolve a lawsuit brought by several persons challenging their dismissal as members of their church. The members had been dismissed because they sued the church over certain decisions that had been made regarding a construction project. The dismissed members argued that their church membership was a valuable right that was being denied by the church's actions. They also claimed that the church bylaws did not authorize the board to dismiss members for suing the church. The church bylaws did authorize discipline or dismissal on the basis of "immoral or un-Christian conduct," but the dismissed members argued that this language did not extend to lawsuits brought against the church. They stressed that the right to go to court for the redress of grievances is a fundamental civil right that was not specifically restricted by the church bylaws. The church asserted that members who sue the church are guilty of "un-Christian" behavior since "there is a basis in Scripture for the exclusion from church membership of those who take church disputes outside the church for resolution." The court agreed with the church, relying on a 1976 decision of the United States Supreme Court holding that the civil courts must accept the decisions of hierarchical churches concerning discipline of members and clergy. Serbian Eastern Orthodox Diocese v. Milivojevich, 426 U.S. 696 (1976). The Ohio court acknowledged that the church in this case was "congregational" rather than hierarchical in structure, but it concluded that there should be no distinction between congregational and hierarchical churches regarding the effect of their decisions to discipline members. It concluded that "a secular court should not resolve disputes over who can be a member of a particular church regardless of whether that church is hierarchical or congregational."[312]

Example. A church convened a disciplinary hearing to determine the membership status of two sisters accused of fornication. Neither sister attended, and neither sister withdrew her membership in the church. Following the hearing, both sisters received letters from the church informing them that their membership had been terminated. The sisters sued the church and its leaders, claiming that the church's actions in delivering the termination letters and disclosing their contents "to the public" constituted defamation, intentional infliction of emotional distress, and invasion of privacy (public disclosure of private facts). The Oklahoma Supreme Court rejected the sisters' claim that the contents of the termination letters had been disclosed improperly to the public. This allegation was based entirely on a conversation between a church board member and another member of the church. The member asked the board member why the board was "going after" the sisters, and the board member replied that it was on account of "fornication." The court concluded that this comment did not constitute a disclosure of the contents of the letters "to the public," and accordingly there had been no defamation of invasion of privacy. In rejecting the sisters' allegation of emotional distress, the court noted that the evidence "does not suggest that the lay leader's conduct was so extreme and outrageous as to justify submission of the claim to the jury." The court then addressed the sisters' claim that the manner in which the church notified them of the results of the disciplinary proceeding was inappropriate. In rejecting this claim, the court observed, "The church court had proper ecclesiastical cognizance when the letters were delivered. The [sisters] had not withdrawn their membership at the time they received notice of their expulsion. Under the first amendment, the procedural norms which govern the exercise of ecclesiastical cognizance are not subject to a secular court's scrutiny." The court then proceeded to announce an absolute consti-

---

[311] Epperson v. Myers, 58 So.2d 150, 152 (Fla. 1952). *See also* Jones v. Wolf, 443 U.S. 595 (1979) (United States Supreme Court suggests that judicial review is permissible if restricted to an analysis based exclusively on "neutral principles" of law devoid of any interpretation of religious doctrine); I. Ellman, *Driven From the Tribunal: Judicial Resolution of Internal Church Disputes*, 69 CAL. L. REV. 1380 (1981) (arguing that judicial review of internal church disputes should be permitted as long as doctrinal interpretation is not required).

[312] Alexander v. Shiloh Baptist Church, 592 N.E.2d 918 (Ohio Com. Pl. 1991). *Accord* Howard v. Covenant Apostolic Church, Inc., 705 N.E.2d 305 (Ohio App. 1998).

tutional protection for the membership determinations of religious organizations (assuming that the disciplined member has not effectively withdrawn his or her membership): "[The relationship between a church and its members] may be severed freely by a member's positive act at any time. Until it is so terminated, the church has authority to prescribe and follow disciplinary ordinances without fear of interference by the state. The first amendment will protect and shield the religious body from liability for the activities carried on pursuant to the exercise of church discipline. Within the context of church discipline, churches enjoy an absolute privilege from scrutiny by the secular authority." However, the court stressed that this constitutional protection does not apply once a person withdraws his or her church membership.[313]

Example. *The Oklahoma Supreme Court refused to resolve the claim of former church members that their dismissal was improper. The court began its opinion by observing that "the courts will not interfere with the internal affairs of a religious organization except for the protection of civil or property rights." The court concluded that "church membership" was not a "civil or property right" that a civil court could enforce: "A civil or property right that justifies the exercise of civil judicial power has long been distinguished from ecclesiastical or spiritual rights that civil courts do not adjudicate. Civil courts in this country recognize that they have no ecclesiastical jurisdiction, and church disciplinary decisions cannot be reviewed for the purpose of reinstating expelled church members." This is true even if a church fails to follow its own constitution or bylaws in dismissing the members. "The issue of whether the church proceeding complied with church rules or custom in expelling members presents no question for our review on a claim for reinstatement," the court observed. The court concluded, "We cannot decide who ought to be members of the church, nor whether the excommunicated have been justly or unjustly, regularly or irregularly, cut off from the body of the church. We must take the fact of expulsion as conclusive proof that the persons expelled are not now members of the repudiating church; for, whether right or wrong, the act of excommunication must, as to the fact of membership, be law to this court."[314]*

Example. *A Minnesota appeals court ruled that church members could not challenge their dismissal in court. The court noted that the first amendment "precludes judicial review of claims involving core questions of church discipline and internal governance." It concluded that the members' claims all involved core questions of church discipline that it was not able to resolve.[315]*

Example. *A federal court in South Dakota ruled that it had no authority to interfere with a decision by a religious organization to oust some of its members. The court noted that it was "unable to envision any set of facts which would more entangle the court in matters of religious doctrine and practice. The religious communal system present in this case involves more than matters of religious faith, it involves a religious lifestyle. An individual Hutterian colony member's entire life—essentially from cradle to grave—is governed by the church. Any resolution of a property dispute between a colony and its members would require extensive inquiry into religious doctrine and beliefs. It would be a gross violation of the first amendment and Supreme Court mandates for this court to become involved in this dispute."[316]*

---

[313] Hadnot v. Shaw, 826 P.2d 978 (Okla. 1992). The court concluded that churches are immune from the civil "discovery" process with regard to their internal disciplinary proceedings. "Discovery" refers to the process of gathering evidence for civil trial, and includes depositions, interrogatories, and motions to produce documents. The court said that churches are immune from these discovery techniques with regard to internal membership disciplinary proceedings (so long as a member is being disciplined prior to withdrawal from membership).

[314] Fowler v. Bailey, 844 P.2d 141 (Okla. 1992), quoting Shannon v. Frost, 42 Ky. 253 (1842).

[315] Schoenhals v. Mains, 504 N.W.2d 233 (Minn. App. 1993).

[316] Wollman v. Poinsett Hutterian Brethren Church, 844 F. Supp. 539 (D.S.D. 1994).

Example. The Iowa Supreme Court ruled that it lacked the authority to resolve a lawsuit brought by an individual challenging his dismissal from church membership. It concluded that the member's dismissal was an internal church matter over which the civil courts have no jurisdiction. It observed, "The general rule is that civil courts will not interfere in purely ecclesiastical matters, including membership in a church organization or church discipline." The court concluded, "[The church's] decision to excommunicate [the member] was purely ecclesiastical in nature, and therefore we will not interfere with the action. Interfering with the decision would contravene both our history of leaving such matters to ecclesiastical officials and the first and fourteenth amendments of the United States Constitution."[317]

Example. A Louisiana court ruled that it could not resolve a lawsuit brought by dismissed church members who claimed that their church acted improperly in dismissing them for suing the church. The church's pastor dismissed the members for filing a legal action against the church, and removed their names from the membership rolls. The pastor acted pursuant to an "essential tenet" of his church that prohibits Christians from taking other Christians to court. The dismissed members sued their pastor and church, claiming that they had been unjustly and illegally dismissed as members of the church. A state appeals court dismissed the dismissed members' claims, noting that, "It is evident to us that this dispute is rooted in an ecclesial tenet of the [church] which prohibits members from suing fellow church members. Certainly, in civil law the [members] had a right to pursue their [initial lawsuit demand seeking inspection of church records]. However, we hasten to add that the religious repercussions that were set into motion as a result of the exercise of their civil right is another matter beyond the reach of judicial authority. In that light, anything we might consider in [resolving this appeal] would require us to apply, interpret, and comment upon the [church's] tenet against the institution of suits among church members. Based upon the Constitution of the United States . . . and the Constitution of the State of Louisiana . . . such action would constitute an impermissible interference in the ecclesiastical matters of the [church]. We decline to do so."[318]

§ 6-10.2 — "Marginal" Civil Court Review

Key point 6-10.2. According to the minority view, the civil courts may engage in "marginal review" of disputes involving the discipline of a church member, in a few limited circumstances if they can do so without inquiring into religious doctrine or polity. For example, a few courts have been willing to review membership dismissals in one or more of the following limited circumstances: (1) the church interfered with a member's civil, contract, or property rights; (2) the disciplining body lacked authority to act; (3) the church failed to comply with its governing documents; (4) the church's decision was based on fraud or collusion; or (5) interpretation of contested terminology in the church's governing documents.

Many courts have been willing to intervene, in limited circumstances, in controversies regarding church membership determinations. This section will review the grounds for "marginal civil court review" most commonly cited by the courts.

1. INTERFERENCE WITH CIVIL, CONTRACT, OR PROPERTY RIGHTS

Although nearly all courts recognize that they have no authority to review purely ecclesiastical matters, some courts have been willing to review the expulsion of a church member if the expulsion affects "civil,

---

[317] John v. Estate of Hartgerink, 528 N.W.2d 539 (Iowa 1995).
[318] Glass v. First United Pentecostal Church, 676 So.2d 724 (La. App. 1996).

contract, or property rights."[319] The precise meaning of the term *civil, contract, or property rights* is unclear. Some courts interpret it broadly. To illustrate, one court concluded that church membership in itself constitutes a "property right" since church members comprise the body of persons entitled to the use and enjoyment of church properties, and therefore the courts have authority to review all expulsions of church members.[320] Another court concluded that civil rights are involved in the expulsion of church members because of "the humiliation and hurt to personality, the injury to character, reputation, feelings and personal rights and human dignity."[321] Similarly, courts have concluded that (1) the expulsion of a member from a church can constitute a serious emotional deprivation which, when compared to some losses of property or contract rights, can be far more damaging to an individual; (2) the loss of the opportunity to worship in familiar surroundings is a valuable right that deserves the protection of the law; and (3) except in cases involving religious doctrine, there is no reason for treating religious organizations differently from other nonprofit organizations, whose membership expulsions are routinely reviewed by the courts.[322]

Other courts take a far narrower view of civil, contract, or property rights. To illustrate, some courts have ruled that church membership in itself does not constitute a property right,[323] a contract right,[324] or a civil right.[325]

One thing is clear—if the civil courts are powerless to resolve internal church disputes involving doctrine or polity, then they should not be permitted to resolve church membership determinations that are essentially ecclesiastical in nature solely because an aggrieved member asserts that his or her discipline or dismissal violated a civil, contract, or property right. The Supreme Court has acknowledged this principle in the context of clergy dismissals. To illustrate, in 1928 the Supreme Court observed, in a case involving the authority of an ecclesiastical organization to discipline a minister, that "the decisions of the proper church tribunals on matters purely ecclesiastical, *although affecting civil rights*, are accepted in litigation before the secular courts as conclusive, because the parties . . . made them so by contract or otherwise."[326]

In 1952, the Supreme Court in the *Kedroff* ruling[327] reaffirmed its pronouncement in *Watson* that civil courts have no authority to resolve "*questions of discipline, or of faith, or of ecclesiastical rule, custom, or law.*" The Court also noted that "in those cases when the *property right* follows as an incident from decisions of the church custom or law on ecclesiastical issues, the church rule controls. This under our Constitution necessarily follows in order that there may be free exercise of religion."[328] The *Kedroff* decision is important since it specifically holds that alleged deprivations or interference with "property rights" cannot serve as a basis for civil court review of ecclesiastical determinations where "the property right follows as an incident from decisions of the church . . . on ecclesiastical issues."

---

[319] First Baptist Church v. State of Ohio, 591 F. Supp. 676 (S.D. Ohio 1983); Church of God in Christ, Inc. v. Stone, 452 F. Supp. 612 (D. Kan. 1976); Chavis v. Rowe, 459 A.2d 674 (N.J. 1983); African Methodist Episcopal Zion Church v. Union Chapel A.M.E. Zion Church, 308 S.E.2d 73 (N.C. App. 1983). *See generally* Annot., 20 A.L.R.2d 421 (1951).

[320] Randolph v. First Baptist Church, 120 N.E.2d 485 (Ohio 1954).

[321] *Id.* at 489.

[322] Baugh v. Thomas, 265 A.2d 675 (N.J. 1970).

[323] Anderson v. Dowd, 485 S.E.2d 764 (Ga. 1997); Sapp v. Callaway, 69 S.E.2d 734 (Ga. 1952).

[324] Cooper v. Bell, 106 S.W.2d 124 (Ky. 1937).

[325] Stewart v. Jarriel, 59 S.E.2d 368 (Ga. 1950). *Accord* Anderson v. Dowd, 485 S.E.2d 764 (Ga. 1997) (church membership "is not a property right"); Fowler v. Bailey, 844 P.2d 141 (Okla. 1992).

[326] Gonzalez v. Roman Catholic Archbishop, 280 U.S. 1, 16-17 (1928) (Justice Brandeis) (emphasis added).

[327] Kedroff v. St. Nicholas Cathedral, 344 U.S. 94 (1952).

[328] *Id.* (emphasis added).

These two rulings indicate that dismissed or disciplined church members will not be able to have their dismissals reviewed by the civil courts merely because they claim that their civil or property rights have been violated. It will be a rare case in which a disciplined or dismissed church member can demonstrate that his or her "civil, contract, or property rights" were violated by the church's action in a manner that does implicate ecclesiastical concerns. Accordingly, this basis for "marginal civil court review" should be used very sparingly. Further, it has no application to hierarchical churches due to the Supreme Court's 1976 ruling in the *Milivojevich* case. Many of the court rulings that have recognized this basis for civil court review occurred prior to 1976.

2. AUTHORITY OF EXPELLING BODY

Some courts have reviewed membership expulsions for the purpose of determining whether members were expelled by the body authorized to do so by the church charter or bylaws. Thus, when certain members of a church were expelled and sought judicial review of their expulsion, a court ruled, over the protests of the church, that it did have jurisdiction to determine whether the expulsions were the act of an authorized and duly constituted body.[329] Another court, in agreeing to review a church's expulsion of certain members, commented:

> [I]f a decision is reached by some body not having ecclesiastical jurisdiction over the matter, then the civil court would not be bound by that decision. . . . Once [a] determination is made that the proper ecclesiastical authority has acted in its duly constituted manner, no civil review of the substantive ecclesiastical matter may take place as this would be prohibited by Amendments I and XIV of the Federal Constitution . . . .[330]

A federal district court that generally agreed with the rule of judicial non-intervention in church membership determinations nevertheless concluded that "[i]t is not beyond the scope of inquiry for a civil court to determine, in a proper proceeding, whether disciplinary action undertaken by [a church] was approved or executed by that body within the church required to take such action under the church covenant, constitution, or bylaws."[331]

> ***Example.*** *An Ohio court ruled that the first amendment guaranty of religious freedom prevented it from resolving a dispute between a dismissed church member and his former church.[332] However, the court concluded that the civil courts retain jurisdiction "to determine whether the proper authority made the decision about church discipline or policy. . . . So long as the appropriate church authority has made the decision, the issue of whether the church followed its internal procedures is a matter of church governance and discipline into which a secular court is prohibited from inquiring."*

3. COMPLIANCE WITH CHURCH CHARTER AND BYLAWS

In 1872, the Supreme Court commented that "[church trustees] cannot be removed from their trusteeship by a minority of the church society or meeting, without warning, and acting without charges, without citation or trial, and in direct contravention of the church rules."[333] In the years that followed, a number of civil courts intervened in church membership determinations to ensure that they were in compliance with a

---

[329] Brown v. Mt. Olive Baptist Church, 124 N.W.2d 445 (Iowa 1963).
[330] Bowen v. Green, 272 S.E.2d 433, 435 (S.C. 1980).
[331] First Baptist Church v. State of Ohio, 591 F. Supp. 676, 683 (S.D. Ohio 1983).
[332] Howard v. Covenant Apostolic Church, Inc., 705 N.E.2d 305 (Ohio App. 1998).
[333] Bouldin v. Alexander, 82 U.S. (15 Wall.) 131 (1872).

church's charter or bylaws. However, this basis for intervening in such disputes came to an abrupt halt in 1976, at least with respect to *hierarchical churches*, when the Supreme Court announced:

> We have concluded that whether or not there is room for "marginal civil court review" under the narrow rubrics of "fraud" or "collusion" when church tribunals act in bad faith for secular purposes, no "arbitrariness" exception—in the sense of an inquiry whether the decisions of the highest ecclesiastical tribunal of a hierarchical church complied with church laws and regulations—is consistent with the constitutional mandate that civil courts are bound to accept the decisions of the highest judicatories of a religious organization of hierarchical polity on matters of discipline, faith, internal organization, or ecclesiastical rule, custom or law. For civil courts to analyze whether the ecclesiastical actions of a church judicatory are in that sense "arbitrary" must inherently entail inquiry into the procedures that canon or ecclesiastical law supposedly require the church adjudicatory to follow, or else into the substantive criteria by which they are supposedly to decide the ecclesiastical question. But this is exactly the inquiry that the first amendment prohibits . . . .[334]

The Court added that "recognition of . . . an arbitrariness exception would undermine the general rule that religious controversies are not the proper subject of civil court inquiry."[335]

Since 1976, a few courts have intervened in the membership determinations of *congregational churches* to determine whether church rules were followed. For example, where former church members complained that they had been removed improperly from the membership roll at a church meeting convened off of church premises without notice to them of either the location of the meeting or the fact that their dismissal would be discussed, a court concluded that it did have jurisdiction to determine whether the members were expelled in accordance with the charter and bylaws of the church.[336] The court cautioned, however, that if the church had complied with its charter and bylaws, the court would have no jurisdiction to proceed in its review.

Expelled church members' allegations that their expulsions deviated from established church procedures have also been reviewed by the courts in the following contexts: (1) members who allegedly were ineligible to vote according to church bylaws were permitted to vote for the expulsion of certain members;[337] (2) a pastor conducted a church meeting without prior notice, and, without a hearing of any kind, members present voted to expel an opposing faction from membership;[338] and (3) members present at a special meeting for which no prior notice had been given voted to summarily expel all members of the church who identified themselves, through attendance or support, with any other church.[339]

Most of the court rulings recognizing noncompliance by a church with its own internal rules as a basis for civil court review either predate the Supreme Court's 1976 ruling in the *Milivojevich* case, or involve congregational churches. Clearly, the civil courts no longer have the authority, since 1976, to review the membership determinations of hierarchical churches on the basis of alleged noncompliance with internal church rules. And, some courts view the constitutional analysis set forth in the *Milivojevich* ruling to be applicable to congregational as well as hierarchical churches.[340]

---

[334] Serbian Eastern Orthodox Diocese v. Milivojevich, 426 U.S. 696, 713 (1976).

[335] *Id.*

[336] Konkel v. Metropolitan Baptist Church, Inc., 572 P.2d 99 (Ariz. 1977); LeBlanc v. Davis, 432 So.2d 239 (La. 1983); Wilkerson v. Battiste, 393 So.2d 195 (La. App. 1980).

[337] Anderson v. Sills, 265 A.2d 678 (N.J. 1970).

[338] Abyssinia Missionary Baptist Church v. Nixon, 340 So.2d 746 (Ala. 1976); Longmeyer v. Payne, 205 S.W.2d 263 (Mo. 1947); Randolph v. First Baptist Church, 120 N.E.2d 485 (Ohio 1954); First Baptist Church v. Giles, 219 S.W.2d 498 (Tex. 1949).

[339] David v. Carter, 222 S.W.2d 900 (Tex. 1949).

Example. The Kansas Supreme Court ruled that the civil courts have limited authority to review decisions by congregational churches to discipline or dismiss members. Twelve persons claiming to be members of a local church attempted to gain information regarding the church's financial affairs and the use of church assets. When their efforts were ignored by church leaders, they filed a class action lawsuit against the pastor, the chairman of the deacon board, the chairman of the trustee board, persons with signature authority over church funds, and other church members who controlled or held title to church assets. The twelve members were expelled some six months after they filed their lawsuit, following a Sunday morning service in which the pastor accused the members of being "anti-Bible" for suing their church. The dismissed members challenged the legality of their dismissal in court. The court concluded, "A congregational church member has a right under common law principles to a fairly conducted meeting on the question of expulsion, and that includes reasonable notice, the right to attend and speak against the proposed action, and the right to an honest count of the vote. In the absence of church law or usage, a majority vote of the members present at a regular Sunday service prevails on expulsion. It does not require formal evidence, the right to counsel, or the right to present witnesses (unless church rules so require)." Since the dismissed members claimed that their expulsions violated their property interests (they had made substantial contributions to the church over many years), and since the church allegedly did not provide them with adequate notice or the right to defend themselves, the civil courts were justified in intervening. This intervention, however, would be limited to a determination of whether or not their allegations were true. If their expulsions violated "fundamental notions of due process," then they were not legally valid, meaning that they were still members who could not summarily be denied the legal right to demand an accounting of church funds.[341]

4. EXPULSION BASED ON FRAUD OR COLLUSION

In 1928, the United States Supreme Court ruled that "[i]n the absence of fraud, collusion, or arbitrariness, the decisions of the proper church tribunals on matters purely ecclesiastical . . . are accepted in litigation before secular courts as conclusive . . . ."[342] However, in 1976 the Court held that ecclesiastical determinations could not be reviewed on account of "arbitrariness," and refused to decide whether or not "fraud" or "collusion" remained permissible grounds for civil court review.[343] The Court observed, "[w]e have concluded that whether or not there is room for 'marginal civil court review' under the narrow rubrics of 'fraud' or 'collusion' when church tribunals act in bad faith for secular purposes, no 'arbitrariness' exception exists." Accordingly, "fraud" and "collusion" *may* constitute grounds for civil court review of internal church determinations regarding membership. That is all that can be said until the Supreme Court provides more guidance.

Some courts have intervened in internal church controversies regarding membership determinations on the basis of fraud or collusion.[344] There are three points to emphasize, however. First, the Supreme Court has expressly refrained from ruling on the viability of civil court review based on fraud or collusion. Second, the higher burden of proof normally required to establish fraud (i.e., clear and convincing evidence) may apply.[345]

---

[340] *See, e.g.,* Burgess v. Rock Creek Baptist Church, 734 F. Supp. 30 (D.D.C. 1990); First Baptist Church v. State of Ohio, 591 F. Supp. 676 (S.D. Ohio 1983).

[341] Kennedy v. Gray, 807 P.2d 670 (Kan. 1991).

[342] Gonzalez v. Roman Catholic Archbishop, 280 U.S. 1, 16 (1928).

[343] Serbian Eastern Orthodox Diocese v. Milivojevich, 426 U.S. 696 (1976). The Court did not pass upon the constitutionality of marginal civil court review of ecclesiastical determinations in cases of fraud or collusion. This remains an open question.

[344] First Baptist Church v. State of Ohio, 591 F. Supp. 676 (S.D. Ohio 1983) (noting that the "higher burden of proof typically applied to cases of fraud" is applicable); Hatcher v. South Carolina District Council of the Assemblies of God, Inc., 226 S.E.2d 253 (S.C. 1976); Presbytery of the Covenant v. First Presbyterian Church, 552 S.W.2d 865 (Tex. 1977).

[345] First Baptist Church v. State of Ohio, 591 F. Supp. 676 (S.D. Ohio 1983).

And third, in 1976 the Supreme Court interpreted "fraud" or "collusion" to imply church actions that are committed "in bad faith for secular purposes." Certainly, it is highly unlikely that any aggrieved member could prove facts satisfying this definition, particularly if the "clear and convincing evidence" standard applies.

5. Interpretation of Contested Terminology

Occasionally a court will agree to review an expulsion based on some vague condition of membership. For example, when a church's bylaws stipulated that failure to attend church or make financial contributions "without a reasonable excuse" would result in termination of membership, a court agreed to resolve the disputed phrase "without a reasonable excuse."[346] Another court agreed to determine whether a church's charter or bylaws made "extending the right hand of fellowship" a condition of membership where this was a disputed question.[347]

The better rule is that churches themselves must interpret their own internal rules regarding member-ship qualifications and expulsions. In the landmark *Watson* case,[348] the Supreme Court observed that "[t]he right to organize voluntary religious associations to assist in the expression and dissemination of any religious doctrine, and to create tribunals for the decision of controverted questions of faith within the association, and for the ecclesiastical government of all the individual members . . . is unquestioned." The Court also observed in *Watson* that:

> Each [religious organization] . . . has a body of constitutional and ecclesiastical law of its own, to be found in their written organic laws, their books of discipline, in their collections of precedents, in their usage and customs, which to each constitute a system of ecclesiastical law and religious faith that tasks the ablest minds to become familiar with. It is not to be supposed that the judges of the civil courts can be as competent in the ecclesiastical law and religious faith of all these bodies as the ablest men in each are in reference to their own. It would therefore be an appeal from the more learned tribunal in the law which should decide the case, to one which is less so.[349]

Similarly, the Court observed:

> The decisions of ecclesiastical courts, like every other judicial tribunal, are final, as *they are the best judges of what constitutes an offense against the word of God and the discipline of the church.* Any other than those courts must be incompetent judges of matters of faith, discipline, and doctrine; and civil courts, if they should be so unwise as to attempt to supervise their judgments on matters which come within their jurisdiction would only involve themselves in a sea of uncertainty and doubt which would do anything but improve either religion or good morals.[350]

In 1952, the Supreme Court ruled that the first amendment guaranty of religious freedom gives reli-gious organizations "independence from secular control or manipulation, in short, power to decide for them-selves, free from state interference, matters of church government as well as those of faith and doctrine."[351]

---

[346] Second Baptist Church v. Mount Zion Baptist Church, 466 P.2d 212 (Nev. 1970).
[347] Honey Creek Regular Baptist Church v. Wilson, 92 N.E.2d 419 (Ohio 1950).
[348] Watson v. Jones, 80 U.S. 679 (1871).
[349] *Id.* at 729.
[350] *Id.* at 732.
[351] Kedroff v. St. Nicholas Cathedral, 344 U.S. 94 (1952).

Further, the Supreme Court's prohibition of civil court interpretation of church doctrine will serve as an additional bar to civil court interpretation of many contested terms contained in church bylaws.[352]

§ 6-10.3 — Preconditions to Civil Court Review

Key point 6-10.3. *The civil courts will not resolve a dispute contesting the discipline of a church member if the member failed to "exhaust" remedies available under the church's own governing documents.*

The courts will not review church membership expulsions unless the expelled members have exhausted all available procedures within their church for obtaining review of their expulsion. To illustrate, one court refused to resolve a lawsuit brought by a dismissed church member challenging his dismissal since he had not pursued all of the remedies provided by his local church and a parent denomination for the review of such actions.[353]

§ 6-10.4 — Remedies for Improper Discipline or Dismissal

Key point 6-10.4. *Courts willing to intervene in disputes challenging the discipline of a church member have granted a variety of remedies to an improperly disciplined member, including reinstatement or monetary damages for defamation or emotional distress.*

1. Decisions Refusing to Recognize a Legal Remedy

Obviously, courts that follow the rule of non-intervention in internal church membership determinations will not provide disciplined or dismissed members with any legal remedy since no cognizable legal harm has occurred.[354] To illustrate, a federal court in New York ruled that it had no authority to stop a religious organization from excommunicating one of its members.[355] The member had been threatened with excommunication because of a lawsuit he had filed against the religious organization. The court observed:

> A long line of Supreme Court cases holds that, where a religious body adjudicates relations among its members, courts will not interfere with the decisions of those bodies made in accordance with those bodies' rules. This line of cases is based on the Court's observation that voluntary religious organizations are much like any other voluntary organization and are in the best position to interpret their own rules. As the Court stated in [a previous decision]: "It is not to be supposed that the judges of the civil courts can be as competent in ecclesiastical law and religious faith . . . as the ablest men in each [faith] are in reference to their own. . . ." Thus, federal courts will not interfere with the decisions of a religious body adjudicating the relationships of members in that body; as a matter of jurisprudence federal courts will defer to the decision of the religious body.[356]

---

[352] Presbyterian Church v. Mary Elizabeth Blue Hull Memorial Presbyterian Church, 393 U.S. 440 (1969).

[353] First Baptist Church v. State of Ohio, 591 F. Supp. 676 (S.D. Ohio 1983); State ex rel. Nelson v. Ellis, 140 So.2d 194 (La. 1962) *aff'd*, 151 So.2d 544 (La. 1963); Rodyk v. Ukrainian Autocephalic Orthodox Church, 296 N.Y.S.2d 496 (1968), *aff'd*, 328 N.Y.S.2d 685 (1972).

[354] *See, e.g.,* John v. Estate of Hartgerink, 528 N.W.2d 539 (Iowa 1995) (defamation, intentional infliction of emotional distress); Glass v. First United Pentecostal Church, 676 So.2d 724 (La. App. 1996) (defamation, intentional infliction of emotional distress); Schoenhalls v. Main, 504 N.W.2d 233 (Minn. App. 1993) (defamation, fraud); Hadnot v. Shaw, 826 P.2d 978 (Okla. 1992) (defamation and intentional infliction of emotional distress).

[355] Grunwald v. Bornfreund, 696 F. Supp. 838 (E.D.N.Y. 1988).

[356] *Id.* at 840.

The court also noted that "[i]n other cases, the Supreme Court has held that it is contrary to the first amendment for a court, either federal or state, to engage in an examination of ecclesiastical doctrine, and unless such examination cannot be avoided, a court must defer to the decisions of a religious body." The court noted that in this case, the member had asked the court "to do something it is not able to do either as a matter of federal jurisprudence or under the first amendment: decide whether [he] should be excommunicated from his religious community for prosecuting this suit . . . ." The court acknowledged that if the member were in fact threatened with imminent physical harm, then "he could come to this court for a remedy." However, "the mere expulsion from a religious society, with the exclusion from a religious community, is not a harm for which courts can grant a remedy." In conclusion, the court permitted the member to pursue a judicial resolution of his dispute with the religious organization, and ruled that the member's threatened excommunication was "beyond the powers of this court to stop, so long as the excommunication results in nothing more than [the member] being excluded from his religious community."

Example. A federal appeals court refused to permit a "disfellowshiped" Jehovah's Witness to sue her former church for defamation, invasion of privacy, fraud, and outrageous conduct. The disfellowshiped member claimed that she had been aggrieved by the Jehovah's Witness practice of "shunning," which requires members to avoid all social contacts with disfellowshiped members. The court, acknowledging that the harm suffered by disfellowshiped members is "real and not insubstantial," nevertheless concluded that permitting disfellowshiped members to sue their church for emotional injuries "would unconstitutionally restrict the Jehovah's Witness free exercise of religion." The constitutional guaranty of freedom of religion, observed the court, "requires that society tolerate the type of harm suffered by [disfellowshiped members] as a price well worth paying to safeguard the right of religious difference that all citizens enjoy."[357]

Example. A Michigan court ruled that it lacked jurisdiction to resolve the claims of parishioners that they had suffered intentional infliction of emotional distress as a result of their priest's actions. Several parishioners withheld their financial support from the church because of their opposition to certain changes that a new priest had initiated. In response to this action, the priest refused to give communion to certain dissident members in the presence of the entire congregation, and verbally criticized others during services. The court observed that "it is well settled that courts, both federal and state, are severely circumscribed by [the state and federal constitutions] in the resolution of disputes between a church and its members. Such jurisdiction is limited to property rights which can be resolved by application of civil law." In rejecting the members' claim that the church had intentionally caused them emotional distress, the court remarked, "This is quite a modern tort not yet recognized by the highest court in this state. Hopefully, it never will be. The awesome flood of litigation has already risen to the gunnels. If the courts were to offer to extract money from everyone who intentionally makes someone else mad, we would surely go under."[358]

Example. A Michigan court ruled that the first amendment guaranty of religious freedom provides churches with substantial protection when disciplining members.[359] This protection extends to statements made by a minister to the church during worship services or in church publications. But when a member resigns from the church prior to being disciplined, a more difficult question is presented. The court drew a distinction between the discipline of members and nonmembers. It concluded that churches

---

[357] Paul v. Watchtower Bible and Tract Society of New York, 819 F. 2d 875 (9th Cir. 1987).
[358] Maciejewski v. Breitenbeck, 413 N.W.2d 65 (Mich. App. 1987).
[359] Smith v. Calvary Christian Church, 592 N.W.2d 713 (Mich. App. 1998).

have limited constitutional protection when disciplining nonmembers, meaning that such individuals are more likely to succeed in pursuing legal action against their former church.

Example. *The Montana Supreme Court ruled that a husband and wife who had been "disfellowshiped" from a Jehovah's Witness congregation could not sue the church for defamation. The couple had been disfellowshiped for marrying contrary to church doctrine. In announcing the decision to the congregation, the overseer remarked that the couple had been living in adultery according to church teachings and had been disfellowshiped for "conduct unbecoming Christians." The overseer added that "we got the filth cleaned out of the congregation, now we have God's spirit." The court concluded that such comments were not defamatory since they were privileged and protected by the constitutional guaranty of religious freedom. As to the defense of privilege, the court remarked that "it is firmly established that statements of church members made in the course of disciplinary or expulsion proceedings, in the absence of malice, are protected by a qualified privilege." The remarks of the overseer were privileged, concluded the court, and did not involve malice since "malice is defined as reckless disregard for the truth [and] does not include hatred, personal spite, ill-will, or a desire to injure." The court added that it "would be violating the [church's] right to free exercise of religion if [it] were to find [the church's] statements actionable under state defamation law."[360]*

2. Decisions Recognizing a Legal Remedy

the Guinn Case

Those courts that have followed the rule of "marginal civil court review" of internal church membership determinations occasionally will recognize that improperly disciplined or dismissed members have a legal remedy against their church. The best illustration of this is a 1989 ruling of the Oklahoma Supreme Court.[361] Because of the significance of this ruling, it will be considered in detail. In 1974, a single woman (the "parishioner") moved with her minor children to Collinsville, Oklahoma, and soon became a member of a local Church of Christ congregation. The first few years of the parishioner's association with the church were without incident. In 1980, however, three "elders" of the church confronted the parishioner with a rumor that she was having sexual relations with a local resident who was not a member of the congregation. According to the elders, they investigated the rumor because of the church's teaching that church leaders are responsible to monitor the actions of church members and confront and discuss problems with anyone who is "having trouble." The Church of Christ follows a literal interpretation of the Bible, which it considers to be the sole source of moral and religious guidance.

When confronted with the rumor, the parishioner admitted violating the Church of Christ prohibition against fornication. As a transgressor of the church's code of ethics, the parishioner became subject to the disciplinary procedure set forth in Matthew 18:13-17. This procedure provides, "If thy brother shall trespass against thee, go and tell him his fault between thee and him alone; if he shall hear thee, thou has gained thy brother. But if he will not hear thee, then take with thee one or two more, that in the mouth of two or three witnesses every word may be established. And if he shall neglect to hear them, tell it unto the church; but if he neglect to hear the church, let him be unto thee as a heathen man and a publican." Pursuant to this procedure, the church elders confronted the parishioner on three occasions over the course of a year. On each occasion, the elders requested that the parishioner repent of her fornication and discontinue seeing her companion. On

---

[360] Rasmussen v. Bennett, 741 P.2d 755 (Mont. 1987).

[361] Guinn v. Church of Christ, 775 P.2d 766 (Okla. 1989). *But see* Hadnot v. Shaw, 826 P.2d 978 (Okla. 1992)(civil courts cannot review a church's discipline of persons who have not withdrawn from church membership).

September 21, 1981, a few days following the third encounter, the elders sent the parishioner a letter warning her that if she did not repent, the "withdrawal of fellowship" process would begin.

Withdrawal of fellowship is a disciplinary procedure that is based on Matthew 18 and carried out by the entire membership in a Church of Christ congregation. When a member violates the church's code of ethics and refuses to repent, the elders read aloud to the congregation those Scripture passages which were violated. The congregation then withdraws its fellowship from the wayward member by refusing to acknowledge his or her presence. According to the elders, this process serves the dual purpose of encouraging transgressors to repent and return to fellowship with other members, and it maintains the purity and holiness of the church and its members. The parishioner had seen one incident of fellowship withdrawal, and was fully aware that such a process would result in the publication of her unscriptural conduct to the entire congregation. Accordingly, she contacted a lawyer who sent the elders a letter signed by the parishioner, and dated September 24, 1981, in which the parishioner clearly stated that she withdrew her membership. The attorney asked the elders not to expose the parishioner's private life to the congregation (which comprised about five percent of the town's population).

On September 25, the parishioner wrote the elders another letter imploring them not to mention her name in church except to tell the congregation that she had withdrawn from membership. The elders ignored these requests, and on September 27 (during a scheduled service) they advised the congregation to encourage the parishioner to repent and return to the church. They also informed the congregation that unless the parishioner repented, the verses of Scripture that she had violated would be read aloud to the congregation at the next service and that the withdrawal of fellowship procedure would begin. The parishioner met with one of the elders during the following week, and she was informed that her attempt to withdraw from membership was not only doctrinally impossible, but could not halt the disciplinary process that would be carried out against her. The parishioner was publicly branded a fornicator when the scriptural standards she had violated were recited to the congregation at a service conducted on October 4. As part of the disciplinary process the same information regarding the parishioner's transgressions was sent to four other area Church of Christ congregations to be read aloud during services.

The parishioner sued the three elders and local church, asserting that their actions both before and after her withdrawal from church membership on September 25, 1981 (the date of her letter to the church), invaded her privacy and caused her emotional distress. The invasion of privacy claim alleged that the elders and church had "intruded upon her seclusion," and in addition, had "unreasonably publicized private facts about her life by communicating her transgressions to the [home church] and four other area Church of Christ congregations." A jury ruled in favor of the parishioner, and awarded her $205,000 in actual damages, $185,000 in punitive damages, and $45,000 in interest. The decision was appealed to the Oklahoma Supreme Court.

The elders and church argued that the first amendment guaranty of religious freedom prevented them from being sued as a result of their exercise of ecclesiastical discipline. The court acknowledged that the United States Supreme Court has banned civil court review of "purely ecclesiastical" matters, but it concluded that the discipline of church members is not always immune from civil court review. It ruled that the first amendment prevented the church and its elders from being sued for their actions *prior* to the parishioner's withdrawal (which, according to the court, occurred on September 24 when the parishioner sent her letter of withdrawal to the church), but that the church and elders *could* be sued for actions occurring *after* the parishioner's withdrawal. With regard to the parishioner's claim for "pre-withdrawal" damages, the court noted that "under the first amendment people may freely consent to being spiritually governed by an established set of ecclesiastical tenets defined and carried out by those chosen to interpret and impose them." The court continued, "Under the first amendment's free exercise of religion clause, parishioner had the right to consent as a participant in the practices and beliefs of the Church of Christ without fear of governmental interference . . . . [H]er willing submission to the Church of Christ's dogma, and the elders' reliance on that submission, collectively shielded the church's pre-withdrawal, religiously-motivated discipline from scrutiny through secular [courts]."

As authority for this proposition, the court quoted from a decision of the United States Supreme Court:

> The right to organize voluntary religious associations to assist in the expression and dissemination of any religious doctrine, and to create tribunals for the decision of controverted questions of faith within the association, and for the ecclesiastical government of all individual members, congregations, and officers within the general association, is unquestioned. *All who unite themselves to such a body do so with an implied consent to this government, and are bound to submit to it.*[362]

The court concluded that "insofar as [the parishioner] seeks vindication for the actions taken by the elders *before* her membership withdrawal, her claims are to be dismissed."

Could the parishioner sue the elders and church for actions occurring *after* her withdrawal? The elders said no, pointing out that the Church of Christ contains no doctrinal provision for withdrawal from membership. Rather, a member remains a part of a congregation for life. Like those born into a family, they may leave but they can never really sever the familial bond. Accordingly, a court determination that the parishioner effectively withdrew from membership and thereby terminated the church's authority to discipline her would amount to "a constitutionally impermissible state usurpation of religious discipline." The elders also emphasized that the disciplinary procedure mandated by Matthew 18:13-17 already had begun at the time of the parishioner's alleged withdrawal (the elders had confronted her on three occasions), and therefore the parishioner could not preempt the disciplinary process by an attempted withdrawal. The parishioner asserted that she had the authority to withdraw from membership in the church, and that her withdrawal terminated the church's authority to discipline her.

The court concluded that the parishioner's September 24, 1981 letter was an effective withdrawal from church membership, and it agreed with the parishioner that the elders and church *could* be sued for their actions following her withdrawal. It observed:

> The first amendment of the United States Constitution was designed to preserve freedom of worship by prohibiting the establishment or endorsement of any official religion. One of the fundamental purposes of the first amendment is to protect the people's right to worship as they choose. Implicit in the right to choose freely one's own form of worship is the right of unhindered and unimpeded withdrawal from the chosen form of worship. . . . [The local church], by denying the parishioner's right to disassociate herself from a particular form of religious belief is threatening to curtail her freedom of worship according to her choice. Unless the parishioner waived the constitutional right to withdraw her initial consent to be bound by the Church of Christ discipline and its governing elders, her resignation was a constitutionally protected right.[363]

---

[362] Watson v. Jones, 80 U.S. (13 Wall.) 679 (1872) (emphasis added).
[363] 775 P.2d at 776-777.

The court concluded that the parishioner had not "waived" her constitutional right to withdraw from church membership. A waiver, observed the court, is a "voluntary and intentional relinquishment of a known right." The parishioner testified that she had never been informed by the church of its teaching that membership constitutes an insoluble bond of lifetime commitment, and accordingly she was incapable of knowingly and intentionally "waiving" such a right.

The court summarized its thinking as follows:

Disciplinary practices involving members of an ecclesiastical association . . . are among those hallowed first amendment rights with which the government cannot interfere. . . . [Nevertheless] first amendment protection does not extend to all religiously-motivated disciplinary practices in which ecclesiastical organizations might engage. By its very nature, ecclesiastical discipline involves both church and member. It is a means of religious expression as well as a means of ecclesiastically judging one who transgresses a church law which one has consented to obey. The right to express dissatisfaction with the disobedience of those who have promised to adhere to doctrinal precepts and to take ecclesiastically-mandated measures to bring wayward members back within the bounds of accepted behavior, are forms of religious expression and association which the first amendment's free exercise clause was designed to protect and preserve. And yet the constitutionally protected freedom to impose even the most deeply felt, spiritually-inspired disciplinary measure is forfeited when the object of "benevolent" concern is one who has terminated voluntary submission to another's supervision and command. While the first amendment requires that citizens be tolerant of religious views different from and offensive to their own, it surely does not require that those like parishioner, who choose not to submit to the authority of a religious association, be tolerant of that group's attempts to govern them. Only those who "unite themselves" in a religious association impliedly consent to its authority over them and are bound "to submit to it." Parishioner voluntarily joined the Church of Christ and by so doing consented to submit to its tenets. When she later removed herself from membership, petitioner withdrew her consent, depriving the church of the power actively to monitor her spiritual life through overt disciplinary acts. No real freedom to choose religion would exist in this land if under the shield of the first amendment religious institutions could impose their will on the unwilling and claim immunity from secular [courts] for their tortious acts.[364]

The court distinguished a federal appeals court decision cited by the elders which held that a dismissed member of the Jehovah's Witness church could not sue her former church for the emotional distress, defamation, and invasion of privacy that it allegedly caused by its practice of "shunning" her.[365] Unlike the conduct of the Church of Christ elders, the practice of shunning the former Jehovah's Witness was "passive." The member abandoned her membership in the church, and the church simply instructed its members to avoid any contact with her. The court observed:

For purposes of first amendment protection, religiously-motivated disciplinary measures that merely *exclude* a person from communion are vastly different from those which are designed to *control* and *involve*. A church is constitutionally free to exclude people without first obtaining their consent. But the first amendment will not shield a church from civil liability for imposing its will, as manifested through a disciplinary scheme, upon an individual who has not consented to undergo ecclesiastical discipline.[366]

---

[364] 775 P.2d at 779.
[365] Paul v. Watchtower Bible & Tract Society, 819 F.2d 875 (9th Cir. 1987).
[366] 775 P.2d at 781.

The court rejected the elders' claim that their statements to the congregations were protected by a "conditional privilege." The court acknowledged that a statement is conditionally privileged if "the circumstances under which the information is published lead any one of several persons having a *common interest* in a particular subject matter correctly or reasonably to believe that there is information that another sharing the common interest is entitled to know." The court concluded that the elders' statements were *not* protected by a conditional privilege since the "parishioner was neither a present nor a prospective church member" at the time of the elders' public statements, and accordingly that the "congregation did not share the sort of 'common interest' in parishioner's behavior" that would render the elders' statements privileged.

The court acknowledged that "communicating unproven allegations of *a present or prospective member's misconduct to the other members of a religious association is a privileged occasion because the members have a valid interest in and concern for the behavior of their fellow members and officers.*" However, it concluded that the elders' claim to a conditional privilege "as it pertains to their actions occurring *after* parishioner's withdrawal from membership, is without merit."

The court acknowledged that churches have a greater interest in receiving information concerning disciplined or dismissed clergy, and accordingly the "common interest privilege" is broader than in the context of lay member discipline. The court concluded that a congregation has "a common interest in being informed about the questionable conduct of one among them who expressed the desire to continue ministering to them or to one of the neighboring [Church of Christ] assemblies. Here, parishioners expressed no interest in continuing her association with [her former church] or with any other Church of Christ [congregation]." Accordingly, the church simply had no "common interest" in her post-withdrawal discipline that would make the elders' statements conditionally privileged.

What is the relevance of the Oklahoma Supreme Court's decision to local churches? Obviously, the court's decision is binding only upon churches in the state of Oklahoma. Nevertheless, the case represents one of the most extensive discussions of church discipline by any court, and accordingly it probably will be given special consideration (and no doubt be followed) by the courts of many other states. For this reason, the case merits serious study by church leaders in every state. With these factors in mind, consider the following:

1. Discipline of church members is constitutionally protected. The discipline of *church members* (i.e., persons who have *not* withdrawn from membership) is a constitutionally protected right of churches. If discipline of church members is a possibility in your church, then you should adopt a disciplinary procedure that is based upon and refers to scriptural references. The procedure should specify the grounds for discipline, and describe the process that will be conducted. Avoid references to loaded phrases such as "due process," which have no legal relevance in the context of church law and only create confusion. The Oklahoma court acknowledged that there might be some pre-withdrawal disciplinary actions which would be so extreme as to lose their constitutional protection. However, it concluded that the elders' conduct did not constitute such a case. Recall that the elders' pre-withdrawal actions were limited to three meetings with the parishioner and involved no public dissemination of her alleged misconduct.

2. No constitutional protection after a member resigns. Discipline of persons who have effectively withdrawn their church membership is not a constitutionally protected activity, and churches that engage in such conduct can be sued under existing theories of tort law. In the Oklahoma case, the parishioner sued the church (and its elders) for both invasion of privacy and intentional infliction of emotional distress. The parishioner asserted that the church invaded her privacy in two ways. First, the actions of the elders "intruded upon her seclusion." Second, the elders' notification of their own congregation (as well as four other local congregations) of the parishioner's misconduct amounted to an unreasonable public disclosure of private facts. Both of these assertions constitute well-recognized variations of the tort of invasion of privacy. The parishioner also claimed that the elders' conduct amounted to an intentional infliction of emotional distress (another well-recognized tort), since their actions were extreme and outrageous and of an intentional and reckless nature which caused her severe emotional distress and shock (particularly since the parishioner's minor children were present at the church service during which the elders publicized her misconduct).

3. Church members have a constitutional right to resign. The court concluded that the constitutional right of a church member to withdraw from church membership is protected by the first amendment guaranty of religious freedom *unless a member has waived that right.* An effective waiver requires the voluntary relinquishment of a known right. In other words, a member can waive the right to resign by a voluntary and intentional act, but not through inadvertence or ignorance. A church wishing to restrict the right of disciplined members to withdraw must obtain a voluntary and knowing waiver by present and prospective members of their constitutional right to withdraw. How can this be done? One approach would be for a church to adopt a provision in its bylaws preventing members from withdrawing if they are currently being disciplined by the church. Obviously, the disciplinary procedure must be carefully specified in the church bylaws so there is no doubt whether the disciplinary process has been initiated with respect to a member. Most courts have held that members are "on notice" of all of the provisions in the church bylaws, and consent to be bound by them when they become members. As a result, the act of becoming a member of a church with such a provision in its bylaws may well constitute an effective waiver of a member's right to withdraw (if the disciplinary process has begun). Such a conclusion is not free from doubt, however. To be as safe as possible, a church could explain to present and prospective members the provision in the bylaws limiting their right to withdraw, and explaining to them that by becoming members they will be waiving their right to withdraw from membership if they are under discipline by the church. The problem in the Oklahoma case was that the church attempted to discipline the parishioner following her withdrawal. According to the court's ruling, the church could have avoided liability by obtaining an effective waiver. Unfortunately, the court did not discuss what forms of waiver it would find acceptable.

4. Passive discipline. The Oklahoma court concluded that a church retains the right to engage in "passive" discipline of former members. It approved a federal appeals court decision rejecting the claim of a former Jehovah's Witness that her former church had defamed her, invaded her privacy, and caused her emotional distress by its practice of "shunning" former members. The court observed that the decision of the Jehovah's Witness church "to turn away from her was protected under the first amendment as a passive exercise of religious freedom, the legitimacy of which was not grounded in her prior acquiescence."

5. Communications of matters of "common interest" to members. The court acknowledged that church members have a right to know about matters in which they have a "common interest," and that this right permits some disclosures to church members concerning the discipline or misconduct of current members. Statements by church leaders to church members concerning the discipline of current members are conditionally privileged—meaning that the disciplined member cannot successfully sue the church for making such disclosures unless the church acted maliciously (i.e., it either knew that the disclosures were false or made them with a reckless disregard as to their truthfulness). It must be emphasized that this privilege only protects disclosures made to *church members* about *church members.* Disclosures made to a congregation during a worship service in which *non-members* are present would not be protected. And, statements about former members are not protected (presumably, non-members would need to be removed from the sanctuary before statements regarding church discipline could be made). The court observed, "Communicating unproven allegations of a present or prospective member's misconduct to the other members of a religious association is a privileged occasion because the members have a valid interest in and concern for the behavior of their fellow members and officers."

Obviously, the safest course of action for a church board that has disciplined a member is to refrain from disclosing any information to the congregation. If the board decides that the congregation should be informed, then a general statement that the individual is "no longer a member" is the safest approach. If the board would like to share more details with the church, then it should do so at a congregational meeting or service only after all non-members have been removed. Members present should be instructed to retain the information presented in the strictest confidence. Churches following the disciplinary procedure outlined in Matthew 18 ultimately may wish to let the church membership make the final determination regarding the guilt or innocence of an accused member (and any penalty to be imposed). If so, the church must be careful to remove all non-members from such a meeting, and to apprise the membership of the confidentiality of the information that is disclosed. It would be appropriate for the congregation to adopt a resolution at such a meeting committing itself to maintaining all confidences shared during the meeting.

6. Discipline of clergy. Churches have greater protection in making statements about current or former *clergy*, since the congregation continues to have "a common interest in being informed about the questionable conduct of one among them who expresses the desire to continue ministering to them or to one of the neighboring assemblies." Accordingly, disciplined clergy may find it more difficult to sue their church or denomination.

7. Arbitration. Churches wishing to reduce the risk of litigation by disciplined members (or any other members) should consider, in addition to the observations made above, the adoption of a binding arbitration policy. Such a policy, if adopted by the church membership at a congregational meeting as an amendment to the church's bylaws, can force church members to resolve their disputes (with the church, pastor, board, or other members) within the church consistently with the pattern suggested by the apostle Paul in 1 Corinthians 6:1-8. While a discussion of arbitration policies is beyond the scope of this text, churches should recognize that arbitration is an increasingly popular means of resolving disputes in the secular world since it often avoids the excessive costs and delays associated with civil litigation and the uncertainty of jury verdicts. Of course, any arbitration policy should be reviewed by an attorney and the church's liability insurer before being implemented. A legally effective and properly adopted arbitration policy can force disgruntled members to take their complaints to a panel of church representatives rather than create a costly and protracted spectacle in the secular courts. Such an approach, at a minimum, merits serious consideration by any church.

On the whole, churches are benefited by the Oklahoma Supreme Court's ruling, since the court recognized that (1) churches have a constitutional right to discipline members, (2) statements made to church members about disciplined members are "conditionally privileged," (3) churches have broad authority to discipline clergy, and (4) churches have a constitutionally protected right to discipline a former member who has withdrawn from membership if the former member has effectively waived his or her right to withdraw from membership. The court's ruling does not go as far as some other court decisions in recognizing a broad authority on the part of churches to discipline persons who have withdrawn from church membership. And, the court failed to adequately refute the elders' claim that the parishioner's right to withdraw was suspended when the elders commenced the church's disciplinary process (a year before the parishioner's withdrawal). Finally, the court acknowledged (on the basis of United States Supreme Court rulings) that "all who unite themselves to [a church] do so with an implied consent to [its] government, and are bound to submit to it." Yet, it greatly limited the effect of this language by permitting the parishioner to completely avoid the church's well-defined disciplinary process (with which she had been familiar) merely because she did not technically "waive" her right to withdraw. This aspect of the court's ruling is unfortunate—particularly since the court provided no guidance whatever to churches regarding the form and contents of an effective waiver.

other decisions

Persons who believe that they have been improperly expelled from membership in a church have a number of potential remedies available to them. First, they may be able to obtain judicial review of the expulsion if they reside in a jurisdiction that permits marginal civil court review of church membership determinations. If a court agrees to review the expulsion and finds that it was deficient on the basis of one of the grounds discussed in this section, it may declare the expulsion void and reinstate the expelled member.[367] Second, wrongfully expelled members may be able to recover monetary damages.[368] Third, they may petition a court for an injunction prohibiting a church from interfering with their rights or privileges as members.[369] Fourth, they may seek a declaratory judgment setting forth their rights.[370] Fifth, in some cases they may sue their church or certain of its members for defamation.

Defamation generally is defined to include the following elements: (1) a public statement, whether oral or in writing; (2) reference to another; (3) that is false; and (4) which injures the reputation of the other. Truth is generally held to be an absolute defense to a defamation action. Thus if the allegedly defamatory statements were true, an expelled member will not be able to sue for defamation even if his reputation has been injured.

Defamation actions are limited in another important way. Most jurisdictions recognize that statements made by a person in a reasonable manner and for a proper purpose to others having a common interest with him in the communication are "qualifiedly privileged" and immune from attack unless they are made with malice. Malice in this context refers to either a knowledge that the communication was false or a reckless disregard concerning its truth or falsity.

The common interest among church members about church matters is likely sufficient to create a qualified privilege for communications between members on subjects relating to the church's interests. To illustrate, where expelled church members had been publicly referred to by other members as "totally unworthy of the continued confidence, respect and fellowship of a great church," as willing to lie in order to harm their church, and as possessed of a vile spirit, a court concluded that the remarks were entitled to a qualified privilege. The court nevertheless considered the remarks defamatory because they had been made either recklessly or with a knowledge of their falsity.[371] In another case, an expelled member alleged that at various times in meetings of his religious group other members had stated that he was a disgrace to his religion, that his conduct was scandalous, that he was guilty of evil conduct and was a man of low character, and that his conduct was so bad that it could not be described publicly. A court, in finding such statements malicious, stated the general rule as follows:

> [M]embers of such bodies may report on the qualifications of applicants, prefer charges against fellow members, offer testimony in support of the charges, and make proper publications of any disciplinary action that may be taken, without liability for any resultant defamation, *so long as they act without malice.* The rule relative to qualified privilege is always subject to the limitation,

---

[367] Ragsdall v. Church of Christ, 55 N.W.2d 539 (Iowa 1952).
[368] Louison v. Fischman, 168 N.E.2d 340 (Mass. 1960).
[369] David v. Carter, 222 S.W.2d 900 (Tex. 1949).
[370] Epperson v. Myers, 58 So.2d 150 (Fla. 1952).
[371] Brewer v. Second Baptist Church, 197 P.2d 713 (Cal. 1948).

as stated, that in connection with such activities the parties must act without malice. When a matter which otherwise would be a qualifiedly privileged communication is published falsely, fraudulently, and with express malice and intent to injure the persons against whom it is directed, the communication loses its qualifiedly privileged character and the parties lay themselves liable to a suit for damages in an action for libel or slander.[372]

§ 6-11   Members — Personal Liability

It is a fundamental characteristic of corporations that individual members will not be personally responsible for the misconduct of other members, so long as they do not participate directly in the misconduct or ratify or affirm it. Members of course are personally responsible for their own misconduct, and the corporation itself may be derivatively responsible for a member's misconduct. But other members of the corporation who were not involved in and did not affirm the wrongful act of another member ordinarily will not be personally responsible for it.

Members who are expelled from a church ordinarily are no longer responsible for the church's debts and liabilities.[373]

§ 6-12   Meetings of Members

Church charters and bylaws typically bestow substantial powers upon a church's membership. Church members may exercise the authority conferred upon them only when acting at a meeting convened according to procedural requirements in the church's charter and bylaws or in applicable state law. Actions taken at irregularly called meetings generally are considered invalid unless subsequently ratified or affirmed at a duly convened meeting.

Church bylaws commonly call for annual general meetings of the church membership, and for such special meetings as the congregation or board of directors considers appropriate.

The pastor of the church, or the senior pastor of a church having more than one pastor on its staff, is legally authorized to preside at membership meetings if authorized by (1) the church charter or bylaws, (2) established church custom, (3) applicable state nonprofit corporation law, or (4) the doctrine of inherent authority.

Although a church is free to determine the order of business to be followed at general or special meetings, the following order is commonly followed:

1. reading and approval of minutes

2. reports of officers, boards, and standing committees

3. reports of special committees

4. special orders

---

[372] Loeb v. Geronemus, 66 So.2d 241, 244 (Fla. 1953) (citations omitted). *See also* Joiner v. Weeks, 383 So.2d 101 (La. 1980), *cert. denied*, 385 So.2d 257 (La. 1980); Moyle v. Franz 46 N.Y.S.2d 667 (1944), *aff'd*, 47 N.Y.S.2d 484 (1944).

[373] Smith v. Lewis, 578 S.W.2d 169 (Tex. App. 1979).

5. unfinished business and general orders

6. new business[374]

Members generally have a right to express their views at church meetings since the very purpose of such meetings is to arrive at decisions through a free and open exchange of ideas. Accordingly, one court ruled that the leaders of two opposing factions within a church had no authority to agree that a church membership meeting would be conducted without discussion.[375]

> *Example. The Georgia Supreme Court ruled that a provision in the state nonprofit corporation law mandating annual membership meetings did not take priority over a provision in a church's bylaws calling for membership meetings once every four years. The court observed that the state nonprofit corporation law itself specifies that if any of its provisions is inconsistent with religious doctrine governing a nonprofit corporation's affairs on the same subject, "the religious doctrine shall control to the extent required by the Constitution of the United States or the Constitution of this state or both." As a result, the issue "is whether the frequency with which the church's membership meets is a matter of religious doctrine having constitutional precedence over inconsistent statutory provisions of [the nonprofit corporation law]." The court noted that the church in this case was "hierarchical" in nature, and that the members had very limited authority to direct church affairs. It concluded, "[A]n annual meeting as contemplated by [the nonprofit corporation law] would be totally inconsistent with the church's fundamental religious freedom, as a hierarchical religious body, to determine its own governmental rules and regulations. Members have no legal right to wrest the governing of the church from [church officials] by obtaining court-ordered annual meetings conducted in accordance with [nonprofit corporation law]."[376]*

§ 6-12.1 — Procedural Requirements

> *Key point 6-12.1. Church membership meetings must be conducted in accordance with the procedural requirements ordinarily specified in the church's governing documents. The most common requirements pertain to notice, quorum, and voting.*

A church's charter or bylaws typically specifies procedures for the convening and conduct of church membership meetings. State nonprofit corporation law may impose additional procedural requirements on incorporated churches, although in most cases state corporation law will apply only if the church's charter or bylaws are silent. If there is no specific charter, bylaw, or statutory provision governing church meetings, the established custom of the church generally will control.[377] For example, where it was the established custom of a church to give notice of the annual church membership meeting by public announcement during Sunday morning services on the two Sundays before the date set for the proposed meeting, a court ruled that the election of officers at a purported annual meeting was invalid since this custom was not followed.[378]

The procedural requirements causing the greatest amount of controversy and confusion are notice, quorum, and voting requirements. These subjects will be considered individually.

---

[374] *See, e.g.,* Robert's Rules of Order 21 (newly revised ed. 1981).
[375] Randolph v. Mount Zion Baptist Church, 53 A.2d 206 (N.J. 1947).
[376] First Born Church of the Living God, Inc. v. Hill, 481 S.E.2d 221 (Ga. 1997).
[377] McDaniel v. Quakenbush, 105 S.E.2d 94 (N.C. 1958).
[378] Coates v. Parchman, 334 S.W.2d 417 (Mo. 1960).

1. NOTICE

The church membership ordinarily must be notified of the date, time, and place of both annual and special membership meetings. This "notice" requirement usually is found in the church's bylaws, but it also may appear in the corporate charter or in the body of parliamentary procedure adopted by the church. For example, *Robert's Rules of Order, Newly Revised*, which has been adopted by many churches, specifies:

> With the possible exception of matters of very minor importance, only business mentioned in the call of a special meeting can be transacted at such a meeting. If, at a special meeting, it becomes urgent in an emergency to take action for which no notice was given, that action, to become legal, must be ratified by the organization at a regular meeting (or, if the ratification cannot wait, at another special meeting properly called for that purpose).[379]

If a church is incorporated and its bylaws do not contain notice requirements, the state nonprofit corporation law ordinarily will contain the applicable requirements. To illustrate, section 14 of the Model Nonprofit Corporation Act, which has been adopted by many states, specifies:

> Unless otherwise provided in the articles of incorporation or the bylaws, written notice stating the place, day and hour of the meeting and, in the case of a special meeting, the purpose or purposes for which the meeting is called, should be delivered not less than ten nor more than fifty days before the date of the meeting, either personally or by mail . . . to each member entitled to vote at such meeting.

Section 7.05 of the Revised Model Nonprofit Corporation Act, which has been adopted by a few states, specifies that "[a] corporation shall give notice consistent with its bylaws of meetings of members in a fair and reasonable manner." The Act goes on to specify that notice is "fair and reasonable" if (1) the corporation notifies its members of the place, date, and time of each annual, regular, and special meeting of members no fewer than 10 (or if notice is mailed by other than first class or registered mail, 30) nor more than 60 days before the meeting date; (2) notice of an *annual or regular meeting* must include a statement of purpose only with respect to any of the following matters—director conflict of interest, indemnification of officers or agents, amendment of the articles of incorporation, amendment of the bylaws, mergers, some sales of corporate assets, dissolution by directors or members; and (3) notice of a *special business meeting* must include "a description of the matters for which the meeting is called."

Unincorporated churches that have no bylaws or written regulations are bound by their established customs regarding notice of church membership meetings. However, some courts have held that notice requirements established by custom can be disregarded if the notice actually given is more likely to provide notice to all church members than the form of notice prescribed by custom.[380]

A church must comply with the manner and method of giving notice prescribed in its charter or bylaws, in applicable state nonprofit corporation law, or by established church custom. Failure to follow applicable notice requirements may render any action taken at the improperly called meeting invalid.

Example. *A church convened a special meeting of the congregation. Notice of the meeting consisted of announcements from the pulpit on the three consecutive Sundays prior to the meeting. These announce-*

---

[379] ROBERT'S RULES OF ORDER 79 (newly revised ed. 1981).
[380] State Bank v. Wilbur Mission Church, 265 P.2d 821 (Wash. 1954).

ments did not indicate that a vote would be taken on the minister's continued employment. At the meeting, a motion was made from the floor to terminate the minister's services. The minister, acting as chairman of the meeting, ruled the motion out of order since there had been no prior notice that such a vote would be taken. A deacon then proceeded to conduct a vote over the minister's objection, and the members present voted to terminate the minister's services. The ousted minister attempted to return to the pulpit on the following Sunday, but was prevented from doing so. The church later obtained a court order prohibiting the minister from attempting to occupy his former position. The minister appealed this decision, arguing that the church had improperly fired him since it had not given proper notice of the business to be transacted at the congregational meeting. A state appeals court agreed. It noted that neither the church's charter nor bylaws specified the type of notice needed for special meetings. And, since the charter and bylaws were silent, the state nonprofit corporation law under which the church was incorporated had to be consulted. A provision in this law specified that "unless otherwise provided in the [charter] or bylaws . . . the authorized person calling a members' meeting shall cause written notice of the time, place and purpose of the meeting to be given to all members entitled to vote at such meeting, at least ten days and not more than sixty days prior to the day fixed for the meeting." Notice of the church's special congregational meeting was defective since it was not in writing (it had been announced from the pulpit), and it failed to specify the purposes of the meeting. "The notice of the meeting was clearly deficient," concluded the court, "and the meeting was therefore invalid."[381]

Actions taken at church membership meetings have been declared void under the following circumstances: (1) notice of a special meeting was read publicly by a church secretary instead of by a church trustee as required by the applicable state nonprofit corporation law;[382] (2) a pastor publicly notified his congregation during a worship service that a special meeting would be convened immediately following the service, though the church's bylaws stipulated that notice of special meetings had to be mailed to members at a prescribed time in advance of a meeting;[383] (3) a pastor convened a special meeting following a Sunday morning service without any notice other than an oral announcement during the service, despite an applicable provision in state nonprofit corporation law requiring written notice to be posted in a conspicuous place near the main entrance of the church for at least seven days before the meeting;[384] (4) a small number of members present at a Wednesday evening church service publicly called a special meeting of the church membership for the following Saturday, in violation of an established church custom requiring notice to be read publicly during at least two Sunday morning services prior to such a meeting;[385] and (5) a church's attempted removal of its trustees at a special business meeting was "null and void" since the church had not fulfilled the legal notice requirements imposed by state law for calling a special business meeting.[386]

One state supreme court has observed that "it is proper for the courts to inquire whether a congregational meeting, at which church business is to be transacted, was preceded by adequate notice to the full

---

[381] Bethlehem Missionary Baptist Church v. Henderson, 522 So.2d 1339 (La. App. 1988). This case is significant for two reasons. First, it emphasizes the significance of giving proper notice of church business meetings. Second, the case illustrates the principle (which is followed in many states) that an incorporated church may be governed by state nonprofit corporation law in the event that it fails to address certain matters of administration and operation in its charter or bylaws. Of course, churches in such states are free to adopt provisions contrary to the nonprofit corporation law in their own charter or bylaws, and such provisions will be controlling. But in the event that they fail (for whatever reason) to address certain issues of church administration in their organizational documents, state law may step in to "fill the void."

[382] Hayes v. Brantley, 280 N.Y.S.2d 291 (1967).

[383] Mount Zion Baptist Church v. Second Baptist Church, 432 P.2d 328 (Nev. 1967).

[384] Bangor Spiritualist Church, Inc. v. Littlefield, 330 A.2d 793 (Me. 1975).

[385] In re Galilee Baptist Church, 186 So.2d 102 (Ala. 1966).

[386] First Union Baptist Church v. Banks, 533 So.2d 1305 (La. App. 1988).

membership, and whether, once called, the meeting was conducted in an orderly manner . . . ." However, "once the court is presented with sufficient evidence regarding the regularity of the meeting, it will then generally refuse to inquire further as to the fruits of the meeting."[387]

The courts have held that action taken at an improperly called meeting will be invalid no matter how many members are present, and that even a majority of church members present at an improperly called meeting cannot "validate" the meeting by waiving the notice requirements.[388] However, action taken at an improperly called meeting can be ratified or affirmed by the church membership at a properly called meeting.[389]

If notice has been given according to a church's bylaws, a meeting may not be challenged by a disgruntled minority. Thus, when oral notice of a special church membership meeting was announced from the church pulpit in accordance with the church's bylaws, a minority of members who had ceased attending the church and therefore did not receive actual notice of the meeting were not permitted to overturn the actions taken at the meeting on the basis of inadequate notice.[390]

2. QUORUM

Churches should and often do prescribe in their charter or bylaws the number of members that must be present at general or special membership meetings in order for business to be transacted. This minimum number is generally referred to as a *quorum*. State nonprofit corporation law ordinarily specifies a quorum for incorporated churches that have not defined this important term in their charter or bylaws. To illustrate, section 16 of the Model Nonprofit Corporation Act provides that

> [t]he bylaws may provide the number or percentage of members entitled to vote represented in person or by proxy, or the number or percentage of votes represented in person or by proxy, which shall constitute a quorum at a meeting of members. In the absence of any such provision, members holding one-tenth of the votes entitled to be cast on the matter to be voted upon represented in person or by proxy shall constitute a quorum.

Established church custom will control in the case of unincorporated churches having no bylaws or written regulations.

Ordinarily, so long as a quorum is present, a majority of members has the authority to act on behalf of the entire membership provided the meeting was properly called and a greater number or percentage of votes is not mandated by church charter or bylaws. This of course means that in some cases a minority of members can bind a church.[391] For example, if a church's bylaws fix the quorum at 50 percent of the voting members, then as few as 26 percent of the total membership can act on behalf of the church. On the other hand, efforts to avoid minority rule by boosting the quorum requirement may result in too few members being present to conduct business.

---

[387] McKinney v. Twenty-fifth Avenue Baptist Church, Inc., 514 So.2d 837 (Ala. 1987).
[388] Hollins v. Edmonds, 616 S.W.2d 801 (Ky. 1981); Bangor Spiritualist Church, Inc. v. Littlefield, 330 A.2d 793 (Me. 1975); Brooks v. January, 321 N.W.2d 823 (Mich. App. 1982); Old Folks Mission Center v. McTizic, 631 S.W.2d 433 (Tenn. 1981).
[389] Hill v. Sargent, 615 S.W.2d 300 (Tex. 1981).
[390] Gelder v. Loomis, 605 P.2d 1330 (Okla. 1980). *See also* Zimbler v. Felber, 445 N.Y.S.2d 366 (1981).
[391] Padgett v. Verner, 366 S.W.2d 545 (Tenn. 1963).

If a church has no bylaw provision or established custom concerning quorums, it is unnecessary to demonstrate that a majority or any other percentage of the total membership attended a particular meeting in order to validate the action taken at the meeting.[392]

3. VOTING

in general

Unless otherwise restricted by charter, bylaw, statute, or custom, every member of a church congregation is entitled to vote at a membership meeting, and a majority of those members present at a duly called meeting at which a quorum is present can take action on behalf of the church. Section 15 of the Model Nonprofit Corporation Act defines the voting rights of members as follows:

> The right of the members . . . to vote may be limited, enlarged or denied to the extent specified in the articles of incorporation or the bylaws. Unless so limited, enlarged or denied, each member . . . shall be entitled to one vote on each matter submitted to a vote of the members.

Church charters, bylaws, customs, and applicable state nonprofit corporation laws occasionally impose limitations on the right to vote. To illustrate, some nonprofit corporation laws restrict the right to vote in church membership meetings to members who have contributed financially to the support of the church.[393] Churches themselves sometimes enact similar resolutions or bylaws. For example, a church can adopt a resolution restricting the right to vote to members who are "paid up" and who do not neglect their offerings for three consecutive months. Such a resolution will prohibit any member from voting who has neglected to pay offerings for three consecutive months even if the failure to pay was a matter of conscience.[394]

If the right to vote is not restricted by charter, bylaw, custom, or statute, then some courts have ruled that all members of a church may vote in a church membership meeting regardless of age[395] or sex.[396] And, where the signing of a church's bylaws was a condition of church membership, a person who joined the church but failed to sign the bylaws was ineligible to vote.[397] Churches occasionally restrict the right to vote to members who have attended the church for a prescribed period, and of course such limitations must be satisfied in order for a member to be eligible to vote.

A member's right to vote may be lost by voluntary withdrawal from a church. Certainly, members who quit attending a church and publicly state that they have quit the church and will never be back have abandoned their membership and no longer are eligible to vote in membership meetings.[398] But in many cases

---

[392] State Bank v. Wilbur Mission Church, 265 P.2d 821 (Wash. 1954).

[393] First Slovak Church of Christ v. Kacsur, 65 A.2d 93 (N.J. 1949) (members held not qualified to vote because they did not satisfy the statutory requirement that they "contribute regularly" to the support of their church); Anthony v. Cardin, 398 N.Y.S.2d 215 (1977) (holding that contributions of ten cents per week were inadequate to satisfy the statutory requirement that voting members contribute to the support of the church).

[394] Sixth Baptist Church v. Cincore, 91 So.2d 922 (La. 1957).

[395] Hopewell Baptist Church v. Gary, 266 A.2d 593, 597 (N.J. 1970) (rejected contention that only members who had attained the age of 21 years be permitted to vote despite fact that almost two-thirds of a church's 900 members were under 21, since "[s]ound policy dictates that this court refrain from establishing such a limitation by judicial fiat"). *See also* In re Galilee Baptist Church, 186 So.2d 102 (Ala. 1966); Randolph v. Mount Zion Baptist Church, 53 A.2d 206 (N.J. 1947).

[396] Smith v. Riley, 424 So.2d 1166 (La. App. 1982).

[397] Kubilius v. Hawes Unitarian Congregational Church, 79 N.E.2d 5 (Mass. 1948).

[398] Lewis v. Wolfe, 413 S.W.2d 314 (Mo. 1967).

determining with certainty whether a member has voluntarily withdrawn from a church is difficult, since withdrawal is often a process that sometimes is temporarily or permanently reversed. Churches can reduce confusion in this area by defining voting membership in terms of prescribed attendance or financial support.

Members wishing to contest some irregularity in a particular election or vote must object to the irregularity at the meeting. One court has ruled that objections to voting procedures must start when a vote is being taken, not months later when the events have passed from peoples' minds and the matters that were voted on have been accomplished.[399]

proxy voting

Section 15 of the Model Nonprofit Corporation Act recognizes proxy voting:

A member entitled to vote may vote in person or, unless the articles of incorporation or the bylaws otherwise provide, may vote by proxy executed in writing by the member or by his duly authorized attorney-in-fact. No proxy shall be valid after eleven months from the date of its execution, unless otherwise provided in the proxy . . . .

Proxy voting refers to voting by means of a substitute. For example, John White, a member of First Church, appoints Jane Brown to vote on his behalf at a membership meeting. Churches rarely intend to permit proxy voting. *Robert's Rules of Order, Newly Revised,* specifically discourages it: "Ordinarily, it should neither be allowed nor required, because proxy voting is incompatible with the essential characteristics of a deliberative assembly in which membership is individual, personal, and non-transferable. . . . [V]oting by proxy should not be permitted unless the state's corporation law . . . absolutely requires it."[400] Few if any state nonprofit corporation laws require proxy voting. Rather, they recognize proxy voting only in the event that a corporation has not eliminated this type of voting by a provision in its charter or bylaws. This can lead to unexpected consequences when an incorporated church's charter and bylaws do not prohibit proxy voting.

Example. *During a regular church business meeting, a member moved to terminate the services of the church's minister. Of the members present, 42 voted to retain the minister, and 32 voted to remove him. In addition, one of the 32 dissidents produced a list of 57 proxy (absentee) votes to remove the minister from office. The moderator of the business meeting refused to recognize the proxy votes, and the attempt to remove the minister failed. The dissident members thereafter filed a lawsuit seeking a court order upholding the validity of proxy votes in church business meetings. A state trial court ruled against the dissidents, and the case was appealed directly to the Alaska Supreme Court. In an important decision, the court reversed the trial court and held that the proxy votes should have been counted. It based its decision on the provisions of the Alaska Nonprofit Corporations Act (under which the church had incorporated) which authorized proxy voting by members of nonprofit corporations absent a contrary provision in an organization's charter or bylaws. The court rejected the church's claim that requiring it to recognize proxy votes violated the constitutional guaranty of religious freedom. Finally, the court observed that a church could easily avoid the recognition of proxy votes by simply amending its charter or bylaws to so state.* [401]

---

[399] Cosfol v. Varvoutis, 213 A.2d 331 (Pa. 1965).
[400] ROBERT'S RULES OF ORDER 360 (newly revised ed. 1981).
[401] Herning v. Eason, 739 P.2d 167 (Alaska 1987). *But see* First Union Baptist Church v. Banks, 533 So.2d 1305 (La. App. 1988).

Example. A Jewish congregation called a special business meeting to determine whether or not to retain its rabbi. The congregation, by a vote of 23 to 21, voted to submit the dispute to a panel of three orthodox rabbis for a final decision. The minority challenged this vote on the ground that four proxy votes (which were not counted at the business meeting and which agreed with the minority) were improperly disregarded at the meeting. Had they been counted, the vote would have been 25 to 23 against submitting the dispute to an arbitration panel. The court observed that the state nonprofit corporation law (under which the synagogue had been incorporated) permits proxy voting unless prohibited by the corporation's charter or bylaws. The court noted that the bylaws adopted "Robert's Rules or Order," which rejects proxy voting. The court concluded that this case perfectly illustrated the reason why proxy voting is discouraged: "It is obvious from the tenor of the membership meeting . . . that the congregation was split almost evenly among those members who 'loved' [the rabbi] or 'disliked' him vociferously. Such a meeting, by its nature, would call for extensive deliberation. Who can tell how many congregants were swayed to vote one way or the other based upon the arguments presented at the meeting?"[402]

Example. A New York court refused to recognize proxy voting in a congregational meeting conducted by a synagogue. The court concluded that proxy voting was not permissible since it was not authorized by the synagogue's charter (articles of incorporation) or bylaws—even if the membership voted at a meeting to permit it. The court observed that unless specifically authorized by state nonprofit corporation law, or a church's articles of incorporation or bylaws, "proxy voting by members of a religious corporation is not authorized." As a result, proxy votes should not have been counted at the synagogue's membership meetings.[403]

Example. An Ohio court ruled that the members of a nonprofit corporation could not vote by proxy at a special business meeting since proxy voting was not authorized in the corporation's articles of incorporation or bylaws.[404] It noted that Ohio's Nonprofit Corporation Law specifies that "unless the articles of incorporation or the regulations otherwise provide, no member who is a natural person shall vote or act by proxy." While the corporation's bylaws allowed amendments by proxy voting, the articles of incorporation did not. Since the proposed amendment involved the definition of "members" in the articles of incorporation, proxy voting was not authorized and was invalid.

Incorporated churches not wanting to recognize proxy voting should review their charter and bylaws to determine if either contains a provision prohibiting it. If not, an amendment would be in order. It should not be assumed that a church's formal adoption of *Robert's Rules of Order* will result in the prohibition of proxy voting.

how many votes are required?

After determining the qualified voting members of a church who are present at a church membership meeting, a church must ensure that all other voting requirements imposed by charter, bylaw, custom, or statute are satisfied. Often there is confusion over the number of votes required to adopt a particular action. For example, if the church bylaws require a particular vote to be by "a majority of members," does this mean a majority of the total church membership or a majority of those members present at a duly convened membership meeting? If only a majority of those present at a membership meeting is required, then it is possible for an action to be adopted by a minority of the total church membership. To illustrate, if 60 percent of the

[402] Frankel v. Kissena Jewish Center, 544 N.Y.S.2d 955 (1989).
[403] Holler v. Goldberg, 623 N.Y.S.2d 512 (Sup. 1995).

total church membership attends a duly convened meeting, and 55 percent of those present vote to take a particular action, then the church has taken an official action even though only 33 percent (*i.e.,* 55 percent of 60 percent) of the total church membership assented to it. Can this be said to constitute a vote by a majority of members?

Of course, a church can and should define the term *majority of members* to avoid this confusion. For example, a provision in a church's bylaws requiring that a particular kind of vote be by majority vote of the church's total membership would preclude action by a majority of members present at a duly called meeting unless they comprised a majority of the church's entire membership. But if a church nowhere defines *majority of members*, or any other term relating to the required number of votes needed to adopt an action, the fraction or percentage of votes needed to adopt an action generally has reference to the members present at a duly called meeting and not to the entire church membership.[405] To illustrate, section 16 of the Model Nonprofit Corporation Act specifies that "[a] majority of the votes entitled to be cast on a matter to be voted upon by the members present or represented by proxy at a meeting at which a quorum is present shall be necessary for the adoption thereof unless a greater proportion is required by . . . the articles of incorporation of the bylaws."

One court was asked to define the term *three-fourths of the voting members present* in a controversy involving the dismissal of a pastor.[406] Certain members of the congregation became dissatisfied with a new pastor, and a special church business meeting was called to determine whether or not he should be discharged. Of the 26 members who attended the meeting, 18 voted to discharge the pastor and 8 did not vote. The church bylaws specified that "a pastor may be terminated by the church congregation . . . but only if . . . the vote equals or exceeds *three-fourths of the voting members present.*" The pastor refused to acknowledge that the vote resulted in his dismissal, since less than "three-fourths of the voting members present" had voted to dismiss him (18 is only 70 percent of 26). Several disgruntled members of the congregation disagreed with this interpretation, and petitioned a court for a ruling recognizing that the congregational vote had resulted in the dismissal of the pastor. The members argued that the phrase "three-fourths of the voting members present" should be interpreted to mean three-fourths of the individuals who actually cast votes at the business meeting rather than three-fourths of all members actually present and eligible to vote. Since all 18 of the persons who actually voted at the meeting voted to dismiss the pastor, 100 percent of the votes were cast in favor of dismissal. A state appeals court ruled that the pastor had not been lawfully dismissed in the meeting in question. The court relied on *Robert's Rules of Order,* which had been adopted by the church (in its bylaws) as the governing body of parliamentary procedure. The following excerpt from *Robert's Rules of Order* was quoted by the appeals court in support of its decision in favor of the pastor:

> Assume, for example, that at a meeting of a society with a total membership of 150 and a quorum of 10, there are 30 members present, of whom 25 participate in a given counted vote. Then, with respect to that vote: a two-thirds vote is 17; a vote of two-thirds of the members present is 20; a vote of two-thirds of the entire membership is 100 . . . . Regarding these bases for determining a voting result, the following points should be noted—voting requirements based on the number of members present, while possible, are generally undesirable. *Since an abstention in such cases has the same effect as a negative vote, these bases deny members the right to maintain a neutral position by abstaining. For the same reason, members present who fail to vote through indifference rather than through deliberate neutrality may affect the result negatively.*[407]

---

[404] Hecker v. White, 688 N.E.2d 289 (Ohio App. 1996).

[405] Mack v. Huston, 256 N.E.2d 271 (Ohio 1970). *See generally* FLETCHER CYC. CORP. § 2020 (perm. ed. 1996).

[406] Blanton v. Hahn, 763 P.2d 522 (Ariz. App. 1988).

[407] *Id.* at 524 (emphasis in original).

According to this language, concluded the court, the phrase "three-fourths of the voting members present" meant three-fourths "of the individuals present and eligible to vote." Accordingly, the pastor had not been dismissed by the congregational vote since less than three-fourths of the members present and eligible to vote had voted to dismiss him.

If a church's charter, constitution, or bylaws do not designate the required percentage of votes for an affirmative action, then there is a presumption of majority rule. The United States Supreme Court has observed that "[m]ajority rule is generally employed in the governance of religious societies."[408] Other courts similarly have concluded that majority representation is presumed to apply to church determinations unless such a presumption is overcome by express provision in the church's organizational documents, or by a provision in the constitution or bylaws of a parent denomination.[409]

Occasionally, a church's charter, bylaws, and, in some cases, its constitution contain conflicting provisions regarding the required number of votes necessary for adoption of a particular action. As has been noted elsewhere, provisions in the charter prevail over provisions in the constitution, bylaws, or resolutions; provisions in the constitution prevail over provisions in the bylaws, or resolutions; and provisions in the bylaws prevail over provisions in resolutions.[410] In most cases, an incorporated church is bound by the provisions of state nonprofit corporation law only where it has not expressly provided otherwise in its own charter, constitution, or bylaws.

Example. The South Carolina Supreme Court ruled that it lacked the authority to resolve an internal church dispute regarding the percentage vote required to retain the pastor in a vote of confidence. The group supporting the pastor argued that the church bylaws required a three-fourths vote of the congregation for a "no-confidence" vote, while the group opposing the pastor argued that only a simple majority vote was needed. The court ruled that it was without legal authority to "dictate procedures for the church to follow in terminating its pastor."[411]

other methods of voting (by hand, secret ballot, absentee voting)

Votes can be cast orally, by show of hands, or by secret ballot. The method used is governed by the church's charter or bylaws. If the charter and bylaws are silent, established church custom will control. The members present at a meeting can also approve of a particular manner of voting if the church charter or bylaws do not speak to the subject. It has been held that a vote will be upheld even if it was not conducted by secret ballot as required by the corporate bylaws if no one objected to the vote during the meeting.[412] *Robert's Rules of Order, Newly Revised*, which has been adopted by many churches, specifies:

The bylaws of the organization may prescribe that the vote be by ballot in certain cases, as in the election of officers and in admission to membership. Any vote related to charges or proposed charges before or after a trial of a member or an officer should always be by ballot. Except as may be otherwise provided by the bylaws, a vote by ballot can be ordered (without debate) by a majority vote—which may be desirable in any case where it is believed that members may thereby be more likely to vote their true sentiments.[413]

---

[408] Jones v. Wolf, 443 U.S. 595, 607 (1979).
[409] Foss v. Dykstra, 342 N.W.2d 220 (S.D. 1983).
[410] *See* § 6-02.2, *supra.*
[411] Knotts v. Williams, 462 S.E.2d 288 (S.C. 1995).
[412] FLETCHER CYC. CORP. § 2017 (perm. ed. 1996).
[413] ROBERT'S RULES OF ORDER 348 (newly revised ed. 1981).

Absentee voting is not ordinarily permitted unless expressly sanctioned by charter, bylaw, custom, or statute. Again, *Robert's Rules of Order, Newly Revised*, specifies:

> It is a fundamental principle of parliamentary law that the right to vote is limited to the members of an organization who are actually present at the time the vote is taken in a legal meeting. Exceptions to this rule must be expressly stated in the bylaws. . . . An organization should never adopt a bylaw permitting a question to be decided by a voting procedure in which the votes of persons who attend a meeting are counted together with ballots mailed in by absentees, since in practice such a procedure is likely to be unfair.[414]

§ 6-12.2 — Minutes

Key point 6-12.2. Written minutes should be maintained for every church membership meeting. Minutes should reference (1) the date of the meeting, (2) the number of members present, (3) the progression of every action from motion to final action, (4) some statement that each adopted action was approved by the necessary number of votes, and (5) a verbatim transcript of each approved action.

The church secretary should prepare written minutes of every church membership meeting, being careful to note (1) the date of the meeting, (2) the number of members present, (3) the progression of every action from motion to final action, (4) some statement that each adopted action was approved by the necessary number of votes (a tally of the votes for and against a particular action should be inserted in the minutes if the vote is close or the action is of an extraordinary nature), and (5) a verbatim transcript of each approved action. Minutes should be signed by the church secretary, but this is not a legal requirement.[415]

The purpose of the minutes is to memorialize in a permanent and official form the actions taken by a church's membership. It has been said that the minutes are the "voice" of the corporation, and that a corporation will be bound by representations contained in its minutes that are relied upon by outsiders, even if the minutes were irregular.[416]

§ 6-12.3 — Parliamentary Procedure

Key point 6-12.3. Every church should adopt a system of parliamentary procedure to govern membership meetings. While Robert's Rules of Order, Newly Revised, is a commonly used system, it is not the only available system and will not apply unless a church has adopted it in its governing documents.

An organization may adopt any procedure that it desires for the conduct of membership meetings. *Robert's Rules of Order, Newly Revised*, or any other body of parliamentary procedure is not applicable unless specifically adopted.[417] Churches can and should select a specific body of parliamentary procedure by an appropriate clause in the church charter or bylaws. If a particular system of parliamentary procedure has been used by common consent long enough to constitute a church practice or custom, then it probably would be considered as binding as if specifically adopted by a provision in the church's charter or bylaws. If no body of parliamentary procedure has been adopted, either expressly or by custom, it has been held that the ordinary

---

[414] *Id.* at 355-56.
[415] *Id.*
[416] Fletcher Cyc. Corp. § 2190 (perm. ed. 1995).
[417] Abbey Properties Co. v. Presidential Insurance Co., 119 So.2d 74 (Fla. 1960). *See also* Blanton v. Hahn, 763 P.2d 522 (Ariz. App. 1988); Frankel v. Kissena Jewish Center, 544 N.Y.S.2d 955 (1989).

rules of parliamentary law should be observed in the conduct of a meeting.[418] It also has been held that the courts may review an action taken at a church membership meeting to ensure compliance with applicable parliamentary procedure.[419]

There are three important considerations for churches to note regarding parliamentary procedure. First, churches should not assume that *Robert's Rules of Order, Newly Revised,* is the only system of parliamentary procedure. It is not. On the contrary, there are dozens of alternative systems of parliamentary procedure, some of which are excellent (some would say superior) alternatives. Second, many churches adopted the original *Robert's Rules of Order,* or one of the earlier revisions. The original text was published in 1876, and it has been revised on seven occasions. The current revision was released in 1981. Obviously, churches that select "Robert's Rules" should be sure to identify this system of parliamentary procedure as "the most recent revision of *Robert's Rules of Order.*" Otherwise, they may have to resort to obsolete rules to resolve parliamentary questions. Third, no system of parliamentary procedure should serve as a substitute for specific provisions in a church's bylaws. In other words, the fact that a church wanting to prohibit absentee voting has adopted *Robert's Rules of Order, Newly Revised,* should not serve as substitute for a bylaw provision prohibiting absentee voting. There is no assurance that a civil court would regard the adoption of "Robert's Rules" as an exception to the general rule that state nonprofit corporation law will control when a church's bylaws are silent.

Once it is determined that a particular body of parliamentary procedure has been adopted by a church, the civil courts have expressed willingness to apply and enforce that procedure on the ground that no doctrine or substantive ecclesiastical question is involved.[420] Similarly, a federal appeals court ruled that the United States Constitution bars the civil courts from resolving disputes over parliamentary rulings.[421] Noting that the contested parliamentary action (made at the 1985 Southern Baptist Convention) had been reviewed and upheld by the highest Southern Baptist tribunal, the court concluded that "where religious organizations establish rules for their internal discipline and governance, and tribunals for adjudicating disputes over these matters, the Constitution requires that civil courts accept their decisions as binding upon them."

§ 6-12.4 — Effect of Procedural Irregularities

Key point 6-12.4. *Most courts refuse to intervene in church disputes concerning the validity of a membership meeting that was not conducted in accordance with the procedural requirements specified in the church's governing documents. However, some courts are willing to intervene in such disputes if they can do so without inquiring into religious doctrine or polity.*

Many courts have concluded that material procedural irregularities—such as disregard of notice, quorum, or voting requirements in a church's charter or bylaws—will invalidate a membership meeting and any actions taken therein, and that the civil courts will uphold the rights of those challenging the validity of such a meeting provided that no interpretation of religious doctrine is necessary.[422] Some courts refuse to permit any judicial interference with the internal affairs of churches, and accordingly hold that civil courts cannot review the determinations of churches even where a lawsuit is brought alleging that the church disregarded its own procedures in the conduct of a meeting.[423] This view generally is based on the assumption that the first

---

[418] Randolph v. Mount Zion Baptist Church, 53 A.2d 206 (N.J. 1947).

[419] Umberger v. Johns, 363 So.2d 63 (Fla. 1978).

[420] Umberger v. Johns, 363 So.2d 63 (Fla. App. 1978).

[421] Crowder v. Southern Baptist Convention, 828 F.2d 718 (11th Cir. 1987).

[422] Third Missionary Baptist Church v. Garrett, 158 N.W.2d 771 (Iowa 1968); Hollins v. Edmonds, 616 S.W.2d 801 (Ky. 1981); Bangor Spiritualist Church, Inc. v. Littlefield, 330 A.2d 793 (Me. 1975); Fast v. Smyth, 527 S.W.2d 673 (Mo. 1975); Atkins v. Walker, 200 S.E.2d 641 (N.C. 1973); Old Folk Mission Center v. McTizic, 631 S.W.2d 433 (Tenn. 1981).

amendment prohibits courts from interfering with the purely internal affairs of churches. Such a rendering of the first amendment would appear to be too broad under the prevailing interpretation of that amendment by the United States Supreme Court.

It is true that there is no room for civil court review of any internal church decision based on the interpretation of religious doctrine. On this point all courts would agree. But, many internal church disputes involve the interpretation of purely secular language in church charters, bylaws, deeds, and trusts. The Supreme Court has suggested that there is room for marginal civil court review of the internal decisions of churches and church tribunals where the reviewing court can resolve the dispute solely on the basis of "neutral principles" of law.[424] The Court specifically held that "neutral principles" of law include nondoctrinal language in charters, deeds, and bylaws. One court in upholding the majority view observed that "we have no hesitancy in holding that this controversy is properly before us, our decisions being controlled entirely by neutral principles of law."[425]

Procedural requirements pertaining to notice, quorums, and voting generally involve no references to religious doctrine and thus actions adopted at a church membership meeting convened or conducted in violation of a church's procedural requirements occasionally are invalidated by a civil court.[426] In the case of incorporated churches, this rule has been justified on the ground that a religious corporation is an artificial entity created by law and capable of acting only in the manner prescribed by state law or its own internal regulations, and therefore compliance with such procedural requirements is a prerequisite to a valid meeting.[427]

The subject of civil court intervention in internal church disputes is addressed more fully in chapter 9.

Example. A New Jersey court held that procedural irregularities in a congregational meeting did not affect the congregation's vote to affiliate with a denomination. A local congregation was duly informed that a vote would be taken at its annual business meeting on whether or not to affiliate with the Catholic Church. The pastor of the church adjourned the business meeting and rescheduled it for a week later to allow representatives of the Catholic Church to speak. At the rescheduled meeting the congregation voted to affiliate with the Catholic Church. Members who voted against the affiliation sought a court order invalidating the vote on the ground that it was conducted at an improperly called meeting. The dissenters pointed out that the church's bylaws specified that only the board of trustees had the authority to adjourn and reschedule congregational meetings. The court concluded it would not invalidate the vote of the congregation despite the fact that the meeting was conducted in violation of the church's bylaws. It based this result on two factors. First, the civil courts have the authority to resolve property disputes within local congregations so long as they can do so without interpreting religious doctrine. There were two property interests involved in this case, the court observed—"the right to worship in a familiar surrounding," and a lease agreement entered into between the congregation and Catholic Church following the vote to affiliate. Second, the court concluded that the subject of the congregational meeting (whether or not to affiliate with the Catholic Church) was religious in nature and therefore the civil courts had no authority to

[423] Rodyk v. Ukrainian Autocephalic Orthodox Church, 296 N.Y.S.2d 496 (1968), *aff'd*, 328 N.Y.S.2d 685 (1972); Hill v. Sargent, 615 S.W.2d 300 (Tex. 1981).
[424] Jones v. Wolf, 443 U.S. 595 (1979). The Court in *Jones* expressly repudiated the apparent holding in Serbian Eastern Orthodox Diocese v. Milivojevich, 426 U.S. 696 (1976), that the courts *must* defer to the determinations of religious tribunals within hierarchical churches by noting that the first amendment did not require such a rule where no issue of religious doctrine is involved.
[425] Bangor Spiritualist Church, Inc. v. Littlefield, 330 A.2d 793 (Me. 1975).
[426] *Id.*
[427] *Id.*

interfere with what was done even though the bylaws had been violated. The court observed, "[T]his court can discern a no more spiritual matter than a determination by the congregation of who should shepherd its flock. The majority of the congregation . . . chose to invite the priests of [the Catholic Church] to be its spiritual leaders. . . . To invalidate [the meeting and vote] would subjugate the will of the majority on the basis of a minor procedural infraction."[428]

Example. *A New York court ruled that a congregational meeting called by members of a synagogue to vote on the rehiring of a dismissed rabbi was not valid since it was not called according to the synagogue's bylaws. The synagogue's membership was bitterly divided over the continued retention of their rabbi. The dispute was submitted to an arbitration panel which ruled that the synagogue's board of trustees was authorized to discontinue the rabbi's employment. In response to this ruling, a group of ten members called for a special meeting "concerning the tenure of our rabbi." At this meeting, the membership voted to rehire the rabbi. Members of the congregation asked a civil court to determine the legality of this special meeting, and the vote that was taken. A court ruled that the meeting was legally invalid because it was not called in accordance with the synagogue's bylaws. The bylaws permit any ten members to call for a special meeting, provided that at least five days notice of the meeting is given to members by the recording secretary. The court concluded that "[s]ince it is clear that the notice was not sent by the secretary of the synagogue, as required by the bylaws, to the members in good standing as of the date of mailing, I declare that the [special business meeting] was not validly held."*[429]

§ 6-12.5 — Judicial Supervision of Church Elections

Key point 6-12.5. Some courts will supervise church elections to ensure compliance with the procedural requirements specified in the church's governing documents, if they can do so without inquiring into religious doctrine or polity.

Some courts have been willing to supervise a church election to ensure compliance with applicable procedural requirements if the church requests such supervision or if certain members allege that the church has disregarded procedural requirements in the past.[430] To illustrate, in one case, former members who had been expelled by their church asserted that the meeting at which the congregation voted to expel them had not been called with adequate notice. The trial court held that the meeting at which the dissidents had been expelled was invalid due to inadequate notice. It also scheduled an election at which the congregation would determine, by majority vote, the proper membership of the church; prescribed the notice to be given; provided for the counting of ballots by a court officer; and ordered an accounting of all church funds. The Alabama Supreme Court upheld the decision of the trial court, noting that "it is proper for the courts to inquire whether a congregational meeting, at which church business is to be transacted, was preceded by adequate notice to the full membership, and whether, once called, the meeting was conducted in an orderly manner and the expulsion was the act of the authority within the church having the power to order it."[431] However, "once the court is presented with sufficient evidence regarding the regularity of the meeting, it will then generally refuse to inquire further as to the fruits of the meeting."

---

[428] Ardito v. Board of Trustees, 658 A.2d 327 (N.J. Super. Ch. 1995).

[429] Holler v. Goldberg, 623 N.Y.S.2d 512 (Sup. 1995).

[430] First Union Baptist Church v. Banks, 533 So.2d 1305 (La. App. 1988); LeBlanc v. Davis, 432 So.2d 239 (La. 1983); Fast v. Smyth, 527 S.W.2d 673 (Mo. 1975); Second Baptist Church v. Mount Zion Baptist Church, 466 P.2d 212 (Nev. 1970); Rector, Church Wardens and Vestrymen of St. Bartholomew's Church v. Committee to Preserve St. Bartholomew's Church, 56 N.Y.2d 71 (1982).

[431] McKinney v. Twenty-fifth Avenue Baptist Church, Inc., 514 So.2d 837 (Ala. 1987).

On the other hand, the same court ruled that it had no authority to determine which members in a Baptist church are qualified to vote in a church election. A dispute arose in a local Baptist church, and certain members petitioned a state trial court to order a church election to resolve the matter. At the election the votes of 35 individuals were challenged and not counted. The result of the ballots counted was a 74 to 74 tie. One group of members petitioned the court to have the challenged votes counted. The trial court refused to grant this request, noting that "if this court ordered the challenged ballots to be counted, it would be determining that they were members who were eligible to vote. This it cannot do . . . ."

The court acknowledged that its refusal to order the challenged ballots to be counted "leaves the [church] without redress in the courts for even arbitrary acts of a preacher in either falsely challenging voters or intentionally bringing in non-members to vote." However, the trial court concluded that "there is nothing this court can do about it" since prior rulings of the state supreme court prohibited courts from resolving church membership issues. The trial court's ruling was appealed to the Alabama Supreme Court, which agreed that its previous rulings "do not authorize courts to determine the eligibility of church members to vote," and that "to order that certain votes be counted, which theretofore were not counted, would have been tantamount to doing that very thing, i.e., determining eligibility." The supreme court concluded, "In each Baptist church the majority of the members of the church control the business of the church. Also, all the members of a Baptist church are entitled to vote at a congregational meeting, regardless of age. However, *the issue as to which members are eligible to vote is a matter within the discretion of the members of the church*. . . . Because each Baptist church is a democratic institution whose membership possesses the right to vote, perforce it is the church itself under its rules that must examine the eligibility of its individual members to participate in that democracy."[432]

Another court ruled that it had the authority to order a church election since the church board refused to call one.[433]

> ***Example.*** *A Texas state appeals court concluded that a trial court had the authority to call a new church election. The court defended the trial court's action by noting that "an election was held which resulted in [the pastor's discharge], that he has refused to accept the termination, that he has since interfered with church services and will continue to do so . . . and will dissipate funds and property owned by the church unless he is restrained from doing so." The court rejected the pastor's claim that the trial court's intervention violated the constitutional guaranty of religious freedom. It noted that "the vote of a majority of the members of a Baptist church is generally binding in any matter touching the church government or affairs," and that "rules and regulations, including election procedures, made by church functionaries or by long usage will be enforced by the civil courts if not in conflict with some civil law bearing upon the subject of such rules and regulations." It concluded that the trial court had "sought to act in accord with church rules and regulations as dictated by long established custom and usage" and accordingly did "not usurp church authority."[434]*

> ***Example.*** *The Alabama Supreme Court ruled that it was proper for a trial court to resolve an internal church dispute over a church election since both sides to the dispute agreed to civil court involvement. The court began its opinion by observing that "civil courts cannot adjudicate religious disputes concerning spiritual or ecclesiastical matters, but the courts can resolve disputes concerning civil or property rights." However, the court noted that "[c]ertainly, in this case, where both sides agreed to let the court determine the eligibility of the voters, this court has the authority to hear the case."[435]*

---

[432] Mount Olive Baptist Church v. Williams, 529 So.2d 972 (Ala. 1988).
[433] Willis v. Davis, 323 S.W.2d 847 (Ky. 1959).
[434] Ex parte McClain, 762 S.W.2d 238 (Tex. App. 1988).
[435] Bacher v. Metcalf, 611 So.2d 1030 (Ala. 1992).

§ 6-12.6 — Who May Attend

Key point 6-12.6. *Whether or not a church can prevent an individual from attending a membership meeting will depend on the provisions of the church's governing documents as well as the system of parliamentary procedure adopted by the church.*

Who is entitled to be present at a church meeting? Who may lawfully be excluded? These questions often cause confusion, particularly in the context of schismatic churches in which one or more factions desire to prevent attorneys, news media personnel, or members of the public from attending. The following considerations will determine to what extent a church can exclude nonmembers from attending church membership meetings:

First, the charter, constitution, and bylaws of the church should be consulted to determine if they address the question. Ordinarily, they do not.

Second, determine what body of parliamentary procedure has been adopted by the church. Many systems of parliamentary procedure permit nonmembers to be excluded from a membership meeting. One authority states the rule as follows:

> Nonmembers, on the other hand—or a particular nonmember or group of nonmembers—can be excluded any time from part or all of a meeting of a society, or from all of its meetings. Such exclusion can be effected by a ruling of the chair in cases of disorder, or by the adoption of a rule on the subject, or by an appropriate motion as the need arises—a motion of the latter nature being a question of privilege.[436]

Third, many states and the federal government have enacted public meeting laws which generally provide that meetings of specified governmental agencies, commissions, and boards, at which official acts are taken, must be open to the public. Such laws, often called sunshine acts, ordinarily do not apply to private, nonprofit organizations,[437] and they certainly do not apply to entities, such as churches, receiving no tax revenues and having no regulatory authority or relationship with any governmental body. The fact that a church is incorporated will not subject it to the provisions of public meeting laws.[438]

§ 6-13 Powers of a Local Church

It often is necessary to determine the nature and extent of a church's powers, for a church's actions may be subject to challenge if they exceed the church's authority. As has been noted elsewhere,[439] unincorporated churches possess only such authority as is granted to them by state law. Many states have enacted legislation enabling unincorporated churches to sue and be sued and to hold property in the name of trustees. But without any specific delegation of authority from the state, an unincorporated church has no legal powers and must act in the name of its members.[440]

---

[436] ROBERT'S RULES OF ORDER 539 (newly revised ed. 1981).

[437] *See, e.g.*, Marston v. Wood, 425 So.2d 582 (Fla. App. 1982) (public meeting law did not apply to a law school committee organized to select a new dean); Perlongo v. Iron River Co-op TV Antenna Corp., 332 N.W.2d 502 (Mich. App. 1983) (state public meeting law did not apply to a nonprofit, nonstock corporation).

[438] Perlongo v. Iron River Co-op TV Antenna Corp., 332 N.W.2d 502 (Mich. App. 1983).

[439] *See* § 6-01, *supra.*

[440] Jacobs v. St. Mark's Baptist Church, 415 So.2d 253 (La. App. 1982).

Most states have enacted some form of corporation law under which churches may incorporate. Often, a church may incorporate under either a general nonprofit corporation law or a religious corporation law. State nonprofit corporation law ordinarily confers several specific powers upon organizations that incorporate. To illustrate, section 5 of the Model Nonprofit Corporation Act states that a corporation has the authority: (1) to exist perpetually; (2) to sue and be sued; (3) to acquire or dispose of property; (4) to lend money to its employees other than its officers and directors; (5) to make contracts, incur liabilities, borrow money, and issue notes and bonds; (6) to lend money; (7) to elect or appoint officers and directors; (8) to adopt bylaws not inconsistent with the articles of incorporation; (9) to indemnify directors or officers against expenses incurred in connection with lawsuits arising because of the performance of their duties (but there is no indemnification if the director or officer is found to have been guilty of negligence or other misconduct); (10) to establish pension plans; (11) to cease its corporate activities; and (12) to have and exercise all powers necessary or convenient to accomplish any of the purposes for which the corporation is organized.

Some courts have recognized that statutes governing religious corporations reflect a public policy of granting religious organizations wide latitude in the conduct of their affairs, both spiritual and temporal.[441]

It is important to recognize that corporations derive their existence and powers from the state. It follows that corporations are without authority to do any act not expressly authorized by statute or implied from a power specifically granted.[442]

Some states place restrictions on the power of religious corporations to own property. These restrictions include limitations on the number of acres a religious corporation may own, limitations on the total dollar value of the property a religious corporation may own, limiting the property a religious corporation may own to only such property as is reasonably necessary for the corporation's purposes, and limiting the kinds of property that a religious corporation may own.[443]

Some states limit the power of religious corporations to sell or encumber property. For example, some states limit the power of churches to sell property without court approval,[444] or without a specified percentage of voter approval.[445] A number of states limit the power of religious corporations to receive testamentary gifts. These restrictions generally fall into two categories: statutes limiting the amount of property that a religious organization may receive under a will, and statutes invalidating any testamentary gift to a religious organization if the will was executed within a prescribed time before the grantor's death. For example, some states prohibit certain testamentary gifts to a church if the will is executed within 90 days before the grantor's death.[446] A few states invalidate certain testamentary gifts that exceed a specified portion of the total value of the grantor's estate.[447] The subject of state limitations on testamentary gifts to charity is discussed in detail elsewhere.[448]

---

[441] Hopewell Baptist Church v. Gary, 266 A.2d 593 (N.J. 1970), aff'd, 270 A.2d 409 (N.J. 1970).

[442] Succession of Fisher, 103 So.2d 276 (La. 1958); Babcock Memorial Presbyterian Church v. Presbytery of Baltimore, 464 A.2d 1008 (Md. App. 1983); Old Folks Mission Center v. McTizic, 631 S.W.2d 433 (Tenn. 1981).

[443] See generally Kauper & Ellis, supra note 7, at 1545-46.

[444] Application of Church of St. Francis De Sales, 442 N.Y.S.2d 741 (1981) (applying section 12 of the New York Religious Corporations Law).

[445] MODEL NONPROFIT CORPORATION ACT § 44 (requiring approval of a two-thirds majority for a sale of all or substantially all of the property of a corporation).

[446] GA. CODE § 53-2-10; MISS. CODE ANN. § 91-5-31.

[447] OHIO REV. CODE § 2107.06.

[448] See § 9-03, infra.

The powers of churches affiliated with religious hierarchies often are restricted or regulated by the parent ecclesiastical body. For example, the local churches of some denominations possess either limited authority or no authority to purchase or sell property, incur obligations, elect officers, or adopt bylaws.[449]

In addition to conferring specific, express powers upon charitable corporations, state nonprofit corporation laws typically contain a provision granting to incorporated charities the power to have and exercise all powers necessary or convenient to effect any or all of the purposes for which the organization is organized. Such a provision enables a church corporation to list in its charter various powers not specifically delegated by state corporation law. Therefore, in determining whether a church is empowered to take a particular action, the church charter must be reviewed in addition to the statute under which the church was incorporated. It is important to note, however, that a church may not include a power in its charter that would contravene law or public policy.[450] It is a well-settled rule of law that religious corporations, like business corporations, also possess *implied authority* to take all actions that are reasonably necessary in order to accomplish those powers expressly granted by charter or statute.[451]

In summary, in determining whether a church corporation possesses the authority to take a particular action, the following analysis should be employed:

1. Review the statute under which the church was incorporated to determine if the power was expressly granted.

2. Review the church's charter to see if the power was expressly granted.

3. If the proposed church action is not expressly authorized by either statute or the church's charter, determine whether the church possesses implied authority to perform the act. Generally, a church possesses implied authority to take any action reasonably necessary to carry out the powers expressly granted by charter or state corporation law.

4. A corporation is never authorized to perform an act that is prohibited by law or public policy.

The courts generally have held that a corporation's bylaws cannot confer powers upon the corporation that are not granted by statute or charter, although the bylaws may regulate the manner in which a corporation's powers are exercised.[452] It is often said that corporations lack the authority to perform any act that is illegal, contrary to public policy, or that would constitute a public nuisance. Thus, it has been held that a church has no authority to exercise powers, even those expressly granted, in such a way as to cause a disturbance of the peace.[453]

Since most church corporations are incorporated under statutes expressly limiting them to nonprofit or religious purposes, churches generally have no authority to engage in substantial commercial enterprises for

---

[449] Babcock Memorial Presbyterian Church v. Presbytery of Baltimore, 464 A.2d 1008 (Md. App. 1983).

[450] *See generally* FLETCHER CYC. CORP. § 2477 (perm. ed. 1996). Molasky Enterprises, Inc. v. Carps, Inc., 615 S.W.2d 83, 86-87 (Mo. 1981) ("[T]he powers and existence of a corporation are derived from the state creating it. It functions under its charter which is a contract between it and the state in which it is organized. The statutory laws of the state applicable to it enter into and become a part of its articles of incorporation.").

[451] Synod of Chesapeake, Inc. v. City of Newark, 254 A.2d 611, 613-614 (Del. 1969). ("[A]ny contemporary church group, to be worth its salt, must necessarily perform nonreligious functions . . . . Accordingly, such activities may not be banned as unrelated to church ritual."); Sales v. Southern Trust Co., 185 S.W.2d 623 (Tenn. 1945).

[452] FLETCHER CYC. CORP. § 2494 (perm. ed. 1996).

[453] *See* § 7-09, *infra*.

profit. An act performed by a church corporation in excess of its express and implied powers is referred to as *ultra vires*. Considerable confusion surrounds the legal status of *ultra vires* actions. A majority of states permit *ultra vires* acts of a corporation to be challenged in only the following three situations:

1. A proceeding by a member or director against the corporation seeking an injunction prohibiting the corporation from doing an unauthorized act.

2. A proceeding by the corporation against the officers or directors of the corporation for exceeding their authority.

3. A proceeding by the state to dissolve the corporation or to enjoin the corporation from performing unauthorized acts.

If the *ultra vires* act was a contract that has already been executed, it is generally held that the parties to the contract are entitled to compensation for the loss or damages sustained by them as a result of a judicial determination setting aside or prohibiting the performance of the contract.[454]

§ 6-14   Merger and Consolidation

> *Key point 6-14. Two or more religious congregations can merge or consolidate. In a merger, one corporation absorbs the other and remains in existence while the other is dissolved, whereas in a consolidation a new corporation is created and the consolidating corporations are extinguished. The procedure for merging and consolidating incorporated churches is specified by state nonprofit corporation law.*

Although the terms *merger* and *consolidation* frequently are used interchangeably, they have separate legal meanings. In a merger, one corporation absorbs the other and remains in existence while the other is dissolved, whereas in a consolidation a new corporation is created and the consolidating corporations are extinguished.

One court has observed that a church's decision to either merge or consolidate is a religious question that should be of concern to no one other than the congregations involved, that the choice is one to be made by the respective members in the exercise of their religious beliefs, and that their freedom to make this choice is guaranteed by the first amendment against federal or state interference.[455] Although the state may not interfere with a church's decision to merge or consolidate, a church must follow those procedures in its own governing documents or in applicable state nonprofit corporation law for a valid merger or consolidation to occur. State nonprofit corporation laws governing mergers and consolidations often are separate and distinct. As a result, a church seeking to merge with another church may not employ a state law governing consolidations, and two churches desiring to consolidate may not use a state law governing mergers. State nonprofit corporation law may contain a single procedure governing both mergers and consolidations, but this must not be assumed. The Model Nonprofit Corporation Act contains separate procedures, and this is the practice in most states.

Unincorporated congregational churches generally are not restricted by state corporation law, and may merge or consolidate whenever the respective congregations of the merging or consolidating churches so

---

[454] *See generally* FLETCHER CYC. CORP. ch. 40 (perm. ed. 1997); Free For All Missionary Baptist Church, Inc. v. Southeastern Beverage & Ice Equipment Co., Inc., 218 S.E.2d 169 (Ga. 1975).

[455] Mount Zion Baptist Church v. Second Baptist Church, 432 P.2d 328 (Nev. 1967).

desire, provided that applicable provisions in each church's bylaws are followed. However, an unincorporated church and an incorporated church will not be permitted to merge under a state nonprofit law requiring that both of the merging churches be incorporated.[456]

Incorporated churches, like any other form of corporation, derive their corporate existence and powers from the state. It follows that an incorporated church has the power to merge or consolidate only if such power is expressly delegated by state corporation law. Most religious and nonprofit corporation laws grant churches the power to merge or consolidate. Such laws typically prescribe the following procedure:

1. Board resolutions. The board of directors of each church desiring to merge or consolidate adopts a resolution approving of the proposed plan and submits it to a vote of members having voting rights at a general or special meeting.

2. Notice. Written notice of the proposed plan is given to each member eligible to vote.

3. Approval. The proposed plan is adopted if at least two-thirds of the votes cast approve of the plan.

4. Articles of merger or consolidation. Upon approval of the plan by the voting members, each corporation executes either *articles of merger* or *articles of consolidation* on a form prescribed by the secretary of state. This document sets forth the plan of merger or consolidation, the date of the meeting at which the plan was approved, and a statement that a quorum was present and that the plan received at least two-thirds voter approval. The articles of merger or articles of consolidation are filed with the secretary of state.[457]

Church charters or bylaws may impose further requirements that must be followed.[458] And, if a proposed merger or consolidation would alter the doctrines of a church, it is essential to the validity of such a merger or consolidation that the church congregation possess the authority to change its doctrine and that the required number of members assent to the change.[459] Church corporations affiliated with religious hierarchies must of course comply with applicable procedures in the constitution or bylaws of the parent ecclesiastical body.

The legal effect of a merger or consolidation generally is determined by state corporation law and the terms of the merger or consolidation agreement. State corporation law typically stipulates that all the properties of a church corporation that merges with another congregation belong to the surviving corporation. Similarly, the properties of two consolidating churches belong to the new corporation resulting from the consolidation. The surviving corporation in the case of a merger or the new corporation in the case of a consolidation is responsible for all the liabilities and obligations of each of the corporations so merged or consolidated. Thus, neither the rights of creditors nor any liens upon the property of such corporations is affected by a merger or consolidation.

§ 6-15   Dissolution

Key point 6-15. *The procedure for dissolving an incorporated church is specified by state nonprofit corporation law.*

---

[456] Trinity Pentecostal Church v. Terry, 660 S.W.2d 449 (Mo. App. 1983).
[457] MODEL NONPROFIT CORPORATION ACT §§ 38-43.
[458] In re Estate of Trimmer, 330 N.E.2d 241 (Ill. 1975); In re First Methodist Church, 306 N.Y.S.2d 969 (1970).
[459] *See generally* FLETCHER CYC. CORP. ch. 61 (perm. ed. 1990).

The dissolution of incorporated churches generally is regulated by state corporation law since the state alone has the authority to dissolve those organizations it has created.[460] Corporate dissolutions may be either voluntary or involuntary. A voluntary corporate dissolution is accomplished by the corporation itself. Most state religious and nonprofit corporation laws contain a specific procedure for voluntary dissolution, which generally consists of the following elements:

1. Board resolution. The board of directors adopts a resolution recommending that the corporation be dissolved and directing that the question of dissolution be submitted to the church membership.

2. Notice to members. All voting members are notified in writing that the question of dissolution will be discussed at a special or general meeting of the members.

3. Approval. A resolution to dissolve the corporation is adopted if it receives at least two-thirds voter approval.

4. Notice to creditors. Notice of the dissolution is mailed to all creditors of the former corporation.

5. Payment of debts. All corporate liabilities are paid. Any assets remaining after payment of liabilities are transferred to the organization or organizations, if any, prescribed in the dissolved corporation's charter or in the controlling rules of a church hierarchy, if any, with which the church is affiliated. If neither the charter nor controlling rules of a religious hierarchy specifies how corporate assets are to be distributed following dissolution, the assets are conveyed to one or more organizations engaged in activities substantially similar to those of the dissolving corporation.

6. Articles of dissolution prepared. The articles of dissolution are executed. The articles set forth the name of the corporation, the date of the meeting of members at which the resolution to dissolve was adopted, and an acknowledgment that a quorum was present, that the resolution was adopted by at least two-thirds of the members present at such meeting, that all debts of the corporation have been paid, and that all remaining assets of the corporation have been transferred to the organization specified in the corporation's charter, or, if no organization is specified, to an organization engaged in activities substantially similar to those of the dissolving corporation.

7. Articles of dissolution filed. The articles of dissolution are filed with the secretary of state. If the articles of dissolution conform to all legal requirements, the secretary of state issues to a representative of the dissolved corporation a certificate of dissolution, which is recorded with the office of the recorder of deeds of the county in which the church had been located.[461]

It is important to recognize that the IRS maintains that every incorporated church must contain a provision in its charter ensuring that in the event of a dissolution the assets of the church will pass to a tax-exempt organization. The IRS has stated that the following provision will suffice:

> Upon the dissolution of the corporation, assets shall be distributed for one or more exempt purposes within the meaning of section 501(c)(3) of the Internal Revenue Code, or corresponding section of any future federal tax code, or shall be distributed to the federal government, or to a state or local government, for a public purpose. Any such assets not so disposed of shall be disposed of by the

---

[460] Fletcher Cyc. Corp. § 7971 (perm. ed. 1995).
[461] Model Nonprofit Corporation Act §§ 45-51.

Court of Common Pleas of the county in which the principal office of the corporation is then located, exclusively for such purposes or to such organization or organizations, as said Court shall determine, which are organized and operated exclusively for such purposes.[462]

A church, of course, may specify in its charter the tax-exempt organization to which its assets will pass upon dissolution. A dissolution clause is necessary in order to ensure the tax-exempt status of a church, since a church will not be considered entitled to tax-exempt status if any part of its net earnings or assets is payable to or for the benefit of any private individual.[463] It is important to emphasize that the property of a dissolved church will be conveyed to a charitable organization having purposes and activities substantially similar to those of the dissolved church if neither the church charter nor controlling rules of an ecclesiastical hierarchy provide otherwise. Thus, the courts have held that the members of a dissolving church had no authority to distribute church assets to a theological seminary or a servicemen's center, since neither organization was substantially related in purpose or activity to the dissolving church.[464] And, if a dissolving church is affiliated with a religious hierarchy whose internal rules require that the assets of a dissolving local church revert to the parent organization, the members of a dissolving church have no authority to distribute the church's assets to another organization.[465] In addition to the procedures specified by state corporation law, church corporations also are bound by the procedural requirements of their own charters and bylaws, or the controlling rules of a parent ecclesiastical body, in a dissolution proceeding.[466]

The corporation law of many states provides that church corporations may be dissolved involuntarily by the attorney general upon the occurrence of one or more of several grounds, including failure to pay fees prescribed by law, failure to file an annual report, fraudulent solicitation of funds, and exceeding the authority conferred by state corporation law.[467] Such laws typically permit church corporations to be dissolved involuntarily by a director or member if the directors are so deadlocked in the management of the corporation that irreparable injury to the corporation is being suffered; the acts of the directors are illegal, oppressive, or fraudulent; the corporation's assets are being wasted; or the corporation is unable to carry out its purposes.[468] To illustrate, one court found that an involuntary dissolution of a church was warranted since dissension over the dismissal of one minister and the hiring of another was so bitter that the church could no longer conduct its operations.[469] However, one court held that riots and violence within a church that lasted for only two weeks was not a frustration of the church's purposes and did not constitute an adequate basis for involuntary dissolution.[470]

Example. *An Illinois appeals court dismissed a lawsuit brought by members of a church seeking to dissolve their church and have a receiver appointed to liquidate church assets. A schism occurred in a Baptist church over the retention of the pastor. Problems worsened due to disagreements over the pastor's plan to use church funds to build a school. Some members opposed placing a mortgage on the debt-free church building to raise construction funds. When efforts to remove the pastor and those deacons who*

---

[462] IRS Publication 557. An abbreviated version of this language, which also is acceptable to the IRS, appears in Rev. Proc. 82-2, 1982-1 C.B. 367.

[463] I.R.C. § 501(c)(3). The income tax regulations also specify that an organization is not organized exclusively for exempt purposes if its assets are payable to individuals or nonexempt organizations upon dissolution.

[464] Metropolitan Baptist Church v. Younger, 121 Cal. Rptr. 899 (1975).

[465] Polen v. Cox, 267 A.2d 201 (Md. 1970); German Evangelical Lutheran St. Johannes Church v. Metropolitan New York Synod of the Lutheran Church in America, 366 N.Y.S.2d 214 (1975), *appeal denied,* 378 N.Y.S.2d 1025 (1975).

[466] Presbytery of the Covenant v. First Presbyterian Church, 552 S.W.2d 865 (Tex. App. 1977).

[467] MODEL NONPROFIT CORPORATION ACT § 51.

[468] *Id.* at § 54(a).

[469] Fuimaono v. Samoan Congregational Christian Church, 135 Cal. Rptr. 799 (1977).

[470] Hill v. Abyssinia Missionary Baptist Church, 370 So.2d 1389 (Ala. 1979).

supported him failed, some of the disgruntled members filed a lawsuit in civil court seeking an order dissolving the church and transferring its assets to a receiver for distribution to another nonprofit organization. Illinois law permits a voting member or director to "involuntarily dissolve" a nonprofit corporation that is unable to carry out its purposes. The disgruntled members claimed that this procedure was available since the church was unable to carry out its purpose of conducting religious worship because of the controversy. A trial court agreed to dissolve the church and turn over its assets to a receiver for distribution to another nonprofit organization, but a state appeals court reversed this ruling on the ground that the persons who brought the lawsuit did not qualify as members of the church and therefore lacked "standing" to sue. The court noted that even if the former members had standing to sue, they could not prevail since the civil courts lack jurisdiction to determine whether or not the church "could carry out its purposes since the court's decision of that issue [would violate] the first amendment's prohibition against civil courts' involvement in religious matters. . . . [T]he underlying dispute, who will be the pastor at [the church], is an ecclesiastical matter which is not within the court's purview."[471]

If a church, in the regular course of its affairs, is unable to pay its debts and obligations as they come due, the nonprofit corporation laws of many states permit an incorporated church to be involuntarily dissolved by a creditor whose claims are unsatisfied.[472]

Unincorporated churches having no affiliation with a religious hierarchy are mere voluntary associations of persons and may dissolve on their own initiative by a vote of the membership, by abandonment of the church, or by withdrawal of all members from the church, assuming that all applicable provisions in the church's bylaws or other internal rules are followed. The property of unincorporated churches generally is in the name of trustees. The IRS maintains that an unincorporated church is not eligible for exemption from federal income taxes unless its organizational document stipulates that all assets held in trust for the use and benefit of the church will pass to another charitable, tax-exempt organization upon dissolution of the church. Obviously, neither the trustees nor former members have any personal claim to trust assets following the dissolution of a church. This requirement is based on the fact that the Internal Revenue Code prohibits tax-exempt status to any organization whose net earnings or assets are payable to or for the benefit of any private individual.[473] If an unincorporated church has failed to include a provision in its organizational document providing for disposition of trust assets following dissolution of the church, a court may nonetheless direct that all trust assets pass to another charitable organization having similar purposes to those of the dissolved church. This power of the courts to determine the status of the trust assets of a dissolved church is known as the *cy pres* doctrine.

---

[471] Hines v. Turley, 615 N.E.2d 1251 (Ill. App. 1993).
[472] MODEL NONPROFIT CORPORATION ACT § 54(b).
[473] I.R.C. § 501(c)(3).

INSTRUCTIONAL AIDS TO CHAPTER 6

Terms

apparent authority

articles of incorporation

books of account

bylaws

certificate of incorporation

charter

Church Audit Procedures Act

church tax examination

church tax inquiry

civil, contract, or property rights

common interest privilege

congregational

consolidation

constitution

corporation sole

cy pres doctrine

de facto corporation

defamation

directors

dissolution

employment taxes

express authority

good faith

hierarchical

implied authority

incorporation

inherent authority

IRS audits

maturity of members

margin of civil court review

meetings

members

membership corporation

merger

minutes

Model Nonprofit Corporation Act

neutral principles of law

nonprofit

notice

officers

proxy voting

quorum

religious activities

resolution

Revised Model Nonprofit Corporation Act

subpoena

tax-exempt

trademark

trustee corporation

trustees

unfair competition

unincorporated association

Uniform Management of Institutional Funds Act

Volunteer Protection Act

Learning Objectives

- Understand the legal differences between an unincorporated and an incorporated church, and explain the advantages of the corporate form of organization.

- Define the terms *charter, constitution, bylaws,* and *resolution,* and explain the legal priorities among these terms.

- Describe the legal authority of church members to inspect church records.

- Explain the purpose and application of the Church Audit Procedures Act.

- Summarize several state and federal reporting requirements that apply to many churches.

- Identify several potential theories of personal legal liability for church officers and directors.

- Explain the application of charitable immunity laws to church officers and directors.

- Describe the two approaches to civil court intervention in church membership determinations.

- Explain the legal effect of church meetings that are conducted in violation of a church's bylaws.

Short-Answer Questions

1. First Church is not incorporated. G, a member, is driving a church van during a church-sponsored activity, and he negligently causes an accident injuring 2 other members in the van and the driver of another vehicle. Answer the following questions, and explain your reasoning:

   a. Can the 2 injured members sue G?

   b. Can the 2 injured members sue First Church?

   c. Can the 2 injured members sue other members of First Church?

   d. Can the injured driver of the other vehicle sue G?

   e. Can the injured driver of the other vehicle sue First Church?

   f. Can the injured driver of the other vehicle sue the members of First Church?

2. Same facts as question 1, except that First Church is incorporated.

   a. Can the 2 injured members sue G?

   b. Can the 2 injured members sue First Church?

   c. Can the 2 injured members sue other members of First Church?

   d. Can the injured driver of the other vehicle sue G?

   e. Can the injured driver of the other vehicle sue First Church?

   f. Can the injured driver of the other vehicle sue the members of First Church?

3. List 3 advantages and 3 disadvantages of the corporate form of organization.

4. Many attorneys say that they would be guilty of "legal malpractice" if they advised a church not to incorporate. What is the basis for this position?

5. A church incorporates under the Model Nonprofit Corporation Act. Its bylaws do not specify a quorum. What percentage of members will constitute a quorum at a church business meeting?

6. A church is incorporated under the Model Nonprofit Corporation Act. It has not sent in its annual report to the Secretary of State's office for the past three years. What is the legal effect of this omission?

7. A religious organization (not a church) incorporates under a state nonprofit corporation law. Does this render it exempt from federal income taxes? Explain.

8. Why do some churches prefer not to incorporate under the Model Nonprofit Corporation Act?

9. What is a corporate charter?

10. Should a church have both a constitution and a set of bylaws? Explain.

11. The charter of Trinity Church specifies that "all church property shall be sold in the event the church ceases to function and the proceeds distributed equally among the former members." Is this clause permissible?

12. What body of parliamentary law governs church business meetings?

13. A church charter recites the church's purpose as "religion, that is, the proclamation of the Gospel through all available means." Why might this purpose clause be inadequate?

14. What is the difference between a resolution and a bylaw?

15. The constitution of Second Church specifies that a quorum consists of one-half of the active membership. The church bylaws specify that a quorum consists of "60 members." The church board, recognizing the disparity, enacted a resolution stipulating that "the bylaws control in matters of quorums." How many members constitute a quorum?

16. A church charter specifies that the church shall have four board members. The church constitution provides for six. The church bylaws are amended to provide for one board member for each 100 church members. The church has 300 members. How many board members does the church have as a matter of law?

17. The IRS has drafted paragraphs that churches can insert in their charter. What do these paragraphs address? Can they be modified, or must the IRS version be used?

18. A member demands to see a church's financial records. The member claims that he has a right to see the church's records, and he cites the following legal grounds for his position. Which, if any, of these grounds would support the member's claim:

   a. The church is incorporated under the Model Nonprofit Corporation Act.

   b. The federal Privacy Act.

   c. The federal Freedom of Information Act.

   d. The church has issued $500,000 of church securities (promissory notes) to members, and the securities were registered under state securities law.

   e. The church bylaws give members the right to inspect church records at reasonable times for reasonable purposes.

19. Same facts as question 18. What (if any) defenses are available to the church in the event it does not want to disclose the records to the member?

20. A church receives a subpoena demanding production in court of various church records. Under what circumstances, if any, may the church disregard this subpoena?

21. Grace Church owns a large parking lot and two homes. It rents the parking lot to employees and patrons of neighboring businesses during the week, and rents the two homes on an annual lease basis. The IRS learns of the rental properties and would like to determine whether the church is engaged in an unrelated trade or business. It sends the church an inquiry notice in which the only explanation of the concerns giving rise to the inquiry is a statement that "you may be engaged in an unrelated trade or business." Is this inquiry notice legally sufficient under the Church Audit Procedures Act? Explain.

22. A church receives an IRS inquiry notice that does not mention the possible application of the first amendment principle of separation of church and state to church audits. Is this inquiry notice legally sufficient under the Church Audit Procedures Act? Explain.

23. Assume that the IRS receives a telephone tip that First Church may be engaged in an unrelated trade or business. Can a telephone tip serve as the basis for a church tax inquiry? Explain.

24. The IRS sends First Church written notice of a church tax inquiry on July 1. As of September 15 of the same year, no examination notice had been sent. The church tax inquiry must be concluded by what date? Why?

25. The IRS sends Second Church written notice of a church tax inquiry on June 10. On June 20 of the same year it sends written notice that it will examine designated church records on July 15. Is the examination notice legally sufficient under the Church Audit Procedures Act? Explain.

26. If the examination notice in question 25 is not legally sufficient, what is the church's remedy?

27. An IRS examination notice specifies that the "religious activities" of First Church will be examined as part of an investigation into a possible unrelated business income tax liability. Is the examination notice legally sufficient under the Church Audit Procedures Act? Explain.

28. The IRS sends an examination notice to First Church on March 20 of the current year. On June 1 of the same year, as part of its examination, the IRS requests several documents that it reasonably believes are necessary. The church refuses to disclose the documents, and the IRS seeks a court order compelling disclosure. This order is issued two years later, on July 1. Must the IRS examination be terminated on the ground that it was not completed within the 2-year statute of limitations? Explain.

29. Three years ago the IRS conducted an examination of the tax-exempt status of a local church. It concluded that the church was properly exempt from federal income taxation. During the current year the IRS initiates an examination of the same church to determine if it is engaged in an unrelated trade or business, and if it has been withholding taxes from nonminister employees. Is such an examination barred by the prohibition against repeated examinations within a five-year period? Explain.

30. The IRS initiates an audit against K, a member of Covenant Church. The audit focuses on the issue of whether or not K in fact made the substantial contributions to the church that she claimed on her tax return. The IRS contacts church officials, and asks to review contribution records. Is this inquiry subject to the Church Audit Procedures Act? Explain.

31. St. Thomas Church operates a separately-incorporated private elementary school. The IRS contacts the school concerning the basis for its tax-exempt status. Is this inquiry subject to the Church Audit Procedures Act? Why or why not?

32. A state attorney general suspects that a church has engaged in fraud in soliciting donations. Can the attorney general subpoena the church's donor list?

33. A church votes to disaffiliate from a denomination. May it continue to use the denomination's name in its title? Explain.

34. Calvary Church is an independent church that was organized in 1940. This year, another independent church calling itself "Calvary Church" opens in the same community. What, if any, legal right does the original church have to prevent the new church from using the same name?

35. Should an incorporated church hold title to property through trustees? Why or why not?

36. Briefly describe the four categories of authority of church officers, directors, and trustees.

37. Many churches use "staggered elections" of board members. What does this mean?

38. Explain the legal difference between an officer and a director of a church corporation.

39. T is a board member (not an officer) of Elm Street Church. T, without express authority, signs a contract on behalf of the church to purchase a new duplicating machine for the church. Answer the following questions:

    a. Did T have apparent authority to execute the contract?

    b. Assume that the machine is delivered to the church, and that the church accepts the machine and uses it for a month. It then finds another machine it likes better. Can it now seek to avoid T's contract on the ground that T had no legal authority to sign the contract?

40. In 1996 Bob donated $5,000 to his church with the stipulation that the money be used exclusively for the building program. This year the church board decides to cancel the building program. Bob demands a full refund of his contribution. If the church refuses to comply, what are Bob's legal rights? Can he ask a court to compel the church to return his designated contribution? Explain.

41. A church asked its members to contribute toward a missions project with a budget of $10,000. Barb donated $1,000 to the project, but learned later that the budget had been reached before she made her contribution. She asks the church to return her contribution. If the church refuses to comply, what are Barb's legal rights? Can she ask a court to compel the church to return her designated contribution? Explain.

42. A church plans to build a home for a low-income family. While much of the work is done by volunteer labor, and some of the materials are donated, the church still must raise $25,000 to complete the project. Bill does not attend the church, but he learns of the project and donates $1,000 to it. Several weeks after making his contribution Bill learns that the budget had been reached before he made his contribution. He asks the church to return his contribution. If the church refuses to comply, what are Bill's legal rights? Can he ask a court to compel the church to return his designated contribution? Explain.

43. A mother informs a member of the church board that her minor child was molested by a volunteer youth worker at a church activity. The board member does nothing about the allegation. The same volunteer later molests another child. Is the board member legally responsible for the injuries suffered by the second victim? Explain.

44. Can a church board take action by a conference telephone call?

45. M, a member of the board of Bethany Church, engages in conduct in violation of the church's moral teachings. The remaining board members vote to dismiss M from the board. M has served only 1 year of a 3-year term of office. He had been elected by the church membership. Do the other board members have the legal authority to remove M from the board? Explain.

46. Same facts as question 45. Does the church membership have the legal authority to remove M from the board? Explain.

47. B, a director at Northside Church, while driving a church vehicle on church business negligently causes an accident that injures C, an occupant of another vehicle. Can C sue B personally? Explain.

48. A child drowns during a church youth activity. The board is sued on the basis of "negligent supervision." Do board members have personal liability?

49. A church board member is not able to attend most meetings of the board, is not familiar with the church's financial statements or with its charter and bylaws, and does not ask questions about apparent irregularities. Has the board member violated any legal duty owed to the church?

50. J operates a carpet store in his community, and also serves as a director of his church. The church needs to recarpet the sanctuary, and J urges the board to let his company do the work. Does this arrangement violate any legal duty?

51. A church decides to raise funds for a new building by selling church bonds that it issues. The pastor and board actively sell the bonds to church members during and after church services. Do they incur any potential legal liability for doing so?

52. Same facts as the previous example. The board members represent to potential investors that the bonds are "as safe as if your money were invested in a bank, because they are invested in God's economy." Do the board members incur any potential legal liability for making such statements? Explain.

53. A financially struggling church fails to withhold payroll taxes from the wages of its employees (in order to meet payroll obligations). The IRS insists that each of the church's three officers is personally liable for the entire amount of unpaid taxes. Can the officers be personally liable in this manner? Explain.

54. Several members ask the church board to institute a program for screening volunteers who work with minors. The board discusses these proposals, but decides that such a program is not necessary. It bases its conclusion on the fact that no incident of child molestation has ever occurred at the church. A few months later, three minors are molested by a volunteer worker. Answer the following questions:

    a. Why might the parents be motivated to sue the board members personally, in addition to the church?

    b. If the board members are sued personally, what is the likely outcome? The board members insist that they are protected against any liability by a "limited immunity" statute in their state. Are they correct?

55. A church hires a new minister. To assist the minister in paying the down payment on a new home, the church board votes to loan the minister $20,000 over a 10-year term at no interest. Have the church board members acted properly? Do they face any potential legal liability? Explain.

56. Many states have enacted laws providing church board members with limited immunity from personal liability. Describe the requirements and exceptions that ordinarily are associated with these laws.

57. Summarize the two approaches the civil courts have taken when asked to intervene in internal church disputes involving discipline and dismissal of members.

58. A church member is accused of engaging in conduct that violates the church's moral teachings. The church board investigates the matter, determines the member is guilty, and dismisses him from membership in the church. The former member sues the church on the basis of a number of alleged wrongs. Evaluate whether any of the following allegations would support civil court review of the dismissal:

    a. "I have attended this church for many years and have made substantial contributions. My church membership is a valuable right that has been denied by the church's actions."

    b. "The church did not follow the procedure outlined in the church bylaws in dismissing me."

    c. "The church board did not have the authority to dismiss me. The church bylaws give this authority to the church membership."

    d. "The church bylaws do not clearly specify that what I did violated the church's moral teachings."

59. A church votes to expel a member, and its vote is upheld by an ecclesiastical commission of the denomination with which the church is affiliated. The member wants to challenge his expulsion in court. Under what circumstances will the civil courts review the membership determinations of ecclesiastical tribunals within hierarchical denominations?

60. The bylaws of First Church specify that notice of special business meetings must be given at the two Sunday morning services preceding the meeting. A special business meeting is called for September 1. Notice is given on only the immediately preceding Sunday morning. At the meeting, Rev. N is voted out of office. He contests the vote. Result?

61. A church's bylaws specify that "a pastor shall be considered elected if elected by a majority of members." At a church election at which a quorum of 52 out of 100 members is present, Rev. D receives 28 votes. Is Rev. D re-elected? Explain.

62. Church services and functions have been disrupted by a disgruntled member. What legal authority, if any, does the church have to exclude this individual from participating in church services and activities?

63. Explain the difference between merger and consolidation.

64. Define the term *dissolution*. What is a *dissolution clause* in a church charter?

Discussion Questions

1. Do you think it would be advisable to incorporate a church under a state nonprofit corporation law that regulated most areas of church procedure and administration in the absence of provisions to the contrary in the church's own charter, constitution, or bylaws? Or, would you prefer to incorporate a church under a nonprofit corporation law that left churches free to govern their own procedure and administration, and that did not "fill in the gaps" in a church's organizational documents. Explain.

2. The civil courts have struggled with the question of whether or not to intervene in internal church disputes involving membership determinations. Do you believe that the courts should have the authority to review church membership determinations in these areas? Explain. How might such disputes be avoided?

7

CHURCH PROPERTY

Chapter summary. There are many legal issues associated with church property. This chapter addresses several of them. For example, assume that a schism occurs in a local church and a dispute arises over ownership of the church's property. How do the civil courts resolve such a case? Which group will be awarded ownership of the property? Another important issue is the application of local zoning laws to religious congregations. Zoning laws specify the permitted uses of property within a community, and these laws sometimes conflict with a church's desire to use property for church purposes. Similarly, most communities have enacted building codes. To what extent do they apply to church buildings? Many communities have enacted "landmarking" ordinances that prohibit historic properties from being demolished or modified without approval. Do such laws apply to historic church buildings? For example, assume that a city designates a church as an historic landmark, and rejects the church's request to expand its building to accommodate a growing membership. Does the city have this authority? What about the church's constitutional right to freely exercise its religion? Other issues addressed in this chapter include title to church property; conveyances of church property; embezzlement of church funds; reversionary and dissolution clauses; restrictive covenants; materialmen's liens; liability for injuries occurring on church property; criminal liability for defacing church property; discrimination in the sale or rental of church property; eminent domain; and the removal of disruptive persons from church services. Most churches will face at least some of these issues, and so a familiarity with them is important.

§ 7-01   Church Property Disputes — In General

Church property disputes can arise in a variety of ways. In some cases, a church congregation splits over a doctrinal issue or the retention of a minister, with both groups claiming ownership of the church property. In other cases, a congregation votes to disaffiliate from a parent denomination, and the denomination asserts that it now owns the church's property. There are many other ways in which such disputes may occur. The courts have developed a number of rules for resolving such disputes, and these rules are described in the following sections.

§ 7-02   Church Property Disputes — Supreme Court Rulings

1. WATSON V. JONES (1871)

A study of the law of church property disputes must begin with the United States Supreme Court's decision in *Watson v. Jones,*[1] for the methodology outlined in *Watson* served as the principal means of resolving such disputes for nearly a century and continues to exert considerable influence. In *Watson,* the Court was faced with the problem of determining which of two factions in the Third or Walnut Street Presbyterian Church of Louisville, Kentucky, which had split in 1863 over the slavery controversy, was entitled to ownership of the church property. The Court began its analysis by observing: "The questions which have come

---

[1]   80 U.S. 679 (1871) [hereinafter cited as *Watson*].

before the civil courts concerning the rights of property held by ecclesiastical bodies, may, so far as we have been able to examine them, be profitably classified under three general heads . . . ."[2]

1. The first of these is when the property which is the subject of controversy has been, by the deed or will of the donor, or other instrument by which the property is held, by the express terms of the instrument devoted to the teaching, support, or spread of some specific form of religious doctrine or belief.

2. The second is when the property is held by a religious congregation which, by the nature of its organization, is strictly independent of other ecclesiastical associations, and so far as church government is concerned, owes no fealty or obligation to any higher authority.

3. The third is where the religious congregation or ecclesiastical body holding the property is but a subordinate member of some general church organization in which there are superior ecclesiastical tribunals with a general and ultimate power of control more or less complete, in some supreme judicatory over the whole membership of that general organization.[3]

As to the first type of case, the Court concluded that "it would seem . . . to be the obvious duty of the Court . . . to see that the property so dedicated is not diverted from the trust which is thus attached to its use,"[4] and

> [t]hough the task may be a delicate one and a difficult one, it will be the duty of the court in such cases, when the doctrine to be taught or the form of worship to be used is definitely and clearly laid down, to inquire whether the party accused of violating the trust is holding or teaching a different doctrine, or using a form of worship which is so far variant as to defeat the declared objects of the trust.[5]

As to the second type of case, the Court concluded:

The Court went on to observe:

> This ruling admits of no inquiry into the existing religious opinions of those who comprise the legal or regular organization; for, if such were permitted, a very small minority, without any officers of the church among them, might be found to be the only faithful supporters of the religious dogmas of the founders of the church. There being no such trust imposed upon the property when purchased or given, the Court will not imply one for the purpose of expelling from its use those who by regular succession and order constitute the church, because they may have changed in some respect their views of religious truth.[7]

In summary, *Watson* held that property disputes in a purely "congregational" church (*i.e.,* "a religious congregation which, by the nature of its organization, is strictly independent of other ecclesiastical associations") are to be decided by majority rule, and that this rule would apply even if the majority had defected from the faith of the church's founders.

---

[2] *Id.* at 722.

[3] *Id.* at 722-23.

[4] *Id.* at 723.

[5] *Id.* at 724.

[6] *Id.* at 725.

[7] *Id.*

As to the third type of case, the Court concluded:

> In this class of cases we think the rule of action which should govern civil courts . . . is, that, whenever the questions of discipline, or of faith, or ecclesiastical rule, custom, or law have been decided by the highest of these church judicatories to which the matter has been carried, the legal tribunals must accept such decisions as final, and as binding on them, in their application to the case before them. . . . All who unite themselves to such a body do so with an implied consent to this government, and are bound to submit to it. But it would be a vain consent and would lead to the total subversion of such religious bodies, if anyone aggrieved by one of their decisions could appeal to the secular courts and have them reversed. It is of the essence of these religious unions, and of their right to establish tribunals for the decision of questions arising among themselves, that those decisions should be binding in all cases of ecclesiastical cognizance, subject only to such appeals as the organism itself provides for.[8]

This third holding of *Watson* became known as the *compulsory deference rule*—courts must defer to the determinations of church tribunals with respect to "questions of discipline or of faith, or ecclesiastical rule, custom, or law," and, by implication, to *any* decision of a church tribunal. This holding applies generally to *hierarchical* churches, which the Court defined as churches that are "subordinate members of some general church organization in which there are superior ecclesiastical tribunals with a general and ultimate power of control more or less complete, in some supreme judicatory over the whole membership of that general organization." Some churches are independent of denominational control for some purposes, but not for others. In other words, they may be "hierarchical" only for some purposes. The analysis for hierarchical churches articulated in *Watson* would apply to such churches only if they are hierarchical with respect to the ownership or control of church property.

Civil courts generally have followed the Supreme Court's classification of churches into two categories—congregational and hierarchical. A few courts and legal commentators have divided churches into three categories. To illustrate, one commentator has observed:

> At least three kinds of internal structure, or "polity," may be discerned: congregational, presbyterial, and episcopal. In the congregational form each local congregation is self-governing. The presbyterial polities are representative, authority being exercised by laymen and ministers organized in an ascending succession of judicatories—presbytery over the session of the local church, synod over the presbytery, and general assembly over all. In the episcopal form power reposes in clerical superiors, such as bishops. Roughly, presbyterial and episcopal polities may be considered hierarchical, as opposed to congregational polities, in which the autonomy of the local congregation is the central principle.[9]

In the years following *Watson*, nearly every court that decided a church property dispute cited *Watson* and claimed to be following its methodology. In cases involving express trusts and hierarchical churches (the first and third "general heads"), the professed adherence to *Watson* was largely real.

But soon after *Watson* was decided, cases involving the ownership of property in divided congregational churches (the second "general head") began to deviate from the rule enunciated in *Watson*—that the majority in such congregations should dictate the ownership of church property whether or not that majority remained faithful to the doctrine of the church's founders. The seeming inequity of this rule prompted many courts to disregard *Watson*. Thus, many courts adopted the *implied trust doctrine*, under which church prop-

---

[8] *Id.* at 727, 729.
[9] Note, *Judicial Intervention in Disputes Over the Use of Church Property*, 75 HARV. L. REV. 1142, 1143-44 (1962).

erties were deemed to be held in trust for the benefit of those members adhering to the original doctrines of the church.[10] The property of congregational churches following a church split thus went to the faction adhering to the original doctrines of the church, whether that faction represented a majority or a minority of the church membership. This obviously was contrary to the spirit if not the letter of *Watson*, wherein the Court had observed: "There being no such trust imposed upon the property when purchased or given, the Court will not imply one for the purpose of expelling from its use those who by regular succession and order constitute the church, because they may have changed in some respect their views of religious truth."[11]

Several other courts held that if a majority of the members of a congregational church voted to change the denominational ties of the congregation, church property would be vested in the minority desiring to remain faithful to the original denomination.[12] Some courts applied the law of corporations to vest ownership of property in a minority faction of a congregational church where the majority had voted to deviate from the original doctrines. To illustrate, one court observed:

> It is the law of all corporations that a mere majority of its members cannot divert the corporate property to uses foreign to the purposes for which the corporation was formed. There is no difference between the church and other corporations in this regard. Where a church corporation is formed for the purpose of promoting certain defined doctrines of religious faith, which are set forth in its articles of incorporation, any church property which it acquires is impressed with a trust to carry out such purpose, and a majority of the congregation cannot divert the property to other inconsistent religious uses against the protest of a minority, however small. The matter of use of the property of the church corporation, within the range of its corporate powers, may be determined by the majority of the congregation, but no majority, even though it embrace all members but one, can use the corporate property for the advancement of a faith antagonistic to that for which the church was established and the corporation formed.[13]

A few courts remained true to the ruling in *Watson* and awarded title to congregational church property to the majority faction without any consideration of church doctrine.[14]

2. PRESBYTERIAN CHURCH IN THE UNITED STATES V. MARY ELIZABETH BLUE HULL MEMORIAL PRESBYTERIAN CHURCH (1969)

The wholesale disregard of *Watson's* holding with respect to congregational churches was reformed by the United States Supreme Court nearly a century after *Watson* in the landmark decision of *Presbyterian Church in*

---

[10] *See, e.g.*, Davis v. Ross, 53 So.2d 544 (Ala. 1951); Holiman v. Dovers, 366 S.W.2d 197 (Ark. 1963); Chatfield v. Dennington, 58 S.E.2d 842 (Ga. 1950); Sorrenson v. Logan, 177 N.E.2d 713 (Ill. 1961); Pentecostal Tabernacle of Muncie v. Pentecostal Tabernacle of Muncie, 146 N.E.2d 573 (Ind. 1957); Ragsdall v. Church of Christ, 55 N.W.2d 539 (Iowa 1952); Huber v. Thorn, 371 P.2d 143 (Kan. 1962); Philpot v. Minton, 370 S.W.2d 402 (Ky. 1963); Davis v. Scher, 97 N.W.2d 137 (Mich. 1959); Protestant Reformed Church v. Tempelman, 81 N.W.2d 839 (Minn. 1957); Mills v. Yount, 393 S.W.2d 96 (Mo. 1965); Reid v. Johnston, 85 S.E.2d 114 (N.C. 1954); Beard v. Francis, 309 S.W.2d 788 (Tenn. 1957); Baber v. Caldwell, 152 S.E.2d 23 (Va. 1967); Anderson v. Byers, 69 N.W.2d 227 (Wis. 1955).

[11] 80 U.S. 679 at 725.

[12] *See, e.g.*, Holt v. Scott, 42 So.2d 258 (Ala. 1949); Ables v. Garner, 246 S.W.2d 732 (Ark. 1952); Wright v. Smith, 124 N.E.2d 363 (Ill. 1955); Hughes v. Grossman, 201 P.2d 670 (Kan. 1949); Scott v. Turner, 275 S.W.2d 421 (Ky. 1954); Blauert v. Schupmann, 63 N.W.2d 578 (Minn. 1954); Montgomery v. Snyder, 320 S.W.2d 283 (Mo. 1958); Reid v. Johnston, 85 S.E.2d 114 (N.C. 1954); Beard v. Francis, 309 S.W.2d 788 (Tenn. 1957).

[13] Lindstrom v. Tell, 154 N.W. 969 (Minn. 1915).

[14] *See, e.g.*, Booker v. Smith, 214 S.W.2d 513 (Ark. 1948); Ennix v. Owens, 271 S.W. 1091 (Ky. 1925); Holt v. Trone, 67 N.W.2d 125 (Mich. 1954).

the United States v. Mary Elizabeth Blue Hull Memorial Presbyterian Church.[15] The question presented in *Hull* was whether a local Presbyterian church could retain title to its property after disassociating itself from the Presbyterian Church in the United States. In 1966, the membership of the Hull Memorial Presbyterian Church of Savannah, Georgia, voted to withdraw from the parent body on the grounds that it had so departed from the original tenets of the Presbyterian faith that it could no longer be considered the true Presbyterian Church. Specifically, the Hull church majority contended that the parent body had departed from Presbyterianism in "making pronouncements and recommendations concerning civil, economic, social and political matters, giving support to the removal of Bible reading and prayer by children in the public schools, . . . causing all members to remain in the National Council of Churches of Christ and willingly accepting its leadership which advocated . . . the subverting of all parental authority, civil disobedience and intermeddling in civil affairs," and also in "disseminating publications denying the Holy Trinity and violating the moral and ethical standards of faith." Accordingly, the local church argued that it had not disaffiliated itself from Presbyterianism, but rather that the Presbyterian Church in the United States had disassociated itself from Presbyterianism, and hence the parent denomination had no right to claim an interest in the property of the local church.

A state trial court ruled that the parent body had indeed abandoned Presbyterianism, and thus the Hull church was entitled to retain title to its property. The Supreme Court of Georgia affirmed. However, the United States Supreme Court reversed both rulings, concluding that

> the first amendment severely circumscribes the role that civil courts may play in resolving church property disputes. It is obvious, however, that not every civil court decision as to property claimed by a religious organization jeopardizes values protected by the first amendment. Civil courts do not inhibit free exercise of religion merely by opening their doors to disputes involving church property. And there are neutral principles of law, developed for use in all property disputes, which can be applied without "establishing" churches to which property is awarded. But first amendment values are plainly jeopardized when church property litigation is made to turn on the resolution by civil courts of controversies over religious doctrine and practice. If civil courts undertake to resolve such controversies in order to adjudicate the property dispute, the hazards are ever present of inhibiting the free development of religious doctrine and of implicating secular interests in matters of purely ecclesiastical concern. Because of these hazards, the first amendment enjoins the employment of organs of government for essentially religious purposes . . . ; the amendment therefore commands civil courts to decide church property disputes without resolving underlying controversies over religious doctrine. Hence, States, religious organizations, and individuals must structure relationships involving church property so as not to require the civil courts to resolve ecclesiastical questions.[16]

Hull thus may be reduced to the following two principles:

1. Civil courts *are forbidden* by the first amendment to decide church property disputes if the resolution of such disputes is dependent upon the interpretation of religious doctrine.

2. Civil courts *can* decide church property disputes consistently with the first amendment if they do so on the basis of principles involving no analysis of religious doctrine. Illustratively, the Court observed that there are "neutral principles of law developed for use in all property disputes, which can be applied without 'establishing' churches to which property is awarded." Unfortunately, the Court neither described what it

---

[15] 393 U.S. 440 (1969) [hereinafter cited as *Hull*].
[16] *Id.* at 449.

meant by "neutral principles of law," nor mentioned other doctrinally neutral and hence acceptable grounds for resolving church property disputes.

In effect, *Hull* wiped away much of the gloss that had been judicially applied to circumvent the second holding of *Watson*: that the majority faction in a congregational church has the right to all church property whether or not it supports or deviates from the original doctrines of the church. No longer could civil courts award congregational church property to a minority faction as a result of a judicial interpretation of religious doctrine. The first ruling in *Watson*—that property received by a church in an instrument expressly limiting the use of such property to the adherents of a particular religious doctrine or belief—was invalidated by *Hull* to the extent that civil courts are called upon to interpret religious doctrine. In many cases, of course, the civil courts could determine the ownership of property conveyed to a church subject to an express trust, for no interpretation of religious doctrine would be involved. Thus, Justice Harlan, concurring in *Hull*, noted:

> I do not . . . read the Court's opinion to . . . hold that the fourteenth amendment forbids civilian courts from enforcing a deed or will which expressly and clearly lays down conditions limiting a religious organization's use of the property which is granted. If, for example, the donor expressly gives his church some money on the condition that the church never ordain a woman as a minister or elder . . . or never amend certain specified articles of the Confession of Faith, he is entitled to his money back if the condition is not fulfilled. In such a case, the church should not be permitted to keep the property simply because church authorities have determined that the doctrinal innovation is justified by the faith's basic principles.[17]

The Supreme Court failed to discuss the effect of its decision on the third ruling of *Watson*—that the decision of an ecclesiastical judicatory is binding upon a local church in a hierarchical denomination. This omission was unfortunate and gave rise to much confusion.

In summary, the Supreme Court's decision in *Hull* was deficient in three respects: (1) it sanctioned a "neutral principles of law" approach to resolving church property disputes, but failed to describe what it meant by this new term; (2) it implied that the neutral principles of law approach was one of many acceptable methods of resolving church property disputes, but it failed to describe any other methods; and (3) it failed to explain the relationship between a neutral principles of law approach and the compulsory deference approach (*i.e.*, civil courts are compelled to defer to the rulings of church tribunals) of *Watson*.

3. Maryland and Virginia Eldership of the Churches of God v. Church of God (1970)

Subsequent cases have provided further clarification. In *Maryland and Virginia Eldership of the Churches of God v. Church of God*,[18] the United States Supreme Court was asked to review the constitutionality of the methodology employed by the courts of Maryland in resolving church property disputes. The Maryland approach involved the inspection by the courts of nondoctrinal provisions in (1) state statutes governing the holding of property by religious corporations; (2) language in the deeds conveying the properties in question to the local church corporations; (3) the terms of the charters of the corporations; and (4) provisions in the constitution of a parent denomination relating to the ownership and control of church property. Maryland courts awarded title to disputed church property according to the wording and effect of such documents, provided that this could be done without any inquiries into religious doctrine. The Supreme Court, in a *per curiam* opinion, summarily approved of the Maryland approach to the resolution of church property disputes.

---

[17] *Id.* at 452.
[18] 396 U.S. 367 (1970) [hereinafter cited as *Maryland & Virginia Eldership*].

In a concurring opinion, Justice Brennan, who had written the Court's opinion in *Hull*, attempted to resolve some of the questions raised by the *Hull* decision. First, Justice Brennan attempted to define the term *neutral principles of law*:

> [C]ivil courts can determine ownership by studying deeds, reverter clauses and general state corporation laws. Again, however, general principles of property law may not be relied upon if their application requires civil courts to resolve doctrinal issues. For example, provisions in deeds or in a denomination's constitution for the reversion of local church property to the general church, if conditioned upon a finding of departure from doctrine, could not be civilly enforced.[19]

Next, Justice Brennan suggested two other acceptable means of resolving church property disputes:

> [T]he States may adopt the approach of *Watson v. Jones* and enforce the property decisions made within a church of congregational polity "by a majority of its members or by such other local organism as it may have instituted for the purpose of ecclesiastical government," and within a church of hierarchical polity by the highest authority that has ruled on the dispute at issue, unless express terms in the instrument by which the property is held condition the property's use or control in a specified manner. . . . [Another] approach is the passage of special statutes governing church property arrangements in a manner that precludes state interference in doctrine. Such statutes must be carefully drawn to leave control of ecclesiastical polity, as well as doctrine, to church governing bodies.[20]

Finally, Justice Brennan emphasized that "a state may adopt *any* one of various approaches for settling church property disputes so long as it involves no consideration of doctrinal matters, whether the ritual and liturgy of worship or the tenets of faith."[21]

Thus, a court can properly resolve a church property dispute if it can do so solely on the basis of nondoctrinal language in deeds, state corporation laws, constitutions and bylaws of local churches or of parent ecclesiastical bodies, or state statutes pertaining to church property arrangements. Accordingly, a court could not intervene in a church property dispute involving a deed containing a reverter clause specifying that title to church property reverts to the parent ecclesiastical body if the local church deviates from the doctrine of the parent body, since the court would necessarily become involved in an interpretation of religious doctrine. But a reverter clause conditioned on a disaffiliation of a local church could be enforced by the courts, since enforcement would involve the nondoctrinal determination of whether or not a disaffiliation had occurred.

Further, a minority faction in a congregational church remaining faithful to the original doctrines of the church can no longer contend that the state law of corporations is violated when a majority votes to divert corporate property to uses foreign to the purposes for which the corporation was formed, since this obviously will necessitate interpretation of religious doctrine. If the constitution and bylaws of a parent ecclesiastical body provide for the reversion of local church property to the parent body itself in the event of a disaffiliation

---

[19] *Id.* at 370.

[20] *Id.* at 369, 370. Note that the concurring opinion emphasized that the civil courts "do not inquire whether the relevant church governing body has power under religious law to control the property in question. Such a determination, unlike the identification of the governing body, frequently necessitates the interpretation of ambiguous law and usage." *Id.* at 369. The concurring opinion concluded that "the use of the *Watson* approach is consonant with the prohibitions of the first amendment only if the appropriate church governing body can be determined without the resolution of doctrinal questions and without extensive inquiry into religious polity." *Id.* at 370.

[21] *Id.* at 368.

by a local church, the civil courts will intervene and enforce such a provision since it would not involve a question of religious doctrine. However, if the reverter clause conditioned reversion upon a departure or deviation from the doctrines of the parent body, an interpretation of religious doctrine would become necessary and accordingly such a clause would not be judicially enforceable.

The Court in *Maryland & Virginia Eldership* commented that civil courts can examine the ecclesiastical rulings of church judicatories in church property disputes to ensure that such rulings are not the product of "fraud, collusion, or arbitrariness."[22]

4. SERBIAN EASTERN ORTHODOX DIOCESE V. MILIVOJEVICH (1976)

In *Serbian Eastern Orthodox Diocese v. Milivojevich*,[23] the Supreme Court strongly affirmed *Watson's* compulsory deference approach to resolving church property disputes:

In short, the first and fourteenth amendments permit hierarchical religious organizations to establish their own rules and regulations for internal discipline and government, and to create tribunals for adjudicating disputes over these matters. When this choice is exercised and ecclesiastical tribunals are created to decide disputes over the government and direction of subordinate bodies, the Constitution requires that civil courts accept their decisions as binding upon them.[24]

The Court also held that civil courts could not review the rulings of church tribunals for arbitrariness, although it did imply that courts could review such rulings for fraud or collusion.

The Court's emphatic endorsement of the compulsory deference rule in *Serbian* caused considerable confusion about the continuing validity of the neutral principles of law approach. What, for example, would be the effect of a church tribunal's ruling in a church property dispute in a jurisdiction that followed the neutral principles of law approach? Would neutral principles supersede the church tribunal's ruling? Once again, the need for clarification was evident.

5. JONES V. WOLF (1979)

In *Jones v. Wolf*,[25] which was decided in 1979, the Supreme Court again turned its attention to church property disputes. Before analyzing *Jones*, it would be helpful to summarize the law of church property disputes as it existed prior to that decision:

1. Express trusts. When property is conveyed to a local church by an instrument that contains an express provision restricting the use of such property, such a restriction will be recognized by the civil courts if this can be

---

[22] In 1976, the Court ruled that the determinations of ecclesiastical judicatories in hierarchical churches involving questions of clergy discipline may not be disturbed by the civil courts on the basis of *arbitrariness*. Arbitrariness was defined as a failure by a judicatory to follow its own ecclesiastical procedure. The Court left unanswered the question of whether *fraud* or *collusion* remain legitimate grounds for civil court review of the disciplinary determinations of hierarchical judicatories. Presumably, arbitrariness is no longer a basis for civil court review of ecclesiastical determinations regarding property ownership, meaning that the civil courts cannot review such determinations even if it is alleged that a judicatory failed to follow its own stated procedures in reaching its result. Serbian Eastern Orthodox Diocese v. Milivojevich, 423 U.S. 696 (1976).

[23] 426 U.S. 696 (1976) [hereinafter referred to as *Serbian*].

[24] *Id.* at 724-25.

[25] 443 U.S. 595 (1979) [hereinafter referred to as *Jones*].

done without any consideration of religious doctrine. If a consideration of religious doctrine would be necessary, then the courts will not be able to resolve the question of ownership on the basis of the restrictive provision.[26]

2. Congregational churches. When a split occurs in a local congregational church, and a dispute arises as to the ownership of such property, courts may resolve the dispute in any of the following four ways:

Method 1. Civil courts may resolve the dispute on the basis of neutral principles of law, provided that this can be done without inquiries into religious doctrine. Neutral principles of law include nondoctrinal language in the following types of documents:

a. deeds[27]

b. local church charters[28]

c. constitution and bylaws of local church, and of parent ecclesiastical body[29]

Method 2. Civil courts may resolve the dispute on the basis of state statutes governing the holding of property by religious corporations, provided that application of such statutes involves no inquiries into religious doctrine.[30]

Method 3. Civil courts may resolve the dispute on the basis of the *Watson* rue of deference to the will of a majority of the members of a congregational church.[31] Ordinarily, this method is used only if method 1 and method 2 do not resolve the question of property ownership.

Method 4. Civil courts may resolve the dispute on the basis of any other methodology that they may devise "so long as it involves no consideration of doctrinal matters, whether the ritual and liturgy of worship or the tenets of faith."[32]

3. Hierarchical churches. When a split occurs in a local hierarchical church, and a dispute arises as to the ownership of church property, courts may resolve the dispute in any of the following three ways:

Method 1. Civil courts may resolve the dispute on the basis of neutral principles of law, provided that this can be done without inquiries into religious doctrine. Neutral principles of law include nondoctrinal language in the following types of documents:

a. deeds[33]

b. local church charter[34]

---

[26] Maryland & Virginia Eldership, 396 U.S. 367, 369 (1970) (Brennan, J., concurring).
[27] Maryland & Virginia Eldership, 396 U.S. 367, 370 (1970) (Brennan, J., concurring).
[28] *Id.*
[29] *Id.*
[30] *See* note 21, *supra,* and accompanying text.
[31] *See* note 6, *supra,* and accompanying text.
[32] Maryland & Virginia Eldership, 396 U.S. 367, 368 (1970) (Brennan, J., concurring).
[33] *See* note 30, *supra,* and accompanying text.
[34] *See* note 31, *supra,* and accompanying text.

c. constitution and bylaws of local church, and of parent ecclesiastical body[35]

Method 2. Civil courts may resolve the dispute on the basis of state statutes governing the holding of property by religious corporations, provided that application of such statutes involves no inquiries into religious doctrine.

Method 3. Civil courts may resolve the dispute on the basis of the *Watson* compulsory deference rule, under which courts defer to the rulings of church tribunals in *all* church property disputes, whether or not questions of religious doctrine and polity are involved.[36]

Method 4. Civil courts may resolve the dispute on the basis of any other methodology that they may devise "so long as it involves no consideration of doctrinal matters, whether, the ritual and liturgy of worship or the tenets of faith."[37]

In *Jones,*[38] the United State Supreme Court was confronted with a dispute over the ownership of property following a schism in a local church affiliated with the Presbyterian Church in the United States (PCUS). The church had been organized in 1904, and had always been affiliated with the PCUS (a hierarchical denomination). In 1973, the church membership voted (164 to 94) to separate from the PCUS. The majority informed the PCUS of its decision, and then united with another denomination, the Presbyterian Church in America. The PCUS appointed a commission to investigate the dispute. The commission ultimately issued a ruling declaring the minority faction to be the "true congregation" and withdrawing from the majority faction "all authority" to continue to hold services at the church. The majority took no part in the commission's inquiry, and did not appeal the ruling to a higher PCUS tribunal.

The minority faction brought suit against the majority, after it became obvious that the majority was not going to honor the commission's ruling. The Georgia courts held that there was no neutral principle of law vesting any interest in the church property in the PCUS, and that as a result the local congregation itself had to determine the disposition of the property. On the ground that religious associations are generally governed by majority rule, the Georgia Supreme Court ultimately awarded the property to the majority faction that wanted to disaffiliate. The minority appealed the matter directly to the United States Supreme Court. The Court accordingly was confronted with a situation in which a church tribunal's decision in a property dispute conflicted with the decision reached by the courts. The Court characterized the issue as "whether civil courts . . . may resolve the dispute on the basis of 'neutral principles of law,' or whether they must defer to the resolution of an authoritative tribunal of the hierarchical church."

The Supreme Court began its opinion by reiterating the principles enunciated in *Hull* and *Watson* that "the first amendment prohibits civil courts from resolving church property disputes on the basis of religious doctrine and practice,"[39] and that civil courts must "defer to the resolution of issues of *religious doctrine or polity* by the highest court of a hierarchical church organization."[40]

---

[35] *See* note 32, *supra,* and accompanying text.
[36] *See* note 8, *supra,* and accompanying text.
[37] *See* note 22, *supra.*
[38] 443 U.S. 595 (1979).
[39] *See* note 16, *supra,* at 449.
[40] *See* note 1, *supra,* at 733-34 (emphasis added).

The Court also prefaced its decision by observing that a hierarchical church was involved, that the controversy was intimately connected with Georgia law, and that "a State may adopt *any* one of various approaches for settling church property disputes so long as it involves no consideration of doctrinal matters . . . ."

Having established these general guidelines, the Court proceeded with an analysis of the methodology applied by the Georgia courts in resolving church property disputes. In essence, the Georgia methodology involved a two-step process. First, the courts determined whether neutral principles of law imposed a trust upon local church property in favor of a parent denomination. If such a trust existed, and its validity was not dependent upon any analysis of religious doctrine or polity, then the courts would give the property in dispute to the parent denomination. If neutral principles of law did not impose such a trust, then the property was subject to control by the local congregation, at least if title to the church property was vested in the local church or church trustees. The second step of the Georgia methodology, employed when neutral principles of law did not impose a trust and the local congregation was divided, permitted courts to award disputed church property to the majority of the church members provided that this presumptive rule of majority representation was not overcome by a showing that neutral principles of law dictated another result.

The Supreme Court approved of this methodology, provided the Georgia courts could demonstrate that Georgia in fact had adopted "a presumptive rule of majority representation, defeasible upon a showing that the identity of the local church is to be determined by some other means." The Court sent the case back to the Georgia courts for proof that Georgia in fact had adopted such a rule.

The Court's decision clarified the scope of the compulsory deference rule, and the rule's relationship to the neutral principles of law approach. The Court ultimately concluded that civil courts are compelled to defer to the rulings of church tribunals only with respect to "issues of religious doctrine or polity." It observed: "We cannot agree . . . that the first amendment requires the States to adopt a rule of compulsory deference to religious authority in resolving church property disputes . . . ."[41] The compulsory deference rule was accordingly limited to matters of religious doctrine and polity.

The four dissenting Justices were distressed by the Court's limitation of the compulsory deference rule to matters of religious doctrine and polity. The dissenters argued that "in each case involving an intrachurch dispute—including disputes over church property—the civil court must focus directly on ascertaining, and then following the decision made within the structure of church governance." By doing so, the dissenters concluded,

> the court avoids two equally unacceptable departures from the genuine neutrality mandated by the first amendment. First, it refrains from direct review and revision of decisions of the church on matters of religious doctrine and practice that underlie the church's determination of intrachurch controversies, including those that relate to control of church property. Equally important, by recognizing the authoritative resolution reached within the religious association, the civil court avoids interfering directly with the religious governance of those who have formed the association and submitted themselves to its authority.[42]

The Court, while emphasizing that the question before it involved a hierarchical church, also stated that the Georgia "neutral principles" methodology was "flexible enough to accommodate all forms of religious

---

[41] 443 U.S. 595, 605 (1979).
[42] *Id.* at 618.

organization and polity." The Court also noted that church property disputes, even in Georgia, need not necessarily be resolved by the courts, for

> the parties can ensure, if they so desire, that the faction loyal to the hierarchical church will retain the church property. They can modify the deeds or the corporate charter to include a right of reversion or trust in favor of the general church. Alternatively, the constitution of the general church can be made to recite and express trust in favor of the denominational church. The burden involved in taking such steps will be minimal. And the civil courts will be bound to give effect to the result indicated by the parties, provided it is embodied in some legally cognizable form. . . . . Through appropriate reversionary clauses and trust provisions, religious societies can specify what is to happen to church property in the event of a particular contingency, or what religious body will determine the ownership in the event of a schism or doctrinal controversy. In this manner, a religious organization can ensure that a dispute over the ownership of church property will be resolved in accord with the desires of the members.[43]

The Supreme Court in *Jones* clarified the law of church property disputes. It affirmed that church property disputes not involving questions of religious doctrine or polity can be resolved on the basis of any doctrinally neutral method, including neutral principles of law or a rule of compulsory deference to the determinations of church tribunals. The Court emphatically declared that no one method is constitutionally required, at least where no question of religious doctrine or polity is involved. Where, as in *Jones*, no question of doctrine is involved and the compulsory deference and neutral principles of law approaches would yield conflicting results, a court or legislature is free to choose either method (or some other doctrinally neutral method). If it chooses the neutral principles of law approach, as did the Georgia courts in the *Jones* case, it is entitled to reach a decision contrary to the decision of a church tribunal, provided that no question of religious doctrine or polity is involved.

The Supreme Court, in *Jones*, expressed a clear preference for the neutral principles approach over the compulsory deference rule, even while recognizing that a state could adopt the compulsory deference rule without violating the federal constitution:

> The primary advantage of the neutral principles approach is that it is completely secular in operation, and yet flexible enough to accommodate all forms of religious organization and polity. The method relies exclusively on objective, well-established concepts of trust and property law familiar to lawyers and judges. It thereby promises to free civil courts completely from entanglement in questions of religious doctrine, polity, and practice. . . . Under the neutral principles approach, the outcome of a church property dispute is not foreordained. At any time before the dispute erupts, the parties can ensure, if they so desire, that the faction loyal to the hierarchical church will retain the church property . . . .The burden involved in taking such steps will be minimal. And the civil courts will be bound to give effect to the result indicated by the parties, provided it is embodied in some legally cognizable form.[44]

Jones did not alter the methodology for resolving church property disputes that had existed previously. It merely clarified the relationship between the available methods of resolution.

---

[43] *Id.* at 606, 604.
[44] *Id.* at 603-04.

§ 7-03   State Court Rulings

How have state courts resolved church property disputes since *Jones*? A few courts have repudiated the neutral principles approach approved by the United States Supreme Court in *Jones*, and have adopted a rule of compulsory deference by the courts to the determinations of ecclesiastical commissions or judicatories in church property disputes, whether or not religious doctrine is implicated.[45] However, a majority of courts have either adopted the principle of *Jones* that the compulsory deference rule is limited to issues of "religious doctrine or polity,"[46] or have applied a neutral principles approach to the resolution of church property disputes involving hierarchical churches.[47] A few courts continue to adhere to the "implied trust" doctrine that was repudiated by the Supreme Court in *Hull*.[48] Such cases illustrate that diversity will characterize states' solutions to these intractable problems. Some of the leading cases representing the major views expressed by the state courts are summarized below.

§ 7-03.1 — Congregational Churches

Key point 7-03.1. The civil courts resolve disputes over the ownership and control of property in a "congregational" church on the basis of one of the following principles: (1) the provisions of an express trust, if any; (2) the application of neutral principles of law involving no inquiry into church doctrine; (3) state laws governing the disposition of church property; or (4) a majority vote of the church membership.

The courts have uniformly resolved property disputes in "congregational" churches by resorting to (1) the express trust rule, (2) the neutral principles of law rule, (3) state laws governing the disposition of church property, or (4) majority rule. The express trust and neutral principles rules are similar in their application, since both determine title on the basis of nondoctrinal provisions contained in a local church's deed, or the charters or bylaws of the church or a denomination with which it is affiliated. The express trust rule focuses on language creating a trust either in favor of the local church or a denomination. The neutral principles approach looks to nondoctrinal language in deeds, charters, and bylaws to determine who holds legal title. A few states have statutes that attempt to resolve church property disputes. In some cases, these rules do not clearly identify the owner of church property. In such cases, the courts have consistently (since *Jones*) resorted to majority rule, meaning that a majority of members within the church determines the question of property ownership.

---

[45] Townsend v. Teagle, 467 So.2d 772 (Fla. App. 1985); Fonken v. Community Church, 339 N.W.2d 810 (Iowa 1983) (rejecting the claim that "the compulsory deference approach is applicable only to purely ecclesiastical matters"); Calvary Presbyterian Church v. Presbytery of Lake Huron, 384 N.W.2d 92 (Mich. App. 1986); *but cf.* Bennison v. Sharp, 329 N.W.2d 466 (Mich. App. 1982); Tea v. Protestant Episcopal Church, 610 P.2d 181 (Nev. 1980); Protestant Episcopal Church v. Graves, 417 A.2d 19 (N.J. 1980), *cert. denied*, 449 U.S. 1131 (1981); Southside Tabernacle v. Pentecostal Church of God, Pacific Northwest District, Inc., 650 P.2d 231 (Wash. 1982); Original Glorious Church of God in Christ v. Myers, 367 S.E.2d 30 (W. Va. App. 1988); Church of God v. Noel, 318 S.E.2d 920 (W. Va. 1984) (dissenting justice urged adherence to *Jones*). *But see* Antioch Temple, Inc. v. Parekh, 422 N.E.2d 1337 (Mass. 1981).

[46] *See, e.g.*, Graffam v. Wray, 437 A.2d 627 (Me. 1981); Beaver-Butler Presbytery v. Middlesex Presbyterian Church, 489 A.2d 1317 (Pa. 1985).

[47] *See, e.g.*, Harris v. Apostolic Overcoming Holy Church of God, Inc., 457 So.2d 385 (Ala. 1984); Bishop and Diocese of Colorado v. Mote, 716 P.2d 85 (Colo. 1986); New York Annual Conference of the United Methodist Church v. Fisher, 438 A.2d 62 (Conn. 1980); Aglikin v. Kovacheff, 516 N.E.2d 704 (Ill. App. 1987); York v. First Presbyterian Church, 474 N.E.2d 716 (Ill. App. 1984); Grutka v. Clifford, 445 N.E.2d 1015 (Ind. App. 1983); First Presbyterian Church v. United Presbyterian Church in U.S., 476 N.Y.S.2d 86 (N.Y. 1984); Orthodox Church of America v. Pavuk, 538 A.2d 632 (Pa. Common. 1988); Foss v. Dykstra, 319 N.W.2d 499 (S.D. 1982); Templo Ebenezer, Inc. v. Evangelical Assemblies, Inc., 752 S.W.2d 197 (Tex. App. 1988).

[48] For example, a New York court ruled in 1985 that the "implied trust" doctrine may be used to the extent that it "involves no interpretation of religious doctrine." It observed that "if the original precepts of a church were known, uncontested and unambiguous, then those precepts could form the basis of a doctrinal trust to which claimants to that church's property must be faithful." Park Slope Jewish Center v. Stern, 491 N.Y.S.2d 958 (N.Y. App. 1985).

§ 7-03.2 — Hierarchical Churches — the Compulsory Deference Rule

***Key point 7-03.2.** Some courts apply the "compulsory deference" rule in resolving disputes over the ownership and control of property in "hierarchical" churches. Under this rule, the civil courts defer to the determinations of denominational agencies in resolving such disputes.*

A few states have adopted the *compulsory deference rule* in resolving church property disputes involving hierarchical churches, and have awarded title to local church property to a denominational agency.[49] The Supreme Court has recognized this as one of many possible options available to the civil courts in resolving church property disputes.

***Example.** The Iowa Supreme Court ruled that the property of a local Presbyterian church that attempted to disaffiliate from the United Presbyterian Church in the United States of America (UPCUSA) belonged to the denomination. It based its decision on the compulsory deference rule (a church judicatory determined that the denomination owned the property), but it also noted that the same result would occur under an application of the neutral principles of law approach. The court observed: "When its provisions are construed together, the Book of Order gives UPCUSA exclusive ultimate control of the uses and disposition of local property. Local church property decisions are subject to general church approval, and the general church may take over local church government, as it did in this case, when it disagrees with the local church handling of church affairs."[50]*

***Example.** A Michigan state appeals court applied the compulsory deference rule to a church property dispute involving an hierarchical denomination (the Protestant Episcopal Church in the United States of America, or simply the "PECUSA"). The court observed: "In the freedom of conscience and the right to worship allowed in this country, the defendants and members of this church undoubtedly possessed the right to withdraw from it, with or without reason. But they could not take with them, for their own purposes, or transfer to any other religious body, the property dedicated to and conveyed for the worship of God under the discipline of this religious association; nor could they prevent its use by those who choose to remain in the church, and who represent the regular church organization. If complainants maintain the allegations of their bill—that they represent the regularly organized body of the church, and are its regular appointees—they are entitled to the relief prayed."[51]*

***Example.** A Texas court awarded title to a local church's property to a denomination following the church's attempt to disaffiliate. The court observed: "[Texas] courts have consistently followed the deference rule in deciding hierarchical church property disputes since the Texas Supreme Court adopted the rule . . . . The deference rule imputes to members 'implied consent' to the governing bylaws of their church. Persons who unite themselves to a hierarchical church organization do so with 'implied consent' that church bylaws will govern . . . ." The court concluded: "Where a congregation of a hierarchical church has split, those members who renounce their allegiance to the church*

---

[49] *See, e.g.,* Cumberland Presbytery v. Branstetter, 824 S.W.2d 417 (Ky. 1992) (Cumberland Presbyterian Church retained title to the property of a local church that voted to disaffiliate, because of a trust provision in the national church's constitution).

[50] Fonken v. Community Church, 339 N.W.2d 810 (Iowa 1983).

[51] Bennison v. Sharp, 329 N.W.2d 466 (Mich. App. 1982). *See also* Calvary Presbyterian Church v. Presbytery, 384 N.W.2d 92 (Mich. App. 1986). A Michigan appeals court ruled that "it would be inappropriate to apply the neutral principles test to determine disputes between people who have agreed, as a part of the establishment of their church, to resolve disputes between themselves within their internal power structure."

lose any rights in the property involved and remain loyal to the church. It is a simple question of identity."[52]

Example. *A West Virginia appeals court awarded the assets of a local church to a national denomination. The congregation voted to secede from a parent denomination and establish a new church. The church's trustees attempted to convey the church's assets to the new organization. This conveyance was challenged by the denomination, which asserted that the church's assets belonged to it. It cited a provision in its constitution dictating that "no church group desiring to leave this body shall have any legal claim on church property if the property in question was purchased and paid for with general funds or if general funds were in any way used in the purchase thereof." Since the denomination produced a copy of a check in the amount of $300 that it had issued to the local church in 1964 to assist with church construction, the court concluded that the church's assets belonged to the denomination and that the attempted conveyance by the local trustees was void. The court further noted that with respect to hierarchical churches the civil courts "should respect, and where appropriate enforce, the final adjudications of the highest church tribunals, provided that such adjudications are not procured by fraud or collusion. If a church has a hierarchical structure and its leaders have addressed a doctrinal or administrative dispute, the civil courts do not intervene, absent fraud or collusion." Since the denomination had addressed the issue of property disputes in its constitution, the civil courts were bound to defer to that document and award the local congregation's assets to the denomination.*[53]

§ 7-03.3 — Hierarchical Churches — Neutral Principle of Law

Key point 7-03.3. *Most courts apply the "neutral principles of law" rule in resolving disputes over the ownership and control of property in "hierarchical" churches. Under this rule, the civil courts apply neutral principles of law, involving no inquiry into church doctrine, in resolving church property disputes. Generally, this means applying neutral legal principles to nondoctrinal language in any one or more of the following documents: (1) deeds to church property; (2) a church's corporate charter; (3) a state law addressing the resolution of church property disputes; (4) church bylaws; or (5) a parent denomination's bylaws.*

Most state courts have adopted the *neutral principles of law* approach in resolving church property disputes involving hierarchical churches. The cases validate the Supreme Court's pronouncement in *Jones* that "[u]nder the neutral principles approach, the outcome of a church property dispute is not foreordained."[54] Both local churches and denominations have been awarded title to contested church property by courts applying the neutral principles approach. Representative cases are summarized below.

1. TITLE AWARDED TO LOCAL CHURCHES

A number of courts, applying the neutral principles of law approach, have awarded property to local churches that have disaffiliated from a denomination.

---

[52] Green v. Westgate Apostolic Church, 808 S.W.2d 547 (Tex. App. 1991).
[53] Original Glorious Church of God in Christ v. Myers, 367 S.E.2d 30 (W. Va. App. 1988).
[54] *Id.* at 603-04.

Example. An Illinois state appeals court awarded ownership of church property to a local church that had disaffiliated from the American-Bulgarian Eastern Orthodox Church. The appeals court chose to apply the "neutral principles" approach and accordingly concluded that it was not compelled to rule in favor of the national church.[55]

Example. The Kentucky Supreme Court rejected the claim of the Protestant Episcopal Church in the United States of America (PECUSA) to the property of a local church that voted unanimously to disaffiliate from the parent body. The church voted to disaffiliate from the PECUSA because of disagreement with certain denominational policies, and a dispute arose between the church and PECUSA regarding ownership of the church's property. The court emphasized that (a) the congregation's withdrawal from the PECUSA "was unequivocal, and there was no dissenting faction," (b) the "church property was acquired exclusively by the efforts of the local congregation," (c) through the years title to the property was held by the church trustees and later by the church when it incorporated, and (d) the church "freely engaged in transactions such as purchase, encumbrance, and sale of its real property without any involvement by PECUSA." Such evidence, observed the court, created an "appearance of absolute ownership" in the local church. However, the PECUSA maintained that certain denominational documents imposed a trust on the local church's property in favor the national church, and that in any event the civil courts were required to defer to the conclusions of a hierarchical denomination such as the PECUSA (under the so-called "compulsory deference rule"). Both of these contentions were rejected by the court. It refused to adopt the "compulsory deference rule," choosing instead the "neutral principles of law" approach to resolving church property disputes. Under this approach, the court concluded that the local church and not the PECUSA was the rightful owner of the property in question since nondoctrinal language in the church's charter and deed clearly vested title in the local church.[56]

Example. A Massachusetts court ruled that a local church could retain its property after disaffiliating from a parent denomination. The members of a local church voted to amend the church's bylaws to remove all reference to a parent denomination. The executive board of the denomination asked a court to declare the congregational meeting illegal and to rule that all of the church's properties were subject to the control of the denomination. A state appeals court conceded that denominational documents "provide considerable force" to the denomination's claim that it is hierarchical in terms of the control of local church property. But the court also noted that there had been "considerable movement in and out of the [denomination] by individual parishes who took with them their own property without claim by the [denomination]." Based on this evidence, the court concluded that the local church was congregational as far as the control and use of its property was concerned, and owned its own property.[57]

Example. The Missouri Supreme Court adopted the neutral principles approach and awarded church property to a schismatic church that disaffiliated from an hierarchical denomination (the United Presbyterian Church in the United States of America, or "UPCUSA"). The court observed that title to the

---

[55] Aglikin v. Kovacheff, 516 N.E.2d 704 (Ill. App. 1987).

[56] Bjorkman v. Protestant Episcopal Church in the United States of America, 759 S.W.2d 583 (Ky. 1988). The court concluded: "It should be remembered that [the church] acquired the property with no assistance from PECUSA; that the property was managed and maintained exclusively by the church; that the church improved and added to its property; and that PECUSA deliberately avoided acquisition of title or entanglement with the property to ensure that it would not be subject to civil liability. The record is clear that PECUSA's relationship with the church was exclusively ecclesiastical and the church was at all times in control of its temporal affairs."

[57] Primate Synod v. Russian Orthodox Church Outside Russia, 617 N.E.2d 1031 (Mass. App. 1993), *aff'd,* 636 N.E.2d 211 (Mass. 1994).

church property was in the name of the local church, and nothing in the church or denominational bylaws or discipline provided any express trust in favor of the denomination. [58]

Example. *A federal appeals court, applying Missouri law, ruled that a Church of God in Christ congregation that voted to secede from the national church retained control of its property. The court noted that Missouri courts had adopted the "neutral principles of law" approach to resolving church property disputes, and concluded that the local congregation retained title to its properties under the neutral principles of law approach on the basis of the following considerations: (1) The national Church contributed nothing to the acquisition of the congregation's property. (2) The local congregation exercised complete control over the property without any interference from the Church. Indeed, the court pointed out that never in the congregation's history, until the events leading to this lawsuit, had the Church attempted to exercise any control over the congregation. (3) The congregation's articles of incorporation explicitly declare its independence from the national Church. (4) The deeds to the congregation's properties vest title and control in the hands of the local congregation. The court rejected the Church's claim that the congregation held its properties "in trust" for the national Church. It noted that "[t]he Church did not automatically provide local pastors with a copy of its manual, nor was it distributed generally to [the congregation's] members. To require the . . . congregation to hold its property in trust for another without proper notice as to that requirement would too severely distort the application of neutral principles of Missouri law. With only its charter and constitution to point to, no evidence that [the congregation] actually acquiesced in that constitution, and all the other considerations pointing in favor of [the congregation] we conclude that the national Church cannot wrest ownership from the . . . congregation under neutral principles of Missouri law."* [59]

Example. *A federal appeals court, applying New Jersey law, refused to recognize a national church body's attempt to gain control over local church properties through amendments in its Book of Discipline. A church was incorporated in 1915 and affiliated with the African Union Methodist Protestant Church (the "national church"). In 1991 the national church held a meeting at which a "church property" resolution was adopted. This resolution specified that "the title to all property, now owned or hereafter acquired by an incorporated local church . . . shall be held by or conveyed to the corporate body in its corporate name, in trust for the use and benefit of such local church and of the African Union Methodist Protestant Church." Another provision in the property resolution directed churches to include a similar "trust clause" in their deeds. The property resolution, as adopted, was incorporated into the national church's governing Book of Discipline. At the same 1991 meeting of the national church, another resolution was adopted authorizing pastors "to sign official documents pertaining to the individual local church." On the basis of these resolutions, the national church directed a number of pastors to sign a quitclaim deed transferring title to their church's property to the national church. One church, whose property was deeded to the national church by its pastor pursuant to such a directive, voted unanimously to secede from the national church. The court concluded that the pastor's attempt to deed his church's property to the national church had to be invalidated on the basis of neutral principles of law. It noted that the church's articles of incorporation allowed conveyances of church property only upon a vote of at least two-thirds of the church's members. It conceded that this provision conflicted with the "property resolutions" in the national church's Book of Discipline, but it concluded that the Book of Discipline "functioned" as the local church's bylaws, and that whenever there is a conflict between a church's articles of incorporation and its bylaws, the articles of incorporation prevail.* [60]

---

[58] Presbytery of Elijah Parish Lovejoy v. Jaeggi, 682 S.W.2d 465 (Mo. 1984).

[59] Church of God in Christ v. Graham, 54 F.3d 522 (8th Cir. 1995).

[60] Scotts African Union Methodist Protestant Church v. Conference of African Union First Colored Methodist Protestant Church, 98 F.3d 78 (3rd Cir. 1996).

Example. The New York Court of Appeals adopted the neutral principles approach in a dispute involving ownership of property owned by a church that disaffiliated from the United Presbyterian Church in the United States of America (UPCUSA), and awarded the church's property to the local church. The court reasoned that there was no neutral principle of law vesting title in the denomination. The court rejected the denomination's argument that "it is presumed that the local church intended to dedicate the property to the purposes of the larger body by voluntarily merging itself with it." The court criticized the "compulsory deference" rule, since this rule "assumes that the local church has relinquished control to the hierarchical body in all cases, thereby frustrating the actual intent of the local church in some cases. Such a practice, it is said, discourages local churches from associating with a hierarchical church for purposes of religious worship out of fear of losing their property and the indirect result of discouraging such an association may constitute a violation of the free exercise clause. Additionally, by supporting the hierarchical polity over other forms and permitting local churches to lose control over their property, the deference rule may indeed constitute a judicial establishment of religion . . . ."[61]

Example. A New York court ruled that a local church that disaffiliated from the Episcopal Church in 1976 retained control of its property. The church was organized in 1859 for the purpose of establishing a church "in communion with the Protestant Episcopal Church in the Diocese of New York, and in the United States of America, and in accordance with its doctrine, discipline, and worship." In 1976 the church disaffiliated from the Episcopal Church in the United States and its New York Diocese on the basis of changes in doctrine and practice approved by the national church at a General Convention held earlier that year. The church then associated with the Anglican Church. The New York Diocese filed a lawsuit asserting ownership and control of the congregation's property. The court ruled that the local congregation retained ownership and control of its property following its disaffiliation from the Episcopal Church. The court observed: "[E]ven though members of a local group belonged to a hierarchical church, they may withdraw from the church and claim title to either personal or real property provided that they have not previously ceded the property to the denominational church. In other words, the facts that this [church] was originally part of a hierarchical body does not necessarily bind a court if it is possible to decide the controversy through the application of "neutral principles of law." The court acknowledged that there can be an implied trust in church property for the denominational church. However, to establish such a trust there must be a sufficient manifestation of the intention to do so. The court concluded that there was insufficient evidence in this case of an implied trust in favor of the diocese or national church. It observed: "[I]t is clear that [the congregation] acquired the property in question on its own and there is no specific evidence either in the deeds which form a part of the record nor by any other evidence . . . that [the congregation] intended to hold the property in trust. When [it] disassociated itself and revised its corporate charter, the [national church's] ecclesiastical law was not in place to govern the disposition of [the congregation's] property." The court pointed out that the "deeds to this [church] contain no forfeiture or significant reversionary clauses. Further, the "in communion with" language was ecclesiastical and accordingly was of no legal significance.[62]

Example. A North Carolina court ruled that title to a local Church of God congregation that disaffiliated from the denomination belonged to the local church rather than to denominational officials. In 1955, the congregation voted to affiliate with the Church of God denomination "for purposes of fellowship." In 1988, the church voted to disaffiliate from the denomination. In response to this action, the "state overseer" of the Church of God dismissed the local church's board of trustees and appointed a

---

[61] First Presbyterian Church v. United Presbyterian Church in the United States of America, 476 N.Y.S.2d 86 (Ct. App. 1984). *Accord* Park Slope Jewish Center v. Congregation B'Nai Jacob, 664 N.Y.S.2d 236 (Ct. App. 1997).

[62] Diocesan Missionary and Church Extension Society v. Church of the Holy Comforter, 628 N.Y.S.2d 471 (Sup. 1994).

successor board consisting of denominational trustees. The successor trustees executed a deed conveying to themselves title to the church's property. When local church members opposed this denominational control of their property, the denominational trustees asked a court to determine the lawful owner of the church property. The denominational bylaws specify that a local board of trustees shall hold title to local church property and that "all such property shall be used, managed, and controlled for the sole and exclusive use and benefit of the Church of God." The court noted that as a general rule the parent body of a "connectional church" has the right to control the property of local affiliated churches. However, a local church "may have retained sufficient independence from the general church so that it reserved its right to withdraw at any time, and, presumably, take along with it whatever property it independently owned prior to and retained during its limited affiliation with the general church." The court concluded that such was the case here. It based its ruling on the fact that "when the local church affiliated with the denominational church, the property was deeded to trustees of . . . the local church, not to the denominational church." [63]

Example. A Pennsylvania state appeals court ruled that a dissident church was entitled to retain its property following its disaffiliation from the Russian Orthodox Church because of a proposed revision by the Orthodox Church in its calendar. The court held that an award of a local church's assets to a parent denomination is possible only if the denomination can demonstrate "(1) an actual transfer of property from the congregation to the hierarchical church body, or (2) clear and unambiguous documentary evidence or conduct on the part of the congregation evincing an intent to create a trust in favor of the hierarchical church body." The court observed that the denomination could not satisfy the first test, since the local congregation "never relinquished its right to possession or legal title to the church property." On the contrary, the church's original affiliation with the Orthodox Church was accompanied by a letter expressing its intent to retain ownership and control of its property. As to the second requirement, the court observed, after reviewing the church's charter, constitution, bylaws, and the bylaws of the Orthodox Church, that none of these documents contained any "clear and unambiguous" language creating a trust in favor of the Orthodox Church. The court also rejected the denomination's claim that its "hierarchical structure" compelled an award in its favor, since "regardless of the form of government of the church in question, we must examine the relevant deeds, contracts, or other evidence to determine ownership of the disputed property." [64]

2. TITLE AWARDED TO DENOMINATIONS

A number of courts that have applied the neutral principles approach have awarded the properties of a dissident church to a parent denomination. [65]

Example. The Alabama Supreme Court ruled that a national denomination owned the property of a local church that voted to disaffiliate from the denomination, since the deed to the local church property vested title in the denomination, and denominational rules specified that "[i]f any members of the [denomination] leave or cease to be members of the [denomination], irrespective of the amount or number thereof, the fact that they leave or cease to be a member of the [denomination] shall not, in any

---

[63] Looney v. Community Bible Holiness Church, 405 S.E.2d 811 (N.C. App. 1991).

[64] Orthodox Church of America v. Pavuk, 538 A.2d 632 (Pa. Common. 1988). *See also* Board of Bishops of the Church of the Living God v. Milner, 513 A.2d 1131 (Pa. Common. 1986) (court awarded property to local church that disaffiliated from hierarchical denomination—on basis of neutral principles).

[65] *See, e.g.,* Fry v. Emmanuel Churches of Christ, Inc., 839 S.W.2d 406 (Tenn. App. 1992) (Assembly of the Emmanuel Churches of Christ).

manner, affect the property of the said church, and said party or parties or persons leaving the congregation or membership of the [denomination], in any manner, cannot and shall not take any property of the [denomination], in any manner, and all church property, irrespective, whether acquired by the local congregation, local church or otherwise, is the property of the [denomination].[66]

Example. *The Alabama Supreme Court was asked to decide whether a local church or a parent denomination owned the church's property following its disaffiliation from the denomination. A local church had been affiliated with the African Methodist Episcopal Zion Church in America since 1908. In 1985, a majority of the church's membership voted to disaffiliate with the parent denomination. The denomination wrote the church a letter acknowledging the disaffiliation, and requesting all dissident members to vacate the premises. Dissident members refused to vacate the property, and the denomination filed a lawsuit seeking to have itself declared the owner of the church's property. In support of its claim, the denomination quoted a provision contained (since 1884) in its Book of Discipline that pertained to local church property: "In trust, that said premises shall be used, kept, maintained, and disposed of as a place of divine worship for the use of the ministry and membership of the African Methodist Episcopal Zion Church in America, subject to the discipline, usage and ministerial appointments of said church as from time to time authorized and declared by the General Conference of said church." The court ruled in favor of the denomination. It surveyed the close ties that had existed between the local church and parent denomination in the 77 years of affiliation, and noted that since 1884 every prospective member of a church affiliated with the denomination had agreed to be "cheerfully governed" by the denomination's Book of Discipline. In light of such evidence, the supreme court concluded: "[The church] has been a member of [the denomination] for three-quarters of a century, by an association that both the national denomination and the local church acknowledge. For the entire time, the [Book of Discipline] provided that the [church's] property be held for the [denomination] by the local church. Individuals who have been members of the [church] the longest acknowledge that, for as long as they can remember, everyone who became a member of [the church] promised to abide by the rules and regulations of the . . . denomination. [The church] cannot now sever the relationship between [the denomination] and itself and unilaterally declare that obligations incumbent upon itself because of three-quarters of a century of association do not exist. [The church's] choice to join [the denomination] means it is obligated to obey all the rules and regulations its members promised to uphold, not just the rules and regulations they prefer; at least in regard to property disputes, the [denomination's Book of Discipline] binds [the local church]."*[67]

Example. *A California court ruled that title to the properties of a local church that voted to disaffiliate from a parent denomination belonged to the denomination rather than to the church. The local church was the oldest Korean immigrant congregation in the Presbyterian Church (U.S.A.) ("PCUSA"). It had participated actively in the Presbyterian Church for more than 80 years. PCUSA had assisted the church in acquiring its first properties, and in obtaining financing for various projects. A schism developed within the church. Attempts by the PCUSA to resolve the problems failed. As a result of the schism, a group (numbering up to 30% of the church's membership) left the church and formed a "church in exile." The pastor thereafter had the remaining congregation vote to disaffiliate from the PCUSA. Acting in accordance with the Presbyterian Book of Order, the PCUSA designated the exiled congregation as the "true church," and as the rightful owner of the church properties. A lawsuit was filed to determine the ownership of the church properties. A state appeals court awarded the church properties to*

---

[66] Harris v. Apostolic Overcoming Holy Church of God, Inc., 457 So.2d 385 (Ala. 1984). *Contra* Haney's Chapel Methodist Church v. United Methodist Church, 716 So.2d 1156 (Ala. 1998).

[67] African Methodist Episcopal Zion Church in America, Inc. v. Zion Hill Methodist Church, Inc., 534 So.2d 224 (Ala. 1988).

the "exiled" congregation designated by the PCUSA as the true church. The court based its decision on the following 3 considerations: (1) "[I]t has long been the law in California that the identification of a religious body as the true church is an ecclesiastical issue," and accordingly the civil courts must accept the decisions of hierarchical denominations that identify a particular faction as the true representative of a local church. (2) When the church voted to disaffiliate from the PCUSA its members in effect renounced any further obligation to be subject to the doctrines or discipline of the PCUSA. This action also resulted in the loss of their church membership since the church's articles of incorporation required adherence to the doctrines and disciplines of PCUSA as a condition of membership. Having abandoned their membership in the local church, they "lost all power and ability to determine its future status." (3) Express trust provisions in the church's deed, as well as the Book of Order of the PCUSA vested title in the exiled group.[68]

Example. *The Colorado Supreme Court ruled that a national denomination owned the property of a local church that voted to disaffiliate from the Protestant Episcopal Church in the United States of America (PECUSA) when the denomination approved the ordination of women. The court acknowledged that title to the church property was vested in the local congregation; that the deeds contained no reference to PECUSA and no language suggesting that the property was held by the local church in trust for the national denomination; and that PECUSA did not provide any financial assistance to the local church in purchasing the property. Nevertheless, the court concluded that "an intent on the part of the local church corporation to dedicate its property irrevocably to the purposes of PECUSA was expressed unambiguously in the combination of the [church's] articles of incorporation, the local church bylaws, and the canons of the general church . . . ." The court noted that the local church's articles of incorporation stated that the church was organized "to administer the temporalities of the Protestant Episcopal Church in the parish," and that the church "does hereby expressly accede to all the provisions of the constitution and canons adopted by the General Convention of the Protestant Episcopal Church in the United States of America, and to all of the provisions of the constitution and canons of the Diocese of Colorado." These provisions, observed the court, "strongly indicate that the local church property was to be held for the benefit of the general church . . . . There are no provisions in the articles implicitly or explicitly expressing an intent to the contrary." This and other evidence convinced the court that there was a "unity of purpose on the part of the parish and of the general church reflecting the intent that property held by the parish would be dedicated to and utilized for the advancement of the work of PECUSA. These provisions foreclose the possibility of the withdrawal of property from the parish simply because a majority of the members of the parish decide to end their association with PECUSA. We hold that the facts . . . establish that a trust has been imposed upon the real and personal property of the [local church] for the use of the general church."[69]*

Example. *The Connecticut Supreme Court ruled that title to a local Episcopalian church reverted to the Episcopal Diocese of Connecticut following its vote to disaffiliate from the Diocese. The church had been affiliated with the Diocese for more than a century, but voted to disaffiliate and join the Anglican Church in 1986. Both the church and Diocese claimed ownership of the church property. The court noted that the national Episcopal Church adopted the following provision at a national conference in 1979 creating an express trust over local church properties in favor of the national church: "All real and personal property held by or for the benefit of any parish, mission or congregation is held in trust for this church and the diocese thereof in which such parish, mission or congregation is located." Because this*

---

[68] Korean United Presbyterian Church v. Presbytery of the Pacific, 281 Cal. Rptr. 396 (Cal. App. 2 Dist. 1991).
[69] Bishop and Diocese of Colorado v. Mote, 716 P.2d 85 (Colo. 1986).

provision was not adopted until 1979, the court concluded that it did not apply in this case since the church's properties were acquired long before 1979. However, the court concluded that the polity of the Episcopal denomination and the historical relationship of local churches with the denomination clearly demonstrated an "implied trust" in favor of the Diocese over the property of local churches. The court based this conclusion on the following factors: (1) Local churches accepted the doctrine of the denomination. (2) The Diocesan canons permit the establishment of a church only with the permission of the bishop. (3) The Diocesan canons permit the disaffiliation of a local church from the diocese only with the permission of the bishop. (4) The Diocesan canons prohibit the transfer of local church property without the permission of the bishop. (5) The local church in this case submitted annual reports to the Diocese, as required by Diocesan canons. (6) The local church in this case sent delegates (both clergy and laypersons) to the annual conventions of the Diocese. (7) The local church in this case paid its annual assessments to the Diocese as required by Diocesan canons. The court concluded that these factors "strongly reflect the polity of the church as one in which the parish is the local manifestation of [the denomination] to be used for its ministry and mission."[70]

Example. A Florida court ruled that the property of a local church that attempted to secede from an hierarchical denomination remained with the denomination. An African Methodist Episcopal church disaffiliated from the parent denomination, and claimed ownership of its property following the disaffiliation. A state appeals court ruled that in Florida the property of such a church reverts to the denomination following the church's disaffiliation. It concluded that a prior ruling of the state supreme court "requires that church property remain with the parent church where, as here, the church is hierarchical in structure. Given the trial court's finding that the AME Church is hierarchical, judgement should have been entered in favor of [the national church] as representative of the original church."[71]

Example. The Louisiana Supreme Court adopted the neutral principles of law approach, but ruled that the property of a local church that disaffiliated from the African Methodist Episcopal Church belonged to the denomination (A.M.E. Church). The court relied on provisions in the denomination's discipline requiring (a) denominational approval of transfers of local church property, and (b) reversion of title in "abandoned" or "disbanded" churches to the denomination. The court observed: "Applying the neutral principles which are evoked by our examination of the documents in purely secular terms, we concluded that it was the intention of the parties . . . that [the church property] not be alienated without A.M.E.'s consent, and will be considered abandoned to A.M.E. upon [the church's] disbanding as an A.M.E. society. Accordingly, because of [the local church's] disaffiliation without a prior valid transfer of [its property], A.M.E. has become vested with the exclusive right to control its use and to compel the transfer of title if necessary.[72]

Example. A Maryland court ruled that a parent denomination retained control of the property of a local congregation that voted to disaffiliate. The congregation of a church affiliated with the African Methodist Episcopal (A.M.E.) Church voted in 1993 to disaffiliate from the parent body as a result of what it perceived to be burdensome financial demands and a decline in moral conditions within the denomination. Both the dissident congregation and the A.M.E. Church claimed the church's property. A state appeals court awarded the church's property to the national church. The court acknowledged that the deed and the A.M.E. Church Discipline did not contain any trust provision or reverter clause.

---

[70] Rector, Wardens and Vestrymen of Trinity-St. Michael's Parish, Inc. v. Episcopal Church in the Diocese of Connecticut, 620 A.2d 1280 (Conn. 1993).

[71] Bethel AME Church v. Domingo, 654 So.2d 233 (Fla. App. 1 Dist. 1995).

[72] Fluker Community Church v. Hitchens, 419 So.2d 445 (La. 1982).

However, the court insisted that these omissions did not mean that the seceding church retained its property. Quite to the contrary, "the absence of an explicit reverter upon withdrawal clause does not necessarily mean that the local church is entitled to retain control of its property." Rather, a court must consider all relevant documents. The court noted that the church's articles of incorporation specified that the "powers and authority of the trustees shall be in subjection to" the national church. It concluded: "Based exclusively on the language in the [articles of incorporation] requiring that the trustees hold the property 'in trust' for the A.M.E. Church, we hold that [the local church] was not entitled to retain control of the land after their departure from the A.M.E. Church."[73]

Example. *A Missouri court ruled that the property of a dissident church belonged to a national church body with which it was affiliated. The local church opposed a 1984 resolution of the national church which permitted the ordination of women into the priesthood. After efforts to work out their differences failed, the national church attempted in install a new minister. When the congregation overwhelmingly voted to retain their original minister, the national church had the locks to the church property changed, barricades erected, and notices posted to keep people off the property. The congregation proceeded to have keys made to the new locks, removed the barricades, and held services on the premises. The national church then sought and obtained a court order banning the minister "and those acting in concert with him" from entering onto church property and from in any way disrupting the worship services conducted on the property. The congregation appealed this order, and a Missouri appeals court ruled in favor of the national church. With regard to the ownership of the church property, the court applied the neutral principles of law approach, observing that the national church owned the property since the deed to the property created an express trust in favor of the national church, as did relevant documents of the national church. Further, such provisions did not require any inquiries into religious doctrine.[74]*

Example. *A Pennsylvania court ruled that a national denomination retained ownership of the property of a local church that seceded from the denomination. A local congregation affiliated with the Conference of African Union First Colored Methodist Protestant Church in 1977. The church's articles of incorporation stated its purposes to include "Christian worship and fellowship subject to the law and usage of the Holy Bible and the Book of Discipline of the African Union First Colored Methodist Protestant Church." The Conference's book of discipline contains the following clause: "All church property and other property belonging to the [Conference] shall be deeded to the members and [Conference], and should the members disband or secede the property shall remain in the possession of the [Conference], and that each local church should be so incorporated that if the members should disband or secede, the said church and property shall remain in the [Conference]." In 1989 the congregation voted to disaffiliate from the Conference. The Conference asked a court to declare that it was the owner of the church's property. A state appeals court ruled in favor of the Conference. The court noted: "A hierarchical denomination claiming a trust in its favor from a local congregation must demonstrate the trust through clear and unambiguous language or conduct evidencing an intent to create the trust. . . . The record fully demonstrates that the Conference met its burden of proof. [The church] accepted and agreed to be bound by the book of discipline, which governs matters related to the use and disposition of property held by a member church and represents a contractual agreement that may be enforced by the courts."[75]*

Example. *The Supreme Court of South Carolina suggested that when a majority of the membership in a local church votes to disaffiliate the church from a parent denomination, a minority desiring to*

---

[73] Board of Incorporators v. Mt. Olive African Methodist Episcopal Church, 672 A.2d 679 (Md. App. 1996).

[74] Reorganized Church of Jesus Christ of Latter Day Saints v. Thomas, 758 S.W.2d 726 (Mo. App. 1988).

[75] Conference of African Union First Colored Methodist Protestant Church v. Shell, 659 A.2d 77 (Pa. Common. 1995).

remain faithful to the parent church will receive title to church property. The court observed: "Counsel . . . argues the lower court should be reversed because neutral principles of law require that the property in question should be in the possession and control of the appellants as representing the majority of the members of the First Presbyterian Church of Rock Hill. . . . For this proposition appellants rely largely on the case of Presbyterian Church in the United States v. Mary Elizabeth Blue Hull Memorial Presbyterian Church. . . . A review of that case convinces us that it is of no comfort to the appellants here . . . . By a determination of this case, this Court exercises no role in determining ecclesiastical questions. We merely settle a dispute on the question of identity, which in turn necessarily settles a dispute involving the control of property. . . . The appellants voluntarily associated themselves with the First Presbyterian Church of Rock Hill and became subject to the discipline and government of the Presbyterian Church in the United States. They voluntarily severed their connection, and when they did they forfeited any right to the use and possession of the property of that church under the long established law of the church and of South Carolina. . . . By joining the First Presbyterian Church of Rock Hill the members did not acquire such an interest in the property that they are entitled to take with them upon seceding. The property belonged to the First Presbyterian Church of Rock Hill before the members joined the church, and it belongs to the same after they have withdrawn. They simply are not now a part of that church. There is nothing in the ruling of the lower court, nor in our ruling today, which establishes, sponsors, advances, or supports either the religious belief of the majority or the minority in this case. This Court has traditionally avoided any intrusion upon religious matters and has confined its rulings in such cases to identifying the faction which represents the church after the schism occurred. . . . In so doing, we applied neutral principles of law referred to in Hull." Identifying the church, when a majority faction votes to disaffiliate, involves no interpretation of religious doctrine. It is a doctrinally neutral act, and therefore is consistent with Hull.[76]

Example. *A South Carolina appeals court ruled that a national church organization was entitled to the property of a local church that withdrew from the organization. The court observed that the local church was bound by the provision in the national church's "decree book" specifying that all local church properties belonged to the national church. The court further explained: "The main issue of this case is whether when the congregation of an hierarchical church withdraws from the church, the congregation is entitled to the church property. The well-settled answer to this question is that the title and right of possession of the church property remains in the hierarchical church . . . . The South Carolina appellate courts have yet to face a situation in which the congregation as a whole withdrew and contended that the church property belonged to it. The law on this question is settled. . . . [W]hen a church splits, the courts will not undertake to inquire into the ecclesiastical acts of the several parties, but will determine the property rights in favor of the party or division maintaining the church organization as it previously existed. We accordingly hold that when the entire congregation withdraws from the hierarchical church, the title to the church property remains in the church and does not follow the congregation.[77]*

Example. *A Texas state appeals court resolved a church property dispute in which a denomination and a local church both claimed title to the church's property. The church was established in 1970, and in the same year was affiliated with the Evangelical Assemblies denomination. Pursuant to the Evangelical Assemblies' constitution, the church paid for its property but title was vested in the name of the denomination. In 1983, a majority of the church's members voted to disassociate the church from the denomination, whereupon a lawsuit was commenced to determine legal ownership of church property.*

---

[76] Adickes v. Adkins 215 S.E.2d 442 (S.C. 1975), *cert. denied,* 423 U.S. 913 (1975).
[77] Dillard v. Jackson, 403 S.E.2d 136 (S.C. App. 1991). *Accord* Fire Baptized Holiness Church of God of the Americas v. Greater Fuller Tabernacle of Fire Baptized Holiness Church, 475 S.E.2d 767 (S.C. App. 1996).

The court concluded that the Evangelical Assemblies was "in every respect" a hierarchical church orga-nization, and accordingly, "as the parent church, Evangelical Assemblies owns and is entitled to posses-sion of the property under the mutually binding constitution."[78]

§ 7-04   Church Property Disputes — Dispute Resolution Procedures

Key point 7-04. *Churches and denominational agencies can avoid church property disputes by adopt-ing appropriate nondoctrinal language in deeds, trusts, local church bylaws, or denominational bylaws.*

How may a denomination ensure that it will retain the property of an affiliated church that votes to disaffiliate? How may an independent church congregation ensure that its property will remain with a par-ticular group in the event of a church split? When can a local church seeking to disaffiliate from a particular denomination safely assume that it will retain the church property? And, how will a faction (a majority or a minority of church members) in an independent church know what its rights are, if any, in church property following a schism? The Supreme Court responded to these concerns in *Jones*:

[T]he neutral principles analysis shares the peculiar genius of private-law systems in general—flexibility in ordering private rights and obligations to reflect the intentions of the parties. Through appropriate reversionary clauses and trust provisions, religious societies can specify what is to happen to church property in the event of a particular contingency, or what religious body will determine the ownership in the event of a schism or doctrinal controversy. In this manner, a religious organization can insure that a dispute over the ownership of church property will be resolved in accord with the desires of the members.[79]

Private resolution of church property disputes may be facilitated in the following ways:

1. Deeds

Deeds to church property can provide for private resolution of church property disputes in a variety of ways.

a. Denomination holds title to local church property. First, a parent denomination can have title to local church property deeded to the parent denomination. This is particularly appropriate when the denomination has contributed significantly toward the purchase or construction of a new church. In such a case, neutral principles of law would ordinarily confirm the denomination's ownership of the property.

b. A trust provision. A deed could specify that a local church holds title in trust for a parent denomination.[80]

c. Reverter clauses. A deed could vest title in the local church, subject to a reversion clause or a possibility of reverter stipulating that in the event a stated condition occurs title will vest in a parent denomination or in a particular faction of the church. The condition must be worded in such a way that a court could enforce it

---

[78] Templo Ebenezer, Inc. v. Evangelical Assemblies, Inc., 752 S.W.2d 197 (Tex. App. 1988).

[79] 443 U.S. 595, 603 (1979).

[80] To illustrate, a Georgia state appeals court awarded contested church property to a parent denomination on the basis of the following provision contained in the deed to a local church's property: "The aforesaid property is conveyed to the trustees above-named as trustees of First Evangelical Methodist Church, Lafayette, Georgia, affiliated with the Evangelical Methodist Church of Abilene, Texas, and other places, it is understood that this conveyance is made to the trustees hereinbefore named as trustees in connection with the affiliations aforesaid and that said connection is to be maintained in the use of the property herein conveyed." First Evangelical Methodist Church v. Clinton, 360 S.E.2d 584 (Ga. 1987).

without inquiring into religious doctrine or polity. Neutral conditions would probably include disaffiliation or a disagreement about who owns church property. In either case, a court would merely be called upon to determine whether a disaffiliation or a property dispute had in fact occurred. Such a determination would not necessarily involve religious doctrine.

Alternatively, a reverter clause could specify that a church's property immediately reverts to a parent religious body upon an attempted conveyance of property by the church. Such a provision would prevent a church from deleting a reverter clause in its deed by reconveying property to itself, either outright or through an intermediary, by a deed not containing the reverter clause. However, any reverter clause conditioned on an attempted conveyance of church property would automatically vest title in a parent denomination upon *any* attempted conveyance, even those unrelated to a disaffiliation. Most conveyances of church property are not associated with a disaffiliation. Rather, they are prompted by a desire for a new location or a larger facility. But unless the church obtains a written release or renunciation of the reverter clause from the parent denomination and has it recorded in the office of the recorder of deeds for the county in which the property is located, the property will automatically revert to the denomination whenever a church conveys its property. Alternatively, in many states the parent denomination could execute a quitclaim deed in favor of the local church. The parent denomination of course could condition the execution of a release or quitclaim deed upon the inclusion of a reverter clause in the deed by which the local church receives title to its new property.

A church deed could contain a reverter clause conditioned on either an attempted conveyance of church property or disaffiliation. Such a clause presumably would be effective if it involved no interpretation of church doctrine.

A church whose property is held subject to a reversion in favor of a parent religious body, whether through a provision in a deed, charter, bylaw, or constitution, ordinarily is not permitted to borrow money from a commercial lending institution unless the parent body signs a "subordination agreement" agreeing to subordinate its interests under the reversionary clause to the mortgage securing the lender's loan. If such an agreement is not signed, a church mortgage may inadvertently trigger the reverter clause in favor of the parent religious body since a mortgage constitutes a conveyance of a church's legal or equitable interest in its property to the lending institution (or, in the case of a deed of trust, to a trustee) until such time as the loan is repaid. In addition, any attempt by the lender to foreclose on a church mortgage may also inadvertently trigger the reverter clause. Many commercial lending institutions remain unaware of the danger of failing to secure a subordination agreement from the beneficiary of a reverter clause.

d. Title held jointly. A parent denomination could have title deeded to itself and the local church as joint tenants or tenants in common. This would normally not be satisfactory, since a majority faction voting to disassociate itself from the denomination could have the property partitioned (the denomination and the local church would each be declared absolute owner of a fraction of the whole).

2. Trusts

The parent denomination can declare that all affiliated churches hold property "in trust" for the denomination. Churches voting to disaffiliate would thereby lose all claim to church property. Such a trust would normally be inserted in the parent denomination's constitution or bylaws. As an example, the Supreme Court in *Jones* cited paragraph 1537 of the Methodist *Book of Discipline*:

[T]itle to all real property now owned or hereafter acquired by an unincorporated local church . . . shall be held by and/or conveyed to its duly elected trustees . . . and their successors in office . . . in trust, nevertheless, for the use and benefit of such local church *and of The United Methodist Church.* Every instrument of conveyance of real estate shall contain the appropriate trust clause as set forth in the Discipline . . . .

Section 2503 of the *Book of Discipline* similarly requires that the following "trust clause" be incorporated in any deed transferring real estate to a church:

In trust, that said premises shall be used, kept, and maintained as a place of divine worship of the United Methodist ministry and members of the United Methodist Church; subject to the Discipline, usage, and ministerial appointments of said church as from time to time authorized and declared by the General Conference and by the Annual Conference within whose bounds the said premises are situated. This provision is solely for the benefit of the grantee, and the grantor reserves no right or interest in said premises.

The *Book of Discipline* also stipulates that in the absence of a trust clause, a trust in favor of The United Methodist Church would be implied if (1) the conveyance is to the trustees of a local church associated with any predecessor to The United Methodist Church, (2) the local church uses the name of any predecessor to The United Methodist Church and is known to the community as a part of The United Methodist Church, or (3) the local church accepts ministers appointed by any predecessor to The United Methodist Church. The Supreme Court inferred that such "implied trusts" would be deemed valid, since they involved no determinations concerning religious doctrine.

Churches that receive title to property subject to an express trust ordinarily must release the trust when the property is sold. For example, if a deed to church property specifies that the property is held by the church in trust for the use and benefit of a particular denomination, this trust attaches to the property and must be released upon a sale of the property in order to relieve the transferee of the terms of the trust.

In 1979, the Protestant Episcopal Church in the United States of America (PECUSA) amended its canons to add the following provision:

All real and personal property held by or for the benefit of any parish, mission or congregation is held in trust for this Church and the Diocese thereof in which such parish, mission or congregation is located. The existence of this trust, however, shall in no way limit the power and authority of the parish, mission or congregation otherwise existing over such property so long as the particular parish, mission or congregation remains a part of, and subject to this Church and its constitution and canons.

The Book of Order of the Presbyterian Church (U.S.A.) (or "PCUSA") contains several paragraphs subjecting local church properties to an express trust in favor of the PCUSA. These include the following:

All property held by or for a particular church . . . whether legal title is lodged in a corporation, a trustee or trustees, or an unincorporated association . . . is held in trust nevertheless for the use and benefit of the Presbyterian Church (U.S.A.).[81]

---

[81] BOOK OF ORDER § G-8.0200.

Whenever property of, or held for, a particular church of the Presbyterian Church (U.S.A.) ceases to be used by that church as a particular church of the Presbyterian Church (U.S.A.) in accordance with this constitution, such property shall be held, used, applied, transferred, or sold as provided by the presbytery.[82]

The relationship to the Presbyterian Church (U.S.A.) of a particular church can be severed only by constitutional action on the part of the presbytery. . . . If there is a schism within the membership of a particular church and the presbytery is unable to effect a reconciliation or a division into separate churches within the Presbyterian Church (U.S.A.), the presbytery shall determine if one of the factions is entitled to the property because it is identified by the presbytery as the true church within the Presbyterian Church (U.S.A.). This determination does not depend upon which faction received the majority vote within the particular church at the time of the schism.[83]

The Cumberland Presbyterian Church denomination amended its constitution in 1984 to include a provision subjecting all local church property to a trust in favor of the denomination. The amendment provides, in relevant part:

3.32 The Cumberland Presbyterian Church is a connectional church and all lower judicatories of the church to-wit: synod, presbytery, and the particular churches are parts of that body and therefore all property held by or for a particular church, a presbytery, a synod, the General Assembly, or the Cumberland Presbyterian Church, whether legal title is lodged in a corporation, a trustee or trustees, or an unincorporated association, and whether the property is used in programs of the particular church or of a more inclusive judicatory or retained for the production of income, and whether or not the deed to the property so states, is held in trust nevertheless for the use and benefit of the Cumberland Presbyterian Church.

3.33 Whenever property of, or held for, a particular church of the Cumberland Presbyterian Church, ceases to be used by the church, as a particular church of the Cumberland Presbyterian Church in accordance with this Constitution, such property shall be held, used, applied, transferred or sold as provided by the presbytery in which that particular church is located.

3.34 Whenever a particular church is formally dissolved by the presbytery, or has become extinct by reason of dispersal of its members, the abandonment of its work, or other cause, such property as it may have shall be held, used, and applied for such uses, purposes, and trusts as the presbytery in which said particular church is located may direct, limit, and appoint, or such property may be sold or disposed of as the presbytery may direct, in conformity with the Constitution of the Cumberland Presbyterian Church. . . .

3.35 A particular church shall not sell, nor lease its real property used for purposes of worship, nurture or ministry, without the written permission of the presbytery in which the particular church is located, transmitted through the session of the particular church.

Trust provisions should be drafted in such a way as to avoid any interpretation of religious doctrine. To illustrate, an Arizona state appeals court refused to recognize or enforce an express trust on the basis of a deed conveying title to the "trustees of The Word Chapel, a religious body," since this

---

[82] BOOK OF ORDER § G-8.0300.
[83] BOOK OF ORDER § G-8.0600.

would require an examination into religious doctrine of [the church], and a determination of who the real [beneficiary] is according to their current beliefs. . . . [S]uch an approach was . . . expressly declared unconstitutional by the United States Supreme Court in [*Hull*]. . . . [W]e hold that any express trust, sought to be enforced in favor of some specific doctrine or belief, must be written so that the court can enforce it on purely secular terms.[84]

3. LOCAL CHURCH CHARTER OR BYLAWS

In the event of a church dispute, the local church charter or bylaws may also provide for the disposition of property. Again, to be effective, such a provision must not be made dependent upon any determinations involving religious doctrine or polity.[85] This means of private resolution is of limited value, since most church bylaws can be amended by vote of the church membership.[86]

4. CONSTITUTION OR BYLAWS OF A PARENT DENOMINATION

The constitution or bylaws of a parent denomination could contain a provision vesting title to church property in the denomination in the event of a dispute or disaffiliation. Again, such a provision must be made dependent upon neutral conditions. Thus, a provision mandating reversion of church property to the denomination in the event that a local church "departs" or "deviates" from the doctrine of the denomination would not be recognized by the courts, for enforcement of such a provision would involve a scrutiny of religious doctrine. As noted above, a number of denominations have adopted provisions attempting to control the disposition of local church property in the event of a disaffiliation. Clauses adopted by the United Methodist Church and the Protestant Episcopal Church are quoted in their entirety in the preceding paragraphs.

5. STATE STATUTES

State legislatures can enact statutes that provide for the disposition of property in the event of a church dispute. Illustratively, the Georgia legislature has enacted a law which provides that "[t]he majority of those who adhere to its organization and doctrines represent the church. The withdrawal by one part of a congregation from the original body, or uniting with another church or denomination, is a relinquishment of all rights in the church abandoned."[87] Pennsylvania adopted a statute several years ago referred to as the "Lay Control of Church Property Act," which provides:

Whensoever any property, real or personal, has heretofore been or shall hereafter be bequeathed, devised, or conveyed to any ecclesiastical corporation, bishop, ecclesiastic, or other person, for the use of any church, congregation, or religious society, for or in trust for religious worship or sepulture, or for use by said church, congregation, or religious society, for a school, educational institution, convent, rectory, parsonage, hall, auditorium, or the maintenance of any of these, the same shall be taken and held subject to the control and disposition of such officers or authorities of such church, congregation, or religious society, having a controlling power according to the rules, regulations, usages, or corporate requirements of such church, congregation, or religious society, which control and disposition shall be exercised in accordance with and subject to the rules and regulations, usages, canons, discipline and requirements of the religious body, denomination or

---

[84] Skelton v. Word Chapel, Inc., 637 P.2d 753, 756 (Ariz. App. 1981).
[85] Clay v. Illinois District Council of the Assemblies of God, 657 N.E.2d 688 (Ill. App. 1995).
[86] York v. First Presbyterian Church, 474 N.E.2d 716 (Ill. App. 1984).
[87] Ga. Code § 22-5504.

organization to which such church, congregation, or religious society shall belong, but nothing herein contained shall authorize the diversion of any property from the purposes, uses, and trusts to which it may have been heretofore lawfully dedicated, or to which it may hereafter, consistently herewith, be lawfully dedicated . . . .[88]

A Pennsylvania court, in commenting on this statute, noted that it "requires that properties attached to seceding local churches formerly in union with hierarchically governed denominations remain with the denomination." The court concluded that the statute was consistent with and anticipated the neutral principles approach—and required that title to a seceding Presbyterian church revert to the denomination.[89]

Such statutes must not involve any determination regarding religious doctrine or polity. The Georgia statute previously quoted involves no doctrinal interpretations. A court has only to determine whether a faction in a particular congregation has withdrawn from the original body or united with another church or denomination. Such determinations normally would involve no interpretation of religious doctrine or polity, and thus would constitute an appropriate means of resolving church property disputes.

6. RESULTING TRUSTS

In many states, a "resulting trust" arises by operation of law in favor of the person who purchases property in the name of another. The law presumes that it ordinarily is not the intention of a person paying for property to make a gift to the one receiving title. This presumption is rebuttable, however. Similarly, if a person contributes only a part of the purchase price of a piece of property placed in the name of another, a resulting trust will arise in favor of the payor on a prorata basis. In such cases, however, the courts often require the payor to demonstrate the precise percentage he contributed toward the entire purchase price.

A local church that acquires property because of the contributions of a parent church body may hold title subject to a resulting trust in favor of the parent body in proportion to the parent's contribution. For example, a parent body contributing all or substantially all of the funds used to purchase a local church property should be entitled to the benefit of a resulting trust interest in the entire property.[90]

> *Example. An Ohio court ruled that a home purchased by a church for its pastor was subject to a "purchase money resulting trust" in favor of the church and therefore the home could not be considered in a property settlement following the pastor's divorce. A pastor and his wife filed for a divorce. While the couple was engaged in dividing their assets, the pastor's church intervened in the divorce action and asserted a legal interest in the couple's home. The court ruled that when property is purchased by one person, but title is vested in another, the person holding title does so subject to a "purchase money resulting trust" in favor of the person who paid for the property—at least if the parties intended that the purchaser have some equitable interest in the property. The court pointed out that the church purchased the home and adjoining property as a site for a new church building. As a result, the pastor and his wife held title to the home in trust for the church, and the home was not marital property that could be divided between the pastor and his wife.[91]*

---

[88] PA. STAT. title 10, §81.

[89] Beaver-Butler Presbytery v. Middlesex Presbyterian Church, 471 A.2d 1271 (Pa. Common. 1984). This case was reversed on appeal by the state supreme court, which ruled in favor of a local church—but with no mention of the state law cited by the lower court. Beaver-Butler Presbytery v. Middlesex Presbyterian Church, 489 A.2d 1317 (Pa. 1985). *See also* New York Annual Conference of the Methodist Church v. Nam Un Cho, 548 N.Y.S.2d 577 (1989).

[90] Grace Evangelical Lutheran Church v. Lutheran Church—Missouri Synod, 454 N.E.2d 1038 (Ill. App. 1983).

[91] Cayten v. Cayten, 659 N.E.2d 805 (Ohio App. 1995).

7. CONSTRUCTIVE TRUSTS

A constructive trust may be imposed whenever it is established that one person holds property which in equity and good conscience should be held by another. A constructive trust may arise as a result of several factors, including misrepresentation, failure to use property or funds for stated purposes, refusal to carry out the terms of an express trust, frustration of the terms of a will, or wrongful conveyance of another's property. It is possible for the law of constructive trusts to apply to church property so long as no inquiries into church doctrine or polity are involved.[92]

8. ARBITRATION

A church could insert a provision in its charter, constitution, or bylaws specifying that any dispute concerning title to any of its properties will be resolved through binding arbitration. Such provisions occasionally are contained in the organizational documents of nonprofit corporations, and they ordinarily are upheld as binding agreements on the part of the membership.

9. BUY-SELL AGREEMENTS

A buy-sell (or "preemption") agreement requires the owner of a specified tract of property to offer the property to a designated person at a stipulated price before selling it to another. Religious denominations wanting to maintain control over the property of dissident churches could require churches to execute such an agreement, giving the parent denomination a preemptive right to purchase the church's property at a specified price at or below market value. Such an agreement obviously would be of no value unless a dissident church wanted to sell its property. Alternatively, a denomination could enter into a purchase agreement with a local church giving the denomination the right to purchase the church's property in the event of a disaffiliation. Such agreements, if supported by adequate consideration, ordinarily will be enforceable.[93]

10. CHARACTERIZATION OF DENOMINATIONAL FINANCING AS A "LOAN"

A denomination that invests funds in a local, affiliated church could have the church execute a promissory note in favor of the denomination, secured by an appropriate mortgage instrument (with a "future advances clause" securing the repayment of any additional advances by the denomination), specifying that payment shall be due in full within a specified number of days (e.g., 30 days) after the church votes to disaffiliate from the denomination. This arrangement could protect the investment of the denomination in the local church. Some rate of interest should be specified to adequately compensate the denomination for the lost opportunity costs associated with the loss of its capital from the time of the "loan" to the time the church votes to disaffiliate.

11. CONCLUSION

If none of these neutral principles of law disposes of church property in the event of a church property dispute, then the courts will be compelled to apply the methodology of resolution that they have developed.

---

[92] *Id.*

[93] *Id. See also* Grace Evangelical Lutheran Church v. Lutheran Church-Missouri Synod, 454 N.E.2d 1038 (Ill. App. 1983), *cert. denied,* 469 U.S. 820 (1984).

In the sixth chapter of the apostle Paul's first letter to the church at Corinth, he wrote:

If any of you has a dispute with another, dare he take it before the ungodly for judgment instead of before the saints? . . . [I]f you have disputes about such matters, appoint as judges even men of little account in the church! I say this to shame you. Is it possible that there is nobody among you wise enough to judge a dispute between believers? But instead one brother goes to law against another—and this in front of unbelievers! The very fact that you have lawsuits among you means you have been completely defeated already. Why not rather be wronged. Why not rather be cheated?[94]

Paul's denunciation of lawsuits involving Christians is clearly based in part upon the fear that such suits will give unbelievers a negative impression of Christianity. This fear is still warranted. In the *Watson* decision, the United States Supreme Court itself remarked:

[W]e have held [the case] under advisement for a year; not uninfluenced by the hope, that . . . charity, which is so large an element in the faith of both parties, and which, by one of the apostles of that religion, is said to be the greatest of all the Christian virtues, would have brought about a reconciliation. But we have been disappointed. It is not for us to determine or apportion the moral responsibility which attaches to the parties for this result.[95]

Similarly, a state court observed:

Any church dispute has a deep effect upon all involved. If we all followed the teachings of Jesus as to turning the other cheek, there would be no need for courts. Likewise, if the teachings of Paul were followed, a religious dispute would never reach the civil courts. However, these disputes have plagued churches from time immemorial. Paul's First Epistle to the Corinthians was written over such a dispute. As long as we are humans, such disputes will arise. In any religious dispute there is no winner; only losers. All sides lose and the cause for which the church was organized must lose.[96]

The decision to take other Christians to court, like most ethical determinations, is thus not a private decision. It is a decision that also affects outsiders' perceptions of the Christian faith. And, it is a decision that, in many cases, will directly contradict Paul's command in First Corinthians 6. Such considerations, at the least, should encourage utilization of the various methods of private resolution promoted by the Supreme Court in *Jones v. Wolf.* In most cases such methods would avoid litigation. Their effect, however, would be cosmetic, covering over real and festering disputes among believers for whom Jesus prayed "that they may be one." Only grace—not courts or neutral principles—can resolve these disputes.

§ 7-05 Transferring Church Property

Key point 7-05. An incorporated church generally can transfer title to church property, following authorization of the transaction pursuant to the church's governing document, by means of a deed that identifies the church by its corporate name and that is signed by one or more authorized officers. In most states, an unincorporated church can transfer title in the same manner as an incorporated church. In some states unincorporated churches must select trustees to hold and transfer title to church property.

---

[94] *1 Corinthians* 6:1, 4-7 (NIV).
[95] *See* note 1, *supra*, at 735.
[96] Board of Trustees v. Richards, 130 N.E.2d 736, 743 (Ohio App. 1954).

Since one of the attributes of a corporation is the ability to hold title in the corporate name, it is a good practice for an incorporated church to identify itself as a corporation in deeds, mortgages, contracts, promissory notes, and other legal documents. For example, identifying a church as "First Church, a nonprofit religious corporation duly organized under the laws of the state of Illinois," ordinarily will suffice. Such a practice will indicate that the church is incorporated and therefore capable of executing legal documents in its name by its officers or other authorized persons.

In some states, an unincorporated church must execute such documents in the name of church trustees since the church itself lacks authority to execute legal documents. Unfortunately, it is a common practice for unincorporated churches to execute such documents in the name of the church with the signatures of only the minister and church secretary. Such documents of course will be invalid in some states absent ratification by the church membership through acceptance of the benefits of the transaction. Deeds to property present the greatest problem, and many title examiners will object to a deed executed by an unincorporated church in such a manner even if it is later ratified.

In most states, a business corporation is required to include terminology in its name identifying itself as a corporation. Such terminology may include such words and abbreviations as *corporation, corp., incorporated,* or *inc.* This practice ordinarily does not apply to religious corporations. The absence of such a requirement, of course, makes it imperative for a church corporation to identify itself as a corporation following reference to its name in legal documents to avoid any suggestion that it might be an unincorporated association and thereby incapable of conveying title to property in its own name.

A few states have statutes restricting the transfer of property by religious organizations. To illustrate, a New York law specifies that "a religious corporation shall not sell, mortgage or lease for a term exceeding five years any of its real property without applying for and obtaining leave of the court . . . ."[97] A New York court upheld the constitutionality of this statute. A church had argued that this requirement not only violated the first amendment's ban on the establishment of religion but also violated the first amendment's guaranty of religious freedom by involving the government in the internal decisions of churches. In rejecting the church's "establishment clause" argument, the court applied the United States Supreme Court's three-part "*Lemon* test" for determining whether or not the New York law constituted an impermissible establishment of religion. Under this test, first announced in a 1971 decision,[98] a law or government practice challenged as an establishment of religion will be valid only if it satisfies the following three conditions—a secular purpose, a primary effect that neither advances nor inhibits religion, and no excessive entanglement between church and state.

The New York court concluded that all of these tests were met. First, the New York law had a secular purpose—"to insure that such [sales are] in the best interest of the corporation and its members and that the proceeds are properly disbursed." The court noted that the New York law was prompted by "several instances of questionable practices resulting in lawsuits to enjoin and set aside transfers of religious property within congregational-type religious churches." Second, the notice requirement did "nothing to convey any message whatsoever that could be construed to advance or inhibit any religion or religious belief." Third, the notice requirement did not result in an excessive entanglement between church and state since it was a mere "routine regulatory interaction" involving "no inquiries into religious doctrine . . . no detailed monitoring and close administrative contact between secular and religious bodies."

---

[97] N.Y. Religious Corporations § 12.
[98] Lemon v. Kurtzman, 403 U.S. 602 (1971).

The court also concluded that the notice requirement did not violate the first amendment guaranty of religious freedom. It noted that a violation of this guaranty requires proof that a law or government practice "burdens the adherent's practice of his or her religion by pressuring him or her to commit an act forbidden by the religion or by preventing him or her from engaging in conduct or having a religious experience which faith mandates." Such was not the case here, the court concluded. It further noted that "any inquiry by the attorney general involves only the terms of a real estate transaction; it involves no inquiry into religious beliefs nor does it involve the regulation or prohibition of conduct undertaken for religious reasons."[99]

§ 7-06 Zoning Law

Key point. The definition of the term "church" and the subject of accessory uses are addressed in chapter 5.

The vast majority of municipalities in the United States have enacted zoning laws. The purpose of a municipal zoning law

is to regulate the growth and development of the city in an orderly manner. Among the objectives to be served is to avoid mixing together of industrial, commercial, business and residential uses; the prevention of undue concentrations of people in certain areas under undesirable conditions; making provisions for safe and efficient transportation; for recreational needs; and for the enhancement of aesthetic values, all in order to best serve the purpose of promoting the health, safety, morals and general welfare of the city and its inhabitants.[100]

It is important to recognize that municipalities have no inherent authority to enact zoning laws. Zoning laws constitute an exercise of the police power—that is, the authority inherent in state governments to enact laws in furtherance of the public health, safety, morals, and general welfare. Unless a state specifically delegates such authority to a municipality, the municipality will have no authority to enact a zoning ordinance. Most states, however, have adopted "enabling acts" which delegate such authority to designated municipalities. The authority of a municipality to enact a zoning ordinance therefore is limited by the terms of the enabling statute. It is also limited by constitutional considerations, for many courts have ruled that the United States Constitution prohibits the enactment of zoning ordinances that are unreasonable, discriminatory, or arbitrary. And, since a state's delegation of zoning power to a municipality constitutes a delegation of state "police power," a municipal zoning ordinance to be valid must in fact further the public health, safety, morals, or general welfare. Further, zoning ordinances that restrict the location of churches in certain areas must not run afoul of the constitutional guarantees of assembly and the free exercise of religion.

The typical zoning ordinance divides a municipality into zones or districts in which only certain activities or uses are permitted. For example, it is common for a municipal zoning ordinance to divide a municipality into residential, commercial, and industrial districts, with the activities and uses permitted in each district described in the ordinance. Nonconforming uses and activities may be authorized in some cases through variances, special use permits, or by the fact that the nonconforming use preceded the enactment of the zoning ordinance.

Historically, churches presented few problems for municipal planners. Churches were allowed in residential districts so that they would be within walking distance of parishioners' residences. It was unthinkable

---

[99] Greek Orthodox Archdiocese v. Abrams, 618 N.Y.S.2d 504 (Sup. 1994).
[100] Naylor v. Salt Lake City Corporation, 410 P.2d 764, 765 (Utah 1966).

to locate churches anywhere else. The vast majority of municipalities still permit churches in residential zones. With the advent of the automobile, churches became more incompatible with residential districts for two reasons. First, most parishioners drive their automobiles to church, making it less essential for churches to locate within "walking distance" of their membership. Second, on at least one day each week the church is the biggest source of traffic congestion, noise, and pollution in many residential neighborhoods. For a growing number of churches, this is becoming true on several days of the week due to additional church services, youth activities, weddings, funerals, child care, rehearsals, civic events, and programs for the elderly. Understandably, many municipalities have reconsidered the traditional view of allowing churches in residential zones without restriction.

COMMUNICATIONS TOWERS ON CHURCH PROPERTY

Many churches have allowed telecommunications companies to construct antennae on church property in exchange for a monthly rental fee. Such arrangements raise a number of legal and tax issues, including those listed below. It is essential for church leaders to discuss these issues with a local attorney before entering into an agreement with a telecommunications company to erect an antenna on church property.

• *Zoning law.* Is the construction of a telecommunications antenna on church property consistent with the classification of the property under local zoning law? The few courts that have addressed this question have suggested that zoning laws would not be violated by such a use of church property.[101]

• *Property tax exemption.* It is possible that the use of church property for a telecommunications antenna would jeopardize the exemption of the property from local property taxes. In many states, an exemption from property taxes is conditioned on the fact that the property is not used for the generation of income. Loss of exempt status ordinarily will be limited to the portion of a church's property that is actually being used for the production of income rather than to the entire premises. However, in some states a church may lose an exemption for all of its property though only a small amount is used for an antenna.

• *Unrelated business income.* Federal law imposes a tax (equal to the corporate income tax) on the net income generated by a tax-exempt organization from any unrelated trade or business that is "regularly carried on." This tax is called the unrelated business income tax (or UBIT for short). There are a number of exemptions, including rental income. However, in order to be exempt from UBIT, the rental income must be from the rental of a debt-free facility. In other words, you would not be subject to the tax on unrelated business income if the premises that you rent are owned by the church debt-free. Rental income derived from debt-financed property generally constitutes unrelated business taxable income unless the property falls within an exception. One exception is if substantially all (85 percent or more) of the property is used for exempt purposes. Consider both physical area and time. Property is not used for exempt purposes merely because income derived from the property is expended for exempt purposes. If less than 85 percent of the use of the property is devoted to exempt purposes, only that part of the property that is not used to further exempt purposes is treated as unrelated debt-financed property. It is unlikely that this exception would apply in your case, if the property is subject to an indebtedness. Even if a church's rental activities are subject to the tax on unrelated business income, there are three additional observations to note. First, the tax is assessed against net earnings. This means that you are entitled to deduct all of the church's expenses incurred in making the rental property available. Second, the tax is a prorated tax—meaning that only that percentage of net rental income that corresponds to the percentage of the property's value that is encumbered by debt is taxable. For example, if the remaining mortgage debt on the rented property corresponds to half the

---

[101] *See, e.g.,* AT&T Wireless PCS, Inc. v. City Council, 979 F. Supp. 416 (E.D. Va. 1997).

This process of reconsidering the proper location of churches within a modern-day community has resulted in a number of views. Most municipalities continue to allow churches in residential zones, but a growing number are requiring churches to obtain a permit prior to obtaining property in a residential zone. The permit procedure gives municipal planners greater control over the location of churches within residential zones. Some municipal zoning ordinances prohibit churches in any residential zone, and a few municipalities have attempted to bar churches from the entire community.

§ 7-06.1 — The Majority View: Churches May Build in Residential Zones

Key point 7-06.1. Most courts have ruled that churches have a legal right to locate in residential districts.

1. IN GENERAL

It is the view of "the long line of cases"[102] or "the wide majority of courts"[103] that churches may not be excluded from residential districts. This conclusion generally rests upon one of two grounds: First, the exclusion of churches from residential districts infringes upon the freedom of religion guaranteed by the first amendment; and second, a total exclusion of churches is an invalid and impermissible exercise of the police power since it cannot be said to further the public health, safety, morals, or general welfare.[104] A few courts have ruled that churches may not be regulated regarding their purchase or use of property within residential zones.[105] However, most courts have concluded that while churches may not be excluded from residential zones, their location within a residential zone can be regulated through a permit application procedure.

To illustrate, a New York court observed that

With respect to zoning restrictions, New York adheres to the majority view that religious institutions are beneficial to the public welfare by their very nature. Consequently, a proposed religious use should be accommodated, even when it would be inconvenient for the community. A religious use may not be prohibited merely because of potential traffic congestion, an adverse effect upon property values, the loss of potential tax revenues, or failure to demonstrate that a more suitable location could not be found. In order to deny a special use permit for a religious use as "detrimental to the public health, safety and welfare," it must be "convincingly shown that the [proposed use] will have a direct and immediate adverse effect upon the health, safety or welfare of the community." A distinction must be drawn between danger to the public and mere public inconvenience. Every effort must be made to accommodate the religious use subject to conditions reasonably related to land use.[106]

---

[102] 5. E. YOKLEY, ZONING LAW AND PRACTICE § 35-14 (4th ed. 1980 and Supp. 1998).

[103] State v. Maxwell, 617 P.2d 816, 820 (Hawaii 1980).

[104] *See generally* A. RATHKOPF, THE LAW OF ZONING AND PLANNING ch. 20 (1998) [hereinafter cited as RATHKOPF]; E. YOKLEY, ZONING LAW AND PRACTICE § 35-14 (4th ed. 1980 and Supp. 1998) [hereinafter cited as YOKLEY]; N. WILLIAMS, AMERICAN LAND PLANNING LAW ch. 77 (1985 and Supp. 1998) [hereinafter cited as WILLIAMS]; Comment, *Zoning the Church: Toward a Concept of Reasonableness,* 12 CONN. L. REV. 571 (1980); Note, *Zoning Ordinances, Private Religious Conduct, and the Free Exercise of Religion,* 76 NW. L. REV. 786 (1981); Note, *Churches and Zoning,* 70 HARV. L. REV. 1428 (1957); Note, *Land Use Regulation and the Free Exercise Clause,* 84 COLUM. L. REV. 1562 (1984); Comment, *Zoning Ordinances Affecting Churches: A Proposal for Expanded Free Exercise Protection,* 132 UNIV. PA. L. REV. 1131 (1984); Pearlman, *Zoning and the Location of Religious Establishments,* 31 CATH. U. L. REV. 314 (1988); Reynolds, *Zoning the Church: The Police Power versus the First Amendment,* 64 B.U.L. REV. 767 (1988).

[105] *See, e.g.,* Community Synagogue v. Bates, 1 N.Y.S.2d 445 (1956).

[106] Holy Spirit Association for Unification of World Christianity v. Rosenfeld, 458 N.Y.S.2d 920 (N.Y.A.D. 1983). *See also* Genesis

Another New York court similarly observed that

[w]e have not said that considerations of the surrounding area and potential traffic hazards are unrelated to the public health, safety or welfare when religious structures are involved. We have simply said that they are outweighed by the constitutional prohibition against the abridgement of the free exercise of religion and by the public benefit and welfare which is itself an attribute of religious worship in a community.[107]

This position often is referred to as the *New York rule*, since the courts of New York have been the most consistent and forceful in upholding the right of churches to locate without restriction in residential zones. The application of this rule can be demonstrated by reviewing a few representative court rulings.

Example. A New York court ruled that a city acted improperly in denying a synagogue's application for a special use permit without making any attempt to accommodate the proposed religious use. The synagogue applied for a special use permit that would have allowed it to operate in a residential property. The city council rejected the permit application, and the synagogue appealed. An appeals court concluded that the city's denial of the permit was "arbitrary, capricious, and an abuse of discretion." The court acknowledged that "there is no exemption from zoning rules for religious uses, nor is there any conclusive presumption that any religious use automatically outweighs its ill effects." However, "where the applicant is a religious institution, more flexibility is required and efforts must be made to accommodate the religious use, if possible." In fact, "every effort must be made to accommodate the religious use subject to conditions reasonably related to land use." The court noted that the city council rejected the synagogue's permit application "without making any attempt to accommodate the proposed religious use." Such an act, concluded the court, was improper. The city had "an affirmative duty to suggest measures to accommodate the proposed religious use." The court found that the synagogue's proposed religious use could have been accommodated by the city: "For example, we observe that the accommodation of the religious use and maintenance of the public's safety, health, and welfare could have been achieved by limiting the number of persons who could attend services or meetings at any given time, and by posting 'no parking' signs along the street to prevent hazardous road conditions, and by limiting the hours during which meetings or instruction could be held . . . ." The court ordered the city council "to issue the permit upon such reasonable conditions as will allow the [synagogue] to establish its house of worship, while mitigating any detrimental or adverse effects on the surrounding community."[108]

Example. A New York court struck down as unreasonable a city's refusal to grant a church's request for a special use permit authorizing it to build a new sanctuary. Noting that churches "enjoy a presumptively favored status with respect to the police powers sought to be protected by zoning laws," the court concluded that "our examination of the reasons enumerated by the [city] for denying [the church] a special use permit discloses that the rejection was unreasonable. No expert evidence was proffered concerning any detrimental effect on traffic or drainage."[109]

Assembly of God v. Davies, 617 N.Y.S.2d 202 (A.D. 2 Dept. 1994) (the court observed that "[I]t is well settled that while religious institutions are not exempt from local zoning laws, greater flexibility is required in evaluating an application for a religious use than an application for another use and every effort to accommodate the religious use must be made").

[107] Application of Covenant Community Church, 444 N.Y.S.2d 415 (N.Y. Sup. 1981).

[108] Harrison Orthodox Minyan v. Town Board, 552 N.Y.S.2d 434 (N.Y. App. 1990).

[109] North Syracuse First Baptist Church v. Village of North Syracuse, 524 N.Y.S.2d 894 (1988).

Example. In another New York case, a municipality denied a congregation permission to construct a church on a two-acre tract of undeveloped property in a residential district on the grounds that the presence of a church and its associated traffic would devalue the adjoining properties, create a fire hazard, and adversely affect the health, safety, and welfare of neighborhood residents. A New York appellate court, in overruling the action of the municipality, held that the potential traffic and safety hazards and property devaluation were outweighed by "the constitutional prohibition against the abridgement of the free exercise of religion and by the public benefit and welfare which is itself an attribute of religious worship in a community."[110]

The courts of several other states have reached similar conclusions.[111] Several illustrative cases are summarized below.

Example. A federal district court in Alabama ruled that a county's practice of prohibiting churches from building new facilities if neighboring residents object violated the churches' constitutional right of religious freedom. A county adopted a new zoning ordinance that limited churches to "institutional districts." The ordinance purposely failed to recognize any land as an institutional district, so that churches would be forced to seek a zoning variance before purchasing property for church use. This procedure was designed to give the county "better site development controls over institutional construction." A Mormon congregation that had outgrown its existing facility attempted to purchase land on which it proposed to construct a new sanctuary. It filed an application to have the property rezoned as an "institutional district," but its application was denied by the county following a hearing in which several neighboring residents expressed "vociferous opposition." The residents lived in an affluent residential district adjacent to the church's proposed building site, and they were horrified by the impact the church would have on the "aesthetics" of the community and the value of existing homes. The county commission based its denial of the church's application on the basis of the "will of the people." The court noted that the church had outgrown its present facility, and that the church had "as a central tenet of its faith the need to assemble together and strengthen the faith of each other and to partake of communion." The court concluded that the church's constitutional right to exercise its religion was violated by the county's procedure: "The court's primary conclusion is that the burden here on religion is that the ability of a church to locate or not is dependent on the acceptability of that church, or any church, to the surrounding community, without there having been any predetermination that churches are allowed to go in any area.[112]

Example. A Connecticut court ruled that a local zoning commission acted improperly in denying a church a special permit to construct a sanctuary in a residential zone. The court observed: "[E]ven though churches may not be completely excluded from residential zones they can be subject to reasonable regulation as to their location without violation of the constitutional guarantee of freedom of religion. . . . Cases from other states have held that it is illegal for a municipality to exclude churches in all zones, from all residential zones, to allow them in the municipality only with a special permit, or have held that there was no compelling reason to deny a special permit. . . . These cases are based on the concept that such zoning restrictions must yield to the right of freedom of religion protected by the . . . United States constitution and comparable provisions in state constitutions where the zoning regulations unreasonably hinder or restrict religious activities. Constitutional provisions do not pre-

---

[110] American Friends of the Society of St. Pius, Inc. v. Schwab, 417 N.Y.S.2d 991, 993 (1979), *appeal denied*, 425 N.Y.S.2d 1027 (1980).

[111] *See, e.g.*, RATHKOPF, *supra* note 100 at § 20.04(1)(b).

[112] Church of Jesus Christ of Latter-Day Saints v. Jefferson County, 741 F. Supp. 1522 (N.D. Ala. 1990).

vent all governmental regulation of churches and religious organizations, and they may be subject to religiously neutral regulation for a secular governmental purpose under the police power, such as, fire inspection and building and zoning regulations." The court concluded that "some increased traffic from construction of a church . . . is not a sufficiently significant factor to warrant limitation of freedom of religion by denial of a special permit."[113]

Example. *An Illinois court ruled that a city's refusal to grant a church's application for a "conditional use permit" violated the church's first amendment guaranty of religious freedom. A Lutheran church in a Chicago suburb experienced explosive growth, but was left with inadequate parking space. To help solve its parking problem, the church sought permission from the city to convert two private residences that it owned on adjoining property into 57 additional parking spaces. The city denied this request on the grounds that the proposed parking lots would adversely affect the value of neighboring properties (the church was located at the entrance to a residential subdivision), and would "injure the use and enjoyment" of the neighborhood. It rejected the church's claim that a limitation on the number of its parking spaces would interfere with the free exercise of its religion. The court concluded that the city had not given due weight to the church's constitutional right to freely exercise its religion. While conceding that city zoning ordinances are presumed to be valid, the court observed that this presumption "diminishes" when an ordinance "limits the free exercise of religion." Significantly, the court concluded: "The location of a church can be regulated by zoning ordinances in proper cases; however, in determining whether this is a proper case for such a restriction, we must take into account that the freedom of religion, and other first amendment freedoms, rise above mere property rights. In addition, first amendment rights and freedoms outweigh considerations of public convenience, annoyance, or unrest." The court concluded that the city had erred in denying the church's request for a permit to convert the two residential properties into additional parking spaces. It rejected the city's claim that the "parking needs of a church should be considered on different legal principles than those applied to the church building itself." This decision represents one of the strongest statements by a court of the right of a church to develop its property despite the complaints of neighboring landowners.*[114]

Example. *An Indiana court, in striking down a municipal ordinance that prohibited churches in residential areas, held that the ordinance constituted "a violation of the fundamental right of freedom to worship protected by the first and fourteenth amendments to the United States Constitution . . . ." The court observed that "[e]arly and modern case law alike has not countenanced the exclusion of churches from residential districts, even though inconveniences may be caused by the influx into a neighborhood of vehicular or pedestrian traffic." The court also acknowledged that churches are subject to such reasonable regulations as may be necessary to promote the public health, safety, and general welfare, but insisted that "[r]easonable restrictions . . . are not tantamount to exclusion."*[115]

Example. *A federal appeals court (with jurisdiction over Louisiana, Mississippi, and Texas) decision strongly supports the right of churches to locate in residential districts. The court ruled that a city's refusal to permit an Islamic center to operate within city limits near a university campus violated the constitutional guaranty of religious freedom. A city zoning ordinance prohibited the use of any building as a church in all areas of the city near a university campus unless a special permit was obtained from*

[113] Grace Church v. Planning and Zoning Commission, 615 A.2d 1092 (Conn. Super. 1992).
[114] Our Saviour's Evangelical Lutheran Church of Naperville v. City of Naperville, 542 N.E.2d 1158 (Ill. App. 2nd Cir. 1989). *See also* Hope Deliverance Center, Inc. v. Zoning Board, 452 N.E.2d 630 (Ill. App. 1983) (church could build, despite allegations of increased traffic, and other adverse effects).
[115] Church of Christ v. Metropolitan Board of Zoning, 371 N.E.2d 1331, 1333-34 (Ind. 1978).

the city council. Twenty-five churches were granted permits to operate in restricted areas. However, the Islamic center's request for a permit was denied. No reason was given for the denial, though a neighborhood spokesman expressed concern over "congestion, parking, and traffic problems." The center sued the city, arguing that the city's action in banishing it from the restricted area near the university campus, while allowing 25 churches to meet in the same area, violated the right of Muslims to the free exercise of their religion. The city denied that the Muslims' rights were violated, since "they can establish a mosque . . . outside the city limits or buy cars and ride to more distant places within the city." The federal appeals court observed that the city's suggestion was "reminiscent of Anatole France's comment on the majestic equality of the law that forbids all men, the rich as well as the poor, to sleep under bridges, to beg in the streets, and to steal bread." The court further observed that "laws that make churches accessible only to those affluent enough to travel by private automobile obviously burden the free exercise of religion by the poor." And, while "the constitution does not forbid all governmental regulation that imposes an incidental burden on worship by making the free exercise of religion more difficult or more expensive," once it is established that a governmental action burdens religious exercise, "the government must offer evidence of an overriding interest" to justify its action. In this case, however, the city "advanced no rational basis other than the neighborhood opposition to show why the [permit] granted all other religious centers was denied the Islamic center. . . . [N]eighbors' negative attitudes or fears, unsubstantiated by factors properly cognizable in a zoning proceeding, are not a permissible basis" for denying a permit. Further, the court concluded that the city had acted improperly in "applying different standards" to the Islamic center than to the "worship facilities of other faiths."[116]

Example. *A New Jersey court ruled that a city cannot totally exclude churches from residential districts. A Jehovah's Witness congregation applied to city officials for approval to build a church in an area zoned for manufacturing use. The city then rezoned much of the community, changed the area where the church was to be built from a manufacturing to a residential district, and then prohibited the building of churches in all residential districts. The congregation challenged the city's action as a violation of the constitutional guaranty of religious freedom. The court agreed: "Municipalities have the power to zone their districts, but to exclude churches and other places of worship from the very areas (residential communities) that they draw their members from and relocate them to a less desirable zone of the township . . . offends the very essence of . . . the New Jersey Constitution."[117]*

A number of courts have concluded that a city cannot exclude churches from residential districts if other non-residential facilities are permitted to locate there. This result generally is based on the federal constitution's guaranty of the "equal protection of the laws."[118] To illustrate a federal district court in Illinois ruled that a city ordinance requiring churches to obtain a special use permit from the city prior to acquiring property in any location violated the constitutional guaranty of the equal protection of the laws since the permit requirement did not apply to certain other organizations (e.g., theaters, funeral homes, hotels, community centers). As a result, the ordinance treated churches differently and less favorably without any apparent basis. The federal district court agreed that the city's permit procedure violated the church's constitutional

---

[116] Islamic Center of Mississippi, Inc. v. Starkville, 840 F.2d 293 (5th Cir. 1988).

[117] Jehovah's Witnesses v. Woolrich Township, 532 A.2d 276, 280 (N.J. Super. 1987). *Accord* Lakewood Residents Association v. Congregation Zichron Schneur, 570 A.2d 1032 (N.J. Super. 1989); Shim v. Washington Township Planning Board, 689 A.2d 804 (N.J. Super. 1997).

[118] *See, e.g.,* Ellsworth v. Gercke, 156 P.2d 242 (Ariz. App. 1949); North Shore Unitarian Society v. Village of Plandome, 109 N.Y.S.2d 803 (1951); Andrews v. Board of Adjustment, 143 A.2d 262 (N.J. App. 1958); Black v. Town of Montclair, 167 A.2d 388 (N.J. App. 1961); Garden Grove Congregation of Jehovah's Witnesses v. City of Garden Grove, 1 Cal. Rptr. 65 (1959) (dismissed on procedural grounds).

right to the "equal protection of the laws," and it awarded the church nearly $18,000 in damages under title 42, section 1983 of the United States Code. This law allows persons and organizations whose constitutional rights are violated to sue the offender for money damages—even if the offender is a city or other government unit. Significantly, the court granted the church a "summary judgment," meaning that it found the church's position so clearly correct that it refused to submit the case to a jury. A federal appeals court later dismissed the case on the technical ground that the church lacked "standing" to challenge the city's permit procedure since the city had never enforced the special permit requirement and accordingly there was no threat of legal consequences if the church disregarded it.[119]

This case is very significant (despite the appeals court's decision) since it illustrates the potential relevance of the equal protection guaranty in the context of zoning, and it illustrates the availability of monetary damages under "section 1983" for a city's violation of a church's constitutional rights. The importance of such rulings cannot be overstated—for they represent a recognition of an extremely potent weapon that is available to churches. To be sure, the federal appeals court dismissed the case, but it did so for technical reasons that in no way diminish the significance of the trial court's decision. Further, the appeals court seemed to concede that it would have affirmed the district court's award of monetary damages had the city ever enforced its permit procedure, or had the church presented more evidence of the unwillingness of landlords to rent to the church. In many cases, these factors will be present, and presumably churches in such cases will be entitled to monetary damages.

Obviously, any attempt by a municipality to totally exclude churches from all districts, whether residential, commercial, or industrial, would be unconstitutional.[120]

2. Special Use Permits

Many courts have ruled that while a city cannot exclude churches from residential zones, it can require them to obtain a special use permit in order to use a particular property for church use. To illustrate, an Indiana court ruled that a city ordinance requiring churches to obtain a "special use permit" before using property for religious purposes did not violate the first amendment guaranty of religious freedom.[121] A city required property owners to obtain a special permit before using their property for any one of 33 different uses, including the operation of a church. A property owner who wanted to use his property as a church obtained a 1-year special use permit. When this permit expired, he filed a lawsuit claiming that the special permit procedure was an unconstitutional interference with the exercise of religion. A state appeals court disagreed. The court provided a useful summary of "special permit" ordinances:

[S]pecial uses are designated because they are necessary to the life and economic health of the community, but have characteristics of operation that do not readily permit classification in the usual residential, commercial, or industrial districts. A property owner may utilize his property to exercise a special use in a traditional zoning district as long as the property owner secures a special use permit and the special use is permitted in that zoning district. A property owner wishing to utilize his property as a school or church is permitted to do so in any residential, commercial, or industrial zoning district. In order to obtain a special use permit, any property owner intending to utilize his property for any of the special uses must comply with the procedure set forth in the special use ordinance.

---

[119] Love Church v. City of Evanston, 896 F.2d 1082 (7th Cir. 1990).
[120] Diocese of Rochester v. Planning Board, 154 N.Y.S.2d 849 (1956).
[121] Area Plan Commission v. Wilson, 701 N.E.2d 856 (Ind. App. 1998).

The purpose of the special use ordinance . . . is the accommodation of desirable land uses which cannot be subject to rigid and restrictive classification into the traditional residential, commercial, and industrial zoning districts. It is the legislative accommodation of special uses which necessitates an administrative review of the impact of the special use at a particular location within a given zoning district. Accordingly, the requirement for a use permit is set out in the ordinance so that the body entrusted with the task of reviewing the application can make certain that it would not adversely affect the public interest if placed in a particular location within the permitted zone.

The court rejected the claim that applying the special use permit procedure to churches violated the first amendment. It noted that the United States Supreme Court has ruled that a government regulation which clearly furthers a secular public purpose does not violate the free exercise clause, though the regulation as applied burdens a religious belief or practice, as long as the regulation is "a valued and neutral law of general applicability." *Employment Division v. Smith, 494 U.S. 872 (1990).* A special permit procedure is such a law, the Indiana court concluded. Regulation of land use "is a secular public purpose, and the special use ordinance carries out this purpose in a manner which is generally applicable to all special uses."

The court also rejected the property owner's claim that the procedure for obtaining a special use permit imposed a substantial and unreasonable burden on the exercise of religion. It concluded that any burden imposed by compliance with the special use procedure was minimal.

§ 7-06.2 — The Minority View: The Government May Restrict Church Construction in Residential Zones

Key point 7-06.2. Some courts permit local zoning commissions to restrict the location of churches in residential areas.

A growing minority of courts are willing to exclude churches from residential zones. Generally, this result has been accomplished in two ways. Most courts have simply upheld municipal decisions denying a church's application for a permit to acquire property in a residential zone. These courts reason that the interests of neighboring residents and the integrity of the residential community as a whole outweigh any interest the church has in locating in the zone. Second, some courts have upheld the legal validity of municipal zoning laws prohibiting churches in residential zones.

In one of the first cases to break from the majority rule, a California state appeals court upheld a city's exclusion of churches from single family residential districts. In defending its conclusion, the court observed:

It is a matter of common knowledge that people in considerable numbers assemble in churches and that parking and traffic problems exist where crowds gather. This would be true particularly in areas limited to single family dwellings. There necessarily is an appreciable amount of noise connected with the conduct of church and youth activities. These and many other factors may well enter into the determination of the legislative body in drawing the lines between districts, a determination primarily the province of the city. A single family residence may be much more desirable when not in an apartment house neighborhood or adjacent to a public building such as a church. The municipal legislative body may require that church buildings be erected to conform to health and safety regulations as provided in its building code and we see no reason to hold that churches may be erected in a single family residential area when a duplex, triplex, or other multiple dwelling can lawfully be excluded therefrom. The provision in the ordinance for a single family residential area affords an opportunity and inducement for the acquisition and occupation of private homes where the owners thereof may live in comparative peace, comfort and quiet. Such a zoning regulation bears a substantial relation to the public health, safety, morals and general welfare because it tends to promote and perpetuate the American home and protect its civic and social value.[122]

In other words, since a city can exclude apartment complexes from single family residential districts to avoid noise and traffic congestion, it can exclude churches for the same reason.

Since California courts pioneered the "minority view," this view occasionally is referred to as the *California rule*.[123] However, even in California there have been court decisions upholding the right of churches to locate in residential districts despite the protests of neighboring residents.[124]

In another early case parting with the majority view, an Oregon state court observed:

Traffic congestion is a phrase comprehending many facets. As used in a matter of this kind, it implies all of the nuisances, inconveniences and hazards to which the public generally, and those residing in the same area, may be exposed. Off-street parking would, no doubt, in some places tend to minimize some of the disadvantages of such congestion, but it cannot be expected to avoid all of its resulting annoyances and potential dangers. The incidents of traffic congestion include, among other things, noise, fumes, the intrusion of automobile lights, the blocking of private driveways by parked cars, and delays in normal travel for those using the highways. But most important are the increased dangers of injury to persons and property. We do not mean to infer that the church-going public is less diligent than others in their respect for the traffic laws. However, even the worthy and cautious persons of that class and their children are too often the victims of the careless.

The test of whether or not the building of a church in a given zone will produce traffic congestion or augment existing traffic conditions to a point of hazard cannot be made solely in terms of what a given number of church members might produce with their probable use of a certain number of automobiles. If a church is perchance, in an area where few people live or travel, then it might be relatively easy for a zoning board to determine, in the absence of other circumstances, that the building of a place of worship at such a given site, within the restricted zone, would not create traffic problems. If so, it would be unreasonable to deny such a religious organization an opportunity to erect its building at that point. On the other hand, if traffic congestion is already a real or threatening problem near the site where a congregation desires to build, and the church would bring to that community enough additional vehicles to definitely establish congestion at that point, then the [city] council would be reasonably warranted, if not duty bound, to deny a permit for its erection.[125]

---

[122] Corporation of Presiding Bishop v. City of Porterville, 203 P.2d 823, 825 (Cal. App. 1949).

[123] *See also* Matthews v. Board of Supervisors, 21 Cal. Rptr. 914 (Cal. App. 1962).

[124] *See, e.g.,* Gray v. Board of Supervisors, 316 P.2d 678 (Cal. App. 1957); McLain v. Planning Commission, 319 P.2d 24 (Cal. App. 1957).

[125] Milwaukee Company of Jehovah's Witnesses v. Mullen, 330 P.2d 5, 18-20 (Ore. App. 1958).

In recent years, many courts have been willing to balance the interests of the church, neighboring residents, and the community as a whole, in deciding whether or not to allow a church to locate on a particular piece of property within a residential zone. In many cases, the courts have concluded that the exclusion of churches from residential districts is justified.

Example. *The federal appeals court for the sixth circuit (comprising the states of Kentucky, Michigan, Ohio, and Tennessee) ruled that a zoning ordinance that prohibited churches from all residential zones did not violate a church's constitutional rights. A church in need of a larger facility found a parcel of vacant land in a residential zone, and applied to the city for a permit to construct a church. The city denied the application on the basis of the zoning ordinance that prohibited churches in all "low density" residential zones. The church sued the city on the ground that the ordinance violated its constitutional right to freely exercise its religion. It stressed that only 10 percent of the community was zoned to accommodate churches, and that available building sites were more expensive and less conducive to worship than residential zones. In rejecting the church's claim, the appeals court noted that while the city's action made the practice of the church's religion more costly and less desirable aesthetically, these "burdens" did not amount to a violation of the first amendment guarantee of religious freedom. The court emphasized that the first amendment only protects governmental interference with a "fundamental tenet" or "cardinal principle" of a church. It observed: "The effect of the [city] ordinance is not to prohibit the congregation or any other faith from worshipping in the city. . . . The lots available to the congregation may not meet its budget or satisfy its tastes but the first amendment does not require the city to make all land or even the cheapest or most beautiful land available to churches. . . . [T]he [city] ordinance does not exclude the exercise of a first amendment right, religious worship, from the city."*[126]

Example. *The federal appeals court for the ninth circuit (comprising the states of Alaska, Arizona, California, Hawaii, Idaho, Montana, Nevada, Oregon, and Washington) ruled that a municipal zoning ordinance prohibiting churches in single-family residential areas without a conditional use permit did not violate the constitutional guaranty of religious freedom. The San Francisco City Code prohibits churches in residential districts unless a conditional use permit is granted. Before granting a permit, the city must determine that the proposed use is necessary, and compatible with the neighborhood, and will not be detrimental to the health, safety, convenience, or general welfare of persons residing in the vicinity. A church desiring to establish a church in a single-family residence applied to the city for a permit. A group of 190 neighboring residents signed a petition in opposition to the permit, based on the following considerations: (1) there already are too many churches in the neighborhood; (2) the church would not maintain neighborhood characteristics; (3) there is a housing shortage in the neighborhood; (4) an additional church would create additional traffic that would create safety hazards for neighbors; (5) inadequate parking spaces; and (6) excessive noise. A city zoning commission denied the church's permit request, and the church filed a lawsuit claiming that the city's actions violated its constitutional rights. The court ruled in favor of the city. It concluded that in evaluating whether a city's denial of a church's zoning permit application violates the constitutional guaranty of religious freedom, the following three factors must be considered: (1) the magnitude of the impact on the exercise of religious beliefs; (2) the existence of a compelling governmental interest justifying the burden on the exercise of religious belief; and (3) the extent to which recognition of an exemption from the permit procedure would interfere with the objectives sought to be advanced by the city. The court*

---

[126] Lakewood, Ohio Congregation of Jehovah's Witnesses v. City of Lakewood, 699 F.2d 303 (6th Cir. 1983). The court suggested that an ordinance that permitted churches but not secular organizations within residential zones would violate the first amendment's nonestablishment of religion clause. The court's first amendment analysis presumably is binding upon the state and federal courts within the sixth circuit, which comprises the states of Kentucky, Michigan, Ohio, and Tennessee.

concluded that the impact of its ruling on the congregation's religious belief was not significant; the city's decision was supported by a compelling interest; and, allowing the church an exemption from the permit procedure would materially interfere with the purpose of that procedure. [127]

Example. *The federal appeals court for the 10th circuit (comprising the states of Colorado, Kansas, New Mexico, Oklahoma, Utah, and Wyoming) ruled that a church's constitutional right to religious freedom was not violated by a county's refusal to permit the church to construct a sanctuary on land not specifically zoned for church uses. The church owned an 80-acre tract of vacant land in an area zoned for agricultural uses. Its application for a special permit to construct a sanctuary was rejected by the county planning commission because of a number of concerns, including access problems, erosion hazards, and inadequate fire protection at the site. The appeals court rejected the church's claim that its right to freely exercise its religion had been violated by the county's action. It found that the county's action did "not in any way regulate the religious beliefs of the church," and did not regulate "any religious conduct of the church or its members." The court concluded that "a church has no constitutional right to be free from reasonable zoning regulations nor does a church have a constitutional right to build its house of worship where it pleases."* [128]

Example. *The federal appeals court for the eleventh circuit (comprising the states of Alabama, Florida, and Georgia) ruled that a city zoning ordinance excluding churches from single-family residential zones did not violate the constitutional guaranty of religious freedom. The zoning ordinance of Miami Beach, Florida, excluded churches from single-family residential zones, but permitted them in other zones comprising 50 percent of the city's territory. An orthodox Jewish rabbi who conducted daily religious services in his residence was ordered by the city to discontinue the services on the ground that his residence was located in a single-family district that did not permit religious services. The rabbi sued the city, arguing that the ordinance violated his constitutional rights to freely exercise his religion. The court rejected the rabbi's claim and upheld the city's ordinance. It concluded that the burden imposed by the zoning ordinance on religious freedom "stands toward the lower end of the spectrum," since the ordinance "does not prohibit religious conduct per se [but rather] prohibits acts in furtherance of this conduct in certain geographical areas." The court stressed that the zoning ordinance permitted churches in over half of the city's territory, and that a permissible zone was located just four blocks from the rabbi's residence. These facts persuaded the court that the balance tipped in favor of the city in this case. The court was quick to add that "all should understand that we have not written today for every situation in which these issues might arise— only that we have done our best . . . in solving this very, very delicate problem."* [129]

---

[127] Christian Gospel Church, Inc. v. San Francisco, 896 F.2d 1221 (9th Cir. 1990). The court's first amendment analysis presumably is binding upon the state and federal courts within the ninth circuit, which comprises the states of Alaska, Arizona, California, Hawaii, Idaho, Montana, Nevada, Oregon, and Washington.

[128] Messiah Baptist Church v. County of Jefferson, 859 F.2d 820 (10th Cir. 1988). The court's first amendment analysis presumably is binding upon the state and federal courts within the tenth circuit, which comprises the states of Colorado, Kansas, New Mexico, Oklahoma, Utah, and Wyoming. One of the three judges who participated in this case dissented from the court's decision. The dissenter insisted that the court had improperly viewed the church's interest as "merely a secular building activity." On the contrary, "places of worship have in almost all religions been as integral to their religion as have Sunday School, preaching, hymn singing, prayer, and other forms of worship . . . . Churches are the situs for the most sacred, traditional exercise of religion: baptisms, confirmations, marriages, funerals, sacramental services, ordinations, and rites of passage of all kinds." Indeed, "if first amendment free exercise rights are not triggered by the impingement on places of worship, the right of free exercise of religion is for practical purposes subject to broad infringement in all of its aspects except perhaps belief." The dissenter further noted that when government agencies seek to encumber the use of buildings for religious worship, they are, in fact, impinging on . . . three different interests recognized by the first amendment itself—speech, assembly, and religious exercise." Because of this significant impact on constitutionally protected rights, the court had erred in too quickly dismissing the church's interest as "merely a secular building activity" that required little judicial deference.

Example. *A federal court in Minnesota ruled that a city's refusal to allow a church to operate in a commercial zone did not violate the church's constitutional rights.[130] A city zoning ordinance permitted churches in residential zones, but not in commercial or industrial zones. A new church congregation began meeting in a pastor's home. As the congregation grew, it began meeting in a public school building, and then in a commercial building. Eventually, the city notified the church that use of the commercial building violated city zoning law. The church unsuccessfully sought to amend the zoning ordinance to permit churches in commercial zones, and then it sought to locate other sites for church services. The church was not able to find suitable accommodations in a residential zone, and continued to meet in the commercial building. When the city ordered the church to vacate the building, the church filed a lawsuit alleging that the city's actions violated the constitutional guaranty of religious freedom. The court rejected the church's position. It noted the constitutional guaranty of religious freedom is not violated unless "something is prohibited because of its religious affiliation or its display of religious belief." This was not the case here, the court concluded, since the city had not barred churches from commercial zones because of their religious character: "The zoning ordinance neither excludes only churches from the commercial and industrial zones nor reveals an anti-religious intent."*

A number of state courts have reached similar results.[131] However, this view still represents a minority position among the states.

§ 7-06.3 — Legal Remedies Available to Churches

Key point 7-06.3. Local zoning commissions may violate a church's first amendment right to the free exercise of religion by imposing unreasonable restrictions on the church's ability to purchase and develop land for church use. Churches whose constitutional rights are violated in this manner may be able to sue for money damages under federal law.

What legal recourse does a church have if its exclusion from a city (or portion of a city) violates its constitutional rights? In the past, churches that have been denied access to certain locations by action of a zoning board generally have been content to seek a reversal of such a determination in the civil courts. In recent years, however, some churches have gone a step further and have sued cities for violating their constitutional rights. The relevant statute is title 42, section 1983, of the United States Code, which specifies:

> Every person who, under color of any statute, ordinance, regulation, custom, or usage, of any State or Territory or the District of Columbia, subjects, or causes to be subjected, any citizen of the United States or other person within the jurisdiction thereof to the deprivation of any rights, privileges, or immunities secured by the Constitution and laws, shall be liable to the party injured in an action at law, suit in equity, or other proper proceeding for redress.

To illustrate, a New Jersey state court ruled that a church could sue a city that had improperly denied its request to build two radio antenna towers on its property.[132] An Assemblies of God church in New Jersey owned 106 acres of land, on which it operated a church and a school with 300 students and a fleet of 35 buses.

---

[129] Grosz v. City of Miami Beach, 721 F.2d 729 (11th Cir. 1983). The court's first amendment analysis presumably is binding upon the state and federal courts within the eleventh circuit, which comprises the states of Alabama, Florida, and Georgia. However, the eleventh circuit ruled in a subsequent case that the first amendment guaranty of religious freedom outweighed a city's interest in enforcing its zoning law. Shuster v. City of Hollywood, 725 F.2d 693 (11th Cir. 1984).

[130] Cornerstone Bible Church v. City of Hastings, 740 F. Supp. 654 (D. Minn. 1990).

[131] *See generally* RATHKOPF, *supra* note 100, at § 20.01; YOKLEY, *supra* note 100, at § 35-14; WILLIAMS, *supra* note 100, at § 77.02.

The church wanted to establish a radio station on its property for broadcasting religious and educational programs. The station required a zoning variance permitting the construction of two 184-foot radio antenna towers. A local zoning board denied the church's request on the grounds that the proposed towers would create a safety hazard and would interfere with radio, television, and telephone usage in the neighborhood. A state court reversed the zoning board's decision, and ordered it to grant the church's request for a variance to construct the towers. The court's ruling did not end the litigation, however, for the church promptly sued the city and zoning board, alleging that they had violated its constitutional right to freely exercise its religion. The church relied on title 42, section 1983, of the United Stated Code. The court not only ruled that the church was entitled to money damages under "section 1983," but it did so by granting the church's motion for summary judgment. This means that the court found the church's demand for money damages to be so clearly authorized by law that it refused to submit the question to a jury.

The court rejected the city's claim that it was "immune" from being sued, noting that "municipalities have no immunity in a suit for damages under the Civil Rights Act" and that "it is clear" that a city that violates a church's constitutional rights "is liable for damages." The court agreed with the church that the radio antenna towers were needed to advance its religious beliefs, and accordingly they served a religious function that was protected by the first amendment guaranty of religious liberty. The court emphasized that the courts of New Jersey have "provided broad support for the constitutional guarantees of religious freedom" and that a city "may not exercise its zoning power in violation of the fundamental tenets of the first amendment." It added: "Churches convey their constitutionally protected religious messages primarily by means of the written and spoken word. In doing so, they are not confined to utterances within a church building but are free to disseminate their beliefs through every avenue of communication. Radio and television facilities are not denied to them."

The court conceded that a zoning board could interfere with a church's constitutional right of religious freedom if an "overriding governmental interest" exists. The court found no compelling interest in this case that outweighed the church's rights under the first amendment. The only two concerns raised by the city were that the antenna towers would create a safety hazard and would cause radio interference in the immediate neighborhood. The court denied that either of these concerns presented a sufficiently compelling interest. As to the safety claim, the court simply observed that the church planned to build the towers on its 106 acres "a good distance from neighboring properties." Further, the evidence demonstrated that the proposed towers were "too well designed" to "give any weight" to the city's concern that they might fall over. As to the city's concern about radio interference, the court noted that the church had obtained a license from the Federal Communications Commission (FCC) to operate the station, and that the FCC had concluded that the station "could be operated at acceptable interference levels." This case is significant in its recognition that churches may sue governmental agencies that deny them their constitutional rights.

A federal district court in Illinois ruled that a church could sue a city for violating its constitutional rights.[133] The city of Evanston, Illinois, adopted a zoning ordinance permitting churches to locate anywhere in the city provided they first obtain a special use permit from the city. To secure a permit, a church must file

---

[132] Burlington Assembly of God Church v. Zoning Board, 570 A.2d 495 (N.J. Super. 1989). *See also* Burlington Assembly of God Church v. Zoning Board, 588 A.2d 1297 (N.J. Super. 1990), in which the same court rejected the church's claim that it was entitled to damages of nearly $800,000, comprised mostly of the projected revenues it lost by not being able to broadcast programs for some four years during the lawsuit. The court concluded that the proper measure of damages was the lost property value resulting from the city's denial of the church's constitutional rights. Since the value of the church's property was in no way diminished by the city's denial of the tower permit, the court refused to award the church any monetary damages.

[133] Love Church v. City of Evanston, 896 F.2d 1082 (7th Cir. 1990).

a detailed plan for the use of the facilities and pay a fee. The city zoning board then holds a hearing and renders a decision. The entire process takes between four and six months. Churches conducting services without a permit are guilty of a misdemeanor and are subject to fines of $25 to $500 per day. A small fundamentalist church began conducting services in Evanston without a permit. The church met in the pastor's apartment, and then in a rented hotel room. It sought a permanent location, but allegedly could not find one since landlords either were unwilling to rent to the church until it obtained a permit, or increased the rent to an unaffordable level. The church filed a lawsuit against the city in federal court, alleging that its constitutional rights were violated by the city's permit procedure. Specifically, it argued that the procedure violated the constitutional guarantees of religious freedom and the "equal protection of the laws." With regard to the equal protection claim, the church claimed that other organizations (e.g., theaters, funeral homes, hotels, community centers) were not required to obtain permits to operate, and thus the permit procedure treated churches differently and less favorably without any apparent basis. The federal trial court dismissed the church's religious claim, but it did agree that the city's permit procedure violated the church's constitutional right to the "equal protection of the laws," and it awarded the church nearly $18,000 in damages under title 42, section 1983 of the United States Code. Significantly, the court granted the church a "summary judgment," meaning that it found the church's position so clearly correct that it refused to submit the case to a jury. The city promptly appealed this decision to a federal appeals court, which dismissed the case on the technical ground that the church lacked "standing" to challenge the city's permit procedure since the city had never enforced the special permit requirement and accordingly there was no threat of legal consequences if the church disregarded it.

This case is significant (despite the appeals court's interpretation of the standing requirement) since it represents another example of a court (in this case, the federal district court) awarding a church monetary damages under "section 1983" for a violation of a church's constitutional rights. The importance of such rulings cannot be overstated—for they represent a recognition of an extremely potent weapon that is available to churches. To be sure, the federal appeals court dismissed the case, but it did so for technical reasons that in no way diminish the significance of the trial court's decision. Further, the appeals court seemed to concede that it would have affirmed the district court's award of monetary damages had the city ever enforced its permit procedure, or had the church presented more evidence of the unwillingness of landlords to rent to the church. In many cases, these factors will be present, and presumably churches in such cases will be entitled to monetary damages.

Example. *The Washington state supreme court ruled that a religious organization is entitled to monetary damages if a city violates its constitutional rights. A religious organization applied for a conditional use permit to construct a building on its property. A city official denied this application, and the organization promptly filed a second application. This application also was denied, and this denial was affirmed by the city council. The organization appealed to a local trial court, which declared the city's actions to be in error. The organization then filed a third application for a conditional use permit, and this application was denied by the same city official. When the city council upheld the denial of this application, the organization filed another lawsuit. This time, the organization demanded monetary damages on the ground that the city's actions had violated its constitutional rights. Specifically, the organization alleged that the city's actions violated its constitutional right to due process of law. The court ruled that the organization's constitutional rights had been violated by the city' actions, and that the organization was entitled to monetary damages. It observed: "Along with the vast majority of federal courts, we recognize that denial of a building permit, under certain circumstances, may give rise to a substantive due process claim. . . . Such a violation is made out, however, only if the decision to deny the permit is 'invidious or irrational' or 'arbitrary or capricious.'" The court concluded that the city's actions in denying the building* *permit satisfied this standard. In particular, it pointed to the fact that the city's decisions were "without consideration and in disregard of the relevant facts and circumstances."[134]*

§ 7-07 Restricting Certain Activities Near Church Property

> ***Key point 7-07.** Many cities have enacted ordinances banning "adult" bookstores and entertainment facilities, and the sale of alcoholic beverages, within a specified distance of a church. These ordinances have been upheld by the courts so long as such businesses are left with a reasonable opportunity to operate in other locations within the city.*

Several courts have upheld municipal zoning ordinances prohibiting the location of "adult theaters" within a prescribed distance of a church, despite the claim that such ordinances constitute an impermissible establishment of religion.[135] To illustrate, the United States Supreme Court ruled in 1986 that cities are free to ban adult bookstores or theaters within 1,000 feet of churches, schools, or residences, provided that such restrictions do not deny such businesses "a reasonable opportunity to open and operate an adult theater [or bookstore] within the city."[136] However, the United States Supreme Court struck down an ordinance giving churches the authority to "veto" applications for liquor licenses by facilities located within a 500-foot radius of a church.[137] The Court concluded that the ordinance substituted the unilateral and absolute power of a church for the decisions of a public legislative body, and thereby "enmeshed" churches in the process of government.

§ 7-08 Building Codes

> ***Key point 7-08.** Most cities have enacted building codes that prescribe minimum standards in the construction of buildings. The courts have ruled that these laws may be applied to churches so long as they are reasonably related to the promotion of public health and safety.*

Many municipalities have enacted building codes prescribing minimum standards in the construction of buildings. Such codes typically regulate building materials, construction methods, building design, fire safety, and sanitation. The validity of such codes has consistently been upheld by the courts.[138]

The courts consistently hold that churches must comply with municipal building codes that are reasonably related to the legitimate governmental purpose of promoting the public health, safety, morals, or general welfare. To illustrate, one court ruled that "the building of churches is subject to such reasonable regulations as may be necessary to promote the public health, safety, or general welfare."[139] In another case, a municipality brought an action against a church in order to prevent the continued use of a church school that did not comply with the building code.[140] The church school was allegedly deficient in several respects, including inadequate floor space, inadequate ventila-

---

[134] Lutheran Day Care v. Snohomish County, 829 P.2d 746 (Wash. 1992).

[135] *See, e.g.,* City of Stanton v. Cox, 255 Cal. Rptr. 682 (4th Dist. 1989); Amico v. New Castle County, 101 F.R.D. 472 (D.C. Del. 1984); City of Whittier v. Walnut Properties, Inc., 197 Cal. Rptr. 127 (1983).

[136] Renton v. Playtime Theaters, Inc., 475 U.S. 41 (1986).

[137] Larkin v. Grendel's Den, Inc., 459 U.S. 116 (1982).

[138] *See* YOKLEY, *supra* note 100, at § 31-2.

[139] Board of Zoning v. Decatur, Ind. Co. of Jehovah's Witnesses, 117 N.E.2d 115, 118 (Ind. 1954). *Accord* City of Solon v. Solon Baptist Temple, Inc., 457 N.E.2d 858 (Ohio App. 1982); City of Sherman v. Simms, 183 S.W.2d 415 (Tex. 1944); Wojtanowski v. Franciscan Fathers Minor Conventuals, 148 N.W.2d 54 (Wis. 1967); Hintz v. Zion Evangelical United Brethren Church, 109 N.W.2d 61 (Wis. 1961).

[140] City of Sumner v. First Baptist Church, 639 P.2d 1358 (Wash. 1982).

tion, no approved fire alarm system, no fire extinguishers, no fire detectors, no sprinkler system, no fire-retardant walls, no exit signs, uneven stairs, and doors that did not open outward. The Supreme Court of Washington acknowledged that application of the building code to the church school would result in a closing of the school, and that this in turn would impair the church members' constitutional right to guide the education of their children by sending them to a church-operated school. However, the court observed that this constitutional right was not absolute, but could be limited by a showing that the building code was supported by a "compelling state interest" and that it was the least restrictive means of accomplishing the state's interest.

Similarly, another court upheld the action of a municipality in ordering substantial renovations in a church-operated school to bring it into compliance with the building code.[141] The court rejected the church's claims that the less stringent building code provisions applicable to church buildings should apply to the school, and that application of the more stringent building code provisions applicable to schools would infringe upon the church's right to freely exercise its religion. The court observed:

> This is not a case where application of the Code forces a choice between abandoning one's religious principles and facing criminal charges. . . . The Code does not restrict or make unlawful any religious practice of the plaintiff; the Code simply regulates the condition of the physical facility if it functions as a school . . . .

It is also clear that state laws establishing minimum standards for the safety of children in child-care facilities and enforcing such standards through inspections and licensing does not violate the religious freedom of a children's home administered by a religious organization.[142]

Sign ordinances regulating the height, size, and number of signs have been applied to churches despite the claim that they violate a church's constitutional right to freely exercise its religion.[143]

Example. *An Alabama court rejected a church's argument that a state law prohibiting it from erecting a sign larger than 8 square feet without a special permit violated its constitutional rights. The Alabama Highway Beautification Act prohibits the erection of signs along a "primary highway" that do not meet certain requirements pertaining to size, location, lighting, and spacing. Among other things, a church sign cannot exceed 8 square feet unless a special permit is issued. A church erected a sign on the property of a private business that was located on a state highway. The sign gave the name of the church, an arrow indicating where motorists should turn to find the church, and three crosses. The state department of transportation ordered the church to remove the sign on the ground that it exceeded 8 square feet. The church protested, claiming that removal of the sign would violate its constitutional right of religious freedom. A state appeals court rejected the church's argument, and upheld the removal of the sign. The court noted that the Highway Beautification Act "makes no reference to the content of the sign. It merely regulates the manner in which churches may display signs . . . by limiting their signs to no more than 8 square feet in area. The [Act] does not attempt to regulate the views of the various churches. It simply regulates the size of the signs."[144]*

---

[141] Faith Assembly of God v. State Building Code Commission, 416 N.E.2d 228 (Mass. 1981).

[142] Roloff Evangelistic Enterprises, Inc. v. State, 556 S.W.2d 856 (Tex. 1977), *appeal denied*, 439 U.S. 803 (1978). *See also* Corpus Christi Peoples' Baptist Church, Inc. v. Texas Department of Human Resources, 481 F. Supp. 1101 (S.D. Tex. 1979), *aff'd*, 621 F.2d 638 (5th Cir. 1980); State Fire Marshall v. Lee, 300 N.W.2d 748 (Mich. 1980); State v. Fayetteville Street Christian School, 258 S.E.2d 459 (N.C. 1979), *vacated*, 261 S.E.2d 908 (N.C. 1980), *appeal dismissed*, 449 U.S. 808 (1980).

[143] Temple Baptist Church v. City of Albuquerque, 646 P.2d 565 (N.M. 1982).

[144] Corinth Baptist Church v. State Department of Transportation, 656 So.2d 868 (Ala. App. 1995). *Accord* Wilson v. City of Louisville, 957 F. Supp. 948 (W.D. Ky. 1997).

§ 7-09   Nuisance

Key point 7-09. A nuisance is any use of property that results in significant annoyance or discomfort to neighboring landowners. Some church activities may constitute a nuisance. The courts will weigh the annoyance and discomfort to neighboring landowners with the church's constitutional right to exercise its religion. In some cases the courts may order a church to limit the activity causing the nuisance, or eliminate it entirely.

In general, the term *nuisance* refers to an activity or use of property that results in material annoyance, inconvenience, discomfort, or harm to others. It is, for example, a nuisance to use one's property in such a way as to cause excessive noise, odor, smoke, vibration, debris, drainage, obstruction, or injury to neighboring landowners. It ordinarily is not a defense that the condition constituting a nuisance existed before the arrival of neighboring residents.

An activity or condition permitted on church property can constitute a nuisance. One court has held:

A church building is as lawful as any other structure. It is not only lawful, but essential to our Christian civilization . . . . It is not, however, above the law. Like any other edifice or structure, however lawful in purpose and use ordinarily, it may become unlawful. The place of its location, and the time and manner of its use, may be such, under the circumstances, as to constitute that interference with the rights of others as to become in law a nuisance . . . .[145]

To illustrate, a church that conducted lengthy revival services punctuated by shouting and singing that could be heard more than a mile away was found guilty of permitting a nuisance.[146]

Another court refused to prevent the construction of a church in a residential district despite the allegations of neighboring landowners that the church consisted of "holy rollers" who would conduct boisterous services until the late hours of the evening, making neighboring homes unfit for habitation.[147] The court reasoned that the existence of a church building close to the homes of neighboring landowners, as well as the noise that might result from an "orderly and properly conducted Christian service therein," were not matters that would constitute a nuisance. The court did acknowledge that it was possible for a church to conduct services with sufficient noise to constitute a nuisance. Nevertheless, the court concluded that it could not prevent the construction of a church in a residential neighborhood based on the mere conjecture of neighboring landowners that the church ultimately would constitute a nuisance.

Another court, in a similar case, concluded that "[s]omething more than the threatened commission of an offense against the law of the land is necessary to call into exercise the injunctive powers of the court."[148] The court also held that a church building itself is not a nuisance, and therefore its construction cannot be enjoined on the ground that it will be the source of unreasonably loud worship services. The proper remedy for unreasonably loud services, concluded the court, would be to halt or abate the excessive noise, and not to prevent the construction of the church.

---

[145] Waggoner v. Floral Heights Baptist Church, 288 S.W. 129, 131 (Tex. 1926).
[146] Assembly of God Church v. Bradley, 196 S.W.2d 696 (Tex. 1946).
[147] Dorsett v. Nunis, 13 S.E.2d 371 (Ga. 1941).
[148] Murphy v. Cupp, 31 S.W.2d 396, 399 (Ark. 1930).

The playing of church bells three times a day and four times on Sundays at regular hours for a period of approximately four minutes has been held not to constitute a nuisance despite the contention of neighboring landowners that the volume of the bells adversely affected their health and serenity. The court held that a material interference with physical comfort must occur before a nuisance can exist, and that the ringing of church bells simply did not constitute a material interference:

> Bells in one form or another are a tradition throughout the world. . . . In the Christian world, every church is proud of its bells. The bells are rung for joy, for sadness, for warnings and for worship. There are people who find total beauty in the . . . daily ritual ringing at the Cathedral of Notre Dame in Paris. There is little question that the sound is often deadening when these bells start to ring, but for the general enjoyment of the public, it is considered acceptable.[149]

One court concluded that the use of church property for school purposes does not amount to a nuisance.[150]

Example. *A federal court in New York ruled that a city did not violate the rights of neighbors by refusing to enforce a noise ordinance against a church that broadcast amplified music from its steeple.[151] For two weeks in 1994 a Congregational church broadcast amplified sounds and music for lengthy periods of time from speakers located in its steeple. Certain neighbors found the volume and duration of these sounds so distressful that they called the state police to advise them of the noises. The state trooper who responded to the call allegedly told the neighbors that the noises were loud enough to constitute a violation of state law. The neighbors also insisted that the church's actions violated a village ordinance relating to "peace and good order," which prohibits persons or organizations from ringing a bell or making other improper noises that disturb the peace, comfort, or health of the community. The city council and district attorney's office both refused to act on the neighbors' complaints. A court eventually directed the church to limit the amount of sounds and music which were being amplified from its steeple. The neighbors later sued the city, claiming that its refusal to enforce the law demonstrated an improper preference for the church that deprived the neighbors of their civil rights, including their constitutional right to equal protection of the law. They further maintain that the city's actions violated the first amendment's nonestablishment of religion clause. A state appeals court rejected the neighbors' claims. First, it ruled that the city had not violated the neighbors' constitutional right to the equal protection of the laws. It pointed out that an equal protection claim requires a showing of intentional discrimination, and this requires proof that "similarly situated persons" have been treated differently. The neighbors failed to present such evidence. Further, the court ruled that the city's failure to enforce state and local law did not violate the first amendment. In particular, it noted that the neighbors failed to explain how a failure to enforce a noise ordinance amounts to state action endorsing religion. It also pointed out that a local court did impose restrictions to reduce the amount of noise coming from the church. The court concluded: "Plaintiffs have alleged that the loudness and duration of the church music was distressful to them, and the town does not deny this accusation. Indeed, although some might consider the church's actions unneighborly or lacking in Christian forbearance, unneighborly behavior is not necessarily unconstitutional behavior. Given the facts and circumstances as plaintiffs have alleged them, there can be no argument that defendants' actions violated plaintiffs' constitutional rights."*

---

[149] Impellizerri v. Jamesville Federated Church, 428 N.Y.S.2d 550 (1979).
[150] Mooney v. Village of Orchard Lake, 53 N.W.2d 308 (Mich. 1952).
[151] Diehl v. Village of Antwerp, 964 F. Supp. 646 (N.D.N.Y. 1997).

§ 7-10   Landmarking

Key point 7-10. Several cities have enacted ordinances permitting certain buildings to be designated as "landmarks" because of their historical or cultural significance. Buildings designated as land-marks generally may not be demolished or renovated without government approval. The Supreme Court has ruled that such laws do no violate a church's first amendment right to the free exercise of religion.

A number of municipalities have enacted ordinances designed to protect and preserve buildings having historic or cultural significance. Such ordinances often are referred to as "landmark" laws. Occasionally, mu-nicipalities attempt to block the sale or demolition of church property on the basis of landmark ordinances. Of course, churches respond by claiming that use of a landmark law in such a context violates the first amendment's guaranty of religious freedom. To illustrate, a federal appeals court ruled that a New York City "landmark" law that prevented a church from developing its property did not violate any of the church's constitutional rights.[152] St. Bartholomew's Church is a Protestant Episcopal Church located in New York City. The church sanctuary was constructed in 1919. Next to the sanctuary is a 7-story community house built by the church in 1928. The community house provides a variety of services, including athletic facilities, a theater, a preschool, meeting rooms, office space, and sleeping quarters for the homeless. In 1967, the church and community house were designated as "landmarks" by the city, meaning that they could not be demolished without city approval. The city may grant approval if it finds that a failure to do so would "seriously interfere" with a charity's ability to carry out its purposes.

In 1983, the church sought permission to tear down the community house and erect in its place a 59-story office tower. This application was denied by the city as inappropriate. In 1984, the church sought permission to tear down the community center and build a 47-story office tower. This application was also denied. The church claimed that the denial of its request to demolish its community center and construct an office building violated its constitutional rights. In particular, it claimed that as a result of the city's actions it could no longer carry out its religious mission and charitable purpose because the existing facility was no longer adequate and the church could not afford the sums necessary to remodel the present building to make it adequate. The court rejected the church's claim that the city's actions violated the first amendment's guaranty of religious freedom, or the fifth amendment prohibition of a "taking" of the church's property without "just compensation." The court acknowl-edged that applying the landmarks law to the church "has drastically restricted the church's abilities to raise revenues to carry out its various charitable and ministerial programs." However, this burden did not constitute a violation of the first amendment's guaranty of religious freedom. The court emphasized that decisions of the United States Supreme Court have clarified that "neutral regulations that diminish the income of a religious organization do not implicate the free exercise clause." The first amendment is violated only if "the claimant has been denied the ability to practice his religion or coerced in the nature of those practices."

The court also rejected the church's claim that the landmark law so severely restricted its ability to use its property that it constituted a confiscation of property without just compensation in violation of the fifth amendment to the United States Constitution. The fifth amendment specifies "nor shall private property be taken for public use without just compensation." The court observed:

[T]he constitutional question is whether the land-use regulation impairs the continued operation of the property in its originally expected use. We conclude that the landmarks law does not effect

---

[152] Rector, Wardens, and Members of the Vestry of St. Bartholomew's Church v. City of New York, 914 F.2d 348 (2nd Cir. 1990).

an unconstitutional taking because the church can continue its existing charitable and religious activities in its current facilities. Although the regulation may freeze the church's property in its existing use and prevent the church from expanding or altering its activities, [Supreme Court rulings] explicitly permit this. . . . [T]he deprivation of commercial value is palpable, but . . . it does not constitute a taking so long as continued use for present activities is viable.[153]

A number of other courts have addressed the application of landmarking laws to religious congregations. Selected cases are illustrated by the following examples.

Example. A federal court in Maryland ruled that a church's first amendment right to the free exercise of religion was violated by a city landmarks ordinance that barred the church from demolishing an old chapel to construct a new facility. The court concluded that the church's decision to demolish the chapel "involves the exercise of the Roman Catholic faith and implicates first amendment free exercise principles." The court conceded, however, that according to the Supreme Court's 1990 decision in the Smith case the church's first amendment rights would not be violated by a "neutral law of general applicability." But the court concluded that the landmarks law was not such a law. It emphasized the fact that the landmarks ordinance "had a series of exemptions" demonstrating a "legislative judgment that the city's interest in historic preservation should, under certain circumstances, give way to other interests." The court then referred to the Supreme Court's conclusion in the Smith case that "where the government enacts a system of exemptions, and thereby acknowledges that its interest in enforcement is not paramount, then the government may not refuse to extend that system [of exemptions] to cases of religious hardship without compelling reason." The court concluded that the city failed to demonstrate such an interest, and therefore its refusal to permit the church to demolish its chapel amounted to a violation of the first amendment.[154]

Example. The Massachusetts Supreme Judicial Court ruled that the City of Boston could not declare a church's interior as a "landmark." Faced with an aging, oversized building, the leaders of a Catholic church adopted a plan to renovate the facility into office, counseling, and residential space. When work began, ten citizens asked the city to designate the interior of the church as a landmark. The city approved the citizens' request, and prohibited permanent alteration of "the nave, chancel, vestibule and organ loft on the main floor—the volume, window glazing, architectural detail, finishes, painting, the organ, and organ case." Church leaders filed a lawsuit, claiming that their constitutional right to freely exercise their religion was violated by the city' action. The court agreed, citing the state constitution's guaranty of religious freedom. In rejecting the city's claim that it was merely addressing a "secular question of interior design," the court observed that "the configuration of the church interior is so freighted with religious meaning that it must be considered part and parcel of [Catholic] religious worship." The court concluded that the state constitution "protects the right freely to design interior space for religious worship, thus barring the government from regulating changes in such places, provided that no public safety question is presented."[155]

Example. The Washington Supreme Court ruled that a municipal landmarking law violated a church's constitutional right to religious freedom. The city of Seattle adopted an ordinance giving the city authority to declare any building to be a landmark. The ordinance was designed to preserve and protect those sites reflecting significant elements of the city's cultural or historic heritage. Buildings designated

---

[153] *Id.* at 356-357.
[154] Keeler v. Mayor and City Council, 940 F. Supp. 879 (D. Md. 1996).
[155] Society of Jesus v. Boston Landmarks Commission, 564 N.E.2d 571 (Mass. 1991).

as a landmark by the city could not be structurally altered without city approval. The city designated a church to be a landmark, and the church sued the city arguing that the landmarks ordinance violated the church's constitutional right to freely exercise its religion. Specifically, the church claimed that its designation as a landmark impaired its religious freedom in the following ways: (1) city approval and bureaucratic "red tape" would be required prior to making any structural alterations in the sanctuary; (2) a secular government had the authority to grant or deny a church's request to develop its worship facility; (3) the value of the church property was decreased significantly by the landmark designation; and (4) the ability of the church to sell its property was diminished. The court agreed with the church's

---

THE CITY OF BOERNE CASE

In 1997 the United States Supreme Court upheld the validity of the landmark law of Boerne, Texas, though the law prohibited an historic church from expanding to accommodate its growing membership. The church claimed that the law violated its rights under the Religious Freedom Restoration Act. The Court concluded that this Act was an unconstitutional attempt by Congress to amend the Constitution by changing the meaning of the guaranty of religious freedom.[157]

The Supreme Court ruled in 1990 that "neutral laws of general applicability" are presumably valid even though they burden the free exercise of religion.[158] The government need not demonstrate that such laws further a "compelling interest." In most cases, a landmarking law will be a neutral law of general applicability, and as a result is presumably valid without the need to prove a compelling government interest. This makes such laws very difficult to challenge.

However, the Supreme Court observed in its 1990 ruling that the compelling government interest test is triggered if a neutral and generally applicable law burdens not only the exercise of religion, but also some other first amendment right (such as speech, press, or assembly). The compelling government interest requirement makes it much more difficult for a city to defend a landmarking law that infringes upon the exercise of religion. The Court observed: "The only decisions in which we have held that the first amendment bars application of a neutral, generally applicable law to religiously motivated action have involved not the free exercise clause alone, but the free exercise clause in conjunction with other constitutional protections, such as freedom of speech and of the press . . . ." In other words, if a neutral and generally applicable law burdens the exercise of religion, then the compelling governmental interest standard can be triggered if the religious institution can point to some other first amendment interest that is being violated. In many cases, this will not be hard to do. For example, the first amendment guaranties of "assembly" and free speech often will be burdened by the designation of a church as a landmark. The Washington state supreme court reached this conclusion, finding that the application of a landmark law to a church (against its will) violated the church's constitutional rights of speech and religion and therefore could be sustained only if it furthered a compelling governmental interest. No such interest existed, the court concluded.[159]

---

[156] First Covenant Church v. City of Seattle, 787 P.2d 1352 (Wash. 1990). This ruling was "vacated" by the United States Supreme Court as a result of its ruling in Employment Division v. Smith, 110 S. Ct. 1595 (1990). But the Washington state supreme court, upon reconsideration, again concluded that the city's landmarking law violated the church's constitutional right to religious freedom. 840 P.2d 174 (Wash. 1992). *See also* First United Methodist Church v. Hearing Examiner, 916 P.2d 374 (Wash. 1996), in which the Washington state supreme court concluded that the mere designation of a church as an historic landmark violated the constitutional rights of churches that were opposed to such a designation.

[157] City of Boerne v. Flores, 117 S. Ct. 2157 (1997).

[158] Employment Division v. Smith, 110 S. Ct. 1595 (1990).

[159] First United Methodist Church v. Hearing Examiner, 916 P.2d 374 (Wash. 1996).

position. It concluded that the city's landmark law placed a substantial burden on the church's religious practices, and that no compelling governmental interest justified the burden: "The practical effect of the [ordinance] is to require a religious organization to seek secular approval of matters potentially affecting the church's practice of its religion." This "creates unjustified governmental interference in religious matters of the church and thereby creates an infringement on the church's constitutional right of free exercise." The court concluded: "We hold that the preservation of historical landmarks is not a compelling state interest. Balancing the right of free exercise [of religion] with the aesthetic and community values associated with landmark preservation, we find that the latter is clearly outweighed by the constitutional protection of free exercise of religion and the public benefits associated with the practice of religious worship within the community."[156]

§ 7-11   Eminent Domain

Key point 7-11. Eminent domain refers to the power of the government to take private property for a public purpose without the owner's consent. A property owner whose property is taken by a governmental exercise of eminent domain is entitled to compensation. Church property is not immune from eminent domain.

Eminent domain refers to the power of the government to take private property for a public purpose without the owner's consent. It often is referred to as *condemnation*. A property owner whose property is taken by a governmental exercise of eminent domain is entitled to compensation. Obviously, attempts to take church property by this process have generated controversy. The relatively few courts that have addressed this issue generally have concluded that church property is not immune from a proper exercise of eminent domain.[160] However, they also have concluded that the government's power of eminent domain must be balanced against the interests of the church, and that in some cases the church will prevail. For example, the Colorado Supreme Court rejected an attempt by a municipal urban renewal authority to condemn a church building that served as "the mother church and fountainhead" of a religious sect.[161] The court observed:

> The first amendment protects freedom of religion which has its roots in the hearts and souls of the congregation, not in inanimate bricks and mortar. Yet, religious faith and tradition can invest certain structures and land sites with significance which deserves first amendment protection. We recognize that church property is private property which can be taken by eminent domain for paramount public use, just as religious conduct is subject to appropriate regulations for the public good. When regulating religious conduct, however, the state may be challenged to justify its infringement of the totally free exercise of religion. We hold that under these circumstances, the state may be so challenged to justify a use of its power of eminent domain. The [trial court] must weigh the plans and goals of the [city] as they bear on the particular land in question, against the right of the [church] to maintain a brick structure which the church claims is unique and does not conform to the general plan for development of the block or the area. . . .

---

[160] *See, e.g.,* First English Evangelical Lutheran Church v. Los Angeles County, 482 U.S. 304 (1987); United States v. Two Acres of Land, 144 F.2d 207 (7th Cir. 1944); Redevelopment Agency v. First Christian Church, 189 Cal. Rptr. 749 (Cal. App. 1983); State Highway Department v. Augusta District of North Georgia Conference of the Methodist Church, 154 S.E.2d 29 (Ga. App. 1967); State Highway Department v. Hollywood Baptist Church, 146 S.E.2d 570 (Ga. App. 1965); First Baptist Church v. State Department of Roads, 135 N.W.2d 756 (Nebr. 1965); Gallimore v. State Highway and Public Works Commission, 85 S.E.2d 392 (N.C. 1955); Trustees of Grace and Hope Mission v. Providence Redevelopment Agency, 217 A.2d 476 (R.I. 1966); Assembly of God Church v. Vallone, 150 A.2d 11 (R.I. 1959).

[161] Pillar of Fire v. Denver Urban Renewal Authority, 509 P.2d 1250 (Colo. 1973).

The only conclusion which we can draw is that we must balance the interests involved in the controversy before us and recognize that the state must show a substantial interest without a reasonable alternate means of accomplishment if the state is to be constitutionally allowed to take the birthplace of the [sect].

The same court later rejected an attempt by a city to condemn the parking lot of a church that had been declared a historic landmark.[162] The court emphasized that the trial court had

a duty to weigh and balance the competing interests, public and religious. Only after such a hearing and upon finding that there is a substantial public interest involved which cannot be accomplished through any other reasonable means, can the court proceed with the condemnation of [church] property.

Assuming that the government has the authority, in a particular case, to take church property through the process of eminent domain, the fifth amendment to the United States Constitution requires that the church be given "just compensation" for its property. The United States Supreme Court has noted that "the fifth amendment provides 'nor shall private property be taken for public use, without just compensation,' and applies to the states through the fourteenth amendment."[163] But what is "just compensation"? In many cases, cities and churches come to widely differing interpretations of this critical term. Most courts have rejected "fair market value" as the standard for computing just compensation. *** The United States Supreme Court has observed that just compensation means "the full and perfect equivalent in money of the property taken," and, that "[w]here, for any reason, property has no market, resort must be had to other data to ascertain its value."[164]

In a leading case, a California state appeals court was asked to determine the value of an old but ornately-decorated, 2,000-seat sanctuary that had been condemned by a city government for urban renewal purposes.[165] The city's appraiser valued the church at $1 million, a figure obtained by reducing the replacement cost of the building by a "depreciation" factor of 75 percent. The appraiser used a 75 percent depreciation factor since the only other comparable church in the community had sold for little more than the value of the land on which it stood. The church's appraiser valued the church at $4.6 million, a figure obtained by reducing the replacement cost by a depreciation factor of 40 percent. The court agreed with the trial court's finding that a fair value of the property was $3 million. It observed:

The ultimate goal in any eminent domain proceeding is of course to determine constitutionally required "just compensation." That compensation is to be measured by what the owner lost and not what the condemnor has gained. . . . Generally speaking, the most widely used and perhaps most easily applied concept is that of "fair market value." But even that test, which is described as what a willing buyer would pay to a willing seller under circumstances totally free from external pressures, may not, in every case achieve a correct result . . . . The economic reality of course is that certain types of buildings such as churches are not, as such, regularly bought and sold in the commercial market and to ordinary buyers of real estate have no greater value than the use which can be made of the land free of the building. The constitutional mandate of just compensation, of course, would not be met if public agencies could thus exercise the power of eminent domain by simply paying for the value of the raw land when it is occupied by some special type of building. . . . Recognized alternatives to the market data approach to valuation are reproduction or replacement costs less

---

[162] Order of Friars Minor v. Denver Urban Renewal Authority, 527 P.2d 804 (Colo. 1974).

[163] First English Evangelical Lutheran Church v. Los Angeles County, 482 U.S. 304, 310 n.4 (1987).

[164] United States v. Miller, 317 U.S. 369, 373-374 (1943).

depreciation or obsolescence. These methods, in reality, provide a more just and equitable approach in evaluating special use buildings such as churches.[166]

Similarly, another court has observed that

Where there is proof that there is no market value of property with a specialized use, such as a church . . . the general rule is that resort may be had to some other method of fixing the value of property. . . . Depending on the nature of the property, the authorities have supported different methods of determining value in these situations. Expert testimony as to reproduction of replacement cost, less depreciation, has been approved in many cases as competent foundation evidence to support an opinion as to valuation.[167]

A federal appeals court has noted that

In the case of nonprofit, religious or service properties, cost of replacement is regarded as cogent evidence of value although not in itself the only standard of compensation. But people do not go about buying and selling country churches. Such buildings have no established market values. Consideration must be given to the elements actually involved and resort had to any evidence available, to prove value, such as the use made of the property and the right to enjoy it.[168]

Occasionally, a church's property is "taken" by a city or governmental agency through a process known as "inverse condemnation." This refers to some regulatory action, short of a formal condemnation proceeding, that has the effect of making a church's property of little or no value. The United States Supreme Court addressed this issue in an important ruling.[169] In 1957, a Lutheran church in California purchased a 21-acre parcel of land in a canyon along the Mill Creek. The church constructed several buildings on the property, including a dining hall, two bunkhouses, a lodge, and a chapel, and used the improved property as a campgrounds known a "Lutherglen." In 1977, a fire destroyed the forest upstream of the campgrounds, creating a serious flood hazard. A severe storm in 1978 flooded Lutherglen and destroyed its buildings. In response to the dangerous conditions in the area, the County of Los Angeles adopted a temporary ordinance prohibiting anyone from building any structure within a flood zone that included Lutherglen. The church thereafter sued the state of California, arguing that the state's prohibition of any further use of the campgrounds violated the fifth amendment to the United States Constitution, which specifies that "private property [shall not] be taken for public use, without just compensation." The fifth amendment, argued the church, does not require that the government seize private property by condemnation. It can also be violated by governmental regulations that effectively deny a landowner the use of his land, even on a temporary basis. The California state courts rejected the church's contention, but the United States Supreme Court agreed that the county's ban on further development of the campgrounds amounted to a "regulatory taking" of the church's property without compensation in violation of the fifth amendment.

---

[165] Redevelopment Agency v. First Christian Church, 189 Cal. Rptr. 749 (Cal. App. 1983).

[166] *Id.* at 753-754. The court added:

We hasten to point out, however, that in our view depreciation and obsolescence should not be used as a "back door" method of nullifying the reproduction and replacement approach to valuation. For example, a large ornate church, as here, because it was used by only a small congregation [average weekly attendance was 200] might be viewed by some as obsolete and having no value beyond that of the land itself. The church, however, does have value to the congregation and the congregation is entitled to compensation therefor. A property owner should not be penalized by application of a concept of locational or functional obsolescence simply because it happens to be in the wrong place at the wrong time when a condemning agency decides to make its move. *Id.* at 754.

[167] State Highway Department v. Hollywood Baptist Church, 146 S.E.2d 570, 759-760 (Ga. App. 1965).

[168] United States v. Two Acres of Land, 144 F.2d 207, 209 (7th Cir. 1944).

EMINENT DOMAIN PROCEEDS AND THE UNRELATED BUSINESS INCOME TAX

Many churches have had their property converted to a public use through eminent domain (sometimes called "condemnation"). For example, a state government acquires property (including church properties) for a new highway. Of course, property holders must be paid a fair amount for their property. Does a charity have to pay the unrelated business income tax on such proceeds? No, said the IRS in a private letter ruling, so long as the charity did not acquire and hold the land for resale.[170]

---

§ 7-12   Defacing Church Property

Key point 7-12. *Federal law makes it a crime to intentionally deface, damage, or destroy religious property because of the religious character of that property. Many states have enacted similar laws.*

Federal law makes it a crime to intentionally deface, damage, or destroy any religious property because of the religious character of that property.[171] The same law makes it a crime to intentionally deface, damage, or destroy any religious property "because of the race, color, or ethnic characteristics of any individual associated with that religious property."[172] Religious property is defined to include "any church, synagogue, mosque, religious cemetery, or other religious real property, including fixtures or religious objects contained within a place of religious worship."

Several states have enacted similar laws, and the courts have upheld their validity against the claim that they favor religious property.

Example. *A Florida court upheld a state law imposing harsher penalties upon persons who damage church property than other kinds of property. A defendant was convicted of defacing church properties by spray-painting them with anti-religious symbols and words. His sentence was harsher because state law imposed increased penalties upon those who deface religious property. The defendant appealed his conviction, arguing that the state law unconstitutionally favored religion. A state court rejected this argument and upheld the validity of the law. It concluded that the purpose of the law was not to advance religion but to deter incidents of vandalism occurring in places of worship and cemeteries. Further, the law's primary effect neither advanced nor inhibited religion. Any "benefit" to religion under the law was indirect and insignificant. Finally, the law did not result in an excessive entanglement between church and state since it did not involve "comprehensive, discriminating and continuing state surveillance" or "administration of religious activities." The court also rejected the defendant's claim that the law violated the constitutional guaranty of "equal protection of the laws" by treating vandalism to church property differently from damage to other kinds of property. The court observed that states may treat criminals differently so long as the classifications are reasonable. The court concluded that this test was met, since the state clearly had a legitimate interest in deterring crime, especially when crimes involving defacement of religious properties and cemeteries was on the rise.*[173]

---

[169] First English Evangelical Lutheran Church v. Los Angeles County, 107 S. Ct. 2378 (1987).

[170] IRS Letter Ruling 9629032.

[171] 18 U.S.C. § 247. The offense must affect interstate commerce.

[172] *Id.*

[173] Todd v. State, 643 So.2d 625 (Fla. App. 1 Dist. 1994).

§ 7-13   Restrictive Covenants

Key point 7-13. A restrictive covenant is a restriction on the use of property. Such restrictions often are noted in deeds to property, but they may appear in other documents as well. Such restrictions apply to a church's use of its property.

A restrictive covenant is a restriction on the use of property. Often, such covenants appear in deeds. Property owners, including churches, are legally bound by such restrictions. As a result, it is important for church leaders to review the deed to their property to be sure they are familiar with any such restrictions. However, as the following examples illustrate, such restrictions are not always legally enforce*able.*

Example. A Connecticut court ruled that a church could construct a parsonage in a subdivision despite a "restrictive covenant" prohibiting any use other than a "strictly private residence."[174] A group of homeowners asked a court to issue an order barring a church from constructing a parsonage in their subdivision. The homeowners asserted that their deeds, and the other deeds to lots in their subdivision, contained a restrictive covenant stating that the lots could not be used for "any business purpose whatsoever, or for any other purpose, other than a strictly private residence." They further insisted that the construction of a parsonage breached the restrictive covenant because church business would be conducted in the residence, violating the requirement that any residence be "strictly private." The homeowners also noted that a parsonage is exempt from property tax under state law if occupied by a minister. They reasoned that the property was exempt from property tax since it is used for "religious purposes," and this demonstrated that the planned use would not be "residential" and therefore the restriction would be violated. A state appeals court ruled that the parsonage might violate the restrictive covenant, and it sent the case back to the trial court for further proceedings. It noted that the church failed to offer any evidence to support its claim that the parsonage would be used solely for residential purposes. On the other hand, the homeowners did produce evidence to support their claim that the parsonage would not be used solely for residential purposes. One document, created by the church and entitled "A Fact Sheet for the Future," discussed the church's need to provide a residence for the pastor. However, this document indicated that the church may use the residence for "smaller church functions." Another document cited by the homeowners was a pamphlet prepared by the church stating that the parsonage "will accommodate various social events to which the [pastor] or spouse invite parishioners, i.e. gatherings in the living room, seated and buffet dinners, teas, parties and cook outs."

Example. A Missouri court ruled that a church was free to remove homes on adjacent property that it owned in order to expand its parking lot, despite a restrictive covenant limiting use of the property to residential purposes. A church purchased two homes adjacent to its property in order to expand its parking lot. Title to the properties was conveyed to the church subject to any "restrictions." Neighboring landowners protested the church's plan, and claimed that the church was barred from demolishing the homes and extending its parking lot by a "restrictive covenant" limiting use of the properties to residential purposes. A state appeals court ruled that the church could remove the homes and extend its parking lot without violating the restrictive covenant. It noted that "restrictive covenants are not favorites of the law, and any doubt is resolved in favor of the free use of land." It concluded that the purpose of the restrictive covenant in this case was to maintain the residential character of the neighborhood, and that the expansion of a church parking lot was consistent with this purpose since churches and their "accessory uses" (including parking lots) were permitted uses in residential areas.[175]

---

[174] Asjes v. Parish of Christ Church, 1997 WL 139450 (Conn. App. 1997).
[175] Fitzwilliam v. Wesley United Methodist Church, 882 S.W.2d 343 (Mo. App. W.D. 1994).

Example. A Texas court ruled that a church was justified in abandoning a rented building upon learning that a restriction in the owner's deed prohibited him from renting the property to a church. A development company developed a tract of property and imposed various deed restrictions on sites that it sold. Those restrictions specified that the property was for the operation and maintenance of any lawful, commercial retail business or offices. Religious facilities were not approved for the location. An individual purchased a site and constructed a building which he later rented to a church, despite his knowledge of the restrictions in his deed. After signing the lease agreement on behalf of his church, the pastor testified that the owner said to him, "by the way, now, I don't know whether there was any truth to this matter, but I heard about the possibility that [the developer] may not allow a church here." A few months later, having learned that the church was operating on the premises, the developer informed the owner that he was in violation of the deed restriction because a church was on the premises. The owner sent a copy of this letter to the church. The church responded by sending the owner a letter informing him that it was vacating the premises and enclosing a check with the notation "final payment, terminating our lease agreement," written on it. The owner later sued the church for breaching the rental contract. A court ruled in favor of the church, concluding that it justifiably abandoned the property after receiving the letter from the developer informing the owner that the church's lease violated the deed restrictions.[176]

§ 7-14   Reversion of Church Property to the Prior Owner

Key point 7-14. Some deeds to church property contain a "reversion" clause stating that title will revert back to the previous owner in the event that a specified condition occurs. The courts will enforce such provisions, so long as they can do so without interpreting church doctrine.

Property owners sometimes sell or give property to a church with a deed specifying that the property will revert to the previous owner if the church violates a specified condition. For example, a deed may convey title to a church "for so long as the property is used for church purposes." Or, a deed may convey title to a church "for so long as the property is used as a Baptist church." Such deeds vest only a "determinable" or "conditional" title in the church, since title will immediately revert back to the previous owner (or such person's heirs or successors) by operation of law upon a violation of the condition. It is essential for church leaders to be aware of any such conditions in the deed to their property. Unfamiliarity can lead to unexpected and harsh consequences.

Example. The Georgia Supreme Court ruled that the property of a church "reverted" to the previous owner when the church moved to another location. In 1947 a landowner transferred property to a local church with a deed that contained a "reverter clause." This clause specified that the church would own the property "only so long as said lot is used for church purposes, it being expressly provided that if said lot of land should ever cease to be used for such church purposes, then the title thereto . . . shall immediately revert to the [previous owner]." The church constructed a building on the property and used it continually as its place of worship. In 1979 the majority of the church's membership voted to move to another location. A minority continued to worship at the original site, with the permission of the majority. Shortly after the majority of members vacated the property, the prior owner filed a lawsuit claiming that the majority's relocation triggered the reverter clause—meaning that neither the majority nor minority of church members had any further right to the property. The supreme court ruled that the reverter clause had been triggered by the majority's relocation, and that the prior owner was entitled to the property. It observed:

---

[176] Ruiz v. Hilley, 1996 WL 580940 (unpublished decision, Tex. App. 1996).

"[T]he language of the reverter clause is clear that the property is to be used for the sole use, benefit and enjoyment of [the church] and the members thereof, the same to be used as a place of divine worship by the congregation of said church, and that title reverts when the property is not used for such church purposes. The use of the property by the minority which formed its own congregation . . . is not a permitted use of the property by [the majority] under the plain language of the reverter clause, even though that use is with the permission of the majority . . . . Accordingly, the property reverted to [the prior owner] in 1979 when it was no longer used by the majority for its church purposes."[177]

Caution. *Many churches received title to their property by means of a deed containing a restriction. It is imperative for church leaders to be aware of such conditions. This can be easily determined by inspecting the deed to the church property. While the language of these conditional deeds varies, it is common to condition a church's ownership of deeded property on continuous use of the property for religious purposes. Such a condition would mean that a church could not sell its property to a buyer who did not plan on using the property for religious purposes. Some of these conditional deeds are even more restrictive, conditioning a church's ownership on continued use of the property as a church of a specified religious denomination. Under such a clause, a church could not sell its property to a buyer other than another church of the same denomination. In some cases a deed conditions a church's ownership on continued use of the property for religious purposes by the congregation that purchased the property. This is even more restrictive, for a church could not sell the property to anyone without triggering a reversion in favor of the previous owner. Obviously, this is a matter that must be taken very seriously. It is possible in some cases to have conditions "released" by the previous owner (if he or she is willing to do so). Often this is done by having the previous owner execute a quitclaim deed. If the previous owner is no longer living (a fairly common circumstance), then the condition can be released only by all of the legal heirs of the deceased owner. This can be a very cumbersome process.*

Example. *An Arkansas court ruled that title to a church's property reverted to a national church when local church trustees attempted to convey the property without permission of the national church as required by a restriction in the deed to the property. In 1973, a couple transferred real estate to the trustees of a Church of God congregation. The deed stated that the trustees could not "sell, convey or encumber" the real estate without the written consent of the national church. In 1993, the trustees conveyed the property by quitclaim deed to a second group of trustees acting on behalf of the local church, and a month later this group of trustees conveyed the property by quitclaim deed to themselves as trustees for an independent church. This conveyance was made for the sole purpose of separating the congregation from the national church. The national church sued the trustees, claiming that their actions amounted to a breach of the restrictions in the church's original deed. A state appeals court declared the two deeds to be void and ruled that the national church owned legal title to the church property. It observed: "[B]y the plain language of the deed, the [trustees] were not authorized to make any conveyances inasmuch as they never obtained the necessary approval to do so."*[178]

§ 7-15   Materialmen's Liens

Key point 7-15. *A company that supplies building materials for a construction project can claim a "materialman's lien" against the property if it is not paid. This means that the company can sell*

---

[177] First Rebecca Baptist Church v. Atlantic Cotton Mills, 440 S.E.2d 159 (Ga. 1994).
[178] Conway v. Church of God of Prophesy, 1996 WL 617274 (unpublished decision, Ark. App. 1996).

the property to enforce its lien and recover the cost of the materials. Churches are not exempt from such liens.

In most states, a company that supplies building materials for a construction project can claim a "materialman's lien" against the property in the event it is not paid. A lien is a security interest in property, much like a mortgage, that gives the supplier the legal right to sell the property to recover the cost of the materials. In many cases, a property owner pays a general contractor for construction materials, but the general contractor fails to pay the supplier. In such a case the owner must pay the supplier in order to avoid the sale of its property to enforce the lien. In other words, the property owner ends up paying twice for the same materials. Of course the owner can sue the general contractor, but in some cases this person cannot be found or is insolvent.

> *Example. A company provided materials for a church construction project. Before delivering the materials, the company wrote the church a letter warning it that if the general contractor failed to pay for the materials, the company could claim a lien against the church's property. When the company failed to receive payment from the general contractor, it sued to enforce its lien. The company sought not only payment in full for the materials it had supplied, but also finance charges and attorney fees. A court ruled that a materialman's lien only allows a supplier to collect the full price of materials that were supplied. The supplier is not entitled to an additional amount, whether for finance charges or attorney fees, unless the contract between the parties specifically provides for it.[179]*

> *Example. A church entered into a contract with a contractor for the purpose of constructing a driveway and parking lot on its property (at a total cost of $12,500, including all labor and materials). The church paid the contractor the full contract price, but the contractor failed to pay the concrete supplier for $6,500 worth of concrete. The concrete supplier sued the church, demanding payment for the concrete. The church in turn sued the contractor (who could not be located). A jury ordered the church to pay the concrete supplier for the concrete, and acknowledged that the church could sue the contractor if he ever was found. An appeals court observed that under North Carolina law the church's full payment of the contract price to the contractor extinguished the concrete supplier's right to a "materialmen's lien" in the church's property, but that the church had failed to raise this defense at either the trial court or on appeal.[180]*

§ 7-16   Religious Discrimination in the Sale or Rental of Church Property

> *Key point 7-16. Federal law prohibits discrimination in the sale or rental of residential property on the basis of race, color, national origin, religion, or sex. However, religious organizations are permitted to discriminate in the sale or rental of residential property in favor of persons of the same religion.*

The Fair Housing Act (Title VIII of the Civil Rights Act of 1968) prohibits discrimination in the sale or rental of residential property on the basis of race, color, national origin, religion, or sex. However, the Act specifically exempts religious organizations from the ban on religious discrimination. The Act provides:

---

[179] Sherman v. Greater Mt. Olive Baptist Church, 678 So.2d 156 (Ala. App. 1996).
[180] Concrete Supply Co. v. Ramseur Baptist Church, 383 S.E.2d 222 (N.C. 1989).

AVOIDING DOUBLE PAYMENT OF CONSTRUCTION MATERIALS

It is important for church leaders to be familiar with the concept of materialmen's liens in order to avoid paying twice for construction materials. There are a various ways to avoid such a predicament. Here are some recommendations:

(1) Only deal with reputable contractors who have been in business in your community for several years and who have an excellent reputation. Many churches use a contractor who is a member of their congregation.

(2) Withhold all payments to a general contractor in any construction project until "lien waivers" (signed by all material suppliers) are presented. The same is true for construction laborers.

(3) Insist upon a construction contract.

(4) Incorporate the lien waiver requirement into the contract.

(5) Be sure that the materialman's lien is restricted to the price of delivered materials, and does not include attorney's fees, finance charges, or other "add ons."

(6) Hold back a portion of the contract price until you are assured that all suppliers and workers have been paid.

(7) Consider asking the contractor to submit bills from suppliers and workers directly to the church, and inform the contractor that the church will pay these bills directly.

(8) Retain a local attorney to draft (or review) the construction contract, and have the attorney review the materialman's lien procedures under your state law. And, if your church is ever sued by a supplier seeking to enforce a materialman's lien, remember that the supplier may not be able to recover attorney's fees or finance charges.

Nothing in this subchapter shall prohibit a religious organization, association, or society, or any nonprofit institution or organization operated, supervised or controlled by or in conjunction with a religious organization, association, or society, from limiting the sale, rental or occupancy of dwellings which it owns or operates for other than a commercial purpose to persons of the same religion, or from giving preference to such persons, unless membership in such religion is restricted on account of race, color, or national origin.[181]

§ 7-17   Removing Disruptive Individuals

Key point 7-17. Churches do not have to tolerate persons who disrupt religious services. Church leaders can ask a court to issue an order barring the disruptive person from the church's premises. If the person violates the order, he or she may be removed from church premises by the police, and may be found to be in contempt of court.

---

[181] 42 U.S.C. § 3607(a).

Does a church have the legal authority to remove disruptive individuals from church services? This issue has been addressed by a number of courts. Generally, the courts have been sympathetic to attempts by churches to deny access to disruptive individuals. To illustrate, a Connecticut court agreed that a church could bar a disruptive individual from entering onto church premises.[182] It noted that "there was ample evidence that the defendant entered church property, on the three occasions charged, as a knowing trespasser. The record reveals that the defendant had been unequivocally informed and understood that his privilege to attend church services had been revoked. . . . The record here is replete with evidence that this defendant knew that he was trespassing upon church property and was unwelcome at services." With regard to the defendant's claim that a church is "public property" and that one cannot be convicted of trespassing for attending services, the court observed that "property does not lose its private character merely because the public is generally invited to use it for designated purposes. . . . The owner or one in lawful possession has the right to determine whom to invite, the scope of the invitation and the circumstances under which the invitation may be revoked." As to the defendant's claim that his constitutional rights were violated by his conviction for attending church services, the court observed that there is "no constitutional right to 'freedom of movement' or 'freedom of worship' on private property where there is no license or privilege to be there."

A Texas appeals court ruled that a trespasser could be ordered off church property.[183] A trespasser entered onto a church's premises just prior to the conclusion of Sunday morning services. He carried a sign and attempted to speak with persons leaving the church services about "taxes" and "civil rights." A security guard asked the trespasser to leave the premises, and when he refused, the police were called in. When the trespasser continued speaking with church members, two security guards physically restrained him and held him in a church building until the police arrived. The trespasser was convicted of criminal trespass and was sentenced to 90 days in jail. The court further ordered the trespasser "not to go onto or within 200 yards of the [church]." He appealed his conviction on the grounds that he had a constitutional right to be on the church's property, and that the requirement that he not go within 200 yards of the church in the future was unreasonable.

A state appeals court rejected both of these arguments. In rejecting the trespasser's claim that his criminal conviction for trespass violated his constitutional right of free speech, the court emphasized that the first amendment guaranty of free speech "is not protected" on private property, and therefore had no application to a church. In concluding that the church's property was private property, the court observed that (1) the trespasser ignored warnings to stay off the property, (2) the church had signs posted on its premises clearly stating that the premises were for church use only, and (3) church policy prohibited picketing or demonstrating on its property. Finally, the court concluded that the trial court's order prohibiting the trespasser from coming within 200 yards of the church property was reasonable: "It significantly contributes to [his] rehabilitation by removing from him the temptation of trespassing on the church's property. The condition also insures that those persons legally using the property will be protected from any unlawful interference."

Example. *A Louisiana court ruled that a church has a legal right to use reasonable force in removing a potentially disruptive individual from its premises. A former pastor attended a business meeting of his former church, even though (1) he was no longer pastor, (2) he was not a member, (3) he had no legal right to be present, and (4) had been notified not to attend. He was asked to leave the church, but refused to do so. In response, a few members took him by each arm and physically removed him from the church. The former pastor later sued the members who removed him claiming that they had committed battery. A state appeals court disagreed. The court defined a battery as "harmful or offensive contact to*

---

[182] State v. Steinmann, 569 A.2d 557 (Conn. App. 1990).
[183] Gibbons v. State, 775 S.W.2d 790 (Tex. App. 1989).

another without that person's consent, done with an intent" to cause the contact. The court concluded that the church members did not intend any offensive or harmful contact with the former pastor when they removed him from the building. It added: "They had a legal right to see that [he] left the church meeting so its business would not be impeded and disrupted by his presence. Their contact with him was a reasonable means of accomplishing that intention. When, with no intent to cause offensive or harmful contact, reasonable force is used by persons in authority against one who has provoked an incident, the resulting contact is not a battery."[184]

Example. *A Minnesota court upheld the legal validity of a restraining order prohibiting a disruptive individual from entering onto a church's premises. A person (the "defendant") disrupted services at a Catholic church. The church's board of directors adopted a resolution authorizing the pastor to send a letter to the defendant banning him from church property, and to enforce the ban through appropriate legal action. This letter was hand-delivered to the defendant. Later, on three separate occasions, the defendant attended services at the church despite being banned from the premises. The church board asked a court to issue a "harassment restraining order." Following a hearing, a court issued a restraining order that provided, "[The defendant] shall not enter upon the premises of the [church] and/or any other church property." The defendant challenged the legality of this order on appeal. A state appeals court ruled that the order was valid and enforceable. The court noted that the first amendment prohibits civil courts from deciding ecclesiastical or doctrinal disputes, but that "civil courts can hear non-doctrinal disputes that can be determined utilizing neutral principles of law." The court concluded that the church board's resolution banning the defendant from the property was a "secular" document that provided the court "with a familiar and neutral basis to decide the harassment action before it." The court also rejected the defendant's claim that the restraining order was too broad.[185]*

Example. *A New York court upheld the convictions of religious protestors who disrupted a church service. As a Catholic church was preparing to conduct a mass in honor of gay pride, a group of protestors began disrupting the service. One protestor grabbed a microphone and shouted at a priest, "You shouldn't be here. You are not fit to be a priest. You should be ashamed of yourself. You're not worthy to sell shoes." Other protestors engaged in similar behavior. The protestors were charged with violating a state law that provides: "A person is guilty of aggravated disorderly conduct, who makes unreasonable noise or disturbance while at a lawfully assembled religious service or within one hundred feet thereof, with intent to cause annoyance or alarm or recklessly creating a risk thereof." The protestors claimed that a mass is "a sacrifice of God to God on behalf of mankind," and that a mass in honor of gay pride "would be in the name of sin and evil, therefore making the mass a sacrilege." They argued that "all Catholics are under an obligation to prevent such a sacrilege from occurring within a church." A court ruled that the protestors could be charged with violating the state law prohibiting disturbance of religious services, and that the law was not unconstitutional. The court concluded that the state may lawfully "protect the rights of those individuals who choose to exercise their fundamental right of freedom of religion." It further observed that "the constitutional guarantees of the free exercise of religious opinion and of the people peaceably to assemble and petition for a redress of grievances, would be worth little if outsiders could disrupt and prevent such a meeting in disregard of the customs and rules applicable to it."[186]*

---

[184] Robinson v. Dunn, 683 So.2d 894 (La. App. 1996).
[185] Naumann v. Zimmer, 1997 WL 10520 (unpublished decision, Minn. App. 1997).
[186] People v. Morrisey. 614 N.Y.S.2d 686 (N.Y. City Crim. Ct. 1994).

§ 7-18   Adverse Possession

Key point 7-18. Churches can lose a portion of their property to a neighboring landowner as a result of "adverse possession," if the neighbor openly and adversely occupies church property for the length of time prescribed by state law.

Churches can lose a portion of their property to a neighboring landowner as a result of "adverse possession," if the neighbor openly and adversely occupies church property for the length of time prescribed by state law.

Example. A neighboring landowner claimed title to 2 portions of a church's property as a result of adverse possession. The first portion of land claimed by the neighbor was land up to a boundary line that was set back several feet onto the church's property. For at least 11 years, the church and neighboring landowner considered this line to be their actual boundary line. The second portion of land claimed by the neighbor was a tract that he maintained for more than 11 years. A New York appellate court concluded that the church had lost its right to both portions of land. With respect to the first portion (land lost by the incorrect boundary line), the court observed, "Testimony shows the practical location of the boundary line and acquiescence thereto by the respective property owners for at least 11 years. Practical location and acquiescence for the statutory period is conclusive as to the location of the boundary line." With respect to the second portion of property (that had been maintained by the neighboring landowner), the court observed that for 14 years the neighboring landowner "cultivated and maintained the subject parcel, mowed it, planted a garden and trees on it, and erected a garage, swimming pool, storage shed and clothes line on it. We find that these facts established that [the neighbor] possessed the parcel hostilely and under claim of right, actually, openly and notoriously, exclusively and continuously for the statutory period." This case demonstrates the potential loss of property that may result from erroneous boundary lines and fences, and the maintenance and use of a portion of a church's property by a neighbor.[187]

§ 7-19   Accounting for Depreciation

Key point 7-19. The Financial Accounting Standards Board (FASB) requires nonprofit organizations to recognize the depreciation of property and assets in their financial statements. As a result, churches that do not report depreciation will not be eligible for an unqualified opinion from a CPA at the conclusion of an audit.

In 1987, the "Financial Accounting Standards Board" (FASB) issued "Statement of Financial Accounting Standards No. 93," which required all nonprofit organizations (including churches) to recognize depreciation in their financial statements. FASB based the new rule on its conclusion that a nonprofit organization has assets that are used up in providing services, and that this "using up" of assets is a real "cost" that should be recognized (as depreciation) in the organization's financial statements in order to fairly present its financial condition. To illustrate, FASB noted that the value of a cathedral "is used up not only by wear and tear in intended uses but also by the continuous destructive effects of pollutants, vibrations, and so forth. The cultural, aesthetic, or historical value of [such assets] can be preserved, if at all, only by periodic major efforts to protect, clean, and restore them, usually at significant cost. Thus, [it was] concluded that depreciation of those assets needs to be recognized."

---

[187] Chavoustie v. Stone Street Baptist Church, 569 N.Y.S.2d 528 (A.D. 4 Dept. 1991).

Stated another way, a nonprofit organization "produces and distributes goods and services by using resources . . . . Some of its resources (assets) are used up in providing services at the time they are received, others are used up at a later date, and still others are used up gradually over time." In any event, "using up assets in providing services *has a cost* whether those assets have been acquired in prior periods or in the current period and whether acquired by paying cash, incurring liabilities, or by contribution." FASB further noted that "even if that organization plans to replace the asset through future contributions from donors, and probably will be able to do so, it has not maintained its net assets during the current period." Not reporting depreciation (the cost of using up assets), on a nonprofit organization's financial statements "produces results that do not reflect all costs of services provided." FASB rejected the argument that depreciation need not be recognized on a nonprofit organization's donated properties since "whether an organization's use of an asset results in an expense does not depend on how the asset was acquired." FASB did concede that "depreciation need not be recognized on individual works of art or historical treasures whose economic benefit or service potential is used up so slowly that their estimated useful lives are extraordinarily long. A work of art or historical treasure shall be deemed to have that characteristic only if verifiable evidence exists demonstrating that (a) the asset individually has cultural, aesthetic, or historical value that is worth preserving perpetually and (b) the holder has the technological and financial ability to protect and preserve essentially undiminished the service potential of the asset and is doing that."

What is the relevance of this rule to churches and religious organizations? Simply this—if your financial statements are audited by a CPA firm each year, you will not receive an "unqualified opinion" if you do not recognize depreciation on your long-lived assets. An unqualified opinion cannot be given because readers of your financial statements will not receive information about the cost of using up your assets, and accordingly they are not presented with information reflecting your organization's true costs. What difference will this make? None, if your financial statements are not audited by a CPA firm. Even if you have an annual CPA audit, the failure to report depreciation will probably result in a "qualified" opinion by your CPA (i.e., an unqualified opinion *except for* your failure to report depreciation). According to FASB, the best reason to record depreciation in your accounting records is to ensure that the readers of your financial statements receive an accurate picture of your financial condition because of the inclusion of all relevant cost information. Whether or not your church or organization will record depreciation is a matter that should be addressed by the church board.

§ 7-20   Premises Liability

Persons can be injured on church premises in a number of ways. Many parishioners have slipped on icy sidewalks or parking lots, fallen down stairs, tripped on wet floors, walked through plate glass windows, or been assaulted on church parking lots. Many churches allow outside groups to use their premises, and it is not uncommon for injuries to occur during such activities. What is a church's liability in such cases?

§ 7-20.1 — Liability Based on Status as Invitee, Licensee, or Trespasser

Key point 7-20.1. In most states, whether a church is liable for injuries occurring on its premises will depend on the whether the victim is an invitee, a licensee, or a trespasser. Churches, like any property owner, owe the highest degree of care to invitees, a lesser degree of care to licensees, and a very minimal degree of care to trespassers. As a result, it is more likely that churches will be liable for injuries to persons who meet the definition of an "invitee."

In most states, the liability of a church for injuries caused on its premises depends upon the status of the victim, since the degree of care which a church must exercise in safeguarding and inspecting its premises depends entirely upon the status of the victim. Most courts hold that a person may be on another's property as an *invitee*, a *licensee*, or a *trespasser*. An *invitee* may be either a public invitee or a business visitor. Section 332 of the Restatement (Second) of Torts, which has been adopted in many states, specifies that:

(a) An invitee is either a public invitee or a business visitor.

(b) A public invitee is a person who is invited to enter or remain on land as a member of the public for a purpose for which the land is held open to the public.

(c) A business visitor is a person who is invited to enter or remain on land for a purpose directly or indirectly connected with business dealings with the possessor of the land.

Landowners owe the greatest duty of care to *invitees*, since invitees by definition are on a landowner's property because of an express or implied invitation. Most courts hold that landowners owe invitees a duty to use reasonable and ordinary care to keep their premises safe, including the responsibility of correcting those concealed hazards of which they know or reasonably should know, or at least warning invitees of such hazards. Even so, a landowner is not a guarantor of the safety of invitees. So long as a landowner exercises reasonable care in making the premises safe for invitees or if adequate warning is given about concealed perils, a landowner will not be responsible for injuries that occur. Many courts have refused to hold landowners responsible for an invitee's injuries caused by an obvious hazard or by a concealed hazard of which the invitee was aware. Some courts have concluded that church members attending church services or activities are invitees because they satisfy the definition of *public invitee*. For example, one court concluded that a church member who was injured when she tripped and fell over a wooden cross that had been used in a skit presented at a church meeting was a public invitee since she had been invited to enter the premises as a member of the public for a purpose for which the property was held open to the public.[188]

A *licensee* generally is defined as one who is privileged to enter or remain on property because of the owner's express or implied consent. It is often said that invitees enter one's property by invitation, either express or implied, and that licensees are not invited but their presence is tolerated or merely permitted. In most states a landowner is responsible for warning licensees of hidden dangers of which the landowner is actually aware and to refrain from willfully or wantonly injuring them or recklessly exposing them to danger. The landowner has no duty to protect a licensee against hidden dangers of which the landowner is unaware. Thus, landowners are under no duty to make their premises safe by inspecting for and correcting hidden conditions that may cause injury.

A *trespasser* is a person who enters another's property without invitation or consent. In general, a landowner owes no duty to an undisclosed trespasser, and thus trespassers have no legal remedy if they are injured by a dangerous condition on another's property.[189] However, landowners who are reasonably apprised of the presence of trespassers ordinarily must refrain from willfully or wantonly injuring them, and, according to some courts, must warn them of concealed hazards of which the owner is actually aware.[190]

---

[188] Stevens v. Bow Mills Methodist Church, 283 A.2d 488 (N.H. 1971). *See also* Hedglin v. Church of St. Paul, 158 N.W.2d 269 (Minn. 1968).

[189] Adams v. Atlanta Faith Memorial Church, 381 S.E.2d 397 (Ga. 1989); Richards v. Cincinnati West Baptist Church, 680 N.E.2d 191 (Ohio App. 1996).

[190] *See, e.g.,* Reider v. city of Spring Lake Park, 480 N.E.2d 662 (Minn. App. 1992) (a church has a duty to warn trespassers of danger on its property if trespassers regularly use portions of the property).

A few states in recent years have abandoned the prevailing view of assessing a landowner's liability for injuries occurring on his premises by focusing on the status of the victim. These states have substituted a simple standard of reasonable care that a landowner owes to all lawful visitors. In determining a landowner's liability, the status of a victim is still relevant but not controlling. For example, the fact that an injured victim was a trespasser will reduce the landowner's duty of care since a reasonable person would not take the same steps to ensure the safety of trespassers that he would for invitees.

The great majority of cases involving accidents on church property have determined the church's liability on the basis of the status of the victim. Often, an accident victim's recovery of monetary damages against the church depends on his or her characterization as an invitee by a court, since this status creates the highest duty of care on the part of the church. If the victim is deemed to be a mere licensee, then often any monetary recovery is precluded. Many courts have concluded that accident victims are invitees of a church.

1. Cases Recognizing Invitee Status

A number of courts have ruled that members and certain other persons who are injured on church property are entitled to recover damages because of their status as invitees.

> ***Example.*** *An Indiana appeals court concluded that a member who tripped over a plastic runner covering an aisle in a synagogue was an invitee rather than a licensee, and accordingly that the synagogue was legally responsible for his injuries. The court concluded that persons who are invited to enter upon premises for a purpose for which the premises are held open to the public or for business dealings with the owner of the premises are invitees who may recover for such injuries. The court concluded that members who attend activities at a church or synagogue are invitees under this test, since they are invited to enter the premises for the purposes for which they are held open to the public. Accordingly, a church or synagogue has a duty to protect them against negligent conditions on the premises, including improperly maintained aisle runners.[191]*

> ***Example.*** *The Iowa Supreme Court ruled that the president of a state organization of church women who was injured when she fell down a darkened church stairway was an invitee of the church because she had been invited to appear and preside over a women's meeting, and her presence was of mutual benefit to herself and the church. Since she was an invitee, the court concluded that the church owed her a duty to exercise ordinary care to keep the premises in reasonably safe condition and that this duty had been breached.[192]*

> ***Example.*** *The Mississippi Supreme Court ruled that a church and its board of trustees could be sued by a member who was injured when she slipped and fell on a waxed floor while leaving a Sunday school class. The member argued that she was an invitee and accordingly that the church had a duty "to exercise reasonable care to keep the premises in a reasonably safe condition and, if the [church] knows of, or by the exercise of reasonable care should have known of, a dangerous condition, which is not readily apparent to the invitee, the [church] is under a duty to warn the invitee of such condition." The member claimed that the church breached this duty of care. On the other hand, the church maintained that the member was merely a licensee to whom it owed a minimal duty of refraining from willfully and wantonly injuring her through active negligence. The state supreme court ruled that the member*

---

[191] Fleischer v. Hebrew Orthodox Congregation, 504 N.E.2d 320 (Ind. App. 1987).
[192] Sullivan v. First Presbyterian Church, 152 N.W.2d 628 (Iowa 1967).

was an invitee at the time of her injury: "Members of religious associations, in general . . . fall within the category of public invitees. Religious bodies do expressly and impliedly invite members to come and attend their services and functions. They hold their doors open to the public. While they do not charge admission fees . . . churches do depend on contributions . . . in order that they may continue to be open to the public. Therefore, a church member who does not exceed the scope of the church's invitation, is an invitee while attending a church for church services or related functions." As a result, the member who slipped and fell on the waxed floor was an invitee to whom the church owed a high degree of care, rather than a mere licensee to whom the church owed only a minimal duty of care.[193]

Example. *The Missouri Supreme Court ruled that a woman who was injured when she slipped and fell on a freshly waxed floor inside a church while on a tour at the invitation of her son was an invitee to whom the church was liable because of its failure to remedy the dangerous condition. The church's contention that the victim was not an invitee because the church received no benefit from her presence was rejected by the court: "Not only was she welcome, but her status as a potential member and future contributor provided a benefit to the church in an economic sense. That benefit so derived is not speculative but is comparable to, and no less than, that where the customer shops but does not buy. This was sufficient to give her all the required attributes of an invitee."[194]*

Example. *The New Jersey Supreme Court rejected a church's claim that a Sunday school teacher who was injured when she slipped and fell on an icy sidewalk in front of the church was not entitled to recovery as an invitee since she was a mere social guest. The court acknowledged that those who enter another's property as guests, whether for benevolent or social reasons, are licensees to whom the landowner owes a very minimal duty of care. The court concluded that the operation of a church is more than a mere social gathering: "To very many people it concerns a business of extreme moment, however unworldly." The court also insisted that the injured teacher's presence on church property was primarily for the benefit of the church, for "despite the voluntary and unrecompensed status of the plaintiff, she entered these premises as a matter of duty to the [church], and for the furtherance of the important interest, albeit a spiritual one, of the church, as distinguished from her own." The court accordingly held that the teacher was a business invitee to whom the church had breached its duty of reasonable care.[195]*

Example. *The Washington state supreme court concluded that a church member who was injured in a fall from a negligently assembled scaffolding while donating his labor in the construction of a church building was an invitee of the church since the business or purpose for which he had entered the premises was of economic benefit to the church. Accordingly, the church was found liable for breaching its duty of exercising reasonable care to render its premises safe from, or at least warn of, dangerous conditions of which the church knew or could discover with reasonable diligence.[196]*

2. CASES RECOGNIZING LICENSEE STATUS

In other cases, courts have concluded that a particular accident victim was present on church premises as a licensee. In most cases, a finding that an accident victim is a licensee will insulate the church from liability, since the only duty that a church owes to a licensee in most states is the duty to refrain from injuring a licensee

---

[193] Clark v. Moore Memorial United Methodist Church, 538 So.2d 760 (Miss. 1989). *Accord* Heath v. First Baptist Church, 341 So.2d 265 (Fla.App.1977), *cert. denied,* 348 So.2d 946 (Fla.1977).
[194] Claridge v. Watson Terrace Christian Church, 457 S.W.2d 785 (Mo. 1970).
[195] Atwood v. Board of Trustees, 98 A.2d 348 (N.J. 1953).
[196] Haugen v. Central Lutheran Church, 361 P.2d 637 (Wash. 1961).

willfully or want only and to exercise ordinary care to avoid imperiling the licensee by any active conduct. In some states, a church also owes a licensee a duty to correct concealed hazards of which it is actually aware or at least to warn a licensee of such hazards. But a church does not owe a licensee a duty to exercise reasonable care in maintaining church premises in a reasonably safe condition, and it does not have a duty to make inspections for dangerous conditions. This latter duty is owed only to invitees.

To illustrate, courts have found the following persons to be licensees and as a result have denied a legal remedy for injuries suffered on church premises: a member of an industrial basketball league that played its games in a church gymnasium;[197] a five-year-old girl who was visiting a church at which her grandmother was employed;[198] a church member who was injured while walking across a church lawn seeking entrance into a church to light a candle for her daughter;[199] a policeman who was investigating a complaint that a church was being broken into;[200] and a child who was burned by a fire while playing on church property.[201]

> *Example. The Alabama Supreme Court ruled that a church was not responsible for injuries sustained by a visiting choir member who slipped and fell on church premises. The court based its decision on the status of the choir member while present as a guest on the other church's property. It concluded that a person attending a church service is a licensee while on the church premises, and not an invitee. It noted that a choir member visiting another church to participate in a special service is not an invitee since the person's presence does not provide a "material benefit" to the other church. It further observed that special church services are common, and that guests who participate in such services are "in much the same position as social guests enjoying unrecompensed hospitality in a private home by invitation." As such, they are licensees. The court concluded that the church did not breach any duty it owed to the choir member as a licensee, since it did not willfully or wantonly injure her, and it was not aware of any condition of the floor that would cause an injury.[202]*

3. Trespassing Children

It is common for neighborhood children to play on church property. This may include skateboarding, bicycling, use of motorized recreational vehicles, basketball, baseball, or several other activities. Some of these activities expose minors to a significant risk of harm. Is the church legally responsible for injuries that may result? The answer depends on whether the victim entered onto church property because of an "artificial condition."

injuries caused by an artificial condition

If a minor is injured because of an artificial condition on church property, then the church's potential liability is described in section 339 of the *Restatement (Second) of Torts*, a respected legal treatise that is recognized in most states:

---

[197] Turpin v. Our Lady of Mercy Catholic Church, 202 S.E.2d 351 (N.C. 1974).

[198] Lemon v. Busey, 461 P.2d 145 (Kan. 1969).

[199] Coolbaugh v. St. Peter's Roman Catholic Church, 115 A.2d 662 (Conn. 1955).

[200] Scheurer v. Trustees of Open Bible Church, 192 N.E.2d 38 (Ohio 1963).

[201] Wozniczka v. McKean, 247 N.E.2d 215 (Ind. 1969).

[202] Hambright v. First Baptist Church, 638 So.2d 865 (Ala. 1994). *Accord* Prentiss v. Evergreen Presbyterian Church, 644 So.2d 475 (Ala. 1994); Davidson v. Highlands Church, 673 So.2d 765 (Ala. App. 1995).

A possessor of land is subject to liability for physical harm to children trespassing thereon caused by an artificial condition upon the land if:

(a) the place where the condition exists is one upon which the possessor knows or has reason to know that children are likely to trespass, and

(b) the condition is one of which the possessor knows or has reason to know and which he realizes or should realize will involve an unreasonable risk of death or serious bodily harm to such children, and

(c) the children because of their youth do not discover the condition or realize the risk involved in intermeddling with it or in coming within the area made dangerous by it, and

(d) the utility to the possessor of maintaining the condition and the burden of eliminating the danger are slight as compared with the risk to children involved, and

(e) the possessor fails to exercise reasonable care to eliminate the danger or otherwise to protect the children.

An artificial condition is any condition that does not naturally exist. For example, the following conditions would be artificial: a basketball court, swimming pool, parking lot, or playground equipment.

Example. A New Jersey court ruled that a church may be liable for injuries sustained by a neighborhood child while playing on church premises. A church was located on a large lot without a fence.[203] The lot contained a low point where rain water accumulated. One day it rained quite heavily and a deep pond-like puddle formed in the low area. A 3-year-old child who lived across the street often played on the church's property. She looked out the window of her home and noticed her tricycle on the church's property and wanted to bring it out of the rain. Her mother (the "victim") instructed the little girl to stay in the house and told her that she would retrieve the tricycle. The mother crossed the street to get the tricycle and noticed the large pond-like puddle that had accumulated on the church's property as a result of the rain. The tricycle was on the other side of puddle and the mother began walking around the puddle to retrieve it. Suddenly, she heard her little girl behind her saying that she would get the tricycle. The mother instantly realized that her daughter had walked into the large puddle and was in the middle of it. The mother was fearful that due to the young age of the child and given the depth of the water that the child was in danger. She immediately walked towards the child, but before she could reach her, she slipped in the mud under the water, fracturing her leg. The mother sued the church. A state appeals court concluded that the church could be sued for the mother's injuries. It quoted the general rule from section 339 of the Restatement (Second) of Torts, and concluded that each of these conditions was met. First, the pastor knew that children played on the church's property. Second, the pastor was aware of the accumulation of water on the property after a heavy rain, and the risk this posed to small children. Third, the pastor should have realized that the flooding condition on the property created an unreasonable risk of serious harm to young children. Fourth, the burden of eliminating the danger was slight compared with the risk to children. The pastor testified that the cost of installing a fence to keep children from walking in the area was approximately $2,000. The court pointed out that the church in fact did install a fence following the incident. Fifth, the church failed to

---

[203] Blackburn v. Broad Street Church, 702 A.2d 1331 (N.J. Super. 1998).

exercise reasonable care to eliminate the danger or otherwise to protect the children. At the time of the incident, "the church had taken no steps to remove the condition or to warn children of the danger." The court noted that the Restatement addresses liability of property owners associated with injuries to children caused by artificial conditions on their property. It concluded that the "ponding effect" was an artificial condition: "The church buildings and the parking lot had been constructed on the property. The engineer testified that rain water from portions of the roof and from the stone driveway area contributed to the accumulation of water in the low area. The church building, with the resulting flow of rain water from the roof and the stoned parking lot were not natural conditions of the land, but instead were artificial conditions contributing to the accumulation of rain water on the property." The court concluded that if a church owes a duty of care to a trespassing child under the Restatement analysis summarized above, it also owes a duty of care to an adult rescuer. As a result, the church could be responsible for the mother's injuries incurred while attempting to save her child from the dangerous condition on the property.

injuries not caused by an artificial condition

Churches owe a minimal degree of care to trespassing children who are injured due to a natural condition (such as a tree or naturally occurring pond or lake). In general, the church must refrain from wantonly or willfully injuring such children.

> **Example.** *An Ohio court ruled that a church was not responsible for injuries sustained by a minor who was injured while trespassing on church property.[204] A church owned a "water drenching machine" that was used at various church activities. The machine was designed to be connected to a hose, and anyone who hit a lever on the machine with a ball caused an individual in the machine to be drenched with water. When not in use, the church stored the machine against a wall in the back of the church. A "no trespassing" sign was posted by the church. In addition, neighborhood children were not permitted to play on church premises during the week. The pastor and his wife frequently chased uninvited children off the property. One day a 6-year-old boy entered the church's premises, walked around to the back of the church, and crawled onto the machine. He was injured when it fell on him. The boy's parents sued the church. They claimed that they were not aware that neighbor children were not allowed to play on church property, although they did acknowledge that they were aware of the "no trespassing" sign. A state appeals court ruled in favor of the church. It noted that the boy was a trespasser, and that a property owner's only duty with respect to a trespasser is to "refrain from wantonly or willfully injuring him." The parents admitted that the church had not acted wantonly or willfully, but they insisted that the church was liable for their son's injuries on the basis of the "dangerous instrumentality" rule. Under this rule, a property owner has a higher duty of care to a child trespasser when it operates hazardous equipment "the dangerousness of which is not readily apparent to children, on or immediately adjacent to a public place." The court concluded that this exception did not apply in this case, since the machine was not "on or immediately adjacent to a public place." To the contrary, the machine was "private property, behind the church building and up against a wall. It was not within easy reach of a child in a public area."*

4. Conclusion

Ultimately, the liability of a church for injuries suffered on its premises depends upon how narrowly or expansively the courts of a particular state define the term *invitee*. As the cases previously discussed illustrate,

---

[204] Richards v. Cincinnati West Baptist Church, 680 N.E.2d 191 (Ohio App. 1996).

there is some difference of opinion regarding the definition of this term. Clearly, however, those states that have adopted the Restatement (Second) of Torts definition of an invitee ordinarily will regard most participants in church activities and services to be invitees. The United States Supreme Court has observed:

> In an effort to do justice in an industrialized urban society, with its complex economic and individual relationships, modern common-law courts have found it necessary to formulate increasingly subtle verbal refinements, to create subclassifications among traditional common-law categories, and to delineate fine gradations in the standards of care which the landowner owes to each. Yet even within a single jurisdiction, the classifications and subclassifications bred by the common law have produced confusion and conflict. . . . Through this semantic morass the common law has moved, unevenly and with hesitation, towards "imposing on owners and occupiers a single duty of reasonable care in all the circumstances."[205]

§ 7-20.2 — Use of Church Property by Outside Groups

Key point 7-20.2. Churches may be legally responsible for injuries occurring on their premises while being used by an outside group, if they maintain sufficient "control" over their premises during such use.

Churches often let outside groups use their premises. Examples include scout troops, preschools, aerobics classes, substance abuse groups, childbirth classes, and music classes. Can a church be legally responsible for injuries occurring on its premises while being used by such groups? Possibly.

Example. An Indiana court ruled that a church was liable for an injury occurring on its premises while being used by an outside group. A church permitted a local community group to use its facilities for an annual one-day celebration. The event was advertised in the church bulletin, and included a religious ceremony. After the ceremony, guests were ushered into another room for a reception where refreshments were served. While refreshments were being served, volunteers disassembled the tables and chairs in the room where the ceremony occurred. Although the guests were asked to proceed to the reception immediately following the ceremony, a few guests remained behind to socialize. As one of these guests proceeded to the reception area a few minutes later, she tripped and fell over some of the disassembled tables. She later sued the church. The church claimed that it was not responsible for the guest's injuries since it had not retained any control over its facilities while they were being used by the community group for its celebration. The church also pointed out that the group was permitted to use the facilities without charge, that it was responsible for cleaning up the facilities following its activities, and that the church did not retain any control over the facilities during the celebration. A state appeals court noted that "the church is correct in observing that control of the premises is the basis of premises liability." However, the court concluded that there was ample evidence of control by the church. It observed: "[The priest] testified . . . that if he chose to do so, he could have decided not to allow the [community group] to hold their function there; that there was a janitor on the premises to make sure the buildings were locked; that the [organization] was not in charge of securing the premises; that the church placed an announcement in the church bulletin regarding when and where the celebration was to take place; that the church conducted a religious ceremony as a part of the celebration; and that he would not say that the church relinquished control over the property. This testimony was enough to create an issue of fact as to whether the church retained control over the premises."[206]

---

[205] Kermarec v. Compagnie Cenerale, 358 U.S. 625, 630-31 (1959).
[206] St. Casimer Church v. Frankiewics, 563 N.E.2d 1331 (Ind. App. 1990).

Example. Can a charity be legally responsible for an injury occurring on its premises while being used by an outside group? That was the question addressed by a Louisiana court in a recent decision. A charity permitted an outside group to use its facility for a Christmas party. During the party, a woman suffered serious injuries when she fell on a slippery floor. As a result of her injuries the woman underwent surgery for a complete hip replacement. She later sued the charity, claiming that it was responsible for her injuries because it had retained control over the premises during the party. She claimed that the floor was unreasonably slippery, and this dangerous condition caused her to fall. One witness testified, "It was obvious that floor was slippery. It was just waxed or something. I mean it wasn't dirty. It was clean. Probably too clean." The charity asked the court to dismiss the case, but its request was denied. On appeal, a state appeals court suggested that there was sufficient evidence that the charity retained control over its premises during the party to send the case to a jury. The court began its opinion by acknowledging that a property owner may be legally responsible for injuries that occur on its premises when they are under its custody or control. The court suggested that the charity had retained control over its premises during the Christmas party on the basis of the following factors: (1) the charity was responsible for setting up tables for the party; (2) the charity provided a custodian during the entire party; and (3) the charity was responsible for opening the premises at the beginning of the party and locking the premises at the conclusion of the party. The charity's custodian admitted that he had cleaned the floor prior to the party and that he was on duty and responsible for cleaning the floor during the party.[207]

§ 7-20.3 — Assaults in Church Parking Lots

Key point 7-20.3. A church may be legally responsible for assaults occurring in its parking lot if there is a history of assaults in the area and the church failed to take reasonable precautions.

Some persons have been assaulted in church parking lots. To illustrate, a member is assaulted and robbed while walking to her car in a church parking lot after leaving an evening function. Is the church liable for such injuries?

Example. A female college student (the victim) worked as a summer waitress in a local restaurant. One evening she left work and walked to the far end of the parking lot where her car was parked. A busboy accompanied her part of the way, but returned to the restaurant when they were in the vicinity of the car. The victim entered her car, started the engine, rolled down her window, and waited several seconds for the engine to "warm up" (the car had been experiencing engine problems). As she waited, an assailant reached through the open window, unlocked the door, and forced his way into the car. The assailant punched the victim in the face and drove off while holding her in a "headlock." He drove to a nearby cornfield, raped her, tied her with jumper cables, and then fled with her car keys. The victim managed to free herself and run to a nearby farmhouse where she called for help. She later sued her employer, claiming that it was responsible for her injuries because of its failure to provide adequate security and lighting in its parking lot. A jury agreed, and awarded her $600,000 in damages. The employer appealed this verdict, and the state supreme court upheld the award. The court noted that other waitresses had complained to the restaurant's owner about the inadequate lighting in the parking lot. It also noted that 14 minor property crimes (mostly vandalism) had occurred on the parking lot in the 4 years preceding the assault. Under these circumstances, the court concluded that it was appropriate to find the employer responsible for the victim's injuries on the basis of negligence.[208]

---

[207] Aufrichtig v. Progressive Men's Club, 634 So.2d 947 (La. App. 2 Cir. 1994).
[208] Koutoufaris v. Dick, 604 A.2d 390 (Del. 1992).

Example. A South Carolina court ruled that a church was not liable for injuries sustained by a person when he was attacked on church property.[209] *A church owned an apartment complex that is used as low income housing. Despite the fact that the apartment building was in a high-crime area, and church leaders were aware of numerous incidents of criminal behavior occurring within the building, the church did not provide a security guard. A man (the "victim") was injured when he was attacked while visiting a friend in the apartment building. The victim sued the church, claiming that it was responsible for his injuries on the basis of negligence. A state appeals court disagreed. The court observed: "A [property] owner has a duty to take reasonable care to protect invitees. However, this duty does not extend to protection from criminal attacks from third persons unless the owner knew or had reason to know the criminal attack would occur. . . . In this case [the victim and his mother] stated they knew of criminal activity that had occurred at [the apartment building] in the past, including an alleged shooting. In addition [the victim] asserted he knew [his attacker] was a violent person and that he had seen [him] involved in other fights at the complex. However, there is no evidence in the record that [the church] was aware of [the attacker's] previous fights or of any incident that day that would put management on notice the attack [on the victim] might occur. Therefore [the church] had no duty to protect [the victim] from an intentional attack."*

REDUCING THE RISK OF ASSAULTS ON CHURCH PROPERTY

Unfortunately, church members occasionally are assaulted on church property. Some members have been assaulted on church parking lots while walking toward their car at night after a service or event at their church. A church may be responsible for such assaults if it was aware of previous assaults on its premises, or in the immediate area. Church leaders should recognize that their church is exposed to a much higher degree of care for the protection of members and visitors if one or more assaults has occurred on church premises or in the immediate vicinity of the church. However, the church can reduce its risk of liability by demonstrating that it used reasonable care in protecting against such attacks. How can a church do so? Churches have used some or all of the following measures:

• Provide adequate illumination of the parking lot.

• Designate "escorts" who will accompany persons to their car upon request. Be sure that this option is communicated to church members and visitors.

• Station volunteers in the parking lot.

• Install a wide-angle video camera on the church roof.

• Have a uniformed security guard, or off-duty police officer, monitor the parking lot. For more suggestions, church leaders should contact their insurance agent.

---

[209] Goode v. St. Stephens United Methodist Church, 494 S.E.2d 827 (S.C. 1998).

§ 7-20.4 — Defenses to Liability

Key point 7-20.4. *A variety of defenses are available to a church that is sued as a result of an injury occurring on its premises.*

Churches have been found innocent of wrongdoing in several cases regardless of the status of the person injured on their property because the condition or activity that caused the injury could not under any circumstances serve as a basis for legal liability. For example, the courts have held that a church is under no duty to illuminate its parking lot when no church activities are in process;[210] to remove oil and grease from its parking lot;[211] to place markings on a sliding glass door;[212] to begin removing snow from church stairways before the end of a snowstorm;[213] or to remove every square inch of snow and ice from its parking lot following a storm.[214] The parents of an infant whose eye was seriously injured in a church nursery during worship services were denied any recovery since no one witnessed the accident and there was no evidence that it was caused by any negligence on the part of the church.[215] Similarly, a church member doing volunteer work for his church was denied recovery for injuries sustained when a ladder fell on him. The court noted that the member was an invitee, and that the church owed him a legal duty to correct or give notice of concealed, dangerous conditions of which it was or should have been aware. However, the court denied recovery on the ground that the member was aware of the unsecured ladder and the danger it presented, and this knowledge excused the church from its duty of correcting the condition or notifying the member of its existence.[216]

One or more defenses may be available to a church that is sued by a person who is injured on church premises. Many of these are addressed in chapter 10.

Example. *The Florida Supreme Court held that a church member who was injured when she fell while walking in a dark hallway connecting the sanctuary with a social hall was precluded from suing the church by her own contributory negligence. The court observed that darkness is in itself sufficient warning to signal caution to one entering an unfamiliar situation, and that if one fails to heed the signal, he is guilty of contributory negligence.[217]*

Example. *A Georgia court ruled that a church was not responsible for injuries suffered by a woman who slipped and fell on church property. The woman had taken her daughter up a wooden ramp to the entrance of a church school, and was injured when she slipped and fell on the way down. It was raining at the time of the accident, and the ramp was wet. Immediately after she fell the woman told the church's pastor that "it's not your fault . . . it was just raining and I was in a hurry and slipped and fell." The woman had slipped before on the same ramp, and was aware that it was slippery even under dry conditions. She later sued the church as a result of her injuries. A state appeals court, in upholding the trial court's dismissal of the lawsuit, observed: "Everyone knows that any wet surface may be slippery. [The woman] has slipped on the ramp when it was dry. She had knowledge of its danger equal and perhaps superior knowledge to [that of the church], and she fell either because she was hurrying or*

---

[210] Huselton v. Underhill, 28 Cal. Rptr. 822 (1963).

[211] Goard v. Branscom, 189 S.E.2d 667 (N.C. 1972), *cert. denied*, 191 S.E.2d 354 (N.C. 1972).

[212] Sullivan v. Birmingham Fire Insurance Co., 185 So.2d 336 (La. 1966), *cert. denied*, 186 So.2d 632 (La. 1966).

[213] Hedglin v. Church of St. Paul, 158 N.W.2d 269 (Minn. 1968).

[214] Byrne v. Catholic Bishop, 266 N.E.2d 708 (Ill. 1971).

[215] Helton v. Forest Park Baptist Church, 589 S.W.2d 217 (Ky. App. 1979).

[216] Fisher v. Northmoor United Methodist Church, 679 S.W.2d 305 (Mo. App. 1984). *Contra* Coates v. W.W. Babcock Co., 560 N.E.2d 1099 (Ill. App. 1990).

[217] Trinity Episcopal Church v. Hoglund, 222 So.2d 781 (Fla. 1969).

because she chose to negotiate the ramp despite the danger which was obvious to her. The mere fact that a dangerous condition exists, whether caused by a building code violation or otherwise, does not impose liability on the [property owner]."[218]

Example. *A Michigan court ruled that a church could be sued by the estate of an individual who was killed as a result of a defective ladder while performing work on church property. The decedent was engaged in performing repair and maintenance of a church building when he fell from a church-owned ladder and was killed. His estate sued the church, claiming that its negligence was the cause of the decedent's death. The court concluded that the decedent was an "invitee" on the church's premises. It noted that "an invitor must warn of hidden defects; there is no duty to warn of open and obvious dangers unless the [property owner] anticipates harm to the invitee despite the invitee's knowledge of the defect." The court concluded that "an extension ladder is an essentially uncomplicated instrument which gains a propensity for danger only because it will allow the user to reach great heights. This danger is most obvious to all but children of tender years . . . ." As a result, a church cannot be legally responsible for injuries suffered by workers who are injured when they fall from a ladder. However, the court cautioned that this rule did not necessarily apply in this case, since the estate of the decedent claimed that the decedent's fall was caused not by the general nature of the ladder itself but rather by a missing or malfunctioning safety latch. The court observed, "The real inquiry is whether this defect must be deemed an open and obvious danger. We think not. The danger that an extension ladder might slip and telescope down because of inadequate bracing at its base . . . is a danger readily apparent to persons of ordinary intelligence and experience. However, the fact that a safety latch is missing or malfunctioning creates a different, or at least an additional, danger that is not so obvious absent specific knowledge of the defect."*[219]

Example. *A Minnesota court concluded that a church member who slipped and fell on an icy stairway while leaving a church service was not entitled to recover damages from the church because her failure to use an available handrail made her contributorily negligent.*[220]

Example. *A Minnesota court concluded that a church was not responsible for injuries sustained by a member who tripped on a dark stairway. The court noted that "evidence of the church's negligence was minimal. [The member] did not establish that the lights were turned off by a person for whose negligence the church could be held vicariously liable."*[221]

Example. *A New York court dismissed a lawsuit brought against a church by a woman who was injured during a church-sponsored activity. The woman and her husband attended a "country fair and*

---

[218] Patterson v. First Assembly of God, 440 S.E.2d 492 (Ga. App. 1994).

[219] Eason v. Coggins Memorial Christian Church, 532 N.W.2d 882 (Mich. App. 1995).

[220] Hedglin v. Church of St. Paul, 158 N.W.2d 269 (Minn. 1968). *But cf.* Davis v. Church of Jesus Christ of Latter Day Saints, 796 P.2d 181 (Mont. 1990). In the *Davis* case, the Montana Supreme Court upheld a jury's award of more than $400,000 to a young woman who was injured when she slipped and fell on an icy church sidewalk. The church argued that it was not responsible for "natural accumulations" of snow and ice and that it had no duty to warn of a danger that was clearly apparent to a reasonable person. The court concluded that "a property owner may be held liable for falls on accumulations of ice and snow where the hazard created by the natural accumulation is increased or a new hazard is created by an affirmative act of the property owner. Even where such a condition is actually known or obvious, a property owner may be held liable if he should have anticipated that injuries would result from the dangerous condition." The court concluded that the church janitor's act of shoveling the sidewalk without applying any salt left the sidewalk covered with a "sheen of ice" that constituted a new hazard different from the natural accumulation of snow and ice that existed previously. It was this hazard, along with the dangerous slope of the sidewalk (without a railing), that constituted negligence on the part of the church.

[221] Thies v. St. Paul's Evangelical Lutheran Church, 489 N.W.2d 277 (Minn. App. 1992).

barbecue" sponsored by her church. Following dinner, the couple took a raft ride on a nearby lake. After the ride, they were directed to walk on a back lawn area to return to the front of the church building. As the woman walked up a sloping lawn around the outside of a large tree, she slipped and fell, injuring her leg. She claimed that she slipped on ice cubes that were on the ground. A state appeals court dismissed the case. The court concluded that "plaintiff was required to demonstrate . . . that the condition was caused by [the church's] agents or existed for a sufficient period of time to require [the church] to have corrected it." Since the woman offered no evidence that an agent of the church caused the ice to be discarded on the lawn, or that the ice had been on the lawn for an unreasonable amount of time without being corrected, the lawsuit had to be dismissed.[222]

Example. *A New York court ruled that a church was not legally responsible for injuries sustained by a woman who slipped on a patch of ice in the church parking lot. The woman had attended a meeting of a local community group on the church's premises. On her way to her car, she slipped and fell on a patch of snow-covered ice and sustained serious injuries. She sued the church. The court ruled that the church was not responsible for the accident, since it was not aware of the ice and snow accumulation (no church employees were present at the time of the meeting) and the church did not have a reasonable opportunity to remove the snow and ice. The icy condition developed only two hours before the accident, and the snow (that concealed the ice) began falling only 15 minutes prior to the accident. Under these circumstances the court concluded, "[The church] as the owner of the premises, had a duty to exercise reasonable care under the circumstances. In order to impose liability upon [the church] there must be evidence that it knew, or in the exercise of reasonable care should have known, that an icy condition existed in its parking lot. Additionally, a party in possession or control of property is afforded a reasonable time after the cessation of the storm or temperature fluctuation which created the dangerous condition to exercise due care in order to correct the situation." There simply was not sufficient time in this case for the church to have removed the snow or ice prior to the accident, and accordingly the church was not legally responsible for the woman's injuries.[223]*

Example. *A Pennsylvania court ruled that a Catholic church and diocese were not responsible for the injuries sustained by a woman who slipped and fell on an icy church parking lot. The woman, who was attending the church to participate in a bingo game, alleged that the parking lot was covered with a sheet of ice and also 5 inches of new snow. She alleged that the church had been negligent in failing to "implement some remedial measure (placing salt or ashes, warning visitors of the presence of ice, or barricading the icy area)," and accordingly the church was responsible for her injuries. A state appeals court ruled that the church was not responsible for the woman's injuries. It observed, "[A]n owner or occupier of land is not liable for general slippery conditions, for to require that one's walks be always free of ice and snow would be to impose an impossible burden in view of the climatic conditions in this hemisphere. Snow and ice upon a pavement create merely a transient danger, and the only duty upon the property owner or tenant is to act within a reasonable time after notice to remove it when it is in a dangerous condition. . . . [I]n order to recover for a fall on an ice or snow covered sidewalk, a plaintiff must prove (1) that snow and ice had accumulated on the sidewalk in ridges or elevations of such size*

---

[222] Torani v. First United Methodist Church, 558 N.Y.S.2d 272 (A.D. 3 Dept. 1990).

[223] Byrd v. Church of Christ, 597 N.Y.S.2d 211 (A.D. 3 Dept. 1993). *But see* Graff v. St. Luke's Evangelical Lutheran Church, 625 N.E.2d 851 (Ill. App. 1993), in which the court concluded that "there is generally no duty to remove natural accumulations of ice and snow" and that "[t]he mere removal of snow leaving a natural ice formation underneath does not constitute negligence." However, a church or other property owner can be legally responsible for injuries in at least two situations: (1) snow is removed in a negligent manner, or (2) "an injury occurred as the result of snow or ice produced or accumulated by artificial causes or in an unnatural way, or by the defendant's use of the premises."

character as to unreasonably obstruct travel and constitute a danger to pedestrians traveling thereon; .) that the property owner had notice, either actual or constructive, of the existence of such condition; (3) that it was the dangerous accumulation of snow and ice which caused the plaintiff to fall." The court concluded that the injured woman had failed to satisfy this test, and accordingly the church was not responsible for her injuries.[224]

Example. *The Rhode Island Supreme Court ruled that a church was not responsible for the death of a parishioner who was killed when she was struck by a vehicle while crossing a street to enter a parking lot. Three adult members of a Catholic church drove to the church to attend midnight mass on Christmas Eve. As was the practice of many parishioners, they parked their car in a small parking lot across the street from the church. The parking lot was owned by a neighboring commercial establishment, but church members were allowed to use the parking lot during church services by common consent. The parking lot was separated from the church by a public street. After mass ended, the three members left the church and proceeded to cross the street to reach their car in the parking lot. While in a crosswalk they were struck by a vehicle driven by a drunk driver. One of the members was killed, and another received severe and permanent injuries. On prior occasions the church had asked the city police to provide a traffic officer to control traffic after church services. The police occasionally provided officers in response to the church's requests if any were available. At no time did the church have a contract with the police to provide traffic officers. No representative of the church had asked the police to provide a traffic officer on the night of the accident. A lawsuit was brought against the church by the injured member and the estate of the member who was killed (the "plaintiffs"). The state supreme court dismissed the lawsuit on the ground that "the duty to control traffic has traditionally rested squarely with the government." Further, "[t]he fact that a landowner may request public traffic control on a public street does not vest in that landowner the personal right or obligation to control such a public way."*[225]

§ 7-21   Embezzlement

Key point 7-21. Embezzlement refers to the wrongful conversion of funds that are lawfully in one's possession. Embezzlement is a common occurrence in churches because of weak internal controls.

1. IN GENERAL

As hard as it may be to believe, embezzlement is a relatively common occurrence in churches. As a result, it is important for church leaders to take this risk seriously.

2. DEFINITION OF EMBEZZLEMENT

The definition of embezzlement varies slightly from state to state, but in general it refers to the wrongful conversion of property that is lawfully in your possession. The idea is that someone has legal control or custody of property or funds, and then decides to convert the property or funds to his or her own personal use.

Most people who embezzle funds insist that they intended to pay the money back and were simply "borrowing" the funds temporarily. An intent to pay back embezzled funds is not a defense to the crime of

---

[224] Harmotta v. Bender, 601 A.2d 837 (Pa. Super. 1992).
[225] Ferreria v. Strack, 636 A.2d 682 (R.I. 1994).

embezzlement. Most church employees who embezzle funds plan on repaying the church fully before anyone suspects what has happened. One can only imagine how many such schemes actually work without anyone knowing about it. The courts are not persuaded by the claims of embezzlers that they intended to fully pay back the funds they misappropriated. The crime is complete when the embezzler misappropriates the church's funds to his or her own personal use. As one court has noted:

> The act of embezzlement is complete the moment the official converts the money to his own use even though he then has the intent to restore it. Few embezzlements are committed except with the full belief upon the part of the guilty person that he can and will restore the property before the day of accounting occurs. There is where the danger lies and the statute prohibiting embezzlement is passed in order to protect the public against such venturesome enterprises by people who have money in their control.

In short, it does not matter that someone intended to pay back embezzled funds. This intent in no way justifies or excuses the crime. The crime is complete when the funds are converted to one's own use—whether or not there was an intent to pay them back.

WHY CHURCH LEADERS SHOULD TAKE THE RISK OF EMBEZZLEMENT SERIOUSLY

• *Removing temptation.* Churches that take steps to prevent embezzlement remove a source of possible temptation from church employees and volunteers who work with money.

• *Protecting reputations.* By taking steps to prevent embezzlement, a church protects the reputation of innocent employees and volunteers who otherwise might be suspected of financial wrongdoing when financial irregularities occur.

• *Avoiding confrontations.* By taking steps to prevent embezzlement, a church avoids the unpleasant task of confronting individuals who are suspected of embezzlement.

• *Avoiding church division.* By taking steps to prevent embezzlement, a church avoids the risk of congregational division that often is associated with cases of embezzlement—with some members wanting to show mercy to the offender and others demanding justice.

• *Avoiding the need to inform donors.* By taking steps to prevent embezzlement, a church reduces the risk of having to tell donors that some of their contributions have been misappropriated by a church employee or volunteer.

• *Protecting the reputation of church leaders.* By taking steps to prevent embezzlement, a church reduces the damage to the reputation and stature of its leaders who otherwise may be blamed for allowing embezzlement to occur.

• *Preserving accountability.* Churches that take steps to prevent embezzlement help to create a "culture of accountability" with regard to church funds.

What if the embezzled funds are returned? The crime of embezzlement has occurred even if the embezzled funds in fact are paid back. Of course, it may be less likely that a prosecutor will prosecute a case under these circumstances. And even if the embezzler is prosecuted, this evidence may lessen the punishment. But the courts have consistently ruled that an actual return of embezzled funds does not purge the offense of its criminal nature or absolve the embezzler from punishment.

> **Key point.** *Even if an embezzler is caught or confesses, and then agrees to "pay back" the embezzled funds, church officials seldom know if all embezzled funds are being returned. They are relying almost entirely on the word of a thief.*

3. WHY CHURCHES ARE VULNERABLE

Many churches refuse to adopt measures to reduce the risk of embezzlement out of a fear that such measures will reflect a lack of trust in those persons who handle church funds.

> **Example.** *Tom has counted the church offering at his church for 25 years. The church board has discussed this arrangement several times, but fails to stop it out of a fear of offending Tom.*

4. HOW EMBEZZLEMENT OCCURS

Let's look at a few cases of actual embezzlement of church funds to see how it can occur.

> **Example.** *An usher collected offerings each week in the church balcony, and pocketed all loose bills while carrying the offering plates down a stairway to the main floor. Church officials later estimated that he embezzled several thousands of dollars over a number of years, before being caught.*

> **Example.** *The same two persons counted church offerings for many years. Each week they removed all loose coins and currency (not in offering envelopes) and split it between them. This practice went on for several years, and church officials later estimated that the two had embezzled several tens of thousands of dollars.*

> **Example.** *A church left its Sunday offering, along with the official count, in a safe in the church office until Monday. On Monday morning a church employee deposited the offering. The employee ignored the official counts, and deposited the offering less loose coins and currency (which she retained). The deposits were never checked against the offering counts.*

> **Example.** *A church child care director embezzled church funds by issuing herself paychecks for the gross amount of her pay (before deductions for tax withholding). The church withheld taxes and paid them to the government, but her paychecks reflected the gross amount of her pay.*

> **Example.** *A pastor had the sole authority to write checks on the church's checking account. He used church funds to pay for several personal expenses, amounting to thousands of dollars each year, until his actions were discovered.*

> **Example.** *A church bookkeeper embezzled several thousand dollars by issuing checks to a fictitious company. He opened an account in the name of a fictitious company, issued church checks to the company for services that were never performed, and then deposited the checks in the fictitious company's*

account. He later withdrew the funds and purchased two automobiles which he gave to a friend. A court ruled that the friend had to give the cars back to the church, since they had been purchased with embezzled church funds. The point here, as noted by the court, is that one who acquires property that was purchased with embezzled church funds may be required to transfer the property to the church.

***Example.** A minister received an unauthorized kickback of 5% of all funds paid by a church to a contractor who had been hired to build a new church facility. The minister received over $80,000 from this arrangement, in exchange for which he persuaded the church to use the contractor. The minister's claim that the $80,000 represented a legal and nontaxable "love offering" was rejected by a federal court that found the minister guilty of several felony counts. This arrangement was not disclosed to the church board, and obviously amounted to an unauthorized diversion of church funds back to the minister.*

***Example.** A church accountant embezzled $212,000 in church funds. This person's scheme was to divert to his own use several designated offerings, and to inflate the cost of equipment that he paid for with his own funds and that the church later reimbursed at the inflated amounts. The interesting aspect of this case was that the accountant was not only found guilty of embezzlement, but he was also convicted for tax evasion because he had failed to report any of the embezzled money as taxable income, and was sentenced to prison.*

***Example.** A court ruled that an insurance company that paid out $26,000 to a charity because of an act of embezzlement could sue the embezzler for the full amount that it paid. This is an important case, for it demonstrates that a church employee who embezzles church funds may be sued by the church insurance company if it pays out a claim based on the embezzlement. In other words, the fact that the church decides not to sue the embezzler does not mean that the person will be free from any personal liability. If the church has insurance to cover the loss, the insurance company can go after the embezzler for a full recovery of the amount that it paid out on account of the embezzlement.*

5. Reducing the Risk of Embezzlement

Can the risk of embezzlement be reduced? If so, how? The good news is that there are number of steps that church leaders can take to reduce this risk, and most of them are quite simple. Consider the following:

1. Implement an effective system of internal control. The first and most effective deterrent to embezzlement is a strong system of "internal control." Internal control is an accounting term that refers to policies and procedures adopted by an organization to safeguard its assets and promote the accuracy of its financial records. What procedures has your church adopted to insure that cash receipts are properly recorded and deposited, and that only those cash disbursements that are properly authorized are made? These are the kinds of questions that are addressed by a church's system of internal control. A table in this chapter addresses a number of common weaknesses in church internal control that increase the risk of embezzlement. The table provides helpful suggestions for responding to these weaknesses.

***Key point.** The most important point to emphasize is "division of responsibilities." The more that tasks and responsibilities are shared or divided, the less risk there will be of embezzlement.*

***Key point.** Many churches refuse to implement basic principles of internal control out of a fear of "offending" persons who may feel that they are being suspected of misconduct. The issue here is not one* *of hurt feelings, but accountability. The church, more than any other institution in society, should set the standard for financial accountability. After all, its programs and activities are rooted in religion, and it is funded entirely with donations from persons who rightfully assume that their contributions are being used for religious purposes. The church has a high responsibility to promote financial accountability. This duty is simply not met when the practices described above are followed.*

2. Screen persons with financial responsibility. Some churches screen bookkeepers, accountants, and other employees who will have access to funds or be involved in financial decisions. Screening can consist of obtaining references from employers, prior employers, and other churches or charities with which the person has been employed or associated.

3. Annual audits. A church can reduce the risk of embezzlement by having an annual audit of its financial records by a CPA firm. An audit accomplishes three important functions:

• An audit promotes an environment of accountability in which opportunities for embezzlement (and therefore the risk of embezzlement) are reduced.

• The CPA (or CPAs) who conducts the audit will provide the church leadership with a "management letter" that points out weaknesses and inefficiencies in the church's accounting and financial procedures. This information is invaluable to church leaders.

• An audit contributes to the integrity and reputation of church leaders and staff members who handle funds.

Key point. Don't confuse an audit with a more limited engagement that CPAs will perform, such as a "compilation."

Key point. Audits can be expensive, and this will be a very relevant consideration for smaller churches. Of course, the time involved in performing an audit for a smaller church will be limited, which will result in a lower fee. Churches can control the cost of an audit by obtaining bids. Also, by staying with the same CPA firm, most churches will realize a savings in the second and succeeding years since the CPA will not have to spend time becoming familiar with the church's financial and accounting procedures.

Key point. Smaller churches that cannot afford a full audit may want to consider two other options: (1) Hire a CPA to conduct a review, which is a simpler and less expensive procedure. If the review detects irregularities, a full audit may be considered worth the price. (2) Create an internal audit committee if there are accountants or business leaders within the church who have the ability to review accounting procedures and practices and look for weaknesses. These people often are very familiar with sound internal control policies, and will quickly correct weaknesses in the church's financial operations. An added bonus—such a committee will serve as a deterrent to those who might otherwise be tempted to embezzle church funds.

4. Bonding of persons who handle funds. Churches can address the risk of embezzlement by bonding the church treasurer and any bookkeeper or accountant that is on staff. You can also purchase a blanket policy to cover all employees and officers. It is important to note that insurance policies vary. Some require that the embezzler be convicted before it will pay a claim, while others do not. The period of time covered by the policy will also vary. These are important points to be discussed by your church board in consultation with your insurance agent.

Key point. Insurance is not a substitute for implementing a sound system of internal control.

6. Responding to Allegations of Embezzlement

Sometimes a person who has embezzled church funds will voluntarily confess—usually out of a fear that he or she is about to be "caught." But in many cases the embezzler does not confess—at least initially. Discrepancies or irregularities may occur which cause church leaders to suspect this person. Consider the following examples.

Example. The same person has counted church offerings for many years. The pastor inadvertently notices that offerings are always higher when this person is absent (due to illness, business, or vacation).

Example. Church officials noticed that a church bookkeeper was living a higher standard of living than was realistic given her income. Among other things, she purchased an expensive home and a luxury car.

Example. Church offerings have remained constant, or increased slightly, despite the fact that attendance has increased.

Example. A church treasurer notices that a church official with sole signature authority on the church checking account has purchased a number of expensive items from unknown companies without any documentation to prove what was purchased and why.

Church leaders often are unsure how to address suspected cases of embezzlement. The suspected embezzler is almost always a trusted member or employee, and church leaders are reluctant to accuse such a person without irrefutable evidence that he or she is guilty. Seldom does such evidence exist. The pastor may confront the person about the suspicion, but in many cases the individual will deny any wrongdoing—even if guilty. This compounds the frustration of church officials, who do not know how to proceed.

Here is a checklist of steps that church leaders can take to help resolve such difficult cases:

1. Confront the suspected embezzler. The pastor and at least one other church leader should confront the suspected embezzler. Inform the person that the church has evidence indicating that he or she has embezzled church funds. Seek a confession. Inform the person that if no one confesses, the church will be forced to call in a CPA firm to confirm that embezzlement has occurred, and to identify the probable embezzler.

Tip. Embezzlement is a criminal offense. Depending on the amount of funds or property taken, it may be a felony that can result in a sentence in the state penitentiary. This obviously would have a devastating impact on the embezzler, and his or her family. If the evidence clearly indicates that a particular member or employee has embezzled church funds, but this person denies any wrongdoing, inform him or her that the church may be forced to turn the matter over to the police for investigation and prosecution.

Tip. Embezzlers never report their illegally obtained "income" on their tax returns. Nor do they suspect that failure to do so may subject them to criminal tax evasion charges! In fact, in some cases it is actually more likely that the IRS will prosecute the embezzler for tax evasion than the local prosecutor will

TABLE 7-1
HOW EMBEZZLEMENT OCCURS:
COMMON EXAMPLES OF POOR INTERNAL CONTROL

example of poor internal control	how embezzlement may occur	preventive action
(1) One person counts church offerings.	This person may remove cash, especially if not in an offering envelope.	Have more than one person count each offering. The more persons that are involved, the lower the risk of embezzlement.
(2) There is not regular turnover or rotation among the persons who count church offerings.	The same two persons count church offerings every week. After a number of years, they agree to remove cash and divide it between them.	A pool of counters should be identified, and each offering should be counted by a randomly selected number of persons from this pool.
(3) One person collects the offerings.	An usher collects offerings in the church balcony during each service, and while carrying offerings down a stairway to a counting room he pockets all loose bills.	There should be at least two persons who collect the offering in the balcony, and they should together carry the offering down the stairs to the counting room. Further, these persons should be rotated.
(4) Offering counts are submitted to the person who deposits the offering.	The counters provide the individual who deposits the offering with a count. This individual disregards the count, withholds several bills unaccom-panied by offering envelopes, and then deposits the lower amount.	Different persons should count and deposit church offerings. A person who neither counts offerings nor deposits them with a bank should be assigned the responsibility of reconciling offering counts with the bank deposit slips.
(5) Only one signature is needed to write a check.	A church employee is given sole signature authority on the church's checking account. The employee pays for a number of personal expenses with this checking account.	At least two signatures should be required for all checks above a nominal amount.
(6) Members who contribute coins and currency (not checks) do not use offering envelopes.	This is one of the major causes of embezzlement. Persons who embezzle church funds often restrict their activities to cash that was not contributed in an offering envelope. Embezzlers assume that it will be more difficult to detect their behavior under these circumstances, since the church cannot provide these donors with a receipt for their contributions (that will reveal discrepancies).	Churches should provide offering envelopes to all members for each week, and also place them in church pews for easy access. Members should be encouraged periodically to use offering envelopes. While they are not required to substantiate charitable contributions, they do reduce the risk of embezzlement. Also, offering counts should note (as a subtotal) loose cash unaccompanied by offering envelopes. This practice will reveal fluctuations that may indicate embezz-lement, and will serve as a deterrent.

example of poor internal control	how embezzlement may occur	preventive action
(7) Offering counts and bank deposit slips are not regularly reconciled.	A church only assigns an employee to reconcile the first offering of each month with a bank deposit slip. The person who deposits offerings is aware of this practice, and embezzles loose cash before depositing offerings from the remaining services of each month.	Offering counts and bank deposit slips should be reconciled for every service. Or, reconcile offering counts with monthly bank statements.
(8) Contribution receipts are not issued to members, or they are issued but members are not encouraged to report discrepancies to the church board.	A church does not provide members with receipts of their contributions. A church employee embezzles cash (whether or not accompanied by an offering envelope), knowing that the risk of discovery is remote. The same risk exists if a church issues contribution receipts but does not actively encourage members to verify the accuracy of these receipts.	Churches should issue a contribution receipt to each donor, and encourage donors to immediately call to the attention of church leaders any discrepancies between their own records and the amount reflected on the church receipt. Discrepancies should not be reported to the person who prepares contribution receipts.
(9) Offerings are not deposited immediately.	When offerings are not promptly deposited, the risk of embezzlement increases since funds are accessible longer. Further, some persons may claim they "reimbursed" themselves out of church funds for unauthorized expenses.	Offerings should be deposited promptly with a bank.
(10) Monthly bank statements are not reviewed by someone having no responsibility for handling cash.	A church bookkeeper writes a check to a fictitious company, then cashes it. The bookkeeper is responsible for reconciling bank statements, and does not disclose the embezzlement.	Monthly bank statements should be reviewed by a church official or employee having no responsibility for handling cash or writing checks (ideally, the statements should be sent to this person's residence). This form of embezzlement also can be avoided by requiring two signatures on all checks.
(11) Reimbursing employees for travel expenses or purchases of church equipment or supplies without requiring adequate substantiation.	A church employee claims to have purchased equipment for church use, and is reimbursed without substantiation. In fact, the purchase was solely for personal use.	Do not reimburse any employee's purchase of church supplies or equipment without first obtaining proof that the purchase was duly authorized; also insist on seeing a receipt documenting what was purchased and its price.

prosecute for the crime of embezzlement. If the evidence clearly indicates that a particular member or employee has embezzled church funds, but this person denies any wrongdoing, inform him or her that the church may be forced to turn the matter over to the IRS for investigation and possible prosecution.

2. Have a local CPA conduct an audit to establish that embezzlement has occurred, and provide an estimate of how much was embezzled. If the suspected embezzler denies any wrongdoing (or if embezzlement is suspected but it is not clear who is guilty), church leaders should consider hiring a local CPA firm to look for evidence of embezzlement. There is a good possibility that the embezzlement will be detected, and that the perpetrator will be identified.

Tip. CPAs can also help the church establish a strong system of internal control to reduce the risk of embezzlement in the future.

Many church leaders have found that turning the investigation over to a CPA firm is much more acceptable than conducting the investigation internally. The CPA firm is completely objective, and ordinarily will not know the suspected embezzler. Further, few church members will object to the church hiring a CPA firm to detect wrongdoing and help establish a sound system of internal control.

3. Contacting the police or local prosecutor. If the suspected embezzler does not confess, or if embezzlement is suspected but it is not clear who is guilty, church leaders must consider turning the matter over to the police or local prosecutor. This is a very difficult decision, since it may result in the prosecution and incarceration of a member of the congregation.

4. The embezzler confesses. In some cases the embezzler eventually confesses. Often, this is to prevent the church from turning the case over to the IRS or the police, or to a CPA firm. Embezzlers believe they will receive "better treatment" from their own church than from the government. In many cases they are correct. It often is astonishing how quickly church members will rally in support of the embezzler once he or she confesses—no matter how much money was stolen from the church. This is especially true when the embezzler used the embezzled funds for a "noble" purpose, such as medical bills for a sick child. Many church members demand that the embezzler be forgiven. They are shocked and repulsed by the suggestion that the embezzler—their friend and fellow church member—be turned over to the IRS or the police! But is it this simple? Should church leaders join in the outpouring of sympathy? Should the matter be dropped once the embezzler confesses?

These are questions that each church will have to answer for itself, depending on the circumstances of each case. *Before forgiving the embezzler and dropping the matter, church leaders should consider the following points:*

(1) A serious crime has been committed, and the embezzler has breached a sacred trust. The church should insist, at a minimum, that the embezzler must:

• disclose how much money was embezzled

• make full restitution by paying back all embezzled funds within a specified period of time, and

• immediately and permanently be removed from any position within the church involving access to church funds

Tip. Closely scrutinize and question the amount of funds the embezzler claims to have taken. Remember, you are relying on the word of an admitted thief. Is it a realistic amount? Is it consistent with the irregularities or discrepancies that caused church leaders to suspect embezzlement in the first place? If in doubt, consider hiring a local CPA to review the amount the embezzler claims to have stolen.

(2) In many cases the embezzler will insist that he or she is not able to pay back the embezzled funds. The embezzled funds already have been spent. This presents church leaders with a difficult decision, since the embezzler has received unreported taxable income from the church. The embezzler should be informed that the embezzled funds must either be returned within a specified time, *or* a promissory note must be signed promising to pay back the embezzled funds within a specified period of time. The embezzler should be informed that failure to agree to either alternative will force the church to issue him or her a 1099 (or a corrected W-2 if the embezzler is an employee) reporting the embezzled funds as taxable income. Failure to do so will subject the church to a potential penalty (up to $10,000) for aiding and abetting in the substantial understatement of taxable income under section 6701 of the tax code.

Tip. An embezzler's biggest problem ordinarily will not be with the church or even with the local prosecutor. It will be with the IRS for failure to report taxable income. There are only two ways to avoid trouble with the IRS: (1) the embezzler pays back the embezzled funds, or (2) the church reports the embezzled funds as taxable income on a 1099 or corrected W-2.

(3) Church leaders must also remember that they owe a fiduciary obligation to the church and that they are stewards of the church's resources. Viewing the offender with mercy does not necessarily mean that the debt must be forgiven and a criminal act ignored. Churches are public charities that exist to serve religious purposes, and they are funded entirely out of charitable contributions from persons who justifiably assume that their contributions will be used to further the church's mission. These purposes may not be served when a church forgives and ignores cases of embezzlement.

Tip. The federal Employee Polygraph Protection Act prohibits most employers from requiring or even suggesting that an employee submit to a polygraph exam. Employers also are prevented from dismissing or disciplining an employee for refusing to take a polygraph exam. There is an exception that may apply in some cases—an employer may require that an employee take a polygraph exam if the employee is suspected of a specific act of theft or other economic loss and the employer has reported the matter to the police. However, the employer must follow very strict requirements to avoid liability. A church should never suggest or require that an employee submit to a polygraph exam, even in cases of suspected embezzlement, without first contacting a local attorney for legal advice.

7. THE CONSEQUENCES OF EMBEZZLEMENT

Persons who embezzle church funds face a number of consequences. Some of them may come as unpleasant surprises. Here are four of them.

• *Felony conviction.* Embezzling church funds is a felony in most states, and conviction can lead to a term in a state penitentiary. The definition of embezzlement varies slightly from state to state, but in general it refers to the wrongful conversion of property that is lawfully in your possession. The idea is that someone has legal control or custody of property or funds, and then decides to convert the property or funds to his or her own personal use.

Key point. It does not matter that the embezzler intended to pay back the embezzled funds. This intent in no way justifies or excuses the crime. The crime is complete when the funds are converted to one's own use—whether or not there was an intent to pay them back.

Key point. Sometimes an embezzler, when caught, will agree to pay back embezzled funds. This does not alter the fact that the crime of embezzlement has occurred. Of course, it may be less likely that a prosecutor will prosecute the case under these circumstances. And even if the embezzler is prosecuted, this evidence may lessen the punishment. But the courts have consistently ruled that an actual return of embezzled property does not purge the offense of its criminal nature or absolve the embezzler from punishment for his or her wrongdoing. Also, note that church officials seldom know if all embezzled funds are being returned. They are relying almost entirely on the word of the thief.

• *Tax evasion.* In many cases the embezzler's biggest concern is not the possibility of being prosecuted for the crime of embezzlement. Rather, it is the possibility of being prosecuted by the IRS for tax evasion. Embezzlers never report their illegally obtained "income" on their tax returns. Nor do they suspect that failure to do so may subject them to criminal tax evasion charges. In fact, in some cases it is actually more likely that the IRS will prosecute the embezzler for tax evasion than the local prosecutor will prosecute for the crime of embezzlement.

Example.A church accountant embezzled $212,000 in church funds. His scheme was to divert to his own use several designated offerings, and to inflate the cost of equipment that he paid for with his own funds and that the church later reimbursed at the inflated amounts. The accountant not only was found guilty of embezzlement, but he was also convicted of tax evasion because he had failed to report any of the embezzled money as taxable income. He was sentenced to a 2-year prison term, followed by 2 years of probation.

• *Recovery of property purchased with embezzled funds.* Here's a real shocker—persons who receive property purchased by the embezzler with embezzled funds may be required to return the property to the church!

Example.A church bookkeeper embezzled several thousand dollars by issuing checks to a fictitious company. He opened an account in the name of a fictitious company, issued church checks to the company for services that were never performed, and then deposited the checks in the fictitious company's account. He later withdrew the funds and purchased two automobiles which he gave to a friend. A court ruled that the friend had to give the cars back to the church, since they had been purchased with embezzled church funds. The point here, as noted by the court, is that one who acquires property with embezzled church funds may be required to transfer the property to the church.

• *Insurance company lawsuits.* As if the three consequences summarized above are not enough, embezzlers face an additional consequence—they may be sued by an insurance company that pays a claim based on the embezzlement. Many churches purchase insurance to cover financial losses due to theft or embezzlement. Insurance companies that pay out claims based on such losses are free to sue the persons responsible.

Example. A court ruled that an insurance company that paid out $26,000 to a charity because of an act of embezzlement could sue the embezzler for the full amount that it paid. Such cases illustrate an important point—a church employee or volunteer who embezzles church funds may be sued by the church insurance company if it pays out a claim based on the embezzlement.

8. CONFIDENTIALITY AND PRIVILEGED COMMUNICATIONS

Sometimes ministers learn of embezzlement through a confession by the embezzler in the course of confidential counseling. This presents the minister with a dilemma—either protect the confidentiality of the confession and refuse to disclose it, or ignore confidentiality and disclose the confession. This dilemma is compounded by the fact that some ministers have been sued for disclosing confidential information without the consent of the other person. Embezzlers may claim that they confessed their crime to their minister in confidence and in the course of spiritual counseling, with no thought that the minister would disclose the information to others.

> *Tip. Ministers who disclose confidential information without permission risk being sued for breaching their duty of confidentiality. When an employee or volunteer approaches a minister and confesses to embezzling church funds, there normally will be an expectation that the minister will keep that information in confidence. There is no sign above the minister's desk that says, "Warning: confessions of criminal activity will be promptly shared with the board or with the civil authorities."[226] Ministers who violate this expectation need to understand that they face potential legal liability for doing so— unless they have the employee's permission, in writing.*

Ministers who receive a confidential confession of embezzlement from a church employee or volunteer should not disclose this information to others, including the church board, without the person's written permission. If the embezzler does not consent to the disclosure of the confession, and refuses to meet with the board, the minister should not disclose the information to any other person. Disclosure under these circumstances could result in a lawsuit being brought against the minister and church.

Does this mean that the minister should drop the matter? Not necessarily. The minister is free to gather independent evidence that embezzlement occurred, so long as this is done without disclosing the confession. For example, the minister could persuade the church board to hire a CPA to conduct an audit of the church's financial records. Such a procedure may reveal that embezzlement has occurred. The minister also should attempt to persuade the embezzler to confess to the board.

> *Key point. Closely related to the concept of confidentiality is the clergy-penitent privilege. Ministers cannot be compelled to disclose in court the contents of confidential communications shared with them in the course of spiritual counseling.*

> *Example.Late one night, a church treasurer arranged a meeting with her priest after informing him that she "had done something almost as bad as murder." The treasurer, after requesting that their conversation be kept confidential, informed the priest that she had embezzled $30,000 in church funds. The priest, with the permission of the treasurer, sought the assistance of the church board. The board decided that the embezzlement had to be reported to the local police. The treasurer was later prosecuted for embezzling church funds, and she was convicted and sentenced to 4 months in jail despite the fact that she fully repaid the church prior to her trial. She appealed her conviction on the ground that it had been based on her confidential statements to the priest which, in her opinion, were "penitential communications" that were privileged against disclosure in court. The appeals court concluded that the statements made by the church treasurer to the priest were not privileged since they involved a "problem-solving entreaty" by the treasurer rather than "a request to make a true confession*

---

[226] *See* Lightman v. Flaum, 687 N.Y.S.2d 562 (Sup. 1999), in which the court observed: "It is beyond peradventure that, when one seeks the solace and spiritual advice and guidance of a member of the clergy, whether it be a priest, rabbi or minister, on such sensitive, personal matters as those involved in our case, this is not done as a prelude to an announcement from the pulpit."

seeking forgiveness or absolution—the very essence of the spiritual relationship privileged under the statute." That is, the treasurer sought out the priest not for spiritual counseling, but to disclose her embezzlement and to seek his counsel on how to correct the problem. The court also emphasized that the treasurer had "released" the priest from his assurance of confidentiality by consenting to his disclosure of the facts of the case to the church board members.

9. INFORMING THE CONGREGATION

Church leaders often refuse to disclose to the congregation any information about an incident of embezzlement for fear of being sued for defamation. This concern is understandable. However, serious problems can occur when the pastor or church board dismisses a long-term employee or volunteer for embezzlement and nothing is disclosed to the membership. Church leaders under these circumstances often are accused of acting arbitrarily, and there is a demand for an explanation. Refusal to respond to such demands may place the church leadership in an even worse light.

There is a possible answer to this dilemma. Many states recognize the concept of "qualified privilege." This means that statements made to others concerning a matter of common interest cannot be defamatory unless made with malice. Statements are made with malice if they are made with a knowledge that they are false, or with a reckless disregard as to their truth or falsity. In the church context, this privilege protects statements made by members to other members concerning matters of common interest. Such communications cannot be defamatory unless malice is proven. Church leaders who decide to disclose why an embezzler was dismissed can reduce the legal risk to the church and themselves by following a few basic precautions:

• Only share information with active voting members of the church—at a membership meeting or by letter. The qualified privilege does not apply if the communication is made to non-members.

• Adopt procedures that will confirm that no non-member received the information.

• Limit your remarks to factual information and do not express opinions.

• Prepare in advance a written statement that is communicated with members, and that is approved in advance by an attorney.

Key point. In some cases, it is helpful to obtain a signed confession from an individual who has been found guilty or who has confessed. If the individual consents to the communication of the confession to church members, then you can quote from the confession in a letter that is sent to members of the congregation, or in a membership meeting. Be sure that this consent is in writing.

Key point. One court ruled that a church could be sued for defamation for sharing suspicions regarding a church treasurer's embezzlement with members in a congregational meeting. The court concluded that the treasurer should have been investigated and dismissed by the board, without informing the congregation. While no other court has reached a similar conclusion, this case suggests that church leaders should disclose cases of embezzlement to the church membership only if (1) absolutely necessary (for example, to reduce congregational unrest), and (2) an attorney is involved in making this decision.

10. Avoiding False Accusations

In some cases it is not certain that embezzlement has occurred, or that a particular individual is guilty. A church must be careful in how it proceeds in these cases to avoid possible liability for defamation or emotional distress.

> ***Example.*** *A church convened a special business meeting at which the church treasurer was accused of embezzling church funds. Following this meeting the treasurer was shunned by church members who viewed her as guilty. This case is tragic, since the treasurer had been a long and devoted member of the church. Her life was ruined by the allegation, and she had to leave the church. It was later proven that she was completely innocent. She later filed a lawsuit, accusing the pastor and members of the church board of defamation. A court agreed with her, and awarded her a substantial verdict. The court pointed out that the accusation of embezzlement was based on flimsy evidence and could have easily been refuted with any reasonable investigation. The court concluded that church leaders are liable for defamation if they charge a church worker with embezzlement without first conducting a good faith investigation. The court also pointed out that the charges should not have been disclosed to the congregation, but rather should have been discussed among the church board and a decision made at that level on whether or not to dismiss the treasurer.*

This case provides church leaders with very helpful guidance in handling suspicions of embezzlement. Do not rush to judgment. Conduct a deliberate and competent investigation, and let the church board resolve the issue without involving or informing the congregation, if possible. In some cases, congregational outrage may occur following the dismissal of an embezzler by the pastor or church board, especially if nothing is communicated to the congregation about the basis for the action. In these cases the board may decide that the membership must be informed. If so, refer to the above discussion on "informing the congregation."

INSTRUCTIONAL AIDS TO CHAPTER 7

Terms

accessory use

building code

compulsory deference rule

congregational

disaffiliation

hierarchical

implied trust doctrine

neutral principles of law

nuisance

polity

reversion clause

Learning Objectives

- Understand the difference between hierarchical and congregational churches.

- Explain the neutral principles of law approach to resolving church property disputes.

- Describe how the courts resolve property disputes involving congregational churches.

- Describe how the courts resolve property disputes involving hierarchical churches.

- Identify several methods of resolving potential property disputes internally without the need for civil court intervention.

Short-Answer Questions

1. First Church is an independent church that was started in 1965 by Rev. S. The church was incorporated in 1966. The church charter recites the church's doctrinal positions, including the infallibility of the Bible. Rev. S left the church in 1995, and Rev. B became pastor. A change in membership occurred. This year, a majority of the church voted to amend the charter to remove the doctrinal position of Biblical inerrancy. A minority of members protested. A schism resulted. Which faction is entitled to the church property?

2. Member J, an elderly member of Trinity Church, died in 1960, leaving a will in which she gave $500,000 of her estate to her local church "to be used exclusively for the construction of a new sanctuary for so long as the church remains affiliated with [a named denomination], and, in the event the church ever disaffiliates from [the denomination], then to said denomination." Trinity Church constructed a new sanctuary in 1961. This year, a new minister convinces a majority of church members to vote to disaffiliate from the denomination. A minority of members claim that the majority is no longer entitled to keep the church property. The majority disagrees. What is the most likely outcome of this case?

3. Grace Church amends its bylaws to read, in part: "In the event that Grace Church shall ever disaffiliate from [a named denomination], its properties shall immediately revert to said denomination." A controversy within Grace Church leads to a division of the congregation. A majority of the members vote to disaffiliate from the denomination. Immediately after taking the vote to disaffiliate, the church membership votes to amend the bylaws by deleting the reverter clause quoted above. A minority of members contend that the property now belongs to the denomination. What is the most likely outcome of this case?

4. The *deed* to Second Church's property vests title in Second Church for so long as it is affiliated with its parent denomination, and if it ceases to be so affiliated, then title reverts to the denomination. The *church bylaws* specify that if the church ever disaffiliates from its parent denomination, then title to all church property immediately reverts to the denomination. The *bylaws of the denomination* specify that the property of any church that "departs from the stated doctrines" of the denomination shall revert to the denomination. A majority of members of Second Church vote to disaffiliate from the parent denomination. They also (1) vote to amend the bylaws by deleting the reverter clause, and (2) authorize the church board to deed the church property back to Second Church without a reverter clause. A minority of members claim that the denomination's bylaw provision requires that all church property revert to the denomination. Second Church disagrees. What is the most likely outcome of this case?

5. A majority of the members of a local church vote to disaffiliate from a parent denomination. The denomination has an ecclesiastical tribunal that rules that title to all church property now belongs to the denomination. The church ignores this ruling on the ground that it is no longer affiliated with the denomination and therefore is not subject to its rulings. Who owns the property?

6. Give four examples of "neutral principles of law."

7. The membership of a small church gradually departs from several of the original doctrinal positions of the church. Only one member is left who adheres to the original doctrines. This member claims that title to the church's property is legally vested in himself, and not in the majority. Do you agree? Explain.

8. A denomination's bylaws contain a provision specifying that the property of a local church reverts to the denomination in the event the church "deviates from the doctrines" of the denomination. Is such a clause an effective way for the denomination to maintain control over the property? Why or why not?

9. A denomination's bylaws contain a provision specifying that the property of a local church reverts to the denomination in the event the church "disaffiliates from" the denomination. Is such a clause an effective way for the denomination to maintain control over the property? Why or why not?

10. A church adopts a bylaw provision stating that the church is affiliated with a particular denomination. This provision further states that it is "not amendable." Would such a clause be legally enforceable?

11. A church adopts a bylaw provision stating that the church is affiliated with a particular denomination. This provision further states that it is amendable only by a 100% vote of all active members. Would such a clause be legally enforceable?

12. A local congregational church splits, and a minority of members who continue to adhere to the original doctrine of the church are expelled from the property. They form their own church and purchase a church building. They want to take whatever steps as are necessary to ensure that those members adhering to the original doctrine of the church will never be ousted from the property. What steps would you recommend?

13. Same facts as question 12, except that the church is hierarchical in structure.

14. A denomination purchases a church building for a mission church. What steps could the denomination take to ensure that title to the property will remain with those members who desire to remain affiliated with it?

15. A church's present facility has become too crowded, and the church decides to purchase an undeveloped lot in a residential zone of the city as a site for a new building. Neighboring landowners oppose construction on the ground that a church would increase traffic congestion, create additional hazards for children playing in the street, cause additional pollution and noise, and depreciate property values in the neighborhood. Will a civil court prohibit the church from constructing a new facility in the residential zone on the basis of the neighbors' arguments? Explain.

16. Can a city exclude a church from building a new facility anywhere within the city limits? Explain.

17. A church wants to open a private elementary school and a child care facility on its property. It is located in an area zoned for residential and church uses. Will the elementary and nursery schools be permitted uses? Explain.

18. A church is designated as a "landmark" by a local board. As a result, the church is not able to expand its present facilities. The church sues the city, claiming that this restriction violates the first amendment guaranty of religious freedom. Will the church prevail? Is there an argument the church could make that would increase its chances of winning?

19. A state office informs a church that the construction of new highway will make it necessary to demolish the church. Is the church entitled to compensation from the state? If so, in what amount?

20. Identify at least two reasons why it is important for church leaders to be familiar with the wording in deeds to church property.

21. What is a materialman's lien? How is it created? Give an example of how such a lien may be imposed on church property. What is the legal effect of such a lien?

22. A church member stumbles on a puddle of water on a tile floor in a church basement prior to a morning worship service.

    a. On the basis of what legal theory would the church most likely be responsible for the victim's injuries?

    b. What defenses are available to the church?

    c. Would such a risk be covered under a standard general liability insurance policy? If so, would the church have to pay for its own legal defense? Explain.

23. On a Saturday afternoon, several neighborhood children are playing on recreational equipment on a church's property. No church employee or member is present. One of the children is injured when she falls off of one piece of equipment. She sues the church.

    a. On the basis of what legal theory would the church most likely be responsible for the victim's injuries?

    b. What defenses are available to the church?

24. A church treasurer confesses to the pastor that he has embezzled $50,000 in church funds. Which of the following actions may expose the church to legal liability:

    a. The pastor immediately informs the board.

    b. The board notifies the police.

    c. The treasurer is prosecuted and convicted, and sentenced to prison.

    d. The pastor informs the congregation following a worship service.

25. What are "internal controls"? Identify three internal controls.

26. A church treasurer confesses to the pastor that she has embezzled $10,000 in church funds. She agrees to pay back the full amount, and resigns from her position. Answer the following questions:

    a. Has the crime of embezzlement been committed if the treasurer in fact pays back the full $10,000?

    b. Should the pastor inform the police or local prosecutor?

    c. Several members of the congregation ask the pastor why the treasurer has been removed. Should the pastor disclose the reason to the congregation? If so, how?

Discussion Questions

1. The Supreme Court has ruled that the courts are free to disregard the rulings of the ecclesiastical tribunals of religious denominations in church property disputes when no question of religious doctrine or polity is involved. For example, courts are now free to apply the "neutral principles of law" approach in resolving church property disputes even if this produces a result contrary to the ruling of a religious denomination, so long as no question of religious doctrine or polity is involved. Do you believe that the Supreme Court has given the civil courts too much authority in this context? Should the courts always be compelled to defer to the ruling of religious denominations? Explain.

2. In 1969, the Supreme Court ruled that the courts no longer can resolve church property disputes on the basis of religious doctrine. Do you agree with this decision? Do you believe that the courts should have the authority to resolve church property disputes in those cases not involving religious doctrine? Explain.

3. A church treasurer confesses to embezzlement, pays back the embezzled funds, and resigns. Should the church turn the matter over to the prosecutor? What considerations would be relevant in reaching a decision?

THE CHURCH AS EMPLOYER

Chapter summary. The employer-employee relationship is heavily regulated by state and federal law. For example, many employers must withhold federal income taxes and FICA taxes from wages paid to church employees; pay unemployment taxes; pay workers compensation insurance based on the number of their employees; refrain from discriminating against employees on the basis of age, race, color, national origin, gender, religion, or disability; pay minimum wage and overtime compensation; and comply with federal immigration requirements in the hiring of new employees. In addition, employers are often sued for wrongfully dismissing employees. Do any of these legal obligations apply to churches? After all, most churches often are employers. In addition to a minister, they may employ a secretary, custodian, bookkeeper, music director, counselor, or business administrator. As an employer, is a church subject to the same legal obligations that apply to secular employers? That is the question addressed in this chapter. Unfortunately, there is no simple answer. Federal immigration reporting requirements clearly apply to church employers. And many states treat churches no differently than secular employers for purposes of workers compensation. This means that they may have to obtain insurance to provide payments to injured employees. On the other hand, there is much confusion concerning the application of various federal employment and civil rights laws to religious organizations. For example, are churches subject to Title VII of the Civil Rights Act of 1964, which prohibits discrimination in employment on the basis of race, color, national origin, sex, or religion? Are churches subject to federal law banning discrimination in employment decisions based on the age or disability of an employee or applicant for employment? Can the employees of religious organizations organize labor unions? Must churches pay the minimum wage and overtime compensation to their employees? All of these questions are addressed in this chapter. This chapter also addresses an employer's liability for wrongful dismissal of employees. The increasingly regulatory character of our government is seen nowhere more clearly than in the context of the employer-employee relationship. Churches must be aware that some of the laws that pertain to this relationship may apply to them, and that first amendment's guaranty of religious freedom may not provide any protection.

§ 8-01   Introduction

Some important aspects of the employer-employee relationship are discussed in other chapters in this text, or in companion texts. For example, the relationship between a church and its minister is addressed fully in chapter 2. A church's payroll reporting obligations under federal law, the obligations of a church under the social security system, unemployment taxes, and compensation planning are discussed in other texts.[1]

§ 8-02   Workers Compensation

Key point 8-02. All states have enacted workers compensation laws to provide benefits to employees who are injured or become ill in the course of their employment. Benefits generally are financed through insurance premiums paid by employers. Churches are subject to workers compensation laws in most states.

---

[1]   R. HAMMAR, CHURCH AND CLERGY TAX GUIDE addresses payroll reporting, social security, and unemployment taxes. J. COBBLE AND R. HAMMAR, CHURCH COMPENSATION HANDBOOK addresses compensation planning for church employees along with the results of comprehensive compensation surveys. Both texts are published annually by the publisher of this text.

1. In General

Workers compensation laws have been enacted in all fifty states. These laws provide compensation to employees as a result of job-related injuries and illnesses. The amount of compensation is determined by law and generally is based upon the nature and extent of the employee's disability. In exchange for such benefits, employees give up the right to sue an employer directly. Fault is irrelevant under workers compensation laws. As one court has observed, "workmen's compensation, like the gentle rain from heaven, falls on the just and unjust alike."[2] The only inquiries are (1) did an employment relationship exist; (2) did the injury occur during the course of employment; and (3) what were the nature and extent of the injuries?

Workers compensation laws were enacted to give injured workers a quicker, less costly, and more certain recovery than was possible by suing an employer directly for negligence. Prior to the general acceptance of workers compensation statutes in the early part of the twentieth century, injured employees were often unsuccessful in collecting damages from their employers. When they did collect, the awards were sometimes so high that they threatened the solvency of the employer. In every case, the costs to the injured employee of suing an employer were high.

Workers compensation laws are founded on the premise that job-related injuries and illnesses are inevitable and should be allocated between the employer and the consumer as a cost of doing business. This is accomplished, in most cases, by the employer purchasing insurance to cover the costs of workers compensation benefits, with the cost of such insurance being passed on to consumers through price adjustments.[3] As a result, the ultimate cost of an employee's work-related injury or illness is borne by the consumers of the product or service that the employee was hired to produce.

2. Treatment of Churches

Churches are exempted from workers compensation laws in a few states.[4] A few more states exempt activities not carried on for monetary gain, and twelve states exempt any employer having fewer than a prescribed number of employees.[5] The crucial inquiry is whether churches are exempt from those workers compensation laws that contain no specific exemption of churches, nonprofit organizations, or organizations employing less than a prescribed number of employees.

Although very few courts have considered the question, the prevailing view is that religious organizations are subject to workers compensation laws unless specifically exempted.[6] One court stated the rule as follows:

---

[2] Thomas v. Certified Refrigerators, Inc., 221 N.W.2d 378 (Mich. 1974).

[3] Gunter v. Mersereau, 491 P.2d 1205 (Ore. 1971).

[4] One commentator states that "[t]hree states, Arkansas, Mississippi, and North Dakota, to some degree expressly exclude charitable or religious employers." A. Larson, The Law of Workmen's Compensation § 50.41 (1998) [hereinafter referred to as Larson].

[5] One authority has noted that 7 states exempt employers having fewer than 3 employees (Alabama, Arkansas, Florida, Georgia, New Mexico, North Carolina, and Virginia); 2 states exempt employers having fewer than 4 employees (Rhode Island and South Carolina); and 3 states exempt employers having fewer than 5 employees (Mississippi, Missouri, and Tennessee). Larson, supra note 4, at § 52.10.

[6] Roman Catholic Archbishop v. Industrial Accident Commission, 230 P. 1 (Cal. App. 1924); Gardner v. Trustees of Main St. Methodist Episcopal Church, 250 N.W. 740 (Iowa App. 1933); Meyers v. Southwest Region Conference Assoc., 88 So.2d 381 (La. App. 1956); Schneider v. Salvation Army, 14 N.W.2d 467 (Minn. App. 1944); Victory Baptist Temple v. Industrial Commission, 442 N.E.2d 819 (Ohio App. 1982), cert. denied 459 U.S. 1086 (1982).

[T]he fact that [a religious organization] is a purely charitable enterprise does not of itself release [it] from the obligations of our workers compensation act, which, unlike the acts of some states, does not except charitable or religious institutions, as such, from its operation, nor exclude their employees from its benefits. Where the relationship of employer and employee actually exists between a charitable institution and an injured workman, the latter is entitled to the benefits of our act, otherwise not.[7]

A federal court in Ohio rejected the claim that subjecting churches to workers compensation laws violates their constitutional rights.[8] A church argued that the state of Ohio, through its workers compensation system, had "assumed lordship over the church in direct contravention to the biblical principle that Jesus is 'head over all things to the church' (Eph. 1:22) and that 'in all things [Christ] might have preeminence' (Col. 1:18)." In addition, the church argued that "it would be a sin to contribute to workers compensation out of church funds designated for biblical purposes and that tithe and offering money . . . belongs to God." The court concluded that these allegations were "sufficient to allege infringement of [the church's] religious beliefs." However, "the mere fact that a religious practice is burdened by a governmental program does not mean that an exemption accommodating the practice must be granted," since "the state may justify a limitation on religious liberty by showing that it is essential to accomplish an overriding governmental interest." The court concluded that a state's interest in assuring the efficient administration and financial soundness of the workers compensation fund, and in protecting the interests of injured workers, amounted to a compelling interest that overrode the church's religious beliefs. The court noted that the Ohio law did exempt clergy from coverage under the workers compensation, and this limited exemption sought "to obviate excessive interference with the religious ministry of churches." Also rejected was the church's claim that the workers compensation program would impermissibly "entangle" government and church, since other courts had upheld even greater reporting requirements as constitutionally permissible. The court observed that exempting churches from coverage under the workers compensation law would force injured workers to sue churches in the civil courts, "an even more undesirable result from a scriptural standpoint."

Similarly, an Ohio state appeals court, in upholding the coverage of church employees under a state workers compensation law, observed:

The workers compensation law has been characterized by the broadest possible coverage with frequent amendments to insure that no class of employers or employees was unintentionally excluded. If the legislature had intended to exclude religious institutions, it had ample opportunity to do so. We believe that the legislature intended for employees of religious institutions to come under the protections of the [law].[9]

The court rejected the church's claim that subjecting it to the workers compensation law violated the constitutional guaranty of religious freedom. It relied on a 1982 decision of the United States Supreme Court rejecting the claim of Amish employers that their constitutional rights were violated by subjecting them to social security taxes.[10] The Supreme Court had agreed that the religious beliefs and practices of Amish employers were burdened by the social security tax, but it concluded that "because the broad public interest in

[7] Schneider v. Salvation Army, 14 N.W.2d 467, 468 (Minn. App. 1944). *See also* Hope v. Barnes Hospital, 55 S.W.2d 319 (Mo. App. 1932).
[8] South Ridge Baptist Church v. Industrial Commission, 676 F. Supp. 799 (S.D. Ohio 1987).
[9] Victory Baptist Temple v. Industrial Commission, 442 N.E.2d 819 (Ohio 1982), *cert. denied* 459 U.S. 1086 (1982). *But see* NLRB v. Catholic Bishop of Chicago, 440 U.S. 490 (1979).
[10] United States v. Lee, 455 U.S. 252 (1982).

maintaining a sound tax system is of such a high order, religious belief in conflict with the payment of taxes affords no basis for resisting the tax." Similarly, the Ohio court concluded:

> [T]he state has an "overriding governmental interest" in compensating workers and their dependents for death, occupational disease, and injury arising out of and occurring during the course of employment. To accomplish this purpose, the state has enacted comprehensive legislation creating a system which requires support by mandatory contributions by covered employers. Widespread voluntary coverage would undermine the soundness of the program and be difficult, if not impossible, to administer with a myriad of exceptions flowing from a wide variety of religious beliefs. The assessments imposed on employers to support the system are uniformly applicable to all, except as the [legislature] provides explicitly otherwise. Thus, we find no constitutionally required exemption for [a church] from the operation of the Workers Compensation Act.[11]

This same rationale has been articulated by many of the courts finding that churches are covered by workers compensation laws. As one commentator has observed: "The basic reason . . . is straightforward. It is that the compensation act expressly covers all employers, then specifically exempts such employers as it wants to exempt, so that if charitable [or religious] employers are not expressly exempted the only possible conclusion is that they are covered."[12]

This logic was directly repudiated by the United States Supreme Court in a significant ruling. In 1979, the Court ruled that in determining whether or not the National Labor Relations Board (NLRB) could assert jurisdiction over parochial school teachers, the courts must first ask whether an assertion of jurisdiction would give rise to serious constitutional questions under the first amendment.[13] If serious constitutional questions would arise, then the agency cannot assert jurisdiction over religious institutions without demonstrating an "affirmative intentions of the Congress clearly expressed" to confer such jurisdiction. This same analysis should apply to the application of workers compensation laws to churches that are opposed, on the basis of doctrinal considerations, to coverage. Obviously, few if any states expressly include churches among the employers who are covered, and accordingly there is no "affirmative intention of [the legislature] clearly expressed" to cover churches. Unfortunately, this argument has not been made by churches opposing coverage under workers compensation laws.

Some have maintained that workers compensation laws were intended to apply only to commercial businesses and thus should not be extended to nonbusiness activities such as the operation of a church. Many courts have rejected this reasoning as a basis for exempting charitable organizations from workers compensation laws, largely on the ground that the term *business* is so broad that it encompasses charitable activities.[14] One court has observed: "[I]t is well to remember that in His earthly career the Head of the Christian Church seriously declared, 'I must be about my Father's business.' Wherefore does not church activity qualify as business? This term has such recognition apart from pecuniary gain."[15] Another court, in holding that a church is engaged in a "business" subject to the state's workers compensation law when constructing a new sanctuary, observed: "The business of a church is not strictly confined to charitable purposes, spiritual uplift,

---

[11] 442 N.E.2d at 822.

[12] *See* LARSON, *supra* note 4, at § 50.42.

[13] NLRB v. Catholic Bishop of Chicago, 440 U.S. 490 (1979). *See* note 178, *infra*, and accompanying text.

[14] LARSON, *supra* note 4, at §§ 50.20-20.25.

[15] Tepesch v. Johnson, 296 N.W. 740, 745 (Iowa App. 1941). *See also* Hope v. Barnes Hospital, 55 S.W.2d 319, 321 (Mo. App. 1932) ("[T]here is nothing about the act as a whole which discloses a legislative purpose to have limited its application solely to industries and businesses within the ordinary sense of the word.").

and the saving of souls. Such, no doubt, is the ultimate object and purpose of all church associations; but it is a matter of common knowledge that, in order to attain such ends, it is also necessary to construct and maintain houses of worship in which the business of the church is carried on."[16] The court also noted that a church could be a *business* under a state workers compensation law since there was no requirement that a business be "profit-seeking."

> *Caution. If a church is not exempt from workers compensation law, what is the effect of its failure to obtain workers compensation insurance? Most workers compensation laws are compulsory. The employer has no prerogative to remain outside the system. In a "compulsory" jurisdiction, a covered employer that fails to obtain workers compensation insurance will ordinarily be subject to a direct action by an injured employee, or may be treated as a "self-insurer" and accordingly be liable for the damages prescribed by the workers compensation law.[17] A few states permit employers to elect coverage under workers compensation law. To coerce employers into electing coverage, these states impose various legal disabilities upon employers that do not elect coverage.*

Workers compensation laws only cover injuries and illnesses suffered by *employees* on the job. The term *employee* generally is defined very broadly to effectuate the objectives of the workers compensation law.[18] As a result, persons whom a church may deem self-employed for income tax purposes may be deemed employees for purposes of the workers compensation law. In some cases, however, a court may conclude that a particular worker in fact is self-employed and accordingly not covered by the workers compensation law. To illustrate, a South Carolina state appeals court ruled that a construction company president who donated his labor in constructing a new church was not eligible for workers compensation benefits following an injury on the job.[19] The court noted that workers compensation benefits are available only to "employees," and that state law defined the term *employee* as one who works for wages under a written or oral contract of hire. The injured worker in this case "donated his labor in the construction of the church. There is no evidence he was paid wages or had a right to demand payment. There is also no evidence [that he] entered into a tithing agreement with [the church] so that his work could be considered as a credit toward his tithe obligation. We find no evidence of an employment relationship between [him and the church]. He was not hired by [the church] and he was not performing any paid service for [the church]." As a result, the court concluded that the worker "was a volunteer and not an employee" under the state workers compensation law. Accordingly, the church, through its workers compensation insurance carrier, was not obligated to pay benefits to the injured worker.

> *Key point. In summary, churches are subject to workers compensation laws in most states. Nevertheless, very few churches have obtained workers compensation insurance. This will render some churches directly liable to injured employees.[20] Churches should review their liability insurance policies to ascertain what, if any, coverage exists for injured employees. Often, general liability policies exclude the insured's employees on the assumption that they are covered under a workers compensation policy. This can create a dangerous gap in coverage.*

> *Example. Is a homeless person who is paid $5 per hour by a church for performing miscellaneous services as part of a "charitable work program" an employee covered by state workers compensation law? Yes, concluded a California appeals court. A church operated a charitable program for homeless or transient*

---

[16] Greenway Baptist Church v. Industrial Commission, 636 P.2d 1264, 1267 (Ariz. App. 1981).
[17] LARSON, *supra* note 4, at §§ 67.21-67.29.
[18] Mill Street Church of Christ v. Hogan, 785 S.W.2d 263 (Ky. App. 1990).
[19] McCreery v. Covenant Presbyterian Church, 383 S.E.2d 264 (S.C. App. 1989).
[20] *See* note 17, *supra*, and accompanying text.

persons. Sometimes, the church made small payments directly to needy individuals. In other cases, when persons "wished to maintain their dignity and asked to do work," the church would attempt to find work for them to do (generally at a rate of $5 per hour). Most persons worked at most a day. However, one individual worked for nearly 4 weeks, performing a variety of tasks including roofing, gardening, digging, drywall work, painting, and laying a carpet. This individual sustained serious injuries when he fell off a ladder while doing roofing work. The victim later asserted that he had been an "employee" of the church and accordingly was entitled to workers compensation benefits. The church vigorously rejected this position, claiming that the victim was a volunteer who was paid an "honorarium" for participating in the church's charitable work program. A state agency ruled in favor of the church, noting that private charities should not be discouraged from providing aid by requiring them to pay workers compensation. The agency noted that "in fact, [the church] has apparently discontinued its benevolence fund program due to the litigation and liability issues raised in this case." The victim appealed, and a state appeals court concluded that he was an employee of the church, and as such was entitled to workers compensation benefits. The court concluded: "[The victim] worked shoulder to shoulder with covered employees, did the same work, received wages, and ran the same risks. . . . He worked at a set hourly rate, for cash wages. . . . They were hourly wages, indistinguishable in any way from the wages paid to any laborer, except that they were probably considered below the prevailing wage rate for the kind of work done."[21]

§ 8-03   Immigration Law Requirements

Key point 8-03. *Employers are required by law to confirm the identity, and eligibility to work, of all new hires. This is done by having each new hire complete Immigration and Naturalization Service Form I-9. Churches are subject to this requirement.*

Every employer in the United States is required to confirm the identity of all new employees and verify that they are either American citizens or aliens legally authorized to work in this country. These rules, enacted by Congress in the Immigration Reform and Control Act of 1986 as a means of stemming the tide of illegal immigration, represent one of the most comprehensive reporting schemes ever adopted by the federal government.[22] Religious organizations are subject to the new rules.

Key point. *One federal court ruled that churches can be forced to comply with the immigration reporting requirements even if compliance would violate their religious convictions.[23]*

The law requires employers to do the following five things:

1. Have all new employees complete the top half of Form I-9 on or before the date they start work.

2. Check original documents establishing every new employee's identity and eligibility to work. These documents ordinarily will be an original state driver's license *plus* either an original social security number card or an original or certified birth certificate. Employees must furnish the required documentation within three business days of starting work. An employee unable to produce the required documentation within three days may produce a receipt showing that he or she has applied for the required documents. The employee may then produce the documents within 21 days of starting work.

---

[21] Hoppmann v. Workers Compensation Appeals Board, 277 Cal. Rptr. 116 (Cal. App. 1991).
[22] 8 U.S.C. § 1324a.
[23] American Friends Service Committee v. Thornburgh, 718 F. Supp. 820 (C.D. Cal. 1989).

3. Complete the bottom half of Form I-9, by certifying that you inspected the original documents verifying the employee's identity and eligibility to work (discussed in the preceding paragraph).

4. Retain every Form I-9 for at least three years. If you employ a person for more than three years, you must retain the form until one year after the person leaves your employment.

5. Present a Form I-9 for inspection to an Immigration and Naturalization Service ("INS") or Department of Labor officer upon request. Note that the Form I-9 is not filed with the government. Rather, it is retained by the employer for presentation to an appropriate government representative upon request.

These reporting requirements do not apply to persons who are self-employed, but this term is defined very narrowly and would not include most ministers who report their federal income taxes as self-employed persons. The law also prohibits employers having four or more employees from discriminating against any individual (other than an alien not legally authorized to work) in hiring because of that individual's national origin.

Violations of these requirements may result in monetary penalties.

It is not certain whether or not the courts will apply the Immigration Reform and Control Act to ministers. Churches should assume that the law applies to both ministers and lay workers, unless an opinion to the contrary is received from legal counsel. Accordingly, churches should comply with the 5 requirements summarized above when hiring both ministers and lay workers.

Some commonly asked questions, with answers, are presented below.

Question. First Church hires a custodian who will be paid a flat fee of $200 per month to perform the church's limited custodial duties. He is free to choose his own hours and perform the work as he wants with no supervision or direction by the church. Must a Form I-9 be completed under these circumstances?

Answer. No. The custodian under these facts is self-employed, and therefore no Form I-9 is required.

Question. Do United States citizens need to prove they are eligible to work?

Answer. Yes. While United States citizens are automatically eligible for employment, they too must provide the required documents and complete the Form I-9.

Question. Does a church have to complete an I-9 for everyone who applies for a job?

Answer. No. A Form I-9 need only be completed for people that you actually hire. A person is "hired" when he or she begins to work for you.

Question. If someone accepts a job with our church but will not start work for a month, can a Form I-9 be completed when the employee accepts the job?

Answer. Yes.

Question. What should an employer do if the person hired is unable to provide the required documents within three days?

Answer. If an employee is unable to provide the required documents within three days, he or she must at least produce a receipt showing that he or she has applied for the documents. The employee must then produce the documents within 21 days.

Question. When do I fill out the Form I-9 if I hire someone for less than three days?

Answer. Some time before the end of the employee's first working day.

Question. What if I rehire someone who previously filled out a Form I-9?

Answer. You do not need to complete a new Form I-9 if you rehire the person within three days of the initial hire, and the person is still authorized to work.

§ 8-04   Termination of Employees

Key point 8-04. *In most states, employees who are hired for an indefinite period are considered "at will" employees. This means that the employment relationship may be terminated at will by either the employer or employee, with or without cause, and with or without notice. The courts and state legislatures have created a number of exceptions to the at will employment rule. These exceptions limit the right of an employer to terminate an at will employee. Employees who are hired for a specific term are not at will employees, and they may be terminated only if the employer has "good cause."*

1. The "At Will" Employment Rule, and Its Exceptions

In most states an employee hired for an *indefinite term* may be discharged by the employer at any time with or without cause.[24] This principle is referred to as the "at will" employment rule. The idea is that either the employer or the employee has the right to terminate the employment relationship "at will." This rule only applies to employees hired for indefinite terms of employment. The "at will" employment rule is subject to a number of exceptions in each state, including some or all of the following:

1. Discrimination based on race, color, national origin, sex, or religion. Title VII of the Civil Rights Act of 1964 is a federal law that makes it unlawful for an employer that is engaged in "commerce" and that has at least 15 employees to discharge any individual on the basis of race, color, national origin, religion, or sex (including both pregnancy and sexual harassment). The Act does permit religious organizations to discharge or otherwise discriminate against employees on the basis of religion. Many states have their own civil rights laws that ban this type of employment discrimination, and they are more likely to apply to churches since there is no "commerce" requirement and the minimum number of employees often is fewer than 15.

2. Discrimination based on age. The federal Age Discrimination in Employment Act makes it unlawful for an employer that is engaged in "commerce" and that has at least 20 employees to discharge any individual on the basis of age (if the person is at least 40 years of age). Many states have their own civil rights laws that

---

[24] *See generally* L. Larson, Unjust Dismissal (1990); W. Holloway and M. Leech, Employment Termination (1985); H. Perritt, Employee Dismissal: Law and Practice (1987).

ban this type of employment discrimination, and they are more likely to apply to churches since there is no "commerce" requirement and the minimum number of employees often is fewer than 20.

3. Discrimination based on disability. The federal Americans with Disabilities Act is a federal law that makes it unlawful for an employer that is engaged in "commerce" and that has at least 15 employees to discharge any individual on the basis of disability—if the employee is able to perform the essential functions of the job with or without reasonable accommodation by the employer (so long as the accommodation would not impose an undue hardship on the employer). The Act does permit religious organizations to discriminate against employees on the basis of religion. Many states have their own civil rights laws that ban this type of employment discrimination, and they are more likely to apply to churches since there is no "commerce" requirement and the minimum number of employees often is fewer than 15.

4. Discrimination based on military status. The Uniformed Services Employment and Reemployment Rights Act of 1994 specifies that a person "who is a member of, applies to be a member of, performs, has performed, applies to perform, or has an obligation to perform service in a uniformed service shall not be denied initial employment, reemployment, retention in employment, promotion, or any benefit of employment by an employer" on the basis of his or her military service or application for service. The law applies to all employers, including churches, whether or not they are engaged in interstate commerce and regardless of the number of their employees. The law defines "service in the uniformed services" to include "active duty, active duty for training, initial active duty for training, inactive duty training, full-time National Guard duty, and a period for which a person is absent from a position of employment for the purpose of an examination to determine the fitness of the person to perform any such duty." The law only protects employees whose military absences from an employer have not exceeded 5 years, with certain exceptions. An employee's reinstatement rights depend upon the time he or she is away on military leave.

5. Discrimination based on sexual orientation. A number of states have enacted laws prohibiting employers from discriminating against employees and applicants for employment on the basis of their sexual orientation. Most of these laws exempt religious organizations. Even without such an exemption, it is unlikely that most courts would apply such a law to the relationship between a church and its ministers.

> **Tip.** *A church should avoid dismissing an employee who is a member of a protected class under a federal or state civil rights law unless there is a legitimate, nondiscriminatory basis for the dismissal. For example, a church should avoid dismissing a 60-year-old employee unless there is clear and convincing evidence of incompetency, incapacity, insubordination, or some other nondiscriminatory basis for dismissal.*

> **Tip.** *Dismissed employees often point to "performance reviews" as proof that their termination was discriminatory. To illustrate, assume that a church conducts annual "performance reviews" for all employees, and that a disabled employee consistently received excellent or above average scores. Within a few months of such a review, the employee is dismissed because of the "poor quality" of his work. The employee sues the church, claiming that it discriminated against him on the basis of his disability. The church insists that the disability had nothing to do with its decision, but the employee points to the annual performance reviews as proof that the church's alleged basis for termination was a "pretext."*

6. Dismissal based on polygraph testing. The federal Employee Polygraph Protection Act prohibits any employer engaged in commerce, regardless of the number of employees, from requiring, requesting, suggesting, or causing any employee or applicant for employment to take a polygraph exam. This law applies to all employers, including religious organizations, engaged in an activity affecting interstate commerce. The law contains a few exceptions that ordinarily will not apply to churches. For example, employers can ask an employee to take a polygraph exam if an incident of theft or embezzlement has occurred and there is evidence pointing to the employee as the perpetrator. Employers relying on this exception must comply with several requirements. The assistance of legal counsel is essential.

7. State laws regulating off-hours conduct of employees. Many states have enacted laws prohibiting employers from disciplining employees for using lawful products (such as tobacco or alcohol) off of the employer's premises during non-working hours. Some of these laws exempt religious organizations.

8. Violation of public policy. A number of courts have protected "at will" employees by permitting them to sue their former employer if their dismissal violated "public policy."[25] To illustrate, employees terminated for refusing to commit perjury or some other crime, for performing jury service, or for filing a workers compensation claim against their employer have been allowed to sue their employer for wrongful discharge.[26] The "public policy" exception to the employer's right to discharge employees hired for indefinite terms has been narrowly construed, and is rejected by some courts. One court has rejected the argument that the "national policy" against religious discrimination is sufficiently compelling to create an exception to the "at will" doctrine in the context of religious employers.[27]

9. Employment handbook exception. Some courts have restricted an employer's right to fire "at will" employees as a result of binding assurances and commitments contained in an employee manual or handbook.[28] This view has been rejected by other courts.[29] Many courts have upheld the validity of "disclaimers" appearing in employment contracts and handbooks, which purport to disclaim any contractual meaning or intent.

10. Invasion of privacy. Some courts have allowed dismissed employees to sue their former employer if their dismissal was based on an "invasion of privacy" by the employer. Examples include dismissals based on evidence obtained through illegal telephone wiretapping, or through unauthorized access to the employee's personal property.

---

[25] *See generally* Note, *Protecting At Will Employees Against Wrongful Discharge: The Duty to Terminate Only in Good Faith,* 93 HARV. L. REV. 1816 (1980).

[26] *Id. See, e.g.,* Merkel v. Scovill, Inc., 570 F. Supp. 133 (S.D. Ohio 1983) (employee terminated for refusal to give perjured testimony); Nees v. Hocks, 536 P.2d 512 (1975) (employee terminated for performing jury duty); Hansrote v. Amer Indus. Technologies, 586 F. Supp. 113 (W.D. Pa. 1984), *aff'd,* 770 F.2d 1070 (3rd. Cir. 1985) (employee terminated for refusal to violate law); Segal v. Arrow Industries Corp., 364 So.2d 89 (Fla. App. 1978) (employee terminated for filing a workers compensation claim); Hughes Tool Co. v. Richards, 610 S.W.2d 232 (Tex. App. 1980) (employee terminated for filing a workers compensation claim).

[27] Amos v. Corporation of Presiding Bishop, 594 F. Supp. 791 (D. Utah 1984), *rev'd on other grounds,* 483 U.S. 327 (1987). *See also* Ogilbee v. Western District Guidance Center, Inc., 658 F.2d 257 (4th Cir. 1981) (employer has absolute right to terminate employees hired "at will" for an indefinite term); Fleming v. Mack Truck, Inc., 598 F. Supp. 917 (E.D. Pa. 1981) (Pennsylvania law permits the termination of "at will" employees at any time for any or no reason); Murphy v. American Home Products Corp., 451 N.Y.S.2d 770 (1982) (New York does not recognize a cause of action for retaliatory or abusive discharge); Rosby v. General Baptist State Convention of North Carolina, Inc., 370 S.E.2d 605 (N.C. App. 1988) (the "authoritative principle . . . grounded in well-established precedent in [North Carolina] is that where a contract of employment, whether oral or written, contains no provision which governs the duration or termination of employment, the employment relationship is terminable at the will of either party"); Maus v. National Living Centers, Inc., 633 S.W.2d 674 (Tex. App. 1982) (employer's right to terminate "at will" employees upheld despite employee's claim that she was wrongfully discharged in retaliation for her complaints to supervisors that patients in the nursing home where she worked were being neglected); Brower v. Homes Transportation, Inc., 435 A.2d 952 (Vt. 1981) ("at will" employees can be discharged by employer at any time with or without cause).

[28] *See, e.g.,* Carter v. Kaskaskia Community Action Agency, 322 N.E.2d 574 (Ill. App. 1975); Hamilton v. First Baptist Elderly Housing Foundation, 436 N.W.2d 336 (Iowa 1989).

[29] *See, e.g.,* Chin v. American Telephone and Telegraph Co., 410 N.Y.S.2d 737 (1978); Rosby v. General Baptist State Convention of North Carolina, Inc., 370 S.E.2d 605 (N.C. App. 1988); Reynolds Manufacturing Co. v. Mendoza, 644 S.W.2d 536 (Tex. App. 1982).

11. "True cause" letters. Although not directly limiting an employer's right to discharge an employee engaged for an indefinite term, some states have enacted laws requiring employers to provide discharged employees with a letter setting forth the "true cause" of the discharge.[30] Ordinarily, however, the employer is not obligated to provide such a letter unless it receives a written request from a discharged employee.

12. Fraud. A few courts have permitted dismissed employees to sue their former employers on the basis of fraudulent representations. For example, an employee who was assured by his employer that his position would be "permanent" was fired. While the court concluded that an employee hired on a "permanent" basis is in fact an "at will" employee who ordinarily can be terminated at any time with or without cause, the employee could sue his former employer on the basis of the fraudulent representation.[31]

13. Statutory elimination of the "at will" rule. At least one state (Montana) has enacted a statute prohibiting employers from dismissing employees except for "good cause."[32] Such a statute in effect repeals the "at will" rule.

14. Covenant of fair dealing. A few courts have ruled that a "covenant of fair dealing" is implied in every contract of employment. A dismissed employee can sue a former employer for violating this covenant.

15. Union activities. The National Labor Relations Act makes it unlawful for an employer engaged in a business or activity "affecting commerce" to discharge an employee on the basis of union activities.[33]

THE MODEL EMPLOYMENT TERMINATIONS ACT

In 1991 the Model Employment Terminations Act was adopted by the Uniform Law Commissioners and offered to the state legislatures for their consideration. So far, no state has adopted the Act, although it is likely that several will. As a result, church leaders should be familiar with the Act's major provisions, which are summarized below:

The Act prohibits employers from dismissing an employee without good cause. However, this limitation only applies to employees who have been employed by the same employer for at least one year.

The Act defines *good cause* as (1) a "reasonable basis" for termination based on such considerations as the employee's job performance or employment record; or (2) an employer's "business judgment" (for example, the reorganization, consolidation, or discontinuation of positions or departments, or "changing standards of performance for positions").

Only those employers with five or more employees are covered by the Act.

The Act does not apply to self-employed persons.

The Act permits employees to waive the Act's requirement that terminations be based on good cause by entering into a severance agreement with their employer. The Act defines the terms that must appear in such an agreement.

---

[30] *See, e.g.,* MO. REV. STAT. § 290.140.

[31] Hamlen v. Fairchilds Industries, Inc., 413 So.2d 800 (Fla. App. 1982); Silver v. Mohasco Corp., 462 N.Y.S.2d 917 (1983).

[32] THE MONTANA WRONGFUL DISCHARGE FROM EMPLOYMENT ACT (1987).

[33] *See* chapter 10, § E, *supra*, for a discussion of the meaning of the term *affecting commerce.*

2. The Dismissal of Employees Hired for a Definite Term

The courts generally hold that employees hired for a definite term may not be discharged before the end of their term of employment unless *good cause* exists. An employer need not demonstrate good cause to justify a failure to rehire an employee upon the expiration of a definite term of employment.

Good cause may include serious illness; abandonment of employment; breach of contract; refusal to perform assigned duties; incompetency; neglect of duties; misconduct; insubordination; intoxication; intemperance; doctrinal deviation; or conduct contrary to the church's moral teachings.

> *Tip. Many churches reserve the right to dismiss an employee for conduct in violation of the church's moral teachings. Unfortunately, this can lead to confusion since dismissed employees often insist that their behavior did not violate such teachings. One way to reduce the likelihood of such disputes is to state (in the church's employee handbook, or in some other appropriate document) that the church board is the sole arbiter of what behavior violates the church's moral teachings.*

An employee who is discharged without good cause before the end of a specified term of employment generally is entitled to recover as damages the salary and other benefits agreed upon for the remainder of the employment term less the amount the employee earned, or with reasonable diligence might have earned, from other employment of the same or a similar nature during the period.

> *Key point. The civil courts generally will not interfere with a church's decision to terminate a minister's services. This subject is covered fully in chapter 2.*

3. Severance Agreements

Churches should consider using a severance agreement when a decision is made to dismiss an employee. Such agreements set forth the terms and conditions of an employee's separation. In most cases, the employer agrees to pay the employee a specified sum of money (often expressed in terms of so many weeks of pay) in exchange for the employee's consent to the termination of the employment relationship and a release of any legal claims against the employer. Such agreements should be drafted by an attorney to ensure their enforceability.

4. Communicating with Other Employees and the Congregation

The dismissal of an employee can be a traumatic experience. When an employee is dismissed who has been employed by the church for many years, there often is a desire by other employees and the congregation itself for information about the dismissal. After all, what could this trusted and faithful employee have done to warrant such harsh treatment? Often, church leaders resist sharing any of the details, fearing they will be sued if they do. This concern is understandable. However, problems can occur when nothing is disclosed to the staff or membership. Church leaders under these circumstances often are accused of acting arbitrarily, and there is a demand for an explanation. Refusal to respond to such demands may place the church leadership in an even worse light.

There is a possible answer to this dilemma. Many states recognize the concept of "qualified privilege." This means that statements made to others concerning a matter of common interest cannot be defamatory unless made with malice. Statements are made with malice if they are made with a knowledge that they are false, or with a reckless disregard as to their truth or falsity. In the church context, this privilege protects statements made by members to other members concerning matters of common interest. Such communications cannot be defamatory unless malice is proven. Church leaders who decide to disclose why an employee was dismissed can reduce the legal risk to the church and themselves by following a few basic precautions:

- Only share information with active voting members of the church—at a membership meeting or by letter. The qualified privilege does not apply if the communication is made to non-members.

- Adopt procedures that will confirm that no non-member received the information.

- Limit your remarks to factual information and do not express opinions.

- Prepare a written statement that will be shared with members, and have it reviewed in advance by an attorney.

Tip. In some cases, it is helpful to obtain a signed confession from an employee who is being terminated because of misconduct. The confession should state that it can be read to the staff and congregation.

Example. A church business administrator, upon returning from a two-month leave of absence, suspected that another church employee had been signing unauthorized church checks. She shared her concerns with the church's finance council. The employee later sued the church, claiming that she had been defamed. A Minnesota appeals court dismissed the lawsuit. It noted that a person who makes a defamatory statement may be protected from legal liability by a "qualified privilege." Statements are protected by a qualified privilege if they address a matter of common concern among church members. This means that they cannot be defamatory. The court cautioned that a qualified privilege may be lost if it is "abused," meaning that the person making defamatory statements did so with "malice." Malice exists if the statements were made out of "ill will and improper motives or . . . wantonly for the purpose of injuring the [victim]." Was the church guilty of malice in this case? The court rejected the employee's claim that malice was established by the church's failure to publish a retraction, and by its failure to investigate fully the facts of the case before making the allegedly defamatory statements. The court cautioned that the following factors may tend to establish malice: (1) exaggerated language; (2) the character of the language; (3) an extensive distribution of the defamatory statements; and (4) "other matters in excess of the privilege." The court concluded: "Employers have legitimate interests in protecting themselves against dishonest employees. Employers are entitled to a qualified privilege if they have reasonable grounds for believing in the validity of a statement, even though hindsight might show the statement to be false. [The business administrator] was understandably bothered by the situation and took steps to address the apparent breach of authority. She spoke to the person who chairs the committee responsible for monitoring church funds and, on his request, to the entire finance council. [Her] actions were reasonable to protect her employer."[34]

Example. A New Jersey court ruled that a church acted properly in dismissing its music director for criminal acts.[35] The music director entered into a one-year employment contract with a church. The contract contained the following provision for termination: "The parties involved shall give notice of termination of employment at least thirty days in advance of the termination. The termination time must be completed by the employee or if the employer does not wish the termination to be completed the employer shall fulfill all

---

[34] Kozar v. Church of St. John the Baptist, 1997 WL 89144 (unpublished decision, Minn. App. 1997).

[35] McGarry v. Saint Anthony of Padua Roman Catholic Church, 704 A.2d 1353 (N.J. Super. 1998) (quoting Restatement (Second) of Agency, § 380 and comment).

contractual financial agreements." After working for the church for a few months, the music director was arrested for possession of illegal anabolic steroids. It was later disclosed that the music director had been taking steroids to assist him with bodybuilding, and that he had previously ordered several shipments of steroids shipped directly to the church to avoid detection. One package recovered by the police contained 290 tablets of methandrostenolone, 240 tablets of oxandrolone, and 9 vials of decadurabolin. A few days later the pastor of the church learned of his music director's arrest from a newspaper article. A few days later, the music director's employment was terminated. The music director sued the church for wrongful termination. A state appeals court, in rejecting the music director's claim, noted that "in every contract there is an implied covenant of good faith and fair dealing." The music director violated this covenant by his behavior: "Even where, as here, the employee performs the duties contracted for satisfactorily, criminal activity by the employee can justify his discharge for breach of an employment contract. . . . It is clear that [the music director] intentionally ordered the anabolic steroids for his personal use and had them shipped to [the church] address. This constituted a breach of the implied conditions of [his] contract of employment. The receipt of anabolic steroids at work indirectly involved [the church] in the commission of a criminal offense and constituted gross misconduct." Second, the court concluded that employees have a "duty of good conduct." It based this duty on the following language from a respected legal treatise: "[An employee] is subject to a duty not to conduct himself with such impropriety that he brings disrepute upon the [employer] or upon the business in which he is engaged . . . . The nature of the business and the position of the agent determine what reputation the agent has agreed to maintain and what conduct can be expected from him. . . . [A]lthough the employer has no control over the conduct of such persons when they are not engaged in his work, he has such interest in the general integrity of his business household that it may be a breach of duty for one of them to acquire a deserved reputation for loose living, or to commit a serious crime." The court concluded that "when the duty of good conduct is violated by an employee, the employer has good cause to terminate a contract and the termination will not support a cause of action for breach of contract."

Example. *An Ohio court ruled that a preschool teacher who was dismissed for striking a child could not sue the preschool for defamation. A preschool director entered a classroom of 2-year-old children upon hearing hysterical crying. A worker informed the director that the teacher had struck the child. The director noticed a hand-mark on the child's face. Upon being questioned, the boy stated (and demonstrated) that the teacher had put her hand over his mouth and shook him. The teacher was confronted with this information, but denied it. However, she offered no other explanation as to the boy's condition. The director was not satisfied that the teacher was being truthful, and dismissed her. The director later reported the incident to the boy's mother, and to the state department of human services. The fired teacher sued the center, alleging that she had been defamed by the director's communications to the boy's mother, to other workers at the center, to the president of the center's board of directors, and to the state. A state appeals court rejected the teacher's claims. It noted that the director was required by state law to report suspected cases of abuse to the department of human services, and so this communication did not constitute defamation. Further, there was no evidence that the director ever informed other workers at the center as to the reason that the teacher had been terminated. With respect to the communications made to the boy's mother, and to the president of the center's board of directors, the court concluded that such communications "enjoyed at least a qualified privilege" since they were matters of "common interest." As such, the communications would not be defamatory unless they were made with "malice." The court observed that "the record is devoid of evidence of actual malice on the part of [the director in communicating] the statements. On the contrary, the record reveals that [she] acted properly and reasonably under the circumstances."[36]*

---

[36] Lail v. Madisonville Child Care Project, 561 N.E.2d 1063 (Ohio App. 1990).

Example. An Ohio court ruled that a former teacher at a church-operated school could not sue school officials for defamation since the allegedly defamatory statements made by the school officials concerned a matter of "common interest" and accordingly were privileged. The teacher was convicted of contributing to the delinquency of a minor for providing alcohol to one of his students. He advised school officials of his conviction, and was permitted to remain on the faculty both as a teacher and yearbook adviser. A few years later, his teaching contract was not renewed. A priest was hired to replace him as teacher and yearbook adviser. When the former teacher continued to associate with student members of the yearbook staff, two priests (who served as administrators at the school) contacted the parents of two of these students and informed them that the former teacher had been convicted of "corrupting a minor," implied that he was a homosexual, and recommended that they not permit their sons to associate with such a person. The former teacher learned of these statements, and sued the priests for defamation. A state appeals court ruled that the statements made by the priests were not defamatory since they were protected by a qualified privilege. It observed: "As a matter of public policy, educators and parents share a common interest in the training, morality and well-being of the children in their care. . . . [S]tatements made by a teacher and a principal which relate to a former teacher's . . . commission of acts which are potentially harmful to the well-being of a student, when made to the parents of the student involved, can be motivated by a common interest in the education or safety of that student."[37]

Example. A Texas court ruled that a church was not liable for defaming a former secretary as a result of statements made to church members claiming that she had misappropriated church funds. A church operated a private school. Its minister of education, who also served as principal of the school, resigned after admitting that he misappropriated church funds, destroyed church records, forged signatures, and committed other criminal acts. He later pleaded guilty to criminal charges for his admitted conduct in misappropriating school funds. He informed the church that a woman who served as a secretary at the school participated in the misappropriations. After an audit confirmed the principal's accusations the church asked the secretary to resign. The church published (1) a letter to its members claiming that the secretary misappropriated school funds; (2) a letter to the school children's parents claiming that the secretary deposited tuition funds into the wrong accounts and later used the funds for her personal benefit; destroyed checks, financial records, and bank records; forged signatures; covered up these indiscretions; received seventy dollars extra per pay period for nearly two years as well as other undocumented "reimbursements"; and (3) a report to the church members reporting the secretary's resignation and claiming that she deposited tuition funds into the wrong account and then used the funds to support programs and individuals outside of and over the budget adopted by the congregation. At a meeting of church members, church officials orally accused the secretary of depositing tuition funds into the wrong account and then using the funds for her personal benefit or for other people or projects as she and the principal saw fit; destroying checks, bank records, and financial records; forging signatures; and covering up many of these indiscretions. The secretary later sued the church and the individual members of the church audit committee, claiming that the church's actions defamed her. A state appeals court rejected all of the secretary's claims. It concluded that words that otherwise might be defamatory may be "legally excused" by a qualified privilege. It observed: "All of the members of [the church] have a common interest in the church's use of their financial contributions to the church; thus, the members have a common interest in information about those funds. The members who made the statements in question reasonably believed that the misappropriation took place and that the board, the members, and the parents shared a common interest in the use of the funds and information about those funds. [The church] reasonably believed that these people were entitled to know of the misappropriation. [It]

---

37 McCartney v. Oblates of St. Francis de Sales, 609 N.E.2d 216 (Ohio App. 1992).

522

had a duty to perform for the board, the members, and the parents. [It] made the communications without actual malice. [The principal] confessed his and [the secretary's] involvement, and [he] later pleaded guilty to criminal charges. [The church's] audit confirmed all of [his] statements. [The secretary] never swore under oath in an affidavit in opposition to summary judgment that the statements were lies. [She] kept the misappropriated funds in a shoe box in her closet and returned the funds when accused. [The principal] testified that the statements were true. [The secretary] admits receiving personal benefit from the misappropriation of funds. [She] admits she destroyed records. [The church] neither entertained serious doubts as to the truth of the statements nor made these statements with a high degree of awareness of their probable falsity. The communications appeared accurate, [the church] reasonably believed [the principal], and church members and parents who received information had an interest in the funds and information about the funds."[38]

§ 8-05   Introduction to Federal Employment and Civil Rights Laws — The "Commerce" Requirement

Key point 8-05. *Congress has enacted a number of employment and civil rights laws regulating employers. These laws generally apply only to employers that are engaged in interstate commerce. This is because the legal basis for such laws is the constitutional power of Congress to regulate interstate commerce. As a result, religious organizations that are not engaged in commerce generally are not subject to these laws. In addition, several of these laws require that an employer have a minimum number of employees. The courts have defined "commerce" very broadly, and so many churches will be deemed to be engaged in commerce.*

Congress has enacted a variety of employment and civil rights laws that apply to some churches and religious organizations. These include Title VII of the Civil Rights Act of 1964, the Age Discrimination in Employment Act, the Americans with Disabilities Act, the Fair Labor Standards Act, the National Labor Relations Act, the Employee Polygraph Protection Act, and the Occupational Safety and Health Act. See Table 8-1 for a summary of the more important laws. Before turning to a direct examination of these laws, it is important to recognize that they all were enacted by Congress under its constitutional authority to regulate interstate commerce. As a result, these laws apply only to employers engaged in a business, industry, or activity "affecting commerce."[39] The National Labor Relations Act defines *affecting commerce* as "in commerce, or burdening or obstructing commerce or the free flow of commerce, or having led to or tending to lead to a labor dispute burdening or obstructing commerce or the free flow of commerce."[40]

Is a church engaged in a business, industry, or activity affecting commerce? This is a complex question for which no simple answer can be given. In general, the answer in a particular case will depend upon how narrowly or expansively a court construes the term *affecting commerce*, and upon the size of the church and the nature of its operations. Small churches employing no more than one or two persons ordinarily are not engaged in an activity affecting commerce. They are not involved in commercial activities; they sell no product or service; they are financed through voluntary contributions; they exist to fulfill noncommercial purposes; and they function outside the economic marketplace. Further, governmental regulation of such churches carries with it the hazard of excessive governmental entanglement with religion, which is prohibited by the

---

[38] Hanssen v. Our Redeemer Lutheran Church, 938 S.W.2d 85 (Tex. App. 1997).

[39] 29 U.S.C. § 142 (National Labor Relations Act); 29 U.S.C. § 203 (Fair Labor Standards Act); 29 U.S.C. § 630(b) (Age Discrimination in Employment Act); 29 U.S.C. § 652 (Occupational Safety and Health Act); 42 U.S.C. § 2000e(b) (Title VII of the Civil Rights Act of 1964). A more limited standard applies under the Fair Labor Standards Act (discussed later in this chapter).

[40] 29 U.S.C. § 152(7).

first amendment.[41] Congress has observed that nonprofit employers in general are "not engaged in 'commerce' and certainly not in interstate commerce . . . [and] frequently assist local governments in carrying out their essential functions, and for this reason should be subject to exclusively local jurisdiction."[42]

Nevertheless, a church or other religious organization engaged in significant commercial activities may be considered to be affecting commerce. To illustrate, a federal appeals court concluded that a church-operated school was engaged in commerce.[43] A disabled woman who was turned down for a job at the school filed a lawsuit claiming that the school discriminated against her in violation of the federal Americans with Disabilities Act. The ADA prohibits employers engaged in an activity "affecting commerce" *and* having at least 15 employees from discriminating in any employment decision on account of the disabled status of an employee or applicant for employment who is able to perform the essential functions of the job with or without reasonable accommodation by the employer. Was the school engaged in an industry affecting commerce? The court noted that the ADA defines this crucial term as "any activity, business, or industry in commerce or in which a labor dispute would hinder or obstruct commerce or the free flow of commerce." The church insisted that it was not an "industry affecting commerce" under this definition, but the court concluded that it was. It relied on an earlier case in which a federal appeals court found that an employer affected commerce since (1) it purchased products and supplies from out of state; (2) its employees traveled out of state on the employer's business; and (3) its employees made interstate telephone calls.[44] The court concluded:

> *The school and its employees have engaged in activities that affect commerce. The school purchased supplies and books from companies outside of the District of Columbia. . . . Approximately five of its employees commuted to the school from outside of the District. Employees made interstate telephone calls and mailed letters to locations outside of the District of Columbia.*

However, the court cautioned that the woman had not provided any evidence that the church had engaged in activities affecting interstate commerce, and so "this issue is inconclusive." The court added that "[we] presume that some of the same factors exist with respect to the church." There is little doubt that the court believed that the church was engaged in commerce.

> *Example. A church is accused of engaging in sex discrimination in violation of Title VII of the Civil Rights Act of 1964. The church insists that it is not covered by Title VII since it is not engaged in commerce. The church operates a web page on the internet. This single factor may persuade a court that the church is engaged in commerce.*

> *Example. A church is accused of engaging in age discrimination in violation of federal law. The church insists that it is not covered by this law since it is not engaged in commerce. The church conducts a weekly 15-minute radio broadcast. This single factor indicates that the church is engaged in commerce.*

> *Key point. The United States Supreme Court issued a ruling in 1997 that defined commerce very broadly. The case is important because it involved a religious organization (a church-affiliated summer camp). This case makes it more likely that churches and other religious organizations will be deemed to be engaged in commerce. The Court observed: "Even though [the] camp does not make a profit, it is unquestionably*

---

[41] NLRB v. Catholic Bishop of Chicago, 440 U.S. 490 (1979).

[42] H.R. Rep. No. 245, 80th Cong., 1st Sess. 12 (1947). *See generally* Laycock, *Towards a General Theory of the Religion Clauses: The Case of Church Labor Relations and the Right to Church Autonomy*, 81 COLUM. L. REV. 1373 (1981).

[43] Equal Employment Opportunity Commission v. St. Francis Xavier Parochial School, 117 F.3d 621 (D.C. Cir. 1997).

[44] Martin v. United Way, 829 F.2d 445 (3d Cir.1987).

IS A CHURCH ENGAGED IN COMMERCE?

There are a number of factors indicating that a church or other religious organization is engaged in commerce. These include any one or more of the following:

• operation of a private school

• sale of products (such as literature or tapes) to persons or churches in other states

• purchase of products (Sunday School literature, office equipment, etc.) from out-of-state vendors

• persons from other states attend your church

• operation of a "web page" on the internet

• operation of a commercial or "unrelated trade or business"

• employees travel out-of-state

• employees make out-of-state telephone calls

• the church sends mail out-of-state

• television or radio broadcasts

engaged in commerce, not only as a purchaser . . . but also as a provider of goods and services. . . . The attendance of these campers necessarily generates the transportation of persons across state lines that has long been recognized as a form of "commerce" . . . . Our cases have frequently applied laws regulating commerce to not-for-profit institutions. . . . The nonprofit character of an enterprise does not place it beyond the purview of federal laws regulating commerce. We have already held that the commerce clause is applicable to activities undertaken without the intention of earning a profit. . . . We see no reason why the nonprofit character of an enterprise should exclude it from the coverage of [the commerce clause]."[45]

The United States Supreme Court has ruled that an evangelistic association was engaged in activities affecting commerce since it was engaged in several commercial enterprises, including advertising, landscaping, service stations, restaurants, manufacture and sale of candy and clothing, record keeping, construction, plumbing, sand and gravel, electrical contracting, hog farms, feed and farm supplies, real estate development, and freight hauling.[46] Similarly, a federal appeals court concluded that a religious organization that operated a hotel on a commercial basis was engaged in a business or activity affecting commerce.[47]

The United States Department of Labor has enacted a regulation specifying that

[a]ctivities of eleemosynary, religious, or educational organizations may be performed for a business purpose. Thus, where such organizations engage in ordinary commercial activities, such as

---

[45] Camps Newfound/Owatonna v. Town of Harrison, 117 S. Ct. 1590 (1997).
[46] Tony and Susan Alamo Foundation v. Secretary of Labor, 471 U.S. 290 (1985).
[47] NLRB v. World Evangelism, Inc., 656 F.2d 1349 (9th Cir. 1981).

operating a printing and publishing plant, the business activities will be treated under the Act the same as when they are performed by the ordinary business enterprise.[48]

The National Labor Relations Board has ruled that the publishing and distribution of Sunday school literature by a religious denomination is an activity affecting commerce.[49] It is also possible that a church that operates a child care facility, an elementary school, a home for the aged, or an orphanage is engaged in an activity affecting commerce.

§ 8-05.1 — Counting Employees

> *Key point 8-05.1. Many federal employment and civil rights laws apply only to those employers having a minimum number of employees. In determining whether or not an employer has the minimum number of employees, both full-time and part-time employees are counted. In addition, employees of unincorporated subsidiary ministries of a church are counted. The employees of incorporated subsidiary ministries may be counted if the church exercises sufficient control over the subsidiary.*

Some federal civil rights and employment laws apply only to employers having a minimum number of employees. To illustrate, employers must have 15 or more employees to be subject to the Americans with Disabilities Act and Title VII of the Civil Rights Act of 1964. An employer must have at least 20 employees to be subject to the federal age discrimination law. Such laws raise two important questions: (1) which employees are counted, and (2) are a parent organization and its affiliates or subsidiaries treated as a single employer? These questions will be addressed separately.

1. Which Employees Are Counted?

Which employees should be counted in determining whether or not an employer has the minimum number of employees specified by a federal employment or civil rights law? Should part-time employees be counted? Hourly workers? Temporary workers? Persons on vacation or sick leave? These laws generally require that an employer have the minimum number of employees "for each working day in each of 20 or more calendar weeks in the current or preceding year." The United States Supreme Court has applied the "payroll method" for counting employees.[50] Under this approach, an "employee" is any person with whom the employer has an *employment relationship* during the week in question. The Court explained: "Under the interpretation we adopt . . . all one needs to know about a given employee for a given year is whether the employee started or ended employment during that year and, if so, when. He is counted as an employee for each working day after arrival and before departure." As a result, the Supreme Court's decision repudiates the argument made by the church, school, and preschool that they did not meet the 15 employee requirement since less than 15 employees were employed on Saturdays and Sundays.

> *Example. A Louisiana court dismissed a Title VII sex discrimination claim brought against a church by a dismissed female choir director. The court noted that the church had fewer than 15 employees and therefore it was not subject to Title VII's ban on sex discrimination.[51]*

---

[48] 29 C.F.R. § 779.214.
[49] Sunday School Board of the Southern Baptist Convention, 92 N.L.R.B. 801 (1950). *But cf.* Lutheran Church Missouri Synod, 109 N.L.R.B. 859 (1954).
[50] Walters v. Metropolitan Educ. Enterprises, Inc., 117 S.Ct. 660 (1997).
[51] Steed v. St. Paul's United Methodist Church, 1999 WL 92626 (La. App. 1999).

TABLE 8-1
APPLICATION OF SELECTED FEDERAL EMPLOYMENT AND CIVIL RIGHTS LAWS TO RELIGIOUS ORGANIZATIONS

Statute	Main Provisions	Covered Employers
Title VII of 1964 Civil Rights Act	bars discrimination in employment decisions on the basis of race, color, national origin, sex, or religion	• 15 or more employees plus interstate commerce • religious employers can discriminate on the basis of religion
Age Discrimination in Employment Act	bars discrimination in employment decisions on the basis of age (if 40 or over)	20 or more employees plus interstate commerce
Americans with Disabilities Act	bars discrimination against a qualified individual with a disability who can perform essential job functions with or without reasonable employer accommodation (that does not impose undue hardship)	• 15 or more employees plus interstate commerce • religious employers can discriminate on the basis of religion
Employee Polygraph Protection Act	employers cannot require, request, suggest, or cause any employee or applicant to take a polygraph exam	interstate commerce (no minimum number of employees)
Immigration Reform and Control Act	I-9 form must be completed by all new employees demonstrating identity and eligibility to work	all employers
Fair Labor Standards Act	requires minimum wage and overtime pay to be paid to employees	employers who employ employees who are engaged in commerce or in the production of goods for commerce, as well as any employee "employed in an enterprise engaged in commerce or in the production of goods for commerce"
Family and Medical Leave Act of 1993	eligible employees qualify for up to 12 weeks unpaid leave per year because of (1) birth or adoption of child, including care for such child, or (2) caring for spouse, child, or parent with a serious health condition, or (3) the employee's serious health condition	50 or more employees plus interstate commerce
Occupational Safety and Health Act	mandates a safe and healthy workplace for covered employees	an organization "engaged in a business affecting commerce who has employees"
Older Workers Benefit Protection Act of 1991	bars employees at least 40 years old from "waiving" their rights under age discrimination law unless the waiver meets strict legal standards	20 or more employees plus interstate commerce

Tip. In summary, in determining whether an employer has 15 or more employees "for each working day in each of 20 or more calendar weeks in the current or preceding year," each week in which an employer has an employment relationship with 15 or more employees is counted.

Tip. The Supreme Court acknowledged that self-employed persons will appear on an employer's payroll, and that they should not be counted. It clarified that in counting employees under the "payroll method," only those persons who in fact are employees are counted.

Key point. One church insisted it was open on Saturdays and Sundays, and that a few of its employees (mostly its ministers) worked on those days. Therefore, if the work week is defined to include Saturdays and Sundays, then it would not have the required number of employees "for each working day" since only a few persons worked on those days. Obviously, many churches have a few employees whose duties require them to work on Saturdays or Sundays. However, since the number of employees who work on these days usually is minimal, such churches could argue that they are not covered by any civil rights law (federal or state) that applies to employers having a specified number of employees "for each working day in each of 20 or more calendar weeks in the current or preceding year." This argument was rejected by a federal appeals court on the basis of the Supreme Court's "payroll method" approach to counting employees.

2. Employees of Affiliated Organizations

Should the employees of an affiliated or subsidiary organization be combined with the employees of a parent organization when counting employees? That is, should the employees of a school, preschool, retirement facility, or other church-affiliated ministry be combined with the employees of the church when counting employees for purposes of applying federal civil rights and employment laws? This is an important question, given the large number of churches that operate affiliated ministries.

A federal appeals court addressed these questions in an important decision.[52] A woman (the "plaintiff") with multiple sclerosis claimed that she was not considered for a position as music director at a church-operated school because of her disability. She filed a complaint with the Equal Employment Opportunity Commission (EEOC), which determined that she had been a victim of discrimination. The EEOC sued the church and its school, claiming that they both had violated the Americans with Disabilities Act (ADA) as a result of their refusal to "accommodate" the plaintiff's disability, and their failure to hire her because of her disability. The church and school argued that they were not covered by the ADA since they each had less than 15 employees. The plaintiff asserted that under the so-called "single employer doctrine" the court should combine the employees of the church, the school, and a preschool to come up with the required 15 employees.

Under the single employer doctrine, separate entities that represent a "single, integrated enterprise" may be treated as a single employer for purposes of meeting the 15 employee test. The plaintiff asserted that the church operated the school and the preschool, and therefore these three entities should be considered as one.

In deciding whether or not the church, school, and preschool were a "single, integrated enterprise," a federal district court applied a four-part test announced by the Supreme Court in 1965.[53] This test focuses on the following four factors:

---

[52] Equal Employment Opportunity Commission v. St. Francis Xavier Parochial School, 117 F.3d 621 (D.C. Cir. 1997).
[53] Radio Union v. Broadcast Services, 380 U.S. 255 (1965).

(1) interrelation of operations

(2) common management

(3) centralized control of labor relations, and

(4) common ownership or financial control

The court clarified that "the absence or presence of any single factor is not conclusive," and that "control over the elements of labor relations is a central concern." The court cautioned that a plaintiff "must make a substantial showing to warrant a finding of single employer status," and that

> there must be sufficient indicia of an interrelationship between the immediate corporate employer and the affiliated corporation to justify the belief on the part of an aggrieved employee that the affiliated corporation is jointly responsible for the acts of the immediate employer.

The court referred to an earlier federal appeals court case finding that the entities must be "highly integrated with respect to ownership and operations" in order for single employer status to be found.

The court's analysis of each of the four factors is summarized below.

(1) interrelation of operations

The court referred to combined accounting records, bank accounts, lines of credit, payroll preparation, telephone numbers, or offices as examples of "interrelated" operations. However, it concluded that there was insufficient interrelationship between the church, school, and preschool to consider them as a single employer. It did acknowledge that the pastor signed the school's budget, that a room in the church occasionally was used for school purposes, and that school children ate in a room that was also used by the preschool. However, the following factors demonstrated that there was insufficient interrelationship among the three entities (church, school, and preschool) to treat them as a single employer: (1) the school had a separate budget; (2) daily operations of the three entities (church, school, and preschool) were independent; (3) hours of operation of the three entities were significantly different (preschool was open earlier and later than the school, and the church alone was open on Saturdays and Sundays); (4) each of the three entities was operated by a different staff; (5) each of the three entities had its own principal or administrator; (6) each entity had different employment contacts and practices; (7) the school was located in a different building from the church and preschool; and (8) while the schoolchildren ate lunch in a room that was also used by the preschool, they did not use the room at the same time.

(2) common management

A second factor to consider in deciding whether or not to treat separate entities as a "single employer" is the presence or absence of common management. The court noted that the "focus of this factor . . . is on the existence of common directors and officers." In other words, are the directors and officers of the separate entities the same? The court concluded that this factor was not present in this case: "Here, there are separate management structures for the church, the day care center, and the school. These structures do not continuously monitor one another. The circumstances present here do not warrant a finding of common management."

The court cautioned that common management will exist when one organization runs another organization "in a direct, hands-on fashion, establishing the operating practices and management practices."

(3) centralized control of labor operations

A third factor to consider in deciding whether or not to treat separate entities as a "single employer" is the presence or absence of "centralized control of labor operations." The court observed that "the control required to meet the test of centralized control of labor relations is not potential control, but rather actual and active control of day-to-day labor practices." This test was not met, the court concluded:

The enterprises here have separate employees, directors, and employment practices. The sole way in which the church is involved with the labor practices of the school is in the final phases of hiring. Plaintiff asserts that the pastor "interviews all applicants for the school," but plaintiff's own exhibits contradict this assertion. Rather, the principal and assistant principal screen resumes and conduct interviews; the pastor does not become involved until the end of the process, after the principal and assistant principal have selected two or three finalists, at which point he gives his input. When there is a disagreement, the pastor makes the final decision. The entities have different administrators and distinct labor pools. Plaintiff does not present adequate evidence of day-to-day active control by the church of the school's labor relations to justify a finding that the entities should be treated as a single employer.

(4) common ownership or financial control

A fourth factor to consider in deciding whether or not to treat separate entities as a "single employer" is the presence or absence of "common ownership or control." The court noted that "there is common ownership of the property and the buildings in which the day care center, the church, and the school are located, and that the pastor must sign the school's budget." On the other hand, the court noted that the church was part of the Archdiocese of Washington, "which is the corporate entity that owns the property and the buildings. Further . . . the Archdiocese has ultimate control over the school's budget." The court cautioned that "even if the Archdiocese were a party, common ownership alone is not enough to establish that separate employers are an integrated enterprise." The court continued:

Even though the Archdiocese, rather than the church, is the owner and locus of financial control, the church does have some intermediary supervisory power over the school. However, given (1) the Archdiocese's ultimate control over the school's budget, (2) the Archdiocese's status as owner of the property and buildings, and (3) the fact that the school, the church, and the day care center have separate budgets, the court finds that this factor does not support a finding that the entities constitute a single employer. Accordingly, the court declines to apply the integrated enterprise doctrine to consolidate defendants into constituting a single employer.

The EEOC appealed the district court's dismissal of the lawsuit. A federal appeals court for the District of Columbia reversed the trial court's dismissal of the case on the ground that there was insufficient evidence to support the trial court's conclusion that the church, school, and preschool should not be treated as a single employer in applying the 15 employee requirement. Of most significance to the appeals court was the fact that the record did not reveal whether or not the church, school, and preschool were one corporate legal entity, or three separate entities. The court observed that "we cannot answer a question of utmost importance--whether the school (and the day care center) are distinct legal entities or whether they are merely parts of one legal entity--the church."

Why was this question so important? Because the Supreme Court's 4 factor test (discussed above) has only been applied in the context of *separate legal entities.* In other words, if the church, school, and preschool were a single corporate entity, with the school and preschool operating under the church's corporate umbrella, then they presumably would be treated as a single employer for purposes of applying the 15 employee requirement. There would be no need to apply the Supreme Court's 4 factor test. This test would be applied only if the three entities were legally distinct—that is, they were each separately incorporated. Only then would the 4 factor test be applied to determine whether or not the three entities were sufficiently related to be treated as a single employer for purposes of the 15 employee requirement.

The court conceded that "the door is at least open to apply the test to entities that have different names (a condition satisfied here)--even if they are not legally distinct (a condition that may or may not be satisfied here)," and that "leaving the door open allows the possibility that a single legal entity could . . . encompass divisions that are sufficiently independent of one another to warrant being treated as distinct employers within the meaning of the employment discrimination statutes." The court added that "such cases are perhaps rare, but we see no reason to think they are non-existent."

> **Key point.** *The court sent the case back to the trial court for further proceedings to determine whether or not the church, school, and preschool were a single entity or three separate legal entities. If they were a single entity, it would be much more likely that they would be treated as a single employer for purposes of applying the 15 employee requirement.*

In summary, the appeals court's analysis can be reduced to the following points:

Church with no affiliated entities. Consider only the church's employees in applying the 15 employee test under the Americans with Disabilities Act (or any other federal discrimination law—see Table 8-1).

Church with one or more affiliated entities that are not separately incorporated. Many churches operate a school, preschool, retirement facility, or other ministry. If these ministries are not separately incorporated, then the church along with its affiliates ordinarily will be treated as a single employer for purposes of applying the 15 employee test under the Americans with Disabilities Act (or any other federal discrimination law—see Table 8-1). In rare cases, this conclusion may not be automatic. For example, if the affiliates have different names, and are "sufficiently independent," then single employer status may not be automatic. Rather, the Supreme Court's 4 factor test (discussed above) may be applied to determine whether or not the church and its affiliates constitute a single employer for purposes of applying the 15 employee test. While such a result will be rare, it is not non-existent.

Church with one or more affiliated entities that are separately incorporated. Many churches operate a school, preschool, retirement facility, or other ministry. If these ministries are separately incorporated, then the Supreme Court's 4 factor test (discussed above) is applied to determine whether the church along with its affiliates should be treated as a single employer for purposes of applying the 15 employee test under the Americans with Disabilities Act (or any other federal discrimination law—see Table 8-1).

> **Example.** *A church with 10 employees is accused of violating the federal age discrimination law by not hiring a job applicant who is 60 years old. Since the church does not have 20 employees, it is not subject to the federal age discrimination law (see Table 8-1).*

Example. Same facts as the previous example, except that the church operates a preschool that has 12 employees. The preschool is not separately incorporated. Since the preschool has no separate legal existence, the church and preschool probably will be treated as a "single employer" for purposes of applying the 20 employee test under the federal Age Discrimination in Employment Act (or any other federal discrimination law—see Table 8-1). This means that the 10 church employees and 12 preschool employees are combined, and therefore the 20 employee requirement is met. In rare cases, this conclusion may not be automatic. For example, if the affiliates have different names, and are "sufficiently independent," then single employer status may not be automatic. Rather, the Supreme Court's 4 factor test may be applied to determine whether or not the church and its affiliates constitute a single employer for purposes of applying the 20 employee test. While such a result will be rare, it is not non-existent. This test focuses on the following four factors: (1) interrelation of operations; (2) common management; (3) centralized control of labor relations; and (4) common ownership or financial control. In applying this test, the absence or presence of any single factor is not conclusive, and "control over the elements of labor relations is a central concern." A plaintiff "must make a substantial showing to warrant a finding of single employer status," and "there must be sufficient indicia of an interrelationship between the immediate corporate employer and the affiliated corporation to justify the belief on the part of an aggrieved employee that the affiliated corporation is jointly responsible for the acts of the immediate employer." This example assumes that the church is engaged in commerce. Finally, note that one court has cautioned that "the cases in which we have applied the [4 factor test] have all involved business corporations. We have found no cases . . . applying the test to a religious corporation. Because a religious corporation can possess unique attributes . . . it may be the case that even where there are multiple religious entities, aggregation (or non-aggregation) of employees in employment discrimination cases should not be resolved under [this test]."[54]

Example. Same facts as the previous example, except that the preschool is separately incorporated. The Supreme Court's 4 factor test is applied to determine whether the church along with its affiliates should be treated as a single employer for purposes of applying the 20 employee test under the federal Age Discrimination in Employment Act (or any other federal discrimination law—see Table 8-1). This test focuses on the following four factors: (1) interrelation of operations; (2) common management; (3) centralized control of labor relations; and (4) common ownership or financial control. In applying this test, the absence or presence of any single factor is not conclusive, and "control over the elements of labor relations is a central concern." A plaintiff "must make a substantial showing to warrant a finding of single employer status," and "there must be sufficient indicia of an interrelationship between the immediate corporate employer and the affiliated corporation to justify the belief on the part of an aggrieved employee that the affiliated corporation is jointly responsible for the acts of the immediate employer." This example assumes that the church is engaged in commerce. Finally, note that one court has cautioned that "the cases in which we have applied the [4 factor test] have all involved business corporations. We have found no cases . . . applying the test to a religious corporation. Because a religious corporation can possess unique attributes . . . it may be the case that even where there are multiple religious entities, aggregation (or non-aggregation) of employees in employment discrimination cases should not be resolved under [this test]."[55]

---

[54] Equal Employment Opportunity Commission v. St. Francis Xavier Parochial School, 117 F.3d 621 (D.C. Cir. 1997).
[55] *Id.*

religious employers

The appeals court acknowledged that no other court has ever addressed the application of the Supreme Court's 4 factor test to religious organizations:

> The cases in which we have applied the [4 factor test] have all involved business corporations. We have found no cases in this circuit or elsewhere applying the test to a religious corporation. Because a religious corporation can possess unique attributes . . . it may be the case that even where there are multiple religious entities, aggregation (or non-aggregation) of employees in employment discrimination cases should not be resolved under [this test]. Although we express no opinion on the question, we note that the question to be answered by the [trial] court on remand may be [the first time any court has addressed this question].

§ 8-06 The "Clergy Exemption" under Federal Civil Rights Laws

Key point 8-06. *The civil courts have consistently ruled that the first amendment prevents the civil courts from applying civil rights laws to the relationship between a church and a minister.*

Many courts have ruled that the first amendment guaranty of religious freedom prevents civil rights laws from applying to the relationship between a church and its ministers. Here are some examples:

Example. A federal appeals court made the following observation in a case involving a dismissed minister's claim of unlawful discrimination: "This case involves the fundamental question of who will preach from the pulpit of a church, and who will occupy the church parsonage. The bare statement of the question should make obvious the lack of jurisdiction of a civil court. The answer to that question must come from the church. The court acknowledged that the government's interest in preventing employment discrimination "is compelling," but it concluded that such an interest "does not override" the protection that the church claims under the constitutional guaranty of religious freedom."[56]

Example. A minister-employee of the Salvation Army alleged that her employer had violated the Civil Rights Act of 1964 by paying female officers smaller salaries than similarly situated males. A federal appeals court concluded that the relationship of the Salvation Army to its officers was a church-minister relationship, and that the application of the provisions of Title VII to the employment relationship existing between a church and its minister would result in an impermissible encroachment by the government into an area of purely ecclesiastical concern.[57]

Example. A female sued a religious denomination alleging sex discrimination in violation of Title VII when her application to serve as an "associate in pastoral care" was rejected. In rejecting this lawsuit, the court observed: "[C]ourts must distinguish incidental burdens on free exercise in the service of a compelling state interest from burdens where the inroad on religious liberty is too substantial to be permissible. . . . This case is of the latter sort: introduction of government standards to the selection of spiritual leaders would significantly, and perniciously, rearrange the relationship between church and state. While an unfettered church may create minimal infidelity to the objective of Title VII, it provides maximum protection of the first amendment right to the free exercise of religious beliefs. In other words,

---

[56] Minker v. Baltimore Annual Conference of the United Methodist Church, 894 F.2d 1354 (D.C. Cir. 1990).
[57] McClure v. Salvation Army, 460 F.2d 553 (5th Cir. 1972), *cert. denied*, 409 U.S. 896 (1972).

in a direct clash of highest order interests, the interest in protecting the free exercise of religion embodied in the first amendment to the Constitution prevails over the interest in ending discrimination embodied in Title VII."[58]

Example. *A black female sued her religious denomination, claiming both sex and race discrimination when her application for appointment as a member of the clergy was denied. A federal appeals court rejected her claim, noting that "religious bodies may make apparently arbitrary decisions affecting the employment status of their clergy members and be free from civil review having done so." The court added: "[The minister's] argument, that Title VII may be applied to decisions by churches affecting the employment of their clergy, is fruitless." The court concluded: "To accept [the minister's] position would require us to cast a blind eye to the overwhelming weight of precedent going back over a century in order to limit the scope of the protection granted to religious bodies by the free exercise clause."*[59]

Example. *A federal appeals court dismissed a lawsuit by a nun claiming that her employer, the Catholic University of America, discriminated against her on the basis of her sex in violation of Title VII of the Civil Rights Act of 1964. The nun was employed as a professor of canon law. She applied for academic tenure after 6 years of teaching, and her application was denied. She sued the University, claiming that its decision to deny her tenure amounted to sex discrimination. The court upheld a federal district court's dismissal of the lawsuit, concluding that it was barred by the first amendment guaranty of religious freedom: "The Supreme Court has shown a particular reluctance to interfere with a church's selection of its own clergy. . . . Relying on these and other cases [a number of federal courts] have long held that the free exercise [of religion] clause exempts the selection of clergy from Title VII and similar statutes and, as a consequence, precludes civil courts from adjudicating employment discrimination suits by ministers against the church or religious institution employing them." The court pointed out that the so-called "ministerial exemption" has not been limited to members of the clergy, but "has also been applied to lay employees of religious institutions whose primary duties consist of teaching, spreading the faith, church governance, supervision of a religious order, or supervision or participation in religious ritual and worship." Employees whose positions are "important to the spiritual and pastoral mission of the church should be considered clergy." The court concluded that "the ministerial exception encompasses all employees of a religious institution, whether ordained or not, whose primary functions serve its spiritual and pastoral mission," and this included a nun who taught in the canon law department of the Catholic University. The court noted that the canon law department performs "the vital function of instructing those who will in turn interpret, implement, and teach the law governing the Roman Catholic Church and the administration of its sacraments."*[60]

Example. *A New Jersey court ruled that a lay teacher could sue a Catholic high school for age and sex discrimination. The teacher had been employed to teach English and history. After several years of teaching, she was informed that her position was being eliminated due to "budget problems." The teacher sued the school, claiming that the real reason she was being terminated was because of her gender and age. As proof, she alleged that the school later replaced her with a younger, male teacher. The school defended itself by insisting that all teaching positions at a Catholic high school are "religious" in nature, and that the first amendment prohibits the civil courts from applying civil rights laws to such positions. In support of its position, the school noted that the contract signed by its teachers stated that all teachers are to "exemplify Christian principles and ideals" in the performance of their duties, and are to*

---

[58] Rayburn v. General Conference of Seventh Day Adventists, 772 F.2d 1164 (4th Cir. 1985).
[59] Young v. Northern Illinois Conference of the United Methodist Church, 21 F.3d 184 (7th Cir. 1994).
[60] E.E.O.C. v. Catholic University of America, 83 F.3rd 455 (D.C. Cir. 1996).

open each class with prayer. Further, the school asserted that "parochial school teachers, no matter what the subject matter being taught, are performing a ministerial function . . . inculcating faith, values, and moral precepts into the students" and that "secular subjects in a parochial school are important vehicles for the propagation of the faith." The court acknowledged that civil rights laws cannot be applied to ministers or lay employees performing ministerial functions for a church or religious school. However, the court concluded that the lay teacher in this case did not satisfy this test. It observed: "[T]he fact that faculty members serve as exemplars of practicing Christians does not automatically make their duties ministerial. . . . A teacher of secular subjects need not be considered a religious leader. Here . . . enforcing the prohibition against discrimination would have no impact on religious belief, doctrine, or practice. . . . Thus, since the underlying dispute does not turn on doctrine or polity, the court should not abdicate its duty to enforce secular rights."[61]

Example. A Wisconsin court ruled that a lawsuit brought by a former church employee claiming that her dismissal constituted unlawful sex discrimination had to be dismissed since the employee's position was "ministerial" and "ecclesiastical."[62] A female employee of a Catholic seminary, who served as "director of field education," claimed that the seminary's decision not to renew her contract of employment was based on her sex in violation of a state civil rights law. The law prohibits discrimination in employment decisions on the basis of an employee's "age, race, creed, color, handicap, marital status, sex, national origin, ancestry, arrest record, or conviction record." A state court rejected the seminary's claim that the civil courts lack jurisdiction to resolve employment discrimination suits brought against religious organizations. The court relied in part on a 1986 decision of the United States Supreme Court finding that the civil courts are not prohibited from "merely investigating" the circumstances of an employee's dismissal by a religious school.[63] The court observed that giving religious organizations immunity from employment discrimination laws "would dangerously encroach upon the [nonestablishment of religion] clause's prohibition against furthering religion by providing a benefit exclusively to a religious association." However, the court ruled that the first amendment's protection of the free exercise of religion provides religious organizations with substantial protections that must be considered. These include the enforcement of state civil rights laws in cases involving employment decisions by religious organizations with respect to employees who perform a "ministerial" or "ecclesiastical" function. If an employee performs such a function, then "further enforcement of the [state civil rights law] against the religious association is constitutionally precluded, and the complaint should be dismissed." The court concluded that the employee in this case performed ministerial functions since her duties consisted of "teaching, spreading the faith, church governance, supervision of a religious order, or supervision or participation in religious ritual or worship."

§ 8-07 Procedure for Establishing a Discrimination Claim

Key point 8-07. Employees and applicants for employment who believe that an employer has violated a federal civil rights law must pursue their claim according to a specific procedure. Failure to do so will result in the dismissal of their claim.

The procedures for filing claims under the federal discrimination laws discussed in this chapter are fairly consistent. Church leaders should be familiar with the following procedures in the event that a discrimination complaint is brought against the church:

---

[61] Gallo v. Salesian Society, Inc., 676 A.2d 580 (N.J. Super. 1996).
[62] Jocz v. Labor and Industry Review Commission, 538 N.W.2d 588 (Wis. App. 1995).
[63] Ohio Civil Rights Commission v. Dayton Christian Schools, Inc., 477 U.S. 619 (1986).

1. Filing a charge with the EEOC. An "aggrieved" individual, a person acting on behalf of an aggrieved individual, or the Equal Employment Opportunity Commission (EEOC) itself may file a "charge" with the EEOC. The charge is a complaint filed on an EEOC form that alleges discrimination by an employer. In most cases, the charge is brought by the aggrieved individual claiming to have been a victim of discrimination in employment.

2. Notification of employer. Within ten days of the filing of the charge, the EEOC sends the employer a "notice" of the charge. The notice includes a summary of the alleged discrimination.

3. Investigations by state or local civil rights agencies. If the aggrieved person files a charge with a state or local civil rights agency, then no charge may be filed with the EEOC until at least sixty days have elapsed since the charge was filed with the state or local agency.

4. Time for filing charges. A charge must be filed with the EEOC within 180 days after the alleged discriminatory practice occurred. If a charge was initially filed with a state or local civil rights agency, then the charge must be filed with the EEOC by the earlier of the following two dates: (1) 300 days after the alleged discriminatory practice occurred, or (2) thirty days after notice from the state or local agency that it has terminated its proceedings regarding the charge.

5. EEOC investigation—no reasonable cause exists. The EEOC investigates the charge. If it determines that there is no reasonable cause to believe that the charge is true, it dismisses the charge and notifies the aggrieved person and employer of its decision. In deciding if reasonable cause exists, the EEOC must give "substantial weight" to the findings of any state or local civil rights agency that conducted its own investigation. If a charge is dismissed by the EEOC, or if the EEOC has not brought a civil lawsuit within 180 days of the filing of the charge, then the EEOC notifies the aggrieved person that he or she may file a civil lawsuit against the employer within ninety days of such notice. This is referred to as a "right-to-sue notice."

6. EEOC investigation—reasonable cause exists. If the EEOC determines that there is reasonable cause to believed that the charge is true, then it attempts to eliminate the alleged discriminatory practice by such informal methods as conferences, conciliation, and persuasion. If an employer accused of discrimination does not enter into a conciliation agreement with the EEOC within thirty days of the filing of the charge, then the EEOC may sue the employer in federal court on account of the alleged violation of the applicable federal civil rights law. Further, if the EEOC determines that reasonable cause exists, and the employer refuses to conciliate, then it sends the aggrieved party a "right-to-sue notice."

7. Federal court procedure. The plaintiff (the aggrieved person) bears the initial burden of proving that the employer engaged in the discriminatory practice. This can be done by direct evidence of discrimination, but more often it is done by showing "disparate treatment"—that is, the aggrieved party was treated less favorably than other employees who were not members of a protected group. The courts have ruled that a plaintiff can meet the initial burden of proof by establishing a "prima facie case" of discrimination by a preponderance of the evidence. This is done by showing that (1) the plaintiff is a member of a class protected by a federal, state, or local civil rights law; (2) the plaintiff suffered an adverse employment decision (such as not being hired if a job applicant, or being dismissed or disciplined if an employee); (3) a direct relationship exists between membership in the protected class and the adverse employment decision.

If the plaintiff is successful in making out a prima facie case of discrimination, then a presumption of discrimination exists, and the burden shifts to the employer to show a legitimate, nondiscriminatory reason for the adverse employment decision. If the employer demonstrates a nondiscriminatory reason for the adverse employment action, then the presumption is rebutted and the plaintiff must prove that the nondiscriminatory reason was a pretext for discrimination.[64]

8. Remedies. A variety of remedies are available to persons who establish that they were victims of employment discrimination. These include money damages and injunctive relief.

> **Example.** *A federal court dismissed a race and sex discrimination claim brought by a black male employee against a church agency on the ground that he failed to demonstrate that his dismissal was discriminatory or that the church treated white employees more favorably.[65] The court noted that the plaintiff "bears the burden of establishing a prima facie case of discrimination," meaning that he must establish that (1) he is in a protected group; (2) he satisfactorily performed the duties of his position; (3) he was subject to an adverse employment action; and (4) the adverse action occurred in circumstances giving rise to an inference of discrimination. Failure to provide some factual support for each of these elements of a "prima facie" discrimination case requires that a court dismiss it. The court noted that the plaintiff "failed to allege, let alone identify, any such incidents of disparate treatment that might give rise to an inference of discrimination in this case." The court concluded, "simply put, the facts that plaintiff was male and black, without more, do not suffice to make out a prima facie case of [sex or race] discrimination . . . ."*

§ 8-08   Title VII of the Civil Rights Act of 1964

> **Key point 8-08.** *Title VII of the Civil Rights Act of 1964 prohibits employers engaged in commerce and having at least 15 employees from discriminating in any employment decision on the basis of race, color, national origin, gender, or religion.*

The Civil Rights Act of 1964 was enacted by Congress "to achieve a peaceful and voluntary settlement of the persistent problem of racial and religious discrimination."[66] Title VII, Section 703(a), of the Civil Rights Act of 1964 specifies:

(a) It shall be an unlawful employment practice for an employer

(1) to fail or refuse to hire or to discharge any individual, or otherwise to discriminate against any individual with respect to his compensation, terms, conditions, or privileges of employment, because of such individual's race, color, religion, sex, or national origin; or

(2) to limit, segregate, or classify his employees or applicants for employment in any way which would deprive or tend to deprive any individual of employment opportunities or otherwise adversely affect his status as an employee, because of such individual's race, color, religion, sex, or national origin.

This general ban on discrimination applies to all employers, including religious organizations, that have 15 or more employees and that are engaged in an industry or activity "affecting commerce." The "commerce" and "15 employee" requirements are discussed earlier in this chapter.

---

[64] McDonnell Douglas Corporation v. Green, 411 U.S. 792 (1973).
[65] Jones v. General Board of Global Ministries, 1997 WL 458790 (S.D.N.Y. 1997).
[66] SEN. REPORT NO. 872, 88TH CONG., 2ND SESS. (1964).

Note that Title VII only addresses discrimination committed by employers against employees or applicants for employment on the basis of any one or more of the following five grounds:

- race

- color

- religion

- sex

- national origin

§ 8-08.1 — Application to Religious Organizations

Key point 8-08.1. Title VII of the Civil Rights Act of 1964 prohibits employers engaged in commerce and having at least 15 employees from discriminating in any employment decision on the basis of race, color, national origin, gender, or religion. Religious organizations are exempt from the ban on religious discrimination, but not from the other prohibited forms of discrimination.

1. RELIGIOUS EDUCATIONAL INSTITUTIONS

Title VII, Section 703(e)(2) of the Civil Rights Act of 1964 specifies:

[I]t shall not be an unlawful employment practice for a school, college, university, or other educational institution or institution of learning to hire and employ employees of a particular religion if such school, college, university, or other educational institution or institution of learning is, in whole or in substantial part, owned, supported, controlled, or managed by a particular religion or by a particular religious corporation, association, or society, or if the curriculum of such school, college, university, or other educational institution or institution of learning is directed toward the propagation of a particular religion.

This provision exempts religious educational institutions, whether at the primary, secondary, or college level, from the prohibition of religious discrimination contained in Title VII of the Civil Rights Act of 1964. Significantly, this provision speaks generally of the right of religious educational institutions to discriminate on the basis of religion in the hiring of employees who will directly promote religious belief, such as teachers, as well as those who will not, such as clerical, custodial, and administrative personnel. The United States Supreme Court has ruled that this exemption does not violate the first amendment's "nonestablishment of religion" clause.[67]

Example. A federal appeals court ruled that a teacher could not sue a church-operated school for discrimination after it refused to renew her contract because of her violation of the church's moral teachings. A divorced teacher at a Catholic school remarried, and was later informed by the school that she would not be rehired for the following school term. The school based its decision on the employment contract which noted that a teacher could be dismissed "for serious public immorality, public scandal,

---

[67] Corporation of Presiding Bishop v. Amos, 483 U.S. 327 (1987). This case is discussed below.

or public rejection of the official teachings, doctrine or laws of the Roman Catholic Church." The school informed the teacher that she would not be rehired because she had remarried without pursuing "proper canonical process available from the Roman Church to obtain validation of her second marriage," and thereby had committed a serious offense against the "Church's teachings and laws on the indissolubility of Christian marriage and the sacramental nature of the marriage bond." The dismissed teacher sued the school, claiming that her dismissal violated Title VII of the Civil Rights of 1964. A federal appeals court rejected the teacher's claim. It concluded: "[I]t does not violate Title VII's prohibition of religious discrimination for a parochial school to discharge a Catholic or a non-Catholic teacher who has publicly engaged in conduct regarded by the school as inconsistent with its religious principles. We therefore hold that the exemptions to Title VII cover the parish's decision not to rehire [the teacher] because of her remarriage."[68]

Example. *A federal appeals court ruled that a church-affiliated university did not commit unlawful discrimination when it dismissed a professor in its divinity school.[69] The professor had been employed to teach at a divinity school associated with Samford University—a Baptist university in Birmingham, Alabama. The professor claimed that he was dismissed by the divinity school's dean because he "did not adhere to and sometimes questioned the fundamentalist theology advanced by the leadership" of the divinity school. The professor sued the university, claiming that it had discriminated against him on account of his religious views in violation of Title VII of the Civil Rights Act of 1964. A federal district court dismissed the case, and the professor appealed. A federal appeals court upheld the district court's decision. It concluded that Title VII's exemption of "religious institutions" from the ban on religious discrimination in employment applied to the school. It based this conclusion on the following considerations: (1) the university was established as a "theological" institution. (2) The university's trustees are all Baptists. (3) Nearly 7 percent ($4 million) of the University's budget comes from the Alabama Baptist Convention (the "Convention")—representing the university's largest single course of funding. (4) The university submits financial reports to the Convention, and its audited financial statements are made available to all Baptist churches in Alabama. (5) All university professors who teach religious courses must subscribe to the Baptist "statement of faith," and this requirement is clearly set forth in the faculty handbook and in faculty contracts. (6) The university's charter states that its chief purpose is "the promotion of the Christian religion." (7) The university is exempt from federal income taxes as a "religious educational institution." The court also concluded that the school qualified for the exemption of "religious educational institutions" from Title VII's ban on religious discrimination in employment since it was "in substantial part" supported by the Convention: "Continuing support annually totaling over $4 million . . . accounting for seven percent of a university's budget, and constituting a university's largest single source of funding is of real worth and importance. This kind of support is neither illusory nor nominal. So, the Convention's support is substantial." The court concluded: "We . . . must give disputes about what particulars should or should not be taught in theological schools a wide berth. Congress, as we understand it, has told us to do so for purposes of Title VII. Also, such a construction allows us to avoid the first amendment concerns which always tower over us when we face a case that is about religion."*

---

[68] Little v. Wuerl, 929 F.2d 944 (3rd Cir. 1991).
[69] Killinger v. Samford University, 113 F.3d 196 (11th Cir. 1997).

2. RELIGION AS A "BONA FIDE OCCUPATIONAL QUALIFICATION"

Title VII, Section 703(e)(1) of the Civil Rights Act of 1964 states:

Notwithstanding any other provision of this title . . . it shall not be an unlawful employment practice for an employer . . . to hire and employ employees . . . on the basis of his religion, sex, or national origin in those certain instances where religion, sex, or national origin is a bona fide occupational qualification reasonably necessary to the normal operation of that particular business or enterprise . . . .

If an employer otherwise subject to the Civil Rights Act of 1964 can demonstrate that religion is a bona fide occupational qualification for a particular position, then the employer may lawfully discriminate on the basis of religion in filling the position.

3. EMPLOYMENT DECISIONS OF RELIGIOUS ORGANIZATIONS

in general

Title VII, section 702, of the Civil Rights Act of 1964 states:

This title shall not apply to . . . a religious corporation, association, educational institution, or society with respect to the employment of individuals of a particular religion to perform work connected with the carrying on by such corporation, association, educational institution, or society of its activities.

This provision permits religious corporations, associations, and educational institutions to discriminate on the basis of religion in the employment of any person for any position. As originally enacted, section 702 permitted religious employers to discriminate on the basis of religion only in employment decisions pertaining to their "religious activities." Congress amended section 702 in 1972 to enable religious organizations to discriminate on the basis of religion in *all* employment decisions. In the years following the 1972 amendment, a number of federal courts suggested that the amendment violated the first amendment's "nonestablishment of religion" clause. To illustrate, one court characterized the amendment as "a remarkably clumsy accommodation of religious freedom with the compelling interests of the state, providing . . . far too broad a shield for the secular activities of religiously affiliated entities with not the remotest claim to first amendment protection . . . ." [70] The court conceded that it would be unconstitutional to prohibit religious organizations from discriminating on the basis of religion in employment decisions pertaining to *religious activities*, but it concluded that allowing religious organizations to discriminate on the basis of religion in *any* employment decision went too far. Other courts reached the same result.[71]

---

[70] Equal Employment Opportunity Commission v. Southwestern Baptist Theological Seminary, 485 F. Supp. 255, 260 (N.D. Tex. 1980), *rev'd on other grounds*, 651 F.2d 277 (5th Cir. 1981), *cert. denied*, 102 S. Ct. 1749 (1982). *See also* Feldstein v. Christian Science Monitor, 555 F. Supp. 974 (D. Mass. 1983) (Christian Science Monitor held to be a religious activity of the First Church of Christ, Scientist, a religious organization, and thus it could discriminate in employment decisions on the basis of religion).

[71] *See, e.g.*, King's Garden, Inc. v. Federal Communications Commission, 498 F.2d 51 (D.C. Cir. 1974), *cert. denied*, 419 U.S. 996 (1974). *But cf.* Equal Employment Opportunity Commission v. Southwestern Baptist Theological Seminary, 651 F.2d 277 (5th Cir. 1981); Equal Employment Opportunity Commission v. Mississippi College, 626 F.2d 477 (5th Cir. 1980), *cert. denied*, 453 U.S. 912 (1981); Ritter v. Mount St. Mary's College, 495 F. Supp. 724 (D. Md. 1980).

In 1987, the United States Supreme Court resolved the controversy concerning the legal validity of section 702 by ruling unanimously that it did not violate the first amendment's nonestablishment of religion clause.[72] The case involved a maintenance employee of a Mormon church-affiliated gymnasium in Salt Lake City, Utah, who was fired because he failed to comply with the church's standards regarding church attendance, tithing, and abstinence from coffee, tea, alcohol, and tobacco. The employee sued the church, alleging that his dismissal violated the ban on religious discrimination in employment decisions contained in Title VII of the Civil Rights Act of 1964. The church asserted that the exception contained in section 702 of the Act permitted it to discriminate in any employment decision on the basis of religion. The employee countered by claiming that the exception violated the first amendment's ban on the establishment of a religion. A federal district court agreed with the employee, and ordered the employee reinstated with back pay. The church appealed directly to the Supreme Court.

The Supreme Court began its opinion by emphasizing that "there is ample room under the establishment clause for benevolent neutrality which will permit religious exercise to exist without sponsorship and without interference." It evaluated the constitutionality of the section 702 exemption on the basis of a three-part test it devised in 1971. Under this test, a law challenged on the basis of the nonestablishment of religion clause is permissible only if it satisfies three requirements—(1) it has a clearly secular purpose, (2) its primary effect is neither the advancement nor the inhibition of religion, and (3) it does not result in an excessive entanglement between church and state.[73] The Court concluded that "the exemption involved here is in no way questionable" under the three-part test. The section 702 exemption met the first part of the test since "under the *Lemon* analysis, it is a permissible legislative purpose to alleviate significant governmental interference with the ability of religious organizations to define and carry out their religious missions." In concluding that the section 702 exemption met the second part of the test, the Court observed that

> undoubtedly, religious organizations are better able now to advance their purposes than they were prior to the 1972 amendment to section 702. But religious groups have been better able to advance their purposes on account of many laws that have passed constitutional muster: for example, the property tax exemption . . . . A law is not unconstitutional simply because it *allows* churches to advance religion, which is their very purpose. For a law to [have the primary effect of advancing religion] it must be fair to say that the *government itself* has advanced religion through its own activities and influence.

The Court also concluded that the section 702 exemption did not result in an excessive entanglement between church and state. On the contrary, "the statute effectuates a more complete separation of the two and avoids . . . intrusive inquiry into religious belief . . . ."

In responding to the dismissed employee's claim that section 702 provided adequate protection to religious employers prior to its amendment in 1972, the Court observed:

> [The dismissed employee argues] that . . . section 702 provided adequate protection for religious employers prior to the 1972 amendment, when it exempted only the religious activities of such employers from the statutory ban on religious discrimination. We may assume for the sake of argument that the pre-1972 exemption was adequate in the sense that the free exercise [of religion] clause required no more. Nonetheless, it is a significant burden on a religious organization

---

[72] Corporation of the Presiding Bishop of the Church of Jesus Christ of Latter-Day Saints v. Amos, 483 U.S. 327 (1987).
[73] Lemon v. Kurtzman, 403 U.S. 602 (1971).

to require it, on pain of substantial liability, to predict which of its activities a secular court will consider religious. The line is hardly a bright one, and an organization might understandably be concerned that a judge would not understand its religious tenets and sense of mission. Fear of potential liability might affect the way an organization carried out what it understood to be its religious mission.[74]

Key point. *Most state civil rights laws exempt religious organizations from a ban on religious discrimination in employment.*[75]

consistency

A number of courts have ruled that Title VII's exemption of religious organizations from the ban on religious discrimination in employment does not apply if a religious organization uses religion as a "pretext" to discriminate against a member of a protected class. This is a very important qualification. Religious organizations can discriminate in their employment decisions on the basis of religion, but they must be consistent. To illustrate, a church that dismisses only female employees on the basis of adultery could not justify this practice on the basis of the Title VII exemption.

Example. *A federal appeals court ruled that a church-operated preschool did not violate federal law when it dismissed an unmarried, pregnant preschool teacher. The school, which was affiliated with the Church of Christ, expects that its teachers will adhere to its religious tenets. All teachers are required to be Christians, and preference is given to those who are Church of Christ members. The school uses as its religious tenets the teachings of the New Testament, including the prohibition against sex outside of marriage. The dismissed worker knew that the school was a church-related school and indicated on her employment application that she had a Christian background and believed in God. The worker insisted that she was never told that she would be terminated if she engaged in sex outside of marriage. However, the school's faculty handbook (given to the worker after she was hired) reads: "Christian character, as well as professional ability, is the basis for hiring teachers at [the school]. Each teacher . . . is expected in all actions to be a Christian example for the students." When school administrators learned that the unmarried worker was pregnant, a decision was made to terminate her employment. However, the woman was informed that she would be eligible for re-employment if she married the father of the child. The school's president claimed that the woman was dismissed not because of pregnancy, but because the facts indicated that she engaged in sex outside of marriage. The woman sued the school, claiming that it committed unlawful sex discrimination when it fired her. The court ruled that the school lawfully dismissed the woman on the basis of her violation of its religious teachings against premarital sex and not because she was pregnant. The court rejected the woman's claim that the school applied its policy against premarital sex in a discriminatory way that was more strict when women were involved. The court observed that "although Title VII requires that [the school's] code of conduct be applied equally to both sexes, [the school] presented uncontroverted evidence . . . that [the administrator] had terminated at least four individuals, both male and*

---

[74] *Id.* at 335-336. The Court noted that the present case illustrated the difficulties of distinguishing between "religious" and "secular" positions. The church maintained that the dismissed maintenance worker was engaged in a religious position, while the district court concluded that the position was entirely secular.

[75] *See, e.g.,* Gabriel v. Immanuel Evangelical Lutheran Church, 640 N.E.2d 681 (Ill. App. 4 Dist. 1994); Porth v. Roman Catholic Diocese, 532 N.W.2d 195 (Mich. App. 1995); Assemany v. Archdiocese of Detroit, 434 N.W.2d 233 (Mich. App. 1988); Geraci v. ECKANAR, 526 N.W.2d 391 (Minn. App. 1995); Sabatino v. Saint Aloysius Parish, 672 A.2d 217 (N.J. Super. 1996); Scheiber v. St. John's University, 600 N.Y.S.2d 734 (A.D. 2 Dept. 1993); Speer v. Presbyterian Children's Home and Service Agency, 847 S.W.2d 227 (Tex. 1993); Jocz v. Labor and Industry Review Commission, 538 N.W.2d 588 (Wis. App. 1995).

female, who had engaged in extramarital sexual relationships that did not result in pregnancy." Further, the court acknowledged that the school's policy occasionally may have been violated because the administrator was unaware of every instance of premarital sex by his staff, but it insisted that "isolated inconsistent application" of the policy "was not sufficient to show that [the school's] articulated nondiscriminatory reason was not the real reason for [the woman's] termination."[76]

Example. *A federal court ruled that a church-affiliated private school could be sued by a former employee who had been dismissed for extramarital sexual relations.[77] The school hired an unmarried woman as a math teacher. When she was hired, the woman signed a statement expressing her agreement with the school's "statement of belief" and agreed that her "lifestyle" would be "in accordance with the will of God and the Holy Scripture." A year later the school learned that the teacher (who was still unmarried) was pregnant. Because sexual activity outside of marriage violated the religious beliefs of the school, the teacher was dismissed. Shortly after being dismissed, the woman sued the school, claiming that the school had discriminated against her on the basis of pregnancy in violation of Title VII of the Civil Rights Act of 1964. She insisted that she was never informed, before her pregnancy, of any school policy against extramarital sexual relations, and she further claimed that she was told "I was terminated due to the fact that I was pregnant and unmarried and therefore a bad role model." The school denied that pregnancy rather than sexual activity was the basis for the teacher's dismissal. It conceded that this was the first case in which it had dismissed an employee for extramarital sex, but it insisted that it would treat male employees no differently if a case arose. The school asked the court to dismiss the lawsuit on the ground that Title VII permits religious employers to discriminate against employees on the basis of religion. The court declined to do so. It acknowledged that "Title VII explicitly provides exceptions for religious entities by allowing them to hire only employees of a given religion" and "permits employment of teachers based on religion if a school is controlled by a particular religion and qualification for employment is a religious requirement." This includes the right to "employ only teachers who adhere to the school's moral code". However, the court cautioned that "these exceptions to Title VII do not sanction gender discrimination" and that "religious codes of morality must be applied equally to male and female teachers." But if religious requirements "are applied equally to both males and females, the court will not evaluate the underlying dogma." The court then drew an important distinction between employment decisions based no pregnancy and those based on sexual activity. A rule that singles out pregnant employees for adverse treatment is not permitted because it is limited to females and therefore is discriminatory by definition. On the other hand, "restrictions on sexual activity, applied equally to males and females, are not discriminatory." The court was unwilling to dismiss the lawsuit because the evidence submitted by the school "does not indicate whether anyone else—male or female—has ever been fired as a teacher by the [school] for sexual intercourse outside of marriage."*

violations of moral teachings

Can a church lawfully discriminate against an employee or applicant for employment on the basis of moral teachings? In some cases, religious organizations will be able to demonstrate that their moral teachings are integral to their religious beliefs, and therefore employment discrimination based on moral teachings is a form of religious discrimination that is permitted by Title VII. To avoid any confusion, religious organizations that take an adverse employment action against an employee or applicant for employment as a result of the organization's moral teachings should word their determination with references to relevant passages from

---

[76] Boyd v. Harding Academy of Memphis, Inc., 88 F.3d 410 (6th Cir. 1996).
[77] Ganzy v. Allen Christian School, 995 F. Supp. 340 (E.D.N.Y. 1998).

scripture. This will make it more likely that a court will view the decision as a protected form of religious discrimination.

> **Example.** *A federal district court in California refused to dismiss a lawsuit brought by a former church employee who was dismissed after church leaders learned that she was pregnant out of wedlock. A church operated a private school, and required all employees to be "born again believers living a consistent and practical Christian life." Employees were required to sign a statement of faith, and to commit themselves to the mission of the church and to a Christian lifestyle that emulates the life of Christ. The school's librarian, a female, signed an annual affirmation agreement in which she agreed that she would be bound by the moral values and religious beliefs of the church. As an employee, the librarian received an employee manual that repeatedly stressed the importance of employees living a life in conformity to the beliefs and values of the church. The librarian was fired when church leaders learned that she was pregnant out of wedlock. The librarian filed a lawsuit in federal court, asserting that the church and school discriminated against her on account of her pregnancy in violation of Title VII. The church and school filed a motion to dismiss, alleging that the librarian had been fired "for the sin of being pregnant without benefit of marriage" (a condition inconsistent with the religious values of the church and school). However, the church and school later asserted that the librarian's dismissal had nothing to do with her pregnancy, but rather was based on her adulterous relationship. Her pregnancy was evidence of the adultery but had nothing to do with the religious reason for her dismissal. A federal court acknowledged that the "new position" of the church and school—that the librarian was fired for adultery, and not on account of her pregnancy—would not give rise to a Title VII claim since Title VII specifically permits religious employers to discriminate on the basis of religion in employment decisions. However, the "old position" of the church and school—that the librarian was fired because she was pregnant and not married—raised the possibility of sex discrimination. This case illustrates the importance of accurately describing the basis for terminating an employee. There is a critical legal difference between dismissing an employee on account of pregnancy (even if out of wedlock) and dismissing an employee on account of adultery (of which pregnancy is merely evidence).[78]*

discrimination based on race, color, national origin, or sex

Religious organizations that are subject to Title VII are exempt only from the ban on religious discrimination in employment. They remain subject to Title VII's ban on employment discrimination based on race, color, national origin, or sex—except, as noted above, with respect to employment decisions involving clergy.

> **Example.** *Religious organizations subject to Title VII are exempt from the ban on religious discrimination in employment, but they remain subject to the ban on employment discrimination based on race, color, national origin, or gender. However, not every allegation of discrimination has merit. To illustrate, a federal court in Pennsylvania ruled that a female employee of a Lutheran synod was not a victim of sex discrimination when her position was eliminated due to the merger of her synod with other synods. It observed: "[T]he 1984 decision of the three national Lutheran churches to merge had a significant impact on the future needs and direction of the Synod. Reflecting on these material changes, and their potential impact on the Synod's operational needs, the executive board of the Synod concluded that the coordinator of planning and communications position held by [the female employee] was expendable. While one may lament the fact that business principles and methods (e.g., budgets, income statements and time reports) have crept into our religious organizations, and regret the economic and*

---

[78] Vigars v. Valley Christian Center, 805 F. Supp. 802 (N.D. Cal. 1992).

DISMISSING AN EMPLOYEE FOR VIOLATION OF A CHURCH'S MORAL TEACHINGS

Before dismissing an employee for violating the church's moral teachings, church leaders should ask the following questions:

(1) Is there sufficient evidence to support our decision?

(2) Did we inform the employee, in an employee handbook or other document, that he or she would be subject to dismissal for engaging in behavior in violation of our moral teachings?

(3) How will we describe the basis for our decision? The best description will refer to the church's doctrinal tenets, and scriptural citations. Stay away from words such as "pregnancy" that can have a "secular" meaning, and that diminish the "religious exemption" available to churches under most federal and state civil rights and employment laws.

(4) How have we treated other employees in the past who were guilty of the same kind of misconduct? Have we treated all employees equally? Or, have we treated some employees less favorably than others. For example, have we dismissed female employees who were guilt of extramarital sexual relations, but only warned or reprimanded males employees guilty of the same behavior? Before dismissing an employee for misconduct, church leaders should review all other known cases involving similar misconduct by other employees. Be sure that the church's actions are consistent with its previous practice, and that an employee who is protected against discrimination by state or federal law not be treated less favorably than other employees.

(5) Have we contacted an attorney before taking final action

---

personal pain that such bottom-line orientation caused the [dismissed employee] in this case, this hand-wringing will not create a cause of action [for sex discrimination] where none exists."[79]

§ 8-08.2 — Sexual Harassment

Key point 8-08.2. *Sexual harassment is a form of sex discrimination prohibited by Title VII of the Civil Rights Act of 1964. It consists of both "quid pro quo" harassment and "hostile environment" harassment. Religious organizations that are subject to Title VII are covered by this prohibition. An employer is automatically liable for supervisory employees' acts of harassment, but a defense is available to claims of hostile environment harassment if they have adopted a written harassment policy and an alleged victim fails to pursue remedies available under the policy. In some cases, an employer may be liable for acts of sexual harassment committed by nonsupervisory employees, and even nonemployees.*

Sexual harassment is a form of "sex discrimination" prohibited by Title VII of the Civil Rights Act of 1964. Equal Employment Opportunity Commission (EEOC) regulations define sexual harassment as follows:

(a) *Harassment on the basis of sex is a violation of Sec. 703 of Title VII.* Unwelcome sexual advances, requests for sexual favors, and other verbal or physical conduct of a sexual nature constitute sexual

---

[79] Yost v. Western Pennsylvania-West Virginia Synod of the Lutheran Church in America, Inc., 789 F. Supp. 191 (W.D. Pa. 1992).

harassment when (1) submission to such conduct is made either explicitly or implicitly a term or condition of an individual's employment, (2) submission to or rejection of such conduct by an individual is used as the basis for employment decisions affecting such individual, or (3) such conduct has the purpose or effect of unreasonably interfering with an individual's work performance or creating an intimidating, hostile, or offensive working environment.

This definition confirms the conclusion reached by numerous state and federal courts that sexual harassment includes *at least two separate types of conduct:*

(1) "quid pro quo" harassment, which refers to conditioning employment opportunities on submission to a sexual or social relationship, and

(2) "hostile environment" harassment, which refers to the creation of an intimidating, hostile, or offensive working environment through unwelcome verbal or physical conduct of a sexual nature.

Key point. *A woman's "consent" is not a defense to an allegation of sexual harassment. The United States Supreme Court has observed: "[T]he fact that sex-related conduct was voluntary in the sense that the complainant was not forced to participate against her will, is not a defense to a sexual harassment suit . . . . The gravamen of any sexual harassment claim is that the alleged sexual advances were unwelcome . . . . The correct inquiry is whether [the victim] by her conduct indicated that the alleged sexual advances were unwelcome, not whether her actual participation in sexual intercourse was voluntary." In other words, a female employee may engage in voluntary sexual contact with a supervisor because of her belief that her job (or advancement) depends on it. While such contact would be voluntary, it is not necessarily welcome. Sexual harassment addresses unwelcome sexual contact, whether or not that contact is voluntary.*

When is an employer liable for sexual harassment? Consider the following rules:

rule #1 – quid pro quo harassment

If a supervisor conditions employment opportunities on an employee's submission to a sexual or social relationship, and the employee's "compensation, terms, conditions or privileges of employment" are adversely affected because of a refusal to submit, this constitutes quid pro quo sexual harassment for which the employer will be legally responsible. This is true whether or not the employer was aware of the harassment.

rule #2 – harassment committed by nonsupervisory employees

EEOC regulations address employer liability for the sexual harassment of nonsupervisory employees as follows:

With respect to conduct between fellow employees, an employer is responsible for acts of sexual harassment in the workplace where the employer (or its agents or supervisory employees) knows or should have known of the conduct, unless it can show that it took immediate and appropriate corrective action.

rule #3 – harassment committed by non-employees

EEOC regulations address employer liability for the sexual harassment of non-employees as follows:

An employer may also be responsible for the acts of non-employees, with respect to sexual harassment of employees in the workplace, where the employer (or its agents or supervisory employees) knows or should have known of the conduct and fails to take immediate and appropriate corrective action. In reviewing these cases the Commission will consider the extent of the employer's control and any other legal responsibility which the employer may have with respect to the conduct of such non-employees.

rule #4 – hostile environment harassment by a supervisor, with a tangible employment decision

If a supervisor creates an intimidating, hostile, or offensive working environment through unwelcome verbal or physical conduct of a sexual nature, this is "hostile environment" sexual harassment for which the employer will be legally responsible if the supervisor takes any "tangible employment action" against the employee. A tangible employment action includes "a significant change in employment status, such as hiring, firing, failing to promote, reassignment with significantly different responsibilities, or a decision causing a significant change in benefits." The employer is liable under such circumstances whether or not it was aware of the harassment.[80]

rule #5 – hostile environment harassment by a supervisor, with no tangible employment decision

If a supervisor creates an intimidating, hostile, or offensive working environment through unwelcome verbal or physical conduct of a sexual nature, this is "hostile environment" sexual harassment for which the employer will be legally responsible even if the supervisor takes no "tangible employment action" against the employee.[81]

rule #6 – the employer's "affirmative defense" to liability for a supervisor's hostile environment sexual harassment not accompanied by a tangible employment decision

If a supervisor engages in hostile environment sexual harassment but takes no "tangible employment decision" against a victim, the employer may assert an "affirmative defense" to liability. This defense consists of two elements:

(i) The employer "exercised reasonable care to prevent and correct promptly any sexually harassing behavior." This generally means that the employer adopted a written sexual harassment policy that was communicated to employees, and that contains a complaint procedure.

(ii) The victim "unreasonably failed to take advantage of any preventive or corrective opportunities provided by the employer or to avoid harm otherwise." This generally means that the victim failed to follow the complaint procedure described in the employer's sexual harassment policy.[82]

---

[80] Burlington Industries, Inc. v. Ellerth, 118 S. Ct. 2257 (1998); Faragher v. City of Boca Raton, 118 S. Ct. 2275 (1998).
[81] *Id.*
[82] *Id.*

It is essential for any church having employees to adopt a sexual harassment policy, since this will serve as a defense to liability for a supervisor's acts of "hostile environment" sexual harassment to the extent that a victim of such harassment does not follow the policy.

Key point. A written sexual harassment policy does not insulate a church from all sexual harassment liability. It will not serve as a defense in any of these situations: (1) a "tangible employment decision" has been taken against an employee; (2) incidents of quid pro quo sexual harassment; or (3) a victim of a supervisor's hostile environment sexual harassment pursues his or her remedies under the employer's sexual harassment policy.

What terms should be included in a sexual harassment policy? Unfortunately, the Supreme Court has not addressed this question directly. However, other courts have. Here is a list of some of the terms that should be incorporated into a written sexual harassment policy:

• Define sexual harassment (both quid pro quo and hostile environment) and state unequivocally that it will not be tolerated and that it will be the basis for immediate discipline (up to and including dismissal).

• Contain a procedure for filing complaints of harassment with the employer.

• Encourage victims to report incidents of harassment.

• Assure employees that complaints will be investigated promptly.

• Assure employees that they will not suffer retaliation for filing a complaint.

• Discuss the discipline applicable to persons who violate the policy.

• Assure the confidentiality of all complaints.

In addition to implementing a written sexual harassment policy, a church should also take the following steps:

• Communicate the written policy to all workers.

• Investigate all complaints immediately. Some courts have commented on the reluctance expressed by some male supervisors in investigating claims of sexual harassment. To illustrate, a federal appeals court observed: "Because women are disproportionately the victims of rape and sexual assault, women have a stronger incentive to be concerned with sexual behavior. Women who are victims of mild forms of sexual harassment may understandably worry whether a harasser's conduct is merely a prelude to violent sexual assault. Men, who are rarely victims of sexual assault, may view sexual conduct in a vacuum without a full appreciation of the social setting or the underlying threat of violence that a woman may perceive."

• Discipline employees who are found guilty of harassment. However, be careful not to administer discipline without adequate proof of harassment. Discipline not involving dismissal should be accompanied by a warning that any future incidents of harassment will not be tolerated and may result in immediate dismissal.

• Follow up by periodically asking the victim if there have been any further incidents of harassment.

Key point. EEOC guidelines contain the following language: "Prevention is the best tool for the elimination of sexual harassment. An employer should take all steps necessary to prevent sexual harassment from occurring, such as affirmatively raising the subject, expressing strong disapproval, developing appropriate sanctions, informing employees of their right to raise and how to raise the issue of harassment under Title VII, and developing methods to sensitize all concerned."

Key point. Most states have enacted their own civil rights laws that bar sexual harassment in employment, and it is far more likely that these laws will apply to churches since there is no "commerce" requirement and often fewer than 15 employees are needed to be covered by the law.

Tip. The assistance of an attorney is vital in the drafting of a sexual harassment policy.

Tip. Church insurance policies generally do not cover employment related claims, including sexual harassment. If your church is sued for sexual harassment, you probably will need to retain and pay for your own attorney, and pay any judgment or settlement amount. This often comes as a shock to church leaders. You should immediately review your policy with your insurance agent to see if you have any coverage for such claims. If you do not, ask how it can be obtained. You may be able to obtain an endorsement for "employment practices." Also, a "directors and officers" policy may cover these claims.

The following examples will illustrate the application of Title VII's ban on sexual harassment to religious organizations.

Example. A church has 4 employees. A female employee believes that she has been subjected to sexual harassment, and threatens to contact the EEOC. Sexual harassment is a form of sex discrimination that is prohibited in employment by Title VII of the Civil Rights Act of 1964. This law applies only to those employers having at least 15 employees and that are engaged in commerce. Since the church in this example has fewer than 15 employees, it is not subject to Title VII, and therefore the EEOC (which has jurisdiction over Title VII claims) will not be able to process the employee's complaint.

Example. Assume that a church is covered by Title VII. A female bookkeeper claims that a male custodian has been sexually harassing her by creating a "hostile environment." She does not discuss the custodian's behavior with the senior pastor or church board. She later threatens to file a complaint with the EEOC, charging the church with responsibility for the custodian's behavior. Since the harassment was not committed by a supervisor having the authority to affect the bookkeeper's terms and conditions of employment, EEOC guidelines addressing employer liability for sexual harassment specify: "With respect to conduct between fellow employees, an employer is responsible for acts of sexual harassment in the workplace where the employer (or its agents or supervisory employees) knows or should have known of the conduct, unless it can show that it took immediate and appropriate corrective action." If the pastor and church board were not aware of the custodian's offensive behavior, then according to this regulation the church will not be legally responsible for it.

Example. Same facts as the previous example, except that the bookkeeper complained on two occasions to the senior pastor about the custodian's behavior. The pastor delayed acting because he did not believe the matter was serious. According to the EEOC regulations quoted in the previous example, it is likely that the church is liable for the custodian's behavior since the pastor was aware of the offensive behavior but failed to take "immediate and appropriate corrective action."

Example. Same facts as the previous example, except that the pastor immediately informed the church board. The board conducted an investigation, determined the charges to be true on the basis of the testimony of other employees, and warned the custodian that one more complaint of harassing behavior would result in his dismissal. This action was based on the bookkeeper's own recommendation. It is doubtful that the church will be liable for sexual harassment under these circumstances, since it took "immediate and appropriate corrective action."

Example. A church is subject to Title VII. A female secretary claims that she was harassed by a man who frequently was on church premises maintaining duplicating equipment. An EEOC regulation specifies that "[a]n employer may also be responsible for the acts of non-employees, with respect to sexual harassment of employees in the workplace, where the employer (or its agents or supervisory employees) knows or should have known of the conduct and fails to take immediate and appropriate corrective action. In reviewing these cases the Commission will consider the extent of the employer's control and any other legal responsibility which the employer may have with respect to the conduct of such non-employees."

Example. A church is subject to Title VII. A male supervisory employee informs a female employee that her continuing employment depends on engaging in sexual relations with him. This is an example of quid pro quo sexual harassment. The church is liable for such harassment by a supervisor whether or not it was aware of it. The fact that it had a written sexual harassment policy that prohibited such behavior will not relieve it from liability.

Example. A church is subject to Title VII. A male employee (with no supervisory authority) repeatedly asks another employee to go to dinner with him. This is not quid pro quo sexual harassment because the offending employee has no authority to affect the terms or conditions of the other employee's work if she refuses to accept his invitations. If the offending employee's behavior becomes sufficiently "severe and pervasive," it may become hostile environment sexual harassment. However, the church generally is not liable for hostile environment sexual harassment by a non-supervisory employee unless it was aware of it and failed to take "immediate and appropriate corrective action."

Example. A church is subject to Title VII. It adopts a written sexual harassment policy that defines harassment, encourages employees to report harassing behavior, and assures employees that they will not suffer retaliation for reporting harassment. A male supervisory employee engages in frequent offensive remarks and physical contact of a sexual nature with a female employee. The female employee is greatly disturbed by this behavior, and considers it inappropriate in a church. In fact, she had sought church employment because she considered it a safe environment and her job would be a ministry. The supervisor eventually dismisses the employee because of her refusal to "go along" with his offensive behavior. Throughout her employment, the employee never informed church leadership of the supervisor's behavior. Several months after her termination, the employee files a sexual harassment complaint with the EEOC. Will the church be liable for the supervisor's behavior under these circumstances? After all, it was not aware of the supervisor's behavior, and it adopted a written sexual harassment policy. The supervisor's behavior constituted "hostile environment" sexual harassment for which the church will be liable. The fact that the church leadership was unaware of his offensive behavior is not relevant. Further, the church's sexual harassment policy is no defense, since the employee suffered a "tangible employment decision" (dismissal) as a result of her refusal to go along with the supervisor's behavior.

Example. Same facts as the previous example, except that the employee was not dismissed and suffered no "tangible employment decision" (firing, failing to promote, reassignment with significantly different responsibilities, or a decision causing a significant change in benefits). The general rule is that an employer is liable for a supervisor's "hostile environment" sexual harassment that does not result in a tangible employment decision against the victim. However, the employer has an "affirmative defense" to liability if (1) it adopted a sexual harassment policy that was adequately communicated to employees, and (2) the victim failed to pursue her remedies under the policy. The church in this case qualifies for the affirmative defense. It adopted a sexual harassment policy, and the victim failed to follow the policy's complaint procedure. As a result, the church probably would not be liable for the supervisor's behavior.

Example. Same facts as the previous example, except that the church is not subject to Title VII (it only has 5 employees). The church still may be liable under a state civil rights law, or under other legal theories (such as "intentional infliction of emotional distress," negligent selection or supervision, assault and battery, invasion of privacy, or false imprisonment).

Example. A church is subject to Title VII. It has not adopted a written sexual harassment policy. A female employee files a complaint with the EEOC, claiming that a supervisor has engaged in hostile environment sexual harassment. She never informed church leadership of the supervisor's behavior before filing her complaint with the EEOC. The church will be responsible for the supervisor's behavior under these circumstances. It does not qualify for the "affirmative defense" because it failed to implement a sexual harassment policy.

Example. Same facts as the previous example, except that the church had adopted a written sexual harassment policy that was communicated to all employees. The church will have an "affirmative defense" to liability under these circumstances, because it adopted a sexual harassment policy and the victim failed to follow it by filing a complaint. These two examples demonstrate the importance of implementing a sexual harassment policy. Such a policy can insulate a church from liability for a supervisor's hostile environment sexual harassment—if no "tangible employment decision" was taken against the victim, and the victim failed to pursue his or her remedies under the policy.

Example. An associate pastor engaged in sexual relations with two female employees in the course of a counseling relationship. The women later informed the senior pastor. As a result, the two women were dismissed, and the associate pastor was forced to resign. The women later sued the church on the basis of several legal theories, including sexual harassment. A trial court threw out the sexual harassment claim, and the women appealed. A federal appeals court concluded that the church was not guilty of "hostile environment" sexual harassment. It noted that in order for the two women to establish "hostile environment" sexual harassment they needed to "produce evidence showing, among other things, that [the church] knew or should have known of the harassment in question and failed to take prompt remedial action." However, since it was established that the church "took prompt remedial action upon learning of [the minister's] misconduct," the two women had to prove that the church should have known of the minister's behavior before it was disclosed. The court concluded that the women failed to do so. The women claimed that the former minister had offended a few other women by complimenting them on their appearances and hugging them. This evidence, even if true, was not enough to demonstrate that the church "knew or should have known" of a "hostile environment." The court also rejected the women's claim that the church had engaged in "quid pro quo" sexual harassment. It noted that for the women to establish quid pro quo sexual harassment, they "were required to produce evidence showing, among other things, that the harassment complained of affected tangible aspects of their compensation, terms, conditions, or privileges of employment. In addition, they were required to develop evidence demonstrating that their acceptance or rejection of the harassment was an express or implied condition to the receipt of a job benefit or the cause of a tangible job detriment. [But the women's] own testimony--that they were subjected to mild criticism of their work and told that they would not be promoted to positions they knew did not exist--indicates that their jobs were not tangibly and detrimentally affected by their decisions to end their sexual relationships with [the minister] . . . . Further, there is no objective evidence in the record supporting the [women's] claims that they engaged in sex with [the minister] under an implied threat of discharge if they did not.[83]

Example. *A federal appeals court ruled that a church-operated school was guilty of sexual harassment as a result of its failure to address its principal's offensive behavior with several female employees. A denominational agency operated a residential school for emotionally and physically impaired children. Over the course of several years, the principal of the school was accused on many occasions of sexual harassment by female employees. There was substantial evidence that school officials were aware of many of these complaints. School officials launched an investigation into the sexual harassment charges. They found that there was a significant basis to the harassment complaints. The school suspended the principal for five days without pay, ordered him to submit to a psychological assessment, and placed him on three months' probation. It also invited an outside consultant to conduct several days of seminars on sexual harassment. Even after this corrective action, there were several instances of inappropriate behavior involving the principal. During this same year, the principal was given a satisfactory performance evaluation and a raise. Several female employees who had been harassed by the principal sued the denominational agency on the ground that it was legally responsible for the principal's acts because of its failure to respond adequately to the accusations against him. A trial court ruled in favor of the women, and awarded them $300,000 in damages. A federal appeals court upheld this ruling. It referred to the "long-term, ostrich-like failure" by denominational and school officials to "deal forthrightly with [the principal's] treatment of female employees." The court observed that "the jury was entitled to conclude that [the agency] not only looked the other way for many years but that its corrective action was woefully inadequate, as demonstrated by [the principal's] later conduct." This case illustrates the importance of dealing promptly with complaints of sexual harassment. Letting years pass without addressing complaints of harassment will only increase significantly a church's risk of liability. After several years of complaints, the agency finally suspended the principal for five days, ordered a psychological assessment, imposed a three-month probationary period, and invited consultants to conduct sexual harassment training. These acts may seem thorough and adequate, but the court concluded that they were not sufficient to avoid liability for sexual harassment, because (1) the complaints against the principal had occurred over so many years; (2) the principal's acts of harassment were so pervasive; (3) the agency waited years before acting; (4) the agency's response was insufficient, since the principal continued to engage in harassment even after he was disciplined; and (5) the principal received a satisfactory employee evaluation and a raise during the same year that he was disciplined for harassment.*[84]

Example. *A federal court in California ruled that a female minister failed to prove that her denomination engaged in sexual harassment. The woman, an ordained Buddhist minister, was employed as national director of a department of a denominational agency (the Buddhist Churches of America or BCA). While attending an annual meeting of Buddhist ministers at a hotel in California, she received*

---

[83] Sanders v. Casa View Baptist Church, 134 F.3d 331 (5th Cir. 1998).
[84] Jonasson v. Lutheran Child and Family Services, 115 F.3d 436 (7th Cir. 1997).

a sexually offensive anonymous telephone call. BCA officials conducted an investigation, and determined that a male Buddhist minister attending the same conference was the likely caller. The woman later sued the BCA, claiming that she had been a victim of sexual harassment. She claimed that BCA engaged in quid pro quo harassment by "the defunding of her department because of her refusal to quietly allow [the accused minister] to talk dirty to her." She claimed that her employment was conditional upon allowing this "sexual favor." The court rejected the woman's claim of sexual harassment, noting that she could not have suffered quid pro quo harassment because the accused minister did not hold any position giving him the power to affect the terms of her employment with BCA. Even if the accused minister held such a position, the contents of the harassing telephone call made at the hotel could not be construed as conditioning job benefits upon the woman's submission to the minister's sexual demands. The court also rejected the woman's claim that BCA was guilty of "hostile environment" sexual harassment. It noted that the telephone call she received while attending the conference "was not physically threatening or humiliating. It was not repeated at plaintiff's place of employment and was not accompanied by any other sexual conduct in the workplace. Moreover, the alleged co-employee who made the phone call was not a person who plaintiff was forced to work with on a daily basis . . . . This single isolated incident does not rise to the level of seriousness required to establish an abusive working environment." Further, the woman's claim that BCA did not quickly and thoroughly investigate her complaint did not by itself prove a hostile environment: "[A]n employer's lack of remedial action is not itself evidence of the hostile work environment. A hostile environment claim requires wrongful verbal or physical conduct of a sexual nature. Thus, although the action or inaction of an employer in response to an allegation of sexual harassment may be probative on the issue of the employer's liability, this evidence is relevant only if the plaintiff first establishes that that incident created a hostile work environment."[85]

Example. *A woman was hired as an associate pastor of a church in Minnesota. A year later, she filed a discrimination charge with the state department of human rights against her supervising pastor. She claimed that her supervising pastor repeatedly made unwelcome sexual advances toward her. He allegedly referred to themselves as "lovers," physically contacted her in a sexual manner, and insisted on her companionship outside the work place despite her objections. The woman informed her local church leaders as well as her synod before filing the complaint with the state. Although the church and synod investigated the woman's allegations, no action was taken to stop the alleged harassment. Less than three months after the complaint was filed with the state, the church held a congregational meeting at which it voted to dismiss the woman as pastor. The reason stated for the discharge was the woman's "inability to conduct the pastoral office efficiently in this congregation in view of local conditions." A state appeals court ruled that the woman could sue her former supervising pastor for sexual harassment. The court also rejected the supervising pastor's claim that the woman was prevented from suing because she had "consented" to the supervising pastor's conduct.[86]*

Example. *A New York court ruled that a charity was liable for an executive officer's acts of sexual harassment.[87] A male executive director of the charity engaged in repeated acts of sexual harassment against female employees. The director was the charity's highest ranking employee. The harassment included inappropriate and demeaning communications, unwelcome sexual overtures, unwanted physical contact, and threats to fire the women (or make their jobs more unpleasant) if they did not submit to his advances. The director repeatedly begged each woman to be his "girlfriend" or "mistress," and to marry*

---

[85] Himaka v. Buddhist Churches of America, 917 F.Supp. 698 (N.D. Cal. 1995).
[86] Black v. Snyder, 471 N.W.2d 715 (Minn. App. 1991).
[87] Father Belle v. State Division of Human Rights, 642 N.Y.S.2d 739 (A.D. 1996).

him or sleep with him. He frequently demanded that the women attend nonwork-related lunches with him. A personnel committee was apprised of these actions, and it conducted an investigation which came to the attention of the governing board. As a result of the investigation, the director was placed on a brief leave of absence. The women later sued the director for sexual harassment. They also sued the charity and each member of the governing board. The court concluded that the charity was liable for the director's acts of harassment. The court ruled that the director's acts constituted both quid pro quo and hostile environment sexual harassment, and it found the charity liable for those acts. The court noted that under federal law an employer is "strictly liable" for quid pro quo harassment, since the harasser has the authority to alter the terms or conditions of the victims' employment based on their response to his advances. Therefore, the charity was liable for the director's quid pro quo harassment. On the other hand, under federal law employers are strictly liable for a hostile work environment created by a victim's supervisor, but not by co-workers lacking supervisory authority. Since the director was the highest ranking supervisory employee, the charity was strictly liable for hostile environment harassment caused to his actions.

Example. *A North Carolina appeals court ruled that the first amendment did not prevent it from resolving a sexual harassment lawsuit brought by three female church employees against their church and denominational agencies. Three female church employees (the "plaintiffs") sued their Methodist church and various Methodist agencies as a result of the sexual misconduct of a pastor. The lawsuit alleged that the pastor "committed inappropriate, unwelcome, offensive and nonconsensual acts of a sexual nature against the plaintiffs, variously hugging, kissing and touching them, and made inappropriate, unwelcome, offensive and nonconsensual statements of a sexually suggestive nature to them." The plaintiffs further alleged that the pastor's actions amounted to sexual harassment and assault and battery, causing them emotional distress, embarrassment, humiliation, and damage to their reputations and career potential. The lawsuit alleged that the local church and Methodist agencies "knew or should have known" of the pastor's propensity for sexual harassment as well as assault and battery upon female employees and that they failed to take any actions to warn or protect the plaintiffs from his wrongful activity. A state appeals court concluded that if a resolution of the plaintiffs' legal claims did not require the interpretation of church doctrine, then "the first amendment is not implicated and neutral principles of law are properly applied to adjudicate the claim."*[88]

Example. *An Ohio court ruled that an Episcopalian minister and his employing church could be sued for the minister's alleged acts of sexual harassment. A woman served some ten years as parish secretary of an Episcopal church prior to the arrival of a new minister. Soon after the arrival of the new minister, the secretary began alleging that the minister was engaging in acts of sexual harassment against her. Initially, the secretary contacted the bishop of the diocese with her complaint. He promised to make an investigation and apparently did, but concluded that, although he believed she was sincere in her allegations, there was nothing that he could do because the minister denied any wrongdoing. The bishop did order the work hours of the minister and secretary to be so staggered that they would not be working at the same time. After hearing that the bishop would take no further action, the woman wrote to the minister in question, the standing committee of the diocese, the vestry, the warden, and the bishop in an attempt to resolve what she called "this terrible problem." Upon receipt of this letter, the minister called the chancellor of the diocese, who advised him to fire the secretary. The minister thereafter was instructed by the vestry of the church to notify the congregation that the secretary had been fired and to give a reason. Accordingly, the minister published in the parish newsletter a statement that the secretary*

---

[88] Smith v. Privette, 495 S.E.2d 395 (N.C. App. 1998).

had been engaging in an open malicious endeavor to discredit him. Following her dismissal, the former secretary filed a lawsuit against the minister, her church, and the diocese. She based her lawsuit on a number of grounds, including sexual harassment. The appeals court ruled that the woman's claims were credible. It rejected the claim that the church could not be responsible for the minister's alleged actions since they were not performed within the "scope of his employment." It noted that "it is quite clear that the alleged sexual harassment did occur within the scope of [the minister's] employment with [the church]. He was the supervisor of [the secretary], and most of the alleged sexual harassment took place during working hours at the work place."[89]

Example. A South Carolina court ruled that a denominational agency and one of its officials were not liable for a pastor's acts of sexual harassment. Three female church members claimed that their pastor sexually harassed and abused them over a period of several months. The pastor resigned from his denomination before it could review the charges of sexual harassment. The denomination accepted the resignation as a "withdrawal under complaint or charges," and discontinued its investigation into the women's charges. It later spent $4,000 for training pastors in handling sex abuse allegations and for sending the three women to a "survivors of clergy sexual abuse" retreat. The women later sued the denomination and one of its officers, claiming that they were responsible for the pastor's sexual harassment. The women asserted that the denomination "had a duty to prevent the sexual harassment of its parishioners by a member of the clergy and to help in healing afterward rather than being indifferent." They insisted that the denomination should be found guilty of negligence for violating this standard. The court disagreed, noting that the women "have cited no precedent and we are aware of none that stands for the proposition a church owes its parishioners a duty of care regarding its handling of their complaints." The court also rejected the women's claim that the denomination was liable for the pastor's harassment on the basis of a breach of a fiduciary duty. First, it concluded that no fiduciary relationship existed between the women and the denomination. It noted that the women had no contact with the denomination other than a single meeting with one official. Further, the women's personal expectation that the denomination would "take action" on their complaints did not create a fiduciary relationship: "The steps taken unilaterally by the [women] do not constitute an attempt on their part to establish the relationship alleged, and there is no evidence that [the denomination] accepted or induced any special, fiduciary bond with any of [the women] under these facts in any event." Even if a fiduciary relationship did exist, it was not violated since "there is no evidence of a breach of that duty. There is no evidence that [denomination] acted other than in good faith and with due regard to [the women's] interests."[90]

§ 8-08.3 — Failure to Accommodate Employees' Religious Practices

Key point 8-08.3. Title VII of the Civil Rights Act of 1964 prohibits covered employers from discriminating against any employee on account of the employee's religion. Employers are required to "reasonably accommodate" employees' religious practices, so long as they can do so without undue hardship on the conduct of their business. Many state civil rights laws have a similar provision.

Title VII of the Civil Rights Act of 1964 makes it unlawful for a covered employer to "discharge any individual, or otherwise to discriminate against any individual with respect to his compensation, terms, conditions, or privileges of employment, because of such individual's . . . religion." Religion is defined to include only those "aspects of religious observance and practice" that an employer is able to "reasonably accommodate

---

[89] Davis v. Black, N.E.2d, 70 Ohio App. 3d 359 (Ohio App. 1991).

[90] Brown v. Pearson, 483 S.E.2d 477 (S.C. App. 1997).

. . . without undue hardship on the conduct of the employer's business." The intent and effect of this definition of "religion" is to make it a violation of Title VII for an employer *not* to make reasonable accommodations, short of undue hardship, for the religious practice of employees.

Courts have implemented a two-step procedure for evaluating claims and allocating burdens of proof under these provisions. First, plaintiff has the burden of establishing a "prima facie case." A plaintiff establishes a prima facie case of religious discrimination by proving that (1) he or she has a bona fide religious belief that conflicts with an employment requirement; (2) he or she informed the employer of this belief; and (3) he or she was disciplined for failure to comply with the conflicting employment requirement. Once a plaintiff has made out a prima facie case, the burden shifts to the employer to show that it was unable reasonably to accommodate the plaintiff's religious needs without undue hardship.

Several courts have ordered employers to make "reasonable accommodations" of the religious needs of employees whose religious beliefs prevented them from working on certain days of the week. Most courts have required employers to attempt scheduling adjustments or reassignments prior to dismissing such employees.[91] If rescheduling, reassignments, or other accommodations would impose undue hardship on the employer, then accommodation of employees' religious practices is not required.[92]

> **Example.** *A county government employed a conservative Christian as director of its data processing department. The director was dismissed because of overtly religious practices, including: (1) his secretary typed Bible study notes for him; (2) he allowed employees to recite prayers in his office prior to the start of the workday and during departmental meetings; and (3) affirming his Christian faith during department meetings. The director sued the county claiming that his dismissal amounted to religious discrimination in violation of Title VII of the Civil Rights Act of 1964. A federal appeals court agreed in part with the director. It noted that Title VII prohibits covered employers from dismissing an employee on account of religion "unless an employer demonstrates that it is unable to reasonably accommodate an employee's religious observance or practice without undue hardship on the conduct of [its] business." The court noted that the county had made no attempt to accommodate the director's religious practices, and therefore it could defend against the charge of religious discrimination only by demonstrating that it would have suffered "undue hardship" had it not dismissed the director. The court cautioned that "undue hardship" must be real rather than speculative, and that it requires more than "some fellow worker's grumbling." An employer must demonstrate "actual imposition on co-workers or disruption of the work routine." The court agreed with the county that allowing the director to have his secretary type Bible study notes would impose an undue hardship on the county, and therefore a dismissal based on this conduct would not violate Title VII. The court reached the same conclusion with regard to the prayer meetings conducted in the director's office prior to the start of the workday. It noted that "nothing in Title VII requires that an employer open its premises for use before the start of the workday." However, the court disagreed that the county would have suffered "undue hardship" by*

---

[91] *See, e.g.,* Tincher v. Wal-Mart Stores, Inc., 118 F.3d 1125 (7th Cir. 1997) (employer found liable); Heller v. EBB Auto Co., 8 F.3d 1433 (9th Cir. 1993) (employer found liable); Shpargel v. Stage & Co., 914 F.Supp. 1468 (E.D. Mich. 1996) (employer found liable); E.E.O.C. v. Arlington Transit Mix Inc., 734 F.Supp. 804 (E.D. Mich. 1990), *rev'd on other grounds,* 957 F.2d 219 (employer found liable); Riley v. Bendix Corp., 464 F.2d 1113 (5th Cir. 1972) (employer found liable); Jackson v. Veri Fresh Poultry, Inc., 304 F. Supp. 1276 (D. La. 1972) (employer found liable); Shaffield v. Northrop Worldwide Aircraft Services, Inc., 373 F. Supp. 937 (D. Ala. 1973) (employer found liable); Claybaugh v. Pacific Northwestern Bell Telephone Company, 355 F. Supp. 1 (D. Ore. 1973) (employer found liable).

[92] *See, e.g.,* Hardison v. Trans World Airlines, 527 F.2d 22 (8th Cir. 1976) (employer proved undue hardship); Reid v. Memphis Publishing Company, 521 F.2d 512 (6th Cir. 1975) (employer proved undue hardship); Dixon v. Omaha Public Power District, 385 F. Supp. 1382 (D. Neb. 1976).

allowing the director to utter occasional and spontaneous prayers during departmental meetings or to make occasional affirmations of religious faith. The court concluded that such expressions were "inconsequential . . . especially since they were apparently spontaneous and infrequent" and no employee complained about them. They did not result in "actual imposition on co-workers or disruption of the work routine." As a result, the court concluded that the director could maintain his religious discrimination lawsuit against the county.[93]

Example. *A federal court in Kansas ruled that an employer committed unlawful religious discrimination by dismissing two employees for engaging in religious speech with customers. The employees frequently greeted customers by saying "God bless you," "Praise the Lord," and other similar phrases. At certain times, because they felt that the Holy Spirit moved them to bless all GM employees, they extended such blessings to all of their food service customers. The employer deemed the employees' greetings to be inappropriate, and it eventually dismissed them. The employees sued the employer, claiming that its actions violated Title VII of the Civil Rights Act of 1964. The employees maintained that they were Christians who felt strongly that because of what God has done for them and the joy He has given them by changing their lives dramatically, they had to say things that were positive, uplifting, and inspirational to people with whom they spoke, and their religious greetings emanated from this belief. Honoring God through their speech, through such greetings, was a deep seated and sincerely held religious belief. The employer claimed that it did not have to tolerate these employees' religious practices if doing so would impose an undue hardship on it. It insisted that allowing them to continue their religious greetings would impose an undue hardship because it would jeopardize their business. The court concluded that the employees had met their "prima facie case" of religious discrimination by proving that (1) they had a bona fide religious belief that conflicted with an employment requirement; (2) they informed the employer of this belief; and (3) they were disciplined for failure to comply with the conflicting employment requirement. Having established a prima facie case, "the burden shifts to the employer to show that it was unable reasonably to accommodate the plaintiff's religious needs without undue hardship." Since the employer did not attempt to accommodate the employees' religious practice of blessing food service customers, the issue was whether its refusal to accommodate the employees' religious speech violated its obligation under Title VII to "reasonably accommodate" its employees' religious practice without undue hardship on the conduct of its business. The court concluded that allowing the employees to continue their religious greetings would not have imposed an undue hardship upon the employer. Allowing such a practice imposed only a "minimal burden" on the employer. It stressed that undue hardship cannot be proven by speculation, and yet this is what the employer was attempting to do.*[94]

Example. *A federal court in Nebraska ruled that an employer violated both state and federal law by dismissing an employee who refused to work on Easter Sunday. The employee, a devout Christian, was employed by a convenience store chain as a cashier. A previous manager accommodated the employee's desire not to work on Easter Sunday by allowing her to work on non-religious holidays (such as New Year's Day) instead. A new manager was not so accommodating. She scheduled the employee to work the evening shift on Easter Sunday even though she had been fully apprised in writing by the employee of her strong religious opposition to working on Easter Sunday. The employee attended church on Easter Sunday evening rather than go to work, and she was promptly fired. She later sued her employer, claiming that she had been unlawfully discharged on account of her religion. The court concluded that*

---

[93] Brown v. Polk County, 61 F.3d 650 (8th Cir. 1995). The court also concluded that the county's actions may have violated the director's first amendment right to freely exercise his religion.
[94] Banks v. Service America Corporation, 72 EPD ¶45,018 (D. Kan. 1996).

the employee proved all three elements of her prima facie case, and therefore the employer violated Title VII by dismissing her. First, it pointed to the employee's long history of church attendance, including attending worship services on Sunday mornings and evenings, as evidence of her bona fide belief that working on Easter Sunday violated her religious beliefs. Second, it noted that the employee had informed her manager in writing of her desire not to work on Easter Sunday. Third, the employee clearly was dismissed because of her religious beliefs. The court rejected the employer's defense that it had offered the employee a "reasonable accommodation." It observed that the employer "knew that the entirety of Easter was of paramount religious significance to [the employee] and was unlike a normal Sunday." The court also rejected the employer's claim that accommodating the employee's religious beliefs would have imposed an undue burden on it. It noted that the previous manager was willing to allow the employee to work on secular holidays in lieu of working on Easter, and that other employees had indicated a willingness to work "at any time."[95]

§ 8-08.4 — The Civil Rights Act of 1991

Key point 8-08.3. *The Civil Rights Act of 1991 permits victims of discrimination under various federal civil rights laws to sue their employer for money damages up to specified limits based on the size of the employer.*

The Civil Rights Act of 1991 permits persons who are victims of intentional gender or religious discrimination under Title VII, or intentional discrimination in violation of the Americans with Disabilities Act, to sue employers for monetary damages. The Act defines these as "compensatory and punitive damages." However, the Act limits the amount of compensatory and punitive damages that are available to discrimination victims. Employers with more than 14 but fewer than 101 employees cannot be liable for more than $50,000 to any one person; for employers with more than 100 but fewer than 201 employees, the maximum damages available to any one person is $100,000; for employers with more than 200 but fewer than 500 employees, the maximum damages available to any one person is $200,000; and for employers with more than 500 employees the maximum damages available to any one person is $300,000.

Example. A denominational agency has 75 employees, and engages in the national distribution of religious literature to affiliated churches. A female sues the agency as a result of alleged intentional sex discrimination in employment. The agency clearly is subject to Title VII, and therefore is subject to "compensatory and punitive damages" not to exceed $50,000 if the woman can prove intentional sex discrimination.

Example. First Baptist Church refuses to hire an applicant for employment because he is not a Baptist. The applicant cannot sue for monetary damages under Title VII since churches are not subject to the prohibition of religious discrimination in employment even if they are covered by Title VII.

The Civil Rights Act of 1991 provides that if an employer is charged with discrimination against a disabled person in violation of the Americans with Disabilities Act, no monetary damages will be available if the employer can demonstrate that it exercised good faith efforts (in consultation with the disabled person) to reasonably accommodate the disabled person.

The Civil Rights Act of 1991 authorizes the award of attorneys fees to prevailing parties.

---

[95] Pedersen v. Casey's General Stores, Inc., 978 F. Supp. 926 (D. Neb. 1997).

§ 8-09   The Age Discrimination in Employment Act

***Key point 8-09.** The federal Age Discrimination in Employment Act prohibits employers with 20 or more employees, and engaged in interstate commerce, from discriminating in any employment decision on the basis of the age of an employee or applicant for employment who is 40 years of age or older. The Act does not exempt religious organizations. Many states have similar laws that often apply to employers having fewer than 20 employees.*

In 1967, Congress enacted the Age Discrimination in Employment Act to prohibit employers engaged in an industry affecting commerce and employing at least 50 employees from making employment decisions that discriminate against individuals from 40 to 65 years old on account of age.[96] Congress later amended the Act to apply to employers employing 20 or more employees for each working day in each of 20 or more calendar weeks in the current or preceding year. Congress also expanded the class of protected employees to include all persons 40 years of age and older.

The Act specifies that "it shall not be unlawful for an employer . . . to observe the terms of . . . a bona fide employee benefit plan such as a retirement, pension, or insurance plan, which is not a subterfuge to evade the purposes of [the Act] . . . or to discharge or otherwise discipline an individual for good cause."[97] Ordinarily, an employee benefit plan will be considered to be "bona fide" if it is genuine and pays substantial benefits.

This ban on age discrimination applies to all employers, including religious organizations, that have 20 or more employees and that are engaged in an industry or activity "affecting commerce." The "commerce" and "employee" requirements are discussed earlier in this chapter. Note that the age discrimination law only addresses discrimination committed by employers against employees or applicants for employment.

***Example.** The United States Supreme Court ruled that an employer cannot necessarily avoid an age discrimination claim by replacing one protected worker with another.[98] A long-term employee of a business corporation was dismissed at the age of 56, and replaced by a worker who was 40 years old. He sued his employer, claiming that it had committed unlawful age discrimination in violation of the federal Age Discrimination in Employment Act. The employer insisted that it could not be guilty of violating the Act if it replaced a worker at least 40 years of age with another worker who also was 40 years of age or older—since both employees are in the protected group of workers under the Act. The Supreme Court rejected this argument, noting that "the fact that one person in the protected class has lost out to another person in the protected class is . . . irrelevant, so long as he has lost out because of his age. Or to put the point more concretely, there can be no greater inference of age discrimination . . . when a 40 year-old is replaced by a 39 year-old than when a 56 year-old is replaced by a 40 year-old." The Court cautioned that "in the age-discrimination context . . . an inference [of discrimination] cannot be drawn from the replacement of one worker with another worker insignificantly younger." However, "the fact that a replacement is substantially younger than the plaintiff is a far more reliable indicator of age discrimination than is the fact that the plaintiff was replaced by someone outside the protected class."*

---

[96] 29 U.S.C. §§ 621-634.
[97] 29 U.S.C. § 623(f).
[98] O'Connor v. Consolidated Coin Caterers Corporation, 116 S. Ct. 1307 (1996).

Example. A federal appeals court ruled that the first amendment guaranty of religious freedom prevented it from resolving a Methodist minister's claim that his dismissal violated federal age discrimination law.[99] The 63-year-old minister was employed by an annual conference of the United Methodist Church. After serving ten years as a counselor, he requested that he be returned to a pastoral appointment. He was assigned to a temporary post at a local church. The minister claimed that the new position paid him less than what a pastor with his qualifications and experience would normally receive. He complained to his district superintendent who, he alleged, assured him that he would be "moved to a congregation more suited to his training and skills, and more appropriate in level of income, at the earliest opportunity." The minister made repeated requests for reassignment, but four years passed without any change in his position. He then filed a lawsuit in federal court, alleging that he had been denied a rightful "promotion" solely on the basis of his age. The court rejected the minister's claim. It based its conclusion on a number of factors, including the following: (1) The Methodist Book of Discipline did mention age as one factor to consider in assigning clergy, and therefore a judicial finding that the church violated a minister's rights under federal age discrimination law could conceivably violate the church's right to freely exercise its religion. (2) The determination of "whose voice speaks for the church" is "per se a religious matter." The court noted that "we cannot imagine an area of inquiry less suited to a temporal court for decision; evaluation of the 'gifts and graces' of a minister must be left to ecclesiastical institutions. This is the view of every court that has been confronted by this [kind] of dispute." (3) The court acknowledged that churches have less protection when it comes to employment decisions involving non-clergy employees. However, cases reaching this conclusion were not relevant in this case, since a minister was involved.

Example. A federal appeals court ruled that federal age discrimination law applied to a church school.[100] A Catholic parochial school did not offer a teaching contract to a math teacher who had taught at the school for 5 years. The school noted that the teacher did not open classes with prayer and did not attend Mass with students. The former teacher sued the school for violating the federal Age Discrimination in Employment Act. The school argued that subjecting it to the provisions of the Act would create an "excessive entanglement" between church and state in violation of the first amendment. The court disagreed, noting that "[t]he majority of courts considering the issue have determined that application of the [Age Discrimination in Employment Act] to religious institutions generally, and to lay teachers specifically, does not pose a serious risk of excessive entanglement. . . . [Age discrimination lawsuits] do not require extensive or continuous administrative or judicial intrusion into the functions of religious institutions. The sole question at issue . . . is whether the plaintiff was unjustifiably treated differently because of his age. . . . The Supreme Court has stated that 'routine regulatory interaction which involves no inquiries into religious doctrine, no delegation of state power to a religious body, and no detailed monitoring and close administrative contact between secular and religious bodies, does not of itself violate the [Establishment Clause's] nonentanglement command.' Application of the [Act] to the case at bar requires just such routine regulatory interaction between government and a religious institution." The court acknowledged that the Act is not applicable to claims brought by members of the clergy against their religious employers, since these cases involve "the pervasively religious relationship between a member of the clergy and his religious employer."

---

[99] Minker v. United Methodist Church, 894 F.2d 1354 (D.C. Cir. 1990). *Accord* Gargano v. Diocese of Rockville Centre, 80 F.3d 87 (2nd Cir. 1996).

[100] DeMarco v. Holy Cross High School, 4 F.3d 166 (2nd Cir. 1993), quoting Hernandez v. Commissioner, 490 U.S. 680 (1989).

Example. A federal appeals court ruled that a hospital chaplain could not sue the hospital for alleged age and sex discrimination following her dismissal.[101] The former chaplain was an ordained Episcopal priest who had served as chaplain of a church affiliated hospital for 10 years. Following her dismissal, the former chaplain sued the hospital on the grounds that her dismissal (1) violated the federal Civil Rights Act of 1964, which prohibits certain employers from dismissing employees on the basis of their sex, and (2) violated the federal Age Discrimination in Employment Act, which bans discrimination in employment against persons 40 years of age and older—on account of age. The court emphasized that the hospital was "without question a religious organization," and that the chaplain position "is primarily a ministerial position." The court concluded: "[W]e believe that the free exercise [of religion] clause of the first amendment also prohibits the courts from deciding cases such as this one. Personnel decisions by church-affiliated institutions affecting clergy are per se religious matters and cannot be reviewed by civil courts, for to review such decisions would require the courts to determine the meaning of religious doctrine and canonical law and to impose a secular court's view of whether in the context of the particular case religious doctrine and canonical law support the decision the church authorities have made. This is precisely the kind of judicial second-guessing of decision-making by religious organizations that the free exercise [of religion] clause forbids."

Example. A Catholic college denied a priest's application for a one-year sabbatical, while at the same time approving the applications of two female professors. The priest sued the college, claiming that its denial of his application amounted to unlawful discrimination based on age, gender, and race (the priest was Asian). A federal appeals court dismissed the priest's claims.[102] It agreed that federal law banning discrimination based on age, race, and gender can be applied to a college's policies regarding sabbatical leave. However, it concluded that the college had demonstrated a "legitimate, nondiscriminatory reason" for denying the priest's application for a sabbatical. In particular, it noted that the college was in the process of upgrading its two-year nursing program into an accredited four-year program, and that it granted the two female professors' requests for sabbaticals since they were involved with the nursing program and needed advanced degrees in order for the nursing program to be upgraded. Unfortunately, the college failed to claim that the priest's discrimination claims were barred by the first amendment guaranty of religious freedom. The appeals court took the extraordinary step of asking the college to address this issue in a supplemental brief. The college eventually did so, but the court ruled that the first amendment did not bar the priest's claims in this case since the college "failed to convince us that our consideration of [the priest's] claims would risk excessive entanglement" between church and state. The lesson is clear—churches and church schools should vigorously and at the earliest opportunity challenge any discrimination claims brought by a member of the clergy, emphasizing the religious role and functions of the minister. As this case illustrates, failure to do so may cause a civil court to reject such a defense.

Example. A federal court in Colorado ruled that a dismissed teacher at a Catholic high school could not bring an age discrimination claim against the school and archdiocese.[103] A teacher was employed to teach theology at a parochial high school. The school did not renew the teacher's contract of employment for two reasons: (1) a need for fewer teachers, and (2) the teacher's skills, abilities, and qualifications were deemed less desirable than other faculty members. The teacher alleged that the archdiocese failed to renew his employment contract on account of his age in violation of the Age Discrimination in Employment Act. In rejecting the teacher's claim, the court observed: "[T]he more pervasively religious the

---

[101] Scharon v. St. Luke's Episcopal Presbyterian Hospitals, 929 F.2d 360 (8th Cir. 1991).
[102] Roxas v. Presentation College, 90 F.3d 310 (8th Cir. 1996).
[103] Powell v. Stafford, 859 F. Supp. 1343 (D. Colo. 1994).

institution, the less religious the employee's role need be to risk first amendment infringement. Conversely, the less religious an organization, the more religious an employee's role need be to risk first amendment infringement. In this case [the teacher] does not challenge [the school's] religious affiliation. And, significantly he does not contest that his teaching role was primarily religious in nature. He taught Roman Catholic theology exclusively and even held some of his classes in [the school's] chapel so that his students could pray as part of his class. There is no genuine dispute that [his] duties were pervasively religious in nature. Courts have consistently held that the ADEA does not apply in cases involving employees performing primarily religious functions. . . . Simply put, there is no teaching position more closely tied to a Roman Catholic school's religious character than teaching Roman Catholic doctrine. I conclude that the archdiocese's free exercise [of religion] rights are substantially burdened by application of the ADEA under the circumstances here."

Example. *A federal court in Indiana rejected the claims of a 61-year-old employee of a church-operated hospital that she had been a victim of age discrimination.*[104] *A woman (the "plaintiff") worked for a church-operated hospital as a full-time cashier. Her position was reduced to part-time as a result of a reduction in force (RIF) caused by budget deficits. Eventually, the position was terminated. The plaintiff sued the hospital, claiming that the elimination of her position amounted to age discrimination in violation of federal law. The court observed: "[We] must determine whether a [jury] could find that the hospital's true reason for reducing her hours was the RIF going on at that time, and not whether that decision was a sound business decision. The evidence on which [the plaintiff] relies does not call into doubt the hospital's proffered reason for eliminating her cashier position. The hospital asserts that [the plaintiff's] position was eliminated because it was the department's only part-time position (and elimination of part-time positions was a suggested method of cutting costs) and other full-time employees had the skills necessary to perform her duties, while she would have required additional training to perform their duties. [The plaintiff's] assertions that she was performing satisfactorily, that her duties still needed to be performed, and that a younger employee continued to perform her duties simply do not refute the specific reason given for her elimination, and therefore could not support a finding that the reason is a pretext for age discrimination."*

Example. *A Michigan court dismissed an age discrimination lawsuit brought against a Catholic church and archdiocese by a 62-year-old employee who was dismissed as a result of economic conditions.*[105] *The number of families in a Catholic parish declined from 1,500 to 1,250. This decline led to a deficit of $200,000. A CPA firm was called in to conduct a financial study and organizational analysis, and it recommended that the parish reorganize its staff and consolidate responsibilities. The pastor of the church responded by terminating five employees including the plaintiff (a 62-year-old custodian); a 40-year-old religious education secretary; a 31-year-old director of religious education; a 63-year-old school librarian; and a 68-year-old school secretary. The dismissed custodian sued the church and archdiocese, claiming that his dismissal violated a state civil rights law banning age discrimination in employment. He relied on the pastor's testimony that his decision to dismiss the custodian was based in part on the fact that the dismissed custodian would be able to retain his pension and medical benefits while two other custodians who were not dismissed would not. The court concluded that the pastor's consideration of the custodian's eligibility for retirement and medical benefits did not automatically constitute unlawful age discrimination. It noted that in an age discrimination case the plaintiff has the burden of proving a "prima facie case" of discrimination by a preponderance of the evidence. It concluded that the custodian failed to meet this burden of proof, noting that "the mere fact that plaintiff*

---

[104] Humphrey v. Sisters of St. Francis Health Services, Inc., 979 F. Supp. 781 (N.D. Ind. 1997).
[105] Plieth v. St. Raymond Church, 534 N.W.2d 164 (Mich. App. 1995).

was eligible for a pension is not enough for this court to infer age discrimination." The court pointed to a second basis for its decision: "When an employer lays off employees for economic reasons, the employee bears a greater burden of proof in establishing discrimination. In such a case, the employee must present evidence that age was a determining factor in the decision to discharge him. At best, plaintiff has offered evidence that his pension eligibility played some part in [the pastor's] decision to terminate him rather than the other two maintenance workers. Plaintiff has made no showing that his pension eligibility— and therefore, in plaintiff's argument, his age—was a determining factor in that decision."

Example. *A federal district court in Missouri ruled that it could not resolve a lawsuit brought against a synagogue by a former business administrator who claimed that he had been dismissed on the basis of age in violation of the Age Discrimination in Employment Act.[106] In deciding that the Act did not apply to the synagogue, the court relied on the Supreme Court's 1979 decision in N.L.R.B. Catholic Bishop of Chicago.[107] In the Catholic Bishop decision, the Supreme Court ruled that in deciding whether or not a federal law applies to religious organizations, a civil court first must ask if applying the law "would give rise to serious constitutional questions." If it would, then the law cannot be applied to religious organizations without a "clear expression of an affirmative intention" by Congress to apply the law to such organizations. The district court concluded that applying the Act to a church or synagogue would "give rise to serious constitutional questions." In reaching this conclusion, the court quoted from the business administrator's job description, and noted that his duties included "implementing Temple policies" and "having a positive attitude towards Jewish life and a Jewish background, enabling the administrator to understand the work of the Temple, its purposes and highest ideals and goals." The court then observed, again referring to the Catholic Bishop decision, that if a "serious constitutional question" exists, the court next must ascertain whether Congress has provided a "clear expression of an affirmative intention" that the Act apply to religious institutions. The court concluded that the Act did not specifically apply to churches of synagogues, and so this test was not met. As a result, the Act could not be applied in this case.*

Example. *A federal court in Missouri ruled that it lacked jurisdiction to resolve a seminary employee's claim that his dismissal violated federal age discrimination law.[108] The court, applying the analysis set forth by the United States Supreme Court in a previous ruling,[109] concluded that in deciding whether or not a federal law applies to religious organizations, a civil court first must ask if applying the law to religious organizations "would give rise to serious constitutional questions." If it would, then the law cannot be applied to religious organizations without an "affirmative expression of congressional intent" to apply the law to such organizations. Would application of the federal Age Discrimination in Employment Act to a seminary create "serious constitutional questions"? Yes, concluded the court. It emphasized that the seminary was "primarily a religious institution" whose objective was the preparation of students for the priesthood and the dissemination of religious values to its students. The court noted that "all faculty members, both lay and clerical, are expected to serve as religious role models, participate in spiritual activities and 'carry religious fervor and conviction' into the classroom." The court concluded that applying the federal age discrimination law to such an institution "would give rise to serious constitutional questions." In particular, discrimination claims would require the courts to determine whether a dismissal was based on religious considerations or age, and such inquiries "are fraught with the sort of entanglement [between church and state] that the Constitution forbids." Further, applica-*

---

[106] Weissman v. Congregation Shaare Emeth, 839 F. Supp. 680 (E.D. Mo. 1993).
[107] 440 U.S. 490 (1979).
[108] Cochran v. St. Louis Seminary, 717 F. Supp. 1413 (E.D. Mo. 1989).
[109] NLRB v. Catholic Bishop, 440 U.S. 490 (1979).

tion of the Act to the seminary would cause the seminary to be more cautious in its religion-based employment decisions, thereby "imposing a chilling effect on the [seminary's] exercise of control over its religious mission." If "serious constitutional questions" would arise by applying a federal law to a religious organization, then the law cannot be applied without an affirmative and clear expression of congressional intent to apply the law to such organizations. The court found no clear indication that Congress intended the Act to apply to religious seminaries.

Example. *A federal district court in Ohio rejected a religious school's claim that it was exempt from federal age discrimination law.[110] Xavier University is a Catholic institution of higher education operated by the Order of Jesuits. An employee brought an age discrimination lawsuit against the University. The University claimed that the court lacked jurisdiction over the case, since, as a religious institution, it was exempt from the antidiscrimination provisions of the federal Age Discrimination in Employment Act. The court agreed with the employee that the Act "gives no indication that religious institutions are exempt from its provisions." However, it also acknowledged that a religious institution could be exempted on the basis of the constitutional guaranty of religious freedom if application of the Act to the institution would "give rise to serious constitutional questions" under the religious freedom clause of the first amendment. The court concluded that no "serious constitutional questions" were implicated by an application of the Act to the University and accordingly the claim of an exemption was rejected.*

Example. *A federal court in Pennsylvania ruled that a religious organization may have violated the Age Discrimination in Employment Act.[111] A Catholic monastery dismissed its chef after ten years of employment. The chef sued the monastery for violating the Act. The monastery asserted that the chef was not protected by the Act since he was not an employee (he owned a food service company that provided meals to the monastery). It also insisted that its decision was based on a deterioration in the quality and variety of food, and had nothing to do with the chef's age. The court refused to dismiss the case and ordered that it proceed to trial. It acknowledged that there was some evidence to support the conclusion that the chef was not an employee, including: (1) he insisted on being treated as an independent contractor for tax purposes, and received a 1099 rather than a W-2; (2) the monastery contracted with the chef's corporation for his services; (3) the monastery did not withhold taxes from the chef's pay; and (4) the monastery did not pay social security taxes for the chef, or extend to him any employee fringe benefit. However, the court concluded that there was evidence that the chef was an employee, and accordingly it could not dismiss the case. It cited the following factors indicating employee status: (1) the monastery provided the chef's equipment; (2) the monastery hired and paid the chef's assistants; (3) the chef had worked for ten years at the monastery, and was required to work five or six days each week; (4) the chef had to comply with various reporting requirements imposed by the monastery; and (5) the chef's work was done at the monastery. The court concluded that from this evidence "there is a genuine issue whether [the chef] was an employee of the [monastery]." The court also rejected the monastery's claim that it dismissed the chef because of poor service. It quoted from a glowing reference letter a monastery representative had issued on behalf of the chef a short time before his dismissal. The letter stated, in part, that "[the chef] will not disappoint the client that entrusts with him their fondest culinary expectations." The court concluded that this letter, praising the chef's performance, and written just a few*

---

[110] Soriano v. Xavier University, 687 F. Supp. 1188 (S.D. Ohio 1988). *See also* Ritter v. Mount St. Mary's College, 738 F.2d 431 (4th Cir. 1984), *aff'd*, 814 F.2d 986 (4th Cir. 1987). Note, however, that while federal law prohibits sex discrimination under "any educational program or activity receiving federal financial assistance," the law does not apply "to an educational institution which is controlled by a religious organization if the application of this section would not be consistent with the religious tenets of such organization." 20 U.S.C. § 1681(a)(3).

[111] Stouch v. Brothers of the Order of Hermits of St. Augustine, 836 F. Supp. 1134 (E.D. Pa. 1993).

months before his dismissal, "creates a genuine issue of fact as to whether the proffered reason for his termination was the true reason." It left to the jury the task of deciding whether the monastery's dismissal was in fact based on unacceptable quality, or upon the chef's age.

Example. *A California court ruled that a hospital affiliated with the Methodist church was a "religious corporation" for purposes of a state civil rights law banning discrimination in employment on the basis of age.[112] A 50-year-old nurse was dismissed by her employer (a hospital) for exceeding four months of medical leave in the same year. She sued the hospital, claiming that it was guilty of age discrimination in violation of a state civil rights law. The hospital claimed that the law exempted "religious corporations" and that it was therefore exempt because of its affiliation with the Methodist church. A state appeals court agreed, on the basis of the following factors: (1) the hospital was "created, organized, and is governed (at least partially) by members of the United Methodist Church"; (2) its articles of incorporation state that upon dissolution, its assets will revert to the United Methodist Church; (3) its bylaws require that a majority of its board members belong to the United Methodist Church, and that at least one other board member must be a Methodist minister; (4) its directors are elected annually by a Methodist agency; (5) it is accredited by the United Methodist Church; (6) a Methodist chaplain ministers to patients, and the hospital broadcasts daily sermons to patients' rooms. The court agreed with the hospital that it was a religious corporation and therefore was exempt from the state age discrimination law. It observed: "[I]t is far from clear that religiously affiliated hospitals serve a primarily secular purpose, as the [nurse] contends. To many religious adherents, the healing of the sick is closely associated with faith in a divine being. Many hospitals, even those without an official religious affiliation, offer on-site chapels and chaplains for the spiritual comfort of their patients and their families. This hospital, in particular, broadcasts daily religious sermons to its patients' rooms. We are not prepared to hold, as a matter of law, that a religiously affiliated hospital may not define and carry out its mission of healing the sick as a primarily religious mission."*

Key point. *Many laws refer specifically to "religious organizations." Examples include zoning ordinances, tax laws, civil rights laws, and copyright law. This case illustrates that an organization may be deemed "religious" for purposes of these laws even though it was created for charitable purposes—so long as it is affiliated with a church and furthers the church's religious mission.*

Example. *A Wisconsin appeals court ruled that a state agency's investigation into a dismissed teacher's complaint of age discrimination did not violate the constitutional rights of a church-operated school.[113] State law prohibits most employers, including church schools, from discriminating in employment decisions on the basis of age. A church school terminated a teacher whom it had employed for 16 years. The school cited "problems with the teacher's classroom management, her professionalism, and her maintenance of a prayerful environment." The teacher felt that she was fired on account of her age (she was 56), and she filed a complaint with the state equal rights agency. The agency concluded that there was reason to believe that the teacher had been a victim of age discrimination, largely on the ground that the school had given the teacher an excellent evaluation less than a year prior to her dismissal. The agency ordered a hearing to resolve the matter, but the school filed a lawsuit seeking to prevent a hearing on the ground that such a procedure would violate its constitutional right to religious freedom. A state appeals court concluded that the school's constitutional rights would not be violated by a hearing addressing the charge of age discrimination. The court relied solely on a 1986 decision of the United States Supreme Court in a similar case. The Supreme Court had ruled that an Ohio civil rights agency "violates no*

---

[112] Kelly v. Methodist Hospital of Southern California, 52 Cal. Rptr.2d 177 (Cal. App. 1996).
[113] Sacred Heart School Board v. Labor & Industry Review Commission, 460 N.W.2d 430 (Wis. App. 1990).

constitutional rights by merely investigating the circumstances of [the employee's] discharge in this case, if only to ascertain whether the ascribed religious-based reason was in fact the reason for the discharge." The court emphasized that the school "is still free to discharge employees for religious reasons," and that the school "will prevail in the [agency] investigation if [the dismissed teacher] cannot prove that the religious-based reason given for her discharge was only a pretext for age discrimination."

§ 8-10 The Americans with Disabilities Act

Key point 8-10. *The federal Americans with Disabilities Act prohibits employers with at least 15 employees, and that are engaged in interstate commerce, from discriminating in any employment decision against a qualified individual with a disability who is able, with or without reasonable accommodation from the employer, to perform the essential functions of the job. Accommodations that impose an undue hardship upon an employer are not required. Religious organizations may give preference to nondisabled members of their faith over disabled persons who are members of a different faith.*

In enacting the Americans with Disabilities Act ("ADA") in 1990, Congress was responding to evidence that disabled persons occupy an inferior status in American life, and face persistent discrimination in employment, transportation, places of public accommodation, and communications. The ADA attempts to eliminate discrimination against individuals with disabilities, by (1) prohibiting covered employers from discriminating in any employment decision against a "qualified individual with a disability," and requiring employers to make "reasonable accommodations" for disabled persons unless doing so would impose an "undue hardship"; (2) prohibiting most places of public accommodation to discriminate against disabled individuals; (3) prohibiting discrimination in public transportation against disabled individuals; and (4) prohibiting discrimination in telecommunications against disabled individuals. The first two of these prohibitions are of the most relevance to religious organizations, and they are discussed separately below.

1. DISCRIMINATION IN EMPLOYMENT

Title I of the ADA prohibits discrimination in any employment decision against a qualified person with a disability. This section of the ADA applies to any employer that is engaged in a business or activity that "affects" interstate commerce and that has 15 or more employees. The prohibition of discrimination applies to all aspects of the employment relationship, including recruitment, advertising, processing of applications, hiring, promotion, awards, demotion, transfer, layoff, termination, right of return following layoff, rates of pay, job assignment, leaves of absence, sick leave, fringe benefits, financial support for training (e.g., apprenticeships, professional meetings and conferences), and employer-sponsored social or recreational programs. The word "discriminate" is defined broadly, and includes:

- segregating or classifying a job applicant or employee on the basis of a disability (if doing so adversely affects the person's job opportunities);

- utilizing standards or criteria that have the effect of discriminating on the basis of disability;

- not making reasonable accommodations to the known physical or mental limitations of an otherwise qualified individual with a disability who is an applicant or employee, unless the employer can demonstrate that the accommodation would impose an undue hardship on the operation of the business of the employer;

- using employment tests or other selection criteria that screen out or tend to screen out disabled individuals, unless the test or criteria is shown to be job-related for the position in question and is consistent with business necessity.

Prohibited discrimination must be against a *qualified individual with a disability*. This important term is defined as follows:

> The term "qualified individual with a disability" means an individual with a disability who, with or without reasonable accommodation, can perform the essential functions of the employment position that such individual holds or desires. For purposes of this title, consideration shall be given to the employer's judgment as to what functions of a job are essential, and if an employer has prepared a written description before advertising or interviewing applicants for the job, this description shall be considered evidence of the essential functions of the job.

This definition contains several important terms. For example, a qualified individual with a disability is someone who, with or without reasonable accommodation by the employer, can perform the essential functions of the job. The regulations interpreting the ADA list the following factors to consider in deciding whether or not a particular function is essential: (1) the employer's judgment; (2) a written job description prepared by the employer before the employee is hired; (3) the amount of time spent on the job performing the function; (4) the consequences of not requiring an employee to perform the function; (5) the essentiality of the function in the work experience of current and former employees in similar positions. It is clear that qualified individuals with a disability cannot be discriminated against simply because they cannot perform marginal job functions. For example, job applicants with a disability that prevents them from using their hands would not be "qualified individuals with a disability" with respect to a clerk-typist position that involves mostly typing, since typing would be an essential function that such persons could not perform. However, these persons would be qualified individuals with a disability with respect to jobs requiring only occasional, light typing, since in such cases typing would be a marginal rather than an essential job function.

The ADA defines the term *disability* to mean "a physical or mental impairment that substantially limits one or more of the major life activities of such individual." The term also includes persons who are "regarded" as being disabled even though they are not. Examples of disabilities include orthopedic, visual, speech, and hearing impairments; cerebral palsy; epilepsy; HIV infection; muscular dystrophy; multiple sclerosis; cancer; heart disease; diabetes; mental retardation; and emotional illness.

The ADA also lists several behaviors and conditions that are *not* disabilities. These include homosexuality; bisexuality; illegal drug use; transvestism; pedophilia; exhibitionism; voyeurism; gender identity disorders and other sexual disorders; compulsive gambling; kleptomania; and pyromania.

Note that the term *qualified individual with a disability* includes persons who can perform the essential functions of a job with reasonable accommodation by the employer. Employers must recognize that they now have an affirmative duty to make reasonable accommodations to the known physical or mental limitations of an otherwise qualified individual with a disability who is an applicant or employee, unless they can demonstrate that the accommodation would impose an undue hardship on the operation of their business. The term *reasonable accommodation* is defined by the ADA as

> making existing facilities used by employees readily accessible to and usable by individuals with disabilities, and job restructuring, part-time or modified work schedules, reassignment to a va-

cant position, acquisition or modification of equipment or devices, appropriate adjustment or modifications of examinations, training materials or policies, the provision of qualified readers or interpreters, and other similar accommodations for individuals with disabilities.

The House Report to the ADA contains the following additional comments regarding reasonable accommodation:

> In [some] cases, the acquisition or modification of equipment, such as adaptive hardware or software for computers, telephone headset amplifiers, and telecommunication devices will enable persons with disabilities to do the job. For some people with disabilities, the assistance of another individual, such as a reader, interpreter or attendant, may be necessary for specified activities. . . .

> A reasonable accommodation should be tailored to the needs of the individual and the requirements of the job. Persons with disabilities have vast experience in all aspects of their lives with the types of accommodations which are effective for them. Employers should not assume that accommodations are required without consulting the applicant or employee with the disability. Stereotypes about disability can result in stereotypes about the need for accommodations, which may exceed what is actually required. Consultations between employers and persons with disabilities will result in an accurate assessment of what is required in order to perform the job duties.

Employers need not accommodate disabled individuals if the accommodation would impose an undue hardship on the operation of their business. The term *undue hardship* is defined by the ADA as

> an action requiring significant difficulty or expense, when considered in light of [the following factors]: (i) the nature and cost of the accommodation needed; (ii) the overall financial resources of the facility or facilities involved in the provision of the reasonable accommodation; the number of persons employed at such facility; the effect on expenses and resources; or the impact otherwise of such accommodation upon the operation of the facility; (iii) the overall financial resources of the covered entity; the overall size of the business of a covered entity with respect to the number of its employees; the number, type, and location of its facilities; and (iv) the type of operation or operations of the covered entity, including the composition, structure, and functions of the workforce of such entity; the geographic separateness, administrative, or fiscal relationship of the facility or facilities in question to the covered entity.

The ADA states that religious organizations (including religious educational institutions) are not prohibited "from giving preference in employment to individuals of a particular religion to perform work" connected with the carrying on by the organization of its activities. The ADA further provides that "a religious organization may require that all applicants and employees conform to the religious tenets of such organization."

The ADA also prohibits pre-employment medical tests, and requires covered employers to post notices to applicants and employees describing the applicable provisions of the Act.

2. Application of Employment Discrimination Provisions to Religious Organizations

What is the relevance to religious organizations of the ADA's prohibition of employment discrimination against qualified individuals with a disability? Consider the following three points:

• The ADA's employment discrimination provisions apply only to employers engaged in a business or activity that "affects" interstate commerce and that have 15 or more employees. Any religious organization with fewer than 15 employees is not covered by the ADA's employment discrimination provisions. Any religious organization having 15 or more employees will be covered only to the extent that it is engaged in a business or activity that "affects" interstate commerce. The application of the "commerce" and "employee" requirements to religious organizations are addressed fully earlier in this chapter.

• The ADA specifically permits religious organizations (including religious educational institutions) to "give preference in employment to individuals of a particular religion to perform work connected with the carrying on by organization of its activities."

• The ADA further provides that "a religious organization may require that all applicants and employees conform to the religious tenets of such organization."

Example. A denominational agency employs D as a maintenance worker. D suffers a heart attack, and is no longer able to shovel snow. D's job description lists snow shoveling as an essential function of his position. Accordingly, the agency terminates D. Assuming that the agency is a covered employer under the ADA, it has violated the law. Consider the following analysis: the first question is whether or not D is a qualified individual with a disability. The term "qualified individual with a disability" is defined by the ADA as an individual with a disability who, with or without reasonable accommodation, can perform the essential functions of the employment position. D is clearly disabled. The ADA lists "heart disease" as a disability (assuming that it substantially limits one or more major life activities). The question then is whether or not D, with reasonable accommodation, can perform the essential functions of the job. Once again, it is clear that D's disability can be accommodated in such a way as to permit him to perform the essential function of snow shoveling. This could simply mean the purchase of a $500 snow blower. The final question is whether or not the reasonable accommodation (purchasing a snow blower) would impose an undue hardship on the employer. Several factors may be considered in answering this question. However, under these facts, it is unlikely that the purchase of a $500 snow blower would impose an undue hardship. Accordingly, the employer must accommodate D's disability. By firing D, the employer failed to reasonably accommodate D's disability, and thereby committed unlawful discrimination.

Example. Same facts as the previous example, except that the employer is a local church with 3 employees. The ADA would not apply, since it applies only to employers having at least 15 employees.

Example. A denominational agency has an opening for a job requiring some use of a computer. K, a blind female, applies for the position. The agency informs K that she is not qualified for the position since she cannot type, and hires someone else. The House Report to the ADA states: "For example, in a job requiring the use of a computer, the essential function is the ability to access, input, and retrieve information from the computer. It is not essential that the person be able to use the keyboard or visually read the information from a computer screen. Adaptive equipment or software may enable a person with no arms or a person with impaired vision to control the computer and access information." Assuming that the agency is a covered employer under the ADA, it has violated the law. K clearly is a qualified individual with a disability. The term "qualified individual with a disability" is defined by the ADA as an individual with a disability who, with or without reasonable accommodation, can perform the essential functions of the employment position. Since the "essential function" of the job is the ability to access, input, and retrieve information from the computer (and not the ability to use the keyboard or visually read the information from a computer screen), K can perform this function with reasonable accommodation. This could simply mean the purchase of an "adaptive equipment or software." The final question is whether or not the reasonable accommodation (purchasing the adaptive equipment or software) would impose an undue hardship on the employer. Several factors may be considered in answering this question. However, under these facts, it is unlikely that the purchase of such equipment or software would impose an undue hardship, if its cost is insignificant in comparison to the agency's total budget. Accordingly, the employer must accommodate K's disability. By refusing to consider K, the employer failed to reasonably accommodate K's disability, and thereby committed unlawful discrimination.

Example. *A denomination conducts a summer camping program for minors. It employs several "counselors" and attendants who help to conduct the program. The denomination requires that all counselors have a valid driver's license. This requirement is based on the fact that it is sometimes necessary for counselors to drive accident victims to a nearby hospital. G applied for a counselor position but was turned down when the denomination discovered that she had epilepsy and did not have a driver's license. The House Report to the ADA states, "While it was necessary that some of the group counselors be able to drive, it was not essential that all group counselors be able to drive. On any given shift, another group counselor could perform the driving duty. Hence, it is necessary to review the job duty not in isolation, but in the context of the actual work environment. . . . The 'essential functions' requirement assures that a person who cannot drive because of his or her disability is not disqualified for these reasons if he or she can do the actual duties of the job." Assuming that the denomination is a covered employer under the ADA, it has violated the law. G clearly is a qualified individual with a disability. The term "qualified individual with a disability" is defined by the ADA as an individual with a disability who, with or without reasonable accommodation, can perform the essential functions of the employment position. Since the "essential function" of the job is the ability to engage in counseling activities, and not the ability to drive a car, G can perform the essential job functions without any accommodation by the employer. Accordingly, the employer must accommodate G's disability. By refusing to consider G, the employer failed to reasonably accommodate G's disability, and thereby committed unlawful discrimination.*

Example. *A denominational agency has a job opening for a warehouse worker. The job description states that the position requires a person capable of lifting 50-pound boxes. R, who suffers from multiple sclerosis, applies for the job although he is not able to lift 50-pound boxes. The House Report to the ADA states, "[Congress] does not intend to limit the ability of covered employers to choose and maintain a qualified workforce. Covered employers continue to have the ability to hire and employ employees who can perform the job. Employers can continue to use job-related criteria in choosing qualified employees. For example, in a job that requires lifting 50-pound boxes, an employer may test applicants and employees to determine whether or not they can lift 50-pound boxes." The ADA itself states that "it may be a defense to a charge of discrimination . . . that an alleged application of qualification standards, tests, or selection criteria that screen out or tend to screen out or otherwise deny a job or benefit to an individual with a disability has been shown to be job-related and consistent with business necessity, and such performance cannot be accomplished by reasonable accommodation." That is, the 50-pound box requirement is a legitimate requirement only if it in fact is job-related (i.e., workers in fact have to lift 50-pound boxes) and consistent with business necessity.*

Example. *A denomination plans to conduct an annual conference of affiliated clergy at Hotel Y. The denomination enters into a contract with Hotel Y for the conference. Assuming that the denomination is a covered employer under the ADA, it has an affirmative duty to investigate the accessibility of Hotel*

Y to disabled persons. The House Report to the ADA states, "Suggested approaches for determining accessibility would be for the employer to inspect the hotel first-hand, if possible, or to ask a local disability group to inspect the hotel. In any event, the employer can always protect itself in such situations by simply ensuring that the contract with the hotel specifies that all rooms to be used for the conference, including the exhibit and meeting rooms, be accessible in accordance with applicable standards. If the hotel breaches this accessibility provision, the hotel will be liable to the employer for the cost of any accommodation needed to provide access to the disabled individual during the conference, as well as for any other costs accrued by the employer."

Example. A religious organization subject to the ADA has a job opening for a typist. One of the essential functions of the job is the ability to type at least 75 words per minute. Two persons apply for the job. One is a disabled person who can type 50 words per minute. The other is a nondisabled person who can type 75 words per minute. The employer is free to hire the nondisabled person. This will not violate the ADA. The House Report to the ADA states: "An employer can continue to give typists typing tests to determine their abilities. [Congress] does not intend that covered employers have an obligation to prefer applicants with disabilities over other applicants on the basis of disability."

Example. A religious organization subject to the ADA has an opening for an accountant. The job description requires that the individual be a college graduate with a degree in accounting. A blind applicant satisfies these requirements. She can perform all the essential functions of the job if she is provided with a part-time reader. If providing a part-time reader is a reasonable accommodation, then the applicant is a qualified individual with a disability, and she cannot be denied the job on the basis of her impairment unless providing the reader would constitute an undue hardship to the employer. Whether or not an undue hardship would exist depends upon an analysis of several factors, including the size, financial resources, and number of employees of the employer. Obviously, the concept of undue hardship will be much narrower for larger employers having substantial financial resources. The House Report to the ADA states, "For some people with disabilities, the assistance of another individual, such as a reader, interpreter or attendant, may be necessary for specified activities."

Example. A denominational agency subject to the ADA restricts its hiring to persons who are members of affiliated churches. J, a disabled person, applies for a position with the agency. J is not a member of an affiliated church. The agency hires T for the position, since T is a member of an affiliated church (even though T had lower test scores than J). This discrimination is permitted under ADA.

Example. Same facts as the previous example, except that both J and T are members of an affiliated church. The denomination may not discriminate against J on the basis of disability.

Example. A federal appeals court ruled that a church-operated school violated the Americans with Disabilities Act by failing to accommodate a disabled job applicant.[114] A church school placed an ad in a local newspaper for a part-time music teacher. A woman with multiple sclerosis and confined to a wheelchair called the school in response to the ad. She claimed that school employees refused to grant her an interview after she asked if the building was "wheelchair accessible." The woman filed a complaint with the Equal Employment Opportunity Commission (EEOC), which determined that the she had been a victim of discrimination on account of her disability. The EEOC sued the church and its school, claiming that they both had violated the Americans with Disabilities Act (ADA) as a result of their

---

[114] Equal Employment Opportunity Commission v. St. Francis Xavier Parochial School, 117 F.3d 621 (D.C. Cir. 1997).

refusal to "accommodate" the woman's disability, and their failure to hire her because of her disability. The church and school argued that they were not covered by the ADA since they were not engaged in "commerce" and had less than 15 employees. A federal appeals court rejected this argument, and ruled that the woman could sue for a violation of the ADA. This case is addressed fully in section 8-05.

Example. *A federal court in Louisiana ruled that a church school did not violate the Americans with Disabilities Act by not rehiring a teacher (the "plaintiff") who had to temporarily quit her job because of pregnancy-related varicose veins.[115] The school accommodated her by providing her with a first floor classroom because of her discomfort in climbing stairs. While pregnant with her fifth child, the plaintiff did not teach and received disability payments from the school. She returned to the school for the next school year but left during the middle of the year when she became pregnant with her sixth child. She received disability payments during this time period. When her doctor released her to return to teaching, the school had no available positions since the release occurred during the middle of the school year. The school's principal informed the plaintiff that she would probably not be hired for the next school year because the school would be retaining her replacement. When the replacement teacher indicated that she would not be returning the next year, the principal hired another teacher from a list of 75 applicants. She chose not to rehire the plaintiff because of her evaluation of the plaintiff's professional capabilities and past attendance record. The principal felt that the new teacher, who had 11 years of teaching experience, was better qualified than the plaintiff. The plaintiff sued the school, claiming that its decision not to rehire her violated the Americans with Disabilities Act (ADA). The court noted that the school offered non-discriminatory reasons for the principal's decision not to rehire the plaintiff. It was then up to the plaintiff to prove that the employer's reason was a "pretext" for discrimination. The court concluded that the plaintiff failed to meet this burden.*

Example. *A woman began her employment as choirmaster of a church and thereafter became the director of music. While employed, she allegedly suffered from a variety of disabilities, including asthma, osteoarthritis of both knees, migraine headaches, and endometriosis. She claimed that the church refused to modify her work schedule to allow full recovery from knee surgery and, after she suffered chemical exposures from cleaning materials, refused to accommodate her chemical sensitivities. Her employment was terminated, and she sued the church and its pastor, claiming that she was discharged in violation of the Americans with Disabilities Act. The pastor insisted that the ADA only applied to employers, and therefore he could not be sued personally for violating it. The pastor and church both claimed that the woman's lawsuit was barred by the first amendment's nonestablishment and free exercise of religion clauses. A federal court in Louisiana agreed with the pastor that the ADA only applied to employers, and therefore the woman could not sue the pastor for violating the ADA since he was not her employer.[116] The church claimed that if a civil court were to apply the ADA to this case, it would constitute an "excessive entanglement" between church and state in violation of first amendment's nonestablishment of religion clause. The court agreed that it had to "avoid disputes that cannot be resolved without entangling the government in questions of religious doctrine, polity, and practice," and that contain issues "which cannot be analyzed in purely secular terms." It concluded that the woman's lawsuit might place the court in just such a position. However, the court ruled that dismissal of the case at this time was premature, since the church had not yet established that its decision to dismiss the woman was based solely on religious grounds. It cautioned that the "bare potential" that an employment discrimination inquiry would impact religious beliefs "does not warrant precluding the*

---

[115] Kent v. Roman Catholic Church, 7 A.D. Cases 884 (E.D. La. 1997).
[116] Starkman v. Evans, 18 F. Supp.2d 630 (E.D. La. 1998).

application" of the law to religious employers. The court agreed with the church that if the woman was a "minister," then the first amendment's "free exercise of religion" clause barred her ADA claim against the church. The court concluded that the woman's position at the church was "within the parameters" of the ministerial exception from civil rights laws. It pointed out that "the Director of Music was responsible for duties squarely within the conventional understanding of ecclesiastical or religious functions, and was not a position mainly performing tasks which are not traditionally ecclesiastical or religious." The court noted that "the ministerial exception has not been limited to members of the clergy," but rather "encompasses all employees of a religious institution, whether ordained or not, whose primary functions serve its spiritual and pastoral mission."

Example. *A Washington state court ruled that a Catholic archdiocese was liable for handicap discrimination.[117] The archdiocese maintains a conference facility that hired a female housekeeper. The housekeeper injured her hand while working, and had to have surgery. Following the surgery, she returned to work for a brief time before she underwent a second surgery. When she left for this second surgery, she alleged that her supervisor assured her that there "would always be a place for her" at the conference facility and that another employee would fill her position only on a temporary basis. Eight months later, the housekeeper was released by her doctor to return to work. When she returned to work, she was informed by her supervisor that her position had been filled after she had been absent for 60 days. She was not notified of any other job openings nor offered any other jobs with the archdiocese, even though there were 3 job openings at the conference facility following her discharge. The housekeeper sued the archdiocese, alleging handicap discrimination. A jury awarded her $150,000 in damages, and a state appeals court affirmed this verdict. The court noted that once the employee demonstrated that she was handicapped, and that she was qualified to fill vacant positions, then the burden "shifted" to the employer "to demonstrate a nondiscriminatory reason for refusing to accommodate" the employee. The court noted that the housekeeper had established that she was handicapped (because of her hand injury), and that 3 job openings later occurred that she was qualified to fill. Accordingly, the archdiocese then had the duty to demonstrate that it had a valid nondiscriminatory reason for not "accommodating" the housekeeper by taking affirmative measures to notify her of the job openings. The court insisted that when an employee becomes handicapped on the job, the employer has a continuing duty to inform the employee of job openings beyond the termination of the employer-employee relationship—until such time as "such attempts to accommodate become an undue burden rather than a reasonable requirement." Since the archdiocese failed to notify the former employee of these job openings, and failed to demonstrate a nondiscriminatory reason for not doing so, the former employee had proven her claim of handicap discrimination.*

3. Discrimination in Public Accommodations

Another major provision (Title III) of the ADA prohibits discrimination against disabled persons by privately-owned places of public accommodation. The ADA states that "no individual shall be discriminated against on the basis of disability in the full and equal enjoyment of the goods, services, facilities, privileges, advantages, or accommodations of any place of public accommodation by any person who owns, leases (or leases to), or operates a place of public accommodation." The ADA defines the term *public accommodation* to include 12 types of facilities, including auditoriums or other places of public gathering, private schools (including nursery, elementary, secondary, undergraduate, and postgraduate), and day care centers.

---

[117] Wheeler v. Catholic Archdiocese of Seattle, 829 P.2d 196 (Wash. App. 1992).

STEPS EMPLOYERS SHOULD TAKE TO COMPLY WITH THE ADA

1. Prepare job descriptions for all employees. Be sure to itemize essential job functions. These are functions that are job-related and required by business necessity. Do not list functions that will not in fact be required in performing the job in question.

2. Review job application forms and eliminate any question that segregates or classifies applicants on the basis of disability.

3. Review all employee selection criteria and procedures to ensure that they (1) provide an accurate measure of an applicant's actual ability to perform the essential functions of the job, and (2) offer disabled applicants a reasonable accommodation to meet the criteria that relate to the essential job functions.

4. Review all pre-employment tests to ensure that they do not discriminate against disabled individuals.

5. Eliminate any pre-employment medical examination requirement.

6. Post required notices informing applicants and employees of their rights under the ADA.

7. Interview procedures and questions should be reviewed carefully. It is not permissible to ask applicants about disabilities. For example, if driving is an essential job function, an employer may ask a job applicant whether or not he or she has a driver's license, but it would be improper to ask whether or not the applicant has a visual impairment.

8. Designate an employee who will be responsible for ensuring ADA compliance, and be sure that this individual receives sufficient training.

9. Educate supervisory personnel regarding ADA requirements and prohibitions.

The ADA defines discrimination in public accommodations broadly to include the following:

• Denying an individual (or class of individuals) the opportunity to use the accommodations on the basis of a disability.

• Providing disabled individuals with use or enjoyment of the accommodations that is not equal to that afforded nondisabled persons.

• Providing disabled individuals with use or enjoyment of the accommodations separate from those afforded nondisabled persons.

• Establishing eligibility criteria that screen out disabled individuals.

• Failure to make reasonable modifications in policies, practices, or procedures, if necessary to make the accommodations available to disabled individuals.

• Failure to take steps to ensure that disabled persons are not denied use of the accommodations because of the absence of "auxiliary aids and services."

• Failure to remove architectural barriers in existing facilities if such removal is "readily achievable." The term *readily achievable* is defined by the ADA to mean "easily accomplishable and able to be carried out without much difficulty or expense." Factors to be considered in making this determination include (1) the nature and cost of the action needed, and (2) the overall financial resources of the facility, the number of employees, and the impact of the removal on the operation of the facility.

• Failure to employ readily achievable alternatives if the removal of architectural barriers is not readily achievable.

Disabled persons are permitted to sue an organization that owns or operates a place of public accommodation that engages in one or more of these discriminatory practices. They can either obtain a court injunction ordering the place of public accommodation to comply with the law, or they can obtain monetary damages (up to $50,000 for a first violation, and up to $100,000 for subsequent violations).

4. APPLICATION OF THE PUBLIC ACCOMMODATION PROVISIONS TO RELIGIOUS ORGANIZATIONS

The ADA specifies that its public accommodation provisions "shall not apply to . . . religious organizations or entities controlled by religious organizations, including places of worship." Accordingly, most types of religious organizations are excluded from the prohibition of discrimination in places of public accommodation. The House Report to the ADA specifies that "places of worship and schools controlled by religious organizations are among those organizations and entities which fall within this exemption." The House Report further specifies that "activities conducted by a religious organization or an entity controlled by a religious organization on its own property, which are open to nonmembers of that organization or entity are included in this exemption."

It is important to note that while religious organizations are not subject to the ADA's public accommodation provisions, they may be subject to similar provisions under state or local law.

> **Example.** *Local churches, denominational agencies, and church-controlled schools do not have to comply with the public accommodation provisions of the ADA. For example, they would not need to remove architectural barriers to make their facilities more accessible to disabled persons. This exemption applies both to existing and future construction.*

§ 8-11 Employer "Retaliation" Against Victims of Discrimination

> **Key point 8-11.** *State and federal civil rights laws generally prohibit employers from retaliating against an employee for filing a discrimination claim or otherwise exercising rights provided by the law.*

Many federal and state civil rights laws that ban discrimination in employment prohibit employers from "retaliating" against employees who oppose discriminatory practices or pursue claims of discrimination. To illustrate, Title VII of the Civil Rights Act of 1964,[118] the federal Age Discrimination in Employment Act,[119] and the Americans with Disabilities Act[120] all prohibit employer retaliation.

---

[118] 42 U.S.C. § 2000e-3(a).
[119] 29 U.S.C. § 623(d).
[120] 42 U.S.C. § 12203.

Example. The Colorado Supreme Court threw out a lawsuit brought by a woman alleging that her church acted improperly and unlawfully when it dismissed her after she made complaints of sexual harassment against another minister. The woman alleged that her stepfather committed various acts of sexual assault against her when she was a minor. Her stepfather was a minister at the time, and later became president of his denomination. The woman pursued ministerial studies and was licensed as a minister. She later learned that her stepfather was harassing female church employees and parishioners in another church, and she reported this to denominational officers. In response, the stepfather filed charges with the denomination against the woman, claiming that her allegations were false and demanding a full investigation. After an investigation, denominational officers revoked the woman's license and denied her the opportunity to open a new church. The woman responded by filing a lawsuit against her stepfather, and her denomination, alleging several theories of liability including illegal retaliation by denominational officials in response to her charges of sexual harassment, in violation of Title VII of the Civil Rights Act of 1964. The court rejected this claim on the ground that it arose from the denomination's decision to revoke her minister's license. The court concluded that it was barred from resolving the woman's lawsuit on the basis of the first amendment's free exercise and nonestablishment of religion clauses.[121]

Example. A male associate pastor engaged in sexual relations with two female church employees. The two women eventually disclosed the affairs to the church's senior pastor. This led to their termination, and the forced resignation of the associate pastor. The women later sued the church, claiming that it committed unlawful "retaliation" against them in violation of Title VII by dismissing them for disclosing the associate pastor's behavior. A federal district court disagreed, noting that the church could not be responsible for retaliation since its decision to dismiss the women was not sex discrimination. This conclusion was affirmed on appeal by a federal appeals court.[122] The court observed: "The [women] did not . . . produce any evidence suggesting that they were fired because of their gender. In fact, the record shows that [the former minister], who also committed adultery, was forced to resign, and that [the church's] position against adultery was neutral with respect to sex, longstanding, and understood by both [women] at the time they engaged in sexual conduct with [the minister]."

Example. A federal court in California ruled that a female minister failed to prove that her denominational agency had engaged in sexual harassment.[123] A woman (the victim) was employed as national director of a department of a denominational agency (the Buddhist Churches of America, or BCA). She was ordained as a Buddhist minister. She alleged that another minister made a sexually harassing telephone call to her during a BCA conference. She filed a complaint with the Equal Employment Opportunity Commission (EEOC) regarding the harassing call. She later sued the BCA in federal court, claiming that it had engaged in unlawful "retaliation" against her by cutting off all funding of her department following the filing of her EEOC claim. The court noted that to prove a "prima facie case" of unlawful retaliation, a plaintiff must establish that she acted to protect her Title VII rights, that an adverse employment action was thereafter taken against her, and that a connection existed between these two events. At that point, the burden of production then shifts to the employer to advance legitimate, non-retaliatory reasons for any adverse actions taken against the plaintiff. The court concluded that it could not resolve the victim's retaliation claim, since "[i]f plaintiff makes out a prima facie case of retaliation, the court would be placed in the position of evaluating whether BCA had any legitimate, non-retaliatory reasons for the defunding of [her] department. . . . Although the financial

[121] Van Osdol v. Vogt, 908 P.2d 402 (Colo. 1996).
[122] Sanders v. Casa View Baptist Church, 134 F.3d 331 (5th Cir. 1998).
[123] Himaka v. Buddhist Churches of America, 917 F.Supp. 698 (N.D. Cal. 1995).

decisions of a church are not, strictly speaking, part of the church's "spiritual function," these decisions remain vital to a religious organization's ministerial and religious planning. Determining whether the decision to eliminate funding from [the victim's] department—a religious education department—was legitimate seems likely to draw this court into judgments on matters of faith and doctrine, as well as matters of general church governance. Because it appears that plaintiff's retaliation claim would result in an intolerably close relationship between church and state both on a substantive and procedural level, plaintiff's retaliation claim is dismissed . . . on first amendment grounds.

§ 8-12   Discrimination Based on Sexual Orientation

***Key point 8-12.** Many state civil rights laws prohibit employers with a specified number of employees from discriminating in any employment decision on the basis of the sexual orientation of an employee or applicant for employment. Such laws generally exempt religious organizations.*

Several states have enacted laws prohibiting employers from discriminating against employees and applicants for employment on the basis of their sexual orientation. All of these laws contain some form of exemption for religious organizations. Examples include California,[124] Connecticut,[125] Hawaii,[126] Massachusetts,[127] Minnesota,[128] New Jersey,[129] Rhode Island,[130] Vermont,[131] and Wisconsin.[132] Even without such an

---

[124] CAL. LABOR CODE § 1102.1 ("employers" subject to a state law banning discrimination in employment on the basis of sexual orientation do not include "a religious association or corporation not organized for private profit, whether incorporated as a religious or public benefit corporation").

[125] CONN. GEN. STAT. § 46a-81p (specifies that the ban on employment discrimination based on sexual orientation "shall not apply to a religious corporation, entity, association, educational institution or society with respect to the employment of individuals to perform work connected with the carrying on by such corporation, entity, association, educational institution or society of its activities, or with respect to matters of discipline, faith, internal organization or ecclesiastical rule, custom or law which are established by such corporation, entity, association, educational institution or society").

[126] HAWAII REV. STAT. § 378-3 (permits a "religious or denominational institution or organization, or any organization operated for charitable or educational purposes, that is operated, supervised, or controlled by or in connection with a religious organization," to give preference "to individuals of the same religion or denomination or [to make] a selection calculated to promote the religious principles for which the organization is established or maintained").

[127] MASS. ANN. LAWS ch. 151B, § 4 (not a specific exemption for religious organizations from the ban on discrimination in employment based on sexual orientation, but it specify that "[n]otwithstanding the provisions of any general or special law nothing herein shall be construed to bar any religious or denominational institution or organization, or any organization operated for charitable or educational purposes, which is operated, supervised or controlled by or in connection with a religious organization, from limiting admission to or giving preference to persons of the same religion or denomination or from taking any action with respect to matters of employment, discipline, faith, internal organization, or ecclesiastical rule, custom, or law which are calculated by such organization to promote the religious principles for which it is established or maintained").

[128] MINN. STAT. ANN. § 336.02.

[129] N.J. REV. STAT. § 10:5-12 ("it shall not be an unlawful employment practice . . . for a religious association or organization to utilize religious affiliation as a uniform qualification in the employment of clergy, religious teachers or other employees engaged in the religious activities of the association or organization, or in following the tenets of its religion in establishing and utilizing criteria for employment of an employee").

[130] R.I GEN. LAWS § 28-5-6(2)(B) ("[n]othing herein shall be construed to apply to a religious corporation, association, educational institution, or society with respect to the employment of individuals of its religion to perform work connected with the carrying on of its activities").

[131] VT. STAT. ANN. title 21, § 495(e) ("[t]he provisions of this section prohibiting discrimination on the basis of sexual orientation shall not be construed to prohibit or prevent any religious or denominational institution or organization, or any organization operated for charitable or educational purposes, which is operated, supervised or controlled by or in connection with a religious organization, from giving preference to persons of the same religion or denomination or from taking any action with respect to matters of employment which is calculated by the organization to promote the religious principles for which it is established or maintained").

[132] WIS. STAT. § 111.337(2)(a) (not a specific exemption for religious organizations from the ban on discrimination in employment based on sexual orientation, but it does permit religious organizations to "give preference to an applicant or employee who is a member of the same or a similar religious denomination").

exemption, it is unlikely that the civil courts would apply such a law to the relationship between a church and its ministers.

Example. A Minnesota appeals court ruled a local civil rights ordinance banning discrimination against homosexuals could not be applied to a religious organization.[133] *A Catholic religious center in Minneapolis rented space to a number of community groups, including Alcoholics Anonymous, Weight Watchers, and Dignity (an organization composed largely of homosexual Catholics). In 1986, the local archbishop was instructed by the Vatican to determine whether or not pastoral practices in the diocese were consistent with the Vatican's "Letter to Bishops on the Pastoral Care of Homosexual Persons." This letter prohibits church facilities from being used by organizations that oppose the Vatican's position on homosexuality. Since Dignity's beliefs were in conflict with the Vatican's position, its lease of space in the religious center was terminated. Dignity filed a complaint with the Minneapolis "department of civil rights," claiming that a municipal civil rights ordinance banning discrimination against homosexuals had been violated by the termination of its lease. It named the center along with the diocese and archbishop as defendants. The complaint was dismissed, and Dignity appealed to an appeals board which concluded that Dignity's civil rights had been violated by the defendants. It assessed fines, and ordered the defendants to refrain from any further discrimination against homosexuals. The defendants appealed this order to a state appeals court. The court ruled that application of the civil rights ordinance to the center, diocese, and archbishop constituted prohibited "entanglement" of the government in religious affairs in violation of the first amendment. It concluded: "In determining whether state action constitutes excessive entanglement, a court must undertake an examination of the character and purposes of the groups involved, the nature of the state's involvement, and the relationship that results between the state and religious authority. In this case, we conclude the nature of the state's activity clearly evinces excessive entanglement. . . . A city or municipality is without jurisdiction to enforce civil rights protections against a religious organization enforcing conformity of its members to certain standards of conduct and morals. We therefore conclude the order of the [appeals board] must be reversed as excessive entanglement in religious affairs contrary to the first amendment of the United States Constitution." This case is one of a few decisions recognizing that the first amendment permits a church to "enforce conformity of its members to certain standards of conduct or morals," notwithstanding a civil rights law to the contrary.*

Example. Georgetown University was sued by various homosexual student groups for its refusal to officially recognize them. The students cited the District of Columbia "Civil Rights Act," which bans discrimination based on sexual orientation by any educational institution within the District. The University (a private Catholic educational institution) argued that recognition of the groups would violate its constitutional right to religious freedom since recognition would imply endorsement of conduct contrary to Catholic doctrine. The court concluded that the District's Civil Rights Act did not require that a private religious university recognize a student group whose beliefs and practices were contrary to church teachings. However, it held that the Act did require equal access to University facilities and services, and, since the University denied the homosexual groups certain services (a mailbox, computer labeling, mailing services, and the right to apply for funding), it was in violation of the Act. The court found that any burden on the University's religious freedom that might result from providing these incidental services was so minimal that it was overridden by the compelling governmental interest of eradicating discrimination.[134]

---

[133] Dignity Twin Cities v. Newman Center and Chapel, 472 N.W.2d 355 (Minn. App. 1991).
[134] Gay Rights Coalition v. Georgetown University, 536 A.2d 1 (D.C. App. 1987).

Example. A city enacts a civil rights ordinance that bans any employer (including churches) from discriminating on the basis of sexual orientation in any employment decision. A church argues that applying such a law to a church that is opposed on the basis of religious doctrine to hiring homosexuals will violate its constitutional right to freely exercise its religion. Under the Supreme Court's 1990 ruling in the Smith case,[135] it is doubtful that the church would prevail. The civil rights law in question clearly is neutral and of general applicability, and accordingly it is presumptively constitutional (without any need of demonstrating a compelling governmental interest). However, a number of federal courts (prior to the Smith case) concluded that the clergy-church relationship is unique and is beyond the reach of civil rights laws. Accordingly, it is doubtful that such an ordinance could be applied to clergy. This of course assumes that the Supreme Court, after Smith, would agree with these previous rulings.

§ 8-13   Discrimination Based on Use of Legal Substances

Key point 8-13. Many states have enacted laws prohibiting employers from disciplining employees for using lawful products (such as tobacco) during non-working hours. Some of these laws exempt religious organizations.

Many states have enacted laws prohibiting employers from disciplining employees for using lawful products (such as tobacco) during non-working hours. Some of these laws exempt religious organizations. Even without such an exemption, it is unlikely that most courts would apply such a law to the relationship between a church and its ministers.

Example. The North Dakota Supreme Court ruled that an employer may have violated a minister's legal rights by dismissing him for engaging in private sexual behavior (masturbation) in a private stall in a public restroom.[136] A state law prohibits an employer from discharging an employee "for participation in lawful activity off the employer's premises during nonworking hours which is not in direct conflict with the essential business-related interests of the employer." Further, employers can dismiss employees who engage in lawful behavior during nonworking hours if "contrary to a bona fide occupational qualification that reasonably and rationally relates to employment activities and the responsibilities of a particular employee . . . ." This law was enacted to prevent employers from "inquiring into an employee's non-work conduct, including an employee's weight and smoking, marital, or sexual habits." The minister acknowledged that state law prohibits masturbation in a public place, but he insisted that a private stall in a public restroom is not a "public place" and therefore his behavior was legal. And, since it was legal, he could not be dismissed for engaging in such behavior. The court noted that several other courts have concluded that "activities conducted in an enclosed stall in a public restroom do not occur in a public place." On the other hand, it acknowledged that state law allows

---

[135] Employment Division v. Smith, 110 S. Ct. 1595 (1990). In the *Smith* case, the Supreme Court ruled that "neutral laws of general applicability" can be applied without offending the first amendment guaranty of religious freedom, even if the religious beliefs or practices of some persons or entities are adversely impacted. The Court observed that the constitutional guaranty of religious freedom "does not relieve an individual of the obligation to comply with a valid and neutral law of general applicability on the ground that the law [prohibits] conduct that his religion prescribes." Congress attempted to overrule the *Smith* case by enacting the Religious Freedom Restoration Act. This Act required a "compelling government interest" to support any law or government practice imposing a substantial burden on the free exercise of religion. In 1997, the Supreme Court ruled that the Act was unconstitutional. City of Boerne v. Flores, 117 S. Ct. 2157 (1997). However, some courts have concluded that the Supreme Court's decision in the *City of Boerne* case only invalidated the Religious Freedom Restoration Act with regard to state and local (as distinguished from federal) legislation. As a result, the Act may protect religious organizations from any future federal legislation prohibiting employment discrimination based on sexual orientation.

[136] Hougum v. Valley Memorial Homes, 574 N.W.2d 812 (N.D. 1998).

DISMISSING AN EMPLOYEE FOR ENGAGING IN LAWFUL ACTIVITIES DURING NONWORKING HOURS

Many states have enacted laws preventing employers from dismissing employees on account of lawful behavior during nonworking hours. These laws vary from state to state. Church leaders should review their own state law and be able to answer the following questions:

(1) Does our state have such a law?

(2) Does it apply to churches? In many states, such laws exempt churches.

(3) If our church is covered, which employees are protected? All employees? Only lay employees? What about clergy?

(4) If our church is covered, what activities are prohibited? This is critical. You need to know how your church can violate the law.

(5) What exemptions exist? It is common for such laws to exempt behavior that is contrary to a "bona fide occupational qualification" that reasonably relates to employment activities and responsibilities. Church leaders need to be familiar with any available exemptions.

---

employers to dismiss an employee for engaging in lawful behavior during nonworking hours if (1) the behavior is in direct conflict with the essential business-related interests of the employer, or (2) is contrary to a bona fide occupational qualification that reasonably and rationally relates to employment activities and the responsibilities of a particular employee. The court conceded that the retirement home might be able to establish either or both of these exceptions, and it sent the case back to the trial court for further consideration.

§ 8-14 Discrimination Based on Military Status

Key point 8-14. Federal law prohibits all employers, including churches, from discriminating against any person on account of military service. This includes discriminating against an applicant for employment, or an employee, who has an obligation to perform services on active duty or in the National Guard.

A federal law enacted in 1994 specifies that a person "who is a member of, applies to be a member of, performs, has performed, applies to perform, or has an obligation to perform service in a uniformed service shall not be denied initial employment, reemployment, retention in employment, promotion, or any benefit of employment by an employer" on the basis of his or her military service or application for service. The law applies to all employers, including churches, whether or not they are engaged in interstate commerce and regardless of the number of their employees. The law defines "service in the uniformed services" to include "active duty, active duty for training, initial active duty for training, inactive duty training, full-time National Guard duty, and a period for which a person is absent from a position of employment for the purpose of an examination to determine the fitness of the person to perform any such duty." The law only protects employees whose military absences from an employer have not exceeded 5 years, with certain exceptions. An employee's reinstatement rights depend upon the time he or she is away on military leave.

This law will have limited application to ministers, who are exempt by federal law from the military training and service. However, some ministers do perform "service in the uniformed services," and the protections of the law may apply to them. Church leaders should assume that the law applies to both ministers and lay workers unless an opinion to the contrary is received from legal counsel.

§ 8-15   The Civil Rights Restoration Act

Key point 8-15. Several federal civil rights laws apply to organizations that receive federal financial assistance, including the Rehabilitation Act, Age Discrimination Act, and Title VI of the Civil Rights Act of 1964. The Civil Rights Restoration Act subjects an entire institution that receives federal financial assistance to these civil rights laws, rather than the specific program or activity that is the actual recipient of the federal assistance.

In 1988, Congress enacted the Civil Rights Restoration Act of 1987 (also known as the "Grove City Bill"). This section will summarize the application of this civil rights law to churches and clergy.

Grove City College is a private college that accepted no direct financial assistance from the federal government. However, the college did enroll students who received federally funded Pell grants and guaranteed student loans. Between 1974 and 1984, students financed their education at Grove City College with more than $1.8 million in Pell grant funds. In 1976, the United States Department of Education asked the college to certify that it was complying with Title IX of the Education Amendments of 1972,[137] which prohibits sex discrimination in any education program or activity receiving federal funds. The college refused to comply with this request on the ground that the receipt of Pell grants and guaranteed student loans by students did not make the college a recipient of federal funds. In 1984, the United States Supreme Court unanimously held that Grove City College was a recipient of federal funds.[138] However, by a 6-3 vote, the Court held that federal financial assistance does not subject an entire educational institution to the Title IX ban on sex discrimination, but rather only the specific "program or activity" that receives the federal funds. Accordingly, Pell grant funding triggered Title IX coverage only of the college's financial aid program. The college remained free to discriminate on the basis of sex in all other programs and activities, including academic instruction and extracurricular activities.

Three other federal anti-discrimination laws were directly affected by the Grove City ruling. The Rehabilitation Act of 1973[139] prohibits discrimination based on handicap in any program or activity receiving federal funding, and the Age Discrimination Act of 1975[140] and Title VI of the Civil Rights Act of 1964[141] ban age and race discrimination, respectively, by any program or activity receiving federal funding. Under the Grove City ruling, only the specific program or activity receiving federal funds, not the institution itself, was subject to these nondiscrimination provisions.

The Civil Rights Restoration Act of 1987[142] was designed to reverse the Supreme Court's Grove City ruling, and to make an entire institution subject to federal anti-discrimination laws rather than just the specific program or activity within an institution that ultimately receives federal funds. Accordingly, the Act amends

---

[137] 20 U.S.C. § 1681(a).
[138] Grove City College v. Bell, 465 U.S. 555 (1984).
[139] 29 U.S.C. § 794.
[140] 42 U.S.C. § 6102.
[141] 42 U.S.C. § 2000d.
[142] Pub. Law 100-259.

Title IX of the Education Amendments of 1972,[143] as well as the Rehabilitation Act,[144] Age Discrimination Act,[145] and Title VI of the Civil Rights Act,[146] to make it clear that these nondiscrimination provisions apply to certain institutions "as a whole" if any of their programs or activities receives federal financial assistance.

How does this new law impact churches, church schools, and religious institutions? Consider the following:

1. CHURCHES

First, it must be emphasized that only recipients of federal financial assistance are covered by the new law. Churches, church schools, and religious institutions that receive no federal funds are simply not affected by the Civil Rights Restoration Act. Since the vast majority of churches receive no federal financial assistance, they need not be concerned about the this law. The contentions that churches are recipients of federal funding if they receive contributions from social security recipients, or if parents pay for church child care services with AFDC payments, are at this time unfounded for two reasons. First, in the Grove City decision the Supreme Court specifically ruled that a school is not made a recipient of federal financial assistance simply because some of its students pay their educational expenses with money received from "food stamps, social security benefits, welfare payments, and other forms of general purpose governmental assistance" since (a) there is no evidence Congress intended that the use of such benefits to pay for school expenses triggered coverage under Title IX; (b) such "general assistance payments, unlike student aid programs, were not designed to assist schools"; (c) "educational institutions have no control over, and indeed perhaps no knowledge of, whether they ultimately receive federal funds made available to individuals under general assistance programs"; and (d) students' "eligibility for general assistance is not tied to attendance at an educational institution."[147] Such language, which was approved unanimously by the Supreme Court and which was neither repudiated nor affected by the Civil Rights Restoration Act, clearly suggests that use of federal benefits received under a general assistance program to pay for church services or benefits does not render the church a recipient of federal financial assistance.

Second, the Act itself (section 7) specifies that it shall not be construed to extend the coverage of any of the four federal anti-discrimination laws affected by the Act to the "ultimate beneficiaries of federal financial assistance."[148] This language means that individuals who receive social security benefits or welfare payments, grocers who accept food stamps, or farmers who receive crop subsidies, will not be subject to federal anti-discrimination law solely on that basis. If that is so, it is hard to imagine how a court could interpret the Act to cover churches to whom such "ultimate beneficiaries" make contributions or payments. No court has ever reached such a conclusion. Many of the senators who sponsored or co-sponsored the bill specifically rejected the notion that churches are covered if any of their members donates money that is attributable, in whole or in part, to social security, veterans benefits, or any other form of federal assistance. Such statements will be directly relevant in any judicial interpretation of the law.

---

[143] 20 U.S.C. § 1687.

[144] 29 U.S.C. § 794(b).

[145] 42 U.S.C. § 6107.

[146] 42 U.S.C. § 2000d-4a.

[147] 465 U.S. at 565 n.13.

[148] Section 7 of the Act specifies that "[n]othing in the amendments made by this Act shall be construed to extend the application of the Acts so amended to ultimate beneficiaries of federal financial assistance excluded from coverage before the enactment of this Act." This section is set forth in a note to 20 U.S.C. § 1687.

Some have suggested that exemption from federal income taxation renders a church a recipient of federal financial assistance. If this were true, nearly every church would be subject to the Act. While several senators publicly scoffed at such a suggestion, it is nevertheless true that one federal court has reached just such a conclusion. In 1972, a federal district court in the District of Columbia concluded that "there is little question that the provision of a tax deduction for charitable contributions is a grant of federal financial assistance.... The charitable contribution deduction is a special tax provision not required by, and contrary to, widely accepted definitions of income applicable to the determination of the structure of an income tax. It operates in effect as a government matching grant...."[149] This radical conclusion has never been endorsed by any other federal court, and indeed it seems to have been rejected by the United States Supreme Court.[150] However, the existence of even one decision reaching such a result is disturbing, and at the least suggests the possibility that other courts might adopt such a view in the future.

Some churches do receive federal financial assistance. Perhaps the most common examples would be church participation in the federal commodities program, the school lunch program, disaster relief, HUD loans, refugee relief, low-income housing, or churches that operate nursing or retirement homes and that receive medicaid or medicare funds. An additional potential source of federal financial assistance to large numbers of churches would be participation in federally subsidized child care. In 1991, Congress enacted legislation authorizing financial assistance to low-income families to provide child care. The assistance (beginning in 1992) will be in the form of "child care certificates" that low-income parents can use to obtain child care services at authorized facilities. Churches that are "registered" or licensed under state law are eligible to participate in the program, if they satisfy various requirements (most of which pertain to health and safety matters). There is little doubt that most churches will qualify as eligible child care providers under this legislation, and accordingly there is the possibility of huge amounts of federal financial assistance flowing to low-income parents and then on to church child care facilities.

Testimony before Congress during the debate leading up to the enactment of this legislation demonstrated that the vast majority of Americans in need of child care would prefer that their children attend church-operated facilities. Obviously, the question arises—will a church become a recipient of federal financial assistance by receiving child care certificates and redeeming them for cash with the state agency administering the program? If so, then a church will be subject to the anti-discrimination provisions of the four federal statutes summarized above (prohibiting discrimination on account of sex, age, handicap, and race). Further, according to the Civil Rights Restoration Act, the anti-discrimination provisions would apply "institution-wide" rather than to the particular program or activity receiving the assistance. In the only reference to this issue, the federal child care law simply states that "child care certificates shall not be considered to be grants or contracts."[151] A joint House-Senate conference committee made the following statement:

> The managers intend that the determination whether any financial assistance provided under this [law], including a ... child care certificate, constitutes federal financial assistance for purposes of title VI of the Civil Rights Act of 1964, title IX of the Education Amendments of 1972, the Rehabilitation Act of 1973, the Age Discrimination Act of 1975, all as amended, and the regulations issued thereunder, shall be made in accordance with those provisions.[152]

Unfortunately, this language holds open the possibility that child care certificates redeemed by a church-operated child care provider will make that church a recipient of federal financial assistance. Congress had the

---

[149] McGlotten v. Connally, 338 F. Supp. 448 (D.D.C. 1972).
[150] Bob Jones University v. Simon, 416 U.S. 725, 731-32 n.6 (1974).
[151] § 658P(2).
[152] HOUSE CONF. REP. NO. 101-964, §§ 5081-5082, *reprinted in* 1991 U.S CODE CONG. & AD. NEWS 2626 *et seq.*

opportunity to repudiate such a view in the child care legislation, and chose to reject it. As a result, this question will be left to the courts to decide on a case-by-case basis. It is entirely possible that a church that accepts and redeems child care certificates will be deemed to be a recipient of federal financial assistance. This question is addressed in further detail in chapter 13.

Under the Civil Rights Restoration Act, complete coverage of all the activities and operations of a church or other religious organization would result under two circumstances. First, if federal financial assistance is extended to the organization "as a whole," the organization as a whole would be required to comply with federal anti-discrimination law. Second, when "principally engaged in the business of providing education, health care, housing, social services, or parks and recreation," an organization is subject "as a whole" to federal anti-discrimination law. However, it is reasonably certain that a church will not be covered "as a whole" on the basis of this second circumstance even if it is engaged in providing child care, nursing home, or other social services, since it will still be "principally engaged" in providing religious services. Except in these two circumstances, a church or other religious organization that receives federal assistance will not be covered in its entirety. Rather, only the specific "plant or other comparable, geographically separate facility to which federal financial assistance is extended" will be subjected to federal anti-discrimination law.

> *Example.* First Church operates a private elementary school in a separate building on the church's premises. The school is a recipient of federal financial assistance. Since the aid is not to the church "as a whole," and the church is principally engaged in religious rather than educational or social services, the church "as a whole" is not subject to federal laws banning discrimination based on age, sex, race, or handicap by recipients of federal aid. Rather, only the "geographically separate facility to which federal financial assistance is extended" (i.e., the school) will be covered.

> *Example.* Same facts as the preceding example, except that the elementary school is not in a geographically separate facility, but is located within the church building. In this case, the Civil Rights Restoration Act would impose all four federal anti-discrimination laws to the church as a whole rather than to just the school, since the church and school are not geographically separate facilities.

Despite the denials of many senators, churches will be covered "as a whole" under the Act if any program or activity receives federal financial assistance and the program or activity is not conducted in a geographically separate facility. In most cases, church programs and activities are conducted in the church facility itself, not in a geographically separate facility. In such cases, the four federal anti-discrimination laws discussed above will apply to the entire church and all of its programs and activities. Substitute bills offered by Senator Hatch and President Reagan would have limited the application of federal anti-discrimination law to only the specific program or activity within a church that receives federal funds, even if that program or activity were not conducted in a geographically separate facility. These substitutes were both rejected.

As noted in chapter 2, the courts have recognized that the first amendment guaranty of religious freedom gives churches the right to select clergy without governmental interference. Accordingly, it is less likely that the Civil Rights Restoration Act, or the four federal anti-discrimination statutes that it amends, will apply to clergy than other categories of church workers.

2. Homosexuals and AIDS Victims

Does the Civil Rights Restoration Act prevent churches from discriminating against homosexuals or AIDS victims? This is a question that several church leaders have asked. The Rehabilitation Act of 1973,[153] as amended by the Civil Rights Restoration Act, forbids discrimination on the basis of handicap by any institution that receives federal financial assistance. In 1987, the Supreme Court ruled that a public school teacher suffering from tuberculosis was a "handicapped individual" entitled to protection under the Act.[154] The Court emphasized that the teacher was handicapped because her tuberculosis caused physical impairment, not because the disease was contagious. "This case does not present, and we therefore do not reach," concluded the Court, "the questions whether a carrier of a contagious disease such as AIDS could be considered to have a physical impairment, or whether such a person could be considered, solely on the basis of contagiousness, a handicapped person." To clarify that a contagious disease (such as AIDS) does not render a person "handicapped" in the absence of physical impairment, the Act was amended to read that the term *handicapped* does not include "an individual who has a currently contagious disease or infection and who, by reason of such disease or infection, would constitute a direct threat to the health or safety of other individuals or who, by reason of the currently contagious disease or infection, is unable to perform the duties of the job."[155] According to this language, an AIDS victim could be classified as handicapped if he or she was physically impaired by the disease and did not constitute a threat to the health or safety of others. A few courts have ruled that under these circumstances AIDS is a handicap.[156]

While it is possible that the federal courts will interpret the term *handicapped* to include homosexuals, such a result is unlikely as a result of the overwhelming expression by Congress that homosexuality is not a handicap. Consider the following sampling of comments (contained in the Congressional Record) of some of the sponsors and co-sponsors of the bill (many other examples could be cited). "[The Act] does not prohibit discrimination against homosexuals and does not give sweeping protection to alcoholics and drug addicts" (Senator Kennedy). "The bill does not change the definition of who is handicapped. There are no Supreme Court rulings which require anyone to consider alcoholics, drug addicts, active homosexuals or transvestites to be handicapped. [Some have suggested that] churches and religious leaders could be forced to hire a practicing homosexual drug addict with AIDS to be a teacher or youth pastor. This is the most blatant untruth of all. No American government has ever had or could ever get the power, under our Constitution, to dictate any choice of pastor in a church—whether it be a youth pastor or any other" (Senator Mitchell). "There is no truth to the charges that the Act would require schools, churches, or any employer to hire homosexuals, alcoholics, drug abusers, or victims of AIDS" (Senator Conrad). "The Civil Rights Restoration Act absolutely does not expand coverage of the civil rights laws to homosexuals" (Senator Ford). "This law will not require churches to hire homosexuals" (Senator Bentsen). "If, for instance, the religious tenets of an organization require it to take disciplinary action against a homosexual because of that person's sexual preference . . . the Act would not protect the individual" (Senator DeConcini). "Is it true that churches and religious schools will have to hire homosexuals as a result of this bill? No, it is not true" (Senator Levin).

One federal court has concluded that transvestites are protected by federal anti-discrimination law. The court concluded that "while homosexuals are not handicapped it is clear that transvestites are, because many experience strong social rejection in the work place as a result of their mental ailment made blatantly apparent

---

[153] 29 U.S.C. § 794.

[154] Arline v. School Board of Nassau County, 107 S. Ct. 1123 (1987).

[155] 29 U.S.C. § 706(8)(C).

[156] *See, e.g.*, Thomas v. Atascadero Unified School District, 662 F. Supp. 376 (C.D. Cal. 1987); District 27 Community School Board v. Board of Education, 502 N.Y.S.2d 325 (1986).

by their cross-dressing life-style."[157] While no other federal court has concluded that transvestites are handicapped, the existence of the one decision certainly makes the acceptance of such a conclusion by other courts a possibility. Again, there is ample testimony in the Congressional Record by the sponsors and co-sponsors of the Civil Rights Restoration Act demonstrating that it was not the intent of Congress to treat transvestites as handicapped. Such testimony will be relevant in future judicial decisions interpreting the term *handicapped*. But again, it cannot be said with certainty that the courts will not treat transvestites as handicapped, and therefore that churches covered by the Act will not be required to hire transvestites.

Finally, note that churches or religious institutions receiving federal funds can discriminate against any handicapped individual for reasons not relating to a handicap (e.g., other applicants were more qualified for the job).

3. Alcoholics and drug addicts

Are alcoholics and drug addicts "handicapped," and therefore entitled to the protections of the Civil Rights Restoration Act? The answer is no, since the Rehabilitation Act of 1973 specifically defines the term *handicap* to exclude "any individual who is an alcoholic or drug abuser whose current use of alcohol or drugs prevents such individual from performing the duties of the job in question . . . ."[158]

4. Handicap Accommodations

Must churches construct ramps and make other structural alterations to accommodate handicapped persons? If a church receives federal financial assistance, then it may be required to make structural alterations to accommodate the handicapped. The Act provides, however, that "small providers (i.e., those with fewer than 15 employees) are not required . . . to make significant structural alterations to their existing facilities . . . if alternative means of providing the services are available."[159]

5. Religious Schools

One of the major objections to the Civil Rights Restoration Act was its treatment of religious schools. Specifically, the Act exempts "an entity which is controlled by a religious organization" from the prohibition of sex discrimination contained in Title IX of the Education Amendments of 1972 if coverage would "not be consistent with the religious tenets of such organization." This exemption restates the exemption of church-controlled educational institutions that has always been available under Title IX, and clarifies that the exemption applies to the entire institution. An amendment offered by Senator Hatch, which would have exempted from the prohibition of sex discrimination any educational institution "controlled by, or closely identified with the tenets of, a particular religious organization," was rejected.

6. Abortion

The Act was amended to include an "abortion neutrality" clause stating that "no provision of this Act or any amendment made by this Act shall be construed to force or require any individual or hospital or any other institution, program, or activity receiving federal funds to perform or pay for an abortion."[160]

---

[157] Blackwell v. United States Department of Treasury, 656 F. Supp. 713 (D.D.C. 1986)
[158] 29 U.S.C. § 706(8)(B).
[159] 29 U.S.C. § 794(c).
[160] Section 8 of Public Law 100-259, set out as a note under 20 U.S.C. § 1688.

7. Conclusion

How will the Civil Rights Restoration Act impact churches? The answer to this question will depend on how the federal courts interpret a few key terms. Specifically, how broadly will the courts interpret "federal financial assistance"? How broadly will they interpret the term *handicapped*? And, will they apply the Act to churches "as a whole" or to only a specific program or activity within a church that receives federal financial assistance? Unfortunately, all attempts to clarify the application of such terms to churches and religious organizations failed. If, as nearly every Senator testified, the Act poses no threat to churches, it is hard to understand why clarifying language was not inserted in the bill.

No one can predict how the federal courts will interpret the law. For a time, the Supreme Court interpreted the word "Congress" to include shopping malls. But the courts, when interpreting legislation, often attach considerable significance to the statements of those members of Congress who sponsored the bill. In the case of the Civil Rights Restoration Act, there are numerous statements in the official record by the chief sponsors of the bill that make a broad interpretation of the Act unwarranted. Such statements were doubtless a result of the outpouring of opposition to the bill that flooded Congress in the days immediately preceding the vote to override the President's veto. But the courts can and do ignore even the most clearly expressed "original intent" of the drafters of both statutory and constitutional provisions. As a result, no one can predict how the courts ultimately will apply the Act to churches and religious organizations. Again, Congress had ample opportunity to clarify the application of the Act to churches, but chose not to do so.

§ 8-16   Display of Posters

> *Key point 8-16. Many federal and state employment and civil rights laws require covered employers to post notices informing employees and job applicants of their legal rights. Many churches are subject to at least some of these notice requirements.*

A variety of federal and state employment and civil rights laws require employers to post notices or posters. Here is a summary of some of the more important provisions under federal law.

1. Federal Law

minimum wage and overtime pay

Every employer that employs workers subject to the federal Fair Labor Standards Act's minimum wage and overtime pay requirements is required by law to post "a notice explaining the Act . . . in conspicuous places in every establishment where such employees are employed so as to permit them to observe readily a copy."[161] The poster describes a covered employee's legal right to receive the minimum wage and overtime pay. The coverage of churches and other religious employers under the Fair Labor Standards Act is described in another section in this chapter.[162]

You can obtain a free copy of a poster from any local office of the United States Department of Labor, Wage and Hours Division.

---

[161] 29 C.F.R. § 516.4.
[162] *See* § 8.16, *infra.*

equal employment opportunity

Every employer covered by the principal federal nondiscrimination laws is required to post on its premises the poster "Equal Employment Opportunity Is the Law." The notice must be posted prominently, where it can be readily seen by employees and job applicants. Employers covered by Title VII of the Civil Rights Act of 1964, the Age Discrimination in Employment Act, and the Americans with Disabilities Act are required to post a notice. The coverage of churches under these statutes is discussed fully earlier in this chapter.[163]

You can obtain a free copy of the poster "Equal Employment Opportunity Is the Law" by contacting any local office of the Equal Employment Opportunity Commission, or by contacting the Equal Employment Opportunity Commission, Communications and Legislative Affairs, 1801 L Street NW, Room 9405, Washington, DC 20507. You also may obtain a free copy of this poster by calling 1-800-669-3362.

Occupational and Safety and Health Act (OSHA)

Employers covered by the Occupational Safety and Health Act are required to display a poster prepared by the U.S. Department of Labor summarizing the major provisions of the Act, and telling employees how to file a complaint. The poster must be displayed in a conspicuous place where employees and job applicants can see it. Federal law requires that any reproductions or facsimiles must be at least 8 1/2 by 14 inches with 10 point type.

You can obtain a free copy of the OSHA poster by contacting any local office of the U.S. Department of Labor, Occupational Safety and Health Administration. Or, you may write the U.S. Department of Labor, Occupational Safety and Health Administration, 200 Constitution Avenue, N.W., Washington, DC 20210.

Employee Polygraph Protection Act

The federal Employee Polygraph Protection Act makes it unlawful for an employer engaged in interstate commerce (regardless of the number of employees) to require or even suggest that an employee or job applicant take a polygraph examination. The concept of commerce is addressed above. Since religious organizations are not exempted by the Act, they are subject to it so long as they meet the commerce requirement.

Federal regulations specify that "every employer subject to the [Act] shall post and keep posted on its premises a notice explaining the Act . . . . Such notice must be posted in a prominent and conspicuous place in every establishment of the employer where it can readily be observed by employees and applicants for employment."[164]

A free copy of the required notice can be obtained from the nearest office of the U.S. Department of Labor, Wage and Hour Division. Or, you can write the U.S. Department of Labor, Employment Standards Administration, Wage & Hour Division, Washington, D.C. 20210.

---

[163] *See* §§ 8.08.01, 8-09, and 8-10, *supra.*
[164] 29 C.F.R. § 801.6.

Family Medical Leave Act

The Family Medical Leave Act provides certain employees with up to 12 weeks of unpaid, job-protected leave a year to give birth or to care for a family member, and requires group health benefits to be maintained during the leave as if the employee continued to work instead of taking leave. The coverage of churches and other religious organizations under this Act is discussed later in this chapter.[165] Employers subject to the Act are required to post notices informing employees and job applicants of their legal rights under the Act.

You can obtain a free copy of a poster from any local office of the United States Department of Labor, Wage and Hours Division.

2. STATE LAW

Many states have their own poster requirements in addition to those mandated by federal law. For example, many states require that employers subject to the following laws post notices described by state law: (1) a state civil rights law; (2) a state minimum wage law; (3) unemployment compensation; and (4) workers compensation.

§ 8-17   Fair Labor Standards Act

Key point 8-17. The Fair Labor Standards Act mandates that employers pay the minimum wage, and overtime compensation, to employees who work for an enterprise engaged in commerce. There is no exception for religious organizations, but there are exceptions for certain classifications of employees.

1. IN GENERAL

In 1938 Congress enacted the Fair Labor Standards Act to protect employees engaged in interstate commerce from substandard wages and excessive working hours. The Act achieves its purpose by prescribing a maximum workweek of 40 hours for an employee engaged in commerce, unless the employee is paid at the rate of one and one-half times the regular rate of compensation for all hours worked over 40, and by prescribing a minimum wage for all employees engaged in interstate commerce. The Act also requires equal pay for equal work regardless of gender, and restricts the employment of underage children. The Act initially covered only those employees "engaged in commerce or in the production of goods for commerce." Congress greatly expanded the Act's coverage in 1961 by amending the Act to cover "enterprises" as well as individual employees. The Act now provides that employers must pay the minimum wage and overtime compensation not only to employees actually engaged in commerce or in the production of goods for commerce, but also to any employee "employed in an enterprise engaged in commerce or in the production of goods for commerce."

In summary, for the minimum wage and overtime compensation requirements to apply to a particular worker, the following two requirements must be satisfied: (1) the worker must either be (a) engaged directly in commerce or in the production of goods for commerce, or (b) employed by an enterprise engaged in commerce or in the production of goods for commerce, and (2) the worker must be an employee.

The more important of these terms are discussed in the following paragraphs, along with pertinent exemptions.

---

[165] *See* § 8.20, *infra.*

enterprises

The Act defines an *enterprise* as "the related activities performed . . . by any person or persons for a common business purpose."[166] The United States Supreme Court has noted that this definition excludes most religious and charitable organizations to the extent that they are not operating for profit and are not pursuing a "business purpose."[167] On the other hand, religious and charitable organizations will be deemed to be an "enterprise" subject to the minimum wage and overtime compensation requirements if they are engaged in commercial or business activities.

In 1966, Congress amended the Act to include within the definition of "enterprise" any "preschool, elementary or secondary school, or an institution of higher education (regardless of whether or not such . . . institution or school is public or private or operated for profit or not for profit)."[168] The Act now provides that schools and preschools, even those operated by churches, are "deemed to be activities performed for a common business purpose."[169]

The fact that a church school or preschool is now deemed to be an "enterprise" does not end the analysis. As noted above, the enterprise must be "engaged in commerce or in the production of goods for commerce," and the worker must be an employee. The Act defines the term *enterprise engaged in commerce or in the production of goods for commerce* to include an enterprise that:

(1) "has employees engaged in commerce or in the production of goods for commerce, or that has employees handling, selling, or otherwise working on goods or materials that have been moved in or produced for commerce by any person, *and* is an enterprise whose annual gross volume of sales made or business done is not less than $500,000"; *or*

(2) "is engaged in the operation of a . . . preschool, elementary or secondary school, or an institution of higher education (regardless of whether or not such . . . institution or school is public or private or operated for profit or not for profit)."[170]

According to this language, church-operated schools and preschools are deemed to be "enterprises engaged in commerce or in the production of goods for commerce."

The United States Department of Labor has issued a number of publications that help to clarify the meaning of key provisions in the Act. For example, the Act covers church-operated preschool employees, but it does not define the term *preschool*. In Publication 1364, the Department addresses this issue by noting:

A preschool is any enterprise . . . which provides for the care and protection of infants or preschool children outside their own homes during any portion of a 24-hour day. The term "preschool" includes any establishment or institution which accepts for enrollment children of preschool age for purposes of providing custodial, educational, or developmental services designed to prepare the children for school in the years before they enter the elementary school grades. This

---

[166] 29 U.S.C. § 203(r).

[167] Tony & Susan Alamo Foundation v. Secretary of Labor, 471 U.S. 290, 302 (1985) ("[t]he Act reaches only the 'ordinary commercial activities' of religious organizations").

[168] 29 U.S.C. § 203(s)(5).

[169] 29 U.S.C. § 203(r).

includes day care centers, nursery schools, kindergartens, head start programs and any similar facility primarily engaged in the care and protection of preschool children.

Employees of preschools employed at central locations where the operations of the centers are administered or serviced and whose work involves duties in connection with the operation of the centers are within the coverage of the Act. For example, coverage extends to clerical workers performing duties in connection with the purchasing or distribution of supplies or equipment for the centers, and to mechanics servicing vehicles or other equipment used in the centers' operations.

This language leaves no doubt that the Department of Labor interprets the term *preschool* to include a church-operated child care facility even if the facility is primarily a custodial rather than an educational institution.

employees

For a worker to be entitled to the minimum wage and overtime compensation, he or she must be an "employee." The Act defines the term *employee* as "any individual employed by an employer," and adds that an employee includes a person who is "suffered or permitted" to work.[171]

volunteers

Are "volunteers" subject to the minimum wage and overtime compensation requirements? The Department of Labor, in its Publication 1364, addresses the issue of volunteer workers:

Individuals who volunteer their services, usually on a part-time basis, to a preschool not as employees or in contemplation of pay are not considered employees within the meaning of the Act. For example, mothers may assist in a preschool as a public duty to maintain effective services for their children, or fathers may drive a bus to take a group of children on a trip without creating an employer-employee relationship. On the other hand, a bookkeeper could not be treated both as an employee and an unpaid volunteer bookkeeper for the same institution. Nuns, priests, lay brothers, ministers, deacons, and other members of religious orders who serve pursuant to their religious obligations in a preschool operated by their church or religious order are not considered to be employees. However, the fact that such a person is a member of a religious order does not preclude an employee-employer relationship with the state or secular institution.

self-employed persons

Only *employees* are covered by the minimum wage and overtime compensation provisions of the Act. Self-employed persons (or independent contractors) are not entitled to the minimum wage or overtime pay. However, note that the term *employee* is defined very broadly. The Department of Labor states in Publication 1297 that "mere knowledge by an employer of work done for him by another is sufficient to create the employment relationship under the Act." This is a very broad definition—much broader than the so-called "common law employee test" that is used to determine whether a person is an employee or self-employed for federal income tax reporting purposes. As a result, churches will seldom be able to demonstrate that child care workers are not covered by the Act on the basis of self-employed status.

---

[170] 29 U.S.C. § 203(s).
[171] 29 U.S.C. §§ 203(e) and 203(g).

exemptions

Certain workers are exempted from coverage under the minimum wage and overtime compensation requirements. Two exemptions are of interest to churches and religious organizations. First, the Act exempts "any employee employed by an establishment which is an . . . organized camp, or religious or nonprofit educational conference center, if (A) it does not operate for more than seven months in any calendar year, or (B) during the preceding calendar year, its average receipts for any six months of such year were not more than [one-third] of its average receipts for the other six months of such year . . . ."[172] Second, the Act exempts "any employee employed in a bona fide executive, administrative, or professional capacity (including any employee employed in the capacity of academic administrative personnel or teacher in elementary or secondary schools)."[173] The definitions of employees "employed in a bona fide executive, administrative, or professional capacity" are complex, and they are contained in regulations issued by the Department of Labor.[174] The key elements of the definitions are set forth below:

Executive employees. The term "employee employed in a bona fide executive capacity" means any employee (a) whose primary duty consists of management level responsibilities, (b) who customarily and regularly directs the work of two or more other employees, (c) who has the authority to hire or fire other employees, or whose recommendations regarding the hiring or firing of other employees is given special weight, (d) who customarily and regularly exercises discretionary powers, (e) who does not devote more than 20% of his or her hours to activities not mentioned in (a) through (d), and (f) who is paid on a *salary basis* at a rate of not less than $130 per week, exclusive of board, lodging, or other facilities.[175]

Administrative employees. The term *employee employed in a bona fide administrative capacity* means any employee (a) whose primary duty consists of either the performance of office or nonmanual work directly related to management policies or general business operations of the employer, or the performance of functions in the administration of a school system in work directly related to the academic instruction or training carried on there, (b) who customarily and regularly exercises discretion and independent judgment, (c) who regularly and directly assists an employee employed in a bona fide executive or administrative capacity, or who performs work along specialized or technical lines requiring special training, experience, or knowledge, or who executes under only general supervision special assignments and tasks, (d) who does not devote more than 20% of his or her hours to activities not mentioned in (a) through (c), and (e) who is paid on a *salary or fee basis* at a rate of not less than $130 per week, exclusive of board, lodging, or other facilities, or who is paid on a salary basis that is at least equal to the entrance salary for teachers in the school system.[176] The regulation further provides that for school employees to be deemed employees employed in an administrative capacity, the employment generally must be in connection with the operation of an elementary or secondary school system or an institution of higher education.[177] Elementary and secondary schools are defined to include those schools that provide elementary and secondary education as determined under state law. In some states, this includes grades 1 through 12. In others, it includes kindergarten through 12.

Professional employee. The term "employee employed in a bona fide professional capacity" means any employee (a) whose primary duty consists of the performance of (i) work requiring knowledge of an advanced

---

[172] 29 U.S.C. § 213(a)(3).
[173] 29 U.S.C. § 213(a)(1).
[174] 29 C.F.R. §§ 541.101 *et seq.* (executive), 541.201 *et seq.* (administrative), 541.301 *et seq.* (professional).
[175] 29 C.F.R. § 541.1.
[176] 29 C.F.R. § 541.2.
[177] 29 C.F.R. § 541.215.

type in a field of science or learning customarily acquired by a prolonged course of specialized intellectual instruction and study, as distinguished from a general academic education, (ii) work that is original and creative in character in a recognized field of artistic endeavor, and that is based on invention, imagination, or talent, or (iii) teaching, tutoring, instructing, or lecturing as a teacher in a school system, (b) whose work requires the consistent exercise of discretion and judgment, (c) whose work is predominantly intellectual and varied in character, (d) who does not devote more than 20% of his or her hours to activities not mentioned in (a) through (c), (e) who is paid on a *salary or fee basis* at a rate of not less than $150 per week, exclusive of board, lodging, or other facilities (this requirement does not apply to teachers).[178] Clergy are included in the list of professional employees.[179]

With respect to the exemption of "executive, administrative, and professional employees," Department of Labor Publication 1364 provides:

> Employees employed in a bona fide executive, administrative, or professional capacity (including any employee employed in the capacity of academic administrative personnel or teacher in elementary or secondary schools) . . . are exempt from the minimum wage and hours provisions of the Act. While preschools engage in some educational activities for the children, employees whose primary duty is to care for the physical needs of the children would not ordinarily meet the requirements for exemption as teachers. This is true even though the term "kindergarten" may be applied to the ordinary day care center. However, bona fide teachers in a kindergarten which is part of an elementary school system are still considered exempt under the same conditions as a teacher in an elementary school.

preschools

Do the Act's minimum wage and overtime pay requirements apply to employees of church-operated preschools? As noted above, the Act applies to any "enterprise engaged in commerce or in the production of goods for commerce." The Act specifically includes church-operated preschools within this definition.

> **Example.** *A federal district court in South Carolina ruled that church-operated preschools are subject to the Act's minimum wage and overtime pay requirements.[180] However, the court concluded that the term preschool suggests a facility that imparts education in an institutional setting, and that this term did not include child care centers that are primarily custodial in nature. The court observed: "A facility operating only as a nursery for babies and small children, such as that portion of [the church's] operation designated as a child care center would not, in the opinion of this court, be considered imparting education." The court rejected the conclusion of the Department of Labor in its Publication 1364 that the term "preschool" included child care facilities. The court concluded: "The [church's] operation of the child care center is primarily designed to provide custodial care which is suitable to the age of the child. This is typical child care which is found in the home and, in the opinion of this court, is not intended by Congress to be within the meaning of 'preschool.' It is not education in an institutional setting." However, the court did conclude that the church's kindergarten was a preschool, and that its employees were entitled to the minimum wage and overtime pay.*

---

[178] 29 C.F.R. § 541.3.
[179] 29 C.F.R. § 541.301.
[180] Marshall v. First Baptist Church, 23 Wage & Hour Cases (BNA) 386 (D.S.C. 1977).

Example. A federal district court in Texas ruled that a church had to provide information to the government in an investigation concerning the alleged failure of the church to pay the minimum wage to its child care workers.[181] The church argued that its operation of a day care center was an integral part of the ministry of the church itself and therefore the subjecting of that center to minimum wage laws violated the constitutional guaranty of religious freedom. The church maintained that its day-care employees were church members who had received a divine call to Christian education and believed that it was their right and duty to serve God by working for minimal compensation. In rejecting the church's position, the court observed that "there is apparently no explicit exemption in the Fair Labor Standards Act for churches or church-related schools. The Court can find none and [the church] has not suggested any. Indeed, the Act specifically defines a covered enterprise to include a pre-school, even if it be private and operated on a non-profit basis." The court then strongly suggested that workers at a church-operated preschool would be covered by the Act. It quoted with approval from an earlier federal appeals court decision noting that "neither the Supreme Court nor this court has held that the employment relationship between a church and all of its employees is a matter of purely ecclesiastical concern." Further, with respect to the church's claim that all of its preschool workers were engaged in "ministry," the court observed: "While religious organizations may designate persons as ministers for their religious purposes free from any governmental interference, bestowal of such a designation does not control their extra-religious legal status."

A few other federal courts have ruled on the application of the minimum wage requirements to workers at secular child care facilities. To illustrate, one court concluded that preschools are covered by the Act, and that the word *preschool* includes child care facilities that are primarily custodial in nature.[182] The child care facility in question was open from 6:00 AM to 6:00 PM, Monday through Friday and accepted children ranging in age from infancy to 12 years, with most children being three to five years of age. Children were accepted on a regular, occasional, or drop-in basis and charges were based on weekly, daily, or hourly periods. Most of the children were brought to the facility by working parents. The center was in a one-story building located within a fenced yard. One room was used as an office and another contained kitchen facilities. The other rooms were equipped with cribs, cots, tables, chairs, pictures, television, and a great variety of toys, books, and games. Playground equipment was in the yard. The center posted a schedule of activities, generally designating time periods for breakfast, morning activities, lunch, naps, snacks, and outdoor play. Occasionally children were taken on field trips. Children of school age were transported from the center to their school and back. The center employed no certified teachers and had no written lesson plans, achievement records, or progress reports.

The center claimed that it was not covered by the minimum wage requirements since it was a purely custodial child care facility rather than a preschool with a primarily educational function. In rejecting this distinction, the court referred to the opinion of a noted expert in child development, who had testified for the government and emphasized the opportunities for learning in child care facilities. The expert testified that children learn from exposure to books, art, and music and from interaction with other children and with adults from outside the family, and that their learning process cannot be formalized because of limited attention spans. The expert defined "preschool" as a facility in which several children unrelated are supervised by adults and in which there are opportunities for learning. She stated that the term *preschool* produces confusion and professional discontent because it simply means "before school" but that professional consensus recognizes that institutions for the care of preschool aged children are generally educational in nature because they

---

[181] Donovan v. Central Baptist Church, 25 Wage & Hour Cases (BNA) 815 (S.D. Tex. 1982).
[182] United States v. Elledge, 614 F.2d 247 (10th Cir. 1980).

provide appropriate learning opportunities for preschool age children in a group setting with adult supervision. The court noted that this is the approach taken by the Department of Labor, and it concluded that it was reasonable. Accordingly, the court concluded that "[a]pplication of the Fair Labor Standards Act may not be avoided by the assertion of primary emphasis on custody and the rejection of the undenied learning opportunities afforded to the children." The court further observed that the Act "was passed for humanitarian and remedial purposes" and accordingly that it "must be liberally construed to apply to the furthest reaches consistent with congressional direction."

A few other courts, while agreeing that secular preschools are automatically covered under the Act, have concluded that the term *preschool* does not include child care facilities that are primarily custodial in nature and that are not licensed or regulated under state law.[183]

schools

As noted above, the Fair Labor Standards Act's minimum wage and overtime pay requirements apply to the employees of any "enterprise engaged in commerce or in the production of goods for commerce." The Act specifically includes church-operated schools within this definition. The coverage of church-operated schools under the Act was affirmed by a federal appeals court in an important decision.[184] The court concluded that a church-operated school violated the Act by paying employees less than the minimum wage and by paying women less than men for comparable work (the Act requires that males and females be paid equally for the same work). The church agreed that it paid women less than men, and that it did not pay some workers the minimum wage. However, it asserted that (1) the school was not covered by the Fair Labor Standards Act, (2) school employees were "ministers" and therefore excluded from coverage under the Act, and (3) applying the Act to the church's school would violate the constitutional guaranty of religious freedom.

A trial court rejected the church's arguments, and ordered it to distribute $177,680 among those female teachers who had been paid less than men, and $16,818 among those workers who had not received the minimum wage. The church appealed, and a federal appeals court upheld the trial court's decision in favor of the government. In rejecting the church's claim that the Fair Labor Standards Act did not apply to a church-operated school, the court noted that the Act was amended in 1966 to specifically cover nonprofit, private schools. The court also rejected without explanation the church's claim that its school employees were really church employees and therefore exempt from the Act. The church had demonstrated that the school was "inextricably intertwined" with the church, that the church and school shared a common building and a common payroll account, and that school employees must subscribe to the church's statement of faith. The court also rejected the church's claim that its school employees were exempt from the Act because they were "ministers" who considered teaching at the school "their personal ministry." It noted that they "perform no sacerdotal functions, neither do they serve as church governors. They belong to no clearly delineated religious order." Further, "the exemption of these teachers would create an exception capable of swallowing up the rule"—since it would mean that all teachers at church-operated schools would be exempt (contrary to the intent of the 1966 amendment to the Act that was designed include them).

The court rejected the church's claim that its constitutional right of religious freedom would be violated by subjecting its school employees to the minimum wage and "equal pay" provisions of the Act. The church claimed that its "head of household" salary supplements (paid to males) "was based on a sincerely-held belief

[183] Marshall v. Rosemont, 584 F.2d 319 (9th Cir. 1978).
[184] Dole v. Shenandoah Baptist Church, 899 F.2d 1389 (4th Cir. 1990).

derived from the Bible," and that employee wages should be fixed by the church acting under divine guidance rather than by the government. The court acknowledged that the church might suffer a burden on the practice of its religion, but it insisted that any burden would be limited. It observed that although the church's head of household salary supplement (for males) "was grounded on a biblical passage, church members testified that the Bible does not mandate a pay differential based on sex. They also testified that no [church] doctrine prevents [the school] from paying women as much as men or from paying the minimum wage. Indeed, the school now complies with the Fair Labor Standards Act . . . ." This limited burden on the church's religious beliefs was outweighed by the government's compelling interest in ensuring that workers receive the minimum wage. The court observed that school employees whose religious convictions were violated by the school's coverage under the Act could simply return a portion of their compensation back to the church. Or, they could volunteer their services to the school.

This ruling indicates that church-operated primary and elementary schools in the fourth federal circuit (which includes the states of Maryland, North Carolina, South Carolina, Virginia, and West Virginia) must comply with the Fair Labor Standards Act's "equal pay" and minimum wage provisions. It is likely that other federal appeals courts will agree with this ruling, meaning that church-operated schools in other states should assume that their employees are protected by the Act. However, note that this ruling only applies to church-operated primary and secondary schools. It does *not* apply to churches themselves.

Other federal courts have concluded that church-operated schools are covered by the Act.[185]

Example. A federal district court in Indiana ruled that the "Equal Pay Act" (a part of the Fair Labor Standards Act) applies to a church-operated school.[186] A Baptist church operated a private school. The federal Equal Employment Opportunity Commission ("EEOC") sued the church for alleged violations of the Equal Pay Act. The EEOC alleged that the church unlawfully paid higher wages and benefits to male teachers than to a class of female teachers performing equal work, and further that the church unlawfully reduced the male teachers' wages in an attempt to comply with the Equal Pay Act. The church claimed that Congress did not intend for the Fair Labor Standards Act, or the Equal Pay Act, to apply to churches or church-operated schools, and therefore neither the EEOC nor the federal court had "jurisdiction over the church." The court noted that the Fair Labor Standards Act does specifically apply to church-operated schools. It "explicitly includes schools (public or private) and other not for profit organizations within the definition of 'enterprises' subject to that statute."

Example. A federal appeals court concluded that the federal minimum wage law applied to the staff of a church-operated school.[187] A church in Little Rock, Arkansas, operated an elementary and secondary school utilizing a self-study program that taught all subjects from a biblical point of view. The school was an integral part of the church. Each class had a supervisor assisted by a classroom "monitor." Both worked with the children but did not conduct formal classroom instruction. Supervisors graded papers, answered students' questions, conducted prayer, and counseled the students. Monitors performed duties equivalent to teachers' aides in the public schools. The school required that all supervisors and monitors be "born again" Christians. Supervisors received compensation of $125 per week ($3.29 per hour for a 38-hour week), while monitors received $100 per week ($2.63 per hour for a 38-hour week). The

---

[185] *See, e.g.,* Equal Employment Opportunity Commission v. Fremont Christian School, 781 F.2d 1362 (9th Cir. 1986).
[186] Equal Employment Opportunity Commission v. First Baptist Church, 56 Fair Empl. Prac. Cases (BNA) 1132 (N.D. Ind. 1991). The court rejected the church's argument that the Supreme Court's "Catholic Bishop" test supported its position. This test is discussed in section 8-17 of this chapter.
[187] DeArment v. Harvey, 932 F.2d 721 (8th Cir. 1991).

Department of Labor charged the church with violating the federal minimum wage law (Fair Labor Standards Act), and sought back wages of some $23,000 for 18 current and former supervisors and monitors. A federal district court upheld the government's position, and the church appealed. A federal appeals court agreed that the federal minimum wage law applied to the school's employees, and it upheld the award of back pay. It emphasized that the minimum wage law specifically applies to church-operated school employees, and it rejected the suggestion that the supervisors and monitors were exempt from coverage on the ground that they are "ministers."

Example. *A federal district court in Ohio ruled that a church-operated school was subject to the Equal Pay Act (a part of the Fair Labor Standards Act).[188] The school, consisting of instruction from preschool through secondary levels, was operated by four Church of Christ congregations. The school adopted a policy of paying its teachers who qualified as a "head of household" an additional allowance of $1,500 per year. A "head of household" was defined as a teacher who was married with dependent children. The sponsoring churches adhered to the conviction that the Bible places the responsibility of the "head of a family" on the husband. Accordingly, the head of household allowance was not paid to a female unless her husband was either absent or unable to work. The Equal Employment Opportunity Commission ("EEOC") charged the school with violating the Equal Pay Act, and demanded that all employees be paid the head of household allowance (regardless of gender). The EEOC also ordered the school to pay "back pay" of $132,000 to female employees who had been denied the allowance in the past. The school maintained that (1) the Equal Pay Act did not apply since the school's alleged discrimination was not based on gender (but rather adherence to a religious principle), (2) the teachers were "ministers" and as such were not subject to the Act, and (3) application of the Act to the school employees violated the first amendment guaranty of religious freedom. The court rejected all of the school's defenses, and ruled in favor of the EEOC. The court began its opinion by noting that the provisions of the Equal Pay Act specifically apply to the employees of church-operated schools. The court then rejected each of the school's 3 defenses. In rejecting the school's first argument, the court insisted that the school's "head of household" allowance policy was in fact based on gender "albeit as a means of giving witness to a religious belief that men and women occupy different family roles." In rejecting the school's second argument, the court acknowledged that the teachers and administrators viewed themselves as teachers of the Christian faith who considered their work religious ministry and a religious calling. The court responded to this perception by noting that the school's "designation of these persons as 'ministers' for religious purposes does not determine their extra-religious legal status. There is no indication that any of the teachers are ordained ministers of the churches, nor do they perform sacerdotal functions. Although it appears undisputed that the principles of the Christian faith pervade the school's educational activities, this alone would not make a teacher or administrator a 'minister' for purposes of exempting that person from the [Fair Labor Standards Act's] definition of 'employee.'" In rejecting the school's third argument, the court concluded that "the compelling interests underlying the Equal Pay Act substantially outweigh its minimal impact on [the school's] religious beliefs .... [The school] remains free to practice its religious beliefs in ways that do not unlawfully discriminate in its wage scales on the basis of gender. Accordingly, the court finds the [school's] free exercise argument is without merit." In support of its decision, the court noted that while the school insisted that the Bible makes a distinction between the familial roles of men and women, "it concedes that the Bible does not mandate that men must be paid more than women for identical tasks."*

---

[188] E.E.O.C. v. Tree of Life Christian Schools, 751 F. Supp. 700 (S.D. Ohio 1990).

other church activities and programs

The Act does not specifically exempt religious organizations from its provisions and accordingly it has been held that the Act covers the employees of such organizations to the extent that they are enterprises engaged in commerce. To illustrate, one court held that the Act applied to the employees of a religious denomination's publishing plant even though the plant was organized "to glorify God, publish the full Gospel to every nation, and promote the Christian religion by spreading religious knowledge."[189] The court observed that the amount of goods sent outside the state where they are produced does not have to be large in order to subject the producer to the provisions of the Act, since the shipment in commerce of "any" goods produced by employees employed in violation of the Act's overtime and minimum wage requirements is prohibited. The plant's interstate shipments were more than sufficient, concluded the court, to involve its employees in interstate commerce. In rejecting the plant's claim that it was engaged in religion and that religion is not commerce, the court observed:

> If we grant that religion itself is not commerce, it still does not follow that a corporation organized for religious purposes may not engage in "commerce" as defined in the Fair Labor Standards Act, that is, by engaging in "trade, commerce, transportation, transmission, or communication among the several states." By engaging in the printing business, as this defendant did, we think it was clearly engaged in "commerce" with the meaning of the Act.[190]

The court also rejected the plant's claim that its first amendment right to freely exercise its religion would be violated by subjecting it to the provisions of the Act. The court noted that first amendment rights are not without limit but may be restricted by the state if it has a sufficiently compelling interest. The objectives underlying the Fair Labor Standards Act, concluded the court, were sufficiently compelling to override a religious organization's first amendment rights under the circumstances of the present case.

In a related case, another court observed that "[o]rganizations affecting commerce may not escape coverage of social legislation by showing that they were created for fraternal or religious purposes."[191]

In 1985, the United States Supreme Court unanimously held that the Fair Labor Standards Acts applied to some 300 "associates" who performed commercial work for a religious organization in exchange for lodging, food, transportation, and medical care.[192] The foundation engaged in several commercial enterprises, including advertising, landscaping, service stations, restaurants, manufacture and sale of candy and clothing, record keeping, construction, plumbing, sand and gravel, electrical contracting, hog farms, feed and farm supplies, real estate development, and freight hauling. Most of the associates who performed such activities were former "derelicts, drug addicts, and criminals" who had been evangelized by the foundation.

The Court observed that the Act would apply to the foundation's commercial activities if two conditions were satisfied: (1) the activities comprised an enterprise engaged in commerce, and (2) the associates were "employees." The Court concluded that both conditions were satisfied, and therefore the foundation's associates were entitled to the protections of the Act. In finding the foundation's commercial activities to be an enterprise engaged in commerce, the Court observed that "[t]he statute contains no express or implied exception for commercial activities conducted by religious or other nonprofit organizations, and the agency

---

[189] Mitchell v. Pilgrim Holiness Church Corp., 210 F.2d 879 (7th Cir. 1944).
[190] *Id.* at 882.
[191] McClure v. Salvation Army, 460 F.2d 553, 557 (5th Cir. 1972).
[192] Tony and Susan Alamo Foundation v. Secretary of Labor, 471 U.S. 290 (1985).

charged with its enforcement has consistently interpreted the statute to reach such businesses." The Court rejected the foundation's assertion that its exemption from federal income taxation constituted governmental recognition of its status as a nonprofit religious and educational organization rather than a commercial one.

As to the second condition, the Court concluded that the foundation's associates were employees despite the foundation's characterization of them as "volunteers" who worked without any expectation of compensation in any form. The Court acknowledged that an individual who "without promise or expectation of compensation, but solely for his personal purpose or pleasure, [works] in activities carried on by other persons either for their pleasure or profit" is not an employee. However, it noted that the Act defines *wages* to include in-kind benefits such as food, lodging, and medical care, and that the associates clearly were compensated employees under this definition. In response to the testimony of several associates that they expected no compensation for their labors and that they considered their work to be "ministry," the Court held that "economic reality" rather than the views of the associates was determinative, and that under this test the associates were employees since they "must have expected to receive in-kind benefits—and expected them in exchange for their services."

The Court rejected the foundation's claim that payment of wages to its associates would violate their right to freely exercise their religion. The Court noted that "[i]t is virtually self-evident that the free exercise of religion clause does not require an exemption from a governmental program unless, at a minimum, inclusion in the program actually burdens the claimant's freedom to exercise religious rights." Since the foundation in fact compensated the associates by providing them with noncash benefits including food and lodging, the Court saw no merit in the associates' assertion that receipt of compensation would violate their religious rights.

The Court emphasized that if a religious organization could engage in a commercial activity in direct competition with ordinary commercial enterprises and remain exempt from the provisions of the Act, it would be free to pay substandard wages and thereby would realize an unfair advantage over its commercial competitors that would jeopardize the right of potentially large numbers of workers to receive minimum wage jobs. The Court also noted that there was no reason "to fear that . . . coverage of the foundation's business activities will lead to coverage of volunteers who drive the elderly to church, serve church suppers, or help remodel a church home for the needy," since none of these activities is commercial in nature and those who perform such services ordinarily do so without any expectation of either cash or in-kind compensation.

A few courts have concluded that the Salvation Army, though a religious organization, is an employer engaged in an industry affecting commerce.[193] However, one federal court ruled that a transient lodge operated by the Salvation Army was not subject to the Act, even though the Salvation Army as a whole was engaged in commerce.[194] The court based this conclusion on the fact that the transient home was not a commercial operation, and the transients were required to perform only incidental services (e.g., making their beds, raking leaves).

> **Example.** *A federal court in North Carolina ruled that a church-operated vocational training program was in violation of federal child labor law.[195] The church used children as young as 11 years of age to work as laborers on a variety of construction projects. The children performed several tasks including remodeling, carpentry, concrete and masonry work, framing, and hanging sheet rock. Children under 16 years of age were not paid for their services, although they generally worked 8 hours each day. The*

---

[193] *See, e.g.,* McClure v. Salvation Army, 460 F.2d 553 (5th Cir. 1972).
[194] Wagner v. Salvation Army, 660 F. Supp. 466 (E.D. Tenn. 1986).
[195] Reich v. Shiloh True Light Church of Christ, 895 F. Supp. 799 (W.D.N.C. 1995).

church attempted to avoid the minimum wage, overtime pay, and child labor provisions of the Fair Labor Standards Act by claiming that the children under age 16 were "vocational trainees" or students rather than employees (the Act applies only to employees). The federal Department of Labor asserted that the children were employees, and that the church had violated the Act. A federal court agreed. The court began its opinion by stressing that the Act applies to all employees employed by an enterprise engaged in commerce, and that the term "employee" is very broadly defined as anyone who is "suffered or permitted to work." The court noted that "a broader or more comprehensive" definition would be difficult to articulate. It also pointed out that the "economic realities" of a position must be considered in deciding whether or not a worker is an employee. The court conceded that in some cases a trainee will not be an employee; but the test to be applied in such cases is whether the trainee or the employer is the "primary beneficiary" of the trainee's labor. If the employer is the primary beneficiary, then the trainee is an employee. The court ruled that this test was met. It conceded that "[t]here is nothing in the federal statutes . . . that prevents church members from arranging for some instruction of their children in vocational pursuits." However, "When the means adopted to serve that end consist of employing children in commercial enterprises that compete with other enterprises fully subject to the labor laws . . . the religious beliefs of the church members cannot immunize the employers from enforcement of the federal statutes. . . . The sectarian purposes of the church members may be served by other means, but their service cannot be sought by putting children to productive work at power saw tables and on brick masons' scaffolding, in violation of the nation's labor laws. Were we confronted merely with violations involving older children or merely with excess hours in non-hazardous environments, this might have been a different case. In the case before us, however, the interest of the United States in prohibiting the employment of children in industrial environments must prevail."

2. CONCLUSIONS

In evaluating the potential application of the Fair Labor Standards Act to religious organizations, consider the following points.

1. The Act's minimum wage and overtime pay requirements only apply to employees who are either (a) engaged directly in commerce or in the production of goods for commerce, *or* (b) employed by an enterprise engaged in commerce or in the production of goods for commerce. Also note that the Act requires covered employers to pay males and females the same compensation for the same work.

2. The Act specifies that church-operated preschools are enterprises engaged in commerce. Accordingly, they are subject to the minimum wage, overtime compensation, and equal pay requirements. The courts have rejected the claim that subjecting church-operated preschools to these requirements violates the constitutional guaranty of religious freedom. Finally, while a few federal courts have concluded that the term *preschool* does not include child care facilities that are primarily custodial rather than educational in nature (*and* that are not regulated or licensed by state law), other courts have rejected this interpretation of the law. It is the position of the Department of Labor that the term *preschool* includes child care facilities that are primarily custodial in nature. Accordingly, churches that operate preschools or child care facilities should recognize that the federal government will consider the employees of such facilities to be covered under the Act. Prudence would dictate that churches follow the minimum wage, overtime compensation, and equal pay requirements of the Act with respect to such employees.

What about workers in a church nursery that is open during worship services, or workers in a church's Sunday School? Many churches operate a nursery for a few hours one day each week or month as an accommodation to mothers (often called "mothers day out"). Must churches pay workers in these programs the minimum wage? Clearly, if the workers are volunteers who work a few hours each week or month with no expectation of compensation, they are volunteers who are not covered by the Fair Labor Standards Act. The Supreme Court observed in the *Alamo* case[196] that while the definition of an *employee* is broad, it does have limits. For example, "an individual who, without promise or expectation of compensation, but solely for his personal purpose or pleasure, works in activities carried on by other persons either for their pleasure or profit, is outside the sweep of the Act." Further, Department of Labor Publication 1364 specifies that "[i]ndividuals who volunteer their services, usually on a part-time basis, to a preschool not as employees or in contemplation of pay are not considered employees within the meaning of the Act." The same rule would apply to volunteer Sunday School teachers. On the other hand, many churches pay their nursery attendants a fee for their services. It would be difficult to argue that such persons are not employees, and accordingly they would be entitled to the minimum wage if they perform services for an enterprise that is engaged in commerce. Is a church such an enterprise? No court has addressed this question. Remember, however, that the definition of an enterprise engaged in commerce includes church-operated preschools. Further, the Department of Labor in its Publication 1364 sets forth a very broad definition of preschool. Whether this definition is broad enough to cover church nursery workers is not clear at this time. Until the federal courts provide clarification, churches must recognize that nursery workers who are compensated for their services may be covered by the Act's requirements (minimum wage, overtime compensation, and equal pay). This apparently is the position of the Department of Labor.

3. The Act specifies that church-operated schools are enterprises engaged in commerce. Accordingly, they are subject to the minimum wage, overtime compensation, and equal pay requirements. The courts have rejected the claim that subjecting church-operated schools to these requirements violates the constitutional guaranty of religious freedom.

4. Churches and religious organizations that are engaged in commercial activities may satisfy the definition of an enterprise. If they further satisfy the definition of an *enterprise engaged in commerce or in the production of goods for commerce*, they will be subject to the minimum wage, overtime compensation, and equal pay requirements of the Act. Note that to be an enterprise engaged in commerce or in the production of goods for commerce, they must not only be engaged in a business or commercial activity, but they also must (1) have two or more employees engaged in commerce or in the production of goods for commerce, or engaged in handling, selling, or otherwise working on goods or materials that have been moved in or produced for commerce, and (2) have annual gross revenues of at least $500,000.

5. Churches that are *not* engaged in commercial or business activities may not be subject to the Act's minimum wage, overtime compensation, and equal pay requirements, for a number of reasons, including the following:

• The authority of Congress (and, by delegation, the Department of Labor) to regulate wages and hours derives from the constitutional authority of Congress to regulate interstate commerce. Activities not affecting interstate commerce are incapable of federal regulation as a matter of constitutional limitation.

• Churches that are not engaged in commercial or business activities can argue that they are not an *enterprise* since a purely nonprofit and noncommercial organization does not have "a common business purpose."

---

[196] *See* note 161, *supra*, and accompanying text.

• Churches that are not engaged in commercial or business activities can argue that they will not satisfy the definition of an *enterprise engaged in commerce or in the production of goods for commerce* since they ordinarily do not have at least two employees who are engaged in commerce, in the production of goods for commerce, or in the handling, selling, or otherwise working on goods or materials that have been moved in or produced for commerce. Further, smaller churches will fail the annual sales volume requirement (currently $500,000).

• The Supreme Court's test for determining the validity of National Labor Relations Board (NLRB) jurisdiction over religious organizations applies to the question of coverage of such organizations under the Fair Labor Standard Act. The test, enunciated in *NLRB v. Catholic Bishop of Chicago*,[197] provides that if the exercise of jurisdiction by a federal agency over a religious organization would give rise to serious constitutional questions under the first amendment religion clauses, then the agency may not exercise jurisdiction without showing an "affirmative intention of the Congress clearly expressed" to confer such jurisdiction. A church could argue that serious constitutional questions would arise under the first amendment's religion clauses by an assertion of jurisdiction by the Department of Labor over local churches that are not engaged in significant commercial activities. At the least, this would constitute an impermissible excessive entanglement between church and state. As noted above, in a few cases the courts have upheld assertions of jurisdiction by the Department of Labor over religious organizations engaged in overtly commercial activities. However, these cases cannot serve as authority for attempted assertions of jurisdiction over most churches and conventions and associations of churches having few if any "commercial" activities. A more pertinent precedent would be the *Catholic Bishop* decision itself, in which the Supreme Court refused to extend NLRB jurisdiction over Catholic parochial schools since (1) the schools were organized exclusively for the propagation of religion and therefore the imposition of NLRB jurisdiction over them would raise serious constitutional questions, and (2) there was no showing by the agency of an "affirmative intention of the Congress clearly expressed" to confer jurisdiction.

Church leaders, and their advisers, must recognize that any claim that a church is not engaged in commerce, and therefore is exempt from the provisions of the Fair Labor Standards Act, is an aggressive position. As noted in section 8-05 of this chapter, the courts have been defining "commerce" very broadly in the context of most federal employment and civil rights laws, and these rulings would be relevant in this context as well.

6. Religious organizations that are covered by the Act's requirements can adjust their liability for overtime compensation and minimum wage payments in a variety of ways. For example, they can reduce the number of hours worked each week; prohibit all unauthorized overtime work (however, they must also ensure that workers in fact do not work overtime, since an employer who "prohibits" overtime is still required to pay overtime compensation to employees that it "allows" to work more than 40 hours each week); reduce hourly compensation (but not below the minimum wage); reduce fringe benefits; or take credit for all indirect and noncash payments made on behalf of employees.

7. All employers having employees covered by the Act must maintain records documenting covered employees' wages, hours, and the other conditions and practices of employment. Included are payroll records, employment contracts, pension plans and other employee benefits, and worktime schedules. If an employer intends to claim credit for noncash payments, it must maintain records documenting the value of such payments.

---

[197] 440 U.S. 490 (1979).

8. The Act does grant a limited exemption in the case of employees of a religious or nonprofit educational conference center if the center does not operate for more than seven months in any calendar year, or if during the preceding calendar year its average receipts for any six months were not more than one-third of its average receipts for the other six months of the year.

9. The Act exempts "any employee employed in a bona fide executive, administrative, or professional capacity" from the overtime and minimum wage provisions of the Act if prescribed income tests are satisfied. The clergy constitutes a learned profession and thus a minister is exempt from the overtime and minimum wage provisions of the Act if his or her annual income exceeds the level prescribed by the government (see the discussion of professional employees discussed earlier). Larger churches and many religious organizations may have employees who qualify as executives or administrators. To qualify, an employee must meet both income and job function tests that are summarized earlier in this section.

10. The Act does not apply to self-employed persons or volunteers. However, note that these terms are interpreted very narrowly, and rarely will apply.

11. The Act only applies to employees. However, this term is interpreted very broadly. It includes persons who are permitted or "suffered" to work. Mere knowledge by an employer of work done for it by another is sufficient to create the employment relationship.

12. The Supreme Court has emphasized that the "the Act must be liberally construed to apply to the furthest reaches consistent with congressional direction,"[198] and that "breadth of coverage is vital to [the Act's] mission."[199] Further, the Supreme Court has noted that the purpose of the Act is to enable workers to receive wages that will sustain a minimum standard of living necessary for health and general well-being. In other words, Congress has determined that the hourly minimum wage is necessary to sustain a minimum standard of living. Many churches not otherwise covered by the Act comply with its provisions in order to ensure that their workers receive what the federal government has determined to be the lowest acceptable hourly wage rate that will sustain a minimum standard of existence.

13. Church leaders must recognize that many states have enacted their own versions of the Fair Labor Standards Act. It is imperative to review the potential application of state minimum wage and overtime compensation laws to church workers.

14. The Act also defines the term *enterprise engaged in commerce* to include a church-operated "hospital, an institution primarily engaged in the care of the sick, the aged, or the mentally ill or defective who reside on the premises of such institution," and a church-operated institution of higher education.[200]

15. Penalties may be imposed for violations of the Act. Employers who violate the minimum wage or overtime pay requirements are liable to their employees for the amount of the unpaid minimum wage or the unpaid overtime pay, and "an additional equal amount as liquidated damages."[201] In addition, employees who are not paid minimum wage or overtime compensation can collect the reasonable cost of their attorney's fees in suing the employer. Employers who "willfully" violate the minimum wage or overtime pay requirements of the

---

[198] Mitchell v. Lubin, McGaughy & Associates, 358 U.S. 207 (1959).
[199] Powell v. United States Cartridge Co., 339 U.S. 49 (1944).
[200] 29 U.S.C. § 203(s).
[201] *Id.* at § 216(b).

Act are subject to a fine of up to $10,000 for each violation. A 2-year statute of limitations applies to the recovery of back wages except in the case of willful violations, in which case a 3-year statute of limitations applies.

§ 8-18   National Labor Relations Act

Key point 8-18. The National Labor Relations Act gives employees the legal right to form labor unions. Some religious organizations are exempt from the provisions of this law.

1. IN GENERAL

In 1935 Congress decided that disturbances in the area of labor relations led to undesirable burdens on and obstructions of interstate commerce, and it passed the National Labor Relations Act.[202] The Act, building on the National Industrial Recovery Act (1933), gave employees a federally protected right to join labor organizations and bargain collectively through their chosen representatives on issues affecting their employment. Congress also created the National Labor Relations Board (NLRB) to supervise the collective bargaining process. The Board was empowered to investigate disputes about which union, if any, represented employees, and to certify the appropriate representatives as the designated collective bargaining agent. The employer was then required to bargain with these representatives, and the Board was authorized to make sure that such bargaining did in fact occur. In general, the Act stipulated that an employer's refusal to bargain was an unfair labor practice. Thus a general process was established that would ensure that employees as a group could express their opinions and exert their influence over the terms and conditions of their employment. The Board would act to see that the process worked. Congress enacted the Labor Management Relations Act in 1947 to adjust and minimize any differences in the rights granted to unions, employees, and employers.

Does the National Labor Relations Act apply to religious organizations? This question has caused considerable controversy. Initially, it should be noted that the stated purpose of the Act was to

eliminate the causes of certain substantial obstructions to the free flow of commerce and to mitigate and eliminate these obstructions when they have occurred by encouraging the practice and procedure of collective bargaining and by protecting the exercise by workers of full freedom of association, self-organization, and designation of representatives of their own choosing, for the purpose of negotiating the terms and conditions of their employment or other mutual aid or protection.[203]

Clearly, then, the Act was designed to apply only to those employment relationships that affect commerce. The Act defines the term *affecting commerce* to mean "in commerce, or burdening or obstructing commerce or the free flow of commerce, or having led or tending to lead to a labor dispute burdening or obstructing commerce or the free flow of commerce."[204] Further, the Act defines *employer* as

any person acting as an agent of an employer, directly or indirectly, but shall not include the United States or any wholly owned Government corporation, or any Federal Reserve Bank, or any State or political subdivision thereof, or any person subject to the Railway Labor Act, as amended from time to time, or any labor organization (other than when acting as an employer), or anyone acting in the capacity of officer or agent of such labor organization.[205]

---

[202] 29 U.S.C. §§ 151-168.
[203] 29 U.S.C. § 151.
[204] 29 U.S.C. § 152(7).
[205] 29 U.S.C. § 152(2).

In summary, the Act covers any employer that is not covered by one of the eight exceptions mentioned in the preceding paragraph. Since religious organizations do not fit within any of the eight exempt categories, the National Labor Relations Board has held that such organizations are covered by the Act at least to the extent that they are engaged in some proprietary activity affecting commerce.[206] To illustrate, the NLRB has asserted jurisdiction over the Sunday School Board of the Southern Baptist Convention since it was engaged in the sale of literature on a nationwide basis and thus could be viewed as being involved in a proprietary activity affecting commerce. The NLRB observed:

> The employer asserts that as it is a nonprofit organization which is engaged in purely religious activities, it is not engaged in commerce within the meaning of the Act. We find no merit in this contention. . . . As this Board and the courts have held, it is immaterial that the employer may be a nonprofit organization, or that its activities may be motivated by considerations other than those applicable to enterprises which are, in the generally accepted sense, commercial.[207]

Similarly, the Board asserted jurisdiction over an evangelistic organization that was engaged in substantial commercial activities that were unrelated, except as a revenue source, to the organization's religious activities.[208]

2. THE "CATHOLIC BISHOP" TEST

A number of religious organizations have challenged the constitutionality of NLRB determinations that they are covered by the Act. In a leading case, the United States Supreme Court was faced with the issue of whether lay teachers in church-operated schools were under the jurisdiction of the NLRB. The Court found that neither the language nor the legislative history of the National Labor Relations Act disclosed "an affirmative intention . . . clearly expressed" that the NLRB have such jurisdiction. Therefore, the Court declined to construe the Act in a manner that would require the resolution of "difficult and sensitive questions arising out of the guarantees of the First Amendment Religion Clauses."[209]

The Court's test for determining the validity of an exercise of jurisdiction by the NLRB over a religious organization may be summarized as follows:

Step #1. Determine if the exercise of jurisdiction by the NLRB over a religious organization would give rise to serious constitutional questions under the first amendment (which guarantees the free exercise of religion).

---

[206] First Church of Christ, Scientist, 194 N.L.R.B. 1006 (1972). Although the NLRB has traditionally assumed jurisdiction over all religious organizations, it has, as a matter of discretion, refused to assert jurisdiction over religious organizations not engaged in commercial activities or religious organizations engaged in commercial activities that earn less than prescribed levels of income. This principle is referred to as the worthy cause doctrine. *See generally* Sherman & Black, *The Labor Board and the Private Nonprofit Employer: A Critical Examination of the Board's Worthy Cause Exemption,* 83 HARV. L. REV. 1323 (1970). *See also* Laycock, *Towards a General Theory of the Religions Clauses: The Case of Church Labor Relations and the Right to Church Autonomy,* 81 COLUM. L. REV. 1373 (1981) (arguing that NLRB assertions of jurisdiction over religious organizations may result in a violation of the first amendment's guaranty of religious freedom).

[207] Sunday School Board of the Southern Baptist Convention, 92 N.L.R.B. 801, 802 (1950).

[208] NLRB v. World Evangelism, Inc., 656 F.2d 1349 (9th Cir. 1981). *See also* Tressler Lutheran Home for Children v. NLRB, 677 F.2d 302 (3rd Cir. 1982) (NLRB jurisdiction over church-operated children's home upheld); Jacobo Marti & Sons, Inc. v. NLRB, 676 F.2d 975 (3rd Cir. 1982) (NLRB jurisdiction over cheese processing plant having a close connection with the Amish faith upheld).

[209] NLRB v. Catholic Bishop of Chicago, 440 U.S. 490, 507 (1979). *See also* NLRB v. Bishop Ford Catholic High School, 623 F. 2d 818 (2nd Cir. 1980), *cert. denied,* 450 U.S. 996 (1980).

Step #2. If a serious constitutional question would arise, then the NLRB may not exercise jurisdiction over the religious organization without a showing of an "affirmative intention of the Congress clearly expressed" to confer such jurisdiction.

Step #3. If serious constitutional questions are not an exercise of jurisdiction by the NLRB over a religious organization, then no inquiry is necessary as to whether Congress clearly expressed an intention to confer jurisdiction.[210]

In applying this test, one court has upheld an exercise of jurisdiction by the NLRB over a Christian evangelistic organization engaged in substantial commercial activities. The court noted that no serious first amendment questions were raised since NLRB jurisdiction resulted in only a "minimal infringement" on the organization's constitutional rights.[211] Serious constitutional questions are raised by an NLRB assertion of jurisdiction over church school teachers, concluded the court, but this is not true of an exercise of jurisdiction over lay employees engaged in the commercial activities of a religious organization.

NLRB assertions of jurisdiction similarly have been upheld over church-affiliated hospitals[212] and nursing homes[213] that (1) receive a substantial percentage of their income from governmental sources; (2) hire employees without regard to religious beliefs; and (3) engage in no specific religious indoctrination of patients or employees. A number of courts have concluded that Congress has "clearly expressed an intention to confer [NLRB] jurisdiction" over church-affiliated hospitals, since in 1974 it removed the pre-existing exemption of all nonprofit hospitals under section 2 of the National Labor Relations Act, and rejected an amendment that would have retained the exemption for church-affiliated hospitals.

Another court reached the same conclusion with respect to employees of a church-operated home for neglected children.[214] The court agreed with the Supreme Court that an exercise of jurisdiction by the NLRB over church-operated schools raised serious constitutional questions since such schools actively propagate religious faith. However, the court did not believe that serious constitutional questions were raised by an assertion of jurisdiction by the NLRB over church-operated homes for neglected children since such institutions are not devoted to the propagation of religion. Since no serious constitutional question was raised, the court concluded that an "affirmative intention of Congress clearly expressed" to confer jurisdiction over church-operated homes for neglected children was not necessary.

Significantly, the court emphasized that (1) governmental funding comprised over half of the home's income; (2) the home hired employees without regard to their religious affiliation; (3) the home accepted only abused children and kept them an average of six weeks during which time they remained wards of the state; (4) all children were referrals from a state agency; and (5) children could not attend religious services contrary to the beliefs of their

---

[210] In *Dole v. Shenandoah Baptist Church*, 899 F.2d 1389 (4th Cir. 1990), a federal appeals court suggested that the Supreme Court may have altered the *Catholic Bishop* test in a 1985 decision. In 1985, the Supreme Court ruled that "because we perceive no `significant risk' of an infringement on first amendment rights, we do not require any clearer expression of congressional intent to regulate these activities." *Tony & Susan Alamo Foundation v. Secretary of Labor*, 471 U.S. 290, 298 n.18 (1985). The federal appeals court observed that the Supreme Court may have intended to replace the *Catholic Bishop* test. If so, this objective is not clear, and has not been clarified in later decisions.

[211] *NLRB v. World Evangelism, Inc.*, 656 F.2d 1349 (9th Cir. 1981).

[212] *St. Elizabeth Community Hospital v. NLRB*, 708 F.2d 1436 (9th Cir. 1983); *Bon Secours Hospital, Inc.*, 248 N.L.R.B. 743 (1980) (Catholic social service agency whose purpose was the provision of social services on a nondenominational basis and that hired employees without regard to religious beliefs held to be subject to NLRB jurisdiction).

[213] *Mid American Health Services, Inc.*, 247 N.L.R.B. 752 (1980).

[214] *NLRB v. St. Louis Christian Home*, 663 F.2d 60 (8th Cir. 1981); *See also* *Tressler Lutheran Home for Children v. NLRB*, 677 F.2d 302 (3rd Cir. 1982).

parents without parental consent. The court concluded that under these facts the home was indistinguishable from a nonreligious institution, and, accordingly, no serious First Amendment questions were implicated.

A federal appeals court ruled that a child care center operated by the Salvation Army was subject to NLRB jurisdiction.[215] The court emphasized that serious constitutional questions were not created by NLRB jurisdiction over the facility, since

> [t]he program's function is primarily to provide care for the children, not education. It involves no religious instruction, indoctrination, or extracurricular activities. Neither the teachers, children, nor parents are chosen for their religious affiliation. Nor do they receive any religious training. The director, who oversees the workplace, need not be, and is not presently, a clergyman. . . . [T]here is not evidence that the [facility] serves anything other than a secular function with respect to the children, parents, and teachers.[216]

The court emphasized that

> if the [facility] provided not just day care for children but also religious instruction and religiously oriented extracurricular activities, a different result might be required. Instead, we have an institution whose primary business is the provision of care and whose operation is indistinguishable from that of secular day care centers. The risk of serious constitutional questions being raised in these circumstances is simply too insignificant and speculative . . . . [W]ere we not to find jurisdiction, we might inadvertently be offering all private day care centers and other private providers of care a formalistic means of circumventing federal labor laws. By articulating some religious affiliation and mission, no matter how little effect it might have on the social programs' functions or operations, providers of care could easily avoid the Board's jurisdiction . . . .[217]

Many children's homes affiliated with churches are not subject to NLRB jurisdiction because their activities are inherently religious. The New Testament itself states: "Pure religion and undefiled before God and the Father is this, To visit the fatherless and widows in their affliction . . . ."[218] Children's homes that are affiliated with and controlled by bona fide churches, that receive all or most of their income from nongovernmental sources, that actively propagate the church's religious tenets to their children, and that require employees to be members of the church, undoubtedly are exempt from NLRB jurisdiction under the Supreme Court's three-part test. However, church-affiliated children's homes that lack most of these characteristics may be subject to NLRB jurisdiction.

3. Conclusion

It is likely that the NLRB will continue to exercise jurisdiction over religious organizations engaged in substantial commercial activities, and that the courts will uphold such exercises of jurisdiction. As one court has observed, when a religious or nonprofit organization operates in the same way as a secular institution, the NLRB may treat such an organization like a secular institution.[219] But NLRB assertions of jurisdiction over religious organizations probably will not be upheld in any of the following situations:

---

[215] NLRB v. Salvation Army, 763 F.2d 1 (1st Cir. 1985).
[216] *Id.* at 6.
[217] *Id.* at 6-7.
[218] James 1:27 (KJV).
[219] NLRB v. St. Louis Christian Home, 663 F.2d 60 (8th Cir. 1981).

a. The organization is not involved in substantial commercial activities.[220]

b. The organization is not engaged in a business or activity affecting commerce. *Commerce* is defined by the National Labor Relations Act as trade, traffic, commerce, transportation, or communication among the several states.[221] A religious organization that purchases all of its supplies from local vendors and sells no product or service to persons residing in other states may not be engaged in any activity affecting commerce. Note, however, that the Act defines *commerce* to include "communication" among the several states. This would include radio or television broadcasts, and may include the operation of a "web page" on the internet. The purchase of electricity and natural gas from a utility company engaged in interstate commerce also may constitute commerce.[222] In general, the discussion in section 8-05 regarding the meaning of "commerce" in the context of federal civil rights laws is relevant here as well.

c. An assertion of NLRB jurisdiction inhibits a religious organization's ability to propagate its beliefs.[223]

d. An assertion of NLRB jurisdiction raises serious constitutional questions under the first amendment and no "affirmative intention of Congress clearly expressed" confers jurisdiction.[224]

§ 8-19   Employee Polygraph Protection Act

> *Key point 8-19. Federal law prohibits employers that are engaged in interstate commerce (regardless of the number of employees) to require or even suggest that an employee or prospective employee submit to a polygraph examination. There is no exemption for religious organizations. A very limited exception exists for "ongoing investigations" into employee theft.*

1. BACKGROUND

The Employee Polygraph Protection Act (EPPA),[225] which was enacted by Congress in 1988, prohibits any "employer" (defined as an employer "engaged in or affecting commerce") from doing any one of the following three acts:

(1) directly or indirectly, to require, request, suggest, or cause any employee or prospective employee to take or submit to any lie detector test

(2) to use, accept, refer to, or inquire concerning the results of any lie detector test of any employee or prospective employee

---

[220] The NLRB claims to possess jurisdiction over all religious organizations, but it declines to assert jurisdiction over religious organizations not engaged in substantial commercial activities. An assertion of jurisdiction over a religious organization not engaged in substantial commercial activities might violate the first amendment. NLRB v. Catholic Bishop of Chicago, 440 U.S. 490 (1979).

[221] 29 U.S.C. § 152(6).

[222] *See generally* NLRB v. St. Louis Christian Home, 663 F.2d 60 (8th Cir. 1981). The expansive interpretation of the term *commerce* has not gone without objection. One judge has commented that "it is virtually unthinkable that the Founding Fathers could have foreseen the extent to which an increasingly expansive interpretation of the Commerce Clause could so infringe local authority." Godwin v. Occupational Safety and Health Review Commission, 540 F.2d 1013, 1017 (9th Cir. 1976) (Ely, J., concurring).

[223] NLRB v. Catholic Bishop of Chicago, 440 U.S. 490 (1979).

[224] *Id.*

[225] 29 U.S.C. § 2001 *et seq.*

(3) to discharge, discipline, discriminate against in any manner, or deny employment or promotion to, or threaten to take any such action against—(A) any employee or prospective employee who refuses, declines, or fails to take or submit to any lie detector test, or (B) any employee or prospective employee on the basis of the results of any lie detector test . . . .

A church is subject to the Act if it is "engaged in or affecting commerce." There is no requirement that an employer have a minimum number of employees. Whether or not churches and other religious organizations are engaged in "commerce" is a question that is addressed in section 8-05 of this chapter.

Tip. The Act not only prohibits covered employers from requiring that employees take polygraph exams, but it also prohibits an employer from requesting or suggesting that an employee or prospective employee take such an exam.

2. An Important Exception for "Ongoing Investigations" into Employee Theft

The Act contains a few narrow exceptions. One permits employers to ask employees to submit to a polygraph exam if they are suspected of theft and there is an ongoing investigation. Here are the details of this exception:

[This Act] shall not prohibit an employer from requesting an employee to submit to a polygraph test if—

(1) the test is administered in connection with an ongoing investigation involving economic loss or injury to the employer's business, such as theft, embezzlement, misappropriation, or an act of unlawful industrial espionage or sabotage;

(2) the employee had access to the property that is the subject of the investigation;

(3) the employer had a reasonable suspicion that the employee was involved in the incident or activity under investigation; and

(4) the employer executes a statement, provided to the examinee before the test, that—(A) sets forth with particularity the specific incident or activity being investigated and the basis for testing particular employees, (B) is signed by a person (other than a polygraph examiner) authorized to legally bind the employer, (C) is retained by the employer for at least 3 years, and (D) contains at a minimum—(i) an identification of the specific economic loss or injury to the business of the employer, (ii) a statement indicating that the employee had access to the property that is the subject of the investigation, and (iii) a statement describing the basis of the employer's reasonable suspicion that the employee was involved in the incident or activity under investigation.[226]

Tip. Know the details of the "ongoing investigation" exception. Under very limited circumstances, you can request that an employee take a polygraph exam if you suspect the employee of theft and you are conducting an ongoing investigation. Do not rely on this exception without fully complying with all of the requirements quoted above. Also, consult with legal counsel to be sure the exception is available to you.

---

[226] 29 U.S.C. § 2006(d).

KNOW WHAT THE LAW FORBIDS

If your church is subject to the Employee Polygraph Protection Act, then the following prohibitions apply:

- You cannot "require, request, suggest, or cause" any employee or prospective employee to take a polygraph exam.

- You cannot "actively participate" with the police in administering a polygraph exam to an employee. You can engage in "passive cooperation." This includes allowing the police to conduct an exam on your premises, or releasing an employee during working hours to take a test at a police station.

- You cannot "use, accept, refer to, or inquire concerning the results" of a polygraph exam.

- You cannot discharge, discipline, discriminate against, or deny employment or promotion to an employee or applicant for employment on the basis of (1) a refusal to take a polygraph exam, or (2) the results of a polygraph exam. Nor can you threaten to do so.

Example. A church board suspects the church's volunteer treasurer of embezzling several thousands of dollars of church funds. The treasurer is called into a board meeting, and is told "you can clear your name if you submit to a polygraph exam." Does this conduct violate the Employee Polygraph Protection Act? Possibly not. The Act only protects "employees," and so a volunteer treasurer presumably would not be covered. However, if the treasurer receives any compensation whatever for her services, or is a "prospective employee," then the Act would apply. Because of the possibility that volunteer workers may in some cases be deemed "employees," you should not suggest or request that they take a polygraph exam without the advice of legal counsel.

Example. Same facts as the previous example, except that the church suspects a full-time secretary of embezzlement. Can it suggest that the secretary take a polygraph exam? Only if all the requirements of the "ongoing investigation" exception apply. These include: (1) the test is administered in connection with an ongoing investigation involving economic loss or injury to the employer's business, such as theft or embezzlement; (2) the employee had access to the property that is the subject of the investigation; (3) the employer had a reasonable suspicion that the employee was involved in the incident or activity under investigation; and (4) the employer executes a statement, provided to the examinee before the test, that—(A) sets forth with particularity the specific incident or activity being investigated and the basis for testing particular employees, (B) is signed by a person (other than a polygraph examiner) authorized to legally bind the employer, (C) is retained by the employer for at least 3 years, and (D) contains at a minimum—(i) an identification of the specific economic loss or injury to the business of the employer, (ii) a statement indicating that the employee had access to the property that is the subject of the investigation, and (iii) a statement describing the basis of the employer's reasonable suspicion that the employee was involved in the incident or activity under investigation.

The EPPA provides that an employer that violates the Act is liable to the employee or prospective employee for "such relief as may be appropriate, including, but not limited to, employment, reinstatement, promotion, and the payment of lost wages and benefits." A court may also award damages based on "emotional distress," and punitive damages.

Key point. Damages awarded for violating the Employee Polygraph Protection Act may not be covered under a church's liability insurance policy. This is another reason for church leaders to assume that the Act applies to their church, and to interpret its provisions prudently.

§ 8-20 Occupational Safety and Health Act

Key point 8-20. The Occupational Safety and Health Act imposes various requirements upon employers in order to achieve safe and healthful working conditions. The Act applies to any employer engaged in commerce, regardless of the number of employees. There is no exemption for religious organizations.

In 1970, Congress enacted the Occupational Safety and Health Act (OSHA) "to assure so far as is possible every working man and woman in the nation safe and healthful working conditions."[227] The Act achieves its aim primarily through imposing various duties upon employers. The Act defines *employer* as any person or organization "engaged in a business affecting commerce who has employees."[228] *Commerce* is defined under the Act as trade, traffic, commerce, transportation, or communication among the several states.[229] In general, the discussion of the "commerce" requirement in section 8-05 of this chapter is relevant in determining the application of OHSA to churches and other religious organizations.

Since religious organizations are not exempted from the Act, they will be deemed subject to it with the same limitations previously discussed in connection with the Fair Labor Standards Act and the National Labor Relations Act.

Example. A North Carolina court ruled that employers, including religious organizations, cannot dismiss an "at will" employee (hired for an indefinite term) for filing a complaint citing his or her employer with a violation of OSHA.[230]

§ 8-21 Family Medical Leave Act

Key point 8-21. The federal Family and Medical Leave Act requires employers with 50 or more employees and engaged in interstate commerce to allow employees up to 12 weeks of unpaid leave each year on account of certain medical and family needs. There is no exemption for religious organizations.

1. IN GENERAL — THE "LEAVE" REQUIREMENT

The Family and Medical Leave Act[231] requires every employer that is "engaged in commerce or in any industry or activity affecting commerce that employs 50 or more employees" to grant eligible employees up to 12 workweeks of unpaid leave during any 12-month period in any one or more of the following situations:

- Because of the birth of a son or daughter of the employee and in order to care for such son or daughter.

- Because of the placement of a son or daughter with the employee for adoption or foster care.

---

[227] 29 U.S.C. § 651(b).
[228] 29 U.S.C. § 652(5).
[229] 29 U.S.C. § 652(3).
[230] Rosby v. General Baptist State Convention of North Carolina, Inc., 370 S.E.2d 605 (N.C. App. 1988).
[231] 29 U.S.C. § 2601 *et seq.*

- In order to care for the spouse, or a son, daughter, or parent, of the employee, if such spouse, son, daughter, or parent has a serious health condition.

- Because of a serious health condition that makes the employee unable to perform the functions of the position of such employee.

An eligible employee (entitled to up to 12 workweeks of leave) is an employee who has been employed for at least 12 months by the employer and who has at least 1,250 hours of service with that employer during the previous 12-month period (an average of 25 hours per week).

Note that only those employers "engaged in commerce or in any industry or activity affecting commerce" and that employ 50 or more employees are covered by the Act. One senator estimated that this restrictive definition has the effect of exempting 95 percent of the employers in this country from the new law, and "leaving over 60 percent of the work force unprotected."

Another important term under the Act is "serious medical condition," since leave is required (1) in order to enable an employee to care for a spouse, son, daughter, or parent if such person has *a serious medical condition*, or (2) if an employee has *a serious health condition* that makes the employee unable to perform the functions of his or her job. What is a "serious medical condition"? The Act defines the term as "an illness, injury, impairment, or physical or mental condition that involves inpatient care in a hospital, hospice, or residential medical care facility; or continuing treatment by a health care provider." Note that the terms "son" and "daughter" include a biological, adopted, or foster child, a stepchild, or a legal ward, who is under 18 years of age or who is 18 years of age or older and incapable of self-care because of a mental or physical disability.

There are a few other provisions of the Act that deserve comment:

intermittent leave

The Act specifies that employees cannot necessarily take their leave "intermittently" or on a "reduced leave" basis. For example, employees entitled to leave because of the birth or adoption (or foster care placement) of a child may not take their leave intermittently or on a reduced leave schedule unless the employee and the employer agree.

unpaid leave

Note that all the Act requires is unpaid leave. Employers are not required to pay employees during their medical or family leave.

effect on existing leave policy

If an employer already makes less than 12 weeks of paid leave available to an employee for the conditions specified in the Act, then "the additional weeks of leave necessary to attain the 12 workweeks of leave required under this Act may be provided without compensation."

employees' duties

Employees have certain duties under the Act. One such duty is the "notice" requirement. The Act specifies that in cases involving the birth or adoption of a child, "the employee shall provide the employer with not less than 30 days' notice, before the date the leave is to begin, of the employee's intention to take leave . . . except that if the date of the birth or placement requires leave to begin in less than 30 days, the employee shall provide such notice as is practicable." Further, if medical care or treatment (for the employee or the employee's spouse, child, or parent) is foreseeable, then the employee is required to "make a reasonable effort to schedule the treatment so as not to disrupt unduly the operations of the employer, subject to the approval of the health care provider of the employee or the health care provider of the son, daughter, spouse, or parent of the employee, as appropriate; and shall provide the employer with not less than 30 days' notice, before the date the leave is to begin, of the employee's intention to take leave . . . except that if the date of the treatment requires leave to begin in less than 30 days, the employee shall provide such notice as is practicable." The Act also clarifies that an employer may require an employee on leave to report periodically to the employer on the status and intention of the employee to return to work.

certification

As an accommodation to employers, the Act contains a provision that permits employers to certify that an employee (or an employee's spouse, child, or parent) has a "serious health condition" warranting leave. The Act specifies that an employer may require that a request for leave under such circumstances "be supported by a certification issued by the health care provider of the eligible employee or of the son, daughter, spouse, or parent of the employee, as appropriate. The employee shall provide, in a timely manner, a copy of such certification to the employer." The certification is sufficient if it states

> (1) the date on which the serious health condition commenced; (2) the probable duration of the condition; (3) the appropriate medical facts within the knowledge of the health care provider regarding the condition; (4) a statement that the eligible employee is needed to care for the son, daughter, spouse, or parent and an estimate of the amount of time that such employee is needed to care for the son, daughter, spouse, or parent, or a statement that the employee is unable to perform the functions of the position of the employee; and (5) in the case of certification for intermittent leave for planned medical treatment, the dates on which such treatment is expected to be given and the duration of such treatment.

The Act permits employers to obtain a "second opinion" concerning the medical condition of an employee or of an employee's spouse, child, or parent. It provides: "In any case in which the employer has reason to doubt the validity of the certification provided [by an employee] the employer may require, at the expense of the employer, that the eligible employee obtain the opinion of a second health care provider designated or approved by the employer concerning any information [in the original certification]." However, an employer may not obtain a second opinion from a health care provider that is "employed on a regular basis by the employer." If a second opinion differs from the original certification, then "the employer may require, at the expense of the employer, that the employee obtain the opinion of a third health care provider designated or approved jointly by the employer and the employee concerning the information certified [in the original certification]. The opinion of the third health care provider . . . shall be considered to be final and shall be binding on the employer and the employee."

The Act further specifies that an employer "may require that the eligible employee obtain subsequent recertifications on a reasonable basis."

returning to work

What happens when an employee who has been on medical or family leave returns to work? Must the employee be returned to his or her former job? This is what the Act says: "Any eligible employee who takes leave . . . shall be entitled, on return from such leave, to be restored by the employer to the position of employment held by the employee when the leave commenced, or to be restored to an equivalent position with equivalent employment benefits, pay, and other terms and conditions of employment." With regard to the accrual of seniority and fringe benefits during periods of unpaid medical or family leave, the Act provides that "the taking of leave shall not result in the loss of any employment benefit accrued prior to the date on which the leave commenced." However, nothing in the Act "shall be construed to entitle any restored employee to the accrual of any seniority or employment benefits during any period of leave, or any right, benefit, or position of employment other than any right, benefit, or position to which the employee would have been entitled had the employee not taken the leave." While an employee is on leave required by the Act, the employer "shall maintain coverage under any group health plan for the duration of such leave at the level and under the conditions coverage would have been provided if the employee had continued in employment continuously for the duration of such leave." If the employee does not return from leave, the employer in some cases is entitled to recover the premium that the employer paid for maintaining coverage for the employee under a group health plan.

If an employee has been on leave because of his or her own medical condition, the Act specifies that "as a condition of restoration . . . the employer may have a uniformly applied practice or policy that requires each such employee to receive certification from the health care provider of the employee that the employee is able to resume work, except that nothing in this paragraph shall supersede a valid state or local law or a collective bargaining agreement that governs the return to work of such employees."

notice

The Act requires employers to "post and keep posted, in conspicuous places on the premises of the employer where notices to employees and applicants for employment are customarily posted, a notice . . . setting forth excerpts from, or summaries of, the pertinent provisions of this Act." The penalty for noncompliance with the notice requirement is $100 for each separate offense.

2. Application to Churches and other Religious Organizations

There is no exemption in the Act for religious organizations. However, the Act will have minimal impact on most churches, since it applies only to employers that are "engaged in commerce or in any industry or activity affecting commerce that employ 50 or more employees." Most churches employ fewer than 50 persons, and these churches will not be affected at all by the new law. A church employing 50 or more persons can establish that it is exempt by demonstrating that it is not engaged in a business or activity "affecting commerce." Whether or not a church or other religious organization is engaged in "commerce" is a question addressed fully in section 8-05 of this chapter.

There is no doubt that some religious organizations will be covered by the Act, including many denominational headquarters, publishers, religious educational institutions, and larger churches. Administrators of such institutions should review this section carefully, and consult with their own legal counsel to discuss coverage and implementation issues.

Some churches will voluntarily comply with the Act, even though they have fewer than 50 employees or are not engaged in commerce. After all, Congress has determined that a 12-week medical and family leave policy is essential to preserve the family. As one senator remarked, "to lose your job and to lose health care coverage when your child is sick or your spouse is ill or a parent you are caring for is in trouble, to lose a job and lose the health care coverage, what more cruel set of facts could strike a family? So this legislation will do an awful lot just to save and protect good people who are trying to hold body and soul and family together at a time when they need it most. . . . The Family and Medical Leave Act establishes a basic standard of human decency."

Churches considering voluntary compliance with the Act should keep in mind the following points:

• The medical and family leave mandated under the Act is unpaid leave. This is a noncash fringe benefit.

• The cost to an employer in granting unpaid leave can be significantly less than the cost of training a permanent replacement for an employee who needs time off due to the birth of a child or an illness in the family. Much congressional testimony was devoted to proving this point.

• Employers who voluntarily comply with the Act will realize a benefit in the form of improved employee morale. Many church employees will expect their church to provide medical and family leave, even though the church may not be subject to the Act. Church employees will expect their church to comply with a law designed to protect the family rather than hide behind the "legal technicality" that they are exempt.

• Recall that employers can require verification that an employee is eligible for the leave. This will reduce the risk that employees will abuse the medical and family leave policy.

Example. *A federal district court in New York ruled that a church agency did not violate the Family and Medical Leave Act by dismissing an employee whose investment decisions resulted in a loss of $8 million in church funds.*[232] *Before dismissing the employee, the agency attempted to work out a severance agreement with the employee. While these negotiations were proceeding, the employee took medical leave. He was later dismissed when efforts to negotiate a severance agreement failed. The employee sued the agency, claiming that his dismissal violated the Family and Medical Leave Act (FMLA), which makes it unlawful for covered employers to "discharge or in any other manner discriminate" against any individual for exercising rights provided by the Act. A federal district court dismissed the lawsuit. It noted that "the FMLA provides that an employee on protected leave is not entitled to any greater rights or benefits than he would be entitled to had he not taken the leave." It further observed that it was undisputed that the church had announced its determination to terminate the director before he went on medical leave, but deferred doing so only to provide an opportunity for the parties to try to negotiate a resignation agreement. Further, the church reserved the right to terminate the director if no such agreement were negotiated. As a result, the director "was not denied any right, for none was preserved." The FMLA "does not require employers to give returning employees any assurances of job security to which they would not have been entitled, prior to taking sick leave." The court also observed that*

---

[232] Carrillo v. The National Council of the Churches of Christ in the U.S.A., 976 F. Supp. 254 (S.D.N.Y. 1997).

"FMLA is not a shield to protect employees from legitimate disciplinary action by their employers if their performance is lacking in some manner unrelated to their FMLA leave."

§ 8-22 New Hire Reporting Requirements

Key point 8-22. *Employers must provide a designated state agency with information about every new hire as a result of federal legislation that seeks to facilitate the enforcement of child support orders and reduce fraud in welfare programs. The "new hire reporting law" does not exempt religious organizations.*

In 1996 Congress enacted the Personal Responsibility and Work Opportunity Reconciliation Act, popularly known as the "welfare reform" bill.[233] The Act has many provisions designed to reduce welfare payments and address welfare fraud. One of these provisions requires employers to report all "new hires" to a designated state agency. The purpose of this requirement is to locate "deadbeat dads" who avoid their child support obligations by changing jobs and their place of residence. Forcing these persons to honor their support obligations will enable many women to go off welfare. Another purpose of the new law is to reduce fraudulent unemployment benefits payments to persons who are working.

Technically, states are not required to mandate new hire reporting. But, if they fail to do so, they will forfeit federal funding under certain programs. To date, all states have enacted legislation mandating new hire reporting, and the laws of all 50 states are summarized in Table 8-2.

1. CHURCH COVERAGE

The new hire reporting requirements apply to all "employers." The new law uses the same definition of "employer" as is contained in section 3401(d) of the tax code. This definition defines an employer as "the person for whom an individual performs or performed any service, of whatever nature, as the employee of such person." This definition contains no exception for religious organizations. And, there is no exception for "small" employers having only one or two employees. But remember—reporting is only for *new hires*, as defined by state law. This generally will be any employee hired after a date specified by state law.

2. HOW IT WORKS

When employers (including churches) report new hire information to their designated state agency, the agency will match the information against its own child support records to locate parents and enforce existing child support orders. Once these matches are done, the information is sent to the "National Directory of New Hires" so other states can compare the information with their own child support records. The information also will be shared with state welfare and unemployment agencies, to detect and prevent fraudulent or erroneous payments.

The federal welfare reform legislation requires that employers include the following information in their new hire reports:

- employee's name

- employee's address

---

[233] 42 U.S.C. § 653a.

- employee's social security number

- employer's name

- employer's address

- employer's federal employer identification number (EIN)

Note that most of this information is contained on the W-4 form ("withholding allowance certificate") completed by each new employee at the time of hire, and as a result most states allow employers to comply with the reporting requirements by sending copies of each new W-4 form completed by a newly hired employee.

Tip. *The employer's federal identification number is inserted on line 10 of Form W-4 only when the form is sent to the IRS. Since this happens infrequently, the employer's identification number generally does not appear on the form. So, for an employer to use W-4 forms to comply with the new hire reporting requirements, it must manually insert its federal employer identification number (EIN) on line 10. The employer's name and address also may need to be manually inserted on line 8.*

Tip. *Some states ask employers to voluntarily report additional information, such as date of hire, or medical insurance information. A summary of each state's law is contained in Table 8-2.*

The deadline for filing a report is specified by state law. However, it may not be later than 20 days after an employee is hired.

Most states allow employers to comply with the new hire reporting requirement in any one of three ways:

(1) electronic or magnetic reporting

Some states permit employers to report by electronic file transfer (EFT); file transfer protocol (FTP); magnetic tape; or 3.5" diskette.

(2) fax or mail

Most states permit employers to fax or mail any one or more of the following:

- A copy of a new employee's W-4. Be sure it is legible, and that the church's federal employer identification number (EIN) is included on line 10. Also be sure that the church's name and address are included on the form.

- A printed list.

- A new hire reporting form provided by your designated state agency.

Tip. *If your church hires new employees infrequently, the easiest way to comply with the reporting obligation may be to use the state reporting form. Simply complete one form with your federal employer identification number, name, and address, and then make several copies. This way, you will only need to add an employee's name, address, and social security number when a new employee is hired.*

(3) voice reporting

In some states, employers can report new hires by leaving a voice message on a special voice response system.

Tip. *Be sure to check with your designated state agency to find out what reporting options are available in your state. Telephone numbers for all state agencies are included in Table 8-2. Use the option that is easiest for you.*

Tip. *Does your church use a payroll reporting service? If so, it may be automatically making the new hire reports for you. Check to be sure.*

3. Penalties

The federal welfare reform law prohibits states from assessing a penalty in excess of $25 for each failure to report a new hire. However, states may impose a penalty of up to $500 if an employer and employee "conspire" to avoid the reporting requirements, or agree to submit a false report.

4. Employees in More than One State

Some denominational agencies and parachurch ministries have employees in more than one state. How do they comply with the new hire reporting rules? They may report newly hired employees to the state in which the employees are working; or, they may select one state to receive all new hire reports. If one state is selected, the employer must submit new hire reports electronically or by magnetic tape. The employer should check with the designated state agency to discuss the technical requirements for such a report.

Key point. *"One state" reporting requires new hire information to be reported twice a month, not less than 12 nor more than 16 days apart.*

Key point. *A multistate employer that elects to report all new hire information to one state must inform the Secretary of the United States Department of Health and Human Services of its decision by writing National Director of New Hires, DHHS-OCSE, Multistate Employer Registration, P.O. Box 509, Randallstown, MD 21133.*

Note: *Explanation of codes used in this table: A (W-4 information, including employee's name, address, social security number, plus the employer's name, address, and employer identification number); B (state employer identification number); C (date of hire); D (date of birth); E (salary); F (employer contact person and phone number); F (medical insurance information). Code letters in brackets (e.g., [A]) refer to information that may voluntarily be reported by an employer, but which is not required by law. Be sure to check with your designated state agency for the most up-do-date information.*

TABLE 8-2
COMPLYING WITH THE NEW HIRE REPORTING REQUIREMENT
A STATE-BY-STATE SUMMARY

state	what to report	when to report (days after hire)	penalty	telephone assistance
AL	A,B	7	$25	334-353-8491
AK	A	20	$10 ($100 for conspiracy)	907-269-6685
AZ	A	30	none	602-252-4045
AR	A	20	none	501-682-3087
CA	A,B,C	20	$24 ($490 for conspiracy)	916-657-0529
CO	A	20	none	303-297-2849
CT	A,B	20	none	860-424-5044
DE	A	20	$25 ($500 for conspiracy)	302-369-2160
DC	A,C,D,E [F,G]	20	$25 ($500 for conspiracy)	888-689-6088
FL	A,C [D]	20	none	904-922-9590
GA	A,B,D	10	written warning	888-541-0469
HI	A	20	$25 ($500 for conspiracy)	808-586-8984
ID	A,B,C	20	none	800-627-3880
IL	A [C]	20	$15 ($500 for conspiracy)	800-327-4473
IN	A	20	$500 for conspiracy	800-437-9136
IA	A,D,F	15	contempt of court	515-281-5331
KS	A	20	none	888-219-7801
KY	A	20	$250 for third and each additional offense, and conspiracy	800-817-2262
LA	A	20	$25 ($500 for conspiracy)	888-223-1461
ME	A,B,D	7	written warning for first offense; up to $200 for additional offenses)	207-287-2886
MD	A,B,C	20	$20 ($500 for conspiracy)	888-634-4737
MA	A,C	14	$25 ($500 for conspiracy)	617-577-7200
MI	A	20	none	800-524-9846
MN	A [D]	20	$25 ($500 for conspiracy)	800-672-4473
MS	A,B,C,D	15	$25 ($500 for conspiracy)	800-866-4461

state	what to report	when to report (days after hire)	penalty	telephone assistance
MO	A [C]	20	$25 ($350 for conspiracy)	800-859-7999
MT	A,C [D,F]	20	none	888-866-0327
NC	A,B	20	$25 ($500 for conspiracy)	888-514-4568
ND	A	20	$25 ($250 for conspiracy)	800-755-8530
NE	A	20	$25	888-256-0293
NH	A,B	20	none	888-803-4485
NJ	A,D	20	$25 ($500 for conspiracy)	609-588-2355
NM	A	20	$20 ($500 for conspiracy)	888-878-1607
NY	A	20	$25 ($450 for conspiracy)	800-972-1233
NV	A	20	$25	888-639-7241
OH	A,C,D	20	less than $25 ($500 for conspiracy)	800-208-8887
OK	A,C	20	none	800-317-3785
OR	A	20	none	503-986-6053
PA	A,C,G	20	warning for first offense; $25 for additional offenses ($500 for conspiracy)	888-724-4737
RI	A,D,F	14	$25 ($500 for conspiracy)	888-870-6461
SC	A	20	$25 for second and additional offenses ($500 for conspiracy)	800-768-5858
SD	A	20	petty offense	888-827-6078
TN	A	20	$20 ($400 for conspiracy)	888-827-2280
TX	A	20	$25 ($500 for conspiracy)	888-839-4473
UT	A	20	$25 ($500 for conspiracy)	801-526-4361
VT	A	20	$25 ($500 for conspiracy)	802-241-2194
VA	A	20	none	800-979-9014
WA	A,D	20	$25 ($500 for conspiracy)	800-562-0479
WV	A [D,E]	14	$25 ($500 for conspiracy)	800-835-4683
WI	A,C,D	20	$25 ($500 for conspiracy)	888-300-4473
WY	A	20	none	800-970-9258

§ 8-23   Reference Letters

Key point 8-23. A reference letter is a letter that evaluates the qualifications and suitability of a person for a particular position. Churches, like other employers, often use reference letters to screen new employees and volunteers. Churches often are asked to provide reference letters on current or former workers. The law generally provides employers with important protections when responding to a reference letter request. However, liability may still arise in some cases, such as if the employer acts with malice in drafting a reference letter.

A "reference letter" is a letter that evaluates the qualifications and suitability of a person for a particular position. There are a number of important legal issues associated with the use of reference letters, and some of them are addressed in this section.

1. REQUESTING REFERENCE LETTERS AS A SCREENING DEVICE

The use of reference letters when hiring employees and selecting volunteer workers is becoming an increasingly common church practice, since it is a way for churches to reduce the risk of liability for "negligent selection" of employees and volunteers. The use of reference letters in screening workers is addressed in chapter 12 of this text.

Tip. The use of reference letters, and several sample forms, is available in several resources available from the publisher of this text.[234]

2. RESPONDING TO REFERENCE LETTER REQUESTS

Many churches have been asked to provide reference letters on a current or former employee or volunteer. Unfortunately, such letters can expose a church to legal liability if not handled properly. While liability ordinarily is associated with negative information disclosed in a reference letter, it also may arise because of positive references. Both kinds of liability are addressed in this section.

Some churches, like many secular employers, refuse to respond to any reference request, other than to confirm the fact that a person worked for the church and the dates of employment or volunteer service. While such an approach certainly reduces if not eliminates a church's liability for providing an inappropriate reference, it does so in some cases at the risk of exposing innocent people to potential harm. To illustrate, assume that First Church dismisses Bill as a volunteer children's worker because of inappropriate sexual contact with children. Bill applies for a similar position at Second Church. Second Church asks First Church for a reference letter describing Bill's suitability for working with children. The pastor and board at First Church refuse to respond because of a fear of legal liability. Within a few months, Bill molests four children while acting as a volunteer worker at Second Church. Are the pastor and board members of First Church morally responsible, at least in part, for the molestation of the four children? Many church leaders would answer yes to this

---

[234] *See, e.g.,* J. COBBLE, R. HAMMAR, AND S. KLIPOWICZ, REDUCING THE RISK OF CHILD SEXUAL ABUSE IN YOUR CHURCH; S. KLIPOWICZ, REDUCING THE RISK OF CHILD SEXUAL ABUSE IN YOUR CHURCH TRAINING MANUAL; J. COBBLE, AND R. HAMMAR, REDUCING THE RISK OF CHILD SEXUAL ABUSE IN YOUR CHURCH AUDIO TRAINING TAPE; J. COBBLE, AND R. HAMMAR, REDUCING THE RISK OF CHILD SEXUAL ABUSE IN YOUR CHURCH VIDEO; J. COBBLE AND R. HAMMAR, SELECTING AND SCREENING CHURCH WORKERS; J. COBBLE AND R. HAMMAR, SELECTION AND SCREENING KIT FOR CHURCH EMPLOYEES; J. COBBLE AND R. HAMMAR, SELECTION AND SCREENING KIT FOR CHURCH VOLUNTEERS; J. COBBLE AND R. HAMMAR, SELECTION AND SCREENING KIT FOR MINISTERS. All of these resources are available from Christian Ministry Resources, the publisher of this text.

question. As a result, many church leaders have a desire to share information about former employees or volunteers with other churches when asked to do so, even if that information involves inappropriate behavior.

While it is possible for churches to be sued, and found liable, for information contained in reference letters that they provide to other churches or employers, there are precautions that church leaders can take to reduce this risk. Several of these precautions are addressed in the following paragraphs.

liability for providing negative references

Church leaders often are reluctant to provide a reference letter containing negative information because of a fear of legal liability. Some churches and secular employers have been sued by former employees or volunteers because of negative information shared in a reference letter. Liability generally is based on defamation, the infliction of emotional distress, or "interference with contract."

> ***Example.*** *An employee of a church-affiliated college was terminated for not returning a paycheck that had been inadvertently issued to him for a time period in which he had performed no services. The employee applied for work at a local business as a security guard. A company supervisor called the college's personnel department for a reference. A supervisor in the personnel department responded to the reference request with laughter, and then advised the caller that the former employee "has a problem of dishonesty concerning money." Because of this negative reference, the company decided not to hire the individual. He later sued the college for slander and "interference with business relations." A Massachusetts appeals court concluded that the college was liable under these circumstances. This case illustrates the legal risks that one assumes in providing negative references to other employers. This is particularly so when "opinions," as opposed to statements of fact, are expressed.[235]*

Many courts and legislatures have recognized a number of legal defenses that are available to employers when responding to a request for a reference letter. These defenses include the following:

(1) truth

Employers cannot be liable for defamation when the information shared in a reference letter is true. Of course, to qualify for this defense, an employer must limit its reference letter to assertions of fact that are verifiable through documents or the testimony of witnesses. Truth is not an absolute defense to claims of emotional distress and interference with contract, but it certainly makes such claims less likely to succeed.

(2) qualified privilege

In many states, employers are protected by a "qualified privilege" when giving references on former employees. This qualified privilege generally prohibits an employer from being guilty of defamation unless the former employee can prove that statements of fact given by the employer in a reference letter were false, and made with malice. Malice in this context generally means that the employer either knew the statements were false, or made them with a reckless disregard as to their truth or falsity. Note that not all states recognize the qualified privilege. As a result, employers should not make potentially defamatory statements about former employees without the advice of a local attorney.

---

[235] St. Clair v. Trustees of Boston University, 521 N.E.2d 1044 (Mass. App. 1988).

The concept of qualified privilege was described by one court as follows:

One who in the regular course of business is asked by a prospective employer . . . for information concerning a person, is entitled to the defense of qualified privilege if his reply would otherwise be regarded as defamatory. . . . The qualified privilege serves an important public function in the employment context. Without the privilege, references would be even more hesitant than they are to provide candid evaluations of former employees. In order to overcome the qualified privilege, the plaintiff must show that the statements were made with malice. Once a communication is deemed privileged, the burden of proof to demonstrate malice rests with the plaintiff. To show malice, the plaintiff must show either that the statements were made with knowing falsity, in bad faith, or with reckless disregard of the truth.[236]

Several states have enacted legislation incorporating the concept of qualified privilege as a matter of law. Such statutes typically protect information shared by employers in reference letters, unless the information is shared with malice.

Example. A federal court in the District of Columbia threw out a lawsuit brought by a worker against his former employer for allegedly defamatory references given to prospective employers.[237] The worker was employed as a bookkeeper for a secular company. His employment was marked by difficulties with fellow employees. Without explanation or advance notice, the worker quit his job. He later applied for another job, and the prospective employer sought references from the former employer. One supervisor stated that the worker was "wholly incompetent" and "not eligible for rehire." Another supervisor stated that the worker was "undesirable as a candidate for rehire," and that he had "personality conflicts" with co-workers. The worker sued his former employer, and these supervisors, for defamation on the basis of these statements. The defendants asked the court to dismiss the case, and the court did so. It emphasized that all of the allegedly defamatory statements were protected by a "qualified privilege" which it defined as follows: "One who in the regular course of business is asked by a prospective employer . . . for information concerning a person, is entitled to the defense of qualified privilege if his reply would otherwise be regarded as defamatory. . . . The qualified privilege serves an important public function in the employment context. Without the privilege, references would be even more hesitant than they are to provide candid evaluations of former employees. In order to overcome the qualified privilege, the plaintiff must show that the statements were made with malice. Once a communication is deemed privileged, the burden of proof to demonstrate malice rests with the plaintiff. To show malice, the plaintiff must show either that the statements were made with knowing falsity, in bad faith, or with reckless disregard of the truth." Applying this standard, the court concluded that the former employer and supervisors were protected by the qualified privilege with regard to information they shared in their references, and that the former worker had the burden of proving that the reference statements were made with malice. The court concluded that the former worker had produced no evidence to demonstrate that any of the statements had been made with malice.

(3) release

Current or former employees and volunteers who are adults can release a church from liability associated with information disclosed in a reference letter. As noted above, it is advisable to obtain such a release

---

[236] Hargrow v. Long, 760 F. Supp. 1 (D.D.C. 1991).
[237] *Id.*

before issuing a reference letter that will contain negative information. Ideally, a release form should require the person's signature to be made before a notary public. At a minimum, a release form should require the signer's signature to be witnessed by one or two other persons whose signatures appear on the form.

Example. A Texas appeals court ruled that a "release form" signed by an employee prevented her from suing a former employer for statements it made about the employee to a prospective employer. An employee who had been terminated by her employer applied to another employer for a job. The new employer had the employee sign a form entitled "authorization for release of information." This form provided, in part: "I hereby authorize any investigator . . . bearing this release to obtain any information from schools, residential management agents, employers, criminal justice agencies, or individuals, relating to my activities. This information may include, but is not limited to, academic, residential, achievement, performance, attendance, personal history, disciplinary, arrest, and conviction records. I hereby direct you to release such information upon request to the bearer. . . . I hereby release any individual, including record custodians, from any and all liability for damages of whatever kind or nature which may at any time result to me on account of compliance or any attempts to comply, with this authorization." The prospective employer contacted the former employer as part of its background check of the employee, and was informed about her negative job performance. On the basis of this information, the prospective employer declined to hire the individual. She promptly sued the former employer for defamation, and a jury awarded her $1 million in damages. The former employer appealed this verdict. A state appeals court reversed the jury's verdict, and ruled that the former employer should pay the employee nothing. The court noted that statements made by a former employer to a prospective employer about a former employee are protected by a "qualified privilege." This ordinarily means that such statements cannot be the basis for defamation unless they are made with "malice." The court concluded, however, that the statements made by the former employer in this case were protected by an absolute privilege because of the release form signed by the former employee, and accordingly it was impossible for the employee to sue her former employer for defamation.[238]

interference with contract

In many states, one who interferes with an existing contract between two other parties can be sued for "interference with contract." To illustrate, assume that a church dismisses a pastor for adultery. The pastor is later hired by another church. After a few months, a denominational official learns of the pastor's new job, and contacts the board members of the new church to inform them of the pastor's previous misconduct. As a result of this unsolicited disclosure, the church board decides to terminate the pastor's employment. The pastor may be able to sue the denominational official for interference with contract. Note that this basis of liability requires the existence of a contract. If the church had asked the denominational official for a letter of reference *prior* to the date the pastor was hired, there can be no interference with contract. The timing of a letter of reference is critical. If it comes before the prospective employee is hired, there can be no interference with contract. If it comes after the employee is hired, there may be liability.

Example. The Alaska Supreme Court ruled that a denominational official in the Presbyterian Church (USA) could be sued on the basis of interference with contract for making disparaging comments about another minister who recently had been hired by a local church.[239] A Presbyterian minister left a pastoral position in Alaska and accepted a call as minister of a Presbyterian church in Tennessee. When

[238] Smith v. Holley, 827 S.W.2d 433 (Tex. App. 1992).
[239] Marshall v. Munro, 845 P.2d 424 (Alaska 1993).

REDUCING RISK WHEN PROVIDING A NEGATIVE REFERENCE

Churches wanting to respond to a request for a reference letter on a former employee or volunteer who did not perform satisfactorily, or who was guilty of some form of misconduct, can reduce the risk of liability in a number of ways, including one or more of the following:

(1) Do not respond.

(2) Respond with a reference letter (or telephone call) that limits the response to statements of fact that can be verified with documents or testimony. So long as there is a factual basis for a reference, a church will be eligible for the "qualified privilege" in most states that makes employers immune from liability for negative references unless they act with malice. In this context, malice means that the employer knew that a statement was false, or acted with reckless disregard or indifference regarding the statement's truth or falsity. In no case should opinions be expressed, since these are difficult to establish in a court of law.

(3) Respond only if you receive, in advance, a "release form" signed by the former employee or volunteer releasing your church and its agents, officers, and employees, from liability based on information shared in the reference letter. Of course, persons with a history of unsatisfactory work or inappropriate behavior often will refuse to sign such a form, which should serve as a warning to the church or other organization that asked you for the reference letter.

Because the availability of these defenses varies from state to state, it is advisable for a church to check with an attorney before making a negative reference.

---

he presented himself to the church to begin his duties, he was informed by church officials that because of derogatory information the church had received from a denominational official (an executive presbyter in Alaska), the church would not hire him. The presbyter had informed church leaders that the minister was divorced, dishonest, unable to perform pastoral duties because of throat surgery, and that he had made an improper sexual advance to a church member in Alaska. The minister sued the presbyter for intentional interference with his employment contract with the Tennessee church. Generally, one who intentionally interferes with a known contract can be sued for damages. The state supreme court concluded that the civil courts can make this determination without any inquiries into internal church discipline. The court drew an important distinction between clergy who are seeking a pastoral position and those who have been hired. If a church official makes derogatory remarks about a minister who already has been hired by a local church, and if those remarks induce local church leaders to terminate the employment agreement, then the church official can be sued for "interference with contract." The court insisted that such claims ordinarily will not involve inquiries into core ecclesiastical issues. This suggests that church officials should be more cautious in making remarks about clergy who already have been hired by a local church or other religious organization.

Example. *A Louisiana court suggested that it could not resolve a priest's claim that a church official was guilty of interference with contract as a result of the contents of a letter of reference.[240] A Catholic priest who had been accused of molesting a child was investigated by church officials. He later filed a lawsuit*

---

[240] Hayden v. Schulte, 701 So.2d 1354 (La. App. 1997).

claiming that a church official interfered with his employment prospects as a Navy chaplain as a result of a letter of reference that referred to "some accusations of questionable behavior and some complaints about [the priest's] ministry." The church official insisted that the letter of reference pertained to the fitness of the priest for assignment to a chaplaincy position—a matter beyond the reach of the civil courts. The court did not address this issue directly, but seemed to acknowledge that internal communications among clergy or church leaders regarding the fitness of a minister cannot give rise to civil liability.

Example. *A New Jersey court ruled that a church acted properly in dismissing its music director for criminal acts.[241] After working for the church for a few months, the music director was arrested for possession of illegal anabolic steroids. It was later disclosed that the music director had been taking steroids to assist him with bodybuilding, and that he had ordered several shipments of steroids shipped directly to the church to avoid detection. The music director was dismissed, and later applied to another church for similar employment. His application was rejected when the church contacted the previous church and was informed by the pastor of what had happened. The music director sued his former church, alleging breach of contract. He also claimed that the pastor, by informing the other church of the music director's criminal activities, had wrongfully "interfered with his prospective economic advantage." The trial court dismissed the music director's assertion that the church had wrongfully interfered with a "prospective economic advantage." It noted that the music director could not show that "there was an intentional, without justification, interference" with his economic advantage. Further, the court pointed out that the pastor had disclosed the information only after it was requested, and the information was of criminal conduct admitted by the music director and covered in the newspaper. Additionally, the pastor was protected by a "qualified privilege" for employment references, meaning that he could not be liable unless his reference contained information that the pastor knew to be false.*

liability for refusing to respond to a request for a reference letter

It is a fundamental principle of law that there can be no liability for a failure to protect another from harm or peril. As one court observed: "One human being, seeing a fellow man in dire peril, is under no legal obligation to aid him, but may sit on the dock, smoke his cigar, and watch the other fellow drown."[242] This principle means that a church cannot be liable for failing to warn another church of the dangerous propensities of a former employee or volunteer. To illustrate, if Jack molests children at First Church while serving as a volunteer worker, and later begins working as a volunteer children's worker at Second Church, First Church is under no legal obligation to warn Second Church of Jack's dangerous behavior. There are practical reasons for this rule. After all, the leadership of First Church cannot be expected to hire an investigator to track Jack down and find out every church that he attends.

Some courts have created a limited exception to the general rule of no liability for a failure to warn others of a former worker's dangerous propensities. If a "special relationship" exists between church leaders and a potential victim, then the church has a legal duty to warn the potential victim of the dangerous propensities of an employee or volunteer. This exception was recognized in the following example.

Example. *A Washington state court ruled that a church and a member of the church board could be sued by three women who had been molested by a volunteer youth worker when they were minors.[243] The board member had received information indicating that the worker was a child molester, but*

---

[241] McGarry v. Saint Anthony of Padua Roman Catholic Church, 704 A.2d 1353 (N.J. Super. 1998).
[242] Evans v. Ohio State University, 680 N.E.2d 161 (Ohio App. 1996).
[243] Funkhouser v. Wilson, 950 P.2d 501 (Wash. App. 1998).

failed to disclose this information for twenty-three years. Because of the board member's failure to disclose this information, the molester was able to molest the sisters over a period of several years. The court found that the church had a "special relationship" with minors that imposed upon it a duty to protect them from the criminal and intentional acts of others. The court acknowledged that "as a general rule, there is no legal duty to protect another from the criminal acts of a third person." However, there is an exception if a "special relationship" exists between a church and a potential victim which imposes upon the church a duty to "protect" the victim from harm. The court concluded that a special relationship exists between churches and children who participate in church programs and activities: "[W]e believe that churches and the adult church workers who assume responsibility for the spiritual well being of children of the congregation, whether as paid clergy or as volunteers, have a special relationship with those children that gives rise to a duty to protect them from reasonably foreseeable risk of harm from those members of the congregation whom the church places in positions of responsibility and authority over them."

The conclusion reached by the court in the previous example is extraordinary. It exposes church leaders to liability for failing to protect children against "reasonably foreseeable risks of harm" by volunteer or paid youth workers. Note that the victims in the example were members of the same church as the molester. But what if the molester began attending a different church? Would church leaders at the former church have a legal duty to warn the second church of the molester's dangerous propensities? Probably not. It is doubtful that the court would have concluded that a "special relationship" existed between the former church and children in the second church that would give rise to a duty to protect them from the molester by notifying the church of his dangerous behavior.

liability for providing positive references

In two historic cases that will be of direct relevance to churches, the supreme courts of Texas and California have ruled that individuals and their employers face potential legal liability for providing positive and unqualified references on former workers *who they know pose a risk of harm to others*. In both cases, positive references were provided on individuals with a known background of sexual misconduct involving minors. The molesters were hired on the basis of these references, and they later molested other minors in the course of their new duties. Both courts ruled that persons who provide positive references under these circumstances, without any disclosure of the negative information, are legally responsible for the harm the worker inflicts on others. It is essential for church leaders to be familiar with both of these rulings. While they apply only in the states of Texas and California, it is likely they will be followed in other states. The cases are summarized in the following two examples.

Example. The Texas Supreme Court ruled that a local Boy Scout council could be liable for a scoutmaster's acts of child molestation because it was aware of rumors suggesting that the scoutmaster had engaged in inappropriate behavior with boys but still recommended him to a leadership position in a local troop.[244] The court concluded that if the council knew or should have known that the molester was "peculiarly likely to molest boys," it had a duty not to recommend him as a scoutmaster. Further, the council's "affirmative act of recommending [the molester] as a potential scoutmaster . . . created a duty on the part of [the council] to use reasonable care in light of the information it had received." It continued: "[W]e hold that if [the local council] knew or should have known that [the molester] was peculiarly likely to molest boys, it had a duty not to recommend him as a scoutmaster." The court concluded:

---

[244] Golden Spread Council, Inc. v. Akins, 926 S.W.2d 287 (Tex. 1996).

"[W]e recognize that there is no way to ensure that this type of conduct will never happen, despite an organization's best efforts. However [the local council] and similar organizations deal with children. The public has a strong interest in protecting children from abuse, and parents put their trust in such organizations. Having undertaken to recommend a potential scoutmaster for the church, [the council] had a duty to use reasonable care in doing so to prevent an unreasonable risk of harm to [the victim] and others who would be affected. [The council] breached that duty if it knew or should have known that [the molester] was peculiarly likely to molest boys. On this record, this is the issue determinative of [the council's] liability."

Example. *The California Supreme Court ruled that the former employers of a teacher who molested an adolescent girl were liable for his actions because they provided his current employer with positive references despite their knowledge of his previous misconduct.[245] A teacher was employed by a public school based in part on the glowing letters of recommendation from the principals of three schools in which he had previously been employed. One of the letters of recommendation stated that "due in large part to [his] efforts, our campus is a safe, orderly and clean environment for students and staff. . . . I recommend [him] without reservation." In fact, each of the principals was aware of prior incidents or reports of sexual misconduct by the teacher. They all failed to disclose the teacher's misconduct in their letters of recommendation. Unfortunately, the teacher sexually molested a 13-year-old girl (the victim) shortly after beginning his new assignment. The victim later sued the three prior schools and their principals, claiming that they were responsible for her injuries because they were aware of prior incidents of sexual misconduct involving the teacher but failed to disclose this information in their letters of recommendation. The three principals (and their schools) insisted that "a rule imposing liability on writers of recommendation letters could have one very predictable consequence—employers would seldom write such letters, even in praise of exceptionally qualified employees." The principals pointed out few persons will provide "full disclosure" of all negative information in reference letters since doing so would expose them to liability for defamation or invasion of privacy. This threat of liability will "inhibit employers from freely providing reference information," and this in turn will restrict the flow of information prospective employers need and impede job applicants in finding new employment. On the other hand, the victim insisted that employers providing references on former employees are protected under California law by a "qualified privilege." The qualified privilege renders employers immune from liability for their communications pertaining to a former employee's "job performance or qualifications" so long as they do not act maliciously and provide the information "to, and upon request of, the prospective employer." The court concluded that this qualified privilege greatly reduces the concerns expressed by the principals (and their schools). The court went so far as to observe that the qualified privilege ordinarily would prevent liability in a case such as this involving negligent misrepresentations made by employers about a former employee. However, the court noted that the qualified privilege did not help the principals in this case since it applies only to communications made "upon request of" a prospective employer. The principals "do not claim that they wrote [their letters of recommendation] in response to [the school's] request, and, accordingly, the privilege is inapplicable." Having concluded that the principals (and their schools) owed the victim a duty of care, the court addressed the question of whether or not they breached this duty by making misrepresentations or giving false information in their letters of recommendation concerning the teacher. The court conceded that there is no liability for "nondisclosure," meaning that an employer cannot be legally responsible for a victim's injuries on the basis of its refusal to disclose information about a former worker. However, the court concluded that this case presented an exception to the general rule: "[T]hese letters, essentially recommending [the*

---

[245] Randi W. v. Muroc Joint Unified School District, 60 Cal. Rptr.2d 263 (Cal. 1997).

teacher] for any position without reservation or qualification, constituted affirmative representations that strongly implied [the teacher] was fit to interact appropriately and safely with female students. These representations were false and misleading in light of [the principals'] alleged knowledge of charges of [the teacher's] repeated sexual improprieties." The court summarized its ruling as follows: "[W]e conclude that [the principals'] letters of recommendation, containing unreserved and unconditional praise for [a former teacher] despite [their] alleged knowledge of complaints or charges of his sexual misconduct with students, constituted misleading statements that could form the basis for . . . liability for fraud or negligent misrepresentation. Although policy considerations dictate that ordinarily a recommending employer should not be held accountable for failing to disclose negative information regarding a former employee, nonetheless liability may be imposed if, as alleged here, the recommendation letter amounts to an affirmative misrepresentation presenting a foreseeable and substantial risk of physical harm to a prospective employer or third person."

Example. *G worked as a volunteer children's worker at First Church. After parents complained to the senior pastor about G's inappropriate touching of a number of children, G is removed from his position. A few months later G leaves First Church and begins attending Second Church. When he applies as a children's worker, Second Church contacts First Church for a reference. First Church sends a letter containing a strong and unqualified recommendation of G. Nothing is disclosed regarding G's inappropriate touching of several children. G later molests a child at Second Church. When the child's parents learn of First Church's recommendation, they sue the church. In Texas and California, or in any state that follows the decisions of the Texas and California supreme courts (summarized above), First Church may be legally responsible for G's acts of molestation occurring at Second Church. It knew that G was "peculiarly likely" to molest minors and therefore had a duty not to recommend him.*

Example. *Same facts as the previous example, except that First Church refused to respond to Second Church's request for a reference regarding G. The Texas Supreme Court ruled that there can be no liability under these circumstances, since First Church has not "recommended" G.*

Example. *B, a former member of First Church, has attended Second Church for a few years and recently applied to work in the church nursery. Second Church asks First Church for a letter of recommendation. The staff at First Church is aware of no information regarding B that would indicate she would be unsuitable for working with minors, and so it sends a letter of recommendation. It does no investigation. B later is accused of abusing a child in the nursery at Second Church. The Texas Supreme Court's ruling would not make First Church legally responsible for B's actions under these circumstances. While it recommended her, it had no knowledge indicating that she posed a risk of harm to others. According to the court's decision, First Church had no independent duty to investigate B on its own.*

Example. *Same facts as the previous example, except that the staff at First Church was aware that B had been accused of child molestation on two different occasions, but it did not believe that the accusations were credible and so ignored them when preparing its letter of recommendation. Under these circumstances, it is possible that a court would conclude that First Church should have known, on the basis of information available to it without an independent investigation, that B posed a risk of harm to children. As a result, it had a duty not to recommend her. In Texas and California, or in any state that follows the decisions of the Texas and California supreme courts (summarized above), First Church may be liable for acts of abuse committed by B at Second Church.*

3. CONFIDENTIALITY

Churches should be careful to treat as confidential any reference letter they receive on a current or former employee or volunteer worker. In some states, employees have a legal right to inspect their personnel records, but this right does not extend to reference letters that may be in their personnel file.[246]

> **Example.** *The Pennsylvania Supreme Court ruled that a state nonprofit corporation law giving members the right to inspect corporate records was "limited by considerations of privacy, privilege and confidentiality." As an example, the court referred to reference letters, noting that releasing "confidential references . . . would infringe upon the legitimate expectations of confidentiality of those who submitted the references. Further, releasing such references would ensure that very few persons in the future would ever respond to requests for references."*[247]

---

[246] *See, e.g.,* MINN. STAT. § 181.961 (employees can inspect their personnel records, but the term "personnel record" does not include "written references respecting the employee, including letters of reference supplied to an employer by another person").

[247] Lewis v. Pennsylvania Bar Association, 701 A.2d 551 (Pa. 1997).

INSTRUCTIONAL AIDS TO CHAPTER 8

Terms

Age Discrimination in Employment Act

Americans with Disabilities Act

"at will" employee

Civil Rights Act of 1964, Title VII

commerce

Employee Polygraph Protection Act

employer

Fair Labor Standards Act

Family and Medical Leave Act

Form I-9

good cause

hostile environment sexual harassment

minimum wage

National Labor Relations Act

Occupational Safety and Health Act

overtime pay

preschool

qualified individual with a disability

quid pro quo sexual harassment

reference letter

sexual harassment

vicarious liability

workers compensation

Learning Objectives

- Understand the meaning of workers compensation, and explain the application of workers compensation laws to religious organizations.

- Understand the application of Immigration and Naturalization Service Form I-9 to religious organizations.

- Explain the "employment at will" doctrine, and identify several exceptions to it.

- Understand the procedure employees follow when filing a discrimination claim under federal civil rights laws.

- Understand the importance of the term "commerce" in the context of federal employment and civil rights laws, and explain its meaning.

- Explain the "clergy exemption" under federal civil rights laws.

- Understand the major provisions of Title VII of the Civil Rights Act of 1964, and explain its application to religious organizations.

- Understand the major provisions of the federal Age Discrimination in Employment Act, and explain its application to religious organizations.

- Understand the major provisions of the Americans with Disabilities Act, and explain its application to religious organizations.

- Understand the major provisions of Employee Polygraph Protection Act, and explain its application to religious organizations.

- Understand the major provisions of Occupational Safety and Health Act, and explain its application to religious organizations.

- Understand the major provisions of Fair Labor Standards Act, and explain its application to religious organizations.

- Understand the major provisions of National Labor Relations Act, and explain its application to religious organizations.

- Understand the major provisions of Family and Medical Leave Act, and explain its application to religious organizations.

- Identify the legal risks associated with the use of reference letters, and explain how these risks may be reduced.

- Understand the application to religious organizations of state laws banning employment discrimination on the basis of sexual orientation.

Short-Answer Questions

1. A church is located in a state that does not exempt churches from workers compensation coverage. A church employee stumbles down a church stairway and receives serious injuries. Answer the following questions:

    a. If the church has workers compensation insurance, what will be the extent of the church's legal liability?

    b. If the church does not have workers compensation insurance, will the employee's injuries be compensated under the church's general liability insurance policy? Why or why not?

    c. Should a church obtain workers compensation insurance, even if it is not legally required to do so? Explain.

2. A church is about to hire a new secretary. What, if any, obligations does it have under federal immigration law?

3. Explain the "at will" employment rule.

4. A church hires a clerical worker. Nothing is said regarding the term of employment. Answer the following questions:

    a. This type of employment relationship is often referred to by what term?

    b. Historically, an employer could terminate such a relationship on the basis of what grounds?

    c. Historically, did an employer have any recourse against an employee who terminated such a relationship?

    d. Do the courts still recognize this rule in most states?

    e. Are there any exceptions to the historical rule that are commonly recognized by the courts today?

5. T is a church employee who has been hired for an indefinite period. The church terminates T's employment because of a "personality conflict" with the pastor. T sues the church for wrongful termination. What is the likely outcome of this case?

6. Same facts as question 5, except that T was hired for a 3-year term, and is terminated after only one year on the job.

7. The church board failed to designate a housing allowance for Rev. B this year. At the end of the year, Rev. B instructs the church bookkeeper to prepare and "backdate" a fraudulent board resolution designating in advance a housing allowance for the entire year. The employee refuses to do so, and is dismissed. The employee sues the church for wrongful termination. The church insists that the worker was an at will employee who could be terminated for any reason. What is the likely outcome of this case?

8. G is a church employee who is injured on the job. She has been awarded workers compensation benefits because of her injury. The church dismisses G because the disability adversely affects her ability to perform her job. G sues the church. The church's defense is that G was an at will employee who could be terminated at any time, with or without cause. Answer the following questions:

   a. What is the likely outcome of this case?

   b. What precautions could Rev. H have taken to reduce the risk of litigation?

9. What is a severance agreement? Give an example of how such an agreement can reduce a church's risk of legal liability when dismissing an employee.

10. J has served as a bookkeeper at his church for more than twenty years. Rev. H learns that J has embezzled over $10,000 of church funds. Rev. H confronts J and obtains a full confession. J's employment is immediately terminated. Members of the staff and congregation immediately notice that J is missing. She no longer shows up at work, and has quit attending the church. People begin asking questions about the reasons for J's sudden departure. Rumors spread that J was fired. In order to respond to these questions, Rev. H informs the staff (at a weekly staff meeting) that J was dismissed because of embezzlement. Rev. H makes a similar disclosure to the congregation following a morning worship service. J learns of these disclosures, and sues Rev. H and the church. Answer the following questions:

   a. What is the likely outcome of this case?

   b. What precautions could Rev. H have taken to reduce the risk of litigation?

11. K is a female who claims that a church did not hire her for an open position because of her sex. She sues the church for unlawful sex discrimination in violation of Title VII of the Civil Rights Act of 1964. The church has 17 employees. It insists that it is not subject to Title VII because it is not engaged in "commerce." Answer the following questions:

   a. Must a church be engaged in "commerce" to be subject to Title VII? If so, what is the basis for this requirement?

   b. The church occasionally purchases Sunday School literature from an out-of-state publisher; sends mail out-of-state; and employees makes out-of-state telephone calls. What is the likelihood that a civil court will conclude that the church is engaged in commerce?

c. In addition to the facts mentioned in paragraph (b), the church occasionally sends staff to out-of-state conferences and has a number of members who live in another state and who cross the state line to attend the church. What is the likelihood that a civil court will conclude that the church is engaged in commerce?

12. Evaluate the likelihood that each of the following churches would be deemed to be engaged in commerce by a civil court:

a. A church operates a private elementary school.

b. A church operates a preschool.

c. A church operates a commercial business (a restaurant).

d. A church occasionally purchases literature and office equipment from out-of-state vendors; sends employees to out-of-state conferences; and has some members who live in another state.

e. A church operates a web page on the internet.

f. A church broadcasts a radio program.

13. M is a disabled male who claims that a church did not hire him for an open position because of his disability. He sues the church for unlawful discrimination in violation of the Americans with Disabilities Act. The church has 10 employees. What is the most likely outcome of this case? Why?

14. Same facts as question 13, except that the church operates a preschool with 8 employees. Are the church's 10 employees and the preschool's 8 employees combined in applying the Americans with Disabilities Act's 15 employee requirement? What factors would a civil court likely consider in deciding this question?

15. Same facts as question 14, except that some of the church's employees are part-time. Are they counted in applying the Americans with Disabilities Act's 15 employee requirement?

16. A church dismisses Rev. K, its senior pastor. Rev. K, who is 68 years of age, believes that the church dismissed him because of his age. He retains an attorney who writes the church a letter threatening to sue for unlawful age discrimination unless the church settles with her client for $100,000. Answer the following questions:

a. Has the church committed unlawful age discrimination? Assume that the main reason it dismissed Rev. K was that it wanted a younger, more dynamic minister.

b. How should the church respond to the attorney's letter?

c. How could the church have minimized the risk of this dispute?

17. Rev. V has served as senior pastor of a church for several years. He has a stroke that permanently affects his speech, making it very slow and unintelligible. The church reluctantly dismisses him. Rev. V retains an attorney who threatens to sue the church for violating the Americans with Disabilities Act. List 4 defenses that may be available to the church.

18. A church has more than 15 employees and is engaged in commerce. Answer the following questions:

    a. An employee claims that she was discriminated against because of her race in violation of Title VII of the Civil Rights Act of 1964. Does Title VII apply to this church? Explain.

    b. An employee claims that he was discriminated against because of his ethnic background in violation of Title VII of the Civil Rights Act of 1964. Does Title VII apply to this church? Explain.

    c. An employee claims that she was discriminated against because of her sex in violation of Title VII of the Civil Rights Act of 1964. Does Title VII apply to this church? Explain.

19. Same facts as question 18. Would any of your answers be different if the church has 12 employees?

20. Same facts as question 18. Would any of your answers be different if the church was not engaged in commerce? Explain.

21. A church has 20 employees, and is engaged in commerce. It is looking for a new youth pastor, and receives an application from an ordained minister of a different religious denomination. The church refuses to consider this application. Answer the following questions:

    a. Has the church committed religious discrimination?

    b. If the church has committed religious discrimination, has it violated Title VII of the Civil Rights Act of 1964? Explain.

22. A church needs a new custodian. It refuses to consider E, a qualified applicant, because E is a member of a different faith. Answer the following questions:

    a. Has the church committed religious discrimination?

    b. If the church has committed religious discrimination, has it violated Title VII of the Civil Rights Act of 1964?

    c. Is a church permitted by Title VII to engage in religious discrimination with respect to custodial positions, or other positions not involving "ministerial" duties? Explain.

23. A church operates a preschool. The pastor learns that an unmarried female employee at the preschool is pregnant. The employee is dismissed because of "pregnancy, out of wedlock." The former employee sues the church for sex discrimination. Answer the following questions:

    a. What is the likely outcome of this case?

    b. What precautions could the church have taken to reduce the risk of litigation?

24. Same facts as question 23, except that the church dismissed the employee for "extramarital sexual relations in violation of the church's religious teachings." The former employee sues the church for sex discrimination, claiming that the church discriminates against women because male employees who were guilty of extramarital sexual relations in the past were not dismissed but rather were warned to discontinue such behavior. Answer the following questions:

    a. What is the likely outcome of this case?

    b. What precautions could the church have taken to reduce the risk of litigation?

25. Distinguish between "quid pro quo" sexual harassment and "hostile environment" sexual harassment.

26. A church has 4 employees. A female employee believes that she has been subjected to sexual harassment, and threatens to contact the EEOC. Answer the following questions:

    a. What civil rights laws does the EEOC enforce?

    b. What federal civil rights law prohibits sexual harassment?

    c. Does the federal law prohibiting sexual harassment apply to the church in this example? Why or why not?

    d. Is it possible that the church could be subject to a state law banning sexual harassment?

27. Assume that a church is covered by Title VII of the Civil Rights Act of 1964. A female bookkeeper claims that a male custodian has been sexually harassing her by creating a "hostile environment." She does not discuss the custodian's behavior with the senior pastor or church board. She later threatens to file a complaint with the EEOC, charging the church with responsibility for the custodian's behavior. Is the church liable for the custodian's sexual harassment? Explain.

28. Same facts as question 27, except that the bookkeeper complained on two occasions to the senior pastor about the custodian's behavior. The pastor delayed acting because he did not believe the matter was serious.

29. A church is subject to Title VII. It adopts a written sexual harassment policy that defines harassment, encourages employees to report harassing behavior, and assures employees that they will not suffer retaliation for reporting harassment. A male supervisory employee engages in frequent offensive remarks and physical contact of a sexual nature with a female employee. The female employee is greatly disturbed by this behavior, and considers it inappropriate in a church. In fact, she had sought church employment because she considered it a safe environment and her job would be a ministry. The supervisor eventually dismisses the employee because of her refusal to "go along" with his offensive behavior. Throughout her employment, the employee never informed church leadership of the supervisor's behavior. Several months after her termination, the employee files a sexual harassment complaint with the EEOC. Will the church be liable for the supervisor's behavior under these circumstances?

30. Same facts as the previous example, except that the employee was not dismissed and suffered no "tangible employment decision" (firing, failing to promote, reassignment with significantly different responsibilities, or a decision causing a significant change in benefits).

31. A church is subject to Title VII. It has not adopted a written sexual harassment policy. A female employee files a complaint with the EEOC, claiming that a supervisor has engaged in hostile environment sexual harassment. She never informed church leadership of the supervisor's behavior before filing her complaint with the EEOC. Will the church be responsible for the supervisor's behavior?

32. Same facts as the previous example, except that the church had adopted a written sexual harassment policy that was communicated to all employees.

33. A 75-year-old person applies for a secretarial position at a local church. The church hires a 35-year-old person (because of better typing skills and familiarity with computers). The 75-year-old person believes that the church practiced illegal age discrimination in not offering her the job. Answer the following questions:

    a. Does the Age Discrimination in Employment Act apply to the church? Assume that it has 5 employees.

    b. Does the Age Discrimination in Employment Act apply to the church? Assume that it has 30 employees.

    c. Assume that the Age Discrimination in Employment Act does apply to the church. Did the church violate it?

    d. Assume that instead of applying to a local church for a secretarial position, the 75-year-old applied to a denominational agency. What difference would this make? Assume that the agency engages in the publication and distribution of literature.

34. Explain the test announced by the United States Supreme Court in the *Catholic Bishop* decision for evaluating the applicability of a governmental regulation to religious organizations.

35. A church has at least 15 employees and is engaged in commerce. It needs to hire a new custodian, and two persons apply. One is a nondisabled member of the church, and the other is a disabled nonmember who could perform the essential functions of the job with reasonable accommodations by the church. The church hires the nondisabled member. Has it violated the Americans with Disabilities Act? Explain.

36. Same facts as question 35, except that the church has only 5 employees.

37. A church has at least 15 employees and is engaged in commerce. It needs to hire a secretary who will need to be able to work with a computer. K, a blind female, applies for the position. The church informs K that she is not qualified for the position since she cannot type, and hires someone else. Has the church violated the Americans with Disabilities Act? Explain.

38. A church has at least 15 employees and is engaged in commerce. It needs to hire a custodian. One of the essential functions of the position is the ability to lift boxes weighing up to 50 pounds. This requirement is noted in a job description for the position. T, who suffers from multiple sclerosis, applies for the job. T is not able to lift 50-pound boxes. The church decides not to hire T. Has it violated the Americans with Disabilities Act?

39. A church has at least 15 employees and is engaged in commerce. It has an opening for a bookkeeper. The job description requires that the individual be a college graduate with a degree in accounting. A blind applicant satisfies these requirements. She can perform all the essential functions of the job if she is provided with a part-time reader. Is the church required to hire a part-time reader to accommodate this applicant and enable her to perform the job? Explain.

40. A church has at least 15 employees and is engaged in commerce. A member who uses a wheelchair insists that the church is required by the Americans with Disabilities Act to install an elevator and wheelchair ramps. Is this true?

41. A church receives charitable contributions from recipients of federal welfare programs. Do these contributions make the church a recipient of "federal financial assistance" for purposes of the Civil Rights Restoration Act? Explain.

42. A church receives direct grants from the federal government for its child care program. The child care program is conducted in the church building (not in a geographically separate facility). Answer the following questions:

    a. Do the provisions of the Civil Rights Restoration Act apply under these circumstances?

    b. Assuming that the Civil Rights Restoration Act does apply, what federal antidiscrimination laws are made applicable to the child care facility?

    c. Do any of these antidiscrimination laws prohibit discrimination on the basis of homosexuality? AIDS? Alcoholism? Addiction to narcotic drugs?

    d. Assuming that the Civil Rights Restoration Act applies, is the church subject to the federal antidiscrimination laws or just the child care facility?

e. What if the child care facility was geographically separate from the church sanctuary? Would this make any difference?

43. A local church has 3 employees—a minister, an office secretary, and a custodian. Must the church pay the minimum wage and overtime pay to its secretary and custodian? Explain.

44. A local church operates a child care facility that is primarily custodial rather than educational in nature. However, the facility does attempt to teach the children stories and principles from the Bible. The church employs 6 persons to work at the facility. Are these persons covered by the federal minimum wage and overtime pay requirements? Explain?

45. A local church operates a private elementary school. Are school employees covered by the federal minimum wage and overtime pay requirements? Explain.

46. A church pays its nursery workers $3 per hour for working in the church nursery during Sunday morning worship services. Some workers accept the pay, while others volunteer their services. Has the church violated the federal minimum wage law with respect to either category of worker? Explain.

47. A church decides to pay its entire staff, including custodians, bookkeeper, and secretaries, a salary in order to avoid the overtime pay requirements. Will this arrangement work?

48. A 10-year-old child informs her mother that a volunteer Sunday School teacher improperly touched her. The mother informs her pastor, who confronts the teacher. The teacher adamantly denies any wrongdoing. The church board is not sure how to proceed. One member suggests that the teacher be asked to take a polygraph exam. The board agrees that this would be a good idea. Answer the following questions:

    a. The church has only 3 employees. Is it subject to the Employee Polygraph Protection Act?

    b. Assume that the church is subject to the Employee Polygraph Protection Act. Would it violate the Act by requiring that the teacher "prove" his innocence by taking a polygraph exam?

    c. Assume that the church is subject to the Employee Polygraph Protection Act. Would it violate the Act by suggesting that the teacher take a polygraph exam?

    d. Assume that the church is subject to the Employee Polygraph Protection Act. Would your answers be different if the teacher were a paid employee of the church? Why?

49. A former member sues a church, alleging that the pastor seduced her in the course of a counseling relationship a few years ago. The pastor adamantly denies any wrongdoing. The woman's attorney has her submit to a polygraph exam, which indicates that the woman is telling the truth. The woman's attorney says that she will drop the lawsuit if the pastor is tested by the same polygraph examiner and is found to be telling the truth. The pastor refuses to do so, insisting that he does not need a test to prove that he is telling the truth. The church board urges the pastor to reconsider, and to take the exam. Assuming that the church is subject to the Employee Polygraph Protection Act, has the church violated the Act? Explain.

50. A church board suspects the church's volunteer treasurer of embezzling several thousands of dollars of church funds. The treasurer is called into a board meeting, and is told "you can clear your name if you submit to a polygraph exam." Does this conduct violate the Employee Polygraph Protection Act? Explain.

51. Same facts as the previous example, except that the church suspects a full-time secretary of embezzlement. What steps can the church take to qualify for the "ongoing investigation" exception under the Employee Polygraph Protection Act?

52. A church is opposed, on the basis of its interpretation of the Bible, to hiring homosexuals. B and C are homosexual men. B applies for a volunteer position as a Sunday School teacher, and C applies for a paid staff position as a business administrator. The church rejects both applications because B and C are homosexuals. B and C retain an attorney who threatens to sue the church. Answer the following questions:

    a. Has the church violated B's rights under Title VII of the Civil Rights Act of 1964? Explain.

    b. Assume that the church is in a state with a civil rights law that bans discrimination in employment on the basis of sexual orientation. Has the church violated B's rights under this law? Explain.

    c. Has the church violated C's rights under Title VII of the Civil Rights Act of 1964? Explain.

    d. Assume that the church is in a state with a civil rights law that bans discrimination in employment on the basis of sexual orientation. Has the church violated C's rights under this law? Explain.

53. A church hires a full-time office secretary in July of 1999. The pastor has learned of the new hire reporting rules, but assumes that the church is exempt. Is this assumption correct? Explain.

Discussion Questions

1. Some local churches are not covered by the federal minimum wage and overtime compensation requirements, and they rely on this exemption to pay less than the minimum wage to their workers and avoid overtime pay for hours worked in excess of 40 each week. Other churches feel strongly that they have a moral duty to honor the minimum wage and overtime compensation rules. What is your opinion? Would you, as a senior pastor, be willing to pay less than the minimum wage to church workers? Why or why not?

2. Many Americans are opposed to the "enforcement of morality" by the government. Yet, is not this what federal civil rights and employment laws seek to do? To illustrate, are federal laws that prohibit discrimination in employment on the basis of race, ethnicity, religion, sex, age, or disability examples of the enforcement of morality by government? And, could it not be argued that such laws are enforcing religious values as well?

3. Some church leaders sincerely believe that the government should not have the authority to force churches to comply with employment and civil rights laws. Do you believe that the government should, or should not, have this authority? Why? What if a law violates a church's religious tenets, such as a law prohibiting employers (including churches) from discriminating in employment decisions on the basis of sexual orientation?

9

GOVERNMENT REGULATION OF CHURCHES

Chapter summary. Over the past several decades the number of laws and regulations enacted by legislative and administrative agencies of federal, state, and local governments have increased enormously. Inevitably, questions have arisen as to the application of these laws and regulations to religious organizations. After all, it is one thing for a statute to apply to a local dry cleaner or fast food restaurant. But it is quite different to apply the same law to a church, since churches are protected by the first amendment guaranty of religious freedom as well as similar provisions in state constitutions. How far, then, can government go in applying legislation and regulations to religious organizations without violating the first amendment?

The amenability of religious organizations to some regulation is not seriously disputed. For example, few protest the application to churches of laws and regulations prohibiting fraud in the sale of securities, requiring donated funds to be expended for the purposes represented, protecting copyright owners against infringement, or prohibiting activities that cause physical harm, property damage, or material disturbance to others. Similarly, churches routinely comply with municipal building codes and zoning regulations in the construction of worship facilities. In summary, most churches have acknowledged that religion should not be used as a means of avoiding laws and regulations that are designed to protect the life, health, or safety of members of the public, or that impose fair and reasonable obligations upon those activities of churches that are not intrinsically religious. But some attempts by the government to regulate the activities of churches are more objectionable. For example, should the government have the authority to invalidate any gift to a church simply because it was contained in a will or deed executed within a prescribed time prior to the donor's death? Should the government have the ability to regulate a church's solicitation of funds? Or, should the government have the authority to apply anti-discrimination requirements to churches? Such governmental assertions of authority are opposed by many churches as unreasonable intrusions into the life of the church. Many of these issues have been addressed in previous chapters. In this chapter, you will study additional examples of government regulation of church activities. Available exemptions from such laws will also be considered. As you read the text, attempt to formulate a rule that will define those instances in which government regulation of church activities may be warranted.

§ 9-01   Introduction

The amenability of churches to some governmental regulation is not seriously disputed. For example, few would protest the application to churches of laws prohibiting fraud in the sale of securities, requiring donated funds to be expended for the purposes represented, protecting copyright owners against infringement, or prohibiting activities that cause physical harm, property damage, or material disturbance to others. Similarly, churches routinely comply with municipal building codes and zoning regulations in the construction and location of worship facilities.

There is much less agreement concerning the extent to which churches should be subject to governmental regulation. The United States Supreme Court has observed:

The [first amendment] embraces two concepts—freedom to believe and freedom to act. The first is absolute but, in the nature of things, the second cannot be. Conduct remains subject to regulation for the protection of society. . . . It is clear that a state may by general and non-discriminatory legislation regulate the times, the places, and the manner of soliciting upon its streets, and of holding meetings thereon; and may in other respects safeguard the peace, good order and comfort of the community, without unconstitutionally invading the liberties protected by the [first amendment]. . . .

Nothing we have said is intended even remotely to imply that, under the cloak of religion, persons may, with impunity, commit frauds upon the public. Certainly penal laws are available to punish such conduct. Even the exercise of religion may be at some slight inconvenience in order that the state may protect its citizens from injury.[1]

---

[1] Cantwell v. Connecticut, 310 U.S. 296 (1940). Similarly, the Supreme Court has stated that (1) "[E]ven when [an] action is in accord with one's religious convictions, it is not totally free from legislative restrictions. The conduct or actions so regulated have invariably posed some substantial threat to public safety, peace or order." Sherbert v. Verner, 374 U.S. 398, 403 (1963), quoting Braunfeld v.

Laws affecting churches consistently are upheld by the courts if they (1) are neutral and of general applicability, (2) avoid excessive governmental entanglement with religion, (3) are the least restrictive means of accomplishing the intended result, and (4) require no judicial determination of the validity of religious belief. To illustrate, the courts consistently uphold reasonable governmental regulation of church securities offerings, labor practices, construction projects, fundraising schemes, child-care and nursing-care facilities, and private schools. One court, in rejecting a religious organization's claim to immunity from governmental regulation on the ground that it was engaged in "God's work," observed that "[n]o court has ever found that conduct, by being so described, is automatically immunized from all regulation in the public interest."[2]

> **Key point.** *Laws that are not neutral toward religion, or that are not of general applicability, must be supported by a compelling government interest in order to be consistent with the first amendment guaranty of religious freedom.*

The application of many laws and regulations to religious organizations has been addressed in previous chapters. These include:

- child abuse reporting laws[3]

- the regulation of church counselors[4]

- nonprofit corporation law[5]

- state and federal reporting requirements[6]

- zoning[7]

- building codes[8]

- landmarking legislation[9]

- eminent domain[10]

Brown, 366 U.S. 599, 603 (1961). (2) "The mere fact that the petitioner's religious practice is burdened by a governmental program does not mean that an exemption accommodating his practice must be granted. The state may justify an inroad on religious liberty by showing that it is the least restrictive means of achieving some compelling state interest. However, it is still true that the essence of all that has been said and written on the subject is that only those interests of the highest order can overbalance legitimate claims to the free exercise of religion." Thomas v. Review Board, 450 U.S. 707, 718 (1981). (3) "Conscientious scruples have not, in the course of the long struggle for religious toleration, relieved the individual from obedience to a general law not aimed at the promotion or restriction of religious beliefs. The mere possession of religious convictions which contradict the relevant concerns of a political society does not relieve the citizen from the discharge of political responsibilities." Minersville School District v. Gobitis, 310 U.S. 586, 594-595 (1940) (Justice Frankfurter).

2   Securities and Exchange Commission v. World Radio Mission, Inc., 544 F.2d 535, 539 n.7 (1st Cir. 1976).

3   *See* § 4-08, *supra.*

4   *See* § 4-10, *supra.*

5   *See* § 6-02, *supra.*

6   *See* § 6-04, *supra.*

7   *See* § 7-06, *supra.*

8   *See* § 7-08, *supra.*

9   *See* § 7-10, *supra.*

10   *See* § 7-11, *supra.*

- workers compensation[11]

- immigration law reporting requirements[12]

- Title VII of the Civil Rights Act of 1964[13]

- the Age Discrimination in Employment Act[14]

- the Americans with Disabilities Act[15]

- the Fair Labor Standards Act (federal minimum wage and overtime pay)[16]

- the Employee Polygraph Protection Act[17]

- the Occupational Safety and Health Act[18]

This chapter will address the application of other federal and state laws and regulations to religious organizations.

§ 9-02   Regulation of Charitable Solicitations

Key point 9-02. Several states have enacted laws regulating the solicitation of charitable contributions. These laws generally do apply to solicitations of contributions by churches from their members. However, in some cases, they may apply to churches that use professional fundraisers, or that actively solicit contributions from nonmembers.

1. State Charitable Solicitation Laws

Several states have enacted laws regulating the solicitation of charitable contributions. The purpose of such laws is "to protect the contributing public and charitable beneficiaries against fraudulent practices in the solicitation of contributions for purportedly charitable purposes."[19] The typical statute requires designated charitable organizations to register with a government agency prior to the solicitation of contributions within the state, and imposes various reporting requirements. Such statutes ordinarily give the state authority to revoke the registration of any charitable organization upon a finding that the organization has engaged in a fraudulent or deceptive practice, or that it has expended more than a prescribed or "reasonable" amount of solicited funds for administrative and fund raising costs, and that the public interests so require.

Key point. Some states have not yet enacted laws regulating the solicitation of charitable contributions.[20]

---

[11] *See* § 8-02, *supra.*
[12] *See* § 8-03, *supra.*
[13] *See* § 8-08, *supra.*
[14] *See* § 8-09, *supra.*
[15] *See* § 8-10, *supra.*
[16] *See* § 8-17, *supra.*
[17] *See* § 8-19, *supra.*
[18] *See* § 8-209, *supra.*
[19] Larson v. Valente, 456 U.S. 228 (1982).
[20] Delaware, Iowa, Idaho, Indiana, Montana, Nebraska, Nevada, South Dakota, Texas, Vermont, and Wyoming have not enacted statutes regulating the solicitation of charitable contributions.

Key point. *Many states have laws requiring registration and regulation of "professional" fund raisers. The validity of such laws was called into question by the United States Supreme Court in a 1988 ruling in which the Court struck down a North Carolina statute requiring professional fund raisers to be licensed by the state, and establishing maximum administrative fees and expenses that could be charged.[21]*

Most state laws that regulate the solicitation of charitable contributions exempt religious organizations.[22] Some restrict the exemption to religious organizations that are exempt from the requirement of filing annual information returns (Form 990) with the IRS.[23] A few states have enacted the Uniform Supervision of Trustees for Charitable Purposes Act.[24]

The application of state charitable solicitation laws to religious and charitable organizations has been challenged in a few important cases. In *Larson v. Valente,*[25] the United States Supreme Court invalidated a section of the Minnesota Charitable Solicitation Act that exempted from registration only those religious organizations receiving more than half of their support from members. The Court emphasized that "the clearest command of the Establishment Clause is that one religious denomination cannot be officially preferred over another,"[26] and concluded that "the fifty percent rule . . . clearly grants denominational preference of the sort consistently and firmly deprecated in our precedents."[27] Such a law, observed the Court, must be invalidated unless (1) it is justified by a compelling governmental interest and (2) it is clearly fitted to further that interest. The "tripartite" establishment clause analysis formulated by the Court in the *Lemon* case[28] was deemed inapplicable in this context, since that analysis was "intended to apply to laws affording a uniform benefit to *all* religions, and not to provisions, like the . . . fifty percent rule, that discriminate among religions."[29]

The Court acknowledged that the State of Minnesota had a significant interest in protecting its citizens from abusive practices in the solicitation of funds for charity, even when the solicitation was conducted by religious organizations. However, it rejected the state's contention that the 50 percent rule was closely fitted to further that interest.

---

[21] Riley v. National Federation of the Blind, 108 S. Ct. 2667 (1988).

[22] *See, e.g.,* CAL. GOVERNMENT CODE §§ 12583 *et seq.* ("any religious corporation or organization that holds property for religious purposes"); FLA. STAT. § 496.406(2)(b) ("bona fide religious institutions"); Ga. Code § 43-17-2 ("religious agencies and organizations"); KY. REV. STAT. § 367.660 ("solicitations by a religious organization for funds for religious purposes such as maintenance of a house of worship, conduct of services, and propagation of its faith and tenets"); MD. CODE ANN. § 6-102(c)(1)(ii)(2) ("a religious organization, a parent organization of a religious organization, or a school affiliated with a religious organization"); N.J. REV. STAT. § 45:17A-26 ("any religious corporation, trust, foundation, association, or organization"); OHIO REV. CODE § 1713-03 ("any religious agencies and organizations, and charities, agencies, and organizations operated, supervised, or controlled by a religious organization"); OKLA. STAT. title 18, § 552.4 ("organizations incorporated for religious purposes and actually engaged in bona fide religious programs, and other organizations directly operated, supervised, or controlled by a religious organization"); R.I. GEN. LAWS § 5-53-3(a)(2) ("churches of recognized denominations and religious organizations, societies and institutions operated, supervised, or controlled by a religious organization or society which solicit from other than their own membership" and "institutions indirectly affiliated with but which are not operated, supervised, or controlled by any religious organizations or religious society which own, maintain, and operate homes for the aged, orphanages, and homes for unwed mothers").

[23] *See, e.g.,* ALASKA STAT. § 45.68.120(a)(1); ARIZ. REV. STAT. § 44-6553.

[24] CAL. GOVERNMENT CODE §§ 12583 *et seq.*; 225 ILL. COMP. STAT. 460/1, ch. 23, ¶ 5100 *et. seq.*; MICH. COMP. LAWS § 400.241 *et seq.*; ORE. REV. STAT. § 128.801 *et seq.*

[25] 456 U.S. 228 (1982). The Court invalidated § 309.515-1(b) of the Minnesota Statutes.

[26] *Id.* at 1683.

[27] *Id.* at 1684.

[28] Lemon v. Kurtzman, 403 U.S. 602, 612-13 (1971). The *Lemon* case is discussed in chapter 12, *infra.*

[29] *Id.* at 1687. While the Court concluded that the tripartite test of *Lemon* was inapplicable, it nonetheless observed that the Minnesota statute did not satisfy that test.

Would a state charitable solicitation law requiring *all* religious organizations to register be constitutionally permissible? Such a law obviously would avoid the "denominational preference" that tainted the Minnesota statute. The Supreme Court even observed in *Larson* that it was not suggesting that "the burdens of compliance with the Act would be intrinsically impermissible if they were imposed evenhandedly."[30] This more difficult question was addressed in 1980 by the Supreme Court of North Carolina in the *Heritage Village* decision.[31]

The Supreme Court of North Carolina, in striking down a state charitable solicitation law exempting all religious organizations except those whose financial support came primarily from nonmembers, concluded that the first amendment (to the United States Constitution) prohibits any state from subjecting religious organizations to the administrative requirements of a charitable solicitation law. The Court noted:

> [F]or a statute to pass muster under the strict test of Establishment Clause neutrality, it must pass the three-prong review distilled by the Supreme Court from "the cumulative criteria developed over many years": First, the statute must have a secular purpose; second, its principal or primary effect must be one that neither advances nor inhibits religion . . . ; finally the statute must not foster an excessive government entanglement with religion.[32]

The court concluded that the first part of the Supreme Court's three-prong test was satisfied, since the Act had a valid secular purpose of protecting the public from fraud. It found, however, that the Act violated both the second and third elements since it inhibited certain religious groups and constituted an impermissible governmental entanglement with religion. As to the second element, the Court observed:

> [T]he Act grants an exemption from the licensing and reporting requirements to a broadly defined class of religious organizations. . . . The proviso, however, which immediately follows in the same section denies the benefits of the exemption to those religious organizations which derive their financial support "primarily" from contributions solicited from "persons other than their own members" . . . . [T]he *effect* of the proviso is to alter the original exemption's religious neutrality. The result is a qualified exemption which favors only those religious organizations which solicit primarily from their own members. The inescapable impact is to accord benign neglect to the more orthodox, denominational, and congregational religions while subjecting to registration those religions which spread their beliefs in more evangelical, less traditional ways. This the state may not do.[33]

As to the third element of the test, the Court observed:

> Considerations of the excessive entanglement between church and state threatened by the Act's substantive requirements additionally compels us to conclude that plaintiffs may not constitutionally be denied an exemption. . . . Should plaintiffs or any other religious organization be subjected to the full panoply of strictures contemplated by the Act, we would be faced with precisely the sort of "sustained and detailed administrative relationships for enforcement of statutory and administrative standards" that have been repeatedly condemned by the Supreme Court.[34]

---

[30] *Id.* at 1688.
[31] Heritage Village Church and Missionary Fellowship, Inc. v. State, 263 S.E.2d 726 (N.C. 1980).
[32] *Id.* at 731.
[33] *Id.* at 732-33.
[34] *Id.*

Both the *Larson* and *Heritage Village* decisions were based on the establishment clause. Neither court directly addressed the applicability of the first amendment's free exercise of religion and free speech clauses in analyzing the constitutionality of applying charitable solicitation laws to religious organizations. The free exercise and free speech clauses have been relied upon by several courts in invalidating municipal charitable solicitation ordinances.[35] In 1980, the Supreme Court observed in the *Village of Schaumburg* decision that

[p]rior authorities, therefore, thoroughly establish that charitable appeals for funds . . . involve a variety of speech interests—communication of information, a dissemination and propagation of views and ideas, and the advocacy of causes—that are within the protection of the first amendment. Soliciting financial support is undoubtedly subject to reasonable regulation but the latter must be undertaken with due regard for the reality that solicitation is characteristically intertwined with informative and perhaps persuasive speech seeking support for particular causes or for particular views on economic, political, or social issues, or for the reality that without solicitation flow of such information and advocacy would likely cease.[36]

Such reasoning buttresses the conclusion reached in *Heritage Village*. Not only would a state charitable solicitation law that applies to religious organizations be constitutionally suspect under the establishment clause, but it also would clash with the free exercise and free speech clauses.[37]

As the Supreme Court noted in *Larson*, a state unquestionably has a significant interest in protecting its citizens from abusive practices in the solicitation of funds for charity. However, such an interest alone does not determine constitutional validity. The state must also demonstrate that its charitable solicitation law is "closely fitted to further the interest that it assertedly serves."[38] As the Court noted in *Village of Schaumburg*, "[t]he Village may serve its legitimate interests, but it must do so by narrowly drawn regulations designed to serve these interests without necessarily interfering with first amendment freedoms."[39] Can a state serve its legitimate purpose of preventing fraud in the solicitation of funds by religious organizations in a less drastic way than by registration under a charitable solicitation law? The answer clearly is yes. In an analogous case, the Supreme Court in the *Village of Schaumburg* decision observed that the government's legitimate interest in preventing fraud can be served by less intrusive measures: "Fraudulent misrepresentations can be prohibited and the penal laws used to punish such conduct directly."[40] Another court has noted that less restrictive alternative means of fulfilling the government's interests include "enforcement of existing laws against fraud, trespass, breach of the peace, and any other substantive offenses which might be committed. The [government] may adopt appropriate registration and identification procedures to protect its residents against wrongdoing by spurious solicitors."[41]

---

[35] *See* Village of Schaumburg v. Citizens for a Better Environment, 444 U.S. 620, 632 (1980).

[36] *Id.* at 632.

[37] In 1990 the Supreme Court observed that the compelling government interest test is triggered if a neutral and generally applicable law burdens not only the exercise of religion, but some other first amendment right (such as speech, press, or assembly) as well. Employment Division v. Smith, 494 U.S. 872 (1990). The Court observed: "The only decisions in which we have held that the first amendment bars application of a neutral, generally applicable law to religiously motivated action have involved not the free exercise clause alone, but the free exercise clause in conjunction with other constitutional protections, such as freedom of speech and of the press . . . ." In other words, if a neutral and generally applicable law or governmental practice burdens the exercise of religion, then the compelling governmental interest standard can be triggered if the religious institution or adherent can point to some other first amendment interest that is being violated. In many cases, this will not be hard to do. For example, the first amendment guaranty of free speech often will be implicated when a law or governmental practice burdens the exercise of religion. The same is true of the first amendment guarantees of free press and assembly.

[38] 456 U.S. 228 (1982).

[39] 444 U.S. at 637.

[40] *Id.*

[41] Alternatives for California Women v. County of Contra Costa, 193 Cal. Rptr. 384, 392 (Cal. App. 1983).

In summary, the *Heritage Village* decision strikes a reasonable balance of the competing interests of church and state. It frees religious organizations from entangling administrative supervision by the government; it acknowledges that the government remains capable of asserting that a particular organization is not in fact a bona fide religious organization entitled to exemption; it does not insulate religious organizations from civil lawsuits or criminal penalties; and it recognizes that the solicitation of funds for the support of religious organizations is often an expression of religious faith.[42]

A similar result has been reached in the related context of securities regulation. Most state securities laws, while designed primarily to prevent fraud, exempt religious organizations from the securities registration requirement. Religious organizations are not exempted from the anti-fraud provisions of such laws, and thus they remain liable for fraudulent conduct even though they are exempt from registration. Further, the state is free to deny an exemption to religious organizations that have engaged in fraud in the past or that are not bona fide religious organizations. Such a balance between the competing interests of church and state serves as a model for the related contexts of state and municipal charitable solicitation laws. The government's interests can be served by less restrictive means than registration.

2. Municipal Charitable Solicitation Laws

Several cities have enacted ordinances regulating the solicitation of charitable contributions. These ordinances often are similar in content and purpose to the corresponding state laws. Such laws typically require the licensing of persons who solicit funds for charity. A number of cities have no charitable solicitation ordinance. Several other cities have adopted charitable solicitation ordinances that exempt certain religious organizations. For example, some cities exempt religious organizations that are exempt from federal income taxation. Other cities exempt properly authorized solicitors of established and organized churches or other established and organized religious organizations, organizations conducting a solicitation among their own membership, solicitations in the form of collections or contributions at a regular assembly or service, and any church which solicits funds for religious purposes. Some cities require religious organizations that use professional fund raisers to register under a charitable solicitation ordinance.

The constitutionality of applying such charitable solicitation ordinances to religious organizations has been challenged in several cases. In *Village of Schaumburg*,[43] the Supreme Court struck down an ordinance prohibiting the solicitation of contributions by charitable organizations that did not use at least 75 percent of their receipts for charitable purposes. The ordinance excluded solicitation expenses, salaries, overhead, and other administrative expenses from the definition of "charitable purpose." The Court conceded that charitable appeals for funds involve a variety of speech interests that are within the protection of the first amendment, and that any ordinance interfering with such interests would be constitutionally valid only if it (1) served a compelling governmental interest and (2) was narrowly drawn to serve that interest without necessarily interfering with first amendment freedoms. The Court acknowledged that a city has a substantial interest in protecting the public from fraud, crime, and undue annoyance. However, it concluded that a municipal ordinance banning solicitations by any charity that did not expend more than 75 percent of solicited funds for charitable purposes could not be upheld, since the city's legitimate interests could be "better served by measures less intrusive than a direct prohibition on solicitation."[44] The Court also noted that there was no

---

[42] *See, e.g.,* Heffron v. International Society for Krishna Consciousness, 452 U.S. 640 (1981); Village of Schaumburg v. Citizens for a Better Environment, 444 U.S. 620, 637-39 (1980); Murdock v. Pennsylvania, 319 U.S. 105 (1943); Heritage Village and Missionary Fellowship, Inc. v. State, 263 S.E.2d 726, 734 (N.C. 1980).

[43] *See* note 35, *supra.*

[44] *Id.* at 637.

evidence that "organizations devoting more than one-quarter of their funds to salaries and administrative expenses are any more likely to employ solicitors who would be a threat to public safety than are other charitable organizations."[45]

In summary, the *Village of Schaumburg* decision may be reduced to the following two principles: (1) The right to solicit funds for religious and charitable purposes is protected by the first amendment's free speech clause, and (2) this right is not unconditional, but may be limited by a municipal ordinance if the ordinance (a) serves a compelling government interest and (b) is narrowly drawn to serve that interest without unnecessarily interfering with first amendment freedoms.

Village of Schaumburg has been followed in several other cases.[46] In most of these decisions, municipal ordinances attempting to regulate charitable solicitations were invalidated. The courts generally concede that a city has a legitimate and substantial interest in preventing fraud, crime, and undue annoyance, but they often conclude that a particular charitable solicitation ordinance too broadly serves that interest since other, less restrictive, alternatives exist which serve the same interest. The Supreme Court in *Village of Schaumburg* noted:

> Frauds may be denounced as offenses and punished by law. Trespasses may similarly be forbidden. If it is said that these means are less efficient and convenient than . . . deciding in advance what information may be disseminated from house to house, and who may impart the information, the answer is that considerations of this sort do not empower a municipality to abridge freedom of speech and press.[47]

In conclusion, a municipal ordinance purporting to regulate the solicitation of funds by some or all religious organizations should presumptively[48] be unconstitutional unless the city can demonstrate that the ordinance serves a legitimate and compelling interest *and* that this interest cannot effectively be protected by less intrusive, more narrowly drawn, alternatives. Several courts have concluded that the availability of private causes of action for fraud and trespass, together with penal prohibitions of such conduct, sufficiently protect a city's legitimate interests in safeguarding its citizens from abusive charitable solicitations by religious organizations. A city also of course may make a determination that a particular "religious" organization is spurious and therefore not entitled to an exemption, and it is free to deny an exemption to otherwise bona fide religious organizations that have been proven to have engaged in frauds upon the public.[49] Further, any municipal charitable solicitation ordinance exempting only some religious organizations from registration would be suspect under the establishment clause, since some religious groups are singled out for favored treatment while others are not. All of these factors indicate that most charitable solicitation laws cannot constitutionally be extended to religious organizations.

---

[45] *Id.* at 638.

[46] *See, e.g.,* ACORN v. City of Frontenac, 714 F.2d 813 (8th Cir. 1983); Pennsylvania Public Interest v. York Township, 569 F. Supp. 1398 (M.D. Pa. 1983); NAACP Legal Defense and Educational Fund, Inc. v. Devine, 567 F. Supp. 401 (D.D.C. 1983); Taylor v. City of Knoxville, 566 F. Supp. 925 (E.D. Tenn. 1982); Optimist Club v. Riley, 563 F. Supp. 847 (E.D.N.C. 1982); Alternatives for California Women v. County of Contra Costa, 193 Cal. Rptr. 384 (Cal. App. 1983).

[47] 444 U.S. 620, 639.

[48] *See, e.g.,* Pennsylvania Public Interest v. York Township, 569 F. Supp. 1398, 140 (M.D. Pa. 1983) ("Because the ordinance impinges on the exercise of free speech, it is presumptively unconstitutional.")

[49] *See* Larson v. Valente, 102 S.Ct. 1673, 1689 n.30 (1982):
Nothing in our opinion suggests appellants could not attempt to compel the Unification Church to register under the Act as a charitable organization not entitled to the religious-organization exemption, and put the Church to the proof of its bona fides as a religious organization. Further, nothing in our opinion disables the State from denying exemption from the Act, or from refusing registration and licensing under the Act, to persons or organizations proved to have engaged in frauds upon the public.

Certainly any charitable solicitation law that gives a licensing body or official effective discretion to grant or deny permission to solicit funds for religious purposes is likewise unconstitutional:

> The solicitation of funds for religious purposes is protected by the first amendment. Any law restricting the exercise of such rights must do so with narrow, objective and definite standards. If a certificate is required for one to solicit funds for religious purposes, the discretion of the official granting the certificate must be bounded by explicit standards. If the decision to issue the certificate "involves appraisal of facts, the exercise of judgment, and the formation of an opinion," the ordinance violates the first amendment. Ambiguities in the application process which give the licensing official effective power to grant or deny permission to solicit funds for religious purposes is likewise unconstitutional. In other words, it is not enough that an official is directed to issue the license forthwith; if the official may deny the application because of unclear requirements in the application process, the law is unconstitutional. Laws allowing an investigation into the financial affairs of religious institutions have been held unconstitutional as an impermissible entanglement of the affairs of church and state. Finally, any prior restraint on the exercise of first amendment freedoms must be accompanied by procedural safeguards designed to obviate the dangers of prior restraint.[50]

The Supreme Court has held that the fund raising activities of religious organizations, "like those of others protected by the first amendment, are subject to reasonable time, place, and manner restrictions."[51] It is doubtful that these restrictions are of any practical relevance in the context of charitable solicitations by religious organizations. One court specifically held that the Supreme Court's decision in *Heffron* "has a rather narrow applicability" because of its "somewhat unusual factual situation" involving solicitation at a state fair.[52] The court observed that "the flow of the crowd and demands of safety are more pressing in the context of the fair."[53] The Supreme Court's decision in *Village of Schaumburg* strongly intimated that "time, place and manner" restrictions do not justify regulation of charitable solicitations.[54]

§ 9-03   Limitations on Charitable Giving

> *Key point 9-03. Historically, several states had laws limiting the right of persons to leave gifts to religious organizations within a specified time prior to their death. In recent years, these laws have been struck down by the courts in nearly all states.*

A few states[55] have laws limiting the right of persons to leave property to religious organizations by a will or deed executed within a specified period prior to death. The purpose of such laws is to prevent "deathbed" gifts to religious organizations by persons who might be unduly influenced by religious considerations. More generally, such laws are intended to protect a donor's family from disinheritance due to charitable gifts made either without proper deliberation or as a result of "undue influence." Several states have had such laws in the past. They often are referred to as "mortmain" laws. Most of these laws either have been rescinded by state legislatures, or invalidated by the courts.

---

[50] Taylor v. City of Knoxville, 566 F. Supp. 925, 929 (E.D. Tenn. 1982).
[51] Heffron v. International Society for Krishna Consciousness, Inc. 452 U.S. 640, 647 (1981).
[52] Pennsylvania Public Interests v. York Township, 659 F. Supp. 1398, 1402 (M.D. Pa. 1983).
[53] *Id.*
[54] 444 U.S. 620, 639-640 (1980).
[55] According to the Florida Supreme Court, there are only three states that have laws invalidating charitable gifts made within a specified time prior to death—Georgia, Idaho, and Mississippi. Shriners Hospital v. Zrillic, 563 So.2d 64 (Fla. 1990).

In a leading case, the Florida Supreme Court struck down a state law that permitted certain heirs to challenge gifts made to churches and other charities in a will executed within six months of a person's death.[56] Prior to this ruling, Florida law permitted a spouse or "lineal descendent" to challenge a will of a decedent who died within 6 months after executing a will leaving all or part of his or her estate to a religious or charitable organization. An elderly Florida resident executed a will leaving most of her estate to a charity. The woman's will left only a token gift to her sole surviving daughter since the daughter "has not shown or indicated the slightest affection or gratitude to me" and since "I have contributed substantially during my life for her education and subsequent monies I have been required to expend primarily due to her promiscuous type of life." The woman died two months later, survived only by her daughter. The daughter immediately challenged her mother's will on the basis of the state law permitting lineal descendants to challenge charitable gifts made in their parents' wills if executed within six months of death. The charity opposed the daughter's action on the ground that the state law violated the constitutional guaranty of the "equal protection of the laws." A trial court agreed with the charity, but a state appeals court agreed with the daughter.

The case was appealed to the state supreme court, which ruled that the state law was unconstitutional. The court began its opinion by observing that statutes restricting charitable gifts originated in feudal England "as part of the struggle for power and wealth between the king and the organized church." As feudalism declined, the justification for these laws became the protection of surviving family members against disinheritance caused by the undue influence of religious organizations. In rejecting this rationale, the court observed that "it is unreasonable to presume, as the statute seems to do, that all lineal descendants are dependents, in need, or are not otherwise provided for."

The court emphasized that state law has ample protections against undue influence and fraud that can be used by disinherited family members without the need for a specific statute. Further, the court observed that "the charitable gift restriction fails to protect against windfalls by lineal descendants who have had no contact with the decedent but who may benefit from the avoidance of a charitable gift." Since the statute was not "reasonably necessary to accomplish the asserted state goals," it violated the state constitution. Further, the statute violated the federal and state constitutional protections of the "equal protection of the laws," since it treated gifts made to charitable and religious organizations within six months of death less favorably than other gifts without any rational justification. The fact that a gift is made within six months of death is not in itself sufficient proof of undue influence, noted the court, since most gifts made within six months of death are not the product of undue influence and some gifts made more than six months prior to death are. Accordingly, the six-month rule was arbitrary and treated charities less favorably than other citizens or organizations without adequate justification.

One dissenting justice cautioned that the law might still serve a valuable purpose in appropriate cases: "Surely one would have to say that, had the [decedent] succumbed to a television evangelist's call to be with the Lord by delivering her property to his church and thus leave unprotected a physically handicapped child, a rationale basis for the statute would exist." In conclusion, note that the court observed that there are only three other states that have laws invalidating charitable gifts made within a specified time prior to death— Georgia, Idaho, and Mississippi.

In another significant decision, the Supreme Court of Pennsylvania struck down a state law invalidating any testamentary gift for religious or charitable purposes included in a will executed within 30 days of the death of the donor.[57] The court reasoned that the fourteenth amendment to the United States Constitution,

[56] Shriners Hospital v. Zrillic, 563 So.2d 64 (Fla. 1990).
[57] In re Estate of Cavill, 329 A.2d 503 (Pa. 1974). *See generally* Annot., 6 A.L.R.4th 603 (1981).

which prohibits states from denying to any persons the "equal protection of the laws," requires that statutory classifications must be "reasonable, not arbitrary, and must rest upon some ground of difference having a fair and substantial relation to the object of the legislation, so that all persons similarly circumstanced shall be treated alike."[58] The Pennsylvania statute, concluded the court, divided donors into two classes, one class being composed of donors whose wills provided for charitable gifts and who died within 30 days of executing their wills, and the other of donors who either made no charitable gifts in their wills or who survived the execution of their wills by at least 30 days. Gifts made by a donor in the first class were nullified by the statute, while gifts made by donors in the second class were permitted.

Such a classification, concluded the court, violated the fourteenth amendment's equal protection clause and therefore was impermissible:

> Clearly, the statutory classification bears only the most tenuous relation to the legislative purpose. The statute strikes down the charitable gifts of one in the best of health at the time of the execution of his will and regardless of age if he chances to die in an accident 29 days later. On the other hand, it leaves untouched the charitable bequests of another, aged and suffering from a terminal disease, who survives the execution of his will by 31 days. Such a combination of results can only be characterized as arbitrary.[59]

The court also observed that although the legislative purpose was to protect a donor's immediate family, the statute sought to nullify testamentary gifts to charity even where the donor left no immediate family. Protection of distant relatives with whom a donor may have had little if any contact during his life was not consistent with the statute's purpose, the court concluded.

Other courts have reached similar results. A District of Columbia statute invalidating any gift to a clergyman or religious organization made in a will executed less than 30 days prior to a donor's death was struck down on the ground that it arbitrarily discriminated against clergymen and religious organizations. A court emphasized that the law did not invalidate gifts to nonreligious charitable organizations that were in an equal position with religious organizations to influence a donor.[60]

One judge has observed that laws limiting the right of religious organizations to receive testamentary gifts are invalid if they are based on a desire to prevent clergy from influencing the dying by holding out "hopes of salvation or avoidance of damnation" in return for generous gifts to further the practice of religion. Such an objective "is precisely what the 'free exercise' of religion clause of the first amendment forbids, for it is premised upon the assumption that such representations are false and hence Congress can enact safeguards against their effect."[61] Another court held that a state's adoption of the Uniform Probate Code by implication repealed a law limiting testamentary gifts to charity.[62]

It seems likely that statutory limitations on the right of charitable organizations to receive testamentary gifts will be viewed with disfavor by courts and legislatures alike. The repeal of such statutes has the salutary effect of abolishing the irrebuttable presumption that certain gifts to charity are the product of undue influence, and of compelling disinherited heirs to prove undue influence in order to invalidate testamentary gifts to charity.

---

[58] *Id.* at 505.
[59] *Id.* at 505-06.
[60] Estate of French, 365 A.2d 621 (D.C. 1976), *appeal dismissed*, 434 U.S. 59 (1977).
[61] *Id.* at 625 (Reilly, C.J., concurring).
[62] Matter of Estate of Holmes, 599 P.2d 344 (Mont. 1979).

§ 9-04   Federal and State Securities Law

Key point 9-04. Federal and state laws regulate the offer and sale of securities for the protection of the investing public. In general, an organization that issues securities must register the securities, and the persons who will be selling the securities, with state and federal agencies. In addition, federal and state laws contain a broad prohibition on fraudulent activities in the sale of securities. Churches are exempt from some of these requirements in some states. However, they remain subject to the prohibition of securities fraud in all fifty states, and under federal law.

Laws regulating the sale of securities have been enacted by the federal government[63] and by all 50 states.[64] The term *security* is defined very broadly by such laws. The Uniform Securities Act, which has been adopted by a majority of the 50 states, defines a *security* as

a note; stock; treasury stock; bond; debenture; evidence of indebtedness; certificate of interest or participation in a profit-sharing agreement; a limited partnership interest; collateral-trust certificate; preorganization certificate or subscription; transferable share; investment contract; voting-trust certificate; certificate of deposit for a security; fractional undivided interest in an oil, gas, or other mineral lease or in payments out of production under a lease, right, or royalty; a put, call, straddle, or option entered into on a national securities exchange relating to foreign currency; a put, call, straddle, or option on a security, certificate of deposit, or group or index of securities, including an interest in or based on the value of any of the foregoing; or, in general, an interest or instrument commonly known as a "security" . . . .[65]

This definition is broad enough to include many instruments utilized in church fundraising efforts.

Securities laws were enacted to protect the public against fraudulent and deceptive practices in the sale of securities and to provide full and fair disclosure to prospective investors. To achieve these purposes, most securities laws impose the following conditions on the sale of securities:

1. registration of proposed securities with the federal or state government in advance of sale

2. filing of sales and advertising literature with the federal or state government

3. registration of agents and broker-dealers who will be selling the securities

4. prohibition of fraudulent practices

Although the federal government and most states exempt securities offered by any organization "organized and operated not for private profit but exclusively for a religious . . . purpose" from registration,[66] it is

---

[63] Securities Act of 1933, 15 U.S.C. §§ 77a-77aa.

[64] Nearly 40 states have enacted all or significant portions of the Uniform Securities Act.

[65] Uniform Securities Act § 101(16).

[66] Section 3(a)(4) of the federal Securities Act of 1933 and section 401(a)(10) of the Uniform Securities Act exempt the securities of nonprofit religious organizations from registration. Section 401(a)(10) of the Uniform Securities Act, which has been adopted by several states, specifies that "[t]he following securities are exempted from the [securities registration and sales literature filing requirements] . . . a security issued by a person organized and operated not for private profit but exclusively for a religious, educational, benevolent, charitable, fraternal, social, athletic, or reformatory purpose, or as a chamber of commerce or trade or professional association."

important to note that some states do not exempt the securities of religious organizations from registration;[67] others impose conditions on the exemption;[68] many require that an application for exemption (or "notice" of exemption) be submitted and approved before a claim of exemption will be recognized;[69] a few states require churches and religious denominations that "issue" their own securities to be registered as issuers or issuer-dealers;[70] and all securities laws subject churches and other religious organizations to the antifraud requirements. Churches therefore must not assume that any securities that they may offer are automatically exempt from registration or regulation. Church securities *always* will be subject to some degree of regulation. The question in each case is how much.

In the minority of jurisdictions in which a church must register its securities, registration ordinarily is accomplished by filing a registration statement with the state securities commission setting forth the following information: the name and address of the church; the date of incorporation; a description of the general character of the church's operations; a description of the church's properties; the name, address, and occupation of each director, and the compensation, if any, that each receives from the church; the kind and amount of securities to be offered; the proposed offering price for each security; estimated commissions and finding fees; and estimated cash proceeds to the church from the sale of registered securities. In addition, the following materials must accompany the registration statement: a copy of any prospectus, offering circular, or other sales literature; a specimen copy of the securities being registered; a copy of the church's articles of incorporation and bylaws; a copy of any trust indenture under which the securities are being offered; a signed opinion of legal counsel as to the legality of the security being registered; written consent of any accountant having prepared or certified a report or valuation which is used in connection with the registration statement; a balance sheet; profit and loss statements for each of the preceding three fiscal years; a check to cover the filing fee; and such other material as the securities commission may require.[71]

The method of registration described above is referred to as registration by *qualification*. Most states provide for two other methods of registration: registration by *coordination* and registration by *notification*. Churches will rarely if ever utilize registration by coordination, since this method assumes registration of an issuer's securities under the federal Securities Act of 1933 and churches are exempt from registration under this Act. Registration by notification is available to securities issued by a corporation that has been in continuous operation for at least five years if the corporation satisfies a minimum net earnings test. A registration

---

[67] As of the date of publication of this text, the following states do not exempt the debt securities (i.e., bonds and notes) of religious organizations from registration: California, Florida, Georgia, Indiana, Louisiana, Minnesota, Oregon, and Wisconsin.

[68] For example, § 451.802(a)(8) of the Michigan Securities Act exempts from registration the securities of nonprofit organizations, including religious organizations, but only if the securities are "part of an issue having an aggregate sales price of $250,000 or less and are sold only to bona fide members of the issuing organization and are sold without payment of a commission or consulting fee." Securities issued by a charity or religious organization that do not meet these conditions are exempt only if (1) ten days before an offer or sale of the security it files with the administrator an offering circular with a filing fee of $50, and the administrator does not disallow the exemption; (2) no commission or consulting fee is paid to any person except a registered broker-dealer in connection with the offer or sale of the security; and (3) it offers and sells the securities only through registered securities broker-dealers or through persons exempted from the definition of the term *agent*. The securities exemption in some states (including Colorado, North Carolina, South Dakota, and Virginia) exempt only those churches that are organized under local law. Many states require churches to notify the state securities commission of a proposed offer or sale of securities as a prerequisite to exemption. Church securities are exempt from registration in some states only if no "commission" or other remuneration is paid to those individuals who offer or sell the securities.

[69] Iowa Code § 502.202.9; Kan. Stat. Ann. § 17-1261(h); Md. Corps. & Ass'ns Code Ann. § 11-601(9); Mo. Ann. Stat. § 409.402(a)(9); Mont. Code Ann. § 30-10-104(8); Nev. Rev. Stat. § 90.520.2(j); N.Y. Gen. Bus. § 359-f(1)(e); N.C. Gen. Stat. § 78A-16(9); Okla. Stat. title 71, § 401(b)(15) (transactional exemption only); Pennsylvania Securities Act of 1972 § 203(p); S.C. Code Ann. § 35-1-310(8); Tenn. Code Ann. § 48-2-103(a)(7); Wash. Rev. Code § 21.20.310(11).

[70] *See, e.g.*, Rule 3E-400.002 of the Rules of the Department of Banking and Finance, Division of Securities, State of Florida.

[71] Uniform Securities Act § 304.

statement similar to that described in connection with registration by qualification must be filed for a registration by notification.

The registration statement ordinarily is prepared on a form provided by the state securities commission. Considerable effort has been expended to standardize securities laws and related forms among the 50 states. Most states now permit issuers to register their securities on a uniform application developed by the American Bar Association. This uniform application is called Form U-1.

Generally, the filing of a registration statement with a state securities commission constitutes registration of the security unless the commission objects to the registration statement within a prescribed period. A state securities commission retains the authority to suspend or revoke a registration of securities on the basis of a variety of grounds, including fraud, unreasonable commissions, illegality, omission of a material fact in the registration statement, and willful violation of any rule, order, or condition imposed by the securities commission.[72] Registration of securities generally is effective for one year, although some state laws stipulate that a registration will expire when the securities described in the registration statement have been sold.

Most securities laws that exempt church securities from registration also exempt churches from the requirement of filing sales and advertising literature with the securities commission. Again, churches must not assume that they are exempt from the filing requirement, since some state securities laws contain no such exemption. Furthermore, even if a church is exempt from the requirement of filing its sales and advertising literature with a state securities commission, it may be deemed to have entered into fraudulent transactions with investors if at or before the time of a sale or an offer to sell it does not provide each investor with a prospectus or offering circular containing sufficient information about the securities to enable an investor to make an informed investment decision.

The North American Securities Administrators Association has developed guidelines for a church to follow in drafting a prospectus or offering circular.[73] In general, these guidelines require certain basic information on the cover page, and in addition require a full description of the history and operations of the church; the church's prior borrowing experience; risk factors associated with investment in the church's securities; how funds will be held during the offering period; anticipated use of proceeds; current financial condition of the church, accompanied by financial statements for the past three years; the church's properties; the type and amount of the securities to be offered, including interest rates, maturity dates, payment dates, and paying agent; the plan of distribution; pending or threatened legal proceedings against the church; tax aspects of ownership of the church's securities; and the church's leadership.

In addition, in 1994 the North American Securities Administrators Association adopted *Guidelines for General Obligation Financing by Religious Denominations*. These guidelines address debt securities offered by denominational agencies that are used to provide resources to affiliated churches and institutions in the form of grants or loans. In general, these guidelines incorporate many of the same standards that are contained in the guidelines for local church securities offerings. They also contain guidelines for evaluating the strength of a loan fund.

It is important to observe that most states require that persons who sell or offer to sell securities be registered with the state securities commission. Registration involves submitting a detailed application[74] and,

---

[72] *Id.* at § 306.

[73] The guidelines are reproduced in Appendix 4 at the end of this book.

[74] Most states accept the uniform Form U-4 prepared by the National Association of Securities Dealers. *See generally* § 4-07, *supra.*

in most cases, the successful completion of a securities law examination. A few states that exempt the securities of religious organizations from registration do not exempt persons selling or offering to sell such securities from the salesman registration requirements.

No state securities law exempts religious organizations from the antifraud provisions. The antifraud provisions of the Uniform Securities Act are set forth in section 501:

> In connection with an offer to sell, sale, offer to purchase, or purchase, of a security, a person may not, directly or indirectly:
>
> (1) employ a device, scheme, or artifice to defraud;
>
> (2) make an untrue statement of a material fact or omit to state a material fact necessary in order to make the statements made not misleading, in the light of the circumstances under which they are made; or
>
> (3) engage in an act, practice, or course of business that operates or would operate as a fraud or deceit upon a person.

This section is substantially the same as section 17(a) of the federal Securities Act of 1933. Section 17 expressly states that the Act's exemption of nonprofit organizations from the registration requirements does not apply to the antifraud provisions.

The antifraud provisions of federal and state securities laws are very broad. They have been construed to prohibit a wide variety of activities, including the following:

- making false or misleading statements about church securities

- failing to disclose material risks associated with securities

- manipulating the church's financial records in order to facilitate the sale of securities

- failing to establish a debt service or sinking fund reserve out of which church securities will be retired

- making false predictions

- recommending the sale of securities to investors without regard to their financial condition

- inducing transactions that are excessive in view of an investor's financial resources

- borrowing money from an investor

- commingling investors' funds with the personal funds of another, such as a salesman

- deliberately failing to follow an investor's instructions; making unfounded guarantees

- misrepresenting to investors the true status of their funds

• representing that funds of investors are insured or "secure" when in fact they are not

• representing that investments are as safe as if they had been made in a bank, when this is not the case

• representing that securities have been approved of or recommended by the state securities commission or that the commission has passed in any way on the merits or qualifications of the securities or of any agent or salesman

> **Key point.** *There are 2 additional considerations that churches should consider before offering securities. First, some securities may be regulated under state and federal banking law. For example, it is possible that the issuance of "demand notes" (notes redeemable by investors "on demand") would violate state and federal banking laws. Demand notes are basically deposit arrangements which may trigger banking regulation. Second, complex accounting principles apply to some securities programs. It is essential for churches to work with a CPA firm with experience in representing nonprofit organizations that issue securities.*

In a leading case, the federal Securities and Exchange Commission brought an action in federal court seeking to enjoin a church and its leader from violating the antifraud provisions of the Securities Act of 1933.[75] The church had solicited funds through investment plans consisting essentially of the sale of interest-bearing notes to the general public. The notes were promoted through advertising literature extolling the security of the investment. For example, one advertisement stated in part:

> You may be a Christian who has committed his life into the hands of God, but left his funds in the hands of a floundering world economy. Financial experts everywhere are predicting a disaster in the economy. They say it is only a matter of time. . . . God's economy does not sink when the world's economy hits a reef and submerges! Wouldn't it be wise to invest in His economy?

The Securities and Exchange Commission argued that the church had defrauded investors by such representations when in fact it had a substantially increasing operating deficit that had jumped from $42,349 to $203,776 in the preceding three years. This fact was not disclosed to investors.

The church argued that religious organizations are protected by the first amendment from the reach of securities laws. In rejecting this contention, the court observed: "Defendants constantly emphasize that they are engaged in 'God's work.' No court has ever found that conduct, by being so described, is automatically immunized from all regulation in the public interest."[76] The court quoted with approval the United States Supreme Court's earlier observation that "[n]othing we have said is intended even remotely to imply that, under the cloak of religion, persons may, with impunity, commit frauds upon the public."[77] The court found it irrelevant that investors had a "religious" motivation, that most investors were "believers," and that the church did not intend to defraud or deceive anyone.

---

[75] Securities and Exchange Commission v. World Radio Mission, Inc., 544 F.2d 535 (1st Cir. 1976).

[76] *Id.* at 539 n.7.

[77] *Id.* at 537 n.3, quoting Cantwell v. Connecticut, 310 U.S. 296, 306 (1940). The court was "surprised . . . by defendants' recitation of the parable of the servants entrusted with their master's talents. We do not question the parable, but insofar as it indicates a duty to make loans, it is to make profitable ones. A servant contemplating lending to a possibly shaky enterprise would do well to note the final verse." *Id.* at 538 n.6.

A number of churches and other religious organizations have been investigated by the federal Securities and Exchange Commission and by state securities commissions. In most cases, the investigation was prompted by the complaint of an investor.[78]

Churches that violate state securities laws face a variety of potential consequences under state and federal securities laws. These include investigations, hearings, subpoenas, injunctions, criminal actions, cancellation of sales, suits for monetary damages by aggrieved investors, monetary fines, and revocation of an exemption, or registration, of securities.

Key point. It is important to recognize that "good faith" (a lack of an intention to deceive, or lack of knowledge that a particular transaction is either fraudulent or otherwise in violation of securities law) does not necessarily protect against liability. To illustrate, some courts have ruled that the sale of unregistered securities in violation of state securities law is punishable despite the innocent intentions of the seller.[79] However, civil lawsuits by investors alleging fraud in the sale of securities must demonstrate an actual intent to deceive or defraud.[80]

Example. A church issues $200,000 in 10-year promissory notes to its members and spends all of the proceeds on a new education building. The failure to establish a "sinking fund" out of part of the proceeds received from the sale of these securities, and out of which the securities will be repaid at maturity, constitutes securities fraud. This is a good example of how churches can unwittingly engage in securities fraud.

Example. A church issues 10-year, 10 percent promissory notes to several of its members. No prospectus, offering circular, or other literature is filed with the state securities commission or made available to investors. The failure to provide prospective investors with a prospectus (also called an "offering circular") constitutes securities fraud. Once again, this illustrates how churches can innocently commit securities fraud.

Example. A church plans to issue $300,000 in promissory notes. It composes a prospectus describing much of the financial background of the church. The prospectus also contains the following four statements: (1) "The membership of the church has increased during each of the past ten years, so it can be expected that membership growth will continue to occur." (2) "These securities have been exempted from registration by the state securities commission and thus you are assured that they have been carefully studied and approved by the state." (3) "A copy of this prospectus shall at all times be maintained in the church office for the benefit of any prospective investor." (4) "Interest on these obligations is guaranteed." Each of these statements may constitute securities fraud.

---

[78] *See, e.g.*, In the Matter of Keep the Faith, Inc., Ariz. Corp. Com., Dec. 54503 (April 25, 1985) (issuer incorrectly stated that its securities program did not involve a donation and did not disclose material information to investors, including the interest rate and term of the securities, and the background and financial condition of the issuer); In the Matter of Johnson Financial Services, Inc., Ga. Securities Div., No. 50-84-9500 (August 6, 1984) (salesperson falsely represented that he was working with a Presbyterian church to help sell its bonds, that he was a licensed salesperson, and that the church bonds he was offering earned 18 percent "tax free" for years); In the Matter of Tri-County Baptist Church, Mich. Corp. and Secs. Bureau, No. 84-32-S (June 11, 1984) (church failed to maintain an escrow account for proceeds of bond sales and did not apply proceeds as described in prospectus).

[79] Moerman v. Zipco, Inc., 302 F. Supp. 439 (E.D.N.Y. 1969), *aff'd*, 422 F.2d 871 (2nd Cir. 1970); Trump v. Badet, 327 P.2d 1001 (Ariz. 1958).

[80] The United States Supreme Court so held in Ernst & Ernst v. Hochfelder, 425 U.S. 185 (1976). While the *Ernst* decision dealt only with proof of an intent to deceive under the antifraud provisions of federal securities law, the decision has been held to apply by implication to private actions under the antifraud provisions of state securities laws. *See, e.g.*, Greenfield v. Cheek, 593 P.2d 293 (Ariz. 1978).

Example. *Same facts as the previous question. The church decides not to include the following information in its prospectus out of a concern that this information might make the church's securities less attractive: (1) A lawsuit is pending against the church alleging malpractice on the part of the pastor. (2) The total dollar value of securities to be offered. (3) A statement that no sinking fund reserve exists. (4) A statement that for two of the past five years the church's expenses exceeded revenues. Omitting any of this information from the church's prospectus may constitute securities fraud.*

Example. *A church finance company failed to comply with the provisions of the Indiana Securities Act regarding the registration of securities prior to the offering and sale of certain securities to Indiana residents. As a result, the company and state securities commission entered into a settlement agreement which required the company to pay a fine and make rescission offers to all Indiana residents who purchased unregistered, non-exempt securities.*[81]

Example. *A business representing itself as a nondenominational, non-sectarian international Christian ministry (formed in the Dutch Antilles Island of Aruba) placed the following advertisement in an entrepreneur magazine with a nationwide circulation: "Need extra income? [We] would like to show Christian families how working together they can become debt free. Call [a toll-free telephone number] and request the Christian program." Persons who responded to the ad were mailed literature that offered financial assistance through participation in a monthly fund-raising project. By providing others with "love gifts" in the amount of $30, $60, or $100 per month, a participant became eligible to receive monetary "gifts of love" from a "3-wide x 7-level deep network." Of the monthly payments, 30% went to the ministry and 70% was for "love gifts" to be forwarded to earlier participants in the program. New participants recruited and sponsored other participants, creating an upline of up to seven levels. A participant received a portion of the monthly "love gift" payments made by those in one's upline. A participant became eligible to receive "love gifts" from others by making monthly payments and by sponsoring others to join the program. The literature represented that it was possible for a participant to receive $10,800 per month from this program. The program was also promoted through radio ads to Kansas residents who needed extra income through a "Christian program." In response to these advertisements, approximately 30 Kansas residents sent for information about the program. The Kansas securities commission concluded that the program was a security, and that it violated securities law in the following ways: (1) neither the securities nor those selling them had been registered; and (2) investors were not informed that the ministry had been issued a cease and desist order by the state securities commission a few years earlier. The commissioner ordered the ministry to discontinue any further offers or sales of its program to residents of Kansas unless the securities are registered in advance.*[82]

Example. *In 1992, the Michigan Corporations and Securities Bureau revoked the exemptions of a denominational church loan fund, and ordered it to discontinue the sale of any securities, because of the offer and sale of unregistered, nonexempt securities from 1987 though 1991 in violation of state securities law. In 1993, the loan fund registered $10 million in securities. Following the expiration of this registration in 1994, the loan fund sold more than $1.3 million in unregistered, nonexempt securities to 95 Michigan residents. Because of this second violation of state securities law, the Bureau took the following steps: (1) It revoked and denied the availability of any exemption for the loan fund's securities for a period of five years. All securities issued during that five-year period would have to be registered under state law. (2) The Bureau ordered the loan fund to give written notice to its investors that they*

[81] In the Matter of Church Extension Plan (Lifeline Extension Pool), 1997 WL 2449 (Ind. Div. Sec. 1997).
[82] In the Matter of Agape International Ministries, 1995 WL 582034 (Kan. Sec. Com. 1995).

may have certain rights to have their money refunded because of the loan fund's violations of state securities law. (3) The Bureau ordered the loan fund to "retain an experienced securities attorney" before any future attempt to register its securities.[83]

Example. *A church engaged in a chain distributor scheme of marketing ministerial credentials was found guilty of a fraudulent practice.*[84] *The church, whose archbishop was an attorney who had been disbarred for tax fraud in connection with the activities of the church, encouraged persons to become members by purchasing ministerial credentials for $3,500. Once the fee was paid, the new minister would name and establish his own church chartered by the parent church. He could then either make donations to his "church" or take a vow of poverty placing all his property in the name of his church and then pay all personal and family expenses through the church's account, thereby avoiding all taxes. Each minister was given the right to act as a "missionary representative" and was entitled to a 10 percent commission for each new member he recruited into the church. After recruiting two fully paid members in one month, the missionary representative was granted advancement to the "missionary supervisor" level and thereby became eligible to receive a special bonus of $500 for each new fully paid minister recruited. After the missionary supervisor level, one could become a "director" and receive a 40 percent commission. Ministers were enticed through a demonstration of number doubling. Two became four, eight became sixteen, thirty-two became sixty-four, and commissions mounted from $350 to a total of $1,023,500 when 2,047 new recruits were added. A chart was prepared to give dramatic visual impact on how to become a millionaire. A court summarily concluded that such a scheme was fraudulent, and that application of state securities law to the church did not violate the first amendment.*

Example. *A securities dealer offered for sale and sold securities in a local church's mortgage bond investment program. The offering materials for such securities contained a letter which indicated that the bonds were "A" rated when, in fact, they had not received any independent rating. The Texas securities commission determined that this representation was misleading, and it ordered the dealer to discontinue any further references to "ratings" unless it obtained an independent rating from a recognized securities rating agency. It also ordered the dealer to pay a fine, and make "rescission offers" to all persons who invested in any securities accompanied by materials containing the misleading representation. A rescission offer is an offer by an issuer of securities to an investor, offering to buy back the investor's securities.*[85]

Example. *The Virginia Division of Securities investigated a church's securities program, and concluded that the church violated state securities law by selling unregistered securities in the form of bonds called "Certificates of Faith," and using unregistered agents in the sale of the securities. The church entered into a settlement offer with the Division, which required it to make a rescission offer to all bondholders including an explanation for the reason for the rescission offer. The church also agreed to offer only securities that are registered under the Virginia Securities Act or are exempted from registration, and to offer and sell such securities only through agents who are registered under the Virginia Securities Act or who are exempted from registration.*[86]

---

[83] In the Matter of the Missions and Church Extension Trust Fund, 1996 WL 173463 (Mich. Corp. Sec. Bureau 1996). *See also* In re Lutheran Association for Church Extension, Inc., 1993 WL 304762 (Fla. Dept. Banking and Finance 1993).

[84] People v. Life Science Church, 450 N.Y.S.2d 664 (1982).

[85] In the Matter of California Plan of Church Finance, Inc., 1997 WL 403287 (Tex. State Securities Board 1998).

[86] Commonwealth of Virginia v. Unity Christ Church, 1996 WL 392586 (Va. Corp. Com. 1996).

Example. A state corporation commission launched an investigation into a church's bond program as a result of the following allegations: (1) the church's prospectus omitted disclosure of defaults by the church on bonds it issued in 1984 and 1987; (2) the financial statements included with the church's prospectus failed to properly reflect the total accrued interest on outstanding bonds; and (3) the prospectus issued to investors falsely represented that the church was current in its sinking fund payments for prior bond offerings. The commission entered into a settlement with the church which contained a number of terms, including the following: (1) payment of a fine; (2) an assurance that the church would not engage in any further practices in violation of state securities law; (3) an audit of the church's financial records; (4) the formulation of a financial plan by which all holders of outstanding bonds will be paid full principal and interest in accordance with the terms of their bond agreements; and (5) distribute to all bondholders a disclosure document, approved by the commission, disclosing all previous omissions, the church's current financial status, and its plan for the full repayment of all outstanding bonds.[87]

§ 9-05   Copyright Law

Resource. The application of copyright law to churches is discussed fully in R. HAMMAR, THE CHURCH GUIDE TO COPYRIGHT LAW (2nd ed. 1990), available from the publisher of this text.

The United States Constitution gives Congress the power to enact laws that "promote the progress of . . . [the] useful arts, by securing for limited times to authors . . . the exclusive right to their respective writings." In 1790, under the power granted by the new Constitution, Congress enacted the first copyright law. Congress enacted several other copyright laws in the ensuing years, and in 1870 enacted the first comprehensive copyright statute. This law was substantially revised in 1909. In 1976, Congress enacted the current copyright act, which became effective on January 1, 1978. It is known as the Copyright Act of 1976.

In commenting on the purpose of the original constitutional provision, the United States Supreme Court has observed:

[The Constitution] describes both the objective which Congress may seek and the means to achieve it. The objective is to promote the progress of . . . the arts. . . . To accomplish its purpose, Congress may grant to authors the exclusive right to the fruits of their respective works. An author who possesses an unlimited copyright may preclude others from copying his creation for commercial purposes without permission. In other words, to encourage people to devote themselves to intellectual and artistic creation, Congress may guarantee to authors . . . a reward in the form of control over the sale or commercial use of copies of their works.[88]

Compensation of authors is thus a secondary purpose of the copyright law.

§ 9-05.01 — Securing Copyright Protection

Key point 9-05.01. Authors and composers receive initial copyright protection as soon as they create an original work in a tangible form.

---

[87] Commonwealth of Virginia v. Zion Apostolic Christian Memorial Church, 1998 WL 514271 (Va. Corp. Com. 1998).
[88] Goldstein v. California, 412 U.S. 546, 555 (1973).

1. INITIAL COPYRIGHT PROTECTION

The objective of copyright law is to promote the progress of the useful arts by granting authors certain exclusive rights in their works. Under the Copyright Act of 1976, authors and composers receive initial copyright protection as soon as they create an original work of authorship that is "fixed" in a "tangible medium of expression."[89] There are then three prerequisites to initial copyright protection in a work: (1) the work must be original, (2) it must be a work of authorship, and (3) it must be fixed in a tangible medium of expression.

A work is *original* if an author created it by his or her own skill, labor, and judgment, and not by directly copying or evasively imitating the work of another. One court has stated that "[o]riginality means that the work owes its creation to the author and thus in turn means that the work must not consist of actual copying."[90] In summary, originality connotes independent creation.

Originality does *not* necessarily mean novelty or creativity. One court observed that "there must be independent creation, but it need not be invention in the sense of striking uniqueness, ingeniousness, or novelty," and that the test of originality "is concededly one with a low threshold in that 'all that is needed . . . is that the author contributed something more than a merely trivial variation, something recognizably his own.'"[91]

For a work to be entitled to initial copyright protection, it must constitute a *work of authorship* as defined by the Copyright Act. Section 102 of the Act provides that works of authorship include

1. literary works, such as books, periodicals, and manuscripts

2. musical works, including any accompanying words

3. dramatic works, including any accompanying music

4. pantomimes and choreographic works

5. pictorial, graphic, and sculptural works

6. motion pictures and other audiovisual works

7. sound recordings

Names and titles are not subject to copyright protection. They may be entitled to protection under federal trademark law if they are affixed to or associated with products or services and serve to identify the source of the products or services in a unique way.

Section 103 stipulates that compilations and derivative works also are entitled to copyright protection. A *compilation* is defined as "a work formed by the collection and assembling of pre-existing materials . . . that are selected, coordinated, or arranged in such a way that the resulting work as a whole constitutes an original work of authorship." A *derivative work* is defined as "a work based upon one or more pre-existing works, such

---

[89] 17 U.S.C. § 102(a).
[90] L. Batlin & Son, Inc. v. Snyder, 536 F.2d 486, 490 (2nd Cir. 1976), *cert. denied*, 429 U.S. 857 (1976).
[91] *Id.*

as a translation, musical arrangement, dramatization, fictionalization, abridgement, condensation, or any other form in which a work may be recast, transformed, or adapted."

For a work to be entitled to initial copyright protection, it must be fixed in some *tangible medium of expression.* Ideas, concepts, and discoveries therefore are not eligible for copyright protection until they are reduced to a tangible form.

2. POST-PUBLICATION COPYRIGHT PROTECTION — WORKS FIRST PUBLISHED BEFORE MARCH 1, 1989

The initial copyright protection that an author receives under the Copyright Act persists until the author publishes his work. The Act defines *publication* as "the distribution of copies . . . of a work to the public by sale or other transfer of ownership, or by rental, lease, or lending."[92] Once an author publishes a work, he or she may have to comply with certain other requirements to perpetuate the initial copyright protection.

For works published prior to March 1, 1989, section 401(a) of the Copyright Act specified:

Whenever a work . . . is published in the United States or elsewhere by authority of the copyright owner, a notice of copyright as provided by this section shall be placed on all publicly distributed copies from which the work can be visually perceived, either directly or with the aid of a machine or device.

This requirement is known as the "notice" requirement, and compliance with it is essential to the continuation of copyright protection following the publication of a work first published prior to March 1, 1989. No registration was necessary to perfect copyright protection in a work first published before March 1, 1989.

3. POST-PUBLICATION COPYRIGHT PROTECTION — WORKS FIRST PUBLISHED ON OR AFTER MARCH 1, 1989

On March 1, 1989, the United States became a party to the "Berne Convention"--an international copyright convention established a century ago and endorsed by nearly 80 nations. Participation by the United States in this significant convention generally will increase the international protections available to American authors. To become a party to the convention, Congress had to make various changes in our copyright law (unwillingness to make the required changes was one of the major reasons that it took the United States a century to join the convention). Perhaps the most important change related to copyright notice. Mandatory notice of copyright has been abolished for works published for the first time on or after March 1, 1989. Failure to place a copyright notice on copies of works that are publicly distributed can no longer result in the loss of copyright. Obviously, this is a significant change in our copyright law, since prior to March 1, 1989, the failure to affix a valid copyright notice to a publicly distributed work could have resulted in loss of copyright protection. While copyright notices are no longer required to obtain copyright protection in works first published on or after March 1, 1989, the Copyright Office "strongly recommends" that publishers place a notice of copyright on such works. One of the benefits of such notices is that an infringer will not be able to claim that he or she "innocently infringed" a work. In summary, while in some cases a copyright notice may no longer be a technical requirement, it should nevertheless always be used.

---

[92] 17 U.S.C. § 101.

The Berne Convention is not retroactive. Accordingly, the notice requirements for works first published prior to March 1, 1989, remain unchanged. To illustrate, works first published between January 1, 1978 and February 28, 1989 without a valid copyright notice (as defined below) generally lost their copyright protection unless they were registered with the Copyright Office within five years of first publication (and a valid notice added to all copies distributed after discovery of the omission). Works first published before January 1, 1978 without a valid copyright notice generally lost all copyright protection immediately (with some exceptions). Obviously, the change in the notice requirement will result in considerable confusion among churches regarding the copyright status of literary or musical works. For example, suppose that a church would like to make copies of a piece of sheet music. The fact that the music does not bear a copyright notice does *not* mean that the work is not copyrighted. Clearly, it will now be more difficult for churches to determine whether or not they are free to make copies of some works. Churches cannot safely assume that a work is "in the public domain" merely because it does not contain a valid copyright notice.

In summary, while copyright notices are no longer technically required for most works first published on or after March 1, 1989, they should still be used.

What, then, is a valid copyright notice? The contents and placement of a valid copyright notice are described in sections 401(b) and (c) of the Copyright Act. A valid notice consists of three elements: (1) the symbol ©, the word "Copyright," or the abbreviation "Copr."; *and* (2) the year of first publication of the work (in the case of compilations and derivative works incorporating previously published material, the year of first publication of the compilation or derivative work is sufficient); *and* (3) the name of the owner of copyright in the work, or an abbreviation by which the name can be recognized, or a generally known alternative designation of the owner.

Section 401(c) provides that the notice shall be affixed to copies of the work "in such manner and location as to give reasonable notice of the claim of copyright." To illustrate, Copyright Office regulations specify that a copyright notice for a work published in book form may be affixed on the title page, the page immediately following the title page, either side of the front or back cover, the first page of the main body of the work, the last page of the main body of the work, or any page between the front page and first page of the main body of the work if there are no more than 10 pages between the front page and the first page of the main body of the work and the notice is prominently displayed and set apart. Similar rules apply to musical works. Other rules apply to single-leaf works, audiovisual works, machine-readable works, and pictorial works. The Copyright Office regulations themselves provide that they merely illustrate acceptable notice placements. They are not exhaustive, and acceptable alternatives probably exist. Of course, it is prudent to follow the Copyright Office guidelines since compliance with them is conclusive evidence that you have affixed your copyright notice in an appropriate position.

What is the effect of a work that is published with a defective or omitted notice? Works first published on or after March 1, 1989, require no copyright notice, so an omitted or defective notice has no legal effect. However, note that section 401(d) of the Copyright Act specifies that if a work first published on or after March 1, 1989 contains a valid copyright notice, "then no weight shall be given" to an "innocent infringement" defense. That is, no infringer can argue that he or she "innocently" infringed on another's work if that work contained a valid copyright notice. If the notice does not satisfy the requirements of sections 401(b) and 401(c), the implication is that an infringer can assert an innocent infringement defense. The same concept applies to phonorecords under section 402(d). What about works first published prior to March 1, 1989? Section 405(a) of the Copyright Act specifies:

With respect to copies and phonorecords publicly distributed by authority of the copyright owner before [March 1, 1989], the omission of the copyright notice described in sections 401 through 403 from copies or phonorecords publicly distributed by authority of the copyright owner does not invalidate the copyright in a work if

(1) the notice has been omitted from no more than a relatively small number of copies . . . distributed to the public; or

(2) registration for the work has been made before or is made within five years after the publication without notice, and a reasonable effort is made to add notice to all copies . . . that are distributed to the public in the United States after the omission has been discovered; or

(3) the notice has been omitted in violation of an express requirement in writing that, as a condition of the copyright owner's authorization of the public distribution of copies . . . they bear the prescribed notice.

Also, note that if someone distributes copies of a copyrighted work without authorization from the copyright owner, and no copyright notice appears on such copies, the copyright in the work is not affected since the copies were made and distributed without authorization.

Can one be guilty of copyright infringement for innocently infringing on a copyrighted work from which the copyright notice had been omitted? For works first published on or after March 1, 1989, the answer is yes--since copyright notices are no longer required to ensure copyright protection. However, the Copyright Act indicates that an infringer can assert the defense of "innocent infringement" to avoid or reduce damages if the infringed work either had no copyright notice or had a defective notice (not meeting the requirements of sections 401(b) and 401(c)). What if the work was first published prior to March 1, 1989? Assuming that the omission of the copyright notice did not invalidate the copyright (i.e., one of the three exceptions referred to above applies), the innocent infringer incurs no liability for any infringing acts "committed before receiving actual notice that registration for the work has been made . . . if such person proves that he or she was misled by the omission of notice."[93] Omission of copyright notice ordinarily will result in loss of copyright protection (in works first published before March 1, 1989) if none of the three exceptions described above applies.

A related question is the effect of an error in the copyright notice. For example, what if a notice has an error in the name of the copyright owner, or in the date of first publication, or either the name or date is omitted? The copyright law specifies that if the name listed in a copyright notice is not the name of the copyright owner, the copyright in the work is not affected. In some cases, innocent infringers are protected if they were misled by the recital of the wrong person in the copyright notice.[94] A copyright notice that recites a year of first publication that is more than one year later than the year in which publication in fact first occurred, the work is considered to have been published without any notice. If the notice recites a year of first publication that is earlier than the actual year of first publication, the copyright in the work is not affected, but any period of time computed from the year of publication for purposes of any provision in the copyright law is computed from the erroneous date.[95] If a copyright notice contains either no name or no date, the work is considered to have been published without any notice.[96]

---

[93] *Id.* at § 405(b).
[94] *Id.* at § 406(a).
[95] *Id.* at § 406(b).
[96] *Id.* at § 406(c).

§ 9-05.02 — The Deposit Requirement

Key point 9-05.2. Copyright owners must "deposit" two copies of their work with the Copyright Office within three months of publication. Failure to do so may result in fines or penalties, but it will not affect the copyright in a work.

Although copyright registration is not required, the Copyright Act establishes a mandatory deposit requirement for works published with notice of copyright in the United States. In general, the copyright owner, or the owner of the exclusive right of publication in a work, has a legal obligation to deposit in the Copyright Office, within three months of publication, two copies (or in the case of sound recordings, two phonorecords) for the use of the Library of Congress. Failure to make the deposit can result in fines and penalties, but does not affect copyright protection. Under section 408(b) of the Act, a single deposit can satisfy both the deposit and registration requirements. This provision requires that the single copy must be accompanied by the prescribed application and registration fee. The Copyright Office regulations exempt various kinds of works from the deposit requirements, including sermons and speeches (when published individually and not as a collection of the works of one or more authors), literary or musical works published only as embodied in phonorecords, computer programs published only in the form of machine-readable copies, and works first published as individual contributions to collective works.

§ 9-05.03 — Copyright Ownership

Key point 9-05.03. Copyright ownership vests initially in the author of a work.

Who owns the copyright in a work, and what difference does it make? Section 201(a) of the Copyright Act states simply that "[c]opyright in a work . . . vests initially in the author or authors of the work." There is very little difficulty in understanding this provision. The copyright law goes on to state that "the authors of a joint work are coowners of copyright in the work." Again, this is straightforward and needs no explanation. There is one aspect of copyright ownership that is more difficult to understand, namely, a "work made for hire." Works made for hire are addressed in the following section.

§ 9-05.04 — Works Made for Hire

Key point 9-05.04. Works created by employees within the scope of their employment are "works made for hire." The employer is deemed to be the "author" of such a work, and owns the copyright in it unless it executes a signed writing assigning the copyright back to the employee.

1. In General

It is common for church employees to compose music or write books or articles in their church office during office hours. What often is not understood is that such persons do not necessarily own the copyright in the works they create. While the one who creates a work generally is its author and the initial owner of the copyright in the work, section 201(b) of the Copyright Act specifies that "[i]n the case of a work made for hire, the employer or other person for whom the work was prepared is considered the author . . . and, unless the parties have expressly agreed otherwise in a written instrument signed by them, owns all of the rights comprised in the copyright."

The copyright law defines "work made for hire" as "a work prepared by an employee within the scope of his or her employment." There are two requirements that must be met: (1) the person creating the work is an employee, and (2) the employee created the work within the scope of his or her employment. Whether or not one is an employee will depend on the same factors used in determining whether one is an employee or self-employed for federal income tax reporting purposes.[97] However, the courts have been very liberal in finding employee status in this context, so it is possible that a court would conclude that a work is a work made for hire even though the author reports his or her federal income taxes as a self-employed person.

The second requirement is that the work must have been created within the scope of employment. This requirement generally means that the work was created during regular working hours, on the employer's premises, using the employer's staff and equipment. This is often a difficult standard to apply. As a result, it is desirable for church employees to discuss this issue with the church leadership to avoid any potential misunderstandings. Section 201(a), quoted above, allows an employer and employee to agree in writing that copyright ownership in works created by the employee within the scope of employment belongs to the employee. This should be a matter for consideration by any church having a minister or other staff member who creates literary or musical works during office hours, on church premises, using church staff and church equipment (e.g., computers, printers, paper, library, secretaries, dictation equipment).

> *Example. Rev. B is senior minister of his church. He is in the process of writing a devotional book. Most of the writing is done during regular church office hours, in his office in the church, using church equipment and a church secretary. Rev. B's contract of employment does not address the issue of copyright ownership in the book, and no written agreement has ever been executed by the church that addresses the matter. Under these facts, it is likely that the book is a "work made for hire." The result is that the church is the "author" of the book, it is the copyright owner, and it has the sole legal right to assign or transfer the copyright in the book.*

> *Example. Rev. T is minister of music at her church. She has composed several songs and choruses, all of which were written during regular office hours at the church, using church equipment (piano, paper, etc.). The church has never addressed the issue of copyright ownership in a signed writing. It is likely that the songs and choruses are "works made for hire." The result is that the church is the "author" of these materials, it is the copyright owner, and it has the sole legal right to assign or transfer the copyright in these works.*

> *Example. Same facts as the preceding example, except that Rev. T composes the music in the evening and on weekends in her home. While she is an employee, she did not compose the music "within the scope of her employment," and therefore the music cannot be characterized as "works made for hire." The legal effect of this conclusion is that Rev. W owns the copyright in the music, and is free to sell or transfer such works in any manner she chooses without church approval.*

> *Example. Same facts as the previous example, except that Rev. T composes many of her works both at home and at the church office. Whether or not a particular work is a work made for hire is a difficult question under these circumstances. The answer will depend upon the following factors: (1) the portion of the work that is composed at the church office, compared to the portion composed at home; (2) the portion of the work created with church equipment, compared to the portion created with Rev. T's personal equipment; (3) the portion of the work created during regular office hours, compared to the*

---

[97] *See* R. HAMMAR, CHURCH AND CLERGY TAX GUIDE chapter 2 (published annually by the publisher of this text).

portion created after hours; and (4) the adequacy of Rev. T's personal records to document each of these factors. Unfortunately, a staff member's records may be inadequate. In such a case, work made for hire status will depend upon the staff member's own testimony, and the testimony of other witnesses (such as other staff members).

2. THE CHURCH'S TAX-EXEMPT STATUS

If a church transfers the copyright in a work made for hire to an employee, this may be viewed by the IRS as "private inurement" of the church's resources to an individual. If so, this could jeopardize the church's tax-exempt status. Neither the IRS nor any court has addressed the tax consequences of such an arrangement to a church. Here are some options:

1. The church transfers copyright ownership to the staff member. This may constitute private inurement. The IRS construes this requirement as follows:

> An organization's trustees, officers, members, founders, or contributors may not, by reason of their position, acquire any of its funds. They may, of course, receive reasonable compensation for goods or services or other expenditures in furtherance of exempt purposes. If funds are diverted from exempt purposes to private purposes, however, exemption is in jeopardy. The Code specifically forbids the inurement of earnings to the benefit of private shareholders or individuals. . . . The prohibition of inurement, in its simplest terms, means that a private shareholder or individual cannot pocket the organization's funds except as reasonable payment for goods or services.

When a church employee writes a book during office hours at the church, using church equipment, supplies, and personnel, the copyright in the work belongs to the church. If the church chooses to renounce its legal rights in the book, and transfers the copyright back to the employee, then it is relinquishing a potentially valuable asset that may produce royalty income for several years. Few if any churches would attempt to "value" the copyright and report it as additional taxable compensation to the employee, and as a result it is hard to avoid the conclusion that such arrangements result in inurement of the church's assets to a private individual. The legal effect is to jeopardize the church's tax-exempt status. This risk must not be overstated, since only a few churches have had their exempt status revoked by the IRS in the last fifty years, and none because of a transfer of copyright to an employee who created a work made for hire. But the consequences would be so undesirable that the risk should be taken seriously.

2. The church retains the copyright. The risk of inurement can be minimized if not avoided if the church retains the copyright in works made for hire, and pays a "bonus" or some other form of compensation to the author.

> ***Example.*** *Rev. G is senior pastor of his church. He writes a devotional book in his office at the church during office hours and using church equipment. He reads an article about works made for hire, and is concerned about the legal implications. He discusses the matter with the church board. In order to eliminate any risk to the church's tax-exempt status, the church board decides that the church will retain the copyright in Rev. G's book. The publisher is contacted, and agrees to list the church as the copyright owner on the title page and to pay royalties from sales of the book directly to the church. The church board agrees to pay Rev. T a "bonus" in consideration of his additional services in writing the book. The bonus is added to Rev. T's W-2 at the end of the year. This arrangement will not jeopardize the church's tax-exempt status.*

3. The church urges employees to do "outside work" at home. Do you have a writer or composer on staff at your church? If so, it is possible that this person is doing some writing or composing on church premises, using church equipment, during office hours. One way to avoid the problems associated with work made for hire status is to encourage staff members to do all their writing and composing at home. Tell staff members that (1) if they do any writing or composing at church during office hours, their works may be works made for hire; (2) the church owns the copyright in such works; and (3) the church can transfer copyright to the writer or composer, but this may constitute "inurement" of the church's assets to a private individual, jeopardizing the church's tax-exempt status. By urging staff members to do all their personal writing and composing at home, the church also will avoid the difficult question of whether works that are written partly at home and partly at the office are works made for hire.

4. Sermons. Are a minister's sermons "works made for hire" that are owned by the employing church? To the extent that sermons are written in a church office, during regular church hours, using church secretaries and equipment, it is possible that sermons would be considered works made for hire since they are created by an employee within the scope of employment. However, this issue has never been addressed directly by any court, and so it is difficult to predict how a court would rule.

A professor's lecture notes provide a comparable example. College professors often prepare their lecture notes in their office on campus, using campus equipment. Are these notes, and the lectures themselves, works made for hire? If so, the college owns the copyright in the notes and lectures, unless it has transferred the copyright back to the professor in a signed writing. Prior to the enactment of the Copyright Act of 1976, it was generally assumed that professors' lectures were an exception to the work for hire doctrine.[98] Perhaps the best example of this view is a decision by a California appeals court in 1969.[99] The court addressed directly the question of whether a professor or his employing university owned the copyright in the professor's lectures. In ruling that the professor owned the copyright, the court observed:

> Indeed the undesirable consequences which would follow from a holding that a university owns the copyright to the lectures of its professors are such as to compel a holding that it does not. Professors are a peripatetic lot, moving from campus to campus. The courses they teach begin to take shape at one institution and are developed and embellished at other. That, as a matter of fact, was the case here. [The professor] testified that the notes on which his lectures were based were derived from a similar course which he had given at another university. If [this] is correct, there must be some rights of that school which were infringed at [the professor's current university]. Further, should [he] leave [his current university] and give a substantially similar course at his next post, [the university] would be able to enjoin him from using the material, which according to [the university], it owns.

The court referred to a federal appeals court decision addressing the copyright ownership in Admiral Rickover's speeches.[100] The speeches in question were prepared by the admiral after normal working hours or while traveling. The California court noted that

> a person in Admiral Rickover's position . . . has no normal working hours any more than a university professor. Whatever distinctions between "on" and "off-duty" hours might be appropriate in the case of an hourly employee who punches a clock, they are quite out of place in cases

---

[98] *See, e.g.,* R. Dreyfuss, *The Creative Employee and the Copyright Act of 1976,* 54 Univ. Chi. L. Rev. 590 (1987).
[99] Williams v. Weisser, 78 Cal. Rptr. 542 (Cal. App. 1969).
[100] Public Affairs Associates, Inc. v. Rickover, 284 F.2d 262 (D.C. Cir. 1960).

such as Rickover and the one at bar. . . . It is thus apparent that no authority supports the argument that the copyright to [professor's] notes is in the university. The indications from the authorities are the other way and so is common sense.

It is important to note that any special exemption professors' notes enjoyed from the work made for hire doctrine was seriously undermined if not abolished by the Copyright Act of 1976. As noted above, the section 201(b) of the Act specifies that "[I]n the case of a work made for hire, the employer . . . is considered the author . . . and, unless the parties have expressly agreed otherwise in a written instrument signed by them, owns all of the rights comprised in the copyright." As a result, cases decided before 1978 (when the Act took effect) are of limited relevance, since prior copyright law contained no provision comparable to section 201. Copyright ownership in a minister's sermons likely will be determined solely by focusing on whether or not the minister created the sermons within the scope of his or her employment.

3. Excessive Compensation

Staff members who retain ownership of a work made for hire because of a written transfer signed by the church may be subject to intermediate sanctions. Intermediate sanctions are excise taxes the IRS can assess against persons who receive excessive compensation from a church or other charity. The point is this—since the church is the legal owner of the copyright in a work made for hire, it is legally entitled to any income generated from sales of the work. By letting the writer or composer retain the copyright, and all rights to royalties, the church in effect is paying compensation to him or her in this amount. If the work generates substantial income, then this may trigger intermediate sanctions. This would expose the writer or composer to an initial excise tax of 25 percent of the amount of taxable compensation that exceeds what the IRS deems to be reasonable. There is an additional 200 percent tax that can be assessed against the writer or composer if he or she does not return the excess amount to the church. Board members who authorized a transfer of the copyright to the writer or composer may be collectively assessed a tax of 10 percent of the excessive compensation up to a maximum of $10,000.

> *Key point. Intermediate sanctions can be imposed only against "disqualified persons" and "managers." IRS regulations define a disqualified person as any person who was in a position to exercise substantial influence over the affairs of the organization at any time during the five-year period ending on the date of the transaction. While a senior pastor ordinarily will meet this definition, other staff members may not. As a result, in many churches the risk of intermediate sanctions will be limited to senior pastors who create works made for hire and are allowed by their church to retain the copyright.*

> *Key point. Church board members are exposed to an excise tax if they authorize a transfer of copyright in a work made for hire to the employee who created it, if the work generates substantial income.*

§ 9-05.05 — Duration of Copyright Protection

> *Key point 9-05.05. The copyright term for most works created after 1977 is the life of the author plus 70 years. The term for works published prior to 1978, and in their initial or renewal copyright term as of October 27, 1998, is 95 years from the date of the original copyright.*

A copyright does not last for an indefinite or unlimited time. The provision in the United States Constitution giving Congress authority to create copyright protection specifies that such protection shall be only "for limited times." The "limited times" vary depending upon the circumstances. Under the copyright law

TABLE 9-1
WORKS MADE FOR HIRE—
A CHECKLIST OF IMPORTANT POINTS

- A "work made for hire" is any book, article, or piece of music created by an employee in the course of employment.

- Factors to consider in deciding whether or not a work was created in the course of employment include the following: (1) Was the work written or composed during office hours? (2) Was the work created on church property? (3) Was the work created using church equipment? (4) Was the work created using church personnel?

- The employer owns the copyright in a work made for hire.

- An employer, by a signed writing, can transfer copyright in a work made for hire to the employee who created it.

- A church that transfers the copyright in a work made for hire to the employee who created it is jeopardizing its tax-exempt status, since this may constitute "inurement" of its assets to a private individual.

- A church that transfers the copyright in a work made for hire to the employee who created it may be exposing the employee to intermediate sanctions.

that was in effect before 1978, copyright was secured either on the date a work was published (with an appropriate copyright notice), or on the date of registration if the work was registered in unpublished form. In either case, the copyright lasted for a first term of 28 years from the date it was secured. During the last (28th) year of the first term, the copyright was eligible for renewal. If renewed, the copyright was extended for a second term of 28 years. If not renewed, the copyright expired at the end of the first 28-year term.

Congress enacted legislation in 1998 amending the duration of copyrights.[101] The current duration rules are as follows:

- *Works created and published before 1978.* The term of copyright protection for any work still in its initial or renewal copyright term as of October 27, 1998 is extended to 95 years from the date that copyright was originally secured.

- *Works created but not published or registered before 1978.* The term of copyright protection is the life of the author plus 70 years, but in no case will copyright expire earlier than December 31, 2002. If the work is published before December 31, 2002, the term will not expire before December 31, 2047.

- *Works created on or after January 1, 1978.* The term of copyright protection will endure for the life of the author plus 70 years. In the case of a joint work, the term lasts for 70 years after the last surviving author's death. For anonymous and pseudonymous works and works made for hire, the term is 95 years from the year of first publication or 120 years from the year of creation, whichever expires first.

---

[101] The Sonny Bono Copyright Term Extension Act, signed into law on October 27, 1998, amends section 302 of the Copyright Act.

Key point. The 1998 legislation extending copyright terms does not restore protection to works that are in the public domain.

§ 9-05.06 — Registration

Key point 9-05.06. Copyright owners may register their works with the Copyright Office. While this is not a legal requirement, it does provide copyright owners with valuable benefits.

The owner of a copyright in a work may register the copyright claim by delivering two complete copies of the best edition of a published work or one complete copy of an unpublished work, along with an application form and the application fee (currently $20) to the Copyright Office.[102] Deposits made to fulfill the deposit requirements of Section 407 may be used to satisfy the deposit requirements for registration if they are accompanied by the appropriate application form and the prescribed fee. Section 408(a) unequivocally states that "registration is not a condition of copyright protection." While registration is not necessary to secure copyright protection, it is advisable in some cases for a variety of reasons, including the following:

1. It is an inexpensive and simple procedure.

2. It establishes a public record or a copyright claim.

3. Section 411 of the Copyright Act provides that "no action for infringement of the copyright in any work shall be instituted until registration of the copyright claim has been made . . . ." This is a significant advantage of registration. If the copyright claim has not been registered, the copyright owner cannot seek redress in the civil courts for acts of infringement. A number of courts have held, however, that a copyright owner of an unregistered work can sue an infringer by simply registering the claim of copyright even though the infringement occurred prior to registration. This rule would not apply if the infringement suit were brought after the limitations period (generally 3 years) following the initial act of infringement.

4. Section 504(c) of the Copyright Act allows a copyright owner to collect "statutory damages" from an infringer in lieu of proving actual damages. Statutory damages ordinarily range from $500 to $20,000 per violation, and they often comprise the only meaningful measure of damages since actual damages are difficult to prove. However, section 412 specifies that "no award of statutory damages . . . shall be made for (1) any infringement of copyright in an unpublished work commenced before the effective date of its registration, or (2) any infringement of copyright commenced after first publication of the work and before the effective date of its registration, unless such registration is made within three months after the first publication of the work."

5. Section 410(c) provides that "[i]n any judicial proceedings the certificate of a registration made before or within five years after first publication of the work shall constitute prima facie evidence of the validity of the copyright and of the facts stated in the certificate." What is the significance of this rule? Simply this--a copyright claimant who has registered a claim of copyright in a work within five years before or after first publication does not have the burden of proving the validity of the copyright claim in an infringement suit.

6. Section 205(c) of the Copyright Act provides that "[r]ecordation of a document in the Copyright Office gives all persons constructive notice of the facts stated in the recorded document, but only if . . . registration has been made for the work." This provision means that the public is "on notice" of any transfers,

---

[102] At the time of publication of this text, a proposal was pending to increase the application fee to $30.

licenses, mortgages, and other documents pertaining to copyrights if such documents are recorded in the Copyright Office and the underlying works are registered.

7. Generally, omission of a valid copyright notice from a work first published before March 1, 1989 invalidates the copyright in the work. However, section 405(a)(2) of the Copyright Act provides that omission of the notice on such a work will not invalidate the copyright if "registration for the work has been made before or is made within five years after the publication without notice, and a reasonable effort is made to add notice to all copies or phonorecords that are distributed to the public in the United States after the omission has been discovered."

8. The Copyright Office reviews every application for registration to ensure that the legal formalities needed to ensure protection are satisfied. Often, the Copyright Office will call to the attention of a copyright owner an error in the registration application or in the copyright notice that can ensure that copyright protection is preserved. This review, however, is limited to the applicant's compliance with technical requirements. The merits of a particular claim of copyright ordinarily are not evaluated.

9. Registration of a copyright in some cases may enhance the marketability of an author's or composer's work. For example, a person checking Copyright Office records on a particular subject may inadvertently find a work, and contact the copyright owner regarding a publishing opportunity.

10. Registration of a musical work may entitle the copyright owner to "compulsory royalty payments" in the event that someone else makes a recording of the work. This provision has special relevance in the context of audio recording of church worship services in which copyrighted music is performed.

Copyright registration is a fairly simple procedure in many cases. To register a work, send the following three items in the same envelope or package to the Register of Copyrights, Copyright Office, Library of Congress, Washington, D.C. 20559:

(a) *A properly completed application form.* Complete the application using black ink or a typewriter, and either an original Copyright Office form or a clear photocopy made on a good grade of white paper. Applications not meeting these requirements will be returned. There are several registration forms. The more commonly used forms include: (a) Form TX for non-dramatic literary works (e.g., compilations, computer programs, contributions to periodicals, dissertations, fiction, lectures, letters, nonfiction, poetry, sermons, song lyrics without music), (b) Form PA for published and unpublished works of the performing arts (musical and dramatic works, choreographic works, motion pictures and other audiovisual works), and (c) Form SR for published and unpublished sound recordings (e.g., music, sermons).

(b) *A nonrefundable filing fee of $20 per application.* At the time of publication of this text, a proposal was pending to increase the filing fee to $30 for most works.

(c) *A nonrefundable deposit of the work being registered.* The deposit requirements vary in particular situations. Generally, two copies of the work must be filed along with the registration application. Section 408(b) of the Copyright Act specifies that the deposit and registration requirements can be satisfied simultaneously.

§ 9-05.07 — The Copyright Owner's Exclusive Rights

Key point 9-05.07. The Copyright Act gives copyright owners the following exclusive rights—reproduction, adaptation, distribution, performance, and display. Anyone who violates one or more of these exclusive rights commits copyright infringement.

Section 106 of the Copyright Act gives a copyright owner the following five "exclusive rights":

(a) to reproduce the copyrighted work in copies or phonorecords;

(b) to prepare derivative works based upon the copyrighted work;

(c) to distribute copies or phonorecords of the copyrighted work to the public by sale or other transfer of ownership, or by rental, lease, or lending;

(d) in the case of literary, musical, dramatic, and choreographic works, pantomimes, and motion pictures and other audiovisual works, to perform the copyrighted work publicly; and

(e) in the case of literary, musical, dramatic, and choreographic works, pantomimes, and pictorial, graphic, or sculptural works, including the individual images of a motion picture or other audiovisual work, to display the copyrighted work publicly.

These five exclusive rights are sometimes referred to as the rights of reproduction, adaptation, publication, performance, and display. They comprise the "bundle of rights" that constitute or define copyright. It is unlawful for anyone to violate any of the exclusive rights of a copyright owner. These rights, however, are not unlimited in scope. The approach of the Copyright Act is to set forth the copyright owner's exclusive rights in broad terms in section 106, and then to provide various limitations, qualifications, or exemptions in sections 107 through 118 of the Act.

§ 9-05.08 — Infringement

Key point 9-05.08. Copyright infringement occurs when one violates any one or more of the exclusive rights of a copyright owner.

Section 501 of the Copyright Act states that "[a]nyone who violates any of the exclusive rights of the copyright owner . . . is an infringer of the copyright." Of the five exclusive rights, the one causing the most difficulties for churches is the copyright owner's exclusive right to reproduce the work (i.e., make copies). Obviously, an infringement occurs when someone makes a verbatim copy of copyrighted material. But what if someone produces a work that is similar but not identical to another's copyrighted work? Can this constitute infringement on the copyright owner's exclusive right of reproduction? The courts generally have resolved this question by applying the following presumption--access by the alleged infringer to the copyrighted material, plus substantial similarity between the allegedly infringing material and the copyrighted work, creates a presumption of infringement. The alleged infringer of course can claim that his work was an independent creation. However, the closer the similarity between the two works, the less likely it is that such a claim will prevail. Other relevant factors to consider in such a case would be the experience and training of the alleged infringer, his previous publishing record, the likelihood that he was capable of independently producing the work, and prior instances of infringement on his part. Some copyright owners intentionally insert errors in their works. The alleged infringer's claim of independent creation will seldom succeed if such errors are duplicated.

The House Report to the Copyright Act of 1976 specifies that "wide departures or variations from the copyrighted work would still be an infringement as long as the author's 'expression' rather than merely the author's 'ideas' are taken."[103]

What about paraphrasing? For example, does infringement occur if a reproduction does not contain any "word-for-word" copying of original material but merely paraphrases it? Probably so, since a number of courts have held that "paraphrasing is tantamount to copying in copyright law."[104] Another court has observed that copying "cannot be limited literally to the text, else a plagiarist would escape by immaterial variations."[105]

Another difficult question is the verbatim copying of only small portions of copyrighted material. When does such use constitute infringement on the copyright owner's exclusive right of reproduction? There is no easy answer to this question. Courts generally evaluate both the quantity of copyrighted material that is copied verbatim, and its quality. That is, what percentage of the copyrighted work was copied, and how much of the allegedly infringing work consisted of the copied material? Further, how significant was the "quality" of the copied material? Was it the essence of the work as a whole, or was it incidental or insignificant? To illustrate, the courts have found copying of the following amounts of copyrighted material to constitute copyright infringement: (1) two identical bars of a musical work;[106] (2) four notes and two words, which comprised the "heart of the composition;"[107] (3) three sentences (that were used for advertising purposes);[108] (4) three sentences;[109] (5) eight sentences;[110] (6) less than one percent of the copyrighted work;[111] and (7) the phrase "put on a happy face."[112]

However, copying of the following portions of copyrighted material was held not to constitute infringement upon the copyright owner's exclusive right of reproduction: (1) a sentence and a half;[113] (2) sixteen words;[114] and (3) two sentences.[115]

Such precedent leaves little doubt that most reproductions of copyrighted materials by churches will constitute an infringement of the exclusive right of copyright owners to reproduce their works. To cite just a few examples--the copying of copyrighted chorus or hymn lyrics onto a transparency or bulletin insert ordinarily will amount to an infringement, since a substantial quantity of the original work is reproduced, the amount reproduced is significant in terms of quality, and the copy serves the same function as the original work. To illustrate, in one case a publisher reproduced the chorus lyrics of two famous copyrighted songs in songsheet pamphlets, maintaining that the reproduction of only chorus lyrics of copyrighted songs was so

---

[103] House Report on the Copyright Act of 1976, p. 61.

[104] *See, e.g.*, Davis v. E.I. duPont de Nemours & Co., 240 F. Supp. 612 (S.D.N.Y. 1965).

[105] Nichols v. Universal Pictures Co., 45 F.2d 119 (2nd Cir. 1930).

[106] Robertson v. Batten, Barton, Durstine and Osborn, Inc., 146 F. Supp. 795 (S.D. Cal. 1956).

[107] Elsmere Music, Inc. v. National Broadcasting Co., 482 F. Supp. 741 (S.D.N.Y. 1980), *aff'd*, 623 F.2d 252 (2nd Cir. 1980).

[108] Henry Holt & Co. v. Liggett & Myers Tobacco Co., 23 F. Supp. 302 (E.D. Pa. 1938).

[109] Amana Refrigeration, Inc. v. Consumers Union of the United States, Inc., 431 F. Supp. 324 (N.D. Iowa 1977).

[110] Martin Luther King, Jr. Center for Social Change, Inc. v. American Heritage Products, Inc., 508 F. Supp. 854 (N.D. Ga. 1981).

[111] Hedeman Products Copr. v. Tap-Rite Products Corp., 228 F. Supp. 630 (D.N.J. 1964).

[112] American Greetings Corp. v. Kleinfab Corp., 400 F. Supp. 228 (S.D.N.Y. 1975).

[113] Toulmin v. The Rike-Kumler Co., 316 F.2d 232 (6th Cir. 1963).

[114] Suid v. Newsweek Magazine, 503 F. Supp. 146 (D.D.C. 1980).

[115] Jackson v. Washington Monthly Co., 481 F. Supp. 647 (D.D.C. 1979).

trivial in nature and amount as to constitute noninfringing fair use. The court found such reproductions to be an infringement, and rejected the publisher's claim that its reproductions constituted fair use. Though only the chorus lyrics were reproduced (and not the regular verse lines or music), the court found that "the chorus of a musical composition may constitute a material and substantial part of the work and it is frequently the very part that makes it popular and valuable."[116] Similarly, another court found the reproduction of chorus lyrics in a song sheet magazine to be an infringement rather than fair use, since the reproduction "met the same demand on the same market" as the original.[117] The courts in each of these two cases gave a narrow interpretation of fair use because the function served by the infringing use directly satisfied a function that was served by the copyright owner's sheet music.

Obviously, verbatim copying of the lyrics and melody of a copyrighted musical work (for use by the choir, a soloist, an accompanist, or an instrumental group) would constitute infringement.

Often overlooked is the fact that both the musical score and lyrics of a hymn or chorus are eligible for copyright protection. Section 102(a) of the Copyright Act states that copyright protection subsists in original "musical works, including any accompanying words," that are reduced to a tangible form. Persons who compose both the music and lyrics of an original hymn are entitled to copyright protection for both. This has important consequences. It means, primarily, that no one can make copies of either the music or lyrics without authorization. To illustrate, a church will infringe upon this copyright protection if it inserts only the words of a particular song in a booklet or on a songsheet, or types them on a piece of paper and projects them onto a screen.

It is also important to recognize that one of the copyright owner's exclusive rights is the right to prepare derivative works based upon the copyrighted work. Derivative works include musical arrangements. Therefore, it is not permissible for anyone other than the copyright owner or one whom the copyright owner has authorized to create an arrangement of a copyrighted musical work. To illustrate, one church choir director who made a choral arrangement of a copyrighted hymn without authorization was found to be guilty of copyright infringement.[118] The director's arrangement consisted of the entire score of the copyrighted hymn plus the insertion of a four-measure introduction. The director made several copies of his arrangement on the church's duplicating machine. Each copy contained the director's name and identified him as the arranger. The copyright owner brought a lawsuit against the director and his church, alleging copyright infringement. A federal appeals court found the director and his employing church jointly liable for copyright infringement. The court found the director's lack of intent to infringe to be irrelevant, and concluded that the copying of all or substantially all of a copyrighted musical work could not be considered "fair use."

It is permissible to make arrangements of preexisting musical works if the preexisting work is in the public domain or if the copyright owner of the preexisting work grants permission. Section 103 of the Act states that lawfully made derivative works are entitled to copyright protection if they otherwise qualify. Section 103 also stipulates that copyright protection in a derivative work extends only to the material contributed by the author of such work as distinguished from the preexisting material employed in the work. Thus, although a musical arrangement of a public domain song is subject to copyright protection, the copyright protection extends only to the new musical score and not to the lyrics of the preexisting work. As a result, churches can copy the lyrics of such arrangements without infringing the arranger's copyright.

---

[116] Johns & Johns Printing Co. v. Paull-Pioneer Music Corp., 102 F.2d 282 (8th Cir. 1939).
[117] Leo Feist, Inc. v. Song Parodies, Inc., 146 F.2d 400 (2nd Cir. 1944).
[118] Wihtol v. Crow, 309 F.2d 777 (8th Cir. 1962).

A federal court has rejected the claim that the first amendment right to freely exercise one's religion immunized from liability for copyright infringement a group of priests who toured the country giving unauthorized performances of the rock opera *Jesus Christ Superstar*.[119]

Example. A religious radio station that broadcast copyrighted religious music without permission was found guilty of "willful infringement" and was assessed statutory damages of $52,500. The station manager admitted that he played copyrighted songs on the radio, and that he had no license or permission to do so. He defended his actions by noting that "the artists have publicly stated their intent to minister through their Christian music" and that "their intent to minister is further accomplished by radio stations broadcasting their music to a listening audience." The court rejected this reasoning and assessed statutory damages of $52,500 against the station for willful copyright infringement. The court based this result on 15 proven infringements at $3,500 each. The court also ordered the station to pay the attorneys fees the copyright owners incurred in maintaining their infringement lawsuit. This case serves as a useful reminder of the consequences associated with the willful infringement of another's copyright. It is common for church leaders to assume that they can infringe upon religious music or literature at will since the writers and composers of such material obviously had a religious motivation and in effect have "donated" their work to the church. Not only is this assumption inappropriate, but as this case demonstrates, it can lead to statutory damages for willful infringement.[120]

Example. A federal court in Massachusetts ruled that a trade show organizer was liable for copyright infringement occurring because of the unauthorized performance of copyrighted music by 6 of 2,000 exhibitors at a national trade show. This was so despite the fact that the organizer's contract with exhibitors contained a statement instructing exhibitors to comply with copyright law. This did not shift liability. The court concluded that the organizer retained sufficient control over the exhibitors to make it responsible for their copyright infringement. Control was demonstrated by (1) the rules and regulations that the organizer had established for exhibitors; (2) agents of the organizer circulated among the exhibitors to "ensure compliance" with the rules and regulations; (3) agents of the organizer were available during the convention to address exhibitor needs and respond to complaints; and (4) the organizer had the authority to restrict exhibits that were objectionable. The court stressed that the organizer could have prohibited exhibitors from playing or performing copyrighted music, but did not. The fact that exhibitors' contracts required them to comply with the copyright law did not prevent the organizer from liability for the exhibitors' copyright infringements, since the organizer "must shoulder responsibility when the instruction is not followed." The court awarded damages of $1,000 for each violation (a total of $6,000).[121]

Example. A federal appeals court ruled that copyright infringement had occurred even though only lyrics were copied. The court observed: "Song lyrics enjoy independent copyright protection as literary works . . . and the right to print a song's lyrics is exclusively that of the copyright holder. . . . A time-honored method of facilitating singing along with music has been to furnish the singer with a printed copy of the lyrics. Copyright holders have always enjoyed exclusive rights over such copies. While projecting lyrics on a screen and producing printed copies of the lyrics, of course, have their differences, there is no reason to treat them differently for purposes of the Copyright Act." Many churches make unauthorized copies of song lyrics. Sometimes the lyrics are printed in a church bulletin. In other cases they are

---

[119] Robert Stigwood Group Limited v. O'Reilly, 346 F. Supp. 376 (D. Conn. 1972), *rev'd on other grounds*, 530 F.2d 1096 (2nd Cir. 1976), *cert. denied*, 429 U.S. 848 (1976).

[120] Meadowgreen Music Company v. Voice in the Wilderness Broadcasting, Inc., 789 F. Supp. 823 (E.D. Tex. 1992).

[121] Polygram International Publishing, Inc. v. NEVADA/TIG, Inc., 855 F. Supp. 1314 (D. Mass. 1994).

duplicated onto a transparency. In either case, or in any other case when lyrics are copied without authorization, copyright infringement has occurred. Church leaders need to understand that lyrics are entitled to copyright protection independently from the musical score.[122]

Example. *A federal appeals court ruled that a church violates the copyright law when it publicly distributes an unauthorized copy of copyrighted materials. The Church of Jesus Christ of Latter-Day Saints (the "Church") acquired a single copy of a copyrighted genealogical text and made several unauthorized copies which were distributed to the Church's "branch libraries." When the copyright owner learned of the Church's actions, it demanded that further distribution be stopped immediately. The Church recalled and destroyed many of the copies that it had made. It was concerned that nine libraries continued to possess unauthorized copies, and it wrote them each a letter asking them to locate and return any offending copies. The copyright owner visited a number of libraries, and found unauthorized copies at two locations. The owner sued the Church for copyright infringement. A federal appeals court ruled that the Church might be liable for copyright infringement. It observed: "A copyright infringement is a violation of any of the exclusive rights of the copyright owner. One of those exclusive rights is the right to distribute copies . . . of the copyrighted work to the public by sale or other transfer of ownership, or by rental, lease, or lending. Generally, as permitted by what is known as the first-sale doctrine, the copyright owner's right to distribute a copyrighted work does not prevent the owner of a lawful copy of the work from selling, renting, lending, or otherwise disposing of the lawful copy. For example, a library may lend an authorized copy of a book that it lawfully owns without violating the copyright laws. However, distributing unlawful copies of a copyrighted work does violate the copyright owner's distribution right and, as a result, constitutes copyright infringement. In order to establish distribution of a copyrighted work, a party must show that an unlawful copy was disseminated to the public." The court agreed with the copyright owner in this case that when a library "adds a work to its collection, lists the work in its index or catalog system, and makes the work available to the borrowing or browsing public, it has completed all the steps necessary for distribution to the public."[123]*

Example. *A federal appeals court ruled that Andrew Lloyd Webber may have engaged in copyright infringement of a religious song composed by Ray Repp, a composer of liturgical music. Ray Repp has written religious music for more than thirty years, and is a leading composer and performer of liturgical folk music. His music is included in many hymnals and songbooks, and has been published by the Lutheran, Episcopal, Presbyterian, and Catholic churches as well as by the Church of the Brethren. In 1978 he wrote the song "Till You." The song is liturgical in nature, and is based on passages from the Book of Luke commonly known as the "Magnificat." It has been distributed on albums and cassettes, as well as 25,000 copies of sheet music. Repp claimed that Andrew Lloyd Webber had access to this song and unlawfully copied it in writing the "Phantom Song" in his musical "The Phantom of the Opera." A federal district court dismissed the lawsuit largely on the basis of Webber's own testimony that he never heard the song, that he disliked "pop church music," and that his interest in church music was limited to the "English choral tradition." Repp appealed, and a federal appeals court reversed the district court's ruling and ordered the case to proceed to trial. The court noted that "if the two works are so strikingly similar as to preclude the possibility of independent creation, copying may be proved without a showing of access." The court continued: "While there was little, if any, evidence demonstrating access, there was considerable evidence that Phantom Song is so strikingly similar to Till You as to preclude the possibility of independent creation and to allow access to be inferred without direct proof."*

---

[122] ABKCO v. Stellar Records, 96 F.3d 60 (2nd Cir. 1996).
[123] Hotaling v. Church of Jesus Christ of Latter-Day Saints, 118 F.3d 199 (4th Cir. 1997).

In support of its conclusion the court referred to two expert musicologists who had testified that there was "no doubt" that Webber's "Phantom Song" was strikingly similar to and based upon "Till You."[124]

§ 9-05.09 — The "Religious Service" Exemption to Copyright Infringement

Key point 9-05.09. *A copyrighted musical or dramatico-musical work of a religious nature may be performed or displayed in the course or services at a place of religious worship or other religious assembly. This is an exception to the copyright owner's exclusive right to publicly perform the work.*

Section 110(3) of the Copyright Act specifies that the "performance of a nondramatic literary or musical work or of a dramatico-musical work of a religious nature, or display of a work, in the course of services at a place of worship or other religious assembly" is not an infringement of copyright. *Performance of a nondramatic literary work* means reading from a book or periodical in a nondramatic manner. Thus, for example, a copyrighted translation of the Bible can be quoted publicly in the course of religious services, as can any book or periodical of a religious nature. Without the exception contained in section 110, such readings might constitute copyright infringement since one of a copyright owner's exclusive rights is the right to perform his work publicly. Similarly, a copyrighted musical work of a religious nature can be performed in the course of services at a place of worship or other religious assembly. Therefore copyrighted hymns, solo materials, orchestrations, and choral arrangements of a religious nature may be performed in religious services. Without the exception contained in section 110, such performances might constitute copyright infringements. Dramatico-musical works of a religious nature may also be performed in the course of religious services. Such works include certain performances of sacred music that may be regarded as dramatic, such as oratorios and cantatas. Also exempted from copyright infringement are displays of works of all kinds in the course of religious services. The exemption is not intended to cover performances of secular operas, musical plays, motion pictures, and the like, even if they have an underlying religious or philosophical theme and take place in the course of religious services.

To be exempted under section 110, a performance or display must be "in the course of services," and thus activities at a place of worship that are for social, educational, fundraising, or entertainment purposes are excluded. Some performances of these kinds may be exempted under section 110(4). This section exempts from copyright infringement certain performances of nondramatic literary or musical works that are performed without admissions charge or that are performed with an admissions charge if the proceeds are used exclusively for educational, religious, or charitable purposes and not for private financial gain, unless the copyright owner has served notice of objection to the performance at least seven days before the performance.

Since the performance or display must also occur "at a place of worship or other religious assembly," the exemption would not extend to religious broadcasts or other transmissions to the public at large, even if the transmissions were sent from a place of worship. Nor would the exemption apply to the public distribution of tape recordings of religious services containing any copyrighted materials. Thus, while a copyrighted religious musical work may be performed at a religious service, publicly distributed tape recordings of the service that reproduce the copyrighted work do not constitute a performance of the work in the course of services at a place of worship and, accordingly, such recordings are not exempt under section 110. On the other hand, as long as services are being conducted before a religious assembly, the exemption would apply even if they were conducted in such places as auditoriums and outdoor theaters.

---

[124] Repp v. Webber, 132 F.3d 862 (2nd Cir. 1997).

The exemption provided by section 110 exempts only religious performances in the course of religious services from copyright infringement. The Act states that to *perform* a work means to recite or render it. Performance of a copyrighted hymn or choral arrangement thus means to sing it, and performance of a copyrighted cantata means to present it. There is therefore no license to copy a copyrighted work, such as by duplicating a single piece of music for all of the members of a choir, since duplication does not constitute a performance even though the duplicated copies may eventually be used in a performance. Only the copyright owner has the right to reproduce a copyrighted work by making copies. Similarly, a church may not assemble a booklet of copyrighted hymns or choruses (lyrics or music) for use by its members in the course of religious services since this would necessitate copying the protected works. Of course, a church can duplicate a musical work or lyrics whose copyright term has expired or that never was subject to copyright protection since such works are considered to be in the public domain.

In 1976, a publisher of religious music sued the Catholic Bishop of Chicago as representative of various churches in the archdiocese of Chicago that allegedly were infringing upon the publisher's copyrights by unauthorized duplication and use of its songs in "homemade or pirated hymnals" prepared for use in worship services. As a result of an agreement between the parties, over 80,000 "homemade" hymnals and song collections containing the allegedly infringing materials were collected from parishes in Chicago and impounded by the court. Thereafter, the publisher investigated other large dioceses and archdioceses in the United States to determine if unauthorized copying was occurring elsewhere. The publisher, claiming to have found copyright violations nationwide, notified the bishop in each area that local parishes were violating the copyright law by reproducing the publisher's copyrighted music without permission in the "pirated" songbooks. The publisher requested the bishops' assistance in determining the extent of the violations, and in voluntarily compensating it for the violations. When no assistance or compensation was offered, the publisher sought a court injunction restraining the National Conference of Catholic Bishops (NCCB) and the United States Catholic Conference (USCC) from further violations of the copyright law.[125] Specifically, the publisher alleged that the NCCB and USCC violated the law by

> [f]ailing to provide adequate direction to the dioceses and parishes concerning the proper use of [the publisher's] copyrighted materials and thereby caused, permitted and materially contributed to the publication, distribution and/or sale in many of the archdioceses and dioceses . . . of songbooks including songs which were copies largely from [the publisher's] aforementioned copyrighted work.[126]

The court, while refusing to grant an injunction, did recognize that the publisher had stated a claim for which relief could be granted.

§ 9-05.10 — Other Exceptions to Copyright Infringement

Key point 9-05.10. There are several exceptions to copyright infringement, including fair use, religious displays, nonprofit performances, and authorization from a copyright owner to use his or her work.

---

[125] F.E.L. Publications v. National Conference of Catholic Bishops, 466 F. Supp. 1034 (N.D. Ill. 1978), *aff'd*, 754 F.2d 216 (7th Cir. 1985).

[126] *Id.* at 1039.

1. FAIR USE

Section 107 of the Copyright Act specifies that

the fair use of a copyrighted work, including such use by reproduction in copies or phonorecords or by any other means specified [in section 106], for purposes such as criticism, comment, news reporting, teaching (including multiple copies for classroom use), scholarship, or research, is not an infringement of copyright. In determining whether the use made of a work in any particular case is a fair use the factors to be considered shall include--(1) the purpose and character of the use, including whether such use is of a commercial nature or is for nonprofit educational purposes; (2) the nature of the copyrighted work; (3) the amount and substantiality of the portion used in relation to the copyrighted work as a whole; and (4) the effect of the use upon the potential market for or value of the copyrighted work.

Fair use is one of the most common defenses invoked by persons charged with copyright infringement. Unfortunately, it is very difficult to define. Even section 107 does not define the term but rather recites "factors to be considered" in determining if a particular use is a fair use.

There is little doubt that many reproductions of copyrighted materials by churches will fail to constitute noninfringing fair use. Certainly any verbatim copying of an entire work will almost never constitute fair use. Examples of this type of copying include the duplication of a musical work for members of the choir, a bulletin insert, a soloist, accompanist, instrumental group, or for use as a transparency or slide. Even copying of a significant portion (in terms of either quantity or quality) of a copyrighted work ordinarily will fail to constitute noninfringing fair use. An example here would be the copying of only the lyrics (and not the melody) of a copyrighted chorus or hymn. In all of these cases, a finding of fair use will be unlikely because (1) such acts of copying constitute mere reproductions of a work in order to use it for its intrinsic purpose; (2) the nature of the work involved does not suggest a broad definition of fair use; (3) the amount of copyrighted material that is copied is significant in terms of both quantity and quality; (4) similar acts of copying by other churches would "adversely affect the market for or value of the copyrighted work." In other words, none of the four fair use factors ordinarily will support a finding of fair use.[127]

One of the most common fair use issues concerns the reproduction of copyrighted materials for educational purposes. In 1975, negotiating teams representing authors, publishers, and the "Ad Hoc Committee of Educational Institutions and Organizations on Copyright Law Revision" met informally in an attempt to reach a "meeting of the minds" as to permissible educational uses of copyrighted material. The parties reached an agreement, known as the Agreement on Guidelines for Classroom Copying in Not-For-Profit Educational

---

[127] *But cf.* New Era Publications International v. Carol Publishing Group, 904 F.2d 152 (2nd Cir. 1990). A federal appeals court ruled that the use of several extended quotations of a religious leader reproduced without permission in an uncomplimentary biography constituted fair use. The court evaluated each of the 4 "fair use factors" and concluded that all of them supported the finding of fair use. With regard to the first factor, the court concluded that biographies, and particularly critical biographies, generally constitute fair use. The proposed book used quotations from the religious leader's published writings "for the entirely legitimate purpose of making his point that [the leader] was a charlatan and his church a dangerous cult." While the author no doubt expected to make a profit, this was a secondary purpose. As to the second factor, the court again emphasized that the proposed book was a biography, and that biographies generally constitute fair use. The court observed that "biographies, of course, are fundamentally personal histories and it is both reasonable and customary for biographers to refer to and utilize earlier works dealing with the subject of the work and occasionally to quote directly from such works." The third fair use factor asks how much of the copyrighted work is quoted—both in terms of quantity and quality. The court concluded that only small portions of several works were quoted, rather than larger selections of any one work. Further, the portions quoted were not "key portions" of any of the books. Finally, the court concluded that the fourth factor led to a finding of fair use, since the biography would have little if any impact on the sale of the copyrighted works.

Institutions with Respect to Books and Periodicals. The House Report on the Copyright Act of 1976 reprinted the Agreement in full, and further noted that the guidelines set forth in the Agreement "are a reasonable interpretation of the minimum standards of fair use."[128] The educational guidelines are very restrictive, and rarely will apply to churches. They apply primarily to copying by teachers in not-for-profit educational institutions for their own research or class preparation, and also to limited copying for classroom use. There are strict requirements as to the amount of material that can be copied under the guidelines for classroom use. For example, in the case of literary works ("prose"), teachers are limited to (a) either a complete article, story or essay of less than 2,500 words, or (b) an excerpt from any prose work of not more than 1,000 words or 10 percent of the work, whichever is less, but in any event a minimum of 500 words. Other requirements apply. The guidelines also warn that "copying shall not substitute for the purchase of books, publishers' reprints or periodicals."

Shortly after the guidelines for books and periodicals were formulated, representatives of music publishers and music educators met to draft guidelines relative to music. It must be emphasized that the stated purpose of the guidelines, as with the guidelines for books and periodicals, was "to state the minimum and not the maximum standards of educational fair use." The parties acknowledged that "there may be instances in which copying which does not fall within the guidelines . . . may nonetheless be permitted under the criteria of fair use." Nevertheless, the House Report on the Copyright Act of 1976 reprinted the guidelines in full,[129] and further noted that the guidelines "are a reasonable interpretation of the minimum standards of fair use." Like the guidelines for books and periodicals, the music guidelines are very restrictive and rarely will apply to churches. Perhaps most importantly, these guidelines permit "emergency photocopying to replace purchased copies which for any reason are not available for an imminent performance provided purchased replacement copies shall be substituted in due course." Clearly, this provision will be of little use to churches, since it requires that (1) copies of music have been purchased, (2) they are unavailable for an imminent performance because they are suddenly destroyed or lost, and (3) the church purchases replacement copies in due course.

Example. A federal appeals court ruled that the use of several extended quotations of a religious leader reproduced without permission in an uncomplimentary biography constituted fair use. The court evaluated each of the 4 "fair use factors" and concluded that all of them supported the finding of fair use. With regard to the first factor, the court concluded that biographies, and particularly critical biographies, generally constitute fair use. The proposed book used quotations from the religious leader's published writings "for the entirely legitimate purpose of making his point that [the leader] was a charlatan and his church a dangerous cult." While the author no doubt expected to make a profit, this was a secondary purpose. As to the second factor, the court again emphasized that the proposed book was a biography, and that biographies generally constitute fair use. The court observed that "biographies, of course, are fundamentally personal histories and it is both reasonable and customary for biographers to refer to and utilize earlier works dealing with the subject of the work and occasionally to quote directly from such works." The third fair use factor asks how much of the copyrighted work is quoted—both in terms of quantity and quality. The court concluded that only small portions of several works were quoted, rather than larger selections of any one work. Further, the portions quoted were not "key portions" of any of the books. The court concluded that the fourth factor led to a finding of fair use, since the biography would have little if any impact on the sale of the copyrighted works.[130]

---

[128] House Report on the Copyright Act of 1976, pp. 68-70. Representatives of the American Association of University Professors and of the Association of American Law Schools strongly criticized the guidelines on the ground that they were too restrictive with respect to classroom situations at the college and graduate level.

[129] *Id.* at pp. 70-71.

[130] New Era Publications International v. Carol Publishing Group, 904 F.2d 152 (2nd Cir. 1990).

Example. A federal district court in New York ruled that a company's practice of making several copies of newsletters to distribute among key employees constituted copyright infringement. While the case involved a secular business, it will be directly relevant to churches and other religious organizations. Texaco Oil Company employs nearly 500 scientists and engineers to engage in research. To support its research activities, Texaco subscribes to several newsletters and journals. Texaco scientists frequently make photocopies of articles in these publications. There are many reasons for doing so. First, making copies "frees" the original publication to circulate among other employees. Second, copying permits employees to keep personal copies of the same materials. This enables employees to maintain their own copies of key articles for future reference, to take articles home and read them at their own convenience, and to make marginal notes on their copies instead of defacing the original. Texaco was sued by a number of publishers who claimed that this photocopying infringed upon their copyrights. Texaco insisted that its photocopying constituted non-infringing "fair use." The court concluded that Texaco scientists did engage in copyright infringement when they made copies of the newsletters and journals, and that the fair use defense was not available. The court evaluated each of the 4 "fair use factors" and concluded that they did not support a finding of fair use. With regard to the first "fair use factor," the court concluded that the purpose and character of the copying was solely to duplicate the original articles, and that this objective is simply not compatible with fair use. The court observed: "Texaco simply makes mechanical photocopies of the entirety of relevant articles. Nor is the copy of the original employed as part of a larger whole, for some new purpose. The dimensions of the original and the copy are identical. The principal purpose of Texaco's copies is to supersede the original and permit duplication, indeed, multiplication. A scientist can make a copy, to be read subsequently and kept for future reference, without preventing the circulation of the journal among coworkers. This kind of copying contributes nothing new or different to the original copyrighted work. It multiplies the number of copies." As to the second factor—the nature of the copyrighted work—the court noted that with respect to scientific newsletters and journals "circulation of such material is small, so that subscriptions must be sold at very high prices. If cheap [copies] could be freely made and sold at a fraction of the subscription price, [the publisher] would not sell many subscriptions, it could not sustain itself, and articles of this sort would simply not be published." The third fair use factor asks how much of the copyrighted work is quoted—both in terms of quantity and quality. The court noted that entire articles and issues were copied, and that the Supreme Court has ruled that reproduction of an entire copyrighted work "militates against a finding of fair use."[131] Finally, the court concluded that the fourth factor (market effect) did not support a finding of fair use. Texaco argued that it would not buy additional subscriptions to the newsletters and journals if its scientists could not make individual copies of articles, and accordingly the "market" for the newsletters and journals was not affected adversely by the copying. The court rejected this reasoning. It noted that Texaco certainly would purchase some additional subscriptions if its scientists could not make individual copies. Further, it observed that Texaco could purchase "blanket licenses" from the newsletter and journal publishers, allowing its scientists to make copies of any articles they chose for an annual fee.[132]

Example. A federal court in California ruled that an instructor who made copies of copyrighted religious books and tapes for instructional purposes was guilty of copyright infringement. The court rejected the instructor's defense of "fair use." It concluded that she failed all four fair use factors. The purpose of the copying was commercial (the copied materials were sold to students); the nature of the copyrighted works were creative and thus entitled to a higher degree of protection; the amount copied (the entire copyrighted works) was substantial; and, the impact of the copying on the copyright owner's rights was

---

[131] Sony Corporation of America v. Universal Studios, Inc., 464 U.S. 417 (1984).
[132] American Geophysical Union v. Texaco, Inc., 802 F. Supp. 1 (S.D.N.Y. 1992).

significant since the instructor's act of unauthorized copying "fulfilled the demand for the original works and [will] diminish or prejudice their potential sale." Finally, the court rejected the instructor's claim that her copying met the standards for "fair use" as set forth in the so-called "fair use guidelines" for classroom copying of educational materials. In 1975, groups of authors and publishers adopted guidelines for classroom copying in nonprofit educational institutions. The House Report on the Copyright Act of 1976 reprinted these guidelines in full, and further noted that they "are a reasonable interpretation of the minimum standards of fair use." The guidelines apply only to educational copying of literary works (books, articles, poetry, charts, etc.). Among other things, the guidelines specify that a teacher may make a single copy of a chapter from a book or an article from a periodical for use in teaching or in preparing to teach. The court observed that the instructor's copying in this case "was not restricted to one copy for her own use in teaching" and therefore was not eligible for a fair use exemption. The guidelines also permit teachers to make multiple copies of a copyrighted work for classroom use, but several restrictions apply. For example, a teacher may make multiple copies of an entire article of less than 2,500 words or an excerpt from a longer work so long as the excerpt is not more than the lesser of 1,000 words or 10 percent of the entire work. Further, the decision to use the work must be "spontaneous" in the sense that it is so close in time to the date the work is to be used that it would be unreasonable to expect a timely reply to a request for permission to reproduce it. There also are strict limitations on the number of times this exception can be used. The court concluded that this exemption did not apply: "[T]he undisputed evidence shows [that the instructor's] copying was not limited and spontaneous, but was extensive and methodical, and consisted of copying from the same author, time after time. This is clearly not within the letter or spirit of the congressional guidelines."[133]

2. RELIGIOUS DISPLAYS

Section 109(c) provides that "the owner of a particular copy lawfully made . . . is entitled, without the authority of the copyright owner, to display that copy publicly, either directly or by the projection of no more than one image at a time, to viewers present at the place where the copy is located." Section 109(d) provides further that the privilege granted under section 109(c) does not, unless authorized by the copyright owner, "extend to any person who has acquired possession of the copy or phonorecord from the copyright owner, by rental, lease, loan, or otherwise, without acquiring ownership of it."

This section is of considerable relevance to many churches, and particularly to those that use transparencies and slides of copyrighted music in the course of worship services. Recall that one of the exclusive rights of a copyright owner is the right to display a copyrighted work publicly. Section 109(c) limits this exclusive right by adopting the general principle that the *lawful owner* of a copy of a copyrighted work should be able to put the copy on public display without the consent of the copyright owner. The House Report to the Copyright Act of 1976 provides that a copyright owner's exclusive right of public display

> would not apply where the owner of a copy wishes to show it directly to the public, as in a gallery or display case, or indirectly as through an opaque projector. Where the copy itself is intended for projection, as in the case of a photographic slide, negative, or transparency, the public projection of a single image would be permitted as long as the viewers are "present at the place where the copy is located" . . . . [T]he public display of an image of a copyrighted work would not be exempted from copyright control if the copy from which the image was derived were outside the

---

[133] Bridge Publications, Inc. v. Vien, 827 F. Supp. 629 (S.D. Cal. 1993).

presence of the viewers. . . . Moreover, the exemption would extend only to public displays that are made "either directly or by the projection of no more than one image at a time."[134]

Perhaps most significantly, the House Report specifies that section 109(d) qualifies the privilege granted in section 109(b) "by making it clear that [it does] not apply to someone who merely possesses a copy or phonorecord without having acquired ownership of it. Acquisition of an object embodying a copyrighted work . . . carries with it no privilege to . . . display it publicly under section 109(b)."[135]

Section 109(c) would authorize the use of an opaque projector to display a copy of a musical work in the course of choir rehearsals or church services since the opaque projector displays an image of a lawfully made copy consisting ordinarily of either sheet music or a page in a hymnal. But if a church makes a transparency of an existing copyrighted musical work without authorization, such a transparency would not be a lawfully made copy and thus could not be displayed without infringing the owner's copyright. Section 109(b) would authorize the display of a transparency in the course of choir rehearsals or church services if the transparency constituted a lawfully made copy. This could occur in three ways. First, a transparency purchased from an authorized vendor would be a lawful copy and could be displayed publicly. Second, a transparency of a public domain work could be fabricated and displayed. Third, a transparency made with the express permission of the copyright owner would be a lawful copy.

Congress has stated that the purpose of section 109 is not only to preserve the traditional privilege of the owner of a copy to display it directly, but also to place reasonable restrictions on the ability of others to display it indirectly in such a way that the copyright owner's market for reproduction and distribution of copies would be affected.[136] Accordingly, it is likely that continued public display of a copyrighted work by a church would tend to result in a loss of the protection afforded by section 109(b). For example, if a church choir director projected a copyrighted musical arrangement on a screen for several weeks in succession in an effort to have his choir memorize the work, the repetitive display of the work might not be eligible for protection under section 109(b).

3. THE NONPROFIT PERFORMANCE EXCEPTION

Section 110(4) contains a general exception to the exclusive right of a copyright owner to publicly perform his or her copyrighted work. It provides:

[P]erformance of a nondramatic literary or musical work otherwise than in a transmission to the public, without any purpose of direct or indirect commercial advantage and without payment of any fee or other compensation for the performance to any of its performers, promoters, or organizers, [does not constitute copyright infringement] if--(A) there is no direct or indirect admission charge; or (B) the proceeds, after deducting the reasonable costs of producing the performance, are used exclusively for educational, religious, or charitable purposes and not for private financial gain, except where the copyright owner has served notice of objection to the performance under the following conditions; (i) the notice shall be in writing and signed by the copyright owner or such owner's duly authorized agent; and (ii) the notice shall be served on the person responsible for the performance at least seven days before the date of the performance, and shall state the reasons for the

---

[134] *Id.* at pp. 79-80.
[135] *Id.* at p. 80.
[136] *Id.*

objection; and (iii) the notice shall comply, in form, content, and manner of service, with require-ments that the Register of Copyrights shall prescribe by regulation.

Let's consider a number of important aspects of this important exemption.

(1) The performance must not have a profit motive.

(2) No fee or compensation can be paid to the performers (or promoters or organizers) for the perfor-mance. This condition does not prevent performers from receiving a salary for duties that include a particular performance. For example, performances by a school band do not lose the benefit of this exemption merely because the band conductor is a music teacher who receives an annual salary for performing his duties, so long as he receives no fee or payment for any particular performance.

(3) There must either be no direct or indirect admissions charge, or alternatively, if an admissions charge is assessed, then any amounts left after deducting the reasonable costs of producing the performance must be used solely for educational, religious, or charitable purposes. If there is an admissions charge, then the copyright owner is given the authority to "veto" the performance by serving upon the person responsible for the performance a notice objecting to the performance. Such a notice must be in a writing that is signed by the copyright owner; it must be served upon the person responsible for the performance at least seven days before the date of the performance; and, it must state the reasons for the objection. The impact of this provision is limited severely by the fact that section 110(4) does not require that the copyright owner be notified that his or her work is going to be performed at a nonprofit event with an admissions charge.

4. AUTHORIZATION FROM COPYRIGHT OWNER

Even if none of the exceptions to copyright infringement discussed above is clearly applicable, a particu-lar use of copyrighted material may be authorized by the copyright owner. For example, assume that a church choir director wishes to perform a particular song during a worship service, that he has a single octavo, and that he cannot obtain additional copies locally and it is too late to order copies by mail. While this "emergency need" to make unauthorized copies is not a recognized exception to copyright infringement, the director is free to contact the copyright owner directly and request permission to make copies. If permission is granted, then the making of copies will not constitute infringement.

Many music publishers have very liberal policies with respect to church music. Some music publishers grant "blanket licenses" to churches, authorizing them to make copies of any song in the publisher's repertory for an annual fee. Occasionally, several publishers and composers will assign the right to license the use of their works to a single company in return for the payment of a royalty. The company acts as a clearinghouse on behalf of the publishers and composers, granting blanket licenses to churches in exchange for a fee that is apportioned among the various publishers and composers. Perhaps the first such arrangement involving reli-gious music was implemented by F.E.L. Publications, Ltd., in the 1970s. F.E.L. obtained the rights to 1400 songs, and offered annual licenses to churches for a fee of $100. The annual license authorized a church to copy any of the listed songs. Further, the purchaser was granted the right to perform the music and text at not-for-profit performances for purposes of worship or classroom use. A church that wanted to use one of F.E.L.'s listed songs could not deal directly with any of the authors or composers whose musical works or copyrights had been exclusively assigned to F.E.L. F.E.L.'s annual license differed from traditional marketing of music in that it did not distinguish between songs, but charged a lump sum for which the licensee received the use rights to all of F.E.L.'s 1400 available compositions, even though the purchaser desired to use only a few of the more popular songs. It also differed from usual marketing practices in that it relied heavily on the licensee to patrol its own use. On the anniversary date of the license, the customer had to destroy all copies made of the virtually unlimited number allowed, unless it elected to pay F.E.L another $100 for an additional annual license.[137]

A federal district court found the F.E.L. blanket licensing scheme to be a "tying contract" that was illegal under the Sherman Antitrust Act. Specifically, the court observed that

> by obtaining assignments of the songs with the right, on behalf of the composers, to license their use for an annual fee, and by obtaining assignment of copyrights for the same purpose, F.E.L. either absolutely controls or has ownership power over copyrights to hymnals, songbooks, and the 1400 religious songs listed in its master title index. A Catholic church or parish that wants to purchase the right to copy and use a song either in one of F.E.L.'s hymnals, songbooks, or those listed in its master title index, cannot deal directly with owners of the copyrighted works listed by F.E.L. In most instances, a church or parish does not desire permission to use all of F.E.L.'s listed songs; there is no interest in all of the songs in F.E.L.'s hymnals, songbooks, and listed in the master index. The most desired are about 25 or 30 of the more popular or "blockbuster" songs. Yet, F.E.L.'s policy has always been "all or nothing"; the church or parish desiring to purchase the right to copy and use some of the listed songs has to pay for permission to use all of them. The songs are different; in many instances, the composers are different, yet purchase of the right to use the more popular has been tied by F.E.L. to the purchase of all, including the less popular. It is now well known that a tying arrangement whereby a party agrees to sell one product but only on condition that the buyer also agrees to purchase a different or tied product is prohibited by the Sherman Act, and by the Clayton Act.

The F.E.L. license was an exclusive license, meaning that a composer gave F.E.L. the sole right to market his or her song. While an in-depth discussion of the legality of such licenses is beyond the scope of this book, it should be noted that a few courts have upheld the legal validity of nonexclusive licenses. For example, ASCAP and BMI operate in much the same manner as F.E.L. in the sense that members give ASCAP and BMI the right to license the performance or broadcast of members' copyrighted works. ASCAP and BMI in turn grant blanket licenses authorizing licensees, for a flat fee, to use any work in the ASCAP or BMI repertory. ASCAP and BMI have been the target of several lawsuits alleging violation of federal antitrust laws (because of "tying arrangements"). So far, ASCAP and BMI blanket licenses have been upheld on the ground that they are nonexclusive. This means that ASCAP and BMI members retain the right to directly license their works to third parties. Churches that obtained a license from F.E.L. were not afforded this right (they granted F.E.L. the exclusive right to license the performance and reproduction of their works).

A similar approach is offered by Christian Copyright Licensing, Inc. (CCLI) of Portland, Oregon. CCLI has attempted to avoid the antitrust issue by having publishers and composers enter into nonexclusive assignments of their musical works with CCLI. While CCLI acts as a clearinghouse for several publishers and composers, the publishers and composers remain free to directly market and license their works to individual churches. Churches that purchase a blanket license from CCLI are authorized to make copies of any song in the CCLI repertory (which includes the works of several publishers and composers) for congregational use, for the duration of the license period (ordinarily one year). This means, for example, that churches are free to make bulletin inserts and transparencies. Churches also are authorized to make audio and video recordings of

---

[137] F.E.L. Publications v. Catholic Bishop of Chicago, 506 F. Supp. 1127 (N.D. Ill. 1981).

services that contain copyrighted music (in the CCLI repertory), provided that copies of the recording are distributed for less than a specified cost, and do not exceed a specified number. The making of certain musical arrangements is also permitted.

Churches must make a record of what songs they sing or perform in the course of a year, and file reports with CCLI. These reports help CCLI allocate royalties to the various publishers and composers. The fee that a church pays is based on a number of variables, including the size of the church and the kind of copying involved. In principle, the CCLI approach has the advantage of making compliance with copyright law much easier. Of course, the success of the project will depend upon four key factors--the number of songs in the CCLI repertory, the number of churches that obtain a CCLI license, the fee that CCLI will charge, and the degree of voluntary compliance by churches with the terms and conditions of the CCLI license. Churches wishing to contact CCLI may write them at the following address: Christian Copyright Licensing, Inc., 17201 NE Sacramento Street, Portland, Oregon 97230-5941. The CCLI toll-free telephone number is 1-800-234-2446. Further, note that CCLI licenses only apply to limited cases of reproduction and performance of religious musical works. They do not convey any authorization with respect to duplication of literary works (books and articles), and they do not apply in all cases to reproduction or performance of music. Accordingly, even if CCLI licenses are widely accepted, they must not be viewed as a solution to all of a church's copyright concerns.

WHAT A CCLI LICENSE DOES AND DOES NOT PERMIT

A CCLI license DOES authorize a church to do the following:

- Print songs and hymns in bulletins, programs, liturgies, and songsheets.

- Create your own customized songbooks or hymnals.

- Create overhead transparencies, slides, or use any other format whereby songs are visually projected, such as computer graphics and projection.

- Arrange, print and copy your own arrangements, vocal and instrumental, of songs where no published version is available.

- Record your worship services by audio or video means, provided you only record "live" music (instrumental and vocal). Accompaniment "tracks" cannot be reproduced. You may also charge up to $4.00 each for audio tapes (cassettes) and $12.00 each for video tapes.

A CCLI license DOES NOT authorize a church to do the following:

- Photocopy or duplicate octavos, cantatas, musicals, handbell music, keyboard arrangements, vocal scores, orchestrations, or other instrumental works.

- Translate songs from English into another language. This can only be done with the approval of the respective publisher.

- Rent, sell, or lend copies made under the license to groups outside the church or to other churches. (It is permissible to distribute tapes to shut-ins, missionaries, or others outside the church.)

- Assign or transfer the license to another church or group without CCLI's approval.

---

§ 9-06   Government Investigations

As has been noted elsewhere,[138] the IRS possesses broad authority to inspect church records. This authority has been upheld on numerous occasions. Government investigations may be initiated by other federal agencies as well. For example, the Postal Service has broad authority to investigate "any scheme or artifice to defraud, or . . . obtaining money or property by means of false or fraudulent pretenses, representations, or promises" in connection with the use of the mail.[139] The Federal Communications Commission is given broad authority to investigate complaints regarding a broadcast licensee's performance, and the Equal Employment Opportunity Commission is invested with authority to investigate the compliance of religious organizations with the Civil Rights Act of 1964.

§ 9-07   Judicial Resolution of Church Disputes

Key point 9-07. The first amendment allows civil courts to resolve internal church disputes so long as they can do so without interpreting doctrine or polity.

1. Decisions of the United States Supreme Court

In *Watson v. Jones*,[140] the United States Supreme Court developed a framework for the judicial review of ecclesiastical disputes that has persisted essentially unchanged until today, more than a century later. The Court began its landmark opinion by acknowledging that "religious organizations come before us in the same attitude as other voluntary associations for benevolent or charitable purposes, and their rights of property, or of contract, are equally under the protection of the law, and the actions of their members subject to its restraints." Though recognizing in principle the authority of civil courts to address the "rights of property, or of contract" of ecclesiastical organizations or officers, the Court proceeded to severely limit this authority. Most importantly, the Court held that "whenever the *questions of discipline, or of faith, of ecclesiastical rule, custom, or law* have been decided by the highest church judicatory to which the matter has been carried, the legal tribunals must accept such decisions as final, and as binding on them . . . ." The Court explained this fundamental limitation on the authority of the courts to review ecclesiastical controversies pertaining to faith or discipline as follows:

> All who unite themselves to such a body do so with an implied consent to its government, and are bound to submit to it. But it would be a vain consent and would lead to the total subversion of such religious bodies, if anyone aggrieved by one of their decisions could appeal to the secular courts and have them reversed. It is of the essence of these religious unions, and of their right to establish tribunals for the decision of questions arising among themselves, that those decisions should be binding in all cases of ecclesiastical cognizance subject only to such appeals as the organism itself provides for.

---

[138] *See* § 6-03, *supra.*

[139] 18 U.S.C. § 1341.

[140] 80 U.S. 679, 722 (1871) [hereinafter cited as *Watson*]. *See also* Bernard, *Churches, Members, and the Role of the Courts: Toward a Contractual Analysis*, 51 Notre Dame Lawyer 545 (1976); Dusenberg, *Jurisdiction of Civil Courts over Religious Issues*, 20 Ohio St. L.J. 508 (1959); Ellman, *Driven from the Tribunal: Judicial Resolution of Internal Church Disputes*, 69 Cal. L. Rev. 1380 (1981); C. Esbeck, *Tort Claims Against Churches and Ecclesiastical Officers: The First Amendment Considerations*, 89 W. Va. L. Rev. 22-23 (1986); Gilkey, *The Judicial Role in Intra-Church Disputes Under the Constitutional Guarantees Relating to Religion*, 75 W. Va. L. Rev. 105 (1972); Patton, *The Civil Courts and the Churches*, 54 U. Pa. L. Rev. 391 (1906); Young and Tigges, *Into the Religious Thicket—Constitutional Limits on Civil Court Jurisdiction over Ecclesiastical Disputes*, 47 Ohio St. L.J. 475 (1986).

Nor do we see that justice would be likely to be promoted by submitting those decisions to review in the ordinary judicial tribunals. Each of these large influential bodies . . . has a body of constitutional and ecclesiastical law of its own, to be found in their written organic laws, their books of discipline, in their collections of precedents, in their usage and customs, which to each constitute a system of ecclesiastical law and religious faith that tasks the ablest minds to become familiar with. It is not to be supposed that the judges of the civil courts can be as competent in the ecclesiastical law and religious faith of all these bodies as the ablest men in each are in reference to their own. It would therefore be an appeal from the more learned tribunal in the law which should decide the case, to one which is less so.[141]

Similarly, the Court observed:

The decisions of ecclesiastical courts, like every other judicial tribunal, are final, as *they are the best judges of what constitutes an offense against the word of God and the discipline of the church.* Any other than those courts must be incompetent judges of matters of faith, discipline, and doctrine; and civil courts, if they should be so unwise as to attempt to supervise their judgments on matters which come within their jurisdiction would only involve themselves in a sea of uncertainty and doubt which would do anything but improve either religion or good morals.[142]

The Court based this fundamental limitation on civil court review of ecclesiastical controversies involving faith or discipline upon jurisdictional grounds:

But it is a very different thing where a subject matter of dispute, strictly and purely ecclesiastical in its character—a matter over which the civil courts exercise no jurisdiction, *a matter which concerns theological controversy, church discipline, ecclesiastical government, or the conformity of the members of the church to the standards of morals required of them*—becomes the subject of its action. It may be said here, also, that *no jurisdiction has been conferred upon the tribunal* to try the particular case before it, or that, in its judgment, it exceeds the powers conferred upon it, or that the laws of the church do not authorize the particular form of proceeding adopted; and, in a sense often used in the courts, all of those may be said to be questions of jurisdiction. But it is easy to see that if the civil courts are to inquire into all these matters, the whole subject of doctrinal theology, the usages and customs, the written laws, and fundamental organization of every religious denomination may, and must, be examined into with minuteness and care, for they would become, in almost every case, the criteria by which the validity of the ecclesiastical decree would be determined in the civil court. This principle would deprive these bodies of the right of construing their own church laws . . . and would, in effect, transfer to the civil courts where property rights were concerned the decision of all ecclesiastical questions.[143]

The *Watson* ruling may be summarized as follows: (1) the civil courts may *never* intervene in ecclesiastical disputes involving questions of ecclesiastical doctrine, polity, discipline, practice, or administration; (2) civil courts may in some cases adjudicate the "rights of property, or contracts" of ecclesiastical organizations and officers; and (3) civil courts have no jurisdiction to adjudicate the "rights of property, or of contracts" if matters of ecclesiastical faith, discipline, or practice are implicated in the controversies and an ecclesiastical body has authority to determine the issue. The third consideration was based on three additional factors: (a) civil judges are incompetent to resolve questions of religious doctrine; (b) church members have voluntarily

---

[141] *Id.* at 729.
[142] *Id.* at 732.
[143] *Id.* at 733 (emphasis added).

joined the church and have given their implied consent to its internal governance; and (c) the structure of our political system requires a severe limit on involvement by the civil courts in the affairs of religious bodies so as to secure religious liberty.

The *Watson* case remains uncompromised today. Indeed, in 1952 the Supreme Court elevated it to the level of first amendment jurisprudence.[144]

One year after the *Watson* ruling, the Supreme Court again emphasized that it had "*no power to revise or question ordinary acts of church discipline*, or of excision from membership," nor to "decide who ought to be members of the church, nor whether the excommunicated have been regularly or irregularly cut off."[145]

In 1928, the Supreme Court observed, in a case involving the authority of an ecclesiastical organization to discipline a minister:

> Because the appointment is a canonical act, it is the function of the church authorities to determine what the essential qualifications of a [clergyman] are and whether the candidate possesses them. In the absence of fraud, collusion, or arbitrariness, the decisions of the proper church tribunals on matters purely ecclesiastical, although affecting civil rights, are accepted in litigation before the secular courts as conclusive, because the parties . . . made them so by contract or otherwise.[146]

The Court's ruling in *Gonzalez* is significant, for it is a specific prohibition of civil court interference in the determinations of ecclesiastical bodies regarding the qualifications of clergy—*even if "civil rights" are involved*—absent fraud, collusion, or arbitrariness. As will be noted later, the Supreme Court subsequently eliminated arbitrariness and severely limited fraud and collusion as available grounds for civil court review.

In 1952, the Supreme Court in the *Kedroff* ruling[147] reaffirmed its pronouncement in *Watson* that civil courts have no authority to resolve "*questions of discipline, or of faith, or of ecclesiastical rule, custom, or law.*" The Court, referring to the *Watson* case, observed that "the opinion radiates, however, a spirit of freedom for religious organizations, and independence from secular control or manipulation, in short, *power to decide for themselves, free from state interference, matters of church government as well as those of faith and doctrine.* Freedom to select the clergy . . . we think must now be said to have federal constitutional protection as a part of the free exercise of religion against state interference." Significantly, the Court also observed:

> There are occasions when civil courts must draw lines between the responsibilities of church and state for the disposition or use of property. *Even in those cases when the property right follows as an incident from decisions of the church custom or law on ecclesiastical issues, the church rule controls.* This under our Constitution necessarily follows in order that there may be free exercise of religion.[148]

The *Kedroff* decision is important since it specifically holds that alleged deprivations or interference with "property rights" cannot serve as a basis for civil court review of ecclesiastical determinations regarding the qualifications or dismissal of clergy where "the property right follows as an incident from decisions of the

---

[144] Kedroff v. St. Nicholas Cathedral, 344 U.S. 94 (1952) [hereinafter cited as *Kedroff*].
[145] Bouldin v. Alexander, 82 U.S. (15 Wall.) 131, 139-40 (1872) (emphasis added).
[146] Gonzalez v. Roman Catholic Archbishop, 280 U.S. 1, 16-17 (1928) (Justice Brandeis) (emphasis added) [hereinafter cited as *Gonzalez*].
[147] 344 U.S. 94 (1952).
[148] *Id.* at 120 (emphasis added).

church . . . on ecclesiastical issues." This important language should be read together with the Court's statement in the *Gonzalez* case that "the decisions of the proper church tribunals [on matters regarding the qualifications of clergy], *although affecting civil rights*, are accepted in litigation before the secular courts as conclusive," except under extraordinary circumstances described below. These two rulings indicate that dismissed clergy will not be able to have their dismissals reviewed by the civil courts merely because they claim that their civil or property rights have been violated.

In 1969, the Supreme Court reaffirmed the principle of judicial nonintervention in church disputes involving ecclesiastical discipline, faith, or practice, citing with approval *Watson, Gonzalez,* and *Kedroff.*[149] The Court did acknowledge, however, that there is room for "marginal civil court review" of ecclesiastical controversies involving the disposition of *church real estate* following a church schism. Nevertheless, even this narrow review is "severely circumscribed" by the first amendment, since the civil courts have "*no* role in determining ecclesiastical questions in the process of resolving church property disputes." The Court added:

> First amendment values are plainly jeopardized when church property litigation is made to turn on the resolution by civil courts of controversies over religious doctrine and practice. If civil courts undertake to resolve such controversies in order to adjudicate the property dispute, the hazards are ever present of inhibiting the free development of religious doctrine and implicating secular interests in matters of purely ecclesiastical concern. Because of these hazards, the first amendment enjoins the employment of organs of government for essentially religious purposes; the amendment therefore commands civil courts to decide church property disputes without resolving underlying controversies over religious doctrine.[150]

In 1976, the Supreme Court again addressed an ecclesiastical controversy.[151] In *Serbian,* however, this issue was not control of church property, but rather the legal right of a defrocked bishop to challenge his expulsion in civil court. The Illinois Supreme Court, citing *Gonzalez,*[152] had reversed the decision of the Serbian Eastern Orthodox Diocese expelling the bishop. The court reasoned that the Diocese had not followed its own bylaws and accordingly its decision to expel was "arbitrary" and, on the basis of *Gonzalez,* subject to civil court review. In reversing the Illinois Supreme Court's ruling, the United States Supreme Court observed:

> The conclusion of the Illinois Supreme Court that the decisions of the [Diocese] were "arbitrary" was grounded upon an inquiry that persuaded the Illinois Supreme Court that the [Diocese] had not followed its own laws and procedures in arriving at those decisions. We have concluded that whether or not there is room for "marginal civil court review" under the narrow rubrics of "fraud" or "collusion" when church tribunals act in bad faith for secular purposes, no "arbitrariness" exception—in the sense of an inquiry whether the decisions of the highest ecclesiastical tribunal of a hierarchical church complied with church laws and regulations—is consistent with the constitutional mandate that civil courts are bound to accept the decisions of the highest judicatories of a religious organization of hierarchical polity on matters of discipline, faith, internal organization, or ecclesiastical rule, custom or law. For civil courts to analyze whether the ecclesiastical actions of a church judicatory are in that sense "arbitrary" must inherently entail inquiry into the

---

[149] Presbyterian Church v. Mary Elizabeth Blue Hull Memorial Presbyterian Church, 393 U.S. 440 (1969) [hereinafter cited as *Presbyterian Church*].

[150] *Id.* at 449.

[151] Serbian Eastern Orthodox Diocese v. Milivojevich, 423 U.S. 696 (1976) [hereinafter cited as *Serbian*].

[152] *See* note 146, *supra,* and accompanying text.

procedures that canon or ecclesiastical law supposedly require the church adjudicatory to follow, or else into the substantive criteria by which they are supposedly to decide the ecclesiastical question. But this is exactly the inquiry that the first amendment prohibits . . . .[153]

The Court rejected an attempt by a defrocked bishop to force civil court review on the basis of an alleged deprivation of a "property right," since the alleged property right was incidental to the underlying issue of ecclesiastical discipline and "the civil courts must accept that consequence as the incidental effect of an ecclesiastical determination that is not subject to judicial abrogation, having been reached by the final church judiciary in which authority to make that decision resides."

Serbian is significant for the following reasons: (a) it reaffirmed the rule of judicial nonintervention in cases of ecclesiastical discipline over which an ecclesiastical organization has jurisdiction; (b) it rejected the claim that civil courts can justify intervention in cases of ecclesiastical discipline on the basis of alleged deprivation of "property rights," if the alleged deprivation is a mere incidental effect of the underlying disciplinary process; and (c) it categorically rejected civil court review of ecclesiastical disciplinary proceedings on the basis of "arbitrariness," and *defined arbitrariness as a failure by a church to follow its own rules and procedures.* The Court based these conclusions on the following grounds: (a) civil courts are forbidden by the first amendment from engaging in "searching inquiry" into the organizational documents of religious organizations; (b) civil judges have no training, experience, or expertise in matters of ecclesiastical law or governance; and (c) "constitutional concepts of due process, involving secular notions of fundamental fairness or impermissible objectives," are not relevant to matters of ecclesiastical cognizance which typically "are reached and are to be accepted as matters of faith whether or not rational or measurable by objective criteria."

The most recent decision of the Supreme Court came in 1979.[154] Like *Presbyterian Church*, *Jones* involved a dispute over control of church real estate following a schism. The Court reaffirmed the long-established principle that "the first amendment prohibits civil courts from resolving church property disputes on the basis of religious doctrine and practice," and that "the amendment requires that civil courts defer to the resolution of issues of religious doctrine or polity by the highest court of a hierarchical church organization." The Court then specifically held that *questions of church membership and ecclesiastical discipline are matters of ecclesiastical doctrine and accordingly are beyond the reach of the civil courts:*

> Issues of church doctrine and polity pervade the provisions of the [Presbyterian] Book of Church Order dealing with the identity of a local congregation. The local church corporation consists of "all the communing members on the active role" of the church. The "active role," in turn, is composed "of those admitted to the Lord's table who are active in the church's life and work." The session is given the power "to suspend or exclude from the Lord's Supper those found delinquent, according to the Rules of Discipline." The session is subject to "the review and control" of the Presbytery's general authority to "order whatever pertains to the spiritual welfare of the churches under its care."[155]

Clearly, on the basis of this language, any determination by a church or denomination agency regarding the qualifications or lack of qualifications of a minister goes to the very essence of religious doctrine, and is not reviewable by a civil court. This result is not affected by a dismissed minister's claim that his or her civil, contract, or property rights were abridged as a result of the disciplinary process. To hold otherwise would be to ignore a

---

[153] *Id.* at 712-713.
[154] Jones v. Wolf, 443 U.S. 595 (1979) [hereinafter cited as *Jones*].
[155] *Id.* at 609 n.7.

century of Supreme Court precedent. The Court in *Jones* did acknowledge that in the context of disputes over *church property*, a civil court may engage in limited review so long as there is "no consideration of doctrinal matters, whether the ritual and liturgy or worship or the tenets of faith." For example, civil courts can resolve church property disputes on the basis of "neutral principles of law" involving no inquiries into religious doctrine, polity, or practice. One authority has aptly summarized *Jones* and its antecedents as follows:

> In short, civil authorities must always forego questions which are essentially religious as a matter of noninterference in the affairs of religious associations. Included in such matters are doctrine, discipline, appointment and removal of religious personnel, church polity, internal administration, and religious practice. In disputes principally over control of real estate, however, states may adopt a neutral principles of law approach so long as civil judges do not become entangled in questions essentially religious in the course of the rule's application.[156]

In summary, the United States Supreme Court over the past century has consistently held that the civil courts are prohibited from interfering in ecclesiastical controversies involving issues of ecclesiastical doctrine, polity, practice, or administration. Determinations of ecclesiastical organizations regarding the standards of church membership or the qualifications of clergy indisputably involve such intrinsically ecclesiastical concerns and accordingly are not reviewable by the civil courts. This is so even if an ecclesiastical determination results in an alleged deprivation of property, contract, or civil rights, and even if the ecclesiastical process was arbitrary in the sense that it was not in accordance with the church organization's own internal rules and procedures. While the Supreme Court has repudiated its 1928 ruling in *Gonzalez* to the extent that "arbitrariness" is no longer an available basis for civil court review of ecclesiastical determinations, it has left open "fraud" and "collusion" as possible grounds for review. However, the Court in *Serbian* severely limited the availability of "fraud and collusion" as grounds for civil court review by limiting their use to those occasions "when church tribunals act in bad faith for secular purposes." The mere assertion of fraud or collusion thus cannot invoke civil court review of ecclesiastical determinations regarding church discipline. A plaintiff also must establish that the alleged fraud or collusion was motivated by "bad faith for secular purposes." It would be extraordinary indeed to ever find a religious organization guilty of such conduct, and, understandably, none has ever been found to be so. The Supreme Court in *United States v. Ballard*,[157] anticipating the *Serbian* limitation, specifically held that frauds perpetrated by religious organizations are not redressable by the civil courts when matters of "religious faith or experience" are involved or implicated. The Court observed:

> Men may believe what they cannot prove. They may not be put to the proof of their religious doctrines or beliefs. Religious experiences which are as real as life to some may be incomprehensible to others. Yet the fact that they may be beyond the ken of mortals does not mean that they can be made suspect before the law. Many take their gospel from the New Testament. But it would hardly be supposed that they could be tried before a jury charged with the duty of determining whether those teachings contained false representations. The miracles of the New Testament, the Divinity of Christ, life after death, the power of prayer, are deep in the religious convictions of many. If one could be sent to jail because a jury in a hostile environment found those teachings false, little indeed would be left of religious freedom.[158]

Similarly, no court has ever found an ecclesiastical organization guilty of the *Serbian* definition of "collusion."

---

[156] C. Esbeck, *Tort Claims Against Churches and Ecclesiastical Officers: The First Amendment Considerations*, 89 W. Va. L. Rev. 22-23 (1986).

[157] 322 U.S. 78 (1944).

[158] *Id.* at 86-87.

2. Decisions of State and Lower Federal Courts

State and lower federal courts have been asked to intervene in a wide variety of internal church disputes. Generally, such courts have followed the analysis developed by the United States Supreme Court in the cases summarized above. To be sure, some state and lower federal court decisions have deviated from the Supreme Court's analysis, but such cases ordinarily can be explained on the ground that they preceded some of the key Supreme Court decisions. Many state and lower courts have deviated from the Supreme Court's analysis because of unfamiliarity or ignorance.

The response by state and lower federal courts to many of the more common forms of internal church dispute are discussed fully in other sections of this text. Examples include: (1) church property disputes following a schism within a local church;[159] (2) clergy dismissals;[160] (3) discipline and dismissal of church members;[161] personal injuries resulting from the negligence or misconduct of church workers;[162] (5) sexual seduction of counselees by clergy;[163] (6) removal of officers and directors;[164] (7) procedural irregularities in church business meetings;[165] (8) access by members to church records;[166] (9) dismissal of church employees;[167] (10) clergy malpractice;[168] and (11) personal liability of officers and directors.[169]

§ 9-08   Political Activities by Churches and Other Religious Organizations

Section 501(c)(3) of the Internal Revenue Code does not allow churches and other organizations exempt from federal income tax to participate in political campaigns or to engage in substantial efforts to influence legislation.

Resource. The prohibition of lobbying and campaign activities by churches is addressed fully in R. Hammar, The Church and Clergy Tax Guide (published annually by the publisher of this text).

§ 9-09 Bankruptcy Law

Key point 9-09. Bankruptcy trustees are prohibited by the federal Religious Liberty and Charitable Donation Protection Act from recovering contributions made by bankrupt debtors to a church or other charity prior to declaring bankruptcy, unless the contributions were made with an intent to defraud creditors. This protection extends to any contribution amounting to less than 15 percent of a debtor's gross annual income, or more if the debtor can establish a regular pattern of giving more. In addition, the Act bars bankruptcy courts from rejecting a bankruptcy plan because it allows the debtor to continue making contributions to a church or charity. Again, this protection applies to debtors whose bankruptcy plan calls for making charitable contributions of less than 15 percent of their gross annual income, or more if they can prove a pattern of giving more.

---

[159] *See* chapter 7, *supra.*
[160] *See* § 2-04, *supra.*
[161] *See* § 6-10, *supra.*
[162] *See* chapter 10, *infra.*
[163] *See* § 4-11, *supra.*
[164] *See* § 6-06.4, *supra.*
[165] *See* § 6-12.1, *supra.*
[166] *See* § 6-03.1, *supra.*
[167] *See* § 8-04, *supra.*
[168] *See* § 4-05, *supra.*
[169] *See* § 6-07, *supra.*

In the past, churches were hurt by federal bankruptcy law in two ways. First, many courts ruled that bankruptcy trustees could recover contributions made to a church by a bankrupt donor within a year of filing a bankruptcy petition. Second, church members who declared bankruptcy were not allowed by some bankruptcy courts to continue making contributions to their church. These harmful restrictions were eliminated last year when Congress enacted the Religious Liberty and Charitable Donation Protection Act. The Act, which is actually an amendment to the bankruptcy code, provides significant protection to churches as well as to church members who file for bankruptcy. This section will review the background of the Act, explain its key provisions, and demonstrate its application with practical examples.

1. AUTHORITY OF BANKRUPTCY TRUSTEES TO RECOVER CHARITABLE CONTRIBUTIONS

background

Section 548(a) of the bankruptcy code authorizes a bankruptcy trustee to "avoid" or recover two kinds of "fraudulent transfers" made by bankrupt debtors within a year of filing for bankruptcy:

(1) Intent to defraud. Section 548(a)(1) gives a bankruptcy trustee the legal authority to recover "any transfer of an interest of the debtor in property . . . that was made or incurred on or within one year before the date of the filing of the petition, if the debtor voluntarily or involuntarily made such transfer or incurred such obligation with actual intent to hinder, delay, or defraud any entity to which the debtor was or became, on or after the date that such transfer was made or such obligation was incurred, indebted."

(2) Transfers of cash or property for less than "reasonably equivalent value." Section 548(a)(2) gives a bankruptcy trustee the legal authority to recover "any transfer of an interest of the debtor in property . . . that was made or incurred on or within one year before the date of the filing of the petition, if the debtor voluntarily or involuntarily . . . received less than a reasonably equivalent value in exchange for such transfer or obligation and was insolvent on the date that such transfer was made or such obligation was incurred, or became insolvent as a result of such transfer or obligation . . . or intended to incur, or believed that the debtor would incur, debts that would be beyond the debtor's ability to pay as such debts matured."

In the past, many bankruptcy trustees contacted churches, demanding that they return donations made by bankrupt debtors within a year of filing for bankruptcy. They argued that charitable contributions made by bankrupt debtors to a church are for less than "reasonably equivalent value," and therefore can be recovered by bankruptcy trustees under the second type of "fraudulent transfer" mentioned above. Donors and churches protested such efforts. They insisted that donors *do* receive valuable benefits in exchange for their contributions, such as preaching, teaching, sacraments, and counseling. Not so, countered bankruptcy trustees. These benefits would be available whether or not a donor gives anything, and so it cannot be said that a donor is receiving "reasonably equivalent value" in exchange for a contribution. Many courts agreed with this logic, and ordered churches to turn over contributions made by bankrupt debtors. This created a hardship for many churches. After all, most churches had already spent the debtor's contributions before being contacted by the bankruptcy trustee, and so "returning" them (especially if they were substantial) was often difficult.

Beginning in 1993, several events occurred that culminated in the enactment of the Religious Freedom and Charitable Donation Protection Act of 1998. Here is a brief summary of what happened.

round 1—the first Young case

In 1993, a federal district court in Minnesota ruled that a church had to turn over contributions made by a couple to their church within a year of filing a bankruptcy petition.[170] The debtors (husband and wife) contributed a total of $13,450 to their church before filing a chapter 7 bankruptcy petition. The bankruptcy trustee opposed the bankruptcy petition on the ground that the contributions were for less than reasonably equivalent value. The court agreed, and concluded that the trustee could recover the contributions so long as the first amendment guaranty of religious freedom was not violated. The court looked to the Supreme Court's decision in *Employment Division v. Smith*[171] in which the Court ruled that a "general law of neutral applicability" can be applied to religious practices without offending the first amendment even if the law is not supported by a "compelling government interest." This ruling repudiated the Supreme Court's longstanding position that a law that offends religious freedom is valid only if it is supported by a compelling government interest. The Court ruled that its prior decisions "have consistently held that the right of free exercise does not relieve an individual of the obligation to comply with a valid and neutral law of general applicability on the ground that the law proscribes (or prescribes) conduct that his religion prescribes (or proscribes)."

The bankruptcy court concluded that the *Smith* decision stood for the proposition that "an individual cannot escape a valid and neutral law of general applicability by merely asserting that the law violates his or her religious beliefs." It further observed that a bankruptcy trustee's authority to deny bankruptcy relief on the basis of "fraudulent transfers" for less than reasonably equivalent value was "a neutral law of general applicability," and that "[t]he purpose of the statute is to enlarge the pool of funds for creditors by recovering gratuitous transfers made on the eve of bankruptcy by insolvent debtors." The court, therefore, dismissed the church's constitutional challenge, and allowed the trustee to recover the debtors' contributions from the church.

round 2—the Religious Freedom Restoration Act

In 1990, the United States Supreme Court ruled that a "neutral law of general applicability" that burdens the exercise of religion need not be supported by a "compelling governmental interest" to be permissible under the first amendment's free exercise of religion clause.[172] In so ruling, the Court repudiated a quarter of a century of established precedent and severely diluted this basic constitutional protection. The results were predictable. Scores of lower federal courts and state courts sustained laws and governmental practices that directly restricted religious practices. In many of these cases, the courts based their actions directly on the *Smith* case, suggesting that the result would have been different had it not been for that decision.

Congress responded to the *Smith* case by enacting the Religious Freedom Restoration Act of 1993. The Act restored the "compelling interest test" through the following provision: "Government shall not burden a person's exercise of religion even if the burden results from a rule of general applicability [unless] it demonstrates that application of the burden to the person (1) is in furtherance of a compelling governmental interest; and (2) is the least restrictive means of furthering that compelling governmental interest." In explaining this provision, the Senate Judiciary Committee commented that the Act "permits government to burden the exercise of religion only if it demonstrates a compelling state interest and that the burden in question is the least restrictive means of furthering the interest."

---

[170] In re Young, 152 B.R. 939 (D. Minn. 1993).
[171] 494 U.S. 872 (1990).
[172] *Id.*

round 3—the second Young case

The church and debtors involved in the original *Young* case (discussed above) appealed the district court's ruling to a federal appeals court. The appeals court acknowledged that the debtors received valuable benefits in exchange for their contributions to the church, including preaching, teaching, and counseling. But, it concluded that these benefits were provided to members whether or not they tithed, and as a result they were not provided "in exchange" for the debtors' contributions. Therefore, under the bankruptcy law the trustee had the authority to recover the debtors' contributions from the church. However, the court further concluded that allowing the trustee to do so would violate the rights of the church and debtors under the newly enacted Religious Freedom Restoration Act. This Act, as noted above, specifies that the government may not "substantially burden" a person's religious practices unless a *compelling governmental interest* exists. In effect, the Act overturned the Supreme Court's decision in the *Smith* case (discussed above). The court noted that the debtors believed in tithing, and faithfully tithed up until the time they filed for bankruptcy. It concluded that the practice of tithing was a religious practice that would be substantially burdened if the trustee could recover the debtors' tithes since it would discourage persons from tithing to their church if they suspected that they might file for bankruptcy within the next year. Further, the court concluded that there was no compelling governmental interest that would justify the substantial burden on the practice of tithing.[173]

round 4—the Supreme Court strikes down the Religious Freedom Restoration Act

In 1997, the United States Supreme Court struck down the Religious Freedom Restoration Act on the ground that Congress exceeded its authority in enacting the law.[174] The Court began its opinion by noting that the federal government "is one of enumerated powers." That is, each branch (legislative, executive, judicial) can only do those things specifically authorized by the Constitution. The Court concluded that nothing in the Constitution gave Congress the authority to enact a law overturning the Supreme Court's interpretation of the first amendment in the *Smith* case. The Court acknowledged that section 5 of the fourteenth amendment gave Congress the authority to "enforce" the provisions of the first amendment, and therefore Congress can enact legislation "enforcing the constitutional right to the free exercise of religion." However, the Court then observed that "[l]egislation which alters the meaning of the free exercise [of religion] clause cannot be said to be enforcing the clause. Congress does not enforce a constitutional right by changing what the right is."

round 5—the third Young case

Following its decision in the *City of Boerne* case striking down the Religious Freedom Restoration Act, the Supreme Court vacated and remanded the federal appeals court ruling in the second *Young* case summarized above. Presumably, the Court assumed that its decision would cause the appeals court to reverse its earlier decision that had been based squarely on the Religious Freedom Restoration Act. On remand, the appeals court reaffirmed its earlier decision rejecting the bankruptcy trustee's attempt to compel the church to return the bankrupt debtors' tithes. The court based its decision on a provision in the Constitution giving Congress broad authority to enact bankruptcy laws. It observed:

> We conclude that RFRA [the Religious Freedom Restoration Act] is an appropriate means by Congress to modify the United States bankruptcy laws. In attempting to [recover the [debtors'] tithes to the church, the trustee relied on an affirmative act of Congress defining which transac-

---

[173] In re Young, 82 F.3d 1407 (8th Cir. 1996).
[174] City of Boerne v. Flores, 521 U.S. 507 (1997).

tions of debtors in bankruptcy may be [recovered]. RFRA, however, has effectively amended the Bankruptcy Code, and has engrafted the additional clause to section 548 . . . that a recovery that places a substantial burden on a debtor's exercise of religion will not be allowed unless it is the least restrictive means to satisfy a compelling governmental interest. The trustee has not contended, and we can conceive of no argument to support the contention, that Congress is incapable of amending the legislation that it has passed. Neither can we accept any argument that allowing the discharge of a debt in bankruptcy and preventing the recovery of a transfer made by insolvent debtors is beyond the authority of Congress. We therefore conclude that Congress had the authority to enact RFRA and make it applicable to the law of bankruptcy. *In re Young, 141 F.3d 854 (8th Cir. 1998).*

The third *Young* case is controlling (unless later reversed by the Supreme Court) in the eighth federal circuit, which includes the states of Arkansas, Iowa, Minnesota, Missouri, Nebraska, North Dakota, and South Dakota. In these states, a bankruptcy trustee cannot recover tithes made by bankrupt debtors to their church—so long as the debtors consider tithing to be an important religious practice that would be "substantially burdened" if bankruptcy trustees had the power to recover debtors' contributions. However, this was a very limited ruling: (1) it only applied in states in the eighth federal circuit; (2) it only applied to debtors who regarded tithing as a central religious practice; and (3) it is a controversial ruling that probably will be reversed at a later time by the Supreme Court.

round 6—the Religious Freedom and Charitable Donation Protection Act of 1998

In response to the developments summarized above, the Religious Freedom and Charitable Donation Protection Act was introduced in the Senate by Senator Grassley and in the House of Representatives by Congressman Packard. In introducing the House bill, Congressman Packard observed:

Mr. Speaker, how much of the work done by your church or favorite charity depends on the generous donations of parishioners and contributors like yourself? Did you know that creditors can take already donated money from them because current bankruptcy law allows them to do so? It's unbelievable, but it's true. In a recent case, a United States Federal Bankruptcy Trustee brought an action against the Crystal Evangelical Free Church of New Hope, Minnesota. In doing so, this unprecedented case reinterpreted the Bankruptcy Code to mean that if an individual gives money to a nonprofit group within one year of declaring bankruptcy, creditors can come after the group to re-claim this money. Why? Because an individual must receive something of "reasonable equivalent value" in return for a monetary donation. Mr. Speaker, current law essentially says that if an individual has filed for bankruptcy, he cannot simply donate money to a charitable organization or to the church. However, because the Bankruptcy Code allows for certain "entertainment exemptions," taking a luxury vacation, purchasing liquor, buying a new car, or making 1-900 calls to psychics, are all reasonable expenditures. This case outraged me and I decided to do something about it. I introduced legislation in early October to protect certain charitable contributions. Known as the *Religious Liberty and Charitable Donation Protection Act,* this legislation will amend U.S. Code to protect our nation's churches and charities from the hands of creditors. Mr. Speaker, H.R. 2604, the *Religious Liberty and Charitable Donation Protection Act,* will allow your church or favorite charity to continue to thrive and prosper. Donations received in good faith from individuals will not be taken from their pockets by creditors. I encourage all of my colleagues to co-sponsor this important legislation. As the holidays quickly approach, we must work to address the needs of our churches, charities and the less fortunate who rely on their vital services. H.R. 2604 will do just that.

The key to the Act was the following provision, which is an amendment to section 548(a)(2) of the bankruptcy code:

A transfer of a charitable contribution to a qualified religious or charitable entity or organization shall not be considered to be a transfer [subject to recovery by a bankruptcy trustee] in any case in which—(A) the amount of that contribution does not exceed 15 percent of the gross annual income of the debtor for the year in which the transfer of the contribution is made; or (B) the contribution made by a debtor exceeded the percentage amount of gross annual income specified in subparagraph (A), if the transfer was consistent with the practices of the debtor in making charitable contributions.

Key point. Note that there are two separate protections here: (1) bankruptcy trustees cannot recover contributions made by a bankrupt debtor for less than reasonably equivalent value within a year prior to filing for bankruptcy if the contributions amount to 15 percent or less of the debtor's gross annual income; and, (2) bankruptcy trustees cannot recover contributions made by a bankrupt debtor for less than reasonably equivalent value within a year prior to filing for bankruptcy if the contributions exceed 15 percent of the debtor's gross annual income, and the amount of the contributions are consistent with the debtor's giving practices.

Key point. It is critical to note that this provision only amends the second type of "fraudulent transfer" described at the beginning of this section—transfers of cash or property made for less than "reasonably equivalent value" within a year of filing a bankruptcy petition. The Act does not amend the first kind of fraudulent transfer—those made with an actual intent to defraud.

Congress enacted the Religious Freedom and Charitable Donation Protection Act by unanimous vote of both houses, and so this important provision is now the law. Its meaning was addressed in a committee report accompanying the Act. The report reads, in part:

[The Act] protects certain charitable contributions made by an individual debtor to qualified religious or charitable entities within one year preceding the filing date of the debtor's bankruptcy petition from being avoided by a bankruptcy trustee under section 548 of the Bankruptcy Code. The bill protects donations to qualified religious organizations as well as to charities . . . [The Act] is not intended to diminish any of the protections against prepetition fraudulent transfers available under section 548 of the Bankruptcy Code. If a debtor, on the eve of filing for bankruptcy relief, suddenly donates 15 percent of his or her gross income to a religious organization, the debtor's fraudulent intent, if any, would be subject to scrutiny under . . . the Bankruptcy Code. This fifteen percent "safe harbor" merely shifts the burden of proof and limits litigation to where there is evidence of a change in pattern large enough to establish fraudulent intent. As Professor Laycock explained during the subcommittee hearing on this bill: "If I have been going along for years putting $5 a week in the collection plate and all of a sudden, before I file for bankruptcy, I clean out my last account and give 15 percent of my last year's income to my church, the trustee and the bankruptcy judge will look at the timing, the amount, the circumstances, the change in pattern, and they will say those are all badges of fraud. They will say I had the actual intent to hinder or defraud my creditors, and that is recoverable under section 548(a)(1). The fraud scenario is not going to happen."

Likewise, Senator Grassley . . . stated: "[T]he bill does not amend section 548(a)(1) of the Bankruptcy Code. This section lets bankruptcy courts recover any transfer of assets on the eve of bankruptcy if the transfer was made to delay or hinder a creditor. Therefore, if the bill is enacted, we don't have to worry about a sudden rash of charitable giving in anticipation of bankruptcy. Such transfers would obviously be for the purpose of hindering creditors and would still be sub-

---

THE RELIGIOUS FREEDOM AND CHARITABLE DONATION PROTECTION ACT—A CHECKLIST

Here is a checklist that will be a helpful resource in applying the new law:

Step #1. Did the bankruptcy debtor make one or more contributions of cash or property to a church within a year preceding the filing of a bankruptcy petition?

• If not, stop here. A bankruptcy trustee cannot recover the debtor's contributions from the church.

• If yes, go to step #2.

Step #2. In making contributions to the church, did the debtor have an actual intent to hinder, delay, or defraud his or her creditors? In deciding if an intent to defraud exists, consider the timing, amount, and circumstances surrounding the contributions, as well as any change in the debtor's normal pattern or practice.

• If yes, a bankruptcy trustee *can* recover from the church contributions made by the debtor within a year prior to the filing of the bankruptcy petition.

• If not, go to step #3.

Step #3. Did the debtor receive "reasonably equivalent value" for the contributions made to the church? Note that reasonably equivalent value will not include such "intangible" religious services as preaching, teaching, sacraments, or counseling.

• If yes, stop here. A bankruptcy trustee cannot recover the debtor's contributions from the church.

• If no, go to step #4.

Step #4. Is the value of the debtor's contributions 15 percent or less of his or her gross annual income?

• If yes, stop here. A bankruptcy trustee cannot recover the debtor's contributions from the church.

• If no, go to step #5.

Step #5. Is the value of the debtor's contributions consistent with the practices of the debtor in making charitable contributions?

• If yes, stop here. A bankruptcy trustee cannot recover the debtor's contributions from the church.

• If no, a bankruptcy trustee can recover from the church contributions made by the debtor within a year prior to the filing of the bankruptcy petition.

ject to the bankruptcy judge's powers. In other words, there really isn't much room for abuse as a result of [this] legislation."

In addition, [the Act] protects the rights of certain debtors to tithe or make charitable contributions after filing for bankruptcy relief. Some courts have dismissed a debtor's chapter 7 case (a form of bankruptcy relief that discharges an individual debtor of most of his or her personal liability without any requirement for repayment) for substantial abuse under section 707(b) of the Bankruptcy Code based on the debtor's charitable contributions. . . .

examples

Let's illustrate the impact of this provision with some practical examples.

Example. *Bob has attended his church for many years. For the past two years, his contributions to his church have averaged $50 per week, or about $2,500 per year. Bob's gross annual income for the current year is about $40,000. On May 15 Bob files for bankruptcy. A bankruptcy trustee contacts the church treasurer, and demands that the church turn over all contributions made by Bob during the year prior to the date he filed for bankruptcy. The Religious Freedom and Charitable Donation Protection Act applies directly to this scenario, and protects the church from the reach of the trustee, since: (1) the amount of Bob's annual contributions in the two previous years in which the contributions were made did not exceed 15 percent of his gross annual income (15 percent of $40,000 = $6,000); and (2) the timing, amount, and circumstances surrounding the contributions, as well as the lack of any change in the debtor's normal pattern or practice, suggest that Bob did not commit intentional fraud, and so the trustee cannot recover contributions on this basis.*

Example. *Same facts as the previous example, except that in addition to his weekly giving Bob made a one-time gift to the church building fund in the amount of $5,000. Bob's total giving for the year preceding the filing of his bankruptcy petition now totals $7,500, or nearly 19 percent of his gross annual income. As a result, he is not eligible for the 15 percent "safe harbor" rule. The trustee will be able to recover the $7,500 in contributions made by Bob to the church within a year of filing the bankruptcy petition, unless Bob can demonstrate that giving 19 percent of his gross annual income is consistent with his normal practices in making charitable contributions. It is unlikely that Bob or the church will be able to satisfy this condition, since the gift to the building fund was a "one time" extraordinary gift for Bob that was unlike his giving pattern in any prior year.*

Example. *Barb believes strongly in giving to her church, and for each of the past several years has given 20 percent of her income. On June 1 of the current year she files for bankruptcy. A bankruptcy trustee contacts the church treasurer, and demands that the church turn over all contributions made by Barb for the year prior to the date she filed for bankruptcy. The Religious Freedom and Charitable Donation Protection Act applies directly to this scenario, and protects the church from the reach of the trustee, since: (1) the amount of Barb's annual contributions for the years in which the contributions were made exceeded 15 percent of her gross annual income, but she had a consistent practice in prior years of giving this amount; and (2) the timing, amount, and circumstances surrounding the contributions, as well as the lack of any change in the debtor's normal pattern or practice, suggest that Barb did not commit intentional fraud, and so the trustee cannot recover contributions on this basis.*

Example. *Bill has attended his church sporadically for the past several years. For the past few years, his contributions to his church have averaged less than $1,000 per year. Bill's gross annual income for the current and previous year is about $80,000. Bill is facing a staggering debt load due to mismanagement and unrestrained credit card charges. He wants to declare bankruptcy, but he has a $15,000 bank account that he wants to protect. He decides to give the entire amount to his church in order to keep it from the bankruptcy court and his creditors. He gives the entire balance to his church on June 1. On July 1, Bill files for bankruptcy. A bankruptcy trustee contacts the church treasurer, demanding that the church turn over the $15,000 contribution. The Religious Freedom and Charitable Donation Protection Act does not protect Bill or the church. The timing, amount, and circumstances surrounding the contribution of $15,000 strongly indicate that Bill had an actual intent to hinder, delay, or defraud his creditors. This conclusion is reinforced by the fact that the gift was contrary to Bill's normal pattern or practice of giving. As a result, the trustee probably will be able to force the church to return the $15,000.*

Key point. *Whenever a donor makes a large gift of cash or property to a church, church leaders should be alert to the fact that a bankruptcy trustee may be able to recover the contribution at a later date if the donor files for bankruptcy within a year after making the gift and none of the exceptions described in this section applies.*

2. Making Charitable Contributions after Filing for Bankruptcy

background

Up until now, this section has addressed the authority of bankruptcy trustees to recover contributions made by bankrupt debtors within a year prior to filing a bankruptcy petition. There is a second bankruptcy issue that is of direct relevance to churches—can church members who file for bankruptcy continue to make regular contributions to their church? This issue was also addressed by the Religious Freedom and Charitable Donation Protection Act of 1998.

Section 707(b) of the bankruptcy code provides for the dismissal of chapter 7 bankruptcy petitions in the case of debtors who can pay their debts from their excess disposable income. Consider the following examples.

• *In re Breckenridge.*[175] A court denied confirmation of a chapter 13 plan because the debtors had not presented the plan in good faith. In determining good faith, the court looked to the overall picture presented by the debtors. The court considered several factors: (1) the "reasonably recent prior bankruptcy of [the debtor], combined with the low percentage dividend to unsecured claimants; (2) retention of imprudently purchased assets; and (3) the devotion of a significant portion of the debtors' income to the payment of an entirely discretionary expenditure, a church tithe . . . ." While stating that tithes are not automatically objectionable, the court stressed that because of the debtors' severe financial condition, they should "devote maximum resources" to the repayment of their obligations and leave tithing to a time when they could better afford it. The court also noted that without the tithing allocation the debtors could propose a chapter 13 plan whose dividend to creditors would be well over 70%. The court, therefore, denied confirmation of the plan.

• *In re Curry.*[176] The debtor presented a chapter 13 plan for confirmation in which he proposed monthly payments of $125 and tithes to his church of $103. The debtor was an ordained minister employed by the church

---

[175] 12 B.R. 159 (S.D. Ohio 1980).
[176] 77 B.R. 969 (S.D. Fla. 1987).

as a teacher. The church did not require the donations. The court emphasized that the contributions constituted almost half of the debtor's disposable income. While the court did not question the sincerity of the debtor's religious convictions and recognized that the contributions had also been made before the bankruptcy, the court held that the contributions were not a necessary living expense. The court reasoned that the contributions would have the effect of requiring the debtor's creditors to contribute to his church and refused to confirm the plan.

• *In re Green.*[177] A debtor's budget included a payment of 10% of her gross monthly income to her church. The debtor testified that "her church and her own religious beliefs require her to tithe." The creditor did not contest the sincerity of the debtor's belief. The court referred to the United States Supreme Court decision in Hobbie v. Unemployment Appeals Commission of Florida, 480 U.S. 136 (1987). In *Hobbie*, an employer discharged an employee who had recently converted to become a Seventh Day Adventist and so could no longer work Friday nights or Saturdays. After the employee's termination, the state refused to grant her unemployment compensation benefits. The Supreme Court found that the state's denial of benefits violated the employee's right to the free exercise of religion because the state required her "to choose between following the precepts of her religion and forfeiting benefits, on the one hand, and abandoning one of the precepts of her religion in order to accept work on the other. Governmental imposition of such a choice puts the same kind of burden upon the free exercise of religion as would a fine imposed against [her] for her Saturday worship." The Supreme Court, in the *Hobbie* case, also held that

> [w]here the state conditions a receipt of an important benefit upon conduct proscribed by a religious faith, or where it denied such a benefit because of conduct mandated by religious belief, thereby putting substantial pressure on an adherent to modify his behavior and to violate his beliefs, a burden upon religion exists. While the compulsion may be indirect, the infringement upon free exercise is nonetheless substantial.

The *Green* court reasoned that chapter 13 relief is at least as important as unemployment benefits. The court held that "[t]o deny confirmation of this plan solely because Mrs. Green tithes would be to deny her the benefits of the Bankruptcy Code because of conduct mandated by her religious beliefs." The court concluded that in the absence of a compelling state interest, it must confirm the plan.

• *In re Navarro.*[178] A court held that tithing was necessary for the support and maintenance of a debtor. A creditor objected to the confirmation of a chapter 13 plan because the plan provided for a tithe to the debtor's church. The debtor testified that she and her family were devoutly religious and that she considered her obligation to tithe "central to her personal beliefs and tenets of her faith." The debtor also stated that "she considered her obligation to tithe to be indispensable so that she would find a way to continue to do so no matter how the court rules in this matter." The court reasoned that religious contributions are not luxury items because the debtors do not obtain a tangible benefit or increased standard of living. Rather the contributions arose "purely out of the debtors' conviction that they are essential for the spiritual and moral well-being of the family." The court also noted the debtor's testimony that "tithing is a family practice of long-standing." The court concluded that religious contributions may be "consistent with expenditures reasonably necessary for the maintenance and support of chapter 13 debtors" and allowed the tithes. The court criticized the *Green* decision (summarized above) for improperly comparing denial of unemployment benefits to a court's decision to confirm a bankruptcy plan. The court reasoned that in chapter 13 bankruptcy proceedings the role of the court is "not to award or deny substantive governmental benefits, but rather to balance the

---

[177] 73 B.R. 893 (W.D. Mich. 1987), *aff'd,* 103 B.R. 852 (W.D. Mich. 1988).
[178] 83 B.R. 348 (E.D. Pa. 1988).

interest of various private parties according to neutral principals [sic] emanating from Congress." More importantly, the court held that the administration of the bankruptcy system and the protection of creditors are sufficiently compelling interests to outweigh the free exercise of religion.

• *In re Bien.*[179] A court allowed a debtor to make religious contributions. The issue again was whether a tithe in a chapter 13 debtor's plan is "reasonably necessary . . . for the maintenance and support of the debtor." The relevant inquiry, the court stated, was "whether the proposed expense fulfills a bona fide personal commitment intended to serve or promote some religious or spiritual purpose, rather than an effort to hinder, delay or defraud creditors." The debtor had been a full tithe-paying member of the Mormon church for five and one-half years. A full tithe-paying member must pay 10% of gross monthly income to the Church and in return may attend services and pray in the central church in Salt Lake City, Utah. Additionally, a full tithe-paying member enjoys eligibility for positions of service within the church. After examining the totality of the circumstances, the court upheld the religious contribution because "(1) [r]eligious participation is a fundamental part of many people's lives . . . (2) [t]he church tithe is a condition precedent to full participation in the debtor's religion, and (3) the . . . expense . . . serves a bona fide religious and spiritual purpose."

• *In re Miles.*[180] Can a debtor who files a "Chapter 13" bankruptcy plan continue to make monthly contributions to his church? No, concluded a federal district court in Florida. The debtor filed a plan under which he proposed to pay only $50 per month for three years (a total of $1,800) against $90,000 in unsecured debts. The plan reflected monthly take-home pay of $1,150 out of which the debtor donated $160 to his church. The bankruptcy trustee objected to the debtor's plan, arguing that by making the monthly contributions of $160 to his church the debtor was not applying all of his "disposable income" toward the payment of his debts. The issue, as stated by the court, was whether "the court, over the objection of the trustee, can confirm a plan which pays only a minimal dividend to unsecured creditors while the debtor continues to devote substantial amounts of his income to the support of his church." The court concluded that the trustee was correct in objecting to the plan, and accordingly it denied the debtor's bankruptcy petition. The court observed: "[We] reject the proposition . . . that the constitutional separation of church and state protects debtors who with the ability to make payments to their creditors choose instead to donate those funds to their church. While church donations may be a source of inner strength and comfort to those who feel compelled to make them, they are not necessary for the maintenance or support of the debtor or a dependent of the debtor," and accordingly the debtor failed to meet the "disposable income test required for confirmation of the plan."

• *In re Tucker.*[181] A bankruptcy court rejected a debtor's bankruptcy petition on the ground that it called for monthly contributions of $100 to his church. The debtor filed a "Chapter 13" (wage-earner's) bankruptcy petition that listed $22,000 in debts. The plan called for only 2% of unsecured debts to be satisfied over the next four years. The largest unsecured creditor (a local bank) objected to the petition on the ground that the plan did not provide for the payment of all of the debtor's disposable income to the bankruptcy trustee. Among other things, the bank pointed out that the debtor's plan called for monthly contributions of $100 to his church. The court observed: "By allowing a debtor to deduct contributions to any organization, the court necessarily is forcing the debtor's creditors to contribute to the debtor's church or favorite charity. Congress could have intended no such result." Accordingly, the court rejected the debtor's bankruptcy petition.

• *In re McDaniel.*[182] The issue was not whether the court would allow the debtor to tithe, but whether the proposed plan contained excessive contributions to his church. While the debtor proposed to pay $540

---

[179] 95 B.R. 281 (D. Conn. 1989).
[180] 20 Collier Bankruptcy Cases 912 (N.D. Fl. 1989). 20 Collier Bankruptcy Cases 912 (N.D. Fl. 1989).
[181] 102 B.R. 219 (D.N.M. 1989).

per month to his church, the proposed monthly chapter 13 plan payment was $600. The court rested its analysis upon the assumption that an absolute ban on tithing would violate the first amendment guaranty of religious freedom. The court reasoned, however, that a determination that the contribution was excessive would not violate the first amendment. In its analysis, the court emphasized that contributions must be made in good faith and not in an effort to divert funds from creditors. The debtors met this requirement with evidence that they had tithed for several years prior to the filing of their petition. The court also noted that the debtors "felt a strong moral obligation to continue" tithing but "would not be denied full participation in their church if they did not tithe." The court held that the debtors' proposed contribution was excessive primarily because the tithe nearly equaled the amount the debtors proposed to pay under their chapter 13 plan. The court ordered that the debtors resubmit a plan with a smaller contribution provision.

• *In re Packham.*[183] A federal court in Utah ruled that a church member's bankruptcy plan could not be approved since he proposed to "tithe" or give 10 percent of his income to his church. The church member had debts of $50,000 and an annual household income of $25,000. He filed a "Chapter 13" wage-earners bankruptcy plan, under which he agreed to pay his creditors 20 percent of their debts. A creditor objected to the proposed plan on the ground that it listed the church member's tithe to his church as a reasonably necessary living expense not available for distribution to creditors. Chapter 13 of the bankruptcy law requires that all of a debtor's "disposable income" be made available for distribution to creditors, except an amount that is reasonably necessary for living expenses. The church member claimed that he believed tithing to be mandatory rather than optional. He testified that tithing "is a commandment from the Lord to pay as a debt to him for what he has done for us, for what God has done for us. . . . I believe that the tithing should be paid before the creditors. I believe that our greatest creditor is the Lord. He is the one that has given us the most." The court rejected this argument, and ruled that the bankruptcy plan could not be approved unless the tithe was canceled and the funds made available to the creditors. The court emphasized that failure to tithe would not prevent the debtor from full participation in the activities of his church, and therefore the practice of his religion would not be adversely affected. The court emphasized that neither the debtor nor his church was "in a position to make the Lord a priority creditor in bankruptcy."

• *In re Lee.*[184] A debtor filed a bankruptcy petition under chapter 7 of the bankruptcy code. His bankruptcy petition showed total unsecured debts of $15,384.71, net monthly income of $3,581.43, and total monthly living expenses of $2,064.00, leaving a net disposal income of $1,517.43. In summary, the debtor had sufficient disposable monthly income to pay off his entire unsecured debts in less than 12 months. As a result, the bankruptcy trustee dismissed the debtor's bankruptcy petition. A court agreed that allowing a discharge of debts in this case would constitute a substantial abuse of the bankruptcy law, since the debtor's disposable income (not reduced by charitable contributions) was sufficient to pay his debts in a timely manner. The court concluded: "In those cases in which courts have found a constitutional right to tithe, the courts premised their decisions on a finding that the debtors had tithed consistently and that either the debtors' church required tithing or the debtors had a strong commitment to continue tithing . . . . In [this] case, [the debtor has] not established a consistent practice of tithing. Neither [has he] introduced credible evidence of strong commitment to tithe. [He] failed to tithe in times of financial difficulty. Additionally, [he has] been a church member since June 1992, but has contributed only since January 1993. . . . This court does not dispute the debtor's commitment to his church or his honest desire to tithe. This court also does not deny the debtor's right to tithe. He may choose to adjust his budget elsewhere and continue to tithe. It is inequitable to

---

[182] 126 B.R. 782 (D. Minn. 1991).
[183] 126 B.R. 603 (D. Utah 1991).
[184] 162 B.R. 31 (N.D. Ga. 1993).

allow him to tithe at the expense of his creditors, when, in the past, he has been able to adjust his moral commitment to tithing to allow for his other financial commitments."

the Religious Liberty and Charitable Donation Protection Act of 1998

The Religious Liberty and Charitable Donation Protection Act of 1998 directly addressed the ability of bankrupt debtors to continue making contributions to their church following the filing of a bankruptcy petition. The bankruptcy code says that a court may not approve a bankruptcy plan unless it provides that all of a debtor's "projected disposable income to be received in the three-year period beginning on the date that the first payment is due under the plan will be applied to make payments under the plan." In addition, a court can dismiss a bankruptcy case to avoid "substantial abuse" of the bankruptcy law. Many courts have dismissed bankruptcy cases on the ground that a debtor's plan called for a continuation of charitable contributions.

The Act clarifies that bankruptcy courts no longer can dismiss bankruptcy cases on the ground that a debtor proposes to continue making charitable contributions. This assumes that the debtor's contributions will not exceed 15 percent of his or her gross annual income for the year in which the contributions are made (or a higher percentage if consistent with the debtor's regular practice in making charitable contributions).

The committee report accompanying the Act states:

In addition [the bill] protects the rights of certain debtors to tithe or make charitable contributions after filing for bankruptcy relief. Some courts have dismissed a debtor's chapter 7 case . . . for substantial abuse under section 707(b) of the bankruptcy code based on the debtor's charitable contributions. The bill also protects the rights of debtors who file for chapter 13 to tithe or make charitable contributions. Some courts have held that tithing is not a reasonably necessary expense or have attempted to fix a specific percentage as the maximum that the debtor may include in his or her budget.

examples

Let's illustrate the impact of this provision with a few practical examples.

Example. Brad files a "chapter 7" bankruptcy petition. Brad's plan states that he will use all available "disposable income" to pay his creditors during the three year period following the approval of his plan. But the plan permits Brad to continue making contributions to his church, which in the past have averaged 10 percent of his income. Some creditors object to the plan, and demand that the court reject it, since Brad will be making contributions to his church rather than using these funds to pay off his lawful debts. The Religious Liberty and Charitable Donation Protection Act of 1998 specifies that the court cannot reject Brad's bankruptcy plan because of the charitable contributions—since the contributions are less than 15 percent of his gross annual income.

Example. Same facts as the previous example, except that Brad's plan proposes to pay contributions to his church in the amount of 25 percent of his gross annual income. Brad would rather that his church receive all available income than his creditors. Several creditors object to this plan. The court probably will deny Brad's request for bankruptcy protection, since the substantial contributions proposed in his plan exceed 15 percent of his gross annual income, and are not consistent with his prior practice of making charitable contributions.

INSTRUCTIONAL AIDS TO CHAPTER 9

Terms

charitable solicitation

copyright

copyright notice

derivative work

infringement

publication

securities fraud

security

testamentary gift

Uniform Securities Act

Learning Objectives

- Recognize that churches are not immune from all forms of government regulation.

- Understand the application of various financial regulations to churches, including regulation of charitable solicitations, limitations on charitable giving, and securities law.

- Understand the basic elements of copyright law, and their application to church practices.

- Understand the application of the Charitable Contribution and Charitable Donation Act to churches.

Short-Answer Questions

1. A church operates a preschool. The preschool is subject to health and safety standards under a state law that is designed to protect children. A state agency learns that the preschool is in violation of a number of safety standards, including the fact that exit doors open inward rather than outward. The agency orders the church to comply with these standards, but the pastor refuses. He insists that the church is subject to the "lordship" of Jesus Christ, and not the state. Is he correct? How would a civil court evaluate the pastor's position?

2. A church is considering the use of a professional fund-raiser to assist in raising funds for a new building. What 2 kinds of state regulation may apply?

3. A state law requires all religious organizations that solicit over half of their financial support from non-members to register with the state. Is this law constitutional? Explain.

4. M, a widow, executes a will on July 1st of this year, leaving $500,000 to her church. She dies on September 15th of this year, and her children contest the gift to the church. The minister of the church asks for your opinion concerning the legal validity of this gift. What would you say?

5. Same facts as question 4, except that M had no surviving children or grandchildren. Would this change your opinion?

6. Why have some states enacted laws invalidating gifts made in a will executed within a prescribed period prior to the donor's death? Do you believe that these laws are necessary? Explain.

7. To raise funds for a new building, a church sells bonds through its minister and board members to church members. The church assumes that it is exempt from any legal restrictions. Is this a prudent assumption? Explain.

8. Are churches automatically exempt from registering their securities under state law? Are they required to "register" those persons who will be promoting and selling church securities?

9. Under what circumstances will a church be exempt from the prohibition of fraudulent activities in the sale of securities?

10. Identify two common forms of security that are issued by churches.

11. A church wants to raise $500,000 for a new building by issuing promissory notes. The pastor learns that churches are exempt from registering their securities under state law, and so he assumes that the church can proceed to issue the notes. Is this a prudent assumption? Explain.

12. A church wants to raise $500,000 for a new building by issuing promissory notes. The securities are not exempt from registration under state law, and so the church retains an attorney who registers the securities. The pastor actively encourages church members to purchase securities. On one occasion, he met with G, an elderly widow of modest means, and persuades her to purchase a $10,000 note. Evaluate the propriety of this transaction.

13. A church issues $200,000 in 10-year promissory notes to its members and spends all of the proceeds on a new education building. Has the church committed securities fraud? Explain.

14. A church issues 10-year, 10 percent promissory notes to several of its members. No prospectus, offering circular, or other literature is filed with the state securities commission or made available to investors. Has the church committed securities fraud? Explain.

15. To help promote the sale of church notes, a minister assures his congregation during a sermon that the notes are as safe "as the Rock of Gibraltar" since they were issued on behalf of the church. Is this statement legally appropriate? Explain.

16. A local church plans to issue $500,000 in promissory notes. It prepares a prospectus describing the securities, the history of the church, and the church's financial condition. The prospectus also contains the following five statements. Indicate whether each statement is legally permissible.

   a. "The membership of the church has increased during each of the past ten years, so it can be expected that membership growth will continue to occur."

   b. "These securities have been exempted from registration by the state securities commission and thus you are assured that they have been carefully studied and approved by the state."

   c. "A copy of this prospectus shall at all times be maintained in the church office for the benefit of any prospective investor."

   d. "Interest on these obligations is guaranteed."

   e. "The church was established in 1935."

17. Same facts as question 16. The church decides *not* to include the following information in its prospectus. Indicate after each statement whether its omission is legally permissible.

   a. A lawsuit is pending against the church alleging that the church is liable on the basis of negligence for the injuries suffered by two minors who were sexually molested by a volunteer church worker. The lawsuit is asking for $5 million.

   b. The total dollar value of securities to be offered.

   c. A statement that no sinking fund reserve exists.

   d. A statement that for three of the past five years the church's expenses exceeded revenues.

   e. A statement that for two of the past three years the church's attendance has declined.

   f. A statement that the pastor was installed one year ago.

18. Can a church be liable for securities fraud if it in good faith did not know that its activities were fraudulent? Explain.

19. To raise funds for a remodeling project, a church solicits 3-year pledge commitments from church members. Is this practice subject to state securities law?

20. What is the Berne Convention? How did it affect copyright law in the United States?

21. A church choir director sees a piece of sheet music that she would like to duplicate for members of the choir. The sheet music contains no copyright notice. Does this necessarily mean that it is in the public domain? Explain.

22. Which of the following is a requirement of current copyright law: (a) affixation of a copyright notice to publicly distributed copies of a copyrighted work first published since March of 1989; (2) registration; (3) deposit of 2 copies with the Copyright Office.

23. Rev. L is minister of music at his church. He composes a religious work during office hours at the church, using church equipment and supplies. Answer the following questions:

    a. Who owns the copyright in this work? Explain.

    b. What is the name used by the Copyright Act for this kind of work?

    c. How could the copyright ownership have been vested in another party?

    d. What is the term of copyright protection?

    e. Define "inurement," and explain the relevance of this term to a church's tax-exempt status.

    f. Does the transaction in this example constitute inurement? Why or why not? If it does, how can this conclusion be avoided?

24. D composes a religious song this year. How long will the copyright last in the work? Are any renewals necessary?

25. List the 5 exclusive rights of a copyright owner.

26. What is copyright infringement?

27. During morning worship services at Grace Church, the following activities occur. Explain whether or not each activity constitutes copyright infringement:

    a. The church congregation sings 2 copyrighted hymns in the church hymnal.

    b. The church choir sings a copyrighted song.

    c. The choir director purchased only one copy of the song the choir performed, and made copies for every member of the choir on church duplicating equipment.

    d. A vocalist sings a copyrighted song as a solo, making a copy of the music for an accompanist.

    e. The church prints the lyrics (not the music) of a religious song in the bulletin.

    f. The church makes an audio recording of the worship service

g. The church makes a video recording of the worship service.

h. The lyrics of a copyrighted religious song are displayed on a screen using an overhead projector (a church employee typed the lyrics on a transparency).

i. A minister reads a chapter from a copyrighted translation of the Bible.

28. Would the so-called "fair use guidelines" excuse any of the activities described in question 27?

29. The music minister of a local church displays chorus lyrics on a wall during worship services by means of an opaque projector. Is this practice legally permissible? Explain.

30. The music minister of a local church composed a new arrangement of a copyrighted hymn and had the choir perform it during worship services. Has the minister, or the church, violated the copyright law? Explain.

31. A church prints the lyrics of a copyrighted song on a bulletin insert and on an overhead transparency. Does either practice constitute "fair use"? Explain.

32. A church conducts a Saturday evening concert featuring a musical group. The church does not charge an admissions fee, but it does pay a fee to the musical group. Does the "nonprofit performance" exemption to copyright infringement apply? The religious services exemption?

33. A church shows video tapes to its youth group. Some of the tapes were purchased by the church, and others were rented at a local video store. Does the showing of these videos to the youth group constitute copyright infringement? What if no admissions fee is charged?

34. A church purchases the current version of a popular word processing program for use on the church computer. A staff member enjoys the program so much that she takes it home and copies it onto her personal computer. Is this permissible?

35. Evaluate the likelihood that a civil court would intervene in each of the following church disputes:

    a. A minister claims that her dismissal violated the church bylaws.

    b. A minister claims that his dismissal was based on fraud and collusion.

    c. A church dismisses a member on the basis of doctrinal deviation. The member challenges the dismissal in court.

    d. A church splits, and both factions claim title to the church's properties.

    e. A church member sues a minister on the basis of malpractice.

    f. A church is sued for copyright infringement.

g. A minister challenges a congregational vote to dismiss him, arguing that the meeting was not called in accordance with church bylaws.

36. J has attended a church for many years. For the past three years, her contributions to the church have averaged $100 per week, or about $5,000 per year. J's gross annual income for the current year is about $50,000. On July 15 J files for bankruptcy. A bankruptcy trustee demands that the church turn over all contributions made by J during the year prior to the date he filed for bankruptcy. How should the church respond?

37. Same facts as the previous example, except that in addition to his weekly giving J made a one-time gift to the church's missions fund of $10,000. Does this change your answer? Explain.

38. T believes strongly in giving to her church, and for each of the past several years has given 20 percent of her income. On July 1 of the current year she files for bankruptcy. A bankruptcy trustee demands that the church turn over all contributions made by T for the year prior to the date she filed for bankruptcy. How should the church respond?

39. D has attended church occasionally over the past several years. For the past few years, his contributions to his church have averaged less than $2,000 per year. D's gross annual income for the current and previous year is about $50,000. D wants to declare bankruptcy, but he has a $20,000 bank account that he wants to protect. He decides to give the entire amount to his church in order to keep it from the bankruptcy court and his creditors. He gives the entire balance to his church on June 1. On July 1, D files for bankruptcy. A bankruptcy trustee demands that the church turn over the $20,000 contribution. How should the church respond?

40. B files a "chapter 7" bankruptcy petition. B's plan states that he will use all available "disposable income" to pay his creditors during the three year period following the approval of his plan. But the plan permits B to continue making contributions to his church, which in the past have averaged 10 percent of his income. Some creditors object to the plan, and demand that the court reject it, since B will be making contributions to his church rather than using these funds to pay off his lawful debts. What is the likely outcome of this case? Will the court accept B's bankruptcy plan?

41. Same facts as the previous example, except that B's plan proposes to pay contributions to his church in the amount of 25 percent of his gross annual income. B would rather that his church receive all available income than his creditors. Several creditors object to this plan. What is the likely outcome of this case? Will the court accept B's bankruptcy plan?

Discussion Questions

1. Persons often uncritically jump to the conclusion that churches should never be subject to government regulation, under any circumstances. Do you agree? If not, what arguments could you make to oppose such an absolutist view? Construct a rule that in your opinion strikes an appropriate balance between legitimate government regulation and a church's right to be free of undue governmental interference.

2. Many churches are offended when they learn that a publisher of religious music has prosecuted a church for copyright infringement. Should Congress amend the Copyright Act to exempt churches from the prohibition against copyright infringement? Explain.

10

CHURCH LEGAL LIABILITY

Chapter summary. Churches are exposed to legal liability as a result of a number of acts and omissions, many of which have been addressed in previous chapters. This chapter addresses church liability based on THE following grounds: (1) vicarious liability for the negligence of employees; (2) negligent selection; (3) negligent retention; (4) negligent supervision; (5) counseling; (6) breach of fiduciary duty; (7) ratification; and (8) defamation. Negligence refers to conduct that creates an unreasonable and foreseeable risk of harm to another's person or property, and that in fact results in the foreseeable harm. Churches can be liable on the basis of negligence in a variety of ways. Four of these are addressed in this chapter. To illustrate, churches can be vicariously liable for the negligence of employees committed within the course of their employment under the legal principle of respondeat superior. Churches also may be liable on the basis of negligence in the selection, retention, or supervision of employees and volunteer workers. In recent years, some courts have found churches liable on the basis of a breach of a fiduciary duty for injuries occurring on their premises or in the course of their activities. This chapter also addresses church liability for defamation, and surveys a number of defenses available to churches that are sued on the basis of these theories of liability. "Risk management" is emphasized, and churches are provided with several suggestions to reduce their risk of legal liability. The chapter concludes with an analysis of the liability of denominational agencies for the activities of affiliated churches and clergy. This is a question of increasing concern to many denominations.

Churches can be sued for a variety of acts and omissions, many of which have been addressed in previous chapters in this text.[1] This chapter will address the following additional bases of church legal liability:

(1) vicarious liability for the negligence of employees

(2) negligent selection

(3) negligent retention

(4) negligent supervision

(5) counseling

(6) breach of fiduciary duty

(7) ratification

(8) defamation

This chapter also will address the legal liability of denominational agencies for the actions of affiliated churches and clergy.

Key point. This chapter has two purposes: (1) to explain several common and significant bases of church liability; and (2) to assist church leaders in adopting strategies to manage or reduce these risks. The good

---

[1] Examples include improper expulsion of ministers (§ 2-04), church members (§ 6-09), and employees (§ 8-04); church property disputes (chapter 7); injuries occurring on church property (§ 7-20); violations of civil rights and employment laws (chapter 8); providing references on former employees or volunteers (§ 8-23); copyright law violations (§ 9-05); and securities law violations (§ 9-04).

news is that by implementing relatively simple precautions, church leaders can significantly reduce the risk of church liability.

§ 10-01 Negligence as a Basis for Liability — In General

Negligence is conduct that creates an unreasonable risk of foreseeable harm to the person or property of another, and that in fact results in the foreseeable harm. The important point to recognize is that negligence need not be intentional. For example, negligence may include conduct that is simply careless, heedless, or inadvertent.

Churches can be liable on the basis of negligence in a number of ways. First, they can be liable for their own negligence. Examples here include the negligent selection or negligent retention of church workers, or the negligent supervision of church activities. To illustrate, a church may be guilty of negligent selection if it hires a convicted child molester or uses a van driver with numerous traffic violations. A church may be guilty of negligent supervision if it uses an inadequate number of qualified adults to supervise a church youth activity.

Churches also can be liable for the negligence of employees and volunteers occurring within the scope of their work. Employers generally are responsible for the negligence of an employee (or volunteer) occurring within the scope or course of employment. This vicarious or imputed liability of an employer for the negligence of an employee is known as respondeat superior *(the "employer responds"). All of these forms of negligence are addressed in the following sections of this chapter.*

§ 10-02 Vicarious Liability (or Respondeat Superior)

Key point 10-02. *The doctrine of respondeat superior imposes vicarious liability on employers for the negligent acts of their employees committed within the scope of their employment.*

Churches are often sued on the basis of respondeat superior for the negligence of church workers. Often, the negligence of church workers is associated with the use of a car, and includes such conduct as excessive speed, disregarding a stop sign or stop light, driving a vehicle with defective brakes, driving a vehicle at night without lights, failing to yield the right of way, or making a turn from an improper lane. While these actions may be intentional, they often are attributable to momentary carelessness or thoughtlessness. Churches also have been sued on the basis of respondeat superior for incidents of sexual molestation committed by a church worker during a church activity.

Why should a church be legally responsible for the negligence of a church worker? After all, the church certainly did not authorize such conduct and ordinarily did not even anticipate that it would occur. Perhaps the most commonly quoted justification for this theory is the following:

> What has emerged as the modern justification for vicarious liability is a rule of policy, a deliberate allocation of risk. The losses caused by the torts of employees, which as a practical matter are sure to occur in the conduct of the employer's enterprise, are placed upon the enterprise itself, as a required cost of doing business. They are placed upon the employer because, having engaged in an enterprise which will, on the basis of all past experience, involve harm to others through torts of employees, and sought to profit by it, it is just that he, rather than the innocent injured plaintiff, should bear them; and because he is better able to absorb them, and to distribute them, through prices, rates or liability insurance, to the public, and so to shift them to society, to the community at large. Added to this is the

makeweight argument that an employer who is held strictly liable is under the greatest incentive to be careful in the selection, instruction and supervision of his servants, and to take every precaution to see that the enterprise is conducted safely.[2]

As we will see later in this chapter, some courts have recognized that this logic has little if any application to churches and other nonprofit organizations.

Under the doctrine of respondeat superior, an employer is responsible for the injuries caused by its employees only if (1) an employer-employee relationship existed at the time of the injury, (2) the injury was caused by an employee's negligence, and (3) the employee was acting in the course of his or her employment at the time of the injury. These three elements will be considered individually.

Key point. A church worker whose negligence or misconduct results in injury to another person is not insulated from personal liability by the respondeat superior doctrine. Church workers whose conduct injures other persons in the course of their church duties can be sued directly by injured victims. Often, both the worker and the church are sued.

§ 10-02.1 — The Requirement of Employee Status

Key point 10-02.1. Employers may be liable on the basis of respondeat superior only for the acts of employees.

Churches can be liable on the basis of respondeat superior for the negligent acts of employees committed within the course or scope of their employment. A number of courts have addressed the question of whether clergy are "employees" for purposes of imposing liability on an employing church. One of the first such cases was a decision by the Supreme Court of California.[3] The case involved a 12-year-old boy who lost a leg and suffered serious injuries to his other leg because of an accident caused by the reckless driving of the pastor of a Presbyterian "missions" church. At the time of the accident, the boy was standing on the "running board" of a car driven by the church's pastor at an excessive rate of speed (he was "racing" a car driven by a seminary student). The boy's family sued the pastor individually, as well as the presbytery of San Francisco (the presbytery overseeing the local missions church). The court was asked to determine whether an ecclesiastical body could be sued on account of the negligence of one of its ministers acting in the course of his employment.

Noting that there was "no compelling reason" why a religious organization should not be liable for the negligence of its employees, the court proceeded to determine whether a minister could be characterized as an employee. In reaching its decision that a minister could be deemed an employee, the court relied on well-established criteria employed by the courts in determining the status of other workers:

> Whether a person performing work for another is an employee or self-employed depends primarily upon whether the one for whom the work is done has the legal right to control the activities of the alleged employee. The power of the employer to terminate the services of the employee gives him the means of controlling the employee's activities. "The right to immediately discharge involves the right of control." It is not essential that the right of

---

[2] *See generally* W. PROSSER, THE LAW OF TORTS § 69 (4th ed. 1971). Quoted in Stevens v. Roman Catholic Bishop of Fresno, 123 Cal. Rptr. 171 (Cal. App. 1975).

[3] Malloy v. Fong, 232 P.2d 241 (Cal. 1951).

control be exercised or that there be active supervision of the work of the employee. The existence of the right of control and supervision establishes the existence of an employment relationship.[4]

The court also found that a minister could be deemed a church employee under the criteria set forth in the Restatement of Agency (an authoritative legal treatise):

(1) An employee is a person employed to perform service for another in his affairs and who, with respect to his physical conduct in the performance of the service, is subject to the other's control or right to control.

(2) In determining whether one acting for another is an employee or self-employed, the following matters of fact, among others, are considered:

(a) the extent of control which, by the agreement, the employer may exercise over the details of the work;

(b) whether or not the one employed is engaged in a distinct occupation or business;

(c) the kind of occupation, with reference to whether, in the locality, the work is usually done under the direction of the employer or by a specialist without supervision;

(d) the skill required in the particular occupation;

(e) whether the employer or the workman supplies the instrumentalities, tools, and the place of work for the person doing the work;

(f) the length of time for which the person is employed;

(g) the method of payment, whether by the time or by the job;

(h) whether or not the work is a part of the regular business of the employer; and

(i) whether or not the parties believe they are creating the relationship of employer and employee.[5]

In concluding that the negligent pastor was an agent of the presbytery (and not an independent contractor), the court noted the following two additional considerations. First, the presbytery exercised significant control over "missions" churches (it held title to all church property, assisted with the churches' finance, and paid a portion of clergy salaries). Second, the presbytery had the authority to approve or disapprove a missions church's selection of its pastor. Following the installation of such a pastor, "he was not responsible to the local church but only to the presbytery. The presbytery, not the church, had the power to remove him. Furthermore, he could not transfer to another pastorate without permission of the presbytery, and in fact he was a member of the presbytery rather than of the local church."

---

4 232 P.2d at 249 (citations omitted). The terms *employer* and *employee* have been used instead of *principal* and *agent.*

5 RESTATEMENT OF AGENCY § 220 (1933). The terms employer and employee have been used instead of the terms principal and agent. Compare the current RESTATEMENT (SECOND) OF AGENCY § 220 (1958) which is identical to the quoted provision except that it adds a further factor: "(j) whether the [employer] is or is not in business."

The court concluded, "The existence of the right of control and supervision establishes the existence of an agency relationship [making the employer legally responsible for the acts of an employee committed within the scope of his or her employment]. The evidence clearly supports the conclusion of the jury that such control existed in the present case. The right of the presbytery to install and remove its ministers, to approve or disapprove their transfer to other jurisdictions, and to supervise and control the activities of the local churches, particularly those in the mission stage, is inconsistent with a contrary conclusion." The court emphasized that "we are not here called upon to determine the liability of the presbytery for negligence in the activities of a fully established and independently incorporated Presbyterian church which has passed from the mission stage." Clearly, the Malloy case would not support liability of the presbytery for the activities of clergy serving such churches, since there would be none of the control by the presbytery over the activities of the local church that in Malloy was deemed sufficient to establish an agency relationship between the presbytery and a pastor of a missions church.

> **Key point.** *Cases addressing the correct reporting status (employee or self-employed) of ministers for income tax reporting purposes are relevant, though not controlling, in deciding whether or not a minister is an employee whose negligence is imputed to his or her employing church under the doctrine of respondeat superior.[6]*

The principle of respondeat superior imposes liability upon churches for injuries caused by the negligence of employees. Some courts have extended this doctrine to cover injuries caused by the negligence of uncompensated volunteers. However, a church generally is not responsible for the misconduct of independent contractors. Independent contractors are persons who offer their services to the public and are generally engaged to do some particular project, usually for a specified sum, and who perform the task with little or no supervision or control. They are not considered to be employees.[7]

In summary, under the doctrine of respondeat superior a church can be liable for the negligent acts of employees committed within the scope or course of their employment. Are clergy "employees" of their church for purposes of this doctrine? If so, their negligent acts committed within the scope of their employment may be imputed to their employing church. What about nonminister church workers? Cases addressing the employee status of both clergy and nonminister workers are summarized in the following examples.

clergy

> **Example.** *The Alabama Supreme Court ruled that a Catholic order was not legally responsible for the actions of a priest who had entered an abortion clinic and injured a woman while destroying several pieces of equipment with a sledge hammer.[8] The priest, a member of the Benedictine Society, had been appointed pastor of a local parish and "pro-life coordinator" for the local diocese by the bishop. The*

---

[6] For a complete discussion of the reporting status of ministers for income tax reporting purposes, see R. Hammar, Church and Clergy Tax Guide, chapter 2 (published annually by the publisher of this text).

[7] *See generally* R. Hammar. Church and Clergy Tax Guide, chapter 2 (published annually by the publisher of this text).

[8] Wood v. Benedictine Society of Alabama, Inc., 530 So.2d 801 (Ala. 1988). This case is significant for the following reasons. First, it recognizes that the mere existence of ecclesiastical authority by a denominational agency over a minister does not, by itself, make the minister an "agent" of the denomination. Second, the court used an interesting analogy to support its conclusion—that of a seminary's relationship with its graduates. The seminary confers a degree upon each graduate, but that action, standing alone, does not make the seminary liable for the subsequent actions of its graduates. Similarly, many denominations confer ecclesiastical credentials upon clergy, but this procedure, by itself, should never authorize persons injured by the actions of a minister to sue the denomination. Third, the state supreme court affirmed a "directed verdict" by the trial court. A directed verdict is a decision by the trial judge, before the case is submitted to the jury, that the plaintiff's case is not supported by any evidence and accordingly that the case need not be submitted to a jury. This is an extraordinary action for a trial court to take, and it is reserved for only the most meritless claims. The fact that such a verdict was involved in this case, and was upheld by the state supreme court, reinforces the position taken by the court.

injured woman sued the Benedictine Society and the priest's immediate superior (an abbot), claiming that the priest was an "agent" of the society and accordingly that the society was legally responsible for his conduct. In particular, she argued that the priest "was a member of the society and, as such, was subject to [his abbot's] orders as it related to his 24-hour life as a monk, including the authority to recall him to the abbey." The supreme court concluded that the woman had produced no evidence demonstrating an agency relationship between the society and the priest: "The Benedictine Order is a clerical order. [The priest] is a monk in that society and [the abbot] is his superior. However, the relationship between [the priest] and the society was ecclesiastical and did not necessarily create a . . . principal/agent relationship. Furthermore, the fact that [the priest] is a monk 24 hours a day does not necessarily mean that his membership in the society makes the society liable for all of his actions." The court further observed that "the law with regard to ecclesiastical orders and religious societies [is] that the relationship is essentially ecclesiastical in nature. I would analogize this to situations where a young man may be in a seminary and the seminary is asked to supply a preacher or a minister for a congregation. The fact that the young minister may have some alma mater does not make the seminary responsible for his behavior in the event he elects to commit a burglary or some other act which he might consider to be ordained by divine aegis or providence. It would not in and of itself make the seminary responsible for his behavior." The court further noted that there was no evidence "that the Benedictine Society was acting in a principal-agency capacity with the [priest]. Further, the court finds there was no employment as that term implies or no employment in the sense required for negligent employment."

Example. A church was sued for injuries and damages caused by the reckless driving of its pastor. The injured victim alleged that the pastor was an employee of his church, and thus the employer-church was vicariously liable for the consequences of the pastor's negligence committed in the course of employment. The church denied liability on the ground that its pastor was self-employed and not an employee, and accordingly his negligence could not be imputed to the church. The California Supreme Court concluded that the pastor was an employee of his church and that his negligence was imputable to the church.[9]

Example. The Colorado Supreme Court concluded that a pastor was an "agent" of his denomination, and as a result the denomination could be liable on the basis of negligent hiring for his sexual relationship with a woman in the course of marital counseling. The court acknowledged that "a prerequisite to establishing negligent hiring is an employment or agency relationship." Did such a relationship exist between the diocese and the assistant pastor? The court said "yes." It defined an agency relationship as one in which one person (the "agent") acts on behalf of another (the "principal") subject to the other's control. The court continued, "At trial, sufficient evidence was presented to establish that the structure of the Episcopal Church was such that the diocese and [the bishop] had and exercised the right of control over the manner of work performed by a priest as well as the hiring, compensation, counseling performed by the priest and discipline of the priest. The evidence was sufficient, in this case, to support the finding of an agency relation between the diocese and [the pastor]." The court noted that in addition to controlling certain aspects of hiring, compensation, and discipline, the diocese also controls and supervises the duties of pastors in their role as counselors. It observed that the bishop had "given talks" about counseling issues to pastors in the diocese. In addition, the diocese "had specific printed regulations on pastoral counseling and that these regulations describe the form counseling should take. The regulations include such details as how appointments are to be kept, what attire is to be worn, where in the room the prayer book and desk should be, and even how the pastor should sit." The court concluded, "All of these facts indicate that a priest is not independent of the diocese but is controlled by the diocese and the

---

9   Vind v. Asamblea Apostolica De La Feen Christo Jesus, 307 P.2d 85 (Cal. 1957). In reaching this decision, the court employed the same criteria used by the California Supreme Court in the *Malloy* case. *See* note 3, *supra*, and accompanying text.

bishop. The priest's education is monitored by the bishop, he is put through a screening for hire by the diocese which includes psychological evaluation. The priest's compensation is affected by the bishop, the priest's discipline is controlled by the bishop, and every part of the form of the priest's counseling is regulated by the diocese. The evidence at trial created a factual issue regarding whether an agency relationship existed. The trial court properly submitted this issue to the jury for determination and the jury found that there was an agency relationship between [the assistant pastor] and the diocese.[10]

Example. *The Kansas Supreme Court concluded that injuries caused by a Catholic priest's negligent driving were not imputable to his diocese since the priest was self-employed rather than an employee.*[11] *In reaching this conclusion, the court applied the "right to control test" under which a worker is considered to be an employee if the employer either controls or has the right to control the person's work. In concluding that the priest was not an employee, the court relied on the following factors: (1) the priest's "day-to-day activities are within his own discretion and control"; (2) the priest is authorized under canon law to do whatever he feels necessary to carry out his duties; (3) he sets his own hours and vacation; (4) he makes out his own paycheck, and hires and fires non-clergy workers; (5) he has complete discretion in purchasing church supplies and paying bills out of parish funds; (6) his work requires a high level of skill and experience and is generally done without supervision; and (7) he was driving his own car at the time of the accident and had obtained his own insurance on the vehicle. Under these facts, the court concluded that the priest was not an employee of the church. Since self-employed persons are not subject to an employer's control with respect to the manner and methods of performing their duties, the diocese was not responsible for the priest's negligence. The court acknowledged that the priest was clearly subject to the "ecclesiastical control" of his bishop, the diocese, and the Catholic Church, but such control was not relevant in determining the issue of legal control for purposes of imputing liability to the diocese on the basis of respondeat superior. The court also noted that the diocese "followed the majority of dioceses in issuing a W-2 form to each priest," but did this practice inconsistent with its conclusion that the priest was self-employed for purposes of respondeat superior. This decision is significant because it recognizes that (1) a church or religious denomination will not necessarily be legally accountable for the negligence of a minister merely because the minister is subject to the "ecclesiastical control" of the church or denomination, and (2) ministers who are treated as employees for federal income tax purposes (and are issued W-2 forms) will not necessarily be considered employees for purposes of holding their church or denomination legally responsible for their actions under the principle of respondeat superior.*

Example. *An Ohio appeals court ruled that churches cannot be responsible for a pastor's defamatory comments unless they are made in the course of employment and in furtherance of the mission and functions of the church. A pastor allegedly made a defamatory statement to a government official, suggesting that a church member had embezzled church funds. The members sued the church, claiming that it was legally responsible for the pastor's defamatory statement on the basis of respondeat superior. The court concluded that the church could not be liable, since the pastor was not an employee. The court observed, "[A] church may now be held liable for its own torts as well as for the tortious acts of its*

---

[10] Moses v. Diocese of Colorado, 863 P.2d 310 (Colo. 1993).

[11] Brillhart v. Scheier, 758 P.2d 219 (Kan. 1988). A dissenting judge felt that the priest was an employee, and that his negligence should have been imputed to the diocese. The dissenter pointed to the following factors: (1) the diocese issued the priest W-2 forms each year; (2) the priest was on call 24 hours a day; (3) the priest's term of employment was indefinite; (4) the priest's work clearly furthered the regular business of the diocese; (5) the priest "was not engaged in an independent occupation in the sense that he contracts with different churches to perform pastoral services on a job-by-job basis; rather, he is engaged solely in his parish and can accept no other assignments without the consent of the bishop."

employees or agents imputed to it by the respondeat superior doctrine. . . . [W]hile plaintiff alleged an employment or agency relationship between the [pastor] and the church in his complaint, obviously to invoke the respondeat superior doctrine, he never developed the precise nature of that relationship from an evidentiary standpoint at trial." In other words, it was not clear that the pastor was a church employee, or that he was acting in the course of his employment when he made the allegedly defamatory remarks, and as a result the church could not be liable on the basis of respondeat superior.[12]

nonminister church workers

Example. *A Louisiana appeals court ruled that a church was responsible for injuries sustained in an automobile accident caused by the negligent driving of a deacon while on church business.*[13] *The deacon was driving his vehicle to pick up supplies for use in a church remodeling project. A bee entered his vehicle through an open window and landed on his arm. He began slapping at the bee, momentarily took his eyes off the road, and ran into two vehicles. The driver of one of the vehicles was killed, and her daughter was severely injured. A lawsuit was filed by the deceased woman's husband and surviving children against the deacon and the church. A state appeals court concluded that the church was responsible for the deacon's negligent driving. It noted that a church will be responsible for the actions of its "servants," and defined a servant as one "employed to perform the services and affairs of another and who is subject to the other's control or right to control with respect to the physical conduct in the performance of the services." The court continued, "In [this] case, the issue involves a religious organization's liability for the negligence of one of its deacons, who is not compensated for his services. An individual who volunteers services without an agreement for or expectation of reward may be deemed the servant of the one accepting those services. Whether the volunteer is to be considered a servant generally depends on the religious organization's right to control the activities of the volunteer." The court concluded that the church had sufficient control over the deacon to make him the church's servant: "[The deacon] was more than a casual volunteer and indeed was a non-employee leader of [the church]. Both the church membership and the board of deacons had the right to exercise and did, in fact, exercise control over him. The membership had the right to discharge him from his position as a deacon if he failed to perform his duties. The deacon board was responsible for the planning and execution of the church remodeling project and [the chairman of the deacon board] had the authority to assign specific tasks to the members of the deacon board. Moreover, regarding the specific task at issue, members of the deacon board directed [the negligent deacon] concerning the materials to purchase, designated the approved places to obtain the specified materials and designated the general time by which delivery was expected. Although the specific time and route for travel were not dictated . . . this [deacon] held one of the highest levels of authority and responsibility within the hierarchy of the church such that precise details were unnecessary."*

Example. *A Louisiana appeals court ruled that a church could not be liable on the basis of respondeat superior for sexual assaults committed by a volunteer worker.*[14] *A volunteer youth worker in a Catholic church provided tutoring services to a teenage girl who was experiencing difficulty with algebra. The volunteer engaged in repeated and unwelcome sexual assaults. The girl's parents later filed a lawsuit on behalf of their minor daughter against the tutor, the local church, the archdiocese, and the youth organization. The church defendants argued that they could not be legally responsible for the volunteer tutor's conduct since a "master-servant" relationship did not exist between the tutor and the church defendants. A*

---

[12] Cooper v. Grace Baptist Church, 612 N.E.2d 357 (Ohio App. 1992).

[13] Whetstone v. Dixon, 616 So.2d 764 (La. App. 1993).

[14] Doe v. Roman Catholic Church, 602 A.2d 129 (La. App.1992).

state appeals court agreed. It observed, "Louisiana's law on vicarious liability based on the respondeat superior doctrine is clear. Under the express provisions of [the Louisiana Civil Code] masters and employers are answerable for the damage occasioned by their servants and overseers, in the exercise of the functions in which they are employed. Under the jurisprudence interpreting this provision, the determination of whether a party may be held vicariously liable for the torts of another depends on whether the [one committing the misconduct] is characterized as a servant. . . . [This] case involves a religious or charitable organization's liability for the torts of a volunteer. Generally, one who volunteers services without an agreement for or expectation of reward may be a servant of one accepting such services. Determination of whether a given volunteer is in fact a servant generally depends on the charitable organization's right to control the activities of the volunteer. Determination of the right to control is a question of fact, based on consideration of the following factors: (1) degree to which the charity orders the volunteer to perform specific actions; (2) degree of contact between the charity and the volunteer; and (3) structural hierarchy of the charity. . . ." This test was not met in this case, the court concluded.

Example. *The Supreme Court of New Hampshire ruled that a church was not responsible for injuries caused by the negligent driving of a volunteer church worker.[15] A man operating a motorcycle sustained permanent injuries when he was struck by a car driven by a church volunteer. The volunteer was a certified public accountant and elected member of the church finance committee, and at the time of the accident was in the process of delivering church financial records to the church treasurer. The motorcycle operator sued the church, arguing that it was responsible for the volunteer's negligence on the basis of the respondeat superior doctrine. The trial court dismissed the lawsuit, ruling that the volunteer "was performing services for the church as an independent contractor. She was not an employee of the church and the church had no control over her actions on the day of the accident, or any other day. . . . Therefore, the [church] is not vicariously liable for the alleged negligence of [the volunteer]." The motorcycle operator appealed, and the state supreme court ruled in favor of the church. The supreme court began its opinion by noting that the question in this case was whether or not to extend the respondeat superior doctrine to volunteer workers. The court did not see any reason why the respondeat superior doctrine should not be applied to volunteer workers, but it insisted that this could occur only if "the community would consider the person an employee." The court concluded that the volunteer in this case would not be considered an employee by the community: "[A]lthough the church may have had control over the tasks assigned to [the volunteer], it had no right to control the physical performance or the details of the accounting services she performed." As a result, the court concluded that the respondeat superior doctrine did not apply, and accordingly the church was not legally responsible for the injuries caused by the volunteer's negligent driving.*

Example. *An Ohio court ruled that a denominational agency was not responsible for a local church elder's actions even though it exercised ecclesiastical control over him.[16] The elder, while driving his car, struck another vehicle. The impact killed the driver of the other vehicle and injured a passenger. The elder served as an elected but uncompensated official of a subdivision ("district") of a state denominational agency, and at the time of the accident was involved in distributing fliers for a district event. A lawsuit was brought by the injured passenger and the family of the deceased driver (the "victims") against national and state denominational agencies on the ground that they were legally responsible for the elder's actions. A trial court dismissed the lawsuit, and the case was appealed. The victims argued that the ecclesiastical control maintained by the church agencies was sufficient to make them liable for the elder's actions on the basis of the legal doctrine of respondeat superior. The court observed that "[r]espondeat superior liability attaches only where the work performed is that of a master, and the*

---

[15] Boissonnault v. Bristol Federated Church, 642 A.2d 328 (N.H. 1994).
[16] Nye v. Kemp, 646 N.E.2d 262 (Ohio App. 1994).

servant is subject to the control of the master in performing the work." The victims claimed that the church agencies had sufficient "control" over the elder to make them liable for his actions since they could revoke his license as an ordained minister if they found that he was not living up to the moral standards required by the denomination. Further, the victims pointed out that the elder was an official with a subdivision of the state denominational agency, and as such he was subject to control by the national and state agencies. The court concluded that these aspects of ecclesiastical control did not make the national or state church agencies liable for the elder's actions. It noted that the elder received no compensation from either the national or state agency, and that he had been elected rather than appointed to his office. It then observed, "[The elder] was not an employee of [the national, state, or district agencies]. [The national and state agencies] had no control over [the district]. [The national and state agencies] had no right to control where the [district] meetings were held, when they were held, who held them, topics that were covered, advertising of the meeting, or any other aspect of these meetings. [The national and state agencies] further had nothing to do with the fliers that [the elder] was distributing at the time of the accident. [The elder] controlled the distribution of the fliers. [He] made the initial decision to deliver the fliers in the first place. [He] also selected who would receive them and when he would deliver them. [He] had no salary, no set hours, no vacation or sick leave, and no bosses or supervisors in his role as chairman of [the district]. Furthermore, [he] supplied his own vehicle and was not reimbursed for gas or mileage. . . . In the instant action, it is clear that [the elder] was not receiving any compensation as an employee. Furthermore, it is also clear that [the state agency] did not supply [him] with the car or the fliers or any of the tools necessary to complete the promotion of this fellowship meeting. [The state agency] did not control the details and quality of [the elder's] work, the hours that [he] worked, the route that he was travelling, or his length of employment. Accordingly . . . this court agrees that reasonable minds could only conclude that [the elder] was not the agent of either [the national or state agency]. Accordingly, the trial court properly found that [these agencies] were not liable for the acts of [the elder]."

In summary, the determination of a minister's status for purposes of imputing liability to an employing church on the basis of respondeat superior is a complex inquiry that requires an analysis of all of the facts of each case. More recent court decisions are less likely to jump to the conclusion that clergy are employees. Some courts have drawn the helpful distinction between ecclesiastical and temporal control. The fact that a church exercises ecclesiastical control over a minister should not be controlling in determining whether or not the minister is an employee for purposes of assigning legal liability to his or her employing church. Courts should focus on aspects of temporal control in determining whether or not a minister is an employee for such purposes.

§ 10-02.2 — Negligent Conduct

The doctrine of respondeat superior imputes an employee's negligence to his or her employer. The term negligence *was defined at the beginning of this chapter. Some courts have expanded respondeat superior to make employers liable for an employee's intentional or even criminal misconduct, if the employee was attempting to serve the employer's interests.*

§ 10-02.3 — Course of Employment

Key point 10-02.3. Churches can be legally responsible on the basis of the respondeat superior doctrine for the actions of their employees only if those actions are committed within the course of employment and further the mission and functions of the church. Intentional and self-serving acts of church employees often will not satisfy this standard.

The doctrine of respondeat superior imputes an employee's negligence to his or her employer only if the negligence occurred in the course of employment. It often is difficult to ascertain whether employees are acting in the course of their employment at the time of a negligent act. Generally, conduct of an employee is in the course of employment if (1) it is of the kind the employee is employed to perform, (2) it occurs during the hours and within the geographical area authorized by the employment relationship, and (3) it is motivated, at least in part, by a desire to serve the employer. An employer generally will not be responsible for the misconduct of an employee that occurs before or after working hours, that occurs an unreasonable distance from an authorized work area, or that occurs while the employee is engaged in personal business.

> *Example. A federal appeals court concluded that a Methodist church was legally responsible for the copyright infringement of a minister of music since "the only inference that reasonably can be drawn from the evidence is that in selecting and arranging the song . . . for use by the church choir [the minister] was engaged in the course and scope of his employment by the church."[17]*

Many persons who have been sexually assaulted by church workers have attempted to sue their church or a denominational agency on the basis of respondeat superior. Most courts have rejected such efforts, on the ground that the offender was not acting within the scope of his or her employment while engaging in such acts. A few courts have interpreted the concept of "scope of employment" more broadly, and have found churches liable on the basis of respondeat superior. Examples of both kinds of cases are presented below.

1. Cases Refusing to Apply Respondeat Superior to Intentional or Criminal Acts

Most courts have refused to hold churches liable on the basis of respondeat superior for the sexual misconduct of employees or volunteers.

> *Example. A California appeals court ruled that a Catholic archdiocese was not responsible on the basis of respondeat superior for the seduction of a 16-year-old girl by several priests. The girl claimed that she had become pregnant through the priests' misconduct, that the priests used their influence to persuade her to remain silent, and that the priests sent her to the Philippine Islands to give birth. The court concluded that for the archdiocese to be liable under the theory of respondeat superior for the priests' conduct, their conduct had to be characteristic of the activities of the church or otherwise reasonably foreseeable. The court observed, "It would defy every notion of logic and fairness to say that sexual activity between a priest and a parishioner is characteristic of the Archbishop of the Roman Catholic Church. . . . Similarly, [the girl] has not pointed out any fact which could lead this court to the conclusion that the Archbishop ratified the concupiscent acts of the priests."[18]*

> *Example. A California court, in ruling that a church was not legally responsible for a Sunday school teacher's repeated rape of a young boy, observed, "Certainly [the teacher] was not employed to molest young boys. There is no evidence the acts occurred during Sunday School. . . . There is no evidence to suggest that [the teacher's] conduct was actuated by a purpose to serve [the church]. Rather, the acts were independent, self-serving pursuits unrelated to church activities. Finally, [the teacher's] acts of sexual molestation were not foreseeable in light of the duties he was hired to perform. There is no aspect of a Sunday School teacher's or member's duties that would make sexual abuse anything other than highly*

---

[17] Wihtol v. Crow, 309 F.2d 777 (8th Cir. 1962).
[18] Milla v. Roman Catholic Archbishop of Los Angeles, 232 Cal. Rptr. 685 (1986).

unusual and very startling. We conclude [the teacher's] acts against [the boy] were neither required, incidental to his duties, nor foreseeable. They were, therefore, not within the scope of his employment.[19]

Example. *A District of Columbia appeals court affirmed a trial court's summary judgment in favor of a church in a case alleging that the church was responsible for the sexual misconduct of a church custodian.*[20] *The court ruled that the sexual misconduct did not grow out of and was not generated by the employment and therefore the acts did not occur while the employee was acting within the scope of his employment. The court relied on the definition of "scope of employment" contained in section 228 of the Restatement of Agency: "(1) Conduct of a servant is within the scope of employment if, but only if: (a) it is of the kind he is employed to perform; (b) it occurs substantially within the authorized time and space limits; (c) it is actuated, at least in part, by a purpose to serve the master; and; (d) if force is intentionally used by the servant against another, the use of force is not unexpectable by the master. (2) Conduct of a servant is not within the scope of employment if it is different in kind from that authorized, far beyond the authorized time and space limits, or too little actuated by a purpose to serve the master."*

Example. *An Illinois court ruled that a church and a parent denomination were not legally responsible for a pastor's sexual assault of three boys.*[21] *The court emphasized that the pastor's assault constituted a deviation from the pastor's "scope of employment." Since the assault did not occur within the scope or course of the pastor's employment, it could not be imputed to the church or parent denomination.*

Example. *A New York court ruled that a Catholic church and diocese could not be liable on the basis of respondeat superior for the sexual molestation of an 11-year-old boy by a Catholic priest. The court noted that "no New York case has been cited in which an employer has been held vicariously liable for intentional sexual misconduct by an employee," and that sexual misconduct by a priest "on its face scarcely seems to fall within the scope of employment of a priest" as would be necessary for the church and diocese to be liable.*[22]

Example. *The Ohio Supreme Court ruled that state and national denominational offices could not be sued on the basis of respondeat superior as a result of the sexual misconduct of clergy.*[23] *The court noted that this doctrine generally does not apply to the intentional misconduct of employees if the misconduct is not designed to further the interests of the employer. The court observed, "It is well-established that in order for an employer to be liable under the doctrine of respondeat superior, the tort of the employee must be committed within the scope of employment. [However] . . . where the tort is intentional . . . the behavior giving rise to the tort must be calculated to facilitate or promote the business for which the [employee] was employed. . . . [The] employer would not be liable if an employee physically assaulted a patron without provocation. . . . [A]n intentional and willful attack committed by an agent or employee, to vent his own spleen or malevolence against the injured person, is a clear departure from his employment and his principal or employer is not responsible therefor. In other words, an employer is not liable for independent self-serving acts of his employees which in no way facilitate or promote his business." The court concluded, "[The denomination] in no way promotes or advocates nonconsensual sexual conduct between pastors and parishioners. The [state and national denominational offices] did not hire [the pastor] to rape, seduce, or otherwise physically assault members of his congregation. Fur-*

---

[19] Scott v. Central Baptist Church, 243 Cal. Rptr. 128 (4th Dist. App. 1988).
[20] Mosely v. The Second New St. Paul's Baptist Church, 534 A.2d 346 (D.C. App. 1987).
[21] Mt. Zion State Bank v. Central Illinois Conference of the United Methodist Church, 556 N.E.2d 1270 (Ill. App. 1990).
[22] Jones by Jones v. Trane, 591 N.Y.S.2d 927 (Sup. 1992).
[23] Byrd v. Faber, 565 N.E.2d 584 (Ohio 1991).

thermore, the [plaintiffs] have alleged no fact indicating that the [denominational offices] should reasonably have foreseen that [the pastor] would behave in this manner toward his parishioners. Consequently, [plaintiffs] have failed to state a claim of respondeat superior or liability on the part of the church, and the trial court was correct in dismissing that portion of their complaint."

Several other courts have concluded that churches cannot be sued on the basis of respondeat superior if church workers were not engaged in the course of their employment at the time their conduct resulted in injuries to others. To illustrate, the following kinds of conduct were deemed not to have occurred within the course of employment: a minister sexually seduced a woman during marital counseling;[24] seven Catholic priests allegedly engaged in a sexual relationship with a female parishioner;[25] a teacher at a church-operated school engaged in sexual relations with a minor;[26] a Catholic nun was driving a car on personal rather than church business.[27]

2. CASES APPLYING RESPONDEAT SUPERIOR TO INTENTIONAL OR CRIMINAL ACTS

A small minority of courts have found churches liable on the basis of respondeat superior for the sexual misconduct of employees and volunteers. In reaching such a conclusion, these courts have interpreted the concept of "course of employment" very broadly.

__Example.__ The Alaska Supreme Court ruled that a pastoral counseling center could be sued on the basis of respondeat superior by a woman who was sexually seduced by a counselor.[28] The woman claimed that she had visited the counselor on several occasions, and that the pastoral counselor "negligently handled the transference phenomenon" by taking advantage of her sexually. She allegedly suffered severe emotional injuries, and as a result sued the center and two of its directors for damages. She claimed that the center was legally responsible for the counselor's misconduct on the basis of respondeat superior. In explaining the "transference phenomenon," the director of the center explained that "transference is a phenomenon that occurs that is similar to a state of dependency in which the client begins to project the roles and relationships and the images and experiences that they have had with other people previously in their life, especially other significant people such as mother, father, brothers, sisters, early teachers and adult models, upon the therapist." The director acknowledged that the transference relationship is very "delicate" and "fragile," and that a counselor has "a professional and ethical responsibility to manage that relationship so that the client is not damaged in any way." A trial court summarily dismissed the lawsuit, concluding that the center was not responsible for the intentional and unauthorized misconduct of a counselor. The case was appealed directly to the state supreme court, which reversed the trial court's decision and ordered the case to proceed to trial. The court announced a very broad interpretation of the respondeat superior doctrine. The court concluded that an employer could be responsible for an employee's sexual misconduct that "arises out of and is reasonably incidental to the employee's legitimate work activities"—even if the misconduct was intentional and unauthorized by the employer. This

---

[24] *See, e.g.,* Destefano v. Grabian, 763 P.2d 275 (Colo. 1988) (the court ruled that the church and a parent denomination might be liable on the basis of negligent hiring or negligent supervision); Schmidt v. Bishop, 779 F. Supp. 321 (S.D.N.Y. 1991); Bladen v. First Presbyterian Church, 857 P.2d 789 (Okla. 1993); Erickson v. Christenson, 781 P.2d 383 (Or. App. 1989) (the court ruled that the church and a parent denomination might be liable on the basis of negligent hiring or negligent supervision); J. v. Victory Baptist Church, 372 S.E.2d 391 (Va. 1988) (the court ruled that the church was not liable on the basis of respondeat superior, but might be liable on the basis of negligent retention or supervision if it were aware of previous incidents of misconduct but did nothing to monitor the employee's behavior); Lund v. Capel, 675 P.2d 226 (Wash. 1984).

[25] Milla v. Tamayo, 232 Cal. Rptr. 685 (1986).

[26] Scott v. Blanchet High School, 747 P.2d 1124 (Wash. App. 1987).

[27] Mattingly v. State Department of Health, 509 So.2d 82 (La. App. 1987). *See also* Ambrosio v. Price, 495 F. Supp. 381 (D. Nebr. 1979).

[28] Doe v. Samaritan Counseling Center, 791 P.2d 344 (Alaska 1990).

ruling ignores the vast majority of court rulings that have rejected an employer's legal responsibility for the intentional misconduct of an employee.

Example. *A Louisiana appeals court found a church-affiliated hospital liable for the sexual misconduct of an employee who had been thoroughly screened and supervised.[29] The hospital hired a male nursing assistant for a psychiatric ward after conducting a thorough background check that showed no criminal record and no unfavorable references from former employers. After working for six months, this employee raped a 16-year-old girl. The victim sued the hospital. The appeals court concluded that the hospital could not be liable for the assault on the basis of negligent hiring, because of the thorough nature of its pre-employment investigation. However, the court concluded that the hospital was legally responsible for the assault on the basis of "vicarious liability." The court noted that when determining whether an employer is responsible for an employee's actions, the following factors must be considered: (1) was the employee's act "primarily employment rooted"; (2) was the employee's act "reasonably incidental to the performance of the employee's duties"; (3) did the employee's act occur on the employer's premises; and (4) did the act occur during normal working hours. Not all of these factors must be present for an employer to be responsible for an employee's actions. The court concluded that the hospital was responsible for the assault in this case because the assault occurred on the employer's premises while the employee was on duty, and the assault was "reasonably incidental to the performance of his duties as a nurse's assistant although totally unauthorized by the employer and motivated by the employee's personal interest." Further, the court observed that the assault was "closely connected to his employment duties so that the risk of harm faced by the young female victim was fairly attributable to his employer."*

Example. *A Washington state appellate court concluded that a Catholic diocese could be sued on the basis of respondeat superior for damages resulting from the alleged sexual molestation of minors by a Catholic priest.[30] A Catholic diocese in Louisiana suspended a priest from performing his "priestly duties" after he admitted to sexual misconduct with minors. The priest was asked to leave the diocese, and he eventually was admitted (with the approval of the diocese) to a rehabilitation program in another state. Just prior to the priest's discharge from this program, the diocese informed him that his "options in the ministry were severely limited if not nil," and that "because of the possibility of legal action and the responsibility on the part of any institution that might hire you, I think realistically that for church employment you are a very poor risk." The diocese further advised the priest that he would not be permitted to perform priestly duties upon his release, and that he was not to return to the diocese. Following his release from the rehabilitation program, the priest accepted a job as a counselor of adolescents in an alcohol and drug rehabilitation center in a private hospital. He was terminated from this job because of complaints of sexual abuse by former patients. Eight adolescents and one adult sued the hospital, the priest, as well as his diocese and bishop. The plaintiffs alleged that the diocese had negligently supervised the priest, and that it should have warned the private hospital of his pedophilia. The appeals court agreed that "an employer may be held liable for acts beyond the scope of employment because of its prior knowledge of the dangerous tendencies of its employee." The diocese argued that it could not be liable for the misconduct of the priest, since his actions did not arise out of his priestly duties and accordingly were not within the scope of his employment relationship with the diocese. In rejecting this claim, the court observed that "the duty of obedience which [the priest] owed the diocese encompassed all phases of his life and correspondingly the diocese's authority over its cleric went beyond the customary employer/employee relationship. . . . Despite his employment with [the hospital], the employment relationship between [the priest] and the diocese continued."*

---

[29] Samuels v. Southern Baptist Hospital 594 So.2d 571 (La. App. 1992).

[30] Does 1-9 v. Compcare, Inc., 763 P.2d 1237 (Wash. App. 1988).

§ 10-02.4 — Inapplicability to Nonprofit Organizations

Key point 10-02.4. The fundamental policy supporting the doctrine of respondeat superior is "risk allocation." That is, an employer can allocate or shift the risk of injuries caused by the operation of its business to the consumers of its products and services by increasing the cost of those products and services to reflect the cost of personal injury claims. This policy has no application to churches and other charities that are incapable of exacting higher "contributions" from their members to cover personal injury claims. Some courts have recognized the impropriety of applying the respondeat superior doctrine to religious organizations.

The policy considerations supporting vicarious liability rest upon the fundamental principle of risk allocation. That is, an employer has the unique ability to allocate the risks of inevitable injuries suffered by the consumers of its products and services through price adjustments.[31] By increasing its prices, the employer allocates the risk of injuries to the consumers of its products and services. As reasonable as this policy may be in the context of "for-profit" employers, it has no application to most nonprofit employers who have no ability to allocate risk to consumers through price increases. Certainly this is true of religious organizations, which would find it difficult if not impossible to compel members to donate larger amounts to "allocate risks" to the "consumers" of its services. For this reason, the rule of vicarious liability should be used sparingly, if at all, in the context of nonprofit employers. Some courts have recognized that the concept of vicarious liability has little if any relevance in the context of nonprofit religious organizations. To illustrate, one judge made the following observation in a case involving the alleged liability of a religious employer for the sexual misconduct of an employee:

> Spreading the cost of therapist-patient sex to the consumers of mental health services is unfair. Therapist-patient sex, although not uncommon, is not an inevitable cost of mental health care. It is a cost imposed by therapists who intentionally disregard the standards of conduct of mental health professionals for personal sexual gratification.[32]

The same judge also rejected the contention that a religious employer can "allocate risk" by purchasing liability insurance:

> Imposing vicarious liability would tend to make malpractice insurance, already a scarce and expensive resource, even harder to obtain. It is also unclear whether malpractice insurance would even cover sexual misconduct. Whether or not mental health employers could insure against this risk, they would have to raise the cost of their services dramatically. Mental health services would be denied to those who are least able to pay. While victims of therapist sexual misconduct may enjoy a greater chance of being compensated, the cost of creating that benefit in reduced access to mental health services is unacceptable.[33]

The California Supreme Court ruled that a public school district was not legally responsible, on the basis of respondeat superior, for the injuries suffered by a 15-year-old boy who was sexually assaulted by his high school math teacher.[34] This case is significant for a couple of reasons. First, the court rejected the application of the respondeat superior doctrine not on the basis of the facts of the case, but rather on the basis of the doctrine's own theoretical justifications. The court observed that

---

[31] *See* note 2, *supra,* and accompanying text.
[32] Doe v. Samaritan Counseling Center, 791 P.2d 344, 354 (Alaska 1990) (dissenting opinion).
[33] *Id.* at 353-354.
[34] John R. v. Oakland Unified School District, 256 Cal. Rptr. 766 (Cal. 1989).

although the facts of this case can be made to fit a version of the respondeat superior doctrine, we are unpersuaded that they should be or that the doctrine is appropriately invoked here. We draw our decision not from the various factual scenarios in which vicarious liability has or has not been imposed on employers for the torts of their employees, but instead from the underlying rationale for the respondeat superior doctrine.[35]

The court stated the rationale for the respondeat superior doctrine as follows:

Three reasons have been suggested for imposing liability on an enterprise for the risks incident to the enterprise: (1) [I]t tends to provide a spur toward accident prevention; (2) it tends to provide greater assurance of compensation for accident victims; and (3) at the same time it tends to provide reasonable assurance that, like other costs, accident losses will be broadly and equitably distributed among the beneficiaries of the enterprises that entail them.[36]

The court rejected all three reasons as a basis for imposing liability on the school district in this case. The court observed:

The first of these three considerations just noted plays little role in the allocation of responsibility for the sexual misconduct of employees generally, and with respect to the unique situation of teachers, indicates that untoward consequences could flow from imposing vicarious liability on school districts. Although it is unquestionably important to encourage both the careful selection of these employees and the close monitoring of their conduct, such concerns are, we think, better addressed by holding school districts to the exercise of due care in such matters and subjecting them to liability only for their own direct negligence in that regard. Applying the doctrine of respondeat superior to impose, in effect, strict liability in this context would be far too likely to deter districts from encouraging, or even authorizing, extracurricular and/or one-on-one contacts between teachers and students or to induce districts to impose such rigorous controls on activities of this nature that the educational process would be negatively affected. . . .

Nor is the second consideration—the assurance of compensation for accident victims— appropriately invoked here. The acts here differ from the normal range of risks for which costs can be spread and insurance sought. The imposition of vicarious liability on school districts for the sexual torts of their employees would tend to make insurance, already a scarce resource, even harder to obtain, and could lead to the diversion of needed funds from the classroom to cover claims.

The only element of the analysis that might point in favor of vicarious liability here is the propriety of spreading the risk of loss among the beneficiaries of the enterprise. School districts and the community at large benefit from the authority placed in teachers to carry out the educational mission, and it can be argued that the consequences of an abuse of that authority should be shared on an equally broad basis. But the connection between the authority conferred on teachers to carry out their instructional duties and the abuse of that authority to

---

[35] *Id.* at 773 (emphasis added).

[36] *Id.* at 773-74, quoting the California Supreme Court's decision in Perez v. Van Groningen & Sons, Inc., 227 Cal. Rptr. 106, 108 (Cal. 1986), which was quoting 5 HARPER, JAMES & GRAY, THE LAW OF TORTS (2nd ed. 1986) § 26.5 n. 21 (citations omitted).

indulge in personal, sexual misconduct is simply too attenuated to deem a sexual assault as falling within the range of risks allocable to a teacher's employer. It is not a cost this particular enterprise should bear, and the consequences of imposing liability are unacceptable.[37]

It is very significant that the California Supreme Court rejected so decisively the application of the respondeat superior doctrine in the context of sexual misconduct of teachers. Surely the same considerations apply to religious organizations.

The court's rejection of the availability of insurance coverage as a justification for extending the respondeat superior principle to charities is important. Insurance coverage is not an effective means for churches to allocate risk, for a few very significant reasons. First, insurance is expensive, sometimes prohibitively so for smaller churches. Second, insurance coverage is becoming increasingly difficult for religious organizations to obtain. Third, insurance policies contain numerous exclusions—in some cases excluding one or more of a church's greatest risks. Fourth, covered risks are subject to the dollar limits of the policy. In some cases, higher risks have reduced coverage. Churches are uninsured for damages claimed in excess of the policy limits.

In a case upholding the validity of a state law limiting the liability of charities, the New Jersey Supreme Court made the following significant observation:

> The principle of charitable immunity was deeply rooted in the common law of New Jersey. The principle is premised on the fact that charitable associations are created to pursue philanthropic goals and the accomplishment of those goals would be hampered if they were to pay tort judgments in cases similar to this matter. . . . [A] person who makes a charitable contribution expects his donation to further the goals of the organization, and not to be used to satisfy lawsuits which bear no direct relationship to those goals.[38]

The court also noted that the state limitation on charity liability reflected the inapplicability of the respondeat superior doctrine to charitable organizations.

§ 10-03 Negligent Selection of Church Workers — In General

One of the most significant legal risks facing churches today is negligent selection. The term negligence means carelessness or a failure to exercise reasonable care. *Negligent selection,* then, means carelessness or a failure to exercise reasonable care in the selection of a worker. Consider the following examples:

Example. *A church employs a pastor without any investigation into his background. The pastor seduces a counselee during marriage counseling. The victim sues the church, claiming that it is responsible for her injuries on the basis of negligent selection. It is later learned that the pastor committed adultery with a member of his prior congregation. No one in his present church asked for any information or references from the former congregation.*

Example. *A church board hires a youth pastor despite its knowledge that the youth pastor engaged in inappropriate sexual relations with an adolescent member of his youth group in a prior church. The board wants to give the youth pastor a "second chance." Six months after being hired, a parent alleges*

---

[37] *Id.* at 774.

[38] Rupp v. Brookdale Baptist Church, 577 A.2d 188, 190 (N.J. Super. 1990), quoting in part from Bottari, The Charitable Immunity Act, 5 Seton Hall Legis. J. 61, 63-64 (1980).

that her adolescent daughter was molested by the youth pastor. The church is later sued by the victim and her mother, who allege that the church is responsible for the youth pastor's misconduct on the basis of negligent selection.

Example. *A church leader asks a church member if he would drive several members of the church youth group to an activity. The member agrees to do so. While driving to the activity, the member is involved in an accident while driving at an excessive rate of speed. Some of the children are injured. Parents later learn that the driver had a suspended driver's license as a result of numerous traffic violations. No one at the church was aware of the member's driving history, and no one ever attempted to find out. The church is later sued by two of the families, who allege that the church is responsible for the driver's actions on the basis of negligent selection.*

Example. *D is a computer technician who feels a "calling" to a counseling ministry. While D is a college graduate, she is not a minister and has never studied psychology or counseling. She is not a licensed counselor. D's church uses D as a part-time volunteer counselor. D counsels with G, a 25-year-old woman with severe emotional problems. D persuades G that her problems are a result of the fact that she was sexually molested by her father when she was a child. G has no recollection of any inappropriate conduct by her father, and at first is repelled by this suggestion. Over the course of several meetings, G comes to believe that D is correct. This results in a complete estrangement from her father. G's father sues the church, claiming that it is responsible for the harm to his family as a result of its negligent selection of D as a counselor.*

Example. *A church takes a group of 25 young children to a local lake for an afternoon of swimming. There are 3 adults who accompany the group. No lifeguards are on duty. One of the children drowns, and no one is able to resuscitate her because none of the adult chaperones is qualified to perform resuscitation techniques. The victim's parents sue the church, claiming that their child's death was caused by the church's negligent selection of the adult chaperones. They assert that the church should have selected at least one adult worker who was qualified to perform resuscitation techniques.*

Example. *A church has difficulty recruiting adults to work in the infant nursery during church services, and so it often uses adolescents. On one occasion, two 13-year-old girls were overseeing several infants. One of the infants broke a leg when she fell off a diaper changing table while one of the 13-year-old girls was changing her diaper. The infant's parents threaten to sue the church on the basis of negligent selection for their child's injuries.*

§ 10-04 Negligent Selection of Church Workers — Sexual Misconduct Cases Involving Minor Victims

> *Key point 10-04. A church may be liable on the basis of negligent selection for a worker's molestation of a minor if the church was negligent in the selection of the worker. Negligence means a failure to exercise reasonable care, and so negligent selection refers to a failure to exercise reasonable care in the selection of the worker. Liability based on negligent selection may be imposed upon a church for the acts of employees and volunteers.*

In recent years, hundreds of churches have been sued as a result of the sexual molestation of minors by church workers on church property or during church activities. Common examples include the molestation of male and female children and adolescents by youth pastors, camp counselors, Sunday school teachers, church custodians, volunteer youth workers, and others. In many of these cases, the victim alleges either or both of the following two theories: (1) the church was negligent in hiring the offender without adequate screening or evaluation, or (2) the church was negligent in its supervision of the offender. The second of these theories ("negligent supervision") is discussed later in this chapter.

As noted earlier in this chapter, the term negligence refers to conduct that creates an unreasonable risk of foreseeable harm to others. It connotes carelessness, heedlessness, inattention, or inadvertence. It is important to recognize that churches are not "guarantors" of the safety and well-being of children. They are not absolutely liable for every injury that occurs on their premises in the course of their activities. Generally, they are responsible only for those injuries that result from their negligence. Negligent selection simply means that the church failed to act responsibly and with due care in the selection of workers (both volunteer and compensated) for positions involving the supervision or custody of minors. Victims of molestation who have sued a church often allege that the church was negligent in not adequately screening applicants. The typical church hires just about anyone who expresses an interest in working in a volunteer capacity with the youth in the church. Even applicants for compensated positions are not screened by many churches. Often, when an incident of molestation occurs the senior minister is later asked to testify in court regarding steps that the church took to prevent the incident. The victim's lawyer asks, "What did you or your staff do to prevent this incident from occurring—what procedures did you utilize to check the molester's background and suitability for work with children?" All too often, the minister's answer is "nothing." The jury's reaction to such a response is predictable.

A single incident of abuse or molestation can devastate a church. Parents often become enraged, the viability of the church's youth and children's programs is jeopardized, and church leaders may be blamed for allowing the incident to happen. But far more tragic is the emotional trauma to the victim and the victim's family, and the enormous potential legal liability the church faces.

There is good news, however. Church leaders can take relatively simple yet effective steps to significantly reduce the likelihood of such an incident occurring. This chapter will review some of the more significant reported court rulings, and then suggest a number of preventive measures that any church can implement in order to reduce the risk of such incidents.

Tip. No one understands or appreciates risk better than insurance companies. Risk evaluation is their business. As a result, it is very important to observe that a number of church insurance companies have reduced the insurance coverage they provide for sexual misconduct, and in some cases they have excluded it entirely. Some companies are suggesting that these incidents are excluded under the provision in most policies excluding damages based on intentional, criminal conduct (most acts of sexual molestation involve criminal activity). Church leaders should immediately review their church liability insurance policy to determine whether the church has any coverage for acts of sexual misconduct, and if so, whether such coverage has been limited in any way. If you fit within either category, the risk management recommendations in this chapter are of even greater relevance.

Key point. Some courts use the term "negligent hiring" instead of "negligent selection." This text uses the term negligent selection since it is a broader term that encompasses the selection of both employees and uncompensated volunteers. Technically, volunteers are not "hired," and so the narrower term "negligent hiring" would not apply to them.

§ 10-04.1 — Court Decisions Recognizing Negligent Selection Claims

Key point 10-04.1. Some courts have found churches liable on the basis of negligent selection for the molestation of a minor by a church worker if the church failed to exercise reasonable care in the selection of the worker.

This section reviews court decisions in which a church or other religious organization was found liable on the basis of negligent selection for a worker's acts of child molestation.

TABLE 10-1
WHY SEXUAL MISCONDUCT IS THE GREATEST
LEGAL RISK FACING CHURCHES TODAY

Church liability for the sexual misconduct of employees and volunteers is the most significant risk facing churches today for a number of reasons, including the following:

(1) Many opportunities. There ordinarily are many opportunities within the church for persons to engage in sexual misconduct with adults or children. Churches have many children involved in a variety of programs, and many pastors engage in extensive counseling.

(2) Trust. Churches are institutions of trust, and many members and leaders cannot conceive of acts of sexual misconduct occurring on their premises. As a result, they do not see a need to institute procedures and policies that will reduce the risk of such behavior.

(3) Money damages. The amount of money damages that courts award in such cases can be substantial.

(4) Limited insurance coverage. Most church insurance policies either exclude sexual misconduct claims, or significantly reduce the amount of coverage. This means that many churches face a potentially large and underinsured risk.

(5) Other damages. The damage that such claims cause to victims, victims' families, offenders, congregations, and church leaders is considerable.

(6) Board liability. Board members face personal liability in such cases if they refused to take steps to address this risk or ignored danger signals, and their conduct amounts to "gross negligence."[39]

(7) Punitive damages. Churches face the possibility of being assessed punitive damages if church leaders willfully refused to address this risk or ignored danger signals. Punitive damages are designed to "punish" wrongdoers for reckless or grossly negligent conduct. They are not covered by church insurance policies.

(8) Polarization. Congregations often are polarized in the aftermath of an incident of sexual misconduct. Some members insist that the offender be forgiven, while others focus on issues of justice, accountability, and protection.

---

[39] *See* § 6-08.1, *supra.*

Example. The Alaska Supreme Court ruled that a church could be legally responsible for the alleged sexual abuse of a 3-year-old child that occurred in a church nursery.[40] The court concluded that the church could be responsible on the basis of "negligent hiring" since it did not exercise a sufficiently high degree of care in selecting the volunteer worker who allegedly committed the abuse. In particular, the court emphasized that the church had not interviewed the volunteer regarding her own history of child abuse, and did not conduct any "background check." The court observed, "[T]he employer, in selecting an employee, must exercise a degree of care commensurate with the nature and danger of the business in which he is engaged and the nature and grade of services for which the employee is intended. In the present case, [the church] was in the business of providing a safe place for the care of young children whose parents were attending church services. It engaged [the attendant] to make sure that those children were properly cared for. We consider it self-evident that the selection of individuals to whom the care and safety of young children will be entrusted requires a relatively high level of care before it may be considered reasonable. [The church] did not interview [the attendant] or conduct a background check, nor has it offered any evidence that [the attendant's] past sexual abuse did not affect her competency." The court rejected the church's claim that it was not required to conduct an interview of background check on the nursery attendant since she was a mere volunteer rather than an employee. It noted simply that a volunteer "may be subject to the same interview and background checks" as any other worker, so long as the volunteer is subject to the control of the employer. The court emphasized that adults who experienced sexual abuse as children are much more likely to be child abusers than the general population. It quoted from an article on child abuse: "One of the predisposing conditions [to child sexual abuse] that has been of considerable interest to clinicians and researchers is an experience of sexual abuse in childhood. Being sexually victimized as a child is a common experience for adult sex offenders and mothers of victims of sexual mistreatment. Moreover, childhood experiences of sexual abuse have been found at higher rates among those who victimize or are mothers of victims than in comparison groups." In summary, the court concluded that a church can be legally responsible on the basis of negligent selection for acts of sexual molestation inflicted by a nursery attendant if the church (1) failed to interview the attendant to determine whether or not the attendant had been a victim of sexual abuse as a minor, and (2) did not conduct any background investigation into the attendant's suitability and fitness as a child care worker.

Example. A California court ruled that a church was responsible on the basis of "negligent hiring" for the sexual molestation of a 13-year-old boy by his pastor.[41] However, the court concluded that the church was not responsible for the victim's molestation of his 6-year-old sister. The pastor was hired after being suspended from the ministry for a number of years because of allegations that he had molested a child. He later molested a 13-year-old boy who attended the church. The court noted that "in California, an employer can be held liable for negligent hiring if he knows the employee is unfit, or has reason to believe the employee is unfit or fails to use reasonable care to discover the employee's unfitness before hiring him." The court noted that the local church's pastoral search committee was aware that the pastor previously had "stepped down" from the ministry for some reason. Yet, the church did not "investigate or make any inquiry" regarding the pastor's fitness to serve. The court observed that the local church's pastoral selection committee was aware of "some difficulty with [the pastor's] reappointment to the active ministry and understood he had been on a sabbatical of some kind. . . . Nevertheless, [the church] did not investigate or make any inquiry regarding [the pastor's] fitness to serve as pastor." The court rejected the sister's claim that the church was liable for her brother's acts of molestation. At the trial, a child psychiatrist testified that the 13-year-old brother had molested his sister because of his experience

---

[40] Broderick v. King's Way Church, 808 P.2d 1211 (Alaska 1991).
[41] Evan F. v. Hughson United Methodist Church, 10 Cal. Rptr.2d 748 (Cal. App. 3 Dist. 1992).

with the pastor. The psychiatrist explained that abused and molested children often abuse and molest others. She noted that the brother had not previously engaged in any incidents of child molestation, and that the pastor's assaults had triggered a premature sexual stimulation and "awakening" of the boy (who was then an early adolescent entering puberty). The psychiatrist concluded that the boy, in molesting his sister, was "re-enacting" or "acting out" his own molestation experience of a larger person overpowering a smaller one. The court, in rejecting the sister's claim, observed, "[T]he theory of negligent hiring here encompasses the particular risk of molestation by an employee with a history of this specific conduct. It does not encompass acts done by non-employees, such as the 13-year-old brother, or consequences involving less particular, even speculative, hazards. To conclude otherwise would impose liability on the person who hired the person who molested the person who molested the person in the sister's position. This convoluted syntax alone argues against imposing liability in this situation."

Example. *A Colorado court dismissed a lawsuit brought by a woman alleging that her church acted improperly and unlawfully when it dismissed her after she made complaints of sexual harassment and child molestation against another minister.[42] The woman alleged that between 1968 and 1975, when she was a minor, her stepfather committed various acts of sexual assault against her when they resided together. Her stepfather was a minister at the time, and later became president of his denomination. The woman pursued ministerial studies and was licensed as a minister. After serving as a minister in the State of Washington she moved to the Denver area to start a new church. She later learned that her stepfather, with whom she had severed all ties, was also pastoring a church in the Denver area. She learned that her stepfather was allegedly sexually harassing women church employees and a woman parishioner in his Denver church. She reported this alleged harassment, as well as the sexual abuse she had suffered from her stepfather as a minor, to denominational officers. In response, the stepfather filed charges with the denomination against the woman, claiming that her allegations were false and demanding a full investigation. After an investigation, denominational officers revoked the woman's license and denied her the opportunity to open a new church. The woman responded by filing a lawsuit against her stepfather and her denomination alleging several theories of liability including illegal retaliation by denominational officials in response to her charges of sexual harassment, and negligent hiring of her stepfather by denominational officials. The court acknowledged that "[a]n employer may be liable for harm to others for negligently employing an improper person for a task that may involve risk to others." The woman claimed that her stepfather had been involved in an extramarital affair with a parishioner at another church prior to his present assignment and that denominational officials failed to investigate this allegation. The court concluded that "the extramarital affair was sufficiently different from [the woman's] allegations against [her stepfather] and, thus, did not create a duty on the part of the church to foresee [his] conduct." Further, the court noted that during the time the woman was allegedly abused as a child, her stepfather was not a minister, and that she did not allege that denominational officials knew or should have known of the stepfather's alleged sexual abuse of his stepdaughter when they hired him."*

Example. *A Florida court ruled that a 27-year-old man who had been molested by a priest when he was a minor was barred by the statute of limitations from suing his church.[43] As a result, the court was not required to decide whether or not the first amendment prevents the civil courts from resolving negligence claims brought against churches for the sexual misconduct of clergy. However, the court did make the following observation: "In any event, we are persuaded that just as the state may prevent a church from offering human sacrifices, it may protect its children against injuries caused by pedophiles by authorizing civil damages against a church that knowingly (including should know) creates a situ-*

---

[42] Van Osdol v. Vogt, 892 P.2d 402 (Colo. App. 1994). Accord Bear Valley Church of Christ v. DeBose, 928 P.2d 1315 (Colo. 1996).
[43] Doe v. Dorsey, 683 So.2d 614 (Fl. App. 1996).

ation in which such injuries are likely to occur. We recognize that the state's interest must be compelling indeed in order to interfere in the church's selection, training and assignment of its clerics. We would draw the line at criminal conduct."

Example. *A New York court ruled that a Catholic church and diocese could be sued on the basis of negligent hiring as a result of the sexual molestation of an 11-year-old boy by a Catholic priest.[44] The victim and his sister were both enrolled in a parochial school operated by the church. An associate pastor at the church (who also served as director of religious education for the school) obtained permission from the victim's mother to take him to an athletic facility at a local college to play racquetball and basketball and go swimming. While in the shower room prior to entering the pool, the pastor allegedly removed all his clothing and made the victim do the same. He then molested the victim. The boy's mother later sued the pastor, church, and diocese, claiming that her son had suffered substantial emotional injuries. She alleged that the church and diocese were liable on the basis of negligent hiring. Specifically, she asserted that the church and diocese were liable for the misconduct of the pastor on the basis of their own negligence in hiring and placing him in contact with boys with inadequate investigation of his background and with actual or "constructive" knowledge of his propensities. The court rejected the argument of the church and diocese that permitting the civil courts to find religious organizations liable on the basis of negligent hiring of clergy would constitute excessive governmental interference with church autonomy in violation of the first amendment guaranty of religious freedom. The court observed, "[If the mother is] successful in establishing that, with knowledge that the priest was likely to commit sexual abuse on youths with whom he was put in contact, his employers placed or continued him in a setting in which such abuse occurred, the fact that the placement occurred in the course of internal administration of the religious units does not preclude holding the institutions accountable to the victim of their neglect in administration. Indeed, a contrary holding—that a religious body must be held free from any responsibility for wholly predictable and foreseeable injurious consequences of personnel decisions, although such decisions incorporate no theological or dogmatic tenets—would go beyond first amendment protection and cloak such bodies with an exclusive immunity greater than that required for the preservation of the principles constitutionally safeguarded."*

Example. *A federal court in Rhode Island ruled that the first amendment did not prevent it from resolving a lawsuit brought by victims of clergy sexual misconduct against church officials.[45] Three adult males sued diocesan officials for injuries they allegedly sustained when they were molested by two priests several years before. The victims claimed that prior to the acts of molestation, the diocese knew that the priests were pedophiles and not only failed to take appropriate preventative action, but also actively concealed the priests' sexual misconduct. The court rejected the diocese's argument that the first amendment guaranty of religious freedom prevents the civil courts from imposing liability on religious organizations for failing to properly screen or supervise clergy: "[T]here is no indication that the reasonably prudent person standard established by tort law and the requirements of Roman Catholic doctrine are incompatible. The [diocese does] not claim that the Roman Catholic Church either condones or tolerates sexual abuse of children. On the contrary, they have made it clear that the Catholic Church considers such conduct to be opprobrious. . . . Briefly stated, there is no indication that, by taking the kind of preventative action required by tort law, the [diocese] would have violated any 'doctrine, practice or law' of the Roman Catholic Church. In the absence of such a conflict, subjecting the [diocese] to potential tort liability does not violate [its] right to the free exercise of religion."*

---

[44] Jones by Jones v. Trane. 591 N.Y.S.2d 927 (Sup. 1992).
[45] Smith v. O'Connell, 986 F. Supp. 73 (D.R.I. 1997).

Example. A federal court in Vermont ruled that an adult who claimed to have been sexually abused by a nun some 40 years earlier could sue a Catholic diocese for his alleged injuries.[46] The lawsuit claimed that the diocese was liable for the priest's acts on the basis of negligence. The court rejected the argument of the diocese that the lawsuit was barred by the first amendment guaranty of religious freedom. Specifically, it argued that by permitting the victim to sue the diocese, the court would be forced to determine what is acceptable behavior by a minister or other religious practitioner in a religious institution such as a church-run orphanage. The court agreed in part with this argument: "The plaintiff's allegations of intentional and negligent conduct on the part of [the diocese] in hiring and supervising [the nun] and in fostering an environment in which sexual and physical abuse could occur give rise to serious constitutional concerns. Inquiry by a court or jury into the policies and practices of a religious organization in supervising and hiring clergy and other religious officials may foster excessive entanglement with religion. On the other hand, if hiring was done with knowledge that a prospective employee had perverted sexual proclivities, the institution might well be held accountable even though the hiring was part of the administration of a religious facility."

Example. The Virginia Supreme Court ruled that a church and its pastor could be sued by a mother whose child was sexually assaulted by a church employee.[47] A mother sued a church and its pastor, alleging that her 10-year-old daughter had been repeatedly raped and assaulted by a church employee. She asserted that the church and minister were legally responsible on the basis of several grounds, including "negligent hiring" (referred to as negligent selection in this chapter). Specifically, she alleged that when the employee was hired, the church and minister either knew or should have known that he had recently been convicted of aggravated sexual assault on a young girl, that he was on probation for the offense, and that a condition of his probation was that he not be involved or associated with children. Despite these circumstances, the individual was hired and entrusted with duties that encouraged him to come freely into contact with children, and in addition was given keys to all of the church's doors. The mother alleged that the employee in fact came into contact with her daughter on the church's premises, and had sexual intercourse with her on numerous occasions. The court ruled that the church could be sued on the basis of negligent selection. It rejected the church's contentions that the theory of negligent selection either was not recognized under Virginia law, or was not recognized in the context of church employers. The court also rejected the church's contention that it could not be responsible for criminal acts of employees: "To say that a negligently hired employee who acts willfully or criminally thus relieves his employer of liability for negligent selection when willful or criminal conduct is precisely what the employer should have foreseen would rob the tort of vitality . . . ." The court also rejected the church's contention that it could not be liable for the employee's acts of molestation since they had not occurred within the scope of employment. It acknowledged that church liability based on respondeat superior required that the employee's acts be committed within the scope of employment. However, "negligent hiring is a doctrine of primary liability; the employer is principally liable for negligently placing an unfit person in an employment situation involving an unreasonable risk of harm to others. Negligent hiring, therefore, enables plaintiffs to recover in situations where respondeat superior's scope of employment limitation previously protected employers from liability.

§ 10-04.2 — Court Decisions Rejecting Negligent Selection Claims

Key point 10-04.2. Some courts have found churches not liable on the basis of negligent selection for the molestation of a minor by a church worker since the church exercised reasonable care in the selection of the worker.

---

[46] Barquin v. Roman Catholic Diocese, 839 F. Supp. 275 (D. Vt. 1993).
[47] J. v. Victory Baptist Church, 372 S.E.2d 391 (Va. 1988).

This section reviews court decisions in which a church or other religious organization was found not liable on the basis of negligent selection for a worker's acts of child molestation. Note that several courts have concluded that the first amendment's "nonestablishment of religion" and "free exercise of religion" clauses prevent the civil courts from resolving negligent selection claims involving clergy misconduct.

> **Example.** *A federal appeals court ruled that an archdiocese was not responsible for the alleged molestation of a minor by a priest.[48] The victim claimed that the archdiocese should have known that the priest had a history of sexual improprieties and that he would continue to pursue those activities when under its employ. He insisted that a minimal background check would have revealed the priest's pattern of sexual activity with minors. The court, in rejecting this argument, observed, "The record, however, permits of no conclusion that the [archdiocese] suspected that [the priest] had engaged in sexual improprieties or might do so in the future. It is doubtful that the archdiocese . . . knew anything about [his] darker side. [He] was diligent in guarding his secrets. He did not disclose his extracurricular activities to anyone at anytime in the course of his employment and, from his perspective, with good reason. No tangible evidence in the form of a criminal history or discipline exists that would have been uncovered in a background check."*

> **Example.** *The Alabama Supreme Court concluded that a church-operated preschool was not responsible for the kidnapping of a three-month-old infant by three adolescent sisters employed by the preschool.[49] At the time of the kidnapping, there was no qualified adult teacher, other than the administrator herself, directly supervising the sisters. The administrator later testified that the other teachers had "gone for the day" and that she thought one of the sisters had intentionally distracted her while the other two slipped the baby out the front door undetected. The local police and the Federal Bureau of Investigation investigated the incident, eventually found the baby, and reunited her with her parents. The parents experienced severe shock as a result of the kidnapping, and later sued the preschool. They claimed that the preschool was legally responsible for the kidnapping on the basis of negligent hiring of the three sisters. They pointed out that the preschool used girls who were only 12, 14, and 17 years of age to care for infants. And, there was evidence that the two older sisters had been physically (and perhaps sexually) abused by members of their family, and that the oldest sister lied to the center's administrator by telling her that she was pregnant. The court rejected the parents' claim that this evidence demonstrated that the preschool had been guilty of negligent hiring.*

> **Example.** *A California court ruled that a Catholic church was not responsible on the basis of negligent hiring for a priest's acts of child molestation, since it had not been aware of any similar incidents of misconduct at the time the priest was employed.[50] The court acknowledged that "an employer may be liable to a third person for the employer's negligence in hiring or retaining an employee who is incompetent or unfit." However, the court qualified this rule by noting that "one who employs another to act for him is not liable . . . merely because the one employed is incompetent, vicious, or careless. If liability results it is because, under the circumstances, the employer has not taken the care which a prudent man would take in selecting the person for the business in hand. . . . Liability results . . . not because of the relation of the parties, but because the employer . . . had reason to believe that an undue risk of harm would exist because of the employment." The court noted that the harm the victim suffered was criminal sexual abuse of a minor by her priest. It observed, "There is nothing in the record to indicate [the priest] had a criminal history or had been previously implicated in sexual abuse of a minor. Thus the*

[48] Tichenor v. Roman Catholic Church, 32 F.3d 953 (5th Cir. 1994).
[49] Hargrove v. Tree of Life Christian Day Care Center, 699 So.2d 1242 (Ala. 1997).
[50] Roman Catholic Bishop v. Superior Court, 50 Cal. Rptr.2d 399 (Cal. App. 1996).

church could not have had antecedent knowledge of [his] purported criminal dangerousness." That is, evidence that the priest had engaged in sexual misconduct with adults did not necessarily make him a risk to children. The court observed that the victim failed to prove any facts "showing an undue risk of harm that [the priest] would commit criminal child sexual abuse if he were employed by the church." But even if evidence of sexual misconduct with adults would be relevant in evaluating a priest's risk of committing similar acts upon children, the church "had no actual knowledge of [his] sexual activity with [her] or anyone else until it heard [her] mother's report and [the priest's] admissions." In other words, the church could not be responsible for the priest's molestation of the victim on the basis of negligent hiring if it had no knowledge of any prior misconduct by the priest at the time he was hired or ordained. The court noted further noted that "the legal duty of inquiry [the victim] seeks to impose on the church as an employer would violate the employee's privacy rights. Privacy is a fundamental liberty implicitly guaranteed by the federal Constitution and is explicitly guaranteed under the California Constitution as an inalienable right. The right encompasses privacy in one's sexual matters and is not limited to the marital relationship. Although the right to privacy is not absolute, it yields only to a compelling state interest. Here there was no compelling state interest to require the employer to investigate the sexual practices of its employee. Moreover, the employer who queries employees on sexual behavior is subject to claims for invasion of privacy and sexual harassment. Similarly [the victim's] contention that the church should have required [the priest] to undergo a psychological evaluation before hiring him is unavailing. An individual's right to privacy also encompasses mental privacy. We conclude the church did not fail to use due care in hiring [the priest]."

Example. *An Illinois court ruled that a church and a parent denomination were not legally responsible for a pastor's sexual assault of three boys.[51] The boys' parents sued the pastor, his church, and a denominational agency, claiming that the boys had suffered severe emotional damage. The parents claimed that the denominational agency negligently assigned the pastor to the church, knowing of a prior assault on another boy several years earlier. A jury returned a verdict against the agency in the amount of $450,000 ($150,000 per boy) on the basis of its alleged negligence. However, a state appeals court reversed the verdict and dismissed the negligence verdict against the agency. It is significant to note that the court observed that "the jury could well have determined that the [agency] took adequate precaution in having [the pastor] counseled and should not have been held to have reasonably foreseen that [he] would be likely to commit the acts of sexual assault." This case suggests that churches and denominations may be legally responsible on the basis of negligent hiring if they hire or retain a minister after learning that he or she was guilty of sexual misconduct in the past. However, the court emphasized that mere knowledge of previous incidents of sexual misconduct does not automatically create legal liability. Liability for negligent hiring or retention requires that the actions of the church or denomination created a foreseeable and unreasonable risk of harm to others.*

Example. *A Louisiana appeals court ruled that a church-affiliated hospital was not liable on the basis of negligent selection for the sexual misconduct of an employee who had been thoroughly screened and supervised. The hospital hired a male nursing assistant for a psychiatric ward after conducting a thorough background check that showed no criminal record and no unfavorable references from former employers. After working for six months, this employee raped a 16-year-old girl. The victim sued the hospital. The appeals court concluded that the hospital could not be liable for the assault on the basis of negligent hiring, because of the thorough nature of its pre-employment investigation.[52]*

---

[51] Mt. Zion State Bank v. Central Illinois Conference of the United Methodist Church, 556 N.E.2d 1270 (Ill. App. 1990).
[52] Samuels v. Southern Baptist Hospital 594 So.2d 571 (La. App. 1992).

Example. A federal district court in Michigan ruled that a church school and various church agencies were not liable on the basis of negligent hiring, supervision, or retention, for the sexual molestation of a minor student by a priest.[53] In rejecting the victim's claim that the school and church agencies had been guilty of "negligent hiring," the court observed, "Questions of hiring and retention of clergy necessarily will require interpretation of church canons, and internal church policies and practices. It is well-settled that when a court is required to interpret canon law or internal church policies and practices, the first amendment is violated because such judicial inquiry would constitute excessive government entanglement with religion. . . . [An] inquiry into the decision of who should be permitted to become or remain a priest necessarily would involve prohibited excessive entanglement with religion. Therefore [the victim's] claims of negligence predicated upon a negligent hiring theory will be dismissed." The court further observed that even if there was not a constitutional bar to recognizing a negligent hiring claim in this case, this claim would still have to be dismissed since "there was absolutely not a shred of evidence in the record that either the [school or any church agency] had any notice of the abuse proclivities of [the offending priests] prior to their 'hiring' of them as priests or teachers . . . ."

Example. A Minnesota court ruled that a church and denominational organization were not legally responsible on the basis of negligent hiring for a pastor's acts of child molestation.[54] The molester served as pastor of a church and was accused of sexually abusing numerous young boys during his tenure. He admitted abusing some of the children, including a 10-year-old boy (the "victim"). The victim later sued the pastor and his former church. The court defined "negligent hiring" as "the negligence of an employer in placing a person with known propensities, or propensities which should have been discovered by reasonable investigation, in an employment position in which, because of the circumstances of employment, it should have been foreseeable that the hired individual posed a threat of injury to others." In ruling that the church had not been negligent in hiring the pastor, the court observed, "There is no evidence [the church] had actual knowledge of [the pastor's] propensities to commit sexual abuse before he was hired. Moreover, it would have been contrary to the evidence for the jury to have concluded that [the church] should have learned of [his] propensities through reasonable investigation. The regional church body had direct knowledge that [the pastor] had sexually abused a child two years before he was hired by [the church]. But it is undisputed that the regional church did not tell [the church] about this incident and took no action against [the pastor] that might have been discovered by [the church]. The record does not permit an inference that [the church] could have learned about [the pastor's] propensities from the regional church, which was unwilling to disclose this information voluntarily. . . . [T]he trial court suggested that if [the church] had simply called [the pastor's] previous employer it might have learned that [he] had been accused of sexual abuse at that church. If this search is reasonably seen as a part of the hiring process in this church organization in 1964, a proposition we do not review, we find no evidence in the record to show that [the pastor's] previous employer was aware of any accusations of sexual abuse against him. [The victim] has not presented any evidence of another source that [the church] might reasonably have investigated to discover [the pastor's] dangerous propensities, so the jury could not have determined that [it] negligently hired [him]."

Example. The Missouri Supreme Court ruled that a diocese could not be liable for the sexual misconduct of a priest.[55] A Catholic priest served as associate pastor of a church. He invited a young boy and one of the boy's friends to spend the night and watch movies in the church parsonage. One of the boys later alleged that

---

[53] Isely v. Capuchin Province, 880 F. Supp. 1138 (E.D. Mich. 1995).

[54] M.L. v. Magnuson, 531 N.W.2d 831 (Minn. App. 1995).

[55] Gibson v. Brewer, 952 S.W.2d 239 (Mo. 1997), citing the United States Supreme Court decision in Kedroff v. St. Nicholas Cathedral of Russian Orthodox Church, 344 U.S. 94 (1952).

the priest sexually molested him. When the boy's parents learned of the allegations, they immediately notified the diocese. Officials of the diocese allegedly told them that "this happens to young men all the time" and that their son "would get over it." Diocese employees urged the parents to meet with the priest to resolve the situation. After hearing of similar incidents between the priest and other young boys, the parents "expressed their concerns to the diocese." They were told that the incident with their son was "an innocent pat on the butt" and that they should "forgive and forget" and get on with their lives. According to the parents, the diocese continued to ignore them until the priest eventually was removed from the diocese. The parents sued the diocese. Among other things, they claimed that the diocese was negligent in "hiring or ordaining" and then retaining the priest. The court noted that "religious organizations are not immune from civil liability for the acts of their clergy," and that "if neutral principles of law can be applied without determining questions of religious doctrine, polity, and practice, then a court may impose liability." However, the court cautioned that "[q]uestions of hiring, ordaining, and retaining clergy . . . necessarily involve interpretation of religious doctrine, policy, and administration. Such excessive entanglement between church and state has the effect of inhibiting religion, in violation of the first amendment. By the same token, judicial inquiry into hiring, ordaining, and retaining clergy would result in an endorsement of religion, by approving one model for church hiring, ordination, and retention of clergy. A church's freedom to select clergy is protected 'as a part of the free exercise of religion against state interference.' Ordination of a priest is a 'quintessentially religious' matter, whose resolution the first amendment commits exclusively to the highest ecclesiastical tribunals of this hierarchical church."

Example. *A Washington state appeals court ruled that a church-operated school was not legally responsible for damages resulting from an alleged sexual relationship between a teacher and a student.[56] The student's parents had sued the school and church for "negligent hiring" and "negligent supervision." The court rejected both allegations. With regard to the school's alleged negligent hiring, the court observed that "the hiring process employed by the school suggests it took reasonable care in hiring [the teacher]. . . . The process appears sufficient as a matter of law to discover whether an individual is fit to teach at [the school]."*

Example. *The Wisconsin Supreme Court ruled that the statute of limitations prevented a woman from suing a Catholic archdiocese for the alleged acts of molestation by a priest nearly 40 years before.[57] The woman claimed that the priest entered into a sexual relationship with her in the late 1950s when she was a high school student, and that as a result of the priest's behavior she "has suffered and continues to suffer from severe emotional distress, causing and contributing to the break-up of her marriage, separation from her children, loss of jobs and other difficulties." The woman's lawsuit claimed that the archdiocese was responsible for her injuries on the basis of negligent hiring. In particular, she claimed that the archdiocese knew or should have known that the priest had engaged in similar acts of misconduct with other parishioners, and yet negligently failed to remove him as a priest. In rejecting this claim, the court noted, "To establish a claim for negligent hiring or retention [the woman] would have to establish that the archdiocese was negligent in hiring or retaining [the priest] because he was incompetent or otherwise unfit. But, we conclude that the first amendment to the United States Constitution prevents the courts of this state from determining what makes one competent to serve as a Catholic priest since such a determination would require interpretation of church canons and internal church policies and practices. Therefore [the suit] against the archdiocese is not capable of enforcement by the courts. . . . Examining the ministerial selection policy, which is 'infused with the religious tenets of the particular sect,' entangles the court in qualitative evaluation of religious norms. Negligence requires the court to create a 'reasonable bishop' norm. Beliefs in penance, admonition and reconciliation as a sacramental*

---

[56] Scott v. Blanchet High School, 747 P.2d 1124 (Wash. App. 1987).
[57] Pritzlaff v. Archdiocese of Milwaukee, 533 N.W.2d 780 (Wis. 1995).

TABLE 10-2
TEN RISKS ASSOCIATED WITH SEXUAL MISCONDUCT

risk	increase risk	decrease risk
#1 negligent selection —inadequate screening	• no screening • inadequate screening (e.g., no contacts with references)	• adequate screening process for all volunteers and employees • reference checks • 6 month rule • criminal checks when indicated
#2 negligent supervision	• inadequate number of trained and screened adults present during youth activities	• develop minimum staffing rules (call other charities for assistance, such as Red Cross or Boy Scouts) • 2 adult rule
#3 negligent retention	• fail to investigate allegations of prior misconduct by a current volunteer or employee	•prompt investigation of any allegation regarding prior misconduct by a current volunteer or employee
#4 inadequate response	• deny allegations of misconduct • minimize the severity • blame the victim and family	• prompt investigation of charges • compliance with state child abuse reporting law •refer to denominational agency if applicable • communication with victim and family • contact legal counsel • contact insurance agent
#5 ratification	• church leaders ignore allegations of sexual misconduct	• church leaders respond immediately to allegations of sexual misconduct • see #4 above
#6 inadequate boundaries in counseling	• no restrictions or limitations on adults who counsel with other adults or minors	• no opposite sex counseling without third person present • opposite sex counseling only when other staff are visible • limit number of sessions • limit length of sessions • women counsel women • video feed to other location • telephone counseling • counseling brochure
#7 inadequate insurance coverage	• coverage for sexual misconduct not addressed during insurance review • church leaders have no idea how much coverage exists • unfamiliarity with exclusions and limitations • failure to notify • no directors and officers coverage	• familiarity with policy and its terms, conditions, and exclusions • prompt notification of any potential claim • directors and officers insurance
#8 inadequate education	• staff and membership not informed why screening and supervisory procedures are followed	• inform staff and membership of magnitude of risk • periodic emphasis • use state child abuse personnel

risk	increase risk	decrease risk
#9 failure to comply with child abuse reporting laws	• church leaders are unfamiliar with the state child abuse reporting law • church leaders handle child abuse allegations "in house"	• church leaders are familiar with state child abuse reporting law (definition of abuse, who are mandatory reporters, clergy privilege) • get updated copy of statute at least annually • become acquainted with someone in state child abuse reporting office
#10 inadequate counsel	• use of legal counsel with no experience in handling such claims	• use of legal counsel with experience in working with churches and with sexual misconduct claims

response to sin may be the point of attack by a challenger who wants a court to probe the tort law reasonableness of the church's mercy toward the offender. . . . The tort of negligent selection of unsuitable teachers has been recognized in civil courts. If negligent selection of a potential pedophile for the religious office of priest, minister or rabbi is a tort as to future child victims, will civil courts also hear Title VII challenges by the non-selected seminarian against the theological seminary that declines to ordain a plaintiff into ministry because of his psychological profile? How far shall the courts' qualitative entanglement with religious selectivity extend?" The court concluded by observing that "the tort of negligent hiring and retention may not be maintained against a religious governing body due to concerns of excessive entanglement" between church and state.

§ 10-04.3 — Risk Management

Key point 10-04.3. *Churches can reduce the risk of liability based on negligent selection for the sexual molestation of minors by adopting risk management policies and procedures.*

Incidents of sexual misconduct involving minor victims can be devastating to the victim, the victim's family, the offender, the church leadership, and the church itself. The good news is that churches can significantly reduce the risk of such incidents by taking a few simple precautions. These precautions are addressed more fully in the resources noted above. Here is a summary of eight risk management strategies:

1. A WRITTEN APPLICATION FORM

Churches can significantly reduce their risk of legal liability for negligent selection (and the likelihood that an incident of abuse or molestation will occur) by having every applicant for youth work (volunteer or compensated) complete a "screening application." At a minimum, the application should ask for the applicant's name and address, the names of other youth-serving organizations in which the applicant has worked as an employee or volunteer, a full explanation of any prior criminal convictions, and the names of two or more references. The application should be completed by every applicant for any position involving the custody or supervision of minors. The application should also be completed by current employees or volunteers having custody or supervision over minors.

There is some confusion regarding the need to ask applicants (who will be working with minors) if they were sexually molested when they were a minor. The confusion stems from a 1991 decision by the Alaska Supreme Court.[58] The court concluded that adults who experienced sexual abuse as children are much more

---

[58] Broderick v. King's Way Church, 808 P.2d 1211 (Alaska 1991).

RISK MANAGEMENT RESOURCES

Churches must exercise reasonable care in the selection of ministers, nonminister employees, and volunteers in order to avoid potential liability based on negligent selection. The publisher of this text has produced several resources to assist church leaders in satisfying the standard of reasonable care in the selection of workers. To order call 1-800-222-1840. These resources include the following:

1) The Selection and Screening of Ministers kit (includes application booklets containing key questions and reference forms, interview booklets containing nearly 200 additional questions to ask during a personal interview of pastoral candidates, and a helpful 100-page book that addresses the selection and screening of church workers).

2) The Selection and Screening of Employees kit (includes application booklets containing key questions and reference forms, and a helpful 100-page book that addresses the selection and screening of church workers).

3) The Selection and Screening of Volunteers kit (includes application booklets containing key questions and reference forms, and a helpful 100-page book that addresses the selection and screening of church workers).

4) The "Reducing the Risk Kit" (includes a 24-minute video, a one-hour audio tape, and two reference books).

5) The 4-Hour Legal Training Kit for Church Boards (4 one-hour audio tapes orient church board members to the critical legal and tax issues that face their church).

likely to become child abusers than the general population. It quoted from an article on child abuse: "One of the predisposing conditions [to child sexual abuse] that has been of considerable interest to clinicians and researchers is an experience of sexual abuse in childhood. Being sexually victimized as a child is a common experience for adult sex offenders and mothers of victims of sexual mistreatment. Moreover, childhood experiences of sexual abuse have been found at higher rates among those who victimize or are mothers of victims than in comparison groups." No other court has followed this decision, and so only in Alaska should churches ask applicants for youth or children's work if they were abused as minors. Churches in other states should consult with a local attorney regarding the use of such a question on their application forms.

2. CONTACT REFERENCES

Having current or prospective employees and volunteers complete an application form does not significantly reduce a church's risk of negligent selection. Significant risk reduction occurs if the church takes the following additional steps:

• If an applicant is unknown to you, confirm his or her identity by requiring photographic identification (such as a state driver's license). Child molesters often use pseudonyms.

• Contact each person and organization listed as a reference in the application, and request a written reference. If you do not receive back the written reference forms, then contact the references by telephone and prepare a written memorandum noting the questions asked and the reference's responses. Sample reference forms (for use by mail or telephone) are contained in the resources mentioned above. Show the date and method of the contact, the person making the contact as well as the person contacted, and a summary of the reference's remarks. Such forms, when completed, should be kept with an applicant's original application. They should be kept permanently.

For pastoral applicants, the best reference will be from a denominational office with which the church is affiliated. If the church is not affiliated with a denomination, then the best reference will be from board members in other churches in which the applicant has served. Sample reference forms are contained in the Selection and Screening of Ministers kit described above.

For nonminister employees and volunteers, the best references will be from other churches or charities in which the applicant has worked with minors. Examples include Boy Scouts, Girl Scouts, Big Brothers/Big Sisters, YMCA, public or private schools, or youth sports. Seek a reference from any such organization in which the applicant has served.

• Be sure you are aware of any additional legal requirements that apply in your state. For example, a number of states have passed laws requiring church-operated child-care facilities to check with the state before hiring any applicant for employment to ensure that each applicant does not have a criminal record involving certain types of crimes. You will need to check with an attorney for guidance.

• The church must treat as strictly confidential all applications and records of contacts with churches or other references. Such information should be marked "confidential," and access should be restricted to those few persons with a legitimate interest in the information.

Churches should keep the following additional considerations in mind when preparing a screening procedure:

The screening procedure should apply to all workers—both compensated and volunteer. Acts of molestation have been committed by both kinds of workers.

• The screening procedure should apply to new applicants as well as current workers. Obviously, churches need to use some common sense here. For example, if your 4th grade Sunday school teacher is a 60-year-old woman with 25 years teaching experience in your church, you may decide that reference checks are unnecessary. The highest risks involve male workers in programs that involve overnight activities or unsupervised activities. Persons in this category should be carefully screened.

• If the screening application and reference forms seem overly burdensome, consider the following: (1) Your church liability insurance policy may exclude or limit coverage for acts of child molestation. If so, you have a potentially enormous uninsured risk. Reducing this risk is worth whatever inconvenience might be generated in implementing a screening procedure. Just ask any member of a church in which such an incident has occurred. (2) The screening procedure is designed primarily to provide a safe and secure environment for the youth of your church. Unfortunately, churches have become targets of child molesters because they provide immediate and direct access to children in a trusting and often unsupervised environment. In order to provide some protection for the youth of your church against such persons, a screening procedure is imperative. (3) The relatively minor inconvenience involved in establishing a screening procedure is a small price to pay for protecting the church from the devastation that often accompanies an incident of molestation. (4) The resistance to screening will diminish as more charities screen volunteer workers. (5) Think of the screening procedure in terms of risk reduction. A church is free to hire workers without any screening or evaluation whatever, but such a practice involves the highest degree of legal risk. On the other hand, a church that develops a responsible screening procedure has a much lower risk. (6) The services of a local attorney should be solicited in drafting an appropriate screening form to ensure compliance with state law. It is also advisable that such forms be shared with a church's insurance company for its comments. You also should consider sharing your form with the state agency that investigates reports of child abuse. (7) Obtain copies of the application forms used by the Boy Scouts, Big Brothers, and similar organizations. As a result of numerous lawsuits, these organizations have developed effective application forms. Review these forms, and use them as resources when preparing your own forms. The state agency responsible for investigating reports of child abuse may have application forms for you to review, and they often are willing to review the application forms that churches prepare.

3. CRIMINAL RECORDS CHECKS

No court has found a church liable for a youth worker's sexual misconduct on the ground that it failed to conduct a criminal records check. But such checks will further reduce a church's risk of being found liable for the negligent selection of youth workers. Some churches conduct criminal records checks on all ministers, all nonminister employees, and volunteers who will have unsupervised access to minors or who will have counseling responsibilities. Note the following additional comments regarding criminal records checks:

• *Different kinds of checks.* There are different kinds of criminal records checks. The two main types are "name checks" and "fingerprint checks." Criminal records checks vary widely in terms of the geographic area covered. In many cases, a criminal records check will only cover records within a particular state or county. The fee for conducting a criminal records check also varies, depending on the type of search. In many states, a "name check" only requires the individual's name (including any aliases or maiden names), date of birth, and address. Some states require the individual's social security number. In any case, a law enforcement agency will not conduct a search without the consent of the individual. This ordinarily is provided in a written release. The screening kits described at the beginning of this section use the Pinkerton Company, which checks county courthouse records. The Pinkerton Company is the largest employment verification service in the world, and it has established a division (with a toll-free telephone number) for assisting churches in conducting criminal records checks. The advantage of these checks is that they are quick and accurate. The disadvantage is that they cover only one county per search. This is not a problem for applicants who have resided in the same county for several years. However, applicants who have lived in several counties in recent years will require multiple checks. While multiple checks can easily be done, the cost is higher. The second type of criminal records check covers state criminal records databases. The advantage of these checks is that they cover a larger geographical area than a county check. The disadvantages are that they are slower, less accurate, may not be available to churches, and are far more intrusive (they often require fingerprinting). In 1998, Congress amended the National Child Protection Act to permit churches and other charities to conduct criminal records checks (based on fingerprints) using the FBI criminal database. This will provide churches with another option.

• *Inconclusive criminal record.* What if you discover that an applicant for youth work was charged with child abuse or molestation but not convicted? Or, what if the applicant was convicted of a lesser offense, such as disorderly conduct. Many churches have learned that an applicant for youth work was charged with child abuse or molestation, but never convicted. In some cases, the applicant has plead guilty to (or been convicted of) a lesser offense. Does the lack of a criminal conviction, or a conviction for a lesser offense, mean that a church is free to use the individual? This is a difficult question. Consider two options:

(1) At a minimum, church leaders should contact the prosecutor's office or the police and ask about the case. Mention that you are considering using the individual in a position in the church that will involve contact with minors. Often, a representative of the prosecutor's office, or a detective or other investigating officer, will respond to inquiries from the church concerning the facts of the case. Such input will be very significant in evaluating an applicant's suitability for working with minors. Remember, there are many reasons why a person may not be convicted of the crime of child abuse or molestation. Often, prosecuting attorneys are consumed with "major" crimes, and do not have the resources to devote to every case of child molestation. In other words, you cannot safely assume that a person who is charged but not convicted of child molestation poses no risk to your church. Further investigation is imperative in such cases.

(2) Request an FBI criminal records check through your designated state agency. The national Volunteers for Children Act, enacted by Congress in 1998, permits churches and other charities that are designated as "qualified entities" by state law to obtain FBI criminal records checks on persons who will be working with minors. Ten sets of fingerprints must be obtained for each applicant. These are delivered to the designated state agency, which will in turn send them to the FBI. Criminal records checks under the Volunteers for Children Act are not mandatory. Rather, they simply offer another option to screen youth workers.

One of the best features of the Volunteers for Children Act is that it relieves churches and other charities of the need to evaluate inconclusive criminal records. The designated state agency reviews the results of the FBI check, and then informs the church or charity whether or not to use the applicant. If an applicant was charged with child molestation but not convicted, or plead guilty to a lesser offense, it is the state's responsibility to determine whether or not the individual should be used. The state does not disclose to the church or charity the nature of the criminal background. Rather, it simply informs the church or charity whether or not it should use the applicant in question. It remains to be seen how many churches will obtain FBI criminal records checks. Obviously, many churches will not want to obtain ten sets of fingerprints on every applicant or worker. However, FBI checks should be viewed as an option that can be used, at a minimum, when an applicant's criminal record is inconclusive.

• *Expunged or sealed criminal records.* In some states it is unlawful for employers to make employment decisions about employees or applicants for employment on the basis of "expunged" or "sealed" criminal records.

• *Arrests.* In some states it is unlawful for employers to make employment decisions about employees or applicants for employment on the basis of arrests.

• *Mandatory criminal records checks.* Some states require criminal records checks for child care workers and teachers.

• *What crimes disqualify an applicant for youth work?* Not all crimes disqualify a person for a position involving contact with minors. A criminal conviction for a sexual offense involving a minor would certainly disqualify an applicant. In the case of pedophilic behavior (molestation of a pre-adolescent child) such a conviction should disqualify an individual no matter how long ago it occurred (because of the improbability that such a condition can be "cured"). Other automatic disqualifiers would include incest, rape, assaults involving minors, murder, kidnapping, child pornography, sodomy, and the physical abuse of a minor. Other crimes would strongly indicate that a person should not be considered for work with minors in a church. Some crimes would not be automatic disqualifiers, because they would not necessarily suggest a risk of child abuse or molestation. Some property offenses would be included in this list, particularly if the offense occurred long ago and the individual has a long history of impeccable behavior.

Key point. Most states have specified those crimes that will disqualify persons from working in licensed child care facilities. Church leaders can reduce the risk of negligent selection by using the same list of disqualifying crimes.

4. Interviews

The final candidates for a church position should be interviewed. This will provide the church with an opportunity to inquire into each applicant's background and make a determination as to each person's suitability for the position under consideration. The "selection and screening kits" described at the beginning of this section contain sample interview questions.

Higher risk individuals (e.g., single males) and persons applying for higher risk positions (e.g., boys groups, scouting groups, camps, overnight or largely unsupervised activities involving either male or female children or adolescents) should be interviewed by a staff member who has been trained to identify child molesters. Law enforcement personnel and local offices of state agencies responsible for investigating reports of child abuse often have materials that can be used to train the staff member who will conduct interviews. Employees of these agencies ordinarily are more than willing to assist a church in learning how to identify potential child molesters during an interview. These resources should be utilized.

5. Six Month Rule

Churches can reduce the risk of incidents of sexual molestation by adopting a policy restricting eligibility for any volunteer position involving the custody or supervision of minors to those persons who have been members in good standing of the church for a minimum period of time, such as six months. Such a policy gives the church an additional opportunity to evaluate applicants, and will help to repel persons seeking immediate access to potential victims.

6. Other Background Checks

There are other aspects of an applicant's background that can be checked. These include (1) educational background (one of the most common misrepresentations that is made on employment application forms); (2) employment (confirming that the applicant worked for prior employers listed on the application form); (3) motor vehicle records; (4) social security number check (confirms identity and residential history); (5) credit history; and (6) professional licenses and certifications. The types of searches selected for any particular applicant will vary depending upon the risks and responsibilities associated with the position.

7. Limit "Second Chances"

Church leaders often "err on the side of mercy" when making employment decisions. This attitude can contribute to a negligent selection claim—if a church gives an applicant a "second chance" despite knowledge of prior sexual misconduct, and the conduct is repeated. What the church views as mercy may be viewed as negligence by a jury.

Should a church hire an applicant for youth work who has been guilty of child molestation in the past? Occasionally, such persons freely admit to a prior incident, but insist that they no longer are a threat because of the passage of time or a conversion experience. There are two options:

• The church could refuse to use the person in any compensated or volunteer position in the church (including, but not limited to, working with minors). This approach eliminates the risk of negligent selection, and it would be appropriate in the case of a pedophile. Pedophiles are persons who are sexually attracted to pre-adolescent children. The FBI "profile" on pedophiles indicates that such persons are "incurable" and predatory. They are always seeking new victims. Obviously, such persons create a significant risk to children and churches.

• The church could encourage such an individual to work in the church, but in a position not involving access to children. This is a reasonable accommodation of the individual's desire to serve the church. A church that permits such an individual to work with children will have a virtually indefensible position should another incident of molestation occur. Some churches have given convicted child molesters a "second chance" by allowing them to work with children—often on the basis that the person has had a religious conversion and no longer is a threat to children. The courts have not been sympathetic to such a defense. To illustrate, one court cited with approval the following testimony of a psychiatrist:

> In the years that I have been doing this work, I probably have treated people from every religious denomination. We have seen priests, ministers, rabbis who have engaged in pedophilic [i.e., child molestation] behavior, so attendance at a church or being high up in a religious hierarchy doesn't contraindicate that a person is a [pedophile]. . . . They tell us that they have repented, that they have found the Lord and no longer have the problem they were accused of having. So we don't see religiosity as solving the problem."[59]

Churches that place a known child molester in a position involving access to children are taking an enormous risk.

8. ARBITRATION POLICY

Consider the adoption of a church "arbitration policy." Such a policy, if adopted by the church membership at a congregational meeting as an amendment to the church's bylaws, may force church members to resolve their disputes (with the church, pastor, board, or other members) within the church consistently with the pattern suggested in 1 Corinthians 6:1-8. While a discussion of arbitration policies is beyond the scope of this section, churches should recognize that arbitration is an increasingly popular means of resolving disputes in the secular world since it often avoids the excessive costs and delays associated with civil litigation and the uncertainty of jury verdicts. Of course, any arbitration policy should be reviewed by a church's liability insurer before being implemented. Such an approach, at a minimum, merits serious consideration by any church.

§ 10-05 Negligent Selection of Church Workers — Sexual Misconduct Cases Involving Adult Victims

Key point 10-05. A church may be liable on the basis of negligent selection for a worker's molestation of an adult if the church was negligent in the selection of the worker. Negligence means a failure to

---

[59] Dutchess County Department of Social Services v. G., 534 N.Y.S.2d 64 (N.Y. 1988).

exercise reasonable care, and so negligent selection refers to a failure to exercise reasonable care in the selection of the worker. Liability based on negligent selection may be imposed upon a church for the acts of employees and volunteers.

In recent years, hundreds of churches have been sued as a result of sexual contact by clergy with adults. Most of these cases have involved sexual contact with church employees or with counselees. Nearly all of the cases have involved sexual contact between male clergy and adult female employees or counselees. The personal liability of ministers for engaging in such acts is addressed in a previous chapter.[60] This section will address the question of whether the minister's employing church can be legally responsible for the minister's acts on the basis of its negligent selection of the minister.

As noted earlier in this chapter, the term negligence *refers to conduct that creates an unreasonable risk of foreseeable harm to others. It connotes carelessness, heedlessness, inattention, or inadvertence. Negligent selection of a minister means that the church failed to act responsibly and with due care in the selection of a minister who later engages in some form of foreseeable misconduct. To illustrate, assume that a church hires a minister without any background check, and fails to discover that the minister had been dismissed by another church because of committing adultery with two women. A year later, it is discovered that the minister has engaged in adultery with a married woman in the course of marital counseling. The woman sues the church, claiming that the minister's conduct caused her emotional and psychological harm, and that her church is legally responsible for the minister's acts on the basis of negligent selection. She insists that had church leaders contacted the other church they would have discovered the minister's background and would not have hired him.*

Church leaders can take relatively simple yet effective steps to significantly reduce the likelihood of such incidents occurring. This section will review some of the more significant reported court rulings, and then suggest a number of preventive measures that any church can implement in order to reduce the risk of such incidents.

Tip. No one understands or appreciates risk better than insurance companies. Risk evaluation is their business. As a result, it is very important to observe that a number of church insurance companies have reduced the insurance coverage they provide for sexual misconduct, and in some cases they have excluded it entirely. Some companies are suggesting that these incidents are excluded under the provision in most policies excluding damages based on intentional, criminal conduct (most acts of sexual molestation involve criminal activity). Church leaders should immediately review their church liability insurance policy to determine whether the church has any coverage for acts of sexual misconduct, and if so, whether such coverage has been limited in any way. If you fit within either category, the risk management recommendations in this chapter are of even greater relevance.

Key point. Be sure to review Table 10-1 and Table 10-2.

§ 10-05.1 — Court Decisions Recognizing Negligent Selection Claims

Key point 10-05.1. Some courts have found churches liable on the basis of negligent selection for the sexual misconduct of a church worker involving another adult if the church failed to exercise reasonable care in the selection of the worker.

---

[60] See § 4-11, supra.

This section reviews court decisions in which a church or other religious organization was found liable on the basis of negligent selection for a minister's sexual contacts with an adult.

Example. *The Colorado Supreme Court ruled that a denominational agency was responsible, on the basis of negligent hiring and supervision, for a pastor's sexual misconduct. A local church board employed a new pastor, who later engaged in a sexual relationship with a woman in the course of marital counseling. At the time the new pastor was hired, the denominational agency failed to provide the church board with any of the information about the pastor contained in its personnel files. Included in the pastor's personnel file were reports of psychological examinations that were conducted as a result of his seeking ordination. These reports indicated that he had problems with depression, low self-esteem, and possessed a "sexual identification ambiguity." The woman claimed that the denominational agency's failure to disclose this information, and its consent to the employment of the pastor by the congregation, amounted to negligent hiring. The state supreme court agreed. It concluded, "[The pastor's] duties included counseling and close association with parishioners at the church. The diocese was in possession of a psychological report which concluded that [the assistant pastor] has a "sexual identification ambiguity." Another psychological report indicated that [the pastor] had a problem with depression and suffered from low self-esteem. An expert testified that a large number of clergy who have sexual relationships with their parishioners do so partially as a result of suffering from depression and low self-esteem. [The pastor's] struggle with his sexual identity and his problems with depression and low self-esteem put the diocese on notice to inquire further whether [the assistant pastor] was capable of counseling parishioners. These reports gave the diocese a reason to believe [the pastor] should not be put in a position to counsel vulnerable individuals and that he might be unable to handle the transference phenomenon. The failure to communicate this knowledge to the vestry and subsequent placement of [the pastor] in the role of counselor breached the diocese's duty of care to [the victim]."*[61]

Example. *A Colorado court ruled that a minister and a denominational agency could be sued by a woman with whom the minister had sexual contacts.*[62] *A woman (the victim) attended a church for a few years, and began to volunteer her services for a variety of activities including the remodeling of a classroom. She engaged in these volunteer services on the recommendation of a therapist who suggested that she work in a "safe environment" to overcome her fears of the workplace. The victim's volunteer work caused her to come in contact with her minister after normal working hours. On one occasion the minister approached her while she was remodeling a classroom, began caressing her back, and told her, "I love you Dianne, you mean so much to me." A few days later, the minister called the victim into his office where the two of them sat next to each other on a small couch. The minister again caressed her and expressed his love for her. Following a third incident, the victim informed two other women in the church about the minister's behavior, and one responded, "Oh my God, not you too." A few months later a denominational agency with which the church was affiliated held a meeting in response to a formal complaint it had received regarding the minister's conduct. Six women attended this meeting, and all described similar incidents of unwelcome verbal comments and physical contact involving the minister. As a result of this meeting, the minister was suspended. The victim later sued her church and a denominational agency on the basis of several theories of liability, including negligent hiring of the minister. She alleged that the agency had been made aware of at least one prior act of sexual misconduct involving the minister, and was aware that he had a problem with alcohol abuse. The court ruled that the agency could be liable on the basis of negligent hiring, despite the agency's argument that the ordina-*

---

[61] Moses v. Diocese of Colorado, 863 P.2d 310 (Colo. 1993).
[62] Winkler v. Rocky Mouton Conference, 923 P.2d 152 (Colo. App. 1995).

tion and discipline of ministers is an ecclesiastical matter involving theological concerns over which the civil courts cannot exercise jurisdiction. The court noted simply that neither the minister nor the agency claimed that the minister's "method of communicating with parishioners by touching, hugging, and expressing affection was based on any religious tenet or belief."

§ 10-05.2 — Court Decisions Rejecting Negligent Selection Claims

Key point 10-05.2. Some courts have found churches not liable on the basis of negligent selection for the sexual misconduct of a minister or other church worker involving another adult since the church exercised reasonable care in the selection of the worker.

This section reviews court decisions in which a church or other religious organization was found not liable on the basis of negligent selection for inappropriate sexual contact with an adult by a minister or other church worker. Note that several courts have concluded that the first amendment's "nonestablishment of religion" and "free exercise of religion" clauses prevent the civil courts from resolving negligent selection claims involving clergy misconduct.

Example. A Florida court ruled that it was barred by the first amendment from resolving a woman's lawsuit claiming that she had been the victim of a priest's sexual misconduct.[63] A woman sought out a priest for marital counseling, and alleged that the priest engaged in sexual contacts with her. The woman sued her church and diocese, claiming that they were aware of prior incidents involving sexual misconduct during counseling by the same priest. Despite this knowledge, nothing was done to address the problem. The church and diocese asked the court to dismiss the lawsuit against them on the ground that a resolution of the woman's claims would result in an "excessive entanglement" of the court with religious beliefs in violation of the first amendment. The court agreed. It began its opinion by noting that the first amendment prohibits any governmental practice (including judicial resolution of internal church disputes) that would lead to an "excessive entanglement" between church and state. The court noted that excessive entanglement occurs "when the courts begin to review and interpret a church's constitution, laws, and regulations." The court concluded that the resolution of a negligent hiring, supervision, or retention claim against a church or diocese would amount to an excessive entanglement in violation of the first amendment: "Our examination of case law presenting both sides of this question leads us to conclude the reasoning of those courts holding the first amendment bars a claim for negligent hiring, retention, and supervision is the more compelling. In a church defendant's determination to hire or retain a minister, or in its capacity as supervisor of that minister, a church defendant's conduct is guided by religious doctrine and/or practice. Thus, a court's determination regarding whether the church defendant's conduct was 'reasonable' would necessarily entangle the court in issues of the church's religious law, practices, and policies. 'Hiring' in a traditional sense does not occur in some religions, where a person is ordained into a particular position in the church, and assigned to one parish or another. A court faced with the task of determining a claim of negligent hiring, retention, and supervision would measure the church defendants' conduct against that of a reasonable employer; a proscribed comparison."

Example. A Georgia court dismissed a lawsuit brought by a woman against her church and a denominational agency as a result of injuries she allegedly sustained during a sexual relationship with her pastor.[64] The woman had received counseling from the pastor on a number of occasions, despite the fact

---

[63] Doe v. Evans, 718 So.2d 286 (Fla. App. 1998).
[64] Alpharetta First United Methodist Church v. Stewart, 473 S.E.2d 532 (Ga. App. 1996).

that the pastor had informed her that she should discontinue the counseling sessions with him and find another counselor because he was sexually attracted to her. Despite this request, the woman did not discontinue the counseling sessions, and the two began having "phone sex" conversations. The woman claimed that the pastor initiated the first such conversation but that at times she would call him. She insisted that while she led him to believe she was participating in the "phone sex," she was, in reality, only pretending. The woman alleged that toward the end of their counseling relationship the pastor called her at home and asked her to come to his office so they could have sex. She drove to his office and the two engaged in intercourse. The woman quit seeing the pastor when she learned that he was engaged to be married to another woman. The woman and her husband sued their church and a denominational agency on the basis of negligent hiring of the pastor. Specifically, they claimed that both the church and denominational agency failed to exercise reasonable care in the selection of the pastor. In rejecting this claim, the court observed, "An employer may not be held liable for negligent hiring or retention unless the [victim] shows the employer knew or should have known of the employee's violent and criminal propensities. Specifically, the [couple] must show that the church and the [denominational agency] knew or should have known of [the associate pastor's] propensity for sexual misconduct. . . . . There is nothing in the record before us to show the church or [denominational agency] should have been on notice prior to ordaining [the associate pastor] that he had a propensity for sexual misconduct." As proof that the church and denominational agency had been negligent in ordaining or hiring the associate pastor, the couple noted that he had been suspended for a year while in seminary for cheating on a Hebrew examination, and that his psychological evaluation indicated certain problems, such as difficulty controlling his impulses, a tendency to use poor judgment, a tendency to disregard the rights of others, and a likelihood to express aggression in a physical manner. The court disagreed that these facts proved that either the church or denominational agency was guilty of negligent selection: "These types of generalized findings, without more, are not sufficient to put the church and [denominational agency] on notice of a propensity for sexual misconduct." The court pointed out that the psychological evaluation (which consisted of the Minnesota Multiphasic Personality Inventory, the Interpersonal Behavior Survey, the Strong-Campbell Interest Inventory, and the Sentence Completion Test) also showed several positive characteristics such as, "He is very social and interested in leadership in service to other people . . . . He shows a pattern of interest moderately like those of successful ministers or social workers." The court also summarized the many precautions that were taken prior to the time the pastor was ordained, including a 2-year internship, letters of recommendation, psychological testing, and extensive interviews by an ordination committee.

Example. *An Indiana court ruled that neither a church nor a denominational agency could be sued on the basis of negligent hiring for injuries suffered by a woman who was molested by her pastor when she was a minor.*[65] *The woman claimed that the pastor began molesting her when she was 7 years old, and that the molestation continued until she was 20. The court concluded that neither the church nor the denominational agency could be liable on the basis of negligent selection of the pastor. The court observed that the pastor was hired by the church in 1954, and that there was no evidence whatsoever that the church or either denominational agency was aware of any misconduct on his part at that time.*

Example. *A Louisiana court ruled that an Episcopal diocese was not legally responsible for the suicide of a woman allegedly caused by a sexual relationship with an Episcopal priest.*[66] *The husband of a woman who committed suicide sued a priest and diocese, claiming that his wife's suicide had been caused by the sexual*

---

[65] Konkle v. Henson, 672 N.E.2d 450 (Ind. App. 1996).
[66] Roppolo v. Moore, 644 So.2d 206 (La. App. 4 Cir. 1994).

misconduct of the priest. The lawsuit alleged that the priest was guilty of malpractice by taking advantage of an emotionally dependent woman and then abusing his position of trust to engage in sexual intercourse with her on numerous occasions. The husband claimed that the priest's behavior violated the teachings of the Episcopal Church as well as the ninth commandment ("thou shalt not covet they neighbor's wife") and the sixth commandment ("thou shalt not commit adultery"). The husband claimed that the diocese was responsible for his wife's suicide on the basis of several grounds, including a failure to adequately investigate the priest as to his emotional, psychological, and moral fitness to be a minister of the Episcopal Church. In dismissing the husband's allegation of "negligent selection" of the priest by the diocese, the court observed, "[A]ny inquiry into the policies and practices of [churches] in hiring or supervising their clergy raises . . . first amendment problems of entanglement . . . which might involve the court in making sensitive judgments about the propriety of [churches'] supervision in light of their religious beliefs."

Example. *The Nebraska Supreme Court ruled that a Catholic diocese could not be liable on the basis of negligent hiring for the sexual misconduct of a priest.[67] The priest had engaged in sexual contact with a woman during marital counseling. The woman sued the priest, claiming that he had been negligent and that his negligence contributed to the sexual relationship and her injuries. Specifically, she claimed that the priest was negligent (1) by failing to properly counsel her concerning her marital and family relationships when he knew or should have known she was having domestic difficulties; (2) by failing to remove himself as parish priest when he knew or should have known that a continuing relationship with her would cause her emotional harm; and (3) by violating his oath of celibacy. The court rejected this theory of liability, noting simply that "[s]o far as we have been able to determine, no jurisdiction to date has recognized a claim for clergy malpractice." The woman also sued her diocese, claiming that it had been negligent in failing to properly investigate the priest's background by inquiring into his relations with other women while he was acting as a parish priest in other parishes when it knew, or should have known, that he had been actively involved in relationships with women in violation of his vows of celibacy on more than one occasion in the past. In rejecting each of these claims of liability against the diocese, the court observed simply that "[i]f there is no tort liability to the [woman] against [the priest] individually, it follows that the diocese cannot be held liable for his conduct."*

Example. *A federal court in New York refused to find a church or denomination agency liable on the basis of "negligent placement, retention, or supervision" for a pastor's sexual contacts with a woman during marital counseling.[68] The court made the following statement in rejecting the woman's claim that the church and denomination had been guilty of negligence: "[A]ny inquiry into the policies and practices of the church defendants in hiring or supervising their clergy raises . . . first amendment problems of entanglement . . . which might involve the court in making sensitive judgments about the propriety of the church defendants' supervision in light of their religious beliefs."*

Example. *The Ohio Supreme Court ruled that state and national denominational offices could not be sued on the basis of negligent hiring as a result of the sexual misconduct of clergy.[69] A woman who had engaged in a sexual relationship with her pastor in the course of marital counseling sued the denominational offices, claiming that they were responsible for her injuries on the basis of negligent hiring. The lawsuit alleged that the state and national denominational offices "knew, or should have known of the inclination of [the pastor] to commit such actions and were reckless or negligent in allowing said [pas-*

---

[67] Schieffer v. Catholic Archdiocese, 508 N.W.2d 907 (Neb. 1993).

[68] Schmidt v. Bishop, 779 F. Supp. 321 (S.D.N.Y. 1991).

[69] Byrd v. Faber, 565 N.E.2d 584 (Ohio 1991). Accord Doe v. Turner, 1994 WL 369956 (Ohio App. 1994), Mirick v. McClellan, 1994 WL 156303 (Ohio App. 1994); Gebhart v. College of Mount St. Joseph, 665 N.E.2d 223 (Ohio App. 1995).

tor] to assume the position of pastor . . . ." The court acknowledged that "if a church hires an individual despite knowledge of prior improper behavior in his former church-related employment, the church may be liable in tort for negligent hiring." However, the court insisted that a lawsuit that merely alleges that a religious organization is guilty of "negligent hiring," but that recites no facts supporting such an allegation, must be dismissed. Since the woman's lawsuit contained no reference whatsoever to any facts to support a claim of negligent hiring, it had to be dismissed. The court observed, "We hold today that . . . greater specificity in pleading is required when a claim is brought against a religious institution for negligent hiring due to the myriad of first amendment problems which accompany such a claim. In order to survive a . . . motion to dismiss, a plaintiff bringing a negligent hiring claim against a religious institution must plead facts with particularity. Specifically, the plaintiff must plead facts which indicate that the individual hired had a past history of criminal conduct, tortious, or otherwise dangerous conduct about which the religious institution knew or could have discovered through reasonable investigation. The mere incantation of the elements of a negligent hiring claim, i.e., the abstract statement that the religious institution knew or should have known about the employee's criminal or tortious propensities, without more, is not enough to enable a plaintiff to survive a motion to dismiss for failure to state a claim [upon which relief can be granted]. . . . While even the most liberal construction of the First Amendment will not protect a religious organization's decision to hire someone who it knows is likely to commit criminal or tortious acts, the mere incantation of an abstract legal standard should not subject a religious organization's employment policies to state scrutiny. Consequently, in order to survive a motion to dismiss, a plaintiff bringing a negligent hiring claim must allege some fact indicating that the religious institution knew or should have known of the employee's criminal or tortious propensities." The court ruled that the woman's lawsuit had to be dismissed, since it "alleged no fact indicating that [the pastor] had a past history of criminal or tortious conduct about which the [denominational offices] knew or should have known."

Example. The Oklahoma Supreme Court ruled that a married couple could not sue their church and former pastor for damages they allegedly incurred as a result of an adulterous affair between the former pastor and the wife.[70] The husband and wife sued the church and former pastor as a result of the pastor's conduct. The lawsuit alleged that the church was negligent in the selection of the pastor since it knew or should have known about the wife's affair and a previous affair in Texas. The church insisted that it did not know of the affair or of the alleged incident in Texas, and that it did not condone such behavior. The court concluded that the church was not responsible for injuries resulting from the minister's conduct. It observed that the first amendment guaranty of religious freedom did not shield churches from liability for personal injuries arising "from acts unrelated to religious practices protected by the first amendment." However, it insisted that all of the couple's claims against the church had to be dismissed. It observed, "Neither the claims by the husband nor the wife against the minister are cognizable in Oklahoma. . . . Because their claims against the minister also serve as the basis for the claims against the church for its negligent hiring and supervision of the minister, that claim is also not cognizable."

§ 10-05.3 — Risk Management

Key point 10-05.3. Churches can reduce the risk of liability based on negligent supervision for sexual misconduct involving adult victims by adopting risk management policies and procedures.

---

[70] Bladen v. First Presbyterian Church, 857 P.2d 789 (Okla. 1993).

Key Resources. Churches must exercise reasonable care in the selection of ministers, nonminister employees, and volunteers in order to avoid potential liability based on negligent selection. The publisher of this text has produced several resources to assist church leaders in satisfying the standard of reasonable care in the selection of workers. These resources include the Selection and Screening of Ministers kit (includes application booklets containing key questions and reference forms, interview booklets containing nearly 200 additional questions to ask during a personal interview of pastoral candidates, and a helpful 100-page book that addresses the selection and screening of church workers). Another useful resource is the 4-Hour Legal Training Kit for Church Boards (4 one-hour audio tapes orient church board members to the critical legal and tax issues that face their church). See Appendix 5 at the end of this text for more information on ordering and of these resources.

This section has addressed church liability on the basis of negligent selection for sexual misconduct by ministers and other church workers with adult victims. Churches can reduce the risk of liability based on negligent selection by adopting some or all of the strategies described in section 10-04.3.

Key point. Many cases of sexual misconduct with adult victims arise out of a counseling relationship. There are a number of steps that churches can take to reduce the risk of such behavior occurring in the course of a counseling relationship, and many of these are addressed later in this chapter.[71]

§ 10-06 Negligent Selection of Church Workers — Other Cases

Key point 10-06. A church may be legally responsible on the basis of negligent selection for injuries resulting from the acts of a minister or other worker not involving sexual misconduct.

Negligent selection claims are not limited to cases involving sexual misconduct. They can arise anytime that a church's failure to exercise reasonable care in the selection of an employee or volunteer leads to a foreseeable injury. Here are some examples:

• Using adolescents as attendants in the church nursery.

• Selecting adult workers without any training in CPR or other resuscitation techniques to accompany a youth group to any event involving swimming or boating.

• Selecting lay counselors with inadequate professional training.

• Selecting drivers for any church-sponsored activity without checking their driving record. For example, if a church uses a driver with a suspended drivers license, or with a history of traffic offenses, then it may be responsible on the basis of negligent selection for injuries caused by the driver's negligence. To reduce the risk of liability in this context, churches should refrain from using any driver without taking the following steps:

(1) Have each prospective driver complete an application form that asks for the person's drivers license number, type of drivers license and expiration date, a description of any driving restrictions, and a history of traffic accidents and moving violations.

---

[71] See § 10-12, infra.

(2) Ask the church's liability insurance carrier to check on the individual's driving record. Often, insurance companies will perform this task if requested, at no charge. The insurance company should be requested to update its research on all drivers of church vehicles periodically, to screen out persons with a recent history of unsafe driving.

(3) Discontinue using any driver if reports are received that he or she is operating a church vehicle in a negligent manner. Fully investigate such reports, and do not use the individual again unless the investigation clearly demonstrates that the complaints were without merit.

(4) If the prospective driver is a new member, then ask for the names and addresses of other churches in which he or she has worked as a driver. Contact those other churches and ask if they are aware of facts that would indicate that the individual should not be used as a driver. Make a written record of such contacts.

(5) Periodically invite a local law enforcement officer to speak to all drivers concerning safety issues.

(6) Require all drivers to immediately inform the church of any traffic convictions.

Key point. The risk management strategies addressed in section 10-04.3 can be used to manage the risk of these other kinds of negligent selection.

§ 10-07 Negligent Retention of Church Workers — In General

Key point 10-07. A church may exercise reasonable care in selecting ministers or other church workers but still be responsible for their misconduct if it "retained" them after receiving information indicating that they posed a risk of harm to others.

A church may use reasonable care in selecting ministers or other church workers but still be responsible for their misconduct if it "retained" them after receiving information indicating that they posed a risk of harm to others.

Example. A visitor attends a church service and recognizes the church's associate pastor as a convicted child molester. No one else in the church is aware of the associate pastor's background. The visitor discloses this fact in a letter to the senior pastor, who shares it with the church board. The board decides not to take any action. It bases its decision on the fact that the associate pastor is well-liked by the congregation, and that the incident of child molestation occurred ten years ago. Several months later, the board learns that the associate pastor molested a child on church premises. The victim and her family sue the church. They claim that the church is responsible for the victim's injuries on the basis of negligent retention. That is, the church retained the pastor after receiving information suggesting that he represented a risk to others.

§ 10-07.1 — Court Decisions Recognizing Negligent Retention Claims

Key point 10-07.1. Some courts have found churches liable on the basis of negligent retention for the sexual misconduct of ministers and other church workers on the ground that the church was negligent in retaining the offender after receiving credible information indicating that he or she posed a risk of harm to others.

Some courts have concluded that churches can be sued on the basis of negligent retention for the sexual misconduct of ministers and other church staff.

Example. A federal appeals court concluded that two female church employees could sue the minister who had seduced them since he had "held himself out" as a qualified marital counselor.[72] However, the court dismissed all of the employees' claims against the church, including negligent retention. The court acknowledged that "an employer that negligently retains in his employ an individual who is incompetent or unfit for the job may be liable to a third party whose injury was proximately caused by the employer's negligence." However, to prove negligent retention, the two women had to show that the church "knew or should have known that [the former minister's] conduct as a supervisor or counselor presented an unreasonable risk of harm to others." The court concluded that there was no evidence that the church "know or should have known" that the former minister was engaging in marital counseling or that he was likely to engage in sexual misconduct or disclose confidences as a marriage counselor.

Example. An Indiana court ruled that the first amendment does not prevent a woman from suing her church and a denominational agency on account of injuries she suffered as a result of being molested by her pastor when she was a minor.[73] The woman claimed that the pastor began molesting her when she was 7 years old, and that the molestation continued until she was 20. The woman sued her church and the regional and national denominational agencies with which her church was affiliated. The court concluded that the national church was not liable on the basis of negligent retention for the actions of the pastor. It observed, "The [national church], which is only affiliated with the local church and [regional agency] through its constitution and judicial procedures, was not informed. The evidence . . . does not indicate that [the woman] invoked the judicial procedures, which is the only mechanism by which the [national church] could have taken action against [the pastor]. According to the judicial procedures, the [regional agency] forms a committee to investigate alleged misconduct upon the submission of a complaint signed by two or more persons. Only after this investigation is completed and the [regional agency] determines that the evidence warrants a trial does the [national church] become involved. [The woman] has not alleged . . . that she or anyone else ever filed a complaint against [the pastor] with the [regional agency]. Therefore, the [national church] could not have disciplined [the pastor]. Accordingly, we conclude that because the evidence does not show that the [national church] was aware of [the pastor's] actions, summary judgment in favor of the [national church] is proper on [the woman's] claims for negligent . . . retention."

Example. A North Carolina court ruled that the first amendment did not prevent it from resolving a sexual harassment lawsuit brought by three female church employees against their church and denominational agencies.[74] Three female church employees (the "plaintiffs") sued their church and various church agencies as a result of the sexual misconduct of a pastor. The lawsuit alleged that the pastor "committed inappropriate, unwelcome, offensive and nonconsensual acts of a sexual nature against the plaintiffs, variously hugging, kissing and touching them, and made inappropriate, unwelcome, offensive and nonconsensual statements of a sexually suggestive nature to them." The lawsuit further alleged that the local church and church agencies "knew or should have known" of the pastor's propensity for sexual misconduct but failed to take any actions to warn or protect the plaintiffs from his wrongful activity. The court began its opinion by noting that the key issue was whether the first amendment

---

[72] Sanders v. Casa View Baptist Church, 134 F.3d 331 (5th Cir. 1998).
[73] Konkle v. Henson, 672 N.E.2d 450 (Ind. App. 1996).
[74] Smith v. Privette, 495 S.E.2d 395 (N.C. App. 1998).

prevents "the filing of a negligent retention and supervision claim against a religious organization, when that claim is based on the conduct of a cleric of that organization." The court concluded that if a resolution of the plaintiffs' legal claims did not require an interpretation of church doctrine, then "the first amendment is not implicated and neutral principles of law are properly applied to adjudicate the claim." The court then noted that North Carolina recognizes negligent supervision and retention as separate bases of legal liability. To support a claim of negligent retention and supervision against an employer, a plaintiff must prove that "the incompetent employee committed a tortious act resulting in injury to plaintiff and that prior to the act, the employer knew or had reason to know of the employee's incompetency." The court concluded, "We acknowledge that the decision to hire or discharge a minister is inextricable from religious doctrine and protected by the first amendment from judicial inquiry. We do not accept, however, that resolution of the plaintiffs' negligent retention and supervision claim requires the trial court to inquire into the church defendants' reasons for choosing [the pastor] to serve as a minister. The plaintiffs' claim, construed in the light most favorable to them, instead presents the issue of whether the church defendants knew or had reason to know of [the pastor's] propensity to engage in sexual misconduct, conduct that the church defendants do not claim is part of the tenets or practices of [their religion]. Thus, there is no necessity for the court to interpret or weigh church doctrine in its adjudication of the plaintiffs' claim for negligent retention and supervision. It follows that the first amendment is not implicated and does not bar the plaintiffs' claim against the church defendants."

Example. A Minnesota court ruled that a church could be sued as a result of the pastor's acts of child molestation.[75] For nearly 20 years, the pastor had served as both pastor and youth program teacher at his church. He lived in an apartment at the church's youth center. An adolescent boy (the "victim") attended confirmation classes at the church, and the pastor was his instructor. The victim so admired the pastor that he wanted to become a pastor himself. The victim often went with the pastor to make calls or visit other churches. He also attended church camp during the summer and at times stayed overnight at the pastor's apartment. When the victim was 13 to 16 years old, he was molested by the pastor. The pastor admitted to engaging in the acts. Prior to his abuse, the victim was a good student and athlete. After the abuse, his grades dropped and he quit playing team sports. During his late teens, he was hospitalized as a result of an attempted suicide. He was married in 1973, and during the marriage he abused alcohol and suffered from social phobia including panic attacks. The court concluded that the church had been negligent in permitting the sexual abuse to occur. This conclusion was based in part on the fact that during the time the victim was being molested (1) A church trustee saw the pastor kissing another adolescent boy on the mouth. The pastor, upon seeing the trustee, blushed and ran back to his apartment. The trustee informed another trustee of this incident, along with two members of the church council. No action was taken. (2) Another church trustee was approached by a local teacher and asked if the pastor was a child molester. This same trustee's uncle told him that he heard something went on at a cabin at church camp and asked if the pastor was "straight." (3) A church trustee's son had to make up some work for confirmation classes at the pastor's home. When he returned home, he told his father that the pastor wanted him "to get under the sheets" with him. (4) A student in the confirmation class testified that during a confirmation class at the church she thought she saw the pastor engage in an act of child abuse. She told her parents and the church's "intern pastor" what she saw. The girl and her parents quit attending the church after this incident. (5) Another confirmation student told the church's intern pastor that the pastor had "put his arm around him all of the time" and showered with the boys. The church claimed that the intern's "knowledge" could not be imputed to the church, since he was not an employee. In rejecting this defense, the court observed, "Regardless of whether [the intern pastor's] knowledge may be imputed to [the church, the church's] own council members

---

[75] Doe v. Redeemer Lutheran Church, 531 N.W.2d 897 (Minn. App. 1995).

and trustees were aware that [the pastor] had been engaging in sexual improprieties, but they turned a blind eye and did nothing to address the problem. The jury clearly could have found that [the church] should have taken action and failure to do so amounted to negligence."

§ 10-07.2 — Court Decisions Rejecting Negligent Retention Claims

Key point 10-07.2. *Many courts have ruled that the first amendment prevents churches from being legally responsible on the basis of negligent retention for the misconduct of ministers.*

Some courts have concluded that the first amendment prevents churches from being sued on the basis of negligent retention for the sexual misconduct of ministers.

Example. A Colorado court threw out a lawsuit brought by a woman alleging that her church acted improperly and unlawfully when it dismissed her after she made complaints of sexual harassment and child molestation against another minister.[76] The woman alleged that when she was a minor, her stepfather committed various acts of sexual assault against her when they resided together. Her stepfather was a minister at the time, and later became president of his denomination. The woman pursued ministerial studies and was licensed as a minister. After serving as a minister in the State of Washington, she moved to the Denver area to start a new church. She later learned that her stepfather, with whom she had severed all ties, was also pastoring a church in the Denver area. She learned that her stepfather was allegedly sexually harassing women church employees and a woman parishioner in his Denver church. She reported this alleged harassment, as well as the sexual abuse she had suffered from her stepfather as a minor, to denominational officers. In response, the stepfather filed charges with the denomination against the woman, claiming that her allegations were false and demanding a full investigation. After an investigation, denominational officers revoked the woman's license and denied her the opportunity to open a new church. The woman responded by filing a lawsuit against her stepfather and her denomination, alleging several theories of liability including negligent retention of her stepfather. In rejecting the woman's claim of negligent retention, the court noted that "[a]n employer may be subject to liability for negligent supervision and retention if the employer knows or should have known that an employee's conduct would subject third parties to an unreasonable risk of harm." The court concluded that any resolution of these theories of liability would involve the civil courts in a church's decision-making processes contrary to the first amendment guaranty of religious freedom.

Example. A federal court in Connecticut dismissed a lawsuit brought by two adult brothers against their church and diocese for injuries they allegedly sustained when they were sexually molested while minors by a priest.[77] The brothers alleged that the church and diocese were legally responsible for the priest's acts on the basis of negligent retention because they were aware that the priest had received treatment sessions for sexual abuse of minors over a 15-year period at Catholic treatment centers in New Mexico and Maryland. The court accepted affidavits from church officials claiming that they had no knowledge (or reason to suspect) that the priest had ever participated in any retreat or treatment for sexual abuse of any kind. The court concluded, based on these affidavits, that the church and diocese had no prior knowledge of any sexual misconduct on the part of the offending priest, and so the negligence claim had to be dismissed.

---

[76] Van Osdol v. Vogt, 892 P.2d 402 (Colo. App. 1994).

[77] Nutt v. Norwich Roman Catholic Diocese, 921 F. Supp. 66 (D. Conn. 1995). *See also* Martinelli v. Bridgeport Roman Catholic Diocese, 989 F. Supp. 110 (D. Conn. 1997).

Example. *A Georgia court dismissed a lawsuit brought by a woman against her church and a denominational agency as a result of injuries she allegedly sustained during a sexual relationship with her pastor.[78] The woman had received counseling from the pastor on a number of occasions, despite the fact that the pastor had informed her that she should discontinue the counseling sessions with him and find another counselor because he was sexually attracted to her. Despite this request, the woman did not discontinue the counseling sessions, and the two began having "phone sex" conversations. The woman claimed that the pastor initiated the first such conversation but that at times she would call him. She insisted that while she led him to believe she was participating in the "phone sex," she was, in reality, only pretending. The woman alleged that toward the end of their counseling relationship the pastor called her at home and asked her to come to his office so they could have sex. She drove to his office and the two engaged in intercourse. The woman quit seeing the pastor when she learned that he was engaged to be married to another woman. The woman and her husband sued their church and a denominational agency on the basis of negligent retention of the pastor. Specifically, they argued that both organizations left the pastor in his position despite knowledge that he posed a risk of harm to women. This knowledge consisted of the following three facts: (1) There were rumors at the church about the pastor's relationship with another woman who was a church employee. (2) A letter to the senior pastor from a prospective church member put the church and denominational agency on notice of the associate pastor's propensity for sexual misconduct. In the letter, a woman claimed that the associate pastor came to her house in an intoxicated condition, made inappropriate comments, and touched her on the knee. (3) The woman informed the church's new associate pastor of her relationship with his predecessor. The court concluded that this evidence did not render the church or denominational agency negligent for retaining the associate minister. With regard to the rumors of an improper relationship with the female church employee, the court noted that (1) the associate pastor later married this woman; (2) the associate pastor denied any inappropriate conduct with this woman when confronted about it by the senior pastor; (3) the senior pastor recommended that the associate pastor be transferred to another church on the basis of these rumors; and (4) the associate pastor's "personal, consensual relationship with [the employee] is totally unrelated to the type of conduct complained of by [the woman in this lawsuit]." With regard to the letter, the court noted that (1) the senior pastor immediately called the woman and met with her to discuss the letter; (2) the senior pastor also discussed it with the associate pastor who denied the events in the letter; (3) the senior pastor conducted a thorough investigation and determined the woman was not telling the truth; (4) the senior pastor testified that at no time did any woman come to him and say she was having a sexual relationship with the associate pastor; (5) the senior pastor testified that he was never, at any time, led to believe that the associate pastor was a threat to women parishioners; and (6) the senior pastor stated, in an affidavit, that "[i]n fact, I believe that [the associate pastor] possibly had an excellent future in the ministry." With regard to the woman's disclosure to the church's new associate pastor of her relationship with his predecessor, the court noted that she also told him she was not ready to come forward and tell anyone else about the relationship. Therefore she "cannot now complain of [his] failure to act when she told him she was not ready to disclose her relationship with [the associate pastor]. The court also noted that the woman's communications to the new associate pastor were privileged and could not be disclosed without her permission. The court concluded, "The record is also devoid of any probative evidence tending to show the church or [denominational agency] were or should have been on notice of a propensity for sexual misconduct after [the associate pastor] became a minister at the church. The [couple] make numerous allegations as to [the associate pastor's] conduct with different women but have submitted no admissible evidence in support of this contention."*

---

[78] Alpharetta First United Methodist Church v. Stewart, 473 S.E.2d 532 (Ga. App. 1996).

Example. A Georgia appeals court dismissed a daughter's lawsuit against a priest and Catholic diocese claiming that her father murdered her mother and then killed himself as a result of an adulterous affair between the mother and a priest.[79] The daughter claimed that her mother had been seduced by the priest, and that her father shot and killed her mother and then shot himself after finding out about it. The daughter claimed that the diocese was responsible for her parent's deaths on the basis of negligent hiring and retention of the priest. She insisted that if the diocese had adequately investigated the matter and "defrocked" the priest, the deaths would not have occurred. The court concluded that the diocese did not have sufficient proof that the priest had acted improperly. It observed, "To the contrary, all signs point to the unreliability of [the mother's] declarations. She told a friend that she did not have an affair with [the priest] and in an official church investigation by the church she denied any involvement with the priest. She wrote a letter to [her] archbishop in which she stated that she had fantasized an affair with [the priest] because her husband was away on business and she was lonely. She asked the archbishop for forgiveness and stated that she was seeking professional help." The court concluded that the priest and diocese "produced evidence demonstrating that [the priest] did not have a sexual relationship with [the mother]. [The daughter] has failed to come up with evidence to the contrary."

Example. A federal district court in Michigan ruled that a church school and various church agencies were not liable on the basis of negligent hiring, supervision, or retention for the sexual molestation of a minor student by a priest.[80] The court, in summarily rejecting the victim's claim that the school and church agencies had been guilty of "negligent hiring," observed, "Questions of hiring and retention of clergy necessarily will require interpretation of church canons, and internal church policies and practices. It is well-settled that when a court is required to interpret canon law or internal church policies and practices, the first amendment is violated because such judicial inquiry would constitute excessive government entanglement with religion. . . . [An] inquiry into the decision of who should be permitted to become or remain a priest necessarily would involve prohibited excessive entanglement with religion. Therefore [the victim's] claims of negligence predicated upon a negligent hiring theory will be dismissed."

Example. A Minnesota court ruled that a church and denominational organization were not legally responsible on the basis of negligent retention for a pastor's acts of child molestation.[81] The molester had served as pastor of a church for nearly 25 years, and was accused of molesting numerous young boys during his tenure. The court defined "negligent retention" as "occurring when, during the course of employment, the employer becomes aware or should have become aware of problems with an employee that indicated his unfitness, and the employer fails to take further action such as investigating, discharge, or reassignment." The victim pointed to the following facts in supporting his claim that the church had been guilty of negligent retention: (1) some church members knew the pastor had an interest in children and youth ministry; (2) some church members knew the pastor was counseling children in private, including discussions of sexual and relationship issues; (3) some church members knew that, as part of his confirmation curriculum, the pastor discussed sexuality with children during the final interview; (4) some church members knew the pastor taught the boys about circumcision in confirmation classes, though a parent was always present during these lectures; (5) other incidents of sexual abuse occurred at the church at a time when other people would normally be around and the pastor took no special precautions to hide the abuse. The court concluded that the church was not guilty of negligent retention, since "[t]here is no evidence [it] had actual knowledge of [the pastor's] propensities to commit

---

[79] Boehm v. Abi-Sarkis, 438 S.E.2d 410 (Ga. App. 1993).
[80] Isely v. Capuchin Province, 880 F. Supp. 1138 (E.D. Mich. 1995).
[81] M.L. v. Magnuson, 531 N.W.2d 831 (Minn. App. 1995). *Accord* Mulinix v. Mulinix, 1997 WL 585775 (Minn. App. 1997).

sexual abuse prior to the time [the victim] was abused." It observed, "There is no evidence that members in 1973 should have foreseen abuse because their clergyperson was interested in youth ministry or counseled children in private. We are mindful that most personal counseling occurs in private. And by itself, evidence of a youth ministry interest and counseling activity does not show that the congregation should suspect the pastor is engaging in sexual abuse. Nor is it reasonable to infer, at least without other evidence, knowledge in 1973 that a pastor will engage in sexual abuse merely because he or she counsels children on sexual issues. There is no evidence that counseling on sexual issues was outside a pastor's purview or so unusual that it should have raised suspicions of sexual abuse. We agree that the details of some of [the pastor's] discussions on sexuality were highly unusual and perhaps would have alerted [the church] to a problem. But there is no evidence that anyone reported the contents of these discussions to [the church's] decisionmakers nor has [the victim] explained how these [church] members could otherwise have learned the details of these conversations. . . . Finally, the jury could not conclude that [the church] should have known about other incidents of abuse simply because they occurred at the church when other people were probably in the building. The incidents all occurred in private, and there is no evidence that people who may have been in the building knew anything more than the fact that counseling sessions occurred. . . . If this evidence alone is sufficient to support a negligent retention verdict, it would appear impossible for a church to avoid liability without prohibiting pastors from counseling children in private or prohibiting discussion of sexual issues. We are not prepared to hold that every church must take these measures to avoid liability for negligent retention, much less that this standard can govern church practices retroactive to a time more than two decades past."

Example. *The Missouri Supreme Court ruled that the first amendment barred it from resolving a lawsuit in which a Catholic diocese was sued as a result of a priest's acts of sexual molestation.[82] An adult male alleged that when he was about 14 years old he went to a Catholic priest for confession and counseling about various concerns, some of a sexual nature. The priest initiated a sexual relationship with the victim that lasted about 10 years. The victim alleged that when the priest was "hired or ordained" the diocese "knew or reasonably should have known of prior sexual misconduct or a propensity to such conduct" by him. The victim sued the diocese on the basis of several theories of liability including negligent retention. The court concluded that a resolution of the victim's claims against the diocese would violate the first amendment.*

Example. *A New York court ruled that a Catholic diocese could not be sued on the basis of negligent hiring for a priest's acts of child molestation, but it could be sued for negligent supervision and negligent retention.[83] The offending priest was ordained in Venezuela and moved to the United States with a letter of reference from his archbishop. He later molested at least one minor (the "victim"). The victim sued the local diocese, claiming that it was legally responsible for the priest's conduct on the basis of negligent hiring, negligent supervision, and negligent retention. He alleged that the diocese became aware of the danger the priest posed to minors after hiring him as a result of comments both he and the priest made to other priests regarding inappropriate behavior. The court noted that if the victim or the priest made such statements to other priests, then the diocese might be legally responsible for the priest's actions on the basis of negligent retention and negligent supervision. The court insisted that imposing liability on the diocese under such circumstances "would not violate constitutional and statutory guarantees of free exercise of religion and separation of church and state" since "there is no indication that requiring increased supervision of [the priest] or the termination of his employment by the [diocese]*

---

[82] Gray v. Ward, 950 S.W.2d 232 (Mo. 1997). *Accord* Gibson v. Brewer, 952 S.W.2d 239 (Mo. 1997).

[83] Kenneth R. v. Roman Catholic Diocese, 654 N.Y.S.2d 791 (N.Y.A.D. 1997).

based upon [his] conduct would violate any religious doctrine or inhibit any religious practice." The court concluded that there was evidence that the retention of the priest by the diocese was dictated by religious doctrine. It insisted that "religious entities have some duty to prevent injuries incurred by persons in their employ whom they have reason to believe will engage in injurious conduct."

Example. *A federal court in New York refused to find a church or denomination agency liable, on the basis of "negligent placement, retention, or supervision," for a pastor's sexual contacts with a woman during marital counseling.[84] The court made the following statement in rejecting the woman's claim that the church and denomination had been guilty of negligence: "[A]ny inquiry into the policies and practices of the church defendants in hiring or supervising their clergy raises . . . first amendment problems of entanglement . . . which might involve the court in making sensitive judgments about the propriety of the church defendants' supervision in light of their religious beliefs. Insofar as concerns retention or supervision, the pastor of a Presbyterian church is not analogous to a common law employee. He may not demit his charge nor be removed by the session, without the consent of the presbytery, functioning essentially as an ecclesiastical court. The traditional denominations each have their own intricate principles of governance, as to which the state has no rights of visitation. Church governance is founded in scripture, modified by reformers over almost two millennia. As the Supreme Court stated [long ago]: 'It is not to be supposed that the judges of the civil courts can be as competent in the ecclesiastical law and religious faith of all these bodies as the ablest men in each are in reference to their own. It would therefore be an appeal from the more learned tribunal in the law which should decide the case, to the one which is less so.'[85] It would therefore also be inappropriate and unconstitutional for this court to determine after the fact that the ecclesiastical authorities negligently supervised or retained the [pastor]. Any award of damages would have a chilling effect leading indirectly to state control over the future conduct of affairs of a religious denomination, a result violative of the text and history of the [first amendment]."*

Example. *The Wisconsin Supreme Court ruled that the statute of limitations prevented a woman from suing a Catholic archdiocese for the alleged acts of molestation by a priest nearly 40 years before.[86] The woman claimed that the priest entered into a sexual relationship with her in the late 1950s when she was a high school student, and that as a result of the priest's behavior she "has suffered and continues to suffer from severe emotional distress, causing and contributing to the break-up of her marriage, separation from her children, loss of jobs and other difficulties." The woman's lawsuit claimed that the archdiocese was responsible for her injuries on the basis of several factors, including negligent retention. Specifically, she alleged that the archdiocese knew or should have known that the priest had a sexual problem and acted "willfully, intentionally and in wanton and reckless disregard of the rights and safety of plaintiff by failing to remove [him] from serving as a priest." In rejecting the woman's claim, the court observed, "To establish a claim for negligent hiring or retention [the woman] would have to establish that the archdiocese was negligent in hiring or retaining [the priest] because he was incompetent or otherwise unfit. But, we conclude that the first amendment to the United States Constitution prevents the courts of this state from determining what makes one competent to serve as a Catholic priest since such a determination would require interpretation of church canons and internal church policies and practices. Therefore [the suit] against the archdiocese is not capable of enforcement by the courts." The court concluded, "Assuming they exist at all, the torts of negligent hiring and retention may not be*

---

[84] Schmidt v. Bishop, 779 F. Supp. 321 (S.D.N.Y. 1991).
[85] Watson v. Jones, 80 U.S. 679 (1872).
[86] *Pritzlaff v. Archdiocese of Milwaukee, 533 N.W.2d 780 (Wis. 1995).*

maintained against a religious governing body due to concerns of excessive entanglement, and that the tort of negligent training or supervision cannot be successfully asserted in this case because it would require an inquiry into church laws, practices and policies."

§ 10-07.3 — Risk Management

Key point 10-07.3. *Churches can reduce the risk of liability based on negligent retention for sexual misconduct involving adult or minor victims by adopting risk management policies and procedures.*

How can churches reduce the risk of liability based on negligent retention of a minister or lay worker who engages in inappropriate conduct with an adult or child? While churches cannot eliminate this risk, they can take steps to reduce it. Consider the following:

1. INVESTIGATE

Whenever a church leader receives credible information suggesting that a church employee or volunteer may represent a risk of harm to others, an immediate and thorough investigation should be initiated. Remember this—once such information is received, the church is "put on notice" of the risk and may be legally responsible on the basis of negligent retention for future acts of misconduct by the church worker if it does nothing to investigate or respond to the information. The investigation should include a thorough review of the accusation. This ordinarily will include some or all of the following procedures:

• Interviews with the victim (and the victim's family, if the victim is a minor).

• Interviews with the alleged perpetrator (and the perpetrator's family, if the perpetrator is a minor).

• Collection of corroborating evidence, such as (1) witnesses; (2) other victims; or (3) documentary evidence including letters and photos.

• Consultation with the church's insurance agent.

• Consultation with the church's attorney.

• Consultation with the denominational officers.

• Consultation with other churches or charities in which the alleged perpetrator has worked, to identify whether any similar acts of misconduct have occurred. If so, this tends to prove a pattern, and supports the inference that the victim's account is correct.

• If the alleged misconduct constitutes a crime, conduct a criminal records check to determine if the worker has a history of such acts. If so, this tends to prove a pattern, and supports the inference that the victim's account is correct.

• If the alleged misconduct constitutes child abuse under state law, then church leaders must comply immediately with applicable reporting requirements. Church leaders can then suspend their own investigation and await the outcome of the state's investigation, or proceed with their own investigation independently of the state. In either case, church leaders should consider suspending the alleged wrongdoer until the investigation is concluded, depending on the nature and severity of the alleged wrongdoing.

Key point. Many churches are associated with denominations that are empowered to investigate allegations of pastoral misconduct. If this is the case, the accusations should be turned over immediately to denominational officials.

Key point. Churches that ignore allegations of wrongdoing by a pastor or lay worker face a number of risks in addition to negligent retention. These include (1) liability based on "ratification" of the minister's actions; (2) punitive damages; and (3) possible personal liability for members of the church board.

2. RESTRICTIONS

If the church's investigation results in credible evidence to support the victim's allegations, then the church can reduce its risk of negligent retention by imposing appropriate restrictions on the alleged wrongdoer. The nature and extent of such restrictions will vary depending on a number of circumstances, including the nature and severity of the alleged wrongs and the strength of the evidence. If a church ignores credible evidence of wrongdoing and imposes no restrictions on the alleged wrongdoer, it is exposed to liability based on negligent retention from the time it learned of the allegations.

Key point. Here is an excellent question to ask when evaluating a church's risk of negligence (in hiring, retention, or supervision): How would a jury view our actions? Would it conclude that our actions were reasonable? If such a conclusion is not certain, then the risk of negligence exists.

§ 10-08 Negligent Supervision of Church Workers — In General

Tip. A number of courts, in addressing the question of whether clergy are employees or self-employed for federal income tax reporting purposes, have observed that churches generally exercise relatively little supervision or control over clergy.[87] Such cases can be used by churches in defending against negligent supervision claims involving clergy misconduct.

Churches can use reasonable care in selecting workers, but still be liable for injuries sustained during church activities on the basis of negligent supervision. The term negligence *means carelessness or a failure to exercise reasonable care.* Negligent supervision, *then, refers to a failure to exercise reasonable care in the supervision of church workers and church activities. Churches have been sued on the basis of negligent supervision in a variety of contexts. Consider the following examples:*

Example. A minor is sexually molested by a volunteer church youth worker on church premises. The minor's parents sue the church, claiming that it is responsible for their child's injuries on the basis of negligent supervision. They claim that the molestation never would have occurred had the church exercised proper supervision over its workers and activities.

Example. A male youth pastor has sexual contact with a 16-year-old female in the church youth group. The incident occurred on a church-sponsored trip. The minor's parents sue the church, claiming that it

---

[87] *See, e.g.,* Weber v. Commissioner, 60 F.3d 1104 (4th Cir. 1995).

is responsible for their child's injuries on the basis of negligent supervision. They claim that the incident never would have occurred had the church exercised proper supervision over its youth pastor.

Example. *A male pastor has sexual contact with an adult female in the course of a counseling relationship. The woman later sues the church, claiming that it is responsible for her injuries on the basis of negligent supervision. She claims that the incident would not have occurred had the church exercised proper supervision over its pastor.*

Example. *An adolescent boy is injured while playing in a church-sponsored basketball game. The minor's parents sue the church, claiming that it is responsible for their child's injuries on the basis of negligent supervision. They claim that the molestation never would have occurred had the church exercised proper supervision over its workers and activities.*

Example. *A 5-year-old girl drowns while participating in a church-sponsored trip to a local lake. The minor's parents sue the church, claiming that it is responsible for their child's death on the basis of negligent supervision. They claim that the death never would have occurred had the church exercised proper supervision over its workers and activities.*

Example. *A 10-year-old boy is injured when he falls off a cliff while participating in a church-sponsored camping trip. The minor's mother sues the church, claiming that it is responsible for her child's injuries on the basis of negligent supervision. She claims that the accident never would have occurred had the church exercised proper supervision over its workers and activities.*

Example. *A 6-month-old infant breaks her leg while in the church nursery. There were two attendants on duty in the nursery, both of whom were 15-year-old girls. The accident occurred when the attendant who was changing the infant's diaper temporarily left the infant unattended. The infant's parents sue the church, claiming that the accident never would have occurred had the church exercised proper supervision over its workers and activities.*

Key point. *Churches are not "guarantors" of the safety and well-being of those persons who participate in their programs and activities. Generally, they are responsible only for those injuries that result from their negligence.*

§ 10-09 Negligent Supervision of Church Workers — Sexual Misconduct Cases Involving Minor Victims

Many of the cases in which churches have been sued for negligent supervision involve incidents of child molestation. A child is molested on church premises, or during a church activity, and the child's parents sue the church. While the parents may allege that the church was negligent in selecting or retaining the offender, they also may assert that the church was negligent in supervising the offender and its premises and activities. One court defined negligent supervision of children as follows:

> The measure of duty of a person undertaking control and supervision of a child to exercise reasonable care for the safety of the child is to be gauged by the standard of the average responsible parent; such person is not an insurer of the safety of the child and has no duty to foresee and guard against every possible hazard. The measure of precaution which must be taken by one having a child in his care, who stands in no relation to the child except that

he has undertaken to care for it is that care which a prudent person would exercise under like circumstances. As a general rule, a person who undertakes the control and supervision of a child, even without compensation, has the duty to use reasonable care to protect the child from injury. Such person is not an insurer of the safety of the child. He is required only to use reasonable care commensurate with the reasonably foreseeable risk of harm.[88]

§ 10-09.1 — Court Decisions Recognizing Negligent Supervision Claims

Key point 10-09.1. *Some courts have found churches liable on the basis of negligent supervision for a worker's acts of child molestation on the ground that the church failed to exercise reasonable care in the supervision of the victim or of its own programs and activities.*

This section reviews court decisions in which a church or other religious organization was found liable on the basis of negligent supervision for a worker's acts of child molestation.

Example. *The Colorado Supreme Court ruled that a church whose pastor molested a young boy could be sued on the basis of negligent supervision of the pastor.[89] A 7-year-old boy (the "victim"), who was experiencing emotional trauma, was encouraged by his pastor to enter into a counseling relationship with him. The boy's mother approved, and the counseling sessions lasted for a number of years. From the very first counseling session the victim claimed that the pastor engaged in sexual contact with him, including having him sit on the pastor's lap while the pastor massaged his thighs and genitals. While these "massages" were occurring the pastor would tell the victim that "your father loves you, your mother loves you, God loves you, and I love you." Two other adult males claimed that the pastor had engaged in similar behavior with them when they were minors, including a physical inspection of their genitals to see if they had been "properly circumcised." The parents of two other boys complained to the church board about the pastor's counseling methods, and in particular his practice of inspecting genitals to check for proper circumcision. Nearly a year later the board responded by directing the pastor to discontinue his counseling of minors. A few months later the pastor was dismissed. The victim and his mother sued the church, claiming that it was responsible for the pastor's acts on the basis of several grounds including negligent supervision. A jury returned a verdict in favor of the victim, and this verdict was affirmed by the state supreme court. The court rejected the church's claim that allowing civil judgments against pastoral counselors and their churches based upon conduct occurring during counseling sessions could so "entangle" the government with religious practices as to violate the first amendment. It acknowledged that "the decision to hire or discharge a minister is itself inextricable from religious doctrine." However, a court must "distinguish internal hiring disputes within religious organizations from general negligence claims filed by injured third parties."*

Example. *In a decision that will be of direct relevance to churches, a Georgia court ruled that a local Boys Club could be sued by the parents of a 5-year-old boy who was abducted and molested when he wandered off the Boys Club premises without adult supervision.[90] The victim was enrolled in a summer day camp conducted by the Boys Club in his community. Boys in the program ranged from 6 to 11 (an exception was made in the case of the victim), and the boys were to be under the direct supervision of an adult worker at all times. An adult was stationed at a desk by the front door of the facility, and no child*

[88] *Wallace v. Boys Club of Albany, Georgia, Inc., 439 S.E.2d 746 (Ga. App. 1993).*
[89] Bear Valley Church of Christ v. DeBose, 928 P.2d 1315 (Colo. 1996).
[90] Wallace v. Boys Club of Albany, Georgia, Inc., 439 S.E.2d 746 (Ga. App. 1993).

was allowed to leave the premised unattended. Nevertheless, the victim was able to walk out the front door and go around the building to look at the swimming pool without adult supervision. While outside, the boy was abducted and sexually molested. No adult staff member was aware of the victim's absence until his big brother brought it to the staff's attention. A search proved fruitless. The boy was later found in a nearby forest by police. The parents later sued the Boys Club and a state appeals court ruled that the parents could sue the Boys Club on the basis of negligent supervision. The appeals court began its opinion by explaining the "duty of care" that is imposed on institutions that care for or work with children: "As a general rule, a person who undertakes the control and supervision of a child, even without compensation, has the duty to use reasonable care to protect the child from injury. Such person is not an insurer of the safety of the child. He is required only to use reasonable care commensurate with the reasonably foreseeable risk of harm." Applying this standard to the facts of this case, the court concluded that the question was "whether a prudent person caring for a five or six-year-old child under similar circumstances would have allowed the child to leave the building without an older person, and thus whether [the Boys Club] breached its duty of care." The Boys Club insisted that it could not be liable since no similar incidents had ever occurred on its premises. The court rejected this argument, noting that in the case of negligent supervision "what is reasonably foreseeable is not exclusively dependent upon what is known about a specific place." The proper question is "what may happen to any child at any place." Based on this standard the court concluded that the risk of abduction was foreseeable.

Example. *An Indiana court ruled that the first amendment does not prevent a woman from suing her church and a denominational agency on account of injuries she suffered as a result of being molested by her pastor when she was a minor.[91] The woman claimed that the pastor began molesting her when she was 7 years old, and that the molestation continued until she was 20. The woman sued her church and regional and national denominational agencies. The court concluded that the national church was not liable on the basis of negligent supervision or retention for the actions of the pastor. It observed, "The [national church], which is only affiliated with the local church and [regional agency] through its constitution and judicial procedures, was not informed. The evidence . . . does not indicate that [the woman] invoked the judicial procedures, which is the only mechanism by which the [national church] could have taken action against [the pastor]. According to the judicial procedures, the [regional agency] forms a committee to investigate alleged misconduct upon the submission of a complaint signed by two or more persons. Only after this investigation is completed and the [regional agency] determines that the evidence warrants a trial does the [national church] become involved. [The woman] has not alleged . . . that she or anyone else ever filed a complaint against [the pastor] with the [regional agency]. Therefore, the [national church] could not have disciplined [the pastor]. Accordingly, we conclude that because the evidence does not show that the [national church] was aware of [the pastor's] actions, summary judgment in favor of the [national church] is proper on [the woman's] claims for negligent hiring, supervision, and retention." The court concluded that there was evidence that the local church and regional agency were aware of the pastor's actions, and therefore they could be sued for negligent supervision and retention. The court sent the case back to the trial court for trial.*

Example. *A Minnesota court ruled that a church could be sued on the basis of negligent supervision as a result of a pastor's acts of child molestation.[92] The pastor served as both pastor and youth program teacher at the church. He lived in a third floor apartment at the church's youth center. The victim attended confirmation classes at the church, and the pastor was his instructor. The victim so admired*

---

[91] Konkle v. Henson, 672 N.E.2d 450 (Ind. App. 1996).
[92] Doe v. Redeemer Lutheran Church, 531 N.W.2d 897 (Minn. App. 1995).

the pastor that he wanted to become a pastor himself. The victim often went with the pastor to make calls or visit other churches. He also attended church camp during the summer and at times stayed overnight at the pastor's apartment. When the victim was 13 to 16 years old, he was molested by the pastor. Prior to his abuse, the victim was a good student and athlete. After the abuse, his grades dropped and he quit playing team sports. During his late teens, he was hospitalized as a result of an attempted suicide. He later suffered from alcohol abuse and social phobia including panic attacks. A jury returned a verdict in favor of the victim, and a state appeals court affirmed this judgment. The appeals court concluded that the church had been negligent in permitting the sexual abuse to occur. This conclusion was based in part on the following facts: (1) During the time the victim was being molested, a church trustee saw the pastor kissing another adolescent boy on the mouth. The pastor, upon seeing the trustee, blushed and ran back to his apartment. The trustee informed another trustee of this incident, along with two members of the church council. No action was taken. (2) During the time the victim was being molested, another church trustee was approached by a local teacher and asked if the pastor was a child molester. This same trustee's uncle told him that he heard something went on at a cabin at church camp and asked if the pastor was "straight." (3) During the time the victim was being molested, a church trustee's son had to make up some work for confirmation classes at the pastor's home. When he returned home, he told his father that the pastor wanted him "to get under the sheets" with him. (4) During the time the victim was being molested, a student in the confirmation class testified that during a confirmation class at the church she thought she saw the pastor engage in an act of child abuse. She told her parents and the church's "intern pastor" what she saw. The girl and her parents quit attending the church after this incident. (5) During the time the victim was being molested, another confirmation student told the church's intern pastor that the pastor had "put his arm around him all of the time" and showered with the boys.

Example. A New York court ruled that a school was liable on the basis of negligent supervision for the rape of a 12-year-old girl that occurred when she left a school outing without permission.[93] The victim and her class of 30 students were attending a school outing at a public park. She left the group to have lunch at a nearby pizza restaurant. Upon returning to the park, she discovered that her class had left. Instead of returning to school, she walked home. While walking home, she was abducted and raped by two adolescent males. The victim sued the school, claiming that her injuries were caused by its negligent supervision of the class outing. A jury found the school negligent, and awarded the victim $3 million in damages. The verdict was based in part on the testimony of an expert in school safety that the school had departed from "safe and common practices." In particular, he noted the following: (1) there should have been at least one more adult supervising the group of 30 elementary-age children (only two adults were present during the outing); (2) students were not "paired off" as buddies; (3) arrangements were not made to have the class meet together at least once each hour while at the park; (4) students were not told that they could not leave the park alone; and (5) students were not told that they would only be dismissed from the outing after they returned to school. The safety expert also testified that the teacher in charge of the outing should have taken several steps immediately upon discovering that a child was missing. These included (1) notifying the school immediately to seek guidance from his superiors; (2) notifying the park police; (3) asking another teacher to take the children back to school so he could continue the search for the missing child; (4) remaining in the park until shortly before dismissal time to give the victim more time to return; and (5) notifying school officials upon his return that the victim was still missing. The case was appealed, and the state's highest court affirmed the trial court's judgment in favor of the victim. The court concluded, "[W]e cannot say that the intervening act of rape was

---

[93] Bell v. Board of Education, 687 N.Y.S.2d 1325 (A.D. 1997).

unforeseeable as a matter of law. A rational jury hearing the trial testimony could have determined, as the jury did in this case, that the foreseeable result of the danger created by [the school's] alleged lack of supervision was injury such as occurred here. A [jury] could have reasonably concluded that the very purpose of the school supervision was to shield vulnerable schoolchildren from such acts of violence. As we have previously recognized, when the intervening, intentional act of another is itself the foreseeable harm that shapes the duty imposed, the defendant who fails to guard against such conduct will not be relieved of liability when that act occurs."

Example. *A New York appeals court ruled that a Catholic church and diocese could be sued as a result of the sexual molestation of an 11-year-old boy by a Catholic priest.[94] The victim and his sister were both enrolled in a parochial school operated by the church. An associate pastor at the church (who also served as director of religious education for the school) obtained permission from the victim's mother to take him to an athletic facility at a local college to play racquetball and basketball and go swimming. While in the shower room prior to entering the pool, the pastor allegedly removed all his clothing and made the victim do the same. He then kissed and fondled the victim against his will. The boy's mother later filed a lawsuit on behalf of her son naming the church and diocese as defendants. She alleged that her son had suffered substantial emotional, mental, and physical injuries, and that she had incurred substantial expenses in providing therapy for him. Specifically, she alleged that the church and diocese were liable for the misconduct of the pastor on the basis of their own negligence in hiring and placing the pastor in contact with boys with inadequate investigation of his background and with actual or "constructive" knowledge of his propensities, and in failing periodically to evaluate his activities. The court rejected the argument of the church and diocese that permitting the civil courts to find religious organizations liable on the basis of negligent hiring or supervision of clergy would constitute excessive governmental interference with church autonomy in violation of the first amendment guaranty of religious freedom. The court observed, "[If the mother is] successful in establishing that, with knowledge that the priest was likely to commit sexual abuse on youths with whom he was put in contact, his employers placed or continued him in a setting in which such abuse occurred, the fact that the placement occurred in the course of internal administration of the religious units does not preclude holding the institutions accountable to the victim of their neglect in administration. Indeed, a contrary holding—that a religious body must be held free from any responsibility for wholly predictable and foreseeable injurious consequences of personnel decisions, although such decisions incorporate no theological or dogmatic tenets—would go beyond first amendment protection and cloak such bodies with an exclusive immunity greater than that required for the preservation of the principles constitutionally safeguarded."*

Example. *A New York court found a school liable on the basis of negligence for the molestation of a kindergarten student in a school restroom.[95] The court's ruling is of direct relevance to churches and church-operated schools. The student was permitted to go to the bathroom alone, where he was molested by an older student. The child's parents sued the school, and a jury found that the child's kindergarten teacher had been negligent in allowing the child to go to the bathroom unaccompanied. The child was awarded $500,000 in damages. The school appealed, and a state appeals court upheld the finding of negligence. The court began its opinion by noting that "[w]hile we recognize the general rule that educational institutions are not the insurers of the safety of their students and cannot be held liable for every instance in which one pupil injures another, schools are, however, under a duty to adequately supervise their students and are liable for foreseeable injuries which are [directly] caused by the absence*

---

[94] Jones by Jones v. Trane, 591 N.Y.S.2d 927 (Sup. 1992).
[95] Garcia v. City of New York, 646 N.Y.S.2d 508 (A.D. 1996).

of such supervision." The court noted that this duty "derives from the fact that the school, once it takes over physical custody and control of the children, effectively takes the place of their parents and guardians." The court noted that in this case the child was sent from his classroom (while class was in session) to the school bathroom, alone and unsupervised, where the assault occurred. Further, "[t]his was done despite two separate school memoranda, circulated amongst the school's staff, which explicitly provided security procedures to the contrary." The first memoranda stated that "teachers are instructed to send all pupils under third grade to the bathroom with a partner." The second memorandum stated that "to further insure security any child leaving your room or corridor area must have a pass. Young children should go in pairs." A school principal testified that the reason for these rules is to make young children more secure from attack by older students. She also stated that she considered the bathroom to be a place where young children "are particularly vulnerable." The court concluded that the school "did not act with ordinary prudence in allowing the five-year old plaintiff to proceed to the bathroom alone." The school insisted that it could not have been negligent since it was not aware of any previous acts of molestation occurring in its bathroom. The court disagreed. It acknowledged that schools generally must have notice of prior similar misconduct to be liable for assaults upon older students, since school personnel "cannot reasonably be expected to guard against all of the sudden, spontaneous acts that take place among students daily." However, in the case of a young child who is sent by his teacher to a public bathroom unescorted, the potential danger to the child "can be reasonably foreseen and could have been prevented by adequate supervision of the school." As a result, "while it would be reasonable to allow high school students to go to a public bathroom unaccompanied, the same practice surely does not apply to a five-year old child, who is unable to resist, is defenseless against attack, and poses an easy target for sexual molestation or other assaults. Stated another way, even the most prudent parent will not guard his or her teen at every moment in the absence of some foreseeable danger of which he or she has notice; but a five-year-old child in a public bathroom should be supervised or, at the very least, be accompanied by another child."

Example. *A New York court ruled that a Catholic diocese could be sued on the basis of negligent supervision for a priest's acts of child molestation.[96] The offending priest was ordained in Venezuela and moved to the United States with a letter of reference from his archbishop. He later molested a minor (the "victim"). The victim later sued the diocese, claiming that it was legally responsible for the priest's conduct on the basis of negligent hiring, negligent supervision, and negligent retention. A trial court dismissed all of the victim's claims against the diocese, and the victim appealed. A state appeals court concluded that the diocese could be sued for negligent supervision and negligent retention. The victim alleged that the diocese became aware of the danger the priest posed to minors after hiring him as a result of comments both he and the priest made to other priests regarding inappropriate behavior. The court noted that if the victim or the priest made such statements to other priests, then the diocese might be legally responsible for the priest's actions on the basis of negligent retention and negligent supervision. The court insisted that imposing liability on the diocese under such circumstances "would not violate constitutional and statutory guarantees of free exercise of religion and separation of church and state." The court conceded that other courts have concluded that the first amendment may bar victims from suing churches or clergy on the basis of conduct "finding its basis in religious beliefs and practices." This was not the case here, however, since "there is no indication that requiring increased supervision of [the priest] or the termination of his employment by the [diocese] based upon [his] conduct would violate any religious doctrine or inhibit any religious practice."*

---

[96] Kenneth R. v. Roman Catholic Diocese, 654 N.Y.S.2d 791 (N.Y.A.D. 1997).

§ 10-09.2 — Court Decisions Rejecting Negligent Supervision Claims

Key point 10-09.2. *Some courts have found churches not liable on the basis of negligent supervision for a worker's acts of child molestation on the ground that the church exercised reasonable care in the supervision of the victim and of its own programs and activities.*

This section reviews court decisions in which a church or other religious organization was found not liable on the basis of negligent supervision for a worker's acts of child molestation.

Example. *A federal appeals court ruled that an archdiocese was not responsible for the alleged molestation of a minor by a priest.[97] An adult male sued a priest, a local Catholic church, and an archdiocese claiming that while he was a minor the priest performed illicit sexual acts upon him. The plaintiff alleged that the archdiocese and church were liable because they knew or should have known that illicit acts were being performed on their premises and at the priest's home. He charged that they failed to protect him or take appropriate measures to ascertain or correct the situation. Moreover, he alleged that they knew or should have known that they were fostering the priest's illicit activities and providing him with the means with which to conduct such activities. In rejecting the plaintiff's claim that the archdiocese was responsible for his injuries on the basis of negligent supervision, the court observed: "[E]mployers do not have a duty to supervise their employees when the employees are off-duty or not working. Employers also are not liable for failure to supervise when the employee engages in independent criminal conduct which results in the plaintiff's injuries. Moreover, an employer's duty to supervise does not include a duty to uncover his employees' concealed, clandestine, personal activities. . . . It is unfortunate, to say the least, that the frequency with which these cases have surfaced suggests that the clergy at [the local church] were naive. There is, however, nothing to indicate that the archdiocese or [church] knew or should have known of what was taking place in [the priest's] private world."*

Example. *The Alabama Supreme Court ruled that a church was not legally responsible for the sexual molestation of a 10-year-old girl.[98] A 10-year-old girl lived near a church that operated a kindergarten at which her aunt was the head teacher. The girl's mother instructed her to walk to the church following school, and then have her aunt escort her home when she quit work at 5:30 p.m. One day, while waiting on the church property for her aunt, the girl was raped by an adolescent male. The girl was raped a second time by the same adolescent several days later. The girl did not disclose the rapes to anyone until, during a routine medical examination, the family physician found evidence of sexual relations. The girl at first denied that she had ever engaged in sexual relations, but later acknowledged that the adolescent male (who was known to her) had raped her on two occasions. The girl's mother later filed a lawsuit against the church, claiming that it had failed to use "due care" in watching and supervising the girl "thereby allowing" the rape to occur. A trial court ruled in favor of the church, and the mother appealed. The state supreme court agreed that the church could not be legally responsible for the girl's injuries. The court acknowledged that there may have been an oral agreement between the mother and the aunt to care for the girl after school. However, the court insisted that "there was no evidence that [the victim] was, in fact, under the care of the church." The court continued, "[T]he mere fact that an injury has occurred is not evidence of negligence and . . . in negligent supervision cases negligence will not be found by inference. Assuming, without deciding, that there was an agreement that [the victim] was to be supervised and cared for by the church, [the victim] failed to produce any*

---

97 Tichenor v. Roman Catholic Church, 32 F.3d 953 (5th Cir. 1994).
98 N.J. v. Greater Emanuel Temple Holiness Church, 611 So.2d 1036 (Ala. 1992).

evidence demonstrating that the church negligently supervised her on the days she says she was assaulted and raped. Thus, a finding that [the girl] was negligently supervised on the days in question could be had only by inference [and] we may not draw that inference here." The court also emphasized that churches ordinarily cannot be found guilty of negligent supervision without some special relationship or special circumstances that were not present in this case: "[T]he general rule is that absent special relationships or circumstances, a person has no duty to protect another from criminal acts of a third person . . . . [A defendant cannot] be held liable for the criminal act of a third party unless the defendant knew or had reason to know that the criminal act was about to occur on the defendant's premises."

__Example.__ A California court ruled that a Catholic church was not responsible on the basis of negligent supervision for a priest's acts of child molestation, since "nearly all" of the acts of molestation occurred when the priest "took the victim from her home to various public places and hotels."[99]

__Example.__ A federal court in Connecticut dismissed a lawsuit brought against a church and diocese by two adults who had been sexually molested by a priest when they were minors.[100] The court ruled that the church and diocese were not responsible for the victims' injuries on the basis of respondeat superior or negligence. The court cautioned that churches and denominational agencies are potentially liable on the basis of negligence for injuries sustained by victims of sexual molestation if they have knowledge of prior sexual misconduct by the molester. However, since the victims could not prove that church officials either knew or should have known of any previous sexual misconduct by the offending priest, the negligence claims had to be dismissed. The court ruled that the first amendment guaranty of religious freedom does not necessarily protect a church or denominational agency from liability in a lawsuit based on negligent hiring, retention, or supervision if the victim's claims do not implicate issues of ecclesiastical concern.

__Example.__ A federal district court in Michigan ruled that a church school and various church agencies were not liable on the basis of negligent hiring, supervision, or retention, for the sexual molestation of a minor student by a priest.[101] The court found that there was no constitutional prohibition to the recognition of a negligent supervision claim against a church school or agency, since such claims "can be decided without determining questions of church law and policies." However, the court refused to find the school or church agencies liable on this basis since "only a few jurisdictions" recognize "negligent supervision" as a basis of liability, and no court in Wisconsin (where the molestation occurred) had ever recognized negligent supervision as a basis of liability. The court made the following additional observation: "The precise issue, as this court sees it . . . is not whether now—20 years after the occurrences upon which plaintiff's claims are predicated—the Wisconsin Supreme Court would adopt the tort of negligent supervision, but rather whether, had the claim been presented to the Wisconsin Court in 1974-78 [when the acts of molestation occurred] would the court have recognized it then? This is consistent with the generally accepted principle that a tort action is to be determined by application of the law which existed at the time of the occurrence of the events upon which the action is predicated. . . . This reflects this court's concern . . . that it would be unfair to juxtapose contemporary mores and contemporary causes of action upon parties for events which occurred in a different era with a different level of social awareness of problems."

__Example.__ The Minnesota Supreme Court ruled that a school was not liable on the basis of negligent supervision for the sexual seduction of a high school student by a female teacher.[102] The teacher used a

[99] Roman Catholic Bishop v. Superior Court, 50 Cal. Rptr.2d 399 (Cal. App. 1996).
[100] Nutt v. Norwich Roman Catholic Diocese, 921 F. Supp. 66 (D. Conn. 1995).
[101] Isely v. Capuchin Province, 880 F. Supp. 1138 (E.D. Mich. 1995).
[102] P.L. v. Aubert, 545 N.W.2d 666 (Minn. 1996).

counseling relationship with a male student as the basis for a sexual relationship that continued for several months. Most of the sexual encounters occurred during regular school hours on school premises. The victim later sued the school, claiming that it was responsible for his injuries on the basis of negligent supervision. In rejecting the victim's claim that the school was guilty of negligent supervision, the court observed: "[The school] performed standard teacher evaluations of [the teacher]. In addition to the evaluations [school officials] made several unannounced visits to [the teacher's] classrooms. Because the school had no public address system, all messages were hand-delivered by staff and students to classrooms throughout the course of the school day. Even with all of this interaction during the school day, the [secret] relationship between teacher and student was never observed. A school cannot be held liable for actions that are not foreseeable when reasonable measures of supervision are employed to insure adequate educational duties are being performed by the teachers, and there is adequate consideration being given for the safety and welfare of all students in the school. The safety and welfare of the students in a school setting is paramount. However, in this case, closer vigilance would not have uncovered the relationship because both participants worked hard to conceal it."

Example. A Minnesota appeals court ruled that a church and denominational organization were not legally responsible on the basis of negligent supervision for a pastor's acts of child molestation.[103] The molester was accused of sexually abusing numerous young boys during his tenure as senior pastor at a church. He admitted abusing some of the children, including a 10-year-old boy (the "victim"). The victim sued the pastor, his former church, and national and regional church bodies. The trial court concluded that the church had been negligent in supervising the pastor, but a state appeals court reversed this judgment. The court defined "negligent supervision" as "the failure of the employer to exercise ordinary care in supervising the employment relationship, so as to prevent the foreseeable misconduct of an employee from causing harm to other employees or third persons." The court added that negligent supervision "derives from the doctrine of respondeat superior" so the victim "must prove that the employee's actions occurred within the scope of employment in order to succeed on this claim." It is important to note that the court stressed the difficulty inherent in supervising clergy: "Even assuming that [the pastor's] abuse of [the victim] occurred within his scope of employment, there was insufficient evidence for the jury to conclude that [the church] failed to exercise ordinary care in supervising [him]. By the nature of the position, a clergyperson has considerable freedom in religious and administrative leadership in a church. The clergy also require privacy and confidentiality in order to protect the privacy of parishioners. There was no evidence that the supervision provided by [the church] differed from the supervision a reasonable church would provide. Nor was there any evidence of further reasonable supervision that could have prevented [the pastor] from abusing [the victim]. There was not enough evidence from which a reasonable jury could conclude that [the church] negligently supervised [the pastor]."

Example. The Missouri Supreme Court ruled that a diocese could not be liable for the sexual misconduct of a priest.[104] A Catholic priest served as associate pastor of a church. He invited a young boy and one of the boy's friends to spend the night and watch movies in the church parsonage. One of the boys later alleged that the priest sexually molested him. The parents sued the diocese, claiming that it was responsible for the priest's acts on the basis of several grounds, including negligent supervision. The parents asserted that after the priest was ordained the diocese had a duty to supervise his activities, which it failed to do. The parents claimed that the diocese "knew or reasonably should have known of prior sexual misconduct and a propensity to such conduct" by the priest. Once again, the court disagreed: "Adjudicating the reasonableness of a

---

[103] M.L. v. Magnuson, 531 N.W.2d 831 (Minn. App. 1995).
[104] Gibson v. Brewer, 952 S.W.2d 239 (Mo. 1997).

church's supervision of a cleric--what the church 'should know'--requires inquiry into religious doctrine .... [T]his would create an excessive entanglement, inhibit religion, and result in the endorsement of one model of supervision. Not recognizing the cause of negligent failure to supervise clergy is not an establishment of religion because it is a 'nondiscriminatory religious-practice exemption.'[105] It achieves 'a benevolent neutrality which will permit religious exercise to exist without sponsorship and without interference.'[106] Nonrecognition of this negligence tort preserves 'the autonomy and freedom of religious bodies while avoiding any semblance of established religion.'"

Example. *An Ohio court ruled that a church was not responsible for the rape of a 6-year-old boy occurring on church property during Sunday school.[107] The boy attended a Sunday school class of about 45 first and second graders. One adult female teacher was present on the day of the rape along with two teenage volunteers (one male and one female). During "story time," the victim became disruptive, and the teacher allowed the male volunteer to "take him back and color" in an unused room. The adult teacher did not check on the boy for the remainder of the Sunday school session. The boy's mother alleged that the male volunteer took her son to an unused room, raped him, and threatened to kill him if he "told anyone." The boy and his mother later sued the church, claiming that the boy's injuries were a result of the church's "negligent supervision" of its agents. The court noted that "negligence does not consist of failing to take extraordinary measures which hindsight demonstrates would have been helpful." The court further observed that a church is "not an insurer of the safety" of persons on its premises, but rather has only a "duty of ordinary care to avoid injury consistent with [existing] facts and circumstances." The court emphasized that the victim and his mother "have presented no evidence that [the church] knew, or in the exercise of reasonable diligence should have known of or anticipated a criminal sexual assault by [the alleged rapist] upon another." The victim and his mother placed great significance upon evidence that "a similar incident had occurred several years earlier." In rejecting the relevance of this evidence the court observed simply that "there is no evidence that the church or its agents knew, or in the exercise of diligence, should have known of such prior activity."*

Example. *An Ohio court ruled that a hospital was not liable on the basis of negligent supervision for a chaplain's acts of child molestation.[108] A Catholic priest was assigned by his religious order to serve both as a hospital chaplain and as a campus minister. On several occasions he sexually molested a minor male. The court emphasized that the acts of molestation occurred in the chaplain's home and were unrelated to any hospital or campus activity. It concluded, "[L]iability under a theory of negligent supervision is premised on the employment relationship. In the case at hand, the alleged attacks did not occur while [the chaplain] was working at the hospital or the college; the alleged assaults occurred in [his] private residence at night. The [victim] failed to come forward with any evidence that the hospital or college had any right or duty to supervise [the chaplain] outside the employment context. Although the employment relationship of a priest is not conducive to an 'office hours' definition, even if one accepts the broader definition of employment as a certain role or capacity, [the chaplain] was acting outside these as well at the time that the alleged assaults occurred. [The victim] was staying with [the chaplain] at the times of the alleged attacks because of the [victim's] family's friendship with their former parish priest. [The chaplain's] interaction with [the victim] was completely unrelated to [his] role as either hospital chaplain or campus minister. Thus, the [victim] failed to establish a duty on the part of the hospital or the college to supervise [the chaplain] at the time of the alleged assaults."*

---

[105] Employment Division v. Smith, 494 U.S. 872, 879 (1990).
[106] Walz v. Tax Commission, 393 U.S. 664 (1970).
[107] Bender v. First Church of the Nazarene 571 N.E.2d 475 (Ohio App. 1989).
[108] Gebhart v. College of Mount St. Joseph, 665 N.E.2d 223 (Ohio App. 1995).

Example. A Pennsylvania court ruled that a church and diocese could not be legally responsible for a priest's repeated acts of child molestation occurring off of church premises.[109] A Catholic priest repeatedly molested a number of boys. His pattern was to befriend young boys, lure them into a sense of trust, and then molest them. He often would take boys out to meals, do special favors for them, and take them shopping or on trips. One victim, who had been molested more than fifty times by the priest, sued the church and diocese on the basis of negligent supervision. The court ruled that the church and diocese could not be guilty of negligent supervision since all of the priest's acts of molestation occurred off of church premises. The court noted that the Restatement of Torts (an authoritative legal text) imposes liability for negligent supervision upon employers only for misconduct occurring on their premises. It pointed out that all of the priest's acts of molestation occurred in motel rooms while on trips, and not on church premises.

Example. A Tennessee court ruled that a church-operated preschool was not legally responsible for a sexual assault committed by a 4-year-old boy on another 4-year-old boy, since the assault was not foreseeable.[110] A 4-year-old boy (the "victim") was enrolled in a church-operated preschool program. One day he asked for permission to use the restroom which was located 40 feet down the hall. The teacher informed the victim that he would have to wait until another 4-year-old boy returned from the restroom. When the other boy returned to the classroom the teacher gave the victim permission to go to the restroom. While the victim was in the restroom, the boy who had just returned asked for permission to "get a drink." The teacher allowed him to do so, but cautioned him not to enter the restroom. The teacher stood in the doorway of the classroom so she could monitor the boy and the classroom at the same time. A few moments later the teacher had to leave the doorway to attend to a crying child. Upon returning to the doorway some 2 or 3 minutes later, she saw the victim and the other boy running together down the hallway toward the classroom. While the teacher was attending the crying child, the boy who had gone to get a drink entered the restroom and sexually assaulted the victim. Neither child was being supervised by an adult while absent from the classroom. The victim's parents sued the church, claiming that it was responsible for their son's injuries on the basis of negligent supervision. A trial court ruled in favor of the church, and the parents appealed. The school conceded that it had a duty to exercise reasonable care in the supervision of children under its control. However, it insisted that a sexual assault between two 4-year-old boys was so unforeseeable that there was no duty to guard against it. The school's director testified that the school had never received a complaint or report about sexual assaults or misconduct among its preschoolers, and that it had never received a complaint concerning the behavior of the boy who committed the molestation. A state appeals court ruled that the school was not guilty of negligent supervision because the sexual assault was not reasonably foreseeable. The court noted that there can be liability for negligence unless a victim's injuries were a reasonably foreseeable result of the negligent behavior. This test was simply not met. The court observed, "[T]he acts alleged in the complaint are unforeseeable as a matter of law. The alleged acts would be considered vile and reprehensible between two adults, but between two four-year-old boys, the alleged acts are even more shocking and appalling. We do not believe that a reasonable person would ever foresee this type of behavior between boys of that age. The possibility of an accident of this general character could not have been foreseen by [the church or school]. [The school] presented affidavits showing that a sexual assault had never occurred in the school, and that the school had no reason to suspect this behavior from [the assailant]. Moreover, we should consider the fact that the teacher could not reasonably foresee that a child that had

[109] Hutchinson v. Luddy, 683 A.2d 1254 (Pa. Super. 1996).
[110] Roe v. Catholic Diocese of Memphis, 950 S.W.2d 27 (Tenn. App. 1996).

just used the restroom facilities would return to the restroom instead of the classroom after getting a drink of water in the school hall."

Example. *A Texas court rejected a parent's claim that a church was responsible on the basis of negligent supervision for the molestation of her daughter by a youth pastor.[111] A mother enrolled her daughter in a private school operated by a local church. A few months later, the mother discovered three sexually explicit letters which she believed were correspondence between her daughter and the youth pastor (who also taught at the school). These letters, along with explicit entries in the daughter's diary, led the mother to believe that her daughter and the youth pastor were engaging in sexual activities. She took the evidence to the senior minister of the church, asking for his assistance. Unsatisfied with the investigation, the mother sued the church and a national denominational agency. She claimed that the national church was responsible for the youth pastor's acts on the basis of negligent supervision. In rejecting this claim, the court noted that negligence requires proof that someone's conduct actually caused injuries to another, and it concluded that the national church's act of ordaining or licensing clergy in no way was the cause of the girl's injuries. Further, in rejecting the plaintiff's claim that the national church used "less than ordinary care" in discharging its "continuing duty" to monitor and supervise its clergy, the court observed that the national church "exercises no supervisory powers over the local ministers" and "is not responsible for the day-to-day oversight of the ministers." Since the national church had no duty to supervise clergy, "it is impossible that lack of supervision . . . was a substantial factor in causing plaintiff's injuries."*

Example. *A Washington state court ruled that a church school was not legally responsible for damages resulting from an alleged sexual relationship between a teacher and student.[112] In rejecting the claim of the victim's parents that the school had been guilty of negligent supervision, the court agreed that "schools have a duty to supervise their students," and to take precautions to protect students from dangers that may reasonably be anticipated. However, "at some point the event is so distant in time and place that the responsibility for adequate supervision is with the parents rather than the school." Such was the case here, concluded the court, since the alleged misconduct occurred off school property during noninstructional hours.*

Example. *A federal district court in Wisconsin ruled that a church was not legally responsible for the molestation of a young boy by a teacher at the church's school.[113] A church hired a full-time teacher at its private school. While the teacher was employed by the school he removed a young boy (the victim) from class and disciplined him on at least ten occasions. On four of these occasions, the teacher engaged in sexual contact with the victim. At the time of these incidents, the school had a written policy that permitted corporal punishment of students to be inflicted only by a parent with a teacher present. The school also had an "unwritten policy" that allowed teachers to administer corporal punishment outside the presence of a student's parents if another adult were present and the parents were later notified. The victim alleged that the church was negligent in failing to properly supervise the teacher, and that this negligence contributed to his injuries. Specifically, the victim argued that the school should have limited the number of times the teacher could have disciplined students, since this would have minimized the risk of molestation. In other words, the victim insisted that a church school has a continuing duty to supervise teachers. The court disagreed that churches or schools have so pervasive a duty of supervision. It based this conclusion on the following considerations: (1) It noted that the right of teachers to disci-*

---

[111] Eckler v. The General Council of the Assemblies of God, 784 S.W.2d 935 (Tex. App. 1990).
[112] Scott v. Blanchet High School, 747 P.2d 1124 (Wash. App. 1987).
[113] *Kendrick v. East Delavan Baptist Church, 886 F. Supp. 1465 (E.D. Wis. 1995).*

pline students is "unquestionably reasonable and done in nearly every educational setting." (2) It "is not unusual for some students to be reprimanded . . . numerous times over the course of a school year." (3) The administrator received no complaints regarding the improper removal of the victim or any other student from class. Accordingly "from the perspective of [church] officials [the teacher] was administering discipline in the same manner as other instructors. While [he] could have been abusing his trust during the process, there is absolutely no indication that [the administrator] or other school officials were notified or should have been aware that child abuse or any violation of the [church's] corporal punishment policies was occurring." The court concluded that "in order to pursue a claim of negligent supervision in this case, the [victim] must show that [church] officials had notice of [the teacher's] improper conduct with [the victim] or other students. What from the outside appeared to be a normal and common exercise of authority in this case may very well have been something quite different; [church] officials, however, had no reason to suspect [the teacher] of wrongdoing at any time prior to the [accusations made by the parents of the other boy]." However, the court ruled that the church was "placed on notice" of the teacher's potential wrongdoing when the parents of the other student communicated their accusations to school officials. The school had a duty to supervise the teacher's actions from this time forward, and as a result any molestation occurring during this period of time could be attributable to the church's negligent supervision. The court concluded, however, that the victim failed to prove that any of the incidents of molestation occurred after the school was made aware of the teacher's alleged violation of policy.

§ 10-09.3 — Risk Management

Key point 10-09.3. *Churches can reduce the risk of liability based on negligent supervision for the sexual molestation of minors by adopting risk management policies and procedures.*

Tip. *A number of courts, in addressing the question of whether clergy are employees or self-employed for federal income tax reporting purposes, have observed that churches generally exercise relatively little supervision or control over clergy.[114] Such cases can be used by churches in defending against negligent supervision claims involving clergy misconduct.*

Churches can reduce the risk of liability, based on negligent supervision, for the sexual molestation of minors by adopting risk management policies and procedures. Here is a listing of policies and procedures that some churches have adopted:

1. Two-Adult Policy

Consider adopting a "two-adult" policy. Such a policy simply says that no minor is ever allowed to be alone with an adult during any church activity. This rule reduces the risk of child molestation, and also reduces the risk of false accusations of molestation.

Example. *A church has a policy requiring two adults to work in the nursery. However, the policy does not prohibit children from being in the custody of less than two adults. On a Sunday morning during worship services, one adult temporarily leaves the nursery for ten minutes to speak with another church member. A few days later the parents of one of the infants in the nursery suspect that their child has been molested. Suspicion is focused on the church nursery. Since the two nursery workers cannot prove that*

---

[114] *See, e.g.,* Weber v. Commissioner, 60 F.3d 1104 (4th Cir. 1995).

they both were present with the child throughout the entire worship service, they cannot "prove their innocence." The worker who was present in the nursery while the other worker was temporarily absent is suspected of wrongdoing, even though she is completely innocent.

Example. A church sponsors a campout for young boys. Some of the boys are accompanied by their fathers, but several are not. One tent is occupied by an adult volunteer worker and one boy. This arrangement violates the two-adult rule.

Example. A youth pastor takes home a group of five teenagers following an activity at church. After taking four of the teenagers to their homes, he is left in his car with a 15-year-old female. This arrangement violates the two-adult rule.

2. NO EARLY RELEASES OF MINORS

Only release minors from church activities to the parent or legal guardian who brought them, or to a third person that the parent or guardian has authorized in writing to receive custody of the child. Churches are legally responsible for the safety of a minor from the time they receive custody until the time they return custody of the minor to his or her parent or legal guardian. As a result, a church may be liable for injuries occurring to a child who is released prematurely.

3. CLAIM CHECK PROCEDURE

Consider adopting a "claim-check" policy for children in the church nursery. As a parent drops a child off at the church nursery, pin a plastic number on the child's clothes and give the parent an identical number. Inform parents that only those persons presenting the corresponding number will be given custody of children. This policy is designed to prevent the kidnapping of children by noncustodial parents, or by child molesters. Numbers should be assigned on a random basis for each service. Unfortunately, in many churches the nursery is staffed by minors who are inclined to transfer custody to anyone who asks for a child. Sets of plastic numbers can be obtained from a variety of manufacturers. Ask a local restaurant that has a "coat check" booth. The concept is the same.

4. GREATER SCRUTINY IF KNOWLEDGE OF PRIOR INCIDENTS

If an incident of child molestation occurs on church premises, or in the course of a church activity off of church premises, the church's duty of supervision increases. The church will be held to a higher standard of supervision because of such knowledge. It is important for church leaders to be aware of this, and to be diligent in implementing some or all of the risk management procedures mentioned in this section.

5. VIDEO TECHNOLOGY

The installation of video cameras in strategic locations can serve as a powerful deterrent to child molesters, and can reduce a church's risk of negligent supervision. Consider the following uses:

• *Nursery areas.* Video cameras are helpful in a church's nurseries, since infants and very young children are present who are incapable of explaining symptoms of molestation. In such cases, innocent nursery workers may be suspected who lack the ability to conclusively prove their innocence. Video cameras can be helpful in documenting how symptoms of molestation may have occurred, and in proving the innocence or guilt of nursery workers.

Example. Shortly after returning home from church on a Sunday morning, a father notices evidence that his infant daughter was molested. He becomes very angry and distraught, and immediately calls his pastor to report the incident. He even mentions a particular nursery worker as the likely offender. The pastor meets with the father at church later that afternoon. The church installed a video camera in the nursery a few years ago, and the pastor replays the tape that was made that morning. The tape reveals no acts of molestation. The father is satisfied that the molestation did not occur at church. He takes his daughter to a doctor the next day, and learns that the child was not molested. The "symptoms" of molestation in fact were caused by a skin disorder. The case is resolved to everyone's satisfaction, because of the video evidence. But consider what might have happened if the church did not have a video camera in the nursery. The father may have been convinced that his daughter was a victim of molestation, and an innocent nursery worker may have been wrongfully accused.

• *Restrooms.* Church restrooms present a unique risk of molestation for both infants and older children. After all, they are frequented by children, they are easily accessible, and they often are in remote locations or are not adequately supervised. A video camera in a hallway outside a restroom that is frequented by minors can be a powerful deterrent to child molesters. It also will provide church leaders and local authorities with evidence in the event that a minor is molested in a church restroom.

6. AN ADEQUATE NUMBER OF QUALIFIED ADULTS

Any activity involving minors should be staffed with an adequate number of qualified adults. This will help to demonstrate that the church exercised reasonable care in the supervision of minors, and reduce the risk of liability based on negligent supervision in the event that a minor is molested.

Tip. It is often helpful to contact other institutions for assistance with staffing ratios. For example, some churches base their adult to child ratio in the nursery to what the state requires of licensed day care facilities. You may also contact the Red Cross, Salvation Army, or similar organizations. The point is this: if you can demonstrate that you based your adult to child ratio on the established practices of other similar organizations in your community, then this will be a strong defense in the event you are accused of liability (for an injury to a child) on the basis of negligent supervision.

7. OFF-SITE ACTIVITIES

Be especially careful of off-site activities such as field trips and camping. These outings can be difficult to control. It is essential that an adequate number of adults are present. While on the trip, precautionary measures must be implemented to assure adequate supervision of the group. For example, some churches group children in pairs, always keep the entire group together, and have frequent "roll calls." Once again, you can call other community-based organizations for guidance.

8. RESTROOMS

As noted above, church restrooms present a unique risk of molestation. They are frequented by children, they are easily accessible, and they often are in remote locations that are not adequately supervised. Church leaders can take steps to reduce this risk. Consider the following:

• *Video technology.* Using video cameras outside of church restrooms is a powerful deterrent to molesters, and provides the church with helpful evidence in the event of an allegation of molestation. This precaution is described above.

• *Designated restrooms.* Restrict young children's restroom breaks to restrooms that have limited access to adults, if this is possible.

• *2-adult rule.* Have two adults accompany children in groups to the restroom, whenever possible. Do not allow one adult to take one or more children to the restroom.

• *"Half doors."* Consider installation of "half doors" that will permit adults to have partial vision into restrooms used by young children.

• *Architecture.* Unauthorized access to nursery areas by outsiders should be discouraged or prevented by the physical layout. Many churches accomplish this with counters staffed by an adult worker or attendant.

• *State regulations.* State regulations that apply to licensed child care facilities ordinarily do not apply to church nurseries, but they will contain a wealth of information that may be useful in adopting policies to reduce the risk of molestation and other injuries. Further, compliance with selected regulations can be cited as evidence that your church should not be legally responsible on the basis of negligent supervision for such incidents.

• *Parental notification.* Churches should discourage parents from allowing their children to wander around unaccompanied on church property. This notification can take place in parents' meetings, in church bulletins or newsletters, or through direct appeals prior to or during worship services. Children who wander unaccompanied on church property often were sitting with a parent during a worship service and were permitted to leave (usually to go to the restroom). In other words, unaccompanied children wandering around on church premises often do so with their parents' permission. Parents should be encouraged to accompany their children to the restroom or any other destination, and not let them leave the service unattended.

• *Restricting access.* The risk of liability can be reduced by restricting access to unsupervised restrooms where molestation may occur. If possible, lock doors to cut off access to remote and unused areas of the church.

• *Ushers.* A church can exercise supervision over its restrooms by having ushers observe access to them during services. For example, if a young child leaves a service to use a restroom, ushers should be alert to others entering the restroom while the minor is present. If an older child or adult enters the same restroom while the unaccompanied minor is present, this is a potential risk that must be addressed. If the minor does not exit the restroom within a brief period of time, an usher may wish to enter the restroom until the minor leaves. Some churches have restrooms that can only accommodate one person, and that can be locked from the inside. Such facilities can reduce the risk of molestation so long as an usher ensures that a minor enters a vacant restroom alone, the door is locked behind him or her, and no one is permitted access to the room until the minor exits. By following such precautions, it soon will be apparent that the church is monitoring access to restrooms, and this will reduce the risk of molestation.

In addition, ushers should be instructed to be alert for minors leaving services or wandering around unaccompanied on church property. Ushers should be informed of the risks associated with such behavior, and should be prepared to confront the minor and direct him or her back to a parent or supervised children's activity.

9. Encouraging Parents to Accompany Their Children

Churches can reduce the risk of liability based on negligent supervision by encouraging parents of younger children to accompany their child to youth programs and activities.

10. Prevent Access to Remote Areas

Acts of child molestation on church premises often occur in remote, unsupervised rooms or areas. A church can reduce its risk of liability based on incidents of molestation occurring in such locations by restricting access to them. If possible, lock vacant rooms that are not being used, or exercise supervision over them. For example, the church could designate a board member or other responsible adult to roam throughout the church during worship services. Such a policy will deter potential molesters, and will help to demonstrate that the church is exercising reasonable care in the supervision of its premises.

11. Windows

Install windows in all doors to classrooms and other areas that are frequented by minors. This will reduce isolation and make it easier to supervise activities.

12. Supervision of Known Molesters

What should church leaders do when they learn that a known child molester is attending their church? This is a complex question. The presence of such a person on church premises creates a substantial risk to the church. If the person molests a child on church premises, or during an off-site church activity, the church will be faced with a very difficult case to defend. The church will need to demonstrate that it exercised a high degree of care and vigilance in the supervision of the individual. Here are some options to consider:

• *Exclusion.* The risk of liability based on negligent supervision can be eliminated by completely excluding known child molesters from church property and activities. Some churches have adopted this policy for persons with a record of multiple acts of molestation, or even one severe act. This is not to say that the person is cut off entirely. Ministers or concerned laypersons can meet with such a person off of church premises on a regular basis, to provide spiritual support.

• *Chaperones.* The risk of liability based on negligent supervision can be eliminated if the church designates a "chaperone" to accompany the molester at all times when present on church premises. To illustrate, the molester can be informed that he is welcome to attend one service each week, provided that he complies with the following restrictions: he will meet a designated church representative (a "chaperone") in the church parking lot, prior to the weekly service; he will be escorted into the church by the chaperone; he will be escorted by the chaperone at all times while in the church, including trips to the restroom; he will be escorted by the chaperone back to his car following the service. The chaperone can be any responsible adult, and it need not be the same person every week. The responsibility can be "rotated" among a number of volunteers.

• *Conditional attendance agreement.* Church leaders may allow a molester to attend church and participate in church activities, subject to specified conditions. These conditions can be set forth in a "conditional attendance" agreement that is signed by the molester. To illustrate, the agreement may specify that the molester is allowed to attend services and other activities so long as he (1) does not work in any official capacity with minors; (2) does not transport minors to or from church or any church activity; (3) does not attend any youth activity; (4) does not sit with a minor during a worship service; (5) is never alone with a minor on church premises; and (6) does not have any contact off of church premises with any minor who attends the church. The nature of these conditions will depend on a number of factors, including the nature and frequency of the previous abuse. Church leaders should be alert to any violations of the agreement. Ignoring a single violation will greatly increase the church's exposure to liability based on negligent supervision.

Key point. *A conditional attendance agreement reduces risk, but does not eliminate it.*

• *If the molester is a minor.* About one in five child molesters is another child—often an adolescent. For example, church leaders learn that a 14-year-old boy molested a 7-year-old girl. What steps can church leaders take to manage the church's risk under these circumstances for future acts by the same boy? Church leaders have a legal duty to protect other children from abuse. Accordingly, they not only should ensure adequate supervision of the abusive child, but they also may want to consider a "conditional attendance agreement." Such an agreement, signed by the parents of the abusive child, permits the abusive child to attend church activities but only on the basis of a number of conditions. The nature of these conditions will depend on a number of factors, including the age of the abusive child and the severity of the abusive behavior. In severe cases, a church may want to prohibit the abusive child from having any access to church property or activities unless accompanied by a parent. On the other hand, far less restrictive conditions would be appropriate if the abusive child is young and the abuse was minor and not repeated.

13. FOLLOW POLICIES

It is absolutely essential to familiarize youth workers with the church's policies and to be sure that these policies are followed. At a minimum, this should be part of an orientation process for all new workers (both paid and volunteer). Periodic training sessions are also desirable to reinforce nursery policies.

14. REVIEW OF POLICIES

It is a good practice to have your risk management procedures reviewed periodically by a local attorney and by your church insurance agent. Such a review will help to ensure that your policies are current and effective.

§ 10-10 Negligent Supervision of Church Workers — Sexual Misconduct Cases Involving Adult Victims

Many of the cases in which churches have been sued for negligent supervision involve incidents of sexual contact with adults. The most common example includes sexual contact between a male pastor and a female counselee in the course of a counseling relationship. While the counselee may allege that the church was negligent in selecting or retaining the pastor, she also may assert that the church was negligent in supervising the pastor.

§ 10-10.1 — Court Decisions Recognizing Negligent Supervision Claims

Key point 10-10.1. Some courts have found churches liable on the basis of negligent supervision for a minister's acts of sexual misconduct involving adult church members on the ground that the church failed to exercise reasonable care in the supervision of the minister.

This section reviews court decisions in which a church or other religious organization was found liable on the basis of negligent supervision for a minister's acts of sexual misconduct.

Example. The Colorado Supreme Court found an Episcopal diocese and bishop legally responsible for a pastor's sexual misconduct with a female parishioner on the basis of a number of grounds, including negligent supervision.[115] The court observed, "An employer may therefore be subject to liability for negligent supervision if he knows or should have known that an employee's conduct would subject third parties to an unreasonable risk of harm. . . . Both the diocese and [the bishop] had previous exposure to the problem of sexual relationships developing between priests and parishioners because the problem had arisen seven times before. The psychological reports gave notice that further supervision may be required. The reports indicate problems of sexual identification ambiguity, depression and low self-esteem. [The pastor's] file also indicated he had problems with authority. [He] had an inability to respond to superior authority. A reasonable person would have inquired further into [his] known difficulty in dealing with superior authority, and would have assumed a greater degree of care in monitoring his conduct. In light of its knowledge, it was reasonable for the jury to determine the [bishop and diocese] should have been alert to the possibility of problems with [the pastor] and taken adequate steps to insure [he] was not in a position where he could abuse the trust he enjoys as a priest conducting counseling."

Example. An Illinois court ruled that a church could be sued by a woman who was sexually seduced by her pastor during marriage counseling.[116] The woman and her husband claimed that during the course of marital counseling the pastor initiated and continued a sexual relationship with the woman, thereby aggravating the problems in her marriage, alienating them from their church and church community, and causing them emotional and psychological damage. The couple sued the church for negligence. Specifically, they claimed that the church was negligent in failing to supervise the pastor despite the fact that it knew or should have known that his previous attractions to female congregation members created an unreasonable risk that his religious and marital counseling would be ineffective and potentially detrimental to those being counseled. The couple insisted that the church had a duty to all members of the congregation to use reasonable care in supervising its pastor with respect to providing religious and counseling services. The couple claimed that the pastor's actions had damaged them in a number of ways, including the wife's contraction of two venereal diseases, medical bills incurred in treating these venereal diseases, psychological damages, counseling expenses, and irreparable deterioration in their marriage. A trial court dismissed the lawsuit on the ground that it was barred by the first amendment guaranty of religious freedom. The couple appealed. A state appeals court reversed the trial court's dismissal of the case and ordered the case to proceed to trial. The court acknowledged that "Illinois courts have generally refused to decide cases that require a judicial interpretation of religious doctrine or church law." However, "where doctrinal controversy is not involved in a church dispute, mandatory deference to religious authority is not required by the first amendment, and the court may choose from a variety of approaches in resolving the dispute." It noted that the courts can resolve disputes over control

---

[115] Moses v. Diocese of Colorado, 863 P.2d 310 (Colo. 1993).
[116] Bivin v. Wright, 656 N.E.2d 1121 (Ill. App. 1995).

of church property so long as they can do so on the basis of "neutral principles of law" requiring no examination of religious doctrine. The court applied the same "neutral principles of law" approach in this case involving alleged church liability for the sexual misconduct of its pastor. It observed, "Although the neutral principles of law approach is usually applied to disputes over church property, we cannot conclude from plaintiffs' complaint that the instant cause cannot be decided using neutral principles of negligence law, developed for use in all negligence disputes, without interpretation of religious doctrine or church law, just as would be a secular dispute in a negligence case. . . . We cannot conclude from plaintiffs' complaint that their cause of action against [the church] will infringe upon, or place a burden upon, the church's freedom to exercise its religion. Inquiring into whether the church was negligent in its failure to protect plaintiffs from the sexual misconduct of its minister may not call into question the church's religious beliefs or practices or subject them to analysis or scrutiny. As we have pointed out, the minister's sexual misconduct was not rooted in the church's religious beliefs and was outside the boundaries of the church's ecclesiastical beliefs and practices. Thus, resolving this dispute may not require any interpretation of church doctrine or any regulation of ecclesiastical activity."

Example. A North Carolina court ruled that the first amendment did not prevent it from resolving a sexual harassment lawsuit brought by three female church employees against their church and denominational agencies.[117] Three female church employees (the "plaintiffs") sued their church and various denominational agencies as a result of the sexual misconduct of a pastor. The lawsuit alleged that the pastor "committed inappropriate, unwelcome, offensive and nonconsensual acts of a sexual nature against the plaintiffs, variously hugging, kissing and touching them, and made inappropriate, unwelcome, offensive and nonconsensual statements of a sexually suggestive nature to them." The plaintiffs further alleged that the pastor's actions amounted to sexual harassment. The lawsuit further alleged that the local church and denominational agencies "knew or should have known" of the pastor's propensity for sexual harassment, but failed to take any actions to warn or protect the plaintiffs from his wrongful activity. A state appeals court noted that the key issue was whether the first amendment prevents "the filing of a negligent retention and supervision claim against a religious organization, when that claim is based on the conduct of a cleric of that organization." The court noted that the local church and denominational agencies asserted that the civil courts were without jurisdiction to resolve plaintiffs' claims against them because the courts' resolution of these claims requires inquiry into religious doctrine. The court disagreed. It noted that the first amendment "does not grant religious organizations absolute immunity from liability. For example, claims against religious organizations have long been recognized for premises liability, breach of a fiduciary duty, and negligent use of motor vehicles." The court concluded that if a resolution of the plaintiffs' legal claims did not require the interpretation of church doctrine, then "the first amendment is not implicated and neutral principles of law are properly applied to adjudicate the claim."

Example. An Oregon court ruled that a woman who was sexually seduced by her minister in the course of a counseling relationship could sue her church on the basis of negligent supervision.[118] The woman alleged that the church "knew or should have known that [the minister] was not adequately trained as a counselor and that it knew or should have known that he had misused his position in the past to take advantage or parishioners and counseled persons . . . [and] failed to investigate claims of his sexual misconduct [or] warn parishioners of his misuse of his position . . . ." The court stressed that it was not finding the church responsible. Rather, it simply was rejecting the trial court's conclusion that the lawsuit failed to state facts for which the law provides a remedy.

---

[117] Smith v. Privette, 495 S.E.2d 395 (N.C. App. 1998).
[118] Erickson v. Christenson, 781 P.2d 383 (Or. App. 1989).

Example. A federal court in Rhode Island ruled that the first amendment did not prevent it from resolving a lawsuit brought by victims of clergy sexual misconduct against church officials.[119] Three adult males sued diocesan officials for injuries they allegedly sustained as minors when they were molested by two priests. The victims claimed that prior to the acts of molestation, the diocese knew that the priests were pedophiles and not only failed to take appropriate preventative action, but also actively concealed the priests' sexual misconduct. The diocese claimed that the first amendment prevented the civil courts from resolving these claims. The court conceded that an internal church dispute cannot be resolved by a civil court if resolution of the dispute would require the court to interpret religious doctrine or ecclesiastical law. But the court rejected the proposition that a secular court lacks jurisdiction over a case simply because it "calls into question the conduct of someone who is a church official." The court rejected the diocese's argument that the first amendment prevents the civil courts from imposing liability on religious organizations for failing to properly screen or supervise clergy: "[T]here is no indication that the reasonably prudent person standard established by tort law and the requirements of Roman Catholic doctrine are incompatible. The [diocese does] not claim that the Roman Catholic Church either condones or tolerates sexual abuse of children. On the contrary, they have made it clear that the Catholic Church considers such conduct to be opprobrious. . . . Briefly stated, there is no indication that, by taking the kind of preventative action required by tort law, the [diocese] would have violated any 'doctrine, practice or law' of the Roman Catholic Church. In the absence of such a conflict, subjecting the [diocese] to potential tort liability does not violate [its] right to the free exercise of religion."

Example. A Washington state court ruled that a Catholic Archdiocese was liable for the negligent supervision of a supervisor who sexually harassed a female employee.[120] A female housekeeper at a conference center owned by the archdiocese claimed that a maintenance director began sexually harassing her shortly after he began his job. The harassment consisted of numerous sexually explicit and offensive statements. The maintenance director eventually was fired. The female employee later sued the archdiocese, claiming that it was legally responsible for his acts on the basis of negligent supervision. A jury ruled in favor of the female employee, and this ruling was affirmed by a state appeals court.

§ 10-10.2 — Court Decisions Rejecting Negligent Supervision Claims

Key point 10-10.2. Many courts have ruled that the first amendment prevents churches from being legally responsible on the basis of negligent supervision for the sexual misconduct of ministers.

This section reviews court decisions in which a church or other religious organization was found not liable on the basis of negligent supervision for a minister's sexual contact with an adult. Many courts have concluded that the first amendment's "nonestablishment of religion" and "free exercise of religion" clauses prevent the civil courts from resolving negligent supervision claims involving clergy misconduct. To illustrate, the United States Supreme Court observed in a landmark case more than a century ago: "It would therefore also be inappropriate and unconstitutional for this court to determine after the fact that the ecclesiastical authorities negligently supervised or retained the defendant Bishop. Any award of damages would have a chilling effect leading indirectly to state control over the future conduct of affairs of a religious denomination, a result violative of the text and history of the establishment clause."[121]

---

[119] Smith v. O'Connell, 986 F. Supp. 73 (D.R.I. 1997).
[120] Wheeler v. Catholic Archdiocese of Seattle, 829 P.2d 196 (Wash. App. 1992).
[121] Watson v. Jones, 80 U.S. 679 (1871).

Some courts have noted the inherent difficulty of supervising ministers in the performance of their duties, and in particular their counseling activities. As one court observed:

> By the nature of the position, a clergyperson has considerable freedom in religious and administrative leadership in a church. The clergy also require privacy and confidentiality in order to protect the privacy of parishioners. There was no evidence that the supervision provided by [the church] differed from the supervision a reasonable church would provide. Nor was there any evidence of further reasonable supervision that could have prevented [the pastor] from abusing [the victim]. There was not enough evidence from which a reasonable jury could conclude that [the church] negligently supervised [the pastor].[122]

Tip. A number of courts, in addressing the question of whether clergy are employees or self-employed for federal income tax reporting purposes, have observed that churches generally exercise relatively little supervision or control over clergy.[123] Such cases can be used by churches in defending against negligent supervision claims involving clergy misconduct.

Example. A federal appeals court ruled that a religious order was not responsible for the alleged seduction of a female parishioner by a Catholic priest.[124] The woman sued the religious order claiming that it was responsible for her injuries on the basis of several grounds, including negligent supervision. The court concluded that the order was not responsible for the priest's misconduct on the basis of negligent supervision, since it had no duty to supervise him. While it was true that the order had received a complaint about the priest's behavior with another woman some 8 years before, the priest performed his duties under the direction and control of the archbishop and was accountable to the archbishop. Accordingly, the order had no duty to supervise the priest's actions.

Example. The Colorado Supreme Court ruled that a diocese was not responsible for a priest's sexual contacts with a woman during counseling.[125] The woman sued the diocese on the basis of a number of grounds, including negligent supervision. Specifically, she alleged that the diocese had knowledge of previous indiscretions by the same priest, which had the effect of imposing upon the diocese a duty to supervise him. The court observed that a religious organization may be liable for negligent supervision if it has reason to know that a minister is likely to harm others. Liability results "because the employer antecedently had reason to believe that an undue risk of harm would exist because of the employment." The court concluded that "a person who knows or should have known that an employee's conduct would subject third parties to an unreasonable risk of harm may be directly liable to third parties for harm proximately caused by his conduct."

Example. A Florida court ruled that it was barred by the first amendment from resolving a woman's lawsuit claiming that she had been the victim of a priest's sexual misconduct.[126] A woman sought out a priest for marital counseling, and alleged that the priest engaged in sexual contact with her. The woman sued her church and diocese, claiming that they were aware of prior incidents involving sexual misconduct during counseling by the same priest. Despite this knowledge, nothing was done to address the problem. She claimed that the church and diocese engaged in negligent hiring, supervision, and reten-

---

[122] M.L. v. Magnuson, 531 N.W.2d 831 (Minn. App. 1995).
[123] See, e.g., *Weber v. Commissioner, 60 F.3d 1104 (4th Cir. 1995).*
[124] Doe v. Cunningham, 30 F.3d 879 (7th Cir. 1994).
[125] Destefano v. Grabian, 763 P.2d 275 (Colo. 1988).
[126] Doe v. Evans, 718 So.2d 286 (Fla. App. 1998).

tion of the priest. The church and diocese asked the court to dismiss the lawsuit against them on the ground that a resolution of the woman's claims would result in an "excessive entanglement" of the court with religious beliefs in violation of the first amendment. The court agreed with the church and diocese, and dismissed the lawsuit against them. It noted that the first amendment prohibits any governmental practice (including judicial resolution of internal church disputes) that would lead to an "excessive entanglement" between church and state. It continued, "Our examination of case law presenting both sides of this question leads us to conclude the reasoning of those courts holding the first amendment bars a claim for negligent hiring, retention, and supervision is the more compelling. In a church defendant's determination to hire or retain a minister, or in its capacity as supervisor of that minister, a church defendant's conduct is guided by religious doctrine and/or practice. Thus, a court's determination regarding whether the church defendant's conduct was 'reasonable' would necessarily entangle the court in issues of the church's religious law, practices, and policies. 'Hiring' in a traditional sense does not occur in some religions, where a person is ordained into a particular position in the church, and assigned to one parish or another. A court faced with the task of determining a claim of negligent hiring, retention, and supervision would measure the church defendants' conduct against that of a reasonable employer; a proscribed comparison."

Example. *A Louisiana court ruled that an Episcopal diocese was not legally responsible for the suicide of a woman allegedly caused by a sexual relationship with an Episcopal priest.[127] The woman's husband claimed that the diocese was responsible for his wife's suicide on the basis of several grounds, including negligent supervision. In rejecting this basis of liability, the court observed, "[A]ny inquiry into the policies and practices of the church defendants in hiring or supervising their clergy raises . . . first amendment problems of entanglement . . . which might involve the court in making sensitive judgments about the propriety of the church defendants' supervision in light of their religious beliefs. . . . The traditional denominations each have their own intricate principles of governance, as to which the state has no rights of visitation. Church governance is founded in scripture, modified by reformers over almost two millennia. As the Supreme Court stated long [ago]: 'It is not to be supposed that the judgment of the civil courts can be as competent in the ecclesiastical law and religious faith of all these bodies as the ablest men in each are in reference to their own. It would therefore be an appeal from the more learned tribunal in the law which should decide the case, to one which is less so.'"[128]*

Example. *The Maine Supreme Court ruled that the first amendment prevented a couple from suing their church as a result of a priest's sexual relationship with the wife.[129] The couple insisted that their claim for negligent supervision against the church could be resolved on the basis of neutral principles of law without violating the first amendment. They claimed that a review of the church's knowledge of any risk presented by the priest and the reasonableness of its supervisory acts would involve "nothing beyond the application of secular legal standards to secular conduct." The court observed that it had never recognized "negligent supervision" as a basis for liability, and that even if it did, the first amendment barred its application to the church in this case. The court observed, "The tort of negligent supervision is based upon the concept that principals have certain duties to supervise those under their control. When a civil court undertakes to compare the relationship between a religious institution and its clergy with the agency relationship of the business world, secular duties are necessarily introduced into the ecclesiastical relationship and the risk of constitutional violation is evident. The exploration of the ecclesiastical relationship is itself problematic. To determine the existence of an agency relationship*

---

[127] Roppolo v. Moore, 644 So.2d 206 (La. App. 1994).
[128] Watson v. Jones, 80 U.S. 679 (1871).
[129] Swanson v. Roman Catholic Bishop, 692 A.2d 441 (Maine 1997).

based on actual authority, the trial court will most likely have to examine church doctrine governing the church's authority over [the offending priest]." The court acknowledged that a few courts in other states have allowed churches to be sued on the basis of the negligent supervision of clergy. It also noted that other courts have recognized negligent supervision claims against churches "when the plaintiff alleges that the defending church knew that the individual clergyman was potentially dangerous." The court rejected all of these cases. It observed, "[T]hese few courts have failed to maintain the appropriate degree of neutrality required by the United States and Maine Constitutions. . . . We conclude that, on the facts of this case, imposing a secular duty of supervision on the church and enforcing that duty through civil liability would restrict its freedom to interact with its clergy in the manner deemed proper by ecclesiastical authorities and would not serve a societal interest sufficient to overcome the religious freedoms inhibited."

Example. *The Nebraska Supreme Court ruled that a Catholic Archdiocese was not legally responsible for damages suffered by a woman who engaged in sexual relations with a priest.[130] The woman began counseling with her priest concerning family matters. At the time she claimed to be "vulnerable" because of prior emotional problems. While she was in this vulnerable state and during the course of pastoral counseling, she alleged that the priest engaged in sexual contacts with her over the course of nine years. The woman later sued the priest and archdiocese on the basis of a number of grounds. Among other things, the woman claimed that the archdiocese had been negligent in failing to supervise the priest in his relations with female parishioners when it knew, or should have known, that he had sexual affairs in the past. The court concluded that the woman had no legal claim against the priest, and as a result the claims against the archdiocese had to be dismissed. It observed simply that "[i]f there is no tort liability to the [woman] against [the priest] individually, it follows that the archdiocese cannot be held liable for his conduct."*

Example. *A federal court in New York refused to find a pastor guilty of malpractice on the basis of his sexual seduction of a church member he had counseled for several years.[131] The woman sued the church and a denominational agency on the basis of several grounds, including negligent supervision. In rejecting this basis of liability, the court observed, "[A]ny inquiry into the policies and practices of the church defendants in hiring or supervising their clergy raises . . . first amendment problems of entanglement . . . which might involve the court in making sensitive judgments about the propriety of the church defendants' supervision in light of their religious beliefs. Insofar as concerns retention or supervision, the pastor of a Presbyterian church is not analogous to a common law employee. He may not demit his charge nor be removed by the session, without the consent of the presbytery, functioning essentially as an ecclesiastical court. The traditional denominations each have their own intricate principles of governance, as to which the state has no rights of visitation. Church governance is founded in scripture, modified by reformers over almost two millennia. As the Supreme Court stated [long ago]: 'It is not to be supposed that the judges of the civil courts can be as competent in the ecclesiastical law and religious faith of all these bodies as the ablest men in each are in reference to their own. It would therefore be an appeal from the more learned tribunal in the law which should decide the case, to the one which is less so.'[132] It would therefore also be inappropriate and unconstitutional for this court to determine after the fact that the ecclesiastical authorities negligently supervised or retained the [pastor]. Any award of damages would have a chilling effect leading indirectly to state control over the future conduct of affairs of a religious denomination, a result violative of the text and history of the [first amendment]."*

---

[130] Schieffer v. Catholic Archdiocese, 508 N.W.2d 907 (Neb. 1993).

[131] Schmidt v. Bishop, 779 F. Supp. 321 (S.D.N.Y. 1991).

[132] Watson v. Jones, 80 U.S. 679 (1872).

Example. The Ohio Supreme Court ruled that a church was not liable on the basis of negligent supervision for a pastor's sexual contact with a woman during counseling.[133] The church had been sued by the former husband of the woman, who claimed that the pastor's conduct resulted in the breakdown of their marriage. The supreme court concluded that the first amendment guaranty of religious freedom did not prevent churches from being sued on the basis of a minister's sexual misconduct since "we find it difficult to conceive of pastoral fornication with a parishioner or communicant as a legitimate religious belief or practice in any faith." The court concluded, however, that the minister could not be liable for any injury suffered by the former husband, since any liability based on "alienation of affections" had been abolished by the legislature several years before. The court concluded that the church could not be liable if the pastor was not: "[A]n underlying requirement in actions for negligent supervision and negligent training is that the employee is individually . . . guilty of a claimed wrong against the employer. Because no action can be maintained against [the minister] in the instant case, it is obvious that any imputed actions against the church are also untenable." The court emphasized that it found the alleged conduct on the part of the minister to be "reprehensible," but concluded that there was no basis for relief available to the husband.

Example. The Oklahoma Supreme Court ruled that a married couple could not sue their church and former pastor for damages they allegedly incurred as a result of an adulterous affair between the former pastor and the wife.[134] The couple claimed that the church was liable for the pastor's acts on the basis of several grounds, including negligent supervision. The court concluded that the church was not responsible for injuries resulting from the minister's conduct, since none of the couple's claims against the pastor were viable. It observed, "Neither the claims by the husband nor the wife against the minister are cognizable in Oklahoma. . . . Because their claims against the minister also serve as the basis for the claims against the church for its negligent hiring and supervision of the minister, that claim is also not cognizable."

Example. The Wisconsin Supreme Court ruled that a Catholic Diocese could not be sued as a result of an alleged sexual relationship that began when a woman initiated a counseling relationship with a priest who served as a hospital chaplain and counselor.[135] The chaplain met with and counseled with a woman (the "victim") with respect to medical and emotional problems she was experiencing after the death of her baby. After her release from the hospital, the victim continued to meet with the chaplain. They dined together, visited art museums, attended pro-life rallies, exchanged gifts, and discussed politics, personal problems, and life in general. The victim viewed the priest as her pastoral counselor during these meetings because he gave her advice to help her cope with stress and depression. On one occasion the priest invited the victim to his family's cabin, where they engaged sexual intercourse. Sexual relations continued for another year, until the victim informed a bishop of the affair. The victim later sued the chaplain and diocese. She claimed that the diocese was legally responsible for the chaplain's misconduct on the basis of negligent supervision. The victim conceded that the diocese was not aware of her affair with the chaplain until she disclosed it to the bishop. The court concluded that the first amendment prohibited it from resolving the victim's negligent supervision claim: "The reconciliation and counseling of the errant clergy person involves more than a civil employer's reprimand of three day suspension without pay for misconduct. Mercy and forgiveness of sin may be concepts familiar to bankers, but they have no place in the discipline of bank tellers. For clergy, they are interwoven

---

[133] Stock v. Pressnell, 527 N.E.2d 1235 (Ohio 1988).
[134] Bladen v. First Presbyterian Church, 857 P.2d 789 (Okla. 1993).
[135] L.L.N. v. Clauder, 563 N.W.2d 434 (Wis. 1997).

in the institution's norms and practices. Therefore, due to the strong belief in redemption, a bishop may determine that a wayward priest can be sufficiently reprimanded through counseling and prayer. If a court was asked to review such conduct to determine whether the bishop should have taken some other action, the court would directly entangle itself in the religious doctrines of faith, responsibility, and obedience. Likewise . . . negligent supervision claims would require a court to formulate a 'reasonable cleric' standard, which would vary depending on the cleric involved, i.e., reasonable Presbyterian pastor standard, reasonable Catholic archbishop standard, and so on. Such individualized standards would be required because . . . church doctrines and practices are intertwined with the supervision and discipline of clergy. . . . This further explains why this court has held that negligent supervision claims are prohibited by the first amendment under most if not all circumstances."

§ 10-10.3 — Risk Management

Key point 10-10.3. *Churches can reduce the risk of liability based on negligent supervision for sexual misconduct involving adult victims by adopting risk management policies and procedures.*

This section has addressed church liability on the basis of negligent selection for sexual misconduct by ministers and other church workers with adult victims. Churches can reduce the risk of liability, based on negligent supervision, by adopting some of the strategies described in section 10-09.3.

Key point. *Many cases of sexual misconduct with adult victims arise out of a counseling relationship. There are a number of steps that churches can take to reduce the risk of such behavior occurring in the course of a counseling relationship, and many of these are addressed later in this chapter.[136]*

Tip. *A number of courts, in addressing the question of whether clergy are employees or self-employed for federal income tax reporting purposes, have observed that churches generally exercise relatively little supervision or control over clergy.[137] Such cases can be used by churches in defending against negligent supervision claims involving clergy misconduct.*

§ 10-11 Negligent Supervision of Church Workers — Other Cases

Key point 10-11. *A church may be legally responsible on the basis of negligent supervision for injuries resulting from a failure to exercise adequate supervision of its programs and activities.*

Other circumstances in which courts have found churches guilty of negligent supervision include a youth activity in which a 9-year-old boy was killed when a utility pole crushed him;[138] a church picnic during which a 15-year-old boy was rendered a quadriplegic when he fell out of a tree;[139] a church picnic at which a child drowned;[140] allowing a dangerous condition to continue in a crowded church service, which resulted in injury to a member;[141] permitting a snowmobile party on farmland without making an adequate

---

[136] *See* § 10-12, *infra.*

[137] *See, e.g.,* Weber v. Commissioner, 60 F.3d 1104 (4th Cir. 1995).

[138] Glorioso v. YMCA of Jackson, 540 So.2d 638 (Miss. 1989).

[139] Logan v. Old Enterprise Farms, Ltd., 544 N.E.2d 998 (Ill. App. 1989).

[140] Herring v. R.L. Mathis Certified Dairy Co., 162 S.E.2d 863 (Ga. 1968), *aff'd in part and rev'd in part,* Bourn v. Herring, 166 S.E.2d 89 (Ga. 1969). *See also* L.M. Jeffords v. Atlanta Presbytery, Inc., 231 S.E.2d 355 (Ga. 1976); Brown v. Church of Holy Name of Jesus, 252 A.2d 176 (R.I. 1969).

[141] Bass v. Aetna Insurance Co., 370 So.2d 511 (La. 1979).

inspection for dangerous conditions;[142] and failing to adequately supervise the activities of a church-sponsored scout troop.[143]

Example. An Arizona court ruled that a church was not responsible for injuries suffered by a 4-year-old child at the church's child care facility.[144] A 4-year-old child broke his leg while in a child care center operated by a church. The injury occurred when the child fell while running, although no employee of the child care center actually saw the boy fall. The boy's parents later sued the church, claiming that their son's injuries were a direct result of the church's negligence in failing to adequately supervise children. Specifically, they alleged that the church has a legal duty to watch and supervise children within its care, and that this duty was breached "as no one saw [the boy] as he fell." A trial court dismissed the lawsuit, and a state appeals court affirmed this decision. The appeals court relied on the following statement by the state supreme court in a previous case: "To hold that [a teacher] had to anticipate [a student's] act and somehow circumvent it is to say that it is the responsibility of a school teacher to anticipate the myriad of unexpected acts which occur daily in and about schools and school premises, the penalty for failure of which would be financial responsibility in negligence. We do not think that either the teacher or the district should be subject to such harassment nor is there an invocable legal doctrine or principle which can lead to such an absurd result."[145] The court noted, "While supervisors of a day nursery are charged with the highest degree of care toward the children placed in their custody, they are nevertheless not the absolute insurers of their safety and cannot be expected or required to prevent children from falling or striking each other during the course of normal childhood play." The court insisted that "a short absence from supervision of a child is not the proximate cause of the child's injury if the supervisor's presence and attention would not have prevented the injury." The court concluded, "[The boy] slipped out of view of the caregiver for a few seconds at most. No evidence has been presented that he would not have been injured had he been in the caregiver's sight." Accordingly, the parents "have failed to present any evidence to support an inference that the caregiver's supervision, whether negligent or not, proximately caused [the boy's] broken leg."

Example. A Louisiana court ruled that a church was liable for injuries sustained by a youth group member who was struck by a vehicle while crossing a busy street.[146] A church's youth minister took a group of 37 teenagers and 4 adult chaperones to an out-of-town youth evangelism conference. Most attendees were high school age. After checking into their motel, the group went to a McDonald's restaurant, which was located on a heavily traveled four-lane road. By then it was getting dark, although the area was well lighted. The arrival of the youth group immediately crowded the McDonald's, filling all serving lines. Some of the boys noticed a small pizza parlor in a strip mall across the street with apparently no waiting. Several of the boys in the group decided they would prefer to eat pizza without the wait. Three of the boys asked the youth minister if they could leave, cross the street, and get pizza. The minister said "yes," and walked them to the street to make sure they crossed safely. He did not lead the boys to a nearby traffic light because he considered that more dangerous. Meanwhile, three younger boys decided they wanted pizza. They assumed it was okay for them to cross the street since they saw the other three older boys doing so. The younger boys exited the McDonald's and ran across the street, passing the first group in the middle of the street in an effort to be first in line for pizza. One of the boys was "buzzed" by a speeding minivan when he was in the middle of the street. One of the members of the

---

[142] Sullivan v. Birmingham Fire Insurance Co., 185 So.2d 336 (La. 1966), *cert. denied*, 186 So.2d 632 (La. 1966).

[143] Kearney v. Roman Catholic Church, 295 N.Y.S.2d 186 (N.Y. 1968).

[144] Ward v. Mount Calvary Lutheran Church, 873 P.2d 688 (Ariz. App. 1994).

[145] Morris v. Ortiz, 437 P.2d 652 (1968).

[146] Bell v. USAA Casualty Insurance Company, 707 So.2d 102 (La. App. 1998).

youth group was a 12-year-old boy with cerebral palsy (the "victim"). When he saw the other boys going to get pizza, he decided he was too hungry to wait at McDonald's. He did not ask the youth minister or any of the chaperones for permission to leave; he just left the restaurant and started across the street, without stopping or looking. In the middle of the street, he saw headlights. He lifted his arm defensively and was knocked to the ground, sustaining serious injuries. The victim and his parents sued their church. They asserted that the accident had been caused by the negligent supervision of the event by the youth minister and church. Specifically, they claimed that the youth minister and the chaperones did not prevent the 12-year-old victim from leaving the group; they did not notice him going out the door, crossing the parking lot and proceeding across the street; and they did not escort the boys to the street to assure safe crossing or lead them to the traffic light where the crossing would be safer. They also claimed that the youth minister and the adult chaperones made no plans for the boys to return safely to McDonald's after they finished their pizza. In essence, they "abandoned" the boys across the street. The court ruled that the church was guilty of negligent supervision. It observed, "Temporary custodians of children, such as school personnel and day care workers, are charged with the highest degree of care towards the children left in their custody, but are not insurers of the children's safety; supervisors must follow a standard of care commensurate with the age of the children under the attendant circumstances. The duty does not require individual supervision of each child at all times and places. However, fairly close supervision is required when students take a walking trip across a major thoroughfare." The court noted simply that "it is negligent for the adult leader to abandon the children."

Example. A New York court ruled that a volunteer who was injured while trimming a tree on church property could sue the church.[147] In response to requests by the pastor (both from the pulpit and in the church bulletin) for volunteers to trim trees on the church property, some 75 men gathered on a Saturday morning. At one point, one of the men was on a ladder cutting off a 30-foot limb with a chain saw. When the limb was cut through, it whipped around and struck the ladder, knocking the man to the ground and injuring him seriously. He sued several of the other volunteers and the church, claiming that they had been negligent in failing to stabilize the limb adequately, in failing to warn him of the need for safety equipment, and in failing to provide him with adequate safety equipment and supervision. The court ruled that the injured volunteer could sue the church for his injuries. It concluded, "As a landowner, [the church] owed a duty of reasonable care under the circumstances to prevent foreseeable injury to [the victim]   . . . . No safety devices were provided, nor was professional supervision provided. An accident of the kind herein could be found to be foreseeable under such circumstances." Under these facts, the court concluded that the victim had presented enough evidence as to the church's alleged negligence to submit the case to a jury.

Example. A North Carolina court refused to dismiss a church from a lawsuit brought by a 13-year-old girl who was locked in a walk-in freezer in the church kitchen.[148] An equipment company sold a walk-in freezer to a church. The freezer was "field assembled" by the seller on the church's premises, and it was tested to be sure that it operated properly. The inside of the freezer door contained a label stating, "You are not locked in! The manufacturer of this unit has equipped it with a . . . latch assembly. You cannot be locked in, even if the door closes behind you and the cylinder is locked. By pushing the inside release on the inside of this unit, you many operate the latch and open the door." One evening, some eight months later, a 13-year-old girl (the "victim") was working as a volunteer at the registration desk in the church's "family life center" (a gymnasium). While on duty, the victim went to the church's kitchen to get

---

[147] Lichtenthal v. St. Mary's Church, 561 N.Y.S.2d 134 (N.Y. Sup. 1990).
[148] Crews v. W. A. Brown & Son, Inc., 416 S.E.2d 924 (N.C. App. 1992).

some ice for a soft drink. She was wearing shorts and a t-shirt, but no shoes. Once inside the kitchen, the victim heard a noise that she thought came from the freezer. She opened the freezer door and stepped inside. When she did, the freezer door closed behind her. She immediately pushed the red release button on the inside of the door, but the door would not open. She repeatedly attempted to open the door, but her efforts were unsuccessful. She began banging on the door with her hands and feet, pushing on the door with her shoulder, and screaming. After an hour of futile attempts to open the door or attract someone's attention, she became tired and sat down. She had lost all feeling in her feet which were completely white. Despite being tired, she continued to kick the door feebly. Later that evening, someone discovered the victim in the freezer. By that time, she had suffered severe frostbite to her feet and legs. Paramedics took her to a local hospital where she remained for nearly two months and where she had five operations. During the first operation, all ten of her toes were amputated. During later operations, she received several skin grafts. The victim and her mother filed a lawsuit against the manufacturer, seller, and church. Among other things, the lawsuit alleged that the church had been negligent in the supervision of the freezer. The court rejected the church's motion to be dismissed from the case.

Example. *A Pennsylvania court ruled that a seminary was responsible for the drowning death of a 12-year-old boy.[149] The victim was swimming with a group of altar boys from a Catholic church at a seminary-owned pool. The victim's mother sued the seminary, alleging that it had been negligent in allowing the boys to use the pool without a qualified lifeguard on duty. At the time of the drowning, the pool was under the supervision of a priest. The jury concluded that both the seminary and church were negligent, and it awarded more than $1 million in damages. A state appeals court affirmed this judgment. The court observed that "it is clear that [the evidence] was sufficient to support the jury's finding that the seminary had breached a duty owed to the minor decedent. The seminary, as owner of the pool, had a duty to exercise those precautions which a reasonably prudent owner would have taken to prevent injury to those persons whom it knew or should have known were using the pool. . . . A jury could have found, in view of the evidence, that the seminary knew or should have known that its pool was being used by children and that it failed to exercise reasonable care to prevent injury to them." The court further observed that "it was for the jury to determine whether the seminary had been negligent in failing to take reasonable precautions to prevent access to its pool when a competent lifeguard was not present and whether the seminary could reasonably rely upon [the priest] to supervise the activities of the boys while they were using the pool."*

§ 10-11.1 — Risk Management

Key point 10-11.1. *Churches can reduce the risk of liability based on negligent supervision for injuries not involving sexual misconduct by adopting risk management policies and procedures.*

Churches can reduce the risk of liability based on negligent supervision for injuries not involving sexual misconduct by adopting risk management policies and procedures. Several risk management strategies addressed in section 10-09.3 are relevant in this context as well, and should be reviewed carefully. Here are some additional risk management strategies:

1. Adequate Number of Qualified Adults

Use an adequate number of adults to supervise all church activities, especially those involving minors. Also, be sure that the adult supervisors are adequately trained to respond to emergencies.

---

[149] Rivera v. Philadelphia Theological Seminary, 580 A.2d 1341 (Pa. Super. 1990).

2. Checking the Policies of Other Charities

Check with the Red Cross, YMCA, Boy Scouts, and similar organizations to obtain guidelines on the number of adults to use, the training of adult workers (based on the type of activity involved), and other safety procedures. Reliance on such standards makes it much less likely that a church will be guilty of negligent supervision. Be sure that you document your research.

3. Swimming and Other Water Sports—Off of Church Premises

If your church sends minors on a trip that will involve swimming (or the possibility of swimming), there are a number of steps that you can take that will reduce the risk of drowning, and the church's risk of liability. They include the following:

• Encourage parents to accompany their children. The court in this case concluded that the charity's duty of care was greater because the victim's mother was not present.

• Have both parents sign a permission form that authorizes their child to participate in the event, and that discloses whether or not the child can swim. In some cases, it is not feasible or possible to have both parents sign (due to divorce, separation, or death). But church leaders should recognize that the best protection comes for having both parents sign.

• If the parental permission form indicates that the child cannot swim, then church leaders must recognize that they are assuming a greater risk by allowing the child to participate. This risk can be avoided by not allowing the child to participate. As one court noted in a case involving the drowning of a 12-year-old girl who could not swim, "the accident could have been prevented by not allowing her into the pool."[150] If parents consent to their child's participation despite his or her inability to swim, then under no circumstances should the child be allowed to attend the event without appropriate restrictions. The nature of these restrictions will depend on a number of factors, including the age of the child, the degree of supervision provided by adults, the availability of trained lifeguards, and the relative risk of the location. For example, lakes generally pose more danger than pools, because (1) the water is not clear, making it more difficult to monitor the activities of children or to quickly locate a missing child; (2) concealed hazards may exist below the surface; (3) emergency medical services often are more distant; and (4) the area is more likely to be unsupervised, with no lifeguards present. Selecting appropriate restrictions is often a very difficult task for the persons in charge of an event. One recommendation that may help is to ask other local charities (Red Cross, YMCA, Boy Scouts, Girl Scouts) what their policy would be under the same circumstances. Be sure to make a record of the person you spoke with, and the suggestion that this person made.

• Go to locations that have certified lifeguards on duty.

• Check with your church insurance agent for additional recommendations.

• Check with your denominational offices for additional recommendations.

---

[150]Turner v. Parish of Jefferson, 721 So.2d 64 (La. App. 1998).

4. Swimming and Other Water Sports—On Church Premises

Some churches have a swimming pool on their property, as do many denominational agencies and parachurch ministries. A pool creates a number of risks, including drowning, slips and falls, and spinal cord injuries as a result of diving accidents. These risks can be reduced in several ways. Churches have used some or all of the following procedures to reduce these risks:

• Most communities have enacted zoning regulations that govern the construction and maintenance of swimming pools. These regulations often address fencing, locks, signs, and depth markings. Be sure the pool complies with all zoning requirements since a failure to do so can result in automatic legal liability for a death or injury.

• Most communities have laws governing the operation of a pool as a place of public accommodation. Check with city health or safety officials, or with a city council member, for details. Again, be sure the pool is in full compliance, since a violation can lead to automatic liability. These requirements often address the number and training of life guards, maximum pool capacity, and hygienic measures. If there are no such laws in your community that apply to your pool, then consider adopting the rules that apply to other kinds of public swimming pools, if any. This will provide a defense to a charge of negligent supervision. If your community has no laws governing public swimming pools, then contact other local charities with pools (such as the YMCA) and consider following their rules.

• Place a water alarm in the pool when it is not in use. Such an alarm is triggered by splashing, and it can alert adults to the unauthorized presence of a child in the pool.

• Place a video camera in the pool area so that the pool can be monitored for unauthorized access when not in use.

• Use certified lifeguards. Local laws may specify the minimum number, based on the number of persons present. If not, check with the YMCA for recommendations.

• Do not install a diving board. Many swimming pool accidents are associated with the use of diving boards.

• Be sure the water is clean and of excellent visibility at all times.

• Install a safety rope separating the shallow from the deep end of the pool.

• Check with your church insurance agent for additional recommendations.

5. Avoid Hazardous Activities

Avoid high-risk activities. Some activities, such as rope-repelling, explosives, and the use of firearms, are so hazardous that a church may be deemed "strictly liable" if an accident occurs, no matter how much care was exercised in supervising the event.

§ 10-12   Counseling — In General

Key point 10-12. *Churches face a number of legal risks when they offer counseling services by ministers or laypersons. These include negligent selection, retention, or supervision of a counselor who engages in sexual misconduct or negligent counseling. A church also may be vicariously liable for a counselor's failure to report child abuse, breach of confidentiality, and breach of a fiduciary relationship.*

Most churches offer some form of counseling services. The most common example would be counseling of church members by a minister. Many churches also offer lay counseling services. Some limit these services to members of the congregation, while others target the general public and promote their counseling ministry in the local media and telephone directory. Some churches use counselors or psychologists who are licensed by the state, while others use unlicensed laypersons with little if any professional training. Counseling ministries can provide an excellent and needed service, and represent a "point of contact" with the community. However, there are a number of important legal concerns that should be considered by any church that offers such services, or that is considering doing so in the future. The more important concerns are summarized in this section.

1. Pastoral Counselors

The legal risks associated with pastoral counseling include malpractice and sexual misconduct. Both risks have been addressed in other sections of this text.[151] Section 10-12.1 reviews several risk management strategies that are designed to reduce the risk of church liability for the acts of pastoral and lay counselors.

2. Lay Counselors

There are several legal concerns for church leaders to consider before offering lay counseling services. The more important concerns are addressed below.

(1) negligent counseling

"Negligent counseling" is a legal risk associated with lay counseling programs. It can arise in a number of ways. Some persons may claim that their emotional problems were aggravated rather than helped by lay counseling. Others may claim that lay counselors have a legal duty to refer suicidal persons to medical professionals having the authority to involuntarily commit such persons, and that they are responsible for the suicide of a counselee who is not referred.

In 1988, the California Supreme Court ruled that "nontherapist clergy" do not have a duty to refer suicidal persons to medical professionals.[152] However, the court emphasized that its ruling applied only to clergy who are not therapists. This ruling has been followed by courts in many other states. The key point is this: there is no assurance that lay counselors working on behalf of a church share the virtual immunity from liability enjoyed by nontherapist clergy counselors. This is so whether or not the lay counselors are licensed counselors or psychologists under state law.

---

[151] See §§ 4-05, 4-11, 10-05, and 10-10.
[152] Nally v. Grace Community Church, 253 Cal. Rptr. 97 (1988).

(2) child abuse reporting

Counselors may receive confessions of child abuse or information giving them a reasonable suspicion that abuse has occurred. It is imperative for church leaders to obtain a copy of their state child abuse reporting statute and ensure that all counselors are aware of their reporting obligations, if any, under state law. Keep in mind that these statutes are amended frequently, so updated copies should be obtained at least annually.

Whether or not the child abuse reporting statute requires a church counselor to report known or reasonably suspected instances of abuse, the counselor (and perhaps the church) would risk potential civil liability for failing to report abuse. For example, a minor who is being abused by a step-parent learns that a church counselor was aware of the abuse but did not report it. The minor may sue the counselor (and the church) arguing that the failure to report the abuse aggravated the injury. The "statute of limitations" on such claims does not even begin to run until the minor reaches the age of majority, meaning that contingent liability for such claims can persist for many years. Further, many states have enacted laws suspending the statute of limitations until an adult survivor of child abuse "discovers" that he or she was injured by the abuse. This can extend the statute of limitations for a significant amount of time.

At least nine states have permitted adults who were abused as children to sue clergy or other adults who were aware of the abuse but chose not to report it. This number will likely grow in the years ahead.

It is essential that any church counselor be apprised of his or her legal obligations under state law with respect to this important issue.

(3) seduction of counselees

There have been a number of lawsuits over the past few years brought by women who were seduced or sexually assaulted by male clergy and mental health professionals. Often the misconduct occurred or started in the course of counseling sessions. As much as we would like to deny it, private counseling sessions involving dependent or emotionally vulnerable persons can present unique and sometimes formidable temptations. If inappropriate sexual contacts are initiated, there can be substantial damage to the victim and the victim's family. But this is not all. The costs of such behavior often devastate the counselor as well, and lead to criminal charges, loss of professional credentials, future unemployability, and unavailability of any insurance coverage for either a legal defense or payment of damages. Clearly, steps must be taken to reduce or eliminate this risk.

But there is another risk associated with counseling—the risk of false accusations of inappropriate behavior. Unfortunately, in some cases false accusations are brought against counselors by persons seeking a legal settlement or pursuing some other ulterior motive. It is imperative for counselors to recognize that a false accusation can be as devastating as a true one.

Because of the unique temptations that counseling can present, and the possibility of false accusations, "defensive measures" should be taken by pastors and others who engage in counseling. There are two highly effective ways to deal with these risks. Some of these are addressed in section 10-12.1.

(4) confidentiality

Another very important consideration in church counseling is the concept of confidentiality. Counselors (and the church) can be sued if they intentionally or inadvertently disclose confidential information to third parties. Obviously, this can occur in several ways—for example, the counselor directly communicates the information, or the counselor's counseling notes are accessible to church staff. Counselors need to be strictly admonished to maintain the confidences shared with them. The one exception relates to child abuse reporting. A legal duty to report known or reasonably suspected cases of child abuse generally overrides the duty to maintain confidences (at least for persons who are required to report under state law).

(5) negligent hiring

The church should carefully screen any candidate for a lay counseling position to ensure, as much as possible, the suitability of the person for a counseling ministry. The screening process should include contacts with former churches with which the member has been affiliated or in which the counselor has worked in a counseling capacity, an appropriate screening form, and communication with a number of references. Of course, all of these contacts must be noted in writing and placed in a confidential file. In some cases, a criminal records check should be considered—for example, if an individual being considered for a counseling position has "no background," or there are unsubstantiated allegations involving prior misconduct. The important consideration is this: the church can be sued for injuries inflicted by a lay counselee if the church either knew or should have known of a dangerous propensity of the counselor.

Churches have been sued by victims of clergy sexual misconduct on the ground that they failed to do an adequate job of screening the minister at the time he or she was hired. Churches wanting to lower this risk will develop screening procedures for clergy applicants.

(6) negligent supervision

The church should consider adopting mechanisms to ensure that unlicensed lay counselors are supervised by appropriately trained and licensed mental health professionals.

The church should also develop a counseling policy setting forth standards on such issues as suicidal counselees, counselees threatening harm to others, counselees who confess to criminal activities, and counselees who are child abusers. Unlicensed lay counselors should understand clearly their responsibilities with regard to these kinds of crises. In most cases they should be advised to refer crisis cases immediately to a designated licensed mental health professional. Of course, this does not mean that the church counselor must sever all ties with the individual. Quite to the contrary, the spiritual counseling offered by the church counselor may continue simultaneously with the counseling provided by the licensed professional.

It is also important for the counseling policy to prohibit lay counselors from engaging in controversial therapies such as "repressed memories" and diagnosis and treatment of multiple personality disorders.

(7) fees

Some churches charge a prescribed fee for counseling services. Are such fees deductible as charitable contributions to the church? The answer is no. The Supreme Court has ruled that prescribed payments for prescribed services are never deductible as charitable contributions.[153] If the counseling is provided free of charge as a ministry of the church, voluntary payments made by counselees to the church probably could be deducted as charitable contributions. However, if the church establishes or even "recommends" a prescribed fee, the IRS

---

[153] Hernandez v. Commissioner, 109 S. Ct. 2136 (1989).

would not recognize such payments as tax deductible. To be deductible, the payments must in fact be voluntary, the counseling services must be available to all without a fixed or suggested charge, and those unable to pay must receive the same consideration as those who are able to pay for the counseling services.

Key point. These are some of the legal considerations that should be addressed before any counseling program is initiated. If conducted on a professional basis, with due regard to the legal environment in which we live, counseling ministries can serve a significant nurturing function.

§ 10-12.1 — Risk Management

Key point 10-12.1. Churches can reduce the risk of liability associated with pastoral or lay counseling by adopting risk management policies and procedures.

Churches can implement a number of risk management strategies to reduce the risk of liability associated with pastoral or lay counseling. These include the following:

1. REDUCING THE RISK OF SEXUAL MISCONDUCT AND FALSE ACCUSATIONS

Churches have adopted a number of precautions to reduce the risk of sexual misconduct by pastoral and lay counselors. These precautions also reduce the risk associated with false accusations. Consider the following:

(1) the "third person" rule

One effective way to deal with these risks is to adopt a policy prohibiting any male minister or counselor on staff from counseling privately with an unaccompanied female (i.e., opposite sex counseling) unless a third person is present. The third person may be the minister's or counselor's spouse, another minister on staff, or a mature and trusted church employee (preferably female).

Key point. Does the presence of a third person negate the "clergy-penitent" privilege for clergy counselors, meaning that either the pastor or counselee can be compelled to answer questions in a court of law regarding the communications? Not necessarily. In some states, the privilege applies so long as no one other than persons "in furtherance of the communication" are present. It is possible that a court would conclude that a third person who is present during a pastoral counseling session as a matter of church policy is present "in furtherance of the communication." As a result, the privilege may be preserved. Further, some courts have ruled that the clergy-penitent privilege is not negated by the presence of a guard during pastoral counseling with prison inmates if the guard's presence is required by law or prison policy. A court may reach the same conclusion in the context of a church policy mandating the presence of a third person during "opposite sex" pastoral counseling sessions.

Key point. Even if the privilege is negated by the presence of a third person, this risk must be weighed against the reduced risk that will occur.

Key point. Some churches that have a ministry to the deaf use a deaf member to serve as the third person. Such a person is ideal, for he or she can observe the entire session but does not apprehend what is said.

Key point. There have been no reported cases involving a claim of sexual seduction of a male counselee by a female counselor. As a result, churches using female counselors are reducing their risks significantly. Of course, there remains the possibility of a male counselee making unfounded accusations against a female counselor, and as a result churches using female counselees may want to consider adopting the same precautions that apply to male counselors.

(2) women counsel women

Since the vast majority of cases of inappropriate sexual behavior involve male counselors and female counselees, churches can significantly reduce their risk by using women to counsel women.

(3) other measures

Churches have implemented a number of other measures to reduce the risk of sexual misconduct, or false claims of sexual misconduct, during pastoral or lay counseling sessions. These include one or more of the following:

• *Windows.* Installing a window in the pastor's office making all counseling sessions clearly visible to office staff. Of course, such a precaution is effective only if other staff are present and visible throughout the counseling session. This means that the church should implement a policy limiting counseling sessions to office hours when other staff are present and visible.

• *Open doors.* Some counselors conduct counseling sessions in a room with an open door, so that office staff can clearly see the counselor or counselee. Of course, such a precaution is effective only if other staff are present and visible throughout the counseling session. This means that the church should implement a policy limiting counseling sessions to office hours when other staff are present and visible.

• *Telephone counseling.* Many smaller churches have no "staff" that is present and visible in the church office during counseling sessions. Some of these churches limit opposite sex counseling sessions to those involving a third person or those that are conducted by telephone.

• *Video cameras.* Some churches have installed a video camera (without audio) in the office where counseling occurs. The video can be transmitted to a monitor in another location in the church where it is observed by a church employee. Or, the camera can simply record the entire session. If sessions are recorded, tapes should be retained indefinitely, or until they are reviewed by two designated church members who prepare a written summary stating whether or not they observed any inappropriate acts. This review can be performed in "fast forward" mode, and should not take long.

• *Boundaries.* Many courts have recognized the psychological principle of "transference." To illustrate, one court defined transference as "a phenomenon that occurs that is similar to a state of dependency in which the client begins to project the roles and relationships and the images and experiences that they have had with other people previously in their life, especially other significant people such as mother, father, brothers, sisters, early teachers and adult models, upon the therapist."[154] Another court defined transference as "a process whereby a patient undergoing psychotherapy for a mental or emotional disturbance (particularly a female patient being treated by a male psychotherapist) develops such overwhelming feelings of warmth, trust, and

---

[154] Doe v. Samaritan Counseling Center, 791 P.2d 344 (Alaska 1990).

dependency towards the therapist that she is deprived of the will to resist any sexual overtures he might make."[155] Similarly, another court observed, "Transference is the term used by psychiatrists and psychologists to denote a patient's emotional reaction to a therapist and is generally applied to the projection of feelings, thoughts and wishes onto the analyst, who has come to represent some person from the patient's past . . . . Transference is crucial to the therapeutic process because the patient unconsciously attributes to the psychiatrist or analyst those feelings which he may have repressed towards his own parents.... [I]t is through the creation, experiencing and resolution of these feelings that [the patient] becomes well. . . . Understanding of transference forms a basic part of the psychoanalytic technique."[156]

Pastoral and lay counselors often are tempted to engage in inappropriate sexual contact with a counselee because of unfamiliarity with this phenomenon. They misinterpret transference as affection, and fail to engage in anti-transference precautions that reduce the risk of inappropriate physical or emotional bonding. These precautions can include one or more of the following: (1) require a third person to be present for any counseling occurring off of church premises; (2) allow one-on-one counseling on church premises only during office hours if other staff members are present and visible; (3) limit counseling sessions to 45 minutes; and (4) permit no more than 5 counseling sessions with the same person during a calendar year.

> **Key point.** *Churches that adopt any of these other measures must recognize that they are not reducing risk as much as if they applied the "third person rule" or required women to counsel women. It is imperative that churches adopting these lesser measures incorporate them into official church policy and strictly monitor them to prevent any deviations. Remember, windows or open doors are of no value if a counseling session extends beyond normal office hours and the church staff leaves.*

2. OTHER RISKS

Another significant risk of lay counseling, when unlicensed counselors are used, is negligence in selecting and using a counselor with little if any formal training. Churches can reduce this risk by adopting a number of risk management strategies. Consider the following:

(1) counseling policy

Churches that use unlicensed lay counselors should prepare a suitable brochure or statement clearly communicating to each counselee that the church considers counseling to be an essential aspect of its ministry, and that it is important for persons seeking counseling to recognize certain legal considerations that apply in the context of counseling. These may include many considerations, including the fact that the counselee understands and agrees that counseling is provided on the basis of the following conditions:

• The counselors are engaged solely in spiritual counseling based on their understanding of the Bible, and they are not engaged in the practice of psychology, professional counseling, or psychotherapy.

• State law may require a counselor to report allegations of child abuse to civil authorities.

• Statements made in confidence to a pastor in the course of counseling ordinarily are "privileged," meaning that neither the counselee nor the pastor can be compelled to disclose in a court of law any state-

---

[155] Alpharetta First United Methodist Church v. Stewart, 473 S.E.2d 532 (Ga. App. 1996).
[156] Bladen v. First Presbyterian Church, 857 P.2d 789 (Okla. 1993).

ments made in the course of the counseling. However, the presence of a third party during a counseling session may jeopardize the privilege, since the counseling may no longer be considered "confidential." To illustrate, statements made in the course of pastoral counseling may not be privileged if a counselee brings a friend along to the counseling session.

• Any statements made in confidence in the course of counseling will be kept in strict confidence by the counselor. As noted above, the duty to maintain confidences may not apply in the context of child abuse. Further, the counselor may reserve the right to disclose confidential information in specified situations (such as threats of suicide, or an intent to harm another person).

(2) avoid controversial therapies

Counselors should be instructed to avoid any controversial counseling techniques that have been associated in recent years with staggering levels of liability (such as age regression therapy or multiple personality disorders).

(3) referrals

Counselors should have a clear understanding of those cases that need to be referred to a professional counselor.

> ***Tip.*** *When referring counselees to a professional counselor, it is important to avoid endorsing the person. Simply inform the counselee that the counselor is state licensed (as a counselor, psychologist, or psychiatrist), and has satisfactorily served a number of other members of the congregation.*

(4) insurance

Does the counselor have counseling insurance? If so, what are the coverage amounts? What exclusions exist? These are questions that should be addressed prior to the time the counselor begins counseling. Also check to see if the church's liability insurance policy covers the counseling activities.

(5) legal agreement

Consider executing a legal agreement with the counselor that expresses the conditions of the arrangement.

(6) disclaimer

Have every counselee sign a form acknowledging that the counselor is not acting as an agent or representative of the church, and that the counselor is not acting under the control or supervision of the church.

(7) use of the term "counselor"

It is unlawful in most states for unlicensed persons to use the term *counselor* or *counseling* in connection with their services. Pastors who engage in counseling of church members in the course of performing their pastoral duties are exempted from this limitation, but lay counselors generally are not even though they are working in a church.

§ 10-13 Breach of a Fiduciary Duty

In recent years, some courts have ruled that certain "special relationships" are "fiduciary" in nature and impose "fiduciary duties." A few courts have concluded that the following relationships are fiduciary in nature: a pastor and a counselee, a lay church counselor and a counselee, and volunteer youth workers and minors. Persons having a fiduciary duty toward another may be legally responsible for injuries they cause to the other person. This basis of liability is addressed in section 4-11.1. In some cases, churches themselves are sued for breaching a fiduciary duty. Cases recognizing and rejecting fiduciary duty claims against churches are summarized below.

§ 10-13.1 — Court Decisions Recognizing Fiduciary Duty Claims

> *Key point 10-13.1. A few courts have found churches and denominational agencies liable on the basis of a breach of a fiduciary duty for the sexual misconduct of a minister. In some cases, the church or agency is found to be vicariously liable for the minister's breach of a fiduciary duty, but in others the church or agency is found to have breached a fiduciary duty that it had with the victim.*

This section reviews court decisions in which a church or other religious organization was found liable on the basis of breaching a fiduciary duty.

> *Example. The Colorado Supreme Court ruled that an Episcopal diocese and bishop were responsible for a pastor's sexual misconduct with a female member of the congregation who had sought him out for counseling. The court concluded that the bishop and diocese breached their "fiduciary duty" to the victim. The court noted that a fiduciary relationship exists when there is a special relationship of trust, confidence, and reliance between two persons, and when one of them assumes a duty to act in the other's best interests. The court acknowledged that the clergy-parishioner relationship "is not necessarily a fiduciary relationship." However, the clergy-parishioner relationship often involves "the type of interaction that creates trust and reliance" and in some cases will constitute a fiduciary relationship. The court concluded that a fiduciary relationship existed between the bishop and the victim on the basis of the following factors: (1) The bishop was in a superior position and was able to exert substantial influence over the victim. An unequal relationship between two parties can be evidence of a fiduciary relationship, since the party with the greater influence and authority often assumes a duty to act in the dependent party's best interests. (2) The bishop, in his meeting with the victim, served as a counselor to the victim and not as a representative of the diocese. If he was acting only as a representative of the diocese, he failed to convey that fact to the victim and led her to believe that he was acting in her interest. The court concluded that the bishop and diocese had breached their fiduciary duty to the victim by not acting in her "utmost good faith" (by taking no action to help her, not assisting her in understanding that she was not solely responsible for the sexual relationship, and not recommending counseling for her).[157]*

> *Example. A Colorado court ruled that a denominational agency could be sued by a woman with whom a minister had sexual contacts.[158] The court noted that the following facts supported the existence of a fiduciary relationship between the victim and the denominational agency: the agency conducted a meeting with six women regarding the minister's inappropriate behavior with them; the agency pro-*

---

[157] Moses v. Diocese of Colorado, 863 P.2d 310 (Colo. 1993). *Accord* DeBose v. Bear Valley Church of Christ, 890 P.2d 214 (Colo. App. 1994), aff'd, 928 P.2d 1315 (Colo. 1996).

[158] Winkler v. Rocky Mouton Conference, 923 P.2d 152 (Colo. App. 1995).

vided a therapist to help the women; the agency sent a letter to the church's membership stating in part that "we are equally concerned for the healing of any persons who have been hurt. They will continue to receive appropriate help for their healing and restoration." The victim claimed that the denominational agency breached its fiduciary duty by failing to provide adequate counseling to the six women with whom the minister had engaged in inappropriate sexual conduct; undermining the credibility of the women by informing their congregation that there was nothing in the minister's personnel file indicating he had problems; failing to protect the women who brought complaints against the minister from verbal attacks; and not informing the congregation that it found the women's complaints credible. The court concluded that sufficient evidence existed for the jury to conclude that the agency breached its fiduciary duty.

§ 10-13.2 — Court Decisions Rejecting Fiduciary Duty Claims

Key point 10-13.2. *Several courts have refused to hold churches and denominational agencies liable on the basis of a breach of a fiduciary duty for the sexual misconduct of a minister. In some cases, this result is based on first amendment considerations.*

This section reviews court decisions in which a church or other religious organization was found not liable on the basis of breaching a fiduciary duty. Many courts have concluded that the first amendment's "nonestablishment of religion" and "free exercise of religion" clauses prevent the civil courts from resolving such claims involving clergy misconduct.

Example. A federal appeals court ruled that a church and denominational agency were not legally responsible for a pastoral counselor's sexual contacts with a female counselee.[159] In rejecting the woman's claim that the church and denominational agency were legally responsible for her injuries on the basis of a breach of a fiduciary duty they owed her, the court observed, "At the outset [we] note that [the woman] cited no Illinois authority establishing that Illinois recognizes such a fiduciary duty. . . . Moreover, given the constitutional difficulties that would be encountered if a cause of action for breach of fiduciary duty were permitted under these circumstances, we ought to be particularly cautious in assuming that Illinois has taken such a step. If the court were to recognize such a breach of fiduciary duty, it would be required to define a reasonable duty standard and to evaluate [the pastor's] conduct against that standard, an inquiry identical to that which Illinois has declined to undertake in the context of a clergy malpractice claim and one that is of doubtful validity under the free exercise [of religion] clause [of the first amendment]. It is clear that Illinois would not entertain a claim for breach of fiduciary obligation under the circumstances alleged here."

Example. A Florida court ruled that it was barred by the first amendment from resolving a woman's claim that her priest and church were responsible on the basis of a breach of a fiduciary duty for the priest's acts of sexual misconduct.[160] The woman had sought out a priest for marital counseling, and alleged that the priest engaged in sexual contacts with her. The woman sued her church and diocese, claiming that they were aware of prior incidents involving sexual misconduct during counseling by the same priest. Despite this knowledge, nothing was done to address the problem. She claimed that the priest breached a fiduciary duty by becoming romantically involved with her, and that the church and diocese had a fiduciary relationship with her (because she reported the priest's misconduct to them) that

---

[159] Dausch v. Rykse, 52 F.3d 1425 (7th Cir. 1994).
[160] Doe v. Evans, 718 So.2d 286 (Fla. App. 1998).

was breached. A state appeals court concluded that resolving the woman's breach of fiduciary duty claims (against the priest, church, and diocese) would constitute excessive entanglement between church and state in violation of the first amendment: "Taking the allegations of [her] complaint as true, [she] alleged the church defendants owed her a fiduciary duty, yet definition of that duty necessarily involves the secular court in church practices, doctrines, and belief. To establish a breach of the fiduciary duty allegedly owed to [her] by the church defendants, [she] would need to establish the church remained inactive in the face of her allegations against [the priest]. However, the church's policies undoubtedly differ from the rules of another employer, and may require the nonsecular employer to respond differently when faced with such allegations. When a secular court interprets church law, policies, and practices it becomes excessively entangled in religion. We align ourselves with those courts finding a first amendment bar to a breach of fiduciary duty claim as against church defendants, concluding resolution of such a claim would necessarily require the secular court to review and interpret church law, policies, and practices."

Example. *The Missouri Supreme Court ruled that a diocese could not be liable on the basis of a breach of a fiduciary duty for the sexual misconduct of a priest.[161] A Catholic priest served as associate pastor of a church. He invited a young boy and one of the boy's friends to spend the night and watch movies in the church parsonage. One of the boys later alleged that the priest sexually molested him. The boy's parents sued the diocese. They alleged that the diocese "stood in a fiduciary relationship" with them and their son because they were the recipients of services that were directed and monitored by the diocese. Further, the diocese "held a fiduciary relationship of trust and confidence" with the family. The court concluded that these "general conclusions" were not sufficient to support the parents' claim of a breach of a fiduciary duty.*

Example. *The North Dakota Supreme Court ruled that a denominational agency could not be liable for a pastor's sexual misconduct on the basis of a breach of a fiduciary duty.[162] A police officer was killed in the line of duty. His widow sought out her pastor for counseling. Within a few months, the pastor initiated a sexual relationship with the widow. The affair lasted for nearly a year, at which time the pastor was assigned to a position in another state. The couple continued their relationship for seven years, meeting four or five times each year at "workshops" around the country. Eventually, the widow informed a denominational official about the pastor's relationship with her. The pastor was promptly removed from his position within the church. The widow later sued the denominational agency, claiming that it owed her a fiduciary duty after it learned of the affair, and that it breached this duty by failing to intervene or respond appropriately. The court concluded that the widow had failed to prove that the denominational agency owed her a fiduciary duty. It observed that a fiduciary duty is based on the existence of a fiduciary relationship, and it concluded that such a relationship exists "when one is under a duty to act or give advice for the benefit of another upon matters within the scope of the relationship." It further noted that a fiduciary relationship "generally arises when there is an unequal relationship between the parties." Did the widow have a fiduciary relationship with her denominational agency on the basis of its alleged knowledge of the affair? No, concluded the court. It observed, "Although there was evidence [the agency and one of its officials] were informed about the intimacy between the [pastor and widow], we are not persuaded that knowledge, by itself and without some other action to assume control of the matter, raises an inference that the [agency] assumed a fiduciary duty to [the widow]."*

---

[161] Gibson v. Brewer, 952 S.W.2d 239 (Mo. 1997).
[162] L.C. v. R.P. 563 N.W.2d 799 (N.D. 1997).

Example. The Ohio Supreme Court rejected a woman's attempt to sue her church and pastor for injuries she allegedly suffered because of a sexual relationship with her pastor.[163] A husband and wife who had been experiencing marital problems went to a Lutheran minister for counseling. They selected him because "he held himself out to the public . . . as a minister and counselor trained and able to provide counseling for marital difficulties." During the final three or four weeks of counseling, the minister allegedly engaged in consensual sexual relations with the wife. These relations, and the counseling, ended when the husband learned of the affair. The husband, who was later divorced from his wife, sued both the minister and his church. The suit against the minister alleged a breach of fiduciary duty, among other things. The state supreme court dismissed all of the husband's claims. It noted that the breach of fiduciary claim, like the husband's other claims, had to be dismissed since they all sought damages based on the minister's seduction of the wife, and as such were barred by the state law prohibiting lawsuits based on "alienation of affections."

Example. A South Carolina court ruled that a denominational agency and one of its officials were not liable on the basis of a breach of a fiduciary duty for a pastor's acts of sexual harassment of three female church members.[164] The court concluded that no fiduciary relationship existed between the women and either the denominational agency or its superintendent. It noted that the women had no contact with the agency and their only direct contact with the superintendent was a single meeting involving one of the women. The court stressed that while the superintendent received the women's initial accusations, "his mere occupation of the position of superintendent did not create a fiduciary relationship with these [women]." Further, the women's personal expectation that the agency or superintendent would "take action" on their complaints did not create a fiduciary relationship: "The steps taken unilaterally by the [women] do not constitute an attempt on their part to establish the relationship alleged, and there is no evidence that [the agency or superintendent] accepted or induced any special, fiduciary bond with any of [the women] under these facts in any event." The court also concluded that even if a fiduciary relationship did exist, it was not violated since "there is no evidence of a breach of that duty. There is no evidence that [the agency or superintendent] acted other than in good faith and with due regard to [the women's] interests."

§ 10-13.3 — Risk Management

Key point 10-13.3. *Churches can reduce the risk of liability based on breach of fiduciary duty by adopting risk management policies and procedures.*

"Breach of fiduciary claims" against churches and other religious organizations are rarely successful. The few exceptions generally have involved claims of sexual misconduct by clergy in the course of a counseling relationship. The risk of such claims can be reduced by implementing the same strategies mentioned in section 10-12.1 in the context of counseling activities.

§ 10-14 Ratification

Key point 10-14. *Churches may be liable on the basis of "ratification" for the unauthorized act of a minister or other church worker if it is aware of the act and voluntarily affirms it.*

---

[163] Stock v. Pressnell, 527 N.E.2d 1235 (Ohio 1988).
[164] Brown v. Pearson, 483 S.E.2d 477 (S.C. App. 1997).

A few courts have found churches liable on the basis of "ratification" for the acts of clergy and lay workers. Ratification is "the affirmance by a person of a prior act which did not bind him but which was done or professedly done on his account, whereby the act, as to some or all persons, is given effect as if originally authorized by him."[165] Stated differently, a church can be liable for the unauthorized acts of an employee or volunteer if it ratifies those acts either expressly or by implication. In order to be liable for unauthorized acts on the basis of ratification, a church must have knowledge of all material facts surrounding the acts and voluntarily affirm them. A church may ratify contracts, promissory notes, deeds, and other legal documents that are signed without authorization, and it may ratify acts causing personal injuries. In many cases, a church ratifies an unauthorized act by accepting or retaining the benefits of the transaction. To illustrate, if a church treasurer without authorization signs a contract to purchase a vehicle on behalf of the church, the church will be liable on the contract on the basis of ratification if it retains and uses the vehicle without objection.

Example. A federal appeals court ruled that an archdiocese was not responsible on the basis of "ratification" for the alleged molestation of a minor by a priest.[166] The court also rejected the victim's claim that the archdiocese "ratified" the priest's actions by not addressing them despite suspicious circumstances. According to the victim, suspicion translates into "constructive knowledge" which is tantamount to a "passive ratification" of the priest's activities. The court noted that "[t]his is a novel proposition to be sure," and it refused to recognize it.

Example. A Colorado court ruled that a church could be sued on the basis of "ratification" for the molestation of a child by a pastor.[167] A 7-year-old boy (the "victim"), who was experiencing emotional trauma, was encouraged by his pastor to enter into a counseling relationship with him. The boy's mother approved, and the counseling sessions lasted for a number of years. From the very first counseling session the victim claimed that the pastor sexually molested him. A jury found the church liable for the pastor's misconduct on the ground that it "ratified" his actions. On appeal, the church insisted that (1) intentional misconduct by a pastor cannot be ratified; (2) it could not ratify actions of the pastor that were outside the scope of his employment; and (3) there was insufficient evidence that it ratified the pastor's actions. The court disagreed with all three objections. In rejecting the church's first objection, the court observed that "[a]n employer can assume liability for the tortious conduct of its employee by approving and ratifying such conduct, irrespective whether that conduct is intentional or negligent." Similarly, in rejecting the church's second objection the court observed that "[a]n employer may ratify the unauthorized act of its employee, i.e., an act not within the scope of the employment, and thereby become obligated to the same extent as if the principal had originally authorized the act." As a result, "it is no defense for the church here that [the pastor's] alleged conduct with the minor fell outside the scope of his defined job responsibilities." Finally, in responding to the church's third objection that there was insufficient evidence that it ratified the pastor's misconduct, the court observed: "In order for an employer to be liable by ratification for the unauthorized act of its employee, the evidence must establish the employer's adoption and confirmation of that act. And, an employer must have full knowledge of the character of the employee's act before it may be said to have ratified that act. The fact that an employer retains an employee after gaining knowledge of the employee's tortious conduct is evidence that may prove ratification of the employee's acts. However, retention of an employee, without more, is not conclusive evidence of such ratification. Further, numerous acts of an employee committed over a period of time can constitute evidence of an implied ratification of that conduct by the employer. . . . Here, the evidence was sufficient to allow the finding that the church elders were aware of [the pastor's] alleged inappropriate

---

[165] Restatement, Agency 2d § 82.
[166] Tichenor v. Roman Catholic Church, 32 F.3d 953 (5th Cir. 1994).
[167] DeBose v. Bear Valley Church of Christ, 890 P.2d 214 (Colo. App. 1994), aff'd, 928 P.2d 1315 (Colo. 1996).

counseling behavior as early as 1986. It began receiving complaints from various parishioners with respect to his conduct, starting in 1986 and continuing through 1987 and 1988. Indeed, the minutes of several church elders' meetings during 1986 and 1987 reflect that the elders were concerned with respect to the church's "liability and responsibility" for [the pastor's] counseling; that [he] might be involved in "medical," rather than religious counseling; and that "many parents are complaining" about [him]. Further, there was evidence, as noted, of specific complaints against [the pastor] made by various parishioners, and there was other evidence that the church failed effectively to respond to such allegations."

§ 10-15 Defamation

Key point 10-15. *The first amendment limits, but does not eliminate, a church's liability for defamation.*

Defamation consists of the following elements:

(1) oral or written statements about another person

(2) that are false

(3) that are "published" (that is, communicated to other persons), and

(4) that injure the other person's reputation

If the words are oral, the defamation is sometimes called slander. If the words are written, the defamation may be referred to as libel. Although this terminology is still widely used, there is a tendency to refer to both slander and libel as defamation.

The courts have been reluctant to subject churches to civil liability on the basis of defamation. In many cases, this reluctance is rooted in the fact that allegedly defamatory statements made by church officials orally or in church publications involve pervasively religious concerns such as the discipline of members or clergy. The courts have responded to defamation claims against churches in the following five ways:

1. No Civil Court Jurisdiction

Some courts have concluded that the first amendment deprives them of jurisdiction to resolve defamation claims against churches, at least if doctrinal or other pervasively religious issues are involved.

Example. *A federal appeals court ruled that civil courts lack authority to resolve disputes between dismissed clergy and their former church or denomination.[168] A minister was dismissed by his denomination. He later sued the denomination, claiming that his dismissal violated established procedures set forth in the denomination's bylaws. He alleged that his dismissal violated various "contract and property rights," and was defamatory. The court concluded that the first amendment guaranty of religious freedom prevents the civil courts from resolving lawsuits brought by dismissed ministers against former churches or denominations "however a lawsuit may be labeled." In other words, the fact that a dis-*

---

[168] Natal v. Christian and Missionary Alliance, 878 F.2d 1575 (1st Cir. 1989). *Accord* Pierce v. Iowa-Missouri Conference of Seventh-Day Adventists, 534 N.W.2d 425 (Iowa 1995).

missed minister alleges breach of contract, defamation, emotional distress, or similar "secular" theories of liability will not enable the civil courts to resolve what in essence is a dispute between a minister and his or her church or denomination. The court observed, "However a suit may be labeled, once a court is called upon to probe into a religious body's selection and retention of clergymen, the first amendment [guaranty of religious freedom] is implicated. . . . The relationship between an organized church and its ministers is its lifeblood. The minister is the chief instrument by which the church seeks to fulfill its purpose. Matters touching this relationship must necessarily be recognized as of prime ecclesiastical concern."

Example. *A federal appeals court refused to allow a "disfellowshiped" Jehovah's Witness to sue her former church for defamation, invasion of privacy, fraud, and outrageous conduct.[169] The disfellowshiped member claimed that she had been aggrieved by the Jehovah's Witness practice of "shunning," which requires members to avoid all social contacts with disfellowshiped members. The court, acknowledging that the harm suffered by disfellowshiped members is "real and not insubstantial," nevertheless concluded that permitting disfellowshiped members to sue their church for emotional injuries "would unconstitutionally restrict the Jehovah's Witness free exercise of religion." The constitutional guaranty of freedom of religion, observed the court, "requires that society tolerate the type of harm suffered by [disfellowshiped members] as a price well worth paying to safeguard the right of religious difference that all citizens enjoy."*

Example. *A Louisiana court ruled that a minister could not sue state and national church officials for defamation.[170] A pastor disciplined certain members of his congregation, who thereafter were accepted as members in a neighboring church of the same denomination. The pastor protested the action of the neighboring church to both national and state denominational officials. These officials declined to assist the pastor, whose congregation thereafter "protested" this result by withholding financial support to the national organization. This prompted the national church to remove the pastor from both state and national offices that he held. The pastor later resigned from the denomination, and sued the state and national offices for defamation. The court, in concluding that it lacked jurisdiction to resolve the dispute, relied upon a 1976 decision of the United States Supreme Court, which held that the United States Constitution "permits hierarchical religious organizations to establish their own rules and regulations for internal discipline and government, and to create tribunals for adjudicating disputes over these matters. When this choice is exercised and ecclesiastical tribunals are created to decide disputes over the government and direction of subordinate bodies, the Constitution requires that civil courts accept their decisions as binding upon them."[171] The Louisiana court concluded that "[i]t would be ludicrous to believe that the constitutional principles upheld by the United States Supreme Court . . . could be satisfied by allowing this intrusion into the disciplinary proceedings of an ecclesiastical board. To allow defamation suits to be litigated to the fullest extent against members of a religious board who are merely discharging the duty which has been entrusted to them by their church could have a potentially chilling effect on the performance of those duties."*

Example. *A Maryland court ruled that a former candidate for the priesthood could not sue his diocese or church officials for defamation.[172] The candidate entered seminary and pursued training in preparation for ordination as a priest. Less than a year before he was to be ordained, he was informed by a church*

---

[169] Paul v. Watchtower Bible and Tract Society of New York, 819 F. 2d 875 (9th Cir. 1987).
[170] McManus v. Taylor, 521 So.2d 449 (La. App. 1988).
[171] Serbian Eastern Orthodox Diocese v. Milivojevich, 426 U.S. 696 (1976).
[172] Downs v. Roman Catholic Archbishop, 683 A.2d 808 (Md. App. 1996).

official that he was being "released" from the diocese and as a result would never be considered for the priesthood. The candidate sued the archbishop on behalf of the diocese and various church officials, claiming that the decision to "release" him was based on defamatory information shared with the diocese. Specifically, the candidate claimed that a priest provided a reference to church officials in which he asserted that the candidate had engaged in "sexually motivated conduct" with certain staff members in a former parish. The candidate claimed that church officials repeated this information with knowledge that it was false and with an intent to harm his chances for ordination to the priesthood. He sought more than $2 million in damages. A Maryland appeals court ruled that the case had to be dismissed. It summed up pertinent decisions of the United States Supreme Court by noting that "the withdrawal of ecclesiastical controversies from civil jurisdiction has been a broad one." The court was not prepared to say that the civil courts can never resolve disputes between a church and its ministers. However, "When the conduct complained of occurs in the context of, or is germane to, a dispute over the plaintiff's fitness or suitability to enter into or remain a part of the clergy . . . it is difficult to see how the forbidden inquiry could be avoided. Questions of truth, falsity, malice, and the various privileges that exist often take on a different hue when examined in the light of religious precepts and procedures that generally permeate controversies over who is fit to represent and speak for the church. . . . It is apparent from these allegations . . . that the very heart of the [lawsuit] is a decision by [the candidate's] clerical supervisors to prevent him from becoming a priest. The allegedly defamatory statements were made by them with that intent, thereby evidencing a determination on their part—whether valid and fair or invalid and unfair—that [the candidate] was not a suitable candidate for the priesthood. That the offensive conduct was so directed is what brings this case squarely within the protective ambit of the first amendment."

Example. A Minnesota court ruled that a female associate pastor could sue her senior pastor for sexual harassment on account of his repeated sexual advances toward her and the "hostile work environment" that he created, but the woman's allegations of breach of contract, defamation, and wrongful dismissal were barred by the first amendment.[173] The court concluded that the woman's defamation claim "is based on the church's stated reason for her discharge as 'inability to conduct her ministry efficiently.' This claim would require a . . . review of the church's reasons for discharging her, an essentially ecclesiastical concern. . . . The impermissible entanglement of doctrinal and disciplinary issues is sufficient to support the dismissal of this claim." The court concluded that "the prohibition against litigating matters at the core of a church's religious practice requires dismissal of [the woman's] discharge-related claims."

Example. A Minnesota court ruled that a church member could not challenge his dismissal in court.[174] The pastor of a church asked two church members (a husband and wife) to sign a document guarantying payment of certain church debts. The pastor represented to them that if the church ever defaulted on its debts the church would sell its property and use the proceeds to pay back any funds the couple advanced pursuant to the guaranty. The couple signed the guaranty agreement. A few months later, they were notified that the church had been late in making several payments on its bank loans. The couple retained an attorney and discontinued their contact with the church. They did not notify the church of any intent to terminate their membership. Their attorney wrote the pastor and requested that the couple be released from their guaranty commitment. The pastor responded by sending the couple a letter dismissing them from membership in the church. The pastor cited the following reasons for terminating their membership: (1) a lack of financial stewardship; (2) a desire to create division and strife in the fellowship; and (3) the dissemination of lies with the intent to hurt the reputation of the church. The

---

[173] Black v. Snyder, 471 N.W.2d 715 (Minn. App. 1991).
[174] Schoenhalls v. Main, 504 N.W.2d 233 (Minn. App. 1993).

pastor's letter was read to the entire congregation. Several months later the pastor met with the couple, and admitted that no proceeds from the sale of church property would be shared with them. The couple then filed a lawsuit against the pastor and church, alleging fraud, defamation, and breach of contract. A state appeals court dismissed the lawsuit. It began its opinion by observing that the first amendment "precludes judicial review of claims involving core questions of church discipline and internal governance." The court concluded that the couple's claims all involved core questions of church discipline that it was not able to resolve. With regard to the couple's defamation claim, the court pointed out that a defamatory statement must be false and that "since an examination of the truth of [the pastor's] statements would require an impermissible inquiry into church doctrine and discipline, the [trial court] did not err in concluding that the defamation claim is precluded by the first amendment." The court added that "the fact that the letter was disseminated only to other members of the church strengthens the conclusion that [the pastor's] statements involved and were limited to church doctrine."

Example. *A federal district court in Minnesota dismissed a minister's lawsuit alleging that church officials had defamed him.[175] A denomination decided not to elevate a congregation to mission status, thereby cutting off all subsidies and in effect terminating the minister who served the congregation. The minister sued his denomination for defamation, alleging that denominational officials published both oral and written defamatory statements about him that damaged his reputation and professional status. The denomination claimed that the civil courts lacked jurisdiction to resolve religious disputes such as this. The court agreed with the denomination and dismissed the lawsuit. It noted that "the United States Supreme Court has determined that civil courts generally may not inquire into a religious organization's activities on matters of religious doctrine or authority and that courts lack subject matter jurisdiction over most disputes stemming from a religious organization's actions." The court rejected the minister's claim that resolving a defamation claim would be permissible: "Although factual scenarios might exist where resolution of a defamation action against a religious organization would not require the court to undertake an inquiry in violation of the first amendment, this case does not present such a situation. [The minister's] defamation claim challenges [the denomination's] authority . . . to comment on [the minister's] actions and abilities as a . . . minister. Resolution of . . . the defamation claim would require the court to review the [denomination's] bases for terminating him, an ecclesiastical concern, and the veracity of the [denomination's] statements. The court determines that such an inquiry would implicate the concerns expressed in the first amendment. Based on that determination, the court concludes that it has no jurisdiction over this matter."*

Example. *The Montana Supreme Court ruled that a husband and wife who had been "disfellowshipped" from a Jehovah's Witness congregation could not sue the church for defamation.[176] The couple had been disfellowshipped for marrying contrary to church doctrine. In announcing the decision to the congregation, the overseer remarked that the couple had been living in adultery according to church teachings and had been disfellowshipped for "conduct unbecoming Christians." The overseer added that "we got the filth cleaned out of the congregation, now we have God's spirit." The court concluded that such comments were not defamatory since they were privileged and protected by the constitutional guaranty of religious freedom. As to the defense of privilege, the court remarked that "it is firmly established that statements of church members made in the course of disciplinary or expulsion proceedings, in the absence of malice, are protected by a qualified privilege." The remarks of the overseer were privileged, concluded the court, and did not involve malice since "malice is defined as reckless disregard for the truth [and] does not include hatred, personal spite, ill-will, or a desire to injure." The court added that*

---

[175] Farley v. Wisconsin Evangelical Lutheran Synod, 821 F. Supp. 1286 (D. Minn. 1993).
[176] Rasmussen v. Bennett, 741 P.2d 755 (Mont. 1987).

it *"would be violating the [church's] right to free exercise of religion if [it] were to find [the church's] statements actionable under state defamation law."*

Example. *An Ohio court dismissed a lawsuit brought by two former ministers against their church and denomination.[177] A church hired a husband and wife as "co-pastors." A few years later, the couple were dismissed. They sued their former church on the basis of several theories of liability, including defamation. In particular, they asserted that the church defamed them by publishing negative comments regarding their ministry and alleged financial misconduct. In rejecting the claim of defamation, the court concluded, "One who falsely and without a privilege to do so publishes a slander which ascribes to another conduct, characteristics, or a condition incompatible with the proper conduct of his lawful business, trade, or profession is liable to the other. However, inquiry by a civil court into the truth or falsity of the statements by [church officials] would require review of subjective judgments made by religious officers and bodies concerning [the co-pastors'] conduct of the pastorate and financial misdealings. Inquiry would be ecclesiastical in nature and constitutionally prohibited."*

Example. *An Ohio court ruled that it could not review a dismissed member's lawsuit claiming that his church had defamed him.[178] The church member sought access to his church's financial records. When church leaders denied this request, the member filed a lawsuit in which he asked a court to order the church to turn over the records. Following the filing of this lawsuit, church leaders attempted to dismiss the member from church membership. The member filed another lawsuit against his church, claiming that the attempt to dismiss him was in violation of the church's bylaws; caused severe emotional distress; and was defamatory. A state appeals court rejected the ousted member's claim that the civil courts could resolve his defamation against the church and its trustees. The ousted member asserted that the church trustees had defamed him by stating that he had lied, that he was "in league with Satan," that he had been "overtaken by a fall," that he was a "defiler of the temple" and an enemy of the church, and that he was "sleeping around," and that a court could resolve the defamation issue without any interpretation of religious doctrine or beliefs. The court disagreed, "In this case, all of the statements alleged . . . to be defamatory arose out of the underlying dispute between him and the church regarding the propriety of his conduct in suing the church to obtain its records and the church's subsequent decision to remove [him] from church membership. [His lawsuit] makes clear that the dispute between the parties regarding [his] lawsuit against the church was based on biblical interpretation. The move to disfellowship [him] therefore arose from a dispute regarding his conformity . . . to the standard of morals required of him by his church. The allegedly defamatory statements made by church members, trustees or agents in terminating [his] membership in the church are therefore inextricably intertwined with ecclesiastical or religious issues over which secular courts have no jurisdiction."*

Example. *The Oklahoma Supreme Court ruled that a church could not be sued for defamation by two church members who had been disciplined because of sexual misconduct.[179] A church convened a disciplinary hearing to determine the membership status of two sisters accused of fornication. Neither sister attended, and neither sister withdrew her membership in the church. Following the hearing, both sisters received letters from the church informing them that their membership had been terminated. The sisters sued the church and its leaders, claiming that the church's actions in delivering the termination letters and disclosing their contents "to the public" constituted defamation, intentional infliction of emotional distress, and invasion of privacy. A trial court dismissed the lawsuit, and the sisters appealed directly to*

---

[177] Salzgaber v. First Christian Church, 583 N.E.2d 1361 (Ohio App. 1991).
[178] Howard v. Covenant Apostolic Church, Inc., 705 N.E.2d 385 (Ohio App. 1997).
[179] Hadnot v. Shaw, 826 P.2d 978 (Okla. 1992).

the state supreme court which upheld the dismissal of the case. The court began its opinion by rejecting the sisters' claim that the contents of the termination letters had been disclosed improperly to the public. This allegation was based entirely on a conversation between a church board member and another member of the church. The member asked the board member why the board was "going after" the sisters, and the board member replied that it was on account of "fornication." The court concluded that this comment did not constitute a disclosure of the contents of the letters "to the public," and accordingly there had been no defamation or invasion of privacy. The court recognized an absolute constitutional protection for the membership determinations of religious organizations (assuming that the disciplined member has not effectively withdrawn his or her membership): "[The relationship between a church and its members] may be severed freely by a member's positive act at any time. Until it is so terminated, the church has authority to prescribe and follow disciplinary ordinances without fear of interference by the state. The first amendment will protect and shield the religious body from liability for the activities carried on pursuant to the exercise of church discipline. Within the context of church discipline, churches enjoy an absolute privilege from scrutiny by the secular authority."

Example. *A Texas court ruled that a bishop and diocese could not be liable on the basis of defamation for statements made about a priest's status within the church.[180] A priest had a history of conflict with his diocese culminating in his association with a dissident Catholic sect. A parishioner asked the priest's bishop about the priest's standing in the Catholic Church, and was informed that "he is not in good standing with his diocese and does not enjoy the [authority] to function as a priest in [this] or any other diocese." The bishop advised another person that the priest was excommunicated, and not in good standing, and "says mass to a small number of people, including elderly women who have been deceived by him." The bishop later sent a memorandum to "all pastors" advising them to refrain from advertising or encouraging a mass being offered by the priest who was described as an "excommunicated priest who has left the Catholic Church." The priest sued the bishop and diocese, claiming that these communications were defamatory. A state appeals court disagreed. The court observed that the first amendment "forbids the government from interfering with the right of hierarchical religious bodies to establish their own internal rules and regulations." As a result the civil courts cannot "intrude into the church's governance or religious or ecclesiastical matters, such as theological controversy, church discipline, ecclesiastical government, or the conformity of members to standards of morality." Furthermore, the court noted, "[C]ourts will not attempt to right wrongs related to the hiring, firing, discipline or administration of clergy. Although such wrongs may exist and may be severe, and although the administration of the church may be inadequate to provide a remedy, the preservation of the free exercise of religion is deemed so important a principle it overshadows the inequities which may result from its liberal application." The court rejected the priest's claim that the dispute did not involve ecclesiastical considerations: "[The priest's] claims arise from his divestiture of priestly authority; thus, his [legal] claims are inseparable from the privileged aura of ecclesiastical exemption. [The bishop's] administrative duties include informing members of the Catholic Church of the status of its clergy. We believe that statements made by a bishop in carrying out his administrative duties concerning an excommunication made before, during or after an excommunication, are all part of an ecclesiastical transaction—the divestiture of priestly authority." The court acknowledged that "there may be circumstances where a bishop or other church authority makes statements which overstep the bounds of [his or her] administrative duties." For example, "when statements are made by a church authority which are clearly intended to defame or inflict emotional distress, the authority has overstepped the bounds of his administrative duties and the state-*

---

[180] Tran v. Fiorenza, 934 S.W.2d 740 (Tex. App. 1996).

ments may fall outside ecclesiastical protection." This was not true in this case, however, since the bishop's statements all related to the priest's standing in the Catholic Church.

2. COMMON INTEREST PRIVILEGE

Many courts have concluded that the law should encourage churches to communicate matters of "common interest" to members without fear of being sued for defamation. These courts have ruled that churches are protected by a *qualified privilege* when communicating with church members about matters of mutual concern or common interest. This means that such communications cannot be defamatory unless made with malice. Malice in this context means that the person who made the allegedly defamatory remark knew that it was false, or made it with a reckless disregard as to its truth or falsity. This is a difficult standard to prove, which means that communications between churches and church members will be defamatory only in exceptional cases.

Tip. *The common interest privilege is addressed in section 4-02.3 in the context of clergy who are sued for defamation,*

Example. *A California court ruled that a national church could not be sued for allegedly defamatory statements made in the course of a doctrinal explanation in one of its publications.[181] A minister of the Worldwide Church of God wrote an article in a church publication that addressed the Church's newly developed and misunderstood doctrine on divorce and remarriage. The article contained statements that allegedly defamed the former spouse of a prominent Church official. The court concluded that "our accommodation of the competing interests of our society—one protecting reputation, the other, the free exercise of religion—requires that we hold that in order for a plaintiff to recover damages for defamatory remarks made during the course of a doctrinal explanation by a duly authorized minister, he or she must show, by clear and convincing evidence, that the defamation was made with 'constitutional malice,' that is with knowledge that it was false or with reckless disregard of whether it was false or not." Such a rule, observed the court, "strikes an appropriate balance between our citizens' reputational interests and our society's interest in protecting the right to free exercise of religion." The court rejected the Church's claim that the constitutional guaranty of religious freedom prevents ministers from ever being sued for defamatory statements made in the course of doctrinal explanations. Such suits are constitutionally permissible, concluded the court, but a plaintiff has the difficult burden of proving "malice" by "clear and convincing evidence."*

Example. *A Louisiana court ruled that a church did not commit defamation when it published derogatory statements in a church newsletter.[182] A Catholic priest became upset when he suspected that a monument company that did work at a church cemetery was guilty of using church utilities without paying for them. He wrote a letter to the owner of the monument company which stated, in part: "Stated simply, your workers entered our property, and used [church] utilities without permission, and that is theft. I could have them arrested and charged, for your information." A copy of the letter was sent to the diocese. A week later, the priest published the following statement in a church newsletter (that was mailed to 362 families): "For your information, I have been obliged [to inform the monument company] that it is forbidden . . . to perform work of any kind in [the cemetery]. The company has persisted in ignoring my cemetery policies, and has a 'come as you please, go as you please' attitude and uses our*

---

[181] McNair v. Worldwide Church of God, 242 Cal. Rptr. 823 (2d App. Dist. 1987).
[182] Redmond v. McCool, 582 So.2d 262 (La. App. 1991).

electrical utilities without permission. The utilities come out of cemetery funds (e.g., your pocket)." The monument company sued the priest, the local church, and the diocese when it learned of the statement in the newsletter. The court rejected the company's claim of defamation. It observed, "The elements of a defamation action are: (1) a defamatory statement, (2) publication, (3) falsity, (4) actual or implied malice, and (5) resulting injury. A statement which imputes the commission of a crime to another is defamatory per se and as a result, falsity and malice are presumed, but not eliminated as requirements." The court concluded that the statements by the priest in the letter and church newsletter were false, but that they were not defamatory since the priest made them with a reasonable belief that they were true and accordingly they were not made with "malice."

Example. *A Minnesota court ruled that the first amendment's "nonestablishment of religion" clause prevented it from resolving a dismissed minister's lawsuit against his former church.[183] A church installed a new pastor. From the beginning, the pastor's relationship with the congregation was strained. When the church council reduced the pastor's salary to less than $4,000, the pastor sued the church and a denominational agency. He alleged several theories of liability, including defamation. Specifically, he claimed that members of the church defamed him by making the following statements about him in public meetings that harmed his reputation and his ability to obtain another call: he did not attend a wedding rehearsal; he made a false statement regarding a church member's attendance at a retirement party; he insisted that his salary should be paid before the church's mortgage; he failed to visit in the hospital a woman with cancer; he failed to respond to a member's telephone call regarding an infant's death; he breached his duty of confidentiality by telling others of a member's abusive father and by stating that the member had a problem with authority; he charged $500 for conducting a wedding; he received eleven weeks of vacation; he had jeopardized the church's insurance policy by taking the church bus to camp; and while out of town, he returned only for the funerals of friends. The court concluded that these statements did not defame the pastor, since they were protected by a "conditional privilege." The court explained that "a communication is conditionally privileged . . . if it is made upon a proper occasion, from a proper motive, and . . . based upon reasonable or probable cause." This principle rests upon the courts' determination that "statements made in particular contexts or on certain occasions should be encouraged despite the risk that the statements might be defamatory." The court concluded that the members' alleged statements about the pastor qualified for this privilege since they all were communicated "at task force meetings or church council meetings and dealt with [the pastor's] actions as a pastor." Further, there was no evidence that the members were acting "out of the kind of malice or ill will that defeats the privilege." The pastor also claimed that he was defamed when a bishop's assistant told a church official that he was "paranoid." This statement was made during a phone conversation in which the church official and the bishop's assistant discussed conflicts in the church, the pastor's position at the church, and the pastor's compensation. The court found these comments to be "within the conditional privilege." Further, there was no evidence that the bishop's assistant made the statement out of malice or ill will.*

Example. *An Ohio court ruled that a letter addressed by a church official to "members and friends" of the church, in which he explained why the church board dismissed a church secretary, might have been defamatory.[184] A woman was employed as an office secretary for her church for approximately eight years. She was informed by church officials that her employment was being terminated. The woman claimed that church officials did not express any dissatisfaction with her work performance. She later*

---

[183] Singleton v. Christ the Servant Evangelical Lutheran Church, 541 N.W.2d 606 (Minn. App. 1996).
*[184]Baker v. Spinning Road Baptist Church, 1998 WL 598094 (unpublished decision, Ohio App. 1998).

received a letter confirming the termination of her employment. The letter did not state any reasons for the termination. A church official later circulated a letter in which he stated that the woman had been "fired" as church secretary. The letter was directed to the "Fellow Members and Friends" of the church. In the letter, the official stated that the church board of trustees had cited "insubordination, some incompetency, and inability to maintain confidentiality" as some of the reasons for the termination. A few months later, the woman sued her church for defamation. A state appeals court threw out the case on the basis of a "qualified privilege." It defined the concept of qualified privilege as follows: "In order to qualify for this privilege, a defendant must establish that (1) he acted in good faith; (2) there was an interest to be upheld; (3) the statement was limited in its scope to the purpose of upholding that interest; (4) the occasion was proper; and (5) the publication was made in a proper manner and only to the proper parties. Once the defendant establishes the defense of qualified privilege, the plaintiff may not recover for defamation unless he can present clear and convincing evidence that the defamatory statement was made with actual malice." Was the letter sent by the church official to "members and friends" of the church protected against defamation by this qualified privilege? The court began its opinion by observing that members of the church would "logically be interested in, and proper parties to, the subject letter. Obviously, the letter concerned a church interest; i.e., [the woman's] ability to perform her duties as secretary for the church. It was written by a church [official], and was limited in scope to informing the members of the reasons for [the woman's] termination." However, the court ordered the case to proceed to trial, because it was not convinced that the letter had been distributed "only to the proper parties, i.e., the church membership." While the church official insisted that the letter had been sent only to members of the church, the woman claimed that "of the approximately 150 persons or households to whom the letter was mailed, seventeen were not members of the church," and that one of the recipients was another church. The court pointed out that the church failed to "indicate that the other church was in any way affiliated with it, and did not provide any evidence to show that the other church had a valid interest in the subject matter of the letter. Therefore, we conclude that a question of fact exists, with regard to the one church on the mailing list, as to whether the publication was limited to proper parties."

3. STATEMENTS MADE AT ECCLESIASTICAL DISCIPLINARY HEARINGS

Some courts have ruled that statements made at church disciplinary hearings are protected by a *qualified privilege*. This means that such communications cannot be defamatory unless made with malice. Malice in this context means that the person who made the allegedly defamatory remark knew that it was false, or made it with a reckless disregard as to its truth or falsity. This is a difficult standard to prove, which means that communications made in the course of church disciplinary hearings will be defamatory only in exceptional cases.

4. DEFAMATION CLAIMS NOT INVOLVING DOCTRINAL INQUIRIES

A few courts have concluded that the first amendment does not prevent them from resolving defamation claims by ministers against churches and denominational agencies to the extent such claims can be resolved without any inquiry into religious doctrine or polity.

Example. *A federal appeals court ruled that a minister could not sue his denomination for allegedly failing to follow its bylaws in suspending him, but he could sue the denomination for defamation.[185] As one of its services for member churches, a denomination prepares and circulates personal information*

---

[185] Drevlow v. Lutheran Church, Missouri Synod, 991 F.2d 468 (8th Cir. 1993).

files on its ministers to churches interested in hiring pastors and advises them on the background and suitability of individual ministers. The denomination placed a document in a minister's file stating that his spouse had previously been married. The minister claimed that the denomination took this action without consulting him or verifying the accuracy of the information, and that the information in fact was untrue. The minister alleged that because churches within the denomination automatically disqualify a minister if his personal file shows that his spouse has been divorced, the denomination effectively excluded him from consideration for employment as a pastor by circulating this false information. At the time the denomination was circulating the erroneous statement about his spouse, the minister was actively, and unsuccessfully, seeking employment in a local church. Even though he was established in his profession and over three hundred churches were in need of a pastor, the minister did not obtain a position with any church. He sued the denomination, seeking monetary damages for his loss of income during the time that it circulated the false information about his spouse. The court concluded that the first amendment did not bar the minister's defamation claim: "The first amendment proscribes intervention by secular courts into many employment decisions made by religious organizations based on religious doctrine or beliefs. Personnel decisions are protected from civil court interference where review by civil courts would require the courts to interpret and apply religious doctrine or ecclesiastical law. The first amendment does not shield employment decisions made by religious organizations from civil court review, however, where the employment decisions do not implicate religious beliefs, procedures, or law. At the present stage of this litigation we are unable to predict that the evidence offered at trial will definitely involve the district court in an impermissible inquiry into the [denomination's] bylaws or religious beliefs. [The minister] has alleged that although over three hundred congregations were in need of a pastor he did not receive an offer of employment from any congregation while the [denomination] was circulating false information about his spouse. [His] fitness as a minister is not in dispute because his name was on the [denomination's] roster of eligible ministers during the relevant period. . . . The [denomination] has not offered any religious explanation for its actions which might entangle the court in a religious controversy in violation of the first amendment. [The minister] is entitled to an opportunity to prove his secular allegations at trial."

Example. *The Alaska Supreme Court ruled that a denominational official could be sued on the basis of defamation and interference with contract for making disparaging comments about another minister who recently had been hired by a local church.[186] A minister left a pastoral position in Alaska and accepted a call as minister of a church in Tennessee. When he presented himself to the church to begin his duties, he was informed by church officials that because of derogatory information the church had received from a denominational official in Alaska, the church would not hire him. The presbyter had informed church leaders that the minister was divorced, dishonest, unable to perform pastoral duties because of throat surgery, and that he had made an improper sexual advance to a church member in Alaska. The minister sued the presbyter for defamation, interference with contract, and breach of contract. A trial court dismissed the lawsuit on the ground that it was without jurisdiction to decide matters of internal church discipline. The minister appealed to the state supreme court. The supreme court ruled that while the civil courts lacked jurisdiction to resolve the breach of contract claim, they could resolve the defamation and interference with contract claims. With regard to the defamation claim the court observed, "The questions raised by the defamation claim concern only the statements made by [the presbyter]. There is no need for the court to involve itself in [the pastor's] qualifications. The court needs to determine only if [the presbyter] actually said: (1) [the pastor] was divorced; (2) [the pastor] was dishonest; (3) [the pastor] had throat surgery disabling him as a pastor; and (4) [the pastor]*

---

[186] Marshall v. Munro, 845 P.2d 424 (Alaska 1993).

made improper advances to a member of the congregation. If [the presbyter] raises the defenses of truth and of privilege, the court need only determine if the facts stated were true and if [the presbyter] made the statements with malice (a reckless disregard for the truth or falsity). There is no need to determine if [the pastor] was qualified to be a pastor or what those qualifications may be." The court rejected the presbyter's claim that this dispute is ecclesiastical in nature because his comments were made in the course of his official duties. The court did acknowledge, however, that "civil common law has long protected this exact type of communication by granting a conditional privilege." The court quoted the general rule as follows, "The common interest of members of religious . . . associations . . . is recognized as sufficient to support a privilege for communications among themselves concerning the qualifications of the officers and members and their participation in the activities of the society. This is true whether the defamatory matter related to alleged misconduct of some other member that makes him undesirable for continued membership, or the conduct of a prospective member. So too, the rule is applicable to communications between members and officers of the organization concerning the legitimate conduct of the activities for which it was organized." That is, the presbyter's statements concerning the fitness of the pastor for the Tennessee church relate to a matter of common interest among members of the church. Accordingly, the presbyter's statements were protected by a qualified or conditional privilege. This means that such statements cannot be defamatory unless they are made with legal malice. In this context, legal malice means either a knowledge that the statements were false, or a reckless disregard as to their truth or falsity. The court noted that "determining whether [the presbyter] acted with actual malice will not require the court to delve into ecclesiastical concerns. Rather, the issue is whether [he] had reasonable grounds for believing the defamatory statements and whether they were motivated by actual malice. This question can be resolved without considering [the pastor's] church related duties and is within the court's jurisdiction."

Example. *A New Jersey court allowed a woman to sue her church on the basis of defamation as a result of an associate pastor's disclosure to the congregation that the woman had engaged in a sexual relationship with the senior pastor.[187]*

5. DEFENSES TO DEFAMATION

There are several defenses available to churches that are sued for defamation. These are reviewed in section 4-02.3 in the context of clergy who are sued for defamation.

Example. *A Georgia court ruled that it could not resolve a lawsuit brought by church members against their church as a result of defamatory statements made by other church members.[188] A church and several of its members were sued by other members who claimed that they had been defamed by several statements made about them. The lawsuit alleged that in the course of a New Year's Eve church service, certain members intentionally and maliciously announced to the congregation that each of the plaintiffs "was a witch and had practiced evil deeds upon family and fellow church members," and that these statements were later repeated to a wider audience at another church service. The "evil deeds" allegedly practiced by the plaintiffs included witchcraft, acts of bodily harm, thievery, causing infertility, stealing United States government files to harm a fellow member, and child abuse. The court concluded that the church could not be liable for defamation: "Although plaintiffs alleged that the church conspired with its members to slander them, the doctrine of respondeat superior [that is, that an organization is responsible for the acts of its*

---

[187] F.G. v. MacDonell, 677 A.2d 258 (N.J. Super. 1996).
[188] First United Church v. Udofia, 479 S.E.2d 146 (Ga. App. 1996).

agents] does not apply in slander cases. Plaintiffs did not allege or show by any record evidence that the church expressly ordered and directed [its members] to say those very words. . . . [A] corporation is not liable for the slanderous utterances of an agent acting within the scope of his employment, unless it affirmatively appears that the agent was expressly directed or authorized to slander the plaintiff. The same would apply to utterances of a church member. Moreover, the complaint does not state an actionable claim against the church. Allegations of slander by individuals and other leaders of the church do not express a claim against the church itself as a separate entity." The court allowed the members to sue those who had uttered the defamatory words. It rejected the defendant members' claim that they were protected by a qualified privilege. Specifically, the members asserted that their remarks concerning the plaintiffs *"were made as testimony or confession during a worship service and thus were a church activity."* As a result, the remarks could not be defamatory unless they were made with legal malice, meaning that the members who uttered the remarks either knew that they were false or did so with a reckless disregard as to their truth or falsity. The court disagreed, noting that the statements *"were not made in a church tribunal in the course of an investigation of alleged misconduct of church members."*

Example. *An Ohio appeals court ruled that a church could be responsible for defamation as a result of information published in a congregational newsletter about a dismissed secretary. However, the court concluded that a denominational agency could not be liable for the defamation, even though an official had suggested to the church that it publish the defamatory statement. A church secretary claimed that a minister sexually harassed her. A denominational official investigated the charges, but took no action because the minister denied any wrongdoing and there was no other evidence supporting the woman's charges. The minister later dismissed the secretary and published in the parish newsletter a statement that the secretary had been engaging in an open malicious endeavor to discredit him. Following her dismissal, the secretary filed a lawsuit against the church and denomination. She asserted several bases of liability, including defamation. The court allowed the secretary to sue the church for defamation, but not the denomination. It concluded, "However, as to the defamation claim, [the former secretary] contends that the diocese, acting through an archdeacon of the diocese, advised [the minister] what to write in the allegedly defamatory newsletter. Nevertheless, that did not make the publication that of the diocese. The publication was that of [the minister and local church]."*

§ 10-16 Defenses to Liability

There are a number of legal defenses that may be available to a church that is sued on the basis of any of the theories of liability addressed in this chapter. Some have been discussed in previous sections, such as the "qualified privilege" defense that is available to a church that is sued for defamation. This section will address several other legal defenses.

§ 10-16.1 — Contributory and Comparative Negligence

Key point 10-16.1. Under the principle of comparative negligence, a church is liable only to the extent of its percentage share of fault for an accident or injury.

Contributory negligence is conduct on the part of a person injured through the negligence of another that itself falls below the standard to which a reasonable person would conform for his or her own safety and protection. Historically, the contributory negligence of an accident victim operated as a complete defense to negligence. Accordingly, accident victims who themselves were negligent could be denied any damages. To illustrate, a woman who was injured when she fell down the back stairway of a church while carrying a large ice chest was denied any monetary damages on the basis of her own contributory negligence.[189] The court concluded that the member "loses because she was contributorily negligent. [T]he fact is she stepped through a doorway, with her vision at least partially obscured by the ice chest she carried, missed her step, and fell. Reasonable prudence required her to be more careful. . . . She had no right to assume that there was a place to land her foot because she could not see where she was going." The absence of a handrail and the width of the top step in no way contributed to the member's injuries, the court concluded.

Most states have attempted to lessen the severity of the rule denying any recovery to an accident victim who was contributorily negligent through the adoption of *comparative negligence* statutes. Under the so-called pure comparative negligence statutes, accident victims whose contributory negligence was not the sole cause of their injuries may recover damages against another whose negligence was the primary cause of the accident, but their monetary damages are diminished in proportion to the amount of their own negligence. Under a pure comparative negligence statute, victims may recover against a negligent defendant even though their own contributory negligence was equal to or greater than the defendant's negligence.

Many other states have adopted the *equal-to or greater-than rule* or the *fifty-percent rule.* Under these statutes, accident victims whose contributory negligence is equal to or greater than the defendant's negligence are totally barred from recovery. But, accident victims whose contributory negligence is less than the defendant's negligence may recover damages, although their damages are diminished in proportion to the amount of their own negligence.

Other states permit a plaintiff to recover damages for the injuries caused by a negligent defendant if his own contributory negligence was slight in comparison to the negligence of the defendant. To illustrate, a woman was injured when she was struck by a church-owned vehicle that was being driven in a negligent manner. The woman sued the church, and a jury found the church negligent, assessing damages at $300,000. However, the jury also found that 80 percent of the woman's injuries were attributable to her failure to wear a seat belt, and accordingly her damages were reduced by 80 percent (or $240,000) to a total of $60,000. At the trial, the church established that the woman's car had a seat belt. The woman herself testified that she was thankful not to have worn the belt because of her belief that a seat belt would have caused additional injuries.[190]

Example. A Colorado court ruled that a jury erred in finding that a young boy who had been molested by his pastor was partly at fault.[191] The jury found the boy to be 4 percent at fault, and reduced the damages it awarded the boy by this amount under the principle of comparative negligence. The court observed, "Here, there was no evidence that would support a finding that the minor unreasonably subjected himself to the risks associated with [the pastor's] counseling. The minor was only seven when he entered counseling, and he continued to see [the pastor] until the time he entered middle school. He entered into the counseling relationship only at [the pastor's] behest and at his mother's direction. Indeed, there was testimony from both the minor and the mother that he was often quite reluctant to see [the pastor] and had to be persuaded to do so. The minor also testified that [the pastor] told him that the counseling was confidential and that the minor should not discuss with others the contents of their sessions. Finally, [the victim's] expert opined that, in situations involving the abuse of a child by an adult in a position of trust, it is common for the child not to report it to others. The church offered no testimony to contradict this view, nor did it offer any testimony respecting the reasonable standard of

[189] Richard v. Church Insurance Company, 538 So.2d 658 (La. App. 1989).
[190] Smith v. Holy Temple Church of God in Christ, Inc., 566 So.2d 864 (Fla. App. 1990). The ruling was reversed on appeal on the basis of a technicality.
[191] DeBose v. Bear Valley Church of Christ, 890 P.2d 214 (Colo. App. 1994).

conduct of a child of the minor's age in such circumstances. We conclude, therefore, that the evidence failed to establish, as a matter of law, any negligence on the part of the minor."

§ 10-16.2 — Assumption of Risk

Key point 10-16.2. *Adults who voluntarily expose themselves to a known risk created by a church program or activity generally cannot sue the church if they are injured as a result of that risk.*

Persons who voluntarily expose themselves to a known danger or to a danger that was so obvious that it should have been recognized will be deemed to have assumed the risks of their conduct. As a result, persons who voluntarily expose themselves to the negligent conduct of a defendant with full knowledge of the danger will be barred from recovery for any injuries resulting from the defendant's negligence. Assumption of risk is closely related to contributory negligence. One court has distinguished the two by noting that assumption of risk connotes "venturousness," whereas contributory negligence connotes a state of carelessness.[192] To illustrate, one court ruled that an adult church member who was seriously injured when he slipped and fell on a wet linoleum floor immediately following his baptism by immersion could sue his church if the church knew or should have known that the floor presented an unreasonable risk of harm. However, the court concluded that the church's negligence might be superseded by the victim's own negligence in carelessly exposing himself to a known hazard.[193]

Example. An Illinois court ruled that a church board member who was seriously injured when he fell off a ladder while installing a ceiling fan in the church was barred from recovering any damages because of his assumption of a known risk.[194] The court observed, "[I]t is well-established that a landowner is not liable for injuries resulting from open and obvious dangers on the premises, including the open and obvious danger of falling from high places. We determine that [the board member's] attempt to install the ceiling fans in the church's high ceiling by positioning his ladder in the church pews was an open and obvious danger, and his injuries are therefore not recoverable . . . ."

Example. The Kansas Supreme Court ruled that a minor who had been rendered a quadriplegic as a result of injuries sustained while playing football for a church-operated high school could not sue the church.[195] "We feel sympathy for the severe injuries suffered by this plaintiff," concluded the court. "However, there are dangers and risks inherent in the game of football and those who play the game encounter these risks voluntarily."

---

[192] Cross v. Noland, 190 S.E.2d 18 (W. Va. 1972).

[193] Huston v. First Church of God, 732 P.2d 173 (Wash. App. 1987).

[194] Coates v. W.W. Babcock Co., 560 N.E.2d 1099 (Ill. App. 1990). However, the court concluded that the board member had presented enough evidence to sue the church for a violation of the state "Structural Work Act," which protects any person employed or engaged on a ladder while undertaking the repair of a building. The court ordered the case to proceed to trial on this basis.

[195] Wicina v. Strecker, 747 P.2d 167 (Kan. 1987). *But see* Locilento v. John A. Coleman Catholic High School, 523 N.Y.S.2d 198 (1987), in which a New York court concluded that voluntary participation in an athletic contest, without more, amounts to only an implied assumption of risk that is not a complete bar to recovery in the event of an accident. It is, however, a factor to be considered in assessing fault.

§ 10-16.3 — Intervening Cause

Key point 10-16.3. A church is not legally responsible for an injury that occurs on its premises or in the course of one of its activities if the injury resulted from the intervention of a new and independent cause that was unforeseeable.

Many courts have ruled that a person's negligence is not the legal cause of an injury that results from the intervention of a new and independent cause that is (1) neither anticipated nor reasonably foreseeable, (2) not a consequence of his or her negligence, (3) not controlled by him or her, and (4) the actual cause of the injury in the sense that the injury would not have occurred without it. If an intervening cause meets these conditions, it is considered a "superseding" cause that eliminates the original wrongdoer's liability.

To illustrate, a superseding, intervening cause was found to have insulated the original wrongdoer from liability for his negligence in the following situations: a bus driver ran a stop sign, causing a car approaching from an intersecting street to abruptly stop, resulting in the car being struck by another car that had been following it too closely;[196] a motorist's negligent driving resulted in a collision with a second vehicle, and a third motorist, whose attention was distracted by the scene of the accident, struck a pedestrian;[197] and a motorist's negligent operation of his automobile caused an accident, and a police officer investigating the scene of the accident was injured when struck by another vehicle being operated in a negligent manner.[198]

Example. A Georgia court ruled that a public school was not legally responsible for the murder of a child who was released by school officials prior to the end of the school day.[199] While the case involved a school, it is directly relevant to churches as well. The school had a written policy addressing early dismissals of students. The policy specified that no student could be released prior to the end of the school day without the consent of a parent. On the day of the murder, the school received two calls from a person with a male voice requesting that the victim be released early. The caller was informed that this was not possible without the consent of a parent. A short time later the school received a call from a person identifying herself as the victim's mother. This person requested that the victim be released early due to a "family emergency." A school secretary authorized the early release of the victim based on this call, and on her way home the victim was abducted and murdered. The victim's parents sued the school, claiming that it was responsible for their daughter's death as a result of its negligent supervision. A state appeals court ruled that the school was not liable for the girl's death. The court conceded that the school may have been negligent, but it concluded that this negligence was not the cause of the girl's death. Rather, the death was caused by an unforeseeable "intervening cause"—the criminal activity of an outsider— which relieved the school from liability. The court observed, "Generally, an intervening criminal act of a third party, without which the injury would not have occurred, will also be treated as the [cause] of the injury thus breaking the causal connection between the defendant's negligence and the injury unless the criminal act was a reasonably foreseeable consequence of the defendant's conduct." The court noted that (1) school officials had no reason to suspect that the murderer posed a risk of harm to the victim; (2) school officials were aware of no threats ever directed to the victim by the murderer or anyone else; (3) no student had ever before been abducted or assaulted after being released before the end of the school day; and (4) the victim expressed no concern for her safety. Based on this evidence, the court concluded that "it was not foreseeable that [the victim] would be murdered after being released from school early." The

---

[196] Seeger v. Weber, 113 N.W.2d 566 (Wis. 1962).
[197] Lewis v. Esselman, 539 S.W.2d 581 (Mo. 1976).
[198] Schrimsher v. Bryson, 130 Cal. Rptr. 125 (1976).
[199] Perkins v. Morgan County School District, 476 S.E.2d 592 (Ga. App. 1996).

court concluded that even if the school had been negligent in properly supervising the victim, its negligence "did nothing more than give rise to the occasion which made her injuries possible." The murder was caused by the intervening criminal act.

Example. *The New York Court of Appeals court ruled that a school was liable on the basis of negligent supervision for the rape of a 12-year-old girl that occurred when she left a school outing without permission.[200] A lower court ruled that the school was not responsible for the victim's injuries. It concluded that even if the school had negligently supervised the outing it could not be responsible for the victim's injuries since "the unforeseeable conduct of [the two rapists] constituted a superseding tortious act that absolved the [school] of any culpability for [the victim's] injuries." The victim appealed this decision, and the state's highest court reversed the lower court's decision and ruled in favor of the victim. The court concluded, "[W]e cannot say that the intervening act of rape was unforeseeable as a matter of law. A rational jury hearing the trial testimony could have determined, as the jury did in this case, that the foreseeable result of the danger created by [the school's] alleged lack of supervision was injury such as occurred here. A [jury] could have reasonably concluded that the very purpose of the school supervision was to shield vulnerable schoolchildren from such acts of violence. As we have previously recognized, when the intervening, intentional act of another is itself the foreseeable harm that shapes the duty imposed, the defendant who fails to guard against such conduct will not be relieved of liability when that act occurs."*

§ 10-16.4 — Statutes of Limitations

Key point 10-16.4. *The statute of limitations specifies the deadline for filing a civil lawsuit. Lawsuits cannot be brought after this deadline has passed. There are a few exceptions that have been recognized by some courts: (1) The statute of limitations for injuries suffered by a minor begins to run on the minor's 18th birthday. (2) The statute of limitations does not begin to run until an adult survivor of child sexual molestation "discovers" that he or she has experienced physical or emotional suffering as a result of the molestation. (3) The statute of limitations does not begin to run until an adult with whom a minister or church counselor has had sexual contact "discovers" that his or her psychological damages were caused by the inappropriate contact. (4) The statute of limitations is suspended due to fraud or concealment of a cause of action.*

1. In General

Statutes of limitation specify the deadline for filing a civil lawsuit. Most states have several of these statutes, with each pertaining to designated kinds of claims. For example, there often are different statutes of limitation for bringing contract, personal injury, and property damage claims, with different deadlines for each kind of claim. Persons who do not file a lawsuit by the deadline specified by law generally have no legal recourse.

2. Extending the Statute of Limitations—Injuries to Minors

The statute of limitations does not begin to "run" in the case of injuries to a minor until the minor's eighteenth birthday. To illustrate, if the statute of limitations for personal injuries is 3 years in a particular state, and a minor is injured in an automobile accident, the minor has until his or her twenty-first birthday to

---

[200] Bell v. Board of Education, 687 N.Y.S.2d 1325 (A.D. 1997).

file a lawsuit seeking damages. The 3-year statute of limitations period begins to run on the minor's eighteenth birthday.

> **Example.** *A 4-year-old child is molested by a volunteer worker at church. The statute of limitations for personal injuries is 3 years. The child has until her twenty-first birthday to file a lawsuit seeking damages for her injuries—a period of nearly 17 years.*

> **Key point.** *Some states have enacted special statutes of limitation for victims of child molestation, and these supersede the statute of limitations for personal injuries.*

3. Extending the Statute of Limitations—the "Discovery Rule"

Some states have adopted, either through legislation or court decision, a limited exception to the statute of limitations known as the discovery rule. Under this rule, the statute of limitations does not begin to run until a person realizes that his or her injuries were caused by a particular event or condition. The discovery rule has been applied most often in the following three contexts:

(1) Medical malpractice. In some cases, medical malpractice is difficult if not impossible to recognize until after the statute of limitations has expired. To illustrate, if a surgeon inadvertently leaves a scalpel in a patient's body during an operation, and the patient does not discover this fact until after the statute of limitations for medical malpractice has expired, he should not be denied his day in court. Under the discovery rule, the statute of limitations begins to run not when the malpractice occurred, but when the patient knew or should have known of it.

(2) Child molestation. Some courts have applied the discovery rule in cases of child molestation. These courts have concluded that young children may "block out" memories of molestation, and not recall what happened for many years. The statute of limitations does not begin to run until the victim's eighteenth birthday, or until the victim knew or should have known that his or her emotional or physical injuries were caused by the acts of molestation. Courts that have applied this rule generally have limited it to victims who were very young at the time of the molestation. Adults who claim that they repressed memories of molestation occurring when they were adolescents have had a very difficult time convincing juries that they are telling the truth.

(3) Seduction of adult counselees. Some courts have applied the discovery rule in cases of sexual contact between a minister and an adult counselee. These courts have concluded that adults who engage in such acts with a minister may attempt to repress their memory of them, or be so intimated by the authority of the minister that they lack the capacity to file a lawsuit.

> **Key point.** *The discovery rule presents extraordinary difficulties for a church that is sued as a result of an alleged incident of sexual misconduct that occurred many years ago. In some cases, church leaders cannot even remember the alleged wrongdoer, much less the precautions that were followed in selecting or supervising this person. Because of these difficulties, a majority of states have rejected the discovery rule, or interpreted it very narrowly.[201]*

---

[201] *See, e.g.,* Tichenor v. Roman Catholic Church, 32 F.3d 953 (5th Cir. 1994) (applying Mississippi law); Cherepski v. Walters, 913 S.W.2d 761 (Ark. 1996); Hertel v. Sullivan, 633 N.E.2d 36 (Ill. App. 1994).

Example. The Supreme Court of Alabama ruled that the statute of limitations prevented an adult from suing a church for damages he allegedly suffered as a minor when he was molested by a priest.[202] The victim asserted that he was unaware that his emotional problems were associated with the abuse until he met with a counselor as an adult. He filed a lawsuit within the next year—some fifteen years after the last act of abuse. The victim sued the church, claiming that it was responsible for his injuries on the basis of negligent hiring and supervision of the priest, and breach of a fiduciary duty. The statute of limitations on such claims is two years under Alabama law, beginning when the victim reaches age eighteen. Since that period had long expired before the victim filed his lawsuit, he claimed that the statute of limitations should be suspended until he first became aware that his problems resulted from the abuse. The victim insisted that he suffered from a "post traumatic stress disorder" that caused him to repress all memory of the abuse until he saw a counselor. A court refused to suspend the statute of limitations, and ruled that the victim's claims against the church had to be dismissed since they were filed too late. It began its opinion by noting that "the controversial question of repressed memory of childhood sexual abuse has been the subject of numerous studies" and that a review of these studies "leads to one conclusion—there is no consensus of scientific thought in support of the repressed memory theory." The court acknowledged that "insanity" may suspend the statute of limitations in some cases, but it rejected the victim's claim that his post traumatic stress disorder and repressed memory qualified as insanity. The court noted that most other courts have reached this same conclusion. It observed, "At its core, the statute of limitations advances the truth-seeking function of our justice system, promotes efficiency by giving plaintiffs an incentive to timely pursue claims, and promotes stability by protecting defendants from stale claims. The essence of the [victim's] claim is that plaintiffs should be able to [suspend the statute of limitations] in any situation where they can demonstrate an inability to comprehend a specific legal right, or to recall events that happened many years before, notwithstanding the fact that they have been capable of living an independent, normal, and productive life as to all other matters. Such an expansive interpretation would undermine the purpose of the statute of limitations." The court noted that allowing alleged victims to sue for incidents of child abuse many years after the statute of limitations ordinarily would have expired would put them "in subjective control" and raise the risk of allowing persons to "assert stale claims without sufficient justification or sufficient guaranties of accurate fact-finding."

Example. A federal court in Connecticut dismissed a lawsuit brought against a church and diocese by two adults who had been sexually molested by a priest when they were minors.[203] The church and diocese insisted that the negligence claims against them were barred by the statute of limitations. They pointed out that negligence claims under Connecticut law must be brought within two years from the date when the injury is first sustained or discovered, but in no event more than three years from the date of the negligent conduct. The court noted that another Connecticut statute specifies that "no action to recover damages for personal injury to a minor, including emotional distress caused by sexual abuse, sexual exploitation or sexual assault may be brought by such person later than seventeen years from the date such person attains the age of majority." The court concluded that this seventeen year statute applied, and that the brothers' lawsuit was filed before seventeen years had elapsed since their eighteenth birthdays.

Example. A court in the District of Columbia ruled that three adults were barred by the statute of limitations from suing an archdiocese for injuries they suffered as a result of being molested by a priest

---

[202] Travis v. Ziter, 681 So.2d 1348 (Ala. 1996).

[203] Nutt v. Norwich Roman Catholic Diocese, 921 F. Supp. 66 (D. Conn. 1995). *See also* Martinelli v. Bridgeport Roman Catholic Diocese, 989 F. Supp. 110 (D. Conn. 1997).

when they were minors.[204] The victims alleged that they had no reason to suspect negligent hiring or retention of the priest until they read a series of articles in a local newspaper when they were in their thirties. The victims insisted that the so-called "discovery rule" applied to their claims and that the archdiocese's "fraudulent concealment" of its wrongdoing delayed the statute of limitations until the publication of the newspaper articles. The appeals court concluded that the statute of limitations barred the victims' claims whether the discovery rule was applied or not. It noted that under both the general rule and the discovery rule exception, the statute of limitations begins to run when a plaintiff either has actual knowledge of a cause of action or is charged with knowledge of that cause of action. The court observed that in the District of Columbia, a plaintiff can be charged with notice of his claims "even if he is not actually aware of each essential element of his cause of action. This court has repeatedly held that a claim accrues when the plaintiff knows of (1) an injury, (2) its cause, and (3) some evidence of wrongdoing." The court concluded that "[a]ccording to their complaints, all three [victims] were aware from the outset that it was the archdiocese that had assigned [the priest] to [their church] and that [the priest's] role was that of a subordinate representative of the archdiocese. It is also undisputed that the alleged acts of abuse occurred on church premises, while [the priest] was functioning as a representative of the archdiocese. In these circumstances, we conclude that a reasonable plaintiff would have investigated his potential claims against the archdiocese at the same time that his claims accrued against its representative. Because there is no evidence of fraudulent concealment by the archdiocese, a reasonably diligent investigation would have revealed at least some evidence of wrongdoing on the part of the archdiocese (assuming arguendo that such wrongdoing had occurred). Consequently, we hold that appellants' claims against the archdiocese accrued simultaneously with their claims against the priest." The court rejected the victims' claim that the statute of limitations should be suspended because of the actions of the archdiocese in concealing from them its responsibility for their injuries. The court conceded that when the party claiming the protection of the statute of limitations has employed "affirmative acts . . . to fraudulently conceal either the existence of a claim or facts forming the basis of a cause of action," such conduct will suspend the statute. But it concluded that the archdiocese did not engage in concealment, noting that "we are unwilling to hold that a failure to disclose information that has not even been requested constitutes fraudulent concealment."

Example. *A Florida court ruled that a 27-year-old man who had been molested by a priest when he was a minor was barred by the statute of limitations from suing his church.[205] The court agreed with the church and bishop that the victim's lawsuit was barred by the statute of limitations. The court noted that the victim was suing the church and bishop for negligence in the hiring and retention of the priest. Under Florida law, the statute of limitations for negligence lawsuits is four years. Since this period is suspended until a minor plaintiff reaches age eighteen, the victim had until age twenty-two to file a lawsuit against the church and bishop. The victim did not sue until he was twenty-seven, but insisted that the statute of limitations should have been suspended further until he became "aware" of his injuries. The court rejected this argument: "This young man knew the identity of the [priest] and the improper conduct engaged in by the [priest] long before he reached the age of majority. This was sufficient knowledge to file an action against the priest for the wrongful sexual battery committed against him and, again assuming such cause of action is available, against the church and bishop for making such conduct possible because of the negligent retention of the priest. . . . [T]he negligent retention of a priest who would commit child abuse, at least insofar as this young man is concerned, must have occurred while he was still a child. Therefore, when [the victim] turned eighteen, he was aware that a*

---

[204] Cevenini v. Archbishop of Washington, 707 A.2d 768 (D.C. 1998).
[205] Doe v. Dorsey, 683 So.2d 614 (Fl. App. 1996).

priest had sexually abused him and that the church had permitted the priest to serve in the parish which made the abuse possible. Sexual abuse of a child in and of itself causes sufficient actual damages, as a matter of law, to support both the intentional tort action against the priest and the negligence action, if one exists, against the church and the bishop. . . . The fact that [the victim] in this case was not immediately aware of all of his resulting emotional problems might create uncertainty as to the amount of his damages but it does not toll the period of limitations."

Example. *An Indiana state court ruled that the statute of limitations prevented two adult survivors of childhood sexual abuse from suing the ministers who allegedly abused them.[206] In 1960, two girls (8 and 9 years of age) were placed as wards in a children's home affiliated with a church. The girls remained in the home for nearly 9 years. While in the home, the girls were repeatedly molested by an ordained minister who served as activities director. The molestation included repeated acts of sexual intercourse. The minister frequently gave the girls quinine pills which caused severe vomiting, bleeding, and diarrhea, in an effort to induce abortions. The girls also were molested by a second ordained minister who was superintendent of the home. The abuse caused the girls to develop severe psychological distress, which manifested itself in the form of shame, guilt, self-blame, denial, depression, nightmares, and ultimately disassociation from their experiences. Through these coping mechanisms, the girls were unable to comprehend that they suffered damages as a result of the abuse. Thirty years later, in 1990, both girls experienced several "flashbacks" of the abuse. It was at this time that the victims began to realize that many of their nightmares were in fact true. The victims separately confronted the ministers. The former activities director admitted to having molested the girls "hundreds of times." The former superintendent also admitted his acts of abuse. The victims filed a lawsuit against the ministers and the children's home in 1990. The ministers and children's home sought to have the lawsuit dismissed on the ground that the statute of limitations had expired many years before. A state appeals court ruled that the statute of limitations did not prevent the victims from suing, even though the abuse occurred thirty years before. The court acknowledged that the statute of limitations for personal injuries under Indiana law requires lawsuits to be commenced within two years "after the cause of action accrues." It noted that this rule is subject to an exception—the statute of limitations does not begin to run in any case involving personal injury until the victim "knew, or in the exercise of ordinary diligence, could have discovered that an injury had been sustained as a result of the tortious act of another." The court observed, "In the case before us the plaintiffs have asserted both that they had repressed knowledge that a number of the acts had occurred such that they had no memory of the act having happened until 1990, and that while they were aware of other acts and of feelings of guilt, depression, low self-esteem, etc. they were without knowledge of any causative connection between their psychological and personality problems and the alleged molestations until 1990." The court found the victims' allegations of repressed memory sufficient to overcome the statute of limitations. However, it did acknowledge that "what knowledge each [victim] might be charged with based upon the exercise of ordinary care remains a disputed question of fact." That is, the case was sent back to the trial court where the women would have to prove that they in fact could not have known prior to 1990, through the exercise of reasonable care, that they had suffered emotional injuries as a result of the acts of molestation that occurred when they were children.*

Example. *A Kentucky court ruled that a 24-year-old adult was barred by the statute of limitations from suing a priest who allegedly molested him when he was a minor.[207] The court also ruled that the victim was barred from suing his church. The statute of limitations in Kentucky for both battery negli-*

---

[206] Shultz-Lewis Child & Family Services, Inc. v. Doe, 604 N.E.2d 1206 (Ind. App. 1992). See also Doe v. United Methodist Church, 673 N.E.2d 839 (Ind. App. 1996); Konkle v. Henson, 672 N.E.2d 450 (Ind. App. 1996).

[207] Rigazio v. Archdiocese of Louisville, 853 S.W.2d 295 (Ky. App. 1993).

gence is one year. However, under Kentucky law (as is true in most states) the statute of limitations does not begin to run for injuries suffered by a minor until the minor's eighteenth birthday. In other words, the statute of limitations for battery and negligence expired one year after the victim's eighteenth birthday, some six years before the lawsuit was filed. The victim argued that there are certain exceptions to the statute of limitations that applied in this case. First, Kentucky law provides that the statute of limitations is suspended if a person is of "unsound mind" when a cause of action accrues. The victim claimed that he had suffered from post-traumatic stress disorder, and that he had repressed the memory of the abuse until shortly before he filed the lawsuit. The court disagreed, noting that the term "unsound mind" under Kentucky law means that a person has been rendered incapable of managing his or her own affairs and accordingly "[t]he mere fact that [the victim] experienced a repression syndrome is not synonymous with being of unsound mind." Second, the victim claimed that the statute of limitations should not begin to run until he "discovered" his injuries, and this did not occur until the day of his suicide attempt (which occurred less than one year before he filed the lawsuit). The court acknowledged that Kentucky has adopted a "discovery rule" in the context of medical malpractice, but "[n]either the Supreme Court nor the General Assembly has further extended the discovery rule." Further, the court observed, "It should again be noted that at the time [the victim's] cause of action accrued, and for sometime thereafter, he was both aware of the abuse and past the age of reason. The fact that his memory of these events was thereafter suppressed, only to return years later, would not seem to present a circumstance falling within the discovery rule which relates to injuries which cannot be discovered with reasonable diligence."

***Example.** A Louisiana court ruled that the statute of limitations prevented an adult woman from suing a Catholic diocese for a priest's acts of molestation when the woman was a minor.[208] The woman sued the diocese claiming that it was responsible for a priest's molestation of her in 1961 when she was fifteen years of age. The applicable Louisiana statute of limitations for incidents of child abuse is one year beginning on the child's eighteenth birthday. The woman claimed that this period should not begin until she discovered that her emotional suffering was caused by the prior act of molestation. The court declined the woman's request. It concluded, "It is clear to us from the testimony that [the woman] recalled the events giving rise to the [lawsuit against the diocese] and knew that it was wrong for [the priest] to engage in such activities. Although the alleged mental and physical abuse administered to [the woman] while under the control of [the priest] may have affected a clear, precise recollection of specific acts of sexual abuse, [the woman] was admittedly aware and cognizant of the abuse once she was out of the control of [the priest]. However, suit was not filed until . . . some 25 years after [her] last contact with [the priest]." The court also pointed out that the woman discussed with others the possibility of filing a lawsuit more than a year before doing so, and this further demonstrated that she was aware of her injuries more than a year before the lawsuit was filed. The court concluded, "[The woman] clearly remembered the alleged abuses suffered at the hands or direction of [the priest]. She was not unable to act, but chose not to do so and allowed her claim to [lapse]. Sympathy we share for the victim of [the priest's] misconduct. The suffering she endured and will continue to endure as a consequence of his unholy acts warrants retribution. With heavy hearts, however, we must affirm the trial court's judgment [dismissing the case]."*

***Example.** The Maryland Court of Appeals (the highest state court) ruled that an adult's "repression" of memories associated with childhood sexual abuse is not a sufficient basis for suspending or delaying the*

---

[208] Doe v. Roman Catholic Church, 656 So.2d 5 (La. App. 1995). *Accord* J.A.G. v. Schmaltz, 682 So.2d 331 (La. App. 1996); Harrison v. Gore, 660 So.2d 563 (La. App. 1995).

statute of limitations.[209] Two female students at a Catholic high school alleged that they were subjected to severe and repeated acts of sexual molestation by a priest to whom they had been sent for counseling. They alleged that the molestation began when they were in ninth grade and continued all the way up until their graduation. The victims claimed that following their graduation from high school, they "ceased to recall" the abuse due to the process of "repression." It was not until twenty years later, during counseling, that they "recovered" their memories of the abuse. They filed a lawsuit against the priest, their former school, and the archdiocese. A state appeals court ruled that the lawsuit had to be dismissed on the basis of the statute of limitations. Maryland law requires such lawsuits to be filed within three years after a minor attains her eighteenth birthday. The court acknowledged that in some cases the "discovery rule" has been applied—meaning that the statute of limitations does not begin to run until the victim "discovers" that his or her injuries were caused by a particular event. However, the court refused to apply the discovery rule to cases of recovered memories of childhood sexual abuse. It reached the following conclusions: (1) The concept of repression is defined as the selective and involuntary forgetting of information that causes pain. Repressed information is not forgotten, but instead is stored in the unconsciousness and may be recovered at a later time if the anxiety associated with the memory is removed. (2) Several professional studies attempt to validate the concept of repression. (3) Several other professional studies discredit the concept of repression. These studies assert that there is absolutely no scientific evidence to support the claim that repression exists. (4) It is impossible to distinguish between repression and "faking." (5) Since serious disagreement exists within the psychological community regarding the validity of repression theory, it would be inappropriate for a court to recognize it. The court concluded that "we are unconvinced that repression exists as a phenomenon separate and apart from the normal process of forgetting." And, because the discovery rule does not help those who merely forget their injuries or legal claims, it should not help those who claim that their memories were repressed and later recovered.

Example. *A Minnesota court ruled that a woman's lawsuit against a denominational agency for her molestation by a priest when she was a minor was barred by the statute of limitations.[210] The woman claimed that a priest sexually abused her over a period of 11 years beginning when she was 15. As their relationship progressed, the priest expressed to the victim his internal conflict over choosing between his love for her and his love for the church. Throughout their relationship, the victim knew that the priest had taken a vow of celibacy and that his conduct with her was inappropriate. As an adult, the victim learned that the priest was engaging in similar behavior with other women. She met another victim, and they shared their experiences. This information was devastating to the victim. She immediately sought professional counseling and experienced radical personality changes. The victim sued the priest and her archdiocese. A state appeals court ruled that the woman's lawsuit was barred by the statute of limitations. Minnesota law provides that "[a]n action for damages based on personal injury caused by sexual abuse must be commenced within six years of the time the plaintiff knew or had reason to know that the injury was caused by the sexual abuse." The victim claimed that not until she received counseling as an adult did she see the situation clearly and recognize that she had been a victim of abuse. Accordingly, she asserted that the statute of limitations began running when she began counseling. The court rejected the victim's argument on the basis of several facts including the following: the victim was*

---

[209] Doe v. Maskell, 679 A.2d 1087 (Md. 1996). *See also* Doe v. Archdiocese of Washington, 689 A.2d 634 (Md. App. 1997).

[210] ABC & XYZ v. Archdiocese of St. Paul and Minneapolis, 513 N.W.2d 482 (Minn. App. 1994). Accord S.E. v. Shattuck-St. Mary's School, 533 N.W.2d 628 (Minn. App. 1995); M.L. v. Magnuson, 531 N.W.2d 831 (Minn. App. 1995); Roe v. Archbishop of St. Paul and Minneapolis, 518 N.W.2d 629 (Minn. App. 1994). Contra Winkler v. Magnuson, 539 N.W.2d 821 (Minn. App. 1995); Doe v. Redeemer Lutheran Church, 531 N.W.2d 897 (Minn. App. 1995); Blackowiak v. Kemp, 528 N.W.2d 247 (Minn. App. 1995).

aware that priests were unable to marry and must remain celibate; she knew that their relationship violated these rules and therefore she tried to keep their relationship secret; she frequently cried after sexual relations or out of town trips with the priest because she was struggling with the situation; and she informed several friends, and eventually her husband, about the priest's actions. The court concluded that this evidence "establishes overwhelmingly that, under a reasonable person standard, [the victim] should have known . . . that she had been abused as a minor and as an adult."

Example. *A New Mexico court ruled that a Catholic diocese could not be sued by a 33-year-old woman who claimed to have been sexually molested by a priest when she was a minor.[211] The woman alleged that her priest initiated sexual contact with her when she began working in the church office at age 15, and that she had sex with the priest weekly thereafter for the next 4 years. During this time the priest informed the girl that he had a venereal disease. She contracted the disease and sought treatment from her family physician. When she was 18, the girl became pregnant and obtained an abortion. The girl quit attending church and began to experience depression and suicidal tendencies. She saw a psychiatrist at this time, but said nothing of her affair with the priest. While the girl often protested to the priest about their relationship, the relationship persisted until the girl was nearly 21. At this time the girl fell in love with the man she would later marry. The priest became furious when she informed him that they no longer could have a sexual relationship. In several emotional conversations she asked him to continue a nonsexual relationship, but he responded that there would be no friendship without sex. She later testified that terminating the relationship was "hideously painful" for her. When she was 21, the woman saw a psychologist for disabling depression. When she was 33 years old, she began seeing another psychologist to whom she disclosed her relationship with the priest. The psychologist identified the relationship as the source of the woman's severe psychological problems. The woman sued her diocese, church, and the former priest that same year. A trial court dismissed the case on the ground that it was barred by the state "statute of limitations." Under New Mexico law, a lawsuit generally must be brought within 3 years of the date of an injury. The court rejected the woman's argument that the statute of limitations did not begin to run until she "discovered" that her psychological problems were caused by the relationship with the priest, and that this did not occur until she began counseling. The woman appealed, and a state appeals court agreed with the trial court that the lawsuit had been brought too late. The court observed, "[The woman's] acquisition of a venereal disease and her pregnancy leading to an abortion were sufficiently substantial injuries that once she knew that they were caused by [the priest] the [statute of limitations] period would no longer be delayed by the discovery rule." The court concluded, "The limitations period is not tolled simply because a plaintiff does not know the full extent of her injuries; the statute begins to run once she knows or should know the sufficient facts to constitute a cause of action."*

Example. *A federal court in New York refused to find a pastor guilty of malpractice on the basis of his alleged sexual seduction of a church member he had counseled for several years.[212] The court noted that neither the legislature nor the courts of New York had ever recognized clergy malpractice as a basis of legal liability. Further, to do so would violate the first amendment guaranty of religious freedom. The court also refused to hold the pastor's church and denomination liable on the basis of "negligent placement, retention, or supervision" and ruled that the woman's lawsuit was barred by the statute of limitations. It noted that the statute of limitations for negligence and malpractice, under New York law, is 3 years. Since the alleged malpractice first occurred nearly 30 years ago, the woman's claims obviously*

---

[211] Martinez-Sandoval v. Kirsch, 884 P.2d 507 (N.M. App. 1994).

[212] Schmidt v. Bishop, 779 F. Supp. 321 (S.D.N.Y. 1991). *Accord* Bassile v. Covenant House, 575 N.Y.S.2d 233 (Sup. 1991); Gallas v. Greek Orthodox Archdiocese, 587 N.Y.S.2d 82 (Sup. 1989).

were barred by the statute of limitations. The woman attempted to avoid the application of the statute of limitations in three ways, each of which was rejected by the court. First, she asked the court to apply the "delayed discovery" doctrine. By this she meant that the statute of limitations should not start until a person "knows or should have known of the injury and the defendant's role in causing that injury." The court acknowledged that some states have adopted such a rule, particularly in the context of child sexual abuse cases. It noted that "the argument for a delayed discovery rule in this context, simply stated, is that victims of child sexual abuse often do not realize until years later either that they have been abused at all or the scope of their injuries." However, the court rejected this view: "Persuasive though this argument may be, there is not authority for the adoption of such a rule in child sex abuse cases in New York. . . . [The New York courts] have steadfastly declined to alter the traditional New York rule that the statute of limitations commences to run when a cause of action accrues, even though the plaintiff is unaware that he has a cause of action." Next, the woman argued that the pastor should be prohibited from relying on the statute of limitations because of his "misrepresentations." The court agreed that the statute of limitations can be suspended if a party's fraud or "active concealment" prevents a plaintiff from filing a timely claim. However, it disagreed that this rule applied in the present case, since the pastor had done nothing to prevent the woman from filing a timely lawsuit. Third, the woman argued that the statute of limitations should be suspended because she was "under duress." The court rejected this claim as well: "This requirement has been applied strictly; courts confronted by facts which might suggest to the layman that duress is present have routinely refused to apply the doctrine. . . . Indeed, the cases are replete with statements . . . to the effect that the statute begins to run irrespective of whether the party seeking to avoid it has enough courage and independence to resist a hostile influence and assert his rights or not. . . . In light of these authorities, it appears that duress is not an element of [the woman's] claims. Even if it were, it is extremely doubtful whether any reasonable juror could find that [she] was under constant legal duress for a 31-year period, during most of which she lived half a continent away from the [pastor]."

Example. *The Ohio Supreme Court dismissed a lawsuit brought by a 25-year-old man who had been repeatedly molested as a minor by a church choir director.[213] The victim had been molested by his church choir director on nearly 300 occasions over a period of three years when he was between fifteen and eighteen years of age. Shortly after his 25th birthday, the victim filed a lawsuit against the choir director and his church. He alleged that the director was guilty of assault and battery, and that the church had been negligent in the selection and supervision of the choir director. Ohio has a one-year statute of limitations for assault and battery, meaning that a lawsuit alleging assault and battery must be brought within one year following the alleged wrongdoing. Ohio has a two-year statute of limitations for bodily injury resulting from negligence. Obviously, these statutes had expired long before the victim brought his lawsuit. However, the victim insisted that the statutes had not expired since he did not "discover" the nature and extent of his injuries until he sought psychological help shortly before filing his lawsuit. The court disagreed. It observed, "Given the facts of this case, even if this court were to adopt, now or in the future, a rule of discovery for cases of sexual abuse, the rule would not apply to toll the periods of limitations beyond [the victim's] eighteenth birthday. Here, the facts clearly establish that at the time [he] reached the age of majority, [he] knew that he had been sexually abused by [the choir director]. [The choir director] allegedly initiated homosexual conduct with [the victim] on two hundred to three hundred separate occasions without [his] consent. During the period of sexual abuse, [the victim] was fourteen to seventeen years of age. Apparently, the last act of sexual battery occurred just months prior to [the victim's] eighteenth birthday. After graduating from high school, [he] became preoccupied with his sexual identity and suffered from*

---

[213] Doe v. First United Methodist Church, 629 N.E.2d 402 (Ohio 1994).

depression, guilt, anger and anxiety. [He] eventually sought psychological help . . . and told his psychologist of the prior sexual encounters with [the choir director]. . . . [U]pon reaching the age of majority, [the victim] knew that he had been sexually abused, and he knew the identity of the perpetrator. Although [he] may not have discovered the full extent of his psychological injuries . . . the fact that [he] was aware upon reaching the age of majority that he had been sexually abused by [the choir director] was sufficient to trigger the commencement of the statute of limitations . . . ."

Example. *A Pennsylvania court ruled that a 27-year-old adult was barred by the statute of limitations from suing a priest and his church on account of the priest's alleged acts of molestation.*[214] *The victim alleged that the priest had molested him when he was an adolescent on numerous occasions. In explaining the delay in filing the lawsuit, the victim claimed that he did not "become aware" of or discover the psychological and emotional injuries he suffered as a result of the abuse for several years after he became an adult. A trial court dismissed the lawsuit, concluding that it was barred by a Pennsylvania statute of limitations which requires that lawsuits be filed within two years of the date of injury. The victim appealed, arguing that the statute of limitations should not begin to run until the date that he "discovered" that he had been injured by the priest's molestation. A state appeals court disagreed, and refused to apply the "discovery" rule in this case. It observed, "In our view . . . it is perfectly clear that this case does not fall within the extremely limited applicability of the Pennsylvania discovery rule. This is simply not a case where the plaintiff, despite the exercise of objectively measured reasonable diligence, could not know of his injury and its cause within the limitations period. [The victim] admits that he knew the abuse was occurring and who was inflicting it, both when it happened and throughout the eight years after the abuse ended and before appellant sued. What he did not know, i.e., that the physical acts allegedly performed on him by [the priest] were abuse and were causing psychological harm, is not relevant to a discovery rule analysis. . . . [The victim] need not have known that what was happening to him was abuse, i.e., was wrongful, or precisely what type of psychological or emotional harm he would suffer as a result. Once he knew what was happening and who was doing it, he had the duty to investigate these questions and to institute suit within the limitations period. Moreover, the affidavit submitted by [the victim] in opposition to summary judgment . . . clearly reveals that he was aware, if not that he had been abused, nevertheless that something very troubling and extraordinary was happening to him. He states that he felt confused about what [his priest] was doing to him, thought 'something was wrong with me,' and 'felt guilty and sinful.' Clearly, he not only knew all the relevant facts regarding the abuse and the abuser, but he also knew that something was very wrong with the situation in which he found himself. . . . [The victim] did recognize that something was amiss, and although he allegedly blamed himself for these feelings, that alone does not relieve him of the duty to investigate and bring suit within the limitations period."*

Example. *A Texas court ruled that a 23-year-old male who was molested by a church music director when he was a minor was barred by a two-year statute of limitations from suing his church.*[215] *The court noted that under the applicable statute of limitations the victim had to bring a lawsuit no later than two years after the date his cause of action accrued. The court noted that in general a cause of action "accrues" when a wrongful act causes a legal injury, even if the injury is not "discovered" until later. However, the statute of limitations does not begin to "run" for a person who was a minor at the time of an injury until his or her eighteenth birthday. Since the victim in this case was a minor when the injuries occurred, he had until his twentieth birthday to file a lawsuit. And, since he did not file his*

---

[214] E.J.M. v. Archdiocese of Philadelphia, 622 A.2d 1388 (Pa. Super. 1993).
[215] Marshall v. First Baptist Church, 949 S.W.2d 504 (Tex. App. 1997).

lawsuit until he was twenty-three years old, his claims were barred by the statute of limitations. The court noted that the discovery rule does not apply unless "the alleged wrongful act and resulting injury were inherently undiscoverable at the time they occurred." The court did not believe that this requirement was met in this case: "Whether or not [the victim] made the complicated connection between the church's conduct and his psychological condition is of no moment because neither the wrongful acts nor the injuries asserted in this case are inherently undiscoverable. In fact, both had rather obvious manifestations long before the limitations period expired. Moreover [the victim] does not argue that he was unaware of the wrongful acts. In addition, he does not contend he was unaware of the psychological and emotional injuries which resulted from those acts. Because [he] was clearly aware of both the wrongful acts and the injury in this case, the [discovery rule does not apply]." The court also rejected the victim's argument that the church's conduct constituted a "continuing tort." Specifically, the victim alleged that because the church failed to report his abuse to the civil authorities, it violated the state's child abuse reporting law. The victim insisted that each day church officials failed to report the abuse constituted "a new wrongful act," initiating a new limitations period. The court disagreed, noting that "the statute only creates a duty to report the abuse or neglect of a child. Thus, the church's duty to report the molestation of [the victim] no longer existed as of the day he turned eighteen."

Example. *A federal court in Vermont ruled that an adult who claimed to have been sexually abused by a nun some 40 years earlier could sue a Catholic diocese for his alleged injuries.[216] An adult male (the plaintiff) began receiving intensive psychotherapy for what he alleges were severe emotional problems. As a result of this therapy, the plaintiff claimed that he discovered he was the victim of "childhood sexual abuse, physical abuse and psychological abuse" allegedly occurring forty years ago when he was a resident of a church orphanage. The plaintiff filed a lawsuit against "Sister Jane Doe," the alleged perpetrator (whose identity was unknown) and various religious organizations allegedly responsible for hiring and supervising Sister Jane Doe. The plaintiff alleged in his lawsuit that he had "used all due diligence, given the nature, extent, and severity of his psychological injuries and the circumstances of their infliction, to discover the fact that he has been injured by the sexual abuse." The diocese urged the court to dismiss the case on the ground that the statute of limitations had expired long before. Under Vermont law, when a plaintiff sues to recover damages for injuries "suffered as a result of childhood sexual abuse," the lawsuit must be brought within "six years of the act alleged to have caused the injury or condition, or six years of the time the victim discovered that the injury or condition was caused by that act, whichever period expires later." The diocese claimed that since the alleged abuse occurred over forty years ago it is reasonable to assume that the plaintiff should have discovered the cause of his injuries long ago. It also argued that forcing it to defend against an alleged injury occurring so long ago violates the very purpose of a statute of limitations—relieving defendants of the difficult if not impossible task of defending against such claims. The court rejected these arguments, and ruled that the statute of limitations had not expired on any of the plaintiff's claims (except for assault and battery, which the court deemed to be unrelated to childhood sexual abuse). The court observed that under Vermont law, the test is when the plaintiff in fact discovered that his injuries were caused by childhood abuse, and not when he reasonably could have made this discovery.*

Example. *A Washington state court ruled that the statute of limitations prevented an adult male from suing his church and a denominational agency for injuries he suffered as a child when he was molested by his pastor.[217] The court noted that under Washington law the victim had until his twenty-first*

---

[216] Barquin v. Roman Catholic Diocese, 839 F. Supp. 275 (D. Vt. 1993).
[217] E.R.B. v. Church of God, 950 P.2d 29 (Wash. App. 1998). See also Funkhouser v. Wilson, 950 P.2d 501 (Wash. App. 1998).

birthday to sue the church and denominational agency for the sexual abuse that occurred while he was a minor. Since the lawsuit was not filed until the victim was twenty-two, it was filed too late. The court noted that even if it applied the discovery rule, the lawsuit was still filed too late: "The common law discovery rule would not apply to [the victim's] claims against the local church and the state office because the record clearly shows, and the trial court so found, that while still a minor [he] clearly knew the facts of the abuse relevant to establish a claim. . . . [He] knew he was being sexually molested by [his pastor]. . . . He knew the molestation was wrong, knew it was causing him substantial harm, as he attempted suicide." The court conceded that the statute of limitations may be suspended or postponed when "plaintiffs could not have immediately known of their injuries due to . . . concealment of information by the defendant." The victim's parents claimed that the statute of limitations did not begin to run on their claims until their son told them the pastor had molested him. The parents argue that before this conversation they could not have learned of their cause of action. The court disagreed, noting that while there was substantial evidence that the pastor concealed important information from the parents and from the church, "there is no evidence that the local church or the state office concealed anything from the [parents]."

Example. *The Wisconsin Supreme Court ruled that the statute of limitations prevented a woman from suing a Catholic archdiocese for the alleged acts of molestation by a priest nearly 40 years before.[218] The woman claimed that the priest entered into a sexual relationship with her when she was a high school student, and that as a result of the priest's behavior she "has suffered and continues to suffer from severe emotional distress, causing and contributing to the break-up of her marriage, separation from her children, loss of jobs and other difficulties." The court began its opinion by noting that the applicable statute of limitations in this case was 3 years. It ruled that the woman filed her lawsuit after this period of time expired, even if the so-called "discovery rule" were applied. Under the discovery rule, the statute of limitations does not begin to run until the victim discovers that his or her injuries were caused by the misconduct of a particular person or organization. The woman in this case argued that she had "suppressed and been unable to perceive the existence, nature or cause of her psychological and emotional injuries" until she sought the assistance of a professional counselor. Therefore, she claimed that her lawsuit was not barred by the statute of limitations. The court concluded that the discovery rule did not help the woman in this case, since the woman by her own admission knew the identity of the priest and was aware of the conduct of the priest. The court pointed out that under the discovery rule the statute of limitations begins to run when a person "has sufficient evidence that a wrong has indeed been committed by an identified person." The court further observed that extending the discovery rule to this case would cause unfairness to a defendant who is forced to attempt to defend a suit for emotional and psychological injuries in which the alleged conduct took place over 40 years ago.*

4. EXTENDING THE STATUTE OF LIMITATIONS—FRAUD AND OTHER GROUNDS

Some courts have permitted the statute of limitations to be suspended in limited circumstances, including fraud or the "active concealment" of the existence of a civil claim by a wrongdoer.

Example. *A Georgia court dismissed a lawsuit brought by a woman against her church and a denominational agency as a result of injuries she allegedly sustained during a sexual relationship with her pastor.[219] The court concluded that the woman's claims were barred by the statute of limitations. The*

---

[218] Pritzlaff v. Archdiocese of Milwaukee, 533 N.W.2d 780 (Wis. 1995). *Accord* Joseph W. v. Catholic Diocese, 569 N.W.2d 795 (Wis. App. 1997); Doe v. Archdiocese of Milwaukee, 565 N.W.2d 94 (Wis. 1997).

[219] Alpharetta First United Methodist Church v. Stewart, 473 S.E.2d 532 (Ga. App. 1996).

woman had two years to file her lawsuit under the Georgia statute of limitations, yet the lawsuit was not filed for nearly three years after the pastor left the church to accept a new assignment. The court also noted that the woman admitted that for more than two years prior to the time the lawsuit was filed she had progressed in her therapy to the point where she was able to tell the associate pastor "no" if he approached her about sexual relations. The court concluded that any acts of sexual intercourse occurring after this time were by her own admission consensual. The court rejected the couple's argument that the statute of limitations was "suspended" due to the woman's depression, noting that "this is not evidence of incompetency sufficient to toll the statute of limitation."

Example. *A Kentucky court ruled that an adult who had been sexually molested as a minor by a teacher at a parochial school could sue the diocese that operated the school for negligent hiring, supervision, and retention. The victim never reported the incidents nor discussed them with anyone until he was 32 years old. It was at that time that he learned from television reports that the teacher had sexually abused other students. These reports brought back memories of his own abuse, and he was hospitalized three days for emotional trauma several months after the programs aired. The programs also prompted him to have several conversations with the diocese concerning the incidents and how they could have occurred. A criminal investigation resulted in the teacher being arrested and convicted of twenty-eight counts of sexual abuse of minors, as well as the filing of several civil suits by the victim and others. The diocese asked the trial court to dismiss the lawsuit on the ground that it was barred by the statute of limitations since it had been brought some seventeen years after the teacher's last act of molestation. The victim insisted that his lawsuit was filed on time due to the "discovery rule," and the fact that the diocese "fraudulently concealed" relevant information. Kentucky law specifies that a personal injury action must be commenced within one year "after the cause of action accrued." Generally, a cause of action is said to accrue when the injury occurs. However, in certain cases, a cause of action does not necessarily accrue when the injury occurs, but rather when the plaintiff first discovers the injury or should have reasonably discovered it. However, the court declined to apply the discovery rule to repressed memories of child molestation. It noted that the victim had not alleged memory loss but was well aware of his injury. Kentucky law also specifies that the statute of limitations is extended during the time that one party through concealment or otherwise "obstructs the prosecution" of a lawsuit. The victim claimed that the diocese should be barred from relying on the statute of limitations due to its failure to report the teacher's multiple acts of child abuse to the authorities, as well as its failure to inform students, faculty, and staff of the teacher's behavior. The diocese vigorously disagreed. It insisted that concealment alone is not enough to suspend the statute of limitations. Rather, the concealment must mislead or deceive the plaintiff so that he or she is lulled into inaction or is otherwise obstructed from investigating or instituting a lawsuit during the limitations period. The court noted that the diocese knew prior to the time when the victim was abused that the teacher had sexually abused students and would continue to be "a problem" and continued to receive reports of his sexually abusing students during at least part of the time period in which the victim was being abused. Nevertheless, the diocese took no action to discipline or sanction him, to inform other students, parents, or employees, or to report the incidents to state authorities. The information was kept secret and confidential in a personnel file, and the victim had no idea that the diocese had prior knowledge of the teacher's propensities until he watched the television programs. Until that time, the victim neither knew nor had reason to know that he had a potential cause of action against the diocese for causing injury to him due to its concealment of its knowledge of the teacher's actions toward other students. The court concluded, "The diocese clearly obstructed the prosecution of [the victim's] cause of action against it by continually concealing the fact that it had knowledge of [the teacher's] problem well before the time [the victim] was abused as well as the fact that it continued to receive reports of sexual abuse of other students during part of the time period in which* *[the victim] was abused. Furthermore, where the law imposes a duty of disclosure, a failure of disclosure may constitute concealment . . . ."* The child abuse reporting statute in effect when these incidents occurred imposed a legal duty on *"any person"* to report child abuse to law enforcement authorities. The diocese failed to comply with this duty, *"and such failure constitutes evidence of concealment."*

Example. An Oregon court ruled that a denominational agency was not legally responsible for a priest's acts of child molestation occurring more than twenty years ago.[220] The victim alleged that when he was a minor he was molested on at least twenty occasions by the priest. However, the victim claimed that it was not until nearly twenty years later that he discovered the connection between the molestation and his emotional damages. He sued his archdiocese, claiming that it was legally responsible for the priest's acts on the basis of negligent selection and supervision. The court dismissed all of the victim's negligence claims on the ground that they were barred by the statute of limitations. While Oregon has an *"ex-tended"* statute of limitations that applies to conduct *"knowingly allowing, permitting or encouraging"* child abuse, this statute did not apply in this case since the victim failed to prove that the archdiocese had any prior knowledge of the priest's behavior. The court rejected the victim's claim that the archdio-cese *"knew enough about child abuse in the church generally that it should have known that [the priest in this case] actually presented a risk to children."*

Example. The South Dakota Supreme Court ruled that the statute of limitations for bringing a lawsuit for acts of sexual molestation may be suspended or delayed through *"fraudulent concealment"* by a denominational agency of the incidents.[221] A former altar boy sued a priest and diocese in 1992 for the priest's acts of molestation that occurred over a 17 year period from 1958 through 1975. The victim claimed that it was not until 1991, in the course of counseling, that he realized that he had been a victim of abuse. The court ruled that the statute of limitations would not be a bar to this lawsuit if the diocese fraudulently concealed from the victim the incidents of abuse, since the statute of limitations is *"suspended"* under these circumstances. The court concluded that there was evidence that the diocese fraudulently concealed from the victim information concerning the incidents. It referred to (1) a letter from the offending priest to his bishop responding to accusations made against him by another priest concerning *"young people"*; (2) the victim, before he graduated from high school, bartended parties for the bishop and several priests, and when the offending priest became drunk he would be openly affec-tionate to the victim in front of the other clergy; and (3) the abuse of the victim occurred over a 17 year period of time during which 17 different priests heard confessions regarding the incidents of molestation involving the victim. The court concluded that if the diocese in fact knew of the acts of molestation but did nothing to warn the victim or his family, then this amounted to *"fraudulent concealment"* of the victim's cause of action that suspended the statute of limitations until he in fact discovered that his emotional injuries were caused by the abuse.

§ 10-16.5 — Charitable Immunity

Key point 10-16.5. The legal liability of churches and their officers, directors, and volunteers, is lim-ited by state and federal *"charitable immunity"* laws.

---

[220] Fearing v. Bucher, 936 P.2d 1023 (Or. App. 1997).
[221] Koenig v. Lambert, 527 N.W.2d 903 (S.D. 1995).

In many states, religious organizations are subject to being sued for the negligence of their employees just like any commercial organization.[222] However, the view that religious organizations should be completely immune from liability was once common. It gradually was rejected by all of the states that had adopted it. The principle of total immunity frequently was criticized. One court observed, "Even the most cursory research makes it apparent that there is no ground upon which this doctrine of nonliability has rested . . . that has not been assailed and criticized at length by some other court . . . ."[223]

While the view that charities should be completely immune from civil liability has been rejected, it is important to recognize that charities are given limited immunity under both state and federal law. The major forms of limited immunity are addressed in this section.

1. LIMITED LIABILITY OF UNCOMPENSATED OFFICERS AND DIRECTORS

This form of charitable immunity is addressed in section § 6-08, as well as in the following subsection addressing the limited liability of volunteers.

2. LIMITED LIABILITY OF VOLUNTEERS

Many states have enacted statutes conferring limited liability upon persons who perform uncompensated volunteer work on behalf of a charity.[224] In addition, Congress enacted the federal Volunteer Protection Act[225] in 1997. This legislation provides substantial protection to volunteers who provide services on behalf of churches and other charities. Here is a summary of the Act's provisions:

- *Congressional "findings."* The Act begins with several "findings," including the following:

---

[222] *See generally* E. FISCH, D. REED, & E. SCHACHTER, CHARITIES AND CHARITABLE FOUNDATIONS ch. 25 (1974 and Suppl. 1990) [hereinafter cited as CHARITIES AND CHARITABLE FOUNDATIONS]; Note, *The Quality of Mercy: "Charitable Torts" and Their Continuing Immunity,* 100 HARV. L. REV. 1382 (1987); Annot., *Tort Liability of Nongovernmental Charities—Modern Status,* 25 A.L.R.4th 517 (1983). One authority lists 21 states in which the concept of charitable immunity (for non-hospital charities) has been totally eliminated: *Arizona,* Roman Catholic Church v. Keenan, 243 P.2d 455 (Ariz. 1952); *California,* Malloy v. Fong, 232 P.2d 241 (1951); *Idaho,* Bell v. Presbytery of Boise, 421 P.2d 745 (Ida. 1966); *Illinois,* Gubbe v. Catholic Diocese of Rockford, 257 N.E.2d 239 (Ill. App. 1970); *Indiana,* Sidle v. Majors, 341 N.E.2d 763 (Ind. 1976); *Iowa,* Sullivan v. First Presbyterian Church, 152 N.W.2d 628 (Iowa 1967); *Kansas,* McAtee v. St. Paul's Mission, 376 P.2d 823 (Kan. 1962); *Kentucky,* Sheppard v. Immanual Baptist Church, 353 S.W.2d 212 (Ky. App. 1961); *Louisiana,* Heirs of Fruge v. Blood Services, 506 F.2d 841 (5th Cir. 1975) (applying Louisiana law); *Minnesota,* Geiger v. Simpson Methodist Episcopal Church, 219 N.W. 463 (1928); *Missouri,* Garnier v. St. Andrew Presbyterian Church, 446 S.W.2d 607 (Mo. 1967); *New York,* Rakaric v. Croatian Cultural Club, 430 N.Y.S.2d 829 (1980); *Ohio,* Albritton v. Neighborhood Centers Association, 466 N.E.2d 867 (Ohio 1984); *Oklahoma,* Gable v. Salvation Army, 100 P.2d 244 (Okla. 1940); *Pennsylvania,* Nolan v. Tifereth Israel Synagogue, Inc., 227 A.2d 675 (Pa. 1967); *Rhode Island,* Brown v. Church of the Holy Name of Jesus, 252 A.2d 176 (R.I. 1969); *South Carolina,* Fitzer v. Greater Greenville South Carolina YMCA, 282 S.E.2d 230 (S.C. 1981); *Texas,* Howle v. Camp Amon Carter, 470 S.W.2d 629 (Tex. 1971); *Vermont,* Foster v. Roman Catholic Diocese, 70 A.2d 230 (Vt. 1950); *Washington,* Friend v. Cove Methodist Church, Inc., 396 P.2d 546 (Wash. 1964); *Wisconsin,* Widell v. Holy Trinity Catholic Church, 121 N.W.2d 249 (Wis. 1963). *See generally* Annot., *Tort Liability of Nongovernmental Charities—Modern Status,* 25 A.L.R.4th 517 (1983).

[223] Gable v. Salvation Army, 100 P.2d 244, 246 (Okla. 1940).

[224] *See, e.g.,* ARK. STAT. ANN. §§ 16-120-102 and 16-6-104 (volunteers may be liable to the extent of liability insurance coverage; no volunteer immunity for negligent operation of motor vehicles); KAN. STAT. ANN. § 60-3601 (no immunity to the extent of any liability insurance carried by the volunteer); NEBR. REV. STAT. § 25-21,191 (immunity does not extend to negligent use of a motor vehicle); N.J. REV. STAT. § 2A:53A-7.1; OHIO REV. CODE § 2305.38; S.C. CODE ANN. § 33-56-180; TEX. CIVIL CODE § 84.004 (no immunity for negligent use of motor vehicles, to the extent of available insurance coverage); WIS. STAT. § 181.0670 (no immunity for negligent operation of motor vehicle).

[225] 42 U.S.C. § 14501

(1) the willingness of volunteers to offer their services is deterred by the potential for liability actions against them; (2) as a result, many nonprofit public and private organizations and governmental entities, including voluntary associations, social service agencies, educational institutions, and other civic programs, have been adversely affected by the withdrawal of volunteers from boards of directors and service in other capacities; (3) the contribution of these programs to their communities is thereby diminished, resulting in fewer and higher cost programs than would be obtainable if volunteers were participating . . . (6) due to high liability costs and unwarranted litigation costs, volunteers and nonprofit organizations face higher costs in purchasing insurance, through interstate insurance markets, to cover their activities . . . .

• *Effect on state laws.* Prior to the enactment of the Volunteer Protection Act, many states had enacted similar laws. What is the legal status of these state laws? The Act addresses this question as follows:

This Act preempts the laws of any state to the extent that such laws are inconsistent with this Act, except that this Act shall not preempt any state law that provides additional protection from liability relating to volunteers or to any category of volunteers in the performance of services for a nonprofit organization or governmental entity.

• *Liability protection for volunteers.* The purpose of the Act is to limit the liability of volunteers. This purpose is accomplished through the following provision:

[N]o volunteer of a nonprofit organization . . . shall be liable for harm caused by an act or omission of the volunteer on behalf of the organization or entity if—(1) the volunteer was acting within the scope of the volunteer's responsibilities in the nonprofit organization or governmental entity at the time of the act or omission; (2) if appropriate or required, the volunteer was properly licensed, certified, or authorized by the appropriate authorities for the activities or practice in the State in which the harm occurred, where the activities were or practice was undertaken within the scope of the volunteer's responsibilities in the nonprofit organization or governmental entity; (3) the harm was not caused by willful or criminal misconduct, gross negligence, reckless misconduct, or a conscious, flagrant indifference to the rights or safety of the individual harmed by the volunteer; and (4) the harm was not caused by the volunteer operating a motor vehicle, vessel, aircraft, or other vehicle for which the state requires the operator or the owner of the vehicle, craft, or vessel to—(A) possess an operator's license; or (B) maintain insurance.

• *Definitions.* The Act defines a nonprofit organization to mean "any organization which is described in section 501(c)(3) of the Internal Revenue Code of 1986 and exempt from tax under section 501(a) of such Code and which does not practice any action which constitutes a hate crime," or "any not-for-profit organization which is organized and conducted for public benefit and operated primarily for charitable, civic, educational, religious, welfare, or health purposes and which does not practice any action which constitutes a hate crime . . . ."

The Act defines a *volunteer* as "an individual performing services for a nonprofit organization . . . who does not receive—(A) compensation (other than reasonable reimbursement or allowance for expenses actually incurred); or (B) any other thing of value in lieu of compensation, in excess of $500 per year, and such term includes a volunteer serving as a director, officer, trustee, or direct service volunteer."

• *No effect on a charity's liability.* The Act clarifies that it does not "affect the liability of any nonprofit organization . . . with respect to harm caused to any person." In other words, the limited immunity provided by the Act extends only to volunteers, and not to charities themselves.

• *Punitive damages.* The Act specifies that punitive damages "may not be awarded against a volunteer in an action brought for harm based on the action of a volunteer acting within the scope of the volunteer's responsibilities to a nonprofit organization or governmental entity unless the claimant establishes by clear and convincing evidence that the harm was proximately caused by an action of such volunteer which constitutes willful or criminal misconduct, or a conscious, flagrant indifference to the rights or safety of the individual harmed."

• *Exceptions.* The "immunity" provided by the Act is limited, meaning that it is not absolute. The Act specifies that it confers no immunity upon volunteers whose misconduct (1) is a crime of violence or act of international terrorism for which the volunteer has been convicted in any court; (2) is a hate crime; (3) is a sexual offense, as defined by state law, for which the volunteer has been convicted in any court; (4) is a violation of a federal or state civil rights law; or (5) occurred while the volunteer was under the influence of intoxicating alcohol or any drug at the time of the misconduct.

• *Amount of liability.* In the event that a volunteer is found liable in any civil action, the Act limits the amount of "noneconomic" damages that can be assessed. Noneconomic damages are defined by the Act as "losses for physical and emotional pain, suffering, inconvenience, physical impairment, mental anguish, disfigurement, loss of enjoyment of life, loss of society and companionship, loss of consortium . . . hedonic damages, injury to reputation and all other nonpecuniary losses of any kind or nature." The Act specifies that a volunteer "shall be liable only for the amount of noneconomic loss allocated to that defendant in direct proportion to the percentage of responsibility of that defendant . . . for the harm to the claimant with respect to which that defendant is liable." In other words, if a volunteer is found to be ten percent at fault, he or she cannot be assessed more than ten percent of the noneconomic damages awarded by a jury.

> *Example.* A child drowns during a church youth activity at a lake. The parents of the victim sue the church, and also a volunteer worker who allegedly was negligent. The volunteer received no compensation for her services. She is protected by the federal Volunteer Protection Act, and cannot be liable unless her actions amounted to "criminal misconduct, gross negligence, reckless misconduct, or a conscious, flagrant indifference to the rights or safety of the individual harmed." The Act does not provide the church with any protection.

> *Example.* Same facts as the previous example, except that the volunteer was paid an "honorarium" of $250 each year by the church. The Act only protects uncompensated volunteers, but it defines "uncompensated" to include volunteers who do not receive annual compensation in excess of $500.

> *Example.* A woman sues her church, claiming that an associate pastor to whom she had gone for counseling engaged in inappropriate sexual contact. Because the church has very limited insurance coverage for such a claim, the woman also sues the members of the church board individually. She claims that they were guilty of negligent supervision. The board members are protected from personal liability by the federal Volunteer Protection Act, unless their actions amounted to "criminal misconduct, gross negligence, reckless misconduct, or a conscious, flagrant indifference to the rights or safety of the individual harmed." The Act does not provide the church with any protection.

Example. Same facts as the previous question, except that the church provides the board with a dinner twice each year in recognition of the services they provide. The value of the meals is approximately $50 per year for each board member. The board receives no other form of remuneration. The Act only protects uncompensated volunteers, but it defines "uncompensated" to include volunteers who do not receive annual compensation in excess of $500. The board members clearly meet the definition of uncompensated, and so are protected against personal liability by the Act.

Example. Same facts as the previous example, except that the church pays each board member an honorarium of $1,000 at the end of each year. The board members do not meet the definition of uncompensated, and as a result are not protected by the Act.

Example. A child is molested by a youth worker while at church. The parents sue the church and members of the board. They allege that the board refused to screen volunteer youth workers, despite numerous requests by parents, because they considered it a waste of time. The Act may not protect the board members, since their actions in refusing to implement any procedures for reducing the risk of child molestation may be viewed by a jury as "gross negligence, reckless misconduct, or a conscious, flagrant indifference to the rights or safety of the individual harmed."

Example. A volunteer church worker causes an accident while driving a church vehicle on church business. An occupant of another car is injured. The victim sues the church, and also sues the volunteer individually. The volunteer is not protected by the Act, since the Act does not extend to harm caused by a volunteer operating a motor vehicle.

Example. A church uses a volunteer "lay counselor" to provide counseling services to members of the church. The counselor also provides services to members of the community as an outreach. The counselor is not licensed. A counselee sues the church and counselor, claiming that she was injured by the counselor's services. The counselor is not protected by the Act if she was required to be licensed by the state to engage in the counseling services she provided.

3. Injuries to beneficiaries

Some states immunize religious organizations from liability for the negligence of agents and employees committed against "beneficiaries" of the organization.[226] This view ordinarily is based upon one of the following grounds: (1) the funds of religious organizations are held in trust for charitable purposes and may not be diverted to the payment of damages; (2) the misconduct of employees should not be imputed to a religious organization when their services are for the benefit of humanity and not for the economic gain of the organization that employs them; (3) a religious organization is engaged in work highly beneficial to the state and to humanity, and its funds should not be diverted from this important purpose to the payment of damages; or, (4) those accepting the benefits of a religious organization implicitly agree not to hold it liable for injuries that they may receive at the hands of its employees.[227]

To illustrate, a woman who visited a church to view the sanctuary and its stained-glass windows was deemed to be a beneficiary of the church and therefore incapable of recovering damages for injuries she

---

[226] *See generally* Charities and Charitable Foundations, supra note 222, at ch. 25; Annot., 25 A.L.R.2d 29 (1952); Bader v. United Orthodox Synagogue, 172 A.2d 192 (Conn. 1961); Parks v. Holy Angels Church, 70 N.W.2d 97 (Neb. 1955); Egerton v. R. E. Lee Memorial Church, 395 F.2d 381 (4th Cir. 1968) (applying Virginia law).

[227] Egerton v. R.E. Lee Memorial Church, 273 F. Supp. 834 (W.D. Va. 1967), *aff'd*, 395 F.2d 381 (4th Cir. 1968).

suffered in the church.[228] Other examples of beneficiaries include a church Sunday school teacher,[229] a non-member who attended a church social,[230] a member of a Girl Scout troop that met on church property,[231] a person attending a religious service,[232] and a guest at a church wedding.[233]

Example. A New Jersey court ruled that a state "charitable immunity" law prevented a church from being sued by the family of a boy who was injured seriously while attending a church day camp.[234] A church operated a summer day camp for grade school children that was designed to "integrate biblical truth into the lives of children through formal teaching and informal activities such as crafts and games." A boy was injured while participating in a camp activity. Though his parents had registered him in the camping program, neither the parents nor the boy attended the church or had any other contact with it. The parents sued the church, alleging that their son's injuries were caused by the church's negligence. The church asked the court to dismiss the lawsuit against it on the basis of a state "charitable immunity" law that prevented charitable organizations from being sued on the basis of negligence by "beneficiaries" of their charitable activities. The New Jersey statute specifies: "No nonprofit corporation . . . organized exclusively for religious, charitable [or] educational . . . purposes shall . . . be liable to respond in damages to any person who shall suffer damage from the negligence of any agent or servant of such corporation . . . where such person is a beneficiary, to whatever degree, of the works of such nonprofit corporation . . . ." The trial court rejected the church's request to dismiss the case, and the church appealed. A state appeals court agreed with the church that the charitable immunity statute prevented the victim's parents from suing the church, and accordingly it dismissed the lawsuit against the church. The court observed that the statute provides legal immunity to nonprofit organizations with respect to injuries caused to their "beneficiaries" by their agents or representatives. The court concluded that these two requirements were satisfied in this case. Clearly, the church was a nonprofit religious organization. And second, the victim was a beneficiary. The court reasoned that one is a beneficiary who participates in an activity of a charity that furthers its charitable objectives. Since the victim was participating in a camp that existed to further the religious objectives of the church, he was a beneficiary of the church and therefore could not sue it on the basis of its alleged negligence.

Example. A Maryland appeals court reaffirmed that state's adherence to the charitable immunity doctrine, and as a result dismissed a lawsuit against a charitable organization seeking money damages for its alleged negligence.[235] An adult was injured during a basketball game at a Jewish Community Center. He sued the center alleging that its negligent supervision of the game resulted in his injury. The center claimed that it was immune from liability as a result of the state's charitable immunity law. A state appeals court agreed with the charity and dismissed the lawsuit. It began its opinion by observing that Maryland has long recognized the doctrine of charitable immunity. While the state legislature enacted a statute permitting charities that carry liability insurance to be sued, "[i]n the absence of such

---

[228] *Id.*

[229] Wiklund v. Presbyterian Church, 217 A.2d 463 (N.J. 1966).

[230] Burgie v. Muench, 29 N.E.2d 439 (Ohio 1940).

[231] Bianchi v. South Park Presbyterian Church, 8 A.2d 567 (N.J. 1939).

[232] Cullen v. Schmit, 39 N.E. 2d 146 (Ohio 1942).

[233] Anasiewicz v. Sacred Heart Church, 181 A.2d 787 (N.J. 1962), *appeal denied,* 184 A.2d 419 (1962).

[234] Rupp v. Brookdale Baptist Church, 577 A.2d 188 (N.J. Super. 1990). In defending the statute, the court observed, "The principle of charitable immunity was deeply rooted in the common law of New Jersey. The principle is premised on the fact that charitable associations are created to pursue philanthropic goals and the accomplishment of those goals would be hampered if they were to pay tort judgments in cases similar to this matter. . . . [A] person who makes a charitable contribution expects his donation to further the goals of the organization, and not to be used to satisfy lawsuits which bear no direct relationship to those goals."

[235] Abramson v. Reiss, 638 A.2d 743 (Md. 1994).

insurance, a negligence action cannot be maintained against a charitable institution." Since the center had no liability insurance coverage, this exception did not apply. The injured basketball player urged the court to follow the lead of most of the other states and reject the doctrine of charitable immunity. The court declined to do so, insisting that it is up to the state legislature to abolish the doctrine. The court noted that the legislature in recent years has expressed no interest in repudiating the doctrine. Quite to the contrary, it has expanded it by granting limited immunity from liability to the directors, employees, and volunteers of charitable organizations. This ruling illustrates the special status enjoyed by churches and other charities in Maryland. While immunity from liability is not absolute (it only applies to acts of ordinary negligence), it is nevertheless a significant protection that is available to churches and other religious organizations in few other states.

Example. *A New Jersey court ruled that a state charitable immunity law that immunizes charities from liability for injuries sustained by "beneficiaries" was not affected by the fact that a charity purchases liability insurance.[236] A drug rehabilitation center was sued by a patient who was injured on the center's premises. The state charitable immunity law clearly prevented the patient (who was a beneficiary of the charity's services) to sue. However, the patient argued that he should be allowed to sue the charity since it carried liability insurance and its assets would not be depleted to the extent that any court judgment did not exceed the insurance policy limits. The court disagreed. It began by describing the purpose of the charitable immunity law: "[If a charity's assets] were used to satisfy the damages suffered by recipients of the charity through the negligence of the agents or servants of the charity, the [assets] would be diverted to purposes not within the charitable intention of the founders and patrons of the charity, and thus the benevolent object would be subverted. The common good and welfare is deemed the better served by the preservation of the [charity's assets] than by [their] diversion to the making of compensation for injury to beneficiaries attending the operation of the charity." The court concluded that this purpose was not affected by the fact that a charity has obtained liability insurance: "Insurance premiums are based on a number of variables, one of which is the nature of the risk to be insured. If a nonprofit charitable organization seeks to purchase insurance, the premiums charged to that organization should be lower than other organizations whose purposes are not charitable in nature due to the immunity status afforded by the Charitable Immunity Act. However, if courts were to hold that the Charitable Immunity Act was inapplicable to insured charitable organizations, then the premiums charged to such charitable organizations would ordinarily be higher due to this greater risk of exposure to liability for negligence claims. Therefore, the court rejects [the patient's] argument because the eventual costs of paying these claims would fall on the charities themselves in the form of higher insurance premiums, thereby depleting the resources of such organizations which are available for the pursuit of their charitable purposes."*

Example. *A New Jersey court dismissed a lawsuit brought against a church by a member injured on church premises on the basis of a state charitable immunity law that immunizes charities from liability for injuries sustained by "beneficiaries."[237] A church elder was injured when she fell down a church stairway. She sued her church, claiming that her injuries were caused by her church's negligence. The church asked the court to dismiss the case on the basis of a New Jersey "charitable immunity" law specifying that "[n]o nonprofit corporation . . . organized exclusively for religious, charitable, educational or hospital purposes shall . . . be liable to respond in damages to any person who shall suffer damages from the negligence of any agent or servant of such corporation . . . where such person is a beneficiary, to whatever degree, of the works*

---

[236] Pelaez v. Rugby Laboratories, Inc., 624 A.2d 1053 (N.J. Super. L. 1993).
[237] George v. First United Presbyterian Church, 639 A.2d 1128 (Super. A.D. 1994).

of such nonprofit corporation . . . ." The trial court dismissed the case on the ground that the elder was a "beneficiary" of the church and accordingly the church could not be liable to her. The elder appealed, and a state appeals court agreed with the trial court's dismissal of the case. The court observed that "we agree . . . that when [the elder] was injured, she was a beneficiary . . . of the defendant church . . . . The statutory language clearly immunizes a charitable organization from the tort claim of a member of the organization who has been injured while working as a volunteer for its benefit."

Example. *A New Jersey court ruled that a state charitable immunity law prevented a church from being sued by a woman who slipped and fell on church property.[238] A woman sustained injuries when she fell while exiting a church. She later sued the church, claiming that her injuries were caused by the church's failure to "maintain the parking lot in a good state of repair." A trial court dismissed the case on the basis of a New Jersey statute that prevents charitable organizations from being sued by "beneficiaries" of their services. The woman appealed, and a state appeals court upheld the trial court's dismissal of the case. It stressed that the "public policy which favors protection of charitable institutions is so strong" in New Jersey that the charitable immunity law must be liberally construed. The court noted that the charitable immunity law protects charities from being sued by their "beneficiaries," and further observed that the term "beneficiary" is broadly construed to include only those persons who are "totally unconcerned in and unrelated to and outside the benefactions of the [charity]." Since the woman had attended services at the church immediately preceding her injury, there was no doubt that she was a "beneficiary" of the church, and accordingly the church could not be sued by her on the basis of negligence. The woman attempted to avoid this law by alleging that the church had been guilty of "gross" negligence. The court rejected this argument, noting that gross negligence is a form of negligence, and accordingly charities cannot be sued even if their conduct constitutes gross negligence. The court observed, "to construe an exception for gross negligence not expressly stated in the Act would disregard this explicit legislative mandate. So, too, to permit a plaintiff to circumvent or avoid the protection given by the Act merely by making unspecified allegations of gross negligence would render the protection of the Act so ineffective as to be virtually meaningless."*

Example. *The Supreme Court of Virginia ruled that a volunteer performing services on behalf of a charity cannot be sued as a result of injuries that occur as a result of those services.[239] A Red Cross volunteer was driving a woman in a Red Cross vehicle to a hospital for medical services. On the way the car was involved in an accident with another vehicle and the woman passenger was injured. The woman later died, and her estate sued the volunteer for negligent driving. The volunteer defended himself by asserting that Virginia recognized the principle of charitable immunity, and that under this doctrine he could not be liable for the woman's injuries since they occurred while he was performing charitable services. Under these circumstances, the volunteer claimed that he was "cloaked with the immunity of the charity." A trial court agreed with the volunteer, and the estate appealed. The state supreme court agreed that the volunteer was not liable for the woman's injuries. The court began its opinion by noting that "[t]he doctrine of charitable immunity adopted in Virginia precludes a charity's beneficiaries from recovering damages from the charity for the negligent acts of its servants or agents if due care was exercised in the hiring and retention of those agents and servants." The woman's estate argued that cloaking a volunteer with charitable immunity would unfairly protect charitable activities at the expense of compensating persons who are injured by those volunteers. The court disagreed, noting that "[w]e struck this balance in*

---

[238] Monaghan v. Holy Trinity Church, 646 A.2d 1130 (N.J. Super. A.D. 1994). See also Loder v. The Church, 685 A.2d 20 (N.J. Super. 1996).
[239] Moore v. Warren, 463 S.E.2d 459 (Va. 1995).

favor of charitable institutions when the doctrine of charitable immunity was adopted and applied in Virginia years ago." This choice, noted the court, was based upon the belief that "it is in the public interest to encourage charitable institutions in their good work." The court observed, "Like any organization, a charity performs its work only through the actions of its servants and agents. Without a charity's agents and servants, such as the volunteer here, no service could be provided to beneficiaries. Denying these servants and agents the charity's immunity for their acts effectively would deny the charity immunity for its acts. If the charity's servants and agents are not under the umbrella of immunity given the institution itself and they are exposed to negligence actions by the charity's beneficiaries, the "good work" of the charity will be adversely impacted. That result is inconsistent with the Commonwealth's policy underlying the doctrine of charitable immunity." The court concluded that "under the doctrine of charitable immunity, a volunteer of a charity is immune from liability to the charity's beneficiaries for negligence while the volunteer was engaged in the charity's work."

4. STATE LAWS IMPOSING "CAPS" ON DAMAGES

Three states have enacted laws limiting the liability of churches (and other charitable organizations). In addition, the federal Civil Rights Act of 1991 places caps on employer damages in some discrimination cases. This section will review these laws, and court rulings applying them.

(1) The Civil Rights Act of 1991

The federal Civil Rights Act of 1991 imposes limits on the amount of monetary damages that can be assessed against employers in discrimination lawsuits. Employers with more than 14 but fewer than 101 employees cannot be liable for more than $50,000 to any one person; for employers with more than 100 but fewer than 201 employees, the maximum damages available to any one person is $100,000; for employers with more than 200 but fewer than 500 employees, the maximum damages available to any one person is $200,000; and for employers with more than 500 employees the maximum damages available to any one person is $300,000. The Civil Rights Act of 1991 is addressed further in section 8-08.04.

(2) Massachusetts

In 1971 the Massachusetts legislature enacted a law limiting the liability of charitable organizations. The statute specifies:

> It shall not constitute a defense to any cause of action based on tort brought against a corporation, trustees of a trust, or members of an association that said corporation, trust, or association is or at the time the cause of action arose was a charity; provided, that if the tort was committed in the course of any activity carried on to accomplish directly the charitable purposes of such corporation, trust, or association, liability in any such cause of action shall not exceed the sum of twenty thousand dollars exclusive of interest and cost. Notwithstanding any other provision of this section, the liability of charitable corporations, the trustees of charitable trusts, and the members of charitable associations shall not be subject to the limitations set forth in this section if the tort was committed in the course of activities primarily commercial in character even though carried on to obtain revenue to be used for charitable purposes.[240]

---

[240] MASS. GENERAL LAWS c. 231, § 85K.

Note the following significant provisions of this law: (1) the liability of charitable organizations for activities carried on to further the organization's charitable purposes is limited to $20,000; (2) there is no $20,000 limit for activities carried on by charitable organizations for "commercial" purposes.

The Massachusetts Supreme Judicial Court unanimously upheld the validity of the Massachusetts law in 1989.[241] The case involved a lawsuit filed against a hospital for its alleged negligent treatment of a minor. A jury awarded the minor $350,000 in damages, and the hospital appealed on the ground that its liability was limited to $20,000 under the Massachusetts law. The minor's attorneys argued that the $20,000 limitation violated the constitutional guarantees of due process, equal protection of the laws, and trial by jury. The Supreme Court conceded that "we are not without misgivings about the paltriness of the $20,000 cap, especially in light of the decline of the dollar since 1971," but it ruled that the law was valid.

The court reasoned that statutes generally should be upheld by the courts so long as they are "rationally related to the furtherance of a legitimate state interest." A statue ordinarily "only needs to be supported by a conceivable, rational basis." The court concluded that the $20,000 limitation was related to a legitimate state interest: "The objective of [the statute] clearly is to protect the funds of charitable institutions so they may be devoted to charitable purposes. That objective is . . . clearly legitimate. If a charity's property were depleted by the payment of damages its usefulness might be either impaired or wholly destroyed, the object of the founder or donors defeated, and charitable gifts discouraged."

The court rejected the claim that the Massachusetts law violated the constitutional guarantees of due process and equal protection of the laws by denying accident victims the ability to recover damages. If also rejected the claim that the law violated the right to a trial by jury. In responding to the argument that the expenses involved in litigating serious personal injury cases often far exceed the $20,000 limit, the court observed that it was "not the court's prerogative to determine whether a more equitable distribution of the burden of negligently inflicted personal injuries could be devised. We cannot say that there is no rational relationship between the cap on damages and the statute's legitimate objective of preserving charitable assets."

(3) South Carolina

Section 33-55-210 of the South Caroline Code contains the following provision:

> Any person sustaining an injury or dying by reason of the tortious act of commission or omission of an employee of a charitable organization, when the employee is acting within the scope of his employment, may only recover in any action brought against the charitable organization for the actual damages he may sustain in an amount not exceeding two hundred thousand dollars. The judgment in an action under sections 33-55-210 through 33-55-230 shall constitute a complete bar to any action by the claimant, by reason of the same subject matter, against the employee of the charitable organization whose act or omission gave rise to the claim. The plaintiff, when bringing an action under the provisions of sections 33-55-210 through 33-55-230 shall only name as a party defendant the charitable organization for which the employee was acting and shall not name the employee individually unless the charitable organization for which the employee was acting cannot be determined at the time the action is instituted. In the event the employee is individually named under the conditions

---

[241] English v. New England Medical Center, 541 N.E.2d 329 (Mass. 1989). *See also* St. Clair v. Trustees of Boston University, 521 N.E.2d 1044 (Mass. App. 1988).

permitted above, the entity for which the employee was acting shall be substituted as the party defendant when it can be so reasonably determined.

Section 33-55-220 further provides that "the bar to any action against an employee, provided herein, shall not apply where the employee is adjudged to have acted recklessly, wantonly, or grossly negligent." Section 33-55-200 specifies that the term *charitable organization* means any organization exempt from federal income taxation under section 501(c)(3) of the Internal Revenue Code. This definition includes most churches and religious organizations.

Here is a summary of the important features of this law. First, it applies to "charitable organizations," a term that covers most churches and religious organizations. Second, persons injured as a result of the negligence (or other wrongful activity) of a church employee may not sue the employee. They must sue the church itself—unless the employee "acted recklessly, wantonly, or grossly negligent," or unless the identity of the church cannot be established. Third, and most significantly, *the church is liable only for actual damages up to but not exceeding $200,000.* Churches are not liable for speculative or punitive damages, and their liability for actual damages (i.e., out-of-pocket expenses that can be substantiated by receipts and other written evidence) cannot exceed $200,000.

The South Carolina Supreme Court unanimously upheld the constitutionality of the statute in a case challenging its validity.[242] In 1985, a woman undergoing routine gall bladder surgery was given a unit of blood containing the AIDS virus. A Red Cross office had collected the infected blood from a volunteer donor four months before a test for detecting the AIDS virus in blood supplies was developed. The victim sued the Red Cross for negligence, and the Red Cross asserted that its liability was limited to $200,000 on the basis of the state law limiting the liability of charitable organizations. The victim argued that the state law violated the "equal protection clause" of the state constitution, which specifies simply that "no person shall be denied the equal protection of the laws." Specifically, she argued that the law impermissibly established a distinction or classification between charitable organizations and non-charitable organizations by limiting the liability of charitable organizations while leaving non-charitable organizations subject to unlimited liability. Further, she argued that the law would affect charities differently depending on their size—i.e., a $200,000 limit on liability would not be of much help to smaller charities (a $200,000 judgment would be catastrophic), but it would be of significant benefit to larger charities.

The South Carolina Supreme Court ruled that a law which treats different classes of persons or organizations differently will satisfy the equal protection clause of the state constitution if the following three requirements are satisfied: "(1) the classification bears a reasonable relation to the legislative purpose sought to be effected; (2) the members of the class are treated alike under similar circumstances and conditions; and (3) the classification rests on some reasonable basis." The court concluded that the law limiting the liability of charitable organizations satisfied all three requirements, and accordingly was constitutional. As to the first requirement, the court noted that the purpose of the law in question was "to encourage the formation of charitable organizations, to promote charitable donations, and to preserve the resources of the charitable organizations." The legislature sought to accomplish this purpose by insulating charitable organizations from liability in excess of $200,000. "It was rational," concluded the court, "for the government to make distinctions between those in business for profit and those who have [nonprofit or charitable] motives. We therefore hold that the limitation on liability [contained in the law] bears a rational relationship to the legislative goal."

---

[242] Doe v. American Red Cross Blood Services, 377 S.E.2d 323 (S.C. 1989).

The court also concluded that the law satisfied the second requirement: "We find that although the impact of a $200,000 damage judgment may vary according to the size of the charitable organization, the varying impact does not violate the equal protection clause [since] we find that potential plaintiffs are not treated disparately because the same monetary cap applies equally to the entire class of plaintiffs."

The court further concluded that the law satisfied the third requirement—that the classification contained in the law rested on a reasonable basis. The statute's classification between charitable and non-charitable organizations "is not arbitrary," the court concluded, "and there is a reasonable relationship between promoting charitable activities and limiting the liability of entities that engage in such activities."

> *Example. The South Carolina Supreme Court ruled that a church member could sue his unincorporated church for injuries sustained while repairing the church sound system, but he could not recover more than the $200,000 "cap" allowed by state law.[243] The member volunteered to enter the church attic to repair the sound system. While in the attic, he fell through the ceiling and landed on a concrete floor some ten feet below. His injuries required him to miss work for nearly a year. The victim sued his church, pastors, and church board members, alleging that they were all negligent and responsible for his injuries. A jury awarded him $300,000, and the defendants appealed. The supreme court ruled that the injured member could sue his church, even though it was unincorporated. But it reduced the jury's award from $300,000 to $200,000 on the basis of a state law that provides: "Any person sustaining an injury or dying by reason of the tortious act . . . of an employee of a charitable organization, when the employee is acting within the scope of his employment, may only recover in any action brought against the charitable organization in an amount not exceeding two hundred thousand dollars." The court concluded that a church fit "squarely within the definition of a charitable organization" for purposes of this law.*

(4) Texas

The Texas legislature also has enacted a law limiting the legal liability of charitable organizations. Section 84.006 of the Texas Code of Civil Procedure specifies:

> Except as provided in section 84.007 of this Act, in any civil action brought against a nonhospital charitable organization for damages based on an act or omission by the organization or its employees or volunteers, the liability of the organization is limited to money damages in a maximum amount of $500,000 for each person and $1,000,000 for each single occurrence of bodily injury or death and $100,000 for each single occurrence for injury to or destruction of property.

The Act defines "charitable organization" to include charitable and religious organizations exempt from federal income taxation under section 501(c)(3) of the Internal Revenue Code. Churches and most religious organizations will satisfy this definition. The Act permits employees of "charitable organizations" to be sued as a result of injuries caused by their negligence in the course of their employment, but their liability is limited to "money damages in a maximum amount of $500,000 for each person and $1,000,000 for each single occurrence of bodily injury or death and $100,000 for each single occurrence for injury to or destruction of property" (i.e., the same limitations that apply to charitable organizations themselves). "Volunteers" (those serving without compensation, including officers and directors) are totally immune from liability (they cannot be sued) for injuries or death resulting from their conduct on behalf of a charitable organization so long as they were acting "in good faith and in the course or scope of [their] duties or functions within the organi-

---

[243] Crocker v. Barr, 409 S.E.2d 368 (S.C. 1992).

zation." The immunity of volunteers does not cover injuries caused by the negligent use of motor vehicles, to the extent of any existing insurance coverage.

The Texas law does *not* apply to (1) "an act or omission that is intentional, willfully or wantonly negligent, or done with conscious indifference or reckless disregard for the safety of others"; or (2) any charitable organization that does not have liability insurance coverage in an amount of at least "$500,000 for each person and $1,000,000 for each single occurrence of bodily injury or death and $100,000 for each single occurrence for injury to or destruction of property."

Here is a summary of the more important features of the Texas law.

• *"Cap" on church liability.* The statute limits the liability of charitable organizations to "money damages in a maximum amount of $500,000 for each person and $1,000,000 for each single occurrence of bodily injury or death and $100,000 for each single occurrence for injury to or destruction of property."

• *"Cap" on personal liability.* Church employees can be sued personally as a result of injuries or damages caused by their negligence in the course of their duties, but their personal liability is subject to the same dollar limitations that apply to charitable organizations.

• *Definition of "charitable organization."* The term charitable organization is defined broadly, and includes most churches and many religious organizations.

• *Definition of "volunteer."* Volunteers (uncompensated workers) cannot be sued personally as a result of injuries or damages caused by their negligent activities, except in the case of negligent operation of a motor vehicle (and then only to the extent of existing liability insurance coverage).

• *Exceptions.* The dollar limits do not apply in the case of "intentional, willfully or wantonly negligent" acts or omissions, or to conduct that shows a conscious indifference or reckless disregard for the safety of others.

• *Necessity of having insurance coverage.* The dollar limits do not apply to a charitable organization that does not have liability insurance coverage in an amount of at least "$500,000 for each person and $1,000,000 for each single occurrence of bodily injury or death and $100,000 for each single occurrence for injury to or destruction of property."

ARE LIMITATIONS ON THE LIABILITY OF CHURCHES AND OTHER CHARITABLE ORGANIZATIONS FAIR?

It certainly could be argued that it is unfair to limit the liability of an innocent person who is seriously injured by the negligence of a church employee. After attorneys' fees and medical expenses are deducted, a $20,000 (or even a $200,000 or $500,000) judgment would be of little value to a person who is rendered a quadriplegic because of the negligence of a church employee. The fact is, however, that serious injuries caused by the negligence of church employees and agents are relatively rare, and that a limitation on liability is necessary to protect churches from the excessive and completely meritless claims for damages that clog the courts. Further, a church in Massachusetts, South Carolina, or Texas is free to voluntarily compensate (over and above the legal limitations) a victim of the church's negligence in the event that the congregation feels that the victim would not otherwise be adequately compensated.

LIMITING A CHURCH'S LIABILITY FOR MONEY DAMAGES

Ministers and lay leaders of churches should be aware of the following considerations:

(1) Legislative initiatives. There is a litigation epidemic in this county, and it is impacting churches. Church leaders can no longer afford to sit back and passively wait to be sued. There are meaningful steps that can be taken that will either reduce the amount of damages for which churches will be liable, or that will reduce the risk of being sued in the first place. One such step, for churches not located in Massachusetts, South Carolina, or Texas, is to encourage state legislators to sponsor legislation imposing dollar caps on damages that can be assessed against charities. The fact that three states have enacted such laws (two of which have been upheld unanimously by the state supreme court) should increase the likelihood of finding sympathetic legislators. The assistance of other charities (e.g., Red Cross, Boy Scouts and Girl Scouts, hospitals, schools, libraries, museums) as well as church insurance companies and other churches and denominations should also be sought.

(2) Locating a religious or parachurch ministry. There are many factors that should be considered in establishing a location for a parachurch ministry or denominational agency. One of those factors is the existence of a charitable immunity law in states under consideration. Any religious organization planning the location of a regional or national office should seriously consider Massachusetts, South Carolina, and Texas as a result of the laws in those states limiting the liability of charitable organizations.

(3) "Charitable" organizations. While churches and religious organizations generally are considered to be "charitable" organizations, it would be prudent for churches and religious organizations in the states of Massachusetts, South Carolina, and Texas to ensure that their charters define their purposes to include charitable as well as religious activities.

(4) Insurance coverage. Should churches in Massachusetts, South Carolina, and Texas reduce their liability insurance coverage to match the maximum amount of liability allowed under state law? This is a difficult question that must be answered by a local attorney and a church's insurance agent. Churches in Texas have much less reason to reduce their insurance coverage than churches in South Carolina and Massachusetts, since (1) the validity of the Texas statute has not been upheld by the state supreme court, and (2) churches and other charitable organizations may be subject to liability in excess of the statute's limitations if their employees cause injury to other persons as a result of willful or wanton conduct. Further, the Texas statute only protects charities that maintain the specified amount of insurance. Even in South Carolina and Massachusetts, the state supreme courts simply found that the state laws limiting the liability of charitable organizations did not violate specific constitutional protections. It is possible that these laws will be attacked in the future on the basis of other provisions in the state or federal constitutions. And, it is conceivable that courts may conclude that churches are religious rather than charitable organizations, and therefore outside the protection of these laws.

§ 10-16.6 — Release Forms

Key point 10-16.6. A release form is a document signed by a competent adult that purports to relieve a church from liability for its own negligence. Such forms may be legally enforceable if they are clearly written and identify the conduct that is being released. However, the courts look with disfavor on release forms, and this has led to several limitations, including the following: (1) release forms will be strictly and narrowly construed against the church; (2) release forms cannot relieve a church of liability for injuries to minors, since minors have no legal capacity to sign such forms and their parents' signature does not prevent minors from bringing their own personal injury claim after they reach age 18; (3) some courts refuse to enforce any release form that attempts to avoid liability for personal injuries on the ground that such forms violate public policy; and (4) release forms will not be enforced unless they clearly communicate that they are releasing the church from liability for its negligence.

Many churches use "release forms," which purport to release the church from legal responsibility for injuries inflicted by the negligence of its employees or workers. Besides being of dubious legal value,[244] such forms primarily protect the church's insurance company. If injuries are caused by the negligence of a church worker, then the liability insurer will pay for such damages up to the policy limits. If the church is not negligent, then it ordinarily will not be assessed any damages. A release form, even if deemed legally valid by a court, would have the effect of excusing the church's liability insurer from paying damages to a victim of the church's negligence.

Release forms that purport to excuse a church or other organization from liability for injuries to a minor are the most likely to be invalidated by the courts, often on the ground that they violate public policy. However, the courts have been less reluctant to recognize release or "assumption of risk" forms signed by competent adults, but even these forms are viewed with disfavor and some courts will go to great lengths to invalidate them, especially if they seek to relieve an organization of liability for personal injuries as opposed to property damage.

PARENTAL PERMISSION AND MEDICAL CONSENT FORMS

Churches should not allow a minor child to participate in any church activity (such as camping, boating, swimming, hiking, or some sporting events) unless the child's parents or legal guardians sign a form that (1) consents to their child participating in the specified activity; (2) certifies that the child is able to participate in the event (e.g., if the activity involves boating or swimming, the parents or guardians should certify that the child is able to swim); (3) lists any allergies or medical conditions that may be relevant to a physician in the event of an emergency; (4) lists any activities that the parents or guardians do not want the child to engage in; and (4) authorizes a designated individual to make emergency medical decisions for their child in the event that they cannot be reached.

Ideally, the form should be signed by both parents or guardians (if there are two), and the signatures should be notarized. If only one parent or guardian signs, or the signatures are not notarized, the legal effectiveness of the form is diminished. Having persons sign as witnesses to a parent's signature is not as good as a notary's acknowledgment, but it is better than a signature without a witness. The form should require the parent or guardian to inform the church immediately of any change in the information presented, and it should state that it is valid until revoked by the person who signed it. The parent or guardian should sign both in his or her own capacity as parent or guardian, and in a representative capacity on behalf of the minor child.

---

[244] *See, e.g.,* Note, *The Quality of Mercy: "Charitable Torts" and Their Continuing Immunity,* 100 Harv. L. Rev. 1382, 1394-95 (1987).

Tip. Churches that send groups of adults to other locations for short-term missions projects should consider having each participating adult sign an assumption of risk form. So long as these forms clearly explain the risks involved, and leave no doubt that the signer is assuming all risks associated with the trip, they may be enforced by the courts. This assumes that the signer is a competent adult. Churches should consult with an attorney about the validity of such forms under state law.

Example. A Michigan court ruled that a release form signed by a competent adult prior to participating in a dangerous activity prevented him from suing as a result of injuries he sustained.[245] As part of an annual historic festival, a city sponsored a "rope climb" contest. A rope was stretched across a river and participants would hang onto the rope with their hands and attempt to cross the river. The winner was the participant who crossed the river in the shortest period of time. Various cash prizes were awarded to the winner and runners-up, and there was a one dollar entry fee paid by all participants. One participant lost his grasp of the rope and fell head first into the river, sustaining permanent and disabling injuries. He sued the city and the individuals who organized the festival. The city and festival organizers claimed that the victim could not sue because he signed a liability release form. Before participating in the rope climb, each participant was required to sign a "waiver of liability" form. A state appeals court ruled that the release prevented the victim from suing. The court rejected the victim's claim that the release was invalid since it did not specifically name every person or organization that was being released from liability. It observed simply that "[i]t was not necessary for the release to individually name each person or entity to be released from liability. The scope of the applicability of the waiver is clear: it waived liability with respect to any person or group responsible for the rope climb event." The court also rejected the victim's claim that the release was unenforceable because he had failed to read it before signing it.

Example. A New York court ruled that a church could not avoid liability for personal injuries suffered by a construction worker on church premises on the basis of a release form that did not specifically release the worker.[246] A church hired a contractor to repair its bell tower and spire, and had the contractor sign an agreement that contained the following "hold harmless" agreement: "The contractor agrees that he undertakes all repairs and renovations as detailed in the proposal at his own risk and he agrees to indemnify and save the church and all its members and officers for damage to property or injury to, or the death of any person, including employees, of any actions arising out of the acts of the contractor and at his own cost and expense; defend any action brought against either the contractor or the church; and promptly pay any adverse judgment in any such action, and hold the church and its members and officers harmless from and against any loss or damage and expense claimed by the church and its members and officers by reason of such claim." The contractor hired a worker who was seriously injured when he fell nearly 30 feet when the scaffolding on which he was working collapsed. The worker sued the church, and the church defended itself by citing the "hold harmless" agreement quoted above. A court ruled that the church could not escape liability on this basis. It noted that New York law imposes absolute liability upon owners and contractors for a failure to furnish and erect safe scaffolding, and that this liability was not avoided by the hold harmless agreement since only the contractor (and not the worker he hired) agreed to release the church from liability.

Example. A Washington court ruled that the family of a college student killed during a scuba diving activity was prevented from suing the college or scuba instructor by a release form signed by the student

---

[245] Dombrowski v. City of Omer, 502 N.W.2d 707 (Mich. App. 1993).
[246] Bain v. First Presbyterian Church and Society, 601 N.Y.S.2d 535 (Sup. 1993).

prior to his death.[247] *The student also signed an "assumption of risk" form that specified: "In consideration of being allowed to enroll in this course, I hereby personally assume all risks in connection with said course, for any harm, injury or damage that may befall me while I am enrolled as a student of the course, including all risks connected therewith, whether foreseen or unforeseen." During one dive the student panicked when he noticed the air in his tank was low, and died of air embolism resulting from too rapid an ascent. His family sued the college and his instructor. A state appeals court ruled that the family was barred from suing as a result of the release and assumption of risk forms signed by the student. The court acknowledged that "a release is a contract in which one party agrees to abandon or relinquish a claim . . . against another party," and that release agreements "are strictly construed and must be clear if the release from liability is to be enforced." The court also stressed that "the general rule is that a pre-injury release of the employer from liability also releases the employee." As a result, the student's release of the college had the effect of releasing the instructor (even if the instructor had not been specifically named in the release). The court agreed with the family that a release will not be enforced if it violates "public policy." However, the court noted that under Washington law, a release agreement does not violate public policy unless it involves a "public interest." Scuba diving did not involve such an interest. The court acknowledged that a release form only releases organizations and individuals from their ordinary negligence, and not from their gross negligence. However, the court added that "evidence of negligence is not evidence of gross negligence; to raise an issue of gross negligence, there must be substantial evidence of serious negligence." The court concluded that there was no evidence of gross negligence in this case other than the unsupported allegations of the family. The court also rejected the family's argument that the assumption of risk form their son signed was unenforceable since he did not specifically assume the risks of negligent instruction and negligent supervision. The court simply noted that the student had signed an assumption of risk form in which he assumed "all risks" associated with his scuba diving class.*

Example. *A West Virginia court refused to recognize a "release form" as a legal defense to an organization's liability.*[248] *A young woman went whitewater rafting as paying passenger on a raft owned and operated by a commercial outfitter. During the trip, the guide who was operating the raft attempted to dislodge another raft that was stuck among some rocks by ramming it with his raft. This maneuver caused the woman to be thrown violently, causing serious injuries. The woman sued the outfitter that owned the raft. The outfitter defended itself by referring to a release form that the woman had signed prior to her trip. The court ruled that the woman could sue the outfitter despite the release. It acknowledged that a release form may be legally enforceable if a person clearly agrees to accept a specified risk of harm. But there are some very important limitations upon this general rule, including the following: (1) The victim must have been aware of and understood the terms of the release. The court observed, "[F]or an express agreement assuming the risk to be effective, it must appear that the [victim] has given his or her assent to the terms of the agreement" and if the agreement is prepared by another person or organization "it must appear that the terms were in fact brought home to, and understood by, the victim, before it may be found that the victim has agreed to them." (2) The release will be effective only with respect to risks that it specifically mentions. For example, a general release exempting an organization from negligence "will not be construed to include intentional or reckless misconduct or gross negligence, unless such intention clearly appears from the circumstances." (3) A release that violates "public policy" will not be enforced by the courts. The court concluded that a release will violate public policy and be unenforceable if it seeks to exempt a person from liability for failure to conform to a standard of conduct prescribed by statute. In this case, state law prescribed a level of care required of whitewater raft operators, and accordingly it was impossible for that duty to be released.*

---

[247] Boyce v. West, 862 P.2d 592 (Wash. App. 1993).
[248] Murphy v. North American River Runners, Inc., 412 S.E.2d 504 (W. Va. 1991).

§ 10-16.7 — Insurance

Key point 10-16.7. A liability insurance policy provides a church with a legal defense to lawsuits claiming that the church is responsible for an injury, and it will pay any adverse settlement or judgment up to the limit specified in the policy. Liability insurance policies exclude a number of claims. For example, some policies exclude injuries based on criminal or intentional acts and claims for punitive damages. A church has an obligation to promptly notify its insurer of any potential claim, and to cooperate with the insurer in its investigation of claims.

Liability insurance may be viewed as a "defense" to church liability in the sense that it will provide the church with a legal defense of a civil lawsuit and pay any portion of a settlement or judgment up to the insurance policy limits. This assumes, of course, that the lawsuit sought damages for an act or occurrence covered by the policy. Listed below are several aspects of church insurance with which church leaders should be familiar:

1. Coverage

An insurance policy will provide a church with a legal defense of a covered claim, and pay any portion of a settlement or judgment up to the policy limit. It is very important for church leaders to be familiar with those claims that are covered under the church's insurance policy or policies.

Churches often engage in activities that are not clearly covered under their insurance policy. Examples include counseling, use of personal vehicles for church-related work, and use of the church facilities by outside groups. Be sure that you check with your insurance agent about coverage for these and other activities.

The issue of directors and officers insurance is addresses in section 6-08.

Key point. Church insurance policies generally do not cover employment-related claims, including discrimination, wrongful termination, and sexual harassment. If your church is sued on the basis of such claims, you probably will need to retain and pay for your own attorney, and pay any judgment or settlement amount. This often comes as a shock to church leaders. You should immediately review your policy with your insurance agent to see if you have any coverage for such claims. If you do not, ask how it can be obtained. You may be able to obtain an endorsement for "employment practices." Also, a "directors and officers" policy may cover these claims.

Key point. In evaluating whether or not an insurance policy provides coverage for a particular claim, the courts generally apply the following principles: (1) the insurance contract is "construed liberally" in favor of the insured and "strictly" against the insurer; and (2) exclusions are interpreted as narrowly as possible, so as to provide maximum coverage for the insured, and are construed most strongly against the insurance company that drafted and issued the policy.

Tip. Does your church have insurance that covers losses caused by embezzlement and employee dishonesty? Ask your insurance agent the following questions: (1) Does our church insurance policy cover employee thefts and dishonesty? (2) If so, what is the coverage amount? (3) Is the coverage amount adequate for our church? If not, how much would additional coverage cost? (4) If our church is not insured against employee theft or dishonesty, what would the cost be for different levels of coverage? (5) Would a series of acts of embezzlement, occurring over more than one year, be a single "occurrence" or separate occurrences under our employee dishonesty policy?

COUNSELING INSURANCE

Does your church carry counseling liability insurance for its ministers? If not, you should give serious consideration to obtaining such coverage. At this time, it is still relatively inexpensive. Do not assume that you are covered simply because your church carries general liability insurance. While the risk of a minister being successfully sued for negligent counseling is remote, the risk that a minister may be sued is increasingly possible. If counseling liability insurance covers an alleged incident, then your insurer ordinarily will provide a church with a complete legal defense to the lawsuit, and pay any resulting damages or settlement up to the policy limits. Since the risk of losing such a suit is remote, the availability of counseling liability insurance will have the effect of a "legal defense" policy. It is true that your church may increase its risk of being sued if it obtains counseling liability insurance (it will become a more attractive "target"). Yet, this consideration should not necessarily be controlling. The risk of being sued without adequate insurance coverage is an equally if not more grave concern.

---

2. EXCLUSIONS

All church insurance policies contain exclusions. An exclusion is a claim that is not covered under an insurance policy. It is important for church leaders to be familiar with the exclusions set forth in their church's liability insurance policy, since these represent potentially uninsured claims that can expose the church to substantial damages. Further, the church would have to retain and compensate its own attorney if it is sued on the basis of an excluded claim.

Common exclusions include intentional or criminal misconduct, injuries occurring outside of the United States, employment-related claims, and injuries caused by exposure to hazardous substances. Some policies exclude claims arising out of incidents of sexual misconduct. Church leaders may want to discuss with their church insurance agent the possibility of obtaining insurance to cover exclusions.

> *Example. A federal appeals court ruled that a church's insurance policy did not cover lawsuits arising from the employment relationship.[249] A pastor dismissed his church's music director. The music director sued the pastor, church, and state denominational agency, claiming that she had been dismissed because she suffered from post-traumatic stress disorder and multiple personality disorder. She insisted that her dismissal amounted to unlawful discrimination based on disability. She also claimed that the pastor had defamed her, and invaded her privacy. The church's insurance carrier insisted that the church insurance policy did not cover the woman's claims, and it refused to provide the church with a legal defense or to pay any portion of a jury verdict or settlement. A federal appeals court agreed that the insurance policy did not cover the woman's claims. It noted that the policy indemnifies the church for damages resulting from "personal injury," including injury from defamation. The policy further obligates the company to defend the church in any suit seeking damages covered by the policy. However, the policy excludes from coverage "personal injury sustained by any person as a result of an offense directly or indirectly related to the employment of such person by the named insured." The court noted that the key question was whether the woman's lawsuit was for "personal injury" sustained "as a result of an offense directly or indirectly related to her employment" by the church. If it was, then the exclusion applied, and the company had no duty to defend the church against the lawsuit. The court concluded that "defama-*

---

[249] The Parish of Christ Church v. The Church Insurance Company, 166 F.3d 419 (1st Cir. 1999).

tory statements providing an explanation for termination or directed to performance are related to employment. Alleged offenses occurring as part and parcel of an allegedly wrongful termination are plainly related to employment. Post-employment defamations can be directly or indirectly related to employment, and thus can fall within an exclusion of the sort at issue here. The statements to which [the lawsuit] refers are comments as to [the woman's] abilities and job performance. They are explanations as to why [the pastor] terminated [her] employment."

Example. *A federal appeals court ruled that an insurance policy covered two denominational agencies that were sued as a result of the sexual misconduct of an affiliated pastor, despite the fact that the policy excluded sexual misconduct claims.*[250] *A learning disabled woman claimed that she had been sexual assaulted by an ordained minister on several occasions at a state school for the mentally handicapped. The minister served as a chaplain at the school. The woman sued the minister for injuries she allegedly suffered as a result of these assaults. She also sued the national denomination (the "national church") with which the minister was affiliated, and a regional denominational agency (the "regional church"). She claimed that the national and regional churches had been negligent in training, supervising, placing, and monitoring the chaplain, who eventually was indicted for alleged sexual contact with three mentally handicapped individuals. The chaplain was never an agent or employee of the national or regional churches, but graduated from a seminary affiliated with the national church and was listed in the national church's "clergy roster" as a retired pastor. The national church had an insurance policy containing both comprehensive general liability and "umbrella" liability provisions. The comprehensive general liability provision provided nationwide coverage for the national church. The umbrella liability provision covered the national church and about 40 regional churches. Both the comprehensive general liability and umbrella liability provisions obligated the insurance company to pay "damages because of bodily injury or property damage to which this insurance applies," but the policies explicitly require that "the bodily injury or property damage must be caused by an occurrence." An "occurrence" is defined as "an accident, including continuous or repeated exposure to substantially the same general conditions." Both policies excluded "bodily injury or property damage expected or intended from the standpoint of the insured." The insurance company asked a federal district court to dismiss the case on the ground that the chaplain's conduct had been "intended" and therefore was excluded from any coverage under the terms of the policy. The district court declined to do so, and ruled that the policies did provide coverage for the national and regional churches. The insurance company appealed. The federal appeals court concluded that under Illinois law (that law applicable to this case) it was clear that the victim's allegations of negligent hiring fell within the definition of "occurrence." It added that "if a complaint potentially supports a ground for recovery, the insurer must defend the entire complaint." The court, in rejecting the insurance company's argument that the exclusion of intentional acts precluded coverage, observed: "Here, negligent training was not an intentional tort, and [the chaplain's] acts are not the insureds' intentional acts. Thus, the insurance policy did not exclude the acts, and [the insurer] has a duty to defend."*

Example. *A federal appeals court ruled that a church insurance policy did not provide for a legal defense of a minister who engaged in sexual relations with two members of his congregation.*[251] *The minister sued the church's insurance company after it refused to pay for his legal defense. The church's comprehensive general liability policy provides coverage for pastoral counseling liability under a provision defining "personal injury" to include "acts, errors or omissions of ordained clergy, acting within the*

---

[250] *Evangelical Lutheran Church in America v. Atlantic Mutual Insurance Company,* 169 F.3d 947 (5th Cir. 1999). See also *D.E.M. v. Allickson,* 555 N.W.2d 596 (N.D. 1996).

[251] Newyear v. The Church Insurance Company, 155 F.3d 1041 (8th Cir. 1998).

scope of their duties as employees of the named insured and arising out of the pastoral counseling activities of these individuals." The minister argued that he was entitled to a defense under the policy since the women's allegations arose out of his duties as a pastoral counselor. A federal appeals court disagreed, and ruled that the church's insurance policy did not cover the minister's actions. The critical question, the court concluded, was whether or not the minister was acting within the scope of his employment when he engaged in sexual relations with the two women. It concluded that "a priest does not act in furtherance of the business or interests of his employer when he engages in sexual misconduct with parishioners." As a result, the minister was not entitled to a defense under the policy "as the alleged acts of sexual misconduct do not fall within the scope of his employment."

Example. *A federal appeals court ruled that a church insurance company was under no legal obligation to provide a legal defense to a church or its board of directors in a lawsuit alleging that a church volunteer had sexually molested a young girl.[252] The church's insurance company refused to provide the volunteer, the church, or the church board with a legal defense to the lawsuit, and denied any obligation to pay any judgment rendered in the case. The insurer based its position on the following language in the church's insurance policy: "This policy does not apply . . . to personal injury arising out of the willful violation of a penal statute or ordinance committed by or with knowledge or consent of any insured." The policy defined the term "insured" to include any duly appointed volunteer. The church and church board conceded that the insurance policy did not protect the volunteer, but they insisted that they were being sued solely on the basis of their negligence and accordingly the insurance policy should cover them. The appeals court rejected the position of the church and church board. It observed, "[T]here is conclusive proof [of a willful violation of penal statutes] by guilty pleas and criminal convictions on both such charges. . . . We cannot agree with the [argument of the church and church board] that the cases can be viewed as involving only the negligence allegations and the negligent entrustment theory. It is, instead, an essential element of [negligence] that [the volunteer] molested the girls and caused them injuries of mind and body. A cause of action for negligence depends not only upon the defendant's breach of duty to exercise care to avoid injury to the plaintiff, but also upon damage or injury suffered by the plaintiff as a consequence of the violation of the duty. The sexual violations and resulting injuries cannot therefore be disregarded. And giving consideration to them, the exclusion in the policy is thus applicable providing that the policy does not apply 'to personal injury arising out of the willful violation of a penal statute or ordinance committed by or with knowledge or consent of any insured.'"*

Example. *An Alabama court ruled that a church's "directors and officers" insurance policy covered a lawsuit brought against a pastor for improperly obtaining money from an elderly member.[253] The daughter of an elderly church member was appointed guardian of her mother's property. The daughter sued the minister of her mother's church, claiming that he improperly obtained funds from her mother by means of conversion, fraud, and undue influence. The minister notified the church's "directors and officers" insurer of the lawsuit and asked the insurer to provide him with a legal defense. The insurer asked a court to determine whether or not the minister's actions were covered under the insurance policy. The court concluded that the insurer had a legal duty to provide the minister with a defense of the lawsuit. It noted that the church's insurance policy provided coverage for officers and directors (including the minister in this case) in any lawsuit brought against them by reason of alleged dishonesty on their part unless a court determined that the officer or director acted with deliberate dishonesty. Since the minister had not yet been found guilty of "deliberate dishonesty," he was covered under the insurance policy. The*

---

[252] All American Insurance Company v. Burns, 971 F.2d 438 (10th Cir. 1992). Contra American Employers Insurance Co. v. Doe 38, 165 F.3d 1209 (8th Cir. 1999).

[253] Graham v. Preferred Abstainers Insurance Company, 689 So.2d 188 (Ala. App. 1997).

court acknowledged that if the minister was found to have acted with deliberate dishonesty in the daughter's lawsuit, the insurer would have no duty to pay any portion of the judgment or verdict.

Example. *A Georgia court found that a general liability insurance policy covered a sexual assault claim at a church-run children's home, despite several exclusions in the policy.[254] A child resident at a church-operated children's home was sexually assaulted by other residents of the facility. The home was sued by the victim and his parents for its alleged negligence in adequately protecting, supervising, controlling, and caring for the residents of the facility. The children's home forwarded the lawsuit on to its insurance company. The insurance company concluded that the insurance policy in this case did not cover claims based on sexual assaults. It relied primarily on the following exclusion: "It is agreed that such coverage as is provided by the policy shall not apply to any claim, demand and causes of action arising out of or resulting from either sexual abuse or licentious, immoral or sexual behavior intended to lead to, or culminating in any sexual act, whether caused by, or at the instigation of, or at the direction of, or omission by, the insured, his employees, patrons or any causes whatsoever." The insurance company also relied on two other exclusions that denied any coverage for "bodily injury or property damage arising out of assault and battery" and "claims, accusations or charges of negligent hiring, placement, training or supervision arising from actual or alleged assault or battery." The court acknowledged that the insurance policy in this case could be construed to exclude any coverage for the victim's claims. However, it concluded that the policy also could be interpreted to require coverage of the victim's claims. With regard to the general sexual abuse exclusion, the court noted that it clearly applied to sexual assaults by "employees and patrons," but it did not necessarily apply to assaults by minor residents. The court concluded that "we do not believe that children residents of [the home] may reasonably be included in the group of individuals specified in the exclusion." The court also rejected the applicability of the other two exclusions relied upon by the insurance company. It noted that the specific sexual abuse exclusion prevented application of the two more general exclusions in deciding the question of insurance coverage for any claims involving sexual abuse, since "a limited or specific provision of a contract will prevail over one that is more broadly inclusive." The court concluded, "[I]nsurance policies are prepared and proposed by insurers. Thus, if an insurance contract is capable of being construed two ways, it will be construed against the insurance company and in favor of the insured. Construing the ambiguity in the sexual abuse exclusion in this case against [the insurance company], the policy did not exclude coverage for sexual abuse perpetrated by the children residents against another resident in the . . . facility."*

Example. *A federal district court in Minnesota resolved a dispute between a church-operated school and its liability insurance company regarding payment of a claim.[255] The school had purchased a policy insuring against wrongful acts of its employees. While the insurance was in force, a female employee notified the school principal that she intended to resign. The principal informed her that her husband (who also was an employee of the school) would be fired if she quit. Soon after this conversation, the wife resigned and the husband was fired. The husband filed a "marital discrimination" claim against the school under a Minnesota human rights law, and the school eventually settled the claim with the husband for $15,000. The insurance company refused to reimburse the school for the amount of the settlement on the grounds that (1) the settlement did not constitute an insurable loss under the policy, (2) the school should not able to insure itself against unlawful actions by its employees, and (3) employers should not be permitted to "shift" their labor costs onto their insurers. The court rejected all of these claims. It concluded that the school's settlement of the discrimination claim was a "loss" under the*

---

[254] Georgia Baptist Children's Homes & Family Ministries, Inc. v. Essex Insurance Company, 427 S.E.2d 798 (Ga. App. 1993).

[255] Convent of the Visitation School v. Continental Casualty Co., 707 F. Supp. 412 (D. Minn. 1989).

insurance policy since it was a liability resulting from an employee's wrongful act. It further noted that the insurance company had "failed to show that unlawful acts relating to termination of employment are uninsurable."

Example. *A Minnesota court ruled that a church insurance policy did not require the insurance company to defend a pastor who was sued by a woman he had seduced.*[256] *The court also ruled that the insurance company would not have to pay any portion of a jury verdict against the pastor. The court noted that the church's insurance policy specified that the insurer was liable for any personal injury "caused by an occurrence to which this insurance applies." The policy defined the term occurrence as an act that "results in bodily injury . . . neither expected nor intended." The court concluded that the pastor's repeated sexual exploitation of the victim resulted in personal injuries that were both "expected and intended," and accordingly they did not constitute an "occurrence" for which insurance coverage was available. The court observed, "We conclude [that the victim's] allegations that [the pastor] used his authority as a pastor and counselor to facilitate his sexual abuse of a psychologically vulnerable person creates an inference of an intent to injure and relieves [the insurance company] of its duty to defend." The court also relied on a provision in the church's insurance policy denying any coverage "to liability resulting from any actual or alleged conduct of a sexual nature, [or] to any dishonest, fraudulent or criminal act or omission of any insured."*

Example. *A federal court in Rhode Island ruled that a diocese's insurance company had a legal duty to defend diocesan officials who were sued as a result of the sexual molestation of several children by Catholic priests.*[257] *Nine lawsuits were brought against the Roman Catholic Diocese of Providence, Rhode Island, and various of its officials, by persons who claimed that they were sexually assaulted by priests of the diocese. The lawsuits were brought against the individual priests accused of perpetrating the assaults, the diocese, and various diocesan officials. The victims claimed that the diocese and its officials were liable for their injuries on the ground that they were negligent in hiring and supervising the priests and that they failed to take appropriate preventive action after learning of the priests' propensities. The diocese's insurance company asked a federal court to rule that it had no duty to defend the diocese or its officials, or to pay any damages awarded to the victims as a result of their lawsuits. The insurance company claimed that it had no duty to defend the diocese or pay any judgments since (1) the diocese had violated the insurance policy by not providing it with timely notice of the claims; (2) the priests' actions were intentional, and the policy excluded any coverage for intentional acts; and (3) the victims sought punitive damages which were excluded under the policy. The court rejected the insurance company's position, and ordered it to defend the diocese and its officials in the lawsuits brought by the alleged molestation victims. The court pointed out that under Rhode Island law "an insurer's duty to defend is broader than its duty to indemnify," and that "a duty to defend arises if the factual allegations contained in the complaint raise a reasonable possibility of coverage. An insurer is not relieved of its duty to defend . . . on the ground that the claim against the insured lacks merit. In short, determining whether an insurer has a duty to defend requires nothing more than comparing the allegations in the complaint with the terms of the policy. If the facts alleged in the complaint fall within the risks covered by the policy, the insurer is obligated to defend. Otherwise, it is not."*

---

[256] Houg v. State Farm Fire and Casualty Company, 481 N.W.2d 393 (Minn. App. 1992).
[257] Aetna Casualty & Surety Company v. Kelly, 889 F. Supp. 535 (D.R.I. 1995).

3. DUTY TO COOPERATE

Most insurance policies impose a "duty to cooperate" on the insured. This means that a church must cooperate with its insurance company in any investigation, or in responding to reasonable requests for information. Church leaders should be aware of this requirement and understand that a failure to cooperate may result in the denial of insurance benefits. There are limits to the authority of an insurance company to investigate. However, churches should never decline an insurance company's request for information without the advice and consent of a local attorney.

> *Example. A church building and its contents were totally destroyed in a fire of suspicious origin. The loss was covered by an insurance policy, and the church promptly filed a claim against its insurance company. The insurance company launched an investigation into the facts and circumstances surrounding the fire. It notified the church that it wanted numerous documents, including (1) a list of monthly expenses for the church, (2) a listing of all income of the church, including the names of donors and the amounts they individually contributed, (3) copies of tax returns filed by the church, (4) copies of tax returns filed by the directors and officers of the church, and (5) a list of the salaries of the directors and officers (from their secular employment). The basis for this request for information was a provision in the insurance policy specifying that the insurance company "may examine and audit the named insured's books and records at any time during the policy period and extensions thereof and within three years after the final termination of this policy, as far as they relate to the subject matter of this insurance." Despite being warned by the insurance company's attorney that a refusal to provide the requested information might lead to a refusal to a denial of any coverage under the policy, the church refused to provide the requested information. A New York court ruled that the church had to provide the documents that were "material and relevant to the issue of [its] financial status at the time of the fire," if the fire loss was to be covered under the insurance policy. However, the court emphasized that "the circumstances presented do not provide a basis for [the insurance company] to be granted access to personal financial information pertaining to [the church's] board of directors and officers, or to the names of church donors . . . ."[258]*

> *Example. A church sustained a $100,000 fire loss, and promptly notified its insurance company. However, the insurance company refused to pay for any portion of the loss because of the church's alleged failure to cooperate in the investigation of the claim. In particular, the insurance company complained that the church refused to allow certain individuals to be examined under oath. The church sued its insurance company, and a state appeals court has ordered the case to proceed to trial. A jury will now decide if the insurance company acted properly in denying coverage.[259]*

4. DUTY TO NOTIFY

Most insurance policies impose on the insured a duty to promptly notify the insurance company of any potential claim. Failure to comply with this condition can result in a loss of coverage. Here are some points to consider:

• *Notifying your broker may not be enough.* Many churches purchase their insurance through a local broker. Sometimes this person is a member of the congregation. Church leaders naturally assume that in the event of an accident or injury they can simply call this individual and everything will be "taken care of." This case illustrates that such a conclusion may not always be correct. A broker may not be deemed to be an "agent"

---

[258] Church of St. Matthew v. Aetna Casualty and Surety Co., 554 N.Y.S.2d 563 (A.D. 1 Dept. 1990).
[259] Bethel Baptist Church v. Church Mutual Insurance Company, 924 S.W.2d 494 (Ark. App. 1996).

of the insurance companies he or she represents, and accordingly when a church provides its insurance broker with notice of an accident or loss it is not necessarily notifying its insurance company.

> *Tip. If you notify your insurance broker of a loss, insist on a written assurance that he or she will notify the insurance company in writing within the period of time specified in the insurance policy. If you do not hear back within a week or so, contact the broker again to follow up. Better yet, the church itself should notify both its broker and insurance company. The insurance company's address will be listed on your insurance policy. Ask the insurance company to provide you with written confirmation of receipt of your notice.*

• *Written rather than oral notice.* If your insurance policy requires written notice, then be sure you provide written rather than oral notice of a loss.

> *Tip. Church leaders should be familiar with the insurance policy's provisions regarding notification of the insurance company. Is written notice required? If so, how soon after a loss? It is essential that these provisions be scrupulously followed in order to prevent a loss of coverage.*

> *Tip. If you change insurance companies, be sure to review the new insurance policy. Do not assume that it will contain the same "notice" provisions as your previous policy.*

• *A reasonable time.* How soon does your church insurance policy require that notice be submitted to the insurance company following an accident or loss? Be sure you know, and that this requirement is followed whenever there is an accident, personal injury, or other kind of loss.

> *Tip. The duty to inform your insurance company of an accident or loss arises when the injury occurs, and not when a lawsuit is filed. The purpose of the notice requirement is to give your insurance company sufficient time to investigate the incident and provide a defense.*

> *Example. The church board at First Church is informed by a parent that her minor child was molested by a church volunteer. The volunteer is questioned, and admits having molested the child. This incident represents a potential "loss" under the church's insurance policy, triggering a duty to inform the church's insurance company of the loss within the period of time specified in the insurance policy. The church should inform its insurance company immediately. It is very important that it not wait until a lawsuit is filed to notify its insurance company. Such a delay not only hinders the insurance company's ability to investigate the incident and defend the case, but it also may result in loss of coverage under the policy. This could have disastrous consequences to the church.*

> *Example. A federal court in Rhode Island ruled that a diocese's insurance company had a legal duty to defend diocesan officials who were sued as a result of the sexual molestation of several children by Catholic priests, despite the insurance company's claim that the diocese had failed to promptly notify it of the potential claims.[260] The court pointed out that for the insurance company to prevail on this claim it would have to prove that the incidents of molestation actually occurred and that the diocese was aware of them. The court noted that these are the very facts that the victims would have to prove to hold the diocese liable for their injuries, and it would be unthinkable for the diocese's own insurance company to attempt to prove the victims' case for them. Such efforts "would be inconsistent with [the insur-*

---

[260] Aetna Casualty & Surety Company v. Kelly, 889 F. Supp. 535 (D.R.I. 1995).

ance company's] obligations as an insurer. The principal purpose of liability insurance is to protect policy holders from claims asserted by third parties based on matters covered by the policy. By taking action that makes a policy holder liable for such claims, an insurer would subvert the purpose of the policy and violate one of the most fundamental duties it owes to its insured."

Example. *A church member was injured when he fell on church property during a funeral.[261] At the time of the injury, the church had a general liability insurance policy that required the church to give the insurance company written notice of any accident "as soon as practicable." Immediately following the accident the pastor instructed the chairman of the board of trustees to notify the church's insurance broker about the accident. The chairman did so by calling the insurance broker's office. An employee of the broker assured the chairman that the insurance company would be duly notified. In fact, the insurance company was not notified. Nine months later the church received a letter from an attorney for the injured member threatening to sue the church unless it paid the member a large amount of money. The church immediately turned this letter over to its insurance broker, who in turn forwarded it to the church's insurance company. The insurance company refused to provide the church with a defense of the lawsuit or pay any amount of money based on the accident since the church had failed to provide it with written notice of the accident "as soon as practicable" as required by the insurance policy. The church responded by suing its insurance company. It sought a court order requiring the insurance company to defend the church under the terms of the policy and to pay for any damages awarded by a jury. A state appeals court ruled that the insurance company had no legal duty to defend the church or pay for any jury verdict since the church had failed to notify it of the accident "as soon as practicable." The court concluded that when the church gave notice of the accident to its insurance broker it was not giving notice to its insurance company as required by the policy. In addition, the insurance policy required that the church provide the insurance company with written notice of any accident. Even if the broker were an agent of the insurance company, the church still failed to comply with the terms of the insurance policy since it provided the broker with oral rather than written notice of the accident.*

5. COVERAGE LIMITS

Insurance policies only provide coverage up to the "limits" specified in the policy. Church leaders should be familiar with the limits in their church insurance policy, and be certain that these limits are adequate. The adequacy of policy limits is a complex question that involves an analysis of several conditions. Most importantly, a church should consider its own net worth, and the frequency and relative risk of its programs and activities. Discuss the adequacy of your limits with your insurance agent, or with an insurance broker.

Some church insurance policies have reduced limits for certain risks, including sexual misconduct. This may expose the board to greater risk, as plaintiffs seek to recover damages in excess of the policy limits by suing board members directly.

Example. *A federal appeals court ruled that several children who were molested over a number of years by two priests represented multiple "occurrences" under a church insurance policy.[262] Two priests molested 31 children over a 7-year period. The priests were sued along with their diocese, and a question arose as to the number of "occurrences" the numerous incidents of molestation represented under the diocese's insurance policies. These policies provided insurance to the diocese on a "per occurrence" basis.*

---

[261] Shaw Temple v. Mount Vernon Fire Insurance Company, 605 N.Y.S.2d 370 (A.D. 2 Dept. 1994)
[262] Society of Roman Catholic Church v. Interstate Fire & Casualty Co., 26 F.3d 1359 (5th Cir. 1994).

The more occurrences that occurred, the more insurance coverage that was available. The court acknowledged that defining this term in the context of multiple acts of molestation occurring over several years is difficult: "An occurrence could be the church's continuous negligent supervision of a priest, the negligent supervision of a priest with respect to each child, the negligent supervision of a priest with respect to each molestation, or each time the diocese became aware of a fact which should have led it to intervene, just to name a few possibilities." The court added that "when a term in an insurance policy has uncertain application [the courts] interpret the policy in favor of the insured." The court concluded that "[w]hen a priest molested a child during a policy year, there was both bodily injury and an occurrence, triggering policy coverage. All further molestations of that child during the policy period arose out of the same occurrence. When the priest molested the same child during the succeeding policy year, again there was both bodily injury and an occurrence. Thus, each child suffered an occurrence in each policy period in which he was molested." To illustrate, a child that was molested several times in each of seven different years represented seven different "occurrences" under the insurance policies. On the other hand, several incidents of molestation occurring within the same year represented only one occurrence.

6. LIABILITY FOR MAINTAINING INADEQUATE INSURANCE COVERAGE

A few churches have been sued for failing to maintain adequate insurance coverage. Such claims have been rejected by the courts.

__Example.__ The Kansas Supreme Court ruled that a student who was rendered a permanent quadriplegic as a result of injuries sustained while playing football for a church-operated high school could not sue church officials for failing to obtain adequate insurance coverage.[263] The victim alleged that the school and church officials had been negligent in "failing to properly insure students for injury incurred as a result of school activities and in failing to properly advise and inform students and their parents . . . of the insurance protection provided to students." In rejecting this claim, the court cited a state law making the purchase of liability insurance coverage by public schools discretionary rather than mandatory. Such a law, reasoned the court, applied "by implication" to private schools as well. Since private schools were not required to purchase insurance, they could not be liable for failure to have enough coverage to cover catastrophic losses. "We feel sympathy for the severe injuries suffered by this plaintiff," concluded the court. "However, there are dangers and risks inherent in the game of football and those who play the game encounter these risks voluntarily. It is fundamental that before there can be any recovery in tort there must be a violation of a duty owed by one party to the person seeking recovery. . . . It is clear under the facts of this case that no . . . duty existed to properly insure or to advise the plaintiff regarding medical insurance purchased by the defendants for the plaintiff."

7. PUNITIVE DAMAGES

Church insurance policies exclude punitive damages. This means that a jury award of punitive damages represents an uninsured risk. As a result, it is important for church leaders to understand the basis for punitive damages. Punitive damages are damages awarded by a jury "in addition to compensation for a loss sustained, in order to punish, and make an example of, the wrongdoer." They are awarded when a defendant's conduct is particularly reprehensible and outrageous. This does not necessarily mean intentional misconduct. Punitive damages often are associated with reckless conduct or conduct creating a high risk of harm. Unfortunately, it is not uncommon for church leaders to ignore significant risks. Church leaders must understand that reckless

---

[263] Wicina v. Strecker, 747 P.2d 167 (Kan. 1987).

inattention to such risks can lead to punitive damages, and that such damages may not be covered by the church's liability insurance policy.

8. What Claims Are Covered

What claims does an insurance policy cover? Assume that a church obtains insurance from Company X for several years, but in the current year it switches to Company Y. The church is sued this year for an incident of child molestation that occurred when the church had insurance with Company X. Which insurance company is obligated to defend and indemnify the church? That depends on the nature of the insurance that the church purchased. Some policies cover claims that occur only during the term of the insurance contract, while others cover claims that are filed during the term of the insurance contract no matter when the actual injury occurred. Church leaders should be familiar with these different types of coverage and understand what kind of insurance their church has obtained.

9. Other Matters

Here are some additional points to note about church insurance:

• *Retaining your policies.* It is important for church leaders to keep church insurance policies permanently, since some claims (such as sexual misconduct) may arise years or even decades later, and a church may need to produce a copy of the insurance contract for the year in which the misconduct occurred in order to obtain coverage.

• *Reservation of rights letters.* It is common for churches to receive a "reservation of rights" letter when they report a claim to their insurance company. Under such a reservation, an insurance company agrees to defend an insured, but reserves the right to deny any obligation to pay an adverse judgment as a result of an exclusion in the policy.

• *Periodic insurance review.* Churches should appoint an insurance committee consisting of persons with some knowledge of insurance who periodically review the church's insurance coverages to ensure they are adequate.

§ 10-16.8 — Other Defenses

> **Key point 10-16.8.** *Churches have various defenses available to them if they are sued as a result of a personal injury. One such defense is an arbitration policy. By adopting an arbitration policy, a church can compel members to arbitrate specified disputes with their church rather than pursue their claim in the civil courts.*

The courts have recognized various other defenses that are available to churches in the event of litigation. Here are some of them:

1. Status of the Person Causing the Injury or Damage

Since a church is liable only for the injuries and damages caused by employees and volunteers, a church generally will not be liable for injuries inflicted by independent contractors.

2. Course of Employment

Since a church is liable only for the injuries and damages caused by employees acting in the course of their employment, a church generally will not be liable for injuries inflicted by employees outside of the course of their employment.

3. Arbitration

Utilizing informal methods of dispute resolution is an idea whose time has come. The civil court system in this nation is deficient in many respects—litigants enter and leave the courtroom as enemies, delays are notorious, expenses are often staggering, and the results often seem unpredictable and arbitrary. As a result, many business organizations are pursuing informal methods of dispute resolution, including binding arbitration. The concept is simple—parties agree in advance to resolve their disputes before one or more arbitrators rather than before the civil courts. Disputes generally are resolved more quickly, with less expense, and with fairer results.

There are two excellent reasons for considering arbitration and mediation in addition to the obvious advantages of speed, cost, and fairness. First, as is obvious from even a casual reading of this text, the vast majority of lawsuits involving churches are brought by "insiders" (i.e., members and adherents). Arbitration is ideal for such disputes. Second, there is scriptural support for arbitration of internal church disputes. In 1 Corinthians 6:1-8 (NIV), the apostle Paul observed:

> If any of you has a dispute with another, dare he take it before the ungodly for judgment instead of before the saints? Do you not know that the saints will judge the world? And if you are to judge the world, are you not competent to judge trivial cases? Do you not know that we will judge angels? How much more the things of this life! Therefore, if you have disputes about such matters, appoint as judges even men of little account in the church! I say this to shame you. Is it possible that there is nobody among you wise enough to judge a dispute between believers? But instead, one brother goes to law against another--and this in front of unbelievers! The very fact that you have lawsuits among you means you have been completely defeated already. Why not rather be wronged? Why not rather be cheated? Instead, you yourselves cheat and do wrong, and you do this to your brothers.

In drafting an arbitration policy, keep the following considerations in mind:

• How will the policy be implemented? There are a number of options, including an amendment to the church's bylaws, or a board-adopted policy that is referenced on each new member's membership card. The most effective means of adopting an arbitration policy is for the church membership to adopt one as an amendment to the church bylaws. Since members are bound by the church bylaws (including any amendments),[264] this approach will have the best chance of binding all members.

• What disputes will be referred to arbitration? Only those disputes relating to church affairs? Disputes between members? What about disputes between a minister and other members, or between a minister and either the church board or the church itself? What about disputes between employees and the church? These are very important questions to resolve.

---

[264] Watson v. Jones, 80 U.S. 679, 729 (1871) ("[a]ll who unite themselves to such a body do so with an implied consent to its government, and are bound to submit to it").

- How will the arbitration process be conducted? Often, each side in a dispute selects an arbitrator, and the two persons so selected choose a third arbitrator. Of course, the third arbitrator must be completely unbiased. Arbitration procedure often is quite informal, and attorneys may or may not be allowed to participate.

- It is essential to consult with the church's liability insurer before implementing any arbitration policy to ensure that it is in complete agreement with the concept and it will honor arbitrators' judgments up to the policy limits. Churches should not change insurers without obtaining the same assurances. The arbitration policy may even contain language conditioning its use on acceptance by the church's liability insurer.

- Enlist the services of an attorney in drafting an arbitration policy.

Example. Maryland's highest court ruled that an arbitration award addressing the composition of a church's board of trustees was not reviewable by the civil courts since any review would require an interpretation of religious doctrine.[265] A dispute arose within a church regarding control of church property. A faction of the church board (the "dissident faction"), headed by the board's president, claimed that the church had become extinct because its minister had died and there were no living members. This group did not recognize the current congregation to be "members." Another faction of the board opposed the dissidents and called a special business meeting to elect a new board. The dissident faction claimed that this election was invalid because the meeting had not been properly called by the president as required by the church's bylaws. The dissident group later authorized the merger of the church with another congregation, and the resulting church elected new trustees including the dissident members and president. As a result, there were two boards of trustees claiming control of the church and its property. In order to resolve this impasse, the parties submitted the dispute to arbitration pursuant to a provision in the Maryland nonprofit corporation law. This provision specifies that "if any contest arises over the voting rights or the fair conduct of an election," then the matter shall be submitted to arbitration and the arbitrators' judgment will be "final." The arbitrators ruled in favor of the board elected at the special business meeting, and the dissident board members immediately appealed to a civil court. The court refused to adopt a rule preventing civil court review of all arbitration awards involving church elections. While conceding that the civil courts could not review such awards if they involve religious doctrine or polity, it noted that not all disputes fall into this category. The court concluded that this dispute did involve religious doctrine and polity, making any judicial review of the arbitration award impermissible: "The root question, then, is whether the [church] was extinct . . . . The church would be deemed extinct if it had no members; the existence of members, conversely, would keep the church alive. It is well-settled in this state that the determination of a membership in a church is a question well embedded in the theological thicket and one that will not be entertained by the civil courts."

Example. A New Jersey court upheld an arbitration award entered in a dispute between a synagogue and its rabbi.[266] The synagogue and its rabbi were embroiled in a "lengthy and destructive dispute" that they agreed to submit to binding arbitration by a panel of ecclesiastical experts (a "Beth Din"). The "arbitration agreement" signed by the parties specified, "This is to certify that we the undersigned fully accept upon ourselves the following judgment of the Beth Din of the Union of Orthodox Rabbis of the United States and Canada . . . to adjudicate between us according to their judicious wisdom, we affirm hereby that we have accepted upon ourselves to obey and fulfill the judgment which shall issue forth from this Beth Din whether it be verdict or compromise, according to the determination of the afore-

---

[265] American Union of Baptists v. Trustees of the Particular Primitive Baptist Church, 644 A.2d 1063 (Md. 1994). *See also* Seat Pleasant v. Long, 691 A.2d 721 (Md. App. 1997).

[266] Elmora Hebrew Center v. Fishman, 570 A.2d 1297 (N.J. Super. 1990), *aff'd,* 593 A.2d 725 (N.J. 1991).

mentioned judges without any appeal whatsoever before any Beth Din under Jewish law or any civil court, but it is incumbent upon us to obey the verdict of the aforementioned Beth Din without any further complaint. All of the above was entered into voluntarily . . . without any reservations whatsoever in a recognizable and legally binding manner and is entered into in a manner so to be completely and lawfully binding." After an extended hearing involving "voluminous documentary evidence" and "lengthy oral testimony," the Beth Din ordered the synagogue to pay the rabbi $100,000, and asked the rabbi to resign "for the sake of peace" (it found no other basis to remove him). The synagogue appealed this arbitration order to a state civil court. A state appeals court upheld the decision of the Beth Din, and rejected the synagogue's appeal. It observed that the "arbitration agreement" was entered into "freely and voluntarily, with an awareness on the part of both sides as to the meaning and significance of that form of religious dispute resolution." The court noted that the authority of a civil court to review an arbitration award is "extremely limited," and is not permissible "absent proof of fraud, partiality, [or] misconduct on the part of the arbitrators . . . ." The court concluded by noting that "the law favors dispute resolution through consensual arbitration, and so the award is presumed to be valid. So it is here. On this record, the Beth Din's decision and award must be confirmed."

§ 10-17 Damages — In General

When a jury finds a church liable in a civil lawsuit, it can award monetary damages to the plaintiff. Monetary damages may be either compensatory or punitive in nature. Compensatory damages are awarded to compensate plaintiffs for the actual injuries or harm they have suffered. They are intended to restore plaintiffs, as much as possible, to their condition before they were injured. Punitive damages are addressed in the next subsection.

§ 10-17.1 — Punitive Damages

Key point 10-17.1. *Punitive damages are monetary damages awarded by a jury "in addition to compensation for a loss sustained, in order to punish, and make an example of, the wrongdoer." They are awarded when a person's conduct is reprehensible and outrageous. Most church insurance policies exclude punitive damages. This means that a jury award of punitive damages represents an uninsured risk.*

Punitive damages are monetary damages awarded by a jury "in addition to compensation for a loss sustained, in order to punish, and make an example of, the wrongdoer." They are awarded when a person's conduct is particularly reprehensible and outrageous. This does not necessarily mean intentional misconduct. Punitive damages often are associated with reckless conduct or conduct creating a high risk of harm. It is critical to note that many church insurance policies exclude punitive damages. This means that a jury award of punitive damages represents an uninsured risk. Accordingly, it is critical for church leaders to understand the basis for punitive damages.

Example. *A Kentucky court ruled that an adult who had been sexually molested as a minor by a teacher at a parochial school could sue the diocese that operated the school for negligent hiring, supervision, and retention.[267] A jury awarded the victim $50,000 in compensatory damages and $700,000 in punitive damages, and it apportioned fault seventy-five percent to the diocese and twenty-five percent to the teacher. An appeals court rejected the claim of the diocese that the jury erred in awarding $700,000 in punitive damages against it. Kentucky law provides that "[a] plaintiff shall recover punitive damages*

---

[267] Roman Catholic Diocese v. Secter, 966 S.W.2d 286 (Ky. App. 1998).

only upon proving, by clear and convincing evidence, that the defendant from whom such damages are sought acted toward the plaintiff with oppression, fraud or malice." The diocese argued that by the plain language of the statute, punitive damages are available only upon a showing that it acted with fraud, malice, or oppression toward the victim and that there was no evidence that it acted in this manner since it had no way of knowing that the teacher had abused the victim or would likely do so. The court rejected this argument.

Example. *A Minnesota appeals court concluded that churches and denominational agencies can be liable for punitive damages (which are meant to punish defendants for shocking and reprehensible conduct).*[268] *The case involved a Catholic priest who repeatedly was placed by church officials in situations in which he could sexually abuse boys, despite knowledge by church officials of the priest's propensities. A jury awarded a victim $855,000 in compensatory damages and $2,700,000 in punitive damages. The court upheld the trial court's reduction in the punitive damages award to approximately $187,000, based on the church's limited resources and the "total effect" of "other punishment" upon the church, including monetary damages in similar lawsuits and the extent of negative publicity generated by the trial. The court rejected the church's claim that subjecting it to punitive damages violated the state constitution, which prohibits interference with religious freedom. However, the court noted that the state constitution further states: "[T]he liberty of conscience hereby secured shall not be so construed as to excuse acts of licentiousness or justify practices inconsistent with the peace or safety of the state." The court concluded, "The church's actions . . . fall within this exclusion. The repeated placement of [the priest] in parishes without restriction arguably condoned acts of licentious behavior and justified practices inconsistent with the peace and safety of the state. Awarding punitive damages furthers the state's interest in protecting its citizens from harm by deterring and punishing such conduct. The state is not only concerned with compensating plaintiffs, but also ensuring that similar conduct does not harm others in the future. Here, the unavailability of criminal sanctions and the ineffectiveness of a punitive damages award against the individuals involved support the trial court's determination that an imposition of punitive damages against the church is appropriate because the state's goals cannot be accomplished through less restrictive means." The court rejected the church's claim that there was insufficient evidence to establish a claim for punitive damages.*

Example. *A federal district court in Michigan ruled that a church school and various church agencies were not liable on the basis of negligent hiring, supervision, or retention, for the sexual molestation of a minor student by a priest.*[269] *The court also noted that neither the school nor any of the church agencies was liable for punitive damages. It noted that under Wisconsin law (the law applicable to the case) punitive damages can be awarded in only two situations: (1) "a defendant desires to cause the harm sustained by the plaintiff, or believes that the harm is substantially certain to follow his conduct"; or (2) the defendant knows, or should have reason to know, not only that his conduct creates an unreasonable risk or harm, but also that there is a strong probability, although not a substantial certainty, that the harm will result, but, nevertheless, he proceeds with his conduct in reckless or conscious disregard of the consequences." The court continued, "Wisconsin courts often use the short-hand term 'outrageous' for the type of conduct which justifies the imposition of punitive damages. This 'outrageous' conduct must be proven by clear and convincing evidence. However, the fact that the conduct on which the suit is based is unlawful and would subject the defendant to criminal prosecution is not itself sufficient to impose punitive damages. Given the 'clear and convincing' evidentiary standard which governs the*

---

[268] Mrozka v. Archdiocese of St. Paul and Minneapolis, 482 N.W.2d 806 (Minn. App. 1992).
[269] Isely v. Capuchin Province, 880 F. Supp. 1138 (E.D. Mich. 1995).

punitive damages, the court finds that the evidence presented is not sufficient to warrant submitting the punitive damages claims to the jury."

§ 10-17.2 — Duplicate Verdicts

Key point 10-17.2. *Juries generally cannot assess monetary damages against two or more organizations for the same wrong. If a jury determines that a personal injury victim has suffered damages of a specified amount, it cannot assess this amount separately against more than one defendant since doing so would result in duplicate verdicts.*

Juries generally cannot assess monetary damages against two or more entities for the same wrong. To illustrate, assume that a victim of sexual misconduct sues a church and a denominational agency, and that a jury determines that the victim's damages amounted to $100,000. If the jury then assesses this amount of damages against both the church and denominational agency, it has rendered duplicate verdicts. Such verdicts are subject to reduction by the trial court or an appeals court.

Example. A Colorado court addressed the liability of a church and denominational agency for a sexual relationship between a youth pastor and a girl in his youth group. The victim sued the youth pastor, her church, and a denominational agency.[270] The jury awarded her $187,500 in compensatory damages against the youth pastor on claims of breach of fiduciary duty and outrageous conduct and another $187,500 in punitive damages. It awarded her $37,500 in compensatory damages against the church on claims of negligent hiring and supervision and breach of fiduciary duty. The jury awarded $150,000 in compensatory damages against the denominational agency on claims of negligent hiring and supervision and breach of fiduciary duty, and an additional $150,000 in punitive damages. The church and denominational agency argued that the jury's various awards of damages were inconsistent. In particular, they argued that it was illogical to award damages against both the youth pastor and church defendants on the basis of the same theories of liability. The court agreed, noting that the jury's award of damages against the youth pastor and church defendants for the same alleged wrongs resulted in "duplication of damages" since the actions of the church defendants did not result in any additional harm to the victim beyond what had been caused by the youth pastor.

§ 10-18 Denominational Liability — In General

Denominational agencies can be liable for their own acts. For example, they may be directly liable for the negligent driving of a denominational official in the course of church business; defamatory statements in denominational publications; or unlawful discrimination or wrongful termination claims involving their own employees.

However, national and regional denominational agencies also have been sued for the acts and obligations of ministers and lay workers at affiliated churches. Such lawsuits often are little more than a search for a "deep pocket" out of which to pay damages when the local church has inadequate insurance coverage or financial resources. Most of these cases fall into one of two categories: (1) incidents of sexual misconduct by clergy or lay church workers, or (2) personal injuries resulting from accidents (on church property, during church activities, or involving a church vehicle).

---

[270] Bohrer v. DeHart, 943 P.2d 1220 (Colo. App. 1996).

The alleged basis for denominational liability in such cases generally will be one or more of the theories of liability addressed previously in this chapter in connection with the liability of local churches. To illustrate, if a denominational agency is sued because of the sexual misconduct of a minister, the agency may be sued on the basis of respondeat superior; negligent selection, supervision, or retention of the minister; or breach of a fiduciary duty. Some plaintiffs have asserted that a denominational agency will be liable in such cases on the basis of an "agency" relationship with the offending minister.

Plaintiffs who sue denominational agencies for injuries resulting from accidents generally assert that the denomination is liable on the basis of "agency" for the acts and obligations of affiliated churches.

The following subsections will address (1) court rulings finding denominational agencies liable for the acts of affiliated ministers and churches; (2) court rulings finding denominational agencies not liable for the acts of affiliated ministers and churches; (3) defenses to liability; and (4) risk management.

§ 10-18.1 — Court Decisions Recognizing Liability

> *Key point 10-18.1. Some courts have found denominational agencies liable for the acts of affiliated ministers and churches on the basis of a number of grounds, including negligence and agency.*

This subsection addresses the "secondary" liability of denominational agencies for the acts and obligations of affiliated churches, ministers, and lay workers. This form of liability is sometimes referred to as "ascending liability." Denominations also are subject to direct liability for their own acts, and these kinds of liability are addressed previously in this and other chapters.

In a small number of cases, the civil courts have found denominational agencies liable for the acts and obligations of affiliated churches, agencies, clergy, and lay workers. Most of the earlier cases involved liability based on the negligent driving of affiliated clergy. To illustrate, in 1951 the California Supreme Court ruled that a presbytery was responsible for injuries caused by the negligent driving of the pastor of an affiliated "mission church."[271] The court concluded that the pastor was an "agent" of the presbytery, since "he was not responsible to the local church but only to the presbytery. The presbytery, not the church, had the power to remove him. Furthermore, he could not transfer to another pastorate without permission of the presbytery, and in fact he was a member of the presbytery rather than of the local church." The court concluded:

> The existence of the right of control and supervision establishes the existence of an agency relationship [making the employer legally responsible for the acts of an employee committed within the scope of his or her employment]. The evidence clearly supports the conclusion of the jury that such control existed in the present case. The right of the presbytery to install and remove its ministers, to approve or disapprove their transfer to other jurisdictions, and to supervise and control the activities of the local churches, particularly those in the mission stage, is inconsistent with a contrary conclusion.[272]

The court emphasized that the presbytery exercised significant control over "missions" churches (it held title to all church property, assisted with the churches' finance, and paid a portion of clergy salaries). It cautioned that "we are not here called upon to determine the liability of the presbytery for negligence in the activities of a fully established and independently incorporated Presbyterian church which has passed from the mission stage."

---

[271] Malloy v. Fong, 232 P.2d 241 (Cal. 1951).
[272] Id. *at 249-50.*

In a similar case, a California appeals court ruled that a trial court had improperly dismissed a lawsuit against a denomination (the International Church of the Foursquare Gospel).[273] The denomination had been sued by a person who was injured as a result of the negligent driving of one of the denomination's pastors (while engaged in church business). The court concluded that there was ample evidence demonstrating that the denomination was legally responsible for the injuries since the pastor was its "agent," and was acting within the scope of church business at the time of the accident. Accordingly, the trial court acted improperly in dismissing the case.

The court based its finding of an agency relationship upon the following factors: (1) The denomination's charter specified that it was incorporated "to supervise the management of the churches of the [denomination]," and to establish and grant charters to churches which would "be subject at all times to the supervision of [the denomination]." (2) The denomination ordained ministers "for the furtherance of the work of the [denomination]." (3) All property or equipment acquired by any local church is required to be held in the name of the denomination. (4) No church is allowed to execute a general contract to build without the written consent of a denominational official. (5) Each church is required to keep books of account and to prepare full and accurate monthly reports of activities in such form as is prescribed by the denomination. (6) The denomination is empowered to remove from office pastors who are not functioning in such a manner as to promote the best interests of their church. (7) Pastors who desire to transfer to a church in another state must secure a letter of transfer from a denominational official. (8) One of the pastor's duties is to see that the local church cooperates in all programs of the denomination.

The court concluded, on the basis of these facts, that "manifestly, this evidence meets every requirement for the establishment of an agency relationship as set forth in Malloy v. Fong.*"[274] Further, the pastor was not only an agent of the denomination, but also was acting within the scope of his duties at the time of the accident. Accordingly, the denomination was legally responsible for his negligence.*

In a third California state court ruling, an appeals court ruled that a Catholic bishop was legally responsible for a death caused by the negligent driving of a priest.[275] The priest was a French citizen who was sent to the United States to minister to the religious and cultural needs of Basque Catholics residing in the western United States. The state appeals court concluded that the priest was an agent of the bishop, and was acting within the scope of his agency at the time of the accident. The "significant test of an agency relationship," observed the court, "is the principal's right to control the activities of the agent." While acknowledging that the "evidence of agency is not strong," the court concluded that there was sufficient evidence to establish that the priest's activities were subject to the control of the bishop. It relied primarily upon the following considerations: (1) The bishop, "had he chosen, could have exercised full authority over [the priest] by extending to him an official, written assignment." While the bishop never took this step, the court concluded that he could have, and this was sufficient. (2) The bishop had jurisdiction over the priest's ministry. (3) In a letter to the Immigration and Naturalization Service, the bishop had stated that the priest was "under the direction of the undersigned bishop of this diocese." (4) In ministering to Basque Catholics, the priest "was performing some of the duties the bishop was responsible for."

In a fourth California case, a state appeals court ruled that the United Methodist Church (UMC) could be sued for the alleged misconduct of a subsidiary.[276] The UMC was sued for the alleged improprieties of a

---

[273] Miller v. International Church of the Foursquare Gospel, Inc., 37 Cal. Rptr. 309 (Cal. 1964).
[274] *See* note 271, *supra,* and accompanying text.
[275] Stevens v. Roman Catholic Bishop of Fresno, 123 Cal. Rptr. 171 (Cal. App. 1975).
[276] Barr v. United Methodist Church, 153 Cal. Rptr. 322 (1979), *cert. denied,* 444 U.S. 973 (1979).

subsidiary corporation that operated fourteen nursing homes in California, Arizona, and Hawaii. When the subsidiary encountered financial difficulties, it raised the monthly payments of residents in violation of the terms of their "continuing care agreements" that guaranteed lifetime nursing and medical care for a fixed price. The subsidiary went bankrupt, and a class of nearly 2,000 residents sued the UMC for fraud and breach of contract. Although the case eventually was settled out of court, a California appeals court did rule that the UMC could be sued for the misconduct of its subsidiary. The court emphasized that the UMC was a hierarchical denomination with control over local churches and subsidiary institutions, ranging from restrictions on the purchase or sale of property to the selection of local church pastors. Such control, observed the court, made the UMC responsible for the liabilities of its affiliated churches and subsidiary institutions. The court also found it relevant that the subsidiary organization that operated the nursing homes was engaged in a commercial enterprise.

The court suggested that the first amendment guaranty of religious freedom might prohibit direct actions against the UMC on account of the actions of subsidiary organizations if the allowance of such actions "would affect the distribution of power or property within the denomination, would modify or interfere with modes of worship affected by Methodists or would have any effect other than to oblige UMC to defend itself when sued upon civil obligations it is alleged to have incurred."[277]

More recent cases involving denominational liability have focused largely on "ascending liability" claims involving sexual misconduct by affiliated clergy or lay workers. Many of these cases are summarized in Table 10-4.

§ 10-18.2 — Court Decisions Rejecting Liability

Key point 10-18.2. Most courts have refused to hold denominational agencies liable for the acts of affiliated ministers and churches, either because of first amendment considerations or because the relationship between the denominational agency and affiliated church or minister is too remote to support liability.

This subsection addresses the "secondary" liability of denominational agencies for the acts and obligations of affiliated churches, ministers, and lay workers. This form of liability is sometimes referred to as "ascending liability." Denominations also are subject to direct liability for their own acts, and these kinds of liability are addressed previously in this and other chapters.

Leading cases addressing denominational liability are summarized in Table 10-4.

§ 10-18.3 — Defenses to Liability

Key point 10-18.3. There are several legal defenses available to a denominational agency that is sued as a result of the acts or obligations of affiliated clergy and churches. These include a lack of temporal control over clergy and churches; a lack of official notice of a minister's prior wrongdoing in accordance with the denomination's governing documents; lack of an agency relationship; the prohibition by the first amendment of any attempt by the civil courts to impose liability on religious organizations in a way that would threaten or alter their polity; and elimination or modification of the principle of joint and several liability.

---

[277] *Id.* at 332.

There are a number of legal defenses available to a denominational agency that is sued as a result of the acts or obligations of affiliated ministers or churches. Some of these are the same that are available to local churches, and they are addressed in previous sections of this chapter. Others are more unique to denominational agencies, and they are addressed in this subsection.

Most attempts to hold denominations legally accountable for the activities of clergy or affiliated churches have failed. The courts have relied on a variety of grounds in reaching this conclusion. The more important grounds are summarized in the paragraphs that follow.

1. Ecclesiastical Rather than Temporal Control

A number of courts have recognized that some denominations have authority to exercise only ecclesiastical control over affiliated clergy and churches, and that this form of control is not enough to warrant the imposition of legal liability upon the denomination for the activities of clergy and churches. In one of the earliest cases, the national conference of the Pentecostal Holiness Church was sued for breach of contract when its Florida regional conference defaulted on a life-care contract with two elderly church members who resided in a nursing home owned by the conference.[278] A state appeals court concluded that the national conference could not be sued for the financial improprieties of a local church or regional conference since local churches and regional conferences were totally independent of the national conference with respect to financial matters.

In a similar case, a Florida court made the following observation in a lawsuit attempting to impute liability to the Central Florida Diocese of the Episcopalian Church for injuries sustained on the premises of a local Episcopalian church:

> [W]e perceive the Constitution and Canons of the Diocese to be in the nature of a contract between it and its missions and parishes. In that circumstance, consistent with the well-settled principle that it is a function of the court to construe and interpret contracts, it was error to grant to the jury the power to interpret the Constitution and Canons in the search for an agency relationship . . . between the Diocese and [the local church]. [W]e conclude that where vicarious liability is sought to be imposed upon one of two ostensibly interrelated entities through the ordinary principles of agency, the imposition of such liability is unwarranted in the absence of evidence revealing that one entity controls the other. Our analysis of the Diocese's Constitution and Canons fails to disclose that quantum of diocesan control, let alone domination, over the everyday secular affairs of [the local church] to sustain the imputation of liability to the Diocese. Indeed, we do not gainsay that the Diocese has impressed upon and demands from [the local church] unfailing obedience to ecclesiastical dogma, discipline and authority. We subscribe, however, to the concept that whenever a religious society incorporates, it assumes a dual existence; two distinct entities come into being—one, the church, which is conceived and endures wholly free from the civil law, and the other, the corporation created through the state prescribed method. Each remains separate although closely allied. The components of the ecclesiastical inter-relationship between the parent church and the subordinate body cannot be permitted to serve as a bridge capable of reaching the nonsecular parent in a civil proceeding.[279]

---

[278] Pentecostal Holiness Church, Inc. v. Mauney, 270 So.2d 762 (Fla. 1972), *cert. denied,* 276 So.2d 51 (Fla. 1973).
[279] Folwell v. Bernard, 477 So.2d 1060, 1063 (Fla. App. 1985).

This language illustrates quite well the difference between ecclesiastical relationship and legal agency. To quote the Florida court, "the components of the ecclesiastical interrelationship between the parent church and the subordinate body cannot be permitted to serve as a bridge capable of reaching the nonsecular parent in a civil proceeding." Further, the Florida court observed that "[w]e find no evidence from which a jury could conclude that the Diocese controlled or regulated the church [or its agents] in the maintenance of its grounds or the manner in which the equipment used to maintain the grounds was either operated or kept in repair." In other words, the Diocese could not be liable on an agency theory for injuries occurring on a local church's premises during mowing activities since the Diocese had no authority to control the church's maintenance activities or the instrumentalities that allegedly caused the injuries in question.

The Alabama Supreme Court ruled that a Catholic religious order was not responsible for the misconduct of a priest.[280] The court noted that "the relationship between [the priest] and the society was ecclesiastical and did not necessarily create a . . . principal/agent relationship." The court further observed that

> the law with regard to ecclesiastical orders and religious societies [is] that the relationship is essentially ecclesiastical in nature. I would analogize this to situations where a young man may be in a seminary and the seminary is asked to supply a preacher or a minister for a congregation. The fact that the young minister may have some alma mater does not make the seminary responsible for his behavior in the event he elects to commit a burglary or some other act . . . . [T]he plaintiff must have evidence in addition to the fact that [the priest] was a member of the Benedictine Society of monks.[281]

The Kansas Supreme Court ruled that the fact that a priest was subject to the "ecclesiastical control" of his diocese was not relevant in determining the issue of legal control for purposes of imputing liability to the diocese on the basis of agency or respondeat superior.[282]

In another case, the United States Tax Court addressed the question of whether a minister (Rev. Shelley), who was ordained by the International Pentecostal Holiness Church (IPHC), was an employee or self-employed for federal income tax reporting purposes.[283] The IRS argued that the fact that Rev. Shelley was expected to comply with the provisions of the IPHC Manual indicated that he was an employee. While the Court conceded that the Manual imposed certain requirements on Rev. Shelley, it viewed these as "more in the nature of an outline of his responsibilities than directions on the manner in which he was to perform his duties. We do not find the Manual or its contents to be determinative of an employer-employee relationship." The IRS noted that the Manual described pastors as "amenable to the quadrennial conference and the conference board," and it insisted that this proved an employer-employee relationship. The Tax Court disagreed:

> While this language suggests an employee-employer relationship, we are not persuaded that it fully defines the relationships between the parties. The Manual provides little guidance as to how this amenability is exercised so as to give this description significance. In addition, testimony and other evidence indicate that the relationships between the parties

---

[280] Wood v. Benedictine Society of Alabama, Inc., 530 So.2d 801 (Ala. 1988).

[281] Id. at 806 (quoting from the trial judge's opinion).

[282] Brillhart v. Scheier, 758 P.2d 219 (Kan. 1988).

[283] Shelly v. Commissioner, T.C. Memo. 1994-432 (1994). See also Weber v. Commissioner, 103 T.C. 378 (1994), aff'd, 60 F.3d 1104 (4th Cir. 1995). In Weber, a case involving the correct reporting status of a Methodist minister, the Tax Court observed that "[w]e recognize that there may be differences with respect to ministers in other churches or denominations, and the particular facts and circumstances must be considered in each case."

are more complicated than the statement suggests. A chart included in the Manual depicts the local church board as amenable or accountable to the pastor. But, similarly, an examination of the record reveals that the relationship between those parties is less hierarchical and more interwoven than the chart indicates. While Rev. Shelley had a place in the structure of the IPHC, that structure was a looser affiliation than the strict hierarchy suggested by the term "amenable."

A federal appeals court reached the same conclusion in a case involving the question of whether an Assemblies of God minister (Rev. Alford) was an employee or self-employed for federal income tax reporting purposes.[284] The IRS insisted, based on language in the Constitution and Bylaws of the national church (the "General Council") and a state agency (the "District Council") that Rev. Alford was an employee. In rejecting this conclusion, the court observed:

> The General Council's and District Council's right to control Alford during the relevant years extended primarily to their function in awarding credentials to ministers like himself. Generally, the church has established certain criteria that must be met for an individual such as Alford to obtain credentials initially and to renew that status annually. . . . Thus it is apparent that, while the regional and national churches had doctrinal authority to exercise considerable control over Alford as regards his beliefs and his personal conduct as a minister of the church, they did not have "the right to control the manner and means by which the product [was] accomplished."

> The [trial court] and the United States make much of the fact that Alford, as a minister holding credentials, was "amenable" to the General Council and to the District Council in matters of doctrine and conduct. But this is not unusual in such a profession, and actually is merely a shorthand way of describing the parent church's doctrinal and disciplinary control discussed above. The control exercised by the regional and national organizations, and their right to control Alford, was no more nor less than most professions require of individuals licensed or otherwise authorized to work in the profession. State bar associations, for example, have certain education requirements and demand a certain level of performance on a bar examination before an individual can be licensed to practice law. On an annual basis, such associations require the payment of dues and often the completion of continuing legal education in order for an attorney to retain his license. State bar associations are empowered to monitor attorneys' behavior and to discipline them as they see fit, including the revocation of an attorney's license to practice law (disbarment). Yet no one would suggest that, by virtue of this right to control an attorney's working life, the bar association is his employer, or even one of his employers.

> Further, we are somewhat concerned about venturing into the religious arena in adjudicating cases such as this one, and interpreting what really are church matters as secular matters for purposes of determining a minister's tax status. The doctrinal and disciplinary control exercised by the General and District Councils, or available for their exercise, "is guided by religious conviction and religious law, not by employment relationships, and . . . should be considered impermissible or immaterial in determining the employment status of a religious minister."

---

[284] Alford v. Commissioner, 116 F.3d 334 (8th Cir. 1997).

Such cases are significant. They recognize that the mere presence of authority to exercise control over some ecclesiastical activities of a minister or church is not enough of a relationship to impose legal liability on the denomination. Unfortunately, the bylaws or other internal rules of many denominations define the relationship with local churches and clergy in a way that suggests far more "control" than actually exists. For example, many denominational documents speak generally of an almost unlimited authority to "control" or "supervise" the activities of affiliated churches or clergy, when in fact no such control was intended. Using unlimited language of "control" or "supervision" should be scrupulously avoided, if such authority does not exist. Words such as *control* or *supervision* have legal connotations, and should not be used without qualification unless unlimited authority in fact exists.

2. NOTICE OF WRONGFUL CONDUCT

In many cases victims of sexual misconduct involving clergy have argued that a denominational agency is legally responsible for the minister's actions because it was aware of, or should have been aware of, the minister's wrongful conduct. Some courts have ruled that denominations often have clearly prescribed internal rules for bringing charges against ministers who engage in inappropriate conduct, and that the only way for such denominations to be "on notice" of a minister's dangerous propensities is if a charge is filed and processed under the denomination's system of clergy discipline. Without a formal charge or complaint being brought, the denomination is not officially on notice and cannot be liable for the minister's subsequent acts.

> *Example. An Indiana court ruled that a denominational agency was not liable on the basis of negligent supervision or negligent retention for the molestation of a minor by a pastor.[285] When the victim was an adult, she sued her church and denomination, claiming that they were responsible for the pastor's actions on the basis of several theories, including negligence. The court concluded that the national church was not liable for the pastor's acts of molestation, even if it had some knowledge of them, if the disciplinary procedure outlined in its bylaws was not activated by the victim. It concluded, "The [national church], which is only affiliated with the local church and [regional agency] through its constitution and judicial procedures, was not informed. The evidence . . . does not indicate that [the woman] invoked the judicial procedures, which is the only mechanism by which the [national church] could have taken action against [the pastor]. According to the judicial procedures, the [regional agency] forms a committee to investigate alleged misconduct upon the submission of a complaint signed by two or more persons. Only after this investigation is completed and the [regional agency] determines that the evidence warrants a trial does the [national church] become involved. [The woman] has not alleged . . . that she or anyone else ever filed a complaint against [the pastor] with the [regional agency]. Therefore, the [national church] could not have disciplined [the pastor]. Accordingly, we conclude that because the evidence does not show that the [national church] was aware of [the pastor's] actions, summary judgment in favor of the [national church] is proper on [the woman's] claims for negligent hiring, supervision, and retention."*

3. LACK OF AN ACTUAL AGENCY RELATIONSHIP

One of the principal grounds cited by plaintiffs' attorneys in seeking access to the "deep pockets" of a denomination is agency. If a minister or lay worker can be classified as an "agent" of a denomination, then the denomination may be legally responsible for his or her acts occurring within the scope of employment. The

---

[285] Konkle v. Henson, 672 N.E.2d 450 (Ind. App. 1996).

courts have consistently rejected agency as a basis for making denominational agencies accountable for accidents occurring in local churches.

Section 1 of the *Restatement of Agency* (an authoritative legal treatise) specifies that "agency is the fiduciary relation which results from the manifestation of consent by one party to another that the other shall act on his behalf and subject to his control, and consent by the other so to act." The *Restatement* further specifies that "the one for whom action is taken is the principal," and "the one who is to act is the agent."

Section 219 of the *Restatement of Agency* specifies that an employer is subject to liability "for the torts of his servants committed while acting in the scope of their employment." This form of vicarious liability was discussed fully earlier in this chapter. The important point here is that clergy serving local churches rarely will be considered to be agents or "servants" (i.e., employees) of a parent denomination, since they will satisfy few if any of the factors indicating an agency relationship enumerated in the *Restatement of Agency*.[286] To illustrate, a Missouri court ruled that a Catholic priest was not an agent of the Archdiocese of St. Louis with respect to his anti-abortion torts. The court observed:

> When questioned about the duty of a priest in the Archdiocese concerning protesting abortions at abortion clinics, the Archbishop stated "there's no such duty prescribed of any priest." Neither was it a priest's duty to "trespass unlawfully on property to express opposition to abortion. . . ."

> [The priest's] activities were not within the direction of his superiors or the Church. Moreover, they were neither authorized, usual, customary, incidental, foreseeable, nor fairly and naturally incidental to his duties. . . . There is nothing in the . . . directions or authorizations of the Archbishop . . . nor under canon law to indicate that it is or was a priest's duty to engage in such activities.[287]

Can a denomination be legally responsible for the obligations of an affiliated church on the ground that the church is its "agent"? Such a conclusion is highly unlikely for many denominations. One authority has observed that

> [g]enerally, absent fraud or bad faith, a corporation will not be held liable for the acts of its subsidiaries. There is a presumption of separateness the plaintiff must overcome to establish liability by showing that the parent is employing the subsidiary to perpetrate a fraud and that this was the proximate cause of the plaintiff's injury. Merely showing control, in the absence of an intent to defraud or escape liability, is insufficient to overcome that presumption. Further, although wrongdoing by the parent need not amount to plain fraud or illegality, the injured party must show some connection between its injury and the parent's improper manner of doing business—without that connection, even when the parent exercises domination and control over the subsidiary, corporate separateness will be recognized. Thus, under ordinary circumstances, a parent will not be liable for the obligations of its subsidiary.[288]

---

[286] *See* note 5, supra, and accompanying text, for a listing of the factors to be considered in determining whether or not a particular individual is a servant of another.

[287] Maryland Casualty Co. v. Huger, 728 S.W.2d 574 (Mo. App. 1987). *See also* Brillhart v. Scheier, 758 P.2d 219 (Kan. 1988); Wood v. Benedictine Society of Alabama, Inc., 530 So.2d 801 (Ala. 1988).

[288] Fletcher Cyc. Corp. § 43 (perm. ed. 1990).

Under general principles of agency law, an agency relationship requires (1) a manifestation of consent by a denomination to its affiliated churches that they shall act on its behalf and subject to its control, (2) consent by the affiliated churches to act as the denomination's agents, and (3) control exerted by the denomination. A fourth requirement that is implicit in the *Restatement's* definition of agency is some direct benefit to the principal.[289]

Those national and regional denominational agencies that have no authority to supervise the activities of affiliated churches obviously cannot be liable for the churches' obligations or activities on the basis of agency. As noted in the preceding section, some denominations retain a limited authority with regard to specified ecclesiastical functions of affiliated churches. This limited "authority" clearly is not an adequate basis for denominational liability for the activities of affiliated churches. As one authority has observed: "Whether the parent so dominates the activities of the subsidiary as to establish an agency relationship is a question of fact determined primarily by the degree of control the parent has over the subsidiary. Generally, for the parent to be held liable for the subsidiary's acts *this control must be actual, participatory, and total.*"[290] Few if any denominations exercise this degree of control over affiliated churches.[291]

A number of courts have rejected the allegation that churches are "agents" of the denomination with which they are affiliated. To illustrate, a federal appeals court rejected the claim that the Assemblies of God denomination exerted sufficient "control" over affiliated churches to warrant denominational liability for the activities of its churches.[292] The national offices and a regional office of the Assemblies of God were sued in 1981 for failure to supervise the fund-raising activities of an affiliated church. The church had created a trust fund in 1973 as a means of financing a new church building and related facilities. The fund consisted of unsecured deposits solicited from both church members and nonmembers. According to the trust agreements and certificates of deposit used in connection with the fund, the deposits could be withdrawn after one year, with interest. Eventually, the fund had assets of over $7,000,000 which had been deposited by some 1,100 persons. In 1978, state banking authorities served the fund with a cease and desist order for operating a bank without a license. A subsequent run on the fund resulted in its collapse. In 1979, the church filed a petition for relief under Chapter 11 of the Bankruptcy Code.

In 1981, a class action suit was filed in federal district court naming the national Assemblies of God offices (the "General Council") and one of its regional divisions ("District Council") as defendants. The suit was brought against the national and regional offices because of an automatic stay by the bankruptcy court prohibiting the plaintiffs from suing the church directly. Specifically, the class action complaint alleged that the church had committed securities fraud in violation of state and federal law by selling securities without proper registration, and that the national and regional offices were derivatively responsible for the securities fraud as "control persons" under section 20(a) of the Securities Exchange Act. Section 20 provides:

---

[289] *See generally* E. Gaffney & P. Sorensen, Ascending Liability in Religious and Other Nonprofit Organizations (1984), in which the authors assert that benefit to the principal is implicit in the definition of agency, presumably because of the fiduciary nature of the relationship.

[290] Fletcher Cyc. Corp. § 43 (1990 perm. ed.).

[291] The most that could be said in such cases is that the denomination may have a limited liability commensurate with its limited authority. In other words, the local church may be a limited agent of the denomination for purposes of those specific activities over which the denomination reserves a right of control. The denomination would have liability, based on agency, only with respect to those activities of the church that the denomination has authority to control. For example, if a denomination's sole authority with respect to affiliated churches is to hold title to real property, then the denomination should have no liability for accidents involving church vehicles.

[292] Kersh v. The General Council of the Assemblies of God, 804 F.2d 546 (9th Cir. 1986).

Every person who, directly or indirectly, controls any person liable under any provision of this title or any rule or regulation thereunder shall also be liable jointly and severally with and to the same extent as such control person to any person to whom such control person is liable, unless the controlling person acted in good faith and did not directly or indirectly induce the act or acts constituting the violation or cause of action.

To substantiate their allegation of control person liability, the plaintiffs cited several factors, including the following: (1) the General Council and District Council issued ministerial credentials to the church's pastor; (2) the General Council and District Council retained control over the pastor's activities by their power to discipline him and withdraw his credentials; (3) the General Council could withdraw the church's certificate of affiliation for improper conduct, and, by failing to do so, it ratified the church's securities fraud; (4) the General Council and District Council and their missionary activities were beneficiaries of some church contributions; (5) by permitting the church to affiliate itself with the Assemblies of God, the General Council and District Council permitted the church to hold itself out as being under their general supervision; and (6) the church was covered by the group federal income tax exemption issued by the IRS to the General Council and all its "subordinate units."

The plaintiffs conceded that the General Council and District Council did not participate in or even know of the church's activities until the state banking authorities issued the cease and desist order in 1978, and therefore were not liable under a strict reading of section 20(a). However, they relied on cases in which the courts have concluded that "broker-dealers" participate in the securities fraud of agents by failing to enforce a reasonable system of supervision.

The General Council and District Council filed motions for summary judgment on a variety of grounds, included the following: (1) they were not "control persons" within the meaning of section 20(a) since (a) under the organizational documents, practice, and theology of the Assemblies of God, they were powerless to exercise control over local churches, (b) their lack of knowledge and participation constituted a "good faith" defense, (c) the stringent broker-dealer standard had no application to religious organizations, and (2) the first amendment's free exercise of religion clause prohibited a civil court from requiring a religious denomination to exercise a degree of control over its affiliated churches contrary to its practices, organization, and theology. The General Council noted that judicial imposition of a duty to supervise the financial affairs of its 11,000 churches in the United States, despite long-established practice and theology to the contrary, would force it to change its polity in order to avoid unlimited liability for the obligations of all of its churches. It noted that the Supreme Court has frequently observed that judicial manipulation of the polity or internal organization of church bodies violates the first amendment.[293]

In 1985, a federal district court granted the motion for summary judgment filed by the General Council and District Council.[294] The court concluded that the defendants could not be guilty as control persons under section 20(a) of the Securities Exchange Act since they did not know of or participate in the activities of the church. The court was not willing to extend the more stringent "broker-dealer" standard (i.e., failure to adequately supervise constitutes participation) to the defendants "since there are some significant differences between the broker-dealer context and the church structure at issue here." In particular, the court observed that "it is generally recognized that broker-dealers have a high degree of control over their agents," unlike the relationship between the defendants and local Assemblies of God churches. Further, the defendants were

---

[293] This contention is discussed in detail later in this chapter.
[294] Kersh v. The General Council of the Assemblies of God, No. C 84-0252 (N.D. Cal., May 17, 1985).

nonprofit entities and thus significantly differed from the typical broker-dealer. Most importantly, however, the court stressed that "the Assemblies of God . . . was founded on the principle that local churches would be sovereign, self-governing units, and are given wide discretion in operating their affairs." This relationship falls short of the "control" contemplated by section 20(a). The plaintiffs appealed this decision, and a federal appeals court agreed with the district court that the Assemblies of God national and regional offices were not responsible for the activities of an affiliated church. The court observed:

> [W]e find the evidence that [plaintiffs] present regarding the power or influence of General Council insufficient to establish "control" under section 20(a). [Plaintiffs] argue that the General Council maintains control by licensing ministers; however, there is no evidence indicating how such control is exercised once a minister has been licensed. [Plaintiffs] contend that the General Council exercises control over a minister's "promotion" to larger congregations; however, each local church has independent power to select its ministers. Moreover, the General Council was not required to approve the [church's] fundraiser. Indeed, there are no facts at all suggesting a nexus between [the church] and General Council regarding the transaction.[295]

The court further noted that the local church "did not act as the agent of the national church in this transaction. [The local church] did not receive compensation from the national church for the sale. More importantly, the sale was solely for the benefit of [the local church] with no direct benefit going to the national church."

The case is important, for it illustrates that a principal may have liability only for those specific activities of an agent over which the principal has the authority to exert control. It also suggests that an agency relationship requires some element of direct benefit to the principal. This is an important observation, since in many cases the activity allegedly creating denominational liability on the basis of agency is of no direct benefit to the denomination.[296]

Several other courts have rejected the contention that local churches or other institutions are agents of a denomination.[297]

4. Lack of an "Apparent Agency" Relationship

Even if a church or minister is not an actual agent of a national or regional denominational agency, it is possible for the denomination to be liable for their activities on the basis of *apparent agency*. Most states recognize the theory of apparent agency. Under this theory, a person or organization can become the "agent" of another though no actual agency relationship in fact exists. Section 267 of the *Restatement of Agency*, which has been adopted by many states, specifies:

> One who represents that another is his servant or other agent and thereby causes a third person justifiably to rely upon the care or skill of such apparent agent is subject to liability to the third person for harm caused by the lack of care or skill of the one appearing to be a servant or other agent as if he were such.

---

[295] 804 F.2d at 549.

[296] *See* note 289, *supra.*

[297] *See, e.g.,* Folwell v. Bernard, 477 So.2d 1060 (Fla. App. 1985); Pentecostal Holiness Church, Inc. v. Mauney, 270 So.2d 762 (Fla. 1972), cert. denied, 276 So.2d 51 (Fla. 1973); Hope Lutheran Church v. Chellew, 460 N.E.2d 1244 (Ind. App. 1244).

An official comment to this section further specifies that

> [t]he mere fact that acts are done by one whom the injured party believes to be the defendant's servant is not sufficient to cause the apparent master to be liable. There must be such reliance upon the manifestation as exposes the plaintiff to the negligent conduct.

Some persons injured by the activities of a local church or pastor have sued a parent denomination on the basis of apparent agency. The argument is that the denomination has "held out" the local church or pastor as its agent, and thus is responsible for injuries or damages that are caused by their activities. This argument has been rejected by a number of courts.[298] To illustrate, an Indiana state appeals court ruled that 65 plaintiffs who brought a class action lawsuit against a federation of Lutheran churches failed as a matter of law to establish apparent agency.[299] The plaintiffs all had purchased "life-care" contracts in a "Lutheran" nursing home organized as a separate nonprofit corporation but actively supported and promoted by the federation of churches. The corporate board consisted of 15 members, including 9 laypersons and 6 ministers—all of whom had to be members of federation churches. The corporate charter stated that the corporation was a "joint agency" of federation churches. Federation churches became members of the corporation, and they approved the articles of incorporation, bylaws, and initial board. The venture never attracted sufficient funding, and the corporation eventually declared bankruptcy.

The court concluded that the individual Lutheran churches in the federation were not legally responsible for the bankrupt corporation's liabilities on the basis of "apparent agency." It noted that the "essential element" of apparent agency is "some form of communication, direct or indirect, by the principal, which instills a reasonable belief in the mind of the third party" that another individual is an agent of the principal. The plaintiffs argued that apparent agency was established by use of the name "Lutheran" in the nursing home title and in promotional literature. Such conduct "led life membership purchasers to believe the [nursing] home had the support and financial backing of the Lutheran Church in general and the participating congregations in particular." In rejecting the application of apparent agency, the court observed that

> use of the word "Lutheran" in the name of the retirement home did not exhibit the degree of control by the churches necessary to create an apparent agency. While delegates from the churches may have been involved in the formation of [the nursing home corporation], it was ultimately the decision and responsibility of [the corporation] and its board of directors to use the word "Lutheran" in the name of the home. The same is true of the promotional materials . . . . Therefore, not only was the evidence insufficient to establish a manifestation by the churches to the plaintiffs, it was devoid of proof that [the nursing home corporation's] operations were controlled by the churches.[300]

In another significant ruling, a Texas state appeals court concluded that the Assemblies of God was not responsible for the activities of local churches or clergy on the basis of apparent authority.[301] An injured plaintiff had alleged that apparent agency was established by the denomination's "holding out" of local churches

---

[298] *See generally* E. GAFFNEY & P. SORENSEN, ASCENDING LIABILITY IN RELIGIOUS AND OTHER NONPROFIT ORGANIZATIONS (1984); Hotz, *Diocesan Liability for Negligence of a Priest*, 26 CATH. LAW. 228 (1981); Note, *Will Courts Make Change for a Large Denomination? Problems of Interpretation in an Agency Analysis in Which a Religious Denomination Is Involved in an Ascending Liability Tort Case*, 72 IOWA L. REV. 1377 (1987).

[299] Hope Lutheran Church v. Chellew, 460 N.E.2d 1244 (Ind. App. 1984).

[300] Id. *at 1251.*

[301] Eckler v. The General Council of the Assemblies of God, 784 S.W.2d 935 (Tex. App. 1990).

and clergy as its agents. The plaintiff claimed that this "holding out" occurred through "the ordination and licensing of ministers, accepting money from local churches, use of the 'Assembly of God' name by local churches, and publishing [a denominational magazine]." The court acknowledged that a national church can be legally accountable for the acts of a local minister or church on the basis of "apparent agency" if the national church "holds out" the church or minister as its agent or otherwise causes third parties to reasonably believe that the local church or minister is in fact an agent of the national church. The court concluded that the alleged methods by which the Assemblies of God "held out" its churches and ministers as its "agents" did *not* establish liability on the basis of apparent agency. With regard to the denomination's ordination and licensing of clergy, the court noted that the authority to ordain and discipline ministers was limited, and that "by plaintiff's close association with the local church and the Assembly of God religion, it is reasonable to believe that she had notice of these limitations on the [national church's] power to ordain and license."

The court rejected the plaintiff's claim that the financial contributions of local churches to the national church demonstrated that the national church was involved in an apparent agency relationship with the local churches (and was therefore responsible for their misconduct). It emphasized that the financial contributions were voluntary, and "would not reasonably lead a prudent person to believe that the local church was an agent of the [national church]." Further, there was no evidence whatever that the plaintiff was even aware that the local church made contributions to the national church, and therefore it was not possible to say that she "relied" on such conduct as indicating an agency relationship.

The court rejected the plaintiff's claim that the local church's use of the "Assembly of God" name demonstrated an apparent agency relationship. The sovereignty granted local churches in the General Council's bylaws rendered it impossible that a reasonable person would conclude that a local church was an agent of the General Council. The court observed that "the local church's autonomy is not affected by the authorized use of 'Assembly of God,' and no apparent agency arises from this use." Similarly, the court rejected the claim that the national church's denominational magazine created an apparent agency relationship with its local churches, since "the bylaws do not indicate that the [magazine] makes representations about the local church in any way, but only publicizes the doctrine of the Assembly of God religion. This does not constitute a sufficient 'holding out' which would generate a reasonable belief that the local church was an agent of [the national church]."

Further, in rejecting the plaintiff's claim that the denomination used "less than ordinary care" in discharging its "continuing duty" to monitor and supervise its clergy, the court observed that the national church "exercises no supervisory powers over the local ministers" and "is not responsible for the day-to-day oversight of the ministers." Since the national church had no duty to supervise clergy, "it is impossible that lack of supervision . . . was a substantial factor in causing plaintiff's injuries."

5. LACK OF AN ALTER EGO RELATIONSHIP

A few attempts have been made to establish denominational liability for the activities of affiliated churches on the basis of the *alter ego* theory. One court, in rejecting the application of this theory to the Catholic Church, described it as follows:

> *The requirements for applying the "alter ego" principle are thus stated: It must be made to appear that the corporation is not only influenced and governed by that person [or other entity], but that there is such a unity of interest and ownership that the individuality, or separateness, of such person and corporation has ceased, and the facts are such that an adherence to the fiction of the separate existence of the corporation would, under the particular circumstances, sanction a fraud or promote injustice. . . .*

Among the factors to be considered in applying the doctrine are commingling of funds and other assets of the two entities, the holding out by one entity that it is liable for the debts of the other, identical equitable ownership in the two entities, use of the same offices and employees, and use of one as a mere shell or conduit for the affairs of the other.[302]

One authority states that the alter ego theory requires " . . . complete domination, not only of the finances, but of policy and business practice with respect to the transaction so that the corporate entity as to this transaction had at the time no separate mind, will or existence of its own; and (2) such control must have been used by the defendant to commit fraud or wrong, to perpetrate the violation of the statutory or other positive legal duty, or dishonest and unjust act in contravention of the plaintiff's legal rights; and (3) the aforesaid control and breach of duty must proximately cause the injury or unjust loss."[303]

Obviously, few if any churches would be deemed an "alter ego" of an affiliated denomination under these tests. One court rejected an attempt to hold a denomination liable for the activities of an affiliated church on the ground that the denomination and its churches were "inextricably intertwined."[304]

6. Parent-Subsidiary Relationship

Some plaintiffs have asserted that denominational agencies are legally responsible for the acts and obligations of affiliated churches, clergy, and lay workers on the basis of a "parent-subsidiary" relationship between the denomination and church. Such arguments will be unsuccessful in most cases because most if not all of the characteristics of a parent-subsidiary relationship are absent. To illustrate, a federal appeals court provided a useful list of factors to consider in determining whether or not a "parent" corporation is legally responsible for the liabilities and obligations of a "subsidiary" or affiliate.[305] While this case involved a parent and subsidiary business corporations, the court's conclusion will be directly relevant to denominational agencies that are sued as a result of liabilities of subsidiary or affiliated corporations. Here is the list of twelve factors to be considered:

(1) the parent corporation owns all or a majority of the stock of the subsidiary

(2) the corporations have common directors or officers

(3) the parent and the subsidiary have common business departments

(4) the parent and the subsidiary file consolidated financial statements and tax returns

---

[302] Roman Catholic Archbishop v. Superior Court, 93 Cal. Rptr. 338, 341-42 (Cal. App. 1971).

[303] Fletcher Cyc. Corp. § 41.10 (1990). This authority lists the following factors to consider in applying the alter ego theory: The factors include whether: (1) the parent and subsidiary have common stock ownership; (2) the parent and subsidiary have common directors and officers; (3) the parent and subsidiary have common business departments; (4) the parent and subsidiary file consolidated financial statements and tax returns; (5) the parent finances the subsidiary; (6) the parent caused the incorporation of the subsidiary; (7) the subsidiary operates with grossly inadequate capital; (8) the parent pays the salaries and other expenses of the subsidiary; (9) the subsidiary receives no business except that given to it by the parent; (10) the parent uses the subsidiary's property as its own; (11) the daily operations of the two corporations are not kept separate; and (12) the subsidiary does not observe the basic corporate formalities, such as keeping separate books and records and holding shareholder and board meetings. *Id.* at § 43.

[304] Eckler v. The General Council of the Assemblies of God, 784 S.W.2d 935 (Tex. App. 1990).

[305] Gundle Lining Construction Corp. v. Adams County Asphalt, Inc., 85 F.3d 201 (5th Cir. 1996). *See also* In re Catfish Antitrust Litigation, 908 F. Supp. 400 (N.D. Miss. 1996) ("[w]e must remember that the alter ego doctrine and piercing of the corporate veil are truly exceptional doctrines, reserved for those cases where the officers, directors or stockholders utilized the corporate entity as a sham to perpetuate a fraud, to shun personal liability, or to encompass other truly unique situations").

(5) the parent corporation finances the subsidiary

(6) the parent corporation caused the incorporation of the subsidiary

(7) the subsidiary has grossly inadequate capital

(8) the parent corporation pays the salaries or expenses or losses of the subsidiary

(9) the subsidiary has substantially no business except with the parent corporation

(10) the parent uses the subsidiary's property as its own

(11) The daily operations of the two corporations are not kept separate

(12) the subsidiary does not observe the basic corporate formalities, such as keeping separate books and records and holding shareholder and board meetings

Denominational agencies are routinely sued as a result of the actions or obligations of affiliated churches. It is important to recognize that "ascending liability" in such cases is not automatic. The person bringing the lawsuit must establish a legal basis for imposing liability on the "parent" organization. The twelve factors mentioned in this case demonstrate that finding a "parent" organization legally responsible for the acts or liabilities of a "subsidiary" can be very difficult.

7. First Amendment Prohibition of Civil Court Manipulation of Ecclesiastical Polity

As formidable as the preceding defenses are, the most significant defense available to many denominations is provided by the first amendment to the United States Constitution. Judicial recognition of a duty on the part of a denomination to supervise the activities of affiliated churches, clergy, and lay workers, where no such authority exists, would violate the first amendment religion clauses since it would amount to governmental manipulation of the polity of a sovereign religious organization. The ultimate question in such cases is whether a civil court, consistently with the first amendment's religion clauses, can impose a duty on a denomination to supervise and control affiliated churches, clergy, or lay workers when the theology, history, practice, and organizational documents of the denomination forbid such control. Stated simply: Can a court "connectionalize" an essentially congregational association of churches? The answer to both questions is no. The United States Supreme Court has often stated that the civil courts may not affect ecclesiastical doctrine or polity:

> • But it is a very different thing where a subject-matter of dispute, strictly and purely ecclesiastical in its character—a matter over which the civil courts exercise no jurisdiction--a matter which concerns theological controversy, church discipline, *ecclesiastical government* or the conformity of the members of the church to the standard of morals required of them—becomes the subject of its action. It may be said here, also, that no jurisdiction has been conferred on the tribunal to try the particular case before it, or that, in its judgment, it exceeds the powers conferred upon it.[306]

---

[306] Watson v. Jones, 80 U.S. 679, 733 (1871) (emphasis added).

• Legislation that regulates church administration, the operation of the churches, the appointment of clergy . . . prohibits the free exercise of religion. . . . *Watson v. Jones* . . . radiates, however, a spirit of freedom for religious organizations, and independence from secular control or manipulation, in short, power to decide for themselves, free from state interference, *matters of church government* as well as those of faith and doctrine.[307]

• First amendment values are plainly jeopardized when church property litigation is made to turn on the resolution by civil courts of controversies over religious doctrine and practice. If civil courts undertake to resolve such controversies in order to adjudicate the property dispute, the hazards are ever present of inhibiting the free development of religious doctrine and of implicating secular interests in matters of purely ecclesiastical concern.[308]

• To permit civil courts to probe deeply enough into the allocation of power within a church so as to decide where religious law places control over the use of church property would violate the first amendment in much the same manner as civil determination of religious doctrine. Similarly, where the identity of the governing bodies that exercises general authority within the church is a matter of substantial controversy, civil courts are not to make the inquiry into religious law and usage that would be essential to the resolution of the controversy. In other words, the use of the *Watson* approach is consonant with the prohibitions of the first amendment only if the appropriate church governing body can be determined without the resolution of doctrinal questions and *without extensive inquiry into religious polity.*[309]

• The fallacy fatal to the judgment of the Illinois Supreme Court is that it . . . impermissibly substitutes its own inquiry into church polity . . . . To permit civil courts to probe deeply enough into the allocation of power within a hierarchical church so as to decide religious law governing church polity would violate the first amendment . . . . For where resolution of disputes cannot be made without extensive inquiry by civil courts into religious law and polity, the First and Fourteenth Amendments mandate that civil courts shall not disturb the decisions of the highest ecclesiastical tribunal within a church of hierarchical polity, but must accept such decisions as binding on them in their application to the religious issues of doctrine of policy before them. . . . In short, the First and Fourteenth Amendments permit hierarchical religious organizations to establish their own rules and regulations for internal discipline and government . . . .[310]

The implication of the above-cited precedent is unequivocal--government action that seeks to manipulate or distort the internal organization and government of a religious denomination violates the constitutional guarantee of free exercise of religion. A civil court is therefore without power to impose a duty of supervision and control upon a congregational association of churches over its affiliated entities contrary to the doctrine, history, and organizational documents of the association in order to redress injuries allegedly caused by the activities of an affiliate. In many cases, a judicial "connectionalizing" of denominational polity would be particularly repugnant since it would present a denomination with the following alternatives: (1) continue to honor its practice of not supervising or interfering with the activities of local churches, even though it will be legally responsible for all such local churches activities; or (2) in fact conform its polity to that of a hierarchical denomination and begin

---

[307] Kedroff v. St. Nicholas Cathedral of the Russian Orthodox Church, 344 U.S. 94, 105-106, 116 (1952).
[308] Presbyterian Church in the United States v. Mary Elizabeth Blue Hull Memorial Presbyterian Church, 393 U.S. 440, 449 (1969).
[309] Maryland and Virginia Eldership of the Churches of God v. The Church of God at Sharpsburg, 396 U.S. 367, 369-70 (1970).
[310] Serbian Eastern Orthodox Diocese v. Milivojevich, 426 U.S. 696, 708-09, 724 (1976).

scrutinizing the activities of churches and clergy. Surely no court could be so insensitive to the constitutional guarantee of free exercise of religion or the principle of separation of church and state.

8. "De Novo" Review for Violations of Constitutional Rights

The United States Supreme Court ruled in 1964 that the courts have a duty to "make an independent examination of the whole record" when constitutional rights are at stake, to be sure that there is no "forbidden intrusion" on the field of first amendment protections.[311] The Court reiterated this principle in a 1984 ruling,[312] in which it observed:

> The simple fact is that first amendment questions of "constitutional fact" compel this Court's de novo review. . . . The requirement of independent appellate review . . . is a rule of federal constitutional law. It emerged from the exigency of deciding concrete cases; it is law in its purest form under our common law heritage. It reflects a deeply held conviction that judges—and particularly members of this Court—must exercise such review in order to preserve the precious liberties established and ordained by the Constitution. . . . Judges, as expositors of the Constitution, must independently decide whether the evidence in the record is sufficient to cross the constitutional threshold that bars the entry of any judgment that is not supported by clear and convincing proof . . . .[313]

This precedent may be more appropriate at the appellate court level. But the implication is clear—courts (presumably even state trial judges) must independently review the record before them and make whatever rulings are required to protect federal constitutional rights. Such rights should not be left to the whim of juries.

9. The "Bar Association" Analogy

In recent years, a number of lawsuits have attempted to hold denominational agencies legally accountable for the acts of ministers that they ordain or license. The argument is that the act of issuing credentials to a minister, and the retention authority to discipline or dismiss a minister for misconduct, constitutes sufficient "control" to make the denomination liable for the minister's actions. In most cases, such efforts will fail. It is true that many denominational agencies ordain or license ministers; require ministerial credentials to be renewed annually; and reserve the authority to discipline or dismiss clergy whose conduct violates specified standards. In some cases, ministers are required or expected to provide annual contributions to the denomination. However, in most cases, the denomination retains no authority to supervise or control the day-to-day activities of ordained or licensed ministers. It may be authorized to discipline or dismiss a minister following an investigation, but ordinarily it has it has no authority to independently monitor or supervise the day-to-day conduct of ministers, and no such authority is ever exercised. It is important to point out that most denominations are "delegated powers" institutions, meaning that they can only exercise those powers that have been delegated to them by their constituent members in their governing documents. If these documents confer no authority to monitor and supervise the day-to-day activities of clergy, the denomination is prohibited from doing so.

The authority of many denominations to license and ordain clergy, require annual renewals of ministerial credentials, and discipline or dismiss clergy found guilty of specified misconduct, is precisely the same authority that is exercised by state professional accrediting organizations such as the bar association. Like such

---

[311] New York Times v. Sullivan, 376 U.S. 254, 285 (1964).
[312] Bose Corporation v. Consumers Union, 466 U.S. 485, 509-10 (1984).
[313] *Id.* at 508 n.27, 510-11.

denominational agencies, the bar association has the authority to license attorneys, require annual renewals, and discipline or dismiss attorneys for proven misconduct in violation of professional standards. In addition, many require annual contributions. However, this limited authority does not give the bar association any right to control or supervise the day-to-day activities of attorneys, and it is for this reason that *no bar association has ever been sued on account of the malpractice or misconduct of a licensed attorney. State bar associations have never been sued or found liable for the numerous incidents of attorney misconduct and malpractice that occur each year, and religious organizations should be treated no differently.*

An identical analogy can be made to any professional licensing organization (*e.g.,* physicians, CPAs, veterinarians, dentists, nurses, morticians), since they all exercise about the same degree of control—they license and retain the right to discipline or dismiss for violations of a professional code of conduct, but they have no authority to supervise the day-to-day activities of licensees.

The civil courts are beginning to recognize this principle. In a leading case, a federal appeals court has recognized the "bar association analogy" directly.[314] The court, in addressing the question of whether Rev. Alford, an Assemblies of God minister, was an employee of the national church ("General Council") and one of its regional agencies ("District Council"), made the following observation:

> The General Council's and District Council's right to control Alford during the relevant years extended primarily to their function in awarding credentials to ministers like himself. Generally, the church has established certain criteria that must be met for an individual such as Alford to obtain credentials initially and to renew that status annually. There are standards for the education a minister must acquire (which he must obtain and pay for himself) and for his performance on certain tests. Other requirements include subscribing to the doctrinal statement of the Assemblies of God, which sets forth the religious beliefs of the church, its ministers, and its members, and to the form of church government. Ordained ministers must preach thirteen times a year, but topics are not decreed by the regional or national organizations. Ministers holding credentials cannot preach in churches other than Assemblies of God churches without permission of the District Council. Ministers may be disciplined for what the church considers failure to follow church doctrine and for lapses in personal conduct, and may, in fact, have their credentials revoked. With some exceptions not relevant here, a minister must tithe to both the regional and national organizations. Attendance at certain meetings is expected, but not required. Thus it is apparent that, while the regional and national churches had doctrinal authority to exercise considerable control over Alford as regards his beliefs and his personal conduct as a minister of the church, they did not have "the right to control the manner and means by which the product [was] accomplished."
>
> The [trial court] and the United States make much of the fact that Alford, as a minister holding credentials, was "amenable" to the General Council and to the District Council in matters of doctrine and conduct. But this is not unusual in such a profession, and actually is merely a shorthand way of describing the parent church's doctrinal and disciplinary control discussed above. The control exercised by the regional and national organizations, and their right to control Alford, was no more nor less than most professions require of individuals licensed or otherwise authorized to work in the profession. State bar associations, for example, have certain education requirements and demand a certain level of

---

[314] Alford v. Commissioner, 116 F.3d 334 (8th Cir. 1997).

performance on a bar examination before an individual can be licensed to practice law. On an annual basis, such associations require the payment of dues and often the completion of continuing legal education in order for an attorney to retain his license. State bar associations are empowered to monitor attorneys' behavior and to discipline them as they see fit, including the revocation of an attorney's license to practice law (disbarment). Yet no one would suggest that, by virtue of this right to control an attorney's working life, the bar association is his employer, or even one of his employers.

Obviously, the importance of this case cannot be overstated. It will effectively refute, in many cases, attempts by plaintiffs to hold denominational agencies accountable for the acts of their ordained and licensed ministers.

> ***Example.*** *The Alabama Supreme Court compared an attempt to impute legal liability to a denomination as a result of the misconduct of a minister "to situations where a young man may be in a seminary and the seminary is asked to supply a preacher or a minister for a congregation. The fact that the young minister may have some alma mater does not make the seminary responsible for his behavior in the event he elects to commit a burglary or some other act which he might consider to be ordained by divine aegis or providence. It would not in and of itself make the seminary responsible for his behavior."*[315]

10. Joint and Several Liability

One of the most unfair aspects of our legal system is the principle of "joint and several liability." Under this principle, which is recognized by most states, any defendant in a lawsuit may be liable for the entire amount of a plaintiff's damages regardless of the degree of fault. This principle often is directed at churches and denominational agencies. To illustrate, assume that Bob drives a church van to a church activity and that several members of the youth group join him. Assume further that Bob's negligent driving results in an accident in which several persons are injured. A lawsuit is filed naming Bob, his church, and a parent denomination as defendants. A jury determines that Bob was 98 percent at fault, and the church and denomination each 1 percent at fault. The jury awards a total of $1 million to the victims. If Bob has no money to pay such an award, the church and the denomination are each individually (or jointly) liable for the entire $1 million judgment even though their respective degree of fault was only 1 percent each. This system is unfair, since legal liability is assigned solely on the basis of the ability to pay without regard to the degree of fault.

The morally inappropriate basis for the rule of joint and several liability has been recognized by several courts. To illustrate, the Kansas Supreme Court observed:

> There is nothing inherently fair about a defendant who is 10 percent at fault paying 100 percent of the loss, and there is no social policy that should compel defendants to pay more than their fair share of the loss. Plaintiffs now take the parties as they find them. If one of the parties at fault happens to be a spouse or a governmental agency and if by reason of some competing social policy the plaintiff cannot receive payment for his injuries from the spouse or agency, there is no compelling social policy which requires the codefendant to pay more than his fair are of the loss. The same is true if one of the defendants is wealthy and the other is not.[316]

---

[315] Wood v. Benedictine Society of Alabama, Inc., 530 So.2d 801 (Ala. 1988).
[316] Brown v. Keill, 580 P.2d 867 (Kan. 1978).

The good news is that several states have limited the principle of joint and several liability. In fact, most states have either eliminated joint and several liability,[317] or have limited it significantly.[318]

11. POLICY REASONS FOR LIMITING VICARIOUS LIABILITY OF NONPROFIT DEFENDANTS

As discussed earlier in this chapter,[319] the policy considerations supporting vicarious liability (under both respondeat superior and agency) rest upon the fundamental principle of risk allocation. That is, a principal or employer has the unique ability to allocate the risks of inevitable injuries suffered by the consumers of its products and services through price adjustments. By increasing its prices, the employer allocates the risk of injuries to the consumers of its products and services. As reasonable as this policy may be in the context of "for-profit" employers, it has no application whatever to most nonprofit employers who have no ability to allocate risk to consumers through price increases. Certainly this is true of religious organizations, which obviously cannot "adjust their prices" to allocate risks to the "consumers" of their products or services. Further, as mentioned earlier in this chapter, religious organizations cannot effectively allocate risks through obtaining liability insurance, since such insurance is increasingly difficult for religious organizations to afford or obtain, and many risks are excluded from coverage or have limited coverage.

§ 10-18.4 — Risk Management

Key point 10-18.4. Denominational agencies can reduce the risk of liability for the acts and obligations of affiliated churches, agencies, clergy, and lay workers by adopting risk management policies and procedures.

There are many ways for denominational agencies to reduce the risk of legal liability. Many of these are the same risk management strategies that may be employed by local churches, and they are addressed in previous sections of this chapter. Other risk management strategies are suggested in the previous subsection in which legal defenses available to denominational agencies are reviewed.

There are some risk management strategies that are unique to denominational agencies. Consider the following:

---

[317] *See generally* A. BEST, COMPARATIVE NEGLIGENCE ch. 13 (1991); ARIZ. REV. STAT. ANN. § 12-2506(A); COLO. REV. STAT. § 13-21-111.5; CONN. GEN. STAT. ANN. § 52-572h(c); IDAHO CODE § 6-803; IND. CODE ANN. § 34-51-2-8; KAN. STAT. ANN. § 60-258a(d); KY. REV. STAT. § 411.182(2); MICH. COMP. LAWS § 600.6304; N.M. STAT. ANN. § 41-3A-1; N.D. CENT. CODE 32-03.2-03; UTAH CODE ANN. § 78-27-40; VT. STAT. ANN. title 12, § 1036; WYO. STAT. § 1-1-109(d).

[318] *See, e.g.,* CAL. CIVIL CODE § 1431.2 (eliminated for "noneconomic damages" for personal injury, property damage, or wrongful death); FLA. STAT. ANN. § 768.81 (for nonecomonic damages only); 735 ILL. COMP. STAT. 5/2-1117; OHIO REV. CODE § 2315,19 (for noneconomic damages only). Many states abolish joint and several liability for defendants whose fault is less than a specified percentage, or permit joint and several liability only up to a specified amount. See, e.g., FLA. STAT. ANN. § 768.81 (joint and several liability abolished for defendants whose fault is less than half of the plaintiff's); IOWA CODE § 668.4 ("the rule of joint and several liability shall not apply to defendants who are found to bear less than 50 percent of the total fault assigned to all parties"); LA. CIV. CODE ANN. art. 2324 (defendants who are less at fault than a plaintiff are severally and not jointly liable); N.J. STAT. ANN. § 2A:15-5.3 (defendants who are 60 percent or more at fault are jointly liable for an entire judgment); N.Y. C.P.L.R. § 1601 (defendants whose fault is less than 50 percent of all defendants cannot be jointly liable for noneconomic damages); OR. REV. STAT. § 18.485 (eliminated for defendants whose fault is 25 percent or less, or is less than the plaintiff's share of fault); TEX. CIV. PRAC. & REM. CODE § 33.013 (eliminated for defendants whose fault is less than 50 percent).

[319] See § 10-02.4, supra.

1. THE DISCIPLINE OF MINISTERS

Many denominational agencies ordain or license ministers, and reserve the authority to discipline ministers for violations of prescribed standards. Deciding whether or not to discipline ministers, and restore them to pastoral ministry, can be difficult questions because imprudent decisions may expose a denominational agency to liability for future misdeeds. Here are some factors that denominational agencies should consider in deciding whether or not to restore a disciplined minister to pastoral ministry:

• *Type of misconduct.* The type of misconduct is an important consideration. Some kinds of misconduct are more severe than others.

• *Duration of misconduct.* The duration of a minister's misconduct is a relevant consideration. The longer the duration, the less likely rehabilitation will be effective.

• *Number of incidents.* The more separate incidents of misconduct, the less likely rehabilitation will be effective.

• *Number of victims.* The more victims, the less likely rehabilitation will be effective.

• *Subsequent misconduct.* Denominational leaders must recognize that the risk of liability increases significantly when a denomination disciplines and restores to pastoral ministry a minister who was previously disciplined for the same kind of misconduct.

• *How the misconduct was discovered.* Did the minister come forward and confess voluntarily? Or was the confession prompted by some external inducement, such as an awareness that the misconduct was about to be revealed.

• *When the incident occurred.* In some cases, the misconduct occurred many years ago and has not recurred. This is a relevant, but not conclusive, factor to consider.

• *Restitution.* If there is a "victim" to the minister's misconduct, has the minister apologized to the victim and made appropriate restitution?

• *Criminal nature of misconduct.* A decision to rehabilitate an employee should take into account the potential for criminal prosecution.

• *The strength of the evidence.* In some cases the evidence of misconduct is not conclusive. In general, the legal risk associated with rehabilitating or reinstating a minister increases if the evidence of guilt is weak and conflicting.

• *A counselor's opinion.* In some cases, denominational agencies have conditioned the discipline of ministers on the receipt of an opinion by a licensed psychologist or counselor that the minister no longer poses a risk of repeating the same kind of misconduct.

• *Limited disclosure agreement.* A number of courts have stated that denominational agencies can avoid legal liability for a disciplined minister's repeat misconduct by disclosing to local churches the minister's prior behavior at the time he or she is employed. To illustrate, one court ruled that a denominational agency was legally responsible for a pastor's sexual misconduct since it was aware of a previous incident and failed to communicate this knowledge to the pastor's employing church.[320] It concluded that "[t]he failure to communicate this knowledge to the [church board] and subsequent placement of [the pastor] in the role of counselor breached the diocese's duty of care to [the victim]." Of course, disclosing information regarding a minister's previous discipline to a local church may expose a denominational agency to liability. This risk can be reduced by having disciplined ministers, as a condition of discipline, sign a "limited disclosure agreement" authorizing designated denominational officials to share with local church boards and pastoral search committees the nature and basis of the disciplined minister's prior discipline. Such an agreement enables a local church to make an informed judgment on whether or not to call a pastor who has completed a rehabilitation program. Lay leaders in a local church are justifiably upset when their minister engages in inappropriate behavior and they later discover that a denominational agency failed to inform them that the minister had committed similar behavior at a previous church. There is no doubt that rehabilitated ministers will have a much more difficult if not impossible time finding employment if churches are advised of the nature of prior discipline. This is one unfortunate consequence of a minister's misconduct. But denominational agencies are under no duty to "protect" a minister's employability by concealing relevant information from local churches. The question is whether a denominational agency should protect a rehabilitated minister's future employment prospects by concealing from prospective churches his or her past, or reduce its own risk of liability through full disclosure.

2. ACCEPTING MINISTERS FROM OTHER ORGANIZATIONS

Denominational leaders must scrutinize carefully any applicant for ministry that comes from another denomination. In some cases, ministers who are disciplined or dismissed in one denomination apply for ministry in another denomination. If such a minister later engages in the same type of misconduct for which he or she was previously disciplined or dismissed, the new denomination may be legally responsible for such misconduct on the basis of negligent selection.

§ 10-18.5 — The Legal Effect of a Group Exemption Ruling

Key point 10-19.5. The tax code permits denominational agencies to obtain a "group exemption" for affiliated churches and organizations that establishes their exemption from federal income tax. While such rulings require the denominational agency to exercise "control" over its affiliates, the IRS and the courts have concluded that this "control" is ecclesiastical in nature and as a result a group exemption ruling does not make a denominational agency liable for the obligations of its affiliates.

Recognition of exemption from federal income tax under section 501(c)(3) of the Internal Revenue Code may be obtained on a group basis for "subordinate organizations" affiliated with and under the supervision or control of a "central organization."[321] This procedure relieves each of the subordinates covered by a group exemption letter of the necessity of filing its own application for recognition of exemption. To be eligible for a group exemption ruling, a central organization must obtain recognition of its own exempt status. It must also submit to the IRS information on behalf of those subordinates to be included in the group exemption letter. The required actions are summarized in Table 10-3.

---

[320] Moses v. Diocese of Colorado, 863 P.2d 310 (Colo. 1993).
[321] Rev. Proc. 80-27, 1980-1 C.B. 677.

TABLE 10-3
GROUP EXEMPTION REQUIREMENTS

1	"central organization . . . must establish that the subordinates to be included in the group exemption letter are affiliated with it . . . ."
2	"central organization . . . must establish that the subordinates to be included in the group exemption letter are . . . subject to its general supervision or control . . . ."
3	"central organization . . . must establish that the subordinates to be included in the group exemption letter are . . . all exempt under the same paragraph of section 501(c) of the Code . . . ."
4	"central organization . . . must establish that the subordinates to be included in the group exemption letter are . . . not private foundations . . . ."
5	"central organization . . . must establish that the subordinates to be included in the group exemption letter are . . . all on the same accounting period . . . ."
6	"each subordinate must authorize the central organization to include it in the application for the group exemption letter"
7	the application for a group exemption must include "a sample copy of a uniform governing instrument (charter, trust indenture, articles of association, etc.) adopted by the subordinates . . . ."
8	the application for a group exemption must include "a detailed description of the purposes and activities of the subordinates . . . ."
9	the application for a group exemption must include "an affirmation that . . . the purposes and activities of the subordinates are as set forth" in #8 and #9
10	the application for a group exemption must include "a list of subordinates to be included in the group exemption letter . . . ."
11	the application for a group exemption must include "the information required by Revenue Procedure 75-50" (pertaining to racially nondiscriminatory policies of schools)
12	the application for a group exemption must include "a list of the . . . employer identification numbers of subordinates to be included in the group exemption letter . . . ."
13	"The central organization must submit with the exemption application a completed Form SS-4 on behalf of each subordinate not having" an employer identification number
14	each year the central organization must provide the IRS with lists of "(a) subordinates that have changed their names or addresses during the year, (b) subordinates no longer to be included in the group exemption letter because they have ceased to exist, disaffiliated, or withdrawn their authorization to the central organization, and (c) subordinates to be added to the group exemption letter . . . ."

The group exemption procedure technically is available only to "connectional," or hierarchical, church organizations consisting of a "central organization" that exerts "general supervision or control" over "subordinate" local churches and church agencies. There are many conventions and associations of churches, however, that exert little if any "general supervision or control" over "subordinate" churches. Up until now, these "congregational" conventions and associations of churches have had to construe the group exemption requirements very loosely in order to obtain the benefits of a group exemption. Many have done so. A potential problem with such an approach is that the association or convention of churches itself may increase its potential liability for the misconduct and improprieties of affiliated churches and clergy, since in pursuing the group exemption the association or convention must affirm that it does in fact exercise "general supervision or control" over its affiliates. Such an affirmation could serve as a possible basis of legal liability.

Any attempt to use a group exemption ruling as evidence of denominational liability for the obligations of affiliated churches faces formidable obstacles, including the following:

1. No court has recognized such a basis of liability. No court in the history of this country has found a denominational agency liable on the basis of a group exemption ruling.

2. One court has rejected this basis of liability. There has been only one reported case in which a group exemption ruling was cited as evidence in support of an ascending liability claim.[322] A federal appeals court upheld a district court's summary judgment in favor of the national Assemblies of God church (the "General Council of the Assemblies of God") in a case claiming that the national church was legally responsible for the alleged securities fraud of an affiliated church.

3. The IRS Tax Guide for Churches and "ecclesiastical" control. In 1994 the IRS issued a "Tax Guide For Churches." The Tax Guide clarifies that "a church or other organization with a parent organization may wish to contact the parent to see if the parent has a group exemption letter." The Tax Guide further explains:

> An organization has a parent if, for example, another organization manages, financially or ecclesiastically, the first organization. If the parent holds a group exemption letter, then the organization seeking exemption may already be recognized as exempt by the IRS. Under the group exemption process, one organization, the parent organization, becomes the holder of a group exemption ruling naming other affiliated churches as included within the ruling. Under these rules, a church is recognized as exempt if it is included in the annual update of the parent organization. If the church is included on such a list, it need take no further action in order to obtain such recognition.

This language is significant, since the IRS concedes that the "control" that is needed to qualify for a group exemption may be *ecclesiastical.* Certainly, it could be said that many national and regional denominational agencies exercise some degree of "ecclesiastical" control over affiliated churches. But this kind of control certainly cannot support legal liability.

4. IRS bias in favor of hierarchical churches. "Congregational" associations and conventions of churches are forced to interpret the "control" language loosely because of the discrimination by the IRS against such organizations in favor of connectional, or hierarchical, church organizations. The current group exemption procedure, granting favored status only to connectional church organizations, is suspect under the Supreme

---

[322] Kersh v. The General Council of the Assemblies of God, 804 F.2d 546 (9th Cir. 1986).

Court's interpretation of the first amendment's nonestablishment of religion clause. In 1982, the Court invalidated a Minnesota law that imposed certain registration and reporting requirements upon religious organizations soliciting more than 50 percent of their funds from nonmembers.[323] The Court observed that "when we are presented with a state law granting a denominational preference, our precedents demand that we treat the law as suspect and that we apply strict scrutiny in adjudging its constitutionality." The Court concluded that any law granting a denominational preference must be "invalidated unless it is justified by a compelling governmental interest, and unless it is closely fitted to further that interest."

Similarly, a federal appeals court, in construing section 6033 of the Internal Revenue Code, observed: "[I]f 'church' were construed as meaning only hierarchical churches such as the Catholic Church—[this] would result in an unconstitutional construction of the statute [IRC 6033] because favorable tax treatment would be accorded to hierarchical churches while being denied to congregational churches, in violation of the first amendment."[324]

There is no conceivable governmental interest that would justify the government's stated preference for connectional church organizations in the present group exemption procedure.

5. Noncompliance with the group exemption requirements. Many denominational agencies that have obtained group exemptions have not fully complied with the requirements summarized in Table 10-3. Some do not even meet a majority of them. Obviously, these "requirements" do not mean much. As a result, little if anything can be made of the "general supervision or control" language.

TABLE 10-4
LIABILITY OF DENOMINATIONAL AGENCIES FOR THE
SEXUAL MISCONDUCT OF AFFILIATED CLERGY AND LAY WORKERS
A STATE-BY-STATE REVIEW OF SELECTED CASES

state	denomination found liable	summary
Alabama		no directly relevant precedent in recent years
Alaska		no directly relevant precedent in recent years
Arizona		no directly relevant precedent in recent years
Arkansas		no directly relevant precedent in recent years
California	no	• A California appeals court ruled that a religious denomination was not responsible for the sexual molestation of a 13-year-old boy by his pastor, or for the boy's subsequent molestation of his 6-year-old sister. Evan F. v. Hughson United Methodist Church, 10 Cal. Rptr.2d 748 (Cal. App. 1992).
Colorado	yes	• The state supreme court ruled that a victim of clergy sexual misconduct could sue the minister directly and also his denomination. The court observed that a denomination may be liable for negligent supervision if it has reason to know that a particular minister is likely to harm others. Destefano v. Grabian, 763 P.2d 275 (Colo. 1988).

[323] Larson v. Valente, 410 U.S. 437 (1982).
[324] Lutheran Social Service of Minnesota v. United States, 758 F.2d 1283 (8th Cir. 1985).

state	denomination found liable	summary
Colorado	yes no	• The state supreme court found a diocese and bishop legally responsible for a pastor's sexual misconduct with a female parishioner. Moses v. Diocese of Colorado, 863 P.2d 310 (Colo. 1993). • A Colorado court ruled that a denominational agency was not liable for injuries associated with a sexual relationship between a youth pastor and a girl in his youth group. It rejected the victim's claim that the denomination breached a fiduciary duty it owed to her, or that it improperly responded to her complaint. Bohrer v. DeHart, 943 P.2d 1220 (Colo. App. 1997).
Connecticut	no possibly yes	• A federal court dismissed a lawsuit brought against a church and diocese by two adults who had been sexually molested by a priest when they were minors. The court ruled that the church and diocese were not responsible for the victims' injuries on the basis of respondeat superior or negligence. The court cautioned that churches and denominational agencies are potentially liable on the basis of negligence for injuries sustained by victims of sexual molestation if they have knowledge of prior sexual misconduct by the molester. However, since the victims could not prove that church officials either knew or should have known of any previous sexual misconduct by the offending priest, the negligence claims had to be dismissed. The court ruled that the first amendment guaranty of religious freedom does not necessarily protect a church or denominational agency from liability in a lawsuit based on negligent hiring, retention, or supervision if the victim's claims do not implicate issues of ecclesiastical concern. Nutt v. Norwich Roman Catholic Diocese, 921 F. Supp. 66 (D. Conn. 1995). • A federal court in Connecticut ruled that the statute of limitations did not necessarily prevent an adult from suing a diocese for injuries he allegedly suffered as a minor when he was molested by a priest. The court noted that the statute can be suspended if a defendant "fraudulently conceals" the existence of a cause of action, and the diocese may have done so by breaching a "fiduciary duty" to warn potential victims of the priest's dangerous propensities. Martinelli v. Bridgeport Roman Catholic Diocese, 989 F. Supp. 110 (D. Conn. 1997). • A Connecticut court ruled that a religious order could be sued on the basis of respondeat superior for the sexual misconduct of a priest. Mullen v. Horton, 700 A.2d 1377 (Conn. App. 1997).
Delaware		no directly relevant precedent in recent years
Dist. Col.	no	• A court in the District of Columbia ruled that three adults were barred by the statute of limitations from suing an archdiocese for injuries they suffered as a result of being molested by a priest when they were minors. Cevenini v. Archbishop of Washington, 707 A.2d 768 (D.C. 1998).
Florida	no	• A Florida court ruled that the first amendment prohibited it from resolving a woman's lawsuit claiming that she had been the victim of a priest's sexual misconduct. The court concluded that the resolution of a negligent hiring, supervision, or retention claim against a church or diocese would amount to an excessive entanglement in violation of the first amendment. Doe v. Evans, 718 So.2d 286 (Fla. App. 1998).
Georgia		no directly relevant precedent in recent years
Hawaii		no directly relevant precedent in recent years
Idaho		no directly relevant precedent in recent years

state	denomination found liable	summary
Illinois	no	• A federal appeals court ruled that a denominational agency was not responsible for the alleged seduction of a female parishioner by a Catholic priest. Doe v. Cunningham, 30 F.3d 879 (7th Cir. 1994).
	no	• A federal appeals court ruled that a church and denominational agency were not legally responsible for a pastoral counselor's sexual contacts with a female counselee. The court stressed that the woman's lawsuit failed "to adequately allege that the church defendants knew or should have known of the improper counseling conduct of [the pastor]." The court also ruled that the church defendants were not liable on the basis of negligent supervision since the lawsuit was "devoid of any allegation that the church defendants were aware or had any knowledge that [the pastor] made improper sexual advances either before or during the time in question." Dausch v. Rykse, 52 F.3d 1425 (7th Cir. 1994).
	no	• An Illinois court ruled that evidence regarding a priest's prior acts of sexual misconduct were not relevant and therefore were not admissible in proving that the priest molested a young boy. The court pointed out that evidence of prior "bad acts" is generally not admissible to prove that a person committed a particular offense —unless the prior bad acts "show a method of behavior that is so distinct that separate wrongful acts are recognized to be the handiwork of the same person." This test was not met in this case. Doe v. Lutz, 668 N.E.2d 564 (Ill. App. 1996).
	no	• An Illinois court ruled that a husband whose wife was seduced by her pastor could not sue the pastor or denominational agencies for malpractice or breach of a fiduciary duty. Amato v. Greenquist, 679 N.E.2d 446 (Ill. App. 1997).
	no	• An Illinois court ruled that a denominational agency was not legally responsible for a priest's acts of child molestation occurring more than 20 years ago. Fearing v. Bucher, 936 P.2d 1023 (Or. App. 1997).
Indiana	no	• A federal appeals court ruled that a denominational agency was not responsible for the alleged seduction of a female parishioner by a Catholic priest. Doe v. Cunningham, 30 F.3d 879 (7th Cir. 1994).
	no	• A federal appeals court ruled that a church and denominational agency were not legally responsible for a pastoral counselor's sexual contacts with a female counselee. The court stressed that the woman's lawsuit failed "to adequately allege that the church defendants knew or should have known of the improper counseling conduct of [the pastor]." The court also ruled that the church defendants were not liable on the basis of negligent supervision since the lawsuit was "devoid of any allegation that the church defendants were aware or had any knowledge that [the pastor] made improper sexual advances either before or during the time in question." Dausch v. Rykse, 52 F.3d 1425 (7th Cir. 1994).
	yes	• An Indiana court ruled that the first amendment does not prevent a woman from suing her church and a denominational agency on account of injuries she suffered as a result of being molested by her pastor when she was a minor. The court noted that a review of the woman's claims "does not require any inquiry into religious doctrine or practice." The court concluded that neither the church nor the regional or national denominational agency could be sued on the basis of negligent selection of the pastor. The court ruled that the national church was not liable on the basis of negligent supervision or retention for the actions of the pastor. It observed, "The [national church], which is only affiliated with the local church and [regional agency] through its constitution and judicial procedures, was not informed. The evidence . . . does not indicate that [the woman] invoked the judicial procedures, which is the only mechanism by which the [national church] could have taken action against [the pastor]. . . . [The woman] has not alleged . . . that she or anyone else ever filed a complaint against [the pastor] with the [regional agency]. Therefore, the [national church] could not have disciplined [the pastor]." The court concluded that there was evidence that the local church and a regional denominational agency were aware of the pastor's actions, and therefore they could be sued for negligent supervision and retention. Konkle v. Henson, 672 N.E.2d 450 (Ind. App. 1996).

state	denomination found liable	summary
Iowa	no	• A federal court in Iowa ruled that a woman who had been seduced by a priest could not sue her church and diocese for violating the federal Violence Against Women Act. Doe v. Hartz, 134 F.3d 1339 (8th Cir. 1998).
Kansas		no directly relevant precedent in recent years
Kentucky	no	• A state appeals court ruled that an adult was barred by the statute of limitations from suing a priest and his church on account of the priest's alleged acts of molestation. The court acknowledged that Kentucky has adopted a "discovery rule" in the context of medical malpractice, but "[n]either the Supreme Court nor the General Assembly has further extended the discovery rule." Further, the court observed, "It should again be noted that at the time [the victim's] cause of action accrued, and for sometime thereafter, he was both aware of the abuse and past the age of reason." Rigazio v. Archdiocese of Louisville, 1993 WL 153206 (Ky. App. 1993) (unpublished opinion).
	yes	• A Kentucky court ruled that an adult who had been sexually molested as a minor by a teacher at a parochial school could sue the diocese that operated the school for negligent hiring, supervision, and retention. In extending the applicable statute of limitations, the court observed, "The diocese clearly obstructed the prosecution of [the victim's] cause of action against it by continually concealing the fact that it had knowledge of [the teacher's] problem well before the time [the victim] was abused as well as the fact that it continued to receive reports of sexual abuse of other students during part of the time period in which [the victim] was abused. Furthermore, where the law imposes a duty of disclosure, a failure of disclosure may constitute concealment . . . ." The child abuse reporting statute in effect when these incidents occurred imposed a legal duty on "any person" to report child abuse to law enforcement authorities. The diocese failed to comply with this duty, "and such failure constitutes evidence of concealment." The court rejected the claim of the diocese that the jury erred in awarding $700,000 in punitive damages against it. Roman Catholic Diocese v. Secter, 966 S.W.2d 286 (Ky. App. 1998).
Louisiana	no	•A Louisiana appeals court reversed a trial judge's decision that a church and religious denomination were legally responsible for the sexual assaults committed by a volunteer youth worker. The court ruled that the church defendants were not responsible for the offender's actions since a "master-servant" relationship did not exist between him and the church defendants. Doe v. Roman Catholic Church, 602 A.2d 129 (La. App. 4 Cir. 1992).
	no	• A federal appeals court ruled that an archdiocese was not responsible for the alleged molestation of a minor by a priest. The court observed: (1) "The record, however, permits of no conclusion that the [archdiocese] suspected that [the priest] had engaged in sexual improprieties or might do so in the future. It is doubtful that the archdiocese . . . knew anything about [his] darker side." (2) "[E]mployers do not have a duty to supervise their employees when the employees are off-duty or not working. Employers also are not liable for failure to supervise when the employee engages in independent criminal conduct which results in the plaintiff's injuries. Moreover, an employer's duty to supervise does not include a duty to uncover his employees' concealed, clandestine, personal activities." Tichenor v. Roman Catholic Church, 32 F.3d 953 (5th Cir. 1994).
	no	• A state appeals court ruled that a diocese was not legally responsible for the suicide of a woman allegedly caused by a sexual relationship with a priest. The court observed, "What it comes down to is that the secular state is not equipped to ascertain the competency of counseling when performed by those affiliated with religious organizations." And, since the priest could not maintain a lawsuit against the priest, "there can be no claim against the Episcopal Diocese based on any theory of responsibility for [the priest's] actions." The court also rejected any liability based on negligent selection, since such a basis of liability when applied to a religious organization would violate the first amendment. Roppolo v. Moore, 644 So.2d 206 (La. App. 4 Cir. 1994).

state	denomination found liable	summary
Louisiana	no no	• A state appeals court ruled that the statute of limitations prevented an adult woman from suing a Catholic diocese for a priest's acts of molestation when the woman was a minor. Doe v. Roman Catholic Church, 656 So.2d 5 (La. App. 3 Cir. 1995). • A Louisiana court ruled that a 32-year-old adult's lawsuit against a diocese and a priest who molested him when he was a minor was barred by the statute of limitations. J.A.G. v. Schmaltz, 682 So.2d 331 (La. App. 1996).
Maine	no	• The Maine Supreme Court ruled that the first amendment prevented a couple from suing their church as a result of a priest's sexual relationship with the wife. The court observed that it had never recognized "negligent supervision" as a basis for liability, and that even if it did, the first amendment barred its application to the church in this case. The court also rejected denominational liability on the basis of agency. Swanson v. Roman Catholic Bishop, 692 A.2d 441 (Maine 1997).
Maryland	no	• A Maryland court ruled that a 34-year-old adult's lawsuit against a diocese and two priests who molested him when he was a minor was barred by the statute of limitations. Doe v. Archdiocese of Washington, 689 A.2d 634 (Md. App. 1997).
Mass.	no	• A Massachusetts court ruled that a diocese probably was not liable for the sexual molestation of a child by a priest more than twenty years ago. The court noted that "the only shred of evidence" that the diocese had notice of the priest's pedophiliac propensities before the time of the victim's molestation was a response to a question in a 1963 confidential investigation of the priest. The question asked, "has he conducted himself with persons of the other sex in such a way as to cause scandal, criticism or suspicion?" The answer to this question was "yes." The court concluded that "it is doubtful that the questionnaire's answer to this question alone would be sufficient to permit a jury to reasonably infer that the diocese had notice of [the priest's] proclivities in regard to possible molestation of a young female child prior to the incidents alleged in this case." Yerrick v. Kelley, 1998 WL 374941 (Mass. Super. 1998).
Michigan	no	• A federal district court ruled that a seminary and denominational agency were not liable on the basis of negligent hiring, supervision, or retention for the sexual molestation of a seminarian by a priest. The court observed, (1) "Questions of hiring and retention of clergy necessarily will require interpretation of church canons, and internal church policies and practices. It is well-settled that when a court is required to interpret canon law or internal church policies and practices, the first amendment is violated because such judicial inquiry would constitute excessive government entanglement with religion. . . . [An] inquiry into the decision of who should be permitted to become or remain a priest necessarily would involve prohibited excessive entanglement with religion. Therefore [the victim's] claims of negligence predicated upon a negligent hiring theory will be dismissed." (2) Few states have recognized "negligent supervision" as a basis of liability. Isely v. Capuchin Province, 880 F. Supp. 1138 (E.D. Mich. 1995).
Minnesota	possibly no	• A state appeals court concluded that churches and denominational agencies can be liable for punitive damages. The case involved a Catholic priest who repeatedly was placed by church officials in situations in which he could sexually abuse boys, despite knowledge by church officials of the priest's propensities. Mrozka v. Archdiocese of St. Paul and Minneapolis, 482 N.W.2d 806 (Minn. App. 1992). • A Minnesota appeals court ruled that a church and pastor could be sued as a result of the pastor's acts of child molestation. However, state and national denominational bodies were found not to have been negligent. Doe v. Redeemer Lutheran Church, 531 N.W.2d 897 (Minn. App. 1995).

state	denomination found liable	summary
Minnesota	no	• A state appeals court ruled that a church and denominational organization were not legally responsible on the basis of negligent hiring for a pastor's acts of child molestation. The court pointed out that "there is no evidence [the church] had actual knowledge of [the pastor's] propensities to commit sexual abuse before he was hired." In rejecting liability based on negligent supervision, the court observed, "Even assuming that [the pastor's] abuse of [the victim] occurred within his scope of employment, there was insufficient evidence for the jury to conclude that [the church] failed to exercise ordinary care in supervising [him]. By the nature of the position, a clergyperson has considerable freedom in religious and administrative leadership in a church. The clergy also require privacy and confidentiality in order to protect the privacy of parishioners. There was no evidence that the supervision provided by [the church] differed from the supervision a reasonable church would provide. Nor was there any evidence of further reasonable supervision that could have prevented [the pastor] from abusing [the victim]. There was not enough evidence from which a reasonable jury could conclude that [the church] negligently supervised [the pastor]. M.L. v. Magnuson, 531 N.W.2d 831 (Minn. App. 1995).
	no	• A state appeals court concluded that a Catholic church was not an "agent" of its diocese and accordingly the diocese was not legally responsible for an injury that occurred on church property. Plate v. St. Mary's Help Church, 520 N.W.2d 17 (Minn. App. 1994).
	possibly	• A state appeals court ruled that a 38-year-old man's lawsuit against a pastor who had molested him when he was a minor may not be barred by the statute of limitations. The court refused to allow the victim to pursue his lawsuit against the church and denominational agency because the victim "has failed to produce any evidence of negligence. It is uncontroverted that no member or employee of the church knew of [the pastor's] abusive conduct with this or any other victim until after the incidents with [the victim] had ended. [The victim] admits that the incidents took place in private and that he himself told no one." Winkler v. Magnuson, 539 N.W.2d 821 (Minn. App. 1995).
	yes	• A federal appeals court ruled that a denominational agency that operated a school was guilty of sexual harassment as a result of its failure to address its principal's offensive behavior with several female employees. The court upheld the trial court's award of $300,000. It referred to the "long-term, ostrich-like failure" by denominational and school officials to "deal forthrightly with [the principal's] treatment of female employees." The court observed that "the jury was entitled to conclude that [the agency] not only looked the other way for many years but that its corrective action was woefully inadequate, as demonstrated by [the principal's] later conduct." Jonasson v. Lutheran Child and Family Services, 115 F.3d 436 (7th Cir. 1997).
Mississippi	no	• A federal appeals court ruled that an archdiocese was not responsible for the alleged molestation of a minor by a priest. The court observed: (1) "The record, however, permits of no conclusion that the [archdiocese] suspected that [the priest] had engaged in sexual improprieties or might do so in the future. It is doubtful that the archdiocese . . . knew anything about [his] darker side." (2) "[E]mployers do not have a duty to supervise their employees when the employees are off-duty or not working. Employers also are not liable for failure to supervise when the employee engages in independent criminal conduct which results in the plaintiff's injuries. Moreover, an employer's duty to supervise does not include a duty to uncover his employees' concealed, clandestine, personal activities." Tichenor v. Roman Catholic Church, 32 F.3d 953 (5th Cir. 1994).
Missouri	no	• The Missouri Supreme Court ruled that the first amendment barred it from resolving a lawsuit in which a Catholic diocese was sued on the basis of respondeat superior, agency, negligence, and breach of fiduciary duty as a result of a priest's acts of sexual molestation. Gray v. Ward, 950 S.W.2d 232 (Mo. 1997).

state	denomination found liable	summary
Missouri	no	• The Missouri Supreme Court ruled that a diocese could not be liable for the sexual misconduct of a priest. The court concluded that the first amendment barred the civil courts from imputing liability to the diocese on the basis of a fiduciary duty, conspiracy, agency, negligent hiring, negligent ordination, negligent retention, negligent supervision, or emotional distress. However, the court allowed the diocese to be sued on the basis of intentional failure to supervise clergy—if the victim could prove that a "supervisor" knew that the priest was likely to harm others but disregarded the risk. Gibson v. Brewer, 952 S.W.2d 239 (Mo. 1997).
Montana		no directly relevant precedent in recent years
Nebraska	no	• The state supreme court ruled that a Catholic Archdiocese was not legally responsible for damages allegedly suffered by a woman who engaged in sexual relations with a priest. Schieffer v. Catholic Archdiocese, 508 N.W.2d 907 (Neb. 1993).
Nevada		no directly relevant precedent in recent years
New Hamp.		no directly relevant precedent in recent years
New Jersey		no directly relevant precedent in recent years
New Mexico	no	• A state appeals court ruled that a Catholic diocese could not be sued by a 33-year-old woman who claimed to have been sexually molested by a priest when she was a minor. The court observed, "[R]egardless of whether [the woman] knew or should have known of the severe psychological damage caused by [the priest's] alleged misconduct [she] knew and should have known well before the limitations expiration date that the alleged misconduct had caused her other substantial injury. The limitations period is not tolled simply because a plaintiff does not know the full extent of her injuries; the statute begins to run once she knows or should know the sufficient facts to constitute a cause of action." Martinez-Sandoval v. Kirsch, 884 P.2d 507 (N.M. App. 1994).
New York	no	• A federal court in New York refused to find a pastor guilty of malpractice on the basis of his alleged sexual seduction of a church member he had counseled for several years. The court also refused to hold the pastor's church and denomination liable on the basis of "negligent placement, retention, or supervision." The court observed, "[A]ny inquiry into the policies and practices of the church defendants in hiring or supervising their clergy raises the same kind of first amendment problems of entanglement discussed above, which might involve the court in making sensitive judgments about the propriety of the church defendants' supervision in light of their religious beliefs." The court also observed, "It would therefore also be inappropriate and unconstitutional for this court to determine after the fact that the ecclesiastical authorities negligently supervised or retained the [pastor]. Any award of damages would have a chilling effect leading indirectly to state control over the future conduct of affairs of a religious denomination, a result violative of the text and history of the [first amendment]." The court also observed, "[The New York courts] have steadfastly declined to alter the traditional New York rule that the statute of limitations commences to run when a cause of action accrues, even though the plaintiff is unaware that he has a cause of action." Schmidt v. Bishop, 779 F. Supp. 321 (S.D.N.Y. 1991).
	no	• A court refused to extend the "statute of limitations" to allow an alleged victim of child sexual molestation to sue the minister who he claimed was the molester. Bassile v. Covenant House, 575 N.Y.S.2d 233 (Sup. 1991).
	no	• A New York state court ruled that the statute of limitations prevented an adult survivor of alleged childhood sexual abuse from suing her church. Gallas v. Greek Orthodox Archdiocese, 587 N.Y.S.2d 82 (Sup. 1989).

state	denomination found liable	summary
New York	possibly	• A New York appeals court ruled that a Catholic church and diocese could be sued as a result of the sexual molestation of an 11-year-old boy by a Catholic priest. The court rejected the argument of the church and diocese that permitting the civil courts to find religious organizations liable on the basis of negligent hiring or supervision of clergy would constitute excessive governmental interference with church autonomy in violation of the first amendment guaranty of religious freedom. Jones by Jones v. Trane. 591 N.Y.S.2d 927 (Sup. 1992).
	no	• A state appeals court ruled that a church and diocese could not be sued on the basis of "malpractice" or "respondeat superior" for the alleged sexual misconduct of a priest. The court observed simply that "the alleged sexual assault was not within the scope of employment and cannot be said to have been in furtherance of the employer's business." Joshua S. v. Casey, 615 N.Y.S.2d 200 (A.D. 4 Dept. 1994).
	no	• A New York court ruled that a Catholic diocese could not be sued on the basis of negligent hiring for a priest's acts of child molestation, but it could be sued for negligent supervision and negligent retention. It noted that "there is no indication that requiring increased supervision of [the priest] or the termination of his employment by the [diocese] based upon [his] conduct would violate any religious doctrine or inhibit any religious practice." The court concluded that there was evidence that the level of supervision exercised over the offending priest, or his retention by the diocese, was dictated by any religious doctrine. It insisted that "religious entities have some duty to prevent injuries incurred by persons in their employ whom they have reason to believe will engage in injurious conduct." Kenneth R. v. Roman Catholic Diocese, 654 N.Y.S.2d 791 (N.Y.A.D. 1997).
	no	• A New York court ruled that it was barred by the first amendment from resolving a woman's claim that she had been injured by a priest's repeated sexual contacts with her. Langford v. Roman Catholic Diocese, 677 N.Y.S.2d 436 (A.D. 1998).
N. Carolina		no directly relevant precedent in recent years
N. Dakota	no	• The North Dakota Supreme Court ruled that a denominational agency could not be liable on the basis of respondeat superior for a pastor's sexual misconduct since the victim had entered into an agreement releasing the pastor from liability. The court also ruled that the agency was not liable on the basis of a breach of a fiduciary duty. The victim insisted that the denomination's "Book of Discipline" imposed a fiduciary duty on the denomination and its officials to investigate and confront clergy for sexual misconduct. The court disagreed, noting that the Book of Discipline "defines the duties and responsibilities of [denominational agencies and officials] and local ministers. [Denominational officials] have no responsibility for the direct pastoral care of parishioners in individual congregations. Such functions are the responsibility of the local church minister." L.C. v. R.P. 563 N.W.2d 799 (N.D. 1997).
Ohio	no	• A state appeals court ruled that a minister and his church, but not his denomination, could be sued for the minister's acts of sexual harassment involving a church secretary. The court observed, "Although [the minister] sought advice from the bishop, and the bishop investigated plaintiff's complaints, this does not make the diocese liable for the conduct of [the minister or church]." Davis v. Black, 70 Ohio App. 359 (Ohio App. 1991).
	no	• The Ohio Supreme Court dismissed a lawsuit brought against a religious institution for negligent hiring because it failed to identify specific knowledge of prior misconduct. Byrd v. Faber, 565 N.E.2d 584 (Ohio 1991).
	no	•A state appeals court ruled that a denominational agency was not responsible for a local church elder's actions even though it exercised ecclesiastical control over him. Nye v. Kemp, 646 N.E.2d 262 (Ohio App. 10 Dist. 1994).

state	denomination found liable	summary
Oklahoma	no	• The state supreme court ruled that a married couple could not sue their church and former pastor for damages they allegedly incurred as a result of an adulterous affair between the former pastor and the wife. The court observed, "Neither the claims by the husband nor the wife against the minister are cognizable in Oklahoma. . . . Because their claims against the minister also serve as the basis for the claims against the church for its negligent hiring and supervision of the minister, that claim is also not cognizable." Bladen v. First Presbyterian Church, 857 P.2d 789 (Okla. 1993).
Oregon	possibly	• A state appeals court ruled that a victim of clergy sexual misconduct could sue her minister, and possibly her church and denomination. It acknowledged that the constitutional guaranty of religious freedom "may provide the [denomination] with an affirmative defense at some later stage of the proceeding." Erickson v. Christenson, 781 P.2d 383 (Or. App. 1989).
Pennsylvania	no no	• A state appeals court ruled that an adult was barred by the statute of limitations from suing a priest and his church on account of the priest's alleged acts of molestation. The court observed, "This is simply not a case where the plaintiff, despite the exercise of objectively measured reasonable diligence, could not know of his injury and its cause within the limitations period. [The victim] admits that he knew the abuse was occurring and who was inflicting it, both when it happened and throughout the eight years after the abuse ended and before appellant sued. What he did not know, i.e., that the physical acts allegedly performed on him by [the priest] were abuse and were causing psychological harm, is not relevant to a discovery rule analysis." E.J.M. v. Archdiocese of Philadelphia, 622 A.2d 1388 (Pa. Super. 1993). • A Pennsylvania court ruled that a church and diocese could not be legally responsible for a priest's repeated acts of child molestation occurring off of church premises. The court noted that the Restatement of Torts (an authoritative legal text) imposes liability for negligent supervision upon employers only for misconduct occurring on their premises. It pointed out that all of the priest's acts of molestation occurred in motel rooms while on trips, and not on church premises. Hutchinson v. Luddy, 683 A.2d 1254 (Pa. Super. 1996).
Rhode Island	possibly	• A federal court in Rhode Island ruled that the first amendment did not prevent it from resolving a lawsuit brought by victims of clergy sexual misconduct against denominational officials. Smith v. O'Connell, 986 F.Supp. 73 (D.R.I. 1997).
S. Carolina	no	• A South Carolina court ruled that a denominational agency and one of its officials were not liable on the basis of negligence, invasion of privacy, fiduciary duty, emotional distress, or fraud for a pastor's acts of sexual harassment. The women claimed that a denominational agency and official "had a duty to prevent the sexual harassment of its parishioners by a member of the clergy and to help in healing afterward rather than being indifferent." They insisted that the agency and official should be found guilty of negligence for violating this standard. The court disagreed, noting that the women "have cited no precedent and we are aware of none that stands for the proposition a church owes its parishioners a duty of care regarding its handling of their complaints." The court also rejected the women's claim that the agency and official breached a fiduciary duty. Brown v. Pearson, 483 S.E.2d 477 (S.C. App. 1997).
S. Dakota	possibly	• The state supreme court ruled that the statute of limitations for bringing a lawsuit for acts of sexual molestation may be suspended or delayed through "fraudulent concealment" by a denominational agency of the incidents. Koenig v. Lambert, 527 N.W.2d 903 (S.D. 1995).
Tennessee		no directly relevant precedent in recent years

state	denomination found liable	summary
Texas	no	• A federal appeals court ruled that an archdiocese was not responsible for the alleged molestation of a minor by a priest. The court observed: (1) "The record, however, permits of no conclusion that the [archdiocese] suspected that [the priest] had engaged in sexual improprieties or might do so in the future. It is doubtful that the archdiocese . . . knew anything about [his] darker side." (2) "[E]mployers do not have a duty to supervise their employees when the employees are off-duty or not working. Employers also are not liable for failure to supervise when the employee engages in independent criminal conduct which results in the plaintiff's injuries. Moreover, an employer's duty to supervise does not include a duty to uncover his employees' concealed, clandestine, personal activities." Tichenor v. Roman Catholic Church, 32 F.3d 953 (5th Cir. 1994).
Utah		no directly relevant precedent in recent years
Vermont	possibly	• A federal court in Vermont ruled that an adult who claimed to have been sexually abused by a nun some 40 years earlier could sue a Catholic diocese for his alleged injuries. Barquin v. Roman Catholic Diocese, 839 F. Supp. 275 (D. Vt. 1993).
Virginia		no directly relevant precedent in recent years
Washington	possibly no	• A Washington court ruled that a church and a member of the church board could be sued by three women who had been molested by a volunteer youth worker when they were minors. The court noted that "as a general rule, there is no legal duty to protect another from the criminal acts of a third person." However, a church may have a duty to prevent a third person from causing physical harm to another if a "special relationship" exists between the church and the victim which imposes upon the church a duty to "protect" the victim from harm. The court concluded that such a relationship did exist: "[W]e believe that churches and the adult church workers who assume responsibility for the spiritual well being of children of the congregation, whether as paid clergy or as volunteers, have a special relationship with those children that gives rise to a duty to protect them from reasonably foreseeable risk of harm from those members of the congregation whom the church places in positions of responsibility and authority over them." However, no special relationship existed between the victims and a denominational agency. Funkhouser v. Wilson, 950 P.2d 501 (Wash. App. 1998). • A Washington state court ruled that the statute of limitations prevented an adult male from suing his church and a denominational agency for injuries he suffered as a child when he was molested by his pastor. E.R.B. v. Church of God, 950 P.2d 29 (Wash. App. 1998).
W. Virginia		no directly relevant precedent in recent years
Wisconsin	no no	• A federal appeals court ruled that a denominational agency was not responsible for the alleged seduction of a female parishioner by a Catholic priest. Doe v. Cunningham, 30 F.3d 879 (7th Cir. 1994). • A federal appeals court ruled that a church and denominational agency were not legally responsible for a pastoral counselor's sexual contacts with a female counselee. The court stressed that the woman's lawsuit failed "to adequately allege that the church defendants knew or should have known of the improper counseling conduct of [the pastor]." The court also ruled that the church defendants were not liable on the basis of negligent supervision since the lawsuit was "devoid of any allegation that the church defendants were aware or had any knowledge that [the pastor] made improper sexual advances either before or during the time in question." Dausch v. Rykse, 52 F.3d 1425 (7th Cir. 1994).

state	denomination found liable	summary
Wisconsin	no	• A state appeals court ruled that the statute of limitations prevented a woman from suing a Catholic archdiocese for the alleged acts of molestation by a priest nearly 40 years before. The court noted that "extending the discovery rule to this case would cause unfairness to a defendant that is forced to attempt to defend a suit for emotional and psychological injuries in which the alleged conduct took place over [40] years ago and increase the potential for fraud." The court also observed, "To establish a claim for negligent hiring or retention [the woman] would have to establish that the archdiocese was negligent in hiring or retaining [the priest] because he was incompetent or otherwise unfit. But, we conclude that the first amendment to the United States Constitution prevents the courts of this state from determining what makes one competent to serve as a Catholic priest since such a determination would require interpretation of church canons and internal church policies and practices. Therefore [the suit] against the archdiocese is not capable of enforcement by the courts." Pritzlaff v. Archdiocese of Milwaukee, 533 N.W.2d 780 (Wis. 1995).
	no	• The Wisconsin Supreme Court ruled that seven adults who were molested as children by parish priests were barred by the statute of limitations from suing the priests, their churches, and a diocese. Doe v. Archdiocese of Milwaukee, 565 N.W.2d 94 (Wis. 1997).
	no	• A Wisconsin court ruled that the statute of limitations barred an adult from suing a church and diocese for injuries he allegedly sustained as a result of a priest's acts of child molestation. The victim argued that he did not "discover" the relationship between his suffering and the priest's assaults until years later, and his claim did not accrue until that date, making his lawsuit timely. The court rejected this attempt to extend the statute of limitations. It concluded, "As a matter of law, [the victim] discovered, or in the exercise of reasonable diligence should have discovered, the cause of his injury at least by the time of the last incident of assault, in May of 1984. Therefore, his claims against the diocese and [church] as well as those against [the priest] accrued no later than the time of the last assault." Joseph W. v. Catholic Diocese, 569 N.W.2d 795 (Wis. App. 1997).
	no	• The Wisconsin Supreme Court ruled that a Catholic Diocese could not be sued as a result of an alleged sexual relationship that began when a woman began a counseling relationship with a priest who served as a hospital chaplain and counselor. The court concluded that the first amendment prohibited it from resolving the victim's negligent supervision claim. L.L.N. v. Clauder, 563 N.W.2d 434 (Wis. 1997).
Wyoming		no directly relevant precedent in recent years

INSTRUCTIONAL AIDS TO CHAPTER 10

Terms

agency

arbitration

apparent agency

ascending liability

assumption of risk

charitable immunity

comparative negligence

contributory negligence

course of employment

"discovery" rule

fiduciary duty

intervening cause

invitee

joint and several liability

licensee

negligence

negligent retention

negligent selection

negligent supervision

punitive damages

ratification

respondeat superior

scope of employment

statute of limitations

trespasser

Learning Objectives

- *Define the term* negligence.

- *Define the term* respondeat superior, *and explain its relevance to churches.*

- Understand the potential legal liability of churches for failing to exercise reasonable care in the selection of workers.

- Understand the potential legal liability of churches for failing to exercise reasonable care in the supervision of workers and activities.

- Understand the potential liability of churches for retaining an employee or volunteer after being made aware of information suggesting that the person represents a risk of harm to others.

- Explain the concept of "fiduciary duty," and its relevance to churches.

- Identify several legal defenses to negligence.

- Understand the legal status of "release forms" that purport to relieve a church of liability for the negligence of its employees and volunteers.

- Explain the concept of risk management, and identify risk management strategies that can reduce the risk of church liability based on negligent selection, negligent retention, and negligent supervision.

- Define "defamation," and explain defenses that are available to churches that are sued for alleged defamation.

- Identify legal risks associated with counseling activities, and explain how those risks may be reduced.

- Describe the potential legal liability of religious denominations for the conduct of affiliated churches and clergy, and identify several defenses that are available to denominations.

Short-Answer Questions

1. Define the term respondeat superior, and explain its relevance to churches.

2. Rev. B, the senior minister of First Church, fails to stop at a red light and collides with another vehicle while driving from the church to visit a church member in the hospital. The driver of the other vehicle was seriously injured. Rev. B has not been charged with a traffic violation in more than ten years. Answer the following questions:

    a. On the basis of what legal theory would the church most likely be responsible for the victim's injuries?

    b. What is the justification for the legal liability of the church for the victim's injuries?

    c. What would the victim have to prove in order for the church to be liable?

    d. What if the minister reports his income taxes as a self-employed person? Would this affect the liability of the church? Explain.

    e. What if the accident occurred on a Friday evening while Rev. B was on his way to buy groceries? Would this affect the liability of the church? Explain.

    f. What if the accident occurred while Rev. B was on his way to watch his daughter participate in a sporting event? Would this affect the liability of the church? Explain.

    g. What if the accident occurred while Rev. B was on his way home from church? Would this affect the liability of the church? Explain.

    h. Assuming that the church is sued by the victim, what legal defenses could the church assert?

    i. Can the victim sue Rev. B personally? Explain.

3. A church hires B to mow its lawn on a weekly basis. B spends about three hours at the church each week during the mowing season. While mowing the yard one day, B's tractor runs over a rock that is thrown across the street and strikes a neighbor. The neighbor sues the church, claiming that it is responsible for her injuries on the basis of respondeat superior. How will a court likely rule? Explain.

4. Some courts refuse to apply the principle of respondeat superior to churches and other charities. Why?

5. G is a volunteer youth worker at a church. He sexually assaults an adolescent female while driving her home following a church activity. The victim sues her church, claiming that it is legally responsible for G's actions on the basis of respondeat superior. Answer the following questions:

    a.   Will a court find the church liable for G's actions on the basis of respondeat superior? Why or why not?

    b.   What other theories of liability could be asserted against the church?

6.   The text states that sexual molestation of minors and adults is the greatest legal risk facing churches today. Why? Do you agree or disagree?

7.   After attending a church for 2 weeks, M volunteers to work as a Sunday School teacher. He begins teaching a class a few weeks later. The church did not ask M to complete any application form and did not ask for or contact any references. Shortly after beginning to teach the class, M is accused of molesting a child on church premises following a class. The child's parents sue M and the church. It is later discovered that M was convicted of the sexual molestation of a minor in another community 5 years previously. Answer the following questions:

    a.   On the basis of what legal theory would the church most likely be responsible for the victim's injuries?

    b.   Church leaders claim that they had no knowledge of the previous conviction, or of any other information suggesting that M would pose a risk of harm to anyone. Would this constitute an effective defense? Why or why not?

    c.   List ways that the church could have reduced the risk of this incident occurring.

    d.   Will the church's liability insurance policy cover the church? What about M?

8.   Assume the same facts as question 7, except that M had not been convicted in the past of sexually molesting a minor. Answer the following questions:

    a.   Would the church be legally responsible for the child's injuries? Explain.

    b.   How should church leaders respond to inconclusive or unresolved criminal records on the part of applicants for youth work in the church?

9.   A church decides to implement a procedure for "screening" persons who work with children. One aspect of its screening procedure is an application form to be completed by all workers. Answer the following questions:

    a.   Should such a form be completed by current workers? Or, should it be completed only by those workers hired in the future?

    b.   Should such a form be completed by paid employees? Uncompensated volunteers? Both?

    c.   Should the church ask applicants whether or not they have been arrested or convicted of a crime? If so, which crimes should be included?

    d.   What other questions would be appropriate on a screening application form?

10. An individual begins attending a church and expresses interest in working with the children's program. The individual indicates that he was convicted of sexually molesting a child and served a 3-year term in a state penitentiary. However, he insists that he no longer presents a risk of harm because of a religious conversion that he experienced while in prison. He is interviewed by several church leaders, who all agree that he seems to have experienced a genuine conversion. They would like to give the person the benefit of the doubt and use him in a volunteer capacity in a children's program. Answer the following questions:

   a. Should the church use this person in a children's program? Why or why not?

   b. Would it matter how long ago the previous conviction occurred? What if the criminal conviction was 10 years ago, and the person has had no other charges or convictions? What if the person was released from prison within the past year?

   c. Are there any other alternatives available to the church in responding to such a person's desire to volunteer his services?

11. Assume that you have been asked by your church to recommend procedures to reduce the risk of child molestation occurring on church premises or in the course of church activities. How would you respond?

12. Many incidents of child molestation have occurred in church restrooms. What are some steps that church leaders can take to reduce this risk?

13. Grace Church selects Rev. J as its minister. Church leaders do not investigate the background of Rev. J, and do not discover that Rev. J was guilty of sexually seducing a church member in a previous church. Rev. J sexually seduces a member of Grace Church during marital counseling. The member sues the church as well as Rev. J. Answer the following questions:

   a. On the basis of what legal theory would the church most likely be responsible for the member's alleged injuries?

   b. Church leaders claim that they had no knowledge of the previous incident of misconduct, or of any other information suggesting that Rev. J would pose a risk of harm to anyone. Would this constitute an effective defense? Why or why not?

   c. How could the church have reduced the risk of this incident occurring?

14. Same facts as question 13. Assume that Rev. J's denomination was aware of the previous misconduct, but did nothing to advise Grace Church at the time it employed Rev. J, and did nothing to supervise or monitor Rev. J's activities.

   a. On the basis of what legal theory would the denomination most likely be responsible for the member's alleged injuries?

   b. What steps could the denomination have taken to reduce its risk of liability?

15. A church lets D drive several members of the church youth group in a church vehicle on a church-sponsored activity. D's reckless driving results in an accident that injures some of the members of the youth group. The victims sue the church, as well as D. They reveal that D had been convicted of several traffic offenses in the year preceding the accident, and that his drivers license had been suspended. Answer the following questions:

   a. On the basis of what legal theory would the church most likely be responsible for the victims' injuries?

   b. Church leaders claim that they had no knowledge of D's poor driving record, or of any other information suggesting that D would pose a risk of harm to anyone. Would this constitute an effective defense? Why or why not?

   c. How could the church have reduced its risk of liability?

16. Several courts have refused to find churches liable on the basis of negligent selection or negligent supervision for the sexual misconduct of ministers. Why?

17. What is negligent retention? Give an example of how a church may be liable on this basis for the molestation of a child by volunteer church worker.

18. An adolescent boy is injured while playing in a church-sponsored basketball game. The minor's parents sue the church, claiming that it is responsible for their child's injuries on the basis of negligent supervision. They claim that the molestation never would have occurred had the church exercised proper supervision over its workers and activities. What factors will a jury consider in reaching a decision in this case?

19. A 10-year-old boy is injured when he falls off a cliff while participating in a church-sponsored camping trip. The minor's mother sues the church, claiming that it is responsible for her child's injuries on the basis of negligent supervision. She claims that the accident never would have occurred had the church exercised proper supervision over its workers and activities. What factors will a jury consider in reaching a decision in this case?

20. Rev. S, a youth minister at First Church, takes 23 children swimming at a nearby lake. There were no other adult supervisors and no life guards were on duty. One of the children drowns. Answer the following questions:

   a. On the basis of what legal theory would the church most likely be responsible for the victim's injuries?

   b. What is the probable outcome of such a lawsuit?

   c. What steps could the church have taken to reduce its risk of liability?

21. A church operates a preschool. Children often are taken to a neighboring park for recreation. A four-year-old child is injured when she falls off a slide while her class is at the park. Is the church responsible for her injuries? Explain.

22. A church's organized children's activity ("children's church") is released prior to the end of the adult worship service. A 6-year-old child wanders out of the church building and is struck by a car while crossing a nearby street. Answer the following questions:

    a. On the basis of what legal theory would the church most likely be responsible for the victim's injuries?

    b. What is the probable outcome of such a lawsuit?

    c. What steps could the church have taken to reduce its risk of liability?

23. A church operates a nursery during morning worship services. During one service, the nursery is staffed by two 13-year-old girls. An infant breaks her leg when she falls off a diaper changing table during a diaper change. Answer the following questions:

    a. On the basis of what legal theory would the church most likely be responsible for the victim's injuries?

    b. What is the probable outcome of such a lawsuit?

    c. What steps could the church have taken to reduce its risk of liability?

24. A youth pastor takes his church youth group to an activity in another city. The group travels in a bus. On the way, the group stops at a fast food restaurant for lunch. A few of the children ask if they can go to another restaurant across the street where they will not have to wait so long to be served. The youth pastor agrees. As they cross the street, one of the children is struck by a car. The child's parents sue the church. What is the most likely basis of liability? Explain.

25. A mother brings her infant child to the church nursery before a morning worship service. During the service, an adult male comes to the nursery and asks a teenage nursery attendant for the same child. The attendant is reluctant, because she has never seen the man before. He assures her that he is an "uncle" visiting from out-of-town. The attendant is satisfied with this explanation and gives the child to the man. Following the morning service the mother goes to the nursery and is shocked to learn that her child is not there. It is later determined that the "uncle" in fact was a former husband who was seeking custody of the child. Answer the following questions:

    a. On the basis of what legal theory would the church most likely be responsible for the victim's injuries?

    b. What is the probable outcome of such a lawsuit?

    c. What steps could the church have taken to reduce its risk of liability?

26. A church has a policy requiring two adults to work in the nursery. However, the policy does not prohibit children from being in the custody of less than two adults. On a Sunday morning during worship services, one adult temporarily leaves the nursery for ten minutes to speak with another church member. A few days later the parents of one of the infants in the nursery suspect that their child has been molested. Suspicion is focused on the church nursery. Since the two nursery workers cannot prove that they both were present with the child throughout the entire worship service, they cannot "prove their innocence." The worker who was present in the nursery while the other worker was temporarily absent is suspected of wrongdoing, even though she is completely innocent. What steps could the church have taken to prevent this from happening?

27. T was a Sunday School teacher for several years. T resigned his position and had no further position in the church involving minors. A few years later it is disclosed that T invited a child from the church to his home and molested her. Church leaders were not aware that T had ever invited a child to his home, or that he ever had any social contacts with children from the church. T's parents sue the church, claiming that it was negligent in supervising T. What is the probable outcome of such a lawsuit?

28. Same facts as the previous example, except that T had been asked to resign as a Sunday School teacher after the pastor learned that he had engaged in inappropriate sexual conduct with another minor. Church leaders were not aware of any contacts or socializing between T and children from the church. What is the probable outcome of the lawsuit?

29. A church adopts a policy requiring reference checks on all persons who volunteer to work in any youth program. B is allowed to work as a volunteer in a youth activity without any reference checks. If B engages in inappropriate sexual contacts with a minor and the church is sued, what is the most likely basis of liability?

30. Answer the following questions regarding criminal records checks:

    a. What is a criminal records check?

    b. Explain the various kinds of criminal records checks.

    c. Has a church ever been found liable for not obtaining a criminal records check on an employee or volunteer?

    d. Should a church ever obtain a criminal records check on an employee or volunteer? If so, under what circumstances, and what kind of check?

    e. Summarize the Volunteers for Children Act and its significance to churches.

31. Rev. J accepts a position as pastor of a church. He plans on counseling church members in his office, but is concerned about reducing the risk of false allegations of inappropriate behavior during counseling sessions. What precautions can Rev. J take to reduce or eliminate the risk of inappropriate behavior and false allegations?

32. A church wants to start a counseling ministry that will be staffed by volunteers. The volunteers are not licensed counselors or psychologists, but they have attended a 3-day training event. List several legal concerns that are associated with this counseling ministry.

33. A 30-year-old woman sues a church, claiming that when she was a 15 years old a youth pastor sexually molested her on church premises. Answer the following questions:

    a. On the basis of what legal theory would the church most likely be responsible for the victim's injuries?

    b. What is the most likely legal defense available to the church? What is the likelihood that this defense will be successful?

34. Same facts as the previous question. Assume that the woman claims that she has suffered severe emotional problems since being molested by the youth pastor, but that she did not "discover" that her problems were caused by the youth pastor's misconduct until she went to a counselor shortly before filing her lawsuit. Will these allegations affect the outcome of the case? Explain.

35. Same facts as the previous question, except that the woman claims that the molestation occurred when she was 3 years old, and that she had "repressed" all memory of it until she went to a counselor shortly before filing her lawsuit. Will this allegation affect the outcome of the lawsuit? Explain.

36. What is "ratification"? Give an example of how a church might be liable on this basis.

37. A pastor announces to the congregation following a worship service that the church board dismissed T from membership in the church because of adultery. T sues the church for defamation. How would a court most likely resolve this case under each of the following assumptions:

    a. T was guilty of adultery.

    b. T was not guilty of adultery.

    c. There were nonmembers present in the congregation when the pastor made the announcement.

    d. There were no nonmembers present in the congregation when the pastor made the announcement.

38. A denominational publication lists ministers who have been "dismissed" as a result of discipline. A dismissed minister sues the denomination for defamation. What is the likely outcome of such a case? Explain.

39. Explain the "qualified privilege" defense that may be available to churches that are sued for defamation.

40. What is charitable immunity? Is it recognized in any states? Explain.

41. A church requires all parents to sign a "release form" before their children can participate in swimming and other sports activities and out-of-town trips. Answer the following questions:

   a. What is a release form?

   b. Assume that the youth group goes on a trip to another city in a church-owned vehicle, and that several children are injured when the driver loses control because of a tire blowout. It is later determined that the tire had been driven for 70,000 miles and had little if any tread left. Several parents threaten to sue the church on behalf of their injured children. Would the release form prevent them from doing so?

   c. How do the courts generally view release forms? Why?

42. What is comparative negligence? Why would this concept be relevant in the event someone is injured on church property or during a church activity?

43. A parent informs two board members at her church that her 5-year-old child was sexually molested by a volunteer children's worker during a church activity. The board members share this information with the entire board, and the board removes the accused worker from his position. However, no one notifies the church's liability insurance company of the potential claim. Two years later, the parent sues the church. The lawsuit claims that the victim has suffered severe psychological problems as a result of the molestation, and that the church is legally responsible for the injuries on the basis of negligent selection and negligent supervision. The church sends the lawsuit to its insurance agent. The insurance company refuses to provide the church with a defense of the case, or pay any judgment or settlement, on the ground that the church failed to provide it with timely notice of the potential claim after the incident occurred. The church asks a court for a ruling on the coverage of this claim under its insurance policy. What is the likely outcome of such a claim?

44. A minister of a local church injures the driver of another car while driving negligently. Answer the following questions:

   a. On the basis of what legal theory would the church most likely be responsible for the victim's injuries?

   b. On the basis of what legal theory would a parent religious denomination most likely be responsible for the victim's injuries?

   c. What defenses are available to the denomination in the event it is sued by the victim?

45. What are punitive damages? Why should church leaders be familiar with this term?

46. The legal doctrine of joint and several liability is being restricted or eliminated in several states. Why is this development of interest to denominational agencies?

47. A woman who is sexually seduced by a minister sues a denomination with which the church is affiliated. The woman argues that the denomination is liable for the conduct of affiliated churches and clergy, since they are all "one big family." Specifically, she alleges that the denomination "held out" affiliated churches to be its agents through (1) local church use of the denominational name, (2) ordination of ministers by the denomination, and (3) denominational authority to discipline clergy. Answer the following questions:

    a. On the basis of what legal theory would the church most likely be responsible for the victim's injuries?

    b. On the basis of what legal theory would a parent religious denomination most likely be responsible for the victim's injuries?

    c. What defenses are available to the denomination in the event it is sued by the victim?

48. A minister confesses to sexual relations with a church member. The minister is disciplined by his denomination, but he is allowed to remain in the active ministry. The minister accepts a call at a church in another community. Does this situation impose any risk for the denomination? Explain.

49. Same facts as question 48, except that the minister is dismissed by his denomination. He applies for ordination in another denomination, which ordains him. The other denomination did not ask the minister if he had previously been ordained with another church, and did not discover that he had been dismissed for inappropriate sexual relations with a church member. Assume that the minister engages in inappropriate sexual relations with a member of his new church. Answer the following questions:

    a. The woman sues the former denomination, claiming that it negligently failed to warn the other denomination of the minister's misconduct. What is the likely outcome of such a claim? Explain.

    b. The woman sues the second denomination. What is the most likely basis of liability? Explain.

    c. Identify any legal defenses that may be available to the second denomination.

    d. What steps could the second denomination have taken to reduce the risk of liability in such a case?

50. A parent informs church leaders that her child was molested by a volunteer youth worker at the church. The church leaders remove the volunteer from his position, but do not inform the church insurance company. Answer the following questions:

    a. Is the church's failure to promptly notify the insurer of any legal significance? Explain.

    b. The church's liability insurance policy excludes any intentional or criminal acts. Does this mean that the church is uninsured if the victim or her parent decides to sue the church? Explain.

Discussion Questions

1. Why do you suppose that churches once were immune from legal liability in many states? Do you agree with the prevailing view that churches should be responsible like any other organization for injuries caused by their employees or by dangerous conditions on their premises?

2. Some argue that the existence of liability insurance only encourages lawyers to file lawsuits, and that the lack of insurance will discourage litigation. Do you agree with this logic? Should churches be uninsured? Explain.

3. Some male clergy have adopted a policy of not counseling with unaccompanied females without a third person being present. Evaluate the effectiveness of such a procedure in reducing the risk of seduction, as well as the risk of false claims of seduction. Is such a procedure going too far? Are there less restrictive means that would be as effective?

4. Many courts have ruled that churches and denominational agencies cannot be liable on the basis of negligent selection or negligent supervision for the sexual misconduct of clergy, since any attempt by the civil courts to resolve such claims would violate the first amendment religion clauses. Do you agree with this position? What considerations support the opposite view?

Part Three
Church and State

11

A SUMMARY OF CONSTITUTIONAL HISTORY

Chapter summary. *"Congress shall make no law respecting an establishment of religion, or prohibiting the free exercise thereof." So begins the first amendment to the United States Constitution. The meaning of these words is apparent to even a casual reader: Congress, our national legislature, can neither establish a religion nor prohibit its free exercise. These provisions were incorporated into the Constitution because of the fear that the new federal government would create an established church, as many of the colonies had done. Since Congress never attempted to establish a church, these constitutional provisions were all but forgotten at the beginning of the twentieth century. However, since 1940, the religion clauses have taken on a new and expanded meaning that is foreign to the objectives of its drafters. The "new" interpretation has caused a significant erosion of religious freedom. This tragic story is the focus of chapter 11.*

Congress shall make no law respecting an establishment of religion, or prohibiting the free exercise thereof . . . .[1]

The first amendment religion clauses were the product of the egalitarian fervor of the fledgling Republic. The federal government—"Congress"—would never be able to commit the sin of many of the colonies: establishment of an official religion. Correlatively, the right of each citizen to "freely exercise" his or her religion was protected from federal encroachment. Justice Stewart, dissenting in the *Schempp* case, observed:

As a matter of history, the First Amendment was adopted solely as a limitation upon the newly created National Government. The events leading to its adoption strongly suggest that the Establishment Clause was primarily an attempt to insure that Congress not only would be powerless to establish a national church, but would also be unable to interfere with existing state establishments.[2]

Justice Reed, dissenting in the *McCollum* case,[3] observed:

---

[1] U.S. CONST. amend. 1 (1791).

[2] School District of Abington v. Schempp, 374 U.S. 203, 309-10 (1963). The *Schempp* case is discussed in chapter 16, *infra. See also* Jaffree v. Board of School Commissioners, 554 F. Supp. 1104 (S.D. Ala. 1983) (extensive historical analysis), *rev'd,* Wallace v. Jaffree, 472 U.S. 38 (1985) (extensive historical analysis by Justice Rehnquist, in a dissenting opinion, is summarized in chapter 16, *infra*); R. CORD, SEPARATION OF CHURCH AND STATE: HISTORICAL FACT AND CURRENT FICTION (1982); Kurland, *The Irrelevance of the Constitution: The Religion clauses of the First Amendment and the Supreme Court,* 24 VILLANOVA L. REV. 3 (1978); McClellan, *The Making and the Unmaking of the Establishment Clause,* in A BLUEPRINT FOR JUDICIAL REFORM (P. McGuigan & R. Rader eds. 1982).

[3] People of State of Illinois ex rel. McCollum v. Board of Education, 333 U.S. 203, 244 (1948).

The phrase "an establishment of religion" may have been intended by Congress to be aimed only at a state church. When the First Amendment was pending in Congress in substantially its present form, Mr. Madison said, he apprehended the meaning of the words to be, that Congress should not establish a religion, and enforce the legal observation of it by law, nor compel men to worship God in any manner contrary to their conscience." Passing years, however, have brought about acceptance of a broader meaning . . . .[4]

Similarly, Justice Powell noted:

At this point in the 20th century we are quite far removed from the dangers that prompted the Framers to include the Establishment Clause in the Bill of Rights. The risk of significant religious or denominational control over our democratic processes—or even of deep political division along religious lines—is remote.[5]

After a comprehensive analysis of the history of the establishment clause, Chief Justice Rehnquist concluded that

[i]t seems indisputable from these glimpses into Madison's thinking, reflected by actions on the floor of the House in 1789, that he saw the amendment as designed to prohibit the establishment of a national religion, and perhaps to prevent discrimination among sects. . . . The framers intended the Establishment Clause to prohibit the designation of any church as a "national" one.[6]

Justice Story, writing early in our nation's history, noted that "the real object of the [first] amendment was . . . to prevent any national ecclesiastical establishment, which would give to an hierarchy the exclusive patronage of the national government."[7]

This construction of the intent of the framers of the religion clauses is supported by the absence of judicial opinions interpreting these clauses for the first one and a half centuries following their enactment. Prayers, Bible readings, and religious instruction in the public schools; rental of public facilities by church groups; religious symbols on public property; tax exemptions for religious organizations; and state assistance to religious education were seldom if ever challenged since such practices were plainly far from the congressional establishment of a national religion prohibited by the first amendment. In a related context, the Supreme Court has observed that "[i]f a thing has been practiced for two hundred years by common consent, it will need a strong case for the Constitution to affect it."[8]

Thomas Cooley, an eminent 19th-century authority on constitutional history, observed that "[n]o principle of constitutional law is violated when thanksgiving or fast days are appointed; when chaplains are designated for the army and navy; when legislative sessions are opened with prayer or the reading of the Scriptures;

---

[4] Justice Douglas, concurring in Engel v. Vitale, 370 U.S. 421, 442 (1962), remarked, "I cannot say that to authorize this prayer is to establish a religion in the strictly historic meaning of those words. A religion is not established in the usual sense merely by letting those who choose to do so say the prayer that the public school teacher leads."

[5] Wolman v. Walter, 433 U.S. 229, 263 (concurring in part and dissenting in part). This statement was quoted with approval by a majority of the Supreme Court in Mueller v. Allen, 463 U.S. 388 (1983).

[6] Wallace v. Jaffree, 472 U.S. 38 (1985) (dissenting opinion).

[7] J. STORY, COMMENTARIES ON THE CONSTITUTION 630 (5th ed. 1891).

[8] Jackman v. Rosenbaum Co., 260 U.S. 22, 31 (1922). See also Coler v. Corn Exchange Bank, 250 N.Y. 136, 138 (1928) (Cardozo, J.) ("[n]ot lightly vacated is the verdict of quiescent years").

or when religious teaching is encouraged by a general exemption of the houses of religious worship from taxation for the support of state government."[9]

In more recent years, other judges have interpreted the historical precedent as supporting a much broader interpretation of the establishment clause.[10] Many would concur with Justice Brennan's conclusion that a too literal quest for the advice of the founding fathers upon these issues is futile and misdirected since "the historical record is at best ambiguous, and statements can readily be found to support either side of the proposition."[11] Nevertheless, Justice Brennan conceded that the framers of the first amendment were "preoccupied" with the "imminent question of established churches."[12]

Three factors have considerably broadened the meaning and effect of the first amendment's religion clauses, and particularly the establishment clause. The first occurred in 1803 when the United States Supreme Court ruled that "an act of the legislature, repugnant to the Constitution, is void," and that the federal judiciary is the ultimate interpreter of the Constitution.[13] Thereafter, federal judges had the power—nowhere given in the Constitution itself—to invalidate legislation they deemed inconsistent with the Constitution. A law that established a religion, violated an individual's right to freely exercise his or her religion, or contravened any other provision of the Constitution could be invalidated by a federal court. The nature of the American polity had been redefined.

The second factor that considerably extended the scope of the first amendment was the judge-made doctrine of *incorporation* expressed in 1937 in the landmark case of *Palko v. Connecticut.*[14] The Supreme Court ruled in *Palko* that those provisions of the Bill of Rights—the first ten amendments to the federal Constitution—that were "implicit in the concept of ordered liberty" were incorporated into the fourteenth amendment's "due process clause" and accordingly became applicable to the states.[15] This decision was of fundamental significance, for the framers of the Bill of Rights never intended these amendments to apply to the states. Chief Justice Marshall himself, the author of *Marbury v. Madison,*[16] observed over a century prior to *Palko* that the provisions of the Bill of Rights "contain no expression indicating an intention to apply them to the state governments. This court cannot so apply them."[17] Marshall's admonition was ignored by a majority of the Supreme Court in *Palko.* In 1940, the Court concluded that the religion clauses of the first amendment were "implicit in the concept of ordered liberty," and accordingly concluded that they were limitations

---

[9] T. COOLEY, CONSTITUTIONAL LIMITATIONS 471 (1851).

[10] Everson v. Board of Education, 330 U.S. 1, 31 (1947) (Rutledge, J., dissenting); People of State of Illinois ex rel. McCollum v. Board of Education, 333 U.S. 203, 212 (Frankfurter, J., concurring).

[11] School District of Abington v. Schempp, 374 U.S. 203, 237 (Brennan, J., concurring).

[12] *Id.*

[13] Marbury v. Madison, 1 Cranch 137 (1803).

[14] 302 U.S. 319 (1937).

[15] The fourteenth amendment provides in part, "nor shall any State deprive any person of life, liberty, or property, without due process of law . . . ." It is important to note that the fourteenth amendment is a limitation on the power of "States." By comparison, the Bill of Rights, including the first amendment, was intended to be a limitation solely upon the power of Congress.

[16] *See* note 13, *supra,* and accompanying test.

[17] Barron v. Mayor and City Council, 32 U.S. (7 Pet.) 243 (1833). *See also* Adamson v. California, 332 U.S. 46 (1947), in which Justice Frankfurter observed:

Those reading the English language with the meaning which it ordinarily conveys, those conversant with the political and legal history of the concept of due process, those sensitive to the relations of the States to the central government as well as the relation of some of the provisions of the Bill of Rights to the process of justice, would hardly recognize the Fourteenth Amendment as a cover for the various explicit provisions of the first eight amendments. . . . The notion that the Fourteenth Amendment was a covert way of imposing upon the States all the rules which it seemed important to Eighteenth Century statesmen to write into the Federal Amendments, was rejected by judges who were themselves witnesses of the process by which the Fourteenth Amendment became part of the Constitution. *Id.* at 63-4.

upon state as well as federal action.[18] Accordingly, since 1940 the states have been prohibited from making any law "respecting an establishment of religion, or prohibiting the free exercise thereof . . . ." And, significantly, the term *state* has been construed to mean any subdivision or agency of a state. The first amendment thereby applies to cities, counties, boards of education, and every other level, department, office, or agency of government.

A federal district court judge, in a notable if futile opinion, openly condemned the Supreme Court for its unwarranted extension of the first amendment religion clauses to the states.[19] Ironically, the Supreme Court publicly derided this historically accurate lower court ruling as "remarkable" and "aberrant."[20]

A third factor that has extended the reach of the first amendment's establishment clause is the willingness of the federal courts, since 1948, to liberalize the concept of "establishment" to such a degree as to prohibit conduct that had been deemed consistent with the first amendment for over a century and a half.

But the establishment clause is not the only religion clause contained in the first amendment. There is another: "Congress shall make no law . . . prohibiting the free exercise [of religion]." This latter clause—the "free exercise clause"—is fundamentally incompatible with the philosophy of disestablishment contained in the establishment clause: disestablishment necessarily restricts the free exercise of religion. Thus, the recent judicial emphasis upon disestablishment has at times collided with free exercise interests and with other express and implied rights (speech, assembly, association) contained in the first amendment. Chief Justice Burger, in *Walz v. Tax Commission*,[21] commented on this underlying tension: "The Court has struggled to find a neutral course between the two religion clauses, both of which are cast in absolute terms, and either of which, if expanded to a logical extreme, would tend to clash with the other." Similarly, Justice Stewart, dissenting in *Schempp*,[22] observed, "[T]here are areas in which a doctrinaire reading of the establishment clause leads to irreconcilable conflict with the free exercise clause." The Supreme Court has attempted to synthesize the religion clauses by emphasizing the concepts of "neutrality" and "accommodation." To illustrate, the Court has observed:

> The general principle deductible from the First Amendment and all that has been said by the Court is this: that we will not tolerate either governmentally established religion or governmental interference with religion. Short of those expressly prescribed governmental acts there is room for play in the joints productive of a benevolent neutrality which will permit religious exercise to exist without sponsorship and without interference.[23]

The Court has also stated:

> [T]his Court repeatedly has recognized that tension inevitably exists between the Free Exercise and the Establishment Clauses . . . and that it may often not be possible to promote the former without offending the latter. As a result of this tension, our cases require the State to maintain an attitude of "neutrality," neither "advancing" nor "inhibiting" religion.[24]

---

[18] Cantwell v. Connecticut, 310 U.S. 296 (1940).
[19] Jaffree v. James, 554 F. Supp. 1130 (S.D. Ala. 1983).
[20] Wallace v. Jaffree, 472 U.S. 38 (1985).
[21] 397 U.S. 664, 668-69 (1970).
[22] *See* note 11, *supra*, at 309.
[23] Walz v. Tax Commission, 397 U.S. 664, 669 (1970).
[24] Committee for Public Education & Religious Liberty v. Nyquist, 413 U.S. 756, 788 (1973).

In *Zorach v. Clauson*,[25] the Court spoke of the need of "accommodating" the religious needs of the people.

Notwithstanding the emphasis upon "neutrality" and "accommodation," there is a marked judicial preference for the establishment clause over the free exercise clause. Justice Rehnquist has observed:

> The Court apparently believes that the establishment clause of the first amendment not only mandates religious neutrality on the part of government but also requires that this Court go further and throw its weight on the side of those who believe that our society as a whole should be a purely secular one. Nothing in the first amendment or in the cases interpreting it requires such an extreme approach to this difficult question, and any interpretation of the establishment clause and constitutional values it serves must also take account of the free exercise clause and the values it serves.[26]

Chief Justice Burger has observed: "One can only hope that, at some future date, the Court will come to a more enlightened and tolerant view of the first amendment's guarantee of free exercise of religion . . . ."[27]

Ironically, the Supreme Court, in the same decision that outlawed voluntary, school-sponsored Bible readings on the ground that they violate the establishment clause, acknowledged that "the state may not establish a 'religion of secularism' in the sense of affirmatively opposing or showing hostility to religion, thus preferring those who believe in no religion over those who do believe."[28]

The continuing frustration by the Supreme Court and lower federal courts of voluntary religious practices that are perceived as legitimate by a substantial majority of the public may one day prompt a reassessment of the meaning of first amendment religion clauses. It is possible that such a reassessment has already begun, for in a few recent decisions the Supreme Court, by narrow majorities, has been willing to tolerate certain religious practices that almost certainly would have been outlawed in the past. Significantly, some Supreme Court justices are even calling for a reconsideration of the Court's present interpretation of the religion clauses.[29]

---

[25] 343 U.S. 306 (1952).

[26] Meek v. Pittinger, 421 U.S. 349, 395 (1975) (Rehnquist, J., dissenting).

[27] Meek v. Pittinger, 421 U.S. 349, 387 (1975) (Burger, C.J., dissenting).

[28] School District of Abington v. Schempp, 374 U.S. 203, 225 (1963).

[29] *See, e.g.*, Wallace v. Jaffree, 472 U.S. 38 (1985) (Justices White and Rehnquist, dissenting).

INSTRUCTIONAL AIDS TO CHAPTER 11

Terms

benevolent neutrality

Congress

establishment clause

free exercise clause

incorporation doctrine

judicial review

Marbury v. Madison

state

Learning Objectives

- Understand the original purpose of the first amendment's "nonestablishment of religion" clause.

- Explain the three factors that have led to the enormous expansion and revision of the original intent of the first amendment's "nonestablishment of religion" clause.

- Understand the significance of the Supreme Court's decision in *Marbury v. Madison.*

- Understand what is meant by the *incorporation doctrine.*

Short-Answer Questions

1. The manager of a large apartment complex prohibits non-residents from entering the premises for evangelistic purposes. The minister of a neighboring church contacts the manager, and suggests that the manager's behavior violates the first amendment right of religious freedom. Is the minister correct? Explain.

2. How can the first amendment, which prevents "Congress" from establishing a religion, be relied on by the courts in striking down the actions of state legislatures and public school boards that promote religion?

3. The author of this text states that the nature of the American system of government was altered by the Supreme Court's 1803 decision of *Marbury v. Madison*. Do you agree or disagree with this statement? Explain.

4. Explain the "incorporation doctrine." What is its relevance to churches?

5. What do you believe was the original purpose for the first amendment religion clauses?

6. Massachusetts was the last state to disestablish an established religion. This occurred nearly a half a century after the ratification of the first amendment. How is this fact relevant in interpreting the original purpose of the first amendment's nonestablishment of religion clause?

7. The Supreme Court has called for a "benevolent neutrality" on the part of government toward religion. What does this mean, and why is this necessary?

Discussion Questions

1. How would the framers of the Constitution and Bill of Rights have viewed the "incorporation doctrine"? Do you believe that it is relevant today to determine the intention of the framers?

2. The Supreme Court has observed that an emphasis on one of the first amendment's two religion clauses inevitably leads to a clash with the other. What did the Court mean?

12

LANDMARK SUPREME COURT DECISIONS INTERPRETING THE FIRST AMENDMENT RELIGION CLAUSES

Chapter summary. Charles Evans Hughes, a former Chief Justice of the United States Supreme Court, once remarked that "we are under a Constitution, but the Constitution is what the judges say it is." These words reflect the holding of the Supreme Court's 1803 decision of Marbury v. Madison, in which the Court ruled that the Constitution is the supreme law of the land, that any act of government in conflict with the Constitution is void, and that the federal judges are entrusted with the responsibility of interpreting the Constitution. Since the United States Supreme Court is the highest court in the federal judicial system, its pronouncements have the ultimate authority. An interpretation of the Constitution by the Supreme Court becomes the supreme law of the land until the court reverses itself or until a constitutional amendment is ratified that alters the Court's interpretation. The importance of Supreme Court interpretations of the first amendment religion clauses should thus be apparent. In this chapter, several Supreme Court decisions will be reviewed. Through a careful study of these decisions, you will

acquire an understanding of how the Supreme Court interprets the religion clauses. Such interpreta-
tions are binding on all other courts, and upon every other organ of government.

The United State Supreme Court in *Marbury v. Madison*[1] held that the United States Constitution is the
"paramount," or supreme law of the land, and that "[i]t is emphatically the province and duty" of the federal
courts to construe the Constitution. Accordingly, federal courts have the ultimate authority to construe provisions in the Constitution.[2] Since the United States Supreme Court is the highest court in the federal judicial
system, its interpretations of the Constitution are entitled to the greatest deference. An interpretation of a constitutional provision by the Supreme Court in effect becomes the supreme law of the land, and must be followed
by all state and lower federal courts until the Supreme Court reverses itself and overrules the earlier decision, or
until the Court's ruling is invalidated by ratification of an amendment to the Constitution. The importance of
Supreme Court interpretations of the first amendment's "religion clauses"[3] should be apparent.

The Supreme Court seldom discussed the religion clauses in the first century and a half following their
enactment. Since 1947, however, the Court has construed the religion clauses on a number of occasions.
Some of the more significant of these decisions will be summarized in this chapter.[4]

§ 12-01 Everson v. Board of Education[5]

A New Jersey statute authorized local school districts to make arrangements for the transportation of
children to and from schools. One township board of education, acting pursuant to this statute, adopted a
resolution authorizing reimbursement to parents of money expended by them for the bus transportation of
their children on buses operated by the public transportation system. Part of this money was for the payment
of transportation of some children in the community to Catholic parochial schools. A taxpayer filed suit
against the board of education, alleging that the state law and board of education resolution constituted a
violation of the first amendment to the United States Constitution insofar as they forced taxpayers to pay for
the transportation of children to Catholic schools.

The New Jersey Court of Errors and Appeals concluded that the statute and resolution did not
violate the first amendment, and the taxpayer appealed directly to the United States Supreme Court. In
upholding the statute and school board resolution, the Supreme Court rendered the first modern interpretation of the first amendment's "establishment clause." After briefly describing the colonial experience of

---

[1] 1 Cranch 137 (1803). *See* chapter 11, note 13, and accompanying text.

[2] "We are under a Constitution, but the Constitution is what the judges say it is." Charles Evans Hughes, Speech, May 3, 1907.

[3] The first amendment provides in relevant part that "Congress shall make no law respecting an establishment of religion or prohibiting
the free exercise thereof . . . ." The first phrase of the amendment—"Congress shall make no law respecting an establishment of
religion"—is referred to as the *establishment clause.* The second phrase—"or prohibit the free exercise thereof"—is referred to as the
free exercise clause.

[4] Some important Supreme Court decisions interpreting the first amendment religion clauses are discussed in other chapters. *See, e.g.,*
Corporation of the Presiding Bishop of the Church of Jesus Christ of Latter-Day Saints v. Amos, 483 U.S. 327 (1987) (chapter 8);
Tony and Susan Alamo Foundation v. Secretary of Labor, 471 U.S. 290 (1985) (chapter 8); Larson v. Valente, 456 U.S. 228 (1982)
(chapter 9); Village of Schaumburg v. Citizens for a Better Environment, 444 U.S. 620, 632 (1980) (chapter 9); Jones v. Wolf, 443
U.S. 595 (1979) (chapter 7); NLRB v. Catholic Bishop of Chicago, 440 U.S. 490 (1979) (chapter 8); Serbian Eastern Orthodox
Diocese v. Milivojevich, 426 U.S. 696 (1976) (chapters 2 and 9); Maryland and Virginia Eldership of the Churches of God v. Church
of God, 396 U.S. 367 (1970) (chapter 7); Presbyterian Church in the United States v. Mary Elizabeth Blue Hull Memorial Presbyte-
rian Church, 393 U.S. 440 (1969) (chapter 7); Kedroff v. St. Nicholas Cathedral, 344 U.S. 94 (1952) (chapters 2 and 9); Cantwell v.
Connecticut, 310 U.S. 296 (1940) (chapter 11); Gonzalez v. Roman Catholic Archbishop, 280 U.S. 1 (1928) (chapter 2); Watson v.
Jones, 80 U.S. (13 Wall.) 679 (1871) (chapters 2, 7, and 9).

[5] 330 U.S. 1 (1947). *See* Justice Rehnquist's dissenting opinion in Wallace v. Jaffree, 472 U.S. 38 (1985), for a devastating critique of
the historical accuracy of this ruling. The *Wallace* case, and Justice Rehnquist's dissent, are discussed later in this chapter.

established religions and persecution of religious dissenters that "found expression in the first amendment," the Court observed:

> The "establishment of religion" clause of the first amendment means at least this: Neither a state nor the Federal Government can set up a church. Neither can pass laws which aid one religion, aid all religions, or prefer one religion over another. Neither can force nor influence a person to go or to remain away from church against his will or force him to profess a belief or disbelief in any religion. No person can be punished for entertaining or professing religious beliefs or disbeliefs, for church attendance or nonattendance. No tax in any amount, large or small, can be levied to support any religious activities or institutions, whatever they may be called, or whatever form they may adopt to teach or practice religion. Neither a state nor the Federal Government can, openly or secretly, participate in the affairs of any religious organizations or groups and vice versa. In the words of Jefferson, the clause against establishment of religion by law was intended to erect "a wall of separation between church and state."[6]

Measuring by this standard, the Court concluded that the first amendment did not prohibit New Jersey from spending tax revenues to pay the bus fares of parochial school pupils as a part of a general program under which it paid the fares of pupils attending public and other schools. "We must be careful," observed the Court, in protecting the citizens of New Jersey against state-established churches, to be sure that we do not inadvertently prohibit New Jersey from extending its general state law benefits to all its citizens without regard to their religious beliefs."[7] The Court acknowledged that payment of the bus fares of parochial school students as well as the protection of parochial school pupils by means of state-paid police officers and firefighters and the use of public streets and sidewalks by parochial school pupils did provide some assistance to such pupils, but the Court insisted that

> cutting off church-schools from these services, so separate and so indisputably marked off from the religious function, would make it far more difficult for the schools to operate. But such is obviously not the purpose of the first amendment. That amendment requires the state to be neutral in its relations with groups of religious believers and non-believers; it does not require the state to be their adversary. State power is no more to be used so as to handicap religions, than it is to favor them.[8]

Finally, the Court observed that the free exercise of religion, also protected by the first amendment, would be abridged by a state law excluding certain citizens on the basis of their religion from receiving the benefits of public welfare legislation.

§ 12-02 People of State of Illinois ex rel. McCollum v. Board of Education[9]

In 1940, interested members of the Jewish, Roman Catholic, and a few of the Protestant faiths formed a voluntary association in Champaign, Illinois, called the Champaign Council on Religious Education. The council obtained permission from the local board of education to offer classes in religious instruction to public school pupils in grades four to nine inclusive. Classes were made up of pupils whose parents signed printed cards requesting that their children be permitted to attend. Classes were held weekly, 30 minutes for the lower grades

---

[6] *Id.* at 15-16.
[7] *Id.* at 16.
[8] *Id.* at 18.
[9] 333 U.S. 203 (1948).

and 45 minutes for the higher. The council employed the religious teachers at no expense to the school authorities, but the instructors were subject to the approval and supervision of the superintendent of schools. The classes were taught in three separate groups by Protestant teachers, Catholic priests, and a Jewish rabbi. Classes were conducted in the regular classrooms of the school building. Students who did not choose to take the religious instruction were not released from public school duties; they were required to leave their classrooms and go to some other place in the school building for the pursuit of their secular studies. Students who were released from secular study for the religious instruction were required to be present at the religious classes.

The constitutionality of this "released time" program was challenged by the parent of a public school student on the ground that it violated the first amendment's prohibition of the establishment of a religion. The state courts of Illinois upheld the constitutionality of the program, and the case was appealed directly to the United States Supreme Court. The Supreme Court struck down the released time program on the ground that it was "beyond all question a utilization of the tax-established and tax-supported public school system to aid religious groups to spread their faith" and thus "falls squarely under the ban of the first amendment."[10] The Court noted in particular that the state's tax-supported public school buildings were used for the dissemination of religious doctrine, and that the state materially aided religious groups by providing pupils for their religious classes through use of the state's compulsory school machinery. "This is not separation of Church and State," the Court concluded.

The Court rejected the argument that the first amendment was intended to forbid only governmental preference of one religion over another, and not impartial governmental assistance of all religions. The Court also rejected the contention that forbidding the use of public school property to aid all religious faiths in the dissemination of their doctrine constituted an impermissible governmental hostility to religion. A manifestation of governmental hostility to religion would be impermissible, the Court agreed, but it found no such hostility under the facts of this case. The Court concluded:

> [T]he first amendment rests upon the premise that both religion and government can best work to achieve their lofty aims if each is left free from the other within its respective sphere. . . . [T]he first amendment has erected a wall between Church and State which must be kept high and impregnable.[11]

Justice Jackson, in a concurring opinion, cautioned that it may be unnecessary if not impossible to cast out of secular education all that some people may reasonably regard as religious instruction:

> Music without sacred music, architecture minus the cathedral, or painting without the scriptural themes would be eccentric and incomplete, even from a secular point of view. Yet the inspirational appeal of religion in these guises is often stronger than in forthright sermon. Even such a "science" as biology raises the issue between evolution and creation as an explanation of our presence on this planet. Certainly a course in English literature that omitted the Bible and other powerful uses of our mother tongue for religious ends would be pretty barren. And I should suppose it is a proper, if not an indispensable, part of preparation for a worldly life to know the roles that religions have played in the tragic story of mankind. The fact is that, for good or ill, nearly everything in our culture worth transmitting, everything which gives meaning to life, is saturated with religious influences, derived from paganism, Judaism, Christianity—both Catholic and Protestant—and other faiths accepted by a large part of the world's peoples. One can

---

[10] *Id.* at 210.
[11] *Id.* at 212.

hardly respect a system of education that would leave the student wholly ignorant of the currents of religious thought that move the world society for a part in which he is being prepared.[12]

In a dissenting opinion, Justice Reed insisted that the first amendment was never intended to prohibit religious instruction of public school children during school hours. He agreed that government cannot "aid" all or any religions, but he construed the word *aid* to mean purposeful assistance directly to a church or religious organization itself. Justice Reed recounted many examples of government accommodation of religious practices, and observed:

> The prohibition of enactments respecting the establishment of religion does not bar every friendly gesture between church and state. It is not an absolute prohibition against every conceivable situation where the two may work together any more than the other provisions of the first amendment—free speech, free press—are absolutes.[13]

Justice Reed concluded that "[t]his Court cannot be too cautious in upsetting practices embedded in our society by many years of experience" and that devotion to the great principle of religious liberty "should not lead us into a rigid interpretation of the constitutional guarantee that conflicts with accepted habits of our people."[14]

§ 12-03 Zorach v. Clauson[15]

Shortly after deciding that released time programs allowing public school students to receive religious instruction on school property were unconstitutional, the Supreme Court was faced with the task of deciding the constitutionality of released time programs that permitted public school children to leave school property to receive religious instruction.

New York City developed a program that permitted its public schools to release students during the school day so that they could leave the school buildings and grounds and go to religious centers for religious instruction or devotional exercises. Students were released upon written request of their parents. Those not released stayed at school. The churches and other religious centers made weekly reports to the schools. All costs of the program were paid by religious organizations.

A group of parents challenged the constitutionality of the program. In particular, the parents argued that the program constituted an establishment of religion in violation of the first amendment since the weight and influence of the school was put behind a program of religious instruction; public school teachers policed the program, keeping track of students who had been released; and classroom activities came to a halt while students who had been released were on leave.

The Court rejected the parents' challenge. While acknowledging that "there cannot be the slightest doubt that the first amendment reflects the philosophy that Church and State should be separated," the Court held that the first amendment "does not say that in every and all respects there shall be a separation of Church and State."[16] A strict separation, observed the Court, would cause the state and religion to be aliens—hostile, suspicious, and even unfriendly. Municipalities would not be permitted to render police or fire pro-

---

[12] *Id.* at 236.
[13] *Id.* at 255-56.
[14] *Id.* at 256.
[15] 343 U.S. 306 (1952).
[16] *Id.* at 312.

tection to religious groups; police officers who helped parishioners to their places of worship would violate the Constitution; and prayers in the nation's legislative halls, the proclamations making Thanksgiving Day a holiday, and the words "so help me God" in courtroom oaths—these and all other references to the Almighty that run through our laws and ceremonies would flout the first amendment.

In one of its most eloquent descriptions of the meaning of *establishment*, the Court observed:

We are a religious people whose institutions presuppose a Supreme Being. We guarantee the freedom of worship as one chooses. We make room for as wide a variety of beliefs and creeds as the spiritual needs of man deem necessary. We sponsor an attitude on the part of government that shows no partiality to any one group and that lets each flourish according to the zeal of its adherents and the appeal of its dogma. When the state encourages religious instruction or cooperates with religious authorities by adjusting the schedule of public events to sectarian needs, it follows the best of our traditions. For it then respects the religious nature of our people and accommodates the public service to their spiritual needs. To hold that it may not would be to find in the Constitution a requirement that the government show a callous indifference to religious groups. That would be preferring those who believe in no religion over those who do believe. Government may not finance religious groups nor undertake religious instruction nor blend secular and sectarian education nor use secular institutions to force one or some religion on any person. But we find no constitutional requirement which makes it necessary for government to be hostile to religion and throw its weight against efforts to widen the effective scope of religious influence. The government must be neutral when it comes to competition between sects. It may not thrust any sect on any person. It may not make a religious observance compulsory. It may not coerce anyone to attend church, to observe a religious holiday, or to take religious instruction. But it can close its doors or suspend its operations as to those who want to repair to their religious sanctuary for worship or instruction. No more than that is undertaken here.[17]

The released time program of New York City was found to be valid under this test. The Court distinguished *McCollum* on the ground that classrooms were used in that case for religious instruction, and the force of the public school was used to promote that instruction. In the present case, the public schools did no more than accommodate their schedules to a program of outside religious instruction. "We follow the *McCollum* case," concluded the Court. "[B]ut we cannot expand it to cover the present released time program unless separation of Church and State means that public institutions can make no adjustments of their schedules to accommodate the religious needs of the people. We cannot read into the Bill of Rights such a philosophy of hostility to religion."[18]

§ 12-04 Engel v. Vitale[19]

The New York Board of Regents, a governmental agency having broad supervisory power over the state's public schools, recommended that the following nondenominational prayer be recited in each public school at the start of every school day: "Almighty God, we acknowledge our dependence upon Thee, and we beg Thy blessings upon us, our parents, our teachers, and our country."

---

[17] *Id.* at 313-14.
[18] *Id.* at 313-14.
[19] 370 U.S. 421 (1962).

A group of parents whose children attended a public school in which the "Regents' prayer" was recited challenged the constitutionality of the practice in state court. The New York state courts upheld the constitutionality of the practice on the condition that no child be compelled to join in the prayer over his own or his parents' objection. The parents appealed to the United States Supreme Court, which ruled that the practice constituted an establishment of religion in violation of the first amendment:

> [W]e think that the constitutional prohibition against laws respecting an establishment of religion must at least mean that in this country it is no part of the business of government to compose official prayers for any group of the American people to recite as a part of a religious program carried on by government.[20]

The Court rejected the contention that the prayer was permissible because it was nondenominational and voluntary, since the establishment clause "does not depend upon any showing of direct governmental compulsion and is violated by the enactment of laws which establish an official religion whether those laws operate directly to coerce nonobserving individuals or not."[21] Furthermore, the Court refused to concede that the Regents' prayer was in fact "voluntary" since when the power and prestige of government is placed behind a particular religious belief "the indirect coercive pressure upon religious minorities to conform to the prevailing officially approved religion is plain."[22]

In rejecting the contention that its decision evidenced a hostility toward religion which itself contravened the first amendment, the Court observed:

> [T]here grew up a sentiment that caused men to leave the cross-currents of officially established state religions and religious persecution in Europe and come to this country filled with that hope that they could find a place in which they could pray when they pleased to the God of their faith in the language they chose. And there were men of this same faith . . . who led the fight for adoption of our Constitution and also for our Bill of Rights with the very guarantees of religious freedom that forbid the sort of governmental activity which New York has attempted here.[23]

The Court acknowledged that governmental endorsement of the Regents' prayer was insignificant in comparison to the encroachments upon religion which were uppermost in the minds of those who ratified the first amendment, but it reasoned that "it is proper to take alarm at the first experiment with our liberties" in order to preclude more substantial violations.

In dissent, Justice Stewart traced the many spiritual traditions of our nation, including the recitation of prayer before legislative and judicial sessions, the references to God in the Pledge of Allegiance and the national anthem, presidential proclamations of national days of prayer, the provision of military and institutional chaplains at government expense, and imprinting the words "In God We Trust" on coins and currency. He concluded that it was arbitrary to deny school children the right to share in this spiritual heritage by forbidding them to voluntarily recite a prayer at the start of each school day.

---

[20] *Id.* at 425.
[21] *Id.* at 430.
[22] *Id.* at 431.
[23] *Id.* at 434-35.

§ 12-05 School District of Abington v. Schempp[24]

The State of Pennsylvania enacted a law that stipulated, "At least ten verses from the Holy Bible shall be read, without comment, at the opening of each public school on each school day. Any child shall be excused from such Bible reading, or attending such Bible reading, upon the written request of his parent or guardian."

A family having two children in the public schools filed suit to halt enforcement of the Pennsylvania law on the ground that it constituted an impermissible establishment of religion in violation of the first amendment. A federal district court agreed that the law violated the establishment clause, and the state appealed directly to the United States Supreme Court. The Supreme Court, in affirming the lower court ruling, stated that "to withstand the strictures of the establishment clause there must be a secular legislative purpose and a primary effect that neither advances nor inhibits religion."[25] The Court concluded that the reading of the Bible at the start of each school day was indisputably a religious practice and as such it violated the first amendment. It did not matter that participation in the readings was voluntary, or that the readings themselves were relatively minor encroachments on the first amendment, since "[t]he breach of neutrality that is today a trickling stream may all too soon become a raging torrent."[26]

The Court agreed that the state "may not establish a 'religion of secularism' in the sense of affirmatively opposing or showing hostility to religion," but it did not believe that its decision in any sense had that effect.[27] The Court also acknowledged that

one's education is not complete without a study of comparative religion or the history of religion and its relationship to the advancement of civilization. It certainly may be said that the Bible is worthy of study for its literary and historic qualities. Nothing we have said indicates that such study of the Bible or of religion, when presented objectively as part of a secular program of education, may not be effected consistently with the first amendment.[28]

Finally, the Court rejected the contention that its decision collided with the majority's right to the free exercise of their religion:

The very purpose of a Bill of Rights was to withdraw certain subjects from the vicissitudes of political controversy, to place them beyond the reach of majorities and officials and to establish them as legal principles to be applied by the courts. One's right to . . . freedom of worship . . . and other fundamental rights may not be submitted to vote; they depend on the outcome of no elections.[29]

Justice Stewart, in dissent, argued that the neutrality mandated by the first amendment required that school children be permitted, on a voluntary basis, to start their day with Bible reading since "a refusal to permit religious exercises is thus seen, not as the realization of state neutrality, but rather as the establishment of a religion of secularism, or at the least, as government support of the beliefs of those who think that

---

[24] 374 U.S. 203 (1963).
[25] *Id.* at 222.
[26] *Id.* at 225.
[27] *Id.*
[28] *Id.*
[29] *Id.* at 226, quoting *West Virginia Board of Education v. Barnette*, 319 U.S. 624, 638 (1943) (Justice Jackson).

religious exercises should be conducted only in private."[30] Justice Stewart also maintained that readings from the Bible unaccompanied by comments and addressed only to those children who chose to be present did not represent the type of support of religion barred by the establishment clause.

§ 12-06 Walz v. Tax Commission[31]

The New York legislature enacted a property tax law that exempted real property owned by nonprofit corporations and associations that were organized exclusively for religious, charitable, benevolent, educational, scientific, or literary purposes. A taxpayer filed suit in the New York state courts to prevent the New York City Tax Commission from granting property tax exemptions to religious organizations for properties used solely for religious worship on the ground that such exemptions required the government to make "contributions" to religious organizations in violation of the principle of separation of church and state embodied in the first amendment. The New York state courts upheld the constitutionality of the exemption, and the case was appealed to the United States Supreme Court.

The Supreme Court, with only one dissenting vote, affirmed the constitutionality of the New York law. After noting that the purpose of the establishment clause is the prevention of "sponsorship, financial support, and active involvement of the sovereign in religious activity,"[32] the Court concluded that the exemption of properties used exclusively for religious purposes did not constitute sponsorship or financial support of religious organizations by the state. "The grant of a tax exemption is not sponsorship," noted the Court, "since the government does not transfer part of its revenue to churches but simply abstains from demanding that the church support the state."[33] In addition, property used for religious purposes was but one of a wide variety of classifications of property that were exempted from tax. The state had not singled out church-owned property for the exemption, but rather it had included such property in a long list of other exempted properties owned by organizations whose activities the state had decided were socially desirable and deserving of protection through exemption from tax.

Finally, the Court emphasized that any practice that leads to an excessive governmental entanglement with religion is prohibited by the establishment clause. It acknowledged that either taxation of churches or exemption occasioned some governmental involvement with religion. However, it concluded that elimination of the exemption would lead to a greater entanglement "by giving rise to tax valuation of church property, tax liens, tax foreclosures, and the direct confrontations and conflicts that follow in the train of those legal processes."[34] On the other hand, the exemption "creates only a minimal and remote involvement between church and state and far less than taxation of churches."[35] The Court also stressed that "an unbroken practice of according the exemption to churches, openly and by affirmative state action, not covertly or by state inaction, is not something to be lightly cast aside,"[36] and it quoted Justice Holmes' earlier observation that "[i]f a thing has been practiced for two hundred years by common consent, it will need a strong case for the [Constitution] to affect it."[37]

---

[30] *Id.* at 313.
[31] 393 U.S. 664 (1970).
[32] *Id.* at 668.
[33] *Id.* at 675.
[34] *Id.* at 674.
[35] *Id.* at 676.
[36] *Id.* at 678.
[37] *Id.*

§ 12-07 Wisconsin v. Yoder[38]

The *Yoder* case involved the constitutionality of applying a state compulsory attendance law to Old Order Amish children who had completed the eighth grade. The principal significance of the decision lies in the Court's construction of the "free exercise clause" of the first amendment. After emphasizing that "only those interests of the highest order and those not otherwise served can overbalance legitimate claims to the free exercise of religion,"[39] the Court enunciated a three-pronged test for assessing the constitutionality of governmental action under the free exercise clause:

1. Is the activity interfered with by the state motivated by and rooted in legitimate and sincerely held religious belief?

2. Is the activity interfered with by the state unduly and substantially burdened to the extent of affecting religious practice?

3. Does the state have a compelling interest in limiting or restricting the religiously motivated activity that cannot be accomplished through less restrictive means?

This test served as the basic analysis for assessing the validity of governmental limitations on the free exercise of religion until 1990. In 1990, the Supreme Court altered this analysis, making it easier for governmental limitations on religious practice to be constitutional.[40]

§ 12-08 Lemon v. Kurtzman[41]

In striking down various provisions of a New York law authorizing state aid to nonpublic school teachers who taught secular subjects, the Court articulated a three-pronged test for evaluating the constitutionality of government action under the establishment clause: "First, the statute must have a secular legislative purpose; second, its principal or primary effect must be one that neither advances nor inhibits religion; finally, the statute must not foster 'an excessive governmental entanglement with religion.'"[42] This is the test that the federal courts have applied, almost without exception, in evaluating whether or not a particular governmental accommodation of religion violates the establishment clause.

§ 12-09 Chambers v. Marsh[43]

For many years, the Nebraska unicameral legislature has begun each of its sessions with a prayer offered by a chaplain chosen biennially and paid out of public funds. This practice was challenged in 1980 by a state senator who claimed that it constituted an establishment of religion in violation of the first amendment. A federal district court found the practice to be permissible, but a federal appeals court ruled that the practice violated the establishment of religion clause.

---

[38] 406 U.S. 205 (1972).
[39] 406 U.S. at 215.
[40] *See* Employment Division v. Smith, 110 S. Ct. 1595 (1990), which is discussed later in this chapter.
[41] 403 U.S. 602 (1971).
[42] *Id.* at 612-13. The Court has observed that the "three-part test that has emerged from our decisions is a product of considerations derived from the full sweep of the establishment clause cases." Committee for Public Education v. Nyquist, 413 U.S. 756 (1973).
[43] 463 U.S. 783 (1983).

In a six to three decision, the Supreme Court reversed the federal appeals court and upheld the constitutionality of the Nebraska legislative chaplaincy program. The Court surveyed the history of legislative chaplains, observing that "[t]he opening of sessions of legislative and other deliberative public bodies with prayer is deeply embedded in the history and tradition of this country," and that this practice "coexisted with the principles of disestablishment and religious freedom." The Court found it especially relevant that the first Congress, which drafted the first amendment religion clauses, adopted the policy of selecting a chaplain to open each session with prayer:

> It can hardly be thought that in the same week members of the First Congress voted to appoint and to pay a chaplain for each House and also voted to approve the draft of the first amendment for submission to the States, they intended the establishment clause of the Amendment to forbid what they had just declared acceptable. In applying the first amendment . . . it would be incongruous to interpret the clause as imposing more stringent first amendment limits on the states than the draftsmen imposed on the Federal Government.[44]

While acknowledging that "no one acquires a vested or protected right in violation of the Constitution by long use," the Court found the historical precedent to unequivocally establish the constitutionality of legislative chaplaincies.

The Court also rejected the claim that the Nebraska practice had to be invalidated since a clergyman of only one religious faith had been selected for 16 consecutive years, the chaplain was compensated at public expense, and the prayers were exclusively in the Judeo-Christian tradition. None of these characteristics, concluded the Court, was materially different from the experience of the first Congress.

The true significance of this decision is the Court's willingness to depart from the three-pronged *Lemon* test in evaluating the constitutionality of a practice challenged on establishment clause grounds. In the *Lemon* case, decided in 1971, the Court had formulated the following test as a device to assist in applying the first amendment's establishment clause: "First, the statute . . . must have a secular legislative purpose; second, its principal or primary effect must be one that neither advances nor inhibits religion; finally, the statute must not foster an excessive governmental entanglement with religion."[45] This test, unfortunately, was used by many state and federal courts as a cudgel to obliterate many forms of religious expression and practice that were not even remotely considered to be establishments of religion by the framers of the first amendment. The willingness of the Court to uphold a religious practice without any reference to the *Lemon* test suggests that not every accommodation of the "religious nature of our people"[46] or acknowledgment of religious belief will be summarily invalidated.

§ 12-10 Wallace v. Jaffree[47]

In 1981, the Alabama legislature enacted a law specifying:

---

[44] This evidence would conclusively establish the legitimacy of legislative chaplains to all but the most doctrinaire disestablishmentarians, or to those who adhere to a "progressive understanding" of constitutional provisions. To illustrate, in a dissenting opinion, Justice Brennan urged the Court to disregard history and the original purpose of the first amendment in favor of a more enlightened view of the proper place of religious exercise. Of course, one of the deficiencies of such an approach is that once the moorings of history are abandoned, any substitute standard is itself immediately vulnerable to revision. Thus, condemnations by Justice Brennan and others of decisions that have departed from the "settled" meaning of the *Lemon* decision are hollow and unprincipled.

[45] Lemon v. Kurtzman, 403 U.S. 602 (1971).

[46] Zorach v. Clauson, 343 U.S. 306 (1952) (Justice Douglas speaking for the Court).

[47] 472 U.S. 38 (1985).

At the commencement of the first class of each day in all grades in all public schools the teacher in charge of the room in which each class is held may announce that a period of silence not to exceed one minute in duration shall be observed for meditation or voluntary prayer, and during any such period no other activities shall be engaged in.[48]

This law was challenged in 1982 by a parent who asserted that it was an impermissible establishment of religion in violation of the first amendment. A federal district court, after a lengthy and accurate historical analysis, concluded that the Supreme Court was misguided in its interpretation and application of the first amendment, and declined to follow its precedents. In particular, the court concluded, correctly, that the first amendment religion clauses were not applicable to the states, and therefore the State of Alabama was free to accommodate or even establish a religion if it so desired.[49] Predictably, this decision was reversed by a federal appeals court, and ultimately by the Supreme Court as well. Ironically, characterizing the district court's thorough and historically indisputable analysis as "remarkable" and aberrant, the Supreme Court saw nothing improper in its application of the first amendment to the states contrary to the expressed intention of the framers of that amendment.[50]

The Court concluded that the Alabama law constituted an impermissible "establishment of religion" since it did not have a clearly secular purpose and therefore failed the first prong of the three-pronged *Lemon* test.

The significance of this decision is not the Court's ruling or its facile "historical analysis." Rather, it is the dissenting opinion of Justice Rehnquist, which presents a compelling and comprehensive historical explication of the establishment clause and in the process calls into question the *Lemon* test, the "wall of separation between church and state" metaphor, and the propriety of applying the first amendment's proscriptions to state governments.

Justice Rehnquist began his opinion by exposing the impropriety of the "wall of separation" metaphor allegedly coined by Thomas Jefferson. Justice Rehnquist pointed out that Jefferson was in France at the time the first amendment was debated, enacted, and ratified, and that his metaphor was contained in a brief letter to the Danbury Baptist Association 14 years after the first amendment was drafted. "He would seem to any detached observer," concluded Justice Rehnquist, "as a less than ideal source of contemporary history as to the meaning of the religion clauses of the first amendment."

Justice Rehnquist then summarized the debates associated with the enactment of the first amendment by Congress and demonstrated that the concern was "the establishment of a national church, and perhaps the preference of one religious sect over another. . . ." James Madison, the chief architect of the amendment, saw no need for it, but proposed it merely as an expedient to satisfy the concerns of those opponents of the Constitution who insisted that without a Bill of Rights the newly-created federal government might become despotic. Justice Rehnquist also cited the early nineteenth-century commentaries of Supreme Court Justice Story and legal historian Thomas Cooley as proof that the purpose of the establishment clause was the prevention of a national

---

[48] ALA. CODE § 16-1-20.1.

[49] *See* chapter 11, *supra.*

[50] As noted in chapter 11, the Court has, since 1940, assumed that the fourteenth amendment's guaranty of "life, liberty and property" against state interference "incorporated" the first amendment religion clauses. Therefore, the Court believes that it is justified in invalidating *state* (and local) legislation even though the first amendment is by its own terms a limitation solely on the power of the federal government ("Congress"). One can only wonder why it took the Court three-quarters of a century to "discover" that the protections of the first amendment were "incorporated" into an amendment ratified at the conclusion of the Civil War and designed to protect newly-freed slaves. This untenable construction is convincingly refuted in a number of scholarly works on constitutional law. *See e.g.,* R. BERGER, GOVERNMENT BY JUDICIARY: THE TRANSFORMATION OF THE FOURTEENTH AMENDMENT (1977).

religion. He condemned the Court's constitutionalization of the "wall of separation" metaphor in its *Everson* decision in 1947, and suggested that this "theory of rigid separation" be "frankly and explicitly abandoned."

Justice Rehnquist denounced the three-pronged *Lemon* test adopted by the Court in 1971, since it "has no more grounding in the history of the first amendment than does the wall theory upon which it rests." He observed that the Court itself had moved away from the *Lemon* formulation:

> [W]e soon began describing the test as only a 'guideline,' and lately we have described it as 'no more than [a] useful signpost'. . . . We have noted that the *Lemon* test is 'not easily applied,' under the *Lemon* test we have 'sacrificed clarity and predictability for flexibility' . . . [and] the *Lemon* test has never been binding on the Court. . . . If a constitutional theory has no basis in the history of the amendment it seeks to interpret, and is difficult to apply and yields unprincipled results, I see little use for it.[51]

In place of the "wall of separation" metaphor or the *Lemon* test, Justice Rehnquist proposed that the religion clauses he interpreted consistently with the principles that "the framers inscribed," for "[a]ny deviation from their intentions frustrates the permanence of [the Bill of Rights] and will only lead to the type of unprincipled decisionmaking that has plagued our establishment clause cases since *Everson*" in 1947. The principles inscribed by the framers on the first amendment's religion clauses were clear:

> The framers intended the establishment clause to prohibit the designation of any church as a "national" one. The clause was also designed to stop the federal government from asserting a preference of one religious denomination or sect over others. Given the "incorporation" of the establishment clause as against the states via the fourteenth amendment in *Everson*, states are prohibited as well from establishing a religion or discriminating between sects. As its history abundantly shows, however, nothing in the establishment clause requires government to be strictly neutral between religion and irreligion, nor does that clause prohibit Congress or the states from pursuing legitimate secular ends through nondiscriminatory means.[52]

Justice Rehnquist concluded that the Court's decision would "come as a shock to those who drafted the Bill of Rights" as well as to "a large number of thoughtful Americans today." Noting that George Washington himself, at the request of the very Congress that passed the Bill of Rights, proclaimed a day of public thanksgiving and prayer, Justice Rehnquist observed that "[history] must judge whether it was the father of his country in 1789, or a majority of the Court today, which has strayed from the meaning of the establishment clause."

§ 12-11 Employment Division v. Smith[53]

The first amendment to the United States Constitution guarantees that "Congress shall make no law . . . prohibiting the free exercise of religion." For many years, the United States Supreme Court has interpreted this language to mean that government cannot impose substantial burdens on the exercise of sincerely-held religious beliefs unless its action is justified by a "compelling state interest" that cannot be served through less restrictive means. In a case of historic proportion, the Supreme Court revised its understanding of the "free exercise" clause. It is unclear at this time what the ramifications will be.

---

[51] 472 U.S. at 112.
[52] *Id.* at 113.
[53] 110 S. Ct. 1595 (1990).

Oregon law prohibits the intentional possession of a "controlled substance," including the drug peyote. Two employees of a private drug rehabilitation organization were fired from their jobs because they consumed peyote for "sacramental purposes" at a ceremony of the Native American Church. The two individuals applied for unemployment benefits under Oregon law, but their application was denied on the grounds that benefits are not payable to employees who are discharged for "misconduct." The two former employees claimed that the denial of benefits violated their constitutional right to freely exercise their religion. The state supreme court agreed with the discharged employees, and the state appealed to the United States Supreme Court.

The Supreme Court reversed the Oregon court's decision, and ruled that (1) the constitutional guaranty of religious freedom did not prohibit a state from criminalizing the sacramental use of a narcotic drug, and (2) the state of Oregon could deny unemployment benefits to individuals who were fired from their jobs for consuming peyote.

The Court began its opinion by noting that "we have never held that an individual's religious beliefs excuse him from compliance with an otherwise valid law prohibiting conduct that the state is free to regulate." On the contrary, the constitutional guaranty of religious freedom "does not relieve an individual of the obligation to comply with a valid and neutral law of general applicability on the ground that the law [prohibits] conduct that his religion prescribes."

The real significance of the Court's ruling was its refusal to apply the "compelling state interest" test as requested by the discharged employees. As noted above, the Supreme Court previously had interpreted the constitutional guaranty of religious freedom to mean that government could not impose substantial burdens on the exercise of sincerely-held religious beliefs unless its action was justified by a "compelling state interest" that could not be served through less restrictive means. The former employees argued that the Oregon law's denial of unemployment benefits to persons using peyote for sacramental purposes was not supported by a "compelling state interest" and accordingly could not be applied without violating the constitution. The Court justified its refusal to apply the "compelling state interest" test by noting that (1) it had not applied the test in a number of its recent decisions, (2) it had never found a state law limiting religious practices invalid on the ground that it was not supported by a compelling state interest, and (3) the compelling state interest test should never be applied "to require exemptions from a generally applicable criminal law." The Court also rejected the former employees' suggestion that the "compelling state interest" test be applied only in cases involving religiously-motivated conduct that is "central" to an individual's religion. This would require the courts to make judgments on the importance of religious practices—and this the civil courts may never do. The only options are to apply the "compelling state interest" test to all attempts by government to regulate religious practices, or to not apply the test at all. Applying the test in all cases involving governmental attempts to regulate religious practices would lead to "anarchy," since it would render presumptively invalid every law that regulates conduct allegedly based on religious belief. This would open the floodgates of claims of religious exemption

> from civic obligations of almost every conceivable kind—ranging from compulsory military service to the payment of taxes, to health and safety regulation such as manslaughter and child neglect laws, compulsory vaccination laws, drug laws; to social welfare legislation such as minimum wage laws, child labor laws, animal cruelty laws, environmental protection laws, and laws providing for equality of opportunity for the races. The first amendment's protection of religious liberty does not require this.[54]

---

[54] *Id.* at 1605-06 (citations omitted).

The Court's ruling represents a clear departure from its previously well-established understanding of the constitutional guaranty of religious freedom. No longer will a state need to demonstrate that a "compelling state interest" supports a law that prohibits or restricts religious practices. This is unfortunate, and will tend to make it more difficult to prove that a state's interference with religious practices violates the guaranty of religious freedom. Four of the Court's nine justices disagreed with the Court's analysis, and with the virtual elimination of the "compelling state interest" test. The minority asserted that the Court's ruling diminished the guaranty of religious liberty by making it more difficult for persons to prove a violation of this fundamental constitutional guaranty. One of the dissenting Justices lamented that the Court's decision tilts the scales "in the state's favor," and "effectuates a wholesale overturning of settled law concerning the religion clauses of our Constitution. One hopes that the Court is aware of the consequences . . . ."

§ 12-12 Board of Education v. Mergens[55]

May a public high school that allows a variety of student groups to meet on school property before or after regular classroom hours deny the same privilege to a student group wanting to meet for prayer and Bible study? No, said the United States Supreme Court in a 1990 decision.

Westside High School is a public high school in Omaha, Nebraska, with a student enrollment of nearly 2,000. Students are permitted to join various student groups and clubs, all of which meet after school hours on school property. Students may choose from among 30 recognized groups on a voluntary basis. The groups include the school band, chess club, cheerleaders, choir, junior rotarians, debate, drill squad, Future Business Leaders of America, photography, and scuba diving. A school board policy recognizes these groups as a "vital part of the total education" of high school students, and it also forbids "political or religious" clubs. In 1985, a student met with the school principal and requested permission to form a Bible study and prayer group. The principal denied this request on the ground that allowing a religious club to meet on school property would violate the first amendment's "nonestablishment of religion" clause. The school board later upheld the principal's decision, and the student filed a lawsuit in federal court seeking a court order requiring the school to recognize the religious club. The lawsuit claimed that the school's policy of outlawing religious groups violated the "Equal Access Act," which provides:

> It shall be unlawful for any public secondary school which receives federal financial assistance and which has a *limited open forum* to deny equal access or a fair opportunity to, or discriminate against, any students who wish to conduct a meeting within that limited open forum on the basis of the religious, political, philosophical, or other content of the speech at such meetings.[56]

A "limited open forum" exists whenever a public high school "grants an offering to or opportunity for one or more *noncurriculum related student groups* to meet on school premises during noninstructional time."

The school argued that the Equal Access Act did not apply in this case, since all of its student groups were "curriculum related" and therefore the school had not created a "limited open forum" that would be available to religious groups. Further, the school maintained that if the Act required religious groups to meet, then it was unconstitutional.

---

[55] 110 S. Ct. 2356 (1990). The *Mergens* case is discussed further in chapter 14, *infra*.
[56] 20 U.S.C. §§ 4071-4074.

A trial court agreed with the school and upheld the ban on student groups. It concluded that the school did not have a "limited open forum" since all of its student groups were curriculum related. A federal appeals court reversed the trial court's decision, and ruled in favor of the student. The appeals court rejected the trial court's conclusion that all student groups were "curriculum related." If the scuba diving club and chess club are "curriculum related" because they are related to logic and physical education (as the school and trial court claimed), then "the Equal Access Act [would be] meaningless" and schools could "arbitrarily deny access to school facilities to any unfavored student club on the basis of its speech." The appeals court concluded that many of the school's student groups were noncurriculum related, and accordingly that the Equal Access Act prohibited the school from banning the proposed Bible club on the basis of the religious content of its speech. The United States Supreme Court agreed to review the decision of the appeals court.

The Supreme Court concluded that the school did have noncurriculum related student groups, and accordingly had created a limited open forum. The Court observed that the term *noncurriculum related student group* "is best interpreted broadly to mean any student group that does not *directly* relate to the body of courses offered by the school."[57] The court emphasized that "groups such as a chess club, a stamp collecting club, or a community service club" ordinarily will be noncurriculum related since they do not directly relate to the body of courses offered by a school. Accordingly, the existence of such groups would create a "limited open forum" under the Act and would prohibit the school from denying equal access to any other student group on the basis of the content of that group's speech.

The school contended that all of its 30 student groups were curriculum related because they furthered the general educational goals of the school. For example, the student government club "advances the goals of the school's political science classes," the scuba club "furthers the essential goals of the physical education department," the chess club "supplements math and science courses," and the junior rotarians "promote effective citizenship—a critical goal of the social sciences department." The Court rejected this analysis, noting:

> Allowing such a broad interpretation of "curriculum related" would make the [Act] meaningless. A school's administration could simply declare that it maintains a closed forum and choose which student clubs it wanted to allow by tying the purpose of those clubs to some broadly defined educational goal. At the same time the administration could arbitrarily deny access to school facilities to any unfavored student club on the basis of its speech content. This is exactly the result that Congress sought to prohibit by enacting the [Act]. A public secondary school cannot simply declare that it maintains a closed forum and then discriminate against a particular student group on the basis of the content of the speech of that group.[58]

The Court concluded that the school had a number of noncurriculum related student groups, including the scuba club and chess club. It did not evaluate any other clubs, but hinted that a number of the other groups also would be noncurriculum related. Because the school clearly allowed one or more noncurriculum related student groups to meet during noninstructional hours, it had created a limited open forum and could not discriminate against students wanting to meet for religious purposes.

Finally, the Court rejected the school's argument that the Equal Access Act violated the first amendment's nonestablishment of religion clause.

---

[57] 110 S. Ct. at 2366.

[58] *Id.* at 2369, quoting from the federal appeals court decision in Board of Education v. Mergens, 867 F.2d 1076, 1078 (8th Cir. 1989).

§ 12-13 Lee v. Weisman[59]

For many years it was the policy of the Providence (Rhode Island) School Committee and the Superintendent of Schools to permit principals to invite members of the clergy to give invocations and benedictions at middle school and high school graduations. Many, but not all, of the principals elected to include prayers as part of the graduation ceremonies. A student and her father objected to any prayers at the student's graduation, but to no avail. The school principal invited a rabbi to deliver prayers at the student's graduation exercises. The principal provided the rabbi with a pamphlet entitled "Guidelines for Civic Occasions," prepared by the National Conference of Christians and Jews, and advised him that the invocation and benediction should be nonsectarian. The school board (and the United States government) argued that nonsectarian prayers at graduation exercises are of profound meaning to many students and parents throughout this country who consider that due respect and acknowledgement for divine guidance and for the deepest spiritual aspirations of our people ought to be expressed at an event as important in life as a graduation. The dissenting student and her father sought a court order prohibiting any further prayers at public high school graduation ceremonies in Providence. A federal district court issued such an order, and this decision was affirmed by a federal appeals court. The case was then appealed to the United States Supreme Court.

The Supreme Court, by a majority of 5 votes to 4, ruled that prayers offered at public high school graduation ceremonies violate the first amendment's "nonestablishment of religion" clause. The Court began its opinion by emphasizing that

> [i]t is beyond dispute that, at a minimum, the Constitution guarantees that government may not coerce anyone to support or participate in religion or its exercise, or otherwise act in a way which establishes a state religion or religious faith, or tends to do so. The state's involvement in the school prayers challenged today violates these central principles. That involvement is as troubling as it is undenied. A school official, the principal, decided that an invocation and a benediction should be given; this is a choice attributable to the state, and from a constitutional perspective it is as if a state statute decreed that the prayers must occur. The principal chose the religious participant, here a rabbi, and that choice is also attributable to the state. . . . The state's role did not end with the decision to include a prayer and with the choice of clergyman. [The school principal provided the rabbi] with a copy of the "Guidelines for Civic Occasions," and advised him that his prayers should be nonsectarian. Through these means the principal directed and controlled the content of the prayer. . . . It is a cornerstone principle of our establishment clause jurisprudence that it is no part of the business of government to compose official prayers for any group of the American people to recite as a part of a religious program carried on by government, and that is what the school officials attempted to do.

The Court concluded that a public high school graduation ceremony that includes prayers exerts a "psychological coercion" or pressure on everyone to conform, even those who are personally opposed to prayer. The Court observed:

> The undeniable fact is that the school district's supervision and control of a high school graduation ceremony places public pressure, as well as peer pressure, on attending students to stand as a group or, at least, maintain respectful silence during the invocation and benediction. This pressure, though subtle and indirect, can be as real as any overt compulsion. Of course, in our culture

---

[59] 112 S. Ct. 2649 (1992).

standing or remaining silent can signify adherence to a view or simple respect for the views of others. And no doubt some persons who have no desire to join a prayer have little objection to standing as a sign of respect for those who do. But for the dissenter of high school age, who has a reasonable perception that she is being forced by the state to pray in a manner her conscience will not allow, the injury is no less real. There can be no doubt that for many, if not most, of the students at the graduation, the act of standing or remaining silent was an expression of participation in the Rabbi's prayer. That was the very point of the religious exercise. It is of little comfort to a dissenter, then, to be told that for her the act of standing or remaining in silence signifies mere respect, rather than participation. What matters is that, given our social conventions, a reasonable dissenter in this milieu could believe that the group exercise signified her own participation or approval of it.

The Court emphasized that "[r]search in psychology supports the common assumption that adolescents are often susceptible to pressure from their peers towards conformity, and that the influence is strongest in matters of social convention."

The Court acknowledged that participation in graduation ceremonies is voluntary, and that students who are opposed to prayers can simply not attend. But it concluded that the voluntary nature of the ceremony did not mean that prayers had to be allowed. It noted:

[T]o say a teenage student has a real choice not to attend her high school graduation is formalistic in the extreme. True, [the student] could elect not to attend commencement without renouncing her diploma; but we shall not allow the case to turn on this point. Everyone knows that in our society and in our culture high school graduation is one of life's most significant occasions. A school rule which excuses attendance is beside the point. Attendance may not be required by official decree, yet it is apparent that a student is not free to absent herself from the graduation exercise in any real sense of the term "voluntary," for absence would require forfeiture of those intangible benefits which have motivated the student through youth and all her high school years. Graduation is a time for family and those closest to the student to celebrate success and express mutual wishes of gratitude and respect, all to the end of impressing upon the young person the role that it is his or her right and duty to assume in the community and all of its diverse parts.

The Court acknowledged that a majority of those attending graduation ceremonies probably have no objection to prayers being offered, and would even prefer that they be. It concluded, however, that "[w]hile in some societies the wishes of the majority might prevail, the establishment clause of the first amendment is addressed to this contingency and rejects the balance urged upon us. The Constitution forbids the state to exact religious conformity from a student as the price of attending her own high school graduation."

The Court acknowledged that

[w]e do not hold that every state action implicating religion is invalid if one or a few citizens find it offensive. People may take offense at all manner of religious as well as nonreligious messages, but offense alone does not in every case show a violation. We know too that sometimes to endure social isolation or even anger may be the price of conscience or nonconformity. But, by any reading of our cases, the conformity required of the student in this case was too high an exaction to withstand the test of the establishment clause.

The Court concluded its opinion with the following statement:

Our society would be less than true to its heritage if it lacked abiding concern for the values of its young people, and we acknowledge the profound belief of adherents to many faiths that there must be a place in the student's life for precepts of a morality higher even than the law we today enforce. We express no hostility to those aspirations, nor would our oath permit us to do so. A relentless and all-pervasive attempt to exclude religion from every aspect of public life could itself become inconsistent with the Constitution. We recognize that, at graduation time and throughout the course of the educational process, there will be instances when religious values, religious practices, and religious persons will have some interaction with the public schools and their students. But these matters, often questions of accommodation of religion, are not before us. The sole question presented is whether a religious exercise may be conducted at a graduation ceremony in circumstances where, as we have found, young graduates who object are induced to conform. No holding by this Court suggests that a school can persuade or compel a student to participate in a religious exercise. That is being done here, and it is forbidden by the establishment clause of the first amendment.

INSTRUCTIONAL AIDS TO CHAPTER 12

Terms

compelling state interest

entanglement

Equal Access Act

judicial review

public welfare legislation

released time

religion of secularism

sponsorship

Learning Objectives

- Understand the Supreme Court's interpretation of the first amendment religion clauses in a variety of contexts, including

- aid to religious schools

- released time programs

- prayer and Bible readings in public schools

- church property tax exemptions

- compulsory attendance requirements

- tax credits to parents with children in private schools

Short-Answer Questions

1. Your state legislature is considering a bill that would reimburse parents for the cost of transporting their children to public and private elementary and secondary schools. A taxpayer claims that such a law would constitute the establishment of a religion in violation of the first amendment. Will a court agree with the taxpayer?

2.   Your public school board adopts a "released time" program whereby students are released from school for one hour each week to receive religious instruction at churches and other facilities located away from school property. A parent claims that the program constitutes the establishment of a religion in violation of the first amendment. Is this claim correct?

3.   Same facts as question 2, except that students are permitted to meet in vacant classrooms in the school building. Does this affect your answer?

4.   A public school adopts a course entitled "The Bible—Its Literary and Cultural Significance." Several books in both the Old and New Testaments are read for purposes of literary and cultural appreciation. No proselytizing occurs. Is this class constitutionally permissible?

5.   All of our coins and currency are required by law to bear the inscription "In God We Trust." Does this practice constitute an impermissible establishment of religion in violation of the first amendment? Explain.

6.   A public high school teacher opens each class with a voluntary prayer. Students not wishing to participate are instructed to remain in the hallway until the prayer is completed. A parent challenges this practice. How would a court rule?

7.   A group of 15 public high school students asks their school principal for permission to conduct a Bible study in an empty classroom building one morning each week prior to the start of the school day. The principal denies the request. The students are considering a lawsuit challenging the principal's action. Would such a lawsuit be successful? What factors would be most important in a court's resolution of such a dispute?

8.   Does the exemption of church sanctuaries from state property taxes constitute an impermissible establishment of religion? Explain.

9.   A state legislature employs a full-time chaplain, who has various duties including the opening of each legislative session with prayer. Is this practice constitutionally permissible? Explain.

10.   A state enacts a law permitting each school day to begin with a minute of silence during which students can pray, meditate, do homework, or occupy themselves in any other manner. Is such a law constitutional?

Discussion Questions

1.   The Supreme Court has outlawed most collective prayers in public elementary and secondary schools, yet Congress continues to open its sessions with prayer. Can you think of a rational basis for this distinction?

2.   A substantial majority of the public favors voluntary collective prayer in public elementary and secondary schools. Yet, since 1962, the courts consistently have disallowed such a practice. Can you think of a legitimate justification for this suppression of the will of the majority? How can the majority's rights be accommodated?

3. In 1963, the Supreme Court held that the practice of reading the Bible in public schools at the start of each school day constituted an impermissible establishment of religion in violation of the first amendment, despite the consistent acceptance of such a practice since the adoption of the first amendment in 1791. Why did it take the Supreme Court nearly two centuries to decide that the reading of the Bible in public schools violated the first amendment? Does this delay raise questions about the legitimacy of the Court's interpretation? What else does the delay tell us?

13

THE PRESENT MEANING OF THE FIRST AMENDMENT RELIGION CLAUSES

Chapter summary. The two previous chapters have addressed the importance of the Supreme Court's interpretation of the first amendment religion clauses. In this chapter, the Court's current interpretation of the religion clauses is addressed. In 1973, the Court held that a law or government action challenged on the basis of the "establishment clause" will be constitutional only if it meets all of the following three conditions: (1) a clearly secular purpose, (2) a primary effect that neither advances nor inhibits religion, and (3) no excessive entanglement between government and religion. This test often is referred to as the "tripartite" establishment clause test. In more recent rulings the Supreme Court has held that the tripartite test is not the only test available under the establishment clause. It is merely a guide that may be helpful in some contexts but not in others. To illustrate, in 1984 the Court upheld the constitutionality of a nativity scene on public property during the Christmas season even though such displays might not pass the tripartite test. The Court was satisfied that the display reflected a deeply-held and widely-accepted religious tradition that did not advance or establish religion in a substantial way. In evaluating whether a particular law or government action violates the "free exercise" clause, the Supreme Court has formulated the following two rules: first, government may never interfere with an individual's right to believe whatever he or she wants. Second, in deciding whether or not a government law, regulation, or practice that burdens religiously motivated conduct violates the free exercise clause, various principles apply. For example, "generally applicable criminal prohibitions" that burden religiously motivated conduct do not violate the free exercise clause. Such prohibitions are presumptively valid and need not be supported by a compelling state interest. In other cases, the courts must consider (i) whether the activity was motivated by and rooted in legitimate and sincerely held religious belief, (ii) whether the activity was unduly and substantially burdened by the government's action, and (iii) whether the government has a compelling interest in limiting the religious activity that cannot be accomplished by less restrictive means.

§ 13-01 The Establishment Clause

The clearest evidence that the framers of the first amendment's establishment clause intended only to prohibit the creation of a national church is the virtual absence of any judicial decisions applying the clause in the first century and a half following its adoption despite countless state and federal accommodations of religion.[1] Prior to 1940, the Supreme Court interpreted the establishment clause on only two occasions. In 1890, it rejected a claim that an Idaho law prohibiting polygamy constituted an impermissible establishment of religion.[2] The Court observed that the purpose of the establishment clause was to prohibit federal legislation

> for the support of any religious tenets, or the modes of worship of any sect. The oppressive measures adopted, and the cruelties and punishments inflicted, by the governments of Europe for many ages, to compel parties to conform in their religious beliefs and modes of worship, to the views of the most numerous sect, and the folly of attempting in that way to control the mental operations of persons, and enforce an outward conformity to a prescribed standard, led to the adoption of the [first] amendment.[3]

In 1918, the Court summarily dismissed a claim that the exemption of ministers from military conscription constituted the establishment of a religion.[4]

In 1940, the Court reaffirmed that the purpose of the establishment clause was to prevent an established church: "[I]t forestalls compulsion by law of the acceptance of any creed or the practice of any form of worship."[5] However, the Court added that the concept of "liberty" protected against state interference by the fourteenth amendment to the federal Constitution "embraces the liberties guaranteed by the first amendment." The significance of this holding cannot be overstated. The first amendment's liberties, including the free exercise and nonestablishment of religion, intended by the framers of that amendment as a limitation on the *federal* government and so interpreted for a century and a half,[6] were now also limitations upon state and local governments. Ironically, shortly after this unwarranted expansion of federal authority over the states, the Court remarked that "[j]udicial nullification of legislation cannot be justified by attributing to the framers of the Bill of Rights views for which there is no historic warrant."[7]

Despite this assurance, the Court largely abandoned the views of the framers of the establishment clause in its landmark *Everson* decision in 1947.[8] In *Everson*, a case involving a constitutional challenge to a state law

---

[1] This construction is also amply supported by historical evidence. *See, e.g.,* Wallace v. Jaffree, 472 U.S. 38 (1985) (dissenting opinion of Justice Rehnquist); R. CORD, SEPARATION OF CHURCH AND STATE: HISTORICAL FACT AND CURRENT FICTION (1982); chapter 11, *supra.*

[2] Davis v. Beason, 10 S. Ct. 299 (1890).

[3] *Id.* at 300.

[4] Aver v. United States, 245 U.S. 366 (1918).

[5] Cantwell v. Connecticut, 310 U.S. 296 (1940).

[6] *See, e.g.,* chapter 11, *supra. See also* Permoli v. Municipality No. 1 of New Orleans, 44 U.S. 589 (1845) (federal Constitution makes no provision for protecting religious liberties against *state* interference).

[7] Minersville School District v. Gobitis, 310 U.S. 586 (1940).

[8] Everson v. Board of Education, 330 U.S. 1 (1947).

authorizing bus transportation for parochial school students at public expense, the Court announced the following interpretation of the establishment clause:

> Neither a state nor the Federal Government can set up a church. Neither can pass laws which aid one religion, aid all religions, or prefer one religion over another. Neither can force nor influence a person to go or to remain away from church against his will or force him to profess a belief or disbelief in any religion. No person can be punished for entertaining or professing religious beliefs or disbeliefs, for church attendance or nonattendance. No tax in any amount, large or small, can be levied to support any religious activities or institutions, whatever they may be called, or whatever form they may adopt to teach or practice religion. Neither a state nor the Federal Government can, openly or secretly, participate in the affairs of any religious organizations or groups and vice versa. In the words of Jefferson, the clause against establishment of religion by law was intended to erect a wall of separation between church and state.[9]

Four dissenting justices similarly remarked that the first amendment's purpose

> was not to strike merely at the official establishment of a single sect, creed or religion, outlawing only a formal relation such as had prevailed in England and some of the colonies. Necessarily, it was to uproot all such relationships. . . . It was to create a complete and permanent separation of the spheres of religious activity and civil authority by comprehensively forbidding every form of public aid or support for religion.[10]

By 1947, the Court not only had expanded the prohibitions of the establishment clause beyond anything contemplated by its framers, but also had imposed its interpretation upon state and local governments by means of the fourteenth amendment.[11]

The Court found in Jefferson's "wall of separation" metaphor the philosophical basis for its interpretation of the establishment clause in *Everson*. However, as Justice Rehnquist demonstrated convincingly nearly 40 years later, Jefferson's metaphor cannot properly be used as evidence of the meaning of the establishment clause.[12]

In the years following *Everson*, several longstanding accommodations of religious belief and practice fell victim to the new interpretation of the establishment clause. In 1948, the Court, relying on *Everson* and Jefferson's "wall of separation" metaphor, struck down a local school board policy that permitted teachers employed by private religious groups to come weekly into public school buildings during regular school hours and impart religious instruction for 30 minutes to students whose parents requested it.[13]

In 1962, the Court struck down a New York law requiring the following prayer to be said aloud in each public school classroom at the beginning of each school day: "Almighty God, we acknowledge our dependence upon Thee, and we beg Thy blessings upon us, our parents, our teachers and our country."[14] The Court

---

[9] *Id.* at 15-16.

[10] *Id.* at 31-32.

[11] Wallace v. Jaffree, 472 U.S. 38 (1985) (dissenting opinion of Justice Rehnquist). The dissenting opinion is an extensive historical analysis that seriously undermines the legitimacy of the Court's *Everson* decision and many subsequent rulings based on that precedent.

[12] *Id. See also* § 12-10, *supra.*

[13] People of State of Illinois ex rel. McCollum v. Board of Education, 333 U.S. 203 (1948). Justice Reed, in dissent, noted that "the 'wall of separation between church and state' that Mr. Jefferson built at the university which he founded [the University of Virginia] did not exclude religious education from that school." *Id.* at 247.

concluded that recitation of this prayer in public schools "breaches the wall of separation between church and state," even though children who were opposed to the prayer were not compelled to participate and could be excused from class until the recitation was completed. Similarly, the Court in 1963 invalidated a Pennsylvania law requiring that "[a]t least ten verses from the Holy Bible shall be read, without comment, at the opening of each public school on each school day."[15] The law permitted children to be excused from attending class during the reading upon the written request of a parent. The Court relied entirely on the expansive interpretation of the establishment clause enunciated in *Everson* in striking down the law.

In 1968, the Court struck down an Arkansas law making it unlawful for public school teachers to "teach the theory or doctrine that mankind ascended or descended from a lower order of animals."[16] The Court, relying on *Everson*, concluded that the first amendment "does not permit the state to require that teaching and learning must be tailored to the principles or prohibitions of any religious sect or dogma."

§ 13-01.1 — The Lemon Test

Key point 13-01.1. The most commonly applied test for evaluating the validity of a law of government practice under the first amendment's nonestablishment of religion clause is the three-part "Lemon" test. Under this test, a law or government practice that conveys some benefit on religion will be constitutional if it (1) has a clearly secular purpose; (2) has a primary effect that neither advances nor inhibits religion; and (3) does not foster an excessive entanglement between church and state. All three parts of the test must be met in order for the law or practice to be constitutional. The Supreme Court has recognized limited exceptions to this test.

In 1971, the Court held that its establishment clause decisions since *Everson* could be embodied in a three-pronged test: "First, the statute must have a secular legislative purpose; second, its principal or primary effect must be one that neither advances nor inhibits religion; finally, the statute must not foster 'an excessive governmental entanglement with religion.'"[17] This test, known as the three-pronged or "tripartite" *Lemon* test, enshrined the dubious interpretation of the establishment clause announced in *Everson*. The Court, in amplifying on this test, has observed that "[t]he purpose prong of the *Lemon* test asks whether government's actual purpose is to endorse or disapprove of religion. The effect prong asks whether irrespective of government's actual purpose, the practice under review in fact conveys a message of endorsement or disapproval. An affirmative answer to either question should render the challenged practice invalid."[18] With regard to the primary effect prong, the Court has further observed that "not every law that confers an 'indirect,' 'remote,' or 'incidental' benefit upon [religion] is, for that reason alone, constitutionally invalid."[19] "Excessive entanglement" between church and state connotes "comprehensive, discriminating, and continuing state surveillance."[20] The Court suggested in *Lemon* that laws or government practices having the potential for "political divisiveness" may violate the entanglement prong. However, the Court later confined this aspect of entanglement to "cases where direct financial subsidies are paid to parochial schools or to teachers in parochial schools."[21]

---

[14] Engel v. Vitale, 370 U.S. 421 (1962). In a dissenting opinion, Justice Steward observed that "the Court's task, in this as in all areas of constitutional adjudication, is not responsibly aided by the uncritical invocation of metaphors like the 'wall of separation,' a phrase nowhere to be found in the Constitution." *Id.* at 445-46.

[15] School District of Abington v. Schempp, 374 U.S. 203 (1963).

[16] Epperson v. Arkansas, 393 U.S. 97 (1968).

[17] Lemon v. Kurtzman, 403 U.S. 602, 612-13 (1971).

[18] Lynch v. Donnelly, 465 U.S. 668 (1984).

[19] Committee for Public Education & Religious Liberty v. Nyquist, 413 U.S. 756, 771 (1973).

[20] Lemon v. Kurtzman, 403 U.S. 602, 619 (1971). *But see* Wallace v. Jaffree, 472 U.S. 38 (1985) (dissenting opinion of Justice Rehnquist).

[21] Mueller v. Allen, 463 U.S. 388, 403 n.11 (1983).

Application of the *Lemon* standard resulted, predictably, in the invalidation of many accommodations of religious practice. For example, the Supreme Court outlawed several programs providing limited assistance to private education;[22] a Kentucky law requiring a copy of the Ten Commandments to be posted in each public school classroom;[23] a state law specifying that each public school day should begin with a minute of silence during which students could pray, meditate, or occupy themselves in any other manner they chose;[24] a state law requiring that public schools present both the theories of evolution and creation science;[25] and a nativity display maintained in a county courthouse building during the Christmas season that was not a part of a larger display containing secular symbols.[26] Lower federal courts invalidated scores of religious practices on the basis of the *Lemon* test.

The Supreme Court has often expressed misgivings about the *Lemon* formulation. In 1971, the Court called the *Lemon* test a mere "guideline."[27] It later described the test as "no more than [a] useful signpost,"[28] and expressed an unwillingness to be "confined to any single test or criterion."[29] Similarly, the Court has noted that the test "is not easily applied"[30] and "sacrifices clarity and predictability for flexibility."[31] The Court has disregarded the *Lemon* test on at least two occasions. In 1982, the Court deviated from the *Lemon* test in striking down a Minnesota statute requiring certain religious organizations to register with the state prior to soliciting contributions.[32] The Court, observing that the *Lemon* test was "intended to apply to laws affording a uniform benefit to *all* religions," announced the following two-part test to be used in assessing the constitutionality of a law that discriminates "*among* religions": (1) The law must be justified by a compelling governmental interest, and (2) it must be closely fitted to further that interest.

In 1983, the Court again deviated from the *Lemon* test in upholding the practice of legislative chaplains,[33] reversing a federal appeals court ruling that invalidated the practice on the basis of the *Lemon* test. The Court, noting that the very Congress that approved the first amendment establishment clause also voted to appoint and pay a chaplain for both houses, concluded that "it would be incongruous to interpret that clause as imposing more stringent first amendment limits on the states than the draftsmen imposed on the federal government." Such cases are a repudiation, at least in part, of the hostility that the Court has shown to religious practice since *Everson*. They suggest that there is hope for a repudiation of *Everson* and the *Lemon* test, and a return to an interpretation of the establishment clause that is faithful to its history and purpose.[34]

Until the three-part *Lemon* test is repudiated, it likely will continue to be the primary analytical tool employed by the courts in establishment clause cases, with the following limitations:

---

22 *See, e.g.*, Meek v. Pittinger, 421 U.S. 349 (1975); Wolman v. Walter, 433 U.S. 229 (1977); Levitt v. Committee for Public Education, 413 U.S. 472 (1973).
23 Stone v. Graham, 449 U.S. 39 (1980).
24 Wallace v. Jaffree, 472 U.S. 38 (1985).
25 Edwards v. Aguillard, 482 U.S. 578 (1987).
26 County of Allegheny v. American Civil Liberties Union, 109 S. Ct. 3086 (1989).
27 Tilton v. Richardson, 403 U.S. 672 (1971).
28 Mueller v. Allen, 463 U.S. 388 (1983).
29 Lynch v. Donnelly, 465 U.S. 668 (1984).
30 Meek v. Pittinger, 421 U.S. 349 (1975).
31 Committee for Public Education v. Regan, 444 U.S. 646 (1980).
32 Larson v. Valente, 456 U.S. 228 (1982).
33 Marsh v. Chambers, 463 U.S. 783 (1983).
34 If the citizens of this country are dissatisfied with the framers' intent, the Constitution itself provides a remedy—amendment. It is the people, through the power to amend the Constitution, that should have determined whether or not the first amendment should be expanded beyond the original intention to prohibit established churches, and whether the first amendment's establishment clause should be applied to state and local governments.

1. Laws that discriminate between religious groups. Laws that discriminate between religious groups will be upheld against a claim that they violate the establishment clause only if (1) they are justified by a compelling governmental interest, and (2) they are closely fitted to further that interest.[35]

2. Certain accommodations of religious custom and practice. Certain accommodations of religious custom and practice may be validated by history. For example, in 1984 the Supreme Court upheld the practice of including a nativity scene on public property as part of a Christmas display.[36] While the Court validated the practice on the basis of *Lemon*, its application of the *Lemon* test was influenced if not controlled by historical precedent. Noting that the nativity scene had the secular purpose of depicting the origins of Christmas, did not have a primary effect of advancing religion, and did not create an excessive entanglement between church and state, the Court concluded, "It would be ironic, however, if the inclusion of a single symbol of a particular religious event, as part of a celebration acknowledged in the Western World for 20 centuries, and in this country by the people, by the Executive Branch, by the Congress, and the courts for two centuries, would so taint' the City's exhibit as to render it violative of the establishment clause." Similarly, the court upheld the constitutionality of legislative chaplaincies in 1983 on the basis of historical precedent without any reference to the *Lemon* test.[37] The Court found controlling the fact that the first Congress, which approved the first amendment establishment clause, also voted to appoint and pay a chaplain for each House.

3. Public welfare legislation. The benefits of public welfare legislation cannot be denied to any group of persons "because of their faith, or lack of it."[38] For example, the establishment clause does not require that a law authorizing free transportation of children to school must exclude children attending private religious schools.

4. Neutrality. As noted in the following section of this chapter, the principles underlying the establishment clause can in some cases conflict with the values embodied in the free exercise of religion clause. Therefore, neither clause should be construed in isolation. The establishment clause, properly construed in light of the free exercise of religion clause, mandates governmental neutrality toward religion. Neither sponsorship nor hostility is permissible.

5. Incidental accommodations religion. "[N]ot every law that confers an 'indirect,' 'remote,' or 'incidental' benefit upon [religion] is, for that reason alone, constitutionally invalid."[39]

§ 13-02 The Free Exercise Clause

The first amendment specifies that "Congress shall make no law . . . prohibiting the free exercise [of religion]." This language generally is referred to as the "free exercise clause." The free exercise clause remained a dormant provision of the Bill of Rights for nearly a century and a half following its adoption. This was based largely on two factors. First, Congress seldom if ever took any action that interfered with the exercise of anyone's religion. Second, in its first decision interpreting the free exercise clause, the Supreme Court ruled in 1878 that while federal laws "cannot interfere with mere religious belief and opinions, they may with prac-

---

[35] Larson v. Valente, 456 U.S. 228 (1982).
[36] Lynch v. Donnelly, 465 U.S. 668 (1984).
[37] Marsh v. Chambers, 463 U.S. 783 (1983).
[38] Everson v. Board of Education, 330 U.S. 1 (1947).
[39] Committee for Public Education & Religious Liberty v. Nyquist, 413 U.S. 756, 771 (1973). *See also* Widmar v. Vincent, 454 U.S. 263, 273 (1981).

tice."[40] According to this interpretation, the free exercise clause would be violated only by congressional legislation that interfered with an individual's religious *beliefs*, and not with religiously-motivated *conduct*.

Two developments significantly increased the relevance and application of the free exercise clause. The first occurred in 1940, when the Supreme Court "incorporated" the first amendment religion clauses into the fourteenth amendment "due process" clause, thereby making the first amendment a limitation upon state (and local) governments as well as Congress.[41] Prior to 1940, only federal legislation could violate the free exercise clause. Since 1940, the same is true of state and local legislation and regulations. Clearly, this had the effect of greatly expanding the application of the free exercise clause. Second, in 1963 the Supreme Court issued a major reinterpretation of the free exercise clause in the case of *Sherbert v. Verner*.[42] In the *Sherbert* case, the Court departed from the simplistic "belief-conduct" standard that it had enunciated in its earlier *Reynolds* decision and announced that a government statute or regulation that imposes a "burden" on the free exercise of one's religion violates the free exercise clause *unless the statute or regulation is justified by a "compelling state interest."* This test was clarified a few years later in *Wisconsin v. Yoder*.[43] The Supreme Court articulated its understanding of the free exercise clause as follows:

1. Government may never interfere with an individual's right to *believe* whatever he or she wants.

2. In determining whether the government may interfere with or restrict religiously motivated *conduct*, the courts must consider (a) whether the activity was motivated by and rooted in legitimate and sincerely held religious belief, (b) whether the activity was unduly and substantially burdened by the government's action, and (c) whether the government has a compelling interest in limiting the religious activity that cannot be accomplished by less restrictive means.

This general understanding of the free exercise clause was applied by the Court in several cases.[44]

§ 13-02.1 — The Smith Case

> *Key point 13-02.1. In the Smith case (1990) the Supreme Court ruled that a neutral law of general applicability is presumably valid and need not be supported by a compelling government interest to be consistent with the first amendment, even if it interferes with the exercise of religion.*

Oregon law prohibits the intentional possession of a "controlled substance," including the drug peyote. Two employees of a private drug rehabilitation organization were fired from their jobs because they consumed peyote for "sacramental purposes" at a ceremony of the Native American Church. The two individuals applied for unemployment benefits under Oregon law, but their application was denied on the grounds that benefits are not payable to employees who are discharged for "misconduct." The two former employees claimed that the denial of benefits violated their constitutional right to freely exercise their religion. The United States Supreme Court ruled that (1) the constitutional guaranty of religious freedom did not prohibit a state from

---

[40] Reynolds v. United States, 98 U.S. 145, 166 (1878). The Court upheld the bigamy conviction of a Mormon under a federal statute, and rejected the claim that the statute violated the free exercise clause.

[41] *See* chapter 11, *supra*.

[42] 374 U.S. 398 (1963).

[43] 406 U.S. 205 (1971). The *Yoder* case is discussed in chapter 12, *supra*.

[44] *See, e.g.*, Hernandez v. Commissioner, 109 S. Ct. 2136 (1989); Hobbie v. Unemployment Appeals Commission, 480 U.S. 136 (1987); United States v. Lee, 455 U.S. 252 (1982).

criminalizing the sacramental use of a narcotic drug, and (2) the state of Oregon could deny unemployment benefits to individuals who were fired from their jobs for consuming peyote.[45]

The Court began its opinion by noting that "we have never held that an individual's religious beliefs excuse him from compliance with an otherwise valid law prohibiting conduct that the state is free to regulate." On the contrary, the constitutional guaranty of religious freedom "does not relieve an individual of the obligation to comply with a valid and neutral law of general applicability on the ground that the law [prohibits] conduct that his religion prescribes."

> ***Key point.*** *The Court did not throw out the "compelling state interest" requirement in all cases involving governmental restrictions on religious freedom. Rather, the Court stated that this requirement does not apply to restrictions caused by a "neutral law of general applicability." A law or other government act that targets or singles out religious organizations must be supported by a compelling state interest. Further, as noted below, the compelling state interest requirement applies if a second constitutional right is burdened by a law or other government act.*

The real significance of the Court's ruling was its refusal to apply the "compelling state interest" test as requested by the discharged employees. As noted above, the Supreme Court previously had interpreted the constitutional guaranty of religious freedom to mean that the government could not impose substantial burdens on the exercise of sincerely-held religious beliefs unless its actions were justified by a "compelling state interest" that could not be served through less restrictive means. The former employees argued that the Oregon law's denial of unemployment benefits to persons using peyote for sacramental purposes was not supported by a "compelling state interest" and accordingly could not be applied without violating the constitution.

The Court justified its refusal to apply the "compelling state interest" test by noting that

• it had not applied the test in a number of its recent decisions

• it had never found a state law limiting religious practices invalid on the ground that it was not supported by a compelling state interest

• the compelling state interest test should never be applied "to require exemptions from a generally applicable criminal law"

The Court rejected the former employees' suggestion that the "compelling state interest" test be applied only in cases involving religiously-motivated conduct that is "central" to an individual's religion. This would require the courts to make judgments on the importance of religious practices—and this the civil courts may never do. The only options are to apply the "compelling state interest" test to all attempts by government to regulate religious practices, or to not apply the test at all. Applying the test in all cases involving governmental attempts to regulate religious practices would lead to "anarchy," since it would render "presumptively invalid" every law that regulates conduct allegedly based on religious belief. This would open the floodgates of claims of religious exemption "from civic obligations of almost every conceivable kind—ranging from compulsory military service to the payment of taxes, to health and safety regulation such as manslaughter and child neglect laws, compulsory vaccination laws, drug laws; to social welfare legislation such as minimum wage

---

[45] 110 S. Ct. 1595 (1990). The *Smith* case is discussed in § 12-11, *supra.*

laws, child labor laws, animal cruelty laws, environmental protection laws, and laws providing for equality of opportunity for the races. The first amendment's protection of religious liberty does not require this."

The Court's ruling represents a clear departure from its previously well-established understanding of the constitutional guaranty of religious freedom. No longer will a state need to demonstrate that a "compelling state interest" supports a law that prohibits or restricts religious practices. This is unfortunate, and will tend to make it more difficult to prove that a state's interference with religious practices violates the guaranty of religious freedom. Four of the Court's nine justices disagreed with the Court's analysis and with the virtual elimination of the "compelling state interest" test. The minority asserted that the Court's ruling diminished the guaranty of religious liberty by making it more difficult for persons to prove a violation of this fundamental constitutional guaranty. One of the dissenting Justices lamented that the Court's decision tilts the scales "in the state's favor," and "effectuates a wholesale overturning of settled law concerning the religion clauses of our Constitution. One hopes that the Court is aware of the consequences . . . ."

The *Smith* case suggests that the Court is moving back towards the old "belief-conduct" analysis articulated more than a century ago in *Reynolds*—religious belief is protected by the free exercise clause, but not religiously-motivated conduct.[46] This shift has generated much criticism and opposition, which will ensure further reinterpretations of the free exercise clause.

§ 13-02.2   The Religious Freedom Restoration Act

Key point 13-02.2. Congress enacted the Religious Freedom Restoration Act to prevent the government from enacting any law or adopting any practice that substantially burdens the free exercise of religion unless the law or practice is supported by a compelling government interest. The compelling government interest requirement applies to any law, including neutral laws of general applicability. The objective of the Act was to repudiate the Supreme Court's decision in the Smith case (1990) in which the Court ruled that neutral laws of general applicability that burden the free exercise of religion do not need to be supported by a compelling government interest in order to satisfy the first amendment. In 1997, the Supreme Court ruled that the Act was unconstitutional. However, other courts have limited this ruling to state and local legislation, and have concluded that the Act continues to apply to federal laws.

The consequences of the Supreme Court's reinterpretation of the first amendment guaranty of religious freedom were predictable. Scores of lower federal courts and state courts upheld laws and other government actions that directly restricted religious practices. In many of these cases, the courts based their actions directly on the *Smith* case, suggesting that the result would have been different had it not been for that decision.

Congress responded to the *Smith* case in an extraordinary way—by enacting the Religious Freedom Restoration Act ("RFRA") by a unanimous vote of both houses. RFRA was signed into law by President Clinton in 1993. It begins by reciting the following "congressional findings":

(1) the framers of the Constitution, recognizing free exercise of religion as an unalienable right, secured its protection in the first amendment to the Constitution;

---

[46] Other decisions of the Court support this view. *See, e.g.*, Goldman v. Weinberger, 475 U.S. 503 (1986) (Air Force regulation prohibiting religious headgear upheld despite claim of Jewish officer that it violated the free exercise of his religion); United States v. Lee, 455 U.S. 252 (1982) (Court rejected an Amish farmer's request to be exempt from social security taxes); Bowen v. Roy, 476 U.S. 693 (1986) (government can deny welfare benefits to an individual who refuses to obtain a social security number, even though the individual's actions are based on religious convictions).

(2) laws "neutral" toward religion may burden religious exercise as surely as laws intended to interfere with religious exercise;

(3) governments should not burden religious exercise without compelling justification;

(4) in Employment Division v. Smith, 494 U.S. 872 (1990) the Supreme Court virtually eliminated the requirement that the government justify burdens on religious exercise imposed by laws neutral toward religion; and

(5) the compelling interest test as set forth in prior federal court rulings is a workable test for striking sensible balances between religious liberty and competing prior governmental interests.

RFRA next states its purposes as follows: "(1) to restore the compelling interest test . . . and to guarantee its application in all cases where free exercise of religion is burdened; and (2) to provide a claim or defense to persons whose religious exercise is burdened by government."

The key provision of RFRA is section 3, which specifies:

(a) IN GENERAL. Government shall not substantially burden a person's exercise of religion even if the burden results from a rule of general applicability, except as provided in subsection (b) . . . .

(b) EXCEPTION. Government may substantially burden a person's exercise of religion only if it demonstrates that application of the burden to the person—(1) is in furtherance of a compelling governmental interest; and (2) is the least restrictive means of furthering that compelling governmental interest.

(c) JUDICIAL RELIEF. A person whose religious exercise has been burdened in violation of this section may assert that violation as a claim or defense in a judicial proceeding and obtain appropriate relief against the government. Standing to assert a claim or defense under this section shall be governed by the general rules of standing under article III of the Constitution.

In practical terms, how did the enactment of RFRA affect local churches and other religious organizations? There is little doubt that it provided significant protections to the exercise of religion. Any law or government practice (whether at the local, state, or federal level) that "burdened" the exercise of religion was legally permissible only if the law or practice (1) was in furtherance of a compelling governmental interest, and (2) was the least restrictive means of furthering that compelling governmental interest. These were difficult standards to meet. As the Supreme Court itself observed in 1993, the concept of a "compelling governmental interest" is a very difficult standard for the government to satisfy:

A law burdening religious practice that is not neutral or not of general application must undergo the most rigorous of scrutiny. To satisfy the commands of the first amendment, a law restrictive of religious practice must advance interests of the highest order and must be narrowly tailored in pursuit of those interests. The compelling interest standard that we apply once a law fails to meet the Smith requirements is not "watered . . . down" but "really means what it says." A law that targets religious conduct for distinctive treatment or advances legitimate governmental interests only against conduct with a religious motivation will survive strict scrutiny only in rare cases. . . .[47]

---

[47] Church of the Lukumi Babaluaye, Inc. v. City of Hialeah, 508 U.S. 520 (1993).

In the years following the enactment of RFRA a number of government attempts to regulate or interfere with religious practices were struck down by the courts on the basis of the Act.

§ 13-02.3 — The City of Boerne Case

Key point 13-02.3. In the City of Boerne case (1997), the Supreme Court ruled that the Religious Freedom Restoration Act was unconstitutional. Other courts have limited this ruling to state and local legislation, and have concluded that the Act continues to apply to federal laws.

In the City of Boerne case, in 1997, the Supreme Court struck down the Religious Freedom Restoration Act on the ground that Congress exceeded its authority in enacting the law.[48] The Court's decision will impact virtually every religious organization in America. Some of those impacts are predictable, but others are not. This subsection reviews the facts of this important case, and the Court's conclusions.

Situated on a hill in the city of Boerne, Texas, some 28 miles northwest of San Antonio, is St. Peter Catholic Church. Built in 1923, the church's structure reflects the mission style of the region's earlier history. The church seats about 230 worshippers, a number too small for its growing parish. Some 40 to 60 parishioners cannot be accommodated at some Sunday services. In order to meet the needs of the congregation the Archbishop of San Antonio gave permission to the parish to plan alterations to enlarge the building.

A few months later, the Boerne City Council passed an ordinance authorizing the city's Historic Landmark Commission to prepare a preservation plan with proposed historic landmarks and districts. Under the ordinance, the Commission must pre-approve construction affecting historic landmarks or buildings in a historic district.

Soon afterwards the Archbishop applied for a building permit so construction to enlarge the church could proceed. City authorities, relying on the ordinance and the designation of a historic district (which, they claimed, included the church), denied the application. The Archbishop filed a lawsuit challenging the city's denial of the permit. The lawsuit relied upon RFRA as one basis for relief from the refusal to issue the permit. A federal district court concluded that by enacting RFRA Congress exceeded the scope of its authority. A federal appeals court reversed this decision, and upheld the constitutionality of RFRA. The city appealed to the United States Supreme Court. The appeal addressed the question of the constitutional validity of RFRA.

The Supreme Court ruled that RFRA was unconstitutional since Congress did not have the authority to enact it. The Court began its opinion by noting that the federal government "is one of enumerated powers." That is, each branch (legislative, executive, judicial) can only do those things specifically authorized by the Constitution. The first amendment specifies that "Congress" cannot enact legislation "prohibiting the free exercise" of religion. Of course, "Congress" refers to the federal legislature, and so the first amendment guaranty of religious freedom, as originally worded, was not a limitation on the power of state or local governments. In 1868, the fourteenth amendment to the Constitution was ratified, which prohibits any state from depriving "any person of life, liberty, or property without due process of law." Then, in 1940, the Supreme

---

[48] It is not clear whether the Supreme Court intended to invalidate the Act as applied to federal law, state law, or both. Some courts have concluded that the Supreme Court only intended to invalidate the Act as applied to state and local legislation, and that the Act still applies to federal legislation that burdens the exercise of religion. *See, e.g.,* In re Young, 82 F.3d 1407 (8th Cir. 1996) (the Act prevented federal bankruptcy law from infringing upon the religious beliefs of church members). The Supreme Court will need to resolve this ambiguity.

Court ruled that the "liberty" protected by the fourteenth amendment against state interference included the first amendment guaranty of religious freedom. For the first time, this limitation upon the power of Congress to prohibit the free exercise of religion now applied to state and local governments as well. The fourteenth amendment contained a section (section 5) which gave Congress "power to enforce, by appropriate legislation, the provisions of this [amendment]." Congress pointed to this section as the source of its authority to enact RFRA. Members of Congress insisted that they were only protecting by legislation one of the liberties guaranteed by the fourteenth amendment that had been diminished by the Supreme Court's ruling in *Smith*.

The Supreme Court ruled that section 5 of the fourteenth amendment did not authorize Congress to enact RFRA. It acknowledged that section 5 authorizes Congress to "enforce" the fourteenth amendment, and therefore Congress can enact legislation "enforcing the constitutional right to the free exercise of religion." However, the Court then observed:

> Congress' power under section 5, however, extends only to enforcing the provisions of the fourteenth amendment. . . . The design of the amendment and the text of section 5 are inconsistent with the suggestion that Congress has the power to decree the substance of the fourteenth amendment's restrictions on the states. Legislation which alters the meaning of the free exercise [of religion] clause cannot be said to be enforcing the clause. Congress does not enforce a constitutional right by changing what the right is. It has been given the power "to enforce," not the power to determine what constitutes a constitutional violation. Were it not so, what Congress would be enforcing would no longer be, in any meaningful sense, the "provisions of [the fourteenth amendment] . . . ."

> If Congress could define its own powers by altering the fourteenth amendment's meaning, no longer would the Constitution be "superior paramount law, unchangeable by ordinary means." It would be "on a level with ordinary legislative acts, and, like other acts . . . alterable when the legislature shall please to alter it." Under this approach, it is difficult to conceive of a principle that would limit congressional power. Shifting legislative majorities could change the Constitution and effectively circumvent the difficult and detailed amendment process contained [therein].

The Court conceded that it is not always clear whether Congress is "enforcing" the fourteenth amendment or making unauthorized substantive changes in the Constitution. However, it insisted that there must be a "proportionality between the injury to be prevented or remedied and the means adopted to that end." The Court concluded that this test was not met in this case, since RFRA was not a "proportional" response to the "injury to be prevented or remedied." Rather, RFRA was an expansive law that was enacted to address minimal threats to religious freedom. The Court noted that

> sweeping coverage ensures [RFRA's] intrusion at every level of government, displacing laws and prohibiting official actions of almost every description and regardless of subject matter. RFRA's restrictions apply to every agency and official of the federal, state, and local governments. RFRA applies to all federal and state law, statutory or otherwise, whether adopted before or after its enactment. RFRA has no termination date or termination mechanism. Any law is subject to challenge at any time by any individual who alleges a substantial burden on his or her free exercise of religion.

Further, this massive response was not warranted by any significant threat to religious freedom:

RFRA's legislative record lacks examples of modern instances of generally applicable laws passed because of religious bigotry. The history of persecution in this country detailed in the [congressional] hearings mentions no episodes occurring in the past 40 years. . . . The absence of more recent episodes stems from the fact that, as one witness testified, "deliberate persecution is not the usual problem in this country." Rather, the emphasis of the [congressional] hearings was on laws of general applicability which place incidental burdens on religion. Much of the discussion centered upon anecdotal evidence of autopsies performed on Jewish individuals and Hmong immigrants in violation of their religious beliefs . . . and on zoning regulations and historic preservation laws (like the one at issue here), which as an incident of their normal operation, have adverse effects on churches and synagogues. . . . It is difficult to maintain that they are examples of legislation enacted or enforced due to animus or hostility to the burdened religious practices or that they indicate some widespread pattern of religious discrimination in this country. Congress' concern was with the incidental burdens imposed, not the object or purpose of the legislation.

The stringent test RFRA demands of state laws reflects a lack of proportionality or congruence between the means adopted and the legitimate end to be achieved. If an objector can show a substantial burden on his free exercise, the State must demonstrate a compelling governmental interest and show that the law is the least restrictive means of furthering its interest. Claims that a law substantially burdens someone's exercise of religion will often be difficult to contest. Requiring a state to demonstrate a compelling interest and show that it has adopted the least restrictive means of achieving that interest is the most demanding test known to constitutional law. If "compelling interest" really means what it says . . . many laws will not meet the test. . . . [The test] would open the prospect of constitutionally required religious exemptions from civic obligations of almost every conceivable kind." Laws valid under Smith would fall under RFRA without regard to whether they had the object of stifling or punishing free exercise. . . . [RFRA] would require searching judicial scrutiny of state law with the attendant likelihood of invalidation. This is a considerable congressional intrusion into the states' traditional prerogatives and general authority to regulate for the health and welfare of their citizens.

The substantial costs RFRA exacts, both in practical terms of imposing a heavy litigation burden on the states and in terms of curtailing their traditional general regulatory power, far exceed any pattern or practice of unconstitutional conduct under the free exercise clause as interpreted in Smith. Simply put, RFRA is not designed to identify and counteract state laws likely to be unconstitutional because of their treatment of religion. In most cases, the state laws to which RFRA applies are not ones which will have been motivated by religious bigotry. . . .

It is a reality of the modern regulatory state that numerous state laws, such as the zoning regulations at issue here, impose a substantial burden on a large class of individuals. When the exercise of religion has been burdened in an incidental way by a law of general application, it does not follow that the persons affected have been burdened any more than other citizens, let alone burdened because of their religious beliefs. (emphasis added)

§ 13-02.4 — Conclusions

The following rules summarize the current interpretation of the first amendment guaranty of religious freedom, in light of the most recent Supreme Court decisions and other relevant precedent.

RULE #1. It will be difficult for religious organizations to challenge neutral laws of general applicability that burden religious practices or beliefs, because such laws are presumably valid whether or not supported by a compelling government interest.

Rule #1 is based on the Supreme Court's decisions in the *Smith* and *City of Boerne* cases. RFRA's attempt to establish a "compelling government interest" requirement in order to justify governmental infringements upon religion was declared unconstitutional by the Court in the *City of Boerne* ruling.

RULE #2. Laws that are not "neutral" towards religion, or that are not of "general applicability," will violate the first amendment guaranty of religious freedom unless supported by a compelling government interest.

The Court's repeal of the "compelling state interest" requirement in the *Smith* case applied only in the context of neutral laws of general applicability. In 1993, the Court clarified the meaning of these important terms.[49] It also clarified the meaning of a "compelling state interest."

neutrality

The Court ruled that a law that is not neutral "must be justified by a compelling governmental interest and must be narrowly tailored to advance that interest." It is very important to define neutrality. The Court noted that "[i]f the object of a law is to infringe upon or restrict practices because of their religious motivation, the law is not neutral." It continued:

There are, of course, many ways of demonstrating that the object or purpose of a law is the suppression of religion or religious conduct. To determine the object of a law, we must begin with its text, for the minimum requirement of neutrality is that a law not discriminate on its face. A law lacks facial neutrality if it refers to a religious practice without a secular meaning discernible from the language or context.

A law may not be neutral even though it is neutral "on its face." The Court observed:

The free exercise clause . . . "forbids subtle departures from neutrality," and "covert suppression of particular religious beliefs." Official action that targets religious conduct for distinctive treatment cannot be shielded by mere compliance with the requirement of facial neutrality. The free exercise clause protects against governmental hostility which is masked, as well as overt. The Court must survey meticulously the circumstances of governmental categories to eliminate, as it were, religious gerrymanders.

In evaluating the neutrality of a government action, the courts should consider "the historical background of the decision under challenge, the specific series of events leading to the enactment or official policy in question, as well as the legislative or administrative history, including contemporaneous statements made by members of the decisionmaking body," to determine if the intent was to single out religious organizations or believers for unfavorable treatment.

---

[49] Church of the Lukumi Babaluaye, Inc. v. City of Hialeah, 508 U.S. 520 (1993).

general applicability

The Court ruled that a law that is not of general applicability "must be justified by a compelling governmental interest and must be narrowly tailored to advance that interest." This is so even if the law is neutral. Neutrality and general applicability are separate considerations. If a law fails either, then it must be supported by a compelling governmental interest in order to justify a negative impact on religious practices. With regard to the concept of "general applicability," the Court made the following clarification:

> All laws are selective to some extent, but categories of selection are of paramount concern when a law has the incidental effect of burdening religious practice. The free exercise clause "protects religious observers against unequal treatment," and inequality results when a legislature decides that the governmental interests it seeks to advance are worthy of being pursued only against conduct with a religious motivation. The principle that government, in pursuit of legitimate interests, cannot in a selective manner impose burdens only on conduct motivated by religious belief is essential to the protection of the rights guaranteed by the free exercise clause.

The court further observed that "in circumstances in which individualized exemptions from a general requirement are available, the government may not refuse to extend that system to cases of religious hardship without compelling reason." In other words, if a law of general applicability contains some non-religious exceptions, it cannot deny an exemption to religious institutions (in cases of religious hardship) without a compelling reason.

compelling state interest

The Court emphasized the high standard that a law or governmental practice must satisfy that burdens religious practice and that is either not neutral or not generally applicable:

> A law burdening religious practice that is not neutral or not of general application must undergo the most rigorous of scrutiny. To satisfy the commands of the first amendment, a law restrictive of religious practice must advance interests of the highest order and must be narrowly tailored in pursuit of those interests. The compelling interest standard that we apply once a law fails to meet the Smith requirements is not "watered . . . down" but "really means what it says." A law that targets religious conduct for distinctive treatment or advances legitimate governmental interests only against conduct with a religious motivation will survive strict scrutiny only in rare cases.

The Court then proceeded to give one of its most detailed interpretations of the concept of a "compelling governmental interest":

> Where government restricts only conduct protected by the first amendment and fails to enact feasible measures to restrict other conduct producing substantial harm or alleged harm of the same sort, the interest given in justification of the restriction is not compelling. It is established in our strict scrutiny jurisprudence that "a law cannot be regarded as protecting an interest of the highest order . . . when it leaves appreciable damage to that supposedly vital interest unprohibited."

RULE #3. *Neutral laws of general applicability that infringe upon a second constitutional right (in addition to religious freedom) will be unconstitutional unless supported by a compelling government interest.*

In the *Smith* case the Supreme Court observed that the compelling government interest test is triggered if a neutral and generally applicable law burdens not only the exercise of religion, but some other first amendment right (such as speech, press, or assembly) as well. The Court observed, "The only decisions in which we have held that the first amendment bars application of a neutral, generally applicable law to religiously motivated action have involved not the free exercise clause alone, but the free exercise clause in conjunction with other constitutional protections, such as freedom of speech and of the press . . . ." In other words, if a neutral and generally applicable law or governmental practice burdens the exercise of religion, then the compelling governmental interest standard can be triggered if the religious institution or adherent can point to some other first amendment interest that is being violated. In many cases, this will not be hard to do. For example, the first amendment guaranty of free speech often will be implicated when a law or governmental practice burdens the exercise of religion. The same is true of the first amendment guarantees of free press and assembly.

RULE #4. *The government may not refuse to extend a system of exemptions to cases of religious hardship without compelling reason.*

In the *Smith* case the Supreme Court observed, "[O]ur decisions in the unemployment cases stand for the proposition that where the state has in place a system of individual exemptions, it may not refuse to extend that system to cases of 'religious hardship' without compelling reason."

RULE #5. *Every state constitution has some form of protection for religious freedom. In some cases, these protections are more comprehensive than under the federal Constitution. State constitutional protections in some cases may provide religious organizations with additional protections.*

Churches and religious adherents whose first amendment right to the free exercise of religion is not violated by a neutral law of general applicability may claim that their state constitution's guaranty of religious freedom has been violated.

Rule #6. *Government may never interfere with an individual's right to believe whatever he or she wants. Only religiously-motivated conduct may be regulated, in accordance with the previous rules.*

These rules are illustrated by the following examples.

Example. *A state law prohibits the issuance of securities by any organization unless the securities are registered with the state securities commissioner. One of the purposes of the law is to prevent fraud. A church would like to sell promissory notes to raise funds for a new sanctuary. When it learns that it cannot do so without registering its securities, it insists that the application of such a law to churches violates the first amendment's free exercise of religion clause. The church will lose. The securities law is neutral and of general applicability, and accordingly rule #1 controls. The law is presumably valid without the need to prove a compelling governmental interest.*

Example. *A number of common church practices may violate copyright law. Does the application of copyright law to churches violate the first amendment's free exercise of religion clause? No. The copyright law is neutral and of general applicability, and accordingly rule #1 controls. The law is presumably valid without the need to prove a compelling governmental interest.*

Example. *A city enacts a civil rights ordinance that bans any employer (including churches) from discriminating on the basis of sexual orientation in any employment decision. A church argues that* *applying such a law to a church that is opposed on the basis of religious doctrine to hiring homosexuals will violate its constitutional right to freely exercise its religion. Under the Supreme Court's ruling in the Smith case, it is doubtful that the church would prevail. The civil rights law in question clearly is neutral and of general applicability, and accordingly rule #1 applies. This means that the law is presumably valid without the need to prove a compelling governmental interest. However, a number of federal courts (prior to Smith) concluded that the clergy-church relationship is unique and is beyond governmental regulation. Accordingly, it is doubtful that such an ordinance could be applied to clergy. This of course assumes that the Supreme Court, after Smith, would agree with these previous rulings.*

Example. *A religious denomination does not ordain women. A female church member sues the denomination, claiming that its ban on female clergy violates a state civil rights law banning discrimination in employment on the basis of gender. Is the denomination's practice legally permissible as a result of the first amendment's free exercise of religion clause? See the preceding example.*

Example. *A city council receives several complaints from downtown business owners concerning homeless shelters that are operated by churches. In response to these complaints, the city council enacts an ordinance banning any church from operating a homeless shelter. This ordinance is neither neutral nor of general applicability, and so rule #2 applies. This means that the city will need to demonstrate that the ordinance is supported by a compelling government interest. It is doubtful that it will be able to do so. First, the law is "underinclusive," meaning that it singles out churches to further its purposes. Further, as the Supreme Court observed in the Hialeah case (discussed above), "[a] law that targets religious conduct for distinctive treatment or advances legitimate governmental interests only against conduct with a religious motivation will survive strict scrutiny only in rare cases."*

Example. *Same facts as the previous example, except that the ordinance bans any homeless shelter in the downtown area, whether or not operated by a church. A downtown church sues the city, claiming that the ordinance violates its first amendment right to freely exercise its religion. The church will lose. The ordinance in this example is a neutral law of general applicability, and so rule #1 controls. This means that the ordinance is presumably valid without the need for demonstrating that it is based on a compelling government interest.*

Example. *A state legislature enacts a law that requires teachers at all public and private elementary and secondary schools, including those operated by churches, to be state-certified. A church challenges this law on the basis of the first amendment guaranty of the free exercise of religion. The church probably will lose. The law in question clearly is neutral and of general applicability, and so rule #1 controls. This means that the law is presumably valid without the need to prove a compelling governmental interest.*

Example. *A state legislature enacts a law imposing a sales tax on purchases made by most organizations, including churches. A church challenges this law on the ground that it violates the first amendment guaranty of the free exercise of religion. It is doubtful that the church will prevail. The law in question clearly is neutral and of general applicability, and so rule #1 controls. This means that the law is presumably valid without the need to prove a compelling governmental interest.*

Example. *A city enacts an ordinance establishing a "landmark commission." The commission is authorized to designate any building as an historic landmark. Any building so designated cannot be modified or demolished without the commission's approval. A church is designated as an historic landmark. A* few years later, the church asks the commission for permission to enlarge its facility in order to accommodate its growing congregation. The commission rejects this request, despite proof that several persons are "turned away" each Sunday because of a lack of room in the current church facility. These were the facts in the City of Boerne case. If the church relies solely on a violation of its first amendment right to religious freedom, it will lose because the ordinance is neutral and of general applicability, and so rule #1 controls. This means that the law is presumably valid without the need to prove a compelling governmental interest. However, note that the first amendment also guarantees the rights of assembly and association, and a strong case can be made that these rights are violated by the commission's action since the right of some members to engage in religious services (assembly and association) is being curtailed. By asserting that these first amendment rights are being violated in addition to the free exercise of religion, the church invokes rule #3. This will force the city to demonstrate a compelling government interest supporting its decision to deny the church permission to expand its facilities. It is doubtful that the city could meet this requirement.

Example. A church is located on a major highway. It constructs a billboard on its property that contains religious messages. The city enacts an ordinance prohibiting any billboards along the highway. Since the ordinance is a "neutral law of general applicability" (it applies equally to all property owners and does not single out religious organizations), it is legally valid though it interferes with the church's first amendment right to freely exercise its religion. There is no need for the city to demonstrate a compelling government interest. However, if the church asserts that its first amendment right to free speech is being violated by the city ordinance (in addition to its right to freely exercise its religion), then rule #3 is invoked. This will force the city to demonstrate a compelling government interest supporting the ordinance. As noted above, this is a difficult (though not impossible) test to meet. Note, however, that if the church can force the city to demonstrate that the ordinance is based on a compelling government interest, then it has obtained the same legal protection that it would have had under RFRA.

Example. Federal tax law forbids most tax-exempt organizations from intervening or participating in political campaigns on behalf of or in opposition to any candidate for public office. A church publicly supports a particular candidate during a campaign, and the IRS revokes its exempt status. The church claims that the law violates its first amendment right to the free exercise of religion. If this is the church's only argument, it will lose since the law is a neutral law of general applicability and therefore need not be supported by a compelling government interest. However, if the church argues that its first amendment rights to speech and press are also violated by the ban on political participation, then rule #3 is invoked. This will force the government to prove a compelling government interest to justify the law. As noted above, this is a difficult (though not impossible) test to meet. Note, however, that if the church can force the government to demonstrate that the law is based on a compelling government interest, then it has obtained the same legal protection that it would have had under RFRA.

Example. A public school adopts a policy prohibiting any outside group to rent or use its facilities for any purpose. A church asks for permission to rent the school gymnasium for a special religious service. The school denies this request. The church claims that its first amendment right to the free exercise of religion has been violated by the school's policy. Since the policy is a neutral law of general applicability, rule #1 controls. The law is presumably valid without the need to prove a compelling governmental interest. However, if the church asserts that its first amendment rights to free speech, assembly, and association are violated by the school policy (in addition to its right to freely exercise its religion), then rule #3 is invoked. This will force the school to demonstrate a compelling government interest supporting its policy. Other decisions by the Supreme Court suggest that the school will be able to demonstrate *a compelling government interest—avoiding the "establishment" of religion (by singling out religious groups for special or favored treatment).*

One additional observation must be made about the free exercise clause. The concept of free exercise is fundamentally incompatible with the philosophy of disestablishment contained in the establishment clause.[50] This tension has been aggravated in the past few decades by judicial emphasis upon disestablishment. Chief Justice Burger, in the *Walz* decision, commented on this underlying tension: "The Court has struggled to find a neutral course between the two Religion Clauses, both of which are cast in absolute terms, and either of which, if expanded to a logical extreme, would tend to clash with the other."[51] Similarly, Justice Stewart, dissenting in *Schempp*, observed, "[T]here are areas in which a doctrinaire reading of the establishment clause leads to irreconcilable conflict with the free exercise clause."[52] The Supreme Court in more recent years has attempted to synthesize the religion clauses by emphasizing the concept of neutrality:

The general principle deducible from the first amendment and all that has been said by the Court is this: that we will not tolerate either governmentally established religion or governmental interference with religion. Short of those expressly proscribed governmental acts there is room for play in the joints productive of a benevolent neutrality which will permit religious exercise to exist without sponsorship and without interference.[53]

---

[50] *See generally* chapter 11, *supra.*
[51] Walz v. Tax Commission, 397 U.S. 664, 669 (1970).
[52] School District of Abington v. Schempp, 374 U.S. 203, 309 (1963).
[53] Walz v. Tax Commission, 397 U.S. 664, 669 (1970).

INSTRUCTIONAL AIDS TO CHAPTER 13

Terms

clearly secular purpose

compelling government interest

excessive entanglement

neutral law of general applicability

primary effect

Religious Freedom Restoration Act

LEARNING OBJECTIVES

- Explain the current meaning of the first amendment's nonestablishment of religion clause.

- Explain the current meaning of the first amendment's free exercise of religion clause.

- Apply the current meaning of both of the first amendment's religion clauses to a variety of circumstances.

SHORT-ANSWER QUESTIONS

1. What three conditions must a law or governmental practice ordinarily satisfy to be consistent with the first amendment's "establishment clause"?

2. What factors must a court consider in determining whether a particular law or governmental action violates the first amendment's "free exercise of religion clause"?

3. A public university denies Christian students the right to use campus facilities for group meetings. It permits several other non-religious organizations to use such facilities. Has the university violated the first amendment's free exercise of religion clause? Explain.

4. A taxpayer is opposed to war on the basis of religious convictions. As a result, she refuses to pay that portion of her federal income taxes that will be allocated to defense. The IRS compels the taxpayer to pay her full income taxes. Has it violated the first amendment's free exercise of religion clause? Explain.

5. The Supreme Court has observed that the concept of free exercise of religion is fundamentally incompatible with the philosophy of disestablishment contained in the establishment clause. What did the Court mean?

6. A bookstore owner sells a wide variety of books and publications, but he refuses to sell any religious literature. Has he violated the free exercise of religion clause? Explain.

7. A public school permits students to meet on school premises before regular school hours to participate in religious exercises. Does this practice violate the establishment clause? Explain.

8. A new religious sect espouses child sacrifice under certain circumstances. A court grants an injunction prohibiting such a practice. The sect complains that its right to freely exercise its religion has been violated. Evaluate the merits of the sect's claim.

9. A small Jewish sect in New York reintroduces animal sacrifice. The Humane Society seeks a court order prohibiting the practice. The sect counters by claiming that it has a constitutional right to practice its religion. How will the court rule?

10. A person charged with the unauthorized possession and use of narcotic drugs claims that his use of such drugs is a religious exercise that is protected by the first amendment. He cites as authority Genesis 1:29, which states, "And God said, 'Behold, I have given you every plant yielding seed which is upon the face of the earth.'" How will a court rule on the religious freedom defense?

11. In 1990, the Supreme Court rendered a highly controversial interpretation of the first amendment's free exercise of religion clause. What did the Court say that was so controversial? Did the decision, as some have suggested, effectively "repeal" the concept of religious freedom? Explain.

Discussion Questions

1. The courts have ruled that it is permissible to inscribe the national motto "In God We Trust" on all of our coins and currency, but that it is not permissible to post a copy of the Ten Commandments in public school classrooms. Can you think of a rational basis for this distinction?

2. The courts have relied on the establishment clause in outlawing most collective prayers in public elementary and secondary schools. But does not the prohibition of such prayers violate the first amendment freedom of certain students to exercise their religion? How should a court balance these competing interests?

SIGNIFICANT FIRST AMENDMENT ISSUES

Chapter summary. *Can persons engage in religious "witnessing" or proselytizing in residential neighborhoods on a door-to-door basis? Can persons use public parks for religious meetings? Under what circumstances can voluntary prayers be uttered on public property? Can a city display a cross or nativity scene on public property during the Christmas season? Can a court display a picture of the Ten Commandments? Can the federal government constitutionally print the national motto "In God We Trust" on all of our nation's currency? Can a public school rent its facilities to a church for religious purposes when the school is not in session? Do Sunday closing laws impermissibly discriminate against religious groups that recognize a Sabbath on another day of the week? Does an adult have the right to refuse medical treatment on the basis of religious beliefs? Can the state compel a sick or an injured child to receive medical treatment against the religious beliefs of his parents? What activities are included within the term "religious"? What activities are excluded? Such questions present the courts with difficult choices. In this chapter, you will learn how the courts have responded to these questions.*

Previous chapters have addressed the application of the first amendment religion clauses to several issues. Examples include the dismissal of clergy, malpractice, church securities, child abuse reporting, church audits, discipline of church members, judicial review of internal church decisions, church property disputes, the application of various labor and discrimination laws to churches, zoning law, government regulation of church-operated schools, and church tax exemptions. This chapter will review the application of the first amendment religion clauses in several other contexts.

§ 14-01 The Right to Witness

Key point 14-01. The courts have affirmed the right of persons to disseminate religious literature and doctrine on a door-to-door basis, and in public places. This right may be limited in order to preserve public safety, health, order, and convenience. Strict safeguards, however, must attend any limitations.

1. Door-to-Door Witnessing

The Supreme Court repeatedly has affirmed the right of persons to solicit religious contributions, sell religious books and merchandise, and disseminate religious doctrine on a "door-to-door" basis.[1] Municipal ordinances that condition the exercise of such a right upon the acquisition of a permit or license or upon the payment of a "tax" or fee generally have been found to be unconstitutional. To illustrate, the Supreme Court struck down a city licensing scheme used by city officials to ban Jehovah's Witnesses from going door-to-door in heavily Catholic neighborhoods playing a phonograph record that attacked the Roman Catholic Church as an "enemy" and the church of the devil.[2] Similarly, the Court invalidated a municipal "license tax" that was imposed upon the door-to-door solicitation and evangelistic activities of Jehovah's Witnesses.[3] The Court observed, "Those who can tax the privilege of engaging in this form of missionary evangelism can close its doors to all those who do not have a full purse. Spreading religious beliefs in this ancient and honorable manner would thus be denied the needy. Those who can deprive religious groups of their colporteurs can take from them a part of the vital power of the press which has survived from the Reformation."[4] The Supreme Court also struck down a municipal ordinance that prohibited anyone engaged in distributing literature to summon the occupants of a home to the door.[5]

The Supreme Court has acknowledged that a city may protect its citizens from fraud by requiring strangers in the community to establish their identity and demonstrate their authority to represent the cause they espouse. Cities also may limit door-to-door proselytizing and solicitation where necessary to preserve public safety, health, order, and convenience. Strict safeguards, however, must attend any such limitations.[6]

Many lower federal court decisions have protected the rights of persons to engage in door-to-door religious activities.[7]

---

[1] *See, e.g.,* Murdock v. Pennsylvania, 319 U.S. 105 (1943); Largent v. Texas, 318 U.S. 418 (1943); Jamison v. Texas, 318 U.S. 413 (1943); Cantwell v. Connecticut, 310 U.S. 296 (1940).

[2] Cantwell v. Connecticut, 310 U.S. 296 (1940).

[3] Murdock v. Pennsylvania, 319 U.S. 105 (1943).

[4] *Id.* at 112.

[5] Martin v. City of Struthers, 319 U.S. 141 (1943).

[6] See the discussion of witnessing in public places later in this section.

[7] *See, e.g.,* Troyer v. Town of Babylon, 483 F. Supp. 1135 (E.D.N.Y. 1980), *aff'd,* 628 F.2d 1346 (2nd Cir. 1980), *aff'd,* 449 U.S. 988 (1980) ("[r]equiring consent of householders before approaching their homes constitutes, in effect, an indirect unconstitutional imposition of a licensing fee; it generates costs which burden the exercise of first amendment rights in direct proportion to the number of persons the speaker wants to reach"); Weissman v. City of Alamogordo, 472 F. Supp. 425 (D.N.M. 1979); McMurdie v. Doutt, 468

2. WITNESSING IN PUBLIC PLACES

The Supreme Court has zealously protected the right to disseminate religious doctrine in public places. The Court has struck down a city ordinance that prohibited the distribution of handbills on city streets as applied to Jehovah's Witnesses who distributed religious handbills to pedestrians in a downtown area.[8] The Court also has invalidated a city ordinance under which a Baptist minister was convicted for holding a religious meeting on city streets without a permit.[9] In striking down the ordinance, the Court held that no ordinance that gives city officials discretionary authority, in advance, to allow or refuse individuals the right to speak publicly on religious matters could ever be constitutionally valid. The Court did emphasize, however, that a carefully worded ordinance that conditions the right to hold public religious meetings in public places on the prior receipt of a municipal permit or license could be constitutionally valid if it (1) removed all discretion on the part of city officials by listing the specific preconditions for issuance of a license, and (2) the specified preconditions were constitutionally permissible, such as the preservation of public peace and order. In another decision,[10] the Court upheld the conviction of five Jehovah's Witnesses who paraded through a city carrying a sign stating "Religion is a Snare and a Racket" in violation of an ordinance prohibiting "a parade or procession" on a city street without a license. The Court observed that the city officials had no discretion to grant or deny a license since the conditions for obtaining a license were specifically and clearly set forth in the ordinance. Also, the stated purpose of the ordinance and its various conditions were permissible: preserving the public safety, convenience, peace, and order by preventing conflicts in scheduling; controlling the time, place, and manner of each use of the public streets; and enabling the police to oversee each use and thus minimize the risk of disorder.

In conclusion, the following principles should be noted:

1. No law or regulation that gives government officials unbridled discretion to permit or disallow a religious meeting or service or any other religious activity on public property can be consistent with the first amendment guarantee of free exercise of religion.

2. A law or regulation that requires a license or permit before a religious meeting or activity may be held on public property can be constitutionally valid if

a. specific guidelines exist for determining whether to grant or disallow a license or permit, and the guidelines remove all discretion from those officials who must evaluate applications

b. guidelines only ensure public order, peace, health, safety, or convenience

c. no less restrictive public remedies to protect the peace and order of the community are appropriate or available

3. A permit or licensing scheme is unconstitutional unless it (a) provides for a ruling on an application within a specified brief period of time, (b) places the burden on the government of showing that the law's guidelines are not satisfied, and (c) makes available prompt, final, judicial resolution of the issue.[11]

F. Supp. 766 (N.D. Ohio 1979); Levers v. City of Tullahoma, 446 F. Supp. 884 (D. Tenn. 1978); Murdock v. City of Jacksonville, 361 F. Supp. 1083 (M.D. Fla. 1973).

[8] Jamison v. Texas, 318 U.S. 413 (1943).

[9] Kunz v. New York, 340 U.S. 290 (1951).

[10] Cox v. New Hampshire, 312 U.S. 569 (1941).

[11] Freedman v. Maryland, 432 U.S. 43 (1977); Walker v. Wegner, 477 F. Supp. 648 (D.S.D. 1979).

Numerous lower federal court decisions have protected the rights of persons to engage in religious activities on public property.[12]

§ 14-02 Prayer on Public Property other than Schools

Key point 14-02. The courts have ruled that the first amendment allows chaplains and other ministers to pray before legislative assemblies.

The Supreme Court has ruled that it is permissible for state legislatures to select and compensate legislative chaplains,[13] and other courts have approved congressional chaplains[14] and the practice of opening county board meetings with prayer.[15]

§ 14-03 Prayer During Public School Activities

Key point 14-03. The first amendment prohibits the recitation of prayers by school officials and clergy in public schools or at public school events, including graduation ceremonies and sports activities. However, some courts have allowed student-initiated prayers during such events.

A number of Supreme Court decisions addressing prayer on public property are reviewed in chapter 12 (see sections 12-02, 12-03, 12-04, 12-05, 12-12, and 12-13). The issue of student-initiated religious activities on public school property is addressed in section 14-07.

Example. A federal appeals court ruled that the first amendment nonestablishment of religion clause would be violated by allowing a prayer to be recited at a public high school graduation ceremony, even though a majority of the graduating class voted to include the prayer in the ceremony and attendance was voluntary.[16] Further, outlawing prayer at the ceremony did not violate the majority's constitutional rights of free speech and freedom of religion, since the ceremony was not an "open forum" and students could exercise their religion outside of the ceremony.

Example. A federal appeals court ruled that allowing public high school seniors to choose student volunteers to deliver nonsectarian, nonproselytizing invocations at their graduation ceremonies does not violate the first amendment's nonestablishment of religion clause.[17] A public school district in Texas

---

[12] *See, e.g.,* Edwards v. Maryland State Fair and Agricultural Society, Inc., 628 F.2d 282 (4th Cir. 1980); International Society for Krishna Consciousness, Inc. v. Bowen, 600 F.2d 667 (7th Cir. 1979); Bacon v. Bradley-Bourbonnais High School District, 707 F. Supp. 1005 (N.D. Ill. 1989); International Society for Krishna Consciousness, Inc. v. City of New York, 501 F. Supp. 684 (S.D.N.Y. 1980); International Society for Krishna Consciousness v. Eaves, 601 F.2d 809 (5th Cir. 1979); International Society for Krishna Consciousness v. Bowen, 600 F.2d 667 (7th Cir. 1979); International Society for Krishna Consciousness v. Rochford, 585 F.2d 263 (7th Cir. 1978).

[13] Marsh v. Chambers, 463 U.S. 783 (1983). The *Marsh* case is discussed in § 12-09, *supra.*

[14] Murray v. Buchanan, 720 F.2d 689 (D.C. Cir. 1983).

[15] Bogen v. Doty, 598 F. 2d 1110 (8th Cir. 1979). The court upheld this practice since no expenditure of funds was involved and the primary purpose and effect of the prayer was public decorum and solemnity at county board meetings. These requirements would not be necessary after the Supreme Court's decision in the *Marsh* case. *See* § 12-09, *supra.*

[16] Harris v. Joint School District, 41 F.3d 447 (9th Cir. 1994).

[17] Jones v. Clear Creek Independent School District, 977 F.2d 963 (5th Cir. 1992). The United States Supreme Court issued an order declining to review the *Jones* case. This may signal the Court's satisfaction with the lower court's resolution of this controversial issue. Regardless of why the Court declined to review this case, the fact remains that the decision of the federal appeals court remains binding in the fifth judicial circuit, which includes the states of Louisiana, Mississippi, and Texas. Other federal courts have rejected the conclusion of this ruling. *See, e.g.,* Ingebretsen v. Jackson Public School District, 88 F.3d 274 (5th Cir. 1996).

adopted the following resolution: "The use of an invocation and/or benediction at high school graduation exercises shall rest within the discretion of the graduating senior class, with the advice and counsel of the senior class principal; the invocation and benediction, if used, shall be given by a student volunteer; and consistent with the principle of equal liberty of conscience, the invocation and benediction shall be nonsectarian and nonproselytizing in nature." Pursuant to this resolution, prayers were offered by graduating seniors at public high school graduation ceremonies within the district. A lawsuit was filed challenging the constitutionality of this practice, and a trial court ruled that the practice did not violate the first amendment. A federal appeals court agreed, concluding that the Supreme Court's decision in the Lee[18] case did not change the result. In the Lee case, the Supreme Court ruled that a public high school principal violated the first amendment by inviting a local clergyman to deliver a nonsectarian, nonproselytizing invocation at a graduation ceremony. The appeals court acknowledged that it was bound by the Supreme Court's decision in Lee, but concluded that the Lee case did not require that the school district resolution at issue in this case be invalidated. The court noted many critical differences in this case that distinguished it from Lee. First, the graduating seniors themselves decided whether or not they wanted an invocation during their graduation ceremony. In Lee, a high school principal made this decision. Second, the invocation (if desired by the graduating seniors) was offered by a student. In Lee, the invocation was offered by a member of the clergy. Third, the student selected to offer the invocation was free to compose it without any participation by the school (other than the requirement that it be nonsectarian and nonproselytizing). There was no requirement that the invocation mention God or contain any other religious references. In Lee, there was some school involvement in the composition of the prayers, and it was understood that the prayers would be "religious." Fourth, and perhaps most importantly, there was little if any of the "psychological pressure" upon students to participate in the invocation that there was in Lee. The court observed, "We think that the graduation prayers permitted by the resolution place less psychological pressure on students than the prayers at issue in Lee because all students, after having participated in the decision of whether prayers will be given, are aware that any prayers represent the will of their peers, who are less able to coerce participation than an authority figure from the state or clergy."

Example. *A federal appeals court ruled that invocations delivered before public high school football games violate the nonestablishment of religion clause.[19] Between 1947 and 1986, a Protestant minister delivered an invocation prior to home games at a public high school in Georgia. When a parent complained that this practice violated the first amendment, the school adopted an "equal access" plan whereby invocation speakers were selected randomly among students, parents, and faculty. Ministers were no longer eligible to give invocations. Even this plan was not acceptable to the complaining parent, who filed a lawsuit challenging the constitutionality of the modified "equal access" plan. A federal district court ruled that the equal access plan was not unconstitutional "on its face," and the parent appealed to a federal appeals court. The appeals court concluded that the equal access approach to pregame invocations violated the nonestablishment of religion clause since it violated both the first and second parts of the Supreme Court's three-part test announced in the Lemon case.[20] The court observed that the school's refusal to employ "wholly secular invocations makes it very clear that [its] actual purpose in having pregame invocations was religious." It added that "the conclusion is inescapable that the religious invocation conveys a message that the school endorses the religious invocation." Further,*

---

[18] 112 S. Ct. 2649 (1992). *See* §12-13.

[19] Jager v. Douglas County School District, 862 F.2d 824 (11th Cir. 1989). *See also* Doe v. Duncanville Independent School District, 70 F.3d 402 (5th Cir. 1995).

[20] *See* § 13-01.1, *supra.* Under this test, a challenged practice is permissible only if it has a secular purpose, a primary effect that neither advances nor inhibits religion, and does not create an "excessive entanglement" between church and state.

"the equal access plan places those attending football games in the position of participating in a group prayer." The school defended the legality of the equal access plan on the grounds that the invocations (1) "occur outside the instructional environment of the classroom," (2) "do not invoke the teacher-student relationship," (3) "are given at public events at which attendance is entirely voluntary," (4) "constitute a de minimis [i.e., insignificant] violation of the establishment clause because they last 60 to 90 seconds," and (5) are similar to the Nebraska practice of opening all sessions of the state legislature with prayer—a practice upheld by the United States Supreme Court in 1983. The appeals court rejected all of these contentions.

Example. A federal appeals court ruled that the constitution was not violated when a public high school choir performed religious songs and conducted a few of its concerts in churches.[21] A non-Christian student who was a member of the choir asked a federal court to issue an order banning the choir from singing religious songs and performing concerts in churches. A federal district court refused to do so, and the student appealed. A federal appeals court concluded that the choir's practices were permissible and violated neither the first amendment's nonestablishment of religion or free exercise of religion clauses. The court applied the Supreme Court's three-part Lemon test in determining whether the choir's practices constituted an impermissible establishment of religion. Under this test, a government practice challenged as an establishment of religion will be valid only if it satisfies the following three conditions—a secular purpose, a primary effect that neither advances nor inhibits religion, and no excessive entanglement between church and state. The court concluded that all of these tests were met.

§ 14-04 Display of Religious Symbols on Public Property

Key point 14-04. The display of religious symbols on public property does not violate the first amendment nonestablishment of religion clause so long as they are part of a larger display that includes secular symbols.

Several courts have ruled on the constitutionality of displaying religious symbols on public property. Many courts have concluded that the maintenance of crosses on public property constitutes an impermissible establishment of religion.[22] One court observed:

The employment of publicly owned and publicly maintained property for a highly visible display of the character of the cross in this case necessarily creates an inference of official endorsement of the general religious beliefs which underlie that symbol. Accordingly, persons who do not share those beliefs may feel that their own beliefs are stigmatized or officially deemed less worthy than those awarded the appearance of the city's endorsement . . . . The government has no business placing its power, prestige, or property at the disposal of private persons or groups either to aid or oppose any religion.[23]

---

[21] Bauchman v. West High School, 132 F.3d 542 (10th Cir. 1997).

[22] *See, e.g.,* American Civil Liberties Union v. Rabun County Chamber of Commerce, Inc., 678 F.2d 1379 (11th Cir. 1982); ACLU v. Mississippi State General Services Administration, 652 F. Supp. 380 (S.D. Miss. 1987) (state office building created a 22-story tall "cross" during the Christmas season by leaving the lights on in designated offices after hours); Fox v. City of Los Angeles, 587 P.2d 663 (Cal. 1978); Eugene Sand and Gravel, Inc. v. City of Eugene, 558 P.2d 338 (Ore. 1976); Lowe v. City of Eugene, 463 P.2d 360 (Ore. 1969).

[23] Lowe v. City of Eugene, 463 P.2d 360, 363 (Ore. 1969).

Other courts have approved of the maintenance of crosses on public property.[24] In one case, a court emphasized that a cross was maintained "to decorate streets and attract holiday shoppers to downtown, rather than establish or create a religious symbol or to promote or establish a religion."[25]

One court ruled that it is constitutionally permissible for public schools to temporarily display children's artwork in school rooms and halls, even though some of the artwork is religious.[26] The court reasoned:

> Are school children to be forbidden from expressing their natural artistic talents through media including religious themes? Or, are the results of their efforts to be excluded from display and recognition merely because they choose to adopt a religious, rather than a secular subject? The answer should be obvious. To impose such a restriction would more nearly approach a restraint upon the exercise of religion than does the present practice of the school board in permitting such displays.[27]

The Supreme Court of New Hampshire upheld a state law requiring that all public school classrooms contain a sign stating "In God We Trust."[28] The court observed that such words "appear on all coins and currency, on public buildings, and in our national anthem, and the appearance of these words as a motto on plaques in the public school need not offend the establishment clause . . . ."[29]

> [i]t would be ironic . . . if the inclusion of a single symbol of a particular historic religious event, as part of a celebration acknowledged in the Western World for 20 centuries, and in this country by the people, by the Executive Branch, by the Congress, and the courts for two centuries, would so "taint" the City's exhibit as to render it violative of the establishment clause.[32]

In a similar case, the Court upheld the practice of permitting a nativity scene in a city park during the Christmas season at virtually no expense to the city.[33] Unlike the situation in the *Lynch* case, the nativity scene was not in the context of a larger display containing numerous "secular" objects. Since the ruling was by an equally divided Court (4-4), it is controlling only in the second federal circuit (New York, Vermont, and Connecticut).

In 1989, the Court again addressed the permissibility of nativity scenes on public property.[34] For a number of years, a county government permitted a Roman Catholic group to display a nativity creche on the main staircase of the county courthouse during the Christmas season. The creche included figures of the infant Jesus, Mary, Joseph, farm animals, shepherds, wise men, and an angel bearing a banner proclaiming "Gloria in Excelsis Deo" (glory to God in the highest). The creche bore a plaque stating, "This display donated by the Holy Name Society." The creche was surrounded by poinsettia plants, but otherwise no other seasonal figures or ornaments were located nearby. A municipal building located a few blocks away presented an annual holiday display each December on a public sidewalk outside the main entrance to the building. The

[24] *See, e.g.,* Paul v. Dade County, 202 So.2d 833 (Fla. 1967); Meyer v. Oklahoma City, 496 P.2d 789 (Okla. 1972).
[25] Paul v. Dade County, 202 So.2d 833-835 (Fla. 1967).
[26] Chamberlin v. Dade County, 143 So.2d 21 (Fla. 1962).
[27] *Id.* at 35-6.
[28] Opinion of the Justices, 228 A.2d 161 (N.H. 1967).
[29] *Id.* at 164.
[30] Lynch v. Donnelly, 465 U.S. 668 (1984).
[31] *See* § 13-01.1, *supra.*
[32] 465 U.S. at 686.
[33] Board of Trustees v. McCreary, 105 S. Ct. 1859 (1985).
[34] County of Allegheny v. American Civil Liberties Union, 109 S. Ct. 3086 (1989).

display included a large (45-foot) Christmas tree decorated with lights and ornaments, an 18-foot Chanukah menorah (a candleholder with eight branches) owned by a Jewish group, and a sign reading "during this holiday season the City of Pittsburgh salutes liberty. Let these festive lights remind us that we are the keepers of the flame of liberty and our legacy of freedom." The American Civil Liberties Union (ACLU) filed a lawsuit claiming that these displays violated the constitutional ban on any "establishment of religion." A trial court permitted the displays, but a federal appeals court prohibited them.

The Supreme Court agreed to hear the case, and ruled that the nativity creche had to be removed but that the Chanukah menorah was permissible. The Court observed that among other things, the constitutional prohibition of any establishment of religion prevented any governmental "endorsement" of religion. The constitution, noted the Court, "precludes government from conveying or attempting to convey a message that religion or a particular religious belief is favored or preferred." Whether or not a particular display violates the constitution depends upon its context. The Court affirmed its earlier decision in *Lynch* upholding the validity of a Christmas creche that was part of a larger seasonal display that included a Santa Claus, reindeer, a talking wishing well, trees, and lights. Here, however, "the creche stands alone—it is the single element of the display." This, combined with the fact that the creche was located inside the main entrance of the "seat of county government," sent an "unmistakable message that [the county] supports and promotes the Christian praise to God that is the creche's religious message." The Court concluded: "The government may acknowledge Christmas as a cultural phenomenon, but under the first amendment it may not observe it as a Christian holy day by suggesting that people praise God for the birth of Jesus. . . . [G]overnment may celebrate Christmas in some manner and form, but not in a way that endorses Christian doctrine."

On the other hand, the Court upheld the validity of the Chanukah menorah, since (1) the menorah, being a mere candleholder, was not an "exclusively religious" symbol but rather "has both religious and secular dimensions"; and (2) the menorah stood next to a Christmas tree and a sign saluting liberty and accordingly was part of a "larger display" that detracted from the menorah's religious message. Justice Kennedy, in dissent, criticized the Court's majority for harboring a "latent hostility" and "callous indifference" toward religion. The Court's majority found such a view "as offensive as it is absurd," adding that "there may be some would-be theocrats who wish that their religion were an established creed . . . but this claim gets no relief, for it contradicts the fundamental premise of the establishment clause itself."

These decisions indicate that nativity displays will be permissible so long as they are incorporated into a larger "seasonal" display containing secular objects. Nativity displays standing alone on public property violate the Court's present interpretation of the establishment clause. A number of lower courts have attempted to apply this distinction. To illustrate, a federal appeals court ruled (by a 2-1 vote) that the annual display of a nativity scene in Chicago's city hall violated the first amendment's nonestablishment of religion clause.[35] For 30 years the city of Chicago had displayed the scene, which consisted of 12-inch figures, in the lobby of city hall. The display had been donated to the city, and no public funds were expended in maintaining or installing it. The display contained 6 disclaimer notices which recited that the display had been donated and that it was in no way sponsored or endorsed by the city government. The American Jewish Congress challenged the display on the ground that it constituted the establishment of religion. In agreeing that the display violated the nonestablishment of religion clause, the court distinguished the Supreme Court's *Lynch* decision. Unlike the Chicago display, the display in *Lynch* was "only one element in a larger display that consisted in large part of secularized symbols and decorations" (e.g., a Santa Claus, reindeer, Christmas trees, lights). The Chicago display was not a part of a larger, secularized display. Further, the display in *Lynch*, while sponsored by the city government, was situated in a park

---

[35] American Jewish Congress v. City of Chicago, 827 F.2d 120 (7th Cir. 1987).

owned by a private nonprofit organization. The Chicago display was situated in "the official headquarters building of the municipal government." Under these circumstances, the Chicago nativity scene impermissibly "advanced religion by sending a message to the people of Chicago that the city approved of Christianity."

A federal district court in Illinois ruled that a nativity scene on city hall property violated the first amendment's nonestablishment of religion clause despite the fact that the display was part of a larger display that contained several traditional (and secular) symbols of Christmas and was accompanied by a written notice in which the city disclaimed any endorsement of Christianity or any other religion.[36] The court attempted to distinguish *Lynch* on the ground that the Supreme Court had been addressing the permissibility of a nativity scene located in a private park rather than at the official headquarters of a city government.

A federal appeals court approved the maintenance of a granite monolith bearing the Ten Commandments on public property.[37] The court reasoned that in applying the three-part establishment clause test

we must strike a balance between that which is primarily religious and that which is primarily secular albeit embodying some religious impact. A tempered approach obviates the absurdity of striking down insubstantial and widely accepted references to the Deity in circumstances such as courtroom ceremonies, oaths of public office, and on national currency and coin . . . Overzealous rigidity may diminish or ultimately destroy the bulwark we have erected against governmental interferences in matters of religion.[38]

The court concluded:

It does not seem reasonable to require removal of a passive monument involving no compulsion, because its accepted precepts, as a foundation for law, reflect the religious nature of an ancient era . . . . The wholesome neutrality guaranteed by the establishment and free exercise clauses does not dictate obliteration of all our religious traditions . . . . We cannot say that the monument, as it stands, is more than a depiction of a historically important monolith with both secular and sectarian effects.[39]

One court ruled that the Smithsonian Institution's physical illustration of the theory of evolution did not constitute the establishment of a "religion of secular humanism."[40] On the contrary, the court concluded that a ban on all references to evolutionary theory in a public museum would itself constitute a violation of the establishment clause.

Use of a county seal depicting a cross, some sheep, and the motto "Con Esta Vencemos" (with this we conquer) was upheld against the claim that it constituted an impermissible establishment of religion.[41] The court concluded that the purpose of the seal was to authenticate documents and to commemorate the Christian, Spanish, and sheepherding heritage of the county; that the seal had only a benign reference to religion and thus did not have a primary effect of advancing religion; and that use of the seal resulted in no entanglements between church and state.

---

[36] Mather v. Village of Mundelein, 699 F. Supp. 1300 (N.D. Ill. 1988).

[37] Anderson v. Salt Lake City Corp., 475 F.2d 29 (10th Cir. 1973).

[38] *Id.* at 33.

[39] *Id.* at 34.

[40] Crowley v. Smithsonian Institution, 462 F. Supp. 725 (D.C.D.C. 1978), *aff'd*, 636 F.2d 738 (D.C. Cir. 1980).

[41] Johnson v. Board of County Commissioners, 528 F. Supp. 919 (D.N.M. 1981).

In another case, however, a federal district court concluded that a city's corporate seal containing a cross and other religious symbols was unconstitutional.[42] The City of Zion, Illinois, was organized in 1902 by Reverend John Alexander Dowie "for the purpose of the extension of the Kingdom of God on earth where God shall rule in every department of family, industry, commercial, educational, ecclesiastical and political life." Dowie presented a proposed seal to the city council the same year (all of the members of whom were of Dowie's Theocratic Party), and it was unanimously approved. The seal, which contains symbols of a dove, sword, cross, and crown, was explained by Dowie at the time as follows: "Look at that dove, which is the emblem of the Holy Spirit bearing the message of peace and love over the seas. The cross represents everything to us in redemption, salvation, healing, cleansing and keeping power. The sword is the sword of the Spirit, which is the Word of God. The crown is the crown of glory, the crown of joy, the crown of righteousness, the crown of rejoicing." The City of Zion uses its seal on its flag, letterhead, city council chambers, city vehicle stickers, police uniforms, and a city water tower. The seal was challenged on the ground that it violated the first amendment's "nonestablishment of religion" clause. A federal district court agreed that the seal was unconstitutional, and prohibited its further use.

The court began its opinion by noting that a city practice which allegedly violates the nonestablishment of religion clause will be upheld only if it has a secular purpose, a primary effect that neither advances nor inhibits religion, and does not create any excessive entanglement between church and state.[43] The court concluded that the Zion city seal had a primary effect of advancing religion, and accordingly was unconstitutional. The court rejected the city's claim that the seal merely commemorated the "rich and unique historical heritage of Zion as an experiment in establishing a twentieth century utopian community" and as such had an historical and therefore secular purpose. The court found this theory "not without merit," since "the city was in fact a religious experiment and the seal [recognizes] that origin." However, the court concluded that the religious intent and purpose of the seal was so sectarian that the seal had to be viewed as advancing religion rather than history. It observed, "As Reverend Dowie indicated, each of the symbols [on the seal] has an independent religious significance. The sum of the individual symbols imparts a decidedly religious, in fact sectarian, message." The religious message is enhanced by the words "God Reigns."

Further, the court noted that it could not "impute complete knowledge of the history to the average observer of the seal. We therefore cannot assume the average member of Zion's political community will have either general or specific knowledge of Zion's unique history." The court concluded that "it is possible that the majority of Zion's 15,000 inhabitants know little of its unique history." Therefore, the original purpose of the seal—which was the advancement of religion—was not neutralized by its historical significance.

The same court, in a parallel decision, concluded that the corporate seal of another Illinois town (Rolling Meadows) was constitutional despite the presence of a cross. The court emphasized that the seal had been designed in 1960 by an eighth-grade student as part of a school art assignment, and that neither she nor the city council in adopting the seal had any intent of advancing religion. Further, the cross was one of many designs on the seal, all the rest of which were secular. The court found the cross to be one aspect of community life, that was permissible on a city seal in the context of several other secular representations of municipal life. The remaining pictures "neutralized" the impact of the cross. This fact, in addition to the secular intent of the creator of the seal, persuaded the court that it was permissible.

The use of the national motto "In God We Trust" on all United States coins and currency has been upheld on the ground that such use "has nothing whatsoever to do with the establishment of religion" since

---

[42] Harris v. City of Zion, 729 F. Supp. 1242 (N.D. Ill. 1990).
[43] See § 13-01.1, supra.

its use "is of a patriotic or ceremonial character and bears no true resemblance to a governmental sponsorship of a religious exercise."[44]

§ 14-05 Recurring Use of Public Property by Religious Congregations for Religious Services

Key point 14-05. The first amendment permits religious congregations to use public property for church services so long as the use is temporary and the congregation pays fair rental value.

May public property ever be utilized for religious services? In a leading decision, the New Jersey Supreme Court held that "religious groups who fully reimburse school boards for related out-of-pocket expenses may use school facilities on a temporary basis for religious services as well as educational classes."[45] The court concluded that such a practice did not violate the first amendment's establishment clause. It applied the three-part test announced by the Supreme Court in the *Lemon* case.[46] First, the court observed that "there was a secular purpose in leasing the school facilities. That purpose was to enhance public use of these properties for the common benefit of the residents of East Brunswick."[47] Second, the court noted that the "primary effect" of the rental arrangement was not the advancement of religion: "While we would be naive in refusing to note the obvious advantages to young congregations in the temporary use of school premises, to hold that this scheme primarily benefits religion would be absurd. The community as a whole is benefited when nonprofit organizations of interest to its members prosper." Finally, the court could find no "excessive entanglement" between church and state:

> [N]o significant administrative function is involved. The processing of an application by a clerk is hardly an act of excessive entanglement. Moreover, inasmuch as no use of school premises is made during regular school hours, there is no need for supervision to insure that no religion seeps into secular institutions. The danger of political fragmentation is minuscule, as appropriations are not involved. The mere fact that some persons in the community oppose the use of the schools by sectarian groups should not prevent these groups from enjoying the benefits of premises which the tax dollars of many of their members helped to construct.[48]

The court cautioned that "truly prolonged use of school facilities by a congregation without evidence of immediate intent to construct or purchase its own building would be impermissible."[49]

In a similar case, a federal appeals court ruled that a church could use public school facilities on a temporary basis (and during noninstructional hours) during the construction or renovation of its own facilities.[50] A church applied for and was granted permission to use a public school building on four consecutive Sundays while its own church facility was being renovated. During the four week period, the church applied for a permit to use the school facilities for an additional "six to eight months." This permit was denied, and a trial court granted the church's request for an injunction forcing the school district to issue the requested permit. On appeal, the school district defended its refusal to grant the permit by pointing to a New York law that prohibits

---

[44] Aronow v. United States, 432 F.2d 242, 243 (9th Cir. 1970).

[45] Resnick v. East Brunswick Township Board of Education, 389 A.2d 944, 960 (N.J. 1978).

[46] *See* § 13-01.1, *supra.*

[47] *Id.* at 954.

[48] *Id.* at 958.

[49] *Id.*

[50] Deeper Life Christian Fellowship v. Board of Education, 852 F.2d 676 (2nd Cir. 1988).

public school properties from being used for "meetings . . . where admission fees are charged . . . if such meetings are under the exclusive control, and said proceeds are to be applied for the benefit of . . . a religious sect or denomination." The court acknowledged that this language was inconsistent with church use of public school property. However, it concluded that the school district had "opened this forum to [the church] through a practice of granting permits to use public school facilities to other religious organizations." The court also rejected the school district's argument that granting the permit to the church would constitute an impermissible "establishment of religion" in violation of the first amendment. It noted that "the semblance of official support is less evident where a school building is used at night as a temporary facility by religious organizations, under a program that grants access to all charitable groups."

However, some courts have indicated that a church's use of public school facilities must be temporary for the usage to be permissible. To illustrate, one court ruled that public high school officials acted properly in denying a church's request to use school facilities as a *permanent* location.[51] A church of about 100 members had been meeting in a privately-owned auditorium. Its pastor asked local school officials if the church could rent the public high school auditorium on Sunday mornings. The school officials declined this request on the basis of a school policy prohibiting use of school facilities for religious uses. The church immediately filed a lawsuit against the school district, seeking a court order permitting use of the public high school auditorium on Sundays. In support of its case, the church argued that the high school permitted many non-religious groups to rent the auditorium, and it thereby had created an "open forum" that could not be denied to any group (including a church). The school district argued that its policy of denying access to its facilities by religious groups was required by the constitutional principle of "separation of church and state." The court agreed that the school district had created an "open forum" by permitting various community groups to rent the high school auditorium. However, the court concluded that the district's refusal to rent the auditorium to the church was justified, since rental of the facility to the church would "have the primary effect of advancing religion" in violation of the nonestablishment of religion clause of the federal constitution. The court stressed that the church desired to use the school auditorium as the "*permanent* site for its church services and activities." It noted that the church "has no building site nor does it have any present plans to acquire a site or construct a church facility." As a result, the high school "will become the physical embodiment of the church," and in this sense the church's request was "significantly different" from the requests of other community organizations to rent the facility, since no other community group sought to "become permanently institutionalized within the school."

> **Example.** *A federal appeals court ruled that a public school violated the constitutional rights of a church by charging it more rent than it charged other community organizations for the use of school facilities.[52] A public school board permitted a wide variety of civic and community groups to use its facilities. Most such groups paid a rental fee substantially less than the commercial rate. Churches were permitted to use school facilities, and they were charged the same rate as other civic and community groups for the first 5 years they rented school facilities. However, after 5 years, churches paid a substantially higher rental fee. No other civic or community group paid the higher fee after 5 years. School officials freely acknowledged that the policy singled out churches for higher rent, but it insisted that the purpose was to encourage churches to go elsewhere out of a concern that continued use by churches of public school facilities might violate the first amendment's prohibition of an establishment of religion. A church began renting school facilities. For 5 years it paid the discounted rate, and later began paying the commercial rate. The church estimated that it paid $290,000 in additional rent because of the school board's policy regarding churches. The church*

[51] Wallace v. Washoe County School District, 701 F. Supp. 187 (D. Nev. 1988).
[52] Fairfax Covenant Church v. Fairfax County School Board, 17 F.3d 703 (4th Cir. 1994).

sued the school board, claiming that the rental policy for churches violated the first amendment guarantees of speech and religion. It also demanded a refund of the excess rent it had paid. A trial court agreed with the church that the school board's policy was unconstitutional, but it refused to award the church the excess rent it paid because of the policy. The church appealed. A federal appeals court agreed with the trial court that the policy was unconstitutional, and it ruled that the church was entitled to sue for a return of the excess rent it paid under the policy. The court rejected the school board's suggestion that allowing a church to rent school facilities at a below-market rate for a long period of time automatically violates the first amendment prohibition of the establishment of religion. Such may be the case, but only if religious use of the public forum is "dominant."

Example. A federal appeals court ruled that a church's constitutional rights were not violated by a public school district rule prohibiting it from conducting religious worship on public school property.[53] The church had asked school officials for permission to use a middle school auditorium for weekly religious services after it outgrew its own facilities. School officials denied this request. School policy allowed school property to be used for a wide variety of outside groups for civic, social, and recreational purposes. However, school property could not be used for religious services. The relevant policy specifies, "No outside organization or group may be allowed to conduct religious services or religious instruction on school premises after school. However, the use of school premises by outside organizations or groups after school for the purposes of discussing religious material or material which contains a religious viewpoint or for distributing such material is permissible." The church challenged the school's denial of its request to use school property for religious services. A federal appeals court upheld the policy. It noted that "freedom to speak on government property is largely dependent on the nature of the forum in which the speech is delivered." The court concluded that the public school in question was a limited public forum since school officials allowed only some groups to use school property for designated purposes. As a result, the exclusion of religious worship from this forum was legitimate only if it was "reasonable in light of the purpose served by the forum" and was "viewpoint neutral." The court concluded that both of these requirements were met, and therefore the school policy was legally permissible. The court noted that religious groups are free to use school property after hours for purposes of discussing religious material or material with a religious viewpoint. It was only the use of school property for religious worship that was excluded.

§ 14-06 Nonrecurring Use of Public Property by Adults for Religious Events and Activities

Key point 14-06. Adults may use public property for religious purposes if the property is used by community organizations for non-religious purposes. Excluding religious speech, while allowing other kinds of speech, violates the first amendment guaranty of free speech.

Several courts have ruled that public school officials cannot deny use of their facilities to religious groups if nonreligious community groups are permitted to use the facilities. In 1993, the United States Supreme Court unanimously ruled that a public high school that allows various community groups to rent its auditorium for "social, civic and recreational meetings and entertainments, and other uses pertaining to the welfare of the community," cannot deny the same privilege to a church that wants to rent the auditorium to show a religiously-oriented film series on family values.[54] Section 414 of the New York Education Law autho-

---

[53] Bronx Household of Faith v. Community School District, 127 F.3d 207 (2nd Cir. 1997).
[54] Lamb's Chapel v. Center Moriches Union Free School District, 113 S. Ct. 2141 (1993).

rizes local school boards to adopt reasonable regulations for the use of school property for ten specified purposes when the property is not in use for school purposes. Among the permitted uses is the holding of "social, civic and recreational meetings and entertainments, and other uses pertaining to the welfare of the community; but such meetings, entertainment and uses shall be non-exclusive and open to the general public." The list of permitted uses does not include meetings for religious purposes, and a regulation interpreting section 414 specifies that "school premises shall not be used by any group for religious purposes."

Lamb's Chapel (the "church"), an evangelical church, twice applied to a local public school district for permission to use school facilities to show a six-part film series advocating traditional, Christian family values as the only deterrent to the undermining influences of the media. The school district denied the first application, saying that "[t]his film does appear to be church related and therefore your request must be refused."

The church brought suit in federal district court, challenging the school district's denial as a violation of the first amendment's guarantees of speech, assembly, and religion. The church argued that since school properties could be used for "social, civic, and recreational" purposes, the school district had opened them to such a wide variety of "communicative purposes" that they were in effect "public forums," like public parks and sidewalks in which few restrictions on free speech are tolerated. The district court summarily dismissed the church's lawsuit, rejecting all of the church's claims. The church appealed this ruling, and a federal appeals court affirmed the judgment of the district court "in all respects."

The Supreme Court unanimously reversed the decisions of the district court and appeals court, and ruled in favor of the church. The Court noted that a public school may be a public forum, a limited public forum, or neither, depending on the circumstances of each case. A public school is an *open forum* if its facilities may be used by any outside organization without limitation. However, a public school becomes a *limited forum* if it may be used by only some outside organizations. This, of course, was the case here, since New York law specified that public school property could be used only for designated purposes including "social, civic and recreational meetings and entertainments, and other uses pertaining to the welfare of the community." The Court acknowledged that a public school could prohibit use of its facilities by any outside organization, in which case it would be neither an open forum nor a limited forum. It observed that "there is no question" that a school district "may legally preserve the property under its control for the use to which it is dedicated," and that the school district in this case "need not have permitted" after-hours use of its property by any community group.

The Court noted that the school district's properties in this case were "heavily used by a wide variety of private organizations." These included a New Age religious group known as the "Mind Center," the Southern Harmonize Gospel Singers, the Salvation Army Youth Band, a Council of Churches concert, the humane society's auction, a dance group, a baseball clinic, the chamber of commerce's "town fair day," a drama club, and both boy scouts and girl scouts. When a public school becomes a limited public forum, open to certain types of outside organizations, school officials cannot deny access to school facilities by a permissible group solely on the basis of the content of its speech. It observed:

> [T]he government violates the first amendment when it denies access to a speaker solely to suppress the point of view he espouses on an otherwise includable subject. The film involved here no doubt dealt with a subject otherwise permissible under [the school district's regulations], and its exhibition was denied solely because the film dealt with the subject from a religious standpoint. The principle that has emerged from our cases "is that the first amendment forbids the govern-

ment to regulate speech in ways that favor some viewpoints or ideas at the expense of others."[55] That principle applies in the circumstances of this case . . . .

The Court rejected as "unfounded" the school district's argument that to permit its properties to be used for religious purposes would be an establishment of religion forbidden by the first amendment. The Court observed:

> The showing of this film would not have been during school hours, would not have been sponsored by the school, and would have been open to the public, not just to church members. The [school district's properties] had repeatedly been used by a wide variety of private organizations. Under these circumstances . . . there would have been no realistic danger that the community would think that the [school district] was endorsing religion or any particular creed, and any benefit to religion or to the church would have been no more than incidental.

The Court also rejected the school district's claim that it had justifiably denied use of its property to a "radical" church for the purpose of proselytizing, since to do otherwise would have lead to threats of public unrest and even violence. The Court noted, "There is nothing in the record to support such a justification, which in any event would be difficult to defend as a reason to deny the presentation of a religious point of view about a subject the [school district] otherwise makes open to discussion on [its] property."

Example. A school district opens its facilities for a limited number of specified uses, including "concerts." Several rock concerts (by outside musical groups) are conducted on school property during the current year. A church requests permission to use a public high school auditorium for a concert by a religious group. School officials deny permission on the ground that this would "promote religion." Such a denial would violate the church's constitutional right to free speech according to the Supreme Court's decision in the Lamb's Chapel case.

Example. A school district adopts a policy denying use of its facilities by any community group. A church requests permission to use a public high school auditorium for a religious service. School officials deny permission. Such a denial would be permissible according to the Supreme Court's decision in the Lamb's Chapel case, since the church is not being treated less favorably than other community groups solely on the basis of the religious content of its message.

Example. A school district opens its facilities for a limited number of specified uses, including "civic and cultural" uses. A church requests permission to rent a public high school auditorium for a baccalaureate service for graduating high school students. School officials deny permission on the ground that this would "promote religion." The Court did not address the legality of such a denial in the Lamb's Chapel case. However, an argument could be made that the school officials' actions violate the first amendment guaranty of free speech based on the following factors: (1) A baccalaureate service is a "civic or cultural" event, and accordingly use of school facilities cannot be denied for such a purpose solely on the basis of the religious content of the speech. (2) If school officials have allowed any religious group to use its facilities in the past, then it would be impermissible to deny use of those same facilities for a baccalaureate service. (3) By creating a limited public forum, public school officials cannot deny access to school facilities solely on the basis of the content of an organization's speech (whether that speech is religious, political, philosophical, or of any other variety). This third argument was not addressed by the Supreme

---

[55] City Council of Los Angeles v. Taxpayers for Vincent, 466 U.S. 789, 804 (1984).

Court in the Lamb's Chapel case, but this does not mean that the Court would not recognize it. Some lower federal courts in fact have recognized this argument. (4) The Court noted in the Lamb's Chapel case that "[a]ccess to a [limited public forum] can be based on subject matter or speaker identity so long as the distinctions drawn are reasonable and viewpoint neutral." An argument could be made that an absolute ban on religious speech does not satisfy this test, particularly if the list of "acceptable" organizations and viewpoints is large. (5) The Court in Lamb's Chapel was impressed with the church's argument that the school district "had opened its property for such a wide variety of communicative purposes that restrictions on communicative uses of the property were subject to the same constitutional limitations as restrictions in traditional public fora such as parks and sidewalks. Hence, its view was that subject-matter or speaker exclusions on district property were required to be justified by a compelling state interest and to be narrowly drawn to achieve that end." While noting that the trial court and appeals court in this case had rejected this argument, the Supreme Court concluded that "[t]he argument has considerable force, for the district's property is heavily used by a wide variety of private organizations . . . ." (6) In Lamb's Chapel, the Court noted that it had previously ruled, in Widmar v. Vincent,[56] that permitting use of public university property for religious services and functions was constitutionally permissible, since the property was open to a wide variety of organizations.

Example. A school district opens its facilities for a limited number of specified uses, including "civic and cultural" uses. A church requests permission to rent a public high school auditorium every Sunday for weekly worship services for a period of 18 months while a new church sanctuary is under construction. School officials deny permission on the ground that this would "promote religion." The Court did not address the legality of such a denial in the Lamb's Chapel case. The church had applied to school authorities for such permission, but permission was denied and the church chose not to appeal this denial in court. An argument could be made that the school officials' actions violate the first amendment guaranty of free speech based on the same factors mentioned in the previous example.

Example. A school district opens its facilities to a wide variety of community groups, and on several occasions has permitted religious groups to use its facilities. A church requests permission to use a public high school auditorium for a one-time religious service. School officials deny permission on the ground that this would "promote religion." Such a denial would violate the church's constitutional right to free speech according to the Supreme Court's decision in the Lamb's Chapel case. In Lamb's Chapel, the Court noted that it had previously ruled, in Widmar v. Vincent,[57] that permitting use of public university property for religious purposes under the university's "open access" policy was constitutionally permissible.

Example. A federal appeals court ruled that a religious group could use a public library's auditorium for prayer meetings since the auditorium was made available to a variety of other community groups.[58] The religious group requested permission to use the library auditorium, but its request was denied because of a library policy prohibiting use of its auditorium by religious or political groups. The religious group promptly sought a court order forcing the library to permit it to use the auditorium on the ground that the library's policy violated the group's constitutionally protected rights of free speech, assembly, and religion. A trial court issued an injunction compelling the library to permit the religious group to meet, and the library appealed. The federal appeals court for the fifth circuit agreed with the trial court's decision in favor of the religious group. The court noted that the library had permitted

---

[56] 454 U. S. 263, 271 (1981).

[57] *Id.*

[58] Concerned Women for America v. LaFayette County, 883 F.2d 32 (5th Cir. 1989).

various groups to use the auditorium, including the American Association of University Women, an association of retired federal workers, the United States Navy, the United Way, American Legion, an adult AIDS program, and a swimming club. It also allowed a young girl to use the auditorium for a piano recital. The court concluded that the library, by allowing these groups to use the auditorium, had created a "public forum" and accordingly could not deny any other group access to the same facility solely on the basis of the content of its speech. Since the library denied the religious group access to the auditorium solely on the basis of the religious content of its speech, the denial violated the group's constitutional rights. "It is elementary," the court concluded, "that the government may not exclude speech on the basis of its content from . . . a public forum." The court also rejected the library's argument that allowing the religious group to use its auditorium would violate the first amendment's "nonestablishment of religion" clause. It observed that "in the absence of empirical evidence that religious groups will dominate use of the library's auditorium, causing the advancement of religion to become the forum's 'primary effect,' an equal access policy will not offend the [nonestablishment of religion] clause."

Example. *A federal appeals court ruled that a city could not refuse to allow an evangelistic film on the life of Christ to be shown at a city-owned "senior citizen center."[59] A city owns and operates six senior centers. The centers are multipurpose facilities that provide forums for lectures, classes, movies, crafts, bingo, dancing, physical exercise, and other activities. People who use the senior centers do not reside there, and all of the programs are voluntary. Many of the programs at the senior centers are organized and sponsored by private individuals or organizations. Senior center policies permit non-member groups to use the centers for classes and other activities if the subject matter is "of interest to senior citizens." Alternatively, groups may use the centers without regard to this subject matter requirement if they are composed of seventy-five percent or more senior citizens. Nonmembers or persons under fifty-five years of age may conduct classes, and people who deliver lectures or teach classes are also permitted to distribute literature. The range of subjects that qualify as being "of interest to senior citizens" is quite broad. The senior centers' activities catalogs list many of the programs that meet this requirement, including a number of classes and presentations in which religion or religious matters are the primary focus, such as Bible as Literature, Myths and Stories About the Millennium, Theosophy, and A Passover Commemoration (an oratorio). The catalogs encourage "ideas for new classes and programs" as well. In 1994 a pastor (over the age of fifty-five) requested permission from the supervisor of one of the centers to show a two-hour film entitled "Jesus." A city official denied the pastor's request, stating that city policy prohibited the use of senior centers "for sectarian instruction or as a place for religious worship." A federal appeals court ruled that the city acted improperly in denying the pastor's request to show the religious film. The court began its opinion by noting that the senior centers were limited public forums because the city limited access to these centers in two ways. First, it imposes an age requirement for participation; and second, it limits the subject matter of presentations to topics "of interest to senior citizens." Restrictions on access to such forums based on speaker identity and subject matter "are permissible only if the distinctions drawn are reasonable in light of the purpose served by the forum and are viewpoint neutral." The city claimed that its policy denying religious instruction is a restriction based upon "content," not viewpoint, because it disallows all religious instruction and worship in its senior centers regardless of the particular religion involved. The court disagreed. It pointed out that the city had already "opened the doors" of its senior centers to presentations about religion. The city allowed speakers to discuss the Bible from a "strictly historical" perspective and to address religion as long as such presentations could be characterized as "a literature discussion or a philosophical discussion." The court con-*

---

[59] Church on the Rock v. City of Albuquerque, 84 F.3d 1273 (10th Cir. 1996).

tinued, "The film ran afoul of city policy . . . by advocating the adoption of the Christian faith. In contrast, a film about Jesus's life that ended on a skeptical note and urged agnosticism or atheism would not have contravened the city's policy. Because the prohibited perspective, not the general subject matter, triggered the decision to bar the private expression, the city's policy is properly analyzed as a viewpoint-based restriction on speech." The court noted that "government bears a particularly heavy burden in justifying viewpoint-based restrictions in designated public forums" since viewpoint discrimination is "an egregious form of content discrimination." At a minimum, to survive strict scrutiny the city's policy must be "narrowly drawn to effectuate a compelling state interest." The court concluded that this test was not met. As a result, the city violated the first amendment guaranty of free speech by refusing to allow the film "Jesus" to be shown.

Example. *Must a public high school rent its auditorium to a church that wants to conduct a baccalaureate service for graduating seniors and their families?[60] Yes, concluded a federal district court in Alabama. The church requested permission to rent the school auditorium since no local church was large enough to accommodate the expected crowd. The school routinely rented its auditorium to a wide variety of community groups at a fee of $200 per day, but the school board rejected the church's request since it would involve a religious service. The church asked a court to issue an order requiring the school to rent its facility to the church for the baccalaureate service. The court agreed. It noted that when public property is opened to a wide range of community groups, it becomes a "public forum," and as such it must be available to any group regardless of the content of its speech. The court concluded that the school had created a public forum by making its auditorium available to a wide range of community groups, and accordingly it could not deny the same privilege to a church solely on the basis of the religious nature of the intended use.*

Example. *The Arizona Supreme Court concluded that the rental of a state university stadium to an evangelist for religious services did not constitute the establishment of a religion.[61] The court concluded, "We do not believe that leasing Sun Devil Stadium for an occasional religious service at a fair rental value is an appropriation or application of public property for religious purposes . . . . The twin keys to the use of the stadium are fair rental value and the occasional nature of the use. The lease to a religious group, on a permanent basis, of property on the University campus, for example, would be an entirely different matter because by the permanency of the arrangement, the prestige of the State would be placed behind a particular religion or religion generally. Also, the lease of campus facilities for occasional use, but not for fair rental value, would violate the provision of our Constitution [i.e., of the State of Arizona] as being an appropriation or application of State property for religious purposes."*

Example. *A federal court in New York ruled that a church could not be denied use of public school property that was made available to other community groups including at least one other religious organization.[62] A Methodist church asked permission to conduct a magic show on public school property. The church's application to the school indicated that the show would be performed by a Christian illusionist, and would include a religious service. The school board denied this request on the basis of a state law banning use of public school property by religious organizations for religious purposes. The church sued the school board, claiming that its actions violated the constitutional guarantees of speech and religion. The church acknowledged that state law banned the use of public school property for religious purposes, but it noted that the school board had permitted a Pentecostal church to conduct a*

---

[60] Verbena United Methodist Church v. Chilton County, 765 F. Supp. 704 (M.D. Ala. 1991).
[61] Pratt v. Arizona Board of Regents, 520 P.2d 514 (Ariz. 1974).
[62] Trinity United Methodist Parish v. Board of Education, 907 F. Supp. 707 (S.D.N.Y. 1995).

"Holy Ghost filled concert" on the same public school property that included singing, a sermon by a pastor, and an "altar call." The court concluded that the school board's denial of the church's application to use the school property violated the constitutional guaranty of free speech. The court noted that the guaranty of free speech does not guarantee "unlimited access to government-owned property for purposes of expression" and that "depending on the nature of the property, the government may regulate access." The court also noted that speech may occur in various contexts. The school board claimed that state law had created a limited public forum that was available only to nonreligious groups. However, the court concluded that even if the school board had created a limited open forum, religious services were a permitted use since the board had previously allowed a church choir to use school property for a concert and religious service. As a result, it could not deny access by any group wanting to use the property for religious purposes. The court rejected the school board's argument that allowing the church to use school property for a religious service would violate the first amendment's nonestablishment of religion clause. It observed: "[The performance] would not have occurred during school hours, would not have been sponsored by the school, and would have been open to the public, not just to church members. In addition, the school facilities have repeatedly been used by a variety of private organizations. [The Supreme Court has ruled] that where a forum is available to a broad class of speakers, allowing religious speech does not confer any imprimatur of state approval on religious sects or practices." The court concluded that "[t]he gospel concert occurred and it created at least a limited public forum for entertainment events including prayer, religious instruction, music and religious testimony. This means that the school board cannot selectively deny access for activities of the same genre . . . ."

§ 14-07 Use of Public School Property by Students for Religious Purposes

Key point 14-07. *Public school property may be used during noninstructional hours by students for religious purposes if noncurriculum-related student groups are permitted to use school property during noninstructional hours.*

Resource. *In 1998, the federal government issued to every public school in America a document entitled "Religious Expression in Public Schools." This document was designed to inform public school administrators of the religious rights enjoyed by public school students while at school. These guidelines are reprinted in full in Appendix 5 at the end of this text.*

In 1990, the Supreme Court upheld the constitutionality of the "Equal Access Act," which prohibits public high schools from denying any group access during noninstructional hours to school facilities if the same right is given to any noncurriculum related student groups.[63] The Equal Access Act provides:

It shall be unlawful for any public secondary school which receives federal financial assistance and which has a *limited open forum* to deny equal access or a fair opportunity to, or discriminate against, any students who wish to conduct a meeting within that limited open forum on the basis of the religious, political, philosophical, or other content of the speech at such meetings.[64]

A "limited open forum" exists whenever a public high school "grants an offering to or opportunity for one or more *noncurriculum related student groups* to meet on school premises during noninstructional time." A school is deemed to offer a *fair opportunity* to students wishing to conduct a meeting on school premises

---

[63] Board of Education v. Mergens, 110 S. Ct. 2356 (1990). The *Mergens* case also is discussed in section 12-12, *supra.*
[64] 20 U.S.C. §§ 4071-4074.

during noninstructional hours if it uniformly provides that (1) the meeting is voluntary and student-initiated; (2) there is no sponsorship of the meeting by the school; (3) employees or agents of the school are present at religious meetings only in a nonparticipatory capacity; (4) the meeting does not materially interfere with the orderly conduct of educational activities within the school; and (5) nonschool persons may not direct, conduct, control, or regularly attend activities of student groups.[65] However, the assignment of a teacher, administrator, or other school employee to a meeting for custodial purposes does not constitute impermissible sponsorship. The term *noninstructional time* refers to time set aside by the school before actual classroom instruction begins or after actual classroom instruction ends.

The Supreme Court began its opinion by noting that the critical question is whether or not a public high school permits "noncurriculum related" student groups to use school facilities during noninstructional hours. If it does, then the school has created a "limited open forum," and the Equal Access Act prevents school officials from denying any other student group access to school facilities during noninstructional hours on the basis of the content of its speech. The Court concluded:

> [W]e think that the term "noncurriculum related student group" is best interpreted broadly to mean any student group that does not *directly* relate to the body of courses offered by the school. In our view, a student group directly relates to a school's curriculum if the subject matter of the group is actually taught, or will soon be taught, in a regularly offered course; if the subject matter of the group concerns the body of courses as a whole; if participation in the group is required for a particular course; or if participation in the group results in academic credit. We think this limited definition of groups that directly relate to the curriculum is a common sense interpretation of the Act that is consistent with Congress' intent . . . . For example, a French club would directly relate to the curriculum if a school taught French in a regularly offered course or planned to teach the subject in the near future. A school's student government would generally relate directly to the curriculum to the extent that it addresses concerns, solicits opinions, and formulates proposals pertaining to the body of courses offered by the school. If participation in a school's band or orchestra were required for the band or orchestra classes, or resulted in academic credit, then those groups would also directly relate to the curriculum. The existence of such groups at a school would not trigger the Act's obligations.
>
> On the other hand, unless a school could show that groups such as a chess club, a stamp collecting club, or a community service club fell within our description of groups that directly relate to the curriculum, such groups would be "noncurriculum related student groups" for purposes of the Act. The existence of such groups would create a "limited open forum" under the Act and would prohibit the school from denying equal access to any other student group on the basis of the content of that group's speech. Whether a specific student group is a "noncurriculum related student group" will therefore depend on a particular school's curriculum, but such determinations would be subject to factual findings well within the competence of trial courts to make.[66]

Public high school officials in the *Mergens* case had attempted to bar religious groups by claiming that the school had not created a limited open forum since all non-religious groups were curriculum related. To illustrate, the school contended that all of its 30 non-religious student groups were curriculum related because they furthered the general educational goals of the school. The student government club "advances the goals

---

[65] 20 U.S.C. § 4071(c).
[66] 110 S. Ct. at 2366-67.

of the school's political science classes," the scuba club "furthers the essential goals of the physical education department," the chess club "supplements math and science courses," and the junior rotarians "promote effective citizenship—a critical goal of the social sciences department." The Court rejected this analysis, noting that

> [a]llowing such a broad interpretation of "curriculum related" would make the [Act] meaningless. A school's administration could simply declare that it maintains a closed forum and choose which student clubs it wanted to allow by tying the purpose of those clubs to some broadly defined educational goal. At the same time the administration could arbitrarily deny access to school facilities to any unfavored student club on the basis of its speech content. This is exactly the result that Congress sought to prohibit by enacting the [Act]. A public secondary school cannot simply declare that it maintains a closed forum and then discriminate against a particular student group on the basis of the content of the speech of that group.[67]

The Court concluded that the school had a number of noncurriculum related student groups under the test that it announced. Examples cited by the Court included the scuba club and chess club. It did not evaluate any other clubs, but hinted that a number of the other groups also would be noncurriculum related. Because the school clearly allowed one or more noncurriculum related student groups to meet during noninstructional hours, it had created a limited open forum and could not discriminate against students wanting to meet for religious purposes.

The Court acknowledged that a school wishing to avoid the obligations of the Equal Access Act could do so by "structuring its course offerings and existing student groups to avoid the Act's obligations." In other words, a school could eliminate all student groups that are not directly related to courses offered at the school. A school that took such action would avoid creating a limited open forum, and accordingly it would have no legal obligation to permit student religious groups to meet. The Court refused to decide whether student groups have a constitutionally protected right to meet on public high school property.

The Act does *not* apply to student groups that meet *during* regular classroom hours. It only applies to schools that permit student groups to meet before or after regular classroom hours.

The Court rejected the school's argument that the Equal Access Act violated the first amendment's nonestablishment of religion clause. The Court applied its 20-year-old "three-part test" for evaluating the constitutionality of a law challenged under the nonestablishment of religion clause—(1) does it have a clearly secular purpose, (2) does it have a primary effect that neither advances nor inhibits religion, and (3) does it avoid an "excessive entanglement" between church and state? All three of these tests must be satisfied for a challenged law to be constitutional. The Court concluded that all three tests were met—the Act had a "secular purpose" of demonstrating neutrality rather than hostility toward religion, and it did not create an excessive entanglement between church and state. The second test—the primary effect of the law does not advance religion—was the most difficult to answer, but the Court unequivocally ruled that this test was satisfied as well. The school had argued that the Act failed this test since it required public schools to "endorse" religious clubs and provide them with an official platform to proselytize other students. The Court rejected this claim, noting that the message of the Act "is one of neutrality rather than endorsement . . . the [Constitution] does not license government to treat religion and those who teach or practice it . . . as subversive of American ideals and therefore subject to unique disabilities." Further, the Court observed that

---

[67] *Id.* at 2369, quoting with approval from the appeals court's decision, at 867 F.2d 1076, 1078 (8th Cir. 1989).

there is a crucial difference between *government* speech endorsing religion, which the establishment clause forbids, and *private* speech endorsing religion, which the free speech and free exercise [of religion] clause protect. We think that secondary school students are mature enough and are likely to understand that a school does not endorse or support student speech that it merely permits on a nondiscriminatory basis. . . . [S]chools do not endorse everything they fail to censor.[68]

The Supreme Court has recognized the right of students to meet for religious purposes on public university property if the same privilege is granted to non-religious student groups. In 1981, the Court struck down a policy of the University of Missouri at Kansas City that made university facilities available generally to all student groups except those wanting to meet for religious worship and religious teaching.[69] The Court stressed that if a university regulation excludes any group from meeting solely on the basis of the content of the group's speech, the university must show that the regulation is necessary to serve a compelling state interest and that it is narrowly drawn to achieve that end. In rejecting the university's claim that the maintenance of a strict separation of church and state constituted a sufficiently "compelling" interest to justify the abridgment of religious expression, the Court observed:

Our cases have required the most exacting scrutiny in cases in which a State undertakes to regulate speech on the basis of content. On the other hand, the State interest asserted here—in achieving greater separation than is already ensured under the establishment clause of the Federal Constitution—is limited by the free exercise clause and in this case by the free speech clause as well. In this constitutional context, we are unable to recognize the State's interest as sufficiently "compelling" to justify the content-based discrimination against students' religious speech.[70]

The Court emphasized that a university can impose reasonable regulations affecting the time and place of group meetings, and can exclude any group that violates reasonable campus rules or substantially interferes with the opportunity of other students to obtain an education. It also held that if a school does not make its facilities available to any student group, it is not required to make them available to religious groups.

Similarly, the Supreme Court of Delaware invalidated an absolute ban by the University of Delaware on all religious activities in school buildings.[71] The university's ban barred Christian students from meeting periodically in the "commons" rooms of campus dormitories for religious worship. The Court concluded that

the University cannot support its absolute ban of all religious worship on the theory that, without such a ban, University policy allowing all student groups, including religious groups, free access to dormitory common areas would necessarily violate the establishment clause. The establishment cases decided by the United States Supreme Court indicate that neutrality is the safe harbor in which to avoid first amendment violation: neutral "accommodation" of religion is permitted, while "promotion" and "advancement" of religion are not. University policy without the worship ban could be neutral toward religion and could have the primary effect of advancing education by allowing students to meet together in the commons rooms of their dormitory to exchange ideas and share mutual interests. If any religious group or religion is accommodated or benefited thereby,

---

[68] *Id.* at 2372.
[69] Widmar v. Vincent, 454 U.S. 263 (1981). *See also* Clergy and Laity Concerned v. Chicago Board of Education, 586 F. Supp. 1408 (N.D. Ill. 1984).
[70] *Id.* at 277 (citations omitted).
[71] Keegan v. University of Delaware, 349 A.2d 18 (Del. 1975).

such accommodation or benefit is purely incidental, and would not, in our judgment, violate the establishment clause.[72]

The court distinguished decisions prohibiting religious exercise by public primary and secondary school students on the ground that such decisions did not, like the present case, involve "activity by adult residents of a living complex in common areas generally set aside for the benefit of such residents."[73]

Example. A federal appeals court ruled that a public school district violated the constitutional rights of a Christian student group by denying it access to school property after school hours while permitting a secular organization with similar purposes to meet on school property.[74] A public school district adopted a policy prohibiting any group to meet on school premises between 3:00 and 6:00 p.m. other than Scouts and athletic groups. A Christian student group sued the school district claiming that this policy violated the first amendment guaranty of free speech. The Christian group was organized to foster the moral development of school students from a Christian perspective. Its activities include singing, skits, Bible reading, prayer, and speeches by community role models. The Christian group claimed that both it and the Scouts had the same purpose of fostering the moral development of youth, and that the school district could not deny it access to school property solely on the basis of the religious content of its speech. A federal appeals court ruled in favor of the Christian group. The court began its opinion by referring to a Supreme Court decision holding that a public school district could not deny a Christian group access to school property to show a family film series solely on the basis of the religious perspective of the films, when the same property was available to secular groups to address similar issues from a secular perspective. The Supreme Court concluded that "the government violates the first amendment when it denies access to a speaker solely to suppress the point of view he espouses on an otherwise includable subject. The film involved here no doubt dealt with a subject otherwise permissible under [the school district's regulations], and its exhibition was denied solely because the film dealt with the subject from a religious standpoint. The principle that has emerged from our cases "is that the first amendment forbids the government to regulate speech in ways that favor some viewpoints or ideas at the expense of others."[75] The appeals court concluded that this principle required the school district in this case to permit the Christian group to meet. It noted that the school made its facilities available to the Scouts to promote the moral development of youth from a secular perspective, and accordingly it could not deny a Christian group the same privilege solely on the basis of the religious content of its speech. Any other result would permit the school district to prefer some viewpoints on the same subject matter over others, and this is precisely what is prohibited by the first amendment's guaranty of free speech. In summary, when a public school (or other public entity) creates a "non-public forum" by opening its property to only some groups to address a limited range of issues, it cannot prohibit other groups from using the same property to address similar issues solely on the basis of the religious content of their speech. The court rejected the school district's argument that banning religious groups served a compelling and legitimate governmental interest of avoiding any violation of the first amendment's prohibition of the establishment of religion.

Example. A federal appeals court ruled that a public high school that allowed several student groups to meet on school premises during the lunch period could not deny the same opportunity to a student group that wanted to meet for religious purposes.[76] All students at the school had the same lunch period each

---

[72] *Id.* at 16 (citations omitted).

[73] *Id.* at 18.

[74] Good News/Good Sports Club v. School District, 28 F.3d 1501 (8th Cir. 1994).

[75] Lamb's Chapel v. Center Moriches Union Free School District, 113 S. Ct. 2141 (1993).

[76] Ceniceros v. Board of Trustees, 106 F.3d 878 (9th Cir. 1997).

day, and so no classes were conducted during the lunch period. School officials permitted several student groups to meet during the lunch period, including a surfing club, conservation club, and various ethnic organizations. A student asked a school official for permission to organize a religious club that would meet during the lunch period in an empty classroom. Permission was denied by school officials who insisted that the Equal Access Act did not apply since the lunch period was not "noninstructional time." The student sued the school, and a federal appeals court ruled in favor of the student. The court concluded that a lunch period is "noninstructional time" since the school had "set aside" the lunch period after morning classes ended and before afternoon classes began. The court noted that the United States Supreme Court had ruled that the Equal Access Act reflected a "broad legislative purpose" and must be given a "broad meaning." The court cautioned that the religious club's right to meet "is defined by the extent to which other groups were permitted to meet." It continued, "Our decision today does not necessarily preclude school districts from disallowing religious groups from using school premises for meetings during lunch periods. The Act is about equal access. If a school district wanted to prohibit religious groups from meeting during lunch, the school need only make its prohibition neutral, so that all noncurriculum-related groups are barred from meeting at lunch." The court summarily rejected the school's claim that the first amendment's nonestablishment of religion clause prohibited public school property from being used for religious purposes. It noted that the Supreme Court rejected this argument in a 1990 ruling.

§ 14-08 Sunday Closing Laws

> **Key point 14-08.** *Local ordinances requiring some or all businesses to be closed on Sundays do not violate the first amendment's nonestablishment of religion clause.*

The Supreme Court has upheld the validity of Sunday closing laws against the claim that they constitute the establishment of the Christian religion.[77] The Court has observed:

> [T]he "establishment" clause does not ban federal or state regulation of conduct whose reason or effect merely happens to coincide or harmonize with the tenets of some or all religions. . . . Sunday is a day apart from all others. The cause is irrelevant; the fact exists. It would seem unrealistic for enforcement purposes and perhaps detrimental to the general welfare to require a State to choose a common day of rest other than that which most persons would select of their own accord.[78]

Numerous state and lower federal court rulings have upheld the validity of Sunday closing laws against the contentions that such laws (1) are unconstitutionally vague and uncertain in describing the activities that are either forbidden or allowed,[79] (2) unconstitutionally discriminate against religions that do not observe a Sunday sabbath,[80] (3) "establish" a religion,[81] (4) constitute an impermissible exercise of the police power,[82]

---

[77] Braunfeld v. Brown, 366 U.S. 599 (1961); McGowan v. Maryland, 366 U.S. 420 (1961).

[78] McGown v. Maryland, 366 U.S. 420, 442, 452 (1961).

[79] *See, e.g.,* Mack Paramus Co. v. Borough of Paramus, 549 A.2d 474 (N.J. Super. 1988); Hechinger Co. v. State's Attorney, 326 A.2d 742 (Md. 1974); Voronado, Inc. v. Hyland, 390 A.2d 606 (N.J. 1978), *appeal dismissed,* 439 U.S. 1123 (1978); Charles Stores Co. v. Tucker 140 S.E.2d 370 (N.C. 1965).

[80] *See, e.g.,* Mack Paramus Co. v. Borough of Paramus, 549 A.2d 474 (N.J. Super. 1988); Raleigh Mobile home Sales, Inc. v. Tomlinson, 174 S.E.2d 542 (N.C. 1970); State v. Giant of St. Albans, Inc., 268 A.2d 739 (Vt. 1970).

[81] *See, e.g.,* Discount Records, Inc. v. City of North Little Rock, 671 F.2d 1220 (8th Cir. 1982); Epstein v. Maddox, 277 F. Supp. 613 (N.D. Ga. 1967), *aff'd,* 401 F.2d 777 (1967); Mandel v. Hodges, 127 Cal. Rptr. 244 (Cal. 1976); People v. Acme Markets, Inc., 372 N.Y.S.2d 590 (1975).

(5) arbitrarily discriminate between those commodities that may be sold and those that may not,[83] (6) deny the equal protection of the laws,[84] (7) violate merchants' constitutional right of "commercial speech,"[85] and (8) are invalid due to lax and inconsistent enforcement.[86]

The Virginia Supreme Court ruled that a state Sunday closing law violated the Virginia Constitution's prohibition against "special laws."[87] Virginia enacted its first Sunday closing law in 1610. During the colonial period, this law had a religious purpose, requiring every person "to repair in the morning to the divine service." During the Revolutionary War, in 1779, a Sunday closing law was substituted that had an entirely "secular" purpose—to "prevent the physical and moral debasement which comes from uninterrupted labor." The 1779 law survived until 1960, when the state legislature enacted a new law. In 1974, the legislature completely rewrote the Sunday closing law. The 1974 law generally prohibited commercial establishments to do business on Sunday, but exempted more than 60 "industries and businesses" from the prohibition, and permitted cities and counties to exempt themselves entirely from the law by a referendum vote. These exemptions left only about 20 percent of the Virginia workers subject to the law.

Under these facts, the state supreme court concluded that the 1974 law violated a provision in the Virginia Constitution prohibiting "special laws" exempting private companies from the reach of any general law unless the exemption bore "a reasonable and substantial relation to the object sought to be accomplished by the legislation." The court noted that the purpose of the law was to provide the people of Virginia with a common day of rest, and concluded that the exemption of 80 percent of the businesses and employees in the state from the reach of the Sunday closing law clearly indicated that the many exemptions did *not* bear a reasonable relationship to the object sought to be accomplished by the law. Accordingly, the law violated the ban on special legislation.

The court further held that the Virginia law did not violate the United States Constitution's guaranty of the "equal protection of the laws," since such a standard was more easily satisfied than the state constitution's "special laws" provision. Accordingly, other states will not be able to rely on the Virginia court's decision unless their state constitutions contain a similar ban on special legislation.

In a related matter, one court has held that the establishment clause was violated by an order of the governor of California granting state employees paid time off on Good Friday,[88] although the same court a year later approved the validity of a Good Friday holiday for public school employees.[89] Another court, in upholding the constitutionality of a Hawaii law declaring Good Friday to be a legal holiday, observed:

> [T]he primary purpose of the statute which establishes Good Friday as a legal holiday was to increase the number and frequency of legal holidays. This purpose is clearly secular. The court also finds that the primary effect of the statute is secular. The Good Friday holiday allows the people of Hawaii to play or pray as they see fit. Even the plaintiffs concede that many more

---

[82] *See, e.g.,* Lockwood v. State, 462 S.W.2d 465 (Ark.1971); State v. Underwood, 195 S.E. 2d 489 (N.C. 1973).

[83] *See, e.g.,* Zayre v. City of Atlanta, 276 F. Supp. 892 (N.D. Ga. 1967); Genesco, Inc. v. J. C. Penney Co., Inc., 313 So.2d 20 (Miss. 1975); State v. K Mart, 359 A.2d 492 (N.J. 1976).

[84] *See, e.g.,* Hames Mobile Homes, Inc. v. Sellers, 343 F. Supp. 12 (N.D. Iowa 1972); Southway Discount Center, Inc. v. Moore, 315 F. Supp. 617 (N.D. Ala. 1970); Supermarkets General Corp. v. State, 409 A.2d 250 (Md. 1979).

[85] *See, e.g.,* Mack Paramus Co. v. Borough of Paramus, 549 A.2d 474 (N.J. Super. 1988).

[86] *Id.*

[87] Benderson Development Co. v. Sciortino, 372 S.E.2d 751 (Va. 1988).

[88] Mandel v. Hodges, 127 Cal. Rptr. 244 (1976).

[89] California School Employees Association v. Sequoia Union High School District, 136 Cal. Rptr. 594 (1977).

people can be found in Hawaii's parks and shopping malls on Good Friday than can be found in its churches. Moreover, this court's finding that Good Friday is similar in nature to Thanksgiving and Christmas provides additional ground for insulating the Good Friday holiday from a successful constitutional challenge. Just as Christmas and Thanksgiving are permissible because of their partially secular observations and because they provide a uniform day of rest and relaxation for Americans, Good Friday has attained a secular position in this nation's traditional fabric and provides citizens of Hawaii with a uniform day of rest.[90]

One court struck down a state law prohibiting the sale of alcoholic liquor on Good Friday on the ground that the law constituted an impermissible establishment of a religion.[91]

§ 14-09 The Right to Refuse Medical Treatment

Key point 14-09. Competent adults have the right to refuse medical treatment on the basis of their religious beliefs, including potentially life-saving treatment. However, they do not have the right to withhold life-saving medical treatment from their minor children.

Several courts have dealt with the right of an individual to refuse medical treatment on religious grounds. Such cases often involve treatment that is apparently necessary to save the diseased or injured person's life. In a majority of cases, courts have upheld the right of an adult to refuse potentially life-saving medical treatment on religious grounds, unless the individual is (1) mentally incompetent, (2) the parent and sole provider of young children, or (3) a pregnant woman. The majority rule was well-summarized by a New York court:

As a general rule, every human being of adult years and sound mind has a right to determine what shall be done with his own body and cannot be subjected to medical treatment without his consent. Specifically, where there is no compelling state interest which justifies overriding an adult patient's decision not to receive blood transfusions because of religious beliefs, such transfusions should not be ordered. Such an order would constitute a violation of the first amendment's freedom of exercise clause.

However, judicial power to order compulsory medical treatment over an adult patient's objection exists in some situations. It may be the duty of the court to assume the responsibility of guardianship for a patient who is not compos mentis [mentally competent] to the extent of authorizing treatment necessary to save his life even though the medical treatment authorized may be contrary to the patient's religious beliefs. Furthermore, the state's interest, as parens patriae [i.e., protector of its citizens] in the welfare of children may justify compulsory medical care where necessary to save the life of the mother of young children or of a pregnant woman.[92]

Such cases generally involve Jehovah's Witnesses who refuse potentially life-saving blood transfusions, Christian Scientists who refuse any form of medical care, or fundamentalist Christians who rely solely on faith healing. The result generally is the same in all three cases: the courts will honor the individual's desire to refuse medical treatment so long as he or she is mentally competent, even if such a decision will result in what

---

[90] Cammack v. Waihee, 673 F. Supp. 1524, 1539-40 (D. Hawaii 1987).

[91] Griswold Inn, Inc. v. State, 441 A.2d 16 (Conn. 1981).

[92] In re Melidio, 390 N.Y.S.2d 523, 524 (1976). *Accord* Holmes v. Silver Cross Hospital, 340 F. Supp. 125 (N.D. Ill. 1972); Montgomery v. Board of Retirement, 109 Cal. Rptr. 181 (1973); In re Osborne, 294 A.2d 372 (D.C. App. 1972); People v. Duncan, 205 N.E.2d 443 (Ill. 1965).

otherwise would have been a preventable death. As the Ohio Supreme Court observed in a case involving a fundamentalist Christian's refusal to receive life-saving medical treatment on the basis of his reliance on prayer, "the state may not compel a legally competent adult to submit to medical treatment which would violate that individual's religious beliefs even though the treatment is arguably life-extending." This is so no matter how "unwise, foolish, or ridiculous" those beliefs may seem to others.[93]

While some courts have limited a competent adult's right to refuse potentially life-saving medical treatment when the individual is a parent of minor children, other courts have rejected such a limitation.

> **Example.** *The Florida Supreme Court ruled that a civil court could not force a mother to receive a life-saving blood transfusion against her will and contrary to her religious beliefs.[94] The woman entered a public hospital suffering from "dysfunctional uterine bleeding," and was informed by doctors that she would die if she did not receive a blood transfusion. The woman, a practicing Jehovah's Witness and mother of two minor children, refused the transfusion on the ground that it would violate her religious beliefs (she was competent at the time of her decision). The hospital asked a civil court to force the woman to undergo a blood transfusion. The court granted the hospital's request and ordered the woman to undergo a transfusion (she was by then unconscious) on the ground that "minor children have a right to be reared by two loving parents, a right which overrides the mother's right of free exercise [of religion] and privacy." Upon regaining consciousness, the woman appealed the court's order to a state appeals court, which ruled in favor of the woman. The hospital appealed the case to the state supreme court, which also ruled in favor of the woman. The court cited four factors to consider in deciding whether or not a patient's constitutional right to religious freedom outweighs the state's interest in requiring potentially life-saving medical treatment: "(1) preservation of life, (2) protection of innocent third parties, (3) prevention of suicide, and (4) maintenance of the ethical integrity of the medical profession." The court disagreed with the hospital's claim that the state's interest in maintaining a home with two parents for minor children outweighed any constitutional right of the mother to terminate her life by refusing medical treatment. It concluded, "[This case involves] a delicate balancing analysis in which the courts weigh, on the one hand, the patient's constitutional right of privacy and right to practice one's religion, as against certain basic societal interests. Obviously, there are no preordained answers to such problematic questions and the results reached in these cases are highly debatable. Running through all of these decisions, however, is the courts' deeply imbedded belief, rooted in our constitutional traditions, that an individual has a fundamental right to be left alone so that he is free to lead his private life according to his own beliefs free from unreasonable governmental interference. Surely nothing, in the last analysis, is more private or more sacred than one's religion or view of life, and here the courts, quite properly, have given great deference to the individual's right to make decisions vitally affecting his private life according to his own conscience. It is difficult to overstate this right because it is, without exaggeration, the very bedrock on which this country was founded."*

The courts have consistently held that life-saving medical treatment can be administered to a minor child despite his or her parents' refusal to consent to such treatment on religious grounds, unless the treatment itself poses a significant danger to the child. One court observed:

> [P]arents . . . have a perfect right to worship as they please and believe what they please. They enjoy complete freedom of religion. The parents also have the right to use all lawful means to

---

[93] In re Milton, 505 N.E.2d 255 (Ohio 1987).
[94] Public Health Trust v. Wons, 541 So.2d 96 (Fla. 1989). *See also* In re Dubreuil, 603 So.2d 538 (Fla. App.1992).

vindicate this right. . . . But this right of theirs ends where somebody else's right begins. Their child is a human being in his own right with a soul and body of his own. He has rights of his own—the right to live and grow up and live without disfigurement. The child is a citizen of the State. While he "belongs" to his parents, he belongs also to his State. Their rights in him entail many duties. Likewise, the fact the child belongs to the State imposes upon the State many duties. Chief among them is the duty to protect his right to live and to grow up with a sound mind in a sound body . . . . When a religious doctrine espoused by the parents threatens to defeat or curtail such a right of their child, the State's duty to step in and preserve the child's right is immediately operative.[95]

Another court has observed that "it does not follow that parents who wish to be martyrs for their religious beliefs have a right to impose such martyrdom upon their offspring . . . ."[96] When a minor child's life is not in danger, some courts have permitted the child's parents to refuse consent to medical treatment on religious grounds. The Supreme Court of Pennsylvania has held, "We are of the opinion that as between a parent and the state, the state does not have an interest of sufficient magnitude outweighing a parent's religious beliefs when the child's life is *not immediately imperiled* by his physical condition."[97] Other courts have reached the opposite conclusion.[98]

> **Example.** *The Massachusetts Supreme Judicial Court ordered an 8-year-old girl suffering from leukemia to receive blood transfusions despite her parents' claim that such procedures violated their religious beliefs.[99] The parents were Jehovah's Witnesses, a religion that prohibits blood transfusions. The court observed, "The state has three interests in having a dangerously sick child receive medical treatment over her parents' religious objections. First, the state has an interest in protecting the welfare of children within its borders. Second, the state has an interest in the preservation of life, especially when the affliction is curable. Finally, the medical profession is trained to preserve life, and to care for those under its control. The state has an interest in maintaining the ethical integrity of the medical profession." These interests outweighed the parents' religious rights, concluded the court.*

Some parents have been prosecuted for manslaughter (or other crimes) when their minor child dies because the parents refused life-saving medical treatment and relied exclusively on divine healing.

> **Example.** *The California Supreme Court ruled that a mother could be prosecuted for manslaughter when her child died of meningitis after being treated by prayer instead of medical therapy.[100] The victim was a 4-year-old girl who fell ill with flu-like symptoms and a stiff neck. Consistent with the tenets of her religion, the child's mother chose to treat the illness with prayer rather than medical care. Members of the mother's church prayed with the child on two occasions. Nevertheless, the child lost weight, grew disoriented and irritable, and her breathing became heavy and irregular. She died of acute meningitis 17 days after her symptoms first appeared. The child's mother was charged with*

---

[95] In re Clark, 185 N.E.2d 128, 132 (Ill. 1962). *Accord* In re Karwath, 199 N.W.2d 147 (Iowa 1972); Muhlenberg Hospital v. Patterson, 320 A.2d 518 (N.J. 1974); In re Sampson, 317 N.Y.S.2d 641 (1970); Matter of Hamilton, 657 S.W.2d 425 (Tenn. App. 1983) ("[w]here a child is dying with cancer and experiencing pain which will surely become more excruciating as the disease progresses . . . we believe is one of those times when humane considerations and life-saving attempts outweigh unlimited practices of religious belief").

[96] Muhlenberg Hospital v. Patterson, 320 A.2d 518, 521 (N.J. 1974).

[97] In re Green, 292 A.2d 387, 392 (Pa. 1972).

[98] *See, e.g.,* In re Sampson, 317 N.Y.S.2d 641 (1970).

[99] Matter of McCauley, 565 N.E.2d 411 (Mass. 1991).

[100] Walker v. Superior Court, 253 Cal. Rptr. 1 (Cal. 1988). *Accord* People in Interest of D.L.E., 645 P.2d 271 (Colo. 1982).

involuntary manslaughter, and she moved to dismiss the prosecution on the ground that her conduct was protected by law. Specifically, the mother argued that involuntary manslaughter is defined as the unlawful killing of a human being without malice "in the commission of an unlawful act . . . or without due caution or circumspection," and that her child had not died "in the commission of an unlawful act." She pointed out that the only "unlawful act" for which she could have been charged was the criminal neglect of a child, and that California law exempted "treatment by spiritual means through prayer alone" from the definition of criminal neglect. The state supreme court rejected the mother's arguments, concluding that she could be prosecuted for involuntary manslaughter. The court reasoned that the exemption of "treatment by spiritual means by prayer alone" from the definition of criminal neglect did not necessarily exempt such treatment from the crime of manslaughter. The court also rejected the mother's claim that her actions were protected by the constitutional guaranty of religious freedom. It observed that the mother's constitutional rights were outweighed by a "compelling state interest" of "unparalleled significance"—the protection of children. It further noted that "parents may be free to become martyrs themselves . . . but it does not follow that they are free . . . to make martyrs of their children."

Example. *A parent was prosecuted for manslaughter when his 5-week-old daughter died from bronchial pneumonia. The parent lived with his wife and 9 children in a small cabin in the mountains. He had been on a "walk of faith," which he described as a total reliance on God for all needs and for healing in times of illness or injury. One of the tenets of his church was healing of the sick through prayer. When the baby developed cold symptoms, her parents and another church member anointed the baby with oil, laid their hands on her head, and prayed for her healing. The next day, the baby's symptoms worsened. Because the mother was exhausted from caring for several sick children, and because the family's wood-burning stove seemed to aggravate the baby's condition, the baby was moved to a neighbor's home. The neighbor (who was a nurse) informed the parents that the baby might be suffering from pneumonia, and she urged them to take the baby to a hospital at once. The father declined, stating that "we can't, this is our walk and this is our life." The next morning, the baby seemed better. Later in the day, however, the symptoms worsened again, and the baby died that evening. An autopsy revealed that the baby had died from "acute necrotizing bronchial pneumonia." The father was later prosecuted for child abuse resulting in death. At the trial, a pediatrician testified that the baby would have survived had she received proper medical care. The father was convicted, and he was sentenced to 6 years of probation. On appeal, the Colorado Supreme Court reversed the father's conviction on the basis of a technicality, and sent the case back to the trial court for another trial.[101] The court noted that state law provided a defense to child abuse in cases of "treatment by spiritual means," and that the trial court had improperly let the jury decide if this defense were available rather than compelling the prosecutor to establish the crime, and the unavailability of the "treatment by spiritual means" defense, with evidence "beyond a reasonable doubt." The court cautioned that the "treatment by spiritual means" defense to child abuse was not available under state law when a child is suffering from a condition that would create a danger to the child's life if left untreated.*

Example. *A Washington state appeals court upheld the first degree manslaughter conviction of a parent who unsuccessfully relied on prayer for the healing of his minor child.[102] The victim's parents were members of a religious group that believed that the medical establishment was "wicked" and that members should rely exclusively upon prayer for healing the sick. A 10-year-old boy whose parents were members of the group began losing weight and exhibiting other abnormal symptoms. A church "elder" determined that*

---

[101] Lybarger v. People, 807 P.2d 570 (Colo. 1991).
[102] State v. Norman, 808 P.2d 1159 (Wash. App. 1991).

the boy's illness was a result of sin, and he ordered the boy to be severely spanked. Following an hour-long session of "ministering" (which consisted of intense interrogation and spanking), the boy's condition continued to worsen. The father continued slapping and spanking the child, and consulting with the elder for guidance. The elder assured the father that the boy would be alright. The boy died the next morning. He was completely emaciated and weighed only 46 pounds. It was determined that he died of untreated juvenile diabetes that had been aggravated by his frequent beatings. The boy's father was prosecuted, and convicted, of first degree manslaughter. The father appealed, claiming that his conviction violated his constitutional right to religious freedom. A state appeals court rejected the father's claim and upheld his conviction. The court observed, "[The father] was free under the Washington State Constitution to believe [his son] could be healed through prayer. He was not free to act on that belief in a manner jeopardizing the health of his child. We find no constitutional violation."

Another court found a mother guilty of neglect who believed that healing of her son's arthritic knee condition was possible only through prayer.[103]

§ 14-10 Definition of "Religion" and "Religious"

Key point 14-10. *The courts have defined the terms "religion" and "religious" broadly.*

Occasionally it is important to know how the courts have defined the term *religion*. The first amendment expressly prohibits the "establishment of religion" and protects its free exercise; the Civil Rights Act of 1964 prohibits discrimination by employers on the basis of an employee's religion; the Internal Revenue Code and several state tax laws exempt certain religious organizations from taxation; and many other federal, state, and local laws and regulations use the term.

The term *religion* is not easily defined.[104] Early court decisions generally limited the term to belief in God. For example, in 1890, the Supreme Court observed that the term *religion* "has reference to one's views of his relations to his Creator, and to the obligations they impose on reverence for his being and character, and of obedience to his will."[105] This view was articulated by numerous lower federal courts and state courts.[106]

The courts eventually interpreted the term *religion* much more broadly. In an early decision expressing the modern view, a prominent judge observed:

Religious belief arises from a sense of inadequacy of reason as a means of relating the individual to his fellow-men and to his universe. . . . It is a belief finding expression in a conscience which categorically requires the believer to disregard elementary self-interest and to accept martyrdom in preference to transgressing its tenets. . . . [Conscientious objection] may justly be regarded as a response of the individual to an inward mentor, call it a conscience or God, that is for many persons at the present time the equivalent of what has always been thought a religious impulse.[107]

---

[103] Mitchell v. Davis, 205 S.W.2d 812 (Tex. App. 1947).

[104] *See generally* Boyan, *Defining Religion in Operational and Institutional Terms*, 116 U. Pa. L. Rev. 479 (1968); Choper, *Defining "Religion" in the First Amendment*, 1982 U. Ill. Law Rev. 579, Note, *Toward a Constitutional Definition of Religion*, 91 Harv. L. Rev. 1056 (1978).

[105] Davis v. Beason, 133 U.S. 333, 342 (1890).

[106] *See, e.g.*, Borchert v. City of Ranger, 42 F. Supp. 577 (N.D. Tex. 1941); Gabrielli v. Knickerbocker, 82 P.2d 391 (Cal. App. 1938); Sunday School Board of the Southern Baptist Convention v. McCue, 293 P.2d 234 (Kan. 1956); Nicholls v. Mayor of Lynn, 7 N.E.2d 577 (Mass. 1937); Taylor v. State, 11 So.2d 663 (Miss. 1943); Kolbeck v. Kramer, 202 A.2d 889 (N.J. Super. 1964); Drozda v. Bassos, 23 N.Y.S.2d 544 (1940).

This broader definition was adopted by the Supreme Court in a series of rulings. In 1961, the Court observed that "religions" need not be based on a belief in the existence of God: "[N]either [a state nor the federal government] can constitutionally pass laws or impose requirements which aid all religions as against nonbelievers, and neither can aid those religions based on a belief in the existence of God as against those religions founded on different beliefs."[108] The Court added that "among religions in this country which do not teach what would generally be considered as a belief in the existence of God are Buddhism, Taoism, Ethical Culture, Secular Humanism and others."[109]

In two succeeding opinions, the Court defined the term *religion* in the context of section 6(j) of the Universal Military Training and Service Act of 1948, which exempts from combatant training and service in the armed forces persons who by reason of their religious training and belief are conscientiously opposed to participation in war in any form. The Act defines "religious training and belief" as "an individual's belief in a relation to a Supreme Being involving duties superior to those arising from any human relation, but [not including] essentially political, sociological, or philosophical views or a merely personal moral code." In *United States v. Seeger*,[110] the Court surprisingly interpreted this definition of "religious training and belief" to include a sincere and meaningful belief that "occupies a place in the life of its possessor parallel to that filled by the orthodox belief in God of one who clearly qualifies for the exemption. Where such beliefs have parallel positions in the lives of their respective holder we cannot say that one is 'in relation to a Supreme Being' and the other is not."[111]

In *Welsh v. United States*,[112] the Court equated purely moral or ethical convictions with "religious" belief:

Most of the great religions of today and of the past have embodied the idea of a Supreme Being or a Supreme Reality—a God—who communicates to man in some way a consciousness of what is right and should be done, of what is wrong and therefore should be shunned. If an individual deeply and sincerely holds beliefs that are purely ethical or moral in source and content but that nevertheless impose upon him a duty of conscience to refrain from participating in any war at any time, those beliefs certainly occupy in the life of that individual "a place parallel to that filled by . . . God" in traditionally religious persons. Because his beliefs function as a religion in his life, such an individual is as much entitled to a "religious" conscientious objector exemption . . . as is someone who derives his conscientious opposition to war from traditional religious convictions.[113]

Lower federal courts and state courts have applied this more liberal definition of *religion* in several cases. To illustrate, one court, in concluding that the Science of Creative Intelligence (Transcendental Meditation) is a religion, observed that "[c]oncepts concerning God or a supreme being do not shed their religiosity merely because they are presented as a philosophy or a science."[114] The court also observed that such elements as "clergy, places of worship or explicit moral code" need not be present for a practice or belief to constitute a

---

[107] United States v. Kauten, 133 F.2d 703, 708 (2nd Cir. 1943) (Judge Augustus Hand).

[108] Torasco v. Watkins, 367 U.S. 488, 495 (1961). In *Torasco*, the Court ruled that a Maryland law requiring notaries public to take an oath professing their belief in God violated the first amendment guaranty of freedom of religion.

[109] *Id.* at 495 n.11.

[110] 380 U.S. 163 (1965).

[111] *Id.* at 166. This remarkable interpretation of the plain meaning of the Act apparently was based on the Court's concern that any legislative preference of believers over nonbelievers would be unconstitutional. It is also interesting to note that the Court relied on the writings of several theologians in reaching its decision, including most notably Paul Tillich. P. TILLICH, DYNAMICS OF FAITH 1-2 (1958).

[112] 398 U.S. 333 (1970).

[113] *Id.* at 340.

[114] Malnak v. Yogi, 440 F. Supp. 1284, 1322 (D.N.J. 1977).

religion.[115] The court concluded that "a belief in the existence of a pure, perfect, infinite, and unmanifest field of life" constitutes a religious belief.[116]

Similarly, other courts have found the following beliefs and practices to be religious: witchcraft;[117] pantheistic beliefs of parents upon which they based their opposition to mandatory inoculations of their children;[118] the Black Muslim faith;[119] Krishna Consciousness;[120] and the Salvation Army.[121]

The concept of religion does have limits. The courts have concluded that the following beliefs and practices are not religious: a federal law that prohibits the use of federal funds for nontherapeutic abortions;[122] beliefs and practices that tend to mock established institutions and that are obviously shams and absurdities and whose members are patently devoid of religious sincerity;[123] refusal to accept a social security number as a precondition to the receipt of government aid;[124] the use of marijuana by an individual who claimed that marijuana "was the fire with which baptisms were conducted by John the Baptist";[125] the consumption of marijuana by an individual who claimed that it extended and intensified his "ability to engage in meditative communication with the Supreme Being, to attain spiritual peace through union with God the Father and to search out the ultimate meaning of life and nature";[126] the consumption of cat food by an individual who claimed that the food was "contributing significantly to [his] state of well-being";[127] the sale of golden eagle feathers by an Indian in violation of the Bald Eagle Protection Act;[128] deeply rooted convictions of Indian heritage;[129] the promotion of a homosexual life-style;[130] racist and antisemitic ideology;[131] publishing and distributing the Bible by an organization without any church affiliation;[132] a foundation engaged in the dissemination of religious and philosophical teachings of a Swedish theologian and philosopher;[133] a church that denied the existence of God and totally relied on human reason;[134] and a foster home controlled by two presbyteries.[135]

---

[115] *Id.* at 1326. *See also* Stevens v. Berger, 428 F. Supp. 896, 900 (E.D.N.Y. 1977) ("neither trappings of robes, nor temples of stone, nor a fixed liturgy, nor an extensive literature or history is required to meet the test of beliefs cognizable under the Constitution as religious, and one person's religious beliefs held for one day are presumptively entitled to the same protection as views of millions which have been shared for thousands of years").

[116] *Id.* at 1324.

[117] Dettmer v. Landon, 799 F.2d 929 (4th Cir. 1986).

[118] Sherr v. Northport-East Northport Union Free School District, 672 F. Supp. 81 (E.D.N.Y. 1987).

[119] Banks v. Havener, 234 F. Supp. 27 (E.D. Va. 1964).

[120] International Society for Krishna Consciousness, Inc. v. Barber, 650 F.2d 430 (2nd Cir. 1981).

[121] McClure v. Salvation Army, 460 F.2d 553 (5th Cir. 1972).

[122] Woe v. Califano, 460 F. Supp. 234 (D.C. Ohio 1978).

[123] Theriault v. Silber, 495 F.2d 390 (5th Cir. 1974).

[124] Callahan v. Woods, 479 F. Supp. 621 (D.C. Cal. 1979). *But cf.* Stevens v. Berger, 428 F. Supp. 896 (S.D.N.Y. 1977).

[125] State v. Brashear, 593 P.2d 63 (N.M. 1979). *But cf.* People v. Woody, 40 Cal. Rptr. 69 (1964) (use of peyote by members of the Native American Church held to be a "religious" practice).

[126] People v. Collins, 78 Cal. Rptr. 151 (1969).

[127] Brown v. Pena, 441 F. Supp. 1382 (D.C. Fla. 1977).

[128] United States v. Top Sky, 547 F.2d 486 (9th Cir. 1976).

[129] Matter of McMillan, 226 S.E.2d 693 (N.C. 1976).

[130] Church of the Chosen People v. United States, 548 F. Supp. 1247 (D.C. Minn. 1982).

[131] Bellamy v. Mason's Stores, Inc., 368 F. Supp. 1025 (E.D. Va. 1973).

[132] American Bible Society v. Lewisohn, 386 N.Y.S.2d 49 (1976).

[133] Swedenborg Foundation, Inc. v. Lewisohn, 386 N.Y.S.2d 54 (1976).

[134] Religious Society of Families v. Assessor, 343 N.Y.S.2d 159 (1973).

[135] N.L.R.B. v. Kemmerer Village, Inc., 907 F.2d 661 (7th Cir. 1990).

INSTRUCTIONAL AIDS TO CHAPTER 14

Terms

discretion

proselytize

public safety, convenience, peace and order

religion

Sunday closing law

time, place, and manner restrictions

Learning Objectives

- Understand the extent to which religious "witnessing" is a constitutionally protected practice.

- Understand the extent to which prayer is a permissible activity on public property.

- Distinguish between those religious displays on public property that are permissible under the establishment clause, and those that are not.

- Describe under what circumstances public property can be used for religious purposes.

- Explain the current status of Sunday closing laws.

- Identify those situations in which the state has the legal authority to mandate medical treatment over the religious objections of the patient or the patient's family.

- Define the terms *religion* and *religious*.

Short-Answer Questions

1. A city ordinance requires all outdoor public meetings in city parks to be approved by the parks commissioner. The ordinance does not give the commissioner any criteria to follow. A religious group requests permission to conduct a meeting in a park, but the commissioner denies the request. Is the city ordinance legally valid?

2. A city ordinance permits city officials to deny parade permits if the public safety, convenience, peace, and order would be materially jeopardized. A controversial religious group applies for a parade permit, and its application is rejected on the ground that the proposed parade would be "disruptive of public peace and quiet, and might cause hostilities." The religious group challenges the permit denial in court. How will the court rule?

3. Can a city pass an ordinance prohibiting door-to-door religious evangelism in residential neighborhoods? Explain.

4. A city council opens each session with prayer. Does this practice violate the establishment of religion clause of the first amendment? Explain.

5. A public courthouse lobby contains a statue of Moses holding the Ten Commandments. Does this display constitute a violation of the establishment of religion clause of the first amendment?

6. A city maintains the lighted cross on top of city hall during the Christmas season. Is this practice permissible?

7. A city decorates street lamps during the Christmas season with wreaths and colored lights, and it places a large display consisting of Santa Clause, a sleigh, and six large reindeer, on the city hall lawn. Is this practice permissible?

8. Same facts as question 7, except that the display contains a nativity scene showing Mary, Joseph, and the baby Jesus. Does the inclusion of the nativity scene affect the constitutionality of the display?

9. A church's sanctuary is lost in a fire. The congregation would like to use a public school gymnasium for Sunday worship services while its sanctuary is being rebuilt. Determine the constitutionality of this use in each of the following situations:

   a. The school board offers the gymnasium to the congregation without charge.

   b. The school board charges the church the same rental fee it charges other community groups that use the gymnasium.

   c. The school board charges the church more than the rental fee it charges other community groups that use the gymnasium, in order to avoid any violation of the first amendment's nonestablishment of religion clause.

10. A church's sanctuary becomes too small to accommodate its growing congregation. The church rents public school facilities for worship services and educational classes on Sunday mornings. At first, the church had plans to build a larger sanctuary. However, after several months, the congregation becomes accustomed to using the school facilities, and loses interest in building a new sanctuary. Evaluate the constitutionality of this arrangement.

11.   A public high school would like to begin basketball games involving both its boys' and girls' teams with a prayer recited by a local minister. Evaluate the constitutionality of this practice.

12.   A church would like to invite a popular Christian author to give a speech on family values as depicted in the Bible. Since the church's sanctuary is too small to accommodate the expected crowd, the church asks public school officials if it can rent a public high school gymnasium for a one-night meeting. School officials reject this request. Evaluate the constitutionality of the school's position in each of the following situations:

    a.   The school has allowed a variety of community organizations to rent its gymnasium in recent years, including some religious groups.

    b.   The school has never rented its gymnasium to any outside group.

    c.   The school permits non-religious community organizations to rent its gymnasium.

13.   A group of Christian students at a public high school asks school officials for permission to conduct a Bible study club after school hours in a vacant classroom. The school permits several other student groups to use classrooms after hours for meetings. School officials refuse to permit the Bible club since it would violate the first amendment's ban on the establishment of religion. Do the Christian students have any recourse? Explain.

14.   Federal employees are given a paid holiday at Thanksgiving and at Christmas. Is this practice permissible? Explain.

15.   A young woman is seriously injured in an accident. She refuses to receive potentially life-saving medical treatment because of her religious convictions. Can the state compel her to receive medical treatment?

16.   Same facts as problem 15, except that the woman's four year old son is also injured in the same accident. Can the woman refuse the administration of medical treatment to her son? Explain.

17.   Has the Supreme Court held that secular humanism is a religion?

18.   Do the courts restrict the term *religion* to those faiths maintaining a belief in a Supreme Being?

Discussion Questions

1.   Do you agree with the Supreme Court's definition of religion, or do you find it too expansive or too restrictive? Formulate your own definition.

2.   Can you think of a rational basis for permitting public university students to conduct group worship and Bible study in school facilities, but denying the same right to students in public elementary and secondary schools?

3. A city enacts an ordinance banning door-to-door religious evangelism because of the disturbance it causes homeowners. Is disturbance to homeowners a sufficient reason for banning door-to-door evangelism? Should it be?

Appendices

APPENDIX 1

ELIGIBILITY TO PERFORM MARRIAGE CEREMONIES

State-by-State Analysis

Note: The relevant portion of each state's statute describing those clergy who are authorized to perform marriage ceremonies is set forth below in alphabetical order. All statutes are subject to change, and accordingly this appendix should not be relied upon. To determine the current text of any statute, you should visit a library containing your state statutes, or consult with an attorney.

ALABAMA

Ala. Code § 30-1-7. Persons authorized to solemnize marriages (1988)

(a) *Generally.* Marriages may be solemnized by any licensed minister of the gospel in regular communion with the Christian church or society of which he is a member, by a judge of the supreme court, court of criminal appeals, court of civil appeals, any circuit court or any district court within this state or by a judge of probate within his county or any retired judge of the supreme court, retired judge of the court of criminal appeals, retired judge of the court of civil appeals, retired judge of the circuit court, retired judge of the district court within this state or a retired judge of probate within his county.

(b) *Pastor of religious society; clerk of society to maintain register of marriages; register, etc., deemed presumptive evidence of fact.* Marriage may also be solemnized by the pastor of any religious society according to the rules ordained or custom established by such society. The clerk or keeper of the minutes of each society must keep a register and enter therein a particular account of all marriages solemnized by the society, which register, or a sworn copy thereof, is presumptive evidence of the fact.

(c) *Quakers, Mennonites or other religious societies.* The people called Mennonites, Quakers, or any other Christian society having similar rules or regulations, may solemnize marriage according to their forms by consent of the parties, published and declared before the congregation assembled for public worship.

ALASKA

Alaska Stat. § 25.05.261. Who may solemnize (1963)

(a) Marriages may be solemnized

(1) by a minister, priest, or rabbi of any church or congregation in the state, or by a commissioned officer of the Salvation Army, or by the principal officer or elder of recognized churches or congregations that traditionally do not have regular ministers, priests, or rabbis, anywhere within the state . . . or

(3) before or in any religious organization or congregation according to the established ritual or form commonly practiced in the organization or congregation.

(b) This section may not be construed to waive the requirements for obtaining a marriage license.

ARIZONA

Ariz. Rev. Stat. Ann. § 25-124. Persons authorized to perform marriage ceremony (1995)

A. The following are authorized to solemnize marriages between persons who are authorized to marry . . . duly licensed or ordained clergymen. . . .

B. For the purposes of this section, "licensed or ordained clergymen" includes ministers, elders or other persons who by the customs, rules and regulations of a religious society or sect are authorized or permitted to solemnize marriages or to officiate at marriage ceremonies.

ARKANSAS

Ark. Stat. § 9-11-213. Persons who may solemnize marriages (1997)

(a) For the purpose of being registered and perpetuating the evidence thereof, marriages shall be solemnized only by the following persons . . . (5) any regularly ordained minister or priest of any religious sect or denomination . . . .

(b)(1) Marriages solemnized through the traditional rite of the Religious Society of Friends, more commonly known as Quakers, are recognized as valid to all intents and purposes the same as marriages otherwise contracted and solemnized in accordance with law.

CALIFORNIA

Cal. Family Law Code § 400

Marriage may be solemnized by any of the following who is of the age of 18 or older: (a) a priest, minister, or rabbi of any religious denomination . . . .

Cal. Family Law Code § 402

In addition to the persons permitted to solemnize marriages under Section 400, a county may license officials of a nonprofit religious institution, whose articles of incorporation are registered with the Secretary of State, to solemnize the marriages of persons who are affiliated with or are members of the religious institution. The licensee shall possess the degree of doctor of philosophy and must perform religious services or rites for the institution on a regular basis. The marriages shall be performed without fee to the parties.

COLORADO

Colo. Rev. Stat. § 14-2-109. Solemnization and registration (1993)

(1) A marriage may be solemnized . . . in accordance with any mode of solemnization recognized by any religious denomination . . .

CONNECTICUT

Conn. Gen. Stat. § 46b-22. Who may join persons in marriage (1979)

(a) [A]ll ordained or licensed clergymen, belonging to this state or any other state, so long as they continue in the work of the ministry may join persons in marriage. All marriages solemnized according to the forms and usages of any religious denomination in this state . . . are valid.

DELAWARE

Del. Code Ann. title 13, § 106. Solemnization of marriages (1995)

(a) A clergyman or minister of any recognized religion . . . may solemnize marriages between persons who may lawfully enter into the matrimonial relation. . . . Marriages may also be solemnized or contracted according to the forms and usages of any religious society.

DISTRICT OF COLUMBIA

D.C. Code Ann. § 30-106. Persons authorized to celebrate marriages (1981)

(a) For the purposes of this section, the term: (1) "Religious" includes or pertains to a belief in a theological doctrine, a belief in and worship of a divine ruling power, a recognition of a supernatural power controlling man's destiny, or a devotion to some principle, strict fidelity or faithfulness, conscientiousness, pious affection, or attachment. (2) "Society" means a voluntary association of individuals for religious purposes.

(b) For the purposes of preserving the evidence of marriages in the District of Columbia, every minister of any religious society approved or ordained according to the ceremonies of his religious society, whether his residence is in the District of Columbia or elsewhere in the United States or the territories, may be authorized by any judge of the Superior Court of the District of Columbia to celebrate marriages in the District of Columbia. . . . Provided, that marriages of any religious society which does not by its own custom require the intervention of a minister for the celebration of marriages may be solemnized in the manner prescribed and practiced in any such religious society, the license in such case to be issued to, and returns made by, a person appointed by such religious society for that purpose. . . .

FLORIDA

Fla. Stat. § 741.07. Persons authorized to solemnize matrimony (1953)

(1) All regularly ordained ministers of the gospel or elders in communion with some church, or other ordained clergy . . . may solemnize the rights of matrimonial contract, under the regulations prescribed by law. . . .

(2) Any marriage which may be had and solemnized among the people called "Quakers," or "Friends," in the manner and form used or practiced in their societies, according to their rites and ceremonies, shall be good and valid in law; and wherever the words "minister" and "elder" are used in this chapter, they shall be held to include all of the persons connected with the Society of Friends, or Quakers, who perform or have charge of the marriage ceremony according to their rites and ceremonies.

GEORGIA

Ga. Code § 19-3-30(c). How granted, returned, and recorded (1996)

The license shall be directed to any . . . minister, or other person of any religious society or sect authorized by the rules of such society to perform the marriage ceremony; such license shall authorize the marriage of the persons therein named and require the . . . minister, or other authorized person to return the license to the judge of the probate court with the certificate thereon as to the fact and date of marriage within 30 days after the date of the marriage.

HAWAII

Hawaii Rev. Stat. § 572-12. By whom solemnized (1974)

A license to solemnize marriages may be issued to, and the marriage rite may be performed and solemnized by any minister, priest, or officer of any religious denomination or society who has been ordained or is authorized to solemnize marriages according to the usages of such denomination or society, or any religious society not having clergy but providing solemnization in accordance with the rules and customs of that society . . . upon presentation to such person or society of a license to marry, as prescribed by this chapter. Such person or society may receive the price stipulated by the parties or the gratification tendered.

IDAHO

Idaho Code § 31-11-6. By whom solemnized (1997)

Marriage may be solemnized by . . . [a] priest or minister of the gospel of any denomination.

ILLINOIS

750 Ill. Comp. Stat. 5/209. Solemnization and registration (1993)

(a) A marriage may be solemnized . . . in accordance with the prescriptions of any religious denomination . . . provided that when such prescriptions require an officiant, the officiant be in good standing with his religious denomination . . . .

(b) The solemnization of the marriage is not invalidated by the fact that the person solemnizing the marriage was not legally qualified to solemnize it, if either party to the marriage believed him to be so qualified.

INDIANA

Ind. Code § 31-7-5-1. Authority to solemnize marriage

1. Marriages may be solemnized by any of the following:

(1) A member of the clergy of a religious organization (even if the cleric does not perform religious functions for an individual congregation), such as a minister of the gospel, a priest, a bishop, an archbishop, or a rabbi. . . .

(6) The Friends Church, in accordance with the rules of the Friends Church.

(7) The German Baptists, in accordance with the rules of their society.

(8) The Bahai faith, in accordance with the rules of the Bahai faith.

(9) The Church of Jesus Christ of Latter Day Saints, in accordance with the rules of the Church of Jesus Christ of Latter Day Saints.

(10) An imam of a masjid (mosque), in accordance with the rules of the religion of Islam.

IOWA

Iowa Code § 595.10. Who may solemnize (1995)

A person ordained or designated as a leader of the person's religious faith.

KANSAS

Kan. Stat. Ann. § 23-104a. Solemnizing marriage

(a) Marriage may be validly solemnized and contracted in this state, after a license has been issued for the marriage, in the following manner: By the mutual declarations of the two parties to be joined in marriage, made before an authorized officiating person and in the presence of at least two competent witnesses over 18 years of age, other than the officiating person, that they take each other as husband and wife.

(b) The following are authorized to be officiating persons:

(1) Any currently ordained clergyman or religious authority of any religious denomination or society;

(2) any licentiate of a denominational body or an appointee of any bishop serving as the regular clergyman of any church of the denomination to which the licentiate or appointee belongs, if not restrained from so doing by the discipline of that church or denomination . . . .

(c) The two parties themselves, by mutual declarations that they take each other as husband and wife, in accordance with the customs, rules and regulations of any religious society, denomination or sect to which either of the parties belong [sic], may be married without an authorized officiating person.

KENTUCKY

Ky. Rev. Stat. § 402.050. Who may solemnize marriage—persons present (1996)

(1) Marriage shall be solemnized only by:

(a) Ministers of the gospel or priests of any denomination in regular communion with any religious society . . . .

(c) A religious society that has no officiating minister or priest and whose usage is to solemnize marriage at the usual place of worship and by consent given in the presence of the society, if either party belongs to the society. . . .

LOUISIANA

La. Rev. Stat. Ann. § 9:202. Authority to perform marriage ceremony (1997)

A marriage ceremony may be performed by: (1) A priest, minister, rabbi, clerk of the Religious Society of Friends, or any clergyman of any religious sect, who is authorized by the authorities of his religion to perform marriages, and who is registered to perform marriages . . . .

MAINE

Me. Rev. Stat. Ann. title 19-A, § 655 (1995)

1. *Persons authorized to solemnize marriages.* The following persons may solemnize marriages in this State . . .

B. Whether a resident or nonresident of this State and whether or not a citizen of the United States:

(1) An ordained minister of the gospel;

(2) a cleric engaged in the service of the religious body to which the cleric belongs; or

(3) a person licensed to preach by an association of ministers, religious seminary or ecclesiastical body.

MARYLAND

Md. Family Law Code Ann. § 2-406. Performance of ceremony (1984)

(a) A marriage ceremony may be performed in this State by: (1) any official of a religious order or body authorized by the rules and customs of that order or body to perform a marriage ceremony . . . .

(g) This section does not affect the right of any religious denomination to perform a marriage ceremony in accordance with the rules and customs of the denomination.

MASSACHUSETTS

Mass. Gen. Laws Ann. ch. 207, § 38. Solemnization of marriage; situs; persons authorized

A marriage may be solemnized in any place within the commonwealth by the following persons who are residents of the commonwealth: a duly ordained minister of the gospel in good and regular standing with his church or denomination, including an ordained deacon in The United Methodist Church or in the Roman Catholic Church; a duly ordained rabbi of the Jewish faith . . . an authorized representative of a Spiritual Assembly of the Baha'is in accordance with the usage of their community; a priest or minister of the Buddhist religion; a minister in fellowship with the Unitarian Universalist Association and ordained by a local church; a leader of an Ethical Culture Society which is duly established in the commonwealth and recognized by the American Ethical Union and who is duly appointed and in good and regular standing with the American Ethical Union; the Imam of the Orthodox Islamic religion; and, it may be solemnized in a regular or special meeting for worship conducted by or under the oversight of a Friends or Quaker Monthly Meeting in accordance with the usage of their Society; and, it may be solemnized by a duly ordained nonresident minister of the gospel if he is a pastor of a church or denomination duly established in the commonwealth and who is in good and regular standing as a minister of such church or denomination, including an ordained deacon in The United Methodist Church or in the Roman Catholic Church; and, it may be solemnized according to the usage of any other church or religious organization which shall have complied with the provisions of the second paragraph of this section.

Churches and other religious organizations shall file in the office of the state secretary information relating to persons recognized or licensed as aforesaid, and relating to usages of such organizations, in such form and at such times as the secretary may require.

MICHIGAN

Mich. Comp. Laws § 551.7. Persons authorized to solemnize marriages (1983)

(1) Marriages may be solemnized by any of the following . . .

(h) A minister of the gospel, anywhere in the state, if the minister is ordained or authorized to solemnize marriages according to the usages of the denomination, and is a pastor of a church in this state, or continues to preach the gospel in this state.

(i) A minister of the gospel, anywhere in the state, if the minister is not a resident of this state but is authorized to solemnize marriages under the laws of the state in which the minister resides.

MINNESOTA

Minn. Stat. § 517.04. Solemnization (1995)

Marriages may be solemnized throughout this state by . . . a licensed or ordained minister of any religious denomination . . . .

Minn. Stat. § 517.05. Credentials of minister (1986)

Ministers of any religious denomination, before they are authorized to solemnize a marriage, shall file a copy of their credentials of license or ordination with the court administrator of the district court of a county in this state, who shall record the same and give a certificate thereof. The place where the credentials are recorded shall be endorsed upon and recorded with each certificate of marriage granted by a minister.

MISSISSIPPI

Miss. Code Ann. § 93-1-17. By whom marriages may be solemnized (1994)

Any minister of the gospel ordained according to the rules of his church or society, in good standing; any rabbi or other spiritual leader of any other religious body authorized under the rules of such religious body to solemnize rites of matrimony and being in good standing . . . may solemnize the rites of matrimony between any persons anywhere within this state who shall produce a license granted as herein directed.

MISSOURI

Mo. Rev. Stat. § 451.100. Marriages solemnized by whom (1996)

Marriages may be solemnized by any clergyman, either active or retired, who is in good standing with any church or synagogue in this state. . . . Marriages may also be solemnized by a religious society, religious institution, or religious organization of this state, according to the regulations and customs of the society, institution or organization, when either party to the marriage to be solemnized is a member of such society, institution or organization.

MONTANA

Mont. Code Ann. § 40-1-301. Solemnization and registration (1985)

(1) A marriage may be solemnized . . . in accordance with any mode of solemnization recognized by any religious denomination . . . .

NEBRASKA

Nebr. Rev. Stat. § 42-108. Marriage ceremony; who may perform (1986)

Every . . . preacher of the gospel authorized by the usages of the church to which he or she belongs to solemnize marriages, may perform the marriage ceremony in this state.

NEVADA

Nev. Rev. Stat. § 122.062. Licensed or ordained ministers and chaplains of Armed Forces to obtain certificates from county clerk; temporary replacements; solemnization by minister licensed or ordained in another state (1997)

1. Any licensed or ordained minister in good standing within his denomination, whose denomination, governing body and church, or any of them, are incorporated or organized or established in this state, may join together as husband and wife persons who present a marriage license obtained from any county clerk of the state, if the minister first obtains a certificate of permission to perform marriages . . . . The fact that a minister is retired does not disqualify him from obtaining a certificate of permission to perform marriages if, before his retirement, he had active charge of a congregation within this state for a period of at least 3 years.

2. A temporary replacement for a licensed or ordained minister certified pursuant to this section and NRS 122.064 to 122.073, inclusive, may solemnize marriages pursuant to subsection 1 during such time as he may be authorized to do so by the county clerk in the county in which he is a temporary replacement, for a period not to exceed 90 days. The minister whom he temporarily replaces shall provide him with a written authorization which states the period during which it is effective.

3. Any chaplain who is assigned to duty in this state by the Armed Forces of the United States may solemnize marriages if he obtains a certificate of permission to perform marriages from the county clerk of the county in which his duty station is located. The county clerk shall issue such a certificate to a chaplain upon proof by him of his military status as a chaplain and of his assignment.

4. A county clerk may authorize a licensed or ordained minister whose congregation is in another state to perform marriages in the county if the county clerk satisfies himself that the minister is in good standing with his denomination or church. The authorization must be in writing and need not be filed with any other public officer. A separate authorization is required for each marriage performed. Such a minister may perform not more than five marriages in this state in any calendar year.

NEW HAMPSHIRE

N.H. Rev. Stat. Ann. § 457:31. Who may solemnize (1969)

Marriage may be solemnized . . . by any minister of the gospel in the state who has been ordained according to the usage of his denomination, resides in the state, and is in regular standing with the denomination; by any clergyman who is not ordained but is engaged in the service of the religious body to which he belongs, resides in the state, after being licensed therefor by the secretary of state; and within his parish, by any minister residing out of the state, but having a pastoral charge wholly or partly in this state.

N.H. Rev. Stat. Ann. § 457:32. Special commission (1925)

The secretary of state may issue a special license to an ordained minister residing out of state authorizing him in a special case to marry a couple within the state. The names and residences of the couple proposed to be married in such special case shall be stated in the license, and no power shall be conferred to marry any other parties than those named therein. The fee for such license shall be $5. The secretary of state shall keep a permanent record of all such special licenses, which record shall contain the names and residences of the couple to be married and the name and residence of the minister to whom the license is issued.

NEW JERSEY

N.J. Revised Stat. § 37:1-13. Who are authorized to solemnize (1998)

[E]very minister of every religion [is] hereby authorized to solemnize marriage between such persons as may lawfully enter into the matrimonial relation; and every religious society, institution or organization in this State may join together in marriage such persons according to the rules and customs of the society, institution, or organization.

NEW MEXICO

N.M. Stat. § 40-1-2. Clergymen or civil magistrates may solemnize; fees (1989)

A. It is lawful, valid and binding to all intents and purposes for those who may so desire to solemnize the contract of matrimony by means of any ordained clergyman or authorized representative of a federally recognized Indian tribe, without regard to the sect to which he may belong or the rites and customs he may practice.

N.M. Stat. § 40-1-3. Ceremony by religious society (1983)

It is lawful for any religious society or federally recognized Indian tribe to celebrate marriage conformably with its rites and customs, and the secretary of the society or the person presiding over the society or federally recognized Indian tribe shall make and transmit a transcript to the county clerk certifying to the marriages solemnized.

NEW YORK

N.Y Dom. Rel. Law Art. 3, § 11. By whom a marriage must be solemnized (1996)

No marriage shall be valid unless solemnized by either:

1. A clergyman or minister of any religion . . . .

7. The term "clergyman" or "minister" when used in this article, shall include those defined in section two of the religious corporation law. . . .

NORTH CAROLINA

N.C. Gen. Stat. § 51-1. Requisites of marriage; solemnization (1977)

The consent of a male and female person who may lawfully marry, presently to take each other as husband and wife, freely, seriously and plainly expressed by each in the presence of the other, and in the presence of an ordained minister of any religious denomination, minister authorized by his church, or of a magistrate, and the consequent declaration by such minister or officer that such persons are husband and wife, shall be a valid and sufficient marriage: Provided, that the rite of marriage among the Society of Friends, according to the form and custom peculiar to themselves, shall not be interfered with by the provisions of this Chapter; Provided further, that marriages solemnized and witnessed by a local spiritual assembly of the Baha'is, according to the usage of their religious community, shall be valid; provided further, marriages solemnized before March 9, 1909, by ministers of the gospel licensed, but not ordained, are validated from their consummation.

NORTH DAKOTA

N.D. Cent. Code § 14-03-09. Who may solemnize marriages (1997)

Marriages may be solemnized . . . by ordained ministers of the gospel, priests, and clergy licensed by recognized denominations pursuant to chapter 10-33, and by any person authorized by the rituals and practices of any religious persuasion.

OHIO

Ohio Rev. Code Ann. § 3101.08. Who may solemnize (1991)

An ordained or licensed minister of any religious society or congregation within this state licensed to perform marriages [sic] . . . or any religious society, in conformity with the rules and regulations of its church, may join together as husband and wife any persons not prohibited by law.

OKLAHOMA

Okla. Stat. title 43, § 7. Solemnization of marriages (1989)

A. All marriages must be contracted by a formal ceremony performed or solemnized in the presence of at least two adult, competent persons as witnesses, by . . . an ordained or authorized preacher or minister of the Gospel, priest or other ecclesiastical dignitary of any denomination who has been duly ordained or authorized by the church to which he or she belongs to preach the Gospel, or a rabbi and who is at least eighteen (18) years of age.

B. . . . 2. The preacher, minister, priest, rabbi, or ecclesiastical dignitary who is a resident of this state shall have filed, in the office of the court clerk of the county in which he or she resides, a copy of the credentials or authority from his or her church or synagogue authorizing him or her to solemnize marriages. 3. The preacher, minister, priest, rabbi, or ecclesiastical dignitary who is not a resident of this state, but has complied with the laws of the state of which he or she is a resident, shall have filed once, in the office of the court clerk of the county in which he or she intends to perform or solemnize a marriage, a copy of the credentials or authority from his or her church or synagogue authorizing him or her to solemnize marriages. The filing by resident or nonresident preachers, ministers, priests, rabbis, or ecclesiastical dignitaries shall be effective in and for all counties of this state; provided, no fee shall be charged for such recording.

C. No person herein authorized to perform or solemnize a marriage ceremony shall do so unless the license issued therefor be first delivered into his or her possession nor unless he or she has good reason to believe the persons presenting themselves before him or her for marriage are the identical persons named in the license, and for whose marriage the same was issued, and that there is no legal objection or impediment to such marriage.

D. Marriages between persons belonging to the society called Friends, or Quakers, the spiritual assembly of the Baha'is, or the Church of Jesus Christ of Latter Day Saints, which have no ordained minister, may be solemnized by the persons and in the manner prescribed by and practiced in any such society, church, or assembly.

OREGON

Or. Rev. Stat. § 106.120. Who may solemnize marriage (1997)

(1)(a) Marriages may be solemnized . . . (2) by any minister of any church organized, carrying on its work and having congregations in this state, who is authorized by such church to solemnize marriages, and who has filed for record with the county clerk of the county in which the minister resides or in which the marriage is solemnized, evidence satisfactory to the county clerk that the minister has been so authorized. A person authorized to solemnize marriages under this paragraph may solemnize a marriage anywhere in this state.

(b) In the case of a nonresident minister, the filing required by paragraph (a) of this subsection must be in any county in which the minister performs any marriage ceremony, but no minister shall be required to file such evidence of authority in more than one county.

(2) The evidence of authority, if approved by the county clerk, shall be recorded by the county clerk in a book called "Authority to Solemnize Marriages," for which the county clerk shall charge a fee for recording and indexing as set by ORS 205.320. Whenever any minister who has filed such evidence of authority with one county clerk solemnizes any marriage in any other county, the minister shall attach to or indorse upon the certificate required by ORS 106.170, a statement over the minister's signature showing place of residence and the county clerk with whom evidence of authority to solemnize marriages is recorded.

PENNSYLVANIA

Pa. Stat. Ann. title 23, § 1503. Persons qualified to solemnize marriages (1990)

(a) *General rule.* The following are authorized to solemnize marriages between persons that produce a marriage license issued under this part . . .

(6) A minister, priest or rabbi of any regularly established church or congregation.

(b) *Religious organizations.* Every religious society, religious institution or religious organization in this Commonwealth may join persons together in marriage when at least one of the persons is a member of the society, institution, or organization, according to the rules and customs of the society, institution or organization.

RHODE ISLAND

R.I. Gen. Laws § 15-3-5. Officials empowered to join persons in marriage (1994)

Every ordained clergy [sic] or elder in good standing . . .may join persons in marriage in any town in this state . . . .

R.I. Gen. Laws § 15-3-5. Marriages after the manner of Friends, according to Jewish rites or spiritual assembly of Baha'is (1970)

Any marriage which may be had and solemnized among the people called Quakers, or Friends, in the manner and form used or practiced in their societies, or among persons profession the Jewish religion, according to their rites and ceremonies, or by a local spiritual assembly of the Baha'is according to the usage of the religious community, shall be good and valid in law; and wherever the words "minister" and "elder" are used in this chapter, they shall be held to include all of the persons connected with the Society of Friends, or Quakers, and with the Jewish religion, and with the Baha'is faith, who perform or have charge of the marriage ceremony according to their rites and ceremonies.

SOUTH CAROLINA

S.C. Code Ann. § 20-1-20. Persons who may perform marriage ceremony (1962)

Only ministers of the Gospel or accepted Jewish rabbis and officers authorized to administer oaths in this state are authorized to administer a marriage ceremony in this state.

SOUTH DAKOTA

S.D. Codified Laws § 25-1-30. Persons authorized to solemnize marriages (1940)

Marriage may be solemnized by . . . any person authorized by a church to solemnize marriages.

TENNESSEE

Tenn. Code Ann. § 36-3-301. Persons who may solemnize marriages (1998)

(a) (1) All regular ministers, preachers, pastors, priests, rabbis and other spiritual leaders of every religious belief, more than eighteen (18) years of age, having the care of souls . . . may solemnize the rite of matrimony. . . .

(2) In order to solemnize the rite of matrimony, any such minister, preacher, pastor, priest, rabbi or other spiritual leader must be ordained or otherwise designated in conformity with the customs of a church, temple or other religious group or organization; and such customs must provide for such ordination or designation by a considered, deliberate, and responsible act.

(3) If any marriage has been entered into by license issued pursuant to this chapter at which any minister officiated before April 15, 1998, such marriage shall not be invalid because the requirements of the preceding subdivision (2) have not been met.

(b) The traditional marriage rite of the Religious Society of Friends (Quakers), whereby the parties simply pledge their vows one to another in the presence of the congregation, constitutes an equally effective solemnization.

TEXAS

Tex. Family Code Ann. § 1.83. Persons authorized to conduct ceremony (1997)

(a) The following persons are authorized to conduct a marriage ceremony:

(1) a licensed or ordained Christian minister or priest;

(2) a Jewish rabbi;

(3) a person who is an officer of a religious organization and who is authorized by the organization to conduct a marriage ceremony . . . .

UTAH

Utah Code Ann. § 30-1-6. Who may solemnize marriages (1997)

(1) Marriages may be solemnized by the following persons only: (a) ministers, rabbis, or priests of any religious denomination who are (I) in regular communion with any religious society; and (ii) 18 years of age or older . . . .

VERMONT

Vt. Stat. Ann. title 18, § 5144. Persons authorized to solemnize marriage (1981)

Marriages may be solemnized . . . by a minister of the gospel residing in this state and ordained or licensed, or otherwise regularly authorized thereunto by the published laws or discipline of the general conference or convention of his denomination or by such a minister residing in an adjoining state or country, whose parish lies wholly or in part in this state, or by a minister of the gospel residing in some other state of the United States or in the Dominion of Canada who is ordained or licensed, or otherwise regularly authorized thereunto by the published laws or discipline of the general conference or convention of his denomination, provided he has first secured from the probate court of the district within which said marriage is to be solemnized a special authorization to said nonresident minister authorizing him to solemnize said marriage if it appear to said probate judge that circumstances seem to make such special authorization desirable. Marriage among the Friends or Quakers, the Christadelphian Ecclesia and the Baha'is faith may be solemnized in the manner heretofore used in such societies.

VIRGINIA

Va. Code § 20-23. Order authorizing ministers to perform ceremony (1981)

When a minister of any religious denomination shall produce before the circuit court of any county or city in this State, or before the judge of such court or before the clerk of such court at any time, proof of his ordination and of his being in regular communion with the religious society of which he is a reputed member, or proof that he holds a local minister's license and is serving as a regularly appointed pastor in his denomination, such court, or the judge thereof, or the clerk of such court at any time, may make an order authorizing such minister to celebrate the rites of matrimony in this State. Any order made under this section may be rescinded at any time by the court or by the judge thereof.

Va. Code § 20-26. Marriage between members of religious society having no minister (1968)

Marriages between persons belonging to any religious society which has no ordained minister, may be solemnized by the persons and in the manner prescribed by and practiced in any such society, One person chosen by the society shall be responsible for completing the certification of marriage in the same manner as a minister or other person authorized to perform marriages; such person chosen by the society for this purpose shall be required to execute a bond in the penalty of $500, with surety.

WASHINGTON

Wash. Rev. Code § 26.04.050. Who may solemnize (1984)

The following named officers and persons, active or retired, are hereby authorized to solemnize marriages, to wit . . . any regularly licensed or ordained minister or any priest of any church or religious denomination . . . .

WEST VIRGINIA

W. Va. Code § 48-1-12. Persons authorized to celebrate marriages (1969)

Any minister, priest or rabbi, over the age of eighteen years, who has complied with the provisions of section [48-1-12a] of this article . . . is authorized to celebrate the rites of marriage in all the counties of the State . . . .

Whenever in this article the terms "minister," "priest" or "rabbi" shall appear, the same shall be understood and held in all respects to include, without being limited to, a leader or representative of a generally recognized spiritual assembly, church or religious organization which does not formally designate or recognize persons as ministers, priests or rabbis.

W. Va. Code § 48-1-12a. Qualifications of minister, priest or rabbi for celebrating marriages (1972)

When any minister, priest or rabbi shall, before the county court of any county in this State, or the clerk of any such court in vacation, produce proof that he is over the age of eighteen, duly licensed by, and being in regular communion with, the religious society of which he is a member, and give bond in the penalty of fifteen hundred dollars, with surety approved by such court or clerk thereof in vacation, such court or clerk may make an order authorizing him to celebrate the rites of marriage in all the counties of the State: Provided, that any minister, priest or rabbi who gives proof before the county court of any county in this State, or the clerk of any such court in vacation, of his ordination or authorization by his respective church, denomination, synagogue or religious society, shall be exempted from the giving of such bond.

WISCONSIN

Wis. Stat. § 765.16. Marriage contract, how made; officiating person (1980)

Marriage may be validly solemnized and contracted in this state only after a license has been issued therefor, and only in the following manner: by the mutual declarations of the 2 parties to be joined in marriage, made before a duly authorized officiating person and in the presence of at least 2 competent adult witnesses other than such officiating person, that they take each other as husband and wife. The following are duly authorized to be officiating persons:

(1) Any ordained clergyman of any religious denomination or society who continues to be such ordained clergyman;

(2) Any licentiate of a denominational body or an appointee of any bishop serving as the regular clergyman of any church of the denomination to which the clergyman belongs, if not restrained from so doing by the discipline of the church or denomination . . . .

WYOMING

Wyo. Stat. § 20-1-106. Who may solemnize marriage (1957)

(a) Every . . . licensed or ordained minister of the gospel, may perform the ceremony of marriage in this state.

APPENDIX 2
CLERGY-PENITENT PRIVILEGE

State-by-State Analysis

Note: The relevant portion of each state's statute or rule of evidence describing the clergy-penitent privilege is set forth below in alphabetical order. All statutes and rules are subject to change, and accordingly this appendix should not be relied upon. To determine the current text of any statute, you should visit a library containing your state statutes, or consult with an attorney.

ALABAMA

Alabama Rules of Evidence, Rule 505. Communications to clergymen

(a) *Definitions.* As used in this rule:

(1) A "clergyman" is any duly ordained, licensed or commissioned minister, pastor, priest, rabbi or practitioner of any bona fide established church or religious organization; the term "clergyman" includes, and is limited to, any person who regularly, as a vocation, devotes a substantial portion of his or her time and abilities to the service of his or her church or religious organization.

(2) A communication is "confidential" if it is made privately and is not intended for further disclosure except to other persons present in furtherance of the purpose of the communication.

(b) *General rule of privilege.* If any person shall communicate with a clergyman in the clergyman's professional capacity and in a confidential manner, then that person or the clergyman shall have a privilege to refuse to disclose, and to prevent another from disclosing, that confidential communication

(c) *Who may claim the privilege.* The privilege may be claimed by the communicating person, by that person's guardian or conservator, or by that person's personal representative if that person has died, or by the clergyman

ALASKA

Alaska Rules of Evidence, Rule 506. Communications to clergymen (1994)

(a) *Definitions.* As used in this rule:

(1) A member of the clergy is a minister, priest, rabbi, or other similar functionary of a religious organization, or an individual reasonably believed so to be by the person consulting the individual.

(2) A communication is confidential if made privately and not intended for further disclosure except to other persons present in furtherance of the purpose of the communication.

(b) *General Rule of Privilege.* A person has a privilege to refuse to disclose and to prevent another from disclosing a confidential communication by the person to a member of the clergy in that individual's professional character as spiritual adviser.

(c) *Who May Claim the Privilege.* The privilege may be claimed by the person, by the person's guardian or conservator, or by the person's personal representative if the person is deceased. The member of the clergy may claim the privilege on behalf of the person. The authority so to do is presumed in the absence of evidence to the contrary.

ARIZONA

Ariz. Rev. Stat. Ann. § 12-2233. Clergyman or priest and penitent (civil) (1939)

In a civil action a clergyman or priest shall not, without consent of the person making a confession, be examined as to any confession made to him in his character as clergyman or priest in the course of discipline enjoined by the church to which he belongs.

Ariz. Rev. Stat. Ann. § 13-4062. Other privileged communications (criminal) (1983)

A person shall not be examined as a witness in the following cases: . . . (3) A clergyman or priest, without consent of the person making the confession, as to any confession made to him in his professional character in the course of discipline enjoined by the church to which he belongs.

ARKANSAS

Arkansas Rules of Evidence, Rule 505. Religious privilege

(a) *Definitions.* As used in this rule:

(1) A "clergyman" is a minister, priest, rabbi, accredited Christian Science Practitioner, or other similar functionary of a religious organization, or an individual reasonably believed so to be by the person consulting him.

(2) A communication is "confidential" if made privately and not intended for further disclosure except to other persons present in furtherance of the purpose of the communication.

(b) *General Rule of Privilege.* A person has a privilege to refuse to disclose and to prevent another from disclosing a confidential communication by the person to the clergyman in his professional character as a spiritual adviser.

(c) *Who May Claim the Privilege.* The privilege may be claimed by the person, by his guardian or conservator, or by his personal representative if he is deceased. The person who was the clergyman at the time of the communication is presumed to have authority to claim the privilege but only on behalf of the communicant.

CALIFORNIA

Cal. Evid. Code §§ 1030-1034. Clergyman-penitent privileges (1967)

Clergyman. As used in this article, "clergyman" means a priest, minister, religious practitioner, or similar functionary of a church or of a religious denomination or religious organization.

Penitent. As used in this article, "penitent" means a person who has made a penitential communication to a clergyman.

Penitential communication. As used in this article, "penitential communication" means a communication made in confidence, in the presence of no third person so far as the penitent is aware, to a clergyman who, in the course of the discipline or practice of his church, denomination, or organization, is authorized or accustomed to hear such communications and, under the discipline or tenets of his church, denomination, or organization, has a duty to keep such communications secret.

Privilege of penitent. Subject to section 912, a penitent, whether or not a party, has a privilege to refuse to disclose, and to prevent another from disclosing, a penitential communication if he claims the privilege.

Privilege of clergyman. Subject to section 912, a clergyman, whether or not a party, has a privilege to refuse to disclose a penitential communication if he claims the privilege.

Cal. Evid. Code § 912. Waiver of privilege (1980)

[T]he right of anyone to claim a privilege provided by . . . section 1033 (privilege of penitent), 1034 (privilege of clergyman) . . . is waived with respect to a communication protected by such privilege if any holder of the privilege, without coercion, has disclosed a significant part of the communication or has consented to such disclosure made by anyone. Consent to disclosure is manifested by any statement or other conduct of the holder of the privilege indicating consent to the disclosure, including failure to claim the privilege in any proceeding in which the holder has the legal standing and opportunity to claim the privilege.

Cal. Evid. Code § 917. Presumption that certain communications are confidential (1967)

Whenever a privilege is claimed on the ground that the matter sought to be disclosed is a communication made in confidence in the course of the . . . clergyman-penitent . . . relationship, the communication is presumed to have been made in confidence and the opponent of the claim of privilege has the burden of proof to establish that the communication was not confidential.

COLORADO

Colo. Rev. Stat. § 13-90-107. Who may not testify without consent

(1) There are particular relations in which it is the policy of the law to encourage confidence and to preserve it inviolate; therefore, a person shall not be examined as a witness in the following cases . . .

(c) A clergyman, minister, priest, or rabbi shall not be examined without both his consent and also the consent of the person making the confidential communication as to any confidential communication made to him in his professional capacity in the course of discipline expected by the religious body to which he belongs.

CONNECTICUT

Conn. Gen. Stat. § 52-146b. Privileged communications made to a clergyman (1967)

A clergyman, priest, minister, rabbi, or practitioner of any religious denomination accredited by the religious body to which he belongs who is settled in the work of the ministry shall not disclose confidential communications made to him in his professional capacity in any civil or criminal case or proceedings preliminary thereto, or in any legislative or administrative proceeding, unless the person making the confidential communication waives such privilege herein provided.

DELAWARE

Delaware Rules of Evidence, Rule 505. Religious privilege (1998)

(a) *Definitions.* As used in this rule:

(1) A "clergyman" is a minister, priest, rabbi, accredited Christian Science Practitioner, or other similar functionary of a religious organization, or an individual reasonably believed so to be by the person consulting him.

(2) A communication is "confidential" if made privately and not intended for further disclosure except to other persons present in furtherance of the purpose of the communication.

(b) *General Rule of Privilege.* A person has a privilege to refuse to disclose and to prevent another from disclosing a confidential communication by the person to the clergyman in his professional character as a spiritual adviser.

(c) *Who May Claim the Privilege.* The privilege may be claimed by the person, by his guardian or conservator, or by his personal representative if he is deceased. The clergyman may claim the privilege on behalf of the person. His authority so to do is presumed in the absence of evidence to the contrary.

DISTRICT OF COLUMBIA

D.C. Code Ann. § 14-309. Clergy (1973)

A priest, clergyman, rabbi, or other duly licensed, ordained, or consecrated minister of a religion authorized to perform a marriage ceremony in the District of Columbia or duly accredited practitioner of Christian Science may not be examined in any civil or criminal proceedings in the federal courts in the District of Columbia and District of Columbia courts with respect to any— (1) confession, or communication, made to him, in his professional capacity in the course of discipline enjoined by the church or other religious body to which he belongs, without the consent of the person making the confession or communication; or (2) communication made to him, in his professional capacity in the course of giving religious or spiritual advice, without the consent of the person seeking the advice; or (3) communication made to him, in his professional capacity, by either spouse, in connection with an effort to reconcile estranged spouses, without the consent of the spouse making the communication.

FLORIDA

Fla. Stat. § 90.505. Privilege with respect to communications to clergy (1995)

(1) For the purpose of this section:

(a) A "member of the clergy" is a priest, rabbi, practitioner of Christian Science, or minister of any religious organization or denomination usually referred to as a church, or an individual reasonably believed so to be by the person consulting him or her.

(b) A communication between a member of the clergy and a person is "confidential" if made privately for the purpose of seeking spiritual counsel and advice from the member of the clergy in the usual course of his or her practice or discipline and not intended for further disclosure except to other persons present in furtherance of the communication.

(2) A person has a privilege to refuse to disclose, and to prevent another from disclosing, a confidential communication by the person to a member of the clergy in his or her capacity as spiritual advisor.

(3) The privilege may be claimed by:

(a) The person.

(b) The guardian or conservator of the person.

(c) The personal representative of a deceased person.

(d) The member of the clergy, on behalf of the person. The member of the clergy's authority to do so is presumed in the absence of evidence to the contrary.

GEORGIA

Ga. Stat. § 24-9-22. Communications to ministers, priests and rabbis (1986)

Every communication made by any person professing religious faith, seeking spiritual comfort, or seeking counseling to any Protestant minister of the Gospel, any priest of the Roman Catholic faith, any priest of the Greek Orthodox faith, any Jewish rabbi, or to any Christian or Jewish minister, by whatever name called, shall be deemed privileged. No such minister, priest, or rabbi shall disclose any communications made to him by any such person professing religious faith, seeking spiritual guidance, or seeking counseling, nor shall such minister, priest, or rabbi be competent or compellable to testify with reference to any such communication in any court.

HAWAII

Hawaii Rules of Evidence, Rule 506. Communications to clergymen (1992)

(a) *Definitions.* As used in this section:

(1) A "member of the clergy" is a minister, priest, rabbi, Christian Science practitioner, or other similar functionary of a religious organization, or an individual reasonably believed so to be by the communicant.

(2) A communication is "confidential" if made privately and not intended for further disclosure except to other persons present in furtherance of the purpose of the communication.

(b) *General rule of privilege.* A person has a privilege to refuse to disclose and to prevent another from disclosing a confidential communication by the person to a member of the clergy in the latter's professional character as a spiritual adviser.

(c) *Who may claim the privilege.* The privilege may be claimed by the communicant or by the communicant's guardian, conservator, or personal representative. The member of the clergy may claim the privilege on behalf of the communicant. Authority so to do is presumed in the absence of evidence to the contrary.

IDAHO

Idaho Code § 9-203(3). Confidential relations and communications (1996)

There are particular relations in which it is the policy of the law to encourage confidence and to preserve it inviolate; therefore, a person shall not be examined as a witness in the following cases: . . . (3) a clergyman or priest cannot, without the consent of the person making the confession, be examined as to any confession made to him in his professional character in the course of discipline enjoined by the church to which he belongs.

ILLINOIS

735 Ill. Comp. Stat. 5/8-803. Clergy (1982)

A clergyman or practitioner in any religious denomination accredited by the religious body to which he or she belongs, shall not be compelled to disclose in any court, or to any administrative board or agency, or to any public officer, a confession or admission made to him or her in his or her professional character or as a spiritual advisor in the course of the discipline enjoined by the rules or practices of such religious body or by the religion which he or she professes, nor be compelled to divulge any information which has been obtained by him or her in such professional character of as such spiritual advisor.

INDIANA

Ind. Code Ann. § 34-46-3.1. Attorneys, physicians, clergymen, spouses (1998)

Except as otherwise provided by statute, the following persons shall not be required to testify regarding the following communications . . .

(3) Clergymen, as to the following confessions, admissions, or confidential communications:

(A) Confessions or admissions made to a clergyman in the course of discipline enjoined by the clergyman's church.

(B) A confidential communication made to a clergyman in the clergyman's professional character as a spiritual adviser or counselor.

IOWA

Iowa Code § 622.10. Communications in professional confidence (1997)

1. A . . . member of the clergy shall not be allowed, in giving testimony, to disclose any confidential communication properly entrusted to the person in the person's professional capacity, and necessary and proper to enable the person to discharge the functions of the person's office according to the usual course of practice or discipline. . . .

2. The prohibition does not apply to cases where the person in whose favor the prohibition is made waives the rights conferred . . . .

KANSAS

Kan. Stat. Ann. § 60-429. Penitential communication privilege (1964)

(a) *Definitions.* As used in this section,

(1) the term "duly ordained minister of religion" means a person who has been ordained, in accordance with the ceremonial ritual, or discipline or a church, religious sect, or organization established on the basis of a community of faith and belief, doctrines and practices of a religious character, to preach and to teach the doctrines of such church, sect, or organization and to administer the rites and ceremonies thereof in public worship, and who as his or her regular and customary vocation preaches and teaches the principles of religion and administers the ordinances of public worship as embodied in the creed or principles of such church, sect or organization;

(2) the term "regular minister of religion" means one who as his or her customary vocation preaches and teaches the principles of religion of a church, a religious sect, or organization of which he or she is a member, without having been formally ordained as a minister of religion, and who is recognized by such church, sect, or organization as a regular minister;

(3) the term "regular or duly ordained minister of religion" does not include a person who irregularly or incidentally preaches and teaches the principles of religion of a church, religious sect, or organization and does not include any person who may have been duly ordained a minister in accordance with the ceremonial rite, or discipline of a church, religious sect or organization, but who does not regularly, as a vocation, teach and preach the principles of religion and administer the ordinances of public worship as embodied in the creed or principles of his or her church, sect, or organization;

(4) "penitent" means a person who recognizes the existence and the authority of God and who seeks or receives from a regular or duly ordained minister of religion advice or assistance in determining or discharging his or her moral obligations, or in obtaining God's mercy or forgiveness for past culpable conduct;

(5) "penitential communication" means any communication between a penitent and a regular or duly ordained minister of religion which the penitent intends shall be kept secret and confidential

and which pertains to advice or assistance in determining or discharging the penitent's moral obligations, or to obtaining God's mercy or forgiveness for past culpable conduct.

(b) *Privilege.* A person, whether or not a party, has a privilege to refuse to disclose, and to prevent a witness from disclosing a communication if he or she claims the privilege and the judge finds that (1) the communication was a penitential communication and (2) the witness is the penitent or the minister, and (3) the claimant is the penitent, or the minister making the claim on behalf of an absent penitent.

KENTUCKY

Kentucky Rules of Evidence, Rule 505. Religious privilege (1992)

(a) *Definitions.* As used in this rule:

(1) A "clergyman" is a minister, priest, rabbi, accredited Christian Science Practitioner, or other similar functionary of a religious organization, or an individual reasonably believed so to be by the person consulting him.

(2) A communication is "confidential" if made privately and not intended for further disclosure except to other persons present in furtherance of the purpose of the communication.

(b) *General Rule of Privilege.* A person has a privilege to refuse to disclose and to prevent another from disclosing a confidential communication between the person and a clergyman in his professional character as spiritual adviser.

(c) *Who May Claim the Privilege.* The privilege may be claimed by the person, by his guardian or conservator, or by his personal representative if he is deceased. The person who was the clergyman at the time of the communication is presumed to have authority to claim the privilege but only on behalf of the communicant.

LOUISIANA

La. Code of Evidence Article 511. Communications to clergymen (1992)

(a) *Definitions.* As used in this Article:

(1) A "clergyman" is a minister, priest, rabbi, or other similar functionary of a religious organization, or an individual reasonably believed so to be by the person consulting him.

(2) A communication is "confidential" if made privately and not intended for further disclosure except to other persons present in furtherance of the purpose of the communication.

(b) *General Rule of Privilege.* A person has a privilege to refuse to disclose and to prevent another from disclosing a confidential communication by the person to a clergyman in his professional character as spiritual adviser.

(c) *Who May Claim the Privilege.* The privilege may be claimed by the person or by his legal representative. The clergyman is presumed to have authority to claim the privilege on behalf of the person or deceased person.

MAINE

Maine Rules of Evidence, Rule 505. Religious privilege (1997)

(a) *Definitions.* As used in this rule:

(1) A "clergyman" is a minister, priest, rabbi, accredited Christian Science Practitioner, or other similar functionary of a religious organization, or an individual reasonably believed so to be by the person consulting him.

(2) A communication is "confidential" if made privately and not intended for further disclosure except to other persons present in furtherance of the purpose of the communication.

(b) *General Rule of Privilege.* A person has a privilege to refuse to disclose and to prevent another from disclosing a confidential communication by the person to the clergyman in his professional character as a spiritual adviser.

(c) *Who May Claim the Privilege.* The privilege may be claimed by the person, by his guardian or conservator, or by his personal representative if he is deceased. The person who was the clergyman at the time of the communication is presumed to have authority to claim the privilege but only on behalf of the communicant.

MARYLAND

Md. Cts. & Jud. Proc. Code Ann. § 9-111. Minister, clergyman, or priest (1973)

A minister of the gospel, clergyman, or priest of any established church of any denomination may not be compelled to testify on any matter in relation to any confession or communication made to him in confidence by a person seeking his spiritual advice or consolation.

MASSACHUSETTS

Mass. Ann. Laws ch. 233, § 20A. Privileged communications; communications with clergymen (1962)

A priest, rabbi or ordained or licensed minister of any church or an accredited Christian Science practitioner shall not, without the consent of the person making the confession, be allowed to disclose a confession made to him in his professional character, in the course of discipline enjoined by the rules or practice of the religious body to which he belongs; nor shall a priest, rabbi or ordained or licensed minister or any church or an accredited Christian Science practitioner testify as to any communication made to him by any person in seeking religious or spiritual advice or comfort, or as to his advice given thereon in the course of his professional duties or in his professional character, without the consent of such person.

MICHIGAN

Mich. Comp. Laws Ann. § 600.2156. Minister, priest, Christian Science practitioner not to disclose confessions (civil) (1962)

No minister of the gospel, or priest of any denomination whatsoever, or duly accredited Christian Science practitioner, shall be allowed to disclose any confessions made to him in his professional character, in the course of discipline enjoined by the rules or practice of such denomination.

Mich. Comp. Laws Ann. § 767.5a(2). Reporters; disclosure of informant identity or information, exception: attorneys, clergy, physicians; privileged and confidential communications (1986)

Any communication between . . . members of the clergy and the members of their respective churches . . . are hereby declared to be privileged and confidential when those communications were necessary to enable the . . . members of the clergy . . . to serve as such . . . member [sic] of the clergy . . . .

MINNESOTA

Minn. Stat. Ann. § 595.02(1)(c). Testimony of witnesses

A member of the clergy or other minister of any religion shall not, without the consent of the party making the confession, be allowed to disclose a confession made to the member of the clergy or other minister in a professional character, in the course of discipline enjoined by the rules or practice of the religious body to which the member of the clergy or other minister of any religion belongs; nor shall a member of the clergy or other minister of any religion be examined as to any communication made to the member of the clergy or other minister by any person seeking religious or spiritual advice, aid, or comfort or advice given thereon in the course of the member of the clergy's or other minister's professional character, without the consent of the person.

MISSISSIPPI

Mississippi Rules of Evidence, Rule 505. Priest-penitent privilege

(a) *Definitions.* As used in this rule:

(1) A "*clergyman*" is a minister, priest, rabbi or other similar functionary of a church, religious organization, or religious denomination.

(2) A communication is "*confidential*" if made privately and not intended for further disclosure except in furtherance of the purpose of the communication.

(b) *General Rule of Privilege.* A person has a privilege to refuse to disclose and prevent another from disclosing a confidential communication by the person to a clergyman in his professional character as spiritual adviser.

(c) *Who May Claim the Privilege.* The privilege may be claimed by the person, by his guardian or conservator, or by his personal representative if he is deceased. The clergyman shall claim the privilege on behalf of the person unless the privilege is waived.

(d) *Other.* A clergyman's secretary, stenographer, or clerk shall not be examined without the consent of the clergyman concerning any fact, the knowledge of which was acquired in such capacity.

MISSOURI

Mo. Rev. Stat. § 491.060. Persons incompetent to testify (1988)

The following persons shall be incompetent to testify: . . . (4) any person practicing as a minister of the gospel, priest, or rabbi or other person serving in a similar capacity for any organized religion, concerning a communication made to him in his professional capacity as a spiritual advisor, confessor, counselor or comforter.

MONTANA

Mont. Code Ann. § 26-1-804. Privileges (1977)

A clergyman or priest cannot, without the consent of the person making the confession, be examined as to any confession made to him in his professional character in the course of discipline enjoined by the church to which he belongs.

NEBRASKA

Neb. Rev. Stat. § 27-506. Communications to clergyman; definitions; general rule of privilege; who may claim the privilege (1975)

(1) As used in this rule:

(a) A clergyman is a minister, priest, rabbi, or other similar functionary of a religious organization, or an individual reasonably believed so to be by the person consulting him; and

(b) A communication is confidential if made privately and not intended for further disclosure except to other persons present in furtherance of the purpose of the communication.

(2) A person has a privilege to refuse to disclose and to prevent another from disclosing a confidential communication by the person to a clergyman in his professional character as a spiritual advisor.

(3) The privilege may be claimed by the person, by his guardian or conservator, or by his personal representative if he is deceased. The clergyman shall claim the privilege on behalf of the person. His authority so to do is presumed in the absence of evidence to the contrary.

NEVADA

Nev. Rev. Stat. § 49.255. Confessor and confessant (1977)

A clergyman or priest shall not, without the consent of the person making the confession, be examined as a witness as to any confession made to him in his professional character.

NEW HAMPSHIRE

N.H. Rev. Stat. Ann. § 516.35. Religious leaders (1979)

A priest, rabbi or ordained or licensed minister of any church or a duly accredited Christian Science practitioner shall not be required to disclose a confession or confidence made to him in his professional character as spiritual adviser, unless the person confessing or confiding waives the privilege.

NEW JERSEY

N.J. Stat. Ann. § 2A:84A-23 Rule 511. Cleric-penitent privilege (1994)

Any communication made in confidence to a cleric in the cleric's professional character, or as a spiritual advisor in the course of the discipline or practice of the religious body to which the cleric belongs or of the religion which the cleric professes, shall be privileged. Privileged communications shall include confessions and other communications made in confidence between and among the cleric and individuals, couples, families or groups in the exercise of the cleric's professional or spiritual counseling role.

As used in this section, "cleric" means a priest, rabbi, minister or other person or practitioner authorized to perform similar functions of any religion.

The privilege accorded to communications under this rule shall belong to both the cleric and the person or persons making the communication and shall be subject to waiver only under the following circumstances:

(1) both the person or persons making the communication and the cleric consent to the waiver of the privilege; or

(2) the privileged communication pertains to a future criminal act, in which case, the cleric alone may, but is not required to, waive the privilege.

NEW MEXICO

New Mexico Rules of Evidence, Rule 506. Communications to clergymen (1993)

A. *Definitions.* As used in this rule:

(1) a "member of the clergy" is a minister, priest, rabbi, or other similar functionary of a religious organization, or an individual reasonably believed so to be by the person consulting that person;

(2) a communication is "confidential" if made privately and not intended for further disclosure except to other persons present in furtherance of the purpose of the communication.

B. *General rule of privilege.* A person has a privilege to refuse to disclose and to prevent another from disclosing a confidential communication by the person to a member of the clergy as a spiritual adviser.

C. *Who may claim the privilege.* The privilege may be claimed by the person or by the person's guardian, conservator or, upon death, personal representative. The member of the clergy may claim the privilege on behalf of the person. The authority to claim the privilege is presumed in the absence of evidence to the contrary.

NEW YORK

N.Y. Civ. Prac. L. & R. § 4505. Confidential communication to clergy privileged (1965)

Unless the person confessing or confiding waives the privilege, a clergyman, or other minister of any religion or duly accredited Christian Science practitioner, shall not be allowed to disclose a confession or confidence made to him in his professional character as spiritual advisor.

NORTH CAROLINA

N.C. Gen. Stat. § 8-53.2. Communications between clergymen and communicants (1984)

No priest, rabbi, accredited Christian Science practitioner, or a clergyman or ordained minister of an established church shall be competent to testify in any action, suit or proceeding concerning any information which was communicated to him and entrusted to him in his professional capacity, and necessary to enable him to discharge the functions of his office according to the usual course of his practice or discipline, wherein such person so communicating such information about himself or another is seeking spiritual counsel and advice relative to and growing out of the information so imparted, provided, however, that this section shall not apply where communicant in open court waives the privilege conferred.

NORTH DAKOTA

North Dakota Rules of Evidence, Rule 505. Religious privilege (1976)

(a) *Definitions.* As used in this rule:

(1) A "clergyman" is a minister, priest, rabbi, accredited Christian Science Practitioner, or other similar functionary of a religious organization, or an individual reasonably believed so to be by the person consulting him.

(2) A communication is "confidential" if made privately and not intended for further disclosure except to other persons present in furtherance of the purpose of the communication.

(b) *General Rule of Privilege.* A person has a privilege to refuse to disclose and to prevent another from disclosing a confidential communication by the person to the clergyman in his professional character as a spiritual adviser.

(c) *Who May Claim the Privilege.* The privilege may be claimed by the person, by his guardian or conservator, or by his personal representative if he is deceased. The person who was the clergyman at the time of the communication is presumed to have authority to claim the privilege but only on behalf of the communicant.

OHIO

Ohio Rev. Code Ann. § 2317.02(c). Privileged communications and acts

The following persons shall not testify in certain respects . . .

(C) A member of the clergy, rabbi, priest, or regularly ordained, accredited, or licensed minister of an established and legally cognizable church, denomination, or sect, when the cleric, rabbi, priest, or minister remains accountable to the authority of that church, denomination, or sect, concerning a confession made, or any information confidentially communicated, the clergyman, rabbi, priest, or minister for a religious counseling purpose in the clergyman's, rabbi's, priest's, or minister's professional character; however, the cleric, rabbi, priest, or minister may testify by express consent of the person making the communication, except when the disclosure of the information is in violation of the clergyman's rabbi's, priest's, or minister's a sacred trust.

OKLAHOMA

Okla. Stat. title 12, § 2505. Religious privilege (1978)

A. As used in this section:

1. A "clergyman" is a minister, priest, rabbi, accredited Christian Science practitioner or other similar functionary of a religious organization, or any individual reasonably believed to be a clergyman by the person consulting him.

2. A communication is "confidential" if made privately and not intended for further disclosure except to other persons present in furtherance of the purpose of the communication.

B. A person has a privilege to refuse to disclose and to prevent another from disclosing his confidential communication made to a clergyman acting in his professional capacity.

C. The privilege may be claimed by the person, by his guardian or conservator, or by his personal representative if he is deceased. The clergyman is presumed to have authority to claim the privilege but only on behalf of the communicant.

OREGON

Or. Rev. Stat. § 40.260 Rule 506. Clergyman-penitent privilege (1981)

(1) As used in this section, unless the context requires otherwise:

(a) "Confidential communication" means a communication made privately and not intended for further disclosure except to other persons present in furtherance of the purpose of the communication.

(b) "Member of the clergy" means a minister of any church, religious denomination or organization or accredited Christian Science practitioner who in the course of the discipline or practice of that church, denomination or organization is authorized or accustomed to hearing confidential communications, and, under the discipline or tenets of that church, denomination or organization, has a duty to keep such communications secret.

(2) A member of the clergy shall not, without the consent of the person making the communication, be examined as to any confidential communication made to the member of the clergy in the member's professional character.

PENNSYLVANIA

Pa. Cons. Stat. Ann. title 42, § 5943. Confidential communications to clergymen (1978)

No clergyman, priest, rabbi or minister of the gospel of any regularly established church or religious organization, except clergymen or ministers who are self-ordained or who are members of religious organizations in which members other than the leader thereof are deemed clergymen or ministers, who while in the course of his duties has acquired information from any person secretly and in confidence shall be compelled, or allowed without consent of such person, to disclose that information in any legal proceeding, trial or investigation before any government unit.

RHODE ISLAND

R.I. Gen. Laws § 9-17-23. Privileged communications to clergymen (1997)

In the trial of every cause, both civil and criminal, no member of the clergy or priest shall be competent to testify concerning any confession made to him or her in his or her professional character in the course of discipline enjoined by the church to which he or she belongs, without the consent of the person making the confession. No duly ordained minister of the gospel, priest or rabbi of any denomination shall be allowed in giving testimony to disclose any confidential communication, properly entrusted to him or her in his or her professional capacity, and necessary and proper to enable him or her to discharge the functions of his or her office in the usual course of practice or discipline, without the consent of the person making the communication.

SOUTH CAROLINA

S.C. Code Ann. § 19-11-90. Priest-penitent privilege (1962)

In any legal or quasi-legal trial, hearing or proceeding before any court, commission or committee no regular or duly ordained minister, priest or rabbi shall be required, in giving testimony, to disclose any confidential communication properly entrusted to him in his professional capacity and necessary and proper to enable him to discharge the functions of his office according to the usual course of practice or discipline of his church or religious body. This prohibition shall not apply to cases where the party in whose favor it is made waives the rights conferred.

SOUTH DAKOTA

S.D. Codified Laws Ann. §§ 19-13-16 to 19-13-18 (Rule 505). Religious privilege (1965)

A. As used in [this section]:

1. A "clergyman" is a minister, priest, rabbi, accredited Christian Science practitioner, or other similar functionary of a religious organization, or any individual reasonably believed so to be by the person consulting him.

2. A communication is "confidential" if made privately and not intended for further disclosure except to other persons present in furtherance of the purpose of the communication.

B. A person has a privilege to refuse to disclose and to prevent another from disclosing a confidential communication by the person to a clergyman in his professional character as spiritual adviser.

C. The privilege . . . may be claimed by the person, by his guardian or conservator, or by his personal representative if he is deceased. The person who was the clergyman at the time of the communication is presumed to have authority to claim the privilege but only on behalf of the communicant.

TENNESSEE

Tenn. Code Ann. § 24-1-206. Clergymen—communications confidential—waiver—penalty (1989)

(a)(1) No minister of the gospel, no priest of the Catholic Church, no rector of the Episcopal Church, no ordained rabbi, and no regular minister of religion of any religious organization or denomination usually referred to as a church, over the age of eighteen (18) years, shall be allowed or required in giving testimony as a witness in any litigation, to disclose any information communicated to him in a confidential manner, properly entrusted to him in his professional capacity, and necessary to enable him to discharge the functions of his office according to the usual course of his practice or discipline, wherein such person so communicating such information about himself or another is seeking spiritual counsel and advice relative to and growing out of the information so imparted.

(2) It shall be the duty of the judge of the court wherein such litigation is pending, when such testimony as prohibited in this section is offered, to determine whether or not that person possesses the qualifications which prohibit him from testifying to the communications sought to be proved by him.

(b) The prohibition of this section shall not apply to cases where the communicating party, or parties, waives the right so conferred by personal appearance in open court so declaring, or by an affidavit properly sworn to by such a one or ones, before some person authorized to administer oaths, and filed with the court wherein litigation is pending.

(c) Nothing in this section shall modify or in any wise change the law relative to "hearsay testimony."

(d) Any minister of the gospel, priest of the Catholic Church, rector of the Episcopal Church, ordained rabbi, and any regular minister of religion of any religious organization or denomination usually referred to as a church, violating the provisions of this section, shall be guilty of a misdemeanor and fined not less than fifty dollars ($50) and imprisoned in the county jail or workhouse not exceeding six (6) months.

TEXAS

Texas Rules of Evidence, Rule 505. Communications to clergymen (1998)

(a) *Definitions.* As used in this rule:

(1) A "clergyman" is a minister, priest, rabbi, accredited Christian Science Practitioner, or other similar functionary of a religious organization, or an individual reasonably believed so to be by the person consulting him.

(2) A communication is "confidential" if made privately and not intended for further disclosure except to other persons present in furtherance of the purpose of the communication.

(b) *General Rule of Privilege.* A person has a privilege to refuse to disclose and to prevent another from disclosing a confidential communication by the person to the clergyman in his professional character as a spiritual adviser.

(c) *Who May Claim the Privilege.* The privilege may be claimed by the person, by his guardian or conservator, or by his personal representative if he is deceased. The person who was the clergyman at the time of the communication is presumed to have authority to claim the privilege but only on behalf of the communicant.

UTAH

Utah Code Ann. § 78-24-8(3). Privileged communications (1990)

There are particular relations in which it is the policy of the law to encourage confidence and to preserve it inviolate. Therefore, a person cannot be examined as a witness in the following cases: ... (3) A clergyman or priest cannot, without the consent of the person making the confession, be examined as to any confession made to him in his professional character in the course of discipline enjoined by the church to which he belongs.

VERMONT

Vt. Stat. Ann. title 12, § 1607. Priests and ministers (1947)

A priest or minister of the gospel shall not be permitted to testify in court to statements made to him by a person under the sanctity of a religious confessional.

VIRGINIA

Va. Code Ann. § 8.01-400. Communications between ministers of religion and persons they counsel or advise (1994)

Communications between ministers of religion and persons they counsel or advise

No regular minister, priest, rabbi, or accredited practitioner over the age of eighteen years, of any religious organization or denomination usually referred to as a church, shall be required to give testimony as a witness or to relinquish notes, records or any written documentation made by such person, or disclose the contents of any such notes, records or written documentation, in discovery proceedings in any civil action which would disclose any information communicated to him in a confidential manner, properly entrusted to him in his professional capacity and necessary to enable him to discharge the functions of his office according to the usual course of his practice or discipline, wherein such person so communicating such information about himself or another is seeking spiritual counsel and advice relative to and growing out of the information so imparted.

WASHINGTON

Wash. Rev. Code Ann. § 5.60.060(3). Who are disqualified—privileged communications (1997)

A member of the clergy or a priest shall not, without the consent of a person making the confession, be examined as to any confession made to him or her in his or her professional character, in the course of discipline enjoined by the church to which he or she belongs.

WEST VIRGINIA

W. Va. Code § 48-2-10a. Communications between clergyman and party (1981)

In any action brought pursuant to the provisions of this article, no priest, minister, rabbi, or other clergyman . . . of any religious denomination or organization who is not a party to said action shall be compelled to testify regarding any communications or statements made to such clergyman in his capacity as spiritual counselor or spiritual adviser by a party to said action, if (a) both the clergyman and the party making such communications or statements claim that the communications or statements were made to the clergyman in his capacity as a clergyman and spiritual counselor or spiritual adviser to such party; and (b) no person, other than the clergyman, such party and the spouse of such party, was present when such communications or statements were made; and (c) the party making such communications or statements does not either consent to their disclosure or otherwise waive the privilege granted by this section: Provided, that the privilege granted by this section shall be in addition to and not in derogation of any other privileges recognized by law.

WISCONSIN

Wis. Stat. § 905.06. Communications to clergymen (1991)

(1) *Definitions.* As used in this section:

(a) A "clergyman" is a minister, priest, rabbi, or other similar functionary of a religious organization, or an individual reasonably believed so to be by the person consulting him.

(b) A communication is "confidential" if made privately and not intended for further disclosure except to other persons present in furtherance of the purpose of the communication.

(2) *General rule of privilege.* A person has a privilege to refuse to disclose and to prevent another from disclosing a confidential communication by the person to a clergyman in his professional character as a spiritual adviser.

(3) *Who may claim the privilege.* The privilege may be claimed by the person, by his guardian or conservator, or by his personal representative if he is deceased. The clergyman may claim the privilege on behalf of the person. His authority so to do is presumed in the absence of evidence to the contrary.

WYOMING

Wyo. Stat. § 1-12-101. Privileged communications and acts (1991)

The following persons shall not testify in certain respects: . . . (ii) a clergyman or priest concerning a confession made to him in his professional character if enjoined by the church to which he belongs.

APPENDIX 3
ELIGIBILITY OF CLERGY FOR JURY DUTY

State-by-State Analysis

Note: The relevant portion of each state's statute describing the status of clergy for jury duty is set forth below in alphabetical order. All statutes are subject to change, and accordingly this appendix should not be relied upon. To determine the current text of any statute, you should visit a library containing your state statutes, or consult with an attorney. Only those states having statutes exempting clergy from jury duty are listed. If a state is not listed, then it does not exempt clergy from jury duty.

HAWAII

Ha. Rev. Stat. § 612-6. Exempt when (1987)

[A] person may claim exemption from service as a juror if the person is . . . a minister or priest following the minister's or priest's profession . . . .

MASSACHUSETTS

Mass. Ann. Laws ch. 234, § 1. Qualifications; exemptions (1987)

A person of either sex qualified to vote for representatives to the general court, whether a registered voter or not, shall be liable to serve as a juror, except that the following persons shall be exempt . . . settled ministers of the gospel . . . .

MISSOURI

Mo. Rev. Stat. § 494.430. Persons entitled to be excused from jury service

Upon timely application to the court, the following persons shall be excused from service as a petit or grand juror . . . [a]ny person actually performing the duties of a clergyman . . . .

OHIO

Ohio Rev. Code Ann. § 2313.16. Discharge of juror (1998)

[T]he court of common pleas shall not excuse a person who is liable to serve as a juror and who is drawn and notified, unless it is shown to the satisfaction of the judge by either the juror or another person acquainted with the facts that one or more of the following applies . . . (F) The juror is a cloistered member of a religious organization. When a person who is liable to serve is excused in a case specified in this section, the juror can be excused only by the judge presiding in the case or a representative of the judge. An excuse approved pursuant to this section shall not extend beyond that term. Every approved excuse shall be recorded and filed with the commissioners of jurors.

TENNESSEE

Tenn. Code Ann. § 22-1-103. Occupational and disability exemptions

(a) The following persons are exempt from liability to act as jurors . . . [all] clergy . . . .

APPENDIX 4

NORTH AMERICAN SECURITIES ADMINISTRATORS ASSOCIATION, INC.

CHURCH BONDS
Adopted April 29, 1981

INTRODUCTION

The Guidelines which follow have been prepared to aid churches which wish to offer and sell Church Bonds. By their nature, guidelines cannot cover every conceivable situation that may arise, and, therefore, if there are questions regarding the applicability of any of the following provisions or questions about matters not addressed, you should contact the Administrators of the states in which you intend to offer and sell the Church Bonds.

Regulation of Securities. Section 3(a)(4) of the Federal Securities Act of 1933, as amended, exempts from registration "Any security issued by a person organized and operated exclusively for religious, educational, benevolent, fraternal, charitable or reformatory purposes and not for pecuniary profit, and no part of the net earnings of which inures to the benefit of any person, private stockholder, or individual." Church Bonds are securities, but no registration of such securities by churches which meet the above exemption need be made with or approved by the Securities and Exchange Commission which is the Federal agency primarily responsible for regulating the offer and sale or securities in the United States.

In addition to the Federal law, however, most of the individual states have adopted their own securities laws to govern the offer and sale of securities within their respective jurisdiction in the United States over the regulation of securities such as Church Bonds, i.e., both the Federal government and the individual states regulate their offer and sale and the laws of each must be complied with. Most of the states, however, have now adopted laws based upon the Uniform Securities Act, as drafted and approved by the National Conference of Commissioners on Uniform State Laws ("Act") and this Act contains an exemption for Church Bonds similar to the exemption contained in the Federal law. In order to determine whether a particular state statute contains provisions similar to the citations from the Act which follow, however, you should consult your attorney or the Administrators of the states in which you intend to sell the Church Bonds. You should also be aware that there are certain states which do *not* (emphasis added) exempt Church Bonds from registration and, therefore, before offering or selling Church Bonds in any state you must carefully check the laws of that state to be sure that you do so in compliance with its laws. The following discussion relates only to states which follow the Act.

Section 301 of the Act provides that:

It is unlawful for any person to offer to sell any security in this state unless (1) it is registered under this act or (2) the security or the transaction is exempted under Section 402.

Section 402(a)(9) of the Act then provides that the following securities are exempted from Sections 301 and 403 (requiring the filing of sales literature) thereof:

(9) any security issued by any person organized and operated not for private profit but exclusively for religious, educational, benevolent, charitable, fraternal, social, athletic or reformatory purposes . . . .

This section means that registration under Section 301 of the Act is not required for securities of Issuers meeting the above exemption but it does not mean that an Issuer of such securities has no other responsibilities under the Act.

Specifically, Section 101 of the Act provides that:

It is unlawful for any person, in connection with the offer, sale or purchase of any security, directly or indirectly: (1) to employ any device, scheme or artifice to defraud; (2) to make any untrue statement of a material fact or to omit to state a material fact necessary in order to make the statements made, in light of the circumstances under which they are made, not misleading; or (3) to engage in any act, practice or course of business which operates or would operate as a fraud or deceit upon any person.

This section essentially requires that full disclosure of all material facts necessary to make an informed investment decision be made to all Investors including purchasers or all securities offered pursuant to Section 402(a) of the Act.

It may, in fact, be deemed by an Administrator to be a fraudulent transaction per se if an Issuer either (i) offers Church Bonds without the use of an Offering Circular substantially conforming to the disclosures contained in the following Guidelines, or (ii) offers Church Bonds which the Issuer cannot adequately demonstrate an ability to repay. The Guidelines which follow have been promulgated to attempt to insure that an Issuer utilizes a suitable disclosure document and meets the requisite financial tests necessary to evidence an ability to repay any Church Bonds offered.

An issuer offering Church Bonds which are not in compliance with the Act and the following Guidelines could be liable under both the civil and criminal sections of the Act which involve both fines and possible imprisonment. This liability could also extend to the officers and directors of the Issuer.

In addition, Section 401(b) of the Act defines the term "Agent" to mean:

. . . any individual other than a broker-dealer who represents a broker-dealer or issuer in effecting or attempting to effect purchases or sales of securities . . .

Section 201(a) provides:

It is unlawful for any person to transact business in this state as a broker-dealer unless he is registered under this act . . .

Thus, the Act requires that any person, including an officer or director of the Issuer, who wishes to offer or sell Church Bonds must either be a registered representative of a licensed securities broker-dealer, or alternately must file for registration as an agent with the Administrators of the states in which he intends to sell securities pursuant to Section 201 of the Act. This is true even if the Church Bonds themselves are exempt from registration under Section 402(a)(9) of the Act. Any person who sells Church Bonds without compliance with the agent registration provisions of the Act could also be liable under both the civil and criminal sections of the Act.

Pursuant to the rule making power contained in Section 412 of the Act, an Administrator may waive the testing requirements for a securities agent's license, provided, however, that the offering is substantially in compliance with the following Guidelines. Even if the Issuer utilizes registered agents, however, it must take the following steps to insure compliance with the anti-fraud provisions of the Act:

(1) Prepare a letter to each Administrator of a state in which the Issuer intends to offer or sell stating that the Issuer wishes to offer or sell Church Bonds, and setting forth the facts necessary to substantiate the exemption under Section 402(a)(9) thereof. These facts should describe the operations of the Issuer and state the basis for its claimed exemption, e.g., establishing that it is a religious organization. The letter should be signed by an authorized officer of the Issuer. If the Issuer wishes to register its agents and not use a broker-dealer, it should also request registration forms for certain specified individuals. The Issuer should attach to this letter the name of each of the individuals, his home address, his business address, and his home and business phone numbers. The letter should also indicate as to each of the individuals whether they have been, or are now, registered securities agents or whether they have been subject to any previous order by any administrative agency or by any Administrator. The letter should also state whether any compensation will be paid or given to the agents for offering or selling the Church Bonds. The Administrator may waive the examination upon a showing of good cause. Significant factors to be considered in determining whether the examination will be waived would include the methods utilized to offer the Church Bonds, including the types of solicitations made by the agent, and the overall nature of the sales materials and efforts. If solicitations are made primarily through mailing of previously filed sales materials rather than by personal solicitations of the investors, the examination should typically be waived.

(2) The Issuer should enclose with the letter the following documents:

A. Issuer's articles of incorporation, charter and any amendments thereto, and a copy of its bylaws, if any. If the Issuer is not a corporation, the equivalent governing instruments should be filed.

B. A copy of the Issuer's latest nonprofit corporation annual report, if any, required by the Issuer's state of domicile.

C. A draft copy of the Church Bond. It is recommended that the certificates not be printed until approval has been secured. Please label the certificates submitted with the words "specimen" or "void."

D. A copy of any proposed agreement or proposed form of agreement with a securities dealer, underwriter, or financing organization. (If there is or will be none, so state in the letter of transmittal.)

E. A copy of the preliminary or definitive Trust Indenture and/or trust agreement, if any.

F. Copies of all advertising materials to be used in connection with the offering.

G. An opinion of counsel attesting to the authority of the Issuer to offer and sell the Church Bonds and stating that after the sale the Church Bonds will be valid, binding obligations of the Issuer in accordance with the Issuer's governing documents.

H. A copy of the Issuer's resolution authorizing issuance of the Church Bonds.

(3) Enclose with the letter two draft copies of the Offering Circular, prepared in accordance with the following Guidelines. The Offering Circular should not be reproduced or distributed to Investors until approval is obtained. An approved Offering Circular may be reproduced in any legible fashion, and need not be printed nor reproduced on glossy paper.

GUIDELINES

Drafting comment. These Church Bond Guidelines are only used to review offerings of Church Bonds by individual congregations or churches. The concern to emphasize that the Guidelines are not to be rigidly applied, but are only general parameters against which an individual Issuer could be measured.

APPLICATION

These Guidelines are only applicable to offerings of debt securities in the form of notes, bonds, or similar instruments ("Church Bonds") issued by a congregation or church (Issuer) the proceeds of which are to be utilized to finance or refinance the purchase, construction or improvement of buildings or related facilities (including the underlying property) of the Issuer, including church buildings, parsonages or church schools. It is not intended that these Guidelines be applied to general obligation financing by national religious denominations; that method of financing will be addressed in the future should the need arise. It is also not intended that an individual church or congregation be permitted to utilize general obligation financing except in the most unusual circumstances. The Guidelines which follow are intended to be broadly interpreted, therefore, certain portions of these Guidelines may be modified or waived at the discretion of the Administrator.

Drafting comment. The intent was primarily to provide broad standards to establish, in a general sense, whether a Church issuing Church Bonds was capable of repaying them and whether the documents describing the offering provided full and adequate disclosure. It was of particular concern that Administrators be willing to waive or modify portions of the Guidelines where good cause can be shown or an alternative safeguard provided.

DEFINITIONS

Act: The Uniform Securities Act, as drafted and approved by the National Conference of Commissioners on Uniform State Laws.

Administrator: The state securities commissioner or administrator of a state.

Audited Financial: Financial statements prepared in accordance with generally accepted accounting principles applied on a consistent basis, and examined and reported upon by independent certified public accountants or qualified public accountants.

Church Bonds: Certificates in the form of notes, bonds or similar instruments issued by a congregation or church which represent an obligation to repay a specific principal amount at a stated rate of interest.

Service Agent: A nominee, independent of the Issuer, designated to monitor a bond issue on a continuing basis and perform record keeping services for the Issuer.

Investor: A person who is offered, or purchases a Church Bond.

Issuer: A church or congregation which offers and sells Church Bonds.

Limited Graduated Payments: A method of amortizing the debt by making payments of principal and interest on Church Bonds in such a manner that the first years of payments may be lower than the later years of payments, provided that the lowest payment is equal to at least the interest on the bonds and the highest payment does not exceed a payment amount 10% higher than the straight line payment, using the same total number of years.

Offering Circular: The disclosure document prepared by the Issuer to permit an Investor to make an informed investment decision with respect to the purchase of a Church Bond.

Paying Agent: A nominee, independent of the Issuer and the broker-dealer, designated by the Issuer to make payments to the Investors on behalf of the Issuer pursuant to a Trust Indenture.

Straight Line: A method of amortizing the payments of principal and interest on Church Bonds in such a manner that all payments are equal (except that principal payments may be deferred until the estimated construction date but not to exceed 18 months from the date of the Offering Circular) and the final payment retires the remaining principal and interest. The period for amortization should typically not exceed 20 years.

Trustee: A corporation, individual, or other entity (independent of the Issuer) granted trust powers by the state, which holds title to the pledged properties securing the Church Bonds and administers the Trust Indenture.

Trust Indenture: The instrument under which the Trustee is given certain powers and controls over assets or property of the Issuer to secure an issuance of Church Bonds.

FINANCIAL GUIDELINES

An Issuer should offer no more Church Bonds than it can reasonably expect to repay. Although each situation must be viewed in context of the individual facts, the following are among the principal standards which an Administrator will consider in reviewing a proposed issue. The issuer has the burden of proving substantial compliance with these principal standards. Issuers of Church Bonds should comply substantially with the following standards in an offering of Church Bonds:

1. (a) Total debt upon completion of the offering should not exceed four times the last twelve months' revenues. Such revenues shall not include nonrecurring bequests and other extraordinary forms of revenues.

Drafting comment. The test of limiting total debt to four times the last 12 months ordinary revenues must be reviewed in light of total expenses. Also excluded were bequests and extraordinary (nonrecurring) items which cannot be assumed to be available from year to year. However, if extraordinary revenues are excluded, "extraordinary" or non-fixed debts should likewise be excluded.

(b) The Offering must be secured by a Trust Indenture pledging the properties acquired to secure the Church Bonds, the Church Bonds must constitute a first lien on the pledged properties (or the Issuer must document the economic soundness of the financing) and the aggregate amount of the offering should not be in excess of 75% of the appraised value of the properties pledged as collateral (after completion of the building project).

Drafting comment. If the Trust Indenture is not a first lien on the property the Issuer should have a heavy burden of proof as to the fairness of the offer.

(c) The Trust Indenture must provide for a Trustee, provide for the assignment or pledge of the Issuer's first receipts for timely payment of the Church Bonds, afford the usual contractual prohibitions including limitations on future offerings of securities (if they would impair the Issuer's ability to repay the Church Bonds) provide insurance coverage, include a provision for maintenance of the properties, contain prohibitions against further encumbrances upon the properties, and provide provisions to protect the rights of Investors.

(d) The Trust Indenture must provide for regular payments to the paying Agent sufficient to service the payments on the Church Bonds.

(e) The Paying Agent Service Agent must immediately report to the Trustee each failure to cure a non-payment after thirty (30) days of the due date from which the non-payment occurred. The Trustee shall give the Administrator timely notice of each failure to cure a non-payment of principal or interest on any maturity date after sixty (60) days of the date from which the non-payment occurred.

Drafting comment. It was anticipated that each administrator would set up a workable system to ensure that the Notice provisions for non-payments would be quickly disseminated. Specific requirements were included only as parameters since it was felt that each Administrator could tailor this to staff needs.

(f) An Issuer may not normally utilize financing other than Straight Line or Limited Graduated Payments. "Balloon payments" or other graduated payments normally will not be deemed acceptable.

Drafting comment. It is felt that this deviation from Straight Line amortization should be permitted only when the Issuer was able to demonstrate that it did not present a material potential risk for Investors. However, other forms of graduated payments could be permitted depending upon the Issuer's financial condition. By defining a graduated payment method it should not be construed that this is the only acceptable means of having graduated payments.

(g) The Issuer should obtain a fixed price contract, completion bond, or other acceptable form of assurance of performance for the completion of the construction of the facilities to be undertaken with the proceeds of the offering.

(h) The Issuer should provide Investors with financial statements for its last three fiscal years. When required, financial statements for the most recent fiscal year should be audited. If the offering commences more than 120 days after the end of such last fiscal year, the financial should be updated with unaudited financial within 120 days of the offering date. An Issuer which does not provide three years of financial statements, and when required, audited financial for the last fiscal year may, at the discretion of the Administrator, be permitted to sell the Church Bonds; however, this shall be deemed a significant factor in determining whether to permit an offering to proceed and shall be weighed heavily in granting waivers from any provisions of the Guidelines.

(Administrators, in exercising their discretion relative to the requirements of audited financial, should consider the impact of the cost of audited financial in requiring substantial compliance.)

Drafting comment. The use of and need for audited financial was debated at great length by the drafters. It was agreed that audited financial should be required to ensure some outside financial review of the Issuer. However, it was recognized that this requirement can be a great time and expense burden on the Issuer and so it was left open to individual Administrators to waive this guideline if he can otherwise satisfy himself as to the financial integrity of the Issuer. This guideline should not, however, be lightly waived. The cost of audit should be weighed against the size of the offering and the class of potential offerees. The problem of attempting to account for the value of historic properties, at cost, appraised value, or fair market value is recognized. If unaudited financial statements are utilized the Administrator should assure himself in each individual case that the balance sheet fairly reflects the financial condition of the Issuer.

(i) Church Bonds offered to refinance obligations of the Issuer which are in default or which will be in default without immediate refinancing will not be permitted unless the aggregate of all indebtedness which is to be outstanding after the current offering is within the standards set forth in the Guidelines.

Drafting comment. The refinancing of Church Bonds in default, with proceeds from other Church Bonds is a practice that the drafters looked upon with great disfavor. However, it was recognized that sometimes this was preferable, with full disclosure, to bankruptcy for the Issuer. This is not a practice that should be freely permitted.

(j) The proceeds of the offering should not be commingled with the Issuer's other funds.

Drafting comment. It was felt important to emphasize that these tests are only evidence of the soundness of the Issuer and should not be utilized as the sole judge of the integrity of the offering. The Administrators should, therefore, be aware of other financial tests which would mitigate or obviate the need for the audited financial, or such other financial problems or needs as would invalidate the test.

OFFERING CIRCULAR

The following information should be included in an Offering Circular in order to insure that Investors receive adequate information to make an informed investment decision.

Drafting comment. The drafters listed that information for inclusion in the Offering Circular which it felt was relevant, but with the strong provision that all other relevant information be included and that all Issuers be encouraged to add any unique or unusual features which are not covered. In addition, any information which an Issuer can demonstrate is not material to its transaction need not be included. Again it was felt that strict adherence to the Guidelines without regard to individual circumstances was a disservice to Investors.

I. COVER PAGE

(a) Name of the Issuer.

(b) Principal Business Address and Telephone Number.

(c) Title of the Church Bonds offered.

(d) Total offering, estimated expenses and net proceeds of the offering to the Issuer.

(e) Brief description of the Church Bonds including interest rate, payment dates, denominations available, offering price and maturity dates.

(f) Name, address and telephone number of the Trustee, if applicable.

(g) Name, address and telephone number of the Paying Agent, if applicable.

(h) Name, address and telephone number of the principal underwriter or Broker-Dealer assisting with the offering of the Church Bonds and statements as to any market-making intentions of the underwriter.

(i) Date of termination of the offering and the Issuer's right to extend the offering, if any.

(j) Minimum amount of sales necessary to complete the offering, if any.

(k) Date of Offering Circular.

(l) Legends—

The Offering Circular should include the following sections, and there should be set out under each section in narrative or descriptive form all of the relevant information pertaining to the Issuer and the Church Bonds. The Issuer should also include any other information not specifically requested which is important to an understanding of the entire transaction and should omit any sections which are not applicable.

II. HISTORY AND OPERATIONS

(a) Provide a brief description of the Issuer, including the name, address of principal business office, state of organization, date of organization, type of legal entity (corporation, unincorporated association, etc.) and religious purposes of the Issuer.

(b) A brief history of the Issuer and its denominational affiliation, if any.

(c) A brief description of the accreditation of the Issuer, if any, and the entities regulating the Issuer, if any.

(d) A brief description of the current operations and functions of the Issuer, including its principal activities and fiscal policies.

(e) A brief description of the number of members of the Issuer and a comparison of the growth or contraction of such membership over the past three years. Set fort in tabular form the average Church attendance, number of families that regularly contribute and the average Sunday school attendance.

III. PRIOR BORROWING EXPERIENCE

This Section should include a description of any defaults in payments of principal or interest on previously issued debt, and whether any proceeds from refinancing or additional offerings were necessary to repay any prior indebtedness. A brief description of the issuer's borrowing experiences and the results thereof should also be included.

IV. RISK FACTORS

The Issuer must describe to the Investors the risks of investing in the Church Bonds. Particular care must be taken with respect to risks associated with the financial condition of the Issuer. Statements to the effect that little or no risk is involved in buying Church Bonds are prohibited, and such statements by most Issuers will be regarded as material misrepresentations. Likewise, comparisons with other investments made solely on the basis of the interest rate paid will be considered misleading, unless other comparative aspects of the investment are also described. Each risk factor should include a page reference to an appropriate disclosure section. It is important that the Issuer fully describe all of the relevant risks which should include, if applicable, the following:

(a) A description of the Issuer's principal sources of revenues for repayment of the Church Bonds and the potential fluctuations, if applicable, in these sources. For instance, if contributions are the primary source of revenues, a risk factor should be included that there are no assurances that membership will increase or remain stable or that per capita contributions will increase or remain stable.

If increased revenues are expected from increased membership upon completion of the facility which is to be constructed from the proceeds of the offering, a statement should be included that there can be no assurance that this will be the case.

If additional financing may be required to repay Investors, a statement should be included that there can be no assurance that such additional financing will be available or will be permitted by the Administrator.

(b) If any restrictions are to be placed on the transfer of the Church Bonds, a statement describing such restrictions should be included, and if no public market will develop for the repurchase and resale of the Church Bonds, that fact should be stated clearly. If the issuer does not permit early redemption, a statement should be included that Investors should only purchase the Church Bonds if they intend to hold them for the full term thereof.

(c) If construction of a proposed building is not pursuant to a fixed price contract, or the contractor does not post a completion bond, a statement should be included as to the risks of noncompliance. A description of the affiliation, if any, between the Issuer and the contractor or any subcontractor should be included. In addition, a statement should be included as to possible delays in completion due to shortages of materials, possible strikes, act of nature, delays in obtaining necessary building permits or architectural certificates, environmental regulations or fuel or energy shortages.

(d) If any portion of the proceeds from the offering are to be used to refinance existing indebtedness, it should be disclosed if this constitutes a risk factor. A statement of the reasons for the need to refinance the previous indebtedness should also be included.

(e) A statement should be included as to any material pending litigation or contingent liabilities affecting the Issuer, including contingent liabilities for the offer or sale of unregistered securities or potential liabilities before any administrative bodies.

(f) If the Trust Indenture permits the Issuer to further encumber the properties securing the Church Bonds through the issuance and sale of additional obligations at some future date, the maximum debt-to-property ratio and the debt-to-receipts ratio, in such event, should be described.

(g) A statement should be included that in the event of default, the church's property may not sell for its appraised value, since the appraised value of the church property is based on its value as a special purposed property, having a limited market due to its being for the most part single purpose (religious and educational).

Drafting comment. The appraised value of the property should relate to the resale value as a single purpose facility, since this is the Investor's only security if the Church is unable to make payments. Appraisals based upon cost or factors other than fair market value for resale purposes should be closely scrutinized. It was intended that the property should be appraised by an independent qualified appraiser.

(h) If the Offering Circular does not contain financial statements for the Issuer's past three years and Audited Financial for the preceding fiscal year, this fact should be prominently disclosed.

(i) Any special risks relating to insurance, encumbrances, title to the properties or other aspects affecting the Investor's security or the Issuer's financial condition should be disclosed.

The above risk factors are only indicative of the types of risk factors which may be generally associated with offerings of this type. However, the Issuer should also include any special risk associated with the specific offering and must take care to be sure that all problems of which it is aware are described.

Drafting comment. The disclosure of potential risks is a very material portion of the disclosure. Therefore, specific care should be taken to assure that statements as to the ability to increase membership or revenues, ability to maintain a stable market for the Church Bonds, or ability to complete construction without bonding or other assurances, should all be closely scrutinized and adequate assurances should be sought from the Issuer to cover such risks. The risk of holding non-marketable bonds should be prominently disclosed, if applicable.

V. ESCROW OF PROCEEDS

Describe the manner in which funds will be held during the offering period. If funds are to be held in a escrow account with a bank or a state or federally regulated financial institution, they should not be disbursed for the project until the minimum proceeds necessary to complete the project have been obtained. If the minimum proceeds are not obtained, the Issuer must describe the manner in which Investor's funds will be repaid and whether or not interest will be paid on such funds.

VI. USE OF PROCEEDS

Include a tabular schedule of the anticipated use of the proceeds based upon the minimum and maximum anticipated proceeds from the offering. If additional funds may be needed to accomplish the purpose of the offering, this should be stated, along with a description of how such funds will be obtained. Every effort should be made to assure that the project will be completed in accordance with the manner set fort in the Offering Circular.

VII. CURRENT FINANCIAL SITUATION

(a) Include a description of the Issuer's current accounting policies and financial structure, including the date of the Issuer's fiscal year.

(b) Include financial statements, for the Issuer's past three fiscal years when required (financial statements for the most recent fiscal year should be audited) consisting of:

(i) Statement of assets and liabilities (Balance Sheet);

(ii) Statement of revenues and expenses (Income Statement or aggregation of fund balances);

(iii) Statement of changes in financial position; and

(iv) Statement of changes in fund balance.

The most recent financial statements should be as of a date not more than 120 days prior to the date of the proposed offering. If the Issuer's last fiscal year ended more than 120 days prior to the date of the proposed offering, unaudited stub prior financial, including comparative income statements from the end of the Issuer's last fiscal year to date not more than 120 days prior to the date of the proposed offering, should be included. If audited financial are not included and the offering is permitted to proceed, this should be prominently disclosed.

In such instance, a statement verifying the accuracy of the financial statements, signed by the chief financial officer or chief executive officer of the Issuer must be included. If the Audited Financial are provided, a copy of the auditor's report should precede the financial statements. The Issuer should state that any adverse material change in the financial condition of the Issuer during the offering prior will be prominently disclosed in a sticker supplement to the Offering Circular.

(c) Each Offering Circular should contain in tabular form a schedule of outstanding and proposed debt.

CERTAIN STATES ADOPTING THESE GUIDELINES MAY NOT PERMIT AN OFFERING WITHOUT AT LEAST THE MOST RECENT YEAR'S FINANCIAL BEING AUDITED. AN ISSUER PREPARING AN OFFERING OF CHURCH BONDS IN ACCORDANCE WITH THESE GUIDELINES SHOULD THEREFORE FIRST CHECK WITH THE ADMINISTRATOR IN EACH STATE IN WHICH THE CHURCH BONDS ARE PROPOSED TO BE OFFERED IF SUCH AUDITED FINANCIAL WILL NOT BE AVAILABLE.

Drafting comment. The lack of audited financial should be closely reviewed and permitted only in limited instances where the Administrator can otherwise assure himself of the Issuer's financial integrity.

VIII. DESCRIPTION OF THE ISSUER'S PRINCIPAL PROPERTIES

(a) Include a statement describing principal properties of the Issuer and any liens or encumbrances thereon.

(b) Describe the proposed facilities to be constructed from the proceeds of the offering and their proposed use.

(c) List all liens and encumbrances of record on the facilities, or to be created on the facilities.

(d) Describe the purchase agreement if the real property is to be purchased with the proceeds of this offering.

IX. DESCRIPTION OF THE TERMS OF THE CHURCH BONDS

(a) Include a statement describing type and amount of the Church Bonds and set forth the interest rate payment date, and Paying Agent. Describe also the date upon which interest will begin to accrue.

(b) Include a statement describing the underlying collateral, if applicable.

(i) A statement should be made concerning whether the sale of additional Church Bonds may be secured by the same underlying security.

(ii) If guarantees of payment are made by affiliates of the Issuer or otherwise, information describing the ability of the guarantor to satisfy the liability must be furnished, including Audited Financial, if available. A description of the guarantee agreement between the Issuer and the guarantor should also be included. If the guarantee is supported by unaudited financial, appropriate disclaimers should be included. The word "guarantee" should not be used to describe the obligation of the Issuer to repay the indebtedness, and it is appropriate only if there is a secondary obligation by another entity. The guarantee, in and of itself, may involve the offering of a second security which may require registration if not exempt.

(c) Describe the terms of the Church Bonds, including the Issuer's right to early redemption of principal, and the basis upon which such redemption may be made. The Issuer or Investor's right to extend the maturity date, if available, should also be described.

(d) Describe whether any consideration for the purchase of Church Bonds other than cash will be acceptable. Describe whether the Church Bonds will be negotiable or transferable.

(e) Include a description of the Trust Indenture describing the Trustee, Paying Agent, events of default, covenants, restrictions upon subsequent issues and rights of the Issuer and Trustee to modify the Trust Indenture.

X. PLAN OF DISTRIBUTION

(a) List the name and addresses of responsible officials of the Church that will offer or sell or underwriters who will offer or sell the Church Bonds. (It should be noted that certain states require the names, addresses and other information about church members who offer or sell church bonds to be submitted separately to the Administrator.)

(b) Describe the compensation to be paid to such individuals for performing the services in connection with the offering.

(c) Describe any fees paid to "finders" or "advisers" in connection with the distribution, and the services rendered by such persons.

(d) Describe the plan of distribution including a description of the class of offerees, the methods of solicitation to be utilized, and the method of subscribing. All advertising materials must be filed with the Administrator prior to use. If less than the full amount subscribed for may be tendered by the Investor during the offering period, it should be stated whether or not the Investor will be personally liable for subsequent payments.

(e) Describe any underwriting or selling agreement between a broker and the Issuer, including whether such agreements are on a "best efforts" or "firm commitments" basis, whether such arrangements are "exclusive" or "non-exclusive" and whether there are provisions for indemnification of the Issuer or broker-dealer for losses sustained as a result of claims based upon violations of applicable securities laws.

(f) State the responsibilities of the broker-dealer, the Issuer, and the membership of the Issuer under the terms of any underwriting agreement.

(g) Disclose all past, present and anticipated future dealings with broker-dealers, investment advisers, or financing organizations participating this offering, including the aggregate remuneration received by such entities. It should also be disclosed whether any executive officer or director of the Issuer is in any way affiliated with the broker or financing organization participating in this offering or with any executive personnel of such organization.

Drafting comment. The method of sales and the class of Investors should be closely scrutinized by the Administrators to be sure that only the proper inducements were being made and that only appropriate offerees were solicited. This would entail obtaining such assurances from the Issuer and the sales people as each Administrator felt was necessary to Insure the foregoing. Disclosure of officer compensation, at least in the aggregate, is a material factor in any securities offering, especially one of this type.

XI. LITIGATION AND OTHER MATERIAL TRANSACTIONS

(a) Describe any pending or threatened material legal proceeding or proceedings known to be contemplated by governmental authorities, administrative bodies or other persons, to which the Issuer is or may be a party or to which any of its property is or may be subject. Include the name of the court or agency in which the proceedings are pending, the date instituted, the principal parties thereto, a description of the factual basis alleged to underlie the proceeding and the relief sought.

(b) Fully disclose any transactions which may materially affect this offering or an Investor's investment decision, and which are not otherwise mentioned herein.

XII. TAX ASPECTS

Describe the general federal tax aspects of ownership of the Church Bonds and include where appropriate:

(a) Whether the Investor will recognize gain or loss or receive a charitable deduction upon the purchase of Church Bonds,

(b) Whether interest paid or accrued on the Church Bonds will be taxable as ordinary income to the Investor, and

(c) The capital gains treatment upon sale or exchange of the Church Bonds.

XIII. CHURCH LEADERSHIP

(a) Describe the organizational structure of the Issuer, including how the members of the legal governing body are chosen and replaced.

(b) List responsible church officers (i.e., chairpersons of the legal governing body, board of trustees, or other similar authority, and their occupations) and describe the functions they perform for the Issuer and the date their term of office expires.

(c) Disclose if any member of the Board of governing office has, during the past 10 years, been convicted in any criminal proceeding (other than for traffic violations and other minor offenses), or is the subject of any pending criminal proceeding, or was the subject of any order, judgment or decree of any court enjoining such person from any activity associated with the offer or sales of securities. If there are a substantial number of members, only those exercising supervisory authority need be described.

(d) State all direct and indirect remuneration paid by the Issuer to its executive officers or members of the Board for preceding fiscal year in the aggregate, and individually if in excess of $30,000. Indirect remuneration includes pension or retirement plans, or the use of the Issuer's assets for personal purposes.

(e) Describe any employment contracts, perquisites of employment or conflicts of interest with any person described in this section.

(f) Describe any direct or indirect remuneration to be received by members of the Issuer in connection with the offering.

(g) List pastors and associate pastors, their biographical histories and length of employment with the Issuer.

XIV. INVESTOR REPORTS

The bond certificate shall contain a statement that current financial statements of the Issuer will be made available to bondholders upon written request.

XV. *EXPERTS*

(a) Describe the authority of the Issuer to sell the Church Bonds, the validity of the Church Bonds when issued and the claim for exemption from registration, if applicable. This statement should be in the form of an opinion from legal counsel.

(b) The person or persons preparing any appraisals must be identified and describe their qualifications for serving as such along with the method of appraisal.

(c) Where required, all experts should file with the Administrator consents to utilize their names in the Offering Circular.

(d) All experts must be independent of the Issuer and the broker-dealer.

APPENDIX 5
RELIGIOUS EXPRESSION IN PUBLIC SCHOOLS

In 1995 President Clinton directed the Secretary of Education, in consultation with the Attorney General, to provide every public school district in America with a statement of principles addressing the extent to which religious expression and activity are permitted in our public schools. In accordance with the President's directive, the Secretary of Education sent every school superintendent in the country guidelines on *Religious Expression in Public Schools*. The purpose of these presidential guidelines was to end some of the confusion regarding religious expression in public schools that had developed over more than thirty years since the U.S. Supreme Court decision in 1962 outlawing state sponsored school prayer. The guidelines were reissued in May of 1998 in response to further legal developments. The new guidelines are reprinted below in full:

• *Student prayer and religious discussion.* The Establishment Clause of the First Amendment does not prohibit purely private religious speech by students. Students therefore have the same right to engage in individual or group prayer and religious discussion during the school day as they do to engage in other comparable activity. For example, students may read their Bibles or other scriptures, say grace before meals, and pray before tests to the same extent they may engage in comparable nondisruptive activities. Local school authorities possess substantial discretion to impose rules of order and other pedagogical restrictions on student activities, but they may not structure or administer such rules to discriminate against religious activity or speech.

Generally, students may pray in a nondisruptive manner when not engaged in school activities or instruction, and subject to the rules that normally pertain in the applicable setting. Specifically, students in informal settings, such as cafeterias and hallways, may pray and discuss their religious views with each other, subject to the same rules of order as apply to other student activities and speech. Students may also speak to, and attempt to persuade, their peers about religious topics just as they do with regard to political topics. School officials, however, should intercede to stop student speech that constitutes harassment aimed at a student or a group of students.

Students may also participate in before or after school events with religious content, such as "see you at the flag pole" gatherings, on the same terms as they may participate in other noncurriculum activities on school premises. School officials may neither discourage nor encourage participation in such an event.

The right to engage in voluntary prayer or religious discussion free from discrimination does not include the right to have a captive audience listen, or to compel other students to participate. Teachers and school administrators should ensure that no student is in any way coerced to participate in religious activity.

- *Graduation prayer and baccalaureates:* Under current Supreme Court decisions, school officials may not mandate or organize prayer at graduation, nor organize religious baccalaureate ceremonies. If a school generally opens its facilities to private groups, it must make its facilities available on the same terms to organizers of privately sponsored religious baccalaureate services. A school may not extend preferential treatment to baccalaureate ceremonies and may in some instances be obliged to disclaim official endorsement of such ceremonies.

- *Official neutrality regarding religious activity:* Teachers and school administrators, when acting in those capacities, are representatives of the state and are prohibited by the establishment clause from soliciting or encouraging religious activity, and from participating in such activity with students. Teachers and administrators also are prohibited from discouraging activity because of its religious content, and from soliciting or encouraging antireligious activity.

- *Teaching about religion:* Public schools may not provide religious instruction, but they may teach *about* religion, including the Bible or other scripture: the history of religion, comparative religion, the Bible (or other scripture)-as-literature, and the role of religion in the history of the United States and other countries all are permissible public school subjects. Similarly, it is permissible to consider religious influences on art, music, literature, and social studies. Although public schools may teach about religious holidays, including their religious aspects, and may celebrate the secular aspects of holidays, schools may not observe holidays as religious events or promote such observance by students.

- *Student assignments:* Students may express their beliefs about religion in the form of homework, artwork, and other written and oral assignments free of discrimination based on the religious content of their submissions. Such home and classroom work should be judged by ordinary academic standards of substance and relevance, and against other legitimate pedagogical concerns identified by the school.

- *Religious literature:* Students have a right to distribute religious literature to their schoolmates on the same terms as they are permitted to distribute other literature that is unrelated to school curriculum or activities. Schools may impose the same reasonable time, place, and manner or other constitutional restrictions on distribution of religious literature as they do on nonschool literature generally, but they may not single out religious literature for special regulation.

- *Religious excusals:* Subject to applicable State laws, schools enjoy substantial discretion to excuse individual students from lessons that are objectionable to the student or the students' parents on religious or other conscientious grounds. However, students generally do not have a Federal right to be excused from lessons that may be inconsistent with their religious beliefs or practices. School officials may neither encourage nor discourage students from availing themselves of an excusal option.

- *Released time:* Subject to applicable State laws, schools have the discretion to dismiss students to off-premises religious instruction, provided that schools do not encourage or discourage participation or penalize those who do not attend. Schools may not allow religious instruction by outsiders on school premises during the school day.

• *Teaching values:* Though schools must be neutral with respect to religion, they may play an active role with respect to teaching civic values and virtue, and the moral code that holds us together as a community. The fact that some of these values are held also by religions does not make it unlawful to teach them in school.

• *Student garb:* Schools enjoy substantial discretion in adopting policies relating to student dress and school uniforms. Students generally have no Federal right to be exempted from religiously-neutral and generally applicable school dress rules based on their religious beliefs or practices; however, schools may not single out religious attire in general, or attire of a particular religion, for prohibition or regulation. Students may display religious messages on items of clothing to the same extent that they are permitted to display other comparable messages. Religious messages may not be singled out for suppression, but rather are subject to the same rules as generally apply to comparable messages.

The Equal Access Act

The Equal Access Act is designed to ensure that, consistent with the First Amendment, student religious activities are accorded the same access to public school facilities as are student secular activities. Based on decisions of the Federal courts, as well as its interpretations of the Act, the Department of Justice has advised that the Act should be interpreted as providing, among other things, that:

• *General provisions:* Student religious groups at public secondary schools have the same right of access to school facilities as is enjoyed by other comparable student groups. Under the Equal Access Act, a school receiving Federal funds that allows one or more student noncurriculum-related clubs to meet on its premises during noninstructional time may not refuse access to student religious groups.

• *Prayer services and worship exercises covered:* A meeting, as defined and protected by the Equal Access Act, may include a prayer service, Bible reading, or other worship exercise.

• *Equal access to means of publicizing meetings:* A school receiving Federal funds must allow student groups meeting under the Act to use the school media—including the public address system, the school newspaper, and the school bulletin board—to announce their meetings on the same terms as other noncurriculum-related student groups are allowed to use the school media. Any policy concerning the use of school media must be applied to all noncurriculum-related student groups in a nondiscriminatory matter. Schools, however, may inform students that certain groups are not school sponsored.

• *Lunch-time and recess covered:* A school creates a limited open forum under the Equal Access Act, triggering equal access rights for religious groups, when it allows students to meet during their lunch periods or other noninstructional time during the school day, as well as when it allows students to meet before and after the school day.

INDEX

Respondeat superior
Course of employment, 728-732
Employee status, 721-728
In general, 720-735
Negligent conduct, 728
Nonprofit organizations, application to, 733-735

Securities law
Churches, coverage, 655-663
Liability of ministers for violating, 183-187
Self-employed, ministers, 31-36
Sexual harassment, 204-205, 545-555
Sexual misconduct, church liability (see Negligent selection, Negligent retention, Negligent Supervision, Respondeat superior, and Fiduciary duty)
Table, why sexual misconduct is the greatest legal risk to churches, 738
Table, ten risks associated with sexual misconduct, 747
Sexual misconduct, by clergy
Liability, theories of
Alienation of affections, 206
Assault and battery, 204
Criminal liability, 205-206
Emotional distress, 202-204
Fiduciary duty, breach of, 198-202
Loss of consortium, 206
Malpractice, 198
Sexual harassment, 204-205
Defenses
Consent, 206-208
Duplicate verdicts, 213
Elimination of loss of consortium statutes, 212-213
First amendment, application of, 209-211
Insurance, 211-212
Statutes of limitation, 208-209
Sexual orientation, discrimination based on, 577-579
Solicitation of charitable contributions, state regulation of, 646-652
Statutes of limitation, 208-209, 830-843
Subpoena, church records, 293-295

Tax-exemption application, public inspection of, 297-298
Termination of ministers
Exhaustion of ecclesiastical remedies, 80
General rule of judicial nonintervention, 59-76
In general, 59-80
Exceptions to the general rule of judicial nonintervention, 76-80
Title VII, Civil Rights Act of 1964 (see Civil Rights Act of 1964, Title VII)

Unincorporated churches
Characteristics, 262-264
Creation and administration, 268
In general, 261-268
Personal liability of members, 264-267
Uniform Unincorporated Association Act, 269

Vicarious liability (see Respondeat superior)
Volunteer Protection Act, 346
Voting, at church business meetings
Absentee voting, 383-384
Proxy voting, 380-381
Secret ballots, 383-384
Voting requirements, 379-384

Workers compensation, 508-513
Works made for hire, 668-673

Zoning law
Accessory uses, 252-255
Church, definition of, 248-255
In general, 441-456